# INTELLECTUAL PROPERTY

# INTELLECTUAL PROPERTY

**Fourth Edition**

## DAVID I BAINBRIDGE

BSc, LLB, PhD, CEng, MICE, MBCS

*Barrister,*
*Reader in Law, Aston Business School,*
*Aston University*

**FINANCIAL TIMES**
PITMAN PUBLISHING

**FINANCIAL TIMES**

# MANAGEMENT

LONDON · SAN FRANCISCO
KUALA LUMPUR · JOHANNESBURG

*Financial Times Management delivers the knowledge,
skills and understanding that enable students,
managers and organisations to achieve their ambitions,
whatever their needs, wherever they are.*

London Office:
128 Long Acre, London WC2E 9AN
Tel: +44 (0)171 447 2000
Fax: +44 (0)171 240 5771
Website: www.ftmanagement.com

*A Division of Financial Times Professional Limited*

---

First published in Great Britain 1992
**Fourth edition 1999**

© David I Bainbridge 1992, 1994, 1996, 1999

The right of David I Bainbridge to be identified as Author
of this Work has been asserted by him in accordance
with the Copyright, Designs and Patents Act 1988.

ISBN 0 273 63156 X

*British Library Cataloguing in Publication Data*
A CIP catalogue record for this book can be obtained from the British Library.

1 3 5 7 9 10 8 6 4 2

Typeset by Pantek Arts, Maidstone, Kent
Printed and bound in Great Britain by Clays Ltd, St. Ives plc

*The Publishers' policy is to use paper manufactured
from sustainable forests.*

# Contents

Contents

# Preface

The law of intellectual property has moved on at a quite amazing rate since the third edition of this book was printed, and the fourth edition fully reflects the many new and recent developments in this fascinating field. As before, in preparing the new edition, I have attempted to keep to the original purpose of the book, being to provide undergraduate students with an accessible and practical, yet reasonably comprehensive, view of intellectual property law. I am pleased to say that many practitioners tell me they find the book helpful and useful. With all that has happened in intellectual property law in the last couple or so years, the task of keeping this book up to date is beginning to feel somewhat like painting the Forth Bridge.

The more important legislation now described and commented on includes the Copyright and Related Rights Regulations 1996, the Copyright and Rights in Databases Regulations 1997 and the European Commission Technology Transfer Regulation. Important recent case law is included such as the Judicial Committee of the Privy Council's decision in *Canon* v *Green Cartridge* throwing some doubt on the scope of the *British Leyland* doctrine, the breach of confidence cases of *Lancashire Fires* v *Lyons* and *Ocular Sciences* v *Aspect Vision Care* (also noteable for what Laddie J had to say on the design right), the important decisions of the House of Lords in the fields of patents and biotechnology in *Biogen* v *Medeva* and *Merrell Dow* v *Norton*, the European Court of Justice's decision in *Merck* v *Primecrown* and the impressive wealth of case law concerning the Trade Marks Act 1994. This has gone a long way to fleshing out the Act and our new trade mark law is maturing very quickly. It seems that many traders and other undertakings value their trade marks so very highly that they will not hesitate to enforce their trade mark rights by bringing a legal action.

The Internet has come of age and presents many issues for intellectual property law of a practical nature and which are academically stimulating. In particular, in this edition, the liability of Internet service providers for copyright infringement is explored, as is the problem of domain names and the Internet in relation to passing off and trade marks. The first United Kingdom case of copyright and the Internet, *Shetland Times* v *Dr Jonathan Wills*, is discussed. As the Internet is now such a useful tool for students and lawyers alike, Appendix 2 of this book gives a number of addresses from which a wealth of valuable information of interest in the field of intellectual property can be obtained.

The implications of the TRIPs (Trade Related Aspects of Intellectual Property Rights) Agreement are described, and there is explanation and discussion of further European initiatives for changes, such as the Directive on the legal protection of biotechnological inventions, the proposals for Directives on copyright and related rights in the information society and the harmonisation of utility model protection (which would introduce this right into the United Kingdom just in time for the Millennium celebrations). Other proposals include that for a Directive on artists' resale right and an amended proposal for a harmonised registered design.

The opportunity has been taken to significantly extend the chapters on patents and trade marks. The sections on groundless threats of infringement proceedings have been substantially enlarged, taking account of the considerable amount of recent case law in this area. Particular features include copyright subsistence in scientific discoveries, genetic sequences and formulae, the registrability of shape marks and famous names, including the *Elvis*, *Remington* and *Lego* cases, and a new section on comparative advertising.

The structure of the book remains as before and I have retained the sequence of the various intellectual property rights in the book, reflecting my preferred order of teaching the subject. I still find students take to copyright law quite readily and this provides a useful platform to discuss some of the concepts and doctrines that apply more generally to intellectual property law.

I have been fortunate to be helped and encouraged by a number of persons, including practising solicitors, barristers and others whose work brings them into contact with intellectual property rights. I continue to learn from my students and from delegates attending the continuing professional development courses I present. I also learn from the growing number of clients I advise as a barrister (not practising). Pat Bond of Financial Times Pitman Publishing has been supportive and helpful as usual. Lorrain Keenan has done excellent work checking the new material and edits and producing new lists, tables and diagrams. My wife Sylvia has been very patient and encouraging throughout. I extend my sincere thanks to them all. I have attempted to state the law as at 1 June 1998.

*David I. Bainbridge*
*1 June 1998*

# Table of cases

# Table of legislation

# Glossary

## TERMS AND PHRASES COMMON IN INTELLECTUAL PROPERTY LAW

**Anton Piller order:** an order of the High Court permitting the aggrieved party to enter the premises of an alleged wrongdoer and remove or copy materials that are important evidentially. Named after the case of *Anton Piller KG v Manufacturing Processes Ltd* [1976] 1 Ch 55. The order must be executed by a solicitor. The applicant must show, *inter alia*, an extremely strong case. Its purpose is the preservation of evidence, that is to prevent the destruction or concealment of evidence by an alleged wrongdoer. The order is common in intellectual property cases, for example to allow a copyright owner to take possession of alleged pirate copies of his work. The successful applicant for an Anton Piller order usually has to give an undertaking in damages to compensate the other person should the applicant lose the case at trial.

**Assignment:** the transfer of the title in a chose in action. For example, ownership of copyright is transferred by means of an assignment in writing which is signed by or on behalf of the previous owner of the copyright, that is the assignor. In intellectual property law, an assignment must be distinguished from an exclusive licence, which is similar in many practical respects, but which does not involve the transfer of the title in the right.

**Character merchandising:** this occurs when the owner of the rights in some popular character or personality grants licences to others allowing them to apply drawings, photographs or other representations of the character to goods and articles which those others make or sell. Typically, the character will be a famous fictitious character popularised by television or film. Examples are Mickey Mouse, the Pink Panther, Denis the Menace, Indiana Jones, Teenage Mutant Hero Turtles, etc.

**Collecting society:** a society that collects revenue in respect of the exploitation of an intellectual property right and distributes that revenue amongst the right owners. In some cases, the owners of the right will assign part of their rights to the collecting society. An important example is the *Performing Right Society* which takes an assignment of the performing rights in music, grants blanket licences and distributes the revenue thus earned between the authors of the music. For example, the owner of premises such as a shop to which the public have access will pay a fee to the *Performing Right Society* which will allow him to play popular music in the shop. The same applies to hotels, restaurants and the like playing background music. This arrangement is much more convenient to the shop owner or hotelier and removes the problem of trying to negotiate separate licences with individual copyright owners.

**Comptroller of Patents, Designs and Trade Marks:** the head of the Patent Office with responsibility for the administration and grant of patents, registered designs and trade marks. Under trade mark legislation and design legislation the Comptroller is referred to as the *Registrar*. The Comptroller has other duties. Examples are: the conduct of hearing and proceedings, the production of statistics and an annual report, increasing public awareness of the work of the Patent Office in addition to working with, advising and participating with the European Patent Office, the World Intellectual Property Organization and the Council of Europe. In 1996, the Patent Office employed over 700 persons and had a turnover of nearly £60 million.

**Exhaustion of rights:** a doctrine emanating from EC law. Basically, the owner of an intellectual property right which relates to articles which have been put into circulation by him or with his consent anywhere within the EC cannot exercise that right to prevent the subsequent import, export or sale of those particular articles. The right is said to be exhausted. This will only apply where trade between member states is likely to be affected.

**Get-up:** a style, mark, appearance, packaging or form of advertising or marketing used in connection with, or applied to, an undertaking's ('trader's') goods or services which may be or become distinctive in relation to that undertaking and which may give rise to, contribute to, or be associated with, the undertaking's goodwill which is protected by the law of passing off. A particular stylised logo, emblem or other form of insignia may, in appropriate circumstances, be registered as a trade mark.

**Infringement:** intellectual property law gives rights to the owner of that property permitting him to do certain acts in respect of the thing in which the right subsists. Any person who does one of these acts without the permission or authority of the right-owner is said to infringe the right unless the act concerned is permitted by law or a defence applies. Thus, it is usual to speak of an infringement of copyright or to say that a patent has been infringed.

**Licence:** a licence is a permission given by the owner of a right (the licensor) to another person (the licensee) allowing that other person to do certain specified things in respect of the subject matter of the right. For example, the owner of the copyright subsisting in a musical work may grant a licence to a publishing company allowing it to print and sell copies of the work in the form of sheet music. Another example is where the proprietor (owner) of a patent grants a licence to another person permitting the working of the invention by that other person. Intellectual property licences are normally contractual in nature and the licensor will usually receive royalties by way of consideration for the permission.

Licences may be exclusive or non-exclusive. An *exclusive licence* is one where the licensee has the exclusive right to do certain things to the exclusion of all others including the licensor. Several *non-exclusive licences* may be granted to different persons in respect of the same work and the same activities For example, the owner of the copyright in a dramatic work may grant several non-exclusive licences to theatre companies permitting each of them to perform the dramatic work live on stage.

Compulsory licences may be granted under the provisions of an Act of Parliament. For example, the Patents Act 1977 gives the Comptroller of Patents, Designs and Trade Marks the power to grant a compulsory licence to an applicant if the patent in question is not, *inter alia*, being worked commercially in the United Kingdom. In some cases, licences are available as of right. This may be the ultimate result of a report from the Monopolies and Mergers Commission (for example, if a patent or design is not being sufficiently worked and this is contrary to the public interest), or because of a statutory provision, for example as regards designs subject to the design right during the last five years of the right, or because the owner has volunteered that such licences be available (in the case of a patent, the proprietor may do this and from then on he will only pay half the usual renewal fees).

If there is a defect in an assignment or a misunderstanding as to the ownership of a right, a court might be prepared to imply a licence. For example, if

a person commissions the making of a work of copyright and there is no express agreement for the assignment of that copyright, the court might be able to imply a licence so that the commissioner can use the work for certain purposes consistent with the purpose of the commission. Alternatively, the concept of beneficial ownership may be used to similar effect.

**Mareva injunction:** an injunction freezing the assets of a defendant thus preventing him removing them out of the jurisdiction of the court. Such an injunction is useful where the defendant is not resident within the United Kingdom. So named after the case *Mareva Compania Naviera SA* v *International Bulk Carriers SA* [1980] 1 All ER 213.

**Moral rights:** the rights that the author of a work of copyright has independent to the economic rights of the copyright owner. The moral rights are: to be identified as the author of the work (or the director of a film) and to be able to object to a derogatory treatment of the work. These rights leave the author with some control over his work even if he does not own the copyright. Any person also has a right, under copyright law, not to have a work falsely attributed to him.

**Public domain:** refers to all material which is available to the public at large (or a portion of it) and which may be freely used and exploited without infringing anyone's intellectual property rights Material may be in the public domain because: (a) it is commonplace, (b) it has been put there deliberately by the 'owner', and (c) the intellectual property rights concerning the material have expired or lapsed. It is possible that material has fallen into the public domain through a breach of confidence, in which case only those persons who have come across the material in good faith without notice of the breach of confidence will be free to make use of it. Such cases will be rare.

**Reverse engineering:** the process where information about the design or construction of an article is determined by an examination of the article itself, frequently after dismantling or measuring the dimensions of the article. Another manufacturer can copy articles by this process without having to inspect drawings and other design documents made for the article. For example, one company copied another's exhaust pipes by removing an exhaust system from a car and measuring it.

**Royalty:** a payment mechanism, normally calculated on a percentage of the income derived from sales of works or articles subject to an intellectual property right. This is a common method of paying for a licence to exploit an intellectual property right. For example, the author of a literary work may grant a licence to a publisher permitting him to print and sell copies to bookshops The publisher may then pay the author 10 per cent of the price he receives from the booksellers Sometimes, royalty figures will have to be agreed by the Comptroller of Patents, Designs and Trade Marks or by the Copyright Tribunal (for example, where a compulsory licence is obtained and the parties cannot agree a royalty). A percentage based on sales is not the only method of payment and a single lump sum or series of sums can be agreed between the parties.

## COMPUTER TERMS AND PHRASES

**Assembly language:** *see* low-level programming language.

**Computer memory:** the storage facilities of a computer. Computers can store vast amounts of data. Some of the computer's storage is internal, such as that provided for by integrated circuits and an internal magnetic disk. Other forms of storage are external, for example, 'floppy' diskettes, magnetic tape, CD ROM discs. Older forms of external storage include punched cards and paper tape. Internal computer memory can be classified as being ROM (read only memory) or RAM (random access memory). ROM contains programs such as the start up program and parts of the computer's operating system. ROM cannot be altered; it is permanent. RAM is transient memory, the contents are alterable. It is used to store application programs and associated data during the operation of a computer program which has been loaded from a disk or tape. When the computer is switched off, the contents of RAM are erased.

**Computer program:** a series of instructions which control or condition the operation of a computer.

**Decompilation and disassembly:** disassembly is an operation whereby the object code of a computer program is converted into assembly language (a low-level programming language). This is relatively easy to do using an appropriate computer program. Much more difficult is decompilation. This is where object code is converted into its original form in a high-level language. For this to be feasible, the type and version of the high-level language in which the program was originally written must be known. Quite often the word decompilation is used to describe disassembly (in essence, the process is the same, retrieving a source code program from an object code version). Reverse analysis of computer programs is usually undertaken using a disassembler program.

**High-level programming language:** a language that resembles natural language more closely than machine code (object code) or assembly language. High-level language is relatively remote from the machine language which can be directly 'understood' by the computer's central processing unit (processor). It is easier to write programs using a high-level language. However, for the program to operate, it must be converted permanently (compiled) or temporarily (interpreted) into machine code. Each statement in a high-level language corresponds to several statements in machine code. From reading a listing of a computer program written in a high-level language, it is possible to obtain a good insight into the ideas used and the program's algorithm. Examples of high-level languages are COBOL, BASIC, PASCAL and FORTRAN.

**Low-level programming language:** (or assembly language) a language which is very close to the machine code directly executable by the computer. Each statement is directly equivalent to a machine code operation. Assembly language is usually written using mnemonics and memory addresses.

**Programming language:** a set of words, letters and numbers which, according to the particular syntax of the language, describe a computer program, directly or indirectly, to a computer.

**Object code:** the machine code resulting from compiling a program written in a high-level language. Alternatively, it is produced by 'assembling' a program written in a low-level language. Object code is directly executable by a computer. Object code is not directly intelligible and must be converted by disassembly before it can be understood by humans. Most computer programs are marketed in object code form. It is processed faster and is far less easy to modify than a source code program.

**Reverse analysis:** this is the computer equivalent of reverse engineering. It is the process where a computer program is analysed by converting object code into assembly language or high-level language to determine features about the program. Reverse analysis can be used to discover interface details, that is information which will enable the writer of another program to make his program (or the files generated by his program) compatible with the other program. Reverse analysis can also be used to determine a program's algorithm and structure and to facilitate the writing of a program which will perform the same task. Hence, the scope and permissibility of reverse analysis are of utmost importance to the computer industry.

**Source code:** a program in a high-level language which must be converted into object code before it can be executed. *See also,* **object code.**

# Table of abbreviations

| | |
|---|---|
| AC | Appeal Cases |
| AIPC | Australian Intellectual Property Cases |
| All ER | All England Reports |
| B & C | Barnewall and Cresswell's King's Bench Reports |
| BCLC | Butterworth's Company Law Cases |
| Beav | Beavon's Reports |
| BGH | Bundesgerichtshof (Criminal) |
| BGHZ | Bundesgerichtshof (Civil) |
| Bro PC | Brown's Parliamentary Cases |
| Burr | Burrow's King's Bench Reports |
| Ch | Chancery |
| Ch App | Court of Appeal in Chancery |
| Ch D | Chancery Division |
| CLSR | Computer Law and Security Report |
| CMLR | Common Market Law Reports |
| Co Rep | Coke's Report |
| CPC | Community Patent Convention |
| Cr App R | Criminal Appeal Reports |
| Crim LR | Criminal Law Review |
| CTM | Community Trade Mark |
| De GJ & S | De Gex, Jones and Smith's Report |
| ECR | European Court Reports |
| EIPR | European Intellectual Property Review |
| EPO | European Patent Office |
| EPOR | European Patent Office Report |
| Eq | Equity Cases |
| F | Federal Reporter (US) |
| FCA | Federal Court of Australia |
| FSR | Fleet Street Reports |
| F Supp | Federal Supplement (US) |
| Godbolt | Godbolt's Reports |
| Hare | Hare's Chancery Reports |
| IIC | International Review of Industrial Property and Copyright Law |
| IRLR | Industrial Relations Law Reports |
| Jur | The Jurists Report |
| KB | King's Bench |
| LJ CH | Law Journal Reports (Chancery) |
| LT | Law Times Reports |
| Mac & G | Macnaghten and Gordon's Chancery Reports |
| MacG CC | MacGillivray's Copyright Cases |
| MLR | Modern Law Review |
| NSWLR | New South Wales Law Reports |
| NZLR | New Zealand Law Reports |
| QB | Queen's Bench |
| OJ | Official Journal of the European Communities |
| Pet | Peter's Supreme Court Reports (US) |
| RPC | Reports of Patent, Design and Trade Mark Cases |
| Russ & M | Russell and Mylne's Chancery Reports |
| S Ct | Supreme Court |
| SI | Statutory Instrument |
| TLR | Times Law Reports |
| USC | United States Code |
| USPQ | United States Patents Quarterly |
| WLR | Weekly Law Reports |
| WPC | Webster's Patent Cases |

# Part One

## PRELIMINARY

# 1

---

# *Introduction*

The content of this chapter goes further than a simple introduction of the subject of intellectual property in which the various forms of intellectual property are briefly described. The chapter also addresses some of the basic principles underlying this area of law, examines the nature of intellectual property law and discusses some cross-cutting themes that transcend boundaries between individual forms of intellectual property rights. Some practical considerations are also dealt with briefly at this stage such as the essential rationale for intellectual property and its importance in a commercial sense. Finally, the nature of the study of intellectual property is discussed. The purpose of this chapter is to give the reader a feel for intellectual property law and to introduce some of the important issues, laying the foundations for the more detailed study which follows.

## WHAT IS INTELLECTUAL PROPERTY LAW?

Intellectual property law is that area of law which concerns legal rights associated with creative effort or commercial reputation and goodwill. The subject matter of intellectual property is very wide and includes literary and artistic works, films, computer programs, inventions, designs and marks used by traders for their goods or services. The law deters others from copying or taking unfair advantage of the work or reputation of another and provides remedies should this happen. There are several different forms of rights or areas of law giving rise to rights that together make up intellectual property. They are:

- copyright
- rights in performances
- the law of confidence
- patents
- registered designs
- design right
- trade marks
- passing off
- trade libel.

This list is not exhaustive and there are other rights, for example, the rights associated with plant and seed varieties protection, but these will not be dealt with in detail in this book.

## Taxonomy of intellectual property rights

Obviously, there are many similarities and differences between the various rights that make up intellectual property law. For example, there is common ground between patents and registered designs, as there is between copyright and rights in performances. Some rights give rise to monopolies, while others merely prevent the unfair use by others of an existing work or article. The various rights are not necessarily mutually exclusive and two or more of the rights can coexist in relation to a certain 'thing'. Sometimes the rights will progressively give protection, one right taking over from another over a period of time during the development of an invention, design or work of copyright.

A practical distinction that can be used to subdivide the various rights is whether there is a requirement for registration, that is whether the right is dependent upon the completion of formalities, or whether it automatically springs into life at a specified time. Another distinguishing feature is the nature of the right, whether it applies to something which is primarily creative or has to do with goodwill in a wide commercial sense. Creative things can be further subdivided into those that are creative in an artistic or aesthetic sense, such as an oil painting, music or literature, or those that are inventive in an industrial context such as a new type of machine or engine, or a new way of making a particular product. Before looking briefly at each type of right, consider Table 1.1 which shows how, somewhat imperfectly, intellectual property rights conform to the above taxonomy. The word 'artistic' is used in an everyday and wide sense and should not be confused with the artistic category of copyright works where the word has a special significance.

**Table 1.1 Taxonomy of intellectual property**

| | Basic nature of the right | | |
| --- | --- | --- | --- |
| | Creative | | Commercial reputation & goodwill |
| *Whether formalities required* | *Artistic* | *Industrial* | |
| Formalities required | Registered designs | Patents Plant varieties | Trade marks |
| Formalities not required | Copyright Rights in performances | Design right | Passing off Trade libel |
| | | The law of confidence | |

## Formalities

Some intellectual property rights, in respect of particular ideas, works or things, are secured by the successful completion of a formal application and registration procedure. The necessary formalities are not simply satisfied by depositing details with an appropriate authority because such rights are not granted lightly. They do, after all, put the owner of the right in a privileged position whereby he can restrain others from doing certain things while exploiting the right for himself. The rights impinge upon the freedom of action of others. The owner has a form of property which he can use as he likes, subject to some constraints, and he can take legal action either to deter would-be trespassers or to obtain damages against those who have trespassed just as the owner of real property can do.[1]

For those rights that require registration, the applicant will succeed in obtaining such registration only if certain rigorous standards are achieved. The rationale for this is that rights subject to formalities are generally monopolistic in nature. Another distinction is between those rights that are provided for and governed by statute and those that derive from the common law (although the latter are given statutory recognition). There is no correlation between the need for formalities and whether the area of intellectual property law is rooted in statute, as a comparison of Table 1.1 above and Table 1.2 shows.

**Table 1.2  Statutory and common law rights**

| *Statute* | *Common law* |
| --- | --- |
| Copyright | Breach of confidence |
| Patent | Passing off |
| Trade marks | Trade libel |
| Registered designs | |
| Design right | |
| Rights in performances | |
| Plant varieties | |

**Industrial property**

Traditionally, a number of intellectual property rights were known collectively as *industrial property*. Such rights include patents, trade marks and designs. This description was used in the Paris Convention for the Protection of Industrial Property 1883. Included in this term by implication are the law of confidence and passing off. When other rights such as copyright are added to industrial property the phrase used to describe the entirety of rights is *intellectual property* and this has become the phrase normally used to describe these individual, and sometimes disparate, rights collectively. Significant moves have been made in terms of the international harmonisation of intellectual property law, but it should be remembered that the early development of copyright, patents and trade mark law in England set the mould that was largely adopted throughout the common law countries of the world. Even before the beginning of the twentieth century, international collaboration and co-operation was well under way, reflecting the world-wide importance of intellectual property.

Before discussing further the nature of intellectual property, it will be useful to describe briefly each right individually using non-technical language.

---

[1] This also extends to other persons having rights under intellectual property law such as an exclusive licensee of a copyright or patent, as it does to lessees and licensees of real property.

## Copyright

Copyright is a property right which subsists (exists) in various 'works', for example literary works, artistic works, musical works, sound recordings, films and broadcasts. The author of a work is the person who creates it[2] and he (or his employer) is normally the first owner of the copyright, which will last until 70 years after the author's death or 50 years after it was created depending on the type of work.[3] Copyright gives the owner the right to do certain things in relation to the work, which includes making a copy, broadcasting or giving a public performance. Anyone else who does any of these things (known as the acts restricted by copyright) without the permission of the owner, infringes copyright and may be subject to legal action taken by the owner for that infringement. Ownership of a copyright is alienable and it can be transferred to another or a licence may be granted by the owner to another, permitting him to do one or more specified acts with the work in question.

Copyright does not protect ideas, only the expression of an idea (that is, its tangible form), and it is free to others to create similar, or even identical, works as long as they do so independently and by their own efforts. In other words, copyright does not create a monopoly in a particular work. In addition, certain things may be done in relation to a work of copyright without the permission of the copyright owner such as making a copy of a work, for example for the purposes of research, private study, criticism or review. Such acts are known as the 'permitted acts' and limit the scope of copyright protection. Copyright gives rise to two forms of rights:

1  the proprietary or economic rights in the work, for example the right to control copying, and
2  moral rights which leave the author (or principal director of a film), who may no longer be the owner of the copyright, with some control over how the work is exploited in the future.

The author (or film director) has a right to be identified as such and has a right to object to derogatory treatment of the work. The moral rights are independent of the economic rights and hence the importance of the distinction between the author of a work and the owner of the copyright subsisting in it. There are some forms of infringement which can be grouped together as being of a commercial nature, such as importing or dealing with infringing copies, that carry criminal penalties.

International protection of copyright works is effected mainly through two international conventions: the Berne Copyright Convention and the Universal Copyright Convention, both of which lay down minimum standards of protection to be attained and for reciprocity of protection between those countries that are signatories to the conventions. The conventions have been partly responsible for the measure of harmony that now exists on the world stage, albeit far from complete. The effect is that a foreign national can take legal action in the United Kingdom for copyright infringement occurring there as if he was a British subject.[4] The UK is a member of both conventions. Further harmonisation has taken place throughout the European Community as a result of a number of harmonising Directives.

2 For some types of works, the author is the person by whom the arrangements necessary for the creation of the work are undertaken.

3 From the end of the calendar year during which the author died or the work was created, as appropriate. The 50-year period has been rasied to 70 years for some forms of works.

4 *Hanfstaengl* v *Empire Palace* [1894] 2 Ch 1. All three judges in the Court of Appeal commented on this then novel state of affairs.

## Rights in performances

Live performances give rise to two different rights: the performer's right and a recording right. Until recently, the former was restricted to a right not dissimilar to the author's moral right in copyright, whilst persons with whom the performer had an exclusive recording contract acquired a right similar to the copyright owner's economic right. However, as a result of the Copyright and Related Rights Regulations 1996,[5] the performer now also has a true property right relating to making copies, the issue of copies and the rental and lending of recordings of his performance. Being property rights, these rights may be assigned or licensed.

The need for specific rights in live performances is that they give the performer, and the person having exclusive recording rights, a means of protecting live performances from persons making illicit ('bootleg') recordings of such performances.[6] Of course, the work being performed may be protected by copyright, but the copyright owner may not wish to take action. These rights are directly enforceable by the performer and the recording company. In some cases, the work on which the performance is based may be an old work in which copyright does not subsist, such as an operatic aria by Mozart. Rights in performances are not restricted to music and are available in respect of a dramatic performance, the reading or recital of a literary work and the performance of a variety act such as by a juggler.

Rights in performances last for 50 years from the end of the calendar year during which the performance took place. Where a sound recording of a performance is published commercially and is played in public or included in a broadcast or cable programme service, the performer is entitled to an equitable remuneration from the owner of the copyright in the sound recording. This right may not be assigned except to a collecting society, which will enforce the right on behalf of the performer.

## The law of breach of confidence

The law of breach of confidence developed in equity as a way of protecting confidential information by preventing its use by persons to whom the information has been divulged in confidence or the further disclosure of the information by such persons. A wide variety of types of information is protected, ranging from industrial or trade secrets to details of a personal nature to secrets about the government or defence of the realm. In the context of intellectual property, it is with trade and industrial secrets that we are primarily concerned. The rationale of the law of confidence is that it stops a person making wrongful use of information beyond the purposes for which it was disclosed to him. The law of confidence protects ideas and is a useful ally to other intellectual property rights, often being the only form of protection when the subject matter is still in an embryonic state.

## Patent law

A patent right, because it gives its owner a monopoly, is the form of intellectual property *par excellence*. A patent may be granted in respect of a new invention capable of industrial application and gives a monopoly right that can last for up

5  SI 1996 No. 2967.

6  Bootleg recordings of performances by Phil Collins and Cliff Richard were the subject of a case before the European Court of Justice in which it was held that German copyright law was contrary to Article 6 of the EC Treaty in that it discriminated against non-German nationals, *Collins* v *Imtrat Handelgesellschaft mbH* [1994] FSR 166.

to 20 years. This very strong form of protection is reserved for inventions that satisfy rigorous standards (for example, novelty and inventiveness) and an application for a patent has to be drawn up precisely and accurately stating the scope of the invention and the claims made in respect of it for which protection is sought. A patent may be for a product such as a new type of longer lasting light bulb or a new type of ignition system for a petrol engine or it may be for a new industrial process, for example a new way of making synthetic rubber tyres or a novel technique for making plate glass.

Patents can be assigned and licences may be granted in respect of them. The owner of a patent is the person who is registered as the proprietor. A large number of inventions are made by employees and usually, in such cases, the employer will be the proprietor although the inventor will be named as such. If the invention turns out to be of outstanding benefit to the employer, the employee may apply for a compensation award. By their nature, patents usually protect ideas, as expressed in the description and claims, but there are several controls on the monopoly status they confer upon proprietors. For example, compulsory licences may be available after the first three years from the grant of a patent, or it may be indicated on the register of patents that a licence is available as of right. A compulsory licence would be appropriate if the patent was not being worked or if the proprietor was limiting supply of a patented product in order to maintain unjustifiably high prices.

It is probably in respect of patents that the greatest strides have been made towards international harmonisation, particularly within Europe. The European Patent Convention permits the application for a bundle of patents covering a specified number of member states including the UK. The administration of the convention, patent applications, patent grant and resolution of patent disputes are within the remit of the European Patent Office, situated in Munich, which has its own Boards of Appeal.[7] The growing significance of this route to international patent protection cannot be underestimated and, before long, it should be possible to obtain a Community-wide patent. Protection in other countries may be obtained through the Patent Co-operation Treaty, a system which facilitates the application procedure where several countries are concerned, although it does not enjoy the level of concordance between members that the European Patent Convention can boast.

A number of the provisions of the UK Patents Act 1977 are framed so as to have, as nearly as practicable, the same effect as the corresponding provisions of the European Patent Convention, the Community Patent Convention (when in force) and the Patent Co-operation Treaty.[8]

[7] Applications can also be made through the Patent Office in London. This would be the normal procedure for a United Kingdom applicant.

[8] Patents Act 1977 s 130(7).

## Design law – registered designs and the design right

A new product or article may be designed but which is not sufficiently novel or inventive to satisfy the exacting requirements for the grant of a patent. Designs that are applied to articles may be protected by design law. There are two systems of design law in place in the UK (some countries use a watered-down version of patent law for designs known as petty patents or utility patents). Of the two UK systems, one requires registration, has some features in common with patent law, in a very broad sense, and applies to designs that have and are intended to have eye-appeal. Examples are household ornaments, toys, display packaging and some electrical appliances. These designs can be described as being aesthetic. The other system of design protection is called the design right and is provided for along copyright lines. This right applies to designs that can be said to be functional in nature such as a new design for an engine cover, fan cowling or plastic printer ink cartridge. It can, however, also apply to many registrable designs and there is a large overlap between the two forms of design rights. Both forms of design right relate to the design aspects of the shape or configuration of an article and, for registered designs only, also to pattern and ornament.

The registered design lasts for up to 25 years, initially granted for five years and then subject to renewal every five years, whereas the design right can last for 15 years, but this will be reduced if the design is applied commercially during its first five years. Confusingly, the creator of a registered design is known as its author, whereas the creator of a design in which the design right subsists is known as the designer. The owner (proprietor for a registered design) will normally be the creator unless the design was created by an employee or under a commission. Both rights are transmissible. There is potential overlap between the two rights themselves and between the two rights and copyright. This is a complex issue which is dealt with in detail in Part 5 of this book.

## Trade marks

Trade marks may not have the glamour of inventions or creative works but they are, nevertheless, of substantial importance in an industrial and commercial sense. Trade marks are closely associated with business image, goodwill and reputation. Goods or services are often requested by reference to a trade mark and the public rely on many marks as indicating quality, value for money or origin of goods or services.

Trade marks are registered in respect of certain classes of goods or services. Service marks have been registrable since 1986 as a result of the Trade Marks (Amendment) Act 1984. However, the separate description of 'service mark' has disappeared and all marks are now known as trade marks. Registrations for trade marks may be renewed indefinitely. Registration for trade marks began in 1876 and some of the first marks registered (including the very first mark, the Bass Red Triangle label mark) are still in use today. In addition to marks applied to or used with goods or services to indicate a connection in the course of trade, there are also certification marks indicating the origin or quality of the goods, for example the 'wool mark', and collective marks, typically used by members of an association. All registered marks must be used and they can be revoked if they are not used for five or more years. A basic principle is that a trade mark should be capable of distinguishing goods or services of one 'undertaking'[9] from those of other undertakings.

Significant changes to trade mark law have been made – the Trade Marks Act 1994 replaced the Trade Marks Act 1938, which was widely recognised as an obscure and difficult piece of legislation, which was out of touch with modern trading practices. In addition to bringing trade mark law up to date, the 1994 Act has allowed the UK to comply with the European Community Directive on the approximation of the laws of member states relating to trade marks and to ratify the Protocol to the Madrid Convention for the international registration of trade marks.

9 The Trade Marks Act 1994, following the language of the EC Directive harmonising trade mark law, uses the term 'undertaking' rather than 'trader'.

## Passing off

The tort of passing off is, in effect, a common law version of trade mark law. Indeed, trade mark law developed from passing off, which in turn developed from the tort of deceit. Being common law, passing off can be more flexible than trade mark law, and can apply to marks that would not be sufficiently distinctive for registration as a trade mark or are otherwise unregistrable. As with trade mark law, passing off is concerned with the protection of business goodwill and reputation, and this has the secondary effect of protecting the buying public from trade deception. One area of interest is character merchandising, usually a massive commercial activity whereby famous and often fictional characters are used to promote the sale of goods: for example by applying pictures of the characters to the goods, such as 'Teletubbies' bubble bath and 'Spice Girl' dolls.

## NATURE OF INTELLECTUAL PROPERTY

### Intellectual property as property

Intellectual property rights give rise to a form of property that can be dealt with just as with any other property, and which can be assigned, mortgaged and licensed. Table 1.3 shows a classification scheme for property and how intellectual property fits in with this scheme.

**Table 1.3  Classification of property and examples**

| Real property | | Personal property | |
|---|---|---|---|
| *Tangible (immovable)* | *Intangible* | *Tangible (movable)* | *Intangible* |
| Land | Easement<br>*Profit à prendre* | Car<br>Desk<br>Book<br>Box of chocolates | Cheque<br>Shares<br>Intellectual property,<br>e.g. copyright |

Intellectual property is property in a legal sense: it is something that can be owned and dealt with. Statutory forms of intellectual property are declared to be property rights, but even common law forms have been recognised as producing a form of property right.[10] Most forms of intellectual property are 'choses in action', rights that are enforced only by legal action as opposed to possessory rights. Channell J described a chose in action in the following terms in *Torkington* v *Magee*:

> 'Chose in action' is a known legal expression used to describe all personal rights which can only be enforced by action, and not by taking physical possession.[11]

This has implications as regards the transfer of rights (assignment) and the requirement for consideration. In many cases, the assignment of intellectual property rights is expressly governed by statute and, where this is so,

10 For example, in the passing off case of *Leather Cloth Co Ltd* v *American Leather Cloth Co Ltd* (1863) 4 De GJ&S 137, the Court of Chancery recognised that the plaintiff had acquired a property in a trade mark which was valid in equity.

11 [1902] 2 KB 427 at 430.

12 *Re Westerton, Public Trustee v Gray* [1919] 2 Ch 104.

13 This has been recognised as extending to equitable choses in action. It is possible to have an equitable assignment of an equitable chose in action.

assignment requires no consideration.[12] Otherwise, assignment of a chose in action (meaning 'thing in action') is governed by the Law of Property Act 1925 s 136, which requires the assignment to be written and signed by the assignor, to be absolute and followed by express notice.[13] However, there is one major exception to the classification of intellectual property rights as choses in action: patents are declared to be personal property without being a thing in action by the Patents Act 1977 s 30(1). This strange anomaly seems to be without purpose or consequence as the provisions for ownership and assignment are contained in detail in the Act itself.

## Jurisprudential character

Intellectual property gives rise to rights and duties. It establishes property rights, which give the owner the right to do certain things in relation to the subject matter. For example, if the right is a copyright and the subject matter is a piece of music, the owner of the copyright has the exclusive right to make copies of the sheet music, to make an arrangement of the music and to control the performance of the music. However, the owner also has the negative right to prevent others from doing such things in relation to the music. The right can arise automatically, on the creation of the thing to which the right pertains, an example being copyright which springs to life automatically upon the recording of a work.[14] In other cases, the right depends on the completion of an application and registration procedure, patents and trade marks being examples of such rights. In one area of intellectual property, the right comes into existence only after goodwill has been established. This is passing off where one trader is attempting to take unfair advantage of another trader's goodwill. The law can only give remedies here if the aggrieved trader has built up goodwill associated with his business, and this could take several years or just a few days, depending on the circumstances.

14 Recording, in this sense, means putting ideas into some tangible form, for example by writing down on paper, recording on magnetic tape or entering into a computer memory.

We have seen that intellectual property law is concerned with rights. Conversely, it must create duties, for according to the legal theorist Hohfeld, every right has an associated duty – there cannot be one without the other. It is instructive to take the Hohfeldian analysis of legal rules further, particularly in terms of his legal correlatives and oppositions as shown in Figure 1.1.

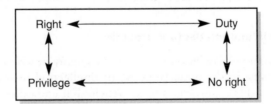

**Figure. 1.1 Hohfeld's correlations and oppositions**

15 Hohfeld, W.N. *Fundamental Legal Conceptions as Applied in Judicial Reasoning*, reprinted in part in Lloyd, Lord (of Hampstead) (1979) *Introduction to Jurisprudence* (4th edn) Stevens, at pp. 260–6.

Rights and duties have a distinct relationship and are called legal correlatives by Hohfeld.[15] In terms of intellectual property, the right is a right to do certain things, such as making copies of a work of copyright, making articles to a design covered by a design right or making products in accordance with a patented invention. The correlative duty is a duty owed by all others not to infringe the right. This duty exists even if the person infringing the right does not know of it.[16] Looking at Hohfeld's scheme again, it can be seen that there are associated privileges and 'no-rights'. The right resulting from the operation of intellectual property law gives the owner of that right a corresponding privilege, that is the privilege to exploit the work. The correlative no-right is to the effect that persons other than the owner do not have this privilege.

In this overall scheme of things, certain provisos must be added. In the area of intellectual property, the law strives to reach a balance between conflicting interests, to reach a justifiable compromise.[17] Therefore, the duty not to infringe is often curtailed by way of exceptions to infringement. For example, the right given by registration of a design does not extend to features dictated solely by function.[18] Copyright law permits many things to be done that would otherwise infringe, for example the 'fair dealing' provisions. Infringement in areas of intellectual property provided for by statute is carefully and precisely defined and any act that falls outside can be freely done by anyone, regardless of the right owner's wishes. An example in copyright law is lending a book to a friend; copyright law does not control such an act, however much the author or the publisher may argue that a sale has been lost as a result.

The honest use by a trader of his own name will not infringe a trade mark comprising the same name. Hohfeld's 'no-right' is also compromised as it is possible, under certain circumstances, to obtain compulsory licences to exploit intellectual property even if the owner of the right is vehemently opposed to this. For example, if may be possible to obtain a compulsory licence to exploit a patent irrespective of the proprietor's wishes. The final limitation on intellectual property rights concerns their duration. Most of the rights are limited in time. As a rule of thumb, it can be said that the duration of the right is inversely proportional to its power. For example, a patent gives a monopoly right which is limited to 20 years maximum, but a copyright, which is not a monopoly right, will last for at least 70 years.[19] Some rights may, however, endure for longer.[20] Trade mark rights are of indefinite duration and last as long as the proprietor of the mark is prepared to continue both renewing his registration and using the mark. The law of passing off will give protection to the goodwill of a trader as long as this still exists. The law of breach of confidence will be available to protect the information concerned for as long as it can be kept confidential.

## Purchasers' rights and intellectual property

The theoretical nature of intellectual property has many practical ramifications. Of particular interest in the understanding of intellectual property law is the question of what rights a purchaser of an article that embodies an intellectual property right obtains. An examination of this question is best carried out by means of an example, and that following is set in the context of copyright law although some of the principles are relevant to other rights. Consider the situation where a person, Georgina, goes to a bookshop to purchase a copy of a best-selling novel. The text of the novel itself will be protected by copyright as a literary work.[21] Georgina picks up a copy of the novel, takes it across to the cash point and buys it. Georgina has become the owner of the book and she now has legal title to it – or does she? She certainly has legal title to the paper,

16 Knowledge of the existence of the right may be relevant in terms of the applicability and measure of some of the remedies for infringement. For example, in an action for infringement of copyright, damages are not available against an 'innocent' infringer: the Copyright, Designs and Patents Act 1988 s 97(1).

17 Justifiable on the grounds of protecting private interests and promoting investment while providing benefits for society at large in terms of increased wealth, knowledge and employment.

18 The Registered Designs Act 1949 s 1(1)(b).

19 In many cases, the period will be significantly longer. However, typographical arrangements of published editions are limited to 25 years' protection.

20 Until 1 August 1989, copyright contemplated perpetual rights in respect of works the copyright in which was vested in the Universities of Oxford and Cambridge and some other colleges.

21 Unless the copyright has expired. Copyright endures for 70 years after the end of the calendar year during which the author dies. The typographical arrangement will also be protected by copyright but this is not considered further in the example.

the cover and the printer's ink which are the physical embodiment of the story. But what are her rights in relation to the literary work expressed in the book – does she own it and can she do with it as she pleases? The answer emphatically is NO, the copyright in the literary work still belongs to the publisher of the novel or the author as the case may be. Georgina can do certain things, such as reading the book, or she may burn it because neither of these acts is controlled by copyright. However, Georgina may not make a copy of the book or translate it into a foreign language because these acts are controlled by copyright.

What if Georgina wishes to lend the novel to her friend John? Non-commercial lending is not a restricted act, so at first sight this would seem to be perfectly lawful. However, if Georgina looks inside the flyleaf of her book she will find a notice stating that certain things cannot be done without the permission of the publisher and lending might be one of them. This brings into question Georgina's status *vis-à-vis* the publisher.[22] The sale of the book was a sale of goods contract between Georgina and the proprietors of the bookshop – there is no privity of contract between Georgina and the publisher. Even if there was, it is extremely doubtful whether the notice was a term of that contract. The only way a contractual link can be forged between Georgina and the publisher would be on the basis of a copyright licence, but this would be unrealistic as Georgina does not need a licence to be able to read the book, she would need a licence only if she intended to perform one of the acts controlled by copyright. Therefore, it would seem that, apart from those parts of the notice that refer to the acts restricted by the copyright, Georgina can ignore it and lend the book to her friend.[23]

Another issue is what remedy Georgina has should the novel turn out to be very poorly written, lacking a good plot. In essence, nothing at all unless there has been some misrepresentation by the bookseller concerning the quality of the novel which is sufficient to make the contract between Georgina and the bookseller voidable.[24] Of course, if the tangible matter is defective, for example the printer's ink is poor and has smudged destroying the legibility of the book, or if the binding is poor and the book falls apart, Georgina may obtain redress from the bookseller under the Sale of Goods Act 1979 s 14(2). However, the absence of a contractual link between Georgina and the publisher robs her of any remedy if the story itself turns out to be very badly written, and it does not appear that the implied terms of satisfactory quality, fitness for purpose and sale by description contained in the Sale of Goods Act 1979 ss 13 and 14 apply to a work of copyright.[25] Lastly, suppose that the book is not a novel but a cookery book and one of the recipes contains a mistake that can lead to food poisoning if that recipe is used. If Georgina suffers as a result, can she sue for negligence, and, if so, who? The bookseller might be liable in negligence on the basis of *Donoghue* v *Stevenson*[26] or on the basis of the contract between them,[27] or the publisher might be liable under the product liability provisions of the Consumer Protection Act 1987. However, the definition of 'product' and 'goods' in the Act would appear not to include intellectual property.[28]

These issues are complex and, in the main, largely unresolved. The problems are compounded tenfold where the transaction includes a licence from the right owner in addition to a normal sale or service contract, for example, where the contract relates to computer software. The 'sale' of computer software must include a licence because using the software will normally require the performance of an act restricted by copyright, unlike the case of reading a book. The licence

---

22 Or the author depending upon which of those two own the copyright.

23 A restriction on lending 'by way of trade or otherwise' is common. The lending of a copy of, *inter alia*, a literary work to the public is now a restricted act: Copyright, Designs and Patents Acts 1988 s 18A(1).

24 A publisher who sold a book written by Alastair MacNeill, based on an outline for a story made by the famous novelist, the late Alistair Maclean, was found guilty of offences under the Trade Descriptions Act 1968 because the relative prominence of Alistair Maclean's name compared to the actual author's name was such that the buying public thought that they were acquiring a book *written by Alistair Maclean*. The publisher was fined £6250: *The Times*, 28 September 1991.

25 By the Sale of Goods Act 1979 s 61(1) 'goods' include all personal chattels other than things in action and money. Copyright is a thing in action, and therefore, outside the provisions of the Act.

26 [1932] AC 562. But is it realistic to expect a bookseller to check the safety of instructions in books which he sells? Even if he wants to check, the bookseller will be ill-equipped to validate the integrity of the contents of many books.

27 For example, compare with the latent defect in a catapult giving rise to damages for breach of contract in *Godley* v *Perry* [1960] 1 WLR 9.

28 *See* the Consumer Protection Act 1987 s 45(1).

may be express, but will otherwise be implied. This may result in a hybrid contract involving a sale of goods contract for the physical items such as floppy disks, together with a licence to use the computer programs included in the package.[29]

The nature of the transaction is far from clear. In Scotland, in the Court of Session, Outer House, Lord Penrose held that a contract for the acquisition of off-the-shelf software was *sui generis*.[30] An Australian case, *Toby Construction Products Pty Ltd* v *Computer Bar (Sales) Pty Ltd*,[31] has been influential in England and Wales in classifying contracts to acquire software as sale of goods contracts. In that case, hardware had been acquired which incorporated defective software. The hardware accounted for most of the overall cost and the court held that the contract was a sale of goods contract with the consequences that entailed, such as the implication of terms relating to quality. In *St Albans City & District Council* v *International Computers Ltd*,[32] at first instance Scott Baker J concluded, *obiter*, that a contract for the writing of computer software was a sale of goods contract, citing *Toby Construction* with approval. However, on appeal, Glidewell LJ accepted that it was not a sale of goods contract as the program was not sold but licensed.[33] Nevertheless, he went on to say that it would be appropriate to imply a term that a program was reasonably capable of achieving its intended purpose.

The better view is that a contract for the acquisition of computer software is or includes a licence between the copyright owner and the person acquiring the software. That licence will be implied if it is not express. If goods are delivered with the software, there may be a collateral sale of goods contract, the importance of which is reflected in the main purpose of the transaction. For example, did the 'buyer' predominantly want to acquire hardware or other things falling in the conventional classification of goods, or were the goods merely the vehicle on which the software was delivered?

As regards liability for defective software, it is now firmly established that the Unfair Contract Terms Act 1977 ss 2–4 apply to the bulk of the terms in software licence agreements and the effect of para 1(c) Sch 1 of the Act, excluding the operation of those sections in relation to contracts for the creation or transfer of a right or interest in any patent, trade mark, copyright, etc., is very limited.[34] In terms of advice contained in a book or provided by computer software, the law of negligent misstatement is very relevant and, as a result of the Unfair Contract Terms Act 1977, it may be difficult to restrict liability for loss occasioned by defective advice generated by computer software.

## CROSS-CUTTING THEMES

Two particular features or aspects permeate through all or most forms of intellectual property rights. The first is concerned with the control of an abuse of the rights, for example by the proprietor of a patent who is unfairly manipulating the market to his own advantage. Obviously, a line will have to be drawn because part of the rationale for intellectual property is that it provides a mechanism for exploiting ideas and the tangible expression of those ideas, but sometimes there is a danger that the exploitation will reach unacceptable levels. The second aspect concerns the international pressures and opportunities presented by intellectual property law, and of particular importance in this respect is the European Community.

29 For a discussion of the nature of a contract for the acquisition of computer software, *see* Bainbridge, D.I. (1996), *Introduction to Computer Law* (3rd edn) Pitman, Chapter 13; Reed, C. (ed.) (1996) *Computer Law* (3rd edn) Blackstone Press, Chapters 2 and 3; and Tapper, C. (1990) *Computer Law* (4th edn) Longman, Part 2.

30 *Beta Computers (Europe) Ltd* v *Adobe Systems (Europe) Ltd* [1996] FSR 367.

31 [1983] 2 NSWLR 48.

32 [1995] FSR 686.

33 [1997] FSR 251 at 266.

34 *See*, for example, *The Salvage Association* v *CAP Financial Services Ltd* [1995] FSR 654 and *St Albans City & District Council* v *International Computers Ltd* [1997] FSR 251.

## Abuse of intellectual property

The owner of an important and prominent item protected by intellectual property law might be tempted to use his position to control a market to the disadvantage of competitors and consumers alike. He can prevent or deter potential competitors from developing products similar to his own, and he can charge high prices for the product. To some extent this is to be expected in a capitalistic society; there must be sufficient rewards for the risks of investment in new products and entrepreneurial creation of employment and wealth. Nevertheless, human nature being what it is, some will try to take an 'unfair' advantage of their status as intellectual property right holders. Some rights, such as patents, give a monopoly and this can lead to obvious abuse. However, there are provisions in domestic UK patent law and in European Community law to control abuse. The Patents Act 1977 s 48 allows any person to apply for a compulsory licence to work the patent after three years of the patent being granted, on the basis of specified grounds, for example when the demand for the product is not being met on reasonable terms. Article 85 of the Treaty of Rome[35] controls restrictive trade practices and Article 86 prohibits the abuse of a dominant position within the European Community where either affects or is likely to affect trade between member states. There seems to be an irreconcilable conflict between the basic monopoly concept of a patent and Article 86. However, European Community law recognises the existence and utility of patents and does not prevent dominant trading situations developing, it only controls abuse of such dominant positions where this affects trade between member states.

Another way in which the owner of an intellectual property right can abuse his position is to threaten potential competitors with legal action. In some cases the threats may be groundless, but the victim might be prepared to cease the relevant activities or pay a royalty rather than risk the court action and its attendant costs. Litigation can be very expensive, and this may deter the person threatened from challenging the validity of the right concerned or otherwise defending the alleged infringement. Patent law, design law and trade mark law contain remedies for groundless threats of infringement proceedings[36] and it is an offence falsely to represent that a trade mark is registered.[37] There is no control over groundless threats of infringement proceedings with respect to an alleged copyright infringement. Bearing in mind the commercial importance of copyright and the possibility of legal tactics by dominant companies to control the market, this seems a serious omission. However, the tort of malicious falsehood (trade libel) might be available in limited cases to provide a remedy.[38]

## European and international considerations

Intellectual property law has long been set upon an international stage, and therefore it is not surprising that the UK's membership of the European Community has had a great influence on copyright, patents, trade marks and the like. Three particular issues mark the impact of the European Community on intellectual property law:

1  the drive towards greater harmonisation of the laws of individual member states;
2  the move to Community-wide intellectual property rights;
3  the impact of the Treaty of Rome on the use and abuse of intellectual property rights.

---

**35** Establishing the European Economic Community, now referred to as the EC Treaty.

**36** The Patents Act 1977 s 70, the Registered Designs Act 1949 s 26, the Copyright, Designs and Patents Act 1988 s 253 and the Trade Marks Act 1994 s 21.

**37** Ibid s 95. There is an equivalent provision for registered designs, the Registered Designs Act 1949 s 35. There are offences as regards false representations in respect of patents; the Patents Act 1977 ss 110 and 111.

**38** *See* Chapter 20.

Each of these aspects is discussed in the context of individual intellectual property rights in the relevant parts of the book. However, a brief overview of basic principles is given below.

### Harmonisation

Trade between member states is facilitated if the intellectual property rights implemented in each member state are alike. The process of harmonisation of national laws in the field of intellectual property has been proceeding for some time and has not been restricted than the European Community. Harmonisation of patent law was effected through the European Patent Convention which has a larger membership than that of the European Community. United Kingdom patent law was changed on 1 June 1978 as a result of this Convention.[39] European Community Directives have been instrumental in changing domestic laws protecting computer programs, semiconductor products, databases and trade marks. Other changes have been made to copyright law and rights in performances. European Community regulations have also had an impact on domestic intellectual property laws.

### Community-wide rights

It would be ideal if identical intellectual property rights were recognised and given effect throughout the European Community. Work has been done towards this goal in respect of patent law and trade mark law. A Community Patent Convention was produced in 1975.[40] The Community patent differs from a patent under the European Patent Convention in that the Community patent system will be a unitary system, granting patents that will take effect throughout the Community, whereas a grant obtained under the European Patent Convention gives a bundle of national patents. The Community patent will be administered by the European Patent Office. The Patents Act 1977 contains the necessary mechanism for recognition of the Community patent.[41]

A Community-wide trade mark system, the CTM, is now underway. A Community Trade Mark Office was established at Alicante in Spain, which started taking applications on 1 January 1996. However, there may be some problems as similar trade marks may be registered and used in different countries by different proprietors and reconciling these conflicts will prove difficult. There is the added difficulty of the impact of the law of passing off in the UK and other similar laws, such as the law of unfair competition in Germany. It is likely that only new and non-conflicting marks can be accepted as Community trade marks.

### Conflicts with the Treaty of Rome   *Read through don't understand*

The control of abuses of intellectual property rights by provisions in the Treaty of Rome has been noted previously. Those provisions are: Articles 30–36 which promote the free movement of goods, Article 85 which prohibits restrictive trade practices and Article 86 which is designed to prevent the abuse of a dominant market position.[42] It must be stressed that these controls are relevant only if trade between member states is affected or is likely to be affected. By their very nature, the rights given by intellectual property law can easily offend

39 The date that the Patents Act 1977 came into force.

40 Convention for the European Patent for the Common Market (Community Patent Convention), (76/76/EEC), OJ, L401, 30.12.89, p.1.

41 The Patents Act 1977 ss 86 and 87.

42 Article 6 (formerly Article 7 EEC) which prohibits discrimination on the grounds of nationality may also be relevant.

against the Treaty of Rome. For example, the proprietor of a patent will wish to exploit that patent to its best advantage, and to do this he may be selective about markets and persons to whom licences are granted and this may operate against the free movement of goods. However, Community law recognises the advantage of intellectual property law and is sufficiently realistic to appreciate the value of licensing arrangements and the like. Article 222 of the Treaty of Rome states that nothing in the Treaty shall prejudice the rules in member states governing the system of property ownership; and, as already mentioned, intellectual property is a form of property. Nevertheless, the worst abuses are struck down without hesitation by the Commission or the European Court of Justice and this has been sometimes controversial, as evidenced by opportunistic parallel importing and the doctrine of exhaustion of rights.[43]

**43** *See* Chapter 9 for an explanation of these terms.

## International aspects

On a wider international stage, it is worth mentioning briefly the importance of uniform laws and reciprocal protection. The vast majority of the world's developed nations play a role and are members of one or more of the various international conventions relating to intellectual property rights. Several of these conventions are administered by the World Intellectual Property Organization (WIPO), which is part of the United Nations. One of the most important and earliest conventions is the Paris Convention for the Protection of Industrial Property 1883, to which there are currently 114 signatories, including the UK. This convention, which is updated and amended occasionally (last revision in 1979), applies to inventions, trade marks, industrial designs, indications of origin and unfair competition. It establishes basic principles for laws in individual countries and reciprocal protection, and also priority rights in respect of patents, trade marks and industrial designs. The WIPO also administers, *inter alia*, the Berne Copyright Convention and the Madrid Agreement which concerns the international registration of trade marks. The UK has recently ratified a protocol to this latter agreement. Another important convention on copyright law is the Universal Copyright Convention. Most countries belong to one of the copyright conventions and in excess of 80 countries are members of the Patent Co-operation Treaty which provides a streamlined method of obtaining a patent internationally.[44]

**44** The membership of this Treaty has increased rapidly over the last few years.

The Uruguay Round of the GATT (General Agreement on Tariffs and Trade) was concluded on 15 December 1993 with a series of agreements including the TRIPs Agreement (Trade Related Aspects of Intellectual Property Rights), now administered by the WTO (World Trade Organization). The TRIPs Agreement lays down minimum standards of protection for intellectual property on the basis that adequate and effective protection must be given in such a way that the enforcement of intellectual property rights does not create barriers to legitimate trade. There is an obligation on members to comply with certain parts of the Paris Convention for the Protection of Industrial Property, the Berne Copyright Convention, the Rome Convention for the Protection of Performers, Producers of Phonograms and Broadcasting Organizations and the Washington Treaty on Intellectual Property in Respect of Integrated Circuits. Part II of the Agreement sets out the standards relating to copyright and related rights, trade marks, geographical indications of origin, industrial design, patents, layout designs of integrated circuits, protection of undisclosed information and the control of anti-competitive practices in contractual licences. There are also measures dealing with enforcement and the resolution of disputes, for example, where a member considers a judicial decision affects its rights under the Agreement.

There are transitional provisions notable in that they grant a period of grace in respect of most of the provisions of the Agreement of four years to developing countries and ten years for the least developed countries. The Agreement came into force on 1 January 1995. TRIPs is, arguably, the most important international initiative in the field of intellectual property since the Paris Convention of 1883. Of course, much of United Kingdom law already complies, but there are differences. However, TRIPs is not of direct effect: *Lenzing AG's European Patent (UK)*.[45] In the United Kingdom, its effects: will be felt through EC legislation, though it has to be said that there are unlikely to be many changes to domestic law in Europe resulting from TRIPs. Members are permitted to grant more extensive protection than that set out in TRIPs provided that it does not conflict with the other provisions of TRIPs. The unregistered design right is an example of such more extensive protection. A submission that it was incompatible with the TRIPs agreement was unsuccessful in *Azrak-Hamway International Inc's Licence of Right*.[46]

45 [1997] RPC 245.

46 [1997] RPC 134.

## PRACTICAL CONSIDERATIONS

### Rationale and justification for intellectual property law

Various justifications have been put forward for the existence of intellectual property law and these have usually been set in the context of patents. A more detailed discussion of the justification for intellectual property rights is, therefore, contained in Chapter 12 concerning patent law. The basic reason for intellectual property is that a man should own what he produces, that is, what he brings into being. If what he produces can be taken from him, he is no better than a slave. Intellectual property is, therefore, the most basic form of property because a man uses nothing to produce it other than his mind.[47] It is claimed that investment should be stimulated by the presence and enforcement of strong laws that provide a framework ensuring that the publication of new works and the manufacture of new products will be profitable, assuming, of course, that they are sufficiently meritorious, useful and commercially attractive to attain a viable level of sales. If investment is stimulated this should lead to increased prosperity and employment, although these days, sadly, this new employment may be outside the UK. Another justification is that the existence of strong laws in this area encourages the publication and dissemination of information and widens the store of available knowledge. For example, details of patents are published and are available for public inspection. In due course, when the patent expires, anyone is free to make the product or use the process, as the case may be. This is ample vindication for offering a monopoly protection in the case of patents.

47 I am indebted to Professor Bryan Niblett for suggesting this simple but powerful reason.

Another reason is that a person who creates a work or has a good idea which he develops has a right, based partly on morality and partly on the concept of reward, to control the use and exploitation of it, and he should be able to prevent others from taking unfair advantage of his efforts. Why should others be able to save themselves all the time and effort required to create or invent the thing concerned? Surely, on this basis, the law should provide remedies against those who appropriate the ideas of others, and a person who has devoted time and effort to create something has a right to claim the thing as his own and also has a right to obtain some reward for all his work. The tendency in the UK has been to encourage innovation through economic incentives, but in other countries stress has been placed on moral aspects although there have been moves in the UK to afford rights to the creator independent from the ownership of the right.

Other considerations come into the study of the place of intellectual property law in modern society. Counterfeiting is a serious problem which should be attacked, not so much to protect the interests of legitimate traders but to protect society from being deceived into buying substandard goods. In some cases, safety is at issue, for example, where the counterfeit is a poorly made toy covered in a paint containing high levels of lead.

## Combination of intellectual property rights NOT IN WRITTEN NOTES

The lifespan of an invention or a work of copyright can comprise several different and distinct stages, and during these stages different intellectual property rights may afford protection to the invention or work. For example, an idea for an invention will be protected by the law of confidence until such time as a patent application is published. Once a patent has been granted in respect of the invention, patent law takes over. Other rights might be appropriate, such as the law of trade marks or passing off, if a mark or name is applied to the product. Intellectual property rights work together to provide legal protection throughout the life of the product until such time as all the rights have expired for one reason or another. Tables 1.4 and 1.5 give examples of how the various intellectual property rights work together to give continuity of protection.

Note that, in the first example, copyright protection might be all but exhausted because, under the Copyright, Designs and Patents Act 1988 s 47, documents submitted in a patent application are open to public inspection and may be copied (with the authority of the Comptroller of Patents, Designs and Trade Marks). Copyright still provides limited protection to these documents, for example if copied without such permission.

In the tables, solid lines represent the duration of the right, and a broken line signifies that the right still exists but in a weaker form.

## The nature of the study of intellectual property

Intellectual property law is a demanding subject, but this is compensated by being one of the most enjoyable and diverse of all substantive law areas. Many aspects of procedural law are also highly relevant. As much as any subject in the study of law, intellectual property law cuts across boundaries and makes the oft-imposed compartmentalisation of legal subjects seem awkward and inappropriate. A study of intellectual property law embraces property law (real and personal), contract law, tort, criminal law, commercial law, competition law, European Community law and evidence. An understanding of the subject is enhanced by a knowledge of the basic principles of equity, some legal philosophy and at least a superficial grasp of other disciplines such as economics, sociology and industrial history. A liking for, or sympathy with, science and technology is also helpful. A number of practitioners in the field of intellectual property, including members of the Chancery bar, solicitors, patent agents and trade mark agents, have science degrees in addition to law degrees, and this

**Table 1.4  The life of an invention**

| Stage in the life of an invention | Form of intellectual property right | | | | |
| --- | --- | --- | --- | --- | --- |
| | *Confidence* | *Copyright* | *Patent* | *Trade marks* | *Passing off* |
| The bare idea, in the inventor's mind only | *** | | | | |
| Discussion with friends and colleagues | Maintain air of confidence | | | | |
| Idea expressed in tangible form, e.g. in writing, on drawings, in a computer memory | | *** | | | |
| Preliminary negotiations with potential manufacturers | Maintain air of confidence | | | | |
| Patent application (assumed successful) | Only in respect of things not disclosed in the patent application | | *** From priority date | | |
| Further negotiations with potential manufacturers | | | | | |
| Put invention into production and sell articles made to it | | | | *** If applied for | |
| Establish a reputation associated with the product | | | | | *** |
| | | Protected for author's life plus 70 years | Up to a maximum of 20 years | For as long as renewed | For as long as reputation associated with article |

*** Signifies the commencement of the right.

**Table 1.5  The life of a play**

| The life of a play | Form of intellectual property right | | | |
|---|---|---|---|---|
| | | Copyright | | |
| | Confidence | Dramatic work | Typographical arrangement | Rights in performance |
| The bare idea for the play in the playwright's mind only | *** | | | |
| Preliminary negotiations with potential publishers | Maintain air of confidence | | | |
| Play is recorded by writing, typing or using word processor, for example | | *** | | |
| Further negotiations with potential publishers | Maintain air of confidence | | | |
| Publish play | Ideas now in public domain | | *** | |
| Performance of play made in public | | | | *** |
| | | Dramatic works protected for author's life plus 70 years | For 25 years from end of year of first publication | For 50 years from end of year of performance |

*** Signifies the commencement of the right.

*Note:* rights in performance are for the benefit of the performers and any person with whom they have a recording contract.

dual educational background can be very much an advantage in the practice of intellectual property law. A command of one or more foreign languages may also be useful. As the demand for specialists in this area of law is high and the number of graduates emerging from educational establishments who have received formal teaching in the subject is still relatively low, though growing rapidly, intellectual property is a good area in which to pursue a career.

## COMMERCIAL EXPLOITATION OF INTELLECTUAL PROPERTY

Intellectual property is a valuable asset which may be exploited in a number of ways. It may be assigned, whereby the ownership in the whole or part of the right is transferred, or licences may be granted in respect of it. As with assignments, licences may be in respect of the whole or part of the right. For example, the owner of the copyright in a dramatic work might grant a licence to a number of theatre companies to perform the work in public for five years, each company being restricted geographically in terms of where it might make the performance.

Licences may be exclusive or non-exclusive. An exclusive licence grants the rights governed by the licence to the licensee who can perform those rights to the exclusion of everyone else including the owner. For example, the proprietor of a patent may grant an exclusive 'world-wide' licence to a manufacturer to work the invention. A non-exclusive licence is appropriate where the owner of the intellectual property right wishes to grant licences to numerous licensees, a good example being in the case of computer software.[48] Sometimes a sole licence is appropriate. This grants permission to perform the particular acts to only one licensee but, unlike the exclusive licence, the owner retains the right to perform the acts himself.

Other forms of exploiting intellectual property include using it as security for loan, such as by way of a mortgage or other charge. Alternatively, it may be acquired as an investment, by paying a capital sum in return for an assignment, the person acquiring it will hope to receive income from it over a number of years by granting licences. In 1996, Enid Blyton's copyrights were sold for £13 million.[49]

It has already been pointed out in this chapter that intellectual property rights are very diverse in nature. Some are informal and arise automatically whilst others can only be acquired by applying for registration. This distinction leads to some persons collectively describing the informal intellectual property rights as 'soft IP' and those subject to registration as 'hard IP'.

It is important to note that even in the case of soft IP, certain formalities must be adhered to in many cases to make the transaction effective at law. For example, in the case of an assignment of copyright, it must be in writing and be signed by or on behalf of the person making the assignment, the assignor.[50] An exclusive licence in respect of a copyright must be in writing signed by or on behalf of the copyright owner.[51]

Most types of transactions involving hard IP must also conform to certain statutory requirements. For example, an assignment of a patent is void unless it is in writing and signed by or on behalf of both of the parties to the assignment.[52] An assignment of a registered trade mark is not effective unless it is in writing signed by or on behalf of the assignor.[53] To be effective, a licence to use a registered trade mark, whether exclusive, non-exclusive or a sub-licence, must be in writing signed by or on behalf of the grantor.[54] It may take some time before the patent is granted or the trade mark is registered and it is possible to deal with the application for a patent or to register a trade mark and similar formalities apply to applications as well as the granted rights.

A further requirement exists with hard IP. Not only must the fact of registration appear on the appropriate register, but most forms of transactions concerning the right must also be notified and placed on the register. Copies of

48 In some cases, the licensee of computer software may require an exclusive licence or even an assignment such as where the software has been written for his specific requirements.

49 *The Times*, 24 January 1996. Enid Blyton died in 1968 and her copyrights will endure until the end of the year 2038.

50 Copyright, Designs and Patents Act 1988 s 90(3).

51 Copyright, Designs and Patents Act s 92(1).

52 Patents Act 1977 s 30(6).

53 Trade Marks Act 1994 s 24(3).

54 Trade Marks Act 1994 s 28(2). References in the Act include sub-licences, s 28(4).

register entries are available to the public on payment of a fee and it is important that the register accurately reflects the fact of proprietorship and what rights have been granted in or under the particular intellectual property. For example, in the case of a patent, the register will include information relating to the proprietor of the patent and, where appropriate, transactions affecting rights in or under the patent such as assignments, the grant or assignment of a licence, sub-licence or mortgage.[55]

Registration of a transaction will be made following application on the appropriate form. For example, for a registrable transaction concerning a patent,[56] Patents Form 21/77 must be used, and must be signed by both parties in the case of an assignment or by the mortgagor or grantor in respect of a mortgage, licence or security.[57] Similar provisions apply to trade marks and to registered designs.

Failure to register a registrable transaction may have serious consequences. There are a number of statutory provisions that can fairly be said to have as one of their main purposes the encouragement of the registration of transactions involving hard IP. A person who takes the right under a transaction may acquire the title to the intellectual property as against someone claiming under an earlier transaction if that earlier transaction had not, at the time of the later one, been registered and the person taking under the later transaction did not know of the earlier one.[58]

A defendant in an infringement action in respect of a patent or trade mark will be able to set up a failure to register a relevant transaction as a partial defence so as to negate the remedies of damages or an account of profits. For example, in respect of a patent, damages and accounts are not be available unless the relevant and registrable transaction, instrument or event was registered within six months or, if it was not practicable to register within six months,[59] it was registered as soon as practicable thereafter.[60] This has been described by Jacob J as being designed to encourage the registration of transactions rather than providing an infringer with a fortuitous defence.[61]

## IP in acquisitions and mergers

Often intellectual property will be acquired as part of a transaction which includes all manner of other property. For example, some or all of the assets of a company may be acquired, the assets comprising tangible property such as premises, plant and equipment in addition to intangible property such as intellectual property. Some of the intellectual property is likely to be soft IP such as copyright in engineering drawings and software, whilst other rights might be in relation to hard IP such as patents, registered designs and trade marks. Many of the points discussed below also apply in the case of mergers and de-mergers.

The organisation making the acquisition is likely to have a number of questions in respect of the various intellectual property rights (IPR). These questions will include:

- what the IPR are and how long will they endure, assuming hard IPs are renewed to the maximum extent, and what is their territorial scope;
- whether the IPR are owned outright or jointly;

55 Patents Act 1977 s 32.

56 Registrable transactions, instruments and events are set out in the Patents Act 1977 s 33(3).

57 Patents Rules 1995 r 46.

58 Patents Act 1977 s 33(1), Trade Marks Act 1994 s 25(3).

59 The court or Comptroller of Patents would have to be satisfied that it was not practicable to register within six months.

60 Patents Act 1977 s 68.

61 *Coflexip Stena Offshore Ltd's Patent* [1997] RPC 179.

- whether any IPR is licensed in (that is, whether they were being exploited under a licence granted by a third party to the company now selling its assets) and, if so, what the scope of the licence is;
- whether any IPR is licensed out (that is, the company now selling its assets granted a licence to a third party enabling it to exploit the IPR) and, if so, what the scope of the licence is;
- whether all registrable transactions were registered in a timely manner, and whether there are any other transactions affecting the IPR;
- whether all renewal fees in respect of hard IPR have been paid on time;
- whether the IPR have been infringed and, if so, what the outcome was;
- whether there have been any instances where the IPR have infringed or have been alleged to infringe IPR belonging to third parties;
- how much the IPR are worth.

These questions can be answered, at least to some extent, by carrying out an audit. This will involve obtaining up-to-date register entries in respect of hard IP, and asking for some evidence of the date of creation of important soft IP. For example, the company may have carried out a policy of depositing copies of its engineering drawings with an independent third party such as the Stationers' Company. Assignments will be scrutinised for form and validity. Licence agreements will be inspected as well as records of royalty payments. In some respects, the organisation acquiring the intellectual property will have to rely on the company now divesting itself of its assets. It will be sensible in such circumstances for the agreement for the transfer of assets to include appropriate warranties, for example, a warranty that a trade mark has been renewed when due and has been in continuous use.[62]

Some information may require more significant detective work such as determining the history of the IPR as regards litigation, or steps taken preliminary to litigation which did not or has not come to fruition. Another problem may be the existence of equitable rights in relation to the IPR. These are not generally registrable in the case of hard IP[63] and, for all forms of IPR, may arise without any written agreement. In other cases, there may be some written agreement which does not comply with the requirements as to form. There may also be an implied licence which is not supported by any direct documentary evidence. Again, the inclusion of warranties in the agreement to transfer the IPR may help, but is no substitute for actual knowledge of all the rights and interests that might affect the value or exploitation of the IPR. The investigative work which is performed to verify and assess the nature, scope and value of IPR is often referred to as 'due diligence'.

It is not unusual for a contract under which IPR are to be transferred to take effect as an agreement to assign the IPR, the formal assignments of the IPR being executed subsequently. If this is the case, the contract should include a term to the effect that the assignor will do everything necessary, including executing the required agreements and completing and submitting the necessary application forms, to give effect to any assignments or other transactions covered by the agreement and ensure their registration.

Assignments of IPR attract stamp duty, currently payable at 1 per cent where the consideration is £60 000 or over.[64] Stamp duty will also be payable on exclusive licences granted for the duration of the right and without provision for

62 If a trade mark has not been put to genuine use in the United Kingdom during the first five years following completion of the registration procedure, or if such use has been suspended for an uninterrupted period of five years, it will be susceptible to revocation, Trade Marks Act 1994 s 46(1).

63 For example, the Trade Marks Act 1994 states that no notice of any trust (express, implied or constructive) shall be entered in the register, s 26(1).

64 There are some savings in respect of Community patents and European patents, see the Patents Act 1977 s 126.

65 If, of course, it is for £60 000 or more.

earlier termination as these are considered to be equivalent in effect to an assignment by the Inland Revenue. Where, for example, a patent has been assigned, the Comptroller of Patents will only register the assignment if it is stamped.[65] Bearing in mind that the initial contract may operate as an agreement to transfer, it is essential that there is a subsequent assignment which is then stamped and submitted to the Comptroller for registration. Failure to do so could result in damages or an account of profits not being available against an infringer as a result of the operation of s 68 of the Patents Act 1977 or, perhaps worse still, the transaction being ineffective as against a third party taking under a later assignment.

66 [1997] RPC 179.

The dangers for persons acquiring patents by assignment associated with registration and stamp duty were highlighted in *Coflexip Stena Offshore Ltd's Patent*.[66] A company agreed to assign to Coflexip Stena Offshore Ltd ('Stena') its assets concerning an offshore pipelaying business which included a ship, onshore facilities, permits, contracts, sales data, etc., as well as many patents, copyrights, designs and know-how. The agreed price was US$31.5m. Subsequently, Stena's patent agent drew up an assignment ('A1') which was signed by both parties and sent for registration to the Patent Office which returned it because it had not been stamped. The patent agent then suggested that the best way forward was to draw up a new assignment ('A2') which was executed, duly stamped in accordance with the Stamp Act 1891 and submitted to the Patent Office where it was entered on the register of patents during November 1992.

Stena brought infringement proceedings against a third party which applied for rectification of the register on the basis that A2 was a nullity and any reference to it should be removed from the register. It argued that A1 complied with the Patents Act 1977 in all respects and was effective to vest the patents in Stena. Therefore, in so far as A2 purported to do this, it was a nullity, as A1 had already conveyed the patent rights to Stena.

The significance of rectification was that the third party would be able to rely on the s 68 defence: that damages or accounts would not be available to Stena. However, the application for rectification was refused and A2 was left on the register. Section 14(4) of the Stamp Act 1891 states that an unstamped instrument shall not be given in evidence or be available for any purpose whatever, except in criminal proceedings. The court could not receive A1 in evidence (the first but unstamped assignment) and without it, it could not be proved that A2 was a nullity.

67 At the time of the assignment, the threshold for stamp duty was lower.

A problem for the patent agent was how to assess the value of the relevant patents for stamp duty purposes. He chose to use an alternative method which was based on the cost of obtaining the patents and this was set at £54 000, leaving stamp duty payable at £540.[67] This was challenged by the alleged infringer, which claimed that the figure should have been over £5 million. However, s 58(1) of the Stamp Act 1891, where property is agreed to be sold for one consideration but is conveyed in separate parts, allows the parties to apportion the consideration as they think fit. As long as the parties act *bona fide* there is no problem with this. In the above case, the business was losing money at the time of sale, and there were no prospective licensees. It was, therefore, impossible to value the patents on the basis of their market worth.

The Patent Office returns unstamped assignments, but apparently acts on such documents to the extent of noting the change of address for service. Section 17 of the Stamp Act 1891 imposes a fine of £10 on the Comptroller of Patents if he registers an unstamped document that is chargeable with duty.

## FRAMEWORK FOR DESCRIPTION OF RIGHTS

In this book, each of the various rights is described, examined and discussed within the following framework:

- overview and history
- nature of the right and its subsistence
- ownership of the right
- infringement of the right
- exceptions and defences
- remedies
- international aspects.

This framework is followed wherever possible, although it has been modified for some of the rights. Because of the nature of these rights, it is usual to speak of infringement rather than breach. You infringe a right, but breach a duty. Breach is suggestive of a pre-existing contractual or tortious duty owed by and to specific persons (though infringing copyright is a tort). Therefore, a person *infringes* a copyright, a patent or a trade mark, he is *not* in breach of copyright, etc. However, many judges talk in terms of breach of copyright and, strictly speaking, this is just as valid an expression. With passing off, it is usual to say that a person has committed the tort of passing off or is guilty of passing off. Breach of confidence is the usual phrase, though it should be noted that this is not a tort as such, as an obligation of confidence is a creature of equity.

*Part Two*

# COPYRIGHT

**(including rights in performances)**

# 2

## Background and basic principles

### WHAT IS COPYRIGHT?

Copyright is a property right that subsists in certain specified types of works as provided for by the Copyright, Designs and Patents Act 1988. Examples of the works in which copyright subsists are original literary works, films and sound recordings. The owner of the copyright subsisting in a work has the exclusive right to do certain acts in relation to the work, such as making a copy, broadcasting or selling copies to the public. These are examples of the acts restricted by copyright. The owner of the copyright can control the exploitation of the work, for example, by making or selling copies to the public or by granting permission to another to do this in return for a payment. A common example is where the owner of the copyright in a work of literature permits a publishing company to print and sell copies of the work in book form in return for royalty payments, usually an agreed percentage of the price the publisher obtains for the books.

If a person performs one of the acts restricted by copyright without the permission or licence of the copyright owner, the latter can sue for infringement of his copyright and obtain remedies, for example, damages and an injunction. However, there are limits and certain closely drawn exceptions are available, such as fair dealing with the work. An example would be where a person makes a single copy of a few pages of a book for the purpose of private study. Other acts may be carried out in relation to the work if they are not restricted by the copyright, for example, borrowing a recording of music to listen to in private.

A broad classification can be made between the various types of copyright work. Some, such as literary, dramatic, musical and artistic works, are required to be original. As will be seen later, this is easily satisfied and the work in question need not be unique in any particular way. Other works such as films, sound recordings, broadcasts, cable programmes and typographical arrangements can be described as derivative or entrepreneurial works and there is no requirement for originality; for example, repeat broadcasts each attract their own copyright.[1] Copyright extends beyond mere literal copying and covers acts such as making a translation of a literary work, performing a work in public and other acts relating to technological developments, such as broadcasting the work or storing it in a computer.

Fundamentally and conceptually, copyright law should not give rise to monopolies, and it is permissible for any person to produce a work which is similar to a pre-existing work as long as the later work is not taken from the first. It is theoretically possible, if unlikely, for two persons independently to produce identical works, and each will be considered to be the author of his work for copyright purposes. For example, two photographers may each take a

1 Under previous copyright legislation, original works were described as Part I works and derivative works were described as Part II works (*see* the Copyright Act 1956). The copyright in a repeat broadcast expires at the same time as the copyright in the original broadcast; the Copyright, Designs and Patents Act 1988 s 14(2).

29

photograph of Nelson's Column within minutes of each other from the same spot using similar cameras, lenses and films, after selecting the same exposure times and aperture settings. The two photographs might be indistinguishable from each other but copyright will, nevertheless, subsist in both photographs, separately. The logical reason for this situation is that both of the photographers have used skill and judgment independently in taking their photographs and both should be able to prevent other persons from printing copies of their respective photographs.

Another feature of copyright law which limits its potency is that it does not protect ideas, it merely protects the expression of an idea. Barbara Cartland does not have a monopoly in romantic novels. Anyone else is free to write a romantic novel, since the concept of a romantic novel is an idea and not protected by copyright. However, writing a romantic novel by taking parts of a Barbara Cartland novel infringes copyright, because the actual novel is the expression of the idea. Just how far back one can go from the expression as formulated in a novel to the ideas underlying the novel is not easy to answer. If a person gleans the detailed plot of a novel and then writes a novel based on that detailed plot, there is an argument that there has been an infringement of copyright even though the text of the original novel has not been referred to further or copied during the process of writing the second novel.[2] A detailed plot, including settings, incidents and the sequence of events can be described as a non-literal form of expression. However, the boundary between idea and expression is notoriously difficult to draw.[3] Suffice it to say at this stage that judges have been reluctant to sympathise with a defendant who has taken a short cut to producing his work by making an unfair use of the plaintiff's work, especially when the two works are likely to compete.

Copyright is also restricted in its lifespan; it is of limited duration, although it must be said that copyright law is rather generous in this respect. For example, copyright in a literary work endures until the end of the period of 70 years from the end of the calendar year in which the author dies.[4] Approximately, therefore, copyright lasts for the life of the author plus 70 years.[5] This temporal generosity can be justified on the basis that copyright law does not lock away the ideas underlying a work.

Ownership of the copyright in a work will often remain with the author of the work, the author being the person who created it or made the arrangements necessary for its creation, depending on the nature of the work. However, if a literary, dramatic, musical or artistic work is created by an employee working during the course of employment, his employer will own the copyright subject to agreement to the contrary. Additionally, copyright, like other forms of property, can be dealt with; it may be assigned; it may pass under a will or intestacy or operation of law, and licences may be granted in respect of it.

Full acknowledgement of moral rights is a relatively recent concept in UK copyright law, though well established in other European countries reflecting differences in the historical development and conceptual foundations of copyright between the UK and continental Europe.[6] These moral rights, such as the right to be recognised as the author of a work and the right to object to a derogatory treatment of the work, remain with the author irrespective of subsequent ownership and dealings with the ownership of the copyright. They recognise the creator's contribution, a way of giving legal effect to the fact that the act of

2 *Corelli* v *Gray* [1913] TLR 570.

3 For example in *Nichols* v *Universal Pictures Corporation* (1930) 45 F 2d 119 the eminent US judge Learned Hand said of the boundary between idea and expression 'Nobody has ever been able to fix that boundary, and nobody ever can' (at 121).

4 This was recently increased from life plus 50 years.

5 For some types of works, the period is 50 years or 25 years.

6 For a discussion of the continental tradition of moral rights, *see* Cornish, W.R. 'Authors in Law' (1995) 58 MLR 1 at 8.

producing a work is an act of creation and that the creator has a link or bond with the work which should be preserved regardless of hard economic considerations. The tort of defamation has, of course, long been available and could provide remedies if an author's work were to be distorted or if a work was falsely attributed to someone, depending on the circumstances, for example, if a dreadful musical composition was falsely attributed to a famous and brilliant composer. But the difficulties of suing in defamation and the attendant expense and uncertainty are good reasons for the author–work nexus to be specifically recognised and enforceable in copyright law.[7] However, just how straightforward the enforcement of moral rights is remains to be seen.[8]

Copyright law adopts a very practical posture and takes under its umbrella many types of works which lack literary or artistic merit and may or may not have commercial importance. Thus, everyday and commonplace items, such as lists of customers, football coupons, drawings for engineering equipment, tables of figures, a personal letter and even a shopping list, can fall within the scope of copyright law.[9] One important reason for this is that such works are likely to be of economic value and usually will be the result of investment and a significant amount of work. Without protection there are many who would freely copy such things without having to take the trouble to create them for themselves and who would be able, as a consequence, to sell the copied items more cheaply than the person who developed or produced the original. If this were to happen, the incentive for investment would be severely limited. Neither is copyright generally concerned with the quality or merit of a work, the rationale being that it would be unacceptable for judges to become arbiters of artistic or literary taste or fashion. Copyright implicitly accepts that tastes differ between people and over a period of time. If the converse were true, many avant garde works would be without protection from unauthorised copying and exploitation.

The pace of technological development over the twentieth century has been unprecedented, but here too, copyright law has striven to keep pace and the current legislation, the Copyright, Designs and Patents Act 1988, has attempted to provide a framework which will be resilient to future changes.[10] A recent example of copyright being adapted to prevent the unfair use of works created by or associated with modern technology is the way that many countries have extended copyright expressly to include computer programs in the fold of copyright works.[11]

## BRIEF HISTORY

Dating back almost to the beginnings of civilization there have been those eager to profit from the work of others. In ancient times, the idea that the author of a work of literature had economic rights to control dissemination and copying was not particularly well established, and yet those who falsely claimed a work were considered contemptible. Most authors were primarily teachers, hence the emphasis on moral rights. The word 'plagiarist', meaning one who copies the work of another and passes it off as his own, is derived from the Latin 'plagiarius' meaning kidnapper. The problems of unauthorised copying of works produced by others stretch back into antiquity.

Copyright law has a relatively long history and its roots can be traced back to before the advent of printing technology, which permitted the printing of multiple

7 Legal aid is not available for defamation, but it may be for false attribution.

8 Although there have been cases on the false attribution right, *see Noah v Shuba* [1991] FSR 14.

9 The protection of design and engineering drawings by copyright law is considerably curtailed by the law of designs as a result of the Copyright, Designs and Patents Act 1988 s 51.

10 However, it has been amended a number of times.

11 For example, in the United Kingdom, the Copyright (Computer Software) Amendment Act 1985 (now repealed); in France, 1985 Law, Article 46 (Law No. 85–660 of 3 July 1985); in the Federal Republic of Germany, BGbl 1985 I 1137 amending the Copyright Law of 1965 and, in the United States, Pub. L. No. 96–517, 12 December 1980, 94 Stat 3028, amending the Copyright Act of 1976.

copies quickly and at relatively little expense. The first record of a copyright case was *Finnian v Columba*.[12] Statutes of the University of Paris in 1223 legalised duplication of texts for use within the university. However, two factors limited the importance of protecting literary works. Before the late fifteenth century, works of literature were mainly religious and were written by scholarly monks who would work painstakingly for considerable periods of time preparing their gloriously illuminated books. Obviously, because of the massive human labour and skill required to produce such works, plagiarism of books was not usually a viable consideration. Additionally, there was not a market for books due to the general illiteracy of the population at large. The religious books which were produced were made mainly for use within the monastery or within churches.

Two inventions in the late fifteenth century changed everything. It could be claimed that printing has had the greatest impact on civilization than any other single invention. Gutenberg invented moveable type, first used in 1455, and Caxton developed the printing press and published Chaucer's *Canterbury Tales* in 1478, the first 'best seller'. An Act of Richard III in 1483 encouraged the circulation of books from abroad. In 1518, the first printing privilege was issued to Richard Pynson, the Royal Printer, which prohibited the printing, for two years, of a speech by anyone else.[13] A copyright notice was appended to the speech.

Until the early sixteenth century, the art of printing was practised freely and England was quickly established as an important centre for printing in Europe.[14] But Henry VIII, desiring to restrict and control the printing of religious and political books, eventually banned the importation of books into England. By an Act of 1529, Henry VIII set up a system of privileges and printing came to be controlled by the Stationers' Company, originally a craft guild. With the backing of the infamous Court of Star Chamber, the government and the Stationers' Company maintained an élite group of printers and regulated publishing. Only registered members of the Stationers' Company could print books, the titles of which had to be entered on the Company's Register before publication. Members of the Company had the right to print their books in perpetuity and this right became known as 'copyright', the right to make copies. The Stationers' Company had powers to enable it to control printing and it could impose fines, award damages and confiscate infringing copies. Following the abolition of the Star Chamber by the Long Parliament in 1640, infringement of copyright was still subject to statutory penalties. For example, in 1649, a penalty of 6s 8d was imposed for reprinting registered books without permission. Eventually, after the lapse of this system, common law copyright was enforced in the Court of Common Pleas which soon recognised that copyright could be assigned.

The system of privileges, registration and control survived, going through phases of varying effectiveness and licensing systems, until its ultimate collapse in 1695; and, following a brief period when piracy of books flourished, the Statute of Anne was passed in 1709,[15] the first true copyright Act in the world. In the period leading up to the Act, many had argued that copyright was a property right

> just the same as houses and other estates and that existing copies [assignments of copyright] had cost at least £50 000, and had been used in marriage settlements and were the subsistence of many widows and orphans.[16]

It was said that Jonathan Swift, the author of *Gulliver's Travels*, who had himself suffered at the hands of copyright pirates, had a hand in drafting the Statute of Anne.

12 Incredibly, in the year 567 AD. Apparently, St. Columba surreptitiously made a copy of a Psalter in the possession of his teacher Finnian: *see* Bowker, R.R. (1912) *Copyright: Its History and its Law*, Houghton Mifflin, at p. 9.

13 Bowker, R.R. ibid at p. 19.

14 As were Germany, France, Venice and Florence.

15 8 Anne c. 19.

16 Bowker, R.R. (1912) *Copyright: Its History and its Law*, Houghton Mifflin, at p. 23.

The effect of widescale piracy of books was described in the Act, in words bordering on the emotional, as being 'to their [authors and proprietors of books and writings] very great Detriment and too often to the Ruin of them and their Families'. The importance of the law as a means of encouraging the dissemination of information was also recognised in the Preamble which described the Act as being for:

> ... the Encouragement of Learning by vesting the Copies of Printed Books in the Authors or Purchasers of such Copies ...

The Statute of Anne gave 14 years' sole right of printing to authors of new books (books already published by 1710 were given 21 years' protection). At the end of that period, the right returned to the author and, if still alive, he was granted an additional 14 years. Infringers were to pay a fine of one penny for every sheet of the infringing book, one moiety of which went to the author, the other to the Crown. By modern standards, this was a considerable fine. In addition, infringing books and parts of books were forfeit to the proprietor who 'shall forthwith damask and make waste paper of them'. A system of registration was still in place and an action could be brought only if the title had been entered in the register book at the Stationers' Company, before publication. The 'copy', by the Act, was the 'sole liberty of printing and reprinting' a book and this liberty could be infringed by any person who printed, reprinted or imported the book without consent. The Act was also the first clear acknowledgement of the legal right of authorship. The 1709 Act did not extend to certain universities and libraries, but some doubt about the scope and effectiveness of this was remedied by the Copyright Act of 1775[17] which gave a perpetual copyright to copies belonging to the Universities of Oxford and Cambridge and the Colleges of Eton, Westminster and Winchester. This survived until the Copyright, Designs and Patents Act 1988 which substituted a period of 50 years from the end of 1989, after which such rights expire.[18]

Later, there was some argument as to whether the author had, apart from statute, a perpetual common law right to print or publish his work (a right that could be assigned to a publisher in perpetuity). Soon after the expiry of the statutory term for previously published cases, there were challenges to the common law copyright. In *Millar v Taylor*[19] the Court of King's Bench held that a perpetual common law copyright existed independent of any statute. That case concerned the copyright to Thomson's *The Seasons* published in four parts from 1726 to 1730.[20] Thomson died in 1748 and his copyright was sold by his executors to Beckett who took legal action against Donaldson, obtaining a permanent injunction from the Lord Chancellor. However, the case was appealed to the House of Lords and was heard before 11 Law Lords. In *Donaldson v Beckett*,[21] it was held that the author did have common law rights that were potentially perpetual (that is, the right of first printing and publishing), but once the work was published, this common law right was extinguished and the author's rights were to be determined solely from the Statute of Anne 1709. On the latter point, the decision was a majority decision of 6:5; a narrow victory that has not gone uncriticised since. For example, Drone points out that many jurists consider that:

> intellectual productions constitute a species of property founded in natural law, recognised by the common law, and neither lost by publication nor taken away by legislation.[22]

**17** 15 Geo. III c.53.

**18** The Copyright, Designs and Patents Act 1988 Sch 1, para 13. The Whitford Committee found that the universities and colleges concerned were not overly anxious to retain perpetual copyright. *Copyright and Design Law*, Cmnd 6732, HMSO, 1977.

**19** (1769) 4 Burr 2303.

**20** James Thomson was a Scottish poet.

**21** (1774) 2 Bro PC 129.

**22** Drone, E.S. (1879) *A Treatise on the Law of Property in Intellectual Productions in Great Britain and the United States*, Little, Brown & Co.

The Statute of Anne was copied by the United States Congress in 1790 and *Donaldson* v *Beckett* followed in the Supreme Court in *Wheaton* v *Peters*.[23] Hence the similarity between the copyright laws of the UK and the USA.

    The scope of copyright was gradually increased to include other works, such as engravings and prints in 1734–35, lithographs in 1734, sculptures in 1798, dramatic works in 1833 and musical works in 1882.[24] Moves were also made to extend the term of copyright, though these changes did not go unchallenged; for example, the historian Macaulay described copyright as 'a tax on readers for the purpose of giving bounty to writers'.[25] In the meantime, it was becoming recognised that copyright was important in an international context, and the Berne Copyright Convention was formulated in 1886 with the purposes of promoting greater uniformity in copyright law and giving copyright owners full protection in all member states. Reciprocal protection was based on the place of publication and not by reference to the nationality of the author. The Berne Convention was remarkable in that it successfully reconciled the fundamentally different nature of UK copyright law with the French tradition of *droit d'auteur*.[26] In the Berlin revision of 1908 (the Berlin Act), *inter alia*, the term of copyright protection was increased to the life of the author plus 50 years and copyright was extended to cover choreographic works, works of architecture and sound recordings. The revision also introduced the compulsory licence and removed formalities (works still had to be registered in the UK). Major changes to UK copyright law were introduced by the Copyright Act of 1911, heavily influenced by the Berlin revision. The 1911 Act formed the basis of copyright law throughout the British Empire and accounts for similarities in copyright law between the UK and countries such as Australia, New Zealand and South Africa.

    Since the Berne Convention and subsequent revisions (and the later Universal Copyright Convention, first promulgated in 1952), the impetus for change in copyright law has been largely the result of the Conventions[27] rather than internal national considerations. The 1911 Act was replaced in the UK by the Copyright Act 1956, which added three new forms of works: cinematograph films, broadcasts and the typographical arrangement of published editions. The Performing Right Tribunal was created.[28] The 1956 Act classified works as being either original works (Part I works – literary, dramatic, musical and artistic works) or Part II works, sometimes known as derivative works or entrepreneurial works (namely, sound recordings, cinematograph films, broadcasts and the typographical arrangement of published editions). These works could be described as derivative as they were usually based on a Part I work. For example, a sound recording may be made of the live performance of a musical work. The link was not essential and a Part II work could be subject to copyright protection without an equivalent Part I work, for example, a sound recording of a bird singing could qualify for copyright protection.

    Finally, in response to major technological developments, the current Act, the Copyright, Designs and Patents Act 1988, was passed. This Act takes due account of *moral rights,* inalienable rights which belong to the author irrespective of the ownership of copyright.[29] These are equivalent to the *droit moral* of the Rome Act of 1928 of the Berne Convention; that is a right to claim authorship of a work and the right to object to any distortion, mutilation or other modification of a work which could be prejudicial to the honour and reputation of the author.[30] This also has the effect of pulling English copyright law closer to that subsisting in most other European countries.

23 (1834) 8 Pet 591.

24 Musical works were protected earlier though the form of protection was unsatisfactory.

25 Hansard, HC Deb vol. 56 (5 February 1841). However, he was not arguing for the abolition of copyright, merely against extending it beyond the author's life.

26 Authors' rights.

27 And, more recently, the European Community.

28 Now replaced by the Copyright Tribunal.

29 With the exception of the *droit de suite*, the author's right to payment on subsequent sale of his work of art or manuscript; Berne Convention, Article 14ᵗᵉʳ.

30 Article 6ᵇⁱˢ of the Berne Convention.

## COPYRIGHT AND ITS RELATIONSHIP TO OTHER INTELLECTUAL PROPERTY RIGHTS

Like other intellectual property rights, copyright does not stand in splendid isolation. The unfair taking or use of the results of the application of human intellect may infringe more than any one single right. An act giving rise to infringement of copyright may be associated with or accompany a breach of confidence. For example, if an employee copies a confidential report belonging to his employer without permission and then passes on the copy to a competitor of the employer, there will be an infringement of copyright by the act of making a copy without permission and a serious breach of confidence by the employee giving the copy to the competitor, and also by the latter if he realises or ought to realise that the report is confidential. Additionally, the employee will be in breach of his contract of employment. The action taken by his employer may depend on the remedies available and, in the example quoted, it is likely that the employer would dismiss the employee (for being in breach of the contract of employment) and an injunction would be sought (for breach of confidence) against the competitor restraining him from using the information and from divulging it further. It is unlikely that there would be much to be gained by suing the employee for infringement of copyright, although this could be a case where 'additional damages' might be appropriate (*see* Chapter 6).

Generally, things that fall within the ambit of copyright law are excluded from the grant of a patent,[31] but preliminary materials such as plans, sketches, specifications, and the like, will be protected, in principle, by copyright. That is, copyright will subsist in each of these items irrespective of any patent granted for the invention with which the items are concerned. However, there are two limitations to this, the first being where the details of the invention represented in drawings fall within the scope of design law[32] and second, copies may be made of patent applications (including the specification) by permission of the Comptroller of Patents, Designs and Trade Marks without infringing copyright.[33] Ideas for a new invention, while outside the scope of copyright until such time as they are given some tangible form of expression, will be the subject matter of the law of confidence. There is also a close relationship between copyright and the law of designs, and many articles that are subject to design law will have been prepared from drawings and written specifications. However, any potential overlap between design law and copyright is expressly removed by the Copyright, Designs and Patents Act 1988.[34]

Sometimes, different rights may be relevant at different times during the life of a work. For example, if a musician has an idea for a piece of music, that idea will be protected by the law of confidence, unless it is already in the public domain. When the music is written down, it will be protected by copyright both before and after publication. After publication, of course, confidentiality will be lost. Live performances of the music will be protected under the Copyright, Designs and Patents Act 1988 Part II which deals with rights in performances (replacing the Performers' Protection Act 1963) and any recordings made will be protected as sound recordings. If a copy is made of a record, cassette tape or compact disc of the music, the copyright both in the sound recording and the original music will be infringed. If the music is a song, the lyrics will be independently protected as a literary work. Thus, it can be seen that a single item

31  The Patents Act 1977 s 1(2). But *see* Chapter 13 for instances when a computer program (which is a literary work under copyright law) can indirectly achieve patent protection.

32  Indirect copying of a drawing of a design by making the article represented does not infringe the copyright in the drawing: the Copyright, Designs and Patents Act 1988 s 51(1).

33  Ibid s 47.

34  With respect to the unregistered design right, *see* ibid s 236. By the Registered Designs Act 1949 s 1(5) (as amended) the Secretary of State may make rules excluding from registration articles of a primarily literary or artistic character (*see* the Registered Designs Rules 1995, SI 1995/2912, r 26).

may be subject to several copyrights. This is essential as different interests may be involved. For example, in the case of a song, the music may have been written by one person, the lyrics by another. The recording company will also require direct protection of the sound recording so that it may take action against anyone making duplicates of the recordings. The performer and, if recorded live, the recording company, also require protection against persons making unauthorised 'bootleg' recordings of the live performance.

## COPYRIGHT AS A MEANS OF EXPLOITING A WORK

Copyright provides a very useful and effective way of exploiting a work economically. It provides a mechanism for allocation of risks and income derived from the sale of the work. For example, if a poet compiles an anthology of poems, this will be protected as a literary work even if unpublished. Copyright provides remedies in respect of published and unpublished works. If an unpublished work is copied and sold by someone without the permission of the copyright owner, remedies such as damages, additional damages, accounts of profits and injunctions are available depending on the circumstances. They are, however, available only to the owner of the copyright or an exclusive licensee. A beneficial owner of the copyright cannot obtain damages or a perpetual injunction without joining the owner of the legal title to the copyright, although a beneficial owner may be able to obtain an interlocutory injunction on his own. If the poet in the example wants his anthology of poems published, he might decide to approach prospective publishers, and if one agrees to publish, the poet might grant an exclusive licence to the publisher allowing him to print and sell copies of the poems in book form. Alternatively, the poet might agree to assign the copyright to the publisher. In either case, the publisher usually takes the risk – he pays the cost of printing, binding, marketing and distributing. In return, the poet will be paid a royalty of, say, 10 per cent of the income obtained by the publisher on sales of the anthology.

An added attraction, in the case of an exclusive licence, for example, a licence granting the exclusive rights of publishing the work in the UK, is that the publisher has the right to sue for infringement, and if the publisher is successful, the poet will be entitled to a share of the damages awarded equivalent to his lost royalties attributable to the infringement.[35] Depending on the terms of the exclusive licence, the poet may be free to make agreements in respect of other modes of expression of the poems, such as a sound recording of the poems being recited by a famous actor. Of course, if the poet assigns the work to the publisher, the publisher will be entitled to sue for infringement as owner of the copyright and the assignment agreement will usually provide for a division of the damages awarded between the author and the publisher. For the author, a major attraction of the exclusive licence, or for that matter an assignment, to a publisher is that copyright actions tend to be fairly expensive and daunting for an individual to pursue, but a reputable publishing company will not hesitate in enforcing its rights under copyright law and, indirectly, the rights of the author.

A copyright can be considered to comprise a bundle of rights, associated with the acts restricted by the copyright. These are the acts that only the copyright owner is allowed to do or authorise. These acts include copying, issuing copies

35 By the Copyright, Designs and Patents Act 1988 s 102 neither the owner nor the exclusive licensee may proceed without the leave of the Court unless the other is joined in the action.

to the public, performing, playing or showing the work in public and broadcasting the work. These can be exploited separately and a copyright owner must be careful not to assign or grant more than necessary. For example, the owner of the copyright in a dramatic work might grant an exclusive right to publish the work in book form to a literary publisher. The owner may then later grant other rights to others, such as the right to perform the work on stage, or even the right to make it into a film. In this way, the income the owner derives from the work can be maximised.

# 3

## *Subsistence of copyright*

### INTRODUCTION

Fundamentally, copyright law exists to prevent others from taking unfair advantage of a person's creative efforts. The courts have displayed very little sympathy for plagiarists and frequently have demonstrated that copyright law ought to be interpreted in such a way as to protect the interests of the copyright owner. This approach is best summed up in the words of Peterson J in *University of London Press Ltd* v *University Tutorial Press Ltd*, where he said:

> ... there remains the rough practical test that what is worth copying is prima facie worth protecting.[1]

1 [1916] 2 Ch 601 at 610.

The Copyright, Designs and Patents Act 1988 is the legislative source of copyright law. This voluminous Act, comprising 306 sections and eight Schedules,[2] also deals with designs, rights in performances and has miscellaneous provisions concerning patent law and trade mark law. The copyright provisions of the Act came into force on 1 August 1989. Although some significant changes were made to copyright law by the Act, it was not intended to change fundamental copyright principles and much of the case law developed prior to the coming into force of the Act may still be used as an aid to the construction of the Act and for determining whether the previous law has been departed from.[3] Also, copyright provisions under the Act which correspond to provisions under the previous law are not to be taken to depart from previous law merely because of a change of expression.[4]

Some of the primary effects of the 1988 Act in terms of copyright law are that it:

2 In its original form. The Act has been amended on a number of occasions.

3 The Copyright, Designs and Patents Act 1988 s 172(3). Statutory references in this chapter are to the Copyright, Designs and Patents Act 1988 unless otherwise stated.

4 Ibid s 172(2).

1 takes account of new technology and it attempts to use definitions that will prove to be sufficiently flexible to take future technological developments in its stride;
2 provides more effectively for 'moral rights' for authors, in accordance with the Berne Copyright Convention;
3 removes some of the anomalies under the old law (for example, under the Copyright Act 1956, the author of the copyright in a photograph was the person who owned the film,[5] not the photographer);
4 attempts to rationalise design law and its overlap with copyright.

5 Copyright Act 1956 s 48(1).

Copyright can subsist only in specified descriptions of works. Section 1(1) lists the works in which copyright can subsist, subject to the qualification requirements (discussed later), as being:

(a) original literary, dramatic, musical or artistic works;
(b) sound recordings, films, broadcasts or cable programmes; and
(c) the typographical arrangement of published editions.

Each of these categories is now examined in detail below.

## ORIGINAL LITERARY, DRAMATIC, MUSICAL OR ARTISTIC WORKS

All of these must be original and must be 'works'. Over the course of time, the courts have attempted to develop tests for showing whether the subject matter is an original work. Apart from defining originality and searching for the threshold that brings the status of a 'work', judges have often engaged in more esoteric exercises, particularly in terms of differentiating between unprotectable idea or copyright expression. It should be noted at once that nowhere in the Act does it state expressly that ideas are not protected by copyright. However, by the Copyright, Designs and Patents Act 1988 s 296A(1)(c), lawful users of computer programs are permitted to gain access to ideas and principles which underlie any element of the program, and the EC Directive on the legal protection of computer programs expressly states that ideas and principles underlying any element of a computer program are not protected by copyright.[6]

Before looking at each of the original works separately, the basic issues relating to subsistence of copyright are discussed.

6  Article 1(2), OJ L122, 17.5.91, p. 42.

### Originality

One can be excused for believing that the word 'original' requires that the work must be new or innovative in some sense, but in copyright law 'original' does not have its ordinary dictionary meaning and the courts have interpreted the concept very loosely. The work does not have to be unique, or even particularly meritorious. Rather, originality is more concerned with the manner in which the work was created and is usually taken to require that the work in question originated from the author, its creator, and that it was not copied from another work. In *Ladbroke (Football) Ltd* v *William Hill (Football) Ltd*, Lord Pearce said that the word original requires:

7  [1964] 1 WLR 273 at 291.

... only that the work should not be copied but should originate from the author.[7]

A drawing of an existing object may not be original because the design of the object was not created by the act of drawing. Harman J came to this conclusion in *The Duriron Company Inc* v *Hugh Jennings & Co Ltd*[8] in the context of an inaccurate drawing of an existing design of an anode, described as being of the most jejune and simple character. It would be unthinkable if this view of originality were applied to drawings made by artists. The act of drawing a representation of a flower or wild bird requires skill and judgment, even if a faithfully accurate reproduction is the purpose. Although the thing drawn already exists, it is in respect of the drawing that the test of originality must be applied. In this respect, the judgment of Harman J is very questionable. It would have been better if he had based his decision on a lack of skill or judgment, or that the drawing was not a 'work'.

8  [1984] FSR 1.

A work in respect of which copyright subsistence is in issue may be preceded by preliminary works, such as sketches made prior to a finished drawing or painting. This does not prejudice the originality of the finished work. In *Bio-trading and Financing Oy* v *Biohit Ltd*[9] it was held that, where an author makes preliminary drawings before producing a final version, the final version does not lack originality merely because it was preceded by the preliminary drawings. In *L A Gear Ltd* v *Hi-Tec Sports plc*,[10] the Court of Appeal thought

9  [1996] FSR 393.

10  [1992] FSR 121.

the point so obvious that it needed no authority, whilst in *Macmillan Publishers Ltd v Thomas Reed Publications Ltd*,[11] the court relied on a sequence of 'chartlets' in successive editions of a nautical almanac. The sense of this approach can be seen when one considers the alternative – it would be curious if a rough sketch were protected by copyright yet the finished drawing was not. The same principle should apply to the other original works, for example, where a written plan for a speech precedes the final printed speech.

In another way, the utility of the rule that the work in question must not have been copied from another work is limited, because if the work is a copy, the very act of copying would most likely infringe the copyright, if any, in the prior work. As a consequence, the maker of the second work would find it difficult, if not impossible, to exploit his work. One situation of more practical import, where originality would be denied on the basis of copying, is where the copyright in the earlier work has expired or it is not a work of copyright at all, for example, a functional article. Otherwise any person, whether a stranger or the owner of the copyright which had subsisted in a work, would be able to extend the duration of copyright simply by making another work which was largely a copy of the prior work, incorporating some minor or trivial alterations. In *Interlego AG v Tyco Industries Inc*[12] small modifications made to existing drawings of 'Lego' bricks were held not to give rise to new works independently protected by copyright, even though the modifications were technically significant. To hold otherwise would result in the possibility that copyright in what was essentially the same work could be extended indefinitely. Thus, half a day's work by a draughtsman making a new drawing by tracing over an existing drawing and making some minor alterations was not sufficient to create a new work of copyright. Originality requires something more than competent draughtsmanship. In *Interlego AG v Tyco Industries Inc*[13] Lord Oliver said that producing a good copy of a painting or an enlarged photograph from a negative would not create an original artistic work, even though the copy painting or positive print would require 'great skill, judgment and labour'. Of course, an artist making a faithful representation of, for example, a still life, uses more than his skill in applying paint to canvas. He also uses compositional and lighting skills, and it is in respect of these that copyright is earned. Some photographers might take issue with Lord Oliver's denial of copyright to photographic enlargements taken from negatives unless, as seems likely, he intended to restrict his comment to those cases where there is no selectivity in cropping the photograph and the entire negative is enlarged without any special effects.[14] Sometimes, originality is equated with the degree of skill, labour and judgment that went into the creation of the work.[15] However, any skill, labour or judgment used merely in the process of copying an existing work cannot be sufficient to make a work original. It is submitted that the requirement for 'skill, labour and judgment' is a test to be used to determine whether the thing concerned is a 'work', rather than a test of originality, and is more concerned with questions of adequacy and the *de minimis* principle, discussed below.

Peterson J gave the issue of originality detailed consideration in *University of London Press Ltd v University Tutorial Press Ltd*, where he said:

> The word 'original' does not in this connection mean that the work must be an expression of original or inventive thought. Copyright Acts are not concerned with the originality of ideas, but with the expression of thought, and, in the case of a 'literary work', with the expression of thought in print or writing. The originality which is required relates to the expression of thought.[16]

11 [1993] FSR 455.

12 [1989] 1 AC 217 (JCPC).

13 [1989] 1 AC 217 at 262.

14 Curiously, in an unreported case, *Manners v The Reject Shop*, June 1994, Bow Street Magistrates' Court, a stipendiary magistrate decided that a photocopy (in this case of a design applied to a ceramic tile) could be an original work; *see* Kinnier-Wilson, J. 'Criminal Copyright Offences under Sections 107 and 110 UK CDPA' [1995] 1 EIPR 46.

15 *See*, for example, the judgment of Whitford J (at first instance) in *LB (Plastics) Ltd v Swish Products Ltd* [1979] RPC 551, where, talking in terms of artistic copyright, he suggested that the question of originality depended upon the amount of labour, skill and judgment expended on the creation of the work.

16 [1916] 2 Ch 601 at 608–9.

He went on to say that the work must not be copied from another work, but that it should originate from the author. The implication of this is that the constituent parts of the work themselves need not be new in any sense and that the work as a whole can be made up from commonplace and pre-existing materials. In a case concerning a street directory, *Macmillan & Co Ltd v K & J Cooper,*[17] it was held that although many compilations have nothing original in their parts, yet the sum total of the compilation may be original for the purposes of copyright. The basic argument for holding that copyright can subsist in such things is that a reasonable amount of work involving judgment and selection has been used in making the compilation.

A formula may be original but its use will not create new works of copyright. In *Bookmakers Afternoon Greyhound Services Ltd v Wilf Gilbert (Staffordshire) Ltd,*[18] Aldous J said that, once a formula has been derived, he did not consider that sufficient skill, labour and judgment is used when calculating, in this case, dividends from starting prices in greyhound races.[19] Aldous J also considered that there was no copyright in a list of 12 such dividends, as it amounted to a mere collocation and not a copyright compilation. There was no skill or judgment and minimal labour in writing them down.

## Meaning of 'work'

As mentioned above, the search for a reasonable amount of effort expended in the creation of a work is one way in which some judges have tested for originality. For copyright to subsist in a literary, dramatic, musical or artistic work, it must qualify as a 'work', and one way of determining this is to consider the amount of skill, labour or judgment which has gone into its creation. Judges have displayed some inconsistency in the formulae they have used: for example, 'work or skill or expense' *per* Lord Pearce in *Ladbroke (Football) Ltd v William Hill (Football) Ltd,*[20] 'knowledge, labour, judgment or literary skill or taste' *per* Lord Atkinson in *Macmillan & Co Ltd v K & J Cooper & Co Ltd*[21] and 'skill and labour' *per* Lord Templeman in *British Leyland Motor Corp Ltd v Armstrong Patents Co Ltd.*[22] Nevertheless, it is clear that some measure of skill or effort must have been expended in the production of the work before it can attract copyright protection. In *Baily v Taylor,*[23] a case concerning the copying of tables of values of leases and annuities, a request for an injunction to restrain publication of a work containing the copied tables was refused partly on the ground that any competent person could have recalculated the tables in a few hours.

It is a misleading to suggest that the creation of a work of copyright should extend over a significant period of time. After all, the time taken might be quite small as in the case of an artist creating a sketch in a matter of minutes or in taking a photograph. However, *Baily v Taylor* is not authority for saying the there can be no copyright in a work which takes but a short time to create. As the plaintiff brought his action in the Court of Chancery, the only remedies available to him were an injunction and/or an account of profits. The Court of Chancery did not say that copyright did not subsist in the tables, and the plaintiff was left to pursue a remedy for damages at law should he wish. What is of greater interest is the position where the information contained in the work is entirely factual such that there is no 'design freedom', as was the case in *Baily v Taylor*. Speaking of factual information in a table containing information such as sunrise and sunset times, Viscount Simon said, *obiter*, in *Cramp (GA) & Sons Ltd v Frank Smythson Ltd:*[24]

17 (1923) 40 TLR 186.

18 [1994] FSR 723.

19 *Quaere* whether a formula would be deemed *de minimis*; *see* post.

20 [1964] 1 WLR 273 at 291.
21 (1923) 93 LJ PC 113 at 121.

22 [1986] 2 WLR 400 at 419.

23 (1829) 1 Russ & M 73.

24 [1944] AC 329 at 336.

The sun does in fact rise, and the moon set, at times which have been calculated, and the utmost that a table can do on such a subject is to state the result accurately. There is so far no room for taste or judgment.

The creation of a new table or compilation containing exclusively factual information may require a significant amount of work and effort in deriving that information, for example, by scientific observation and measurement. It seems unduly harsh to deny protection against another wishing to copy the information to save himself the trouble and expense of deriving the same information independently, particularly if his purpose is to produce a competing work. Of course, there may be copyright in the manner in which the information is presented, for example, in the design and layout of the table itself or in annotations, but that does not protect the information.

It may be that the person recording or calculating the information has done so imperfectly. What if the table contains a number of mistakes and someone copies the table without permission? Notwithstanding that the presence of common mistakes may be potent evidence of copying, is there a copyright in mistakes? Another way of looking at the situation where there is no freedom of expression is to argue that the issue is not one of subsistence of copyright, but is rather a matter of evidential value in an infringement action. The fact that two persons create works containing the same information which must, by necessity, be identical is not evidence of copying; something further is needed.

The question is whether the application of sheer effort alone is sufficient to bestow copyright upon the resulting work. The United States Supreme Court held not in *Feist Publications Inc v Rural Telephone Service Co Inc*[25] in denying copyright protection to purely factual compilations, laying to rest the 'sweat of the brow' doctrine.[26] In that case it was held that the 'White Pages' in a telephone directory were not protected by copyright because that section of the directory was the result of effort only and did not require the application of skill and judgment. It was basically a question of arranging names in alphabetical order and including address and telephone numbers. On the other hand, 'Yellow Pages' in telephone directories could be copyright material because of the skill and judgment expended in selecting the classification system and the fact that other copyright materials such as advertisements were also included.[27]

This approach is not necessarily at odds with the position in the United Kingdom and, apart from the wooliness of some judgments on this point, it appears that the same principle applies. For example, in *Cramp (GA) & Sons Ltd v Frank Smythson Ltd,*[28] a diary containing the usual information printed in diaries, such as a calendar, tables of weights and measures and postal information, failed to attract copyright in respect of the work of selecting and arranging the information. The reason was that the commonplace nature of the information left no room for taste or judgment in the selection and organisation of the material.

However, in *Waterlow Directories Ltd v Reed Information Systems Ltd*[29] the subsistence of copyright in legal directories containing lists of names and addresses of firms of solicitors and barristers was not put in issue. The defendant simply denied infringement. In *Cobbett v Woodward*[30] it was suggested that a Post Office directory which was purchased by the public could be subject to copyright, although it was held that there could be no copyright in a trade catalogue, a fact that must be seriously doubted now. Though there must be

25 (1991) S Ct 1282.

26 According to this doctrine copyright was a reward for the hard work that went into compiling facts.

27 However, in *Bell South Advertising and Publishing Corp v Donnelly Information Publishing Inc* (unreported) 11th Cir September 2, 1993, it was held that copying factual information from yellow pages did not infringe copyright.

28 [1944] AC 329.

29 [1992] FSR 409.

30 (1872) 14 Eq 407 LR.

some doubt about the copyright status of compilations which require no skill or judgment in their making, as soon as some additional material is included by reason of the application of skill or judgment by the compiler, then copyright will subsist in the compilation. That additional material may be a set of headings for a classification scheme,[31] or a credit rating appended to each client in a database of customers. This approach accords with German copyright law, which requires a work to be a 'personal intellectual creation'[32] and the European Community approach which requires a copyright computer program to be the author's 'own intellectual creation'.[33] Where the creation of the work itself does not require skill or judgment, it may still attract copyright if there is sufficient skill or judgment expended in the work carried out in preparing for its creation. Aldous J so held in *Microsense Systems Ltd* v *Control Systems Technology*[34] in relation to a list of mnemonics designed to control pelican crossings. He said it was at least arguable that the skill and labour in devising the functions and operations of the controller should be taken into account.

Scholars who carry out research into old works are concerned about the copyright status of the results of their research. For example, if a literary scholar, by his research, attempts to piece together the true text of a medieval sonnet, does he gain a copyright in his finished work? It would seem entirely possible, especially if the approach of Aldous J in the *Microsense* case above is accepted as representing the true position. Indeed, in Israel it has been held that a scholar, who by his extensive knowledge of the Hebrew language, history and culture, pieced together fragments of one of the Dead Sea Scrolls, filling in missing pieces based on his research, created a work of copyright.[35] However, there must be a limit to this approach and the new work must be more than a mere copy of the original. Logically, if a scholar manages to reproduce an old work exactly as it was originally written he can have no copyright. A long-since expired copyright cannot be resurrected.[36]

One way of looking at the requirement for skill or judgment to have been used in the creation of a work of copyright is to consider it as an example of the basic principle, as alluded to by Peterson J in the *University of London Press* case, that copyright does not protect ideas, merely the expression of ideas.

## Idea/expression

The United States of America has a well-defined legal principle that copyright protects expression but not ideas; indeed the Copyright Act of 1976 specifically states that ideas, procedures, processes, systems, methods of operation, concepts, principles and discoveries are excluded from copyright protection.[37] Blank forms for accounts were denied protection by the Supreme Court in *Baker* v *Selden*[38] and the idea/expression dichotomy has been developed to high levels of sophistication by the US courts ever since. The distinction is important in two respects:

1 some things can be expressed only in one way, the expression is dictated by its function or external factors; and
2 if copyright were limited only to the actual words used (in a literary work), it would be too easily circumvented by re-writing the work using different words.

Therefore, as a direct result of these points, some forms of expression are not protected as being ideas (or equivalent to, or dictated by, ideas) and some forms of expression are not directly perceivable (they are non-literal forms of expression).

---

**31** It was held that there was copyright in a set of headings in a trade catalogue in *Lamb* v *Evans* [1893] 1 Ch 218.

**32** German Copyright Act 1965 s 2(2).

**33** Article 1(3) Council Directive on the legal protection of computer programs, OJ L122, 14.5.91, p. 42.

**34** (Unreported) 17 July 1991.

**35** *Elisha Kimron* v *Hershel Shanks* [1993] 7 EIPR D-157.

**36** Except where the term of copyright is increased by legislative action, as happened under the Copyright Act 1911 and the Duration of Copyright and Rights in Performnces Regulations 1995, SI 1995/3297.

**37** United States Copyright Act of 1976, 17 USC § 102 (a). The EC Directive on the legal protection of computer programs, OJ L122, 17.5.91, p. 42 also adheres to the idea/expression distinction as, by Article 1(2), underlying ideas and principles are not protected by copyright.

**38** 101 US 99 (1880).

United Kingdom law does not explicitly make the distinction between idea and expression, either in legislation or in case law.[39] It has been pointed out that use of the aphorism 'there is no copyright in an idea' is likely to confuse.[40] Indeed, as Lord Hailsham observed in *LB (Plastics) Ltd v Swish Products Ltd,* agreeing with the late Professor Joad, it all depends on what you mean by 'ideas'.[41] However, English judges have decided cases in such a way as to produce similar results. In *Page v Wisden*[42] (which was cited in *Baker v Selden*) it was held that a cricket scoring sheet was not protected by copyright. In *Kenrick v Lawrence*[43] effective protection was denied to a drawing showing a hand holding a pen and marking a ballot paper. The intention of the person commissioning the drawing was that it could be used to show persons with poor literacy skills how to vote. It was held that a similar drawing did not infringe because it was inevitable that any person who attempted to produce a drawing to show how to vote would create a similar drawing. In other words, it was an unprotectable idea.[44] Conversely, non-literal expression has been recognised as being within the scope of copyright protection in *Rees v Melville*[45] and *Corelli v Gray*[46] concerning the plot of a play taken from a novel.

Even if one accepts the idea/expression rule of subsistence as having merit, it has proved, and will continue to prove, very difficult to apply as the boundary between idea and expression is notoriously difficult to discover.[47] This factor, and the idea/expression dichotomy in general, has become highly relevant in terms of computer programs and is discussed at more length in Chapter 8.

## *De minimis* principle

It is clear that it would be ridiculous to afford copyright protection to works that are trivial in the extreme or so small as to be entirely insignificant. However, a line has to be drawn separating works that are the proper subject matter of copyright from those that are not. The courts will often, though not always, use the principle *de minimis non curat lex,*[48] that is, that the work is insufficiently significant to be afforded copyright protection. For example, in *Sinanide v La Maison Kosmeo,*[49] it was held that to quote a bit of a sentence of a literary work was too small a matter on which to base a copyright infringement action. *A fortiori* a name cannot be subject to copyright. For example, the name of the fictional television detective 'Kojak' was not protected by copyright.[50] Nor is there any copyright in a single word such as 'Hitachi'.[51] In the *Sinanide* case, the plaintiff had used an advertising slogan 'Beauty is a social necessity, not a luxury' and complained about the defendant's use of the phrase 'A youthful appearance is a social necessity'. Generally, copyright will not subsist in advertising slogans and titles because they are usually fairly brief, and the song title 'The Man who Broke the Bank at Monte Carlo' was held to be insufficiently substantial for copyright purposes.[52] Nevertheless, there may be circumstances where a title is of such an extensive nature and important character that it will be the proper subject matter of copyright.

In *Shetland Times Ltd v Dr Jonathan Wills,*[53] the Court of Session, Outer House, in Scotland considered that headlines on an Internet website could be a literary work. Some of the headlines consisted of eight or more words put together for the purpose of imparting information. This seems to be inconsistent with the line of cases mentioned above, though it should be noted that, in the

39 Judges may sometimes recognise the principle; for example Whitford J in *Geo Ward (Moxley) Ltd v Sankey* [1988] FSR 66 and Ferris J, applying US authorities, in *John Richardson Computers Ltd v Flanders* [1993] FSR 497.

40 Jacob J in *IBCOS Computers Ltd v Barclays Mercantile Highland Finance Ltd* [1994] FSR 275.

41 [1979] RPC 551 at 629.

42 (1869) 20 LT 435.

43 (1890) QBD 93.

44 However, the judge went on to say that if the drawing had been an exact duplicate, there would have been an infringement of copyright. In other words, exact copies would infringe, inexact copies would not.

45 [1911–1916] MacG CC 168.

46 [1913] TLR 570.

47 For a recent example involving 'Fantasy Football', *see Bleiman v News Media (Auckland) Ltd* [1994] 2 NZLR 673, discussed in Brown, B. 'The Idea/Expression Dichotomy and the Games that People Play' [1995] 5 EIPR 259.

48 The law does not concern itself with trifles. In *Exxon Corporation v Exxon Insurance Consultants International Ltd* [1981] 3 All ER 241, it was held that the word 'EXXON' could not be an 'original literary work' without recourse to the *de minimis* principle.

49 (1928) 139 LT 365.

50 *Tavener Routledge Ltd v Trexapalm Ltd* [1977] RPC 275. Nor is 'ELVIS' protected by copyright; *ELVIS PRESLEY TRADE MARKS* [1997] RPC 543.

51 *Hitachi Ltd v Zafar Auto & Filter House* [1997] FSR 50, Copyright Board, Karachi, Pakistan.

52 *Francis Day & Hunter Ltd v Twentieth Century Fox Corporation Ltd* [1940] AC 112.

53 [1997] FSR 604.

*Shetland Times* case, the defendant had conceded the point. The basic question should remain – can the subject matter be claimed to be a *work*? It is arguable that a small number of words may so qualify if they are the result of a significant amount of work involving the exercise of skill and judgment. Nevertheless, the Court of Appeal was not attracted by an argument that the considerable amount of market research that had gone into the selection of the word 'EXXON' could, by itself, mean that the word was an original literary work.

If a name or title is represented in a particular way it seems possible that copyright might subsist in it. It was held in *News Group Newspapers Ltd v Mirror Group Newspapers (1986) Ltd*[54] that the use by one newspaper·in its advertisements of the logo of another newspaper (the *Sun*) gave rise to an arguable case of copyright infringement. Of course, unauthorised use of a name or title could infringe a trade mark or be actionable as passing off.

54 *The Times*, 27 July 1988.

## Tangibility

We have seen that copyright does not protect ephemeral things such as an idea for a novel or a play.[55] As such, ideas may have some protection under the law of confidence, depending upon the circumstances. Copyright law is, because of the nature of the drafting of the current Act and previous Acts, directed to the expression of ideas rather than to the ideas themselves.[56] The method used by copyright law is to require that the work has some tangible form. In the case of some works, such as sound recordings and films, their very existence implies tangibility. The same applies to artistic works. For example, according to Lawton LJ in *Merchandising Corp of America v Harpbond*[57] a painting is not an idea: it is an object. However, literary, dramatic and musical works clearly can exist without any material form. For example, a person may compose a poem and recite it from memory without ever having written it down. A musician may devise a tune while sitting at a piano keyboard without recording it in some way. Therefore, for literary, dramatic and musical works the Copyright, Designs and Patents Act 1988 declares that copyright does not subsist in such works unless and until they are recorded, in writing or otherwise.[58] 'Writing' is defined in s 178 (the interpretation section)[59] as including any form of notation or code, whether by hand or otherwise and regardless of the method by which, or medium in which, it is recorded. These definitions are deliberately couched in language which should ensure that copyright will not be defeated by technological advances, hence the use of the phrase 'or otherwise'. The requirement for some tangible existence is also important in that it dates the creation of the work, that is, the work is deemed to have been made when it is recorded.

55 Provided that they are not so detailed to be considered a non-literal form of expression.

56 This distinction is evident in the Berne Copyright Convention, *see* Chapter 9.

57 [1983] FSR 32.

58 The Copyright, Designs and Patents Act 1988 s 3(2).

59 Ibid s 178 contains several important definitions, but other definitions are scattered throughout the Act. However, the Act is very helpful in that an index is provided to assist in the location of definitions: s 179. Other indexes are provided for the parts of the Act dealing with rights in performances and the design right.

Of course, one would expect that the record is made by the author or with the author's permission, but this is not essential, and s 3(3) states that it is immaterial whether the work is recorded by or with the permission of the author. Therefore, if a person delivers an impromptu unscripted speech without having made any notes previously, and a member of the audience writes the speech down verbatim, then the speaker will be the author of the written work for copyright purposes. If the member of the audience uses skill and judgment and makes a selective record of the speech, perhaps adding his own comments and interpretation, then it is arguable that he may be considered to be the author of the notes for copyright purposes. In *Walter* v *Lane*,[60] it was held that copyright subsisted in a newspaper report of a speech by Lord Roseberry prepared from a reporter's shorthand notes and that the newspaper for whom the reporter worked, *The Times*, owned that copyright.[61]

## Shifting standards of copyright subsistence

We have seen that there are several ways in which works in the original category of copyright may fail to attract copyright protection. The 'thing' concerned may not be original, or it may not be the result of skill, labour or judgment. It may be deemed to be a mere idea, or it may be too small or trivial for copyright. The traditional English approach of readily granting copyright protection has a lot to be said for it. After all, why should the creator of a work be deprived of the right to control its future use because of the application of some ill-conceived test? For example, take the idea/expression dichotomy and the apparent denial of copyright for 'ideas'. This is based on the false premise that, otherwise, ideas would be monopolised. However, copyright does not create monopolies. Copyright infringement requires some act to be done in relation to the first work. The independent creation of a new work, no matter how similar it may be to existing works, does not trespass on the property rights of other copyright owners. Thus, the purported justification of denying copyright to ideas is unfounded.

The courts in the United States, since *Baker* v *Selden*,[62] have fallen into a trap from which they cannot escape in a dignified manner. The simple truth is that the idea/expression dichotomy should not be an issue of subsistence of copyright. Its relevance is entirely a matter of evidence. Indeed, this is how the court in *Kenrick* v *Lawrence*[63] rightly interpreted it. The fact that the expression of a work is dictated by, or at least severely constrained by, its underlying idea does not and should not affect the subsistence of copyright one way or another. It simply means that any similarity between the first and second work cannot raise a presumption of copying. The independent act of creating a new work based on the same idea inevitably would result in a similar expression. That is not the same as saying that deliberately copying will not infringe. If such copying results in an exact duplicate of the first work, it is likely that a court will accept that there has been infringement of copyright, in the absence of any other explanation.[64]

By falling into the idea/expression trap and using other misguided tests such as *de minimis* (again, this is probably more concerned with infringement than subsistence) it is easy to lose sight of the basic legislative provisions dealing with subsistence. Parliament has sought to endow copyright on qualifying original literary, dramatic, musical and artistic works. The first three are also required to be recorded in writing or otherwise. We have seen that a work is original if it is its author's own work and not simply a copy of an existing work. For the thing to be a work, it must be the result of skill, judgment or labour. This accords with the ordinary meaning of 'work'.

The Act does not expressly deny protection to ideas or, provided they are the result of skill, judgment or labour, small works. Why should we further curtail copyright by imposing additional criteria not in the Act? For example, if I spend some time and effort in compiling a list of customers or in calculating the sun's inclination in the sky at a given time and at a given geographical location based on well-known formulae, why should I be denied copyright? Should I not have a remedy against someone who copies my list or calculations, without my permission, saving himself the trouble of finding the information for himself?

60 [1900] AC 539.

61 At the time of this case there was no requirement for originality. It may depend on whether the person making the record exercises some skill thus bringing some originality to the report, *see Roberton* v *Lewis* [1976] RPC 169 and Cross J's comments on *Walter* v *Lane*. In *Express Newspapers plc* v *News (UK) Ltd* [1990] 1 WLR 1320 it was held that *Walter* v *Lane* was still undeniably good law.

62 101 US 99 (1880)

63 (1890) 25 QBD 99.

64 In *Kenrick* v *Lawrence* it was said, *obiter*, that a slavish copy would infringe.

65 Article 1(3), EC Directive on the legal protection of computer programs, OJ L122, 14.5.91, p. 42.

66 Article 3(1), EC Directive on the legal protection of databases, OJ L77, 27.3.96, p. 20.

67 For example, the judgment of Ferris J in *John Richardson Computers Ltd v Flanders* [1993] FSR 497.

68 [1964] 1 WLR 273 at 291.

The UK is in danger of moving from the reward for work theory to a position whereby more hurdles are placed along the route to copyright subsistence. This danger comes from two fronts. First, there are pressures from European Community legislation, which uses standards such as 'the author's own intellectual creation'[65] and which envisages that many databases will fail to attract copyright protection.[66] The second danger stems from the USA and the readiness of some English judges to treat copyright precedents from there with a respect that is a little too generous.[67]

Lord Devlin, in *Ladbroke (Football) Ltd v William Hill (Football) Ltd*,[68] spoke of copyright in the following terms:

> The law [of copyright] does not impinge on freedom of trade; it protects property. It is no more an interference with trade than is the law against larceny. Free trade does not require that one man should be allowed to appropriate without payment the fruit's of another's labour, whether they are tangible or intangible. The law has not found it possible to give full protection to the intangible. But it can protect the intangible in certain states, and one of them is when it is expressed in words and print. The fact that that protection is necessarily limited is no argument for diminishing it further; and it is nothing to the point to say that either side of the protective limits a man can obtain gratis whatever his ideas of honesty permit him to pick up.

The basic rationale of copyright is the grant of property rights in works created by the human mind which are expressed in some way. It should not matter if the finished work is constrained by its underlying idea or if it requires only effort in its execution. In both of these cases, what is being rewarded is the mental decision to create the work coupled with the toil or labour to bring it to fruition. Why should a work that requires skill in its execution be better protected than one in which the creative element lies in the conception of the work in the human mind? Because we are being drawn into unnecessary or unduly stringent tests for the subsistence of copyright, we are in grave danger of further diminishing copyright law. The élitism of art over labour is becoming subsumed in copyright law.

## Literary work

69 Preparatory design material was added by the Copyright (Computer Programs) Regulations 1992, SI 1992/3233 and databases were added by the Copyright and Rights in Databases Regulations 1997, SI 1997/3032.

The Copyright, Designs and Patents Act 1988 s 3(1) defines a literary work as any work, other than a dramatic or musical work, which is written, spoken or sung, and includes a table or compilation other than a database, a computer program, preparatory design material for a computer program and a database.[69] It should already be clear that a literary work does not have to be a work of literature, and this is implied by the inclusion of tables, compilations, computer programs, preparatory design material for computer programs and databases in the category of literary works. The courts have long since been prepared to take a very wide view of what constitutes a literary work, for example, Peterson J said in *University of London Press Ltd v University Tutorial Press Ltd*:

> It may be difficult to define 'literary work' as used in this Act [Copyright Act 1911], but it seems to be plain that it is not confined to 'literary work' in the sense in which that phrase is applied, for instance, to Meredith's novels and the writings of Robert Louis Stevenson ... In my view the words 'literary work' cover work which is expressed in print or writing, irrespective of the question whether the quality or style is high. The word 'literary' seems to be used in a sense somewhat similar to the use of the word 'literature' in political or electioneering literature and refers to written or printed matter.[70]

70 [1916] 2 Ch 601 at 608.

This must be expanded nowadays to cover material recorded on modern storage media. For example, a report produced using a word processor is a literary work the moment it is stored on a computer disk because it is then recorded 'in writing or otherwise'.

Examples of works afforded literary copyright are books of telegraphic codes,[71] examination papers,[72] football coupons,[73] consignment notes,[74] headings in a trade directory[75] and business letters.[76] Tables and compilations expressly fall within the meaning of literary work, examples of tables being railway timetables, company balance sheets, actuarial tables and mileage charts. Compilations include things like lists of customers, directories, listings of television programmes and the 'Top Twenty' best-selling records. Although it has been accepted in the past that a compilation can comprise both literary and artistic materials,[77] a change in terminology in the 1988 Act may mean that there is no copyright protection in a compilation of artistic works only because a literary work must be written, spoken or sung, and it can be argued that artistic works are not written.[78] Of course, the artistic works may be protected in their own right.

In *Anacon Corp Ltd* v *Environmental Research Technology Ltd,*[79] Jacob J was prepared to accept that circuit diagrams from which circuit boards were made, in addition to being artistic works, were also literary works as a circuit diagram has writing on it which is intended to be read rather than simply being appreciated by the eye. The writing may be in code, for example, the value of a component. Nevertheless, the written information forms a table or compilation and the fact that it is scattered about and joined by lines does not prevent it being so. The headnote to the law report states that the circuit diagrams were literary works. This goes too far. They are artistic works that contain information protected by literary copyright. The graphic elements such as representations of components and connecting lines are not subject to literary copyright. Laddie J considered this to be the correct view of *Anacon* in *Electronic Techniques (Anglia) Ltd* v *Critchley Components Ltd*[80] where he dismissed an application for summary judgment. Part of the basis for his decision was that, ignoring the graphic elements of the diagrams, as a literary work, the circuit diagram was little more than a list of five or six components. Consequently, the defendant had a significant defence that the diagram was not sufficiently substantial to qualify as an original work.

The Copyright, Designs and Patents Act 1988 affords copyright protection to computer programs and preparatory design material for computer programs as literary works. The Act, very wisely, does not attempt to define what a computer program is.[81] In view of the rate of development of computer technology, any precise legal definition could prove to be inappropriate in the future or, at least, could unduly inhibit flexibility in the law. Where the Act does contain definitions, they tend to be very widely drawn. The classification of computer programs as literary works follows international developments and is in line with European Community developments on the subject. Computer programs, preparatory design material for computer programs, databases and other items of computer software are considered more fully in Chapter 8.

For a work to be an 'original literary work', it must accord with that phrase taken as a whole. It is not sufficient that a work satisfies each word individually. This is another limitation on the scope of copyright, the effect of which is similar to the *de minimis* principle. In particular, the word 'original' should not be

71 *Ager* v *Peninsula & Oriental Steam Navigation Company* (1884) 26 ChD 627 and *DP Anderson & Co Ltd* v *Lieber Code Co* [1917] 2 KB 469.

72 *University of London Press Ltd* v *University Tutorial Press Ltd* [1916] 2 Ch 601.

73 *Ladbroke (Football) Ltd* v *William Hill (Football) Ltd* [1964] 1 WLR 273.

74 *Van Oppen & Co Ltd* v *Van Oppen* (1903) 20 RPC 617.

75 *Lamb* v *Evans* [1893] 1 Ch 218.

76 *British Oxygen Co Ltd* v *Liquid Air Ltd* [1925] 1 Ch 383.

77 For example, *Purefoy Engineering Co Ltd* v *Sykes Boxall & Co Ltd* (1955) 72 RPC 89, concerning a trade catalogue containing literary and artistic materials.

78 Neither are they spoken or sung. Monotti, A. 'The Extent of Copyright Protection for Compilations of Artistic Works' [1993] 5 EIPR 156.

79 [1994] FSR 659.

80 [1997] FSR 401.

81 Neither does the Computer Misuse Act 1990 define 'computer program'. The Banks Committee described a computer program as 'a series of instructions which control or condition the operation of a data processing machine' (*Committee to Examine the Patent System and Patent Law*, 1970, Cmnd 4407, para 471, p. 140). The USA has a statutory definition: being 'a set of statements or instructions to be used directly or indirectly in a computer to bring about a certain result', 17 USC § 101. This gives rise to the question 'what is a computer?'!

82 [1981] 3 All ER 241.

looked at in isolation. In *Exxon Corporation* v *Exxon Insurance Consultants International Ltd*,[82] the plaintiff was a multinational oil company. It decided to choose a new corporate name, and after considerable research and consultation the word 'Exxon' was decided upon. The plaintiff contended that the word 'Exxon', being first used by it, was *original*, that it was *literary* because it was expressed in letters and that it was a *work*, being the result of considerable research and effort. Therefore, the plaintiff argued that the word 'Exxon' was an 'original literary work' within the Copyright Act 1956 s 2(1). However, it was held that the term 'original literary work' was a composite expression denoting a literary work intending to offer information, instruction or pleasure in the form of literary enjoyment.[83] For a word or expression to be within the meaning of 'original literary work', it was not enough that the work could be described as 'original', 'literary' and a 'work'. Although 'Exxon' could be described thus separately, it was not an original literary work because it conveyed no information, provided no instruction and gave no pleasure in the form of literary enjoyment. There was, therefore, no copyright in the word 'Exxon'.[84] However, the requirement for literary enjoyment must be questioned now because of the addition of computer programs to the categories of literary works.

83 Based on the definition of a literary work given by Davey J in *Hollinrake* v *Truswell* [1894] 3 Ch 420 at 427–8. This seems to be a narrower definition than that adopted by Peterson J in *University of London Press Ltd* v *University Tutorial Press Ltd* [1916] 2 Ch 601.

84 The word 'Exxon' was registered as a trade mark both within the United Kingdom and elsewhere.

## Dramatic work

85 The Copyright, Designs and Patents Act 1988 s 3(1).

A dramatic work includes a work of dance or mime.[85] Under previous law, it was possible, theoretically, for a work to be both a dramatic work and a literary work, for example, a script for a play could fall into both of these categories. This was of no consequence as the rights provided for were identical for both types of work. Under the Copyright, Designs and Patents Act 1988, this sterile overlap is removed and a literary work is defined to exclude a dramatic work. Dramatic works, in common with literary and musical works, must be recorded for copyright to subsist in them. In *Tate* v *Fullbrook*[86] it was held that a visual skit for a music hall sketch involving the use of a firework was not the subject matter of copyright because it had not been reduced to writing.[87] More recently, in *Green* v *Broadcasting Corporation of New Zealand*,[88] it was held that the dramatic format of a television show had to be certain for that format to be entitled to copyright protection. The appellant, Hughie Green, devised the television show 'Opportunity Knocks' and claimed copyright in the scripts and dramatic format of the show. The latter comprised catch phrases, the use of a 'clapometer' and sponsors to introduce competitors. Finding for the respondents, Lord Bridge said that the protection which copyright gave was a monopoly, and that there had to be certainty in the subject matter of such a monopoly. However, Lord Bridge erred in this respect because copyright certainly does not give a monopoly, it being free to anyone else to produce a similar work as long as they do so independently. A better rationale is that Mr Green's dramatic format could not be protected either because it lacked certainty for want of material form, or because the respondent had copied only the ideas and not the expression of those ideas. It is difficult to reconcile this case with earlier cases such as *Rees* v *Melville*[89] concerning the plot of a dramatic work, in which it appears that the plot of the play, in addition to the written expression, may be afforded some protection. It depends on the level of abstraction from the literal expression: the closer it is the more likely it can be considered to be protected. The further away it is the more likely it will be considered to be an unprotected idea.[90]

86 [1908] 1 KB 821.

87 *See also Tate* v *Thomas* [1921] 1 Ch 503.

88 [1989] RPC 700.

89 [1911–1916] MacG CC 168.

90 Legislative action is needed to clarify the protection of the dramatic format of 'game shows'. An opportunity to include suitable measures in the Broadcasting Act 1990 was not taken advantage of.

## Musical work

A musical work is one consisting of music, exclusive of any words or action intended to be sung, spoken or performed with the music. A song will, therefore, have two copyrights, one in the music and one in the words of the song, the latter being a literary work. This is convenient as it is common for different persons to write the music and the lyrics. Once again, the work must be reduced in writing or otherwise. The Copyright, Designs and Patents Act 1988 gives no guidance as to what a musical work is, but in practice this does not seem to cause any problems; what is beautiful music to one man might be a dreadful cacophony to another. It would seem that a relatively small number of notes and chords are sufficient for copyright protection as a dispute as to the ownership of the copyright in a previous piece of Channel 4 logo music, comprising a four note theme in an orchestral setting, demonstrated.[91]

Making an arrangement of an existing piece of music may attract its own copyright in addition to, and running alongside, the copyright subsisting in the prior work. For example, a musician who expends a reasonable amount of skill in arranging and adapting a piece of music originally written for a rock group so that it is suitable for an traditional orchestra will have a copyright in the orchestral work.[92] Of course, he could be guilty of infringing the copyright in the earlier piece of music, should copyright still subsist in it, if he makes his arrangement without the permission of the copyright owner.[93]

91 *Lawson v Dundas, The Times,* 13 June 1985.

92 *Wood v Boosey* (1868) LR 3 QB 223.

93 This falls within the meaning of making an adaptation, one of the acts restricted by copyright: the Copyright, Designs and Patents Act 1988 s 21(3)(b).

## Artistic works

The artistic work category is a diverse one and includes several different types of works. It is a category that causes special problems because it overlaps with design law and the relationship between copyright and design law is not at all clear-cut. The Copyright, Designs and Patents Act 1988 s 4(1) defines 'artistic work' as meaning:

(a) a graphic work, photograph, sculpture or collage, *irrespective of artistic quality*,
(b) a work of architecture being a building or a model *for* a building, or
(c) a work of artistic craftsmanship.

[emphasis added]

As copyright is stated to subsist in the first category irrespective of artistic quality, a painting of coloured rectangles by Mondrian or a Jackson Pollock painting made up of coloured squiggles is as deserving of copyright protection as is a portrait or a landscape painted in a traditional manner. This formula ensures that personal taste or preference is no bar to copyright protection, and it also safeguards utilitarian and functional works such as drawings for engineering equipment, photographs made for scientific or record purposes, weather charts and plans for civil engineering and building works. However, it appears that for works falling into the last category, that is, works of artistic craftsmanship, some qualitative characteristic is required, as will be discussed later.

The Copyright, Designs and Patents Act 1988 s 4(2) expands on the definitions and states that a graphic work includes:

(a) any painting, drawing, diagram, map, chart or plan, and
(b) any engraving, etching, lithograph, woodcut or similar work.

The scope of some artistic works is very difficult to fix with any certainty. For example, the meaning of 'sculpture' could be particularly wide. Section 4(2) provides a non-exhaustive definition stating that sculpture includes a cast or model made for the purpose of sculpture. While a three-dimensional object carved from a block of wood or stone and bronze or porcelain figures are obviously sculptures, it is doubtful that any three-dimensional article would qualify. Presumably the collection of bricks laid out in the Tate Gallery is a sculpture, but a casing for a gearbox, a moulded plastic chair and a bath are not. What about a moving sculpture such as a 'mobile' or Chinese windcharms? Dictionary definitions of 'sculpture' are suggestive of works of art, but this contradicts the phrase 'irrespective of artistic quality'. If we require the work to have been produced by a sculptor, this is difficult to reconcile with the fact that graphic works are not required to be made by an artist as engineering drawings qualify as artistic works.

There is relatively little case law on sculptures. In *J & S Davis (Holdings) Ltd v Wright Health Group Ltd*[94] it was held that a cast for making a denture was not a sculpture because it was not made for the purposes of sculpture. A generous view of the meaning of sculpture was taken in the New Zealand case of *Wham-O Manufacturing Co v Lincoln Industries Ltd*,[95] in which it was held that a wooden model, from which moulds were made in order to produce plastic flying discs known as Frisbees, was a sculpture.[96] The moulds were held to be engravings, following the decision of Judge Paul Baker in *James Arnold & Co Ltd v Miafern Ltd*,[97] in which he said that the term 'engraving' encompassed not only the final image made by the engraved plate but the plate itself. Correspondingly, in *Breville Europe plc v Thorn EMI Domestic Appliances Ltd*[98] plaster shapes made for die-cast moulds for the heating plates of sandwich toasters were held to be sculptures.

This generous application of the artistic copyright in sculptures may owe something to the lack of any requirement for artistic quality. Does the absence of artistic quality as a threshold for protection mean that any person, whether an artist or not, may make an artistic work? Certainly in the case of a draughtsman preparing an engineering drawing or a plan for a house that would seem to be the case (even more so perhaps in these days of computer-aided design). Does this mean a sculpture can be made by someone who is not a sculptor in the artistic sense? Is an 'Anglepoise' lamp a sculpture? Or a domestic heating radiator? Or a 'desk tidy' made up of a number of tubes to hold pencils, pens and other bits and pieces? In *Metix (UK) Ltd v G H Maughan (Plastics) Ltd*,[99] Laddie J accepted that it was not possible to say with precision what is and what is not a sculpture. However, he considered that counsel's submission that a sculpture is a three-dimensional work made by an artist's hand was near to the mark. The test does not seem to be whether the object is permanent or transient, and an ice sculpture is no less a sculpture because it will melt as it gets warm, assuming that a chef is an artist.[100]

There are, however, limits to what can be a sculpture. An arrangement of objects and people, including a white Rolls-Royce car lowered into a swimming pool, for the purpose of taking a photograph of the scene for the album sleeve for a new recording by the band 'Oasis' was held not to be a sculpture in *Creation Records Ltd v News Group Newspapers Ltd*.[101] Nor was it a collage. Such a work involved, as an essential element, the sticking of two or more items together. Also, as the arrangement was ephemeral, its continued existence being as represented in the photograph, it was distinguishable from Carl Andre's bricks and installation art generally.

94  [1988] RPC 403.

95  [1985] RPC 127.

96  The provisions of the New Zealand Copyright Act 1962 s 2, defining artistic works, were equivalent to those under the United Kingdom Copyright Act 1956.

97  [1980] RPC 397.

98  [1995] FSR 77.

99  [1997] FSR 718.

100  Laddie J approved of this example in *Metix (UK) Ltd v G H Maughan (Plastics) Ltd* [1997] FSR 718, where he disapproved of Whitford J's distinction between a carved wooden model and a model fashioned in plasticine in *J & S Davis (Holdings) Ltd v Wright Health Group Ltd* [1988] RPC 403.

101  *The Times*, 29 April 1997. Although the plaintiff failed to show a sufficiently arguable case on the basis of copyright, an interlocutory injunction was granted on the ground of breach of confidence.

A photograph means a recording of light or other radiation on any medium on which an image is produced or from which an image may by any means be produced, and which is not part of a film. Copyright may subsist in a photograph of a painting provided skill and judgment has been expended, for example, by selecting part of the painting only and/or choosing lighting conditions, aperture settings, etc. In *Groves' Case*[102] it was held that copyright subsisted in a photograph of an engraving taken from a picture – three potential copyrights! The definition of 'photograph' is particularly wide, presumably to keep pace with future technological change.

Like literary, dramatic and musical works, artistic works must be 'original'. However, there is no requirement for them to be recorded as their very existence implies some form of tangibility.

A building includes any fixed structure, and a part of a building or fixed structure.[103] Buildings effectively have double protection, as works of architecture and through the plans drawn up for the buildings. Models for buildings, such as a model made for a proposed building to show to prospective investors and clients, are specifically protected, but models of buildings are not. However, if a model made of an existing building is copied, the copyright in the building itself and in the drawings made for the construction of the building will be infringed. With the exception of works of artistic craftsmanship, artistic copyright is very generous in what it can protect and in the scope of the protection. Some fairly simple things have been afforded artistic copyright, such as a bare design of a hand,[104] chartlets (simplified coastal maps), a simple label,[105] a working sketch of machinery,[106] a label for a whisky bottle[107] and an inverted 'R' with a dot in the loop which looked like a rabbit's head.[108]

Typefaces are not specifically mentioned among the categories of artistic works in the Copyright, Designs and Patents Act 1988 s 4. Nevertheless, it is beyond doubt that a typeface is an artistic work. Indeed, there are references in the Act to typefaces as a form of artistic work. For example, ss 54 and 55 (permitted acts in relation to typefaces) are stated in terms of the 'copyright in an artistic work consisting of the design of a typeface'. In the past, typefaces could have been within the ambit of registered designs (common features such as a new design of serif would have been registrable), but now typefaces are usually stored as computer software and not applied to metal type. Thus, copyright protection is more appropriate.

### Artistic craftsmanship

Works of artistic craftsmanship give rise to the greatest difficulty amongst artistic works. Normally, one might expect this category to include such things as jewellery to a special design, 'designer' goods such as furniture and clothing, and quality hand-made items intended to appear attractive or 'rustic' in some way and as found in craft shops.[109] Certainly, the phrase 'artistic craftsmanship' conjures up items made by hand by skilled workers which are bought because of the quality of workmanship and because of their eye-appeal. Better examples of hand-carved cuckoo clocks made in Switzerland should clearly be works of artistic craftsmanship. But where is the line drawn? What about mass-produced cuckoo clocks which are crudely assembled from machine jigged plywood, incorporating a cheap timepiece and a plastic cuckoo? And what

102 (1869) LR 4 QB 715.

103 *MacMillan Publishers Ltd v Thomas Reed Publications Ltd* [1993] FSR 455.

104 *Hildesheimer and Faulkner v Dunn & Co* (1891) 64 LT 452. But see also *Kenrick v Lawrence* (1890) 25 QBD 93 involving a simple design of a hand showing voters how to cast their votes.

105 *Charles Walker Ltd v The British Picker Co Ltd* [1961] RPC 57.

106 *B O Morris Ltd v F Gilman (BST) Ltd* (1943) 60 RPC 20.

107 *William Grant & Sons Ltd v McDowell & Co Ltd* [1994] FSR 690.

108 *Hutchison Personal Communications Ltd v Hook Advertising Ltd* [1996] FSR 549.

109 In some cases, an article which might properly be considered to be a work of artistic craftsmanship might also qualify for protection as a sculpture. For example, a three-dimensional wood carving.

about a mock-up for furniture to be mass-produced, roughly made with a light timber frame held together with nails and covered in upholstery but too flimsy to be able to support a person sitting on it? The case of *George Hensher Ltd* v *Restawhile Upholstery (Lancs) Ltd*[110] concerned such a prototype made for a suite of furniture, described as 'boat-shaped'. The House of Lords held that the prototype was not a work of artistic craftsmanship and that for something to fall into this category it must, in addition to being the result of craftsmanship, have some artistic quality. None of their Lordships seemed able to lay down a workable test for the required artistic quality, but agreed that the work must be viewed in a detached and objective manner. The question of whether a particular item possesses that quality is one of fact and evidence; in particular, expert evidence is an important factor in reaching a decision. Lord Reid said that a work of artistic craftsmanship would have the necessary artistic quality if any substantial section of the public genuinely admired and valued the thing for its appearance even though others may have considered it common or vulgar.

110  [1976] AC 64.

Lords Reid and Kilbrandon considered that the intention of the maker of the article was an important though not conclusive issue. While Viscount Dilhorne considered that mass-produced articles could not be works of artistic craftsmanship, Lord Simon of Glaisdale said that the word 'artistic' was not incompatible with machine production. However, the claim of copyright infringement concerned the appellant's prototype, not the furniture made from it, and the real obstacle standing in the way of copyright protection for it was that the appellant was unable to convince any of their Lordships that the prototype was, in any sense, artistic. It was likely that the design of the mock-up chair would have been accepted for registration under the Registered Designs Act 1949 because it was new and designed for eye-appeal, albeit somewhat vulgar, and the failure to apply for this relatively inexpensive form of protection against copying reduces the sympathy one can feel for the appellant. Nevertheless, a substantial amount of thought lay behind the design, aimed at reviving falling sales, and the respondent simply copied the appellant's furniture made in accordance with the prototype, saving itself the trouble of designing furniture that would appeal to the public and sell in large numbers. The respondent took unfair advantage and the decision in the House of Lords is difficult to square with Peterson J's oft-quoted dictum that a thing worth copying is worth protecting.[111]

111  *University of London Press Ltd* v *University Tutorial Press Ltd* [1916] 2 Ch 601 at 610.

The *Hensher* case did nothing to clarify the meaning of 'artistic craftsmanship', and while items such as Chippendale chairs, hand-crafted jewellery and fashion clothing are clearly within the meaning, utilitarian and mass-produced works are left vulnerable in terms of copyright protection even though they will often be subject to large commercial investment and risk. For once, the pragmatic and commercially sound approach of copyright law founders on the rock of taste, and one might ask why atrocious or feeble paintings and sculptures are protected by copyright law while other things, such as furniture, that have proven visual appeal, fail to attract protection, and why the *Hensher* principles have not been discarded by the Copyright, Designs and Patents Act 1988. The one saving grace is that many of the articles that will fail to be classed as works of artistic copyright will be protected either as registered designs or under the unregistered design right. However, the former requires registration and the payment of a fee, and both rights require a standard of novelty which is probably higher than is the case for copyright.

The question of artistic craftsmanship was considered again later in the High Court in *Merlet* v *Mothercare plc.*[112] Walton J, applying *Hensher*, held that a prototype cape for a baby, called a 'Raincosy', was not a work of artistic craftsmanship. He said that the test was whether the thing itself was a work of art and, consequently, the garment had to be considered by itself and not as worn or containing a baby. The 'Raincosy' was a work of craftsmanship only and not a work of artistic craftsmanship because the garment itself was not aesthetic, although seeing the ensemble of mother, child and garment may have given an onlooker some sense of aesthetic satisfaction. On the issue of the maker's intention, he said that the purpose of the garment was to protect a child from the rigours of the Scottish climate and the plaintiff had not been concerned with the creation of a work of art.

112 [1986] RPC 115. The case went to the Court of Appeal, but only on the issue of whether there had been an infringement of the copyright in the drawings of the garment concerned.

In the New Zealand case of *Bonz Group (Pty) Ltd* v *Cooke*[113] Tipping J noted that the expression 'artistic craftsmanship' was a composite one. The notion of craftsmanship relates more to the execution of the work rather than its design and, conversely, the requirement that the work be artistic relates more to its design than its execution. Thus, the author of the work must be both an artist and a craftsman, an inconsistently high standard. However, Tipping J did recognise, contrary to the accepted view (albeit implicit) in the English authorities, that the author would usually be a single person, that one person could provide the artistic element while another provided the craftsmanship.

113 [1994] 3 NZLR 216.

## SOUND RECORDINGS, FILMS, BROADCASTS OR CABLE PROGRAMMES

These are the derivative works. They are usually based on original literary, dramatic, musical and artistic works, for example, a recording of pop tunes, where the record is protected as a sound recording and each tune will have musical copyright and literary copyright in any lyrics. Sometimes, however, a derivative work is not based on one of the 'original' works. For example, a recording of the Flying Scotsman building up steam will be a sound recording but there is no other underlying work. Sound recordings, films, broadcasts and cable programmes[114] need protection so that the investors and entrepreneurs involved in such works can take direct action in case of infringement. The fact that several different original works may be encapsulated in a single film or sound recording makes it much more convenient for the owner of the rights in the latter to sue directly for any infringement. To take an example, consider a musical film such as *South Pacific*; there may be separate copyrights in the music, the lyrics to the songs and the dramatic parts of the film. If a part of the film is copied without permission, the owner of the copyright in the film can sue, otherwise it would be necessary to identify which rights were affected and who owned those rights and what the relationships were between those persons and the owner of the film. The situation could become very complex and this could work to the detriment of the film industry, the ensuing confusion making it easier for film piracy to flourish. Of course, if the owner of the copyright in a film successfully sues for infringement of copyright, he may distribute part of the award in damages to the various copyright owners in accordance with pre-existing contractual arrangements. In the case of an award of account of profits in respect of concurrent rights under an exclusive licence, the court will apportion the profit between the licensor and licensee.[115]

114 Note the spelling 'programme'; this is presumably to distinguish these from computer programs. The spelling 'program' has become accepted in terms of computer technology. However, in spite of the common view to the contrary, the '-am' ending is the better and accords with the traditional English spelling. It is not an 'Americanism', the '-amme' ending was adopted in the nineteenth century when French words and spelling were popular.

115 The Copyright, Designs and Patents Act 1988 s 102(4).

Compared to the 'original' works of copyright, these derivative works give rise to far fewer problems relating to the question of copyright subsistence. There is no requirement that these works be original because many would fail; for example, in a broadcast of a play, the play may be an original dramatic work in the copyright sense, but the broadcast cannot be original in the popular sense.

## Sound recordings

Under the Copyright, Designs and Patents Act 1988 s 5A(1), a sound recording is:

(a) a recording of sounds, from which the sounds may be reproduced, or
(b) a recording of the whole or any part of a literary, dramatic or musical work, from which sounds reproducing the work or part may be produced, regardless of the medium on which the recording is made or the method by which the sounds are reproduced or produced.

Under s 5A(2) copyright does not subsist in a sound recording which is, or to the extent that it is, a copy taken from a previous sound recording.[116]

Note that the language of the Act talks of 'sound' not music, so that recordings of non-musical sounds will come within the definition and a recording of a person reciting a passage from a book or a poem falls within the meaning of a sound recording. The definition is very wide in terms of storage media to take account of changes in technology. There is nothing to prevent several persons making recordings of the same thing at the same time and each having their own copyright. For example, if several persons make a sound recording of Concorde passing through the sound barrier, each will own the copyright in their own recording, and can sue for infringement if someone makes a copy of *their* recording without permission.

## Films

Films are defined in s 5B(1) and are a recording on any medium from which a moving image may by any means be produced. Again, notice the width of the definition – 'any medium' and 'by any means'. Until 1 January 1996, the definition only referred to the image and a film sound track was not included. Now, however, by s 5B(2), the sound track accompanying a film shall be treated as part of the film. It may also have a separate copyright as a sound recording.[117] Merely copying an old film does not bring about a new copyright, for, under s 5B(4), copyright does not subsist in a sound recording or film which is, or to the extent that it is, a copy taken from a previous sound recording or film.

## Broadcasts

Copyright subsists in broadcasts and cable programmes. Under the Copyright, Designs and Patents Act 1988 s 6, a broadcast, which consists of visual images, sounds or other information, is a transmission by means of wireless telegraphy of visual images, sounds or other information which is capable of being lawfully received by members of the public, or which is transmitted for presentation to members of the public.[118] Before the 1988 Act, this was limited to the BBC and the IBA. Now, even satellite television, such as BSkyB, is covered. Under s 6(2), if a transmission is encrypted it is still regarded as capable of

**116** Ibid s 5A was inserted by the Duration of Copyright and Rights in Performances Regulations SI 1995/3297. The definition is identical to the previous one in the old s 5.

**117** The Copyright, Designs and Patents Act 1988 s 5B(5) states that nothing in this section affects any copyright subsisting in a film sound track as a sound recording.

**118** In *Australian Performing Right Association Ltd v Telstra Corp Ltd* [1994] RPC 299, the Federal Court of Australia held that transmissions to mobile telephones from base stations were not broadcasts for the purposes of the Australian Copyright Act 1968.

being lawfully received by members of the public if decoding equipment has been made available to the public by or with the authority of the person making the transmission or the person providing the contents of the transmission. An example of a transmission for presentation to the public is where a boxing match is transmitted to a sporting arena in a different part of the country from where the match is held, to be displayed on a large screen to members of the public who pay an entrance fee. Under s 6(6), copyright does not subsist in a broadcast which infringes (or to the extent that it infringes) the copyright in another broadcast or cable programme.

Wireless telegraphy is defined in s 178 as meaning the sending of electromagnetic energy over paths not provided by a material substance constructed or arranged for that purpose, *but does not include the transmission of microwave energy between terrestrial fixed points.*[119]

It is important to know where the broadcast is made from as this will determine whether it attracts UK copyright. This could be an issue where the broadcast is made by satellite; s 6(4) states that a broadcast is made from the place where, under the control and responsibility of the person making the broadcast, the programme-carrying signals are introduced into an uninterrupted chain of communication. Where the transmission is via a satellite, that includes the chain leading to the satellite and down towards earth.[120]

The area of reception of a broadcast, its 'footprint', is likely to overlap national boundaries and further complications arise where a broadcast originates from another country, particularly if it is outside the European Economic Area (EEA). There are some special provisions, inserted by the Copyright and Related Rights Regulations 1996, which are designed to give rights to persons involved in the broadcast who are located in the EEA where the country from which the broadcast originates does not provide adequate protection in terms of broadcast rights, performers' rights and rights of authors of sound recordings and performers to share in a single equitable remuneration in respect of the broadcasting of sound recordings.

[119] The italicised words were added by the Copyright and Related Rights Regulations 1996, SI 1996/2967, r 8.

[120] This is a slight change in definition made by the Copyright and Related Rights Regulations 1996, SI 1996/2967 r 5, as from 1 December 1996. These regulations implement, *inter alia*, the EC Directive on the coordination of certain rules concerning copyright and rights related to copyright applicable to satellite broadcasting and cable retransmission, OJ L248, 6.10.93, p. 15.

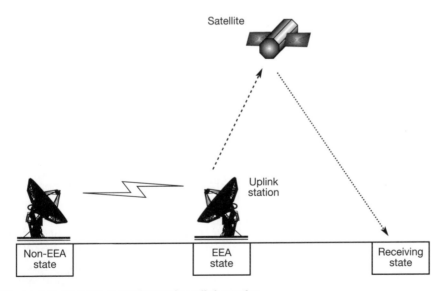

**Figure 3.1 Satellite broadcast via uplink station**

These special provisions (termed 'safeguards') are contained in s 6A. Figure 3.1 shows a typical situation covered by the safeguards. The signals are broadcast from a non-EEA country and are received by a station in an EEA country from where they are transmitted to a satellite to be received in that and/or other countries. That station is known as the uplink station. Where, as in the example, the broadcast is made from a country outside the EEA and which does not afford an adequate level of protection as described above, if the uplink station is located in an EEA state, that state is treated as the place from where the broadcast is made, and the person making the broadcast is deemed to be the person operating the uplink station: s 6A(2). Where the uplink station is not located in an EEA state then, under s 6A(3) a broadcast may still qualify for the protection of the appropriate EEA state if it was commissioned by a person established in an EEA state. The person so established is deemed to be the person making the broadcast, and the place from which the broadcast is treated as having been made is the place in which he has his principal establishment within the EEA. For example, a company registered and established in England commissions a broadcast transmitted from Israel. It is received in Turkey where it is instantaneously retransmitted to satellite from where it can be received in a number of EEA states. The English company is deemed to be the maker of the broadcast, and it is deemed to have been made in the United Kingdom and subject, therefore, to United Kingdom copyright.

### Cable programmes

The content of a broadcast is defined as visual images, sounds or other information. A cable programme service is similar, consisting wholly or mainly in sending visual images, sounds or other information. The difference between a broadcast and a cable programme service is that a broadcast is a transmission by wireless telegraphy, that is, over the airwaves, whereas a cable programme service is a transmission by means of a telecommunications system other than wireless telegraphy, for example, by cables laid in the ground. Therefore, the two are mutually exclusive. It is the cable programme which is protected by copyright (not the cable programme service), and this is defined in s 7(1) as meaning any item included in a cable programme service. There are certain exceptions in s 7(2) which can be added to or modified by the Secretary of State. These exceptions include interactive systems, that is where visual images, sounds or other information can be transmitted back to the person providing the service, and certain 'closed' systems which are not connected to any other telecommunications system.

A 'website' on the Internet could be deemed to be a cable programme service and items contained within that website could be cable programmes. So it was held in *Shetland Times Ltd v Dr Jonathan Wills*[121] in the Court of Session, Outer House in Scotland in granting an interim interdict to the plaintiff which published a newspaper called *The Shetland Times* and which also made it available on the Internet. Even though the information passively awaits access by callers to the website, Lord Hamilton considered that there was an arguable case that the process involved the sending of information as required by s 7(1). Additionally, although the service had an interactive element in that callers to the site could send comments and suggestions, this was not within s 7(2)(a) which excludes from the definition of 'cable programme service' services (or

121 [1997] FSR 604.

part of a service) an essential feature of which is that while visual images, sound or other information are being conveyed by the person providing the service there will or may be sent from each place of reception, by means of the same system (or same part of it), information (other than signals sent for the operation or control of the service) for reception by the person providing the service or other persons receiving it. In other words, the interactive element has to be an essential feature of the service to be excluded from the definition. Lord Hamilton considered that the interactive element was not an essential feature of the service, the primary purpose of which was to distribute news and other items. In any case, even if it was, it was arguable that it was a severable feature.

Under s 7(6), if the cable programme included in a cable programme service merely involves the reception and immediate re-transmission of a broadcast, it is not protected by copyright, although the broadcast itself will be. Also, copyright is declared not to subsist in a cable programme if it infringes, or to the extent that it infringes, the copyright in another cable programme or broadcast.

## TYPOGRAPHICAL ARRANGEMENT OF PUBLISHED EDITIONS

The Copyright, Designs and Patents Act 1988 s 8 defines a published edition, in the context of a typographical arrangement of a published edition, as the whole or any part of one or more literary, dramatic or musical works. Copyright in the typographical arrangement of published editions gives some protection to the publisher of a work which is itself out of copyright, and also gives some recognition to the skill expended in work such as selection of typestyles, format and typesetting. Artistic works are not included. If a publisher produces a book from a literary work which is still in copyright and a person copies a substantial part of the book, say by photocopying, then both the copyright in the literary work and the copyright in the typographical arrangement will be infringed.[122] If the copyright in the content of the book has expired, for example in the case of a Shakespeare play, copying the book will infringe the typographical arrangement only.

This form of copyright is increasingly important because of the recent advances in photocopying technology. To prevent publishers extending the life of their typographical arrangement copyright indefinitely, copyright is declared not to subsist in the typographical arrangement of a published edition if, or to the extent that, it reproduces the typographical arrangement of a previous edition.

## QUALIFICATION

For copyright to subsist in a work, under the Copyright, Designs and Patents Act 1988 s 1(3), the qualification requirements must be satisfied. This can be achieved in the following ways: either by reference to the author of the work, or by reference to the country of first publication or, in the case of a broadcast or cable programme, the country of first transmission.[123] In most cases, qualification will be easily satisfied, such as where the work is created by a UK citizen (or an individual domiciled or resident in the UK) or is first published in the UK. Also, international copyright conventions will give protection to works that would not

122 However, if the person types the book into a computer, there will be an infringement of the literary work but not of the typographical arrangement. Scanning the book into a computer will infringe, however, as this will create a facsimile copy: s 17(5).

123 The Copyright, Designs and Patents Act 1988 s 153. In relation to Crown Copyright, the qualification requirements are waived in the case of a work made by an officer or servant of the Crown in the course of his duties: s 163(1)(a). Similarly in respect of Parliamentary copyright: s 165(1).

otherwise qualify. Basically, these conventions, of which there are two, afford reciprocal protection to member countries, and most developed countries belong to one or other or both. The UK is a signatory to both the Berne Copyright Convention and the Universal Copyright Convention. As a result, if a work is first published in or transmitted from a convention country, or if the author of the work is a citizen of or is domiciled in a convention country, the owner will be able to take action for infringement in the UK. Similarly, works first published or transmitted in the UK, or having an author who is British or is domiciled in the UK will be protected in all the other convention countries.[124]

### Qualification by reference to the author

As will be seen in the following chapter, authorship and ownership of copyright are two distinct concepts and it is quite common for copyright to be owned by artificial legal persons, such as corporations. However, it is self-evident that the author of a literary, dramatic, musical or artistic work will be a living (or lately deceased) person. In the case of computer-generated literary, dramatic, musical and artistic works and sound recordings, films, broadcasts and cable programmes, the Copyright, Designs and Patents Act 1988 still defines the author in terms of a 'person', that is the person who makes the arrangements necessary for the creation of the work, makes the work or the broadcast or provides the service, but in relation to these works it would seem that all forms of legal persons, including artificial persons such as corporations, can be the author of the work. The author of the typographical arrangement of a published edition is the publisher and this will often be a corporation such as a limited company. For this reason, the qualification requirements cover the situation where the author is a corporate body.

Under s 154(1) a work will qualify for copyright protection if the author comes within any of the following categories:

(a) a British citizen, a British Dependent Territories citizen, a British national (Overseas), a British subject or a British protected person within the meaning of the British Nationality Act 1981;
(b) an individual domiciled or resident in the UK or another country to which the relevant copyright provisions apply;
(c) a body incorporated under the law of a part of the UK or another country to which the relevant copyright provisions apply.

The countries to which these provisions apply can be extended by Order in Council to the Channel Islands, the Isle of Man or any colony.[125] A work also qualifies if at the 'material time' the author was a citizen of or a subject of or domiciled or resident in another country, or if the author was a body incorporated under the law of another country to which the provisions have been extended.[126] Parties to the Berne Copyright Convention, the Universal Copyright Convention and countries which otherwise give adequate protection under their law are included.

The 'material time' is defined in s 154(4) as being, in the case of an unpublished literary, dramatic, musical or artistic work, the time it was made; or, if it was made over a period of time, a substantial part of that period. If published, the material time is the time of first publication. If the author dies before first publication, the material time is the time immediately before the author's death.

124 *See* Article 5, Berne Copyright Convention. Authors from another Convention country shall enjoy the same rights which are granted to nationals. The Copyright (Application to Other Countries) Order 1993, SI 1993/942, as amended, makes the necessary legislative provisions.

125 The Copyright, Designs and Patents Act 1988 s 157.

126 Ibid s 159. *See* the Copyright (Application to Other Countries) Order 1993, SI 1993/942 as amended.

For sound recordings, films and broadcasts, the material time is the time they were made. For cable programmes it is the time they were included in a cable programme service, and for a typographical arrangement of a published edition it is the time when the edition was first published.

A work of joint authorship qualifies for copyright protection if, at the material time, any of the authors satisfies the requirements for qualification by reference to the author, and only those who do satisfy those requirements are to be taken into account for the purpose of first ownership of copyright and duration of copyright.[127]

127 The Copyright, Designs and Patents Act 1988 s 154(3).

 NOT READ

### Qualification by reference to country of first publication or transmission

There is a distinction between transmitted works, namely broadcasts and cable programmes, and all other forms of works. In the case of the latter, under s 155, they qualify for protection if they are first published in the UK, any convention country or any country to which the copyright provisions are extended by Order in Council. A publication can still be a first publication even if it is simultaneously published elsewhere, and a period not exceeding 30 days is considered simultaneous. As an example, if a musical work is made by an author who fails to meet the qualification requirements (such as an Iranian living in Teheran) and the work is first published in Iran but is then published in the UK within the following 30 days, the music will attract UK copyright protection under the provisions contained in s 155. The music will be deemed to have been simultaneously published in Iran and the UK.

The meaning of 'publication' is central to these provisions and it is defined in s 175 as being the issue of copies to the public, including by means of electronic retrieval systems in the case of literary, dramatic, musical and artistic works. The construction of a building is equivalent to publication of the work of architecture it represents and any artistic works incorporated in the building.[128] In order to clarify the meaning further, some specified acts are declared not to amount to publication, for example, a performance of a literary, dramatic or musical work, an exhibition of an artistic work, the playing or showing of a sound recording or film in public, or the broadcast of or inclusion in a cable programme service of a literary, dramatic, musical or artistic work or a sound recording or film. Also excluded are the issue to the public of copies of a graphic work (for example, a sketch) representing, or photographs of, a work of architecture in the form of a building or a model for a building, a sculpture or a work of artistic craftsmanship.[129]

128 Ibid s 175(3).

129 Ibid s 175(4).

Thus, selling sheet music or video films to the public will be regarded as publication, but selling photographs depicting an original sculpture will not be. Whether the sale of the original sculpture to a member of the public is to be regarded as publication is a moot point and it may be stretching the language of s 175 too far, especially as it talks in terms of the plural. This is reinforced by s 175(5) which excludes publication which is 'merely colourable and not intended to satisfy the reasonable requirements of the public'. This means that a non-qualifying author who intends to sell copies of his work to the public in large numbers in a non-convention country cannot obtain the international benefits of the conventions simply by putting a few copies on sale at the same time in a convention country. However, selling or offering for sale small numbers of copies may still be deemed to be publication if the intention is to satisfy public demand, as in *Francis Day & Hunter Ltd* v *Feldman & Co*[130] in which the sale

130 [1914] 2 Ch 728.

of six copies of the song 'You Made Me Love You (I Didn't Want To Do It)' was deemed to be good publication because of the publisher's intention from the outset to satisfy public demand in the UK. Section 175(6) states that no account is to be taken of any unauthorised acts, therefore publication by a person without the permission of the copyright owner will not have any consequences as regards the qualification requirements for the work involved.

For transmitted works, broadcasts and cable programmes, the qualification requirements are satisfied if the works etc. are sent from the United Kingdom or any country to which the copyright provisions are extended by Order in Council. Qualification is determined by reference to the country of transmission and not the country or countries of reception. There is no provision here for dealing with simultaneous transmissions within a 30-day period.

It can be seen that qualification for copyright protection will rarely be in issue, particularly as a result of the operation of the Berne Copyright Convention and the Universal Copyright Convention and the reciprocity they provide for. In case there are any shortcomings in the protection offered for British works in another country, the Copyright, Designs and Patents Act 1988 s 160 permits, by Order in Council, the restriction of rights conferred to authors connected with that country.

## DURATION OF COPYRIGHT

The Copyright, Designs and Patents Act 1988 simplified the provisions relating to the duration of copyright. For example, under the Copyright Act of 1956 there were three rules for the duration of copyright in artistic works, depending on which variety of artistic work they were.[131] There were also different rules for works published or unpublished at the time of the author's death.[132] Things are now much clearer, although the transitional arrangements which apply to works in existence at the time when the 1988 Act came into force are not particularly straightforward.[133] Recently, the duration of copyright in most of the 'original works' and in films has been extended to 'life plus 70 years' by the Duration of Copyright and Rights in Performances Regulations 1995 (the '1995 Regulations').[134]

The rules for determining the duration of copyright depend on the nature of the work in question but, as a basic rule of thumb, copyright lasts for the life of the author plus 70 years for literary, dramatic, musical and artistic works (the 'original works') and films, and at least 50 years for sound recordings, broadcasts and cable programmes and 25 years for typographical arrangements of published editions. Copyright in certain types of artistic works that have been commercially exploited is also limited to 25 years. There are also special rules for the duration of Crown Copyright, that is in respect of works of which Her Majesty the Queen is the first owner of the copyright, and Parliamentary copyright. Perpetual copyright previously enjoyed by the Universities of Oxford and Cambridge and the Colleges of Eton, Winchester and Westminster in relation to certain works under the Copyright Act 1775 is abolished and such works existing at the time the Copyright, Designs and Patents Act 1988 came into force are given a 50-year copyright, commencing at the end of 1989.[135]

The recent changes to the duration of copyright in the 'original works' and films have a number of implications, especially in terms of extending the duration of existing copyright and reviving copyright in some works which had

131 The Copyright Act 1956 s 3.

132 Ibid s 2.

133 *See* the Copyright, Designs and Patents, Act 1988 Sch 1, para 12.

134 SI 1995/3297, implementing the EC Directive harmonising the term of copyright and certain related rights OJ L290, 29.10.93, p. 9.

135 The Copyright, Designs and Patents Act 1988 Sch 1, para 13.

fallen into the public domain in the UK. One feature of the new provisions on duration of copyright is that they are set in the context of the European Economic Area (EEA) and not just the European Community.[136] Thus, Iceland, Norway and Liechtenstein are included in the provisions.

Apart from the new rules for determining the duration of copyright for the original works and films, extended and revived copyright and some other aspects of the 1995 Regulations are described towards the end of this chapter.

### Literary, dramatic, musical and artistic works

As a rule, the identity of the author of a work will be known and commonly the author will have produced his work on his own, not in collaboration with another author. The copyright in a literary, dramatic, musical or artistic work of known authorship, having a single author, expires at the end of the period of 70 years from the end of the calendar year during which the author dies.[137] Therefore, when the work is made it is impossible to pinpoint the exact time when the copyright will expire; a work created by a relatively young author should have a long copyright, perhaps close to or even exceeding 120 years. If the work is the result of the collaboration of two or more authors and the contribution of each is not distinct from the other or others, it is a work of joint authorship and, under s 12(4), the 70-year period runs from the end of the calendar year during which the last surviving author dies. If the identities of all the authors is not known, the period is calculated by reference to the end of the calendar year during which the last surviving known author dies.

If the country of origin of the work is a non-EEA state and the author is not a national of an EEA state, the duration of copyright is limited to that in the country of origin provided it is not greater than life plus 70 years.[138] Thus, if the country of origin is Australia and the author is Australian, the duration of copyright as far as the countries within the EEA are concerned remains at life plus 50 years, the present term in Australia.

It is conceivable, though unlikely, that a work might be created by a person unknown.[139] The work may still qualify for protection on the basis of the country of first publication and s 12(2) makes provision for the duration of copyright for works of unknown authorship. Copyright expires at the end of the period of 70 years from the end of the calendar year in which the work was made or, if made available to the public during that period, the 70-year period runs from the end of the calendar year in which the work was first made available to the public.[140] 'Making available to the public' includes, in the case of a literary, dramatic or musical work, a public performance, broadcast or inclusion in a cable programme service. For artistic works, it includes public exhibitions, showing a film including the work in public or inclusion in a broadcast or cable programme service. The definitions are not exhaustive and should also cover acts such as selling or offering to sell to the public copies of the work. In determining whether the work has been made available to the public, no account is taken of any unauthorised act, so that the period of 70 years does not start to run if the work has been performed in public without the permission of the copyright owner. Before the changes made by the 1995 Regulations, copyright in a work of unknown authorship potentially was perpetual, that is if the work was not made available to the public, which seemed to be an anomaly difficult to justify. Even so, the practical effect of this was

136 An EEA state is a state which is a contracting party to the EEA Agreement signed at Oporto on 2 May 1992, adjusted by the Protocol signed at Brussels on 17 March 1993: the 1995 Regulations reg 2.

137 The Copyright, Designs and Patents Act 1988 new s 12(1) (substituted by the Duration of Copyright and Rights in Performances Regulations 1995, SI 1995/3297).

138 The meaning of 'country of origin' is described near the end of this chapter in the section on extended and revived copyright.

139 Of course, there may be situations when, for reasons of his own, the author does not want to be identified and his identity remains a secret between the author and his publisher. In such circumstances, it would appear that the work would be one of unknown authorship for copyright purposes.

140 The Copyright, Designs and Patents Act 1988 new s 12(3).

diluted because, under s 57(1), the copyright in a literary, dramatic, musical or artistic work was not infringed if it was not possible, by reasonable enquiry, to ascertain the identity of the author and it was reasonable to assume that the copyright had expired or that the author died 50 years or more before the beginning of the calendar year in which the relevant act was done.[141] If the work involved is truly anonymous, there may be considerable difficulties regarding the ownership and enforcement of the copyright, although in such circumstances s 104(4) contains a presumption that the publisher of the work as first published was the owner of the copyright at that time. If the identity of the author becomes known before the expiry of the copyright, then the normal rule applies under new s 12(2).

The final form of literary, dramatic, musical or artistic work having special provision is where the work is 'computer-generated', being a work generated by computer in circumstances such that there is no human author.[142] Without the life of a human author to measure the term of copyright, the starting date for the 50-year period is sensibly calculated, under new s 12(7), from the end of the calendar year in which the work was made.[143] Apart from works of unknown authorship, this is the only form of literary, dramatic, musical or artistic work in which the actual time the work was made is relevant to the duration of copyright.

The duration of protection of certain types of artistic work will be considerably shortened if they are 'commercially' exploited. Under s 52, where an artistic work has been exploited by or with the licence of the copyright owner by making articles which are copies of the work by an industrial process and marketing them, the copyright subsisting in the artistic work will be largely ineffective from the end of the period of 25 years from the end of the calendar year during which the articles were first marketed. The copyright in the artistic work still runs its full course notionally but, after the 25-year period, the work may be copied by making articles of any description or doing anything for making such articles without infringing the copyright. The fine detail has been left to the Secretary of State, and by the Copyright (Industrial Processes and Excluded Articles) (No. 2) Order 1989[144] an artistic work is deemed to have been exploited for the purposes of s 52 if more than 50 articles have been made or goods manufactured in lengths or pieces not being hand-made have been produced.[145] Certain types of artistic work are excluded from this provision, for example, works of sculpture, wall plaques, medals, medallions and printed matter primarily of a literary or artistic character. Typically, works of artistic craftsmanship will be caught by this reduction in terms of copyright, if exploited. It is intended to reduce the effective term of copyright in designs that qualify as artistic works but which are also potentially registrable as designs under the Registered Designs Act 1949. This limitation is further discussed in Chapters 7 and 17.

## Sound recordings

Until 1 January 1996, both sound recordings and films were governed by the same rules and, for either, the duration of copyright depended on when the work was made or, in some circumstances, when it was released. Now, for sound recordings, under new s 13A(3) of the Act, a sound recording is 'released' when it is first published, played in public, broadcast or included in a cable programme service.[146] As regards what constitutes a public showing, this can have a wide meaning and is discussed further in Chapter 6. The duration of

141 This presumption still applies but now by reference to the 70-year period; the Duration of Copyright and Rights in Performances Regulations 1995, SI 1995/3297, reg 5(2).

142 The Copyright, Designs and Patents Act 1988 s 178. Computer-generated works are fully explained and discussed in Chapter 8.

143 Unchanged by SI 1995/3297, though previously s 12(3).

144 SI 1989/1070.

145 SI 1989/1070 reg 2.

146 For the meaning of 'publication' *see* the Copyright, Designs and Patents Act 1988 s 175, discussed above. Section 13A (sound recordings) and s 13B (films) substituted the old s 13 by SI 1995/3297. Previously 'released' for the purposes of duration did not include playing in public.

copyright for a sound recording is unchanged and copyright expires 50 years from the end of the calendar year in which it is released with the proviso that, if it is not released, the copyright will expire at the end of the period of 50 years from the end of the calendar year in which it is made.[147] Therefore, the duration of copyright can be extended by delaying the release of the sound recording and can be, potentially, around 100 years if released just before the completion of 50 years from the end of the calendar year in which it is made.

147 The Copyright, Designs and Patents Act 1988 s 13A(2).

## Films

Until 1 January 1996, the duration of copyright in films was as for sound recordings but the changes wrought by the Duration of Copyright and Rights in Performances Regulations 1995 include a similar means of determining copyright in films as applies to the original works, that is, based on life plus 70 years. A number of different persons who make a creative contribution to the film are used to provide the relevant 'life'. Under new s 13B, copyright in a film expires at the end of the period of 70 years from the end of the calendar year during which the death of the last to die of the following occurs:

- the principal director
- the author of the screenplay
- the author of the dialogue, or
- the composer of music specially created for and used with the film.

There are provisions for cases where all or some of those persons are unknown. If all are unknown the duration is 70 years from the end of the year of making or, if made available to the public during that period, 70 years from the end of year in which it was so made available. If one or more of the persons is known, the duration is based on the last to die. In the unlikely event that there is no person in the above list (that is, where the film was made without a director, screenplay, dialogue or specially written music) the period is 50 years from the end of the calendar year during which the film was made.

## Broadcasts and cable programmes

A period of 50 years is part of the formula for calculating duration. In this case, the Copyright, Designs and Patents Act 1988 s 14(1) states that the copyright expires at the end of the period of 50 years from the end of the calendar year in which the broadcast was made or the programme included in a cable programme service.[148] Copyright is deemed to exist in a repeat broadcast or cable programme but expires at the same time as the original, subject to there being no copyright in a repeat broadcast or cable programme made after the expiry of the copyright in the original. Copyright in repeats may seem unnecessary as the concept of indirect copying has been accepted by the courts for some time[149] and is now given statutory effect under s 16(3). At first sight, copyright in repeats might seem useful when no tangible copy is made, such as where a person without permission receives a broadcast and simultaneously relays it to others, but broadcasting a work or including it in a cable programme service are amongst the acts restricted by copyright.

Section 14(3) states that a repeat broadcast or cable programme is one which is a repeat of either a broadcast previously made or a cable programme previously

148 Ibid s 14(2).

149 For example, *see British Leyland Motor Company Ltd* v *Armstrong Patents Co Ltd* [1986] 2 WLR 400 and *Purefoy Engineering Ltd* v *Sykes Boxall Ltd* (1955) 72 RPC 89.

included in a cable programme service. This means that a repeat broadcast can be made from a cable programme and will qualify for copyright protection as a repeat, expiring at the same time as the original cable programme and vice versa.

### Typographical arrangements of published editions

The copyright in a typographical arrangement of a published edition expires at the end of the period of 25 years from the end of the calendar year in which the edition was first published.[150] Under s 175(1)(a), first publication for typographical arrangements of published editions occurs when copies were first issued to the public.

NOT READ

### Crown and parliamentary copyright

Crown copyright subsists in works made by Her Majesty or by an officer or servant of the Crown in the course of his duties. Crown copyright in a literary, dramatic, musical or artistic work lasts until the end of the period of 125 years from the end of the calendar year in which the work was made or, if the work is published commercially before the end of the period of 75 years from the end of the calendar year in which it is made, copyright continues to subsist until the end of the period of 50 years from the end of the calendar year in which it was first published commercially.[151] Therefore, if a work of Crown copyright is published in the first year it was created, it will have copyright protection for only 50 years from the end of that year. Commercial publication in relation to a literary, dramatic, musical or artistic work, means, under s 175(2), issuing copies to the public at a time when copies made in advance of the receipt of orders are generally available to the public or when the work is available to the public by means of an electronic retrieval system.

There are no special provisions for Crown copyright as regards the other types of copyright work, so the usual rules will apply. In the case of a work of joint authorship where one or more of the authors, but not all, fall within the requirement for Crown copyright, the provisions in s 163 apply only in relation to those authors and the copyright subsisting by virtue of their contribution to the work.[152] Does this mean that the rights of the other joint author(s) are unaffected by Crown copyright? This could be problematical as s 10(1) provides that, by definition, a work of joint authorship is a collaborative one in which the work of each joint author is not distinct. Taken to its logical conclusion, this could mean that the copyright subsisting in such a work of joint authorship would have, theoretically, two durations, which is a nonsense.

Acts of Parliament and Measures of the General Synod of the Church of England are protected by copyright from Royal Assent until the end of the period of 50 years from the end of the calendar year in which the Act or Measure received the Royal Assent.[153] Parliamentary copyright in a literary, dramatic, musical or artistic work continues to subsist until the end of the period of 50 years from the end of the calendar year in which the work was made.[154] Works within this category include reports of select committees. The duration of copyright in sound recordings, films, live broadcasts or cable programmes is in accordance with the usual rules. Parliamentary Bills are separately provided for under s 166, and copyright in a Bill expires when the Bill receives the Royal Assent, at which time the copyright in the new Act commences, or, if the Bill does not receive Royal Assent, copyright expires when the Bill is withdrawn or rejected or at the end of the Session.

**150** The Copyright, Designs and Patents Act 1988 s 15.

**151** Ibid s 163(3).

**152** Ibid s 163(4).

**153** Ibid s 164(2).

**154** Ibid s 165.

Providing for copyright in Acts of Parliament and other legislative material is a controversial issue, especially as Her Majesty's Stationery Office appears to be more active in enforcing that copyright.[155] It could be argued that such works should be in the public domain, as it is in the public interest that Her Majesty's subjects are aware of the law. No less than Laddie J has recently suggested that such materials should be freely available.[156]

There has been some relaxation in HMSO's approach to use of Crown copyright material by publishers. A 'Dear Publisher' letter was placed on the Internet by HMSO, dated 1 March 1996. It allows reproduction without permission or charge of Acts of Parliament, Statutory Instruments and Statutory Rules and Orders and certain Press Releases (though not for providing a commercial Crown Press Release Service). This is all subject to the text being 'value-added' (for example, where the publisher has included annotations or comments), the source being acknowledged as Crown copyright and the material being reproduced accurately and in such a way as not to be misleading. Reproduction can be world-wide and by electronic means.

### 'Peter Pan' by Sir James Matthew Barrie

As a special concession to the Great Ormond Street Hospital for Sick Children, to which Sir James Barrie donated his copyright in the play 'Peter Pan', a *sui generis* right to continue to receive royalties beyond the life of the copyright was provided for in the Copyright, Designs and Patents Act 1988. This was the result of an amendment moved by Lord Callaghan. The copyright in the play 'Peter Pan' expired on midnight 31 December 1987, and under s 301 and Sch 6 to the Act, royalties are payable to the Hospital for Sick Children, Great Ormond Street, London in respect of any public performance, commercial publication, broadcasting or inclusion in a cable programme service of the whole or a substantial part of the play or an adaptation of it. The right is not absolute and will come to an end if the hospital ceases to have a separate identity or no longer cares for sick children. However, as a result of the Duration of Copyright and Rights in Performances Regulations 1995,[157] discussed below, it would appear that the copyright in 'Peter Pan' has been revived and will now expire at the end of the year 2007. Presumably, the above provisions are suspended until that time as the Hospital now has full rights of ownership, as any owner of revived copyright, in relation to the work. Indeed, the special jurisdiction of the Copyright Tribunal to determine the royalty in the absence of agreement has been removed by reg 24(2)(b) of the Copyright and Related Rights Regulations 1996.[158] However, as the copyright has been revived, it will be subject to licences as of right following notice and, in the absence of agreement as to royalty, referable to the Copyright Tribunal under reg 25 of the 1995 Regulations instead. Although achieved in a different manner, the result is the same.

### Extended copyright, revived copyright and other aspects of the 1995 Regulations

The Duration of Copyright and Rights in Performances Regulations 1995 increase the term of copyright for original literary, dramatic, musical and artistic works and films.[159] There are some important transitional provisions to deal with cases where existing copyright is extended, for example, as to who will own the extended

155 The Stationery Office Ltd now controls the former HMSO bookshops. A residual HMSO administers Crown copyright.

156 Gibb, F. 'Attack on Copyright', *The Times*, 5 December 1995, at p. 41.

157 SI 1995/3297.

158 SI 1996/2967.

159 There are some changes in respect of rights in performances also for which *see* Chapter 10.

copyright and the position in respect of pre-existing licences, and where copyright is revived. Before looking at these provisions and other aspects of the Regulations, it is important to note the appropriate definitions which are contained in regs 12 and 14.

An 'existing work' is one made before commencement of the Regulations (1 January 1996) and an 'existing copyright work' is one in which copyright subsisted immediately before commencement (that is, 31 December 1995). '1988 provisions' means the provisions of the Copyright, Designs and Patents Act 1988 immediately before commencement of the Regulations. The 'new provisions' are those of the Act as amended by the Regulations.

Under reg 15(1), copyright in an existing copyright work will continue to subsist until the date it would have expired under the 1988 provisions if that date is later than provided for under the Regulations. This preserves the duration of works that were, prior to the Copyright, Designs and Patents Act 1988, works of perpetual copyright or unpublished works or where the work was published after the author's death. For example, perpetual copyright was conferred on works of certain universities and colleges by the Copyright Act 1775 and this was reduced to 50 years from the end of the year of commencement of the 1988 provisions. As regards works published after an author's death, consider an author of a literary work who died in 1958. His work was not published until 1987. Under the Copyright Act 1956, his copyright would not expire until the end of 2037 (50 years after publication).[160] The 1988 provisions maintained this rule with a cut off from the end of the year of commencement.[161] Under the new provisions, copyright would be based solely on the year of the author's death and would expire at the end of 2028. Because of the transitional provisions, the copyright will continue until the end of 2037.

Under reg 15(2), there is a saving such that where the above rule applies the provisions in s 57 (assumptions as to expiry of copyright in anonymous or pseudonymous works) are unmodified (that is, where it reasonable to assume that the author died 50 years ago). The Regulations increase that period to 70 years in other cases.

The new provisions as to duration, as described earlier, apply to:

- copyright works made after commencement;
- existing works which first qualify for copyright protection after commencement (for example, where the author, being a Taiwanese citizen, created the work in 1992, but the work is first published in the UK after 1 January 1996);
- existing copyright works (subject to reg 15 above);
- existing works in which copyright expired before 31 December 1995 but which, on 1 July 1995, were protected in another EEA state (1 July 1995 is that date the Directive on harmonising the term of copyright and certain related rights should have been complied with).

### Extended and revived copyright

Regulation 17 defines 'extended copyright' and 'revived copyright' as follows:

- extended copyright is any copyright which subsists by virtue of the new provisions after the date on which it would have expired under the 1988 provisions;

**160** The Copyright Act 1956 s 2(3).

**161** The Copyright, Designs and Patents Act 1988, Sch 1 para 1.

- revived copyright is any copyright which subsists by virtue of the new provisions after having expired under the 1988 provisions or any earlier copyright enactment.

Regulation 18 states the rules for determining who the owner of extended copyright is and it is the person owning the copyright immediately before commencement of the new provisions. However, if that person did not own the copyright for the full term under the 1988 provisions, the extended copyright is part of the reversionary interest. For example, if Mary owns the copyright in a literary work and the copyright was to expire at the end of 1999, it will continue to subsist until the end of 2019 and Mary will continue to be its owner. If, on 31 December 1990, Mary assigned the copyright to Jacob for seven calendar years, on 1 January 1998 the copyright will revert to her and she will be the owner of the remaining term of copyright (that is, from 1 January 1998 to 31 December 2019, when it expires).

The owner of revived copyright is, under reg 19, the owner at the time the copyright expired. If the former owner died before commencement of the new provisions (or ceased to exist if a corporation), the revived copyright vests in:

- for films – the principal director or his personal representatives
- for other works – the author or his personal representatives.

The personal representatives hold the revived copyright for the benefit of the person who would have been entitled to it had it been part of the director's or author's estate immediately before his death and devolved as part of that estate.

There are provisions for prospective ownership of extended or revived copyright which are similar to those applying to prospective ownership of future copyright, as discussed in the following chapter. Under reg 20, where by an agreement made before commencement of the new provisions, the prospective owner of extended or revived copyright purports to assign that copyright wholly or partly, in writing and signed by the prospective owner, then if on commencement the assignee or person claiming through him would be entitled as against all other persons to require the copyright to be vested in him, the copyright shall so vest in the assignee or successor in title.

Any licence granted by the prospective owner will, as under normal copyright rules, bind every successor in title of his except a purchaser in good faith for valuable consideration without actual or constructive knowledge of the licence. Persons deriving title from such a person will also take free of the licence.

There has to be provision for dealing with pre-existing licences and other rights and obligations. Under reg 21, any copyright licence, term or condition of an agreement relating to the exploitation of a copyright work or waiver or assertion of moral rights will continue to have effect during the extended term of copyright, subject to agreement to the contrary, provided:

- the licence, term, waiver, etc. existed immediately before commencement of the new provisions in relation to an existing copyright work, and
- it is not to expire before the end of the copyright period under the 1988 provisions.

There is an equivalent provision regarding licences, terms or conditions imposed by order of the Copyright Tribunal, subject to any further order of the Copyright Tribunal. Revived copyright could cause particular concern. For example, what about a person who, *bona fide*, performs acts within the scope of copyright in relation to a work in which copyright has expired in the UK. Suddenly, that person could be prevented from doing something he was previously doing quite lawfully. Regulation 23 contains some savings to cover such a situation to the effect that:

- no act done before commencement infringes revived copyright;
- it is not an infringement of revived copyright
  - to do anything after commencement in pursuance of arrangements made before 1 January 1995 at a time copyright did not subsist in the work, or
  - to issue to the public after commencement copies of a work made before 1 July 1995 at a time copyright did not subsist in the work;
- there are equivalent provisions for literary, dramatic, musical, artistic works and films containing copies or adaptations of works in which revived copyright subsists;
- it is not an infringement of revived copyright to do after commencement anything which is a restricted act in relation to the work if the act is done at a time when (or in pursuance of arrangements made at a time when) the name and address of a person entitled to authorise the act cannot by reasonable enquiry be ascertained;
- it is not an infringement of a moral right to do anything which, by the above provisions, does not infringe copyright.

Where these savings do not apply, licences are available as of right in relation to revived copyright (unless a licensing body could have granted the relevant rights) under reg 24. The licence as of right is subject to payment of a reasonable royalty, to be fixed by the Copyright Tribunal in default of agreement. However, the person intending to take advantage of the licence of right provisions must give reasonable notice of his intention to the copyright owner, stating when he intends to begin the acts concerned. Absence of a notice will mean the carrying out of the acts will not be treated as licensed.

Revived copyright could apply in many cases. Before the changes resulting from the Directive on the term of copyright, Germany already granted protection for life plus 70 years.[162] One hypothetical example of revived copyright could be where Hans, a German composer, wrote a piece of music in 1935. He published it both in Germany and in the United Kingdom (within a few days of the German publication) during that year, hence gaining German and United Kingdom copyright. Hans died in 1944. The United Kingdom copyright expired at the end of 1994, but the German copyright was still in existence at 1 July 1995. Therefore, the United Kingdom copyright was revived on 1 January 1996 and will continue to subsist until the end of 2014.

Now imagine that the music was created instead by Edward, a British citizen, who also died in 1944. The work was not published in Germany within the 30-day rule,[163] so he had no German copyright. Say that Edward's work was copied without permission in Germany during 1997 and his estate brought an action in Germany on the basis of the Berne Copyright Convention. If the German court held that the action must fail because the United Kingdom copyright had expired, this could be deemed to be discrimination on the ground of nationality contrary to Article 6 of the EC Treaty. The reason is that, had Edward been a German citizen, his copyright would still subsist and be enforceable in Germany. One of the implications of *Collins v Imtrat Handelsgesellschaft mbH*[164] is that such discrimination is not permissible and, on that basis, it is at

**162** Spain granted life plus 80 years.

**163** Under the Copyright Act 1911 s 35(3), the publication in the other country would have to be within 14 days, not 30 days.

**164** [1994] FSR 166. This case is discussed in Chapter 9.

least arguable that Edward's United Kingdom copyright also should be revived. In other words, all works in which copyright expired in the United Kingdom between 1 January 1975 and 31 December 1995 should be revived, whether or not they had copyright in another EEA state on 1 July 1995.

### Other aspects

The country of origin of a work may be important in some cases in the determination of duration of copyright. Basically, if the country of origin is an EEA state, the provisions on duration in the Regulations will apply. If the country of origin is a non-EEA state, then the duration will be that provided for by the country of origin though not longer than set out in the Regulations. The test for country of origin is not a simple one.

Country of origin is defined in the Copyright, Designs and Patents Act 1988 s 15A (inserted by reg 8), being:

- if first published in a Berne country and not published simultaneously elsewhere, that country;
- if first published simultaneously in two or more countries, one of which is a Berne country, the Berne country is the country of origin;
- if first published simultaneously in two or more Berne countries
  - if any is an EEA state, that country;
  - if none is an EEA state, the country of origin is the Berne country providing the shortest term of protection;
- if first published in a non-Berne country:
  - if a film and the maker has his headquarters or is domiciled in or resident in a Berne country, that country;
  - if the work is a work of architecture constructed in a Berne country or an artistic work incorporated in such a building, the Berne country is the country of origin;
  - in any other case, the country of origin is the country of which the author is a national.

Although the provisions as to duration of sound recordings, broadcasts and cable programmes are as before there are now equivalent provisions as to works from non-EEA states.

There is a new permitted act in relation to films, the Copyright, Designs and Patents Act 1988 s 66A.[165] The copyright in a film is not infringed if:

- it is not possible by reasonable inquiry to ascertain the identity of any of the persons (by reference to whom duration can be fixed), and
- it is reasonable to assume that copyright has expired or the last of those persons has been dead for 70 years or more before the beginning of the calendar year during which the relevant act was done or arrangements are made.

[165] Inserted by the Duration of Copyright and Rights in Performances Regulations 1995, SI 1995/3297 reg 6(2).

This is equivalent to s 57 (assumptions on expiry of copyright in anonymous or pseudonymous literary, dramatic, musical or artistic works).

Regulation 13 deals with the case where a film is protected but not as a film. Where a film is protected not as a film, but as an original dramatic work or by virtue of photographs forming part of the film, reference to copyright in a film include references to other such copyrights.

The sound track of a film is now considered as part of the film and the definition of 'film' is amended accordingly.[166] References in the Act to showing a film now include playing the sound track, though playing a sound recording does not include playing the film sound track to accompany the film. There are some further provisions in terms of moral rights and amendments to the law relating to rights in performances (*see* Chapters 5 and 10).

Appropriate consequential amendments are made to the Copyright, Designs and Patents Act 1988 to account for the new term of copyright and the new definitions.

## PUBLICATION RIGHT

A person may own an old original manuscript which is out of copyright, the author having died more than 70 years ago. Perhaps the manuscript has never been published, but the current owner would like to publish it and sell copies, or grant a licence to a publisher to do so. With no copyright to protect against unauthorised copies being made and sold, the economic incentive to publish would be limited. To overcome this problem, a new publication right was introduced by the Copyright and Related Rights Regulations 1996.[167] It has some of the appearances of a copyright and, under reg 16(1), is declared to be a property right equivalent to copyright. The publication right applies where a literary, dramatic, musical or artistic work or a film is, after the expiry of copyright, published for the first time. It then endures for 25 years from the end of the calendar year during which it was first published. Publication includes any communication to the public, in particular:

- the issue of copies to the public
- making the work available by means of an electronic retrieval system
- the rental or lending of copies to the public
- the performance, exhibition or showing in public, or
- broadcasting the work or including it in a cable programme service.[168]

Unauthorised acts, being without the consent of the owner of the physical medium in or on which the work is embodied or recorded, are not taken into account. Consequently, the publication right can only belong to a person who makes the publication subject to such consent. As the right cannot arise until there has been first publication (with the consent of the owner of the physical medium), any prior unauthorised act cannot infringe the publication right. There may, however, be other legal remedies, such as breach of confidence, or even under the Theft Act 1968 s 1. Unauthorised copying and publication could be deemed to be an assumption of the rights of the owner, and even if the physical medium is only 'borrowed', the circumstances could be such to be equivalent to an intention permanently to deprive the owner.

As with normal copyright, there are some qualification requirements being that the first publication must take place in the European Economic Area (EEA) and the publisher is, at that time, a national of an EEA state or, in the case of a joint publication, at least one of the joint publishers is. There is no provision for the 30-day period of grace which applies to qualification for copyright protection under the Copyright, Designs and Patents Act 1988 s 155 (simultaneous publication). The right cannot arise in relation to works which were subject to Crown copyright or parliamentary copyright.

**166** The Copyright, Designs and Patents Act 1988 new s 5B. Section 5A defines a sound recording which is as before.

**167** SI 1996/2967. The publication right came from the EC Directive harmonising the term of protection of copyright and certain related rights, OJ L290, 24.11.93, p. 9, Article 4.

**168** Regulation 16(2).

Under reg 17, most of the copyright provisions will apply to the publication right as they do to copyright,[169] subject to some omissions and modifications. In particular:

- there are no moral rights in respect of the publication right;
- a small number of the permitted acts do not apply (ss 57, 64, 66A and 67);
- the presumptions as to the identity of the author, owner, director, producer, etc. in ss 104 to 106 do not apply;
- the exception to the licensing-scheme provisions in Chapter VII (for licences or licensing schemes covering works of more than one author for licences or schemes covering only for single collective works or collective works of which the authors are the same, or works made by, or by employees of or commissioned by, a single individual, firm, company or group of companies) does not apply to the publication right;
- the maximum penalty for the offences of making or dealing with infringing articles is only three months and/or a fine not exceeding level five on the standard scale.

Other relevant provisions, including Chapter VIII of the Copyright, Designs and Patents Act 1988 on the Copyright Tribunal, apply *mutatis mutandis*, and other enactments relating to copyright apply in relation to the publication right as they do to copyright, unless the context requires otherwise.

The publication right provisions came into force on 1 December 1996. No act done before this date can infringe the right, nor can anything done in pursuance of an agreement made before 19 November 1992 (the date of adoption of the rental-right Directive, which was also implemented by the 1996 Regulations).

The publication right could encourage the greater dissemination of old works where, until now, the owner of the physical medium has declined to publish because of concerns about unauthorised copying or piracy. It could now be worth considering publishing a book of old legal documents such as wills, deeds of conveyance, leases and even copyright assignments. Anyone discovering an old, hitherto unknown, music score by a great composer might similarly be tempted to publish.

Table 3.1 shows the duration of copyright as it applies to the various types of works, including the publication right.

169 Thus, infringement of the publication right is the same as for copyright.

## Table 3.1  Duration of copyright

| Type of work | Event | Duration: from end of year of event |
| --- | --- | --- |
| **Literary, dramatic, musical, artistic** | | |
| Known author | Author dies | 70 years |
| Unknown author | Work made | 70 years — made available |
| | Or, if made available to the public in above period | 70 years, from end of calendar year of making available |
| Computer-generated work | Work made | 50 years |
| Joint authors | Death of last author to die | 70 years |
| **Sound recordings** | Sound recording made | 50 years — release |
| | Or, if released within above period | 50 years, from end of calendar year of release |
| **Films** | Last to die of principal director, screenplay author, dialogue author, music composer | 70 years |
| **Broadcasts and cable programmes** | Broadcast made or cable programme included in a cable programme service | 50 years |
| **Typographical arrangements of published editions** | First publication | 25 years |
| **Crown & parliamentary copyright etc.** | | |
| Literary, dramatic, musical, artistic | Work made | 125 years — commercial publication |
| | Or, if published commercially within first 75 years | 50 years, from end of calendar year of commercial publication |
| Acts and Measures | Royal Assent | 50 years |
| Parliamentary copyright | Work made | 50 years |
| Bills | Bill made (presumably) | (until Royal Assent/ — rejection) |
| **Publication right** | First publication with consent of owner of medium containing work | 25 years |

*Notes:*
1.  Duration is measured from end of the calendar year in which the event occurred.
2.  Copyright subsists before the commencement of the period shown, from the time at which the work is made.
3.  In effect, copyright in certain types of artistic works which have been exploited is reduced to 25 years.

# 4

## Authorship and ownership of copyright

### INTRODUCTION

As copyright is a property right, this raises important questions about ownership and the mechanisms for exploiting copyright. Authorship and ownership are, in relation to copyright, two distinct concepts, each of which attracts its own peculiar rights: the author having moral rights, and the owner of the copyright possessing economic rights. Sometimes, the author of a work will also be the owner of the copyright in the work, but this is not always so, and many works have separate authors and owners as far as copyright is concerned. Ownership flows from authorship; the person who makes the work is normally the first owner of the copyright in the work, provided that he has not created the work in the course of employment, in which case his employer will be the first owner of the copyright.[1] The owner of the copyright in a work may decide to exploit the work by the use of one or more contractual methods. He may grant a licence to allow another person to carry out certain acts in relation to the work, such as making copies, in which case he retains the ownership of the copyright. Alternatively, the owner may assign the copyright to another, that is transfer the ownership of the copyright to a new owner, relinquishing the economic rights under copyright law. One point to bear in mind is that a third party can carry out certain acts in relation to the whole or a part of a work protected by copyright without the permission of the owner of the copyright in the work and without infringing the copyright in the work, for example, by performing one of the acts falling within the fair dealing provisions, or because the act is not restricted by the copyright. There is little that the owner of the copyright can do about these limitations and exceptions to copyright protection apart from denying access to the work itself, for example, by refusing to publish the work.

Consider a single work in which copyright subsists. There may be several relationships and activities connected with the work and the copyright to the work. Figure 4.1 shows the relationships that might exist in relation to a work.

1 The author is the person who has created the work in question.
2 The copyright in the work is owned by a person who might be the author or the author's employer or a person who has become the owner of the copyright because the title to the copyright has been transferred to him.
3 With respect to the work, there are certain acts which are restricted by the copyright. These 'restricted acts' (an example is making a copy of a work) can be carried out only by the owner of the copyright or by someone having the owner's permission, such as a licensee. Otherwise, subject to certain exceptions, the copyright in the work will be infringed.

1 There are other exceptions, see later.

74

4 The copyright owner can grant licences in respect of the work which will allow the licensee to do all or some of the restricted acts, in accordance with the terms of the licence. Sometimes, a licensee will be permitted to grant sub-licences to others.

5 The copyright owner and any licensees and sub-licensees, subject to the terms of the licence agreement, will be able to carry out all or some of the restricted acts.

6 A third party, for example a member of the general public, can carry out a restricted act *only* if it is permitted by copyright law (for example, the permitted acts of fair dealing for criticism or review) or some other defence applies, such as the public interest.

7 Any person can carry out acts in relation to the work that are *not* acts restricted by copyright, such as lending to a friend a book or a music cassette, or reading a book. There may, however, be contractual restrictions affecting such acts.

8 All persons, including the owner of the copyright, licensees, sub-licensees and members of the public generally, must respect the author's moral rights. The author may be able to enforce his moral rights irrespective of the identity of the present owner of the copyright (provided that author has asserted his right to be identified as author and has not otherwise waived it).

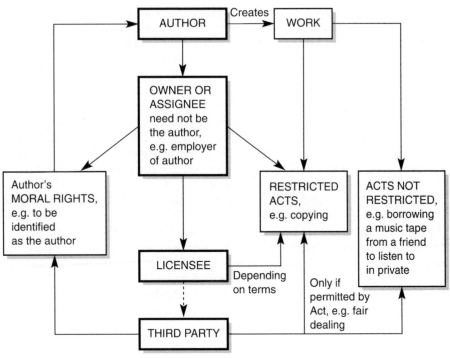

Note:
1. The third party may be a member of the general public or a sub-licensee.
2. The licensee may also carry out the permitted acts and any acts not restricted by the copyright, subject to the terms of the agreement.
3. A licence may impose obligations on the licensor preventing him from doing certain acts himself.

**Figure 4.1 Mechanism of copyright**

## AUTHORSHIP

The author of a work is the person who creates it.[2] In terms of some types of works this will be self-evident: for example, the author of a work of literature is the person who writes it; the author of a piece of music is its composer; the author of a photograph is the photographer and so on. The author of a compilation is the person who gathers or organises the material contained within it and who selects, orders and arranges that material.[3] The author does not have to be the person who carries out the physical act of creating the work, such as by putting pencil to paper. An amanuensis taking down dictation is not the author of the resulting work. In *Cala Homes (South) Ltd v Alfred McAlpine Homes East Ltd*,[4] drawings were made by draughtsmen, but another person had told them what features were to be incorporated in the designs for new houses. In some cases, that information was imparted by means of sketches, in other cases, verbally. The person giving the instructions also marked up the preliminary drawings with alterations he required to be incorporated in the finished drawings. Laddie J said that what is protected by copyright is more than just the skill of making marks on paper or some other medium, and that it was wrong to think that only the person who performs the mechanical acts of fixation is the author. He held that the person giving the instructions was a co-author of the drawings and, hence, the plaintiff for whom he worked as design director, was a joint owner of the copyright.

With some types of works, further explanation of authorship is required and this is furnished by the Copyright, Designs and Patents Act 1988. Under s 9(2), the author of a broadcast is the person making the broadcast, including, in the case of a broadcast relaying another broadcast by reception and immediate retransmission, the person making that other broadcast; the author of a cable programme is the person providing the cable programme service in which it is included. The publisher of the typographical arrangement of a published edition is considered to be its author. If the work is a computer-generated literary, dramatic, musical or artistic work, which is generated by computer in circumstances such that there is no human author, the author is deemed to be the person by whom the arrangements necessary for the creation of the work are undertaken,[5] a formula similar to that for sound recordings.

The author of a sound recording or film used to be simply the person by whom the arrangements necessary for its making are undertaken. Now, as a result of the Copyright and Related Rights Regulations 1996,[6] the author of a sound recording is the producer[7] and the author of a film is the producer and principal director.[8] Unless the producer and principal director are one and the same, a film is treated as a work of joint authorship under s 10(1A). The term 'producer' is new and is defined in s 178, in relation to a sound recording or film, as the person by whom the arrangements necessary for the making of the sound recording or film are undertaken. Hence, for sound recordings the result is the same as before, but for films this is a major change. Previously, a film director was not the author or one of the authors, although film directors did enjoy moral rights in respect of their films. This change applies as from 1 December 1996 in relation to films made on or after 1 July 1994. The reason for the latter date is that the EC Directives on rental and lending rights and on the term of copyright, both of which contained this provision, allowed member states to choose not to apply it to films made before that date.

2 The Copyright, Designs and Patents Act 1988 s 9(1). Unless otherwise stated, statutory references are to the Copyright, Designs and Patents Act 1988.

3 *Waterlow Publishers Ltd v Rose* [1995] FSR 207, which concerned, *inter alia*, the authorship of *The Solicitors' Diary and Directory*.

4 [1995] FSR 818.

5 The Copyright, Designs and Patents Act 1988 s 9(3).

6 SI 1996/2967.

7 Copyright, Designs and Patents Act 1988 s 9(2)(aa).

8 Ibid s 9(2)(ab).

Because copyright protects only the expression of an idea, there may be occasions when the originator of the information that forms the basis of the work in question will not be considered to be the author of the work. For example, in *Springfield* v *Thame*[9] the plaintiff, a journalist, supplied newspapers with information in the form of an article. The editor of the *Daily Mail*, from that information, composed a paragraph which appeared in the newspaper. It was held that the plaintiff was not the author of the paragraph as printed in the newspaper. Similarly, a person making a speech in public will not be the author of a report of the speech made by reporters. In *Walter* v *Lane*,[10] reporters for *The Times* made reports of the speeches of Lord Roseberry which were printed verbatim after they had been corrected and revised. It was held that the reporters were the authors of the reports and, as a result of the terms of the reporters' employment, the copyright in the reports belonged to *The Times*. In the latter case, it can be argued that the reporters had used skill and judgment in making, correcting and revising the reports. However, as noted above, if a person is simply writing down dictation, the person dictating will be the author for copyright purposes, as the person doing the writing is simply the agent by which the work is made.[11] The distinction is a fine but important one, as authorship will usually determine first ownership of the copyright.

In principle, there is nothing to prevent a corporate body being the author of a work, as s 154(1)(c) recognises that a work may qualify for copyright protection if the author is a body incorporated under the law of the United Kingdom. This may apply in the case of a sound recording, where the work in question is the result of arrangements made by senior officers of a music company,[12] in which case the company can be deemed to be the author. If the person who makes the arrangements in practice is lower down in the company hierarchy so that his actions are not automatically deemed to be the actions of the company, the company will probably still *own* the copyright (as opposed to being the author) on the basis of the employer/employee relationship or because of some contractual provision. The identification of the author is important for determining the first ownership of copyright and also for measuring the duration of the copyright. In the case of many of the original works, the copyright expires at the end of the period of 70 years from the end of the calendar year during which the author died.[13]

The Copyright, Designs and Patents Act 1988 recognises that the identity of the author may not always be known. A work is of 'unknown authorship' if the identity of the author is unknown meaning that it is not possible for a *person* to ascertain the identity of the author by reasonable enquiry.[14] It is not clear who the 'person' referred to might be. One possibility is that it is the person wishing to copy the work, making the test subjective;[15] on the other hand, it may be the ubiquitous 'reasonable man', an objective test. The work may be truly anonymous or it may be pseudonymous, that is the author does not wish his identity to be disclosed. The Berne Copyright Convention, by Article 15, makes presumptions in the case of anonymous and pseudonymous works and there is no requirement under UK copyright law that the identity of the author be disclosed to ultimate purchasers of material incorporating the copyright work, for example purchasers of books written by the author. This has little significance, other than with respect to the duration of the copyright in the work concerned, and may be relevant in terms of infringement,[16] and evidentially as regards ownership.

9 (1903) 19 TLR 650. Originality would be in issue now.

10 [1900] AC 539.

11 The principle cannot apply when a person at a seance produces a work under the influence of a person long since dead. In *Cummins v Bond* [1927] 1 Ch 167, the medium who had written down the work was the author, not the extraterrestrial psychic being. The judge said he must confine his inquiry to persons alive at the time the work was made.

12 An analogous principle in criminal law is that of corporate liability, where a company can be criminally liable on the basis of acts or omissions of its senior officers who are deemed to be the brains of the company. See the judgment of Lord Denning MR in *H.L. Bolton (Engineering) Co Ltd v TJ Graham & Sons Ltd* [1957] 1 QB 159 at 172.

13 The Duration of Copyright and Rights in Performance Regulations 1995.

14 *See* the Copyright, Designs and Patents Act 1988 s 9(4) and 9(5). Section 9(5) further states that once the author's identity is known, it cannot subsequently be regarded as unknown.

15 *See* Merkin, R. (1989) *Copyright, Designs and Patents: The New Law*, Longman, at p. 50.

16 The Copyright, Designs and Patents Act 1988 s 57(1) provides for permitted acts on the basis of certain assumptions as to the expiry of copyright or death of the author in relation to anonymous and pseudonymous works. *See* Chapter 7.

Frequently, a work will be the result of the efforts of more than one person. Several employees may work together to produce a written report, a team of computer programmers and systems analysts together may produce a computer program, two or more persons may collaborate in the writing of a work of literature, a piece of music or the painting of a landscape in oils. Collaboration between two or more persons will result in a work of joint authorship only if their respective contributions to the finished work are not distinct from each other, under s 10(1). That is, the work cannot be broken down so that each author's contribution can be separately identified. Thus, an abstract oil painting created by two painters applying paint to create an effect previously agreed by them would be a work of joint authorship. A book comprising separate chapters written by different authors is not a work of joint authorship, neither is a song where one person has written the music and another has written the words, as in a Gilbert and Sullivan operetta. In the latter cases, each person involved will the author of his own distinct work, and in the case of a song, the person writing the music will be the author of the musical work while the person writing the lyrics will be the author of those lyrics, as a literary work. Two copyrights will exist in the song, each having different authors (and, possibly, different owners) and the duration of the copyright in the music and the lyrics will differ according to the dates when the composer and lyricist die. A film is now a work of joint authorship, the producer and principal director being the joint authors, unless they are the same person.[17]

17 Section 10(1A).

In the case of a broadcast, s 10(2) provides that it will be treated as a work of joint authorship where more than one person is to be taken to be making the broadcast. The person making the broadcast is, under s 6(3), the person transmitting the programme if he has any responsibility to any extent for the content of the broadcast and any person providing the programme who makes, with the person transmitting it, the arrangements necessary for its transmission.

## OWNERSHIP

The Copyright, Designs and Patents Act 1988 s 11 states the basic rule that the author of a work is the first owner of the copyright. This will apply in a good number of cases, for example to persons creating works for their own pleasure or amusement, independent persons not employed under a contract of employment and even to employed persons if the work in question has not been created in the course of their employment. However, there are some exceptions to this basic rule, and where a literary, dramatic, musical or artistic work is made by an employee in the course of his employment, his employer is the first owner of the copyright subsisting in the work subject to any agreement to the contrary.[18] In *Noah v Shuba*[19] it was held that the copyright in a work created by an employee in the course of his employment could still belong to the employee on the basis of a term implied on the ground of past practice. If the employee's name appears on the work or copies of the work, there is a presumption that the work was not made in the course of employment.[20]

18 Ibid s 11(2).
19 [1991] FSR 14.

20 The Copyright, Designs and Patents Act 1988 s 104(2).

Other exceptions relate to Crown copyright and parliamentary copyright. Her Majesty the Queen is the first owner of the copyright in her own works and in works produced by an officer or servant of the Crown in the course of his duties, and of the copyright subsisting in Acts of Parliament and Measures of the General Synod of the Church of England.[21]

21 Ibid ss 163 and 164.

One issue in respect of Crown copyright is whether works created by some types of organisation, such as NHS Trusts, can be regarded as being Crown copyright. Can persons working for such organisations be properly described as officers or servants of the Crown? Under the 1956 Act, the test was wider in that it required the work to be made under the direction or control of the Crown, or was so published.[22] This could have applied to a situation where a body was exercising powers devolved from the appropriate Secretary of State. There seems to be no relevant authority under copyright law, but there are some patent cases. For example, in *Pfizer Corp* v *Minister of Health*,[23] use of a patented drug to treat patients in an NHS hospital was deemed to be use for the services of the Crown, and in *Dory* v *Sheffield Health Authority*[24] it was accepted that a health authority was a government department for the purposes of the Patents Act 1977 s 55,[25] exercising powers of the Secretary of State on his behalf. However, the test under patent law is more widely expressed than under the 1988 Act, being in relation to acts done 'for the services of the Crown'. Determination of this issue may be important where an NHS Trust has created a work, for example computer software, for its own purposes, but then realises that it can exploit it commercially, by licensing its use to other NHS Trusts.

If a work is made by or under the direction or control of either or both Houses of Parliament, the first owner of the copyright is the appropriate House or Houses.[26] This includes Bills, public, private and personal.

A final exception to the general rule applies to original literary, dramatic, musical or artistic works made by an officer or employee of certain international organisations, or published by the organisation and which do not otherwise qualify for copyright by reference to the author or country of first publication. In such cases, under s 168(1), copyright is declared to subsist in the work and the organisation concerned is deemed to be the first owner of the copyright in the work. The relevant international organisations are designated by Order in Council and include the United Nations and the Organization for Economic Co-operation and Development. Unlike the position under the Copyright Act 1956, the copyright in certain commissioned works no longer vests in the first instance in the commissioner of the work.[27]

The ownership of the copyright subsisting in anonymous works can present problems, as there is no author available or willing to give evidence as to the ownership. To cope with the evidential difficulties associated with anonymous works, s 104(4) contains a presumption that the publisher of an anonymous work is the owner of the copyright in the work at the time of first publication unless the contrary is proved, provided that the work qualifies for protection by reason of the country of first publication and the name of the publisher appears on copies of the work as first published. In *Warwick Film Productions Ltd* v *Eisinger*,[28] the plaintiff failed to rebut the equivalent presumption under the Copyright Act 1956 in relation to an anonymous work *Oscar Wilde: Three Times Tried*, first published in or around 1911.

If a work is a work of joint authorship, unless they are employees acting in the course of employment, the joint authors will automatically become the joint first owners of the copyright in the work. They will own the copyright as tenants in common and not as joint tenants: *Lauri* v *Renad*.[29] This means that effectively each owner's rights accruing under the copyright are separate from the others, and he can assign his rights to another without requiring the permission of the other owners, and on his death his rights will pass, as part of his

22 Copyright Act 1956 s 39.

23 [1965] AC 512.

24 [1991] FSR 221.

25 Use of patented inventions for services of the Crown.

26 Copyright, Designs and Patents Act 1988 s 165.

27 This applied to commissioned photographs, portraits (painted or drawn) and engravings provided they were made for money or money's worth: the Copyright Act 1956 s 4(3).

28 [1967] 3 All ER 367.

29 [1892] 3 Ch 402. However, where the co-owners have some relationship such as husband and wife, it may be reasonable to infer that they hold the copyright as joint tenants and not as tenants in common: see *Mail Newspapers plc* v *Express Newspapers plc* [1987] FSR 90. On the death of one joint tenant, the other automatically takes the whole copyright.

estate, to his personal representatives. Where the whole or a part of a copyright is assigned to two or more persons, they will hold as tenants in common, unless the agreement states otherwise. As copyright can be considered as a bundle of rights, an assignment might be partial. For example, the owner, C, of a copyright in a dramatic work might assign the right to perform the work in public to new joint owners X and Y, and the right to publish paper copies of the work to W and Z jointly. The original owner, C, will remain the sole owner of the remainder of the copyright which will include, *inter alia*, the right to translate the work. However, simply granting one right to one person and another right to another person does not make them joint owners. Each will be the sole owner of that part of the copyright, for example, where there is an assignment of the paper publication right to X and an assignment of the public performance right to Y. One co-owner of a copyright may not perform or authorise infringing acts to be done in relation to the work without the permission of his co-owners.[30] Where the copyright is owned by more than one person (or a certain aspect such as the right to perform in public is jointly owned), references in Part I of the Act are to all the owners. In particular, this means that where there are joint owners, the licence of all of them is required.[31]

As an example, consider the copyright subsisting in a sound recording that has joint owners either because it was created by joint authors, or because the copyright has been assigned to more than one person. The sound recording is to be reproduced and sold commercially and each joint owner will be entitled to an agreed share of the profits arising from the sales. One joint owner may be anxious to obtain some immediate capital. To do this, he will be able to 'sell' his future share of the profits to a third party for a lump sum, assigning his copyright interest to that person. He can do this without having to seek or obtain the permission of the other co-owners. However, the co-owner cannot grant a licence to a third party allowing that third party to make and sell copies of the sound recording without the agreement of all the other co-owners. Another example is where a co-owner of a copyright dies leaving all his property to his widow. In such a case, his copyright interests pass to his widow who will, from then on, be entitled to a share of the royalties or profits accruing from the sale or other commercial exploitation of the work.

### Employees

The main difficulty with the ownership provisions concerns the employer/employee relationship and the meaning of 'in the course of his employment', or, in the case of Crown copyright, 'in the course of his duties'. There will be many situations where it will be obvious that the work has been made by an employee in the course of his employment, for example a sales manager who, during his normal working hours, writes a report on the last quarter's sales figures for the board of directors of the company he works for. However, difficulties arise if an employee has created the work in his own time, whether or not using his employer's facilities, or if the nature of the work is not that which the employee is normally paid to create. To some extent the expectations of the employee and employer as manifested in the contract of employment are important, for example, the employee's job description and whether the nature of the thing produced sits comfortably with that job description, either expressly or by implication. To take an extreme

30 *Cescinsky v George Routledge & Sons Ltd* [1916] 2 KB 325. This restriction on co-owners should be compared to patent law, where one co-patentee can exploit the patent without the permission of his co-patentees, but cannot licence, assign or mortgage his share without the consent of the others: Patents Act 1977 s 36.

31 Section 173(2).

example, say that a person who is employed as a cleaner writes some music during his own time. He will be the first owner of the copyright in the musical work because he is employed as a cleaner, and not as an author of musical works. Even if our cleaner writes the music during the time he should be performing his employment duties, he still will be the first owner of the copyright, but may have to answer to his employer for this breach of the contract of employment.[32]

32 A soldier in the SAS is not employed to write a book describing his experiences in the Falklands war. However, the Ministry of Defence sought to claim copyright in such a book as a means of preventing publication: Alberge D. 'MoD Will Claim Copyright on SAS Book if Ban Fails', *The Times*, 5 August 1995, at p. 3.

The situation changes if the employee is employed under a contract with a very wide job description, for example as a research and development engineer, and he prepares a work of copyright which is useful to his employer's business. The copyright will probably belong to his employer, even if the employee created the work on his own initiative outside normal working hours. A complicating factor may be that the employee's formal job description no longer completely and accurately describes his present duties, in which case the actual type of work carried out by the employee will be relevant. A basic test is whether the skill, effort and judgment expended by the employee in creating the work are part of the employee's normal duties (express or implied) or within any special duties assigned to him by the employer. If the answer is 'no', then the employee will be the first owner of the copyright, even if he has used his employer's facilities or assistance. In *Stephenson Jordan & Harrison Ltd v MacDonald*,[33] an employed accountant gave some lectures, which he later incorporated into a book. It was held that, even though his employer had provided secretarial help, the copyright in the lectures belonged to the accountant because he was employed as an accountant to advise clients, and not to deliver public lectures. However, part of the book was based on a report that the accountant had written for a client of his employer, so the copyright in this part belonged to his employer.

33 [1952] RPC 10.

Employees sometimes perform work which is outside the contract of employment, that is, a contract of service. In such a case, the work is created under a contract for services rather than a contract of service, and the employee will be the first owner of the copyright. The point is illustrated well by Lord Denning in *Stephenson Jordan & Harrison* where he said:

> [In] *Byrne* v *Statist* [1914] 1 KB 622 ... a man on the regular staff of a newspaper made a translation for the newspaper in his spare time. It was held that the translation was not made under a contract of service but under a contract for services. Other instances occur when a doctor on the staff of a hospital, or a master on the staff of a school, is employed under a contract of service to give lectures or lessons orally to students. If he, for his own convenience, puts the lectures into writing, then his written work is not done under a contract of service. It is most useful as an accessory to his contracted work but it is not really part of it. The copyright is in him and not in his employers.[34]

34 [1952] RPC 10 at 22.

Thus, an academic teacher, such as a university lecturer, will own the copyright in the notes he has prepared for the purpose of presented lectures and will be able to exploit those notes, for example, by granting a licence to a publisher, provided there is not an express term in his contract of employment to the contrary. Presumably, the same can be said in respect of 'handouts' distributed to students during lectures, unless these could be seen as an integral part of the lecturing duties.

If the employer wishes, he may allow the employee to be the first owner of the copyright, as s 11(2) includes the phrase 'subject to any agreement to the contrary'. Normally, transfer of ownership of copyright must be in writing and signed by or on behalf of the copyright owner,[35] but in this case it would appear that a verbal or even implied agreement will suffice because this is not a case of assignment, since the copyright does not exist until the time it has a first owner.[36] On the other hand, if an employee produces a work, the creation of which lies outside his normal duties (that is, it is not created in the course of his employment), any agreement that the employer will be the owner of the copyright must comply with s 90(3) and must be in writing and signed by or on behalf of the employee. The reason is that the employee automatically will be the first owner and the copyright must, therefore, be assigned to the employer. If there is such an agreement, but the formalities are not complied with, the employer may have an implied licence or may be deemed to be the equitable owner of the copyright.

Freelance workers and consultants may be difficult to classify as employees in the normal sense of the word. Under s 178 'employed', 'employee', 'employer' and 'employment' refer to employment under a contract of service or of apprenticeship. The categorisation of a person as an employee or self-employed person is so crucial to the question of ownership of copyright that it requires further exploration, and employment law may provide some guidance as to how the distinction may be made. A person's status as employee or self-employed is important in employment law as many of the statutory safeguards, such as the right to claim unfair dismissal and the entitlement to redundancy pay, depend upon this question. Although the case law on this subject is far from satisfactory, questions such as who controls the work, whether the person is entitled to sick pay, who provides a pension, the method of payment (for example, weekly or monthly or on the basis of a lump sum for an agreed item of work), whether tax is deducted at source and financial responsibility (for example, for faulty work) may combine to provide an overall test.[37] In *Beloff* v *Pressdram Ltd*[38] the question of ownership of a memorandum written for the editor of the *Observer* newspaper had to be determined. The plaintiff, the author of the memorandum and who worked for the *Observer*, sued the publisher of *Private Eye* for infringing the copyright in the memorandum. The plaintiff could sustain the action only if she were the owner of the copyright in the memorandum. She would be the owner only if she was not an employee of the *Observer*.[39] Ungoed-Thomas J referred to a number of indicia which could be used to determine whether the contract was a contract of service (in which case the plaintiff would be an employee) or a contract for services. He decided that the former was the case.

Factors in favour of the arrangement being a contract of service were that the *Observer* provided the plaintiff with office space, equipment and resources, including a secretary; she did not use her own capital and her remuneration was not affected by the success or otherwise of the newspaper; deductions from her earnings were made in respect of PAYE and a pension scheme and, finally, the plaintiff's job was an integral part of the newspaper's business. The fact that the editor did not have full control over her work was not particularly relevant, and the judge pointed out that the greater an employee's skill, the less significant the question of control becomes. Control might be a more important determining factor in the case of employees carrying out lowly tasks under supervision. None of the above factors can be considered to be conclusive as such. In *Hall* v *Lorimer*[40] Mummery J said that the court could not run through a check list of items pointing one way or the other. He went on to suggest that a whole picture

35 The Copyright, Designs and Patents Act 1988 s 90(3).

36 *Noah* v *Shuba* [1991] FSR 14 provides an example of an implied agreement that the employee owned the copyright in a work created during normal working hours.

37 *Market Investigations Ltd* v *Minister of Social Security* [1969] 2 QB 173 *per* Cooke J at 185.

38 [1973] 1 All ER 241.

39 A purported assignment of the copyright to the plaintiff was ineffective, *see* p. 77.

40 *The Times*, 4 June 1992.

should be painted and viewed from a distance to reach an informed and qualitative decision. Emphasis has been placed on 'mutuality of obligation', described by Kerr LJ in *Nethermere (St Neots) Ltd* v *Taverna*[41] in the following terms:

> [The alleged employees] must be subject to an obligation to accept and perform some minimum, or at least reasonable, amount of work for the alleged employer.

Because of the difficulty of predetermining the status of a person carrying out work for another, it is preferable, if there is any doubt whatsoever, to provide contractually for the ownership of copyright subsisting in anything produced by the worker. Certainly, there is a good deal of confusion about the ownership of commissioned works, the commissioner often believing, mistakenly, that he will automatically own the copyright subsisting in the work created.[42] In these situations, the person commissioning the work should insist that the contract contains provisions for the assignment of the future copyright.[43] Of course, in terms of the relationship between employers and employees and between client and consultant, there is the additional factor of the obligation of confidence owed by one to the other.[44] The law of confidence may help the employer or the client prevent the subsequent use of commissioned material by the employee or consultant, regardless of the question of copyright ownership.

## Consultants

There may be occasions when the operation of the basic rule regarding first ownership results in an injustice. For example, a consultant may produce a work for a client in circumstances in which the client expects that he will own the copyright in the finished work and pays the consultant accordingly. However, if there is no provision for the assignment of the copyright and the consultant cannot be classed as an employee working in the course of his employment, the consultant will be the first owner of the copyright. The consultant may realise the implications of this position and may decide later either to interfere with the client's exploitation of the work or to deal with the work himself without the client's permission. The first possibility, that is where the consultant attempts to interfere with the client's use or marketing of the work, should be defeated on the basis of non-derogation from grant,[45] or alternatively on the basis of an implied licence. Both the first and second possibility can be overcome if the court is willing to use equitable principles to infer beneficial ownership. This was done in the case of *Warner* v *Gestetner Ltd,*[46] in which Warner, who was an expert in the drawing of cats, agreed orally to produce some drawings to be used by Gestetner to promote a new product at a trade fair. Gestetner subsequently used the drawings for promotional literature, and Warner complained that this went beyond the agreement and infringed his copyright. Warner remained the owner of the copyright in the drawings because it had not been assigned to Gestetner. However, Whitford J found that he could imply a term granting beneficial ownership of the copyright to Gestetner. Thus, the copyright had two owners, one at law and one at equity, and Gestetner, as beneficial owner, could deal with the work as it wished, Warner's legal interest in the copyright being of little practical significance (although infringement actions are much less effective if brought by a beneficial owner without the legal owner being joined as a party).[47]

[41] [1984] IRLR 240.

[42] This problem came to light as regards the ownership of the 'Lightman Report' commissioned by the National Union of Mineworkers. A publisher intended to publish the report with the permission of Mr Lightman QC, in the face of strong objection by the Union which believed it owned the copyright in the report – *see The Times*, 1 October 1990, p. 3. However, unless there was a signed written assignment of the copyright, the person commissioned, Mr Lightman, would be the first legal owner of the copyright in the report, although the Union might have had some rights as beneficial owner of the copyright in equity.

[43] The Copyright, Designs and Patents Act 1988 s 91 provides for prospective ownership of copyright.

[44] *See* Chapter 11 for a discussion of the operation of the law of confidence as regards employees.

[45] *See British Leyland Motor Corp Ltd* v *Armstrong Patent Co Ltd* [1986] 2 WLR 400.

[46] [1988] EIPR D-89.

[47] Generally, on his own, a beneficial owner will be entitled to interlocutory relief only. *See also Bookmakers' Afternoon Greyhound Services Ltd* v *Wilf Gilbert (Staffordshire) Ltd* [1994] FSR 723, *per* Aldous J at 735–7. In that case, equitable title to copyright in race cards was based on an intention to assign copyright.

The concept of two owners, one legal and one beneficial, is used extensively in the law of real property, but there have been other examples of its application to intellectual property law. For example, in *Ironside v Attorney-General*[48] it was held that an agreement for the design of the reverse face of coins gave rise to an assignment in equity, or alternatively an implied licence.[49] Of course, to be able to imply beneficial ownership, the creator of the work should have been paid a fixed sum rather than a royalty, as the latter is inconsistent with a transfer of ownership. Both the above cases involved a lump sum payment.

The use of beneficial ownership has to be consistent with the overall tenor of the agreement. *Warner v Gestetner* was distinguished in *Saphena Computing Ltd v Allied Collection Agencies Ltd*[50] where a software developer had developed new computer software under the agreement. It is common for software developers to licence their software to other customers in the future. The grant of non-exclusive licences in respect of computer software, even if written for a particular client, is common and this is inconsistent with beneficial ownership. Furthermore, the Court of Appeal considered that, in order to give the agreement business efficacy, there was no reason to imply a term that beneficial interest should pass to the client. This is not to say that beneficial ownership can never arise in relation to computer software. It depends on the circumstances. If the common intention is that the client will be the only person using the software, such an implied term might be appropriate. For example, in *John Richardson Computers Ltd v Flanders*,[51] computer software developed by an ex-employee acting as a consultant to his former employer gave rise to beneficial ownership in favour of the latter.

A less contrived approach than implying beneficial ownership which would, in many cases, have the same effect in practical terms, would be for the court to imply a term to the effect that the commissioner of a work has a licence to continue to use the work. This approach was taken by Lord Denning MR in *Blair v Osborne & Tomkins*[52] in which an architect was commissioned to draw building plans for the purpose of obtaining planning permission for some houses. The site for which the plans had been drawn was then sold with the benefit of the planning permission and the plans were transferred to the purchaser, who employed his own surveyors who modified the plans for building regulations approval and put their name on the plans. Eventually, houses were built in accordance with the plans, and the architect sued for infringement of copyright. It was held that the architect owned the copyright in the plans and there had been an infringement by the surveyors who had submitted the plans to the council in their own name, but only nominal damages were appropriate as no harm was suffered by the architect as a result of this.[53] On the issue of the building of houses by the purchaser of the land in accordance with the architect's plans, it was held that the purchaser had an implied licence to use the plans for this purpose. The person who commissioned the architect had such an implied licence which extended to the making of copies of the plans to be used in respect of that site only and not for any other purpose, and this implied licence extended to any purchaser of the site. The rationale for thus deciding this case was that the architect had received his fee once, and failure to imply a licence would have meant that the architect would have been able to charge a second fee to the purchaser of the site without having to carry out any further work. It must be noted that the scope of the licence was limited to building the houses on that site only, and the purchaser would have been prevented from building further houses in accordance with the plans on other sites.

48 [1988] RPC 197.

49 *See also Performing Right Society Ltd v London Theatre of Varieties Ltd* [1924] AC 1, discussed later.

50 [1995] FSR 616.

51 [1993] FSR 497.

52 [1971] 2 WLR 503.

53 Nowadays, the architect would have an action under the Copyright, Designs and Patents Act 1988 s 77 for infringement of his right to be identified as the author, provided he had asserted this right.

The concept of the implied licence can be criticised because it may destroy the copyright owner's control of the use of the work by others. The initial agreement is for the person paying for the work to have the right to use it for a particular purpose, and its use by others is outside this agreement. An implied licence could operate unfairly in some circumstances. For example, a builder (Acme Construction Ltd) has agreed to design and build a factory for a client (Rapid Developments plc). It was agreed that Acme would prepare all the drawings and specifications for the building work. Two-thirds of the way through the contract, Rapid Developments go into receivership. The receiver decides to engage another company (Quickbuild Ltd) to complete the factory and he hands over the plans and specifications to Quickbuild. The receiver, in his wisdom, considers that he can obtain the best deal for the creditors of Rapid Developments by completing the factory and that Quickbuild will do this at less expense than Acme, even though the latter wishes to continue with the construction work. The use of the plans and specifications in this way seems grossly unfair, and it may be that in these special circumstances the courts will not be prepared to extend an implied licence to the second builder. In terms of tactics, Acme might be well advised to apply immediately for a *quia timet* injunction on the basis that the intended use of the materials will almost certainly involve copyright infringement.

## Complexity of rights

For the derivative works of copyright there will usually be several rights associated with the work, and the exploitation of works in which numerous rights exist can be fairly complex, although collecting societies such as the Performing Right Society bring some simplification. As an example of the number of rights that can subsist in a work, consider a song which has been recorded as a sound recording. The following rights can exist:

● musical copyright
● literary copyright
● copyright in the sound recording
● performance rights (these are neighbouring rights to copyright – the performer and recording company have rights)
● rental and lending rights
● the composer's moral rights, and
● the lyricist's moral rights.

The exploitation of the sound recording must take account of all these rights by way of assignments, licences or waivers. The rights themselves can be subdivided, for example in the above case the following cross-cutting rights are important:

● the right to make copies of the sound recording
● the right to play the sound recording in public
● the right to permit rental of copies of the sound recording.

A film may be subject to many rights. The screenplay will be a dramatic work and may be based on a novel produced as a book. The novel will have literary copyright which will initially be owned by the novelist. The copyright in the film itself will be owned, in the first instance, by the producer and principal director unless they are employees making the film in the course of employment. Even so they will be joint authors and will consequently, have a right to authorise or prohibit rental or lending.[54] Add to this the various rights associated with the sound track, performance rights and moral rights and it becomes clear that lawyers will be kept busy in drawing up all the necessary agreements and consents. Mechanisms for exploiting works of copyright are described in the subsequent sections of this chapter.

## DEALING WITH COPYRIGHT

As has been previously mentioned, copyright is a property right, and as such the owner of that right can deal with it. He can transfer the right to another, or he can grant licences to others, permitting them to do some or all of the acts restricted by copyright in relation to the work. However, it must be remembered that the author of a work has certain moral rights, and the owner of the copyright and his assignees or licensees, indeed the public in general, must take notice of and respect these moral rights.[55] Therefore, the ultimate owner of a copyright is not entirely free to do as he wishes with the work that is the subject matter of the copyright. Nevertheless, in most cases, respecting the author's moral rights will not be a hindrance to the economic exploitation of copyright.

Why should the owner of a copyright wish to transfer his ownership of the copyright or grant licences in respect of it? Bearing in mind that the author of a work of copyright will often be the owner of the copyright, the owner may not be in the best position to exploit the work commercially. For example, the author of a work of literature such as a romantic story (if he is the first owner of the copyright, as will usually be the case), will find it more advantageous in terms of the balance between financial reward and the degree of risk involved to approach a well-established publisher who will arrange for the printing, marketing and sale of books of the story. Not only that, but the publisher will also be better placed to take legal action against persons infringing the copyright. Similarly, the composer of a piece of music may approach a record company which might arrange for the recording of the music by a well-known orchestra and for the manufacture, distribution and sale of records, cassettes and compact discs on a world-wide scale. Copyright can also be a form of investment. A lump sum can be invested to acquire the copyright in works which will continue to provide income over many years.[56] Alternatively, copyright may be used as security for a loan or other financial transaction. Finally, transfer of ownership of copyright will occur on the death of the owner or a part-owner of the copyright.

Two main ways of dealing with copyright are considered below: by assignment and by licensing. Licences may be exclusive or non-exclusive. In the case of an assignment of copyright or an exclusive licence, the transaction, to be effective, must be in writing and signed by or on behalf of the present copyright owner.[57] Although this can be seen as a safeguard for the copyright owner, who may be negotiating with powerful publishing organisations from an unequal bargaining position, it can lead to difficulties in the case of commissioned works because it clearly means that the commissioner cannot have any legal rights of ownership under copyright law unless a written signed agreement exists.[58] Because the language of the statute is very clear on this point, the implication by the courts of terms into the contract for the commissioned work which deal with ownership is unlikely, though not an impossibility.[59]

54 *See* Dworkin, G. 'Authorship of Films and European Commission Proposals for Harmonising the Term of Copyright' [1993] 5 EIPR 151.

55 The right to be identified as the author must, however, have been asserted: the Copyright, Designs and Patents Act 1988 s 78. Questions of author's consent and waiver may also be relevant: s 87.

56 This may be advantageous in terms of tax liabilities. For the tax implications of intellectual property *see* Gallafent, R.J., Eastaway, N.A. and Dauppe V.A.F. (1992) *Intellectual Property: Law and Taxation* (4th edn) Longman.

57 The Copyright, Designs and Patents Act 1988 ss 90(3) and 92(1).

58 However, under s 85(1), the commissioner of a photograph or film made for private and domestic purposes has certain rights, for example a right not to have the work issued to the public.

59 *See* the discussion above on *Warner v Gestetner Ltd* [1988] EIPR D-89.

## Assignment and transmission of copyright

One point that must be made at this stage is that physical possession of an object containing or representing a work of copyright or a copy of such a work does not by itself give any rights under copyright law. For example, mere possession of a book does not give a right to perform any of the restricted acts such as making copies of the book. The same principle applies to a painting, and the sale of a painting, no matter how expensive, does not automatically assign the copyright in it. The purchaser obtains a property right in the physical object but, in the absence of an assignment or licence, no interest in the copyright. This may be inconvenient and the courts will construe any documents, such as a receipt, generously to keep the two forms of property together. For example, in *Savory (EW) Ltd* v *The World of Golf Ltd*,[60] it was held that a written receipt for card designs 'inclusive of all copyrights' was sufficient to assign the copyright to the purchaser.

There is a convention or custom amongst artists that where an artist creates a work in a medium such that multiple copies may be made and the artist limits the number actually made, such as in a limited-edition print, the artist has a right to make and retain or sell up to two additional copies. However, that convention usually applies where an artist sells to purchasers and, in *Danowski* v *The Henry Moore Foundation*,[61] the Court of Appeal declined to imply such a term into a contract of service, between employer and employee. Additionally, referring to Ungoed-Thomas J in *Cunliffe-Owen* v *Teather & Greenwood*,[62] for a practice to amount to recognised usage, it must be notorious. That was not the case here, nor was the convention certain. Anyway, an implied term based on such a convention would be inconsistent with the express terms of the agreement and its overall tenor.

An assignment of copyright can be thought of as a disposal of the copyright by way of sale or hire, or by will. The present owner (the assignor) can assign the copyright to another and, under s 90(3), such an assignment must be in writing signed by or on behalf of the assignor. However, the assignment, and other transmission, of the copyright need not be total and absolute, it can be partial. Under s 90(2), the assignment or other transmission of copyright can be limited either in terms of the things the copyright owner can do, or in terms of the period of subsistence of copyright. As an example, consider a play, a dramatic work, the copyright in which will expire in 40 years' time (William, the author, having died some 30 years ago). The current owner, William's wife Ann (the assignor), may decide to assign the total copyright in the play to another person, Frances. Alternatively, she might decide to assign only the public performance right to Frances for the remainder of the duration of the copyright while retaining the other rights, allowing her to make and issue printed copies of the play either personally or by granting a licence to Richard to do this. Finally, she might decide to assign all the rights to Frances for a period of five years only, after which the copyright will revert to her.

Assignments limited in time need careful thought as to what happens to any copies of the work that have not been sold at the time of the reversion of the copyright. In *Howitt* v *Hall*[63] it was held that the defendant who had been assigned the copyright in a book for four years could continue to sell copies printed during those four years after the copyright reverted to the original owner.

60 [1914] 2 Ch 566.

61 *The Times*, 19 March 1996.

62 [1967] 1 WLR 1421.

63 (1862) 6 LT 348.

If the formalities of the Act are not complied with, it may be that a court will be prepared to infer that there has been an assignment of the copyright in equity only: see *Warner v Gestetner*, above. In these circumstances, there will be a legal owner of the copyright and an equitable owner, the legal owner being the purported assignor; and he will still be the legal owner because of some defect in the formalities, for example the written assignment was not signed by him or on his behalf, or the attempted assignment was made orally.[64] Being an owner in equity only does have some disadvantages. In *Performing Rights Society Ltd v London Theatre of Varieties Ltd*,[65] it was held that the owner of an equitable interest in the performing rights of a song entitled 'The Devonshire Wedding' could not obtain a perpetual injunction without joining the legal owner of the copyright as a party to the action. This case was applied in *Weddel v JA Pearce & Major*,[66] a bankruptcy case, in which it was held that although an equitable assignee could sue in his own right, he could not obtain damages or a perpetual injunction without joining as a party the assignor in whom the legal title of a chose in action was vested.[67] Normally, joining another party in an action would mean both appearing as co-plaintiffs, but it is sufficient if the other party is the defendant. For example, in *John Richardson Computers Ltd v Flanders*[68] the owner in equity sued the legal owner.

The rationale for the rule that a beneficial owner cannot obtain a permanent injunction or damages is based on the principle of double jeopardy.[69] If the beneficial owner obtained damages without joining the legal owner, the latter could come along subsequently and bring a fresh action for damages. Of course, apart from joining the legal owner in the action, another way around the difficulty is for the beneficial owner to take an assignment of the copyright. It appears that this will be effective at any time before judgment provided the assignment includes preceding rights of action.[70]

Of course, the person who executes the assignment may be acting as the agent of the assignor and the general rules of agency apply. It is in the intended assignee's interests to satisfy himself as to the authority of the agent. The case of *Beloff v Pressdram Ltd*[71] involved the publication of a memorandum written by the plaintiff (an employee of the *Observer* newspaper) by *Private Eye*. The memorandum referred to a conversation between the plaintiff and a prominent member of the government, in which the latter said that if the Prime Minister were to run under a bus, he had no doubt that a certain Mr M would take over as Prime Minister. The *Observer* owned the copyright in the memorandum and the editor attempted to assign it to the plaintiff so that the plaintiff could sue the publishers of *Private Eye*. However, as the editor had never before executed an assignment on behalf of the *Observer* and had no express authority to do so, the purported assignment was ineffective. Neither could there be any imputed authority because any representation made by the editor that he had authority had not induced the plaintiff to enter into the assignment or take any relevant step.[72]

Sometimes, there may be an assignment of copyright in a work which has not yet come into existence. Such prospective ownership of copyright and its assignment is provided for under s 91. If an author decides to write a play, he will be the first owner of the copyright in the play when it is written, provided he is not writing the play as an employee in the course of his employment. The author is the prospective owner of the future copyright, and he can deal with that future copyright by assigning it to another. Under s 91(2), 'future copyright' means copyright

---

64 In some cases, it is possible that equitable ownership may arise in the absence of agreement, *see Massine v de Basil* [1933–1945] MacG CC 223 and Lea, G. 'Expropriation of Business Necessity?' [1994] 10 EIPR 453.

65 [1924] AC 1.

66 [1987] 3 All ER 624.

67 Copyright is, of course, a chose in action.

68 [1993] FSR 497.

69 *Batjac Productions Inc v Simitar Entertainment (UK) Ltd* [1996] FSR 139.

70 *Weddell v J A Pearce & Major* [1987] 3 All ER 624.

71 [1973] 1 All ER 241.

72 *Freeman & Lockyer v Buckhurst Park Property* [1964] 1 All ER 630 applied.

which will or may come into existence in respect of a future work or class of works or on the occurrence of a future event. The prospective owner can assign the copyright by an agreement signed by him or on his behalf and the actual assignment will take effect automatically when the copyright in the work in question comes into existence. The assignment can be whole or partial. Before the Copyright Act 1956, it was not possible to assign a future copyright, even if in writing and signed by the prospective owner.[73] This was changed by the 1956 Act and in *Chaplin v Leslie Frewin (Publishers) Ltd*[74] it was held that a contract for writing an autobiography between the infant son of Charlie Chaplin and a publisher was effective to transfer the copyright in the work when it came into existence.[75]

An assignment may be declared by the court to be unenforceable if it is unconscionable or contrary to public policy being in restraint of trade. In *Schroeder Music Publishing Co Ltd v Macauay*[76] a young and unknown song writer assigned the worldwide copyright in any musical composition produced by him for five years to a music publishing company. The agreement was very one-sided, the company did not undertake to publish any of the writer's work and could terminate by giving one month's notice. The song writer could not terminate and was paid only £50 (although he would receive royalties on any of his songs actually published). The House of Lords held that the agreement was unenforceable, being in restraint of trade.[77] It required total commitment from the song writer, but virtually no obligation was placed upon the company. Lord Diplock said that it was not without significance that successful and established song writers were not offered the standard form agreement given to the respondent in this case.

It has been common for an assignment to include the formula 'X, as beneficial owner, hereby assigns ...'. The use of the phrase 'beneficial owner' was thought to imply covenants contained in the Law of Property Act 1925 by virtue of s 76.[78] The Law of Property (Miscellaneous Provisions) Act 1994, which came into force on 1 July 1995, has made some changes to the content of the implied covenants, repealing s 76 of the 1925 Act. Now, an assignment of copyright (or other intellectual property right) should take account of the new formulae of full title guarantees and limited title guarantees. Under s 8(1) of the 1994 Act, the parties are free to extend or limit the implied covenants. The phrase 'as beneficial owner' should now be replaced by the appropriate title guarantee.[79]

## Licensing of copyright

A licence is, in essence, a permission granted by the owner of a right or interest to another person allowing him to do something in respect of that right or interest. For example, it may be a licence to enter land for some purpose, such as for accommodation or to take a short cut across a field. Licences may be contractual, in which case they can be enforced in a court of law, for example the owner of a field allows a neighbour to graze his sheep there in return for an annual fee of £100. In relation to copyright, a licence is an agreement between the owner of the copyright (the licensor) and another person (the licensee) whereby that person is permitted to do certain acts in connection with the work involved that would otherwise infringe the copyright in the work. In return for this arrangement, the licensee will pay the licensor either by way of a lump sum, or by making royalty payments. For example, the owner of the copyright in an

**73** *Performing Rights Society Ltd v London Theatre of Varities Ltd* [1924] AC 1. An attempted assignment of a future copyright could take effect in equity only, regardless of the formalities used in practice.

**74** [1966] Ch 71.

**75** The son was 19 years old at the time, but still classed as an infant for legal purposes. The son tried to avoid the contract, fearing passages in the work might be libellous, but it was held that the contract was analogous to a beneficial contract of service and was, therefore, not voidable at the infant's option.

**76** [1974] 3 All ER 616.

**77** But there are limits to the doctrine, such as where the individual is fully aware of the doctrine and has expert legal advice: *see Panayiotou v Sony Music Entertainment (UK) Ltd, The Times*, 30 June 1994 (Chancery Division) (the 'George Michael' case).

**78** Anderson, M. 'Applying Traditional Property Laws to Intellectual Property Transactions' [1995] 5 EIPR 237.

**79** The assignment is likely to contain express warranties. *See* Stokes, S.'Covenants for title in IP dispositions' [1995] 5 EIPR D-138.

artistic painting might agree with a publisher of art works that the publisher can make and sell prints made of the painting, and in return the publisher will pay the copyright owner £5 for each print he sells. Normally making the prints would be an infringement of copyright, being an act restricted by copyright, that is making a copy of the work.[80]

Like an assignment of copyright, a licence can be limited in terms of either the scope or the duration, or both. Scope can be limited either in terms of the acts the licensee is permitted to do or territorially. The licence may be for the whole of the remainder of the period during which copyright will continue to subsist in the work, or may be for a shorter period. There will usually be provisions in the licence agreement for its earlier termination, for example, if one of the parties is in breach of an important obligation under the agreement or on the insolvency of one of the parties.

A licence may be exclusive. Under s 92(1), an exclusive licence is a licence in writing signed by or on behalf of the copyright owner authorising the licensee, to the exclusion of all other persons *including the owner*, to exercise a right that would otherwise be exercisable exclusively by the copyright owner. The licensee is exclusively granted rights to do certain things in relation to the work and the owner (licensor) will not grant those equivalent rights to anyone else, or even exercise them himself. For example, the owner of the copyright in a work of literature may grant an exclusive licence to a book publisher for the purpose of publication of the work. The owner of the copyright will not grant the right of publication to anyone else while the exclusive licence is in existence, and indeed if he attempts to do so, he will be in breach of the exclusive licence. However, although the licence is exclusive, it need not apply to all the acts restricted by copyright and may encompass only one or some of them, such as publishing a book, and the owner will be free to deal with other rights, such as the broadcasting of extracts of the work recited by a famous actor. In the case of a non-exclusive licence, the licensor may make several agreements in respect of the same acts restricted by copyright. For example, the owner of the copyright in a play may allow several theatrical companies to make public performances of the play.

Under s 90(4), a licence granted by a copyright owner is binding on every successor in title to his interest in the copyright, except a purchaser in good faith for valuable consideration without actual or constructive notice and persons deriving title from such a person. So, 'equity's darling', the bona fide purchaser for value without notice, is given protection that overrides the interests of licensees, which is one reason why a commercial organisation, such as a publisher, wishing to exploit a work of copyright might prefer to take an assignment of the copyright rather than to operate on the basis of an exclusive licence. However, in practice it would be very difficult for a purchaser of the copyright to show that he did not have constructive notice, especially if the work had already been exploited commercially. Note that only a purchaser of the copyright is protected, and a person who receives the copyright as a gift or on the death of the owner must respect any existing licences covering the work regardless of knowledge.

Future copyright can be licensed by the prospective owner under s 91(3), but again protection is given to a purchaser in good faith for valuable consideration without actual or constructive notice as against a licensee. Thus, when a work is eventually created that is subject to a previously executed licence agreement, the owner of the copyright will be bound by the terms of the licence. If the

80 For infringement generally *see* Chapter 6. Making a copy of a literary, dramatic, musical or artistic work is defined as reproducing the work in any material form: the Copyright, Designs and Patents Act 1988 s 17(2).

owner later dies and, for example, the copyright passes to the surviving spouse, he or she will also be bound. If that person then assigns the copyright to Andrew, a person who knows about the licence, he will be bound. If Andrew then gives the copyright to Bernard who does not know, or could not be expected to know of the licence, Bernard will be bound by the licence because he has not purchased the copyright but has taken under a gift. However, if Bernard then assigns the copyright to Cyril, who acts in good faith and does not know of the licence and could not be expected to know of it, Cyril will take free of the licence. Furthermore, if Cyril, later disposes of the copyright to Duncan, who knows of the licence and is acting in bad faith, Duncan can take free of the licence because he has derived his title from a purchaser in good faith. The licence is effectively destroyed by the intervention of the purchaser in good faith for valuable consideration without notice. It may be, however, that the licensee has a remedy against his licensor under the original agreement, as there may be a contractual provision in the agreement requiring successors in title of the owner to be given notice before the copyright is assigned. However, this measure can be really effective only until the chain of notification of the licence between assignors and assignees is broken.

As an example of the exploitation of the various rights associated with the copyright in a particular work, consider the author (and owner of the copyright) of a dramatic play. He decides to deal with the play in terms of its publication, its performance in public and also, because of the popularity of the play, is able to negotiate the making of a film based on the play and the making of sound recordings of famous actors and actresses reading the play. Figure 4.2 shows the types of relationships in terms of assignments and licensing that could ensue. In the case of a work such as a computer program, the use of which normally involves a restricted act, the ultimate 'purchaser' of a copy will usually receive a non-exclusive sub-licence.

### Differences between assignments and licences

An exclusive licence agreement can appear, at first sight, to look like an assignment and it is sometimes difficult to distinguish between the two.[81] Both an assignment and a licence agreement may provide for the payment of royalties, which might be thought of normally as being associated with a licence. In *Jonathan Cape Ltd* v *Consolidated Press Ltd*,[82] there was an agreement between the author (being the first owner of the copyright) and the plaintiff publishing company, granting the latter, its successors and assigns 'the exclusive right to print and publish an original work ... provisionally entitled "A Mouse is Born" in volume form'. The agreement was partial in terms of the copyright acts (printing and publishing) and in the territorial scope (a specified area including Australia). The defendant substantially reproduced the work, but argued that the agreement was a licence and that, as a result, the plaintiff could not bring an action without joining the author. It was held that the question of whether an agreement was an assignment or a licence was a matter of construction and, in this case, the words used implied that the agreement was a partial assignment of the copyright. Even the use of the words 'licensor' and 'licensee' in an agreement is not conclusive that it is a licence.[83]

81 The implied covenants under the Law of Property (Miscellaneous Provisions) Act 1994 will not apply to a licence agreement.

82 [1954] 3 All ER 253.

83 *See*, for example, *Messager* v *British Broadcasting Co Ltd* [1929] AC 151.

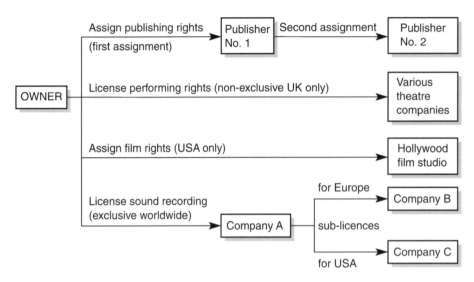

**Figure 4.2 Assignment and licensing**

The payment of royalties is inconsistent with an assignment and is, therefore, highly suggestive of a licence. Indeed, the owner of a copyright would be foolish to assign that copyright in return for royalty payments. If the copyright is subsequently re-assigned to a third party, the terms providing for royalty payments will be unenforceable against that third party, on the basis of privity of contract. It was held in *Barker v Stickney*[84] that a person acquiring a copyright is not bound by mere notice of a personal covenant by a predecessor in title.

Other differences between assignments and licences are that only the owner has a right to sue (although an exclusive licensee may sue after joining the owner or by leave of the court) and a right to alter,[85] subject to the author's moral rights. In the absence of express provisions to the contrary, an assignment will generally be assignable, but a licence will not be assignable unless expressly provided for. There are also differences as regards the effect of the insolvency of the assignee or licensee.[86]

## New forms of exploitation

In time, new ways of exploiting a work of copyright might be discovered and the effect on existing licence agreements may be disputed, for example whether the new form of exploitation falls within the scope of the licence. It will be a question of construction of the licence on the basis of what was properly regarded as being in the contemplation of the parties when the agreement was made. In *Hospital for Sick Children v Walt Disney Productions Inc*[87] the question arose as to whether a licence granted in 1919 by Sir James Barrie in respect of all his literary and dramatic works was limited to silent films or extended to sound films.[88] More recently, in the United States of America, Peggy Lee was awarded $3.8 million in respect of her contributions to the Walt Disney cartoon film *The Lady and the Tramp* on the basis that her contract with Walt Disney did not extend to selling videos of the film.[89] The contract was drawn up before video technology existed.

84 [1919] 1 KB 121.

85 *Frisby v British Broadcasting Corporation* [1987] Ch 932. A licensee, expressly or by implication, may not be allowed to alter the work.

86 For a fuller description of these aspects *see* Skone-James, E.P. *et al* (1991) *Copinger and Skone-James on Copyright* (13th edn) Sweet and Maxwell, at pp. 470–8.

87 [1966] 1 WLR 1055.

88 The first sound film shown to cinema audiences was *The Jazz Singer* in 1927.

89 *The Times,* 7 October 1992, at p. 16.

## COLLECTING SOCIETIES

It may be inconvenient for the owner of copyright to agree licences and collect fees, or alternatively the copyright owner may want the backing of a powerful body to help to defend his rights in a court of law, if it comes to that. On the other hand, it is much more convenient if a user of copyright material can negotiate a single licence with respect to a range of works rather than having to agree separately with all the individual owners. Therefore, a proprietor of a hairdressing salon can obtain a licence from the Performing Right Society (PRS) and Phonographic Performance Ltd (PPL), to be able to play music to the shop's clients. Of course, there is a danger that bodies such as the PRS and PPL may abuse their positions. The PRS operates by taking an assignment of the copyright in the performance and broadcasting of musical works, administering that copyright, collecting fees and distributing them amongst its members.[90] Normally, the person wishing to play or broadcast musical works will obtain a blanket licence to do so in respect of all the works managed by the PRS. Because of the very large number of works administered by the PRS, it clearly has a dominant position and might be tempted to try to control the proportion of music played during a broadcast or the relative proportions of live and recorded work, or to charge high fees. To prevent such abuse, the Performing Right Tribunal was set up by the Copyright Act 1956 to regulate the licensing of performing rights, and this has now become the Copyright Tribunal, having extended jurisdiction and powers in comparison with the Performing Right Tribunal.

## LICENSING SCHEMES

The provisions in the Copyright, Designs and Patents Act 1988 concerning licensing schemes are designed to prevent abuse of monopoly powers by copyright owners. The Copyright Tribunal is given control over licensing schemes and over licences granted by licensing bodies. The Tribunal can also grant compulsory licences, discussed later. A *licensing scheme* is, under s 116(1), a scheme setting out the classes of case in which the operator of the scheme, or the person on whose behalf he acts, is willing to grant copyright licences, and the terms on which licences would be granted in those classes of case. That is, it is a scheme concerning the licence fees to be charged in respect of specific types of works, for example a tariff of licence fees to be charged for performing musical works in public. A *licensing body* is a society or other organisation that has as its main object, or one of its main objects, the negotiation or granting of copyright licences, including the granting of such licences covering the works of more than one author. The body will be negotiating or granting licences either as owner or prospective owner of the copyright, or as the agent of the owner or prospective owner.[91]

The provisions for references and applications in respect of licensing schemes apply, under s 117,[92] to schemes operated by licensing bodies covering the work of more than one author (or publisher in relation to the publication right), so far as they relate to licences for:

(a) copying the work
(b) rental or lending copies of the work to the public

**90** Other collecting societies include the Copyright Licensing Agency, operating in the field of copying. The need for such as scheme can be equated with developments in the technology of photocopying and other means of copying. The issue of a blanket licence is one way that copyright owners can obtain at least some recompense for the vast amount of reproduction of copyright material that takes place nowadays.

**91** The Copyright, Designs and Patents Act 1988 s 116(2).

**92** This is a new section substituting the old s 117, by virtue of the Copyright and Related Rights Regulations 1996, SI 1996/2967.

(c) performing, showing or playing the work in public, or

(d) broadcasting the work or including it in a cable programme service.

The copyright licensing provisions apply generally to the publication right as they do to copyright. However, the exception to the licensing provisions in s 116(4) in relation to a single collective work or collective works of which the authors are the same, or certain commissioned works, does not apply to the publication right. Hence, a collective work comprising previously unpublished works of one author which is out of copyright will, on publication, be subject to the publication right and to the licensing provisions of the Act, unlike the case of a collective work of one author which is still in copyright.

Any of the above schemes can be referred to the Copyright Tribunal. In the case of a proposed scheme to be operated by a licensing body, referral to the Tribunal can be made by an organisation claiming to be representative of users of the copyright material to which the scheme would apply under s 118.[93] If a licensing scheme is already in operation and there is a dispute between the operator of the scheme and a person claiming that he requires a licence under the scheme or an organisation representing users, under s 119, that person or organisation may refer the matter to the Tribunal. The Tribunal may, in either case, confirm or vary the scheme (existing or proposed) as the Tribunal thinks reasonable in the circumstances. There are also provisions for reference to the Tribunal if a person has been refused a licence by the operator of the scheme, or the operator has failed to procure a licence for him, for example if the person is seeking a licence for a work that is in a category of case excluded from the scheme.

The Copyright, Designs and Patents Act 1988 ss 124–128 apply to licences such as those in s 117 above granted by a licensing body but otherwise than in pursuance of a licensing scheme, for example, the Copyright Licensing Agency's licence with education authorities. The provisions are very similar to those for licensing schemes in respect of the works covered and the scope of the licences.[94] However, reference must be by a prospective licensee in the case of a proposed licence or, in the case of an existing licence, by the licensee on the ground that it is unreasonable that the licence should cease to be in force. That is, if the licence is due to expire under the terms of the licence. An application by an existing licensee cannot be made until the last three months before the licence is due to expire. The Tribunal may confirm or vary the terms of a proposed licence or may, in the case of an existing licence, extend the licence either for a fixed period or indefinitely.

The Copyright Tribunal has to make its determinations on the basis of what is reasonable in the circumstances, and under s 129 this means that the Tribunal shall have regard to the availability of other schemes, or the granting of licences to other persons in similar circumstances and the terms of those schemes or licences. Furthermore, the Tribunal shall exercise its powers so that there is no unreasonable discrimination between licensees (existing or prospective) under the scheme or licence that is subject to the referral, and licensees under other schemes operated by, or other licences granted by, the same person. Further guidelines relating to specific works or forms of use are given in ss 130–134. For example, s 130 covers the reprographic copying of published literary, dramatic, musical or artistic works or the typographical arrangement of published editions. With respect to such works, the Tribunal shall have regard to the extent to which published editions of the works are available, the proportion of the work

93 *See,* for example, *The British Phonographic Industry Ltd* v *Mechanical Copyright Protection Society Ltd (No. 2)* [1993] EMLR 86.

94 The Copyright, Designs and Patents Act 1988 s 124.

to be copied and the nature of the use to which the copies are to be put. Also, for these types of works, under s 137 the Secretary of State can extend a licensing scheme under ss 118–123 operated by a licensing body, or a licence under ss 125–128 to works of a description similar to those covered by the scheme or licence that have been unreasonably excluded from the scheme or licence. This is provided that making them subject to the scheme or licence would not conflict with the normal exploitation of the works or unreasonably prejudice the legitimate interests of the copyright owners. Appeal from s 137 orders lies with the Copyright Tribunal which can confirm, discharge or vary the order.

Section 140 gives the Secretary of State powers of investigation as to the need for a licensing scheme or general licence to authorise educational establishments to make for the purposes of instruction reprographic copies of published literary, dramatic, musical or artistic works or the typographical arrangement of published editions. The Secretary of State may within one year of making a recommendation under s 140 grant a statutory licence free of royalty if provision has not been made in accordance with the recommendation.

Additionally, under s 143, the Secretary of State may certify licensing schemes on application from the person operating or proposing to operate the scheme in question.[95] The Secretary of State shall certify the scheme by way of statutory instrument, if he is satisfied that the scheme enables the works to which it relates to be sufficiently identified by persons likely to require licences, and clearly sets out the terms of the licences and charges payable, if any. Such schemes cover some of the acts permitted under copyright, such as the educational recording of broadcasts or cable programmes, or the making of copies of abstracts of scientific or technical articles, so that, if a certified licensing scheme is in operation, anyone carrying out one of the particular permitted acts included in the certified licensing scheme will infringe copyright, unless covered by the scheme. Some of the permitted acts can thus be nullified by certification.[96]

## COMPULSORY LICENCES AND LICENCES AS OF RIGHT

Compulsory licences may be granted by order of the Secretary of State in respect of the lending to the public of copies of literary, dramatic, musical or artistic works, sound recordings or films under s 66, unless there exists a certified licensing scheme under s 143. In its previous form, s 66 was restricted to rental to the public of copies of sound recordings, films or computer programs. Should s 66 ever be used, under s 142, the Copyright Tribunal has the power to settle the royalty payable if the parties cannot agree on a royalty.

Licences as of right may become available following a report by the Monopolies and Mergers Commission. Under s 144, if the public interest is or has been or may be prejudiced because of conditions in licences, restricting the use of the work or the right of the copyright owner to grant further licences, or because the copyright owner refuses to grant licences on reasonable terms, a Minister may act on the Commission's report and cancel or modify the conditions or provide that licences shall be available as of right. The terms of the licence will be settled by the Copyright Tribunal in the absence of agreement. A proviso is that the relevant Minister may exercise his powers under s 144 only if he is satisfied that to do so will not contravene the conventions to which the UK is a party, that is the Berne Copyright Convention and the Universal Copyright Convention.

**95** For the purposes of ss 35, 60, 66, 74 and 141. An example being the Copyright (Certification of Licensing Schemes for Educational Recording of Broadcasts) (Open University Educational Enterprises Limited) Order 1993, SI 1993/2755.

**96** This is acknowledged in the Copyright, Designs and Patents Act 1988, Chapter III the part dealing with the permitted acts. See, for example, ss 35(2), 60(2) and 66(2).

There are provisions under s 144A for the compulsory exercise of rights in literary, dramatic, musical or artistic works, sound recordings or films in respect of cable re-transmission of broadcasts from another EEA member state in which the work is included.[97] The right is referred to as the 'cable re-transmission right', and it may be exercised against a cable operator only through a licensing body. If the copyright owner has not acted to transfer this right to the appropriate licensing body, it will be deemed to be transferred, but such a person must claim his rights within three years from the date of the relevant cable re-transmission. A 'cable operator' means a person providing a cable programme service, and 'cable re-transmission' means the reception and immediate re-transmission by way of a cable programme service of a broadcast.

Sections 135A–C provide a right to use certain sound recordings in broadcasts and cable programme services, being recordings where the appropriate licence could have been granted by or procured by a licensing body. Either one of two conditions must be present, being (a) refusal to grant or procure a licence at terms acceptable to the person including the recordings (or at terms set by the Copyright Tribunal) and which permits unlimited 'needletime' or such as demanded by that person or (b) where the person holds a licence, but the needletime is limited. There are requirements for the person desiring to include the sound recording in the broadcast or cable programme to give notice to the licensing body and to the Copyright Tribunal. Section 135D covers application to the Copyright Tribunal to settle terms of payment and further provisions as to references and applications for review are contained in s 135E–G.[98]

## THE COPYRIGHT TRIBUNAL

The Copyright Tribunal is the old Performing Right Tribunal with more powers and a much wider scope of operation, as has been noted above.[99] Section 145 states that the Performing Right Tribunal, which was established under the Copyright Act 1956 s 23 to regulate the licensing of performing rights, is renamed the Copyright Tribunal. The Copyright Tribunal is made up of a chairman and two deputy chairmen appointed by the Lord Chancellor after consulting the Lord Advocate, and between two and eight ordinary members appointed by the Secretary of State. Persons appointed as chairman or deputy chairmen must be barristers, advocates or solicitors of at least seven years' standing, or who have held judicial office. The Copyright, Designs and Patents Act 1988 s 146 contains provisions for the resignation or removal of members of the Tribunal and provision is made for the payment of members in s 147, as well as for the appointment of staff for the Tribunal.

The constitution of the Tribunal for the purpose of proceedings is to comprise a chairman, either the chairman or a deputy chairman, and two or more ordinary members.[100] Voting on decisions is by majority, with the chairman having a further casting vote if the votes are otherwise equal. The jurisdiction of the Tribunal is set out in s 149 as being to hear and determine proceedings under:

1   the determination of royalty or other remuneration to be paid with respect to re-transmission of a broadcast including the work;
2   applications to determine amount of equitable remuneration where rental right is transferred;

97 Inserted by the Copyright and Related Rights Regulations 1996, SI 1996/2967.

98 These provisions were inserted by the Broadcasting Act 1990.

99 For a criticism of the Tribunal's decision making, *see* Arnold, R. 'Inconsistency in the Copyright Tribunal' [1993] 5 EIPR 179.

100 The Copyright, Designs and Patents Act 1988 s 148.

3 the reference of a proposed or existing scheme, for example by an organisation representing persons claiming they require licences which are covered by the scheme;

4 an application with respect to entitlement to a licence under a licensing scheme, for example, where a person has been refused a licence by the operator of a licensing scheme;

5 the reference or application with respect to licensing by a licensing body, for example, as regards the terms of a proposed licence or the expiry of an existing licence in the case of certain types of works and acts;

6 applications or references with respect to use as of right of sound recordings in broadcasts or cable programme services;

7 appeals against the coverage of a licensing scheme or licence as regards the power of the Secretary of State to extend the coverage of schemes and licences relating to the reprographic copying by educational establishments;

8 applications to settle royalty payments in respect of compulsory licences granted by the Secretary of State in respect of lending of certain works;

9 applications to settle the terms of licences available as of right as a consequence of a report of the Monopolies and Mergers Commission;

10 applications under s 135D in respect of the statutory licence to broadcast sound recordings or include them in a cable programme service.[101]

Other areas of jurisdiction of the Copyright Tribunal are provided for elsewhere, for example, with respect to rights in performances.

The Copyright, Designs and Patents Act 1988 has further provisions as regards the making of procedural rules for the Tribunal[102] and fees to be charged, and under s 151, the Tribunal can make orders as to costs. Finally, under s 152, appeals may be made to the High Court, or to the Court of Session in Scotland, on any point of law arising from a decision of the Tribunal. It should be noted that the Tribunal is not a proactive body and can only respond to applications and references made to it.

**101** Ibid ss 135A–135G were inserted by the Broadcasting Act 1990 as a result of a Monopolies and Mergers Commission report proposing compulsory licensing of broadcasts of sound recordings and the abolition of the Phonographic Performance Ltd's imposition of restrictions on 'needletime'. In *AIRC v PPL and BBC* [1994] RPC 143, the Tribunal set royalty value rates and rejected the rates proposed by PPL. The Tribunal also pointed out that ss 135A–G had deprived PPL of injunction relief.

**102** Copyright Tribunal Rules 1989, SI 1989/1129, as amended.

# 5

## *Moral rights*

### INTRODUCTION

In tardy recognition of parts of the Berne Copyright Convention[1] and in acknowledgement of the importance with which moral rights are regarded in much of the rest of Europe, the Copyright, Designs and Patents Act 1988 gives overt recognition and legal effect to such rights given to the creator of a work in which copyright subsists. United Kingdom copyright law has a tradition of emphasising the economic rights associated with copyright, while the French model stresses the author's rights to control and be identified with his work regardless of the ownership of the economic rights. The Copyright, Designs and Patents Act 1988 bundles a collection of rights together under the appellation 'moral rights', even though some might not be thought to fall within this description, an example being the false attribution right and the right to privacy in certain photographs and films. There are four rights within the 'moral right' designation, being:

1  the right to be identified as the author of a work or director of a film, the 'paternity right' (ss 77–79);
2  the right of an author of a work or director of a film to object to derogatory treatment of that work or film, the 'integrity right' (ss 80–83);
3  a general right, that every person has, not to have a work falsely attributed to him (s 84);
4  the commissioner's right of privacy in respect of a photograph or film made for private and domestic purposes (s 85).

Until recently, a film director only had moral rights and no other rights of authorship. Now, the principal director of a film is a joint author along with the producer unless, of course, they are the same person, in which case the principal director will be the sole author.

In typically half-hearted fashion, these moral rights do not apply globally to all types of copyright work and, additionally, there are many exceptions to the application of the rights. The rights can be waived, or even fail for lack of positive assertion on the part of the author or director. That the rights can be waived at all is unsatisfactory bearing in mind the economic pressure the creator of a work may be subject to. Others may argue that the United Kingdom is wise to take a cautious approach to these rights on the basis of experience elsewhere, particularly in France where the exercise of moral rights forced a television channel to complete making a series of programmes against its wishes and where any objectionable treatment of a work is likely to attract a claim that it infringes the integrity right.[2] Although authors seem keen on enforcing their moral rights in France, there has been very little activity here.

1 The Rome Act 1928 added the *droit moral* to the Berne Convention, being the right to claim first authorship of a work and the right to object to any distortion, mutilation or other modification which would be prejudicial to the honour or reputation of the author. *See* Stewart, S.M. (1989) *International Copyright and Neighbouring Rights* (2nd edn) Butterworths, at pp. 106–7.

2 *See* Cornish, W. R, 'Authors in Law' (1995) 58 *MLR* 1.

To supporters of moral rights, the way in which they have been dealt with by the Act seems to be very much a compromise. Often there will be a conflict between a moral right and an economic right, an example being in the case of employee-authors. Bearing in mind that, as regards a literary, dramatic, musical or artistic work made by an employee in the course of his employment, the employer will be the first owner of the copyright under s 11(2), the Act effectively overrides the author's right to be identified as the author in relation to anything done by or with the authority of the copyright owner.

Moral rights have been hailed as a novelty in United Kingdom copyright law.[3] However, this is not really so – other areas of law could give remedies to the author. A licence agreement or an assignment of copyright can contain terms requiring that the author's name be placed prominently on copies of the work and that the work must not be modified. A treatment of an author's work which is derogatory or the false attribution of a work might give rise to an action in defamation. For example, an eminent and distinguished author, Edward, might write a serious and noble play about love conquering adversity and assign the copyright to a television company. If that television company then rewrites the play and changes it into a smutty farce and broadcasts it, and Edward's name appears in the credits as being associated with the writing of the play, Edward will have an action in defamation on the basis that his reputation would be significantly harmed by this.[4] The same might apply if an inferior and tasteless musical work has been falsely attributed to a celebrated and highly regarded composer with an international reputation.

An author's moral rights can be protected indirectly because the act complained of might also involve a normal infringement of copyright. For example, if another person, without permission of the copyright owner, makes a parody of the work, the author might feel aggrieved and the copyright owner might decide to sue for infringement because the parody contains a substantial part of the original work. However, only the copyright owner could bring a legal action and an author who did not own the copyright in his work would have to stand by helplessly unless the treatment of the work was defamatory. It should be noted that the right to object to a derogatory treatment of the work is likely to be actionable in wider circumstances than would be the case in defamation because it extends to treatment which distorts or mutilates the work without necessarily affecting the author's reputation. In fact, a distortion or mutilation of a work is, from the language of s 80(2)(b), prejudicial to the honour or reputation of the author or director *per se*.

## RIGHT TO BE IDENTIFIED AS THE AUTHOR OR DIRECTOR OF A WORK (THE PATERNITY RIGHT)

The right to be identified as the author of a literary, dramatic, musical or artistic work, or as the director of a film is a recent innovation for United Kingdom copyright law. But it is not as wide-ranging as it should be, and there are a number of exceptions to it. Additionally, the author or director must assert the right for it to be effective. The right does not apply to other types of works, such as sound recordings and broadcasts where it would be inappropriate in any case; neither does the right apply to works in which copyright does not subsist – the work must be a 'copyright' work. Furthermore, the right does not apply to all forms of the works included – for example, the right does not apply to computer programs, even though these are literary works.

3 De Freitas, D. 'The Copyright, Designs and Patents Act 1988 (2)' (1989) 133 *Solicitors Journal* 670 at 675. De Freitas recognises correctly that the right not to have a work falsely attributed to a person is of older vintage, *see* the Copyright Act 1956 s 43.

4 That is, it would be likely to lower him in the estimation of right-thinking people generally.

The Copyright, Designs and Patents Act 1988 s 77(1) states that the right to be identified as author or director applies to literary, dramatic, musical and artistic works, and to films. However, the right is not infringed unless it has been asserted in accordance with s 78 so as to bind the person who carries out an activity which gives rise to the right to be identified. Under s 78(2), the right may be asserted generally or in relation to specified acts either:

(a) on assignment, by including a statement in the instrument effecting the assignment – for example, a term in the assignment stating that the author or director asserts his moral right to be identified as such (an assignment must, of course, be in writing and signed by or on behalf of the assignor by s 90); or

(b) by written instrument signed by the author or director – for example, by including a suitable term in a licence agreement. However, it may simply be a written notification of the right and not part of some contractual document.

There is no requirement that the right must be asserted before or at the time of any assignment or licence, and it would appear that the right may be asserted at any time even subsequent to the transfer of the economic rights in the work. However, there may be a term in an assignment or licence agreement to the effect that the author or director must not at some future date assert this right. If this is so, the author or director will be in breach of contract if he subsequently asserts the right.[5] The Act does not make clear whether the effect of any written notice is retrospective, that is whether an author or director can make this right apply to things done prior to the assertion. This could be extremely awkward for an assignee or licensee but for the fact that the Act does allow a court to take into account any delay in asserting the right when considering remedies.[6] As s 78(2) refers to signature by the author, it would seem that the right to be identified as author cannot be brought to life after the author's death, say by the author's widow.

Under the transitional arrangements contained in the Copyright, Designs and Patents Act 1988 Sch 1, paras 22–24, the right to be identified as author applies to literary, dramatic, musical and artistic works made before the commencement of the 1988 Act if the author was still alive at that date.[7] Therefore, the right to be identified as author can be asserted in respect of a pre-existing work, by a written instrument signed by the author. There are certain safeguards – for example, nothing done before the commencement date is actionable as an infringement of moral rights, and assignees and licensees may continue to perform acts covered by an assignment or licence granted before the commencement date.

There are additional means of asserting the right to be identified that apply in relation to public exhibitions of artistic works. Under s 78(3), when the author or first owner of copyright parts with possession of the original, or a copy is made under his direction or control, the right may be asserted by identifying the author on the original or copy, or on a frame, mount or other thing to which it is attached. Also, in relation to a public exhibition of an artistic work made in pursuance of a licence agreement, the right may be asserted by including in a licence authorising the making of copies of the work a statement to that effect.

It is one thing to assert a right, but quite another to enforce it against third parties, and therefore there must be provisions for determining whether a person is bound by the assertion and whether notice, actual or constructive, is required. In terms of the paternity right, the formula depends on the mode of

5 It might also be a breach of an express or implied term in respect of quiet enjoyment.

6 The Copyright, Designs and Patents Act 1988 s 78(5).

7 The commencement date of the copyright provisions of the Copyright, Designs and Patents Act 1988 is 1 August 1989.

assertion, and s 78(4) states the circumstances in which assignees, licensees and the like are bound by an assertion of the right to be identified as the author or director. In the case of an assignment, the assignee and anyone claiming through him are bound by the right regardless of notice. For example, if a person takes an assignment of the copyright in a literary work and the agreement includes a statement to the effect that the author asserts his right to be identified as author, and that person, the original assignee, subsequently assigns the copyright to a third person, then the latter will be bound by the right even if he has no knowledge of it and could not reasonably be expected to know of its existence. This will apply also to subsequent licensees, and even to a situation where a person obtains ownership of the copyright by way of a gift. Any person without knowledge of the assertion subsequently obtaining rights in the copyright will be bound even if he is acting in good faith, provided that he derives his right or interest in the copyright through the original assignee. If observing the right to identification is likely to be inconvenient, a person acquiring a licence or assignment of copyright in a literary, dramatic, musical, artistic work or film should, if at all possible, have sight of the original assignment of the rights he now wants to acquire before concluding the agreement.[8]

Where the assertion is other than by assignment, only persons to whom notice of the assertion is brought are bound by it. The plain language of s 78 seems to be to the effect that the notice must be actual notice and that constructive or imputed notice will not suffice to bind the person with respect to the right. It is clear, therefore, that as far as the author or director is concerned, the right to be identified is far better asserted through an assignment than by any other means. Of course, if the author or director is also the first owner of the copyright, he may make contractual provision safeguarding this right, for example by including a term that infringement of the right is to be considered a breach of condition and that sublicences may not be granted except with the owner's consent and such sublicences must include a term asserting the right. Least effective of all is the position where the right is asserted by a written and signed non-contractual document.

In relation to public exhibitions of artistic works, terms in licences asserting the right to be identified as author bind everyone, regardless of notice, into whose hands a copy made in pursuance of the licence comes. In the case of identification placed on the original or copy, frame, mount or other thing to which the artistic work is attached, any person into whose hands the original or copy comes is bound even if the identification is no longer present or visible. Therefore, the right is not to be defeated simply because an intermediate possessor of the artistic work deliberately or accidentally removed the identification.

### Scope of the right to be identified as the author or director

The right to be identified as the author or director does not apply to every act that can be performed in relation to the work. For example, the right does not apply when a dramatic work is performed privately, say to a group of friends, or in the case of non-commercial publication. The scope of the right varies according to the nature of the work, as is to be expected and is provided for in s 77. It is interesting to note that the classification of copyright works given in s 1 is not followed precisely and some regrouping is required to make sense of the scope of the right. In particular, a literary work consisting of words intended to be sung or spoken with music is treated the same as a musical work.[9]

8 Of course, in most circumstances, applying the author's name to copies of the work will not be onerous.

9 The Copyright, Designs and Patents Act 1988 s 77(3).

101

In relation to literary works (other than words intended to be sung or spoken with music) and dramatic works, the author has the right to be identified whenever:

(a) the work is published commercially, performed in public, broadcast or included in a cable programme service, or
(b) copies of a film or sound recording including the work are issued to the public.[10]

10  Ibid s 77(2).

The right also applies to these acts in respect of adaptations. That is, the author has the right to be identified as the author of the work from which the adaptation was made. For example, if an author, Florence Smith, writes a story in English and another person later translates the story into German and publishes copies of the German translation commercially, then, provided that Florence has asserted her paternity right, copies of the German version must contain a clear and reasonably prominent notice to the effect that the story has been translated from the original English version written by Florence Smith.

The author of a musical work or literary work consisting of words intended to be spoken or sung with music, for example the lyrics of a song, has the right to be identified as the author of the work whenever:

(a) the work is published commercially, or
(b) copies of a sound recording of the work are issued to the public; or
(c) a film of which the soundtrack includes the work is shown in public or copies of such a film are issued to the public.[11]

11  Ibid s 77(3).

As with dramatic works and the remainder of literary works, the right also applies to the above events in relation to an adaptation, namely that the original author has the right to be identified as the author of the work from which the adaptation was made.

The author of an artistic work has, under s 77(4), the right to be identified whenever:

(a) the work is published commercially or exhibited in public, or a visual image of it is broadcast or included in a cable programme service, or
(b) a film including a visual image of the work is shown in public or copies of such a film are issued to the public, or
(c) in the case of a work of architecture in the form of a building or model for a building, a sculpture or a work of artistic craftsmanship, copies of a graphic work representing it, or of a photograph of it are issued to the public.

Also, under s 77(5), the author of a work of architecture in the form of a building (that is, the architect) has the right to be identified on the building as constructed or, where more than one building is constructed to the design, on the first to be constructed. However, it is unlikely that names of architects will be found on the first example of a mass-produced design, such as on a speculative builder's housing estate, because, as will be seen below, all moral rights can be waived. It is likely that a property developer commissioning an architect will press for a waiver of this moral right unless, of course, the architect is very famous and the fixing at or near the entrance of the finished building of a suitable plaque upon which the architect's name is inscribed would be a good selling point. Alternatively, the fame and reputation of the architect may be such that he is in a strong bargaining position and can insist on exercising his right to be identified. There is no provision for the right in respect of adaptations of artistic works, the reason being that it is not an infringement of an artistic work to make an adaptation of it.[12]

12 *See* ibid s 21.

Section 77(6) gives the director of a film the right to be identified whenever the film is shown in public, broadcast or included in a cable programme service, or copies of the film are issued to the public. An example of the last would be when video recordings of the film are made available to the public by way of sale or rental.

The Act provides that the right to be identified applies in relation to the whole or any substantial part of the work.[13] For example, if a short extract from a literary work is printed and published commercially, the right still applies provided that the extract represents a substantial part of the whole work. It would be ridiculous if the copying and publication of a short extract would infringe the economic right but not the moral right, and therefore it is to be expected that 'substantial' in the context of moral rights will have the same meaning developed by the courts for economic rights, remembering that under s 16(3)(a) acts restricted by copyright apply in relation to the work as a whole or any substantial part of it. The transitional provisions in Sch 1 confirm this approach in that para 23(3) links infringement of moral rights to infringement of the economic rights under copyright, although this is in the context of things permitted under assignments or licences. It would seem sensible that infringement of moral rights should be on all fours with the infringement of economic rights concerning the requirement for substantiality.

13 Ibid s 89(1).

### Method of identification

Having the right to be identified as the author or director would be greatly diluted if there were not also provisions relating to the prominence of the notice containing the identification. Section 77(7) deals with this important matter and requires that the identification must be clear and reasonably prominent. The manner of identification depends to some extent on the nature of the act making the work available. In the case of the commercial publication of the work or the issue to the public of a film or sound recording, the author or director (or both if appropriate) should be identified on each copy or, if that is not appropriate, in some other manner likely to bring his identity to the notice of a person acquiring a copy. Where the identification relates to a building, it should be by appropriate means visible to persons entering or approaching the building, for example, by means of a plaque on the wall adjacent to the entrance. In any other case, the author or director should be identified in such a manner likely to bring his identity to the attention of a person seeing or hearing the performance, exhibition, showing, broadcast or cable programme in question. For example, if a play is performed in public, notices, advertisements and the like, and programmes or brochures sold to the audience should contain the author's name in a prominent place. If there are no written or printed materials, the author's name should be clearly stated to the audience prior to the performance.

Under s 77(8), the author or director may specify a pseudonym or initials, or some other form of identification, and if he does that form shall be used as the means of identification. In all other cases, any reasonable form of identification may be used.

Some forms of works may pose serious problems in terms of identifying authors or directors. For example, a multimedia product such as an encyclopaedia on CD-ROM. There may be thousands of authors and directors involved in making such a product. If the credits had to be 'rolled' as is common in the case of a cinematograph film or television drama, this could take several minutes before the person consulting the encyclopaedia could proceed. There are ways of overcoming this problem, the first being to ensure that all moral rights have been waived. Another way is to give the person using the CD-ROM an option to see details of the contributors should he choose to do so. Whether this is likely to bring the identity of the authors and directors to the notice of the person acquiring a copy is debatable, as few may elect to view this information, at least all the way through. It does, however, accord with pragmatism. A further approach might be to include details of contributors in any printed matter supplied with the multimedia product. However, under s 79(6) there is an important exception to the right to be identified where the work has been made for the purpose of publication in, *inter alia*, an encyclopaedia or where it has been made available with the consent of the author for the purposes of such publication. Note: it is the consent of the author and not the owner of the copyright which is important, and the statutory exception does not cover films (multimedia encyclopaedias contain numerous film clips), presumably because the draftsman of these provisions was thinking of paper publication only. Therefore, although the exception may be useful, it is not a universal exception in the case of electronic publication.

### Exceptions to the right to be identified

The exceptions to the right to be identified as the author or director are contained in s 79. These exceptions have the effect of significantly weakening the paternity right in respect of certain types of works or as regards authors with a particular status. Coupled with the fact the right must be asserted and that the right, in common with the other moral rights, is capable of being waived by the person entitled to it, this reduces the practical importance of the right to what is, perhaps, a regrettable extent.[14] If an author has been commissioned to create the work, he might be under pressure to waive his moral rights by his pay-master, who may be of the view that moral rights are an undesirable hindrance to the commercial exploitation of the work, or just plain inconvenient.

The exceptions to the right to be identified as the author or director of a relevant work are classified by reference to:

1 *The type of work* (s 79(2)). Computer programs, designs of typefaces and computer-generated works are excluded from the province of the paternity right. This confirms the uncomfortable categorisation of computer programs as literary works. However, other items of computer software such as databases,[15] preparatory design material and other works stored in computers may be subject to moral rights. A typeface includes an ornamental motif used for printing and would normally fall within the graphic work category of artistic works. If justification is required for these first two exceptions, it may be on the basis that a large number of persons could be involved in the design, development and subsequent modification of the program or typeface and that it would be inconvenient to allow the right.[16] Another argument

14 Waiver of moral rights is provided by ibid s 87.

15 But not in respect of the database right.

16 This could also be true for many works of architecture.

17 A nice conundrum is that a computer-generated work is one created in circumstances such that there is no human author (s 178), yet s 9(3) states that the author for computer-generated works is the person making the arrangements necessary for the creation of the work. This will often be a human being (it could also be an artificial legal person such as a corporation). If the author, so defined, is a human then surely the work cannot, by definition, be computer-generated because it has a human author after all.

could address the fact that they are more of a commercial character and less of an 'artistic' nature than the other works to which the right applies. As computer-generated works have no human author by definition (s 178), it seems reasonable that they must be excluded.[17]

2 *The employment status of authors and directors* (s 79(3)). If the first owner of the copyright in the work is the author's employer by virtue of s 11(2), or the first owner of the copyright is the director's employer by virtue of s 9(2)(a), then the right does not apply in respect of acts done by or with the authority of the copyright owner. The provision relating to film directors should have been modified, as the principal director is now the author or joint author of a film under new s 9(2)(ab). The reference to s 11(2) should apply to authors and directors, as s 11(2) was modified to include films. This appears to be an omission in the Copyright and Related Rights Regulations 1996.

3 *The permitted acts.* There are exceptions relating to some specific permitted acts which are:

(a) s 30, fair dealing to the extent that it relates to the reporting of current events by means of a sound recording, broadcast or cable programme;

(b) s 31, incidental inclusion of a work in an artistic work, sound recording, film, broadcast of cable programme. It would obviously be troublesome and difficult to give credits identifying the author or director, for example if, in a live television news report, some music could be heard playing in the background;

(c) s 32(3), examination questions. However, it is normal practice for the author of a work quoted in an examination paper to be acknowledged;

(d) s 45, parliamentary and judicial proceedings and ss 46(1) and 46(2), Royal Commissions and statutory inquiries. Again, it is unlikely that the author or director would not be acknowledged as a matter of courtesy;

(e) s 51, permitted acts in relation to design documents and models and s 52, relating to copyright in artistic works that have been exploited in a commercial sense; and

(f) s 57, in respect of acts permitted on assumptions as to the expiry of copyright, or the death of the author in the case of anonymous or pseudonymous works.

4 *Works made for the purpose of reporting current events* (s 79(6)). A matter of convenience again. To some extent, the difficulty in identifying the author depends on the nature of the work involved. In the case of newspaper reports, there should be no real difficulty except in so far as the report has been 'taken' from another source, such as a rival newspaper, or if the original report has been edited and rewritten by one or more other persons. The problem is worse in the case of a television newscast that will include a good number of reports written by different individuals or teams of individuals, and may have been edited or modified by others. While long credits may be acceptable in the case of feature films, it would be burdensome to have to identify all the various authors (and film directors), and the time taken to roll the credits might be nearly as long as the newscast itself.

5 *Publication in various types of publications* (s 79(6)). This exception applies to literary, dramatic, musical and artistic works that are published in newspapers, magazines or other similar periodicals and in an encyclopaedia,

dictionary, yearbook or other collective work of reference. However, for the exception to apply, the author must have created the work for the purpose of such publication or have made the work available with the consent of the author for the purposes of such publication. In many works falling into these categories, authors tend to be identified anyway, if only by way of a list of contributors. However, if there are many authors, identifying each would be onerous, especially if their contributions are interleaved in any way. A question arises as to whether this provision is limited to materials published in paper form as many of the works described are available, additionally or alternatively, in electronic form. If it is so limited then presumably the exception will not apply to these things if they are published in electronic form. For example, certain journals are available using the LEXIS computer-based legal information retrieval system.[18] If the exception extends only to hard-copy publications, the author must be identified in the case of works stored electronically, including computer storage, magnetic storage and compact discs, an irrational and absurd result. The exception does not apply to films.

6 *Crown and parliamentary copyright* (s 79(7)). As might be expected, works in which Crown or parliamentary copyright subsists are excepted from the author's or director's right to be identified. Also excluded are works in which the copyright originally vested in an international organisation by virtue of s 168. This exception does not apply if the author or director has previously been identified as such in or on published copies of the work.

## RIGHT TO OBJECT TO DEROGATORY TREATMENT OF THE WORK

In addition to having a paternity right (subject to exceptions and conditions), the author of literary, dramatic, musical or artistic work and the director of a film has an 'integrity right', a right to object to derogatory treatment of the author's or director's work. It has always been possible for a copyright owner to limit the extent and nature of alterations that can be made to a work by a licensee. A copyright owner who is also the author can thus provide for the continuing integrity of the work by contractual means. Before the right to object to derogatory treatment existed, in the absence of express or implied terms in a licence agreement, the licensee had the right to make alterations, but this was not necessarily an absolute right and in *Frisby* v *British Broadcasting Corp*[19] it was said that the court would, in appropriate circumstances, limit that right to make alterations.[20]

The integrity right is described in s 80(1) as the right belonging to the author or director not to have the work subjected to derogatory treatment. For the right to apply, the work must be a 'copyright' work, that is a work in which copyright subsists; furthermore, the right is subject to exceptions and applies only as regards certain acts carried out in relation to the work. As with all other moral rights, the right can be waived with the consent of the person entitled to the right, who might be the author or director, or a person taking the right after the death of the author or director. The integrity right also applies to works which existed prior to the commencement date of the Copyright, Designs and Patents Act 1988, subject to certain conditions.[21]

'Derogatory treatment' is described in s 80(2) as being a treatment which amounts to distortion or mutilation of the work, or is otherwise prejudicial to

18 Some publishers of journals seek the agreement of authors to the inclusion of the author's article in such a computer database.

19 [1967] Ch 932.
20 The BBC wished to remove words from a script which it considered would be offensive to a large proportion of the viewing public, even though the plantiff author considered that the words were important.

21 *See* the Copyright, Designs and Patents Act 1988 Sch 1, paras 22–25. The provisions are similar to those for the right to identified as author or director.

the honour or reputation of the author or director. If the treatment does injure the honour or reputation of the author or director, it is possible that it may give rise to a claim in defamation in addition to an action for infringement of the moral right. 'Treatment' is defined as meaning the addition to, deletion from or alteration to or adaptation of the work, but not including a translation of a literary or dramatic work or an arrangement or transcription of a musical work involving no more than a change of key or register. Notice that the meaning of 'treatment' is not the same as the very technical meaning of 'adaptation' given in s 21. In some respects, treatment is wider than adaptation because it includes additions and deletions, but narrower in the sense that translations and arrangements are not included. The definition of 'treatment' is directed towards the activities that could offend the author, whereas a straightforward translation of a literary work should not upset any author. The right to object applies in relation to the whole or any part of the work under s 89(2). There is no stipulation that the part must be substantial and, theoretically, the right could arise in relation to a small part (in terms of quality or quantity), although the smaller the part, the less likely it is that its treatment would be considered to be derogatory.

An important aspect of the integrity right is the question of what amounts to a derogatory treatment of a work. Certainly, reducing the aesthetic content or damaging the literary style of the work by altering it – in other words, reducing the merit or quality of the work – would probably fulfil the requirements; for example, where a parody is made of music intended to be taken seriously, or in the case of a performance of a send-up of a worthy drama. An indication of the meaning can be gleaned from the French case of *Rowe* v *Walt Disney Productions*,[22] heard in the *Cour d'Appel* in Paris. In this case it was argued that moral rights under French law had been infringed, including the author's right to integrity. The plaintiff, a citizen of the USA resident in France, had written a story about an aristocratic family of cats living in one of the better, more elegant areas of Paris, believing that a film would be made using live animals. Eventually, the defendant made a film based on the story, not using live animals but in the form of an animated cartoon, called *The Aristocats*. The plaintiff, the author of the story, claimed, *inter alia*, damages for the harm done to the integrity of his work.[23] The plaintiff's various claims failed because of a number of factors, not the least being that the original assignment was subject to English law, and the then current English copyright legislation, the Copyright Act 1956, did not expressly recognise moral rights.[24]

Unfortunately for the descendants of Victor Hugo, they could do nothing but protest when Walt Disney made an animated version of *The Hunchback of Notre Dame*.[25] Victor Hugo died in 1885 and, consequently, the copyright in his works has expired together with his moral rights. Perhaps this demonstrates that moral rights ought to last longer, possibly as long as there are still direct descendants who could be upset by a derogatory treatment of a work.

### Scope of the right to object to derogatory treatment

There are, as might be expected, some similarities in the scope of this right when compared to the right to be identified. However, the scope of this particular right is expressed in terms of a classification of works which is more faithful to that given in s 1. In the case of literary, dramatic and musical works, the right is infringed by a person who:

22 [1987] FSR 36.

23 Initially, the author had asked for further payment in respect of his authorship of the story.

24 A citizen of the USA resident in France enjoys the same moral rights as French authors. However, the law of the country in which the contract is signed becomes the law of the parties, and neither the Universal Copyright Convention nor any other provisions of international law could give the plaintiff moral rights afforded by French law which were denied to him under the law of contract. The assignment had been signed in London.

25 *The Times*, 11 March 1997 at p. 17.

(a) publishes commercially, performs in public, broadcasts or includes in a cable programme service a derogatory treatment of the work, or

(b) issues to the public copies of a film or sound recording of, or including, a derogatory treatment of the work.[26]

26 The Copyright, Designs and Patents Act 1988 s 80(3).

In the case of an artistic work, under s 80(4), the right is infringed by a person who:

(a) publishes commercially or exhibits in public a derogatory treatment of the work, or broadcasts or includes in a cable programme service a visual image of a derogatory treatment of the work;

(b) shows in public a film including a visual image of a derogatory treatment of the work or issues to the public copies of such a film; or

(c) in the case of a work of architecture in the *form of a model for a building*, a sculpture or a work of artistic craftsmanship, issues to the public copies of a graphic work representing, or of a photograph of, a derogatory treatment of the work.

However, unlike the paternity right, this right does not apply to works of architecture in the *form of a building*.[27] Nevertheless, under s 80(5), where the author is identified on the building and the building is subjected to a derogatory treatment, the author has the right to have the identification removed. Other remedies will not, therefore, be applicable in this latter situation.

27 The consequences of failing to provide for this can be seen in a Swiss case reported in [1994] 10 EIPR D-267.

As regards films, the right to object to a derogatory treatment is infringed by a person who:

(a) shows in public, broadcasts or includes in a cable programme service a derogatory treatment of the film;

(b) issues to the public copies of a derogatory treatment of the film.

Section 80(7) provides that the right extends to apply to the treatment of parts of a work resulting from a previous treatment by a person other than the author or director, if those parts are attributed to, or are likely to be regarded as, the work of the author or director. Thus, derogatory treatments of versions of the work that have already been altered by a third party are covered by the right. For example, an author, Joe Brown, writes a story in English and assigns the copyright to a publishing company. The story becomes well known. Another person is engaged by the 'lishing company to translate the story into French. The publishing company grants a licence to a French theatre company permitting the latter to perform the French version in public. The French theatre company decide to perform a send-up of the story in the form of a farce. If this treatment is judged to be derogatory and the work is likely to be attributed to him, Joe Brown's moral right has been infringed. Ironically, the enhanced position given to authors and directors by the paternity right increases the possibility that the author or director will have his integrity right infringed. The stronger the association between the author or director and the work, the greater the likelihood of the integrity right, as regards treatments of previous treatments, being infringed, as indeed is the likelihood that a treatment will harm the honour or reputation of the work. Some authors and directors may find it embarrassing to be so clearly identified as such.

**Exceptions and qualifications to the right to object to the derogatory treatment of a work**

The right is limited in its scope by exceptions and qualifications provided for under ss 81 and 82, respectively. The right to object to derogatory treatment of a work is subject to exceptions as follows.

1  *The right does not apply to computer programs and computer-generated works* (s 81(2)). Although there may be a great deal of creative effort involved in computer programs and, indirectly, in computer-generated works, any right to integrity could be seen as an unwanted potential restriction on the future modification of the work. Nevertheless, professional reputation will be associated with computer programs particularly and it seems anomalous to omit computer programs from the ambit of this right and, indeed, the right to paternity. Computer programs are the result of a great deal of skill, judgment and experience and the author-work bond will be as great as with any other form of literary work, and in many cases it will be greater.[28] As regards computer-generated works, it is accepted that the right, at first sight, seems inappropriate. Computer-generated works are defined as being created in circumstances such that there is no human author under s 178, and there should not be a human author to feel aggrieved if the work is subsequently subjected to derogatory treatment. However, under s 9(3), a computer-generated work does have an author who may be a living individual and who may feel angry or distressed by the treatment of the work by a subsequent copyright owner or licensee. For example, the work may be subjected to treatment which makes it derisory and this reflects on the author.

2  *The right does not apply in relation to any work made for the purpose of reporting current events* (s 80(3)). As with the paternity right, this reflects worries expressed by the media during the passage of the Copyright, Designs and Patents Bill through Parliament, that providing for moral rights in such circumstances would be very onerous.

3  Under s 80(4), *the right does not apply in relation to the publication of a literary, dramatic, musical or artistic work* in:

(a) a newspaper, magazine or other similar periodical, or
(b) an encyclopaedia, dictionary, yearbook or other collective work of reference.

However, for the exception to apply, the author must have made the work for the purposes of such publication, or the work must have been made available with the consent of the author for the purposes of such publication. Furthermore, the right does not apply to any subsequent exploitation elsewhere of such a work without modification of the published version. As the author's work will be one of many in the publication, the purpose of this exception is to facilitate the modification of the works included in the publication and, for example, later storage in a computer database. If only one author could object on the basis of his right to integrity, it could hamper or delay the subsequent publication of the entire work. In many cases, editors of collective works reserve the right to modify the author's original manuscript to produce the finished version for publication. An example of a case in which a single author could hamper publication is where the editor of the

28 Some computer programs and suites of programs are the result of many years of work.

compendium work wishes to reduce the length of a submitted article by leaving out a few paragraphs against the wishes of the author. This exception can be seen as recognising the editor's role, his skill and judgment, and allows the editor the discretion he needs to carry out his work.

4 *The right is not infringed by an act which by virtue of s 57 would not infringe copyright* (s 80(5)). Section 57 deals with permitted acts based on assumptions as to the expiry of copyright or the death of the author in the case of anonymous or pseudonymous works.

5 Under s 80(6), *the right is not infringed by anything done for the purpose of*:

(a) avoiding the commission of an offence;

(b) complying with a duty imposed by or under an enactment; or

(c) in the case of the British Broadcasting Corporation (BBC), avoiding the inclusion in a programme broadcast by them of anything which offends against good taste or decency, or which is likely to encourage or incite crime, or to lead to disorder or to be offensive to public feeling.

If the author or director is identified at the time of the relevant act or has previously been identified in or on published copies of the work, there must be a sufficient disclaimer. One of the main purposes of this exception is to allow the BBC to censor parts of works which are to be broadcast without falling foul of the integrity right. The last exception applies only to the BBC, therefore the independent television companies, and, for that matter, satellite broadcasters and proprietors of cable programme services, must choose whether to run the risk of being sued for infringement of the right if they make cuts, whether to screen the work in full or whether to refuse to use the work at all.[29] A sufficient disclaimer would be to the effect that certain scenes which, for example, would be offensive to many people, have been omitted. Examples of scenes that could fall within this provision are:

29 Alternatively, the author or director may be asked to waive his integrity rights.

- explicit or pornographic sex
- showing how a terrorist makes bombs
- violence at a demonstration.

Section 82 is described in the sub-heading as 'qualification of right in certain cases'. It is really just another list of exceptions to the right and applies to employee works (where the first owner of the copyright is the author's or director's employer), Crown and parliamentary copyright and works in which the copyright originally vested in an international organisation under s 168. In respect of these works, the right to object to derogatory treatment does not apply to anything done by or with the authority of the copyright owner unless the author or director:

(a) is identified at the time of the relevant act, or

(b) has previously been identified in or on published copies of the work.

In other cases concerning the works included in the provisions of s 82, that is where the right still does apply (for example, if the author is not and has not been identified), the right is not infringed if there is a sufficient disclaimer.

## Infringement by possession of or dealing with an infringing article

Almost as a parallel to the secondary infringements of copyright, the right to object to derogatory treatment can be infringed by possessing or dealing with infringing articles. An infringing article is defined under s 83(2) as a work or a copy of a work that has been subjected to derogatory treatment and that has been or is likely to be the subject of any of the acts within the scope of the right in circumstances infringing that right.[30] Under s 83(1), a person also infringes the integrity right if he:

(a) possesses in the course of business, or

(b) sells or lets for hire, or offers or exposes for sale or hire, or

(c) in the course of business exhibits or distributes, or

(d) distributes otherwise than in the course of business so as to affect prejudicially the honour or reputation of the author or director,

an article which is, and which he knows or has reason to believe is, an infringing article.

These activities are the same as or very similar to those relating to some of the secondary infringements of copyright and the associated criminal offences. However, the above activities do not, in terms of the integrity right, give rise to criminal liability, but there is a requirement for knowledge on the part of the person infringing the right. The criminal penalties provided under s 107 are expressed in terms of an 'infringing copy' and it therefore would seem that the criminal penalties do not apply to infringement of the integrity right alone, as this is expressed in terms of an 'infringing article'.[31]

## FALSE ATTRIBUTION OF A WORK

Any person could be angered or distressed if a work of poor quality or a work containing scandalous or outrageous comment were falsely attributed to him. For example, an artist with a high standing in the art world would be likely to object if another person painted a substandard work in the artist's style and tried to pass it off as being made by the artist. Obviously, the artist's reputation could be harmed by this unless the painting was an obvious 'fraud'. Of course, the law of defamation may be available to give some remedy to the person to whom an inferior work is attributed, and substantial damages may be available in appropriate cases.[32] In cases such as the one described, an action in defamation may be the most attractive route to follow for the aggrieved person, especially as such cases tend to attract considerable publicity.

However, the ingredients necessary for an action in defamation may be missing. The work that has been falsely attributed might be of a high standard. The person who has created it may be hoping to 'cash in' on the reputation and standing of a famous person, or may be intending to embarrass some other persons.[33] An example of the latter situation is the work of the exceptionally skilled artist, the late Tom Keating, who produced many paintings in the style of important artists such as Constable, Turner and Palmer. The paintings were not copies of original paintings, but Mr Keating adopted the style used by famous artists and his work was of such a high standard that several reputable art dealers and art collectors were fooled.[34] Mr Keating later appeared in a television series showing how he created his 'masterpieces'.

30 Note that the definition is different to that for 'infringing copies' as given by the Copyright, Designs and Patents Act 1988 s 27(2) which relates to secondary infringement of copyright.

31 An infringing article is defined in ibid s 83(2).

32 Defamation cases usually are heard before a jury and the amount awarded to a successful plaintiff can be seen as being something of a lottery, as it is the jury which decides the measure of damages.

33 In such circumstances, there may be an action in passing off.

34 Criminal proceedings against Mr Keating in respect of his activities were halted because of his ill-health.

It is difficult to know whether the 'false attribution right' is a moral right in the true sense, as it does not concern any work created by the person to whom the right accrues. Nevertheless, the Copyright, Designs and Patents Act 1988 places the right firmly amongst the other moral rights, and includes another right which is somewhat out of place in terms of traditional moral rights, that is a right to privacy in relation to certain photographs and films. The false-attribution right is not new and was originally provided for in the Copyright Act 1956 s 43. For example, in *Moore v News of the World Ltd*,[35] the plaintiff, Mrs Edna May Moore (known professionally as Dorothy Squires), alleged that an article which appeared in the *News of the World* falsely attributed authorship to her and was defamatory. The article was entitled 'How My Love For The Saint Went Sour' and was claimed to be by Dorothy Squires talking to a reporter, Weston Taylor. The plaintiff claimed that the article implied that she was an unprincipled woman who had prepared sensational articles about her private life for substantial payment. The case was heard before a jury which awarded £4300 for the libel and £100 for false attribution.

Where there is a court action which involves a claim in defamation together with a claim in respect of false attribution, the general rule is that double damages, will not be awarded – there can be no duplication of damages, but the jury might properly take the defamation award into account in quantifying damages. In the above case, Lord Denning considered that the jury had decided upon an overall figure of £4400 and had split this between defamation and false attribution in the proportions £4300 and £100 respectively.

There must be a work that has been attributed, and in *Noah v Shuba*[36] it was held that two short sentences by themselves could not be a work for copyright purposes. The defendant had quoted, with acknowledgement in a magazine article, the whole of a passage from a guide on hygiene and sterilisation procedures with respect to electrolysis (a method of hair removal) written by the plaintiff. Two sentences in the passage had not been written by the plaintiff and they gave the impression that the plaintiff agreed with the defendant's view, that if proper procedures were followed, there would be no risk of viral infections after treatment. It was held that the whole of the quoted passage had been attributed, and because it was not taken verbatim from the plaintiff's work the *whole of the passage* had been falsely attributed even though the differences were small. Even a slight change in wording can significantly alter the meaning of a written work. The plaintiff was awarded £250 for the false attribution and a further £7250 in respect of defamation.[37]

Persons quoting extracts from the works of others must be careful to use verbatim extracts only and check carefully for typographical errors. For example, if the word 'not' is omitted from a quoted passage and the author's name is acknowledged, it would seem that the whole passage has been falsely attributed. The omission of the word would change the meaning of the passage or part of it and would, therefore, amount to a distortion of the work, making an action on the basis of the integrity right an alternative or additional claim.

The false-attribution right applies to the same categories of works as do the other moral rights, but there are no exceptions. Therefore, unlike the paternity right, it applies to computer programs, typefaces and computer-generated works. A 'person', which presumably can also be an artificial legal person, has the right not to have a literary, dramatic, musical or artistic work falsely attributed to him as author, or to have a film falsely attributed to him as director.[38] Attribution means an express or implied statement as to who is the author or director of the work. The right is infringed in a number of circumstances as follows:

---

35 [1972] 1 QB 441. The case was notable in that it was the first to come before the United Kingdom courts on the question of false attribution.

36 [1991] FSR 14.

37 There was a further award of £100 for copyright infringement. The judge refused to award additional damages in respect of the copyright infringement. A company which has a work falsely attributed to it could, presumably, also have an action in malicious falsehood.

38 The Copyright, Designs and Patents Act 1988 s 84.

39 The false attribution may
be in or on the offending copy
of the work.

1 issuing copies of a falsely attributed work to the public (s 84(2)(a));[39]
2 exhibiting a falsely attributed artistic work or copy thereof in public (s 84(2)(b));
3 performing in public, broadcasting or including in a cable programme service a literary, dramatic or musical work as being the work of a person, knowing or having reason to believe that the attribution is false (s 84(3)(a));
4 showing in public, broadcasting or including in a cable programme service a film as being directed by a person, knowing or having reason to believe that the attribution is false (s 84(3)(b));
5 with respect to the above acts, issuing to the public or publicly displaying material containing a false attribution (s 84(4)) – this would include publicity materials such as leaflets distributed informing the public of a performance or posters advertising some event;
6 possessing or dealing with a copy of a falsely attributed work (a work with a false attribution in or on it) in the course of business, knowing or having reason to believe that there is such an attribution and that it is false (s 84(5)). In the case of artistic works, possessing and dealing with the work itself is caught. Dealing is defined in s 84(7) as selling or letting for hire, offering or exposing for sale or hire, exhibiting in public, or distributing; or
7 in the case of an artistic work, dealing with a work, which has been altered after the author parted with possession of it, as being the unaltered work of the author or dealing with a copy of such a work as being a copy of the unaltered work of the author, knowing or having reason to believe that the work or the copy is not unaltered (s 84(6)). 'Dealing' has the same meaning as above.

The false attribution provisions also apply to adaptations of literary, dramatic and musical works and to copies of artistic works that are falsely represented as being copies made by the author of the artistic work: s 84(8). Under s 89(2), the right of a person not to have a work falsely attributed to him applies in relation to the whole or any part of a work. As regards false attribution before the commencement date of the 1988 Act, the Copyright Act 1956 s 43 applies.[40]

As before, it is unlikely that many persons will feel the need to turn to the false-attribution provisions except as an alternative or additional cause of action, as in serious cases the law of defamation is more appropriate and, if the false attribution has affected the commercial sales of some article incorporating a copyright work, an action in passing off might be relevant and provide greater recompense.

With the assistance of computer technology it is now possible to re-use and manipulate old film clips and photographs to create 'new' images and film action including deceased persons. For example, it is possible to make a new film starring Marilyn Monroe, or a new television advertisement with Alfred Hitchcock or an advertising hoarding featuring Sid James. Relatives and persons who were friends with such celebrities might feel aggrieved at the use of their images (and voices) in this way. The following points can be made about exploiting the characteristics and appearance of deceased persons:

1 there can be no false attribution right actionable by their personal representatives because there is no work in respect of which authorship is falsely attributed to them;
2 there is no action in defamation as deceased persons cannot be defamed;

3 the photographer or director of the original photographs or film clips used to make the new work could have an action for false attribution if the new work is indeed attributed to either of them;

4 the owner of the copyright, if any, subsisting in the original photograph, film or broadcast may be able to use his economic rights, bearing in mind that a single frame is a substantial part of a film;

5 in some cases, if the original work is a recording of a film or sound recording of a live performance, there will be rights in that performance which last for 50 years from the end of the calendar year during which the performance took place. The person entitled to the performer's rights on his death should be able to obtain injunctive relief and/or damages, as too should the person having an exclusive recording contract with the performer.

In some cases, there will be no way in which close relatives of deceased performers can prevent the making of the new work including images of the deceased person. It is possible that the owner of the economic copyright will be happy to licence the use of the original work for such purposes. Of course, the copyright owner may be the person making the new work. It is arguable that a *sui generis* right ought to be introduced to control the use of old images of deceased persons for a substantial period of time after their death.

## RIGHT TO PRIVACY IN PHOTOGRAPHS AND FILMS

English law recognises no general right to privacy. Prior to the 1988 Act, the right to privacy in relation to photographs or films could be achieved only through the application of the economic rights, for example by obtaining an injunction to prevent publication. In *Mail Newspapers plc v Express Newspapers plc*,[41] an injunction was granted to prevent the publication of wedding photographs of a married couple. The wife had suffered a brain haemorrhage when 24 weeks pregnant and was kept on a life support machine in the hope that the baby could be born alive. The husband had granted exclusive rights to the plaintiff in respect of the photographs, together with an undertaking that he would pose for photographs with the baby within 24 hours of its birth. The defendants had intimated that they would also publish copies of the couple's wedding photographs.[42]

The inclusion of the right to privacy in photographs and films was considered necessary because of the power of visual media and the danger that photographs and films made for private purposes would later be published against the wishes of the persons who commissioned them, as happened in the case of *Williams v Settle*.[43] One reason this right is required is that the first owner of the copyright in, for example, a commissioned photograph is the photographer and not the commissioner.[44] The owner of the copyright in a film is the director (and producer if a different person) unless an employee making the film in the course of employment, in which case the employer will be the first owner of the copyright. Therefore, commissioners of films and photographs, in common with other works of copyright, will not be able to control the subsequent use of the work through the medium of ownership. Of course, it is open to the commissioner to make contractual arrangements to protect privacy, or by taking an assignment of the copyright or becoming an exclusive licensee. How-

41 [1987] FSR 90.

42 The case hinged on whether the husband could grant exclusive rights, as it appeared that the husband and wife were joint owners of the copyright in the wedding photographs. However, it was questionable whether the wife was alive or clinically dead. If the former, her consent would be required for the exclusive licence, but plainly she was not in a position to give it.

43 [1960] 1 WLR 1072. *See* Chapter 6 for a discussion of this case.

44 The Copyright Act 1956 had a different rule. Under s 4(3), a person commissioning a photograph for money or money's worth would be entitled to the copyright.

ever, it will often be the case that the person commissioning the photograph or the film gives no thought to this matter. This new right gives him some safeguards to prevent a publication that would be an unwelcome invasion of his privacy or that of the persons appearing in the photograph or film, or at least to provide him with some legal redress.

Under s 85, the right to privacy applies in the case of a copyright photograph or film which has been commissioned for private and domestic purposes. The scope of the right is not to have:

(a) copies of the work issued to the public (here the difficulty with the scope of this phrase is unlikely to be a problem as it will usually be the first issue to the public that causes the complaint);
(b) the work exhibited or shown in public; or
(c) the work broadcast or included in a cable programme service.

45 The relevant permitted acts are those under the Copyright, Designs and Patents Act 1988 ss 31, 45, 46, 50 and 57.

46 Ibid s 89(1).

The right may be infringed indirectly, such as where a person authorises the act complained of. There are some minor exceptions to the application of the right connected with a number of the permitted acts.[45] However, the right does not apply to photographs and films made before the commencement of the 1988 Act. The right does apply in relation to a substantial part of the film or photograph, as well as the whole of it.[46] This will include a single frame from a film.

## JOINT WORKS

47 Ibid ss 10 and 88(5).

The fact that many works are the result of the effort of joint authors (or joint directors), defined as being collaborative works where the respective contributions of the authors or directors are not distinct from the others,[47] requires that the moral-rights provisions in the Act have to contain some rules to be applied in such cases. Not only does the Act have to address infringement of the paternity and integrity rights associated with joint works, but it also has to consider the possibility that a work might be falsely attributed to joint authors or that a photograph or film may be subject to a joint commission. Section 88 deals with joint works and briefly makes the following provisions:

1 for a joint author (or director) to take advantage of the paternity right, he must assert the right himself. An assertion by one joint author will not benefit the other;
2 the right to object to derogatory treatment applies to each joint author or director individually. The consent of one to the treatment does not prejudice the right of the other;
3 the false attribution right is infringed by any false statement as to the authorship of a work of joint authorship and by falsely attributing joint authorship to a work of sole authorship. Similar provisions apply to the directorship of films; and
4 the right to privacy in certain films and photographs applies to each commissioner individually. The consent of one to the relevant act does not prejudice the right of the other.

A principal director of a film will now be a joint author of the film with the producer, where the producer is a different person. However, film producers do not have moral rights.

## DURATION AND TRANSMISSION ON DEATH

The duration of moral rights is provided for in a fairly straightforward way by s 86. In all cases except the false attribution right, they endure as long as copyright subsists in the work in question. As the duration of copyright is, in most cases where moral rights are likely to be in issue, the life of the author plus 70 years this can be seen as fairly generous. However, it could be argued that the rights of paternity and integrity should have no time limit. Why should a person be able to subject a play written by Shakespeare to a derogatory treatment and yet be prevented from doing the same in respect of a work written by an author who is still living or who died not more than 70 years ago? One possible answer is that, given the passage of time, it is less likely that anyone would feel aggrieved personally (others might feel angered simply because the work of a great author was being debased). If the rights were perpetual, eventually it would be difficult to say who had a right of action, that is *locus standi*; it might no longer be clear who could enforce the right. Finally, the law tends to dislike perpetual property rights, as evidenced by the development of technical rules to prevent perpetual rights, for example, in the law of real property, and especially as exhibited in the Act itself which removes perpetual copyright from certain universities and colleges granted under the Copyright Act 1775.[48]

48 The Copyright, Designs and Patents Act 1988, Sch 1, para 13.

After the author's (or director's, or commissioner's) death, the paternity right, integrity right or the right to privacy in relation to certain photographs and films will pass as provided for in the testamentary disposition; or, in the absence of an appropriate direction, the rights pass with the copyright, should it form part of his estate or, failing this, the rights will be exercisable by the author's personal representatives: s 95(1).

Where the copyright is part of the person's estate but is divided, for example, by passing one part to one person and another part to another person, any moral right which passes with the copyright is correspondingly divided under s 95(2). An example is where Bernard is the author of and owns the copyright in a dramatic work and he dies leaving the publication rights to Angela and the remaining rights to Claire. Similarly the copyright could be left to two or more persons consecutively, such as where Bernard leaves his entire copyright to Lynne for five years, after which it reverts to his estate. Lynne will be able to enforce the moral rights for the five-year period, following which the rights will be exercisable by whoever took under Bernard's estate.

As regards the right not to have a work falsely attributed to a person, this continues to subsist for a period of 20 years after the person's death.[49] Of course, in this case there is no copyright of which the person concerned is the author to measure the duration of the right. It is questionable whether 20 years is sufficient to give the widow or children of the person falsely attributed an action to prevent or claim damages for false attribution. There seems to be no good reason why this right should not endure for a longer period of time, say 50 years, after the person's death.

49 This was the period provided for under the Copyright Act 1956 s 43.

Any infringement of the false attribution right is, following the person's death, actionable by his personal representatives: s 95(5). Any damages recovered by personal representatives in respect of this and the other moral rights will devolve as part of the person's estate (as at the time of his death): s 95(6).

## CONSENT AND WAIVER

Under s 87(1) it is not an infringement of a moral right do any act to which the person entitled to the right has consented. Such consent may be implied and the law of estoppel may be relevant.

The major chink in the armour in moral rights in the UK is that they may be waived by the author or director by whom they are owned. It is very likely that copyright owners (unless the owner is the author or director), assignees and licensees will seek to avoid the inconvenience of having to respect the author's or director's moral rights and that pressure may be brought to bear in the hope of obtaining a waiver. Those authors and directors who are in a weak bargaining position may be tempted to acquiesce.

One safeguard for the author or director is that the waiver must be by written instrument signed by the person giving up the right by s 87(2), and the waiver may be conditional or unconditional and may be expressed to be subject to revocation (s 87(3)(b)). The waiver may relate to a specific work or specified description of works or to works generally and may cover existing and future works. For example, an author of plays (dramatic works) may agree in writing to waive his moral rights in:

1  a play entitled *A Long Summer*, or
2  all the existing plays in a series written for television, or
3  all his works up to 31 December 1999, or
4  a play, yet to be written, entitled *A Short Winter*.

If the author or director intends to waive all or some of his moral rights in an assignment or licence agreement, he would be wise to insist on a term to the effect that the waiver is to be revoked if the assignor or licensee commits a breach of the agreement.

There is a presumption that a waiver, made in favour of the owner or prospective owner of the copyright in the works affected by the waiver, extends to licensees and successors in title unless a contrary intention is expressed. The author or director will be bound, in respect of the waiver, as regards third parties who subsequently acquire economic rights in the work or works involved unless there is a term in the agreement to the contrary effect. If the formalities required for a waiver are imperfect, for example, a written unsigned waiver coupled with an oral agreement, the general law of contract or estoppel may be available. An example would be where the author was the first owner of the copyright and he assigned the copyright to another person who was acting in good faith, and the author orally assured the other that he would waive his moral right to be identified as author. If the author later attempted to exercise that right, he might be estopped by the courts on the basis of his conduct.[50] Generally, a waiver by a joint author or joint director does not affect the moral rights of the others.[51]

50 For examples of the doctrine of promissory estoppel in contract law, *see Central London Property Trust Ltd v High Trees House Ltd* [1947] KB 130 and, in the context of a non-exclusive licence in respect of a patented process, *Tool Metal Manufacturing Co Ltd v Tungsten Electric Co Ltd* [1955] 2 All ER 657.

51 The Copyright, Designs and Patents Act 1988 s 88(3) and (6).

## REMEDIES

An infringement of a moral right is actionable as a breach of statutory duty owed to the person entitled to that right.[52] Mandatory injunctions will be relevant, such as where a judge orders that the author's name is added to copies of the work remaining in stock and to future copies, or that an architect's name is placed in a prominent place at or near to the entrance of a building. Prohibitory injunctions may be granted to prevent subsequent infringement of the integrity right and a *quia timet* injunction may be appropriate to prevent the planned publication of, or broadcast of, a derogatory treatment of the work.

Normally damages are available for a breach of a statutory duty, and in the case of infringement of moral rights this would appear to include damages for non-economic loss for the simple fact that moral rights are not economic in nature. Whether aggravated or exemplary damages are available is difficult to say with any certainty. Additional damages were granted in *Williams* v *Settle*,[53] a case involving the publication of a photograph showing a man who had been murdered. Although the effect of the case was to give a remedy for compromising privacy in relation to a photograph, it was done on the basis of an infringement of the economic rights of copyright for which the remedy of additional damages was clearly available, and this remains so under s 97(2).[54] However, the case of *Moore* v *News of the World Ltd*,[55] indicates that damages for false attribution may be slight, certainly in comparison with those available for defamation.

The final point on remedies is that a court has a discretion, in a case involving the alleged infringement of the right to object to derogatory treatment, conditionally to grant a prohibitory injunction requiring that a disclaimer is made dissociating the author or director from the treatment of the work, the disclaimer being in such terms and in such manner as may be approved by the court.[56] This could be appropriate where the copyright owner intends to broadcast a much abbreviated version of a play and the author objects, complaining that this is a mutilation of his original work. This power is unlikely to be used if the nature of the version subjected to the treatment complained of is such that, despite the disclaimer, the reputation of the author is at some risk, however small. One reason is that the long-term effectiveness of even a strong disclaimer may be doubtful, and that in years to come the author may be causally linked to the work as so treated.

## MORAL RIGHTS AND REVIVED COPYRIGHT

In some cases, copyright which had expired in the UK has been revived as a result of the Duration of Copyright and Rights in Performances Regulations 1995.[57] The Regulations contain some provisions as to moral rights in respect of works in which copyright has been revived. The duration of the moral rights to be identified, to object to a derogatory treatment and in respect to privacy of certain photographs and films is declared by the Copyright, Designs and Patents Act 1988 s 86(1) to subsist as long as copyright subsists in the work. In terms of duration, therefore, those moral rights are affected in the same way as copyright and will be revived along with the copyright. However, by reg 22(6), the provisions of paras 23 and 24 in Sch 1 to the Act still apply (no moral rights in

52 Ibid s 103(1).

53 [1960] 1 WLR 1072.

54 In principle, exemplary damages are more appropriate for infringement of moral rights than they are in respect of infringements of economic rights.

55 [1972] 1 QB 441.

56 The Copyright, Designs and Patents Act 1988 s 103(2).

57 SI 1995/3297, implementing the EC Directive on the harmonisation of the term of copyright and certain related rights OJ L290, 29.10.93, p. 9. For the main effects of this, *see* Chapter 3.

respect of which the author died or the film or photograph was made before commencement, 1 August 1989).

By reg 22(3), moral rights are exercisable by the author (or director of film) in relation to revived copyright, or if the author or director died before commencement, by his personal representatives. Any waiver or assertion subsisting immediately before the expiry of copyright will continue to have effect during the revived period.

Any damages recovered by personal representatives for infringement after the author's/director's death devolve as part of his estate as if the right of action had subsisted and been vested in him immediately before his death: reg 22(5).

# 6

## *Rights, infringement and remedies*

### RIGHTS OF COPYRIGHT OWNERS

The Copyright, Designs and Patents Act 1988 marks out the rights of copyright owners by reference to certain acts which only the owner can do or authorise; he is given exclusive rights in respect of these acts. These are the *acts restricted by copyright*. Other activities, which are mainly of a commercial nature, such as dealing with infringing copies of a work, if they are done without the licence of the copyright owner, are described as secondary infringements. Anyone who does one of the acts restricted by the copyright, including the secondary infringements, without the permission or licence of the copyright owner, infringes copyright, unless a defence or any of the exceptions known collectively as the *permitted acts* apply.[1] Strictly speaking, the permitted acts, although so described in the 1988 Act, are better described as exceptions to copyright infringement. This is because any activity in relation to a copyright work which is neither a restricted act nor a secondary infringement of copyright can be performed by anyone without the permission of the copyright owner. For example, lending a book to a friend does not infringe copyright, neither does making an artistic work from a literary work.[2] Therefore, unless there is an issue of infringement, the relevance of the permitted acts does not enter into the equation. If there is no infringement, there is no need to rely on the permitted acts to excuse the particular activity concerned.

Copyright may be infringed vicariously, where a person without the permission of the copyright owner *authorises* another to do a restricted act.[3] Simply playing a major role in selecting material to include in the infringing work is not, by itself, sufficient to make a person liable by authorising infringement.[4] 'Authorise' means to grant or purport to grant to a third person the right to do the act complained of.[5]

As well as giving an aggrieved copyright owner civil remedies for copyright infringement, the Act also provides for criminal offences which generally, though not exactly, mirror some of the secondary infringements of copyright. Offences will normally be dealt with by the Crown Prosecution Service on reference from the police or by Trading Standards Officers. Of course, private prosecutions may be possible, and there are signs that more will be brought, for example, by collecting societies as in *Thames & Hudson Ltd* v *Design and Artists Copyright Society Ltd.*[6]

### THE ACTS RESTRICTED BY COPYRIGHT

The copyright owner has, under the Copyright, Designs and Patents Act 1988 s 16(1), the exclusive right:

1 *See* Chapter 7.

2 *Brigid Foley* v *Ellott* [1982] RPC 433. It was held that a literary work comprising the words and numerals in a knitting guide was not infringed by the making of garments by the defendant using the knitting guide. But see the section on making an adaptation later in this chapter.

3 The Copyright, Designs and Patents Act 1988 s 16(2). Statutory references in this chapter are, unless otherwise stated, to the Copyright, Designs and Patents Act 1988.

4 *Keays* v *Dempster* [1994] FSR 554.

5 *CBS Songs Ltd* v *Amstrad Consumer Electronics plc* [1988] AC 1013.

6 [1995] FSR 153. The Director of Public Prosecutions has certain powers in respect of private prosecutions, including a power to intervene and undertake the conduct of proceedings even if the purpose is to offer no evidence and thereby abort those proceedings. The Prosecution of Offenders Act 1985 s 6.

- to copy the work
- to issue copies of the work to the public
- to rent or lend the work to the public
- to perform, show or play the work in public
- to broadcast the work or include it in a cable programme
- to make an adaptation of the work or do any of the above in relation to an adaptation.

The copyright subsisting in a work is infringed by any person who does or authorises another to do any of these acts restricted by copyright without the licence (that is, without permission, contractual or otherwise) of the copyright owner.[7] Copyright may be infringed if the act complained of relates to only a part of the work for, under s 16(3), the doing of an act restricted by copyright includes doing it to any *substantial* part of the work. The question of substantiality has been taken by the courts as referring to the quality of what has been taken rather than its quantity in proportion to the whole. In *Ladbroke (Football) Ltd* v *William Hill (Football) Ltd*, Lord Pearce said:

> Whether a part is substantial must be decided by its quality rather than its quantity. The reproduction of a part which by itself has no originality will not normally be a substantial part of the copyright and therefore will not be protected.[8]

However, to speak of the reproduction of a part which has no originality *per se* is misleading. Many works have nothing original, if viewed in terms of their constituent parts, yet it is clear that compilations of commonplace material may still be works of copyright; the rationale is that sufficient skill, effort or judgment has been expended in making the compilation.[9]

In *Ladbroke* v *William Hill*, Lord Evershed alluded to the substantial significance of the part taken and suggested that the question of substantial reproduction is incapable of precise definition but is, rather, a matter of fact and degree.[10] On this basis it is clear that copying a small portion of a work can infringe copyright if that part is important in relation to the whole work. For example, in *Hawkes & Sons (London) Ltd* v *Paramount Film Service Ltd*,[11] a newsreel contained 28 bars comprising the main melody of the well-known march 'Colonel Bogey'. This portion lasted only 20 seconds, whereas the full march lasted for some four minutes. Nevertheless, the newsreel was held to infringe the copyright in the march. It was said that what is substantial is a matter of fact, and value as well as quantity must be considered.

In evaluating substantiality, the court should focus on the parts of the plaintiff's work reproduced by the defendant where the defendant's work contains other materials. In *Spectravest Inc* v *Aperknit Ltd*,[12] Millet J said (at 170):

> In considering whether a substantial part of the plaintiff's work has been reproduced by the defendant, attention must primarily be directed to the part which is said to have been reproduced, and not to those parts which have not.

The test seems to be, therefore, to identify the parts taken by the defendant, to then isolate them from the remainder of the defendant's work and then, finally, to consider whether those parts represent a substantial part of the plaintiff's work. That comparison will be based on a test that is, according to Millet J, qualitative and not, or not merely, quantitative.

7 The Copyright, Designs and Patents Act 1988 s 16(2).

8 [1964] 1 WLR 273 at 293.

9 For example, *see Macmillan & Co Ltd* v *K & J Cooper* (1923) 40 TLR 186.

10 The Copyright Act 1956 contained a restricted act of reproducing a work in a material form, broadly equivalent to copying a work under the Copyright, Designs and Patents Act 1988. Indeed, for literary, dramatic, musical and artistic works, copying is defined in s 17(2) as reproducing the work in any material form.

11 [1934] Ch 593.

12 [1988] FSR 161.

An alternative and, at first sight, very attractive test is to consider whether the act complained of is likely to harm the copyright owner's economic interests. In *Cooper v Stephens*,[13] it was said that copying even a small portion of an author's work would be restrained if used in a work which competed with the author's work or with a work that the author might publish in the future. However, such a test, taken literally, would be very difficult to apply and could mean that copying even a small unimportant part could infringe copyright, which plainly is not the result intended by the Act. Basically, if the part taken is significantly important, regardless of actual size, it is very likely to be detrimental to the copyright owner's interests. Another point is that, in a number of situations, the copyright owner may not wish to exploit the work commercially. For example, the work may have been produced for personal pleasure or interest, such as in the case of a private diary.

The Copyright, Designs and Patents Act 1988 explicitly provides for indirect infringement of copyright under s 16(3), regardless of whether any intervening acts themselves infringe copyright. This is particularly valuable in the context of articles made to drawings, so that a person making copies of the articles will indirectly infringe the copyright subsisting in the drawings. In *LB (Plastics) Ltd v Swish Products Ltd*,[14] the plaintiff manufactured a plastic 'knock-down' drawer system of furniture, known as 'Sheer Glide', in accordance with working drawings. The House of Lords upheld the plaintiff's claim that the copyright subsisting in the drawings had been infringed by the defendant who had copied the drawers. There was some evidence that the defendant had directly used the drawings in question, but the trial judge, Whitford J, based his judgment on indirect copying of the drawings by the defendant's use of the plaintiff's drawer as a model for making similar drawers, and this approach was affirmed in the House of Lords.

Recalling that copyright subsists in drawings as artistic works irrespective of artistic quality, even functional articles sometimes were afforded protection through their working drawings under the Copyright Act 1956. However, the 1988 Act, while expressly reinforcing the notion of indirect infringement of copyright, reduces its scope because of an overlap with design law.[15] The Copyright, Designs and Patents Act 1988 s 51(1) states that the copyright in a design document (or model recording or embodying a design) is not infringed by making articles to the design unless the design is, itself, an artistic work. A design document is, under s 263, any record of a design, whether in the form of a drawing, a written description, a photograph, data stored in a computer or otherwise.[16]

The individual infringing acts will now be considered in more detail. Sections 17–21 of the Act expand upon the meaning and scope of the acts restricted by copyright. Infringements of the rights associated with the restricted acts were described in the 1956 Act as 'primary infringements'. They are no longer so called, although the Act still classifies some activities as secondary infringements and some writers still refer to primary infringements to distinguish them from the secondary infringements. It should be noted at this stage that the scope of the acts restricted by copyright vary according to the nature of the work involved.

---

13 [1895] 1 Ch 567.

14 [1979] RPC 551.

15 Designs created before 1 August 1989 may still be protected through their drawings as a result of the transitional provisions. In *Valeo Vision SA v Flexible Lamps Ltd* [1995] RPC 205 it was held that there was an infringement of the copyright subsisting in drawings of vehicle lamp clusters.

16 This definition applies to the Copyright, Designs and Patents Act 1988 Part III which concerns the design right subsisting in original designs.

## Copying

Making a copy of a work is the act which most people think of in terms of copyright infringement, for example, making a photocopy of pages in a book or duplicating a music cassette. But 'copying' has a technical meaning which varies depending on the nature of the work in question. Section 17 of the 1988 Act comprehensively deals with the concept of copying, and generally copying is a restricted act for all categories of copyright works.[17] When considering the definitions of copying, it is essential to recognise that many of the words and terms used are themselves widely defined in the Act.

Section 17(2) defines copying, in relation to a literary, dramatic, musical or artistic work, as reproducing the work in any material form.[18] This does not extend to taking the idea underlying the work. For example, in *Breville Europe plc* v *Thorn EMI Domestic Appliances Ltd*,[19] it was held that taking the idea of using triangular dividers in a sandwich toaster would not infringe the copyright in the plaintiff's drawings. The defendant's toaster was created independently and no use was made of the skill, labour and effort expended in creating the drawings.[20]

Reproducing in a material form is stated by s 17(2) to include storing the work in any medium by electronic means. Thus, recording a copy of any of the 'original' works of copyright in modern computer storage media falls within the meaning of copying, acknowledging the fact that a work can be stored electronically in an intangible form and copied without the need for paper. 'Electronic' has an extremely wide meaning going well beyond an engineer's understanding of the word. Under s 178, 'electronic' means actuated by electric, magnetic, electro-magnetic, electro-chemical or electro-mechanical energy. However, s 17(2) is phrased in terms of storing the work *in* any medium rather than storing the work *in or on* any medium, although this is unlikely to cause problems in practice because the phrase 'reproducing the work in any material form' should be wide enough in its own right to include any form of storage, given the spirit of the Act.

The inclusion of electronic storage as a means of reproducing a work in a material form means that a musical work recorded on magnetic tape or CD will infringe unless the recording was made with the copyright owner's licence. In the past, there have been problems with some forms of storing works. For example, in *Boosey* v *Whight*[21] it was held that the manufacture of a paper roll with perforations in it so that it could be used to play music on a mechanical organ did not infringe the copyright in the music so represented. However, this case was decided under the Copyright Act 1842 s 15, which was in terms of the author's right being to prevent copying sheet music regarded as a book. That is, it envisaged copying sheet music as sheet music. It is submitted that making a 'piano roll' will infringe under the current legislation. By analogy, storing a work on punched card or paper is no different to storing the work as magnetic pulses on a disc. Music on punched tape is reproduced in a material form.

As regards films, television broadcasts and cable programmes, copying includes making a photograph of the whole or any substantial part of any image forming part of the film, broadcast or cable programme.[22] Therefore, taking a single photograph of a substantial part of one frame of a film or a photograph capturing a substantial part of a momentary display on a television monitor, being the result of either a broadcast or cable programme, infringes copyright. In

*Spelling-Goldberg Productions Inc* v *BPC Publishing Ltd*,[23] the plaintiff made a 'Starsky and Hutch' film and the defendant copied and published a photograph of one frame of the film. It was held that the making of a copy of a single frame of the film was an infringement of the copyright in the film because a single frame was a part of the film within the meaning of the Copyright Act 1956 s 13(10). The generous definition of 'photograph' contained in the 1988 Act should be considered in relation to this form of copying and the fact that photographs and films are mutually exclusive.[24] It should also be noted that s 17(4) states that copying includes making a photograph, and that making a film of a film or a film of a television broadcast will probably be deemed to fall within the act of copying. It is possible in such examples that photographs of some kind may be used in an intermediate process, in which case there will be an infringement in respect of the intermediate copies as, under s 17(6), copying includes the making of copies which are transient or incidental to some other use of the work.

Copying in relation to a typographical arrangement of a published edition simply means making a facsimile copy of the arrangement.[25] Section 178 offers some assistance with the meaning of 'facsimile copy', stating that it includes a copy which is reduced or enlarged in scale. It is reasonable to assume that the word 'facsimile' has its ordinary dictionary meaning, an exact copy or duplicate of something, especially in relation to printed material. This is obviously intended to catch copying by the use of photocopying technology. It will also apply to copies transmitted using 'fax' machines (facsimile transmission machines). Not only can the copyright in the typographical arrangement of published editions be infringed by use of a fax machine, but also copyright in other works, especially the original works. For example, a person faxing a drawing will infringe the copyright in the drawing because he has made a copy

23 [1981] RPC 283.

24 The Copyright, Designs and Patents Act 1988 s 4(2) states that a photograph cannot be a part of a film.

25 Ibid s 17(5).

## Table 6.1 The restricted act of copying

| Work | Restricted act |
|---|---|
| Literary, dramatic, musical, artistic: s 17(2) | Reproducing the work in any material form, including storing the work in any medium by electronic means. |
| Artistic (additional): s 17(3) | Includes making a copy in 3-D of a 2-D work and making a copy in 2-D of a 3-D work, for example, making a painting of a sculpture or constructing a building from an architectural drawing. |
| Film, TV broadcast, cable programme: s 17(4) | Includes making a photograph of the whole or any substantial part. |
| Typographical arrangement of a published edition: s 17(5) | Making a facsimile copy of the arrangement. |
| All works: s 17(6) | Includes the making of copies which are transient or are incidental to some other use of the work. |

*Note:* 'Photograph' has the meaning given in s 4(2), 'material form' is not defined but should include invisible means of storage such as on compact discs, magnetic tape, computer disks and integrated circuits.

of it, unless, of course, he has permission from the copyright owner to do this. Facsimile transmission is carried out by the sender's machine scanning a document and converting the data contained in the document into digital codes which are then transmitted over the telecommunications system to the receiving machine, which converts the digital data back to an image. The person receiving a facsimile will obtain a faithful copy of the original although there may be some degradation in print quality. Table 6.1 summarises the scope of the restricted act of copying as it applies to different categories of works. It should be recalled that, generally, copying is a restricted act for all types of work.

### Copying – an accumulation of insubstantial taking

A defendant may have taken small parts of a work over a period of time where each small part would not, by itself, be regarded as substantial. In *Cate* v *Devon & Exeter Constitutional Newspaper Co*,[26] the defendant extracted and reproduced small amounts of material from the plaintiff's newspaper on a regular and systematic basis. The defendant's purpose was to include the material in his own newspaper. It was held that he had infringed copyright, even though the amount taken each week was small.

The logical problem of holding that the regular taking in insubstantial parts being, eventually, considered to be a substantial taking was highlighted by Laddie J in *Electronic Techniques (Anglia) Ltd* v *Critchley Components Ltd*[27] where he said, criticising *Cate* v *Devon* (at 409):

> At its most extreme it could be put this way: a competitor who, because he only took insubstantial amounts, did not infringe yesterday, does not infringe today and will not infringe tomorrow, will be held to infringe if he continues not infringing for long enough.

Laddie J's sentiment holds true where each insubstantial taking is in relation to a different work of copyright, as in *Cate* v *Devon*. However, in respect of a single work, that approach is flawed. What if, over a period of time, the defendant takes the entire work? A better way to look at an accumulation of insubstantial takings is to consider them as part of a continuing act, as was recognised as a possible explanation by Laddie J in *Electronic Techniques*. That case involved applications for summary judgment only and Laddie J did not come to any firm conclusion on the matter, although he did suggest it might be timely if *Cate* v *Devon* was reconsidered. A line of authorities, including this case, appear to take the defendant's behaviour into account when determining substantiality. That is, a deliberate and repeated taking of small parts might be held to infringe. However, the language of s 16 of the Act does not suggest any such thing.

Copyright is concerned, *inter alia*, with securing the economic rights of owners and, consequently, the test for substantiality should be related in some way to the issue of whether the plaintiff's economic rights have been prejudiced by the defendant's acts. Perhaps more than anything else, that explains why quality has been important in determining substantiality. The systematic taking of small parts can, in some circumstances, injure the plaintiff's economic advantage in owning the copyright in the work. A computer database is an example. Indeed, reg 16(2) of the Copyright and Rights in Databases Regulations 1997 specifically accepts that the repeated and systematic extraction or re-utilistation of insubstantial parts of a database may amount to the extraction or re-utilisation of a substantial part.

26 (1889) 40 Ch D 500.

27 [1997] FSR 401.

## Copying – dimensional shift

In respect of artistic works, copying is extended to include the making of a copy of a two-dimensional work in three dimensions and vice versa.[28] Thus, making a three-dimensional model from a drawing is copying, as is making a drawing of a three-dimensional sculpture. As mentioned earlier, copyright can be infringed indirectly and this means that the process of 'reverse engineering',[29] copying an article by inspecting it, taking measurements and examining details of its construction and using the knowledge thus gained to make the copies, may infringe the copyright in any original drawings of the article concerned. In *British Leyland Motor Corp Ltd* v *Armstrong Patents Co Ltd,*[30] the plaintiff designed and made motor cars and also made spare parts for its cars. The plaintiff also granted licences to other companies permitting them to copy and sell spare parts for the plaintiff's cars in return for a royalty payment. The defendant refused to obtain a licence and manufactured replacement exhaust pipes for the plaintiff's cars by copying the shape and dimensions of the exhaust pipes made by the plaintiff for the Morris Marina car. The defendant simply bought a Morris Marina and removed the exhaust pipe and examined it to see how it was made, what its contours were, etc. The plaintiff claimed that the defendant's exhaust pipes infringed the copyright in the original drawings of the exhaust pipes. It was held that the defendant had infringed the copyright subsisting in the drawings of the exhaust pipes by the process of reverse engineering, but the plaintiff would not be allowed to assert its rights under copyright law. It was said, in the House of Lords, that car owners have an inherent right to repair their cars in the most economical way possible, and for that purpose it was essential that there was a free market in spare parts. This required the adoption of the non-derogation from grant principle in *Browne* v *Flower*[31] in which Parker J said (at 225):

> ... the implications usually explained by the maxim that no one can derogate from his own grant do not stop short with easements.

Lord Templeman thought this principle could apply to a car just as easily as to land. He said:

> The principle applied to a motor car manufactured in accordance with engineering drawings and sold with components which are bound to fail during the life of the car prohibits the copyright owner from exercising his copyright powers in such a way as to prevent the car from functioning unless the owner of the car buys replacement parts from the copyright owner or his licensee.[32]

Therefore, although there had been a technical infringement of copyright, the plaintiff was not allowed to derogate from or interfere with the car owner's right to a free market in spare parts. This case is important because it shows how the courts are prepared to control actual or potential abuse of a copyright, but changes to copyright and design law have removed the possibility of infringing artistic copyright by copying an article made to a drawing if the article is subject to a design right and is not itself an artistic work.[33] However, this does not apply until 1 August 1999 to design documents and models which were created before 1 August 1989.[34] Nevertheless, it is clear that the *British Leyland* defence survives the 1988 Act, both in respect of the transitional provisions[35] and in relation to infringements occurring thereafter: see *Flogates Ltd* v *Refco Ltd.*[36]

28 The Copyright, Designs and Patents Act 1988 s 17(3).

29 Sometimes referred to as 'reverse analysis', especially in terms of computer programs. *See* Chapter 8.

30 [1986] 2 WLR 400.

31 [1911] 1 Ch 219.

32 [1986] 2 WLR 400 at 430.

33 *See* Chapter 18 on the Design Right.

34 *See* the transitional provisions in the Copyright, Designs and Patents Act 1988 Sch 1 para 19(1). An example of the working of these provisions is the case of *Valeo Vision SA* v *Flexible Lamps Ltd* [1995] RPC 205.

35 *See* the Copyright, Design and Patents Act 1988 Sch 1 para 19(9).

36 [1996] FSR 935.

The *British Leyland* principle, that the owner of a complex article that will require replacement parts cannot be deprived of a free market in such parts, can be criticised in that it interferes with and curtails a clear statutory right, particularly as the Act contains numerous permitted acts, excusing what would otherwise infringe. The principle should be applied, therefore, only sparingly. The Judicial Committee of the Privy Council, indicating that the principle should not be extended in its application and scope, went so far as to direct some criticism at it, saying that it was constitutionally questionable for a judicially-declared head of public policy to override or qualify an express statutory provision. In *Canon Kabushiki Kaisha* v *Green Cartridge Co (Hong Kong) Ltd*,[37] which concerned the spare-parts market ('aftermarket') for cartridges for laser printers and photocopiers, it was held the principle could not be regarded as being founded upon any principle of the law of contract or property, but was based on an overriding public policy. Lord Hoffmann, delivering the judgment of their Lordships, said (at 826):

> Their Lordships consider that once one departs from the case in which the unfairness to the customer and the anti-competitive nature of the monopoly is as plain and obvious as it appeared to the House in *British Leyland*, the jurisprudential and economic basis for the doctrine becomes extremely fragile.

A number of factors in the *Canon* case distinguish it from *British Leyland*. The toner cartridges would normally be replaced when nothing was wrong with the printer or copier that could be described as requiring repair. It would have simply run out of toner. The cost is more like a normal running cost, such as servicing a car, rather than a repair. The aftermarket itself was different in that the cost of new cartridges was a much higher proportion of the cost of the printer or copier compared with the cost of an exhaust pipe in relation to the cost of a car. Cartridges are replaced much more frequently than exhaust pipes. Basically, the decision is a triumph for market forces. Lord Hoffmann accepted that customers are likely to calculate the lifetime cost of a printer or copier, taking into account the cost of cartridges, in comparing different manufacturers' products. If customers do this, it cannot be said that controlling the aftermarket is anti-competitive[38] and a manufacturer who charges too much for his cartridges is likely to sell fewer machines.

The Judicial Committee of the Privy Council in *Canon* also directed some criticism at a line of authorities including *Dorling* v *Honnor Marine Ltd*[39] and *LB (Plastics) Ltd* v *Swish Products Ltd*[40] on copying by reproducing an article represented in a drawing or other graphic work. The Committee had been invited to depart from these authorities and decide that copying a functional three-dimensional object is not an indirect reproduction of the drawings. Lord Hoffmann said that such cases did not sufficiently distinguish between the reproduction of an artistic work (whether in two-dimensional form or three-dimensional form) and the use of the information contained in an artistic work, such as a drawing together with additional text as the instructions for making a three-dimensional object. Although plainly derived from the drawing, the object does not reproduce the drawing. For example, in *Burke and Margot Burke Ltd* v *Spicers Dress Designs*[41] it was held that a frock made by the defendant (whether spread out or held up to view) was not a reproduction of the plaintiff's sketch of the frock. However, as the sketch showed the frock worn by

37 [1997] FSR 817, an appeal from the Court of Appeal in Hong Kong.

38 There was no evidence of any abuse of the monopoly position.

39 [1965] Ch 1.
40 [1979] RPC 551.

41 [1936] Ch 400.

...auson J said that there might have been an infringement had the
...een that the frock had been worn by a woman posing as in the
...he Committee declined to depart from previous law, partly because
...d changed and, in *British Leyland*, the House of Lords decided after
...sideration to follow the earlier cases.

...previous law, there was a defence under the Copyright Act 1956 s 9(8)
to the effect that there was no infringement of artistic copyright by a
'dimensional shift' if the alleged infringing object would not appear to persons,
not being experts in relation to such objects, to be a reproduction of the artistic
work. In other words, for an infringement, the object copied in a different
number of dimensions from an artistic work would have to look like the artistic
work in the eyes of the layman. He should have been able to recognise the artistic
work in the copy. This test became known as the 'lay recognition test', and was
neither easy nor fair to apply as many drawings, particularly engineering drawings, do not appear to be much like the objects they represent in the eyes of a
layman.[43] For example, in *Merlet v Mothercare plc*[44] the defendant had copied a
baby's rain cape designed by the plaintiff. On the question of infringement of the
drawings made by the plaintiff for the cape, it was held in the Court of Appeal
that the s 9(8) defence succeeded because the layman would not recognise the
plaintiff's drawing by comparison with garments made by the defendant. The
drawing was in the form of a cutting plan and it was not permissible for the purposes of applying the 'lay recognition test' to unstitch the defendant's garment.[45]
However, that test, which limited the strength of protection in relation to three-
dimensional articles offered primarily through the medium of drawings, has now
been abandoned by the 1988 Act. The test itself was criticised by senior judges
and clearly had failed to achieve its purpose of limiting the scope of copyright. It
also provided some indefensible anomalies. For example, simple objects produced
from simple drawings would be protected, while complex equipment produced
from engineering drawings, difficult for the layman to comprehend, would fail to
attract such protection because the notional non-expert would fail to recognise
one from the other. Judges had even shown an inclination to fail to take account
of differences in scale when applying the test. For example, in *Guildford Kap-
wood Ltd v Embsay Fabrics Ltd*,[46] although the defendant's fabric, greatly
magnified, did resemble part of the plaintiff's lapping diagram, Walton J, regarding himself as the notional non-expert, did not think that the fabric appeared to
be a reproduction of the lapping diagram.

The 'lay recognition test' emphasised visual appearance. In *Interlego AG v
Tyco Industries Inc*[47] it was said that what mattered in relation to artistic works,
especially drawings, is that which is visually significant. Indeed, in *Anacon Corp
Ltd v Environmental Research Technology Ltd*[48] Jacob J held that making a
printed circuit board from a circuit diagram did not infringe the artistic copyright in the diagram because the finished board did not look anything like the
diagram.[49] However, Jacob J failed to note that, under s 17(2), 'reproducing in a
material form' includes storage by electronic means which cannot, by its nature,
have any relevant visual significance. It is submitted that, in respect of that part
of the judgment, Jacob J was unduly influenced by the 1956 Act.

'Dimensional shift' copying applies only to artistic works. For example, in
*Bradbury, Agnew & Co v Day*,[50] the plaintiff owned the copyright in a cartoon
in *Punch* magazine. Some actors who enacted the cartoon on stage by dressing

42 On the basis of *Bradbury,
Agnew & Co v Day* (1916) 32
TLR 349, where a *tableau
vivant* infringed the copyright in
cartoons from *Punch* magazine.

43 In *Merchant Adventurers v M
Grew & Co Ltd* [1971] 2 All ER
657, it was held by Graham J that
the test was whether the drawings
were such that, after inspecting
them, a man of reasonable and
average intelligence would be able
to understand them to such a
degree that he could visualise in
his mind what a three-dimensional object made from the
drawings would look like.

44 [1986] RPC 115.

45 The plaintiff also failed
to show that the finished
garment was a work of artistic
craftsmanship.

46 [1983] FSR 567.

47 [1989] AC 217.

48 [1994] FSR 659.

49 Jacob J went on to hold
that the circuit diagram was
also a literary work because it
was intended to be read and,
by making a 'net list', a list
of components and their
interconnections, the defendant
had infringed the literary
copyright.

50 (1916) 32 TLR 349.

up and posing to look like the cartoon were held to have infringed the copyright in the cartoon. The actors formed a three-dimensional representation of a two-dimensional artistic work, that is, the cartoon. However, in *Brigid Foley Ltd v Ellott*,[51] it was held that converting a two-dimensional literary work, a knitting pattern, into a three-dimensional object, a woolly jumper, was not an infringement of the copyright subsisting in the knitting pattern, and was not a reproduction in a material form for the purposes of copyright.

## Copying and alteration

Significant difficulties may arise in infringement actions if the defendant has produced his work based on a previous original work but has made considerable alterations. Two approaches are possible: first, it is a question of whether the second work is sufficiently the result of skill and labour so that it becomes itself an original work of copyright; second, the distinction between idea and expression may be relevant to this situation. A person might freely admit that he has used another work during the preparation of his own, but may claim that he has not copied the expression of the first work and that his use of it was simply to determine the unprotected ideas contained therein. In other words, he has not made use of the copyrightable elements of the work, but only of the underlying ideas. *Glyn v Weston Feature*[52] provides an example of the former approach, that is whether the second person has used sufficient skill and effort to produce a new and distinct original work of copyright. In that case, a film entitled *Pimple's Three Weeks (without the Option)*, which was a send-up of a risqué play *Three Weeks*, was held not to infringe copyright in the play because very little of the original remained. It could not be said that the film was a reproduction of a substantial part of the incidents described in the play.

Judges are generally unsympathetic to a person who has created a work by making use of a prior work of copyright. It seems wrong in principle that someone can take a short-cut to producing his own work by relying on the skill and effort of others. If there is evidence that the defendant has used the plaintiff's work in some way, judges appear to be reluctant to find for the defendant, regardless of fine distinctions between idea and expression. For example, in *Elanco Products Ltd v Mandops (Agrochemical Specialists) Ltd*,[53] the defendant started to sell a herbicide invented by the plaintiff and called 'Trifluralin' after the expiry of the patent. The defendant sold the herbicide together with a leaflet and label which were partly identical to those used by the plaintiff. After the plaintiff complained, the defendant produced a second leaflet using a different format and language. The plaintiff still complained, and eventually the defendant started using a third version based on the second one, claiming that the information in the plaintiff's leaflet was in the public domain and that, although copyright protected the expression of language, it did not protect the content of it. As a matter of fact, it was found that most of the information in the defendant's leaflet could be traced to the public domain. Nevertheless, it was held that there was an arguable case of infringement of copyright, although the plaintiff was refused an injunction. Plainly, if the defendant had simply taken the trouble to locate and use information in the public domain in the preparation of its leaflet there would have been no infringement. But the fact that the defendant had used the plaintiff's original leaflet did not help its case and Buckley LJ said that, concerning infringement, the question was whether, by using the plaintiff's literature, the defendant was making use of the skill and judgment of the plaintiff.

51 [1982] RPC 433. However, in *Autospin (Oil Seals) Ltd v Beehive Spinning* [1995] RPC 683, Laddie J suggested that, in principle, there was no reason why a literary work could not be infringed by making a three-dimensional reproduction of it, in spite of authority to the contrary.

52 [1916] 1 Ch 261.

53 [1980] RPC 213, an interlocutory hearing.

Of course, if there is a substantial amount of language copying and the same characters and incidents are used, then the fact that the two works may have other differences will not help the defendant's cause. In *Ravenscroft* v *Herbert*,[54] the defendant wrote a work of fiction but had used the plaintiff's non-fictional work as a source to provide credibility in relation to historical facts. The plaintiff's work concerned a spear reputed to have been the one used on Christ at the crucifixion, and to have been a source of inspiration for Nazi Germany. The spear is part of the Hapsburg treasure in the Hofburg Museum in Vienna. The defendant's claim to have used only historical facts from the plaintiff's work was rejected on the basis of substantial copying, particularly in terms of language copying, incidents and in the interpretation of events. Altogether, it was held that the infringing part represented only 4 per cent of the defendant's work, but in assessing damages that 4 per cent was rated as being worth 15 per cent in terms of its value to the whole of the work.

Copyright owners have occasionally complained about parodies of their works, that is satirical or comic send-ups. A parody usually involves a fair amount of alteration, but the link with the first work is quite blatant since the effect of the parody might largely be lost otherwise. Of particular importance, since the passing of the 1988 Act, in addition to the question of whether a substantial part of the first work has been copied, is that infringement of the author's moral rights may also be a significant issue.[55] In *Joy Music Ltd* v *Sunday Pictorial Newspapers (1920) Ltd*,[56] a song entitled 'Rock-a-Billy' was parodied in another song which used the words 'Rock-a-Philip, Rock' in the chorus, but otherwise, the words of the two songs were different. It was held that the parody did not infringe the copyright in the original song. However, in *Schweppes Ltd* v *Wellingtons Ltd*,[57] the defendant produced a label for a bottle which was very much like the plaintiff's famous bottle labels, except instead of using the word 'Schweppes' the defendant used the word 'Schlurppes'. Even though it was accepted that the defendant's label was a parody, it was held that the plaintiff's copyright had been infringed. There is no reason why parodies should be treated any differently to other works which are derived from or based on prior works, although they do seem to have been looked on more kindly by the judiciary. Any difference in treatment runs counter to the Act and confirmation that the same principles apply to parodies as to other copies of works was indicated in *Williamson Music Ltd* v *The Pearson Partnership Ltd*,[58] a case involving a parody of the Rodgers and Hammerstein song 'There is Nothin' Like a Dame' for the purpose of advertising a bus company on television. It was held that the test for determining whether a parody amounted to an infringement of the parodied work was whether the parody made substantial use of the expression of the original work. In other words, to find an infringement by the restricted act of copying, the second work must contain a reproduction in a material form of a qualitatively substantial part of the first work. To this must be added the fact that the 'author' of the second work must have made use of the first work in creating the second, that is there must be some causal connection between the works.[59]

54 [1980] RPC 193.

55 Especially the right to object to derogatory treatment and the right not to have a work falsely attributed to the author. Cases on parodies prior to the 1988 Act must be viewed in the light of subsequent strengthening of the author's moral rights.

56 [1920] 2 QB 60.

57 [1984] FSR 210.

58 [1987] FSR 97.

59 For the 'original' works of copyright, the act of copying is defined as reproducing the work in any material form. 'Reproduction' implies some creative relationship between the works, a casual link.

### Copying – causal connection

In an action for copyright infringement by copying, proof of copying and the question as to which party bears the burden of proof are frequently important issues. Of course, the plaintiff has the burden of proving that the defendant has copied but, having discharged that burden, it can fairly be said that the burden of proof then shifts to the defendant in that he then is given the opportunity to rebut the inference of copying by offering an alternative explanation of the similarities between his work and the plaintiff's work.[60] In *Francis, Day & Hunter Ltd* v *Bron*,[61] it was alleged that the defendant had reproduced the first eight bars of the song 'In a little Spanish Town' in his song 'Why' ('I'll never let you go, Why, because I love you'). The case is also of interest because it deals with the possibility of subconsciously infringing copyright. Willmer LJ accepted counsel's submission that in order to constitute reproduction:

**60** *Creative Technology Ltd v Aztech Systems Pte Ltd* [1997] FSR 491, Court of Appeal, Singapore.

**61** [1963] Ch 587.

1  there must be a sufficient objective similarity between the two works (an objective issue, that is, would the 'reasonable man' consider the two works sufficiently similar), and
2  there must also be some causal connection between the two works (a subjective question but not to be presumed as a matter of law merely upon proof of access).

In his judgment, Diplock LJ described the issue of proof of copying in very clear terms:

> The degree of objective similarity is, of course, not merely important, indeed essential, in proving the first element in infringement, namely, that the defendant's work can properly be described as a reproduction or adaptation of the copyright work; it is also very cogent material from which to draw the inference that the defendant has in fact copied, whether consciously or unconsciously, the copyright work. But it is not the only material. Even complete identity of the two works [i.e. the works are identical] may not be conclusive evidence of copying, for it may be proved that it was impossible for the author of the alleged infringing work to have had access to the copyright work. And, once you have eliminated the impossible (namely, copying), that which remains (namely, coincidence) however improbable is the truth; I quote inaccurately, but not unconsciously, from Sherlock Holmes.[62]

**62** [1963] Ch 587 at 627.

As indicated by Diplock LJ, factual similarity coupled with proof of access does not raise an irrefutable presumption of copying, at most it raises a *prima facie* case for the defendant to answer. Thus, in such cases, the burden of proof will shift to the defendant who will then have to satisfy the court, on a balance of probabilities, that he had not copied the first work and that any similarity is the result of coincidence, not copying. This approach was later accepted by the House of Lords in *LB (Plastics) Ltd v Swish Products Ltd*[63] where it was held, *inter alia*, that a striking similarity combined with proof of access raised a *prima facie* case of infringement that the defendant had to answer.

**63** [1979] RPC 551.

The nature of the similarities is also important. If the information copied is incorrect in its original form, this may be excellent proof of copying. For example, in *Billhöfer Maschinenfabrik GmbH v T H Dixon & Co Ltd*,[64] Hoffman J said (at 123):

**64** [1990] FSR 105.

> ... it is the resemblances in *inessentials*, the small, redundant, even mistaken elements of the copyright work, which carry the greatest weight. This is because they are least likely to have been the result of independent design. (original emphasis)

131

This is a very good reason why authors may deliberately include redundant material, mistakes or dummy entries in their work. It will be very hard for a defendant to give a plausible reason for their existence in his work. Unless admitted by the defendant, the plaintiff has to prove his work is a work in which copyright subsists, that he is the owner of that copyright (or the exclusive licensee), that the defendant has copied from it and that he has taken a substantial part. The inclusion of a few 'deliberate mistakes' in his work will remove one of those barriers. As subsistence and ownership will not frequently be in issue, the outcome will be determined solely on the issue of whether a substantial part has been taken unless the defendant is relying on a particluar defence to infringement. *IBCOS Computers Ltd v Barclays Mercantile Highland Finance Ltd*[65] clearly demonstrates the effectiveness of errors and redundant material in proving copying. It also shows that the amont of such material does not have to be great to convince a judge that copying has occurred.

[65] [1994] FSR 275. This case is discussed in Chapter 8.

The possibility of subconscious copying has already been mentioned above. Musical works are particularly susceptible to this form of copying, where the author of the second piece of music has heard the first music some time before, but has no contemporary conscious recollection of the first piece of music and certainly does not deliberately set out to copy it. This is what was alleged in the *Francis, Day & Hunter Ltd v Bron* case, where it was accepted by the judge at first instance that there had been no conscious copying. Nevertheless, the first eight bars of each song were virtually identical (these are reproduced in the law report). Even so, there must be some causal link between the works – truly independent and coincidental similarity is not copyright infringement. In the Court of Appeal, Willmer LJ said (at 614):

> ... in order to establish liability [on the grounds of subconscious copying] it must be shown that the composer of the offending work was in fact familiar with the work alleged to have been copied.

At first sight, the notion of subconscious copying might appear bizarre, but it appears to be accepted also in the law of breach of confidence.[66] Of course, if the first song has been popular, it will be difficult for a defendant to claim that he has not heard of it and has truly written his work independently in ignorance of it. In terms of music and, to some extent also, computer programs, the author should consider taking deliberate measures to make sure that his work does not appear to be similar to an existing work.

[66] *Seager v Copydex Ltd* [1967] RPC 349.

The ultimate safeguard against allegations of subconscious copying is for the author to cut himself off from the rest of society, or that part of society knowledgeable about the particular class of works, and to create his work in a 'clean-room' environment. But, surely, copyright law does not and should not intend that authors should have to take such extreme measures. Nevertheless, proof that the defendant has taken such measures will help his argument that he has not infringed copyright. In *Plix Products Ltd v Frank M Winstone (Merchants)*[67] the fact that the defendant had instructed his designer to work alone without talking to others involved in the design of kiwifruit packs and without referring to existing packs showed that there had been no direct copying. However, it was held that the defendant had copied through the medium of the New Zealand Kiwifruit Authority's specification for kiwifruit packs which was, in turn, derived from the plaintiff's design. This New Zealand

[67] [1986] FSR 63.

case is also notable in that it accepts that copyright can be infringed by copying from a verbal description, as is, in principle, also a possibility under United Kingdom law as s 16(3)(b) admits infringement by indirect copying.[68]

Certainly, the restricted act of copying should be construed as being concerned with an intentional act. The remedies available for copyright infringement give some support to this approach because, by s 97(1), the plaintiff is not entitled to damages if it is shown that the defendant did not know and had no reason to believe that copyright subsisted in the first work at the time of the infringement. The difficulty is that, if the burden of proof shifts to the defendant, he may find it almost impossible to show that he did not base his work on a previous work which has become very well known, even though it was popular several years earlier.

### Issuing copies of the work to the public

The doctrine of exhaustion of rights, discussed in Chapter 9, is concerned with the freedom of movement of goods. Thus, a person who has put his goods into circulation cannot prevent someone, who lawfully acquires them, from reselling them or importing them into another country for resale. The doctrine is a cornerstone of the Common Market. The market would be too easily distorted if a company could sell identical products in different member states at different prices. Of course, exhaustion of rights should not and does not prejudice the right of a person to put goods into circulation for the first time.

Issuing copies of a work to the public is a restricted act that applies to all categories of works. It is defined by s 18(1)[69] as the issue to the public of copies of the work. Under s 18(2) this means (a) putting into circulation in the European Economic Area (EEA)[70] copies not previously put into circulation in the EEA by or with the consent of the copyright owner, or (b) putting into circulation outside the EEA copies not previously put into circulation in the EEA or elsewhere. This does not include any subsequent distribution, sale, hiring or loan of copies previously put into circulation,[71] or any subsequent importation of such copies into the United Kingdom or another EEA state except so far as (a) above applies to putting into circulation in the EEA copies previously put into circulation outside the EEA.

The main thrust of these complicated provisions is that the copyright owner can take action against anyone who issues a copy of his work to the public for the first time without his consent. However, as in the exhaustion of rights doctrine, in respect of copies already put into circulation by or with the consent of the owner, he loses effective control over them. He cannot, for example, take action against someone who has lawfully bought copies of his work in France and who now wishes to import them into the United Kingdom for the purpose of selling them to the public. The precise application of these provisions depends to some extent on whether the relevant act takes place in the EEA.

It should be noted that this act applies to each and every copy of the work and, under s 18(4), includes the original. Thus, the issue to the public of some copies of a work does not exhaust the right in respect of other copies not yet issued to the public.

As an example of the workings of s 18 consider the following possibilities in respect of 100 copies of a book:

68 As, at the time, only the plaintiff's design had been accepted by the Authority (giving the plaintiff a monopoly in kiwifruit packs), the application of the idea/expression merger doctrine from United States copyright law, discussed in Chapter 8, would probably deny copyright protection to the plaintiff's packs. However, the law of designs and passing off could also apply to this type of situation.

69 Section 18 has been amended on two occasions, most recently by the Copyright and Related Rights Regulations 1996, SI 1996/2967.

70 An EEA state is a state which is a contracting party to the EEA Agreement signed at Oporto 2 May 1992, adjusted by a protocol signed at Brussels 17 March 1993; Copyright and Related Rights Regulations, reg 2. EEA states are the EC countries plus Norway, Iceland and Liechtenstein.

71 Subject to s 18A: infringement by rental or lending.

1 if they are infringing copies – issuing them to the public anywhere will infringe under s 18;
2 if they are copies made for the copyright owner, but he has not consented to their sale (expressly or impliedly) – issuing them to the public anywhere will infringe under s 18;
3 if the owner consented to their sale in the UK – the buyer can resell them or export them for resale anywhere;
4 if the owner consented to their sale in Norway (an EEA state) – as 3 above;
5 if the owner consented to their sale in the USA – the buyer can resell them or export them anywhere except to an EEA state.

The subsequent acts that can be done include hiring or loan, but this may infringe under s 18A which controls rental or lending.

It can be seen from the examples above that the owner's right to issue to the public is not restricted to the issue of infringing copies, and it is possible to infringe by issuing to the public copies which were authorised by the copyright owner.[72] This will be rare as in most cases the person in possession of the copies will have the copyright owner's express or implied consent to issue the copies to the public, for example, in the case of a publishing agreement. One example where the issue of authorised copies may infringe under s 18 is where copies have been made by a printer on behalf of the copyright owner, but an employee of the printer has stolen some and sold them surreptitiously.

### Rental and lending right

The Copyright and Related Rights Regulations 1996[73] introduced, as from 1 December 1996, comprehensive rental and lending rights in relation to copies of works. Previously, only sound recordings, films and computer programs enjoyed specific protection in relation to rental.

Renting or lending copies of a work to the public is now a restricted act, the scope of which is set out in s 18A. The right applies to the 'original' works of copyright (literary, dramatic, musical or artistic works), films and sound recordings. However, there is an exception as regards some of the artistic works and the right does not apply to works of architecture in the form of a building or model for a building nor to works of 'applied art'. This latter phrase derives from Article 2(3) of the Directive (no further indication of its meaning is given there either). It is likely to cover those commercially exploited artistic works falling within s 52.

'Rental' and 'lending' are defined in s 18A(2). Rental is 'making a copy of the work available for use, on terms that it will or may be returned, for direct or indirect economic or commercial advantage', and 'lending' is 'making a copy of the work available for use, on terms that it will or may be returned, otherwise than for direct or indirect economic or commercial advantage, through an establishment which is accessible to the public'. There are some exceptions to the definitions. Neither includes making available for the purpose of public performance, playing or showing in public, broadcasting or inclusion in a cable programme service, exhibition in public or for on-the-spot reference use. Furthermore, lending does not cover making available between establishments accessible to the public (for example, where a library obtains a copy of a book from another library although, of course, the ultimate loan to the borrower is still within the meaning of lending). A charge may be made for lending which,

72 As noted by Laddie J in *Willaim Nelson v Mark Rye and Cocteau Records Ltd* [1996] FSR 313.

73 SI 1996/2967, implementing, *inter alia*, Directive 92/1001/ EEC on rental right and lending right and on certain rights related to copyright in the field of intellectual property, OJ L346, 27.11.92, p. 61 and Directive 93/83/EEC on the coordination of certain rules concerning copyright and rights related to copyright applicable to satellite broadcasting and cable re-transmission, OJ L248, 6.10.93, p. 15.

provided it does not go beyond the operating costs of the establishment, will not take the transaction out of the meaning of lending. A higher charge will result in the act being considered to be rental. The rights apply to the original work as well as to copies of the original.

Under s 36A lending by educational establishments does not infringe, and s 40A contains an appropriate exception where lending is in respect of a book under the public lending right scheme or lending by prescribed libraries or archives (other than public libraries) which are not conducted for profit. Section 66, which provided for compulsory rental of sound recordings, films and computer programs by order of the Secretary of State, is substituted with a new section, which has similar provisions, but in respect of lending of copies of original works, sound recordings or films. No order had been made under the old s 66.

The opportunity was taken to repeal the old s 66(5), which provided that copyright in a computer program was not infringed by the rental of copies to the public 50 years after the program was first issued to the public in electronic form. Now, unless otherwise permitted, such rental will infringe copyright.

Films and sound recordings usually include other works of copyright. For example, the dialogue of a film may be based on a novel or have been written as a screenplay. Music may be included in the sound track. Where an author of an original work agrees with a film producer to its inclusion in the film, unless the agreement provides otherwise, there is a presumption that the author has assigned his rental rights in relation to that film under s 93A. The right is replaced by a right to an equitable remuneration on the transfer of the right. However, the presumption does not apply in respect of any dialogue, screenplay or music *specially* created for and used in the film and, in such cases, express assignment would be required. Where the presumed assignment operates, the absence of any signature on the part of the author does not prevent the operation of s 91(1) (purported assignment of future copyright). If a film producer and principal director make an agreement with the author of a pre-existing piece of music to include the music in the film and the agreement is silent on rental rights, and before the film is made the producer and director sign an agreement with a third party assigning to that third party the copyright in the film, the copyright will automatically vest in the third party and include the relevant rental rights in relation to the music.

Section 93B deals with the detail in relation to the right to equitable remuneration. The right arises where there has been a transfer of the rental right concerning a sound recording or film (including presumed transfer in respect of the inclusion of a copy of a work in a film) and applies to authors of original works and the principal director of a film.[74] The right itself may only be assigned to a collecting society, although it is transmissible by testamentary disposition or operation of law as personal property[75] and may then be assigned by the person into whose hands it passes. The restriction on assignment to a collecting society only no longer seems to apply in such cases. The remuneration is payable by the person for the time being entitled to the rental right. Any purported agreement excluding or restricting the right to an equitable remuneration is to that extent of no effect. The Copyright Tribunal is given the power to determine the amount payable in default of agreement and to vary the amount, and its jurisdiction is modified accordingly.[76] Under s 93C(4), a remuneration shall not be considered inequitable merely because it is made in a single payment, or at the time of the transfer of the rental right.

[74] Although the producer and the principal director are now considered co-authors of a film, this right does not apply to film producers.

[75] In Scotland, moveable property.

[76] Section 93C and s 149(zb).

## Public performance, showing or playing a work in public

Public performances and the public playing or showing of certain types of works infringe copyright unless done with the permission of the copyright owner. These performing rights are, in a great many cases, administered by the Performing Right Society which grants 'blanket' licences to persons wishing to perform, play or show copyright works in public. The performance of a work in public is an act restricted by the copyright in literary, dramatic and musical works. It does not apply to other forms of works. Section 19(2) expands upon the meaning of performance and states that it includes delivery of lectures, addresses, speeches and sermons and, in line with modern technology, it includes in general any mode of visual or acoustic presentation, including by means of a sound recording, film, broadcast or cable programme. Under s 19(3), playing or showing a sound recording, film, broadcast or cable programme in public is an act restricted by the copyright in the work. Therefore, playing music to members of the public, for example background music in a café or restaurant to which the public have access, is a restricted act.

An important element is that the performance, showing or playing must be in 'public', a word which has been responsible for much judicial consideration. A consistent strand in the courts' interpretation has been the question of whether the copyright owner's interests have been harmed by the performance complained of. For example, would the copyright owner expect to be paid a royalty for the performance? Does the performance satisfy part of the public demand for the work and thereby reduce the copyright owner's potential income? In *Duck* v *Bates*,[77] the defendant performed a dramatic piece in a room in a hospital for the entertainment of nurses, attendants and other hospital workers without the consent of the copyright owner. No admission charge was made, but approximately 170 persons attended each performance. It was held that the room where the drama was presented was not a place of public entertainment and that, consequently, the defendant was not liable to the copyright owner in damages. Brett MR said that such a private representation of the drama would not harm the copyright owner, although a public representation in any place where the public were freely admitted with or without payment would.

However, any distinction which might be drawn in this case between the public at large and an audience limited by vocation or membership does not provide a workable formula as there have been several cases involving an audience limited in such a way in which the performance has been deemed to be a performance in public. For example, in *Ernest Turner Electrical Instruments Ltd* v *Performing Right Society Ltd*,[78] the owner of a factory relayed music broadcast by the British Broadcasting Corporation and from gramophone records to his 600 employees. Strangers were not allowed access to the factory. Nevertheless, it was held that the performance was a performance in public for the purposes of the Copyright Act 1911 s 1(2). Lord Greene MR suggested that it was important to consider the relationship between the audience and the copyright owner rather than the relationship between the audience and the person arranging the performance, that is the employer. Economic considerations were also important in that the 'statutory monopoly' granted by the Copyright Act would be, in Lord Greene's opinion, largely destroyed if performances to such groups of persons were permitted.

77 (1884) 13 QBD 843.

78 [1943] 1 Ch 167. *See also Jennings* v *Stephens* [1936] Ch 469 concerning the performance of a play in which the audience was limited to members of a Women's Institute.

Some performances can be said to be in the copyright owner's best interests because they publicise his work and whet the public appetite and, as a result, increase ultimate sales of the work. Such an argument can be raised in terms of radio and television broadcasts of pop music. For example, 'Top of the Pops' and similar programmes can influence sales of particular pieces of music. Nevertheless, broadcasters have to pay for such broadcasts. Since 1976, as a result of a change in policy, even record shops have to pay fees for playing recordings of works written by members of the Performing Right Society over loudspeakers in the shops. In *Performing Right Society Ltd v Harlequin Record Shops Ltd,*[79] the owner of some record shops refused to pay the requisite fee, arguing that playing the records over loudspeakers in the shops promoted sales and increased the composer's royalties and that this playing of recordings did not constitute a performance in public and, consequently, was not an infringement of copyright. However, injunctive relief was granted to the plaintiff and it was held that the performances were in public. The audience comprised members of the public present in shops to which the public at large were permitted and encouraged to enter. Furthermore, it was shown that a prudent record shop owner would pay the society's fee rather than discontinue playing the recordings.

For a performance not to be deemed to be a public performance, it must be to an audience of a domestic nature. It is clear that playing a video film to a group of friends or relatives will not be 'playing the work in public' and enacting a play in the presence of a few friends will not be a performance of the play in public, but the habitual playing of recordings to employees in a factory will be in public even though the employees are not charged anything for this benefit. There are, however, some instances where it is more difficult to draw a line. For example, a private hospital may transmit video films to its patients from a central machine to television monitors in individual rooms. A hotel may provide a similar service for its guests. It is probable, in these circumstances, that the performance or playing will be in public if the service is provided for all the guests or patients and, taken together, they can be said to form part of the public at large, even though only a proportion of them take advantage of the service. If a charge is made, then the question is beyond doubt.

Section 19(4) limits the personalities who can be liable for infringement by performance, showing or playing a work in public. The performers taking part in a public performance are not themselves to be regarded as being responsible for the infringement. In the case of the performance, playing or showing of the work in question by means of apparatus for receiving visual images or sounds conveyed by electronic means, the person by whom the visual images or sounds are sent is not to be regarded as responsible for the infringement. Therefore, a disc jockey at an unlicensed disco will not be liable to be sued for infringement of the public performance right. The language of the subsection appears to be difficult and inconsistent with s 19(2)(b), which is expressed in terms of 'any mode of visual or acoustic presentation', whereas s 19(4) deals only with presentation by electronic means and uses the word 'sound' rather than 'acoustic'. Taking a strictly literal interpretation of s 19(4) could produce absurd results. For example, what is the position where the performers have also arranged the infringing public performance? Section 19(4) appears to excuse their infringement, as it clearly states that the performers shall not be regarded as responsible for the infringement. It is unlikely that the courts will take this interpretation, as it plainly runs

79 [1979] 2 All ER 828.

counter to the spirit of the Act. However, the draftsmen of the Copyright, Designs and Patents Act 1988 have been subject to judicial criticism. In *BBC Enterprises Ltd* v *Hi-Tech Xtravision Ltd*,[80] Scott J said that in his view:

> ... section 298 [of the Copyright, Designs and Patents Act 1988], on any footing, represented inept legislation. The language of the section justified the suspicion that the legislature was under a misapprehension as to the law.

It is inevitable that, given the size and complexity of the Act, there will be interpretational difficulties and it would have been better if, towards the end of s 19(4), the words 'to the extent that the infringement relates to their activity as performer' were added to put the matter beyond doubt.

## Broadcasting or inclusion in a cable programme service

Under the surprisingly brief s 20, the broadcasting of a work or its inclusion in a cable programme service is an act restricted by the copyright in all categories of work except typographical arrangements of published editions. 'Broadcast' is defined in s 6 and the meaning of 'cable programme service' is to be found in s 7; these meanings are discussed in Chapter 3. They are of vital importance because, if the activity concerned falls outside the definitions, such as a cable programme service run for the purposes of business or an interactive service,[81] then there is no infringement of copyright and therefore no need to obtain licences.[82] In many respects, the restricted acts of broadcasting and inclusion in a cable programme service are a wider form of the restricted acts relating to public performance, playing or showing, especially as the meaning of 'broadcast' is expressed in terms of reception by or presentation to members of the public. Similarly, a cable programme service may be one directed at members of the public, although this is only one possibility.

Operating a website on the Internet was held to be operating a cable programme service in *Shetland Times Limited* v *Dr Jonathan Wills*.[83] The defendant had included headlines from the plaintiff's website in articles published on the Internet. The headlines fell within the meaning of a cable programme, being any item included in a cable programme service. Lord Hamilton found that the defendant infringed copyright by including cable programmes in a cable programme service. As a cable programme service is defined as a ' ... service which consists wholly or mainly in sending visual images, sounds or other information ...', this form of infringement is very wide, as it would appear that the inclusion of information infringes, whether or not it is a work of copyright. Thus, including a small amount of information, too trivial to be protected by copyright as a work in its own right, should infringe if done without permission. Even a small amount of information can be described as an item. Lord Hamilton also considered that the headlines could be protected as literary works and that it was arguable, therefore, that there was an infringement by copying under s 17. However, he failed to note the possible double infringement under s 20, for if the headlines were also literary works, there would also be an infringement of copyright by including them as literary works as well as cable programmes in a cable programme service.

80 *The Times*, 28 November 1989. However, the judgment of Scott J was reversed on appeal to the Court of Appeal, *see* [1990] 1 Ch 609.

81 *See* the definitions in the Copyright, Designs and Patents Act 1988 ss 6 and 7 and, especially, the exceptions to the definition of 'cable programme service' in s 7(2).

82 However, there may be other restricted acts involved in the activity such as the making of copies, including transient and incidental copies. This also includes, importantly, storing the work in any medium by electronic means, ibid s 17(2). There may also be a secondary infringement – *see* post.

83 [1997] FSR 604.

## Making an adaptation

In terms of the Copyright, Designs and Patents Act 1988, the word 'adaptation' has some very special meanings, depending on the nature of the work concerned, and should not be taken in its usual sense. Making an adaptation does not simply mean the same as modifying a work. The restricted act of making an adaptation applies only to literary, dramatic and musical works. Of the original works, artistic works are not covered by the act of making an adaptation. Therefore, if a person represents an existing drawing by producing a list of co-ordinates, he is not making an adaptation of the drawing and does not infringe the copyright in the drawing unless the list of co-ordinates can be considered to be a copy of the drawing.[84] If the drawing contains information to be used in the manufacture of an article, it may also be deemed to be a literary work, in which case taking a list of co-ordinates from the drawing will infringe: see *Anacon Corp Ltd* v *Environmental Research Technology Ltd*.[85]

An adaptation is made when it is recorded in writing or otherwise, under s 21(1). 'Writing' is defined in s 178 as including any form of notation or code, whether by hand or otherwise, regardless of the method by which, or medium in or on which it is recorded. This definition is very wide and should present no problems in the context of making an adaptation. 'Adaptation' is defined in s 21(3) and means:

(a) in relation to a literary work other than a computer program or a database, or in relation to a dramatic work:
  (i) a translation of the work;
  (ii) a version of a dramatic work in which it is converted into a non-dramatic work or, as the case may be, of a non-dramatic work in which it is converted into a dramatic work;
  (iii) a version of the work in which the story or action is conveyed wholly or mainly by means of pictures in a form suitable for reproduction in a book, or in a newspaper, magazine or similar periodical;
(ab) in relation to a computer program, means an arrangement or altered version of the program or a translation of it;[86]
(ac) in relation to a database, means an arrangement or altered version of the database or a translation of it;[87]
(b) in relation to a musical work, an arrangement or transcription of the work.

A 'translation' would typically include a work of literature or a play that has been translated from French to English. But, as literary works include computer programs, the word takes on a special meaning in relation to computer programs, and under s 21(4):

> ... a 'translation' includes a version of the program in which it is converted into or out of a computer language or code or into a different computer language or code [, otherwise than incidentally in the course of running the program].[88]

The significance of making an adaptation in terms of computer programs and databases is considered further in Chapter 8.

The dramatic/non-dramatic conversion covers situations such as where a biographical book or a true story is dramatised or, alternatively, where the script for a play is reworked as a novel. For example, in *Corelli* v *Gray*,[89] the

---

84 If the existing work is a sculpture and a person produces a set of co-ordinates describing its form, that will infringe because a 'dimensional shift' has occurred which brings s 17(3) into play. Note that by s 21(5) no inference is to be drawn from s 21 as to what does or does not amount to copying.

85 [1994] FSR 659.

86 Inserted by the Copyright (Computer Programs) Regulations 1992, SI 1992/3233.

87 Inserted by the Copyright and Rights in Databases Regulations 1997, SI 1997/3032.

88 The words in square brackets were repealed by the Copyright (Computer Programs) Regulations 1992, SI 1992/3233.

89 [1913] TLR 570.

defendant was found to have written a dramatic sketch by taking material from the plaintiff's novel. The third form of adaptation in relation to literary and dramatic works is where the story or action has been changed to a form which mainly comprises pictures. An example is where a story has been converted into a strip cartoon. To do the converse is not to make an adaptation, however. To change a cartoon or other graphical means of portraying a story into a written work does not fall within the meaning of making an adaptation; it may, however, fall within the meaning of copying. The rationale for this apparent inconsistency is that, presumably, to convert a story told mainly by pictures to a written work requires a great deal of skill, effort and judgment and all that is really taken is the plot or the idea underlying the pictorial work.[90] The wordsmith has many gaps to fill in. On the other hand, to draw pictures depicting a written work leaves less to the imagination of the artist in terms of the telling of the story, although, of course, he will have free rein to express that story in his preferred way. The Act presumably considers artistic licence to be more constrained than literary licence.

As far as musical works are concerned, arrangements and transcriptions of existing works are adaptations and will, if copyright subsists in the existing work, infringe that copyright. An example of an arrangement is where a piece of music written for one instrument is rewritten so that it is suitable for another, or an operatic aria is re-written as an orchestral piece. If there is a sufficient amount of skill and judgment involved in the arrangement, it too might attract its own copyright,[91] although the permission of the owner of the copyright in the first piece of music would be required before the arranged piece could be exploited.[92]

Under s 21(2), the doing of any of the other restricted acts, described in ss 17–20, in relation to an adaptation, is also an act restricted by the copyright in a literary, dramatic or musical work. This extends to s 21(1), so that making an adaptation of an adaptation also infringes copyright if done without the permission or licence of the copyright owner. For example, if Albert writes a novel in English and Barry, without Albert's permission, translates the novel into French, Barry is making an adaptation and infringes Albert's copyright. If Celia then makes copies of Barry's translation, Celia also infringes the copyright in the original novel (regardless of whether or not she has Barry's permission to do so). Finally, if Duncan translates Barry's French version of the novel into German, Duncan infringes copyright by making an adaptation of an adaptation. In addition to the economic rights, Albert's moral rights might be infringed by the above actions, for example if he is not identified as the author. Albert will have the right to object to derogatory treatment of his work only if the translations have some additions or deletions and the treatment amounts to a distortion or mutilation of the work, or is otherwise prejudicial to Albert's honour or reputation.

## SECONDARY INFRINGEMENTS OF COPYRIGHT

In addition to infringement of copyright through the acts restricted by the copyright in the work, there are certain other infringements known as secondary infringements. Some of the criminal offences provided for under the Act

90 However, *see* the discussion on the requirement for tangibility in Chapter 3.

91 For example, *see Wood v Boosey* (1868) LR 3 QB 223.

92 Apart from infringing the copyright owner's rights, the moral rights of the author must be considered. By the Copyright, Designs and Patents Act 1988 s 80, the author of, *inter alia*, a musical work has a right not to have his work subjected to derogatory treatment. 'Treatment' in relation to a musical work does not include an arrangement or transcription involving no more than a change of key or register.

closely follow the equivalent secondary infringements and the same level of knowledge is required, for example, in some cases knowing or having reason to believe that the article concerned is an infringing copy. The distinction between primary infringement and secondary infringement is that the former involves making the infringing copy or making the infringing performance, while the latter involves 'dealing' with those copies, providing the premises or apparatus for the performance or making an article for the purpose of making infringing copies. If a secondary infringement has been committed, there will almost certainly have been a corresponding infringement of one or more of the acts restricted by copyright.[93] For a secondary infringement the person responsible must have knowledge or reason to believe that the copies are infringing copies or whatever. It would seem from the wording that the person involved must have either actual knowledge or, at least, a subjective reasonable belief that the relevant activity involves a secondary infringement. Under the Copyright Act 1956, only actual knowledge was sufficient for the corresponding secondary infringements, but nevertheless the courts tended to take a liberal view of this and in *Columbia Picture Industries v Robinson*[94] it was held that, *inter alia*, the knowledge required extended to the situation where a defendant deliberately refrained from enquiry and shut his eyes to the obvious. The phrase 'has reason to believe' in the Copyright, Designs and Patents Act 1988 ss 22–26 is new and, in *LA Gear Inc v Hi-Tec Sports plc*,[95] it was said that it could not be construed in accordance with the 1956 Act. The test must be objective in that it requires a consideration of whether the reasonable man, with knowledge of the facts known to the defendant, would have formed the belief that the item was an infringing copy. In the trial at first instance, Morritt J suggested that, once apprised of the facts, the defendant should be allowed sufficient time to evaluate those facts so as to be in a position to draw the conclusion that he is dealing with infringing copies.[96] This is not inconsistent with an objective approach – the reasonable man also may need time for the facts to 'sink in'.[97] Situations where it may be plausible for a defendant not have 'reason to believe' include where he believes that the copyright has expired, where copyright does not subsist in the work or where the copies have been made with the copyright owner's permission.[98]

Where legal proceedings have been initiated against a defendant alleging secondary infringement of copyright, this fact alone does not necessarily mean that he has reason to believe that he is, for example, making or selling infringing copies. Nor does the fact that the defendant had put money aside for a fighting fund for the pending litigation show that he has the requisite knowledge: *Metix (UK) Ltd v G H Maughan (Plastics) Ltd*.[99] After all, the defendant may consider that he has a good chance of successfully defending the action because he does not think that the copies are infringing copies or that he did not have reason to believe that he was infringing at the relevant time.

The need to show a mental element on the part of a secondary infringer must be contrasted with the acts restricted by copyright under ss 16–21, in which the question of the infringer's mental element does not arise. If he commits one of the acts, he infringes copyright regardless of whether he knows that copyright subsists in the existing work and regardless of whether or not it is reasonable for the infringer to suspect that copyright subsists in the work. The strictness of this state of affairs is tempered by the fact that the availability of the remedy of damages is dependent upon the infringer's mental state.[100]

93 But, the 'primary infringement' may have been carried out by another person, hence the need for the secondary infringements. This is especially useful when the primary infringer in outside the jurisdiction of the United Kingdom courts.

94 [1987] 1 Ch 38. *See also Infabrica Ltd v Jaytex Shirt Co Ltd* [1978] FSR 457.

95 [1992] FSR 121.

96 [1992] FSR 121 at 129.

97 Where secondary infringement is planned in the future the plaintiff does not have to wait to see if it is actually carried out when seeking a *quia timet* injunction: *Linpac Mouldings Ltd v Eagleton Direct Export Ltd* [1994] FSR 545.

98 Putting a person on notice that his actions may infringe is not sufficient. The question is whether the reasonable man would believe that he was a secondary infringer: *Hutchinson Personal Communications Ltd v Hook Advertising Ltd* [1995] FSR 365.

99 [1997] FSR 718.

100 On the basis of the same formula, the Copyright, Designs and Patents Act 1988 s 97(1).

Secondary infringement of copyright involves any of the following activities:

1 importing an infringing copy into the United Kingdom, other than for private or domestic use (s 22);
2 possessing or 'dealing' with an infringing copy; this includes possession in the course of business, selling, letting for hire, offering or exposing for sale or hire,[101] exhibiting or distributing in the course of business or distributing (otherwise than in the course of business) to such an extent as to affect prejudicially the owner of the copyright (s 23);
3 making, importing into the UK, possessing in the course of business or selling, letting for hire, offering or exposing for sale or hire an article specifically designed or adapted for making infringing copies of a work (s 24(1));
4 transmission of the work by means of a telecommunications system (excluding by broadcast or inclusion in a cable programme service) without the licence of the copyright owner, knowing or having reason to believe that infringing copies of the work will be made in the UK or elsewhere (s 24(2));
5 permitting the use of premises, being a place of public entertainment, for an infringing performance; a 'place of public entertainment' includes places that are only occasionally made available for hire for the purposes of public entertainment, for example, a room in a public house which is hired out from time to time for functions such as weddings (s 25);
6 where copyright is infringed by a public performance of the work, or by playing or showing the work in public, supplying the apparatus or a substantial part of it for the playing of sound recordings, the showing of films or the receiving of visual images or of sounds conveyed by electronic means (s 26);
7 an occupier of premises who gives permission for the apparatus to be brought onto those premises may also be liable for the infringement (s 26(3));
8 supplying a copy of a sound recording or film used to infringe copyright (s 26(4)).[102]

In all cases, apart from those involving public performances, to be liable the person concerned must have actual knowledge or have had reason to believe, for example, that the copy is an infringing copy or that the copy supplied by him is to be used in such a way so as to infringe copyright. However, there is a subtle difference in the mental element required for the infringement under s 25 in that the person giving permission for the premises to be used for the performance will be liable unless, at the time he gave permission, he believed on reasonable grounds that the performance would not infringe copyright. A similar expression is used in s 26(2) in terms of providing apparatus the normal use of which involves a public performance. Therefore, for these two instances, the test is a blend of the subjective and the objective. It is plain from the wording that the defendant will carry the burden of proof. He will have to show that he did not believe that copyright would be infringed, and furthermore that this belief was based on reasonable grounds. This might be an onerous burden, but the activities involved give rise to civil liability only, which accounts for the difference in the mental element compared to the other secondary infringements.[103]

Some of the secondary infringements involve 'infringing copies' of the work, and the meaning of this phrase is given in s 27 as being:

101 Exposing an article for sale is an invitation to treat and modern statutes use this or a similar formula to overcome the problem that this does not constitute a contractual offer, as identified in cases such as *Fisher* v *Bell* [1961] 1 QB 394 and *Partridge* v *Crittenden* [1968] 2 All ER 421.

102 Strangely, this provision does not extend to computer programs.

103 Under s 107(3), the criminal offences relating to public performances are available only against persons who 'caused' the work to be performed, played or shown. Furthermore, the mental element is stated to be that the person knew or had reason to believe that copyright would be infringed. It is arguable whether a person providing premises or apparatus 'causes' the work to be performed.

1 an article, the making of which constituted an infringement of copyright, or
2 an article which has been or is proposed to be imported into the UK and its making in the UK would have infringed copyright or would have been a breach of an exclusive licence agreement, or
3 copies which are infringing copies by virtue of several provisions relating to the 'acts permitted in relation to copyright works'.[104]

Under s 27(5), the provisions relating to imported copies are abrogated in favour of any enforceable Community right within the meaning of the European Communities Act 1972 s 2(1). This provision is not really necessary and only restates the effects of the UK's obligations as a member of the EC. Community obligations are separate from and prevail over inconsistent national law.[105] Therefore, if the importation into the UK of an otherwise infringing copy is permitted by European Community law (for example, under the exhaustion of rights principle), that copy will not be deemed to be an infringing copy and the persons involved in its importation and subsequent dealings with it will not be liable for secondary infringement. However, if a person then makes copies from the imported copy once it is within the UK that person will have infringed copyright, unless this also is permitted by prevailing Community law.

There is a presumption, under s 27(4), that an article is an infringing copy in any proceedings where the question arises. If it is shown that the article is a copy of the work and copyright subsists or has subsisted at any time in the work, it is presumed that the article was made at a time when copyright subsisted in the work unless the contrary is proved. A person copying or dealing with a copy of any type of work should not only satisfy himself that copyright in the work had expired at the time the copy was made, or that copyright did not otherwise subsist in the work at that time, but should also be able to adduce evidence to that effect to the satisfaction of the court. Bearing in mind that, in this matter, regardless of whether the proceedings are civil or criminal, proof on a balance of probabilities will suffice.[106]

## Publication right

From 1 December 1996 a person who publishes for the first time a literary, dramatic, musical or artistic work of a film in which copyright has expired acquires a publication right, equivalent to a copyright.[107] The provisions of Chapter II of the Act apply to the publication right as they do to copyright and, therefore, infringement of the publication right is the same as for any other work of copyright under ss 16–21. However, the presumptions in ss 104–106 do not apply. These are discussed later in this chapter.

## REMEDIES FOR INFRINGEMENT OF COPYRIGHT

The remedies for copyright infringement and supplemental provisions are set out in ss 96–115 of the 1988 Act. The remedies available include civil remedies and criminal penalties. The main differences in the remedies now available compared to those under the Copyright Act 1956 are the apparent abolition of

104 The acts permitted in relation to copyright works are described and discussed in Chapter 7.

105 *See*, for example, *Costa* v *ENEL* [1964] ECR 585; and Lasok, D. and Bridge, J. W. (1994) *Law and Institutions of the European Union* (6th edn) Butterworths.

106 In criminal proceedings, the prosecution must prove the accused's guilt beyond reasonable doubt and the onus is usually also on the prosecution to negative any defence put up by the accused. However, in some circumstances the accused bears the burden of proving that the defence applies on the balance of probabilities. These circumstances include express or implied statutory provision.

107 *See* the discussion of this right in Chapter 3.

conversion damages and some easing of the knowledge required for the criminal offences, but there are also some minor changes and both the scope and availability of some of the remedies need to be given careful consideration. Before looking at the remedies, it is appropriate to consider first the problem of obtaining evidence, particularly in civil matters. The following discussion is also relevant for other intellectual property rights. (Search and seizure provisions are available for the criminal offences and are discussed later.)

### Obtaining evidence for civil proceedings

In terms of all the forms of intellectual property, the question of obtaining evidence is of vital importance. If the person infringing the right discovers that he is to be sued for that infringement, he may be tempted to destroy materials and articles, such as pirate copies of video tapes, that would incriminate him. There is a limited power given by the Act to a copyright owner to seize infringing articles, but this will apply only in a small number of cases. Normally, if a copyright owner believes that his rights are being infringed and there is a real danger that the person involved will dispose of the evidence before the trial, the copyright owner should apply to the High Court for an *Anton Piller* order which will enable him, accompanied by his solicitor, to enter the premises where the offending materials and articles are kept and remove them, or have copies made, so they can be produced at the trial.

The *Anton Piller* order takes its name from a case involving the alleged disclosure of confidential information concerning frequency converters for computers. In *Anton Piller KG v Manufacturing Processes Ltd*,[108] it was held that, in exceptional circumstances, where the plaintiff has an extremely strong *prima facie* case, where the actual or potential damage to the plaintiff is very serious, where it was clear that the defendant possessed vital evidence and where there was a real possibility that he might destroy or dispose of such material so as to defeat the ends of justice, the court had the jurisdiction to order the defendant to 'permit' the plaintiff's representatives to enter the defendant's premises and inspect and remove such materials. The object of the *Anton Piller* order is the preservation of evidence. When an order is granted, the plaintiff has to give an undertaking in damages in case the plaintiff is wrong and the defendant suffers damage as a result of the execution of the order. However, before the court will grant an *Anton Piller* order, the plaintiff must be able to convince the court that he has a strong case and that the order is indeed essential to the ends of justice.[109] In *Systematica Ltd v London Computer Centre Ltd*,[110] Whitford J said that 'too free a use is being made of the *Anton Piller* provision'. In this case, the defendant was carrying on his business quite openly and there was only a mere suspicion that he was infringing the plaintiff's copyright. There was nothing to stop the plaintiff from simply walking into the defendant's shop and buying the articles in question over the counter. Sometimes, there is a suspicion that the motives for applying for the order are not to obtain evidence, but to remove so much material that the alleged infringer is, effectively, put out of business.

It is very important that the plaintiff does not exceed the provisions of an *Anton Piller* order. In *Columbia Picture Industries v Robinson*,[111] the plaintiffs (there were 35 of them) alleged that the defendant was a video pirate and

108 [1976] 1 Ch 55.

109 In *Jeffrey Rogers Knitwear Productions Ltd v Vinola (Knitwear) Manufacturing Co* [1985] FSR 184, Whitford J, in discharging an *Anton Piller* order, said that it was improper to rely on stale evidence used in other proceedings in making application to the court for an order. The applicant must prepare his application to a very high standard, especially if it is made *ex parte*, as will usually be the case.

110 [1983] FSR 313.

111 [1987] 1 Ch 38.

claimed that he had copied 104 films, infringing copyright, registered trade marks and, additionally, being guilty of the tort of passing off. The plaintiffs sought and obtained an *Anton Piller* order and a *Mareva* injunction, the purpose of the latter being to freeze the defendant's assets, preventing him from removing them from the jurisdiction of the court. But the plaintiffs were excessive in their execution of the *Anton Piller* order and they took more material than was identified in the order, virtually emptying the defendant's premises, apparently taking even the defendant's divorce papers and private correspondence. It appeared that the plaintiffs' real motive in obtaining the order was to shut down the defendant's business. It was held that the method of execution was an abuse of the order. While accepting that the defendant had been infringing copyright and awarding an injunction and damages to the plaintiffs, Scott J awarded the sum of £10 000 in compensatory and aggravated damages to the defendant under the plaintiffs' cross-undertaking in damages.

Scott J identified five criteria essential to the execution of an *Anton Piller* order as follows.

1 The order must be drawn so as to extend no further than the minimum extent necessary to achieve its purpose, that is the preservation of documents or articles which might otherwise be destroyed or concealed. After inspection and copying by the plaintiff's solicitors, the materials should be returned to the owner.
2 A detailed record should be made by the solicitors executing the order of the materials to be taken before removal from the defendant's premises.
3 Only materials clearly covered by the order should be taken.
4 If the ownership of seized material is in dispute, it should be handed over to the defendant's solicitors on their undertaking for its safe custody and production.
5 The affidavits in support ought to err on the side of excessive disclosure. In the case of material falling in the grey area of possible relevance, the judge, not the plaintiff's solicitor, should be the arbiter.

Because *Anton Piller* orders have been abused in their exercise in the past, they are granted sparingly. Further guidelines were suggested by Nicholls VC in *Universal Thermosensors Ltd* v *Hibben*[112] which concerned the execution of an order at a private house at 7.15am. The house was occupied at the time by a woman and her children. The Vice-Chancellor made the following points:

(a) the order should be executed during normal office hours so that the defendant could take immediate legal advice;
(b) if the order was to be executed at a private dwelling and there was a chance that a woman might be alone there, the solicitor executing the order should be accompanied by a woman;
(c) a list of items taken should be made, giving the defendant an opportunity to check it;
(d) if the order contained an injunction restraining the defendant from informing others (for example, co-defendants), the period should not be too long;
(e) in the absence of good reason otherwise, orders should be executed at business premises in the presence of a responsible officer or representative of the defendant's company;

(f) provision should be made to prevent the plaintiff going through all the defendant's documents (for example, where the parties were competitors and the plaintiff could thereby gain useful and sensitive information about the defendant's business unrelated to the alleged infringement);

(g) ideally, the order should be executed by a neutral solicitor who was experienced in the execution of *Anton Piller* orders.

A standard form has been developed for *Anton Piller* orders.[113] A copy of the form, which should be used except where the judge hearing the application considers there is good reason for using a different form, is contained in the *Practice Direction: Mareva Injunctions and Anton Piller Orders*.[114] The order requires the addressee to allow the persons listed to enter the named premises, to hand over articles and provide information as required. It also states that the addressee may insist that, apart from the plaintiff's solicitor, any person who could gain commercially from what he might read or see is not present and that entry may be refused before 9.30am or after 5.30am, or on Saturday or Sunday.

The *Practice Direction* itself stresses the use of an independent supervising solicitor who is familiar with the operation of *Anton Piller* orders and, *inter alia*, requires a woman to be present when the order is served if it is likely that the premises are occupied by an unaccompanied woman and, where appropriate, that items removed under the order are insured by the plaintiff.

Although the *Practice Direction* should make the use of *Anton Piller* orders more satisfactory, controversy about *Anton Piller* orders and their execution remains. The Lord Chancellor's Department issued an advisory paper suggesting, *inter alia*, that the order be placed on a statutory footing.[115]

The Copyright, Designs and Patents Act 1988 does provide the copyright owner with a limited power of seizure. Bearing in mind that pirated copies of copyright works frequently are sold at 'unofficial' markets, car boot sales and the like, s 100 gives the copyright owner a right of seizure of infringing articles at such places. Notice of the proposed seizure must be given to a local police station and the premises at which the infringing articles are located must not be a permanent or regular place of business. Additionally, the copyright owner must leave a prescribed form giving particulars of the person making the seizure and the grounds for the seizure.[116] Force may not be used in effecting the seizure. It is unlikely that this provision will be used frequently because of the limited circumstances in which it is available and because of the attendant conditions.

### *Anton Piller* orders and the privilege against self-incrimination

Infringing intellectual property rights, in some circumstances, may also involve criminal offences. For example, making copies of a work of copyright without permission and selling those copies, knowing or having reason to believe the copies are infringing copies is a criminal offence under the Copyright, Designs and Patents Act 1988 s 107, as well as a civil infringement of copyright under s 16 and, indeed, a secondary infringement under s 23. Making or dealing with counterfeit articles may also attract criminal liability in a number of ways, under specific intellectual property legalisation, trade descriptions and related legislation or, where two or more people are involved, as common law conspiracy to defraud. In many cases, civil wrongs will also be committed, such as under the Trade Marks Act 1994.

113 Standard forms have also been made for notice of *Mareva* injunctions.

114 [1994] RPC 617.

115 *Anton Piller Orders: A Consultation Paper*, Lord Chancellor's Department, November 1992.

116 The form is contained in the Copyright and Rights in Performances (Notice of Seizure) Order 1989, SI 1989/1006.

The rule against self-incrimination is firmly rooted in English law. However, because of the overlap between the civil and criminal law in intellectual property matters, a defendant complying with a court order, such as an *Anton Piller* order, may find that he is asked to hand over documents or other materials tending to show that he has committed criminal offences. In *Rank Film Distributors Ltd* v *Video Information Centre*,[117] the House of Lords upheld the Court of Appeal's decision to the effect that the privilege against self-incrimination could be invoked in such cases, pointing to practical difficulties including the fact that *Anton Piller* orders are intended to take effect immediately. To overcome this decision, which could have significantly weakened if not destroyed the effectivemess of *Anton Pillers* orders, the Supreme Court Act 1981 s 72 withdrew the privilege in civil proceedings relating to infringement of intellectual property rights and passing off. In terms of proceedings for intellectual property infringement or passing off, to obtain disclosure of information relating to intellectual property infringement or passing off or to prevent any apprehended infringement of any intellectual property right or for passing off, it states that:

> ... a person shall not be excused, by reason that to do so would tend to expose that person, or his or her spouse, to proceedings for a related offence or for the recovery of a related penalty –
> (a) from answering any question put to that person in the first-mentioned proceedings; or
> (b) from complying with any order made in those proceedings.

The section goes on to say that statements or admissions made in answering questions or complying with an order are not admissible in proceedings for related offences or the recovery of related penalties, except in proceedings for perjury or contempt or court.

The scope of the rule against self-incrimination and the impact of s 72 are very important in terms of intellectual property matters, particularly in terms of whether the protection in s 72 is available in respect of civil contempt. Civil contempt may be relevant in terms of failure to comply with a court order, for example, an *Anton Piller* order or undertakings given to the court, for example, in a consent order. Distinguishing civil contempt from criminal contempt, it was held in *Cobra Golf Inc* v *Rata*[118] that civil contempt was a related penalty and s 72 applied. In that case, the alleged contempt was in relation to a consent order given by the defendants in an action for trade mark infringement and passing off concerning golf clubs bearing a snake device.

### Civil remedies

The Copyright, Designs and Patents Act 1988 provides an ample range of remedies for copyright infringement. Section 96 states that infringement is actionable by the copyright owner but this is not exhaustive as, under s 101, an exclusive licensee has, except as against the copyright owner, the same rights and remedies as the copyright owner which run concurrent with those of the owner.[119] Of course, an exclusive licensee will be able to take action only if the infringement concerns the subject matter of the licence agreement. For example, if an exclusive licence is granted with respect to the public performance rights in

117 [1982] AC 380.

118 [1997] FSR 317.

119 The Copyright, Designs and Patents Act 1998 s 102 deals with the exercise of concurrent rights. Normally, the copyright owner or an exclusive licensee may not proceed alone without joining the other except with the leave of the court. Section 102 also deals with the matter of remedies in cases involving exclusive licensees and copyright owners having concurrent rights.

a dramatic work, the licensee will be able to sue a person who performs the dramatic work in public, but will not be able to sue a person who simply makes copies of the work.

The civil remedies available for infringement of copyright are damages, injunctions, accounts (of profits), 'or otherwise'. These are stated by s 96(2) as being available in respect of a copyright infringement as they are available in respect of any other property right (remembering that s 1(1) describes copyright as a property right). Although the previous legislation included conversion damages, it is conceivable that the addition of the phrase 'or otherwise' still permits the use of conversion damages, as they are available as a general rule in tort for wrongfully dealing with another person's property.[120] The phrase will include an order for specific performance, such as an order for a written signed assignment of copyright in a situation where a purported assignment has turned out to be defective in some way. However, it should be noted that injunctions and accounts of profits are equitable in nature and factors that might be important are whether the plaintiff acted promptly, whether injustice would be done to innocent third parties and whether the plaintiff came to the court with 'clean hands'. Other remedies available are additional damages (s 97(2)) and delivery up (s 99).

Where the alleged infringing work is a work of architecture, it may be possible to register a caution against dealing with land under the Land Registration Act 1925 s 54(1).[121] This may be particularly useful in the case of a house being built for sale which is alleged to infringe the copyright in architect's drawings, as the limitation on injunctions under the Copyright Act 1956 s 17(4) (no injunction or other order shall be made to prevent a building from being completed or to require its demolition) has no equivalent under the 1988 Act. Whilst it would be extremely unlikely that an infringing buiding would be ordered to be demolished, registering a caution could focus the alleged infringer's mind wonderfully. However, the lawfulness of registering a caution in respect of copyright infringement has not been tested in the courts and, in any case, there are provisions for compensation under the Land Registration Act 1925 s 56(3). Nevertheless, in limited cases, it could prove a useful alternative approach to applying for an interlocutory injunction, especially where it is doubtful that the court will grant an injunction, for example, where the balance of convenience lies in favour of the defendant.

The plaintiff has to elect between damages and an account. At one time, the plaintiff would have had to make that election without knowing what profits the defendant made from the infringement. This was very unsatisfactory and explained why accounts were rarely sought. However, in *Island Records Inc v Tring International plc*,[122] Lightman J said that a plaintiff should not have to make such a decision in the dark. Rather, it should be an informed decision. Thus, it might be appropriate to require the defendant to supply affidavit evidence setting out sufficient information to allow the plaintiff to decide. The information does not have to be enormously detailed, imposing a substantial amount of work on the defendant, and, in *Brugger v Medicaid*,[123] it was held that an affidavit setting out numbers of alleged infringing articles made and sold, the sums received or receivable and an approximate estimate of costs, together with a statement as to how that estimate was made would be sufficient. This development is likely to result in an increase in the proportion of cases in which a plaintiff elects for an account rather than damages.

120 Conversion damages were specifically provided for by the Copyright Act 1956 s 18. Section 18 does not apply after commencement of the 1988 Act unless the proceedings began before, the Copyright, Designs and Patents Act 1988 Sch 1, para 31(2). Conversion damages could result in a windfall for the plaintiff, for example if the subject matter of the plaintiff's rights was incorporated in some larger material or item.

121 Arnold, R. 'A New Remedy for Copyright Infringement?' [1997] EIPR 689.

122 [1995] FSR 560.

123 [1996] FSR 362.

There are special provisions in respect of infringements of a copyright for which a licence is available as of right under s 144 (powers exercisable in consequence of a report of the Monopolies and Mergers Commission).[124] In such a case, no injunction shall be granted, there may be no order for delivery up under s 99 and the amount recoverable by way of damages or an account of profits shall not exceed double the amount which would have been payable under the licence as of right provided the defendant undertakes to take a licence on terms to be agreed or, failing agreement, on terms to be settled by the Copyright Tribunal under s 144.[125]

## Damages

The copyright owner (or exclusive licensee) will usually ask the court for damages, which can be expected to be calculated, as with other torts, on the basis of putting the plaintiff in the position he would have been had the tort not been committed, that is to compensate him for the actual loss suffered in so far as it is not too remote.[126]

In *Claydon Architectual Metalwork Ltd v D J Higgins & Sons*[127] it was said that the normal measure of damages for copyright infringement is the amount by which the value of the copyright as a chose in action has been depreciated.[128] Consequential damages are available in the usual way provided that they arose directly and naturally from the tort. In the *Claydon* case, secondary damages associated with cash flow problems caused to the plaintiff by the defendant's acts were said to be too remote. Therefore, merely showing a causal link between the act and the loss is not enough.[129]

Some forms of damages might be available in patent cases where they would not be in a copyright case. This is a result, not of the existence of different rules on remoteness for patents and copyright, but of the different nature of the rights. In *Work Model Enterprises Ltd v Ecosystem Ltd*,[130] the defendant copied text from the plaintiff's brochure for office partitions. The plaintiff's claim for damages for lost sales of partitions and for price depression was held to be the result of the defendant's competition rather than the copyright infringement and, as a consequence, unrecoverable. Similarly, in *Paterson Zochonis & Co Ltd v Merfarken Packaging Ltd*,[131] the fact that a printer infringed the copyright in the design of packaging did not make him liable for the subsequent passing off by the customer for which he had carried out the printing work. In patent cases, there may be much more of a nexus between the infringement and, for example, lost sales in non-patented products sold alongside the patented product or in the sale of spare parts for such products.[132]

Damages might be assessed as the amount of royalties the copyright owner would have secured had the infringer obtained and paid for a licence to perform whatever the infringing act was.[133] Alternatively, depending on the circumstances, they might be based on the profit the copyright owner would have derived from sales lost as a result of the infringement. It will generally depend on whether the infringement relates to an 'original' work (for example, a literary work), or to a derivative work such as a film or sound recording; calculation by reference to lost royalties is more appropriate to the former. Although knowledge on the part of the defendant is not required for establishing liability for the 'primary' infringements of copyright, there is such a requirement before the plaintiff can be entitled to

124 Copyright, Designs and Patents Act 1988 s 98.

125 Similar provisions apply to designs and patents.

126 Apart from the criminal offences, infringement of copyright is in the nature of a tort.

127 [1997] FSR 475.

128 *Per* Lord Wright in *Sutherland Publishing Co Ltd v Caxton Publishing Co Ltd* [1936] 1 All ER 177 at 180.

129 *Cambridge Water Co v Eastern Counties Leather plc* [1994] 2 AC 224.

130 [1996] FSR 356.

131 [1986] 3 All ER 522.

132 *See Gerber Garment Technology Inc v Lectra Systems Ltd* [1997] RPC 443, discussed in Chapter 14.

133 *See*, for example, *Redwood Music v Chappell* [1982] RPC 109.

damages. Section 97(1) states that if it is shown that at the time of the infringement the defendant did not know, and had no reason to believe, that copyright subsisted in the work to which the action relates, the plaintiff is not entitled to damages against the defendant. This is without prejudice to other remedies that might be available to the plaintiff, such as an injunction or an account of profits. The formula for the defendant's knowledge is the same as for secondary infringements, and what has been said in that context above should apply here also. An award of damages will usually go hand in hand with the granting of an injunction ordering the infringer to cease carrying out the infringing activities. There may also be an order for delivery up, discussed later, for example of pirate copies of sound recordings in the infringer's possession. A wise copyright owner will apply a prominent copyright notice to copies of his work so that infringers cannot claim to be ignorant of the subsistence of copyright in the work.

## Injunctions

An injunction is an order of the court which prohibits an act or the continuance of an act. Alternatively, the injunction might order a person to perform some act.[134] For example, an injunction may be granted by the court ordering a person to cease making infringing copies of a work of copyright, or to destroy some article in his possession which is used for making infringing copies. Injunctions are equitable and therefore discretionary. They will not generally be granted if ordinary damages would be an adequate remedy. However, in terms of intellectual property rights, injunctions are very commonly asked for and frequently granted.

In a situation where a person is marketing unauthorised copies of articles in which copyright subsists, it is vital that the aggrieved party takes action as quickly as possible.[135] Many items in which copyright subsists have a limited commercial lifespan, for example, records, cassettes and compact discs of 'pop tunes', best-selling novels and computer software. Unless the person infringing the copyright can be stopped quickly the damage will be considerable, and it may be some years before a full civil action can be heard, after which time the person responsible for the infringement may have disappeared or dissipated his assets and be a 'man of straw'. Therefore, the availability and use of interlocutory injunctions is extremely important in terms of all intellectual property rights, including copyright. An interlocutory injunction is an interim or temporary injunction which is intended to take effect pending the full trial. The plaintiff must undertake to pay the defendant's losses resulting from the interlocutory injunction should the defendant succeed at the full trial. Interlocutory injunctions are often sufficient to dispose of a case which never comes to a full trial, either because the defendant loses heart and realises he has little chance of eventual success or because the effects on his business are crippling; therefore, such injunctions are not lightly granted.

Certain criteria are used by the courts in determining whether or not to grant an interlocutory injunction. In *American Cyanamid Co v Ethicon Ltd*,[136] a case concerning an alleged infringement of the patent relating to a surgical suture, the basis for granting an interlocutory injunction was discussed. Lord Diplock said (at 406):

**134** Injunctions are classified as 'prohibitory injunctions' and 'mandatory injunctions'; the latter orders the person to whom it is addressed to carry out some act, such as demolishing a dangerous wall.

**135** The doctrine of laches is relevant here.

**136** [1975] AC 396.

The object of an interlocutory injunction is to protect the plaintiff against injury by violation of his right for which he could not be adequately compensated in damages recoverable in the action if the uncertainty were resolved in his favour at the trial; but the plaintiff's need for such protection must be weighed against the corresponding need of the defendant to be protected against injury resulting from his having been prevented from exercising his own legal rights for which he would not be adequately compensated under the plaintiff's undertaking in damages if the uncertainty were resolved in the defendant's favour at the trial. The court must weigh one need against another and determine where the 'balance of convenience' lies.

Obviously, the court must be satisfied that there is a serious issue to be tried. If there is, then the court must weigh the plaintiff's and the defendant's needs in the balance of convenience. In a wide sense, this will call for a consideration of whether damages would adequately compensate the plaintiff if the injunction were refused and the plaintiff succeeds at the trial, and whether the plaintiff's undertaking in damages to an injuncted defendant would be adequate to protect him should he succeed at the trial. If there is some doubt as to whether damages would adequately compensate either party, depending on the outcome at the trial, a narrow balance of convenience is used involving a variety of factors. This will usually call for a consideration of the impact of granting or refusing the injunction on each of the parties. For example, if the interlocutory injunction would result in the closure of a factory, resulting in unemployment, it would be less likely to be granted.

The test was later modified for cases where the granting or refusal of the injunction would have the effect of finally disposing of the matter (for example, where it would completely close down the defendant's entire business operation). In such cases, in *NWL Ltd* v *Woods*,[137] which concerned a shipping trade dispute, Lord Diplock said that the likelihood of the plaintiff succeeding in his claim for an injunction at the full trial was a factor that should be brought into the 'balance of convenience' by the judge in considering the risks of injustice from his deciding the application one way rather than another. The *American Cyanamid* approach is not of universal application. For example, if the complaint concerns an alleged breach of covenant in restraint of trade, an interlocutory injunction may be inappropriate if the covenant is *prima facie* valid.[138] To grant the injunction would be to deprive the covenantee completely of the benefit of the covenant.

Until recently, it was thought that, except in exceptional cases like *NWL* v *Woods*, all the plaintiff had to show was a serious issue before the court engaged in a consideration of the balance of convenience. Interlocutory injunctions can be traced back to the Court of Chancery and, before *American Cyanamid*, the courts usually adopted a flexible approach. For example, in *Hubbard* v *Vosper*,[139] Lord Denning said (at 96):

> The remedy by interlocutory injunction is so useful that it should be kept flexible and discretionary. It must not be made the subject of strict rules.

Whilst the sentiment was approved by the House of Lords in *American Cyanamid*, many thought that Lord Diplock had intended that a consideration of the relative strength of the parties' cases should not be made. Of course, one justification for this was that the court would not, in an application for an interlocutory injunction, have the benefit of all the evidence and argument that would be present in a full trial. Nevertheless, Laddie J disagreed with this inter-

137  [1979] 1 WLR 1294.

138  *Office Overload Ltd* v *Gunn* [1977] FSR 39.

139  [1972] 2 QB 84.

pretation of Lord Diplock's judgment in *Series 5 Software Ltd* v *Philip Clarke*.[140] After looking again at *American Cyanamid*, Laddie J said that, when deciding whether to grant interloctory relief, the court should bear the following matters in mind:

(a) the grant of an interlocutory injunction was a matter of discretion and depended on all the facts of the case;
(b) there were no fixed rules;
(c) the court should rarely attempt to resolve complex issues of disputed fact or law;
(d) major factors to be taken into account are:
    (i) the extent to which damages would be likely to be an adequate remedy and the ability of the other party to pay,
    (ii) the balance of convenience,
    (iii) the maintenance of the status quo, and
    (iv) any clear view the court may reach as to the relative strength of the parties' cases.

This approach of taking the relative strength of the parties' case into account was followed in *EMAP Publications Ltd* v *Security Publications Ltd*.[141] An interlocutory injunction was granted which prohibited the defendant from using a magazine cover format bearing some similarities to that of the plaintiff. The grant of the injunction would have been decisive, as the defendant would not have returned to its original design of cover even if it won at full trial. In such circumstances, the court was entitled to take a view as to the strength of the respective cases of each party.

An interlocutory injunction will not be granted if the plaintiff's claim is frivolous or vexatious, or if there is some doubt about whether the plaintiff would be granted an injunction and substantial damages at the full trial. It was so held in *Entec Pollution Control Ltd* v *Abacus Mouldings*,[142] in which it was alleged that the defendant had indirectly infringed the plaintiff's copyright in sketches for flask-shaped septic tanks. It was doubtful that the defendant would have been able to pay substantial damages, but it was equally doubtful whether the plaintiff would indeed be awarded substantial damages. As the plaintiff did not have a strong case, the issue would have to be tried at a full trial and not preempted. In some cases, the public interest may be relevant, and in *Secretary of State for the Home Department* v *Central Broadcasting Ltd*[143] it was held that the public interest did not require an interlocutory injunction to prevent the showing of a film, alleged to infringe copyright, which included an interview with the serial killer Nilsen. The appellant's argument that the trial judge had taken too narrow a view of the balance of convenience and had failed sufficiently to consider the risk of distress to the relatives of the killer's victims was rejected by the Court of Appeal.

As mentioned above, an injunction, including an interlocutory injunction, will not usually be granted by the court if it appears to the court that damages will fairly compensate the plaintiff. Two questions are relevant in this respect:

1 Will the loss to the plaintiff be adequately compensated for by damages awarded later?
2 Is the defendant likely to be able to pay such damages?

140 [1996] FSR 273.

141 [1997] FSR 891.

142 [1992] FSR 332.

143 *The Times*, 28 January 1993.

The speed with which the plaintiff seeks the injunction may be relevant, because if the infringement complained of has been tolerated for some time, the assumption is that the effects cannot be that serious. Additionally, failure to apply for an interlocutory injunction may seriously prejudice the plaintiff's chances of obtaining a permanent injunction at the full trial.[144]

144 *Jaggard* v *Sawyer* [1995] 1 WLR 269.

## Accounts (of profits)

An account of profits may be a useful alternative for the plaintiff in that the infringer may have made a profit from his actions which exceeds in value what would be the normal award of damages. The purpose of the remedy is to prevent unjust enrichment of the defendant.[145] The quantum of an account is the profit, that is the gain, made by the defendant attributable to the infringement and not the wholesale or retail value of the offending articles or materials. Consider the following hypothetical example which, for the sake of simplicity, ignores income tax and value added tax. Arthur makes 2000 pirate copies of a popular sound recording, the copyright in which is owned by Zenith Ltd., and has sold the copies to a retailer, Nadir Music Ltd. Arthur charged Nadir £3.00 for each one and Nadir sells them at £5.50 each. The cost to Arthur of making the pirate copies, packaging and delivery, etc., is £3750. If Arthur is successfully sued by Zenith for the infringement by making copies, and Zenith asks for an account of profits, Zenith should be entitled to the following sum:

145 *Potton Ltd* v *Yorkclose Ltd* [1990] FSR 11 *per* Millett J.

|  | | £ |
|---|---|---|
| Arthur's income: | 2000 × £3.00 | = 6000.00 |
| Arthur's expenditure: | | = 3750.00 |
| Profit made by Arthur | | = 2250.00 |

Therefore, an account of profits should yield Zenith £2250. This may be better than claiming damages, which will not be available in some cases (although it is almost certain in the example that Arthur would have known that copyright subsisted in the original sound recording). Damages could be based on the fact that Zenith has been deprived of 2000 sales, and if its profit margin is usually 10 per cent and the normal retail price is £7.50, damages would amount to £1500: 2000 × £7.50 × 10% = £1500.00. Damages based on a notional lost royalty might amount to only: 12.5 per cent of 2000 × £3.00 = £750.00, assuming a typical royalty of 12.5 per cent.

Attractive though an account of profits might appear, there are likely to be great practical difficulties in determining what the profit was in relation to the infringement, and it may be well nigh impossible to isolate this profit from the other profits made concurrently by the defendant in other, legitimate, dealings. Nevertheless, because, unlike ordinary damages, accounts are available regardless of the defendant's knowledge as to whether copyright subsisted in the work, an account of profits may be the only way in which the copyright owner can recover some monetary compensation for the infringement if the defendant's knowledge is likely to be in issue. In practice, the remedies of damages and accounts should be considered to be alternatives, assuming damages are available. The Act does not expressly make any statement to this effect so that it is, theoretically, possible for the plaintiff to ask for both. However, if this should happen and an account is ordered, the plaintiff will be awarded nominal damages only.

## Additional damages

Additional damages are a form of punitive damages and such an award may be fitting if the defendant has acted scandalously or deceitfully, or if ordinary damages or an account of profits is not appropriate, for example where the defendant has published a work of a personal nature such as a diary which the copyright owner wished to keep private. The court has a discretion to award additional damages, and in exercising its discretion must have regard to all the circumstances and in particular to:

(a)  the flagrancy of the infringement, and
(b)  any benefit accruing to the defendant by reason of the infringement.[146]

Additional damages are awarded only rarely, but seem to be asked for more frequently nowadays. In one recent example, *Cala Homes (South) Ltd v Alfred McAlpine Homes East Ltd*,[147] additional damages were awarded for infringement of architect's drawings of houses. It was said that neither flagrancy nor benefit accruing to the defendant were precursors in the decision to award additional damages.

Following this, in *Cala Homes (South) Ltd v Alfred McAlpine Homes East Ltd (No. 2)*,[148] Laddie J said that additional damages were quite distinct from ordinary damages, so it was possible to claim to additional damages together with an account of profits. However, in the Court of Session, Inner House, Scotland in *Redrow Homes Ltd v Betts Brothers plc*,[149] it was held that a claim to additional damages under s 97(2) was not a free-standing *sui generis* right and 'additional' means additional to normal damages under s 96(2). Therefore, additional damages could only be claimed if normal damages were claimed. Otherwise, it would mean that an infringer could be sued for additional damages even if ordinary damages were not available, for example, because of lack of knowledge. Although Laddie J talked of ss 96 and 97 as being distinct, s 96(3) states that s 96 has effect subject to the following provisions of this Chapter, including, of course, s 97.

Additional damages may resemble, but are not, exemplary damages. Rather, they are the result of a specific statutory provision. Unlike exemplary damages, a claim for additonal damages can be added in after pleadings, by way of amendment. The Rules of the Supreme Court 1965, Ord 18 r 8(3), prevent this in the case of exemplary damages.

Flagrancy was described in terms of deceitful and treacherous conduct in order to steal a march on the plaintiff in *Nichols Advanced Vehicle Systems Inc v Reese & Oliver*,[150] in which the defendants, including the chief designer and a racing driver who had held positions of responsibility with the plaintiff's company, had made use of the plaintiff's working drawings for a Formula One racing car to build their own cars. The defendants had inflicted humiliation and loss on the plaintiff that was difficult to compensate and difficult to assess. In the later follow-up case it was held by Whitford J that the award of additional damages (£2000) should take account of the damages awarded for infringement (£1000) and conversion (£11 000).[151]

The Copyright Act 1956 required that the court also considered whether effective relief was otherwise available, but this has disappeared from the 1988 Act. This may lead the courts to make more use of additional damages to be

146  The Copyright, Designs and Patents Act 1988 s 97(2).

147  [1995] FSR 818.

148  [1996] FSR 36.

149  [1997] FSR 828. Affirmed, House of Lords, [1998] FSR 345.

150  [1979] RPC 127. In *Ravenscroft v Herbert* [1980] RPC 193, Brightman J described flagrancy thus ' ... in my view implies the existence of scandalous conduct, deceit and such like; it includes deliberate and calculated copyright infringements'.

151  [1988] RPC 71. The Court of Appeal reduced the interest rate from 15 per cent to 10 per cent over seven years.

used where the defendant's behaviour has been particularly despicable or immoral in some way. An example is provided by the case of *Williams* v *Settle*,[152] in which the defendant, a professional photographer, was commissioned by the plaintiff to take photographs at his wedding, the copyright in the photographs vesting in the plaintiff. The father of the plaintiff's wife was later murdered and the defendant sold photographs of the wedding group, showing the murdered man, to the press. On the basis of additional damages as provided under the Copyright Act 1956 s 17(3), or alternatively because of the court's power to award punitive damages, the plaintiff was awarded damages of £1000, which were far in excess of the measure of ordinary damages that would have been awarded, as the defendant received a relatively small sum from the newspaper proprietors for the photographs.

## Delivery up

Under s 99, upon application by the copyright owner, a court may order that infringing copies, or articles designed or adapted for making copies of the copyright owner's work, are delivered up to him or such other person as the court may direct.[153] Delivery up is available where a person has an infringing copy of the work in his possession, custody or control in the course of a business, or has in his possession, custody or control an article specifically designed or adapted for making copies of a particular copyright work. In relation to articles, there is an added requirement that the person knows or has reason to believe that the article has been or is to be used to make infringing copies.

There is a time limit which applies to applications for delivery up, as provided under s 113, which corresponds to limitation of actions. Under s 113(1) the time limit is six years from the time the infringing copy or article was made. However, this may be extended if the copyright owner had been under a disability (for example, a minor or person of unsound mind) as in the Limitation Act 1980.[154] Another cause for extension of the period is if the copyright owner is prevented by fraud or concealment from discovering the facts entitling him to apply for the order.

A further requirement before an order for delivery up can be made is that the court also makes, or it appears to the court that there are grounds for making, an order under the Copyright, Designs and Patents Act 1988 s 114, being an order for the disposal of the infringing copies or other articles. The order may state that the infringing copies or other articles be forfeited to the copyright owner or destroyed, or otherwise dealt with as the court thinks fit, but the court shall consider whether other available remedies would be adequate to compensate the copyright owner and protect his interests. If the order under s 114 is not made immediately, the person to whom the infringing copies or other articles are delivered shall retain them pending the making of the order. If a decision is taken not to make an order under s 114, the items are to be delivered to the person who had them in his possession, custody or control immediately before being delivered up.[155] Rarely will it be necessary, or even desirable, to deliver up offending articles to the copyright owner – he will normally be fairly compensated by the other remedies. However, an order for destruction of the offending articles under s 114 is a likely proposition, for example, in circumstances where the defendant has a stock of pirate video tapes in his possession.

152 [1960] 1 WLR 1072.

153 The order is not based upon any notion that the property in the copies has passed to the plaintiffs, *see Chappell & Co Ltd* v *Columbia Graphophone Co* [1914] 2 Ch 745 *per* Swinfen Eady LJ at 756.

154 *See* the Limitation Act 1980 s 38. In Scotland, disability means legal disability within the meaning of the Prescription and Limitation (Scotland) Act 1973 and, in Northern Ireland, has the same meaning as in the Statute of Limitations (Northern Ireland) 1958.

155 The Copyright, Designs and Patents Act 1988 s 114(5).

## PRESUMPTIONS

The 1988 Act provides for certain presumptions which will apply in proceedings for copyright infringement for the purposes of facilitating those proceedings. Because copyright can endure for a considerable period of time, some presumptions as to the identity of the author, director or publisher of the work are also helpful. Presumptions are made in terms of three classes of works:

(a) literary, dramatic, musical and artistic works (s 104)
(b) sound recordings, films and computer programs (s 105)
(c) works subject to Crown copyright (s 106).

### Presumptions relating to literary, dramatic, musical and artistic works

Where a name purporting to be that of the author appeared on copies of the work as published or on the work when it was made, the person by that name shall be presumed to be the author of the work and to have been the first owner of the copyright in the work.[156] That is, the work was not made in circumstances relating to employees in the course of employment, Crown or parliamentary copyright or copyright of certain international organisations.[157] Similar presumptions apply in the case of works of joint authorship. Even where the identity of the owner is not in dispute, the identity of the author is important for establishing the duration of the copyright and, possibly, its territorial scope.

Where there is no name purporting to be that of the author on copies of the work then, under s 104(4), if the work otherwise qualifies for copyright protection by reference to the country of first publication[158] and a name purporting to be that of the publisher appeared on copies of the work as first published, then that named publisher shall be presumed to have been the owner of the copyright at the time of publication.[159] Although this deals with the question of ownership of the copyright, the identity of the author is still important and s 104(5) provides that if the author is dead, or his identity cannot be ascertained by reasonable enquiry, it shall be presumed in the absence of evidence to the contrary that the work is an original work and the plaintiff's allegations as to what was the first publication of the work and as to the country of first publication are correct. Therefore, in all these matters, if the defendant wishes to challenge any of them, it is he who bears the evidential burden; he must adduce evidence to the contrary. Of course, in many actions for infringement, the defendant will not wish to dispute these matters, but may base his defence on another point, for example that he has not, in the circumstances, copied a substantial part of the work. Although the Act recognises the subsistence of copyright in literary, dramatic, musical and artistic works that are computer-generated, there are no presumptions specifically directed to such works.

### Presumptions relating to sound recordings, films and computer programs

Because computer programs are literary works, the presumptions relating to literary works above apply in addition to the presumption in s 105.[160] In the case of sound recordings, where copies are issued to the public bearing a label or other mark stating that a named person was the owner of the copyright in the recording

156 Ibid s 104(2).

157 This presumption was used in *Noah* v *Shuba* [1991] FSR 14 and the defendant was unable to adduce evidence to rebut it.

158 By virtue of the Copyright, Designs and Patents Act 1988 s 155.

159 For an example, under the 1956 Act, *see Waterlow Publishers Ltd* v *Rose* [1995] FSR 207. In that case the presumption was not rebutted.

160 Interestingly, the heading to the Copyright, Designs and Patents Act 1988 s 105 does not mention computer programs, even though they are specifically dealt with in s 105(3).

**161** Ibid s 105(1). Under the Copyright Act 1956 s 12(6), sound recordings had to be date-stamped to qualify for copyright protection. This is no longer essential, but it is obviously prudent to attach a copyright notice including the year of publication as this fixes would-be infringers with knowledge of the subsistence of copyright and may be important in terms of the availability of damages.

**162** [1997] FSR 580.

at the date of issue of the copies, or that the recording was first published in a specified year or in a specified country, that label or mark shall be admissible as evidence of the facts stated, and shall be presumed to be correct until the contrary is proved.[161] Similar provisions apply in respect of films where copies are issued to the public bearing statements as to the director or producer of the film, the owner of the copyright in the film, and the year and country of first publication: s 105(2).

Where, under s 105(3), computer programs are issued to the public in electronic form bearing a statement that a named person was the copyright owner at the date of issue, or that the program was first published in a specified country or that copies were first issued to the public in electronic form in a specified year, that statement is also admissible as evidence of the facts stated and shall be presumed to be correct until the contrary is proved.

The utility of this presumption was seen in *Microsoft Corp* v *Electro-wide Ltd*.[162] The plaintiff applied for summary judgment under the Rules of the Supreme Court 1965, Ord 14 in respect of an allegation that the defendant was selling computers loaded with unlicensed copies of the plaintiff's MS-DOS and Windows software. The defendant argued that discovery might show some hitherto defect in the plaintiff's title to the copyright. This argument was described by Laddie J, in granting summary judgment, as an unfounded and Micawberish hope. He said that it would be wholly improbable that a company the size of Microsoft, which was clearly alert to the importance of copyright protection, would fail to take the elementary precautions necessary to ensure that it owned the copyrights in its major assets.

All these presumptions apply equally to infringements alleged to have occurred before the date on which the copies were first issued to the public.

A final presumption in s 105 concerns the public showing, broadcast or inclusion in a cable programme service of a film, and s 105(5) provides that if the film bears a statement

(a)  that a named person was the director or producer of the film, or
(aa)  that a named person was the principal director of the film, the author of the screenplay, the author of the dialogue or the composer of music specifically created for and used in the film, or
(b)  that a named person was the owner of the copyright in the film immediately after it was made,

then that statement shall be admissible as evidence of the facts stated and shall be presumed to be correct until the contrary is proved.

This presumption applies equally in proceedings relating to an infringement alleged to have occurred before the date on which the film was shown in public, broadcast or included in a cable programme service. For the purposes of s 105, a statement that a person was the director of a film shall be taken, unless a contrary intention appears, as meaning that he was the principal director of the film.

### Presumptions relevant to Crown copyright

The final presumption is contained in s 106 and relates to literary, dramatic and musical works in which Crown copyright subsists. Where there appears on printed copies of a work a statement of the year in which the work was first published commercially, that statement shall be admissible as evidence of that fact and presumed correct until the contrary is proven.

## CRIMINAL OFFENCES

The Copyright, Designs and Patents Act 1988, in line with the Copyright Act 1956, makes provision for certain criminal offences associated with copyright infringement. Although it would be reasonable to assume that the criminal offences are suitable only for copyright pirates, there is nothing in the wording of the provisions to so limit them. In *Thames & Hudson Ltd v Design and Artists Copyright Society Ltd*[163] the Design and Artists Copyright Society (DACS) served summonses under s 107 of the 1988 Act on a reputable publishing company and on its directors, who now applied to have the prosecutions stayed as being vexatious and an abuse of process. The application was unsuccessful. Evans-Lombe J said (at 160):

> Parliament has elected to provide that breach of copyright can in certain circumstances constitute an offence and that where such an offence is committed by a body corporate the directors of that body corporate who connive at such commission are themselves guilty of an offence. No qualification appears in the statute limiting the types of offender capable of committing the offence to 'pirates'.

In this case, because DACS did not take an assignment of copyright from its members, there was no other way in which it could protect its members' interests.

The criminal offences reflect very closely the secondary infringements of copyright, but there are some omissions. For example, there is no equivalent criminal penalty for the secondary infringement of permitting the use of premises for an infringing performance of a literary, dramatic or musical work. Conversely, the criminal offence of making copies for sale or hire relates to the act restricted by copyright of copying and not a secondary infringement.

The offences are not of strict liability and an element of *mens rea* is required, and this mitigates the harshness of making directors of respectable companies potentially liable for infringement under criminal law. Thus, for a person to be guilty of any of the offences he must possess actual knowledge, or have reason to believe that copyright would be infringed or that he was, for example, dealing with infringing copies. The penalties available have been strengthened in some cases, for example, with respect to literary works where, by the 1956 Act, the maximum penalty available was a fine of 40 shillings.[164] There is evidence that magistrates and judges now are prepared to take piracy and counterfeiting of copyright works seriously. For example, in *R v Carter*[165] the Court of Appeal confirmed a sentence of imprisonment of nine months suspended for two years for a conviction of making and distributing infringing copies of video films contrary to s 107. It was observed that such an activity was really an offence of dishonesty. The offences are contained in s 107 of the 1988 Act and are set out below.

### Making, dealing, etc. (s 107(1))

A person commits an offence who, without the licence of the copyright owner:

(a) makes for sale or hire; or
(b) imports into the UK otherwise for his private and domestic use; or
(c) possesses in the course of a business with a view to committing any act infringing the copyright; or

163 [1995] FSR 153.

164 Some intermediate stiffening of penalties and extension of their scope was undertaken, for example, by the ridiculoously titled 'Copyright Act 1956 (Amendment) Act 1982' and the Copyright (Amendment) Act 1983.

165 [1993] FSR 303.

(d) in the course of a business, sells or lets for hire or offers or exposes for sale or hire or exhibits in public or distributes; or

(e) distributes otherwise than in the course of business to such an extent as to affect prejudicially the owner of the copyright;

an article which is, and which he knows or has reason to believe is, an infringing copy of a copyright work.

These activities are all commercial in nature with the exception of (e), which would apply, for example, to the situation where a private individual makes a large number of copies of a copyright work and distributes them freely, perhaps acting out of misguided social, political or moral beliefs. Some of the offences in this category are triable either way, that is they can be tried either in the Crown Court or in a magistrates' court. These are the offences relating to making, importing or distributing (whether or not in the course of a business). The maximum penalty available if tried in a Crown Court is a term of imprisonment not exceeding two years, or a fine or both. There is no upper limit on the fines which can be imposed by the Crown Court. If the offence is tried in a magistrates' court, the maximum penalty is six months' imprisonment, or a fine not exceeding the statutory maximum (presently £5000) or both. All the other offences are triable summarily only, that is in a magistrates' court, and carry a maximum of six months' imprisonment, or a fine not exceeding level 5 on the standard scale (presently £5000) or both.[166]

For some of the offences, namely (c) and (d) above, there is a specific requirement that they were committed in the course of a business. The meaning of this might be important if the person involved has other legitimate full-time employment and is carrying out his infringing activities in his spare time or as a hobby. However, it would appear that, in terms of the Trade Descriptions Act 1968, for goods to be dealt with in the course of a trade or business, there must be a degree of regularity in such dealing as part of the normal practice of a business.[167] It would appear, therefore, that if the person involved was carrying out the offending activities on a regular basis, it would be considered that he was operating in the course of a business, even if he was doing it in his spare time. However, if the person did whatever it was, regardless of the scale, as a one-off activity, there would be no regularity, and it would appear that the relevant offences would not apply.

### Articles specifically designed or adapted to make copies (s 107(2))

A person commits an offence if he makes an article specifically designed or adapted for making copies of a particular copyright work, or has such an article in his possession knowing or having reason to believe that it is to be used to make infringing copies for sale or hire or for use in the course of a business. This would include making a plate for printing artistic works, or a master copy of a sound recording from which many duplicates could be made. The offence applies only if the article is intended to be used for making copies of a particular copyright work and not for copying works generally. Therefore, the manufacture or possession of a dual cassette tape deck is not caught, as it is not intended to be used to copy a particular work but may be used to copy all sorts of works (some of which may be copied legitimately). The offence is triable summarily only and carries a maximum of six months' imprisonment, or a fine not exceeding level 5 on the standard scale or both.

**166** The penalties are laid out in the Copyright, Designs and Patents Act 1988 s 107(4) and (5).

**167** *See Davis v Sumner* [1984] 3 All ER 831, adapting the test laid down in *Havering London Borough v Stevenson* [1970] 3 All ER 609.

## Public performances, etc. (s 107(3))

This applies where copyright is infringed, otherwise than by the reception of a broadcast or cable programme, by a public performance of a literary, dramatic or musical work, or by the playing or showing in public of a sound recording or film. Any person who caused the work to be so performed, played or shown is guilty of an offence if he knew or had reason to believe that copyright would be infringed. The person who caused the work to be performed, played or shown will normally be the person who made the arrangements necessary and organised the performance. It is unlikely that a person who supplies the equipment necessary or provides the premises will be deemed to be the person 'causing'. Of course, such persons may be charged with being accomplices. An offence under this subsection carries a maximum of six months' imprisonment, or a fine not exceeding level 5 on the standard scale or both, being triable summarily only.

## Liability of officers of corporate bodies

By virtue of s 110, where an offence under s 107 has been committed by a corporate body, for example a limited company, and it is proved that the offence was committed with the consent or connivance of a director, manager, secretary or other similar officer of the body, then that person is also guilty of the offence and is liable to be prosecuted.[168] This also applies to persons holding themselves out to act in such a capacity. Therefore, in the case of an offence by a corporate body, there may be two prosecutions, one against the body itself and another against a high-ranking officer of the body who has been implicated in the offending conduct. This is to prevent persons hiding behind a corporate identity in order to escape prosecution. Normally, in terms of vicarious liability in criminal law, the action of a high-ranking officer of the company will be deemed to be the action of the company, thereby fixing the corporate body with liability.[169] Therefore, there should be no difficulty in a finding of corporate guilt if the activity complained of has been done under the instructions or guidance of a director or company secretary, but there would be difficulty in attaching liability to the individual concerned and this provision in the Act overcomes that problem.

## Search warrants and delivery up

Search warrants are available under s 109[170] and now extend to all types of copyright work. Search warrants can be obtained by a constable from a justice of the peace if the latter is satisfied by information given on oath by the constable that there are reasonable grounds for believing that any of the triable either-way offences under s 107 have been committed or are about to be committed and that evidence of this is on the premises to which the search warrant will apply. The warrant will authorise the constable to enter and search the premises using such reasonable force as is necessary. The warrant remains in force for 28 days and may authorise persons to accompany the constable in his execution of the warrant. It should be noted that warrants are not available for the offences that are triable summarily only, which significantly weakens the effectiveness of these particular offences. Of course, evidence required to secure a conviction may be obtainable in other ways, for example by simply purchasing an infringing copy which is openly on sale. In exercising his duties under the

168 Criminal proceedings were initiated against directors of a reputable publishing company in *Thames & Hudson Ltd v Design and Artists Copyright Society Ltd* [1995] FSR 153.

169 *See* the judgment of Lord Denning MR in *HL Bolton (Engineering) Co Ltd v TJ Graham & Sons Ltd* [1957] 1 QB 159 at 172.

170 Search warrants were first provided for by the Copyright Act 1956 s 21A, an amendment made by the Copyright (Amendment) Act 1983.

warrant, a constable may seize any article he reasonably believes to be evidence that an offence under s 107(1) has been or is about to be committed. Thus, the scope of the powers of seizure do not reflect exactly the availability of search warrants. If a constable obtains a search warrant for a suspected offence under s 107(1)(a) (making an infringing copy for sale or hire) the constable can seize infringing copies in the possession of the suspect (and made by others) in the course of a business – a summary offence under s 107(1)(c) – even though the constable could not obtain a search warrant in relation to that particular offence. The word 'premises' in the context of search warrants includes land, buildings, moveable structures, vehicles, vessels, aircraft and hovercraft.

It seems strange that the availability of search warrants under s 109 does not extend to all the criminal offences, although there is always the danger of over-zealousness coupled with the suspicion that justices of the peace issue search warrants to the police too readily. However, this fear could be overcome by adopting the approach taken in the Computer Misuse Act 1990, in that search warrants in respect of the unauthorised access offence, the basic 'computer hacking' offence, must be obtained from a circuit judge.[171]

Under s 107A (inserted by the Criminal Justice and Public Order Act 1994 s 165) local weights and measures authorities are given duties and powers in relation to offences under s 107 as they have under the Trade Descriptions Act 1968.[172] These include making test purchases and powers of entry and seizure. Obstructing an authorised officer is an offence, and there are provisions for compensation for loss of goods wrongly seized. It is likely that trading standards officers will make significant use of these provisions, and the enactment of them is further evidence that Parliament now takes copyright piracy seriously.

The Copyright, Designs and Patents Act 1988 s 108 also provides for delivery up in criminal proceedings similar in nature to the civil delivery up provisions under s 99. An order for delivery up may be made by the court before which the proceedings are brought if it is satisfied at the time the accused was arrested or charged that:

1 he had in his possession, custody or control in the course of a business an infringing copy of the work; or
2 he had in his possession, custody or control an article specifically designed or adapted for making copies of a particular copyright work, knowing or having reason to believe that it had been or was to be used to make infringing copies.

The order may be made by the court on its own motion or on the application of the prosecutor, irrespective of whether the accused is convicted of the offence with which he was charged. The provisions contained in s 113 (limitation period) and s 114 (order as to disposal) also apply to delivery up in criminal proceedings. The general provisions as to forfeiture contained in the Powers of Criminal Courts Act 1973 s 43 are unaffected.[173]

The Act contains some controls over the importation of infringing copies along the lines of the previous Act. Section 111 extends the class of prohibited goods to infringing copies of literary, dramatic and musical works (printed copies of these three types of works) and sound recordings and films. The Commissioners of Customs and Excise must be given notice in writing by the copyright owner to the effect that he is the copyright owner. As regards literary, dramatic and musical works, the notice must also specify the period, not exceed-

171 Computer Misuse Act 1990, s 14.

172 The relevant provisions are the Trade Descriptions Act 1968 ss 27-29 and s 33.

173 Of course, there are some differences in terms of search, seizure and delivery up in Scotland and Northern Ireland, but the overall effect is generally the same.

ing five years or beyond the duration of the copyright, for which the printed copies are to be treated as prohibited goods. For sound recordings and films the action is pre-emptive in nature and the notice must also specify the time and place at which the infringing copies are expected to arrive and that the copyright owner requests the Commissioners to treat the copies as prohibited goods.[174]

## Other offences

A person infringing copyright (and, for that matter, infringing a trade mark or a patent) may commit criminal offences other than those contained in the part of the Copyright, Designs and Patents Act 1988 dealing with copyright. For example, there may be an offence under the Trade Descriptions Act 1968 s 1. It is an offence, in the course of business, to apply a false trade description to any goods, or to supply or offer to supply goods to which a false trade description has been applied. A trade description is widely defined in the Trade Descriptions Act 1968 s 2 and includes direct or indirect indications as to the person by whom manufactured and the place and date of manufacture. Therefore, making or supplying a duplicate copy of a work such as a sound recording or video film in which copyright subsists without permission of the copyright owner will be an offence under the Trade Descriptions Act if it is done in the course of business and if the copy is dressed up to look like the genuine article.

Under the Theft Act 1968 s 25(1), a person is guilty of an offence if, when not at his place of abode, he has with him any article for use in the course of or in connection with any burglary, theft or *cheat*. 'Cheat' means the same as obtaining by deception. This would cover someone travelling to, say, a market in possession of pirated sound recordings, video films or computer games. However, there may be a difficulty with this offence in that, in such circumstances, the purchasers of these items are unlikely to have been deceived, as they will realise that the articles are not legitimate copies. The cost will be considerably lower and the printed materials and covers probably will be of an inferior quality.

Another offence that could be charged is forgery under the Forgery and Counterfeiting Act 1981 s 1, of which states that a person is guilty of forgery if he makes a false instrument, with the intention that he or another shall use it to induce somebody to accept it as genuine, and by reason of so accepting it, to do or not to do some act to his own or any other person's prejudice. It is also an offence to use a false instrument in such a way. Under s 8 of the 1981 Act, a false instrument includes any 'disc, tape, sound track or other device on or in which information is recorded or stored by mechanical, electronic or other means'. This definition would include sound recordings, films, computer programs and other copyright works stored in or on computer storage media, such as a copy of a computer database. Also covered would be a copy of a work such as the *Encyclopaedia Britannica* stored on CD-ROM discs. However, again there may be problems associated with whether a person would be induced to accept the article as genuine.

If legitimate copies of the original copyright work have a registered trade mark attached to them, anyone making infringing copies who also attaches a sign to his infringing copies, which is identical to, or likely to be mistaken for, the registered mark without permission of the proprietor of the trade mark, may commit an offence under the Trade Marks Act 1994 s 92. This offence is triable either way and carries a maximum penalty, if tried on indictment in the Crown Court, of imprisonment for a term not exceeding ten years, or a fine or both.

174 The Copyright, Designs and Patents Act 1988 s 112 gives power to the Commissioners of Customs and Excise to make regulations concerning the service of notices, payment of fees, providing, securing and indemnifying the Commissioners against liability or expense as regards the detention of the articles or things done to the articles in consequence of the notice.

It does not appear to be possible to steal a copyright by making copies because the owner of the copyright will still have the original.[175] The copyright owner has not been permanently deprived of the copyright and can still make and license the making of copies. The fact that the copyright owner has been deprived of some of the potential income from the work is not sufficient for theft. In *R v Lloyd*,[176] a projectionist at a cinema, in league with some other persons, surreptitiously removed films from the cinema for a few hours so that they could be copied. The infringing (pirated) copies of the films were then sold, making a considerable profit for the video pirates. It was held that a charge of conspiracy to steal was inappropriate. Obviously, there was no intention to permanently deprive the owners of the films, neither was the copyright in the films stolen. Although borrowing sometimes can be regarded as theft if the period and circumstances are equivalent to an outright taking or disposal, by the Theft Act 1968 s 6(1), this would apply only if the 'goodness' or 'virtue' in the borrowed article had been exhausted by the time it was returned. An example is where a person borrows a radio battery intending to return it when its power is expended, or where a person borrows a football pass intending to return it to the rightful owner at the end of the football season. But in the case of the films, there was still virtue in them when they were returned; they were still capable of being used and shown to paying audiences, so the convictions were quashed. The fact that the owner of the copyright in the films had been deprived of potential 'sales' of the films by the circulation of pirate copies was not relevant to the offence of theft.

Whether copyright can be stolen in any circumstances is a moot point.[177] For the purposes of the offence of theft, defined as the dishonest appropriation of property belonging to another with the intention of depriving the other of it permanently,[178] 'property' is defined as including money and all other property, real or personal, including things in action and other intangible property.[179] Theoretically theft of copyright is a possibility because copyright, certainly in the context of the acts restricted by the copyright in the work, is a chose in action and thus falls within the meaning of 'property'. However, the question really hinges on whether the owner has been permanently deprived of the copyright. One plausible scenario is where a rogue obtains a written assignment of copyright from the previous owner, perhaps as a result of some fraud or trick, and then assigns the copyright to a bona fide third party without notice of the fraud or trick. Even though the legal assignment to the rogue would be void or voidable for fraud, the original owner of the copyright may be unable to exploit his work because of the third party who may have obtained equitable ownership of the copyright.[180] Perhaps in these circumstances the rogue could be prosecuted for theft, or alternatively for obtaining property by deception under the Theft Act 1968 s 15.

A final attempt to extend the reach of the criminal law into copyright issues concerned the electronics company Amstrad Consumer Electronics plc and its twin-deck cassette recording machines. The record industry argued unsuccessfully that the sale and advertising of these machines was authorising copyright infringement or was an incitement to infringe copyright. The way the machines were advertised did nothing to reassure the industry, using phrases such as 'You can even make a copy of your favourite cassettes'. It is certainly true that the great majority of purchasers of these machines use them to make unauthorised

---

175 *See Oxford v Moss* [1979] Crim LR 119.

176 [1985] 2 All ER 661.

177 It is unlikely because the owner will not ususally have been deprived of the right, *see* Griew, E. (1995) *The Theft Acts 1968 and 1978* (7th edn) Sweet & Maxwell, at p. 81.

178 The Theft Act 1968 s 1.

179 Ibid s 4(1).

180 Alternatively, the original assignment to the rogue may not have been avoided at the time of the second assignment and the third party may obtain the legal title to the copyright. This is analogous to the exceptions to the *nemo dat quod non habet* rule contained in the Sale of Goods Act 1979, especially under s 23, sale by a seller with a voidable title. *See also Lewis v Avery* [1972] 1 QB 198.

copies of sound recordings and computer games. In *Amstrad Consumer Electronics plc* v *The British Phonograph Industry Ltd*[181] it was held that supplying machines which would be likely to be used unlawfully to copy pre-recorded cassettes subject to copyright protection was insufficient to make the manufacturer or supplier an infringer of copyright. Neither could Amstrad be said to be authorising infringement of copyright because it had no control over the way its machines were used once sold.[182] In the second case, *CBS Songs Ltd* v *Amstrad Consumer Electronics plc*,[183] it was claimed that Amstrad, by its advertising literature, was inciting others to commit an offence under the Copyright Act 1956 s 21(3), which made it an offence to make or be in possession of a plate to make infringing copies, similar to s 107(2) of the 1988 Act. However, it was held that, since s 21(3) of the 1956 Act did not confer the right to sue for breach of that section on a copyright owner, the defendant's incitement, if it were proved, did not confer upon the plaintiff the right to sue for an injunction or damages.[184]

In the subsequent consolidated appeal to the House of Lords, it was held that Amstrad was not liable under several heads including authorising infringement, joint infringement with purchasers of its machines, incitement and negligence for failing to prevent, discourage or warn purchasers against infringement.[185] As to authorisation, Lord Templeman agreed with the definition of authorisation given by Atkin LJ in *Monckton* v *Pathé Frères Pathephone Ltd*,[186] where he said (at 499):

> ... to 'authorise' means to grant or purport to grant to a third person the right to do the act complained of, whether the intention is that the grantee shall do the act on his own account, or only that of the grantor ...

Lord Templeman considered the difficulties of controlling home taping and accepted that little could be done against those who copy privately. Some countries impose a levy on blank tape, notably Germany, to recoup some of the losses caused by private copying, but this solution has yet to find favour in the United Kingdom. The difficulty is that it could be seen as a licence to copy and encourage a greater amount of copying.

---

**181** [1986] FSR 159.

**182** By the Copyright, Designs and Patent Act 1988 s 16(2), copyright is infringed by a person who, without the licence of the copyright owner does, or authorises another to do, any of the acts restricted by the copyright.

**183** [1987] 3 All ER 151.

**184** Amstrad had printed a small warning about infringing copyright in its literature.

**185** *CBS Songs Ltd* v *Amstrad Consumer Electronics plc* [1988] AC 1013.

**186** [1914] IKB395.

# 7

## *Defences to copyright infringement*

### INTRODUCTION

The Copyright, Designs and Patents Act 1988 contains some express defences to copyright infringement known as the acts permitted in relation to copyright works or, more simply, the 'permitted acts'. These are acts that can be performed without attracting liability for copyright infringement, but this is without prejudice to other legal rights or obligations.[1] Therefore, even though something may be done in relation to a copyright work that does not infringe by reason of being a permitted act, it may still result in a breach of confidence or in the tort of passing off, for example. Defences to copyright infringement are not restricted to the permitted acts, and there are other defences that may excuse or justify an act which at first sight infringes copyright. Of course, a person sued for infringement may claim that copyright does not subsist in the work in question,[2] that the courts in the United Kingdom do not have jurisdiction to hear the action, that the act done does not fall within the scope of the restricted acts or that the act complained of was not done to a substantial part of the work. As regards the secondary infringements of copyright, some form of knowledge is required on the part of the alleged infringer, or there may be some dispute as to whether the copy dealt with is an infringing copy within the meaning assigned by s 27.

Other issues are whether the copyright owner authorised or consented to the alleged infringement, or whether the defence of public interest is relevant, or whether it is a case of non-derogation from grant. If none of the above points applies, then the defendant may attempt to justify his actions by claiming that they fall within the meaning of the permitted acts. Finally a 'Euro-defence' might be applicable.[3] The flowchart in Figure 7.1 indicates a rational way of looking at the question of infringement and the defences.

### COPYRIGHT OWNER AUTHORISED OR CONSENTED TO THE ACT

Copyright in a work is infringed by a person who performs or authorises another person to perform one of the acts restricted by the copyright unless the licence of the copyright owner has been obtained.[4] Under s 173, in the case of a work having joint copyright owners the licence of all the joint owners is required. The meaning of 'licence' should be considered in terms of the authority of the copyright owner or his permission to carry out particular restricted acts. It would appear that the licence does not have to be formal or contractual , so that the absence of consideration, *per se*, does not affect the status of the authorisation. Of course, if the licence is not contractual, there is the problem that it may be revoked at any time subject to equitable rules and principles, such as the doctrine of estoppel.

1 The Copyright, Designs and Patents Act 1988 s 28(1). Unless otherwise indicated, in this chapter statutory references are to this Act.

2 A claim that the plaintiff's work itself infringes copyright is no defence if it is subject to its own copyright, *ZYX Music* v *King* [1995] FSR 566.

3 *See* Chapter 9.

4 The Copyright, Designs and Patents Act 1988 s16(2).

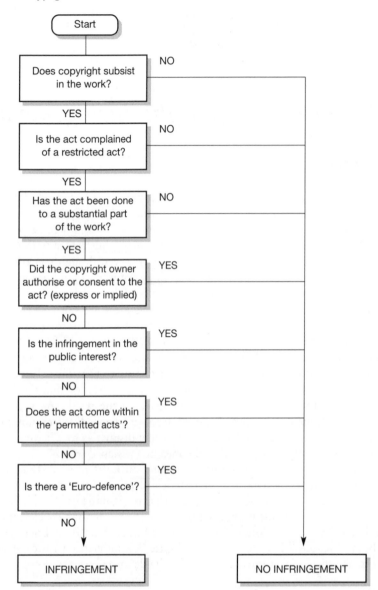

**Figure 7.1 Infringement and defences**

Under normal circumstances, the licence given by the copyright owner will be formal and contractual in nature, for example a non-exclusive licence in respect of a computer software package for a licence fee of £250. Alternatively, it may be informal and/or non-contractual. If there is no express permission or authority to carry out the restricted act concerned, it may be that the courts will be prepared to imply the copyright owner's licence. This will usually be limited to adding terms to an existing agreement. For example, if a person obtains a licence to use a computer program, the court might imply a term in the licence agreement that the licensee will be the beneficial owner of the copyright in any reports produced by running the program. Of course, it becomes impossible or difficult to imply the copyright owner's authorisation or permission in the face of express terms to the contrary in an agreement, or if the remaining rights of the owner are prejudiced in some way. An implied licence may overcome difficulties resulting from misunderstandings about the future ownership of copyright, for example, where a person commissioning a work of copyright later discovers that he does not own the copyright and the person commissioned to create the work is trying to interfere with the subsequent use of the work.[5] Implying the copyright owner's licence may also be a way of curbing any unconscionable conduct that is proposed by the owner, such as taking advantage of an imperfect assignment or a badly drafted licence agreement.

5 *See*, for example, *Warner* v *Gestetner Ltd* [1988] EIPR D-89 and *Blair* v *Osborne & Tomkins* [1971] 2 WLR 503, discussed in Chapter 4.

## PUBLIC INTEREST

'Public interest' is a nebulous concept which can, in some cases, provide a defence for copyright infringement. Cases where the public interest is at issue often concern the publication of information, and frequently questions of confidence also will be raised. Typically, a person will, without authority of the copyright owner, publish something which embarrasses the copyright owner or some other person. For example, in *Lion Laboratories Ltd* v *Evans*,[6] the defendant, a newspaper editor, wished to publish information concerning doubts about the reliability of the Lion Intoximeter 3000, a device used to measure levels of intoxication by alcohol. The device had been used to 'breathalyse' approximately 700 motorists suspected of being unfit to drive through drink. The plaintiff had obtained an injunction preventing the defendant from publishing the information on the basis that the information was confidential, and because publication would infringe copyright. The defendant appealed against the injunction.

6 [1984] 2 All ER 417.

The defendant's appeal was allowed. The defence of public interest applied to both the confidence and the copyright issues because it was in the public interest that the information be published; further, the operation of the defence was not limited to cases where there had been any wrongdoing on the part of the plaintiff. The court identified matters relevant to the application of the defence of public interest as follows:

1 there was a difference between what was interesting to the public and what was in the public interest;
2 it was a fact that the media, for example newspaper proprietors, had a private interest to increase circulation by publishing what appealed to the public;
3 the public interest might be best served by giving the information to the police or some other responsible body rather than to the press;
4 the public interest did not arise only when there was an iniquity to be disclosed, and the defendant ought not to be restrained solely because what he wanted to publish did not show misconduct on the part of the plaintiff.

If the defence of public interest is raised, the court should weigh up the competing interests. In this particular case, it was unquestionable that it was in the public interest that the information be published. The third point above is a little worrying. Surely something either is or is not in the public interest, and this test suggests that publication for gain might injure the prospects of the defence succeeding. Surely the motive for publication should be irrelevant – it is the nature of the information that is crucial. In any case, giving the information to a 'responsible body' might lead to a 'cover-up' – if there is some matter which the public should be aware of, the press can serve a very useful function, albeit financially motivated. In *Initial Services Ltd* v *Putterill*,[7] Salmon LJ recognised that there was very little authority on the status of the person to whom documents or information were given. It was suggested by counsel for the plaintiff that information should have been given to the Registrar appointed under the Restrictive Trade Practices Act 1956[8] and not to the press. However, Salmon LJ said that the law should not lend assistance to anyone proposing to commit or committing a clear breach of statutory duty imposed in the public interest.

Public interest will cover situations involving the disclosure of criminal conduct, both past and contemplated,[9] or matters prejudicing the nation's security.[10] In *A-G* v *Guardian Newspapers Ltd*[11] it was indicated in the House of Lords that the copyright in the *Spycatcher* novel would not be enforced by the courts because of the conduct of the book's author, Peter Wright, in divulging national secrets. It could be said that Peter Wright had harmed the public interest in keeping secret the activities of 'secret agents' and the like, and the nation's security could have been harmed as a result of his disclosures. As the law of confidence could provide no remedies, the book having been published elsewhere and being widely available, the House of Lords was punishing Mr Wright the only way it could. The implication was that anyone could publish the book or extracts from it without being liable for copyright infringement.

Freedom of speech can be said to lie within the public interest and as such will not be restrained by way of an interlocutory injunction if the defence of fair dealing is likely to be raised. In *Kennard* v *Lewis*[12] the plaintiff had published a pamphlet entitled *30 Questions and Answers about CND* and the defendant had published a pamphlet called *30 Questions and Honest Answers about CND*, using a layout which was substantially similar. The plaintiff sought an interlocutory injunction to restrain publication of the defendant's pamphlet and the defendant raised a defence of fair dealing. It was held that, as a principle, interlocutory injunctions should not be used to restrain free speech and, *a fortiori*, should not be used to restrain political controversy.[13]

## NON-DEROGATION FROM GRANT

The exercise of an intellectual property right could unduly interfere with the subsequent use of an article in which such rights subsist. We can see the way in which the law balances the rights of the intellectual property owner with those of persons using or acquiring articles in the doctrine of exhaustion of rights, or in the way in which the law has implied a 'right to repair' in relation to patented products.[14] The nature of copyright law is such that the exercise of a copyright is less likely to conflict with the subsequent use or sale of articles. For example, if I wish to repair a book, I can do this without the copyright owner's permission (unless, of course, I wish to photocopy an old, moth-eaten copy of a book). However, even with copyright there must be some ultimate control of the owner's rights where these could be unfairly used. In *British Leyland Motor Corp Ltd* v *Armstrong Patents Co Ltd*,[15] discussed in Chapter 6, the House of Lords, while accepting that there had

7 [1968] 1 QB 396.

8 Now repealed. Replaced by the Restrictive Trade Practices Act 1976.

9 *Per* Lord Denning in *Initial Services Ltd* v *Putterill* [1968] 1 QB 396. This case involved the disclosure of the operation of a price-fixing ring between laundries.
10 *Per* Ungoed-Thomas J in *Beloff* v *Pressdram Ltd* [1973] 1 All ER 241.
11 [1988] 3 All ER 567.

12 [1983] FSR 346.

13 *See also Hubbard* v *Vosper* [1972] 2 QB 84.

14 This is on the basis of an implied licence: *see Solar Thomson Engineering Co Ltd* v *Barton* [1977] RPC 537.

15 [1986] 2 WLR 400.

been a technical infringement of the copyright subsisting in the plaintiff's drawings, refused to enforce that copyright on the basis of non-derogation from grant. That is, once an article has been sold by the rights owner, he can no longer use those rights to interfere with the purchaser's 'right' to a free market in spare parts.

The *British Leyland* case was concerned with spare exhaust pipes, and the law has changed so that design law is more appropriate to deal with such matters. Nevertheless, the non-derogation from grant principle survives the 1988 Act[16] and may be relevant in terms of some types of copyright work. In particular it should still be relevant for works incorporated into articles where further use or modification will involve a restricted act. One obvious example is a computer program that has errors contained within it. Although the copyright owner may be prepared to correct errors, to allow him to prohibit error correction by the licensee or a third party would be to deprive the licensee of a free market in software maintenance. This principle may also apply to more traditional types of works, such as sound recordings, photographs or films, and could allow the owner of a copy to re-record it to reduce or eliminate the presence of some defect caused by, for example, fair wear and tear. Whether this would extend to enhancing the original, for example, by digitally re-recording an old scratchy vinyl sound recording or improving a photographic image by means of computer technology, is less likely, as this probably would compromise the copyright owner's interests.

It could be argued that the principle of non-derogation from grant is inconsistant with copyright law, except in the context of a licence agreement, where a term in the agreement contradicts or is inconsistent with the general rights granted by the licence. As the permitted acts provisions in the Act are comprehensive, the courts should be slow to enlarge or extend defences to copyright infringement by judical decision-making only. It might be fairly thought that Parliament gave detailed consideration to defences to copyright infringement during the passage of the Bill and any further development of the *British Leyland* principle should be eschewed. This was recognised in *Canon Kabushiki Kaisha* v *Green Cartridge Co (HK) Ltd*[17] by the Judicial Committee of the Privy Council, which said that the principle was based on overriding public policy. Neverthless, the Committee considered it to be questionable in a constitutional and jurisprudential sense for such a policy to override a clear, express statutory right and, consequently, any prospect of extending the principle should be treated with some caution.

## THE PERMITTED ACTS

The acts permitted in relation to copyright works are contained in the Copyright, Designs and Patents Act 1988 Chapter III. The permitted acts are complex and wide-ranging in their scope and application, occupying over 50 sections of the Act, but at least the Act conveniently classifies them by using appropriate sub-headings such as 'Education', 'Libraries and archives', etc., and this classification will be retained in the following description of the permitted acts. At the end of this chapter Table 7.2 shows the basic elements of the permitted acts. The rationale for the permitted acts, allowing what would otherwise be an infringement of copyright, can be seen as a way of limiting the strength of the rights associated with copyright. The justification for this restric-

16 *Flogates Ltd* v *Refco Ltd* [1996] FSR 935.

17 [1997] FSR 817.

tion is that it provides a fair balance between the rights of the copyright owner and the rights of society at large. Generally, the permitted acts excuse activities which, although technically infringing the copyright in a work, do not unduly interfere with the copyright owner's commercial exploitation of the work. For example, a person writing an academic article is able to include quotations from the writings of other authors. The permitted acts are, therefore, on the whole relatively restricted in their effect on commercial exploitation.

It should be noted that the application of some of the permitted acts depends on the amount of the first work that has been copied or otherwise used, whereas in other cases the permitted act relates to the whole work. For example, in terms of the permitted act of fair dealing for the purposes of criticism or review it appears that it would not be fair dealing to copy the whole of an existing work of copyright, that fair dealing is limited by some measure which is based on quality or quantity, or perhaps a combination of the two. On the other hand, it is permissible to perform the whole of a dramatic work before an audience of teachers and pupils at an educational establishment.[18]

18 The Copyright, Designs and Patents Act 1988 s 34.

## FAIR DEALING

The notion of permitting some use of a copyright work which is considered to be 'fair' is common in many jurisdictions. For example, in the USA, copyright law has its 'fair use' provisions. In the UK, 'fair dealing' is allowed in relation to a copyright work. It must be noted at once that this has nothing to do with 'dealing' in a trade sense. It can be roughly equated to 'use'. Thus, fair dealing covers research or private study, criticism, review and reporting current events. The fair dealing provisions allow the copying or other use of the work which would otherwise be an infringement, and in many circumstances the amount of the original work used is very relevant. It may be fair dealing to include five per cent of another work for the purpose of criticism or review. It would not normally be fair dealing to incorporate the whole of the other work. Because the proportion of work taken can be relevant to whether the second author can successfully plead the fair dealing provisions, this immediately brings into question the relationship between fair dealing and the taking of a substantial part of a work. If the part taken is not substantial, then there is no infringement of copyright and no need to rely on the permitted acts.

It may be that, in some cases, the existence of the permitted acts is illusory. The problem lies in the determination of the relative thresholds of substantiality and the permitted act in question. In *Independent Television Publications Ltd v Time Out Ltd*,[19] Whitford J said:

19 [1984] FSR 64.

> Indeed, once the conclusion is reached that the whole or a substantial part of the copyright work has been taken, a defence under sections 6(2) or (3) [of the Copyright Act 1956, some of the fair dealing provisions] is unlikely to succeed.

If this is true, then there is no such thing as a defence of fair dealing. If the part taken is not substantial, there is no infringement and fair dealing is irrelevant, but if the part taken is substantial then, according to Whitford J, the defence will rarely excuse the defendant's use of the work. It is respectfully submitted that this is wrong and that the whole purpose of the fair dealing provisions is to permit, in appropriate circumstances, the taking of a substantial part of a copyright work. It is, however, difficult to say where the boundaries circumscribing substantiality and fair dealing lie.[20]

Consider the case where an author wishes to write a learned article for an academic journal. The author wishes to discuss and critically analyse the work of an eminent professor in the appropriate field. To do this, the author will wish to include extracts from the writings of the eminent professor. But how much does fair dealing allow him to take? Lord Denning gave a good description of the scope of fair dealing for the purposes of criticism or review in *Hubbard* v *Vosper*, where he said:

> You must first consider the number and extent of the quotations ... Then you must consider the use made of them. If they are used as a basis of comment, criticism or review, that may be fair dealing. If they are used to convey the same information as the author, for a rival purpose, they may be unfair. Next you must consider the proportions. To take long extracts and attach short comments may be unfair. But short extracts and long comments may be fair. Other considerations may come to mind also. But it must be a matter of impression.[21]

Apart from the purpose of the inclusion of copyright materials, their overall proportion to the whole must be considered. Although substantiality is determined by a qualitative test, it appears from the above quote that the scope of this particular permitted act is determined at least partly by means of a quantitative test. Hence the difficulty. Consider the following in connection with hypothetical journal articles: the author of the new article is called Aristotle and the author of the earlier article is called Plato. Aristotle uses extracts from Plato's article and quotes and discusses them in his own article. Table 7.1 indicates different proportions of the total volume of the extracts used in relation both to Plato's original article and to Aristotle's new article.

**20** In the New South Wales case of *Copyright Agency Ltd* v *Haines* [1982] FSR 331 it was suggested that fair dealing does not permit as much copying as a licensing scheme permitting photocopying by educational establishments.

**21** [1972] 2 QB 84 at 94.

**Table 7.1  Proportions of extracts and fair dealing**

| Total of extracts: percentage of article written by: | |
|---|---|
| Plato | Aristotle |
| 5 | 5 |
| 5 | 10 |
| 5 | 20 |
| 10 | 5 |
| 10 | 10 |
| 10 | 20 |
| 20 | 5 |
| 20 | 10 |
| 20 | 20 |
| 35 | 5 |
| 35 | 20 |
| 35 | 50 |

For example, in the second entry in Table 7.1, Aristotle has copied 5 per cent of Plato's article and this occupies some 10 per cent of Aristotle's work. (In this case, Aristotle's article must be about half the length of Plato's.) It should be apparent from the table that it is not easy to decide which, if any, of these examples represents an infringement of copyright, even assuming a good motive on the part of Aristotle. In some cases, for example, where the total of the extracts represents 5 per cent of both works, it might be considered to be fair dealing, yet this might be irrelevant because a substantial part of Plato's work has not been taken. In other cases, such as the last one in the table where the extracts amount to 35 per cent of Plato's work and 50 per cent of Aristotle's work, it can be said with some certainty that a substantial amount of Plato's work has been taken and that this does not fall within the scope of the permitted act of fair dealing. However, there is a range of cases in between where it is difficult to say with any certainty. It depends on other things such as motive and the nature of the two works. In some cases it may be that the minimum percentage representing a substantial part is the same as the maximum percentage falling within the fair dealing provisions. In other words, there is coincidence in the infringement and permitted-act thresholds and, thus, the permitted act is of no consequence.[22]

In some circumstances fair dealing may allow the copying of an entire work. For example, it may be fair dealing for criticism or review to publish a photograph of a painting if the purpose is to criticise the painting in terms of its style, content or composition. There is nothing in the Act to prevent fair dealing from being relied upon in respect of copying the whole work. However, such taking is unlikely to be deemed to be fair if it seriously prejudices the commercial value of the copyright work, not because of any criticism of course, but because of the widespread publication of the work.

'Fair dealing' is not defined in the Copyright, Designs and Patents Act 1988 and it is only by reference to case law that the factors that might be considered by a court can be determined. Only sometimes will the factors identified below be said to be conclusive one way or the other; in most cases it will be a matter of combining and weighting the factors. The only thing that can be said with any degree of certainty is that whether a particular act falls within the meaning of 'fair dealing' depends very much upon the circumstances surrounding that act.

1 *Purpose.* Conceivably, it might be fair dealing to take a copy of an entire work, such as a journal article, for the purposes of research or private study. But it will not normally be fair dealing to take a large amount of another's work for the purpose of criticism or review.[23]

2 *Proportion.* Within a particular form of fair dealing, proportion might be important. For example, it may be fair dealing for the purposes of criticism or review to take five per cent of a work, but not to take 40 per cent.[24]

3 *Motive.* If the motive for the act was to compete with the other work, this is unlikely to be fair dealing.[25]

4 *Status of other work*, that is whether confidential or published. It is unlikely to be fair dealing if the work taken has not been published, or in the case of a 'leak'.[26]

One thing to note is that an interlocutory injunction will not normally be granted if the defendant is going to raise the defence of fair dealing and has at least an arguable case. This reluctance to grant interlocutory injunctions stems

22 Of course, it is unsatisfactory to talk in terms of percentages as substantiality is a mainly qualitative measure. This is one reason why it is so difficult to map out the start of infringement and the end of the permitted acts.

23 *See*, generally, *Hubbard v Vosper* [1972] 2 QB 84 and Lord Denning's judgment in particular, and the quote earlier in this chapter. *See also Walter v Steinkopff* [1892] 3 Ch 489.

24 *Walter v Steinkopff* [1892] 3 Ch 489.

25 *Weatherby v International Horse Agency & Exchange Ltd* [1910] 2 Ch 297. Parker J said that the issue of competition is often important and may even be a determining factor in some cases, although he did say that unfair use was wider than this.

26 *British Oxygen Co Ltd v Liquid Air Ltd* [1925] 1 Ch 383; *Beloff v Pressdam Ltd* [1973] 1 All ER 241.

from the desire of the courts to protect freedom of speech, particularly as regards the press, or in a political or quasi-political sphere.[27] However, there has to be genuine conflict and a danger that freedom of speech will be prejudiced. For example, in *Associated Newspapers Group plc* v *News Group Newspapers Ltd*,[28] an injunction was granted because there had been no interference with the press's freedom of speech which would only be interfered with when someone was prevented from saying the truth. The principle that interlocutory injunctions should not be granted when the defendant raises the fair dealing defence was questioned by Dillon LJ in *BBC* v *British Satellite Broadcasting Ltd*,[29] a case concerning excerpts from broadcasts of World Cup football matches made by the BBC, which BSB intended to include in its broadcasts. Nevertheless, the BBC's application for an interlocutory injunction was refused.

### Fair dealing for the purposes of research or private study

The defence of fair dealing for research or private study is available in relation to literary, dramatic, musical or artistic works and also applies to the typographical arrangement of published editions of such works.[30] It is not fair dealing to perform the acts permitted in relation to computer programs in s 50B (decompilation), and fair dealing with a database for research or private study requires an indication of the source.[31] Although this permitted act excuses indirect infringement of typographical arrangements, this fair dealing provision is expressly stated by s 29(2) to apply directly to typographical arrangements of published editions. This might apply in the case of a published edition of a literary work, the copyright in which has expired. There were calls for fair dealing to be limited to private research, but the formula used in the 1956 Act has been retained, that is research and private study.[32] Therefore, fair dealing for the purposes of commercial or industrial research is a distinct possibility, although each case will turn on its particular facts. For example, it would not be considered to be fair dealing to perform an act restricted by the copyright in a work for the purposes of producing a competing work. In *Independent Television Publications Ltd* v *Time Out Ltd*,[33] the defendant copied details of forthcoming television programmes from the *TV Times* and the *Radio Times*. The defence of fair dealing (in this case under the head of fair dealing for criticism and review) failed because the purpose was to provide a television programme listing service and had nothing to do with criticism or review.[34]

The financial motive behind making a copy of a work or part of a work for research or private study surely must be considered in determining whether or not it falls within the scope of fair dealing. To this can be added other factors, such as the nature of the research or study and the funds available to the researcher or student. Questions such as whether the person concerned is copying simply to save himself the expense of buying a copy of the work, or whether it is reasonable to expect a copy to be purchased, are important. Take, for example, a postgraduate research student. He will need to refer to hundreds of different journal articles and books. The student will not be able to purchase more than a handful of these, he will have to be selective. The student may decide to purchase those materials which he will need to use over and over again during the research. But many of the articles and books will be used less

27 For example, *Hubbard* v *Vosper* [1972] 2 QB 84; *Kennard* v *Lewis* [1983] FSR 346. It should be noted that *Hubbard* v *Vosper* pre-dates the *American Cyanamid* guidelines.

28 [1986] RPC 515.

29 (Unreported) 29 June 1990 (an appeal against a decision not to grant interim relief). In the subsequent full trial, *BBC* v *British Satellite Broadcasting Ltd* [1991] 3 WLR 174, it was held by Scott J that the defence of fair dealing was available.

30 The Copyright, Designs and Patents Act 1988 s 29(1).

31 Section 29(1A), inserted by the Copyright and Rights in Databases Regulations 1997, SI 1997/3032.

32 It is so limited in the respect of the database right: Copyright and Rights in Database Regulations, reg 20, SI 1997/3032.

33 [1984] FSR 64.

34 But now, as a result of the Broadcasting Act 1990 s 176, there is a duty to make information about forthcoming programmes available to other publishers. European Community law also may be appropriate here, especially the Treaty of Rome Article 86, *see RTE & ITP* v *Commission of the European Communities* [1995] FSR 530.

frequently and only small portions will be referred to. It would not be realistic to expect the student to purchase a book when he wants to refer to only a small part of it. Similarly, in the case of an article in a journal – the student would not be expected to buy the issue of the journal or have to subscribe to the journal just to have access to one particular article.[35]

It is difficult to draw the limits of fair dealing for research or private study; perhaps it can be suggested, partly on the basis of the permitted acts in respect of librarians, that copying the whole of one article from an academic journal would be fair dealing, or the copying of part of a book, say, no more than one chapter.[36] Any more would not be fair dealing. However, it must be noted that a great deal of copying in relation to private study is carried out by students, and it is difficult to control and monitor the use that students make of photocopying facilities in libraries. Of course, in many cases, the charges made for photocopying (usually around 10p per sheet) mean that it is not economically viable to copy a whole book – in many cases purchasing the book would be cheaper than copying it. Although photocopying immediately springs to mind, it should be remembered that copyright can be infringed by making a hand-written copy. It is less likely that a substantial part will be taken because of the effort and time required. Making hand-written notes is a selective process, and only the materials that are of direct use to the student are likely to be copied out in this way. Also, the materials are read and, usually, analysed by the student during the process. It may be that the notes taken by the student have their own copyright because of the student's expenditure of skill, effort or judgment in adding comments and supplemental notes.

The act involved in fair dealing can be done by another, such as where a librarian makes a copy of an article in a periodical for a student who requires the copy for the purposes of research or private study. However, this is limited under s 29(3), which restricts the making of copies to cases where there are not multiple copies being made or supplied to more than one person at a similar time for purposes that are substantially the same. For example, in *Sillitoe v McGraw-Hill Book Co (UK) Ltd*,[37] the defendant had published 'study notes' intended to assist students taking GCE 'O' level examinations in literature, and had reproduced a substantial part of the plaintiff's works in the study notes. The defendant contended, *inter alia*, that the study notes fell within the fair dealing provisions under the Copyright Act 1956 s 6(1), that is fair dealing for the purposes of research or private study. This submission failed to find favour, as the defendant was not engaged in research or private study, but was merely facilitating this for others, that is the students purchasing copies of the study notes.

### Fair dealing for the purposes of criticism, review and reporting current events

Fair dealing for the purpose of criticism or review applies to any form of work or a performance of a work and does not infringe copyright provided a sufficient acknowledgement is given.[38] Section 178 contains a definition of 'sufficient acknowledgement' and requires that it identifies both the work by its title or other description, and the author. However, if the work is published anonymously, or if the work is unpublished and the author's identity cannot be ascertained by reasonable enquiry, there is no requirement for the author's

35 In some cases, a blanket licence scheme will be in operation allowing more extensive copying, such as that administered by the Copyright Licensing Agency.

36 *See* the Copyright, Designs and Patents Act 1988, ss 38 and 39, post.

37 [1983] FSR 545.

38 The Copyright, Designs and Patents Act 1988 s 30(1). Criticism may be positive or negative: *David Geva v Walt Disney Corp* (Supreme Court of Israel) [1995] 2 EIPR D–39.

name to be included in the acknowledgement. In *Sillitoe* v *McGraw-Hill Book Co (UK) Ltd*[39] it was held that a sufficient acknowledgement must recognise the position or claims of the author.

In giving a sufficient acknowledgement, it is not necessary to give the author's full name or even any name at all provided the acknowledgement is sufficient to convey to a reasonably alert member of the audience to which the work including the copyright work is directed. So it was held in *Pro Sieben Media AG* v *Carlton UK Television Ltd*,[40] where the defendant had included in its television programme a 30-second video of a woman who was then pregnant with eight foetuses. The extract contained the initials of the plaintiff's television programme, TAFF, and its logo, a pale, stylised number 7. It was also held in that case that it is not necessary for criticism or review to be the only or the predominant purpose, provided that it was a significant purpose. The purpose itself is something to be tested subjectively from the point of view of the person relying on the permitted act. However, in *Pro Sieben*, the defendant's purpose was to show that the defendant was above the cheque-book journalism allegedly carried on by the plaintiff.

Section 30(1) allows fair dealing with one work in order to criticise or review another work. For example, it is fair dealing to include extracts from a work by T. S. Eliot in a work which is a critical analysis of the work of E. M. Forster.[41] But otherwise the work must be subjected to criticism or review. The equivalent defence under the Copyright Act 1956 was held not to apply when correspondence between the Duke and Duchess of Windsor was published without any such criticism or review.[42]

Criticism can be scathing and can involve a substantial part of another work, and yet still be fair dealing. In *Hubbard* v *Vosper*,[43] the defendant had been a member of the Church of Scientology for some 14 years. After leaving, he wrote a book which was highly critical of the cult of Scientology and used in his book substantial extracts from books, bulletins and letters, some of which were confidential, written by the plaintiff. The defence of fair dealing for the purposes of criticism and review was successfully raised as regards the copyright issues.

The motive behind the use of the plaintiff's work is an important factor. As Lord Denning confirmed in *Hubbard* v *Vosper*, it would not be fair dealing for a rival to take copyright material belonging to someone else to use as his own. In *Time Warner Entertainments Co Ltd* v *Channel 4 Television Corp plc*[44] the plaintiff obtained an injunction to prevent the screening of a programme entitled 'Forbidden Fruit' which contained extracts of scenes from the notorious film 'Clockwork Orange', which was withdrawn in the UK some 20 years earlier for fears of copycat violence. The defendant's programme was based on a criticism of the decision to continue to refuse to allow the film to be shown. The Court of Appeal lifted the injunction on the basis that the defendant could rely on the defence of fair dealing for criticism or review under s 30 of the Act. The Court held that the criticism or review need not be directed primarily at the work itself, and this is confirmed in s 30(1). Although the copy of the film had been obtained, in the plaintiff's words, 'in an underhand manner' (it had been bought legitimately in Paris), this was not a case where it had been obtained in breach of confidence. In any case, of more relevance was how the work was treated, not how it had been obtained. An argument by the plaintiff for limiting

---

**39** [1983] FSR 545.

**40** [1998] FSR 43.

**41** Both authors are deceased but literary copyright still subsists in their works.

**42** *Associated Newspaper Group plc* v *News Group Newspapers Ltd* [1986] RPC 515.

**43** [1972] 2 QB 84.

**44** [1994] EMLR 1. For a discussion of this case *see* Benson, C. 'Fair Dealing in the United Kingdom' [1995] 6 EIPR 304.

review by third parties to a total of four minutes' duration failed to impress the Court which confirmed that, in order to criticise a film seriously, sufficient time must be spent showing extracts from the film.

Fair dealing for the purpose of reporting current events does not apply in the case of a photograph. It is common practice for newspapers to copy extracts from stories in other newspapers. For example, one newspaper may have an 'exclusive' in its early morning issue and other newspapers carry the story in their later editions giving, of course, a sufficient acknowledgement. This they may do, provided a photograph is not copied without permission. Lightman J confirmed that the practice of newspapers of copying a photograph from another newspaper with the intention of obtaining a licence retrospectively was clearly unlawful.[45] Nor could such use of a photograph be considered to be fair dealing for criticism or review, such a proposition being described as totally unreal.

The fair dealing provisions are wider than under the previous Act because, apart from the exception of photographs, they are not limited to any particular type of work and can, therefore, apply to broadcasts and cable programmes. Indeed, according to Scott J in *BBC v British Satellite Broadcasting Ltd*,[46] this fair dealing provision is not limited to general news bulletins and could apply to a major sporting event such as the World Cup football competition. In this case, there had been an acknowledgement given by BSB as to the source of the film, but according to s 30(3) there is no need to give an acknowledgement in the case of reporting current events by means of a sound recording, film, broadcast or cable programme. It seems strange that an exception is made in the case of photographs but not broadcasts.

## Incidental inclusion of copyright material

The use of movie and video cameras, still cameras and live broadcasts mean that, frequently and inevitably, copyright works will be included in the films, photographs or broadcasts whether by design or accident. To facilitate the making of photographs (and other artistic works), films, broadcasts and cable programmes, the incidental inclusion of a copyright work does not infringe the copyright subsisting in that work: s 31(1). Otherwise, it would be very difficult arranging to make a film or whatever, because it would be necessary to avoid the chance inclusion of copyright works. For example, in the case of a television broadcast made in the streets of a city, the copyright subsisting in buildings (artistic works) would be infringed,[47] as might be the copyright in advertising hoardings. The broadcast may also include a glimpse of the front page of a newspaper on sale and pick up the strains of a popular tune being played loudly further down the street.

The exception goes further in that the copyright in the work incidentally included is not infringed by other acts, such as issuing copies to the public, playing, showing, broadcasting or including in a cable programme anything that was made without infringing copyright under s 31(1). However, as regards musical works and works embodying musical works, incidental inclusion does not extend to deliberate inclusion. This also applies to words spoken or sung with music, for example the lyrics of a song. *Hawkes & Sons (London) Ltd v Paramount Film Service Ltd*,[48] concerning infringement of musical copyright by the inclusion of 28 bars of 'Colonel Bogey' in a newsreel, lives on.

45 *Banier v News Group Newspapers Ltd* [1997] FSR 812.

46 [1991] 3 WLR 174.

47 A work of architecture is an artistic work by the Copyright, Designs and Patents Act 1988 s 4(1)(a). Section 62 would also excuse – *see* post. As with other works except typographical arrangements, the copyright in an artistic work can be infringed by broadcasting or inclusion in a cable programme service, s 20.

48 [1934] Ch 593.

## EDUCATION

Education is treated as a special case by copyright law, and there are several exceptions to infringement contained in the Act.[49] Some control is retained – for example, reprographic copying is permitted only in limited circumstances, and some of the permitted acts can be done only for or at educational establishments.[50] Section 174 of the Act defines 'educational establishments' as being any school and any other establishment specified by order of the Secretary of State. By the Copyright (Educational Establishments) (No. 2) Order 1989,[51] other establishments include universities established by Royal Charter or Act of Parliament, most institutions for further or higher education and theological colleges. 'School' is defined by reference to the appropriate legislation – for example, in England and Wales, it is as defined in the Education Act 1944.[52] The expressions 'teacher' and 'pupil' include, respectively, any person who gives and any person who receives instruction. Another control is that, in some circumstances where it is permitted to make copies of copyright works, if those copies are subsequently dealt with they are treated as infringing copies. 'Dealt with' means sold or let for hire, or offered or exposed for sale or hire.

Section 32 deals with things done either for the purpose of instruction, or for examination purposes. Unusually, for the 'education permitted acts' there is no requirement for the instruction or examination to be done by or on behalf of an educational establishment. It is wider and extends to other institutions such as private colleges for adults and correspondence colleges. Copying in the course of instruction or in preparation for instruction of a literary, dramatic, musical or artistic work is permitted as long as the copying is done by the person giving or receiving the instruction, for example the teacher or the pupil, and the copying is not by a reprographic process.[53] For example, it is permissible for a teacher to ask a pupil to write out by hand a substantial extract from a work of literature. Another example is where a teacher reproduces an artistic work on a blackboard in a classroom for the purpose of instruction. Copying by making a film or a film soundtrack in the course of, or in preparation for, instruction in the making of films or film soundtracks does not infringe the copyright in a sound recording, film, broadcast or cable programme. Again, the copying must be done by a person giving or receiving instruction. As might be expected, examinations are also privileged in that anything may be done for the purposes of the examination by way of setting questions, communicating questions to candidates or answering the questions without infringing copyright. However, there is an exception to this in the case of reprographic copies of musical works for use by an examination candidate in performing the work. Therefore, if the examination requires the candidates to play some music, authorisation to make copies must be obtained from the copyright owner or additional copies of the sheet music purchased. The Act prohibits the subsequent dealing with copies made under s 32 by considering such copies to be infringing copies.

Anthologies are dealt with under s 33, which permits the inclusion of a short passage from a published literary or dramatic work in a collection provided that the collection is intended for use in educational establishments and consists mainly of material in which no copyright subsists. Such material would include works in which the copyright has expired.[54] The collection must be described in its title and in any advertisements as being for use in educational establishments. Furthermore, a sufficient acknowledgement is required. But how short is

49 The Copyright, Designs and Patents Act 1988 ss 32–36.

50 Reprographic copying has a wider meaning than simply making photocopies of a work, *see* ibid s 178.

51 SI 1989/1068.

52 *See* the Copyright, Designs and Patents Act 1988 s 174(3) for the meaning of 'school' in Scotland and in Northern Ireland.

53 The dangers of not so limiting educational copying in New Zealand is apparent in Katz, J. 'Reprography and Fair Dealing – Copying for Educational Use: *Longman* v *Carrington* [1991] 2 NZLR 574' [1993] 2 EIPR 67.

54 It could also cover material published in a country which is not a member of the copyright conventions and fails otherwise to attract protection in the United Kingdom.

a short extract? If it is not substantial in copyright terms, then there can be no infringement anyway, and the requirements of the exception are meaningless. A further requirement is that no more than two excerpts from the copyright works by the same author can be included in anthologies published by the same publisher over any period of five years. It would seem that this permitted act is extremely parsimonious. Presumably, if there is some criticism or review of the extracts the fair dealing provisions would come into play and larger extracts could be used. Just to place a final and unnecessary imposition, s 33(4) limits the provision to the educational purposes of the educational establishment.

Performances of literary, dramatic and musical works are permitted provided the audience is made up of teachers and pupils at the educational establishment and other persons directly connected with the activities of the establishment.[55] A parent of a pupil is not to be taken as directly connected with the school by reason of being a parent only. Therefore, a play performed by pupils before an audience of parents will fall outside the scope of this permitted act. The performance may be by a teacher or pupil in the course of the school's activities, or by any person for the purposes of instruction. For the latter it is required that the performance takes place at the school, but as far as teacher and pupil performances are concerned, this limitation does not apply. However, the wording of s 34 seems to suggest that only sole performances fall within the section. The section is termed in the singular as regards the performers. There are similar provisions in respect of the playing or showing of a sound recording, film, broadcast or cable programme for the purposes of instruction before such an audience as described above. Recordings of broadcasts and cable programmes and copies of such recordings can be made by or on behalf of educational establishments for their educational purposes without infringing copyright in the broadcast or cable programme provided there is not an appropriate licensing scheme under s 143.[56] However, subsequent dealing is not permitted. Some licensing schemes have been certified, for example in respect of the Open University.[57]

Section 36 permits the reprographic copying of passages of published literary, dramatic or musical works by or on behalf of educational establishments for the purposes of instruction. Neither is the copyright in the typographical arrangement of the published edition infringed. However, the amount that can be copied is extremely small, being not more than 1 per cent of any work in any quarter, and the authority to copy given by s 36 is subject to the availability of licences and the actual or constructive notice of the person making the copies as regard such licences. A licence may not attempt to reduce the portion that can be copied under s 36. Again, this provision must be considered in the light of what is a substantial part of a work. It is submitted that in most cases, a substantial part of a work will exceed 1 per cent of the total quantity of a work. If this is so, s 36 has no effect whatsoever, it is just so many empty words. Of course, it is very difficult to predict how a court will decide the issue of substantiality, the test being based mainly on quality. However, it would be unlikely that a mere 1 per cent would capture the essence of a work. In *Hawkes & Sons (London) Ltd* v *Paramount Film Service Ltd*[58] around 8 per cent was adjudged to be substantial, but here the basic melody had been taken. Perhaps a better test would be to look at the effect, if any, on the copyright owner's interests. Has the extent of the copying been such that it would be reasonable to expect that copies of the original work be purchased instead? However, the rapid improvements made in recent times to copying technology perhaps account for the attempts to limit unauthorised copying to tiny amounts only.

55 The Copyright, Designs and Patents Act 1988 s 34. Such performances are deemed not to be public performances.

56 Ibid s 35.

57 Copyright (Certification of Licensing Scheme for Educational Recording of Broadcasts) (Open University Educational Enterprises Limited) Order 1993, SI 1993/2755.

58 [1934] Ch 593.

## LIBRARIES AND ARCHIVES

These provisions apply only to 'prescribed' libraries and archives, that is those prescribed by statutory instrument, which may also provide that, in some cases (also prescribed), a librarian or archivist may make a copy only if the person requesting the copy makes a signed declaration in the prescribed form.[59] In such cases, a librarian or archivist may rely on a signed declaration by a person requesting a copy of part or whole of a work in which copyright subsists, unless he is aware that the declaration is false in a material particular. A signed declaration will usually contain a statement to the effect that the copy is required for the purposes of research or private study and that the person requesting the copy has not previously been supplied with a copy from the same work. If a signed declaration is false in a material particular, the copy supplied is considered to be an infringing copy and the person requesting the copy is liable for infringement of copyright as if he made the copy himself. The Act acknowledges that a librarian or archivist may delegate his duties and responsibilities to others.[60] In general, where the copying is permitted of certain types of work, there will be no infringement of accompanying illustrations or in the typographical arrangement. A reproduction of one of the photocopy declarations used by the British Library is shown in Figure 7.2.

Under s 38, a librarian may make and supply a copy of an article in a periodical to a person requiring the copy for the purposes of research or private study. The person supplied must pay at least the attributable cost, which includes a contribution to the general expenses of the library, that is overheads. No person may be supplied with more than one copy of the same article, or with more than one article from the same issue of the periodical. Similar provisions in s 39 permit the

59 The Copyright (Librarians and Archivists) (Copying of Copyright Material) Regulations 1989 specify prescribed libraries and archives and expand on the prescribed conditions, and also contain the forms to be used for declarations and written statements required in the Copyright, Designs and Patents Act 1988 ss 38–43. For example, the prescribed conditions generally include a requirement for a signed declaration or statement.

60 These preliminary issues are contained in s 37.

**THE BRITISH LIBRARY**  DOCUMENT SUPPLY CENTRE

Photocopy Declaration to be retained by the registered BLDSC Customer.

To be obtained by the Librarian of the user library when a declaration or similar undertaking has not otherwise been obtained.

To the Librarian of the _____ Library

(name of user Library or Library Stamp)

1. I hereby request you to supply me with a copy of item specified on Request Number ...............................
........................................................................
   which I require for the purpose of research or private study.
2. I have not previously been supplied with a copy of the same material by you or any other librarian
3. I will not use the copy except for research or private study and will not supply a copy of it to any other person
4. to the best of my knowledge, no other person with whom I work or study has made or intends to make at about the same time as this request, a request for substantially the same material for substantially the same purpose.
5. I understand that if this declaration is false in a material particular the copy supplied to me by you will be an infringing copy and that I shall be liable for infringement of copyright as if I had made the copy myself.

Signature ...................................   Address ...................................

Name ...................................
(BLOCK LETTERS)

Date ...................................

N.B the signature must be the personal signature of the person making the request.

**Figure 7.2 Photocopy declaration**

(Reproduced by permission of the British Library Document Supply Centre)

making and supplying of a copy of a part of a published edition of a literary, dramatic or musical work. The section refers to copying a part of a work without giving any guidance as to the maximum proportion that may be copied. Section 40 of the Act seeks to restrict the making or supplying of multiple copies of the same material by way of regulations made for the purposes of ss 38 and 39.

Provisions also exist so that one prescribed library may make and supply copies to other prescribed libraries of:

(a) articles in periodicals, or
(b) the whole or part of a published edition of a literary, dramatic or musical work.[61]

61 Section 41.

However, (b) does not apply if, at the time the copy is made, the librarian making it knows or could by reasonable enquiry ascertain the name and address of the person entitled to authorise the making of copies of the work. In the vast majority of cases this will be so – most published editions contain the name of the publisher and the author; and whichever of these is the copyright owner, the librarian should be able, without undue difficulty, to make contact in order to ask permission.

Subject to certain conditions, the making for another prescribed library or archive of replacement copies of literary, dramatic or musical works which have been lost, destroyed or damaged is permitted under s 42. Making copies in order to preserve the original is also permitted, for example so that the copy may be displayed and the original placed in safe storage. However, such copying is not permitted if it is reasonably practicable to purchase a copy of the item. The copying of certain unpublished works for the purposes of research or private study is also permitted,[62] as is the making of copies of articles of cultural or historical importance or interest which are to be exported from the UK, it being a legal requirement that such a copy is made.[63]

62 Section 43.

63 Section 44.

## PUBLIC ADMINISTRATION

Copyright is not infringed by certain things done in connection with what might loosely be described as in the course of public administration. This includes parliamentary and judicial proceedings, Royal Commissions and statutory inquiries, and materials open to public inspection, on a statutory register or contained in a public record. Further, acts done under statutory authority do not infringe copyright, unless the relevant Act of Parliament provides otherwise, and the Crown may copy and issue copies to the public of materials communicated to the Crown in the course of public business.

Thus, the copying of documents for a court trial does not infringe copyright, neither does playing a piece of music in court as part of the proceedings, for example if the case concerns a dispute involving an alleged infringement of copyright in a piece of music. Copyright is not infringed by doing anything for the purpose of reporting parliamentary and judicial proceedings, or the proceedings of Royal Commissions or statutory inquiries that are held in public. This does not, of course, authorise the copying of published reports of such proceedings. It is permissible to make copies of entries in registers such as the Data Protection Register, the Register of Patents and the Trade Marks Register, to make copies of information contained in electoral registers or to obtain copies of birth, marriage and death certificates, etc. without infringing copyright. The Copyright (Material Open to Public Inspection) (Marking of Copies of Plans and Drawings) Order 1990 contains the text of a statement to be applied to copies of plans and drawings supplied under s 47.[64] Further details of the public administration exceptions to copyright infringement are given in Table 7.2 at the end of this chapter.

**64** SI 1990/1427. The statement is contained in reg 2.

## COMPUTER PROGRAMS AND DATABASES

**65** SI 1992/3233.

The Copyright (Computer Programs) Regulations 1992[65] inserted ss 50A–50C providing for some specific exceptions to copyright infringement. Under certain conditions, lawful users of computer programs may make back-up copies of computer programs, decompile programs to achieve interoperability and copy or adapt a computer program. There is also a non-derogation from grant exception in relation to databases in s 50D, inserted by the Copyright and Rights in Databases Regulations 1997.[66] These exceptions are dealt with fully in the following chapter.

**66** SI 1997/3032.

## DESIGNS, TYPEFACES AND WORKS IN ELECTRONIC FORM

The provisions relating to designs are discussed in Part Five which deals with design law; however, these provisions are still contained in Table 7.2 at the end of this chapter for completeness. Basically, the typeface provisions are to limit artistic copyright protection for the design of a typeface[67] which will fall within the graphic work category of artistic works. Using a typeface in the ordinary course of typing, composing text, typesetting or printing, possession of an article for such use or doing anything in relation to the material so produced does not infringe the artistic copyright subsisting in the design of a typeface even if the article is an infringing article.[68] However, s 54(2) goes on to apply certain provisions, including secondary infringement of copyright, to persons making, importing, dealing or possessing for the purpose of dealing with articles specifically designed or adapted to produce material with a particular typeface.[69] Section 55 of the Act limits the duration of copyright in an artistic work consisting of the design of a typeface to 25 years from the end of the calendar year during which articles specifically designed or adapted for producing material in that typeface have been marketed by or with the permission of the copyright owner.[70]

**67** A typeface includes an ornamental motif used in printing: the Copyright, Designs and Patents Act 1988 s 178.

**68** Ibid s 54.

**69** 'Dealing with' means selling, letting for hire, offering or exposing for sale or hire, exhibiting in public or distributing.

**70** 'Marketed' means sold, let for hire or offered or exposed for sale or hire anywhere in the world.

Many works are now made available in electronic form, which is defined in s 178 as being in a form usable only by electronic means, 'electronic' having a wide meaning. For example, computer programs, sound recordings, films, information and data are frequently made available in this form. The provision contained in s 56 raises a legal presumption that where a copy of work in electronic form is transferred, the transferee may do anything the original purchaser could do without infringing copyright. Before the provision can apply, the terms under which the copy had been purchased must have allowed, whether expressly, by implication or by operation of law, the purchaser to make copies, to adapt the work or make copies of the adaptation. Furthermore, there must be no express terms interfering with the transfer of the copy or with transferee's rights. Any copies, whether or not adaptations or copies of adaptations, that were made by the purchaser and not transferred are treated as being infringing copies of the work. The provisions also apply to subsequent transfers of the copy of the work. As an example of the workings of s 56, imagine that a person, George, obtains a copy of a word-processing computer program to use on his computer. He may make a back-up copy if the licence agreement permits this, or if necessary to his lawful use. Suppose the licence allows George to assign it in the future. After a year or two, George wants to obtain a more powerful word processor program and wants to 'sell' his old one to Robert.[71] George may then:

1  give Robert the original disk containing the word processing program and the back-up copy (duplicate), or
2  give Robert the original disk and destroy the back-up copy.

If George retains the back-up copy, this will be treated as an infringing copy. Once Robert receives the original disk, he will be able to make his own back-up copy of the program.

## MISCELLANEOUS – LITERARY, DRAMATIC, MUSICAL AND ARTISTIC WORKS

Sections 57–65 contain a hotch-potch of provisions relating to various permitted acts in relation to literary, dramatic, musical and artistic works. Section 57 applies to anonymous and so-called 'pseudonymous' literary, dramatic, musical and artistic works and covers the situation where it is not possible by reasonable enquiry to trace the author, it being reasonable to assume that the copyright has expired or that the author died at least 70 years ago. In such a case, copyright is not infringed even if it is later discovered that copyright continues to subsist in the work. Notice that it is the identity of the author and not the owner of the copyright which is at issue. This provision does not apply to works of Crown copyright or in respect of designated international organisations. If a work is of joint authorship, the provision does not apply if any one of the authors could have been traced by reasonable enquiry, or if it is not reasonable to assume that all of the joint authors died at least 70 years ago.

Other permitted acts include:

1  the use or copying of a record of spoken words or material from it for the purposes of reporting current events, or broadcasting or including in a cable programme service subject to certain conditions (s 58);
2  the public reading or recitation of a reasonable extract of a published literary or dramatic work, subject to a sufficient acknowledgement (s 59);
3  copying and issuing to the public abstracts of scientific or technical subjects published in periodicals, subject to the existence of a statutory licensing scheme (s 60);
4  recording songs for the purpose of inclusion in an archive maintained by a designated body (s 61);[72]

71  Strictly speaking, George does not sell the system to Robert: instead, he assigns the benefit of his licence to Robert. For assignment generally *see* Chapter 4.

72  A list of designated bodies is given in the Copyright (Recordings of Folksongs for Archives) (Designated Bodies) Order 1989, SI 1989/1012. The Copyright, Designs and Patents Act 1988 s 61 is headed 'Recordings of Folksongs' but the Act nowhere defines a 'folksong' except that, from reading s 61, it appears that a folksong is a song where the words are unpublished and of unknown authorship. In many cases, although they may have qualified under the 1956 Act, such songs will be too old for copyright protection under the 1988 Act.

5 making drawings, paintings, photographs, films, etc. of buildings and, if accessible by the public, sculptures, models for buildings and works of artistic craftsmanship (s 62);

6 copying an artistic work and issuing copies to the public in order to advertise the forthcoming sale of the work, for example, to distribute photographs of an oil painting to be sold at an auction (s 63);

7 the making of subsequent artistic works by the author of a previous work (permits an artist to use and develop his style and technique for future works) (s 64);[73]

8 reconstructing buildings (s 65).

**73** It would be unlikely that copyright would be infringed if the artist did not repeat or imitate the main design as required by ibid s 64.

## MISCELLANEOUS – OTHER WORKS

A miscellany of permitted acts is provided for in ss 66–75. Previously, s 66 concerned rental of sound recordings, films and computer programs, and gave the Secretary of State power to order the rental to be treated as licensed, subject to the payment of a reasonable royalty. A more curious provision in s 66(5) was that copyright in a computer program was not infringed by rental to the public after 50 years from the end of the calendar year during which the program was first issued to the public. Section 66 conflicted with the Directive on rental and lending rights, and was replaced by a new s 66 by the Copyright and Related Rights Regulations 1996 [74] with effect from 1 December 1996.

**74** SI 1996/2967

The new s 66 gives the Secretary of State power to order, in such cases as are specified in the order, that the lending of copies of literary, dramatic, musical or artistic works, sound recordings or films are to be treated as licensed by the copyright owner, subject only to the payment of reasonable royalty. No order will be made if, or to the extent that, there is a licensing scheme under s 143 providing for the grant of licences.

The playing of a sound recording will not infringe copyright if done for charitable, religious, educational or social welfare purposes if the organisation is not established or conducted for profit, and the proceeds of any charge for admission are applied solely for the purposes of the organisation: s 67.

Incidental recording for the purposes of broadcasting or providing a cable programme service is permitted under certain circumstances. It is possible to make a sound recording or film of a literary, dramatic or musical work, or an adaptation of such a work, or to make a photograph of an artistic work, or to make a copy of a sound recording or film. Such activities are treated as licensed by the owner where a person is authorised to broadcast the work or include it in a cable programme service by virtue of a licence or assignment of copyright. The recording, film, photograph or copy in question must not be used for any other purpose, and must be destroyed within 28 days of its first being used in the broadcast or cable programme service. Failure to adhere to either of those conditions results in the recording, film, photograph or copy being considered to be an infringing copy.

The BBC, IBA or Cable Authority do not, under s 69, infringe copyright by making recordings as part of their supervision and control over programmes.

A large number of video recorders are used domestically to record television programmes for viewing at a later, more convenient time. This is known as 'time-shifting' of broadcasts and cable programmes, and is permitted by s 70 if done for private and domestic use. There is no time limit, although one of 28 days was proposed at one stage during the passage of the Bill through Parliament, but this was finally dropped because it was totally unenforceable. Strangely, s 71 permits the making, for private and domestic use, of a photograph of an image which is part of a broadcast or cable programme, stating that the copyright in the broadcast, cable programme or any included films will not be infringed. Presumably, copyright in other works could still be infringed, such as taking a photograph of a television screen when it is showing a painting or some other artistic work. It is unclear why anyone would want to take photographs from screen images on a television set, although such photographs could be used in advertising and promotions.

The free public showing or playing in public of broadcasts or cable programmes is permitted under s 72, for example to the residents of an old people's home or to members of clubs or societies (unless this is not incidental to the main purpose of the club or society). Reception and immediate retransmission of broadcasts and cable programmes is permissible under certain circumstances under s 73. Designated bodies may, under s 74, modify copies of broadcasts or cable programmes for persons who are hard of hearing or disabled, for example by adding sub-titles, subject to the existence of statutory licensing schemes; and, under s 75, recordings of certain broadcasts or cable programmes may be made by bodies such as the British Film Institute and the British Library for archival purposes.[75]

75 The other bodies are the Music Performance Research Centre and the Scottish Film Council: Copyright (Recording for Archives of Designated Class of Broadcasts and Cable Programmes) (Designated Bodies) Order 1989, SI 1989/2510.

## ADAPTATIONS

It is possible for the permitted acts to apply to a work which is an adaptation of another work. In these cases, the copyright in the first work (that is, the work from which the adaptation was made) is not infringed. This is the effect of s 76, which prevents infringement of the underlying work from which the adaptation (being a literary, dramatic or musical work) was made, provided the act in relation to the adaptation is permitted.

## STATUTORY LICENCE TO USE SOUND RECORDINGS IN BROADCASTS AND CABLE PROGRAMME SERVICES

The United Kingdom ratified the Rome Convention for the Protection of Performers, Producers of Phonograms and Broadcasting Organisations in 1963. One provision of the Rome Convention was that ephemeral fixations of phonograms could be made by broadcasting organisations for their own broadcasts. This led to s 68 of the Copyright, Designs and Patents Act 1988 which allows the incidental recording of sound recordings by persons authorised under a licence or assignment of copyright to broadcast a sound recording or include it in a cable programme service. In order to comply with the Rome Convention, a condition was that the copy was destroyed within 28 days of first being used for the broadcast or cable programme service.

Later a report of the Monopolies and Mergers Commission was critical of the way in which licensing bodies such as Phonographic Performance Limited (PPL) exercised the rights assigned to them by copyright owners in relation to royalty rates, common tariffs and imposing restrictions on performances. From this followed the introduction of a statutory licence scheme, allowing the use as of right of sound recordings in broadcasts and cable programme services, contained in ss 135A–G of the Act.[76] The right is available where a licensing body could grant a licence or procure the grant of a licence and the person making the broadcast or including the sound recording in a cable programme service gives notice to the licensing body. A further condition is that the person does not have a licence and the licensing body refuses to grant or procure the grant of a licence on acceptable terms, or to comply with an order of the Copyright Tribunal, allowing unlimited needletime, or that the person holds a licence which limits needletime and the licensing body refuses to substitute or procure the substitution of the term with one which does allow unlimited needletime. 'Needletime' is the time in any period that the sound can be included, whether calculated by hours or by a proportion of the period or otherwise.

Section 135C contains the conditions for the exercise of the right. The person making the broadcast or the cable programme service must comply with any reasonable condition or notice given to him by the licensing body, providing that body with such information as it may reasonably require and making payments to the licensing body at not less than quarterly intervals in arrears.

In *Phonographic Performance Ltd v AEI Rediffusion Music Ltd*,[77] the defendant claimed that s 135C(1) gave him a right to keep copies longer than the 28 days under s 68. The main reason was that it was inconvenient and troublesome for the defendant to stay within the 28-day period. It was held that the purpose of s 135C(1) was to grant a right to make broadcasts of sound recordings or include them in cable programme services and which did not extend to making copies. Any other construction would put the United Kingdom in breach of the Rome Convention and, in any case, it was not necessary to make a copy to make the broadcast. Lightman J said that the court should be slow to imply a term which encroached upon the rights of copyright owners beyond that which was clearly provided for by the Act.

## SUMMARY

Table 7.2 provides a summary of the permitted acts discussed in detail in this chapter.

**Table 7.2 The permitted acts: outline**

| Permitted act | Types of works covered by permitted act | Comments |
|---|---|---|
| **Fair Dealing, etc.** | | |
| Fair dealing – research and private study: s.29 | Literary, dramatic, musical or artistic works, typographical arrangements | Decompilation of computer programs is not fair dealing but provided for under s 50B. For databases, the source must be indicated. |

76 Inserted by the Broadcasting Act 1990.

77 [1997] RPC 729.

▶

**Table 7.2 cont'd**

| Permitted act | Types of works covered by permitted act | Comments |
|---|---|---|
| Fair dealing – criticism or review: s 30(1) | Any work or performance | Must be accompanied by a sufficient acknowledgement. |
| Fair dealing – reporting current events: s 30(2) | Any work other than a photograph | Must be accompanied by a sufficient acknowledgement except in the case of a sound recording, film, broadcast or cable programme. |
| Incidental inclusion in an artistic work, sound recording, film, broadcast or cable programme: s 31(1) | Any work | But musical work, words spoken or sung with music must not be deliberately included. |
| Issuing to the public, playing, showing, broadcasting, including in a cable programme service: s 31(2) | Anything, the making of which was not an infringement by virtue of s 31(1) above | |

**Education**

| | | |
|---|---|---|
| Copying in the course of instruction or preparation for instruction: s 32(1) | Literary, dramatic, musical or artistic work | Must be done by person giving or receiving instruction and not copied by means of a reprographic process. |
| Copying by making a film or a film soundtrack in the course of, or in preparation for, instruction in the making of films or film soundtracks: s 32(2) | Sound recording, film, broadcast or cable programme | Must be done by a person giving or receiving instruction. |
| Anything done for the purpose of examination by way of setting questions, communicating questions to candidates or answering the question: s 32(3) | Any work | Making a reprographic copy of a musical work for use by an examination candidate in performing the work is not permitted: s 32(4). |
| Inclusion of a short passage in a collection intended for use in educational establish-ments and so described in advertisements. The collection must consist mainly of material in which copyright subsists: s 33 | Published literary or dramatic works | Must be accompanied by a sufficient acknowledgement, and the work itself must not be intended for use in such establishments, and not more than two excerpts from copyright works of the same author may be included in collections published by the same publisher over any period of five years. |

**Table 7.2 cont'd**

| Permitted act | Types of works covered by permitted act | Comments |
|---|---|---|
| Performances before an audience of teachers and pupils at an educational establishment and other persons directly connected with the activities of the establishment: s 34(1) | Literary, dramatic or musical works (such performance is not considered to be a public performance) | Performance must be by a teacher or pupil in the course of the activities of the establishment or the performance may be by any person at the establishment for the purposes of instruction. A person is not 'directly connected' simply because he is a parent of a pupil. |
| Playing or showing before an audience of teachers and pupils at an educational establishment and other persons directly connected with the activities of the establishment for the purposes of instruction: s 34(2) | Sound recording, film, broadcast or cable programme (such playing or showing is not considered to be a playing or showing in public) | A person is not 'directly connected' simply because he is a parent of a pupil. |
| Making a recording by or on behalf of an educational establish-ment or making a copy of such a recording for educational purposes of that establishment: s 35 | Broadcast or cable programme and any included work | Does not apply if or to the extent that there is a certified licensing scheme under s 143. |
| Reprographic copying of passages not exceeding 1% of a work in any quarter by or on behalf of an educational establishment for the purposes of instruction: s 36 | Published literary, dramatic or musical works including typographical arrangements of such works | Does not apply if or to the extent that licences are available and the person making the copies knew or ought to have been aware of that fact. |
| Lending copies by an educational establishment: s 36A | Any work | |

**Libraries and archives**

| | | |
|---|---|---|
| Librarians of a prescribed library may, if the prescribed conditions are complied with, make and supply: | | *Prescribed conditions:*<br>(a) person supplied must satisfy librarian that he requires the copies for his own research or private study; |

▶

**Table 7.2 cont'd**

| Permitted act | Types of works covered by permitted act | Comments |
|---|---|---|
| (a) a copy of an article in a periodical: s 38 | Literary work (text) and accompanying artistic works (illustrations) including the typographical arrangement | (b) not more than 1 copy of periodical article (or copies from more than 1 article in the same issue) is supplied or, with respect to published literary, dramatic or musical works, not more than 1 copy of the same material or a copy of more than a reasonable proportion of any work is supplied; |
| (b) a copy of part of a published edition: s 39 | Literary, dramatic or musical works including the typographical arrangement of such works | (c) the person to whom the copies are supplied must pay at least the cost of making and supplying the copies. |
| Lending of a book by a library if the book is in the public lending right scheme: s 40A | Any work | |
| Librarian of a prescribed library may make and supply to another prescribed library, a copy of:<br>(a) an article in a periodical, or<br>(b) the whole or part of a published edition: s 41 | An article in a periodical or literary, dramatic or musical works, including the typographical arrangement of such works | The prescribed conditions above must be complied with.<br>(b) does not apply if the librarian knows or could by reasonable inquiry ascertain the name and address of the person entitled to authorise the making of the copy. |
| Librarian or archivist of a prescribed library or archive may, if the prescribed conditions are complied with, make a copy from any item in the permanent collection of that library or archive<br>(a) in order to preserve or replace the item<br>(b) to replace a lost, destroyed or missing item in the permanent collection of another prescribed library or archive: s 42 | Literary, dramatic or musical works plus accompanying illustrations (artistic works) and including the typographical arrangement | Prescribed conditions include restricting the making of such copies to cases when it is not reasonably practicable to purchase a copy of the item to fulfil the purpose. |

**Table 7.2 cont'd**

| Permitted act | Types of works covered by permitted act | Comments |
|---|---|---|
| Librarian or archivist of a prescribed library or archive may, if the prescribed conditions are complied with, make and supply a copy of the whole or part of a work from an unpublished document, provided that the copyright owner has not prohibited copying to the actual or constructive knowledge of the person making the copy: s 43 | Literary, dramatic or musical works | Prescribed conditions: (a) person supplied must satisfy the librarian or archivist that he requires the copies for research or private study; (b) no person is supplied with more than 1 copy of the same material; (c) the person to whom the copies are supplied must pay at least the cost of making and supplying the copies. |
| Making a copy of an article of cultural or historical importance or interest which cannot be exported from the United Kingdom unless a copy is made and deposited in an appropriate library or archive: s 44 | Any work | |

**Public administration**

| | | |
|---|---|---|
| Anything done for the purposes of parliamentary or judicial proceedings or for the purposes of reporting such proceedings: s 45 | Any work | Does not authorise copying a work which is itself a published report of the proceedings. |
| Anything done for the purposes of the proceedings of a Royal Commission or statutory inquiry or for the purpose of reporting such proceedings held in public or issuing to the public copies of the report of a Royal Commission or statutory inquiry: s 46 | Any work | Does not authorise copying a work which is itself a published report of the proceedings. |

▶

**Table 7.2 cont'd**

| Permitted act | Types of works covered by permitted act | Comments |
|---|---|---|
| Copying material open to public inspection pursuant to a statutory requirement, or on a statutory register, e.g. entries in the Data Protection Register or the Trade Marks Register: s 47 | Any work | Does not include issuing copies to the public except when material contains information about matters of general scientific, technical, commercial or economic interest or to enable the material to be inspected at a more convenient time or place. Includes EPO (European Patent Office) and WIPO (World Intellectual Property Organization) materials. |
| Copying and issuing copies to the public of works which have been communicated to the Crown by or with the licence of the copyright owner and an item containing the work is in the custody or control of the Crown providing the work has not previously been published otherwise. Communication must have been in the course of public business, which includes any activity carried on by the Crown: s 48 | Literary, dramatic, musical or artistic works | Applies only as regards the purpose or related purposes for which the work has been communicated. |
| Copying and supplying a copy of material contained in public records: s 49 | Any work | Must be by or with the authority of any officer appointed under the Public Records Act 1958 (for England & Wales). |
| Acts specifically authorised by an Act of Parliament unless the Act provides otherwise: s 50 | Any work | This does not exclude any defence of statutory authority otherwise available under or by any enactment. |

**Table 7.2 cont'd**

| Permitted act | Types of works covered by permitted act | Comments |
|---|---|---|
| **Computer programs** | | |
| Making back-up copy necessary for lawful use: s 50A | Computer program | Must be by a lawful user. A lawful user is a person having a right to use the program (whether under a licence or otherwise). |
| Decompiling a computer program by a lawful user: s 50B | Computer program | A number of conditions apply, e.g. it must be necessary to decompile to obtain the information necessary to create an independent program that can be operated with the program decompiled or another program. |
| Copying or adapting by a lawful user: s 50C | Computer program | For example, for the purposes of error correction. Unlike the 2 permitted acts above, this can be restricted or prohibited by a term in a licence agreement. |
| **Databases** | | |
| Doing anything necessary for the purposes of access to and use of the contents of a database or part of a database by a person having a right to use the database: s 50D | Databases | Any term or condition purporting to prohibit or restrict this is void. |
| **Designs** | | |
| Making an article to a design or copying an article made to that design. The exception extends to issuing to the public, including in a film, broadcast or cable programme such an article or copy: s 51 | Design document or model recording or embodying the design for anything other than an artistic work or typeface. A design document could be a drawing, written description, photograph or data stored in a computer | Relates to articles which are in the province of registered designs (though not all) or the design right. |

▶

191

**Table 7.2 cont'd**

| Permitted act | Types of works covered by permitted act | Comments |
|---|---|---|
| Copying by making articles, doing anything for the purpose of making articles and doing anything in relation to articles, 25 years from end of calendar year in which articles first marketed: s 52 | Certain artistic works that have been exploited by making articles by an industrial process and marketing the articles in the UK. Films are not 'articles' for s 52. *See* Copyright (Industrial Processes and Excluded Articles) (No. 2) Order 1989 for meaning of 'exploitation' | Effectively limits copyright in certain types of artistic works (e.g. works of artistic craftsmanship) that are commercially exploited by making articles which will normally be taken to be copies of the artistic work. Marketing means selling, letting for hire or offering or exposing for sale or hire. |
| In respect of a design registration:<br>(a) things done in pursuance of an assignment or licence granted by the proprietor of a corresponding design<br>(b) things done in good faith in reliance of the registration without notice of proceedings for cancellation or rectification of registration: s 53 | Artistic work | 'Corresponding design' means a design which if applied to an article would be treated as a copy of an artistic work. |

**Typefaces**

| Permitted act | Types of works covered by permitted act | Comments |
|---|---|---|
| Using a typeface in typing, composing, typesetting or printing; possessing an article for such use; doing anything in relation to material produced by such use: s 54 | Artistic work consisting of the design of a typeface | But making, importing, dealing with, possessing articles specifically designed or adapted for producing material in a particular typeface still infringes – *see* s 54(2). |
| Copying by making further such articles, etc. after 25 years from the end of the calendar year in which articles for producing material in a typeface have been first marketed: s 55 | Artistic work consisting of the design of a typeface | Limits duration of copyright where the design has been commercially exploited anywhere. |

**Table 7.2 cont'd**

| Permitted act | Types of works covered by permitted act | Comments |
|---|---|---|
| **Works in electronic form** | | |
| Transferee of a work in electronic form may do anything purchaser was allowed to do if the terms of the original purchase allowed the purchaser to copy, adapt or copy adaptations and there are no express terms prohibiting transfer or otherwise interfering with the transferee's rights: s 56 | Any work in electronic form | Terms of original purchase may be express, implied or by virtue of any rule of law. Copies and adaptations not transferred are treated as infringing copies. |
| **Miscellaneous – literary, dramatic, musical and artistic works** | | |
| Acts done in relation to works which are anonymous or pseudonymous where it is not possible to trace the author and it is reasonable to assume that copyright no longer subsists in the work: s 57 | Literary, dramatic, musical or artistic works | Note: effects of longer duration of copyright, e.g. Crown copyright, on the assumption as to the time since the author died. Special provisions also for works of joint authorship. |
| Use of a record of spoken words or material from it, copying the record or material taken from it and use of that copy, subject to conditions: s 58 | Literary work (recording, in writing or otherwise, of spoken words for purpose of reporting current events or broadcasting or including in a cable programme service) | Conditions: direct records only, making of which is not prohibited by speaker and did not infringe copyright, use made not of a kind prohibited by speaker or copyright owner, use is by or with authority of lawful possessor of record. |
| Public reading or recitation of a reasonable extract and also the making of a sound recording or broadcasting or including in a cable programme service of such a reading or recitation: s 59 | Published literary or dramatic work | Must be accompanied by a sufficient acknowledgement. |

▶

**Table 7.2 cont'd**

| Permitted act | Types of works covered by permitted act | Comments |
| --- | --- | --- |
| Copy abstracts of scientific or technical subjects published in periodicals or issue copies to the public: s 60 | Literary works (abstracts are almost certain to be literary works) | Does not apply if and to the extent that there is a licensing scheme under s 143. |
| Making a sound recording of a performance of a 'folksong' for inclusion in an archive and subsequent supply of copies for research or private study: s 61 | Literary works (words) and musical works (accompanying music) | Certain conditions must be met, words unpublished and of unknown authorship, no other copyright is infringed and not prohibited by any performer. |
| Making a graphic work representing it, making a photograph or film of it, broadcasting or including in a cable programme service a visual image of it. Also issuing copies to the public, broadcasting or including in a cable programme service in relation to the above: s 62 | Artistic works being buildings and sculptures, models for buildings and works of artistic craftsmanship if permanently sited in a public place or premises open to the public | |
| Copying and issuing copies to the public advertising the sale of a work: s 63 | Artistic works | For example, in an auction catalogue. However, subsequent dealing excepted. |
| The making of another work by the author, not being the owner of the copyright in the first work, by copying the first work: s 64 | Artistic works | Provided the main design of the earlier work is not repeated or imitated. |
| Reconstructing a building: s 65 | Artistic works, that is, the building itself and drawings and plans from which building constructed | As regards the drawings and plans, the building was originally constructed in accordance with them by or with the licence of the copyright owner. |

**Table 7.2 cont'd**

| Permitted act | Types of works covered by permitted act | Comments |
|---|---|---|
| **Miscellaneous – lending of works and playing of sound recordings** | | |
| Lending to the public of copies of works by order of the Secretary of State: s 66 | Literary, dramatic, musical or artistic works, sound recordings or films | Such lending is treated as licensed subject only to payment of a reasonable royalty. This permitted act does not apply if and to the extent there is a licensing scheme under s 143. |
| **Miscellaneous – films and sound recordings** | | |
| Acts done in relation to films where it is not possible by reasonable inquiry to ascertain the identity of persons referred to in s 13B(2) (e.g. principal director, etc) and it is reasonable to assume that copyright no longer subsists in the work: s 66A | Films | Inserted by the Duration of Copyright and Rights in Performances Regulations 1995. |
| Playing a sound recording as part of the activities of, or for the benefit of, a club, society or other organisation, subject to conditions: s 67 | Sound recordings | Main objects of organisation must be charitable or for advancement of religion, education or social welfare and proceeds applied solely for the purposes of the organisation. (Organisation not established or conducted for profit.) |
| **Miscellaneous – broadcasts and cable programmes** | | |
| Incidental recording for the purposes of broadcasting or inclusion in a cable programme service:<br>(a) making a sound recording or film of the work or an adaptation<br>(b) taking a photograph or making a film<br>(c) making a copy: s 68 | (a) Literary, dramatic or musical work or adaptation of such a work<br>(b) Artistic works<br>(c) Sound recording or film | Applies where person is authorised to broadcast or include work in a cable programme by virtue of a licence or assignment of copyright. Such recording is treated as if licensed by the copyright owner. Recording, film, photograph or copy must not be used for any other purpose and shall be destroyed within 28 days of being first used. |

▶

**Table 7.2 cont'd**

| Permitted act | Types of works covered by permitted act | Comments |
| --- | --- | --- |
| Making or use of recordings, etc. for the purpose of maintaining supervision and control over programmes by the BBC, IBA or Cable Authority: s 69 | Any work | IBA purposes – *see* Broadcasting Act 1981: s 4(7) Cable Authority – *see* Cable and Broadcasting Act 1984, Pt I ss 16 and 35. |
| Time shifting broadcasts and cable programmes to view or listen to at a more convenient time: s 70 | Broadcasts, cable programmes and included works | Only for private and domestic use. |
| Making a photograph of the whole or any part of an image forming part of television broadcast or cable programme or making a copy of such a photograph: s 71 | Broadcasts, cable programmes and included films | Only for private and domestic use. |
| Showing or playing in public to a non-paying audience: s 72 | Broadcasts, cable programmes and included sound recordings and films | Section 72 gives guidance as to when an audience has or has not paid admission. |
| Reception of broadcast made from a place in the UK and immediate retransmission in a cable programme service: s 73 | Broadcasts and included works | If and to the extent that the broadcast is made for reception in the area in which the cable programme service is provided and is not a satellite transmission or an encrypted transmission. |
| Making copies of television broadcasts and cable programmes, issuing copies to public if a designated body for purpose of providing people who are deaf, hard of hearing, physically or mentally handicapped in other ways with copies subtitled or modified for their special needs: s 74 | Broadcasts, cable programmes and included works | But not if there is a licensing scheme under s 143. |
| Recording and making a copy of such recording for placing in an archive: s 75 | Broadcasts, cable programmes and included works | Only with respect to designated classes and only for designated archives. |

**Table 7.2 cont'd**

| Permitted act | Types of works covered by permitted act | Comments |
| --- | --- | --- |
| **Adaptations** | | |
| Any of all of the above acts in respect of an adaptation: s 76 | Literary, dramatic or musical works | Does not infringe copyright in the work from which the adaptation was made. |
| **Statutory licensing** | | |
| Including in a broadcast or cable programme service a sound recording: s 135C | Sound recordings | Subject to conditions in ss 135A–C. |

# 8

## New technology and copyright[1]

1 For definitions relating to computer technology *see* the Glossary at the beginning of the book.

### INTRODUCTION

Copyright law has a history of development that can partly be explained by reference to technological change. Examples of advances in science that have in the past been addressed by copyright law include photography, sound recordings, films and broadcasting. The Copyright, Designs and Patents Act 1988[2] was an attempt to keep abreast of developments in technology coupled with an intention to enact legislation that would take future change in its stride. The phrase 'new technology' conjures up thoughts of computer technology, and it is to this exciting and important area that a large part of this chapter is devoted. However, new technology is not restricted to computer systems and other technical advances have been made that need to be examined in the light of copyright law. Two points are worth mentioning at this stage: first, computer technology is not new – universal programmable computing machines have existed for over 50 years; secondly, the vast majority of new technical developments involve computer technology, even if the developments themselves do not appear at first sight to be connected with such technology. Modern photocopiers, facsimile transmission machines, electronic mail, draughting and design tools, even the humble automatic washing machine, all owe something to computer science.

2 Unless otherwise stated, in this chapter statutory references are to the Copyright, Designs and Patents Act 1988.

There is no doubting that the new technology stretches the law which is sometimes slow to react, and one problem has been the manner in which it has been attempted to adapt existing legal paradigms to deal with the problems posed by technological development. Nowhere can this be seen more strikingly than in the way in which copyright has been used as the main vehicle for the protection of computer programs. Whether copyright is an appropriate method of protection has been a long running debate that still rages on.[3] There is one great difference between computer programs and other works protected by copyright that sets them apart. Conventional works of copyright are passive. They await our attention to be read, viewed or listened to. Computer programs, on the other hand, are active – they do things – they manipulate symbols, transform, modify and retrieve digitally stored information. Even though we now have substantial experience of dealing with computer technology, it continues to cause problems, and not just in terms of substantive law. Evidence and discovery are other areas in which problems may arise. For example, in *Dun & Bradstreet Ltd* v *Typesetting Facilities Ltd*,[4] an application for inspection of the defendant's computer database under the Rules of the Supreme Court Ord 29 r 2 was held to be inappropriate as inspecting the computer disks on which a copy of the database was stored would not give the applicant what he really wanted, which was access to the information stored electronically on the disk.[5]

3 For a recent example, *see* Gordon, S.E. 'The Very Idea!; Why Copyright is an Inappropriate Way to Protect Computer Programs' [1998] EIPR 10.

4 [1992] FSR 320.

5 The court allowed inspection as if the application had been made under Ord 24 r 10 instead.

'Computer software' is a phrase that, like many phrases in the computer industry, is incapable of precise definition, but it is usually taken to include computer programs, databases, preparatory material and associated document-ation (in printed or electronic form) such as manuals for users of the programs and for persons who have to maintain the programs. It can also include all manner of other works stored in digital form, interfaces (for example, with the user or hardware or other software), programming languages and software tools to be used to develop software systems.

Computer programs are considered in detail in this chapter in terms of the extent and scope of copyright protection for them and for the effects that they produce.[6] Particular issues are the 'look and feel' of computer programs in the context of non-literal copying, the decompilation of computer programs, back-up copies, and copying and adapting computer programs in manners consistent with their lawful use. After looking at computer programs, the copyright posi-tion of programming languages, databases and other information stored in computer systems and computer-generated works is discussed. Other areas of interest considered are satellite broadcasting, copying technology, scientific dis-coveries, genetic sequences and formulae and, finally, electronic publishing in relation to the Internet and multimedia.

## COPYRIGHT PROTECTION FOR COMPUTER PROGRAMS

### Background

It has already been seen that copyright subsists in computer programs as a form of literary work by the Copyright, Designs and Patents Act 1988 s 3(1)(b).[7] The same prerequisites of originality and qualification must be present as with other forms of literary works for a computer program (or preparatory design material for a computer program) to be the subject matter of copyright. At one time it was not at all clear whether computer programs were protected by copyright. The Copyright Act 1956 made no mention of computers or computer pro-grams. Although at the time that Act was passed computers had been around for a few years, unauthorised copying of computer programs had not become a serious problem. There were only a few computers in existence and they were expensive and costly to operate and maintain, and there was no black market in application programs.[8] Many such application programs were specially written and maintained by the staff of computer departments for an organisation's own particular needs and would probably have been unsuitable for use by others. However, in spite of the omission of computer programs from the 1956 Act, many writers considered that they were protected as literary works. For exam-ple, Laddie *et al.* suggested that:

> ... a computer program expressed in writing or other notation on a piece of paper is a 'literary work' within the meaning of [s 2 of the 1956 Act] ... and if produced as a result of substantial independent skill or useful labour will be 'original' and so qualify for copyright protection.[9]

The issue may have been fairly straightforward and uncontroversial in the case of computer programs that had been printed out, that is listed on paper. After

**6** *See* Chapter 13 for the position of computer programs in patent law.

**7** Preparatory design material for a computer program is also a form of literary work, the Copyright, Designs and Patents Act 1988 s 3(1)(c).

**8** Application programs are designed to perform a specific task such as processing data, producing reports, word processing, etc. They can be distinguished from operating system programs which supply the basic working environment in which the application programs operate.

**9** Laddie, H., Prescott, P. and Vittoria, M. (1980) *The Modern Law of Copyright* (1st edn), Butterworths, at p. 93.

all, if copyright had been extended to books of telegraphic codes as early as 1884, why should copyright be refused for computer programs printed out on paper?[10] However, if this view was accepted, it did not give any assistance in terms of computer programs that were stored in a computer, especially if those programs were in object code form having been compiled from source code programs.[11] A committee, known as the Whitford Committee, after its chairman Whitford J, was set up to examine copyright law generally, and its report was published in 1977 at a time when the problems of unauthorised copying of computer programs were beginning to be perceived.[12] The report recognised that copyright law was unsatisfactory as regards computer programs and the committee made recommendations to improve the law in this area and to put it beyond doubt that computer programs and works produced with the aid of a computer were protected by copyright. A Green Paper was published in 1981 covering copyright and related matters, and included recommendations that copyright law be amended expressly to afford protection for computer programs.[13]

Copyright law remained unchanged after the Whitford Committee report, and during the first few years of the 1980s the problem of computer software piracy[14] became a major concern for the computer industry with the loss attributable to piracy being estimated at some £150 million.[15] There was a handful of interlocutory actions brought alleging infringement of copyright subsisting in computer programs; these actions invariably proceeded on the basis that computer programs were protected by copyright and interlocutory relief was invariably granted. For example, in *Sega Enterprises Ltd v Richards*,[16] the plaintiff owned a computer game called 'FROGGER' which was effected by means of computer programs. The defendant produced a similar program, admitting that his was based on the plaintiff's program. The defendant argued that he had done much work on the program and that, in any case, copyright did not subsist in computer programs under English law. Goulding J said:

> ... I am clearly of the opinion that copyright ... subsists in the assembly code program of the game 'FROGGER'.

He went on to say that the object code derived from the assembly code program (source code) was either a reproduction or an adaptation of the assembly code version and, as a result, also protected by copyright. However, these cases were interlocutory hearings only. Not a single case concerning the issue of the subsistence of copyright in computer programs went to full trial and the computer industry remained nervous.

The industry's fears appeared to be justified when, in 1984, the large and successful Apple Computer Corporation sued in Australia an importer of 'clones' of its computers. Appropriately enough, the clones were called 'WOMBATS'. At first instance, in *Apple Computer Inc v Computer Edge Pty Ltd*,[17] it was held that literary copyright did not subsist in the computer programs in question, being the object code programs in the ROM chips in the Apple II computer.[18] A great deal of reliance was placed by the judge on the old English case of *Hollinrake v Truswell*,[19] in which Davey LJ said that a literary work is one intended to 'afford either information and instruction, or pleasure, in the form of literary enjoyment'. Although the appeal by the plaintiff to the Federal Court of Australia was allowed, reversing the decision at first instance, on the basis that the object code programs were adaptations of the source code pro-

10 For example, in *Ager v Peninsular & Oriental Steam Navigation Co* (1884) 26 ChD 637, a book of telegraphic codes was recognised as being suitable subject matter for literary copyright. *See also D P Anderson & Co Ltd v Lieber Code Co* [1917] 2 KB 469 on the same point.

11 A source code program may be written in a computer programming language, such as COBOL or BASIC, which is fairly easy for computer programmers to understand and write programs in. This source code version will usually be written down on paper or printed out. The source code will then be converted into the language of the computer, that is compiled into object code so that it can run on the computer. The object code will, if printed out in that form, be an apparently meaningless collection of numbers and letters representing binary code.

12 *Copyright – Copyright and Design Law*, Cmnd 6732 (London: HMSO, 1977).

13 *Reform of the Law Relating to Copyright, Designs and Performers' Protection*, Cmnd 8302 (London: HMSO, 1981), cl.2.

14 The unauthorised copying and selling of computer programs including, in some cases, documentation. The United States of America was the first country to enact specific legislation directed towards the copyright protection of computer programs, Computer Software Copyright Act 1980, 17 USC §101,117.

15 The estimate was produced in 1984 by the Federation Against Software Theft (FAST). A more recent estimate, for the United Kingdom alone, is £540m, Jervis, J. 'DTI Fires a Shot across Software Pirates' Bows', *Computing*, 1 August 1996 at p. 4.

16 [1983] FSR 73. *See also Gates v Swift* [1982] RPC 339; *Thrustcode Ltd v W W Computing Ltd* [1983] FSR 502; *Apple Computer Inc v Sirtel (UK) Ltd* (unreported) 27 July 1983.

17 [1984] FSR 246.

18 A ROM chip is a read only memory integrated circuit which contains, typically, operating system programs. The defendant attacked the copyright in the Apple II programs after it was shown that the names of some of the programmers of the Apple II computer were present in the equivalent programs in the defendant's computer. This raised an almost irrefutable presumption of copying.

19 [1894] 3 Ch 420, approved in *Exxon Corporation v Exxon Insurance Consultants International Ltd* [1981] 3 All ER 241.

grams, the dissenting judgment by Shepherd J was the most elegant and well argued.[20] He said that an adaptation of a literary work should be capable of being seen or heard. To put the matter beyond doubt, the Australian Parliament very quickly enacted the Australian Copyright Amendment Act 1984.

The *Apple* case had serious repercussions for the United Kingdom, as Australian copyright law was, at the time, very similar to UK law. While in the United States of America the issue was the scope of the protection offered by copyright, in the UK doubts about whether copyright could subsist in a computer program, whatever its form, increased. Eventually, after vociferous outbursts by a worried but powerful industry, amending legislation was passed in the UK, but only by way of a Private Member's Bill. The Copyright (Computer Software) Amendment Act 1985 made it quite clear that computer programs were protected by copyright as literary works. When it was passed, this piece of legislation was seen as being a temporary measure and did not directly deal with some of the copyright issues related to computer technology, such as the ownership of works produced by or with the aid of a programmed computer.[21] One reason for the brevity and lack of consideration given to the amending legislation was that a wholesale review of copyright and design law was contemplated. That review took place and culminated in the White Paper *Intellectual Property and Innovation*, published in 1986.[22] Many of the recommendations contained in the White Paper found their way into the Copyright, Designs and Patents Act 1988, and it is to this Act and its implications that we will now turn.

## COMPUTER PROGRAMS – BASIC POSITION

The Copyright, Designs and Patents Act 1988 does not attempt to define 'computer program'.[23] This is probably sensible and at least allows the courts to develop the meaning of the phrase in the light of future technological change. In the Irish case of *News Datacom Ltd* v *Satellite Decoding Systems*[24] it was accepted that a 'smartcard' decoder for use with scrambled satellite television broadcasts was a computer program.[25]

In Australia, in *Powerflex* v *Data Access Corp*[26] it was accepted, at first instance, that a single word in a computer program, being derived from the programming language used, could itself be a computer program. In a high-level language, a single statement, such as the word 'PRINT' in the BASIC programming language, is equivalent to and triggers a whole set of instructions in machine language. As such, it is arguable that it is a program. Fortunately, on appeal, the Federal Court saw the fallacy of this proposition, describing such a word as a cipher. It is not the set of instructions, merely the key to access them.[27]

It may sometimes be difficult to distinguish between 'hardware' and 'software', such as where a computer program is permanently hard-wired in a microprocessor in the form of 'microcode' or 'microprograms'. The view in the United States is that such programs or code still fall within the meaning of 'computer program' for the purpose of copyright law. In *NEC Corp* v *Intel Corp*[28] it was held that, even though the computer programs were permanently stored in 'read only memory' (ROM), the programs were still capable of copyright subsistence. The mode of storage did not change the nature of a computer program. In

20  [1984] FSR 481.

21  HC Deb, 19 April 1985 at col. 558.

22  Cmnd 9712 (HMSO, 1986).

23  Nor is 'computer' defined.

24  [1995] FSR 201, Irish High Court.

25  The Irish Copyright Acts of 1963 and 1987 were amended by the European Communities (Legal Protection of Computer Programs) Regulations 1993, SI 1993/26.

26  [1997] FCA 490.

27  The copyright position of programming languages is discussed later in this chapter.

28  645 F Supp 1485 (D Minn 1985).

a later hearing between the parties in 1989,[29] an argument that the microcode embedded within a microprocessor was a defining element of a computer and could not, therefore, also be a computer program failed to find sympathy. In the UK, it is beyond doubt that microcode will be considered to be a computer program or part of a program and will be protected by copyright.

The Copyright, Designs and Patents Act 1988 does not elaborate upon the meaning of originality in respect of computer programs. However, the European Directive on the legal protection of computer programs[30] describes originality in terms of a program being the author's own intellectual creation.[31] This approximates to the requirement under German copyright law that a work be the author's personal intellectual creation[32] and appears to be more stringent than the UK's test of originating from the author. It has been rigorously applied in Germany in the past, and in *Sudwestdeutsche Inkasso KG v Bappert und Burker Computer GmbH*[33] it was held that, to be protected by copyright, a computer program must result from individual creative achievement exceeding the average skills displayed in the development of computer programs.[34] However, recent case law suggests that the hurdle to subsistence has been significantly lowered, as in the *Buchhaltungsprogram* case[35] in which the German Federal Supreme Court confirmed that copyright could subsist in an accounting program, taking the opportunity to signal a lowering of the standard, though, strictly speaking, this part of the decision was *obiter*.

The two most important acts restricted by copyright in relation to computer programs are those of copying and making an adaptation. Other acts may be relevant in the context of a computer program, such as issuing to the public and the secondary infringements, but it is copying and making adaptations that are of particular interest as regards the scope of protection afforded by copyright. Following the uncertainty as to the copyright protection of computer programs which was finally put to rest by the Copyright (Computer Software) Amendment Act 1985, it is possible that the pendulum has swung too far in the other direction and the protection now offered by copyright may be too extensive. As a result, innovation and competition within the computer software industry could be unjustifiably inhibited. The problem of finding a balance between conflicting interests has taxed even the European Community in its search for a balanced Directive on copyright protection for computer programs.

As with any other literary work, the copyright in a computer program is infringed by making, without the copyright owner's licence, a copy of the program or of a substantial part of it.[36] Substantiality is an issue of quality and therefore the copyright subsisting in a computer program can be infringed if the 'essence' of the program is copied, even if the part copied is relatively small quantitatively. Arguably, even a tiny part of a program could be regarded as substantial as the program probably will not function, at all or properly, without it. However, a better approach is to consider whether the part taken was the result of at least a minimal amount of skill on the part of the programmer. In other words, would the part taken, when looked at in isolation, satisfy the basic requirements for copyright subsistence?

Plaintiffs alleging copying of parts of their programs may have difficulty in convincing a judge that a substantial part has been taken because of some judges' lack of technical knowledge. In *Total Information Processing Systems Ltd v Daman Ltd*[37] Judge Paul Baker considered that the data division of a

29  *NEC Corp v Intel Corp* (1989) 10 USPQ 2d.

30  OJ L122, 17.5.91, p. 42.

31  Ibid Article 1(3). This is the test for originality for databases, *see* post.

32  German Copyright Act 1965 s 2(2).

33  (1985) Case 52/83, BGHZ 94, 276.

34  For the background to the Directive, *see* Wilkinson, A., 'Software Protection, Trade, and Industrial Policies in the European Community' in Lehmann, M. and Tapper, C.F. (1993) *A Handbook of European Software Law*, Clarendon Press pp. 28–38 at pp. 28–9.

35  BGH, 14 July 1993. See Günther, A. and Wuermeling, U., 'Software Protection in Germany – Recent Court Decisions in Copyright Law' [1995] 11 CLSR 12.

36  Section 16. In *M S Associates Ltd v Power* [1988] FSR 242, there was an arguable case that substantial part of the original program for converting BASIC into C, had been copied. The second program had 43 line similarities out of a total of 9000 lines, although there were structural similarities and the same errors were present in both programs.

37  [1992] FSR 171.

COBOL program did not represent a substantial part of the program because it did not itself produce executable code or tell anything about the program. The data division in a COBOL program defines the nature and structure of files used by the program, and defines variables used. To many programmers, the data division is considered to be an important and essential part of the program and should certainly be considered to be worthy of protection, at the very least, as a non-literal element of the program. Fortunately, in *IBCOS Computers Ltd* v *Barclays Mercantile Highland Finance Ltd*,[38] Jacob J disagreed with Judge Paul Baker, and he said that there may be considerable skill involved in setting up the data division of a COBOL program such that it could be considered to be a substantial part of the program as a whole.[39] Judge Paul Baker's judgment is flawed in several other respects: for example, he said that the considerable steps taken to preserve confidentiality of the file details were suggestive that copyright did not subsist in that element of the program. This bizarre view is totally unfounded, either in legal principle or in policy, and is another aspect of the judgment in the *Total Information* case which Jacob J criticised.

In relation to literary works, 'copying' is defined by s 17 as a reproduction in any material form; this includes storage in any medium by electronic means and making copies which are transient or incidental to some other use of the work. Thus, loading a computer program (or, for that matter, any other form of work) into a computer's volatile memory (RAM) is copying.[40] That is why a licence is required to use a computer program, in contrast to most other forms of works for which use in private does not involve an act restricted by copyright. Because of the wide definition of 'electronic' in s 178 there should not be any difficulties concerning existing and future media in or on which a computer program is stored.

## Preparatory design material

The finished code of a computer program is the culmination of a long process involving the creation of a number of preparatory (and intermediate) works. For example, the analysts and programmers working on the development of a new program usually will produce specifications, flowcharts, diagrams, layouts for menus, screen displays, and reports and other materials. Prior to the amendments made to the Act by the Copyright (Computer Programs) Regulations 1992 in compliance with the computer program Directive, all these materials would have been protected in their own right as literary or artistic works as appropriate. In *Japan Capsules Computers (UK) Ltd* v *Sonic Game Sales*[41] Whitford J accepted that these and other ancillary materials, such as music generated by a program, could be protected by copyright.[42]

The separate protection of preparatory design material as a literary work by s 3(1)(c) conflicts with the wording of the Directive, which states that the term 'computer programs' shall *include* their preparatory design material.[43] In practice, this should not be troublesome, though it does mean that the special exceptions for computer programs (ss 50A–50C) do not apply to preparatory design material. For example, it is not permissible to make a back-up copy of a computer manual unless the other permitted acts generally available for literary works allow this. Why the 1992 Regulations chose to treat preparatory design material separately is inexplicable and unforgivable, given that certainty and

38 [1994] FSR 275.

39 *See also Autodesk Inc* v *Dyason* [1992] RPC 575, which concerned the copying of a hardware device (a 'lock') without which a particular program (AutoCAD) would not run. It was accepted that copying a table of codes contained in the program in the lock infringed copyright.

40 As it is also in the USA, *Advanced Computer Services of Michigan Inc* v *MIA Systems Corp* (unreported) 14 February 1994, discussed in [1994] CLSR 213.

41 (Unreported) 16 October 1986.

42 For a detailed discussion of this *see* Bainbridge, D. (1992) *Intellectual Property* (1st edn) Pitman Publishing, pp. 172–7.

43 Article 1(1) of the Directive on the legal protection of computer programs, OJ L122, 17.5.91, p. 42.

predictability are so important to the computer industry.[44] Preparatory design material will include works that would previously have been considered to be artistic works, such as flowcharts and other diagrams.[45] These are now literary works notwithstanding the resulting implications. For example, there is no requirement for an artistic work to be recorded, and infringement and the permitted acts are not precisely the same for literary and artistic works.

## LITERAL COPYING OF COMPUTER PROGRAMS

Copying of a computer program can be literal, where the program code itself is copied, in which case the two programs are written in the same computer programming language. Alternatively, copying can be non-literal, where elements of the program such as its structure, sequence of operations, functions, interfaces and methodologies are copied but the program code is not directly copied. The two programs may be written in the same language or in different computer programming languages. The law's recognition of non-literal copying is important because otherwise it would be too easy to defeat copyright protection of computer programs. Non-literal copying is considered later in this chapter. Literal copying occurs where a person copies an existing program by disk to disk copying (a duplicate is made onto another computer disk), or by writing out or printing the program listing, perhaps to key it into another computer at a later date. In either case, the person making the copy may make some alterations to the copy. These may be to disguise its origins or to enhance the program, for example, by adding some additional functions.

Literal copying is relatively easy to test for infringement. In essence, there are three axiomatic questions for the court. First, does copyright subsist in the plaintiff's program? Second, has the defendant copied from the plaintiff's program? Finally, does the part taken by the defendant represent a substantial part of the plaintiff's program? If the answer to these questions is in the affirmative then, unless the defendant has a defence or his actions fall within the permitted acts, infringement is proved. In practice, the answer to the first question will seldom be negative. Even relatively small programs will be the result of the programmer's skill, experience and judgment. The following case is the first to seriously consider the issues relating to literal copying of computer programs and lays down some important precedents for software copyright.

In *IBCOS Computers Ltd* v *Barclays Mercantile Highland Finance Ltd*,[46] the second defendant, a computer programmer called Mr Poole, wrote a suite of programs for accounts and payroll. He owned the copyright in the programs and eventually developed a Mk 3 version. Then, with another person, he set up a firm, PK Computer Services, to provide software for agricultural machinery dealers. When Mr Poole left the company, he signed a note recognising that the company owned all the rights in the software which contained the Mk 3 suite of programs. Mr Poole was then engaged by the first defendant to write similar software. Both suites of programs were written in variants of the same programming language and there was a degree of literal similarity between them. PK Computer Services transferred its assets to the plaintiff which learnt of Mr Poole's activities, obtained a 'door step *Piller*'[47] and sued for infringement of the copyright in its suite of computer programs.

44 *See* Chalton, S. 'Implementation of the Software Directive in the United Kingdom: The Effects of the Copyright (Computer Programs) Regulations 1992' [1993] 9 CLSR 115.

45 An electronic circuit diagram was held to be a literary work as well as an artistic work in *Anacon Corp Ltd* v *Environmental Research Technology Ltd* [1994] FSR 659.

46 [1994] FSR 275.

47 An order requiring the defendant to deliver up relevant materials, as opposed to an *Anton Piller* order which requires the defendant to allow the plaintiff to search his premises for evidence.

Jacob J held that there had been an infringement of the plaintiff's copyright. Not only were the individual programs protected by copyright, but also the suite of programs was protected as a compilation, being the result of sufficient skill and judgment (the plaintiff's computer software comprised 335 programs, 171 record layout files and 46 screen layouts). From the defendant's point of view, there were some unfortunate coincidences. Both suites of programs contained many common mistakes in the 'comment' lines (these are lines that are not executed by the computer and are inserted merely to make a program more easy to understand from the programmer's point of view). Both suites contained the same redundant code. In the mind of Jacob J, and in the absence of any plausible explanation from Mr Poole, this proved that there had been disk to disk copying.[48] Jacob J said that copying was a question of fact and could be proved by showing that something trivial or unimportant had been copied.

The issue of substantiality was considered and Jacob J stressed the importance of expert evidence in this respect. In the event, he decided that 28 out of 55 of the defendant's programs infringed the plaintiff's copyrights. He also found that a later version of the defendant's programs infringed (11 of the defendant's programs infringed and the copyright in the plaintiff's suite of programs as a compilation was also infringed). Furthermore, Mr Poole was in breach of confidence, the source code to the plaintiff's program being confidential. He had also signed a note when leaving PK Computer Services which contained a covenant in restraint of trade. However, Mr Poole was not in breach of the covenant which was construed narrowly by Jacob J.

Jacob J made a number of other interesting points which are set out below with comments:

- fresh copyright could be created when a program was modified. This is a question of whether sufficient skill, labour or judgment has been expended in making the modifications;
- a file record may not be a program within the Act, but it will be a compilation. Thus, the data division of a COBOL program may be protected by copyright acknowledging the work of designing the data structures used by the programs;
- the inclusion of functional elements that could be expressed in only one, or a limited number of ways, does not affect the fact of copyright subsistence;
- the *British Leyland* right to repair principle did not allow copying of a file transfer program. This is a program to convert the structure of a file so that it can be used with other software. However, the decompilation permitted act may allow the necessary information to be discovered to allow the independent writing of a file transfer program.[49]

The case gave Jacob J an opportunity to make a number of criticisms of previous cases. He pointed out that UK copyright law is not the same as US copyright law and questioned the appropriateness of US precedents which Ferris J had found so helpful in *John Richardson Computers Ltd v Flanders*.[50] The judgment in *IBCOS* is comprehensive and is to be welcomed for its realistic approach. Jacob J should be congratulated for his grasp of computer technology and for his application of copyright law to the facts. Of particular importance is the recognition of the work underlying the design of computer software, including the design of the data structures used and the skill and

48 Mr Poole had argued that the similarities were the result of programming style, but this failed to impress the judge.

49 The Copyright, Designs and Patents Act 1988 s 50B.

50 [1993] FSR 497, *see* post.

judgment in developing the overall structure of a suite of programs. However, his comments on non-literal copying and the use of US precedents (particularly in the *John Richardson* case) should be treated with caution. *IBCOS* and *John Richardson* are distinguishable, the former being primarily concerned with literal copying. Of course, US precedents can never be binding on the courts in the UK, but they should certainly be treated with due respect in this field where the US experience of litigation is much more extensive, after making due allowances for differences from UK law.

Merely being in possession of a disk on which a copy of a copyright work is recorded is not a restricted act, *per se*.[51] So it was held in *Ocular Sciences Ltd* v *Aspect Vision Care Ltd*[52] where evidence that a reference to the predecessor of the plaintiff in the program in question had been changed to a reference to the defendant proved that the program must have been saved at some time in its modified form and that act of storing infringed the copyright in the program.

### Indirect copying

It has already been seen that copyright law accepts the notion of indirect copying.[53] Does indirect copying apply to computer programs? Of course there must be copying, which in the *British Leyland* case was done through the medium of a finished exhaust pipe. But consider the position of a person who, having seen a computer program in operation, decides to write a new computer program to perform the same function as the original program. Does that person infringe the copyright subsisting in the original program or preparatory design material even though he has not seen a listing of the program itself or the preparatory materials? In three ways, the Act recognises that copyright can be infringed indirectly: first, by s 16(3)(b) it recognises that the acts restricted by copyright may be done indirectly; second, by s 16(3) the Act contemplates that a work may be infringed even though intervening acts do not infringe copyright; and, third, by s 17(6) the Act states that copying includes the making of copies which are transient or are incidental to some other use of the work. However, the program code in the second program would most likely be significantly different from that in the original, especially if it is written using a different programming language. For this reason, the District Court in *Digital Communications Associates* v *Softklone Distributing Corp*[54] held that the copyright in the underlying program was not infringed by copying a screen display generated by running the program.

## NON-LITERAL COPYING OF COMPUTER PROGRAMS

With some works of copyright, it is an easy matter to distinguish between the literal and non-literal elements. For example, with a work of literature, perhaps in the form of an historical novel, the literal element comprises the words, sentences and paragraphs as expressed in print, while the non-literal element can be said to consist of the detailed plot, sequence of events, characters and scenes. In some cases, the author of the novel will produce written materials or diagrams expressing these non-literal elements, in which case they may have their own copyright independent of the copyright subsisting in the finished novel.

51 It could be relevant to secondary infringement, however, such as where a person possesses an infringing copy in the course of business: s 23; or if he possesses an article specifically designed or adapted to make infringing copies: s 24(1), subject to the necessary knowledge.

52 [1997] RPC 289.

53 *See* Chapter 6, particularly the case of *British Leyland Motor Corp Ltd* v *Armstrong Patents Co Ltd* [1986] 2 WLR 400.

54 659 F Supp 449 (ND Ga 1987).

55 *See,* for example, *Corelli* v *Gray* [1913] TLR 570; *Glyn* v *Weston Feature Film* Co [1916] 1 Ch 261.

However, in the absence of such materials, it is clear that taking the non-literal elements can infringe.[55] One proviso is that at a certain stage of abstraction from the literal text of the work, the non-literal elements will be no more than mere idea, though determining the threshold between the protected and the unprotected is not an easy matter. As Lord Hailsham said in *LB (Plastics) Ltd* v *Swish Products Ltd*, after remarking that it is trite law that there is no copyright in ideas, 'But, of course, as the late Professor Joad used to observe, it all depends on what you mean by "ideas"'.[56]

56 [1979] RPC 551 at 629.

57 45 F 2d 119 (2nd Cir 1930).

Non-literal copying is not a problem restricted to computer programs, and the courts in the United States also have struggled to separate unprotectable ideas from protected expression, including non-literal elements. In *Nichols* v *Universal Pictures Co*[57] Judge Learned Hand recognised the importance of protecting non-literal elements of copyright works, saying (at 121):

> It is of course essential to any protection of literary property ... that the right cannot be limited literally to the text, else a plagiarist would escape by immaterial variations.

He then went on to discuss the various levels of abstraction, from the text to the most general statement of the play (possibly its title only), and the difficulty in determining where, along this spectrum of abstractions, the boundary between copyright and non-copyright material lay. Somewhat discouragingly, he then said 'Nobody has ever been able to fix that boundary and nobody ever can'. In other words, it must depend on the facts of each individual case.

58 For an argument that the law of passing off may provide some protection to computer programs, in particular screen displays, *see* Lea, G. 'Passing Off and the Protection of Program Look and Feel' [1994] 10 CLSR 82.

The same principles apply to computer programs. Copyright must not be limited to a comparison of the code of the original and alleged infringing programs. If that were so, copyright law would be easily defeated.[58] It would simply be a matter of re-writing the program in a different computer programming language or, provided changes are made to variable names, remark lines, line numbering etc., using the same programming language. In other words, it would be a simple matter to defeat copyright by making a duplicate of the original program to which a number of cosmetic alterations could be applied. The United States was the first in the field in developing tests for non-literal copying of computer programs, and before looking at the position in the UK it will be instructive to look at litigation in the US. Of course, US copyright law is not exactly the same as that in the UK, though there are many similarities and most of the basic principles are common. It should be noted that copyright law in both jurisdictions has a common ancestor, the Statute of Anne 1709.

## Developments in the United States of America

59 101 US 99 (1880).

If anything, the idea/expression dichotomy is even more ingrained in USA copyright law, going back at least to *Baker* v *Selden*[59] where it was held that copyright subsisting in a book describing a method of book-keeping did not extend to protect the method so described and illustrated. If copyright protects expression but not idea, it is obviously important for a court to be able to distinguish between them, particularly where the law gives protection to certain non-literal elements of copyright works. However, US law goes further than that in the UK in denying protection to tangible form if it is deemed to be so closely associated with the idea underlying the work that there is no alternative way of expressing it. Hence, it is even more important in the United States to distinguish between protected expression and unprotected idea.

This issue was considered in the context of computer programs in the case of *Whelan Associates Inc v Jaslow Dental Laboratory Inc*,[60] the first so-called 'look and feel' case. It was said that, in relation to a computer program designed to carry out a mundane task (running dental laboratories in that case), anything that was essential to the task was 'idea' while anything that was not essential and could have been written in different ways was 'expression'. If these latter parts were copied, then the copyright would be infringed because the expression had been copied. If the programmer had no option but to write a part of the program the way he did because the task to be achieved dictated its form and content then that part was 'idea' and not protected by copyright. Similarly, the purpose of a utilitarian program was 'idea' and the structure of the program, if there were several different possible structures that could have been adopted, was 'expression'. Consequently, not just the actual program code but the structure of a computer program can be protected by copyright if, because of similar structure, the 'look and feel' of the programs are similar.

*Whelan* was considered in numerous later cases. In *Plains Cotton Cooperative v Goodpasture Computer Service*,[61] an apparent rejection of the *Whelan* case can be explained by concluding that the structure of the plaintiff's program was 'idea' and not 'expression' because the application itself dictated the structure of the program. The program's application was to assist in the marketing of cotton and this, by its very nature, could be expressed only in computer programs exhibiting a substantially similar structure; it left no room for alternative structures.[62] Other cases have dealt with screen displays. In *Broderbund Software v Unison World*,[63] the court held that, as there were several means by which the screens could have been structured, sequenced and arranged, the actual way selected by the plaintiff was copyrightable expression.[64] The court also appears to have confirmed that copying the format, structure and sequence of screen displays infringes the copyright in the underlying programs. However, in *Digital Communications Associates v Softklone Distributing Corp*[65] this view was rejected on the basis that a screen display cannot be a copy of part of the program because the same screen display can be produced by various programs in different ways. Nevertheless, the court did afford protection to the screen display in its own right, and differentiated between 'idea' and 'expression' by regarding the idea of a screen display as being the concept of the screen, whereas the means used to communicate the screen's manner of operation, that is, the arrangement of terms, highlighting and capitalisation, was the expression of the screen display.[66]

## Spreadsheets

A spreadsheet program is, in essence, one which comprises a grid of cells (usually two-dimensional, but three-dimensional grids now exist) into which the user can enter text, numbers and/or formulae. A spreadsheet is useful for preparing an easily updated table of calculations from which graphs and bar-charts can be derived. Non-literal elements of spreadsheet software include its menu system, by which the user interacts with the spreadsheet, and the system for denoting cell references, for example, C7, H21, etc.

60 [1987] FSR 1.

61 807 F 2d 1256 (5th Cir 1987).

62 For an argument that *Plains Cotton* is not inconsistent with *Whelan, see* Taylor, W.D. 'Copyright Protection for Computer Softwar after *Whelan Associates v Jaslow Dental Laboratory*' (1989) 54 *Missouri Law Review* 121.

63 648 F Supp 1127 (ND Cal 1986).

64 The argument by the defendant that there was no other way to structure the screens or design the input formats was quickly overcome by the plaintiff who produced another competing program which performed a similar function (to design greetings cards, signs, banners and posters) but which had screen displays and screen sequences that were very different. Taylor, W.D., *op cit,* at 151.

65 659 F Supp 449 (ND Ga 1987).

66 Some commentators argue for strong copyright protection of screen displays subject to a higher standard of originality. *See* Benson, J.R. 'Copyright Protection for Computer Screen Displays' (1988) 72 *Minnesota Law Review* 1123.

**67** 740 F Supp 37 (D Mass 1990).

**68** A 'macro' is a list of commands that are stored in a separate executable file. The purpose usually is to save time. For example, the user might want to combine several spreadsheets, total them, find the average and change the display format and, rather than having to enter a whole series of commands each time he wants to do this, he can store the instructions in a macro which he can call up and execute in the future at a keystroke. The command language of VP-Planner would have to be the same as that in Lotus 1-2-3 for macros to be compatible.

**69** At the beginning of 1991, in the United Kingdom, Lotus 1-2-3 was available at around £200–£300 (depending on the version) while VP-Planner was available (for educational use only) at around £8. It must be noted that this version of VP-Planner had a limited overall spreadsheet size compared to Lotus 1-2-3.

**70** For example, *Shipman* v *RKO Radio Pictures* 100 F 2d 533(2d Cir 1938).

**71** [1997] FSR 61. Lotus claimed the Borland's Quattro spreadsheet infringed the copyright in the Lotus 1-2-3 menu system.

In *Lotus Development Corp* v *Paperback Software International*[67] the defendant had developed a spreadsheet program called VP-Planner. The defendant had realised that, because of the success of the plaintiff's famous Lotus 1-2-3 spreadsheet program, it was desirable that VP-Planner was compatible with Lotus 1-2-3. To this end, the defendant ensured that the arrangement of commands and menus in VP-Planner conformed to those in Lotus 1-2-3, and this meant that it was possible to transfer spreadsheets from VP-Planner to Lotus 1-2-3 without losing the functionality of any macros in the spreadsheet.[68] Another reason for compatibility and similarity in screen displays and command language was that Lotus 1-2-3 users could transfer to VP-Planner without the need for any further training. When the difference in cost between the two spreadsheets is considered, it is not surprising that Lotus sued the owners of VP-Planner.[69] The defendant claimed that he had not copied the program code of Lotus 1-2-3, so this was a case of 'non-literal copying'. The central issues, therefore, were whether the non-literal elements of the plaintiff's program were protected by copyright, that is the overall organisation of the program (structure), the structure of the command system, the screen displays and, especially, the user interface.

Judge Keeton held that the user interface of Lotus 1-2-3, in particular the two-line moving cursor menu, was protected by copyright and that the defendant had infringed that copyright. The menu command system was said to be copyrightable because it was effected in different ways in different spreadsheet programs. For example, some use a list of letters (Visicalc uses 'BCDEFGIMPRSTVW-'), others use a three-line menu or pull-down menus. The two-line moving cursor menu used by Lotus 1-2-3 was said to be original and non-obvious and, thus, protected by copyright. Other features such as the rotated 'L' used to contain the grid reference letters and numbers, and the use of certain keys to call up commands and perform arithmetical functions, for example the '/,' '+,' '-' and '*' keys, were held not to be protected because they were common to spreadsheets, even though they were not essential.

It was accepted by the judge that disentangling idea from expression was not an 'either/or' or 'black and white' matter but a matter of degree, and a distinction must be made between the generality and specificity of conceptualising an idea. A legal test for copyrightability was suggested based on constructing a scale of abstraction from the most generalised conception at one end to the most particularised conception at the other end. The expression being considered was placed on this scale and a decision made based on choice and judgment, but earlier judgments by Judge Learned Hand had suggested that this could be done only in an *ad hoc* way.[70]

Useful as Judge Keeton's judgment is in terms of non-literal copying generally, it has been overturned in *Lotus Development Corp* v *Borland International Inc*[71] by the First Circuit Court of Appeals. However, the reason was not so much connected with any disagreement with the way of testing for idea or expression, but a direct consequence of the United States Copyright Act s 102(b) which denies copyright protection to '... any idea, procedure, process, system, *method of operation*, concept, principle or discovery ...' (emphasis added). It was held by the First Circuit Court of Appeals that the menu system of Lotus 1-2-3 was a method of operation and, hence, not protected by copyright. This decision has serious implications for the computer industry in that it effectively puts user interfaces into the public domain. The subsequent appeal to the Supreme Court was unsatisfactory in that, whilst the decision of the Court of Appeals was affirmed, it was the result of a split decision and, in such cases, the Supreme Court gives no substantive judgment.[72] The reasoning of the Court of Appeals therefore stands.[73]

Certainly, *Lotus v Borland* goes much further than any case in the UK has ventured or is likely to do in the near future.[74] On the one hand, it can be said to be a liberating influence, facilitating the development of compatible interfaces, but, on the other hand, it could rob the designer of a new interface technique of any real protection from copying. The World Intellectual Property Organisation Copyright Treaty states in Article 2 that copyright protection extends to expression and not ideas, procedures, methods of operation or mathematical concepts as such.[75] Similar exceptions to protection are also present in European Directives, for example, in the Directive on the legal protection of computer programs, Article 1(2) states that ideas and principles which underlie any element of a computer program, including those which underlie its interfaces, are not protected by copyright under the Directive.[76]

### A new test for non-literal copying

*Whelan* and subsequent cases can be explained by the need to deal with non-literal copying of computer programs, where the first program has been unfairly used as a basis for a second program but there is no literal similarity in the actual program code because different programming languages have been used. Although the *Whelan* test proved troublesome to apply in practice, it has been superseded by a more sophisticated test which still does nothing to aid predictability. The New York Court of Appeals strongly criticised *Whelan* in *Computer Associates International Inc v Altai Inc*[77] as taking insufficient account of computer technology. In *Computer Associates*, the defendant had produced a program known as 'Oscar', a job scheduling program for controlling the order in which tasks were carried out by a computer. It had a common interface component allowing the use of different operating systems, and this part had been added by a former employee of the plaintiff which had a similar program and interface. The former employee was very familiar with the plaintiff's program and had even taken parts home to work on. As soon as the defendant company realised the problem, it agreed to pay $364 444 in damages and engaged other programmers to re-write the infringing parts of its program. The plaintiff still sued in respect of the defendant's new version, but the judge held there was no infringement. The judgment of the court was given by Judge Walker, who laid down a new three-stage test for non-literal copying as follows and as shown in Figure 8.1.

1 *Abstraction* – discovering the non-literal elements by a process akin to reverse engineering, beginning with the code of the plaintiff's program and ending with its ultimate function. This process retraces and maps out the designer's steps and produces, *inter alia*, structures of differing detail at varying levels of abstraction.

72 *See* footnote in [1997] FSR 61 and *Computing*, 25 January 1996, p. 8.

73 Some earlier judgments based on *Lotus v Paperback*, such as *Autoskill Inc v National Education Support Systems Inc* (1993) 994 F 2d 1476 (10th Cir) on the use of a keying procedure using the 1, 2 and 3 keys and *Brown Bag Software v Symantec Corp* (1992) F 2d 1465 (9th Cir), suggesting menus and keystrokes could be protected by copyright, must be viewed with some suspicion.

74 In the United Kingdom, program interfaces may be determined by decompilation, but it is at least arguable that user interfaces are protected, see *John Richardson Computers Ltd v Flanders* [1993] FSR 497, discussed post.

75 Geneva, 2–20 December 1996.

76 OJ L122 17.5.91, p. 42. See also the Copyright, Designs and Patents Act s 296A(1)(c), discussed later in this chapter.

77 (1992) 20 USPQ 2d 1641.

sys. that runs the program

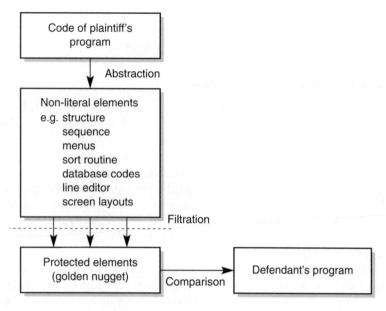

**Figure 8.1  Test for non-literal copying**

2 *Filtration* – the separation of protectable expression from non-protectable expression material. Some elements will not be protected being ideas, dictated by or incidental to ideas, required by external factors (*scènes a faire* doctrine) or taken from the public domain. These elements are filtered out leaving a core of protectable material – the program's 'golden nugget'.

3 *Comparison* – a determination of whether the defendant has copied a substantial part of the protected expression – whether any aspect has been copied and, if so, whether this represents a substantial part of the plaintiff's program.

The judge recognised that the test will be difficult to apply, but expressed the hope that it would become less so with further case law.[78] At first sight, it seems significantly to weaken copyright protection for computer programs. Many programs contain parts taken from the public domain (such as commonly used routines to extract data from files, to perform complex arithmetical operations or to sort data into alphabetical order) and other parts will be significantly constrained by ideas or external factors. It would appear that, in some cases, there will be no golden nuggets left after filtration. The plaintiff's gold prospecting will result in bitter disappointment!

### Merger of idea/expression

There may be occasions when it is impossible to separate idea from expression because of the constraints which severely limit the ways in which the ideas contained in a computer program can be expressed. In *NEC Corp* v *Intel Corp*,[79] such merger of idea and expression was said not to affect the copyright status of a computer program but was an issue of infringement. Even though Intel's microcode programs were declared to be copyrightable material in principle, this case reinforces the look and feel approach in its practical effect because, as

[78] It has been used subsequently. *See*, for example, *The Gates Rubber Co* v *Bando Chemical Industries Ltd* (unreported) 19 October 1993, 10th Circuit Court of Appeals, discussed in [1994] 10 CLSR 101.

[79] (1989) 10 USPQ 2d.

Intel's programs were dictated by the instruction set of the microprocessors involved and because there were no alternative ways of expressing the ideas, reverse analysis of the programs did not infringe copyright.[80]

## Non-literal copying in the United Kingdom

*John Richardson Computers Ltd* v *Flanders*[81] is the first case in the UK to fully address the look and feel of computer programs and is exceptional in that the test used in the USA for non-literal copying was expressly approved and applied, at least in part, by Ferris J in a comprehensive judgment. Both parties were in the business of developing and marketing computer programs to be used by pharmacists for the purpose of producing labels for prescriptions and for stock control. The judge found the facts of the case difficult to determine (there were a number of disputed points) and the case provides a good example of the need to document the development of copyright works carefully and to make suitable arrangements for ownership.[82]

Mr Richardson, the chairman and managing director of the plaintiff company, who was a pharmacist and self-taught computer programmer, developed a program written in BASIC to produce labels suitable for the Tandy computer. He was not an expert at writing programs and he, therefore, engaged a self-employed programmer to help complete the program and make it more reliable. In 1983, Mr Flanders joined the plaintiff company as an employee to write an equivalent program in machine code that would have the same look and feel as the original program for the BBC computer. In 1986, Mr Flanders left the employment of the plaintiff company, but did further work for it as a self-employed consultant, during which time he re-wrote the program in assembly language, a low-level language, adding some new features. Later, Mr Flanders wrote a new version of the program (in the Quick*BASIC* language) for the *IBM* personal computer. The plaintiff was also working on a version for the *IBM* computer and sued for infringement of its copyright in the *BBC* version of the program and for breach of confidence.[83]

The general approach in the *Computer Associates* case attracted Ferris J, who remarked that there was nothing in any English decision which conflicted with it. However, rather than seeking the 'core of protectable expression', an English court would first decide whether the plaintiff's program as a whole was subject to copyright and then decide whether any similarity in the defendant's program was the result of copying a substantial part of the plaintiff's program. In particular, Ferris J directed his attention to the non-literal elements of the programs, finding *Computer Associates* helpful in separating idea from expression.

In the event, Ferris J held that there was a limited infringement of the copyright subsisting in the plaintiff's program based on the non-literal elements of the program. A literal comparison was not helpful as both programs had been written in different languages and bore no literal similarity. He identified 17 objective similarities in the non-literal elements and then went on to consider the reasons for the similarities. The similarities and the reasons for them were classified as follows:

1 Similarities that were the result of copying a substantial part of the plaintiff's program, being the line editor, amendment routines and dose codes. It was in respect of these parts that copyright infringement was found.

80 This should be compared to the Australian case of *Autodesk Inc* v *Dyason* (unreported), Federal Court of Australia, 7 August 1989, in which the reverse analysis of a computer lock (a hardware device, sometimes called a 'dongle', which must be plugged into the computer before a particular computer program can be used) was held to infringe copyright in the computer program contained within the lock. *See* Glodblatt, M. 'Copyright Protection for Computer Programs in Australia: the Law since Autodesk' [1990] 5 EIPR 170. On appeal, the *Autodesk* decision was reversed, *see* Anon, 'Appellate Court gives Green Light to Reverse Engineering' (1991) 2 *Intellectual Property in Business Briefing* 3. However, finally in *Autodesk Inc* v *Dyason* [1992] RPC 575 the High Court of Australia reinstated the decision at first instance.

81 [1992] FSR 497.

82 The defendant may have been the legal owner of the copyright in parts of the program. The plaintiff was the owner in equity of that copyright and the difficulty beneficial owners can experience in obtaining remedies was overcome here because the legal owner was joined in the action – as defendant.

83 The breach of confidence claim was dropped.

2 Similarities that were the result of copying, but not in relation to a substantial part of the plaintiff's program. These were the date option, daily figures reset, operation successful message plus double bleep, data entry by quantity first, four out of eight of the pre-printing options and best day's stock control.

3 Similarities that *might* have been the result of copying but, in any case, related only to an insubstantial part of the plaintiff's program. These were the vertical arrangement of prompts and entries and the entry of data within the label routine.

4 Similarities that were not the result of copying, being the date entry, use of the escape key, position of label on screen, drug entry routine, secondary access to the full list of drugs on screen and label entry sequence.

The line editor, amendment routines and dose codes were deemed to have been copied and to represent a substantial part of the plaintiff's program. This approach affects the test of substantiality which has long been accepted as being a question of quality not quantity.[84] As adopted by Ferris J, it implies that relatively trivial elements of a program could be used in the comparison process. The manner of Ferris J's application of the test from *Computer Associates* can be criticised because he did not carry out the second stage.[85] He did not filter out those elements that might have been unprotected, such as ideas or public domain routines. Essentially, the only significant use he made of the *Computer Associates* case was in his acceptance that non-literal elements of computer programs may be protected by copyright. He did not need to rely on United States precedents to do this. In the *IBCOS* case, Jacob J criticised the use of US precedents, but agreed with Ferris J that consideration must not be restricted to the actual code of the programs in question.

A concern remains with the judgment of Ferris J in that it may result in the protection of relatively trivial and mundane parts of computer programs. It should be noted that the programs in *Richardson* were by no means exceptional. They performed relatively simple functions. Additionally, both programs made substantial use of what might be termed public domain materials, or at least techniques and methods commonly used by programmers. For example, there is a limited number of ways to correct mistakes using a line editor and these are dictated to some extent by the programming language used and other features relating to the type of computer used and its operating system. It is common for standard routines to perform commonly required operations like line editing to be published in textbooks, computer journals and magazines.[86] Even if a line editor could be considered to be protectable expression, there is no doubt that, in terms of the program's function, it could never be said to form a substantial part of the program. Nevertheless, that is what the judge found.

The consideration of a program as a collection of disparate and relatively small and discrete non-literal elements could make it very difficult for ex-employees to write computer programs that perform functions similar to those performed by programs they have written for their previous employers. In this respect, copyright could now become so strong that it operates as a form of restraint of trade. It is also out of step with the law of breach of confidence which is relatively benign as regards mundane information and which generally will permit an employee to make use of what he remembers as long as he does not copy, provided the information concerned is not a trade secret.[87] Computer programs designed to perform mundane functions such as producing labels for pharmacists and handling stock control can hardly be classed as trade secrets.[88]

84 *Ladbroke (Football) Ltd* v *William Hill (Football) Ltd* [1964] 1 WLR 273.

85 In fairness to Ferris J, he did not profess to follow the *Computer Associates* test precisely.

86 However, some of the features in the plaintiff's program were described by Ferris J as idiosyncratic.

87 The position is best summarised by Neill LJ in *Faccenda Chicken Ltd v Fowler* [1986] 1 All ER 617.

88 The phrase 'trade secret' lacks precise definition but has been considered in *Lansing Linde Ltd v Kerr* [1991] 1 WLR 251. *See also* Coleman, A. (1992) *The Legal Protection of Trade Secrets*, Sweet & Maxwell, at pp. 4–28.

## The idea/expression merger doctrine

The idea/expression merger doctrine takes on a different significance in the context of UK copyright law. In a case of suspected non-literal copying, the person who wrote the alleged copy is simply likely to deny that he copied, and both the look and feel test and the merger doctrine become important in an evidential sense. The question that falls to be resolved is whether the defendant copied a substantial part of the original computer program. If the look and feel of the two programs are similar, the fact that there are several different ways in which the program could have been written is persuasive evidence that there has been copying; while the fact that because the function dictates the program code or structure there is only one way the program could have been written, significantly weakens the claim that there has been, in fact, copying. Of course, other factors may be relevant, such as whether the defendant had access to the plaintiff's program. Nevertheless, as current UK copyright law declares without *caveat* that copyright subsists in original computer programs and the fact that one of the acts restricted by the copyright is copying a substantial part of a program, even copying a program or significant part of a program which is dictated by function will infringe copyright. On the other hand, two independently created programs may be similar because function dictates the program (or simply because of coincidence) and there will be no infringement of copyright. In *Total Information Processing Systems Ltd v Daman Ltd*[89] it was accepted that where there is only one way of expressing an idea, the idea and expression merged and were not the subject of copyright.[90] But this is to confuse the question of subsistence with evidence of copying. In *Kenrick v Lawrence*[91] it was said that a duplicate copy of a simple drawing would infringe.

## Limits of look and feel

Perhaps the original program is simply altered in an attempt to disguise its origins or to improve it. Nevertheless, the question of copying still arises, as opposed to adaptation which has a precise legal meaning in terms of computer programs. In many cases, the two programs will be similar enough to raise a presumption of copying, which can shift the burden of proof, as already discussed. But if the alterations are numerous, it may be more difficult to draw this conclusion. It is a relatively simple matter to change constituent parts of a program, for example the screen displays, the names given to variables used in the program and the line numbering. If this is done, a line for line similarity between the two programs will be obscured. If the changes are merely cosmetic, it will still be possible to use a test of objective similarity based on the structure of the programs, for example whether the flow of the program and the relative positioning of its constituent parts are similar. But even here, a determined programmer can rearrange the parts of the program to defeat this test.

Even more difficult is the situation where the new program is written using a totally different programming technique, using software tools and languages that are fundamentally different from those used to create the original program. In particular, the use of 'fourth generation' languages is relevant to this discussion as they are dissimilar to the older, more traditional programming languages, such as *BASIC* and *COBOL*, in a way that goes beyond mere syntax.

89 [1992] FSR 171.

90 Disapproved of by Jacob J in *IBCOS Computers Ltd v Barclays Mercantile Highland Finance Ltd* [1994] FSR 275.

91 (1890) 25 QBD 99.

A program written in a traditional programming language is written subroutine by subroutine and line by line. A fourth generation language is effectively a tool which automates the process of developing a computer system to a great extent. It is like a shell into which the developer specifies attributes of the required system, such as the structure of database files and the operations to be carried out by the finished system. The file-handling and other operations are then performed by the fourth generation system itself.

In *Computer-Aided Systems (UK) Ltd* v *Bolwell*,[92] some of the plaintiff's ex-employees devised a computer program using a fourth generation language to carry out a similar function to the programs they had written in *COBOL* for the plaintiff. The *Whelan* case was cited as authority for the notion that the structure of a computer program was a form of literary expression protected by copyright. However, Hoffmann J did not believe that a seriously triable issue was raised on the questions of copying or the misuse of confidential information. The plaintiff had argued that the output formats and input layouts of the two computer programs would be very similar, especially as the defendants had designed the new system so that it was compatible with the plaintiff's system. The defendants had refused to allow the plaintiff to inspect their program, but it would be highly unlikely that there would be a sufficient similarity in the programs to infer that copying had taken place because of the conceptually different nature of the languages used. Even the structure of the programs would be different.[93] The only plausible similarity might have been in the structure of the databases used by the systems because of the efforts to achieve compatibility in this respect. However, Hoffmann J expressed the opinion that the plaintiff's application for inspection of the defendants' program was little more than a 'fishing expedition' and he refused the application. This decision seems eminently sensible in the context of restraint of trade; after all, computer programmers and analysts should be free to exercise their skill and knowledge for other employers subject to copyright and limited confidentiality issues.[94] However, the potentially wide scope of adaptation may catch even the change from a traditional programming language to a fourth generation language.

## MAKING AN ADAPTATION

The second act restricted by copyright which is highly relevant to computer programs is that of making an adaptation. An adaptation of a computer program is defined by s 21(3)(ab) of the 1988 Act as an arrangement or altered version of the program or a translation of it. For computer programs, a translation includes (by s 21(4)):

> ... a version of the program in which it is converted into or out of a computer language or code or into a different computer language or code[, otherwise than incidentally in the course of running the program].[95]

To understand fully the legal issues concerning this definition, it is important that the basic meaning of some computer terms is understood, and the definitions given in the Glossary at the beginning of the book should be referred to again. The following definitions should also be noted. *Compiling* a computer program means converting a high-level language source code program into

92 (Unreported) 23 August 1989, Chancery Division.

93 It is not really appropriate to talk of computer systems developed using fourth generation languages (4GLs) as computer programs. 4GLs are more akin to system development tools. The 4GL provides a set of all-purpose computer programs and the system designer develops a set of specifications concerning file structures, calculations and reports which the programs incorporate to produce the finished system.

94 For example, in the South African case of *Northern Office Micro Computers (Pty) Ltd* v *Rosenstein* [1982] FSR 124 where it was held, *inter alia*, that an ex-employee would not have to 'wipe the slate of his mind clean'. *See also Printers and Finishers Ltd* v *Holloway* [1965] RPC 239.

95 The words in brackets were repealed by the Copyright (Computer Programs) Regulations 1992, SI 1992/3233.

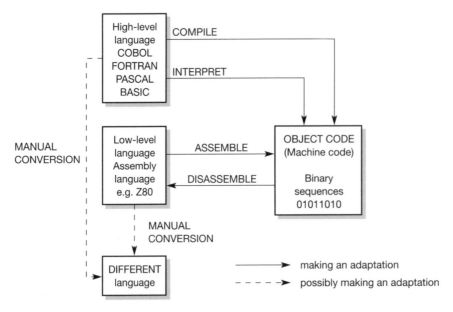

**Figure 8.2 Making an adaptation in relation to a computer program**

object code, being the machine code that can be directly understood by the computer. A permanent version of the program in object code is created which can then be operated without the source code version. This must be contrasted with *interpreting*, a process by which a high-level source code computer program is temporarily converted, line by line, into object code during the operation of the program. This is not as efficient as running a compiled version of the program. *Assembling* a computer program means converting a low-level assembly language program into object code. The process of *disassembly* produces assembly language from an object code version of a computer program. Disassembly unlocks the ideas and techniques contained in the object code version of the program.

What, then, in the context of making an adaptation, does this mean? Figure 8.2 shows the relevant acts that can be done in relation to a computer program. Suppose that a computer program has been written, either in a high-level programming language such as *BASIC* or in a low-level language such as Z80 assembly language.[96] The legal meaning of 'making an adaptation' would certainly seem to cover the act of compiling or assembling the computer program. If the object code version of a program, produced by compiling or assembling a source code program, is later disassembled, to derive an assembly language version, that too falls within the meaning of making an adaptation.

Now that an adaptation includes an arrangement or altered version of a program, this should cover the situation where a program is manually rewritten in a different computer programming language. The meaning of 'translation' may also extend to a manual translation. There seems to be no reason why translating a computer program cannot be done manually by using a knowledge of grammatical rules and a dictionary of commands and functions. This is highly analogous to translating a work of literature from one natural language into another which is, of course, making an adaptation.

96 Not all computer programming languages are capable of being operated in interpreted form.

## PERMITTED ACTS IN RELATION TO COMPUTER PROGRAMS

In terms of the permitted acts under copyright law, computer technology may be indirectly relevant in many cases. For example, as a computer program is a literary work, all the provisions affecting literary works apply to computer programs, unless the contrary is stated. For example, a teacher can write a listing of part of a computer program on a blackboard for the purposes of instruction. (Obtaining the listing in the first place might, however, infringe.) A design document includes data stored in a computer for the purposes of s 51 which effectively suppresses copyright in design documents where an article is made to a design.

Although the main purpose of the Directive on the legal protection of computer programs,[97] in pursuance of which the regulations were passed, was the harmonisation of copyright protection for computer programs, the aspect that stimulated a most heated debate and controversy was the 'decompilation right'.[98] This is a permitted act under copyright which allows lawful users of computer programs to reverse engineer other computer programs for the purpose of achieving 'interoperability' with that or another program. In other words, it allows the act of converting a computer program (the target program) into a form easier to understand (expressed in a higher level language) so that details of its interfaces can be discovered enabling the new program to be compatible with the target program or any other program. Prior to the amendments made by the Copyright (Computer Programs) Regulations 1992,[99] the most important permitted act in terms of achieving the same result was undoubtedly fair dealing for the purposes of research or private study, s 29. It has been seen in Chapter 7 that the scope of this provision is difficult to predict, but it was possible that it would extend to the type of situation mentioned above. Indeed, this seems to be the case in the United States, where the equivalent act of fair use has been relied on successfully to allow reverse engineering of computer programs to discover details of interfaces.[100]

The Directive provided for other specific exceptions to copyright infringement. These have been included in the Copyright, Designs and Patents Act 1988 (amended by the 1992 Regulations) and came into force on 1 January 1993. They are all subject to conditions. Altogether, the special permitted acts for computer programs are:

- decompilation of computer programs
- making back-up copies of computer programs
- making copies or adaptations of computer programs.

New ss 50A–50C are inserted into the Copyright, Designs and Patents Act 1988 under the heading 'Computer programs: lawful users'. These exceptions to infringement apply only to acts done by lawful users of computer programs.

A further 'permitted act' is buried deep in the Act in s 296A(1)(c). This makes void any term in an agreement under which a person has the use of a computer program which purports to prohibit or restrict the use of any device or means to observe, study or test the functioning of the program in order to understand the ideas and principles which underlie any element of the computer program.

97 OJ, L122, 17.5.91, p. 42.

98 Strictly speaking, this is not a right but an exception to infringement.

99 SI 1992/3233.

100 *Sega Enterprises Ltd v Accolade Inc* (1992) 977 F 2d 1510.

### Lawful users

Although the Directive uses the terms 'licensed user', 'person having the right to use' and 'lawful acquirer', depending on the exception concerned, the Act as amended uses the term 'lawful user' for all three exceptions. A lawful user is under s 50A(2):

> a person who has a right to use the program, whether under a licence to do any acts restricted by the copyright subsisting in the program or otherwise.

This will extend to licensees and, presumably, to persons acting for the licensee such as employees. Unless prohibited by the licence agreement, it should also apply to agents and independent consultants working for the licensee and to many other persons, such as students in respect of a site licence granted to an educational establishment or voluntary workers for a charity that has an institutional licence. Others, too, could fall within the definition of 'lawful user'. It may include a receiver of a company, an external auditor or anyone acting in pursuance of a legal requirement (for example, a policeman executing a search warrant or a solicitor executing an *Anton Piller* order).

The addition of the words 'or otherwise' should cause the copyright owner to consider carefully how to exploit the program. For example, it could apply to a person who has obtained a copy of a program by rental or loan. A person who has been given a copy of a program for evaluation purposes should also fall within this category. Of course, if a copy has been made in accordance with the exceptions, at the end of the rental or loan period when the right to use the program ceases, subsequent use will infringe copyright. However, the retained copy will not be an infringing copy because s 27 was not amended to cover this possibility.[101] Selling that copy will not, therefore, be a secondary infringement of copyright.[102] This does not apply where the arrangement by which the person concerned obtained the copy falls within the meaning of s 56 (where a copy of a work in electronic form has been purchased) because any retained copies are treated as infringing copies.[103]

### Decompilation of computer programs

The decompilation right[104] allows (subject to certain conditions) a lawful user of a copy of a computer program expressed in a low-level language:

(a) to convert it into a version expressed in a higher level language, or
(b) incidentally, in the course of so converting the program, to copy it.[105]

While it is up to the legislatures of individual member states to choose their own form of wording to give effect to a Directive, the differences between the language of the modifications made by the regulations and that of the Directive, which is expressed in terms of reproduction of the code and translation of its form, a much wider rubric, are unfortunate. The Directive does not use the terms 'low-level language' and 'high-level language', nor are they defined in the Act. Although someone wanting to gain access to information about the program's algorithm or its detailed workings would almost certainly want to convert from a low-level language version to a higher-level language version, the Directive is more generous, allowing translation, adaptation, arrangement or alteration. The 'decompilation right' as enacted does not expressly cover the conversion of a binary object code program into hexadecimal code, something which is commonly known as per-

**101** The Copyright, Designs and Patents Act 1988 s 27(6) includes as infringing copies any copies made in pursuance of some of the permitted acts but that are subsequently dealt with. The omission of copies made in pursuance of ss 50A–50C is clearly an oversight.

**102** The primary infringement of issuing to the public could apply in some cases: ibid s 18.

**103** It is not clear that this could apply in any case because 'purchase' is not the same as obtaining a copy under a licence. This provision may be more appropriate in terms of sound and video recordings.

**104** So described in the Directive (Article 6) and in the marginal note to the Copyright, Designs and Patents Act 1988 s 50B, though it is an exception to infringement and not a right as such.

**105** Ibid s 50B (inserted by reg 8).

forming a 'hex dump', as there is no higher level language involved at that stage. This would be within the exception as expressed in the Directive.[106]

The conditions that must apply for decompilation to be permitted by s 50B of the 1988 Act are stated in s 50B(2) and are that:

(a) it is necessary to decompile the program to obtain the information necessary to create an independent program which can be operated with the program decompiled or with another program ('the permitted objective'), and

(b) the information so obtained is not used for any purpose other than the permitted objective.

The purpose of decompilation is to obtain, typically, interface details. For example, Ace Software may wish to develop a new word processing program. Ace will need to know details of various computer operating systems (these systems are a collection of computer programs) so that it can work in the computer's operating environment. Ace must determine how the operating system uses the computer's memory so that its new program can run properly. Also, to stand any chance of being successful, the new program must be compatible with existing programs. Ace's new program must be able to accept (import) word processed files produced using other word processing programs (and export them in the appropriate format); it would be even better if Ace's new program could accept files from other types of program such as a spreadsheet program or a graphics program. Hence the need for this interface information. Not only does the exception allow decompilation for the purpose of creating a new compatible program (for example, a new word processing program that is compatible with an existing spreadsheet program), it also allows, in principle, the creation of new competing programs (for example, a new word processing program that can import and export files from and to an existing word processing program). Figure 8.3 shows the concept of interoperability.

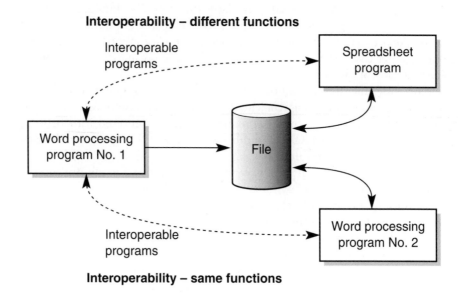

**Figure 8.3 Interoperability of computer programs**

219

The decompilation permitted act, in essence, gives a 'right' to information concerning interfaces so that interoperability can be achieved. It does not give a right to take the interface itself. For example, if an interface is expressed in a number of lines of computer code, that code, provided that it meets the requirements for copyright protection (and that it represents a substantial part of the program or is itself deemed to be a computer program), may not be copied because of this permitted act. Thus, taking a copy of a compression table, used to compress data so as to occupy less storage space, for the purposes of file compatability was deemed to infringe in *Powerflex* v *Data Access Corp.*[107] This is confirmed by s 50B(3)(d) which states that the permitted act does not apply, *inter alia*, where the information is used to do any act restricted by copyright. Once the information is acquired by the process of decompilation, any interface code written must be done so as not to infringe copyright. This may be difficult in the extreme when the interface detail is in the form of a protocol and no design freedom is permissible.[108] It may be that in such circumstances the courts may be prepared to excuse infringement on policy grounds, otherwise the decompilation permitted act would be defeated. However, it is far from certain that the courts would so decide, given their reluctance to override a statutory provision.

The conditions cannot be met if the lawful user has readily available to him the information necessary to achieve the permitted objective, or if he does not confine the act of decompiling to that objective, if he supplies the information to any person to whom it is not necessary to supply it in order to achieve that objective, or if he uses the information to create a program which is substantially similar in its expression to the decompiled program, or to do any act restricted by copyright.[109] Most of these conditions are reasonable, and indeed the last two are probably redundant in most cases. However, it is what constitutes having the information readily available that could be difficult. Of course, the first step that a person who requires interface details of another's program should take is to ask for those details. Sometimes, the information may be freely given. In other cases, it may even be published in documentation accompanying a licensed copy of the program.

Importantly, the 'decompilation right' cannot be prohibited or restricted by any term or condition in an agreement.[110] Any term in a licence agreement purporting to do this is void, unless the agreement was entered into before 1 January 1993.[111] A considerable number of standard form software licences have been amended as a result of this.

Apart from the decompilation exception, fair dealing for the purposes of research or private study still exists in relation to computer programs.[112] Therefore, it may be permissible for a person to list, copy, inspect and study a program in use for the purposes of understanding the operation of the program and the techniques represented within it for research, including commercial research, and private study. However, the prospective author of an academic journal article cannot disassemble the computer program in order to include an extract of the program expressed in a higher-level language. That does not fall within the permitted objective of decompilation.

107 [1997] FCA 490, Federal Court of Australia, discussed in FitzSimons, J. 'Powerflex v Data Access Corporation (Reverse Engineers Beware!)' [1998] 14 CLSR 45.

108 Assuming the protocol is protected by copyright.

109 Copyright, Designs and Patents Act 1988 s 50B(3).

110 Section 296A (1)(b).

111 Regulation 12(2).

112 The Copyright, Designs and Patents Act 1988 s 29(1) and (4).

## Back-up copies of computer programs

Section 50A of the 1988 Act permits the making of back-up copies if necessary for the purposes of the lawful use of a copy of a computer program by a lawful user. As with the decompilation right, this right cannot be taken away by any term or condition in an agreement and any such term, in so far as it purports to prohibit or restrict the exercise of this right, is void[113] provided the agreement was made on or after 1 January 1993. Prior to this amendment, there was no equivalent statutory provision, although the courts may have been prepared to imply an appropriate term into a software licence where the making of a back-up copy was necessary to the use of the program in question.[114] Of course, many software companies make express provision allowing the user to make one or more back-up copies. It is common for the installation instructions to ask the licensed user to make a copy of the program first and use this as the working copy, placing the original disks in a safe place in case the working disks become damaged or corrupted.

Each lawful user within an organisation that has a site licence or a multiple-user licence is entitled under s 50A to make his own copy if necessary for his lawful use. In such a situation, it is difficult to predict just how many back-up copies would be deemed to be 'necessary'. If the program is available on a network of computers, presumably the effect of s 50A is to allow the making of one back-up copy only, to be held by the network manager. Of course, the licence agreement may make specific provision for the making of a greater number of back-up copies.

## Copying and adapting

A licence in respect of a computer program will normally state the acts that may be done by the licensee in relation to the program. If it is silent about some particular act which is within the spirit of the agreement, then the courts will imply the appropriate terms permitting that act. Section 50C, in effect, puts this on a statutory footing by allowing a lawful user of a copy of a computer program to copy it or adapt it[115] if that is necessary for his lawful use.[116] Copying or adapting for the purpose of error correction may fall within this exception to infringement and is given as a particular example in s 50C(2).

It is common for agreements regulating the lawful use of computer programs to contain a term prohibiting modification by the client, and such terms are not controlled by the Act as amended unlike the case with the other two exceptions. However, terms seeking to prevent modification by or on behalf of the licensee might be controlled in other ways. The Court of Appeal, in *Saphena Computing* v *Allied Collection Agencies*,[117] had an opportunity to consider the position at common law with respect to modification and error correction of licensed computer programs. In that case, the licensee had been given a copy of the source code by the licensor and there was, consequentially, an implied undertaking that the licensee could use it for error correction. While the licensor was still testing and modifying the software, the agreement was determined, and it was held that the licensee could continue to use the source code for the purpose of error correction but could not use it for other modifications and improvements to the program. It was said, *obiter*, that there was not an implied duty on a licensor to supply the source code if the agreement provided only for the supply of the object code.

113 Section 296A (1)(a).

114 However, s 56 recognises the possibility that back-up copies may have been made. It makes copies of works purchased in electronic form that are not transferred along with the original, in the case of it being transferred to a third party, infringing copies. However, whether it is right to speak in terms of the purchase of a computer program is uncertain.

115 'Adaption' in relation to computer programs, by new s 21(3)(ab), means an arrangement or altered version or translation of it. 'Translation' is further defined by s 21(4) in terms of conversion into or out of a computer language or code.

116 This can be seen as a non-derogation from grant provision.

117 [1995] FSR 616.

If the supplier is no longer able or willing to provide error correction, the principle of non-derogation from grant may be applicable, with the result that the client can maintain the program himself or approach third parties with a view to their maintaining it. Even if the supplier is prepared to maintain the program and correct errors (for example, by including an obligation to maintain the program in the licence agreement, or by offering a collateral maintenance contract), the licensee may be able to approach others for this service as the non-derogation principle could still apply. For example, in *British Leyland Motor Corp Ltd v Armstrong Patents Co Ltd*,[118] the House of Lords applied the principle to prevent restriction on a free market in spare parts, and extended their refusal to enforce copyright to the manufacturers of spare parts and not just to the purchaser. Their Lordships spoke in terms of articles which, by their nature, would require the fitting of replacement parts during their normal lifespan. This principle is most apposite in terms of computer programs. Virtually all computer programs contain errors, a number of which might not be discovered for some considerable time, and the lawful user of the program will require work to be done to it in order to correct those errors. The owner of the copyright subsisting in the program should not be able to use his right to prevent the lawful user asking other persons to repair the program otherwise the copyright owner could charge exorbitant prices for this work and the lawful user would have little option but to pay.[119] However, the Judical Committee of the Privy Council has shown its reluctance to extend the *British Leyland* principle further in *Canon Kabushiki Kaisha v Green Cartridge Company Hong Kong Ltd*.[120]

### Underlying ideas and principles

Computer programs are unlike other works of copyright. Ideas and principles underlying or incorporated into or expressed in computer programs are, in most cases, not transparent. They are not readily available to a person using the program. In the case of a literary or dramatic work or an artistic work such as a painting, for example, the underlying ideas and principles are available to a person reading, watching or studying work. The plot, idea, concept or message that the author of the work intended to develop or convey is apparent, albeit in some circumstances with difficulty, for example, in the case of abstract art.

As copyright does not protect ideas (notwithstanding the difficulties associated with determining the scope of such a sweeping aphorism), it is important that they are also made available to persons who have lawful access to computer programs. Otherwise, the monopoly granted by copyright could be perceived as being too strong. In the normal run of things, ideas and principles underlying computer programs can only be gleaned by performing an act restricted by the copyright, unlike the case with traditional works of copyright. The plot underlying a play or story can be determined simply by reading it. If the copyright owner were to be allowed to use his exclusive rights to prevent access to underlying ideas and principles, this would hinder fair competition and make it considerably more difficult for a competitor to create a new computer program to perform the same function, bearing in mind that the function itself, in most cases, will not have its own protection unless it is confidential.

118 [1986] 2 WLR 400.

119 In *Digital Equipment Corp v LCE Computer Maintenance Ltd* (unreported) 22 May 1992, it was accepted that there was an arguable case that the non-derogation from grant principle applied to maintenance of computer programs. EC competition law may also be relevant to this question.

120 [1997] FSR 817.

121 OJ L122, 17.5.91, p. 42.

Implementing the Directive on the legal protection of computer programs, [121] Article 1(2) of which denied protection to ideas and principles underlying any element of a computer program including those which underlie its interfaces, the Copyright (Computer Programs) Regulations 1992[122] inserted s 269A into the Copyright, Designs and Patents Act 1998. Subsection (1)(c) makes void any term in an agreement under which a person has the use of a computer program which purports to prohibit or restrict the use of any device or means to observe, study or test the functioning of the program in order to understand the ideas and principles which underlie any element of the computer program.

122 SI 1992/3233.

We have seen the special permitted act of decompilation which, in effect, gives lawful users a means of accessing interfaces. What s 296A(1)(c) does is wider than this and applies to any underlying idea or principle. Consider some examples where this provision will apply:

- a licensee of a computer program attaches an oscilloscope to his computer to monitor the output to a peripheral device in order to determine the protocol used by the program to send data to the device;[123]
- a licensee of a computer program uses another program[124] to record the sequence of operations in the target program, for example, to determine the algorithm used in a sub-routine of the program used to sort data into alphabetic or numeric order;
- a licensee of a computer program submits a batch of carefully prepared test data to the program to determine the logic of a calculation routine.

123 Although it is not clear whether a protocol is an idea or principle or form of expression.
124 Is another computer program a 'device' or is it a 'means'?

Current examples of where the 'right' granted by s 296A(1)(c) might be particularly valuable is where a computer program contains a 'fix' for the 'Millenium time-bomb' (the problems with computer dates when the year 2000 is reached because of the tendency in the past for computer programmers to use only the last two digits of the year) or in relation to the first computer program to have an effective method of triangulation built into it to deal with currency conversions in respect of the Euro.

It may turn out that the denial of protection to ideas and principles is far more important than the other permitted acts for computer programs. Certainly, it is very wide in scope. Although the 'right' cannot be restricted by the agreement under which a person has the use of a program, one limiting factor is that, where the program is licensed to a client, the licence may contain a term prohibiting the publication or dissemination of the ideas or principles. This could effectively stifle the use of the same ideas and principles by others, particularly in the case of bespoke software,[125] where the client is not in the business of writing software for commercial exploitation himself.

125 Software specially written for a client's particular requirements.

In many respects the effect of s 296A(1)(c) is analogous to the exception from the patent system of discoveries, scientific theories and mathematical methods, as such.[126]

126 Patents Act 1977 s 1(2).

## COMPUTER PROGRAMMING LANGUAGES

Considerable research effort, investment and skill goes into the development of computer languages and instruction sets. Yet, as it could be argued that these are ideas, there is some doubt about their protection by copyright. However, in the United States, an argument that microcode embedded in a microprocessor representing the computer's instruction set was a defining element of the computer, and therefore an idea, failed to find sympathy (*NEC Corp* v *Intel Corp*).[127] In the UK, the question of copyright protection for an instruction set was considered in *Microsense Systems Ltd* v *Control Systems Technology Ltd*.[128] The plaintiff made traffic control systems and a controller for pelican crossings, these being programmed using a set of *mnemonics* (a set of three letter symbols, for example SUN for Sunday, MON for Monday),[129] and these were also used to monitor the controllers. The defendant made similar controllers and used a total of 49 of the plaintiff's mnemonics, arguing that there was no copyright in them because once the functions had been decided, there was no room for skill and labour in devising the mnemonics. Judge Paul Baker thought that there was an arguable case that the list of mnemonics was protected by copyright because of the work in devising the functions and operations of the controller in the first place. He refused an injunction but ordered the defendant to pay a 2 per cent royalty into a joint bank account, this being a case where damages would be an adequate remedy for the plaintiff should it be determined at full trial that copyright subsisted in the list of mnemonics and that the defendant had infringed that copyright. The defendant had argued that it was important, in terms of safety, that there was some degree of standardisation in instruction sets for traffic controllers. This is an attractive argument, but is the public interest best served by denying a modest royalty to the person who devises a new and original work?

The Directive on the legal protection of computer programs recognises that programming languages, at least to the extent that they comprise ideas and principles, should not be protected by copyright. Given that this is so, one might wonder wherein lies the incentive to create a new language. The answer lies in the fact that, usually, the program, once written, can be run in a computer only if it is converted into object code, whether temporarily, using an interpreter program, or permanently, using a compiler program. The licensing of these interpreter and compiler programs, together with appropriate documentation describing the syntax, semantics and use of the language, is the method by which financial reward is usually sought. These interpreter and compiler programs are, of course, protected by copyright.

## DATABASES[130]

A computer database is a collection of data stored in or on computer media usually in the form of a computer file or files. The variety and scope of databases is enormous. For example, a computer database can contain information which relates to and represents things such as:

- lists of clients and their addresses
- schedules of parts or articles and their rates or prices
- lists of bibliographical references
- engineering or architectural drawings
- works of art, photographs and other images
- music and sounds

127 (1989) 10 USPQ 2d.

128 (Unreported) 17 June 1991.

129 Not all the mnemonics were obvious. For example, LIT was used to determine the aspect status of the controller. The instruction set was designed so that the engineer could communicate with, monitor or modify the controller or the way it operated.

130 For a good discussion of the problems of database protection see Lea, G. 'Database Law – Solutions beyond Copyright' [1993] 9 CLSR 127.

- the texts of documents
- mixed text and graphics
- films and film extracts
- computer programs or routines
- a combination of two or more of the above.

Databases are accessed, manipulated, modified, dispayed and printed using computer programs and usually have associated indexes, dictionaries, format and layout files. Anything can be stored on computer media as long as it can be reduced to a digital form, and almost anything can be. In the case of text, this is done by using codes to symbolise the letters of the alphabet, for example using ASCII codes.[131] Types of storage media include magnetic disks and tape, compact discs and silicon 'chips'. In earlier times, punched card and paper tape were commonly used. There is nothing particularly unusual about computer databases compared with collections of information that are written down, typed or printed on paper or index cards. The major difference is that, in the case of a computer database, the information is not stored in its original form, but is translated into a digital representation for the purposes of storage, whereas in the case of traditional paper files, the information is stored in its original form.[132] A rapidly growing number of computer databases are available on-line, that is they are stored on a central computer and are accessible remotely using a computer with a modem connected to a telecommunications system; in which case, they may fail to be treated, *inter alia*, as cable programmes.[133] Computer programs accessing a computer database convert the digital representation to a form from which it can be displayed or printed in readable form.

Whether a computer database generated by computer can be a copyright work is not beyond doubt. In principle, there should be no problem as the Copyright, Designs and Patents Act 1988 s 9(3) contains the rule for determining the identity of the author for copyright purposes of a computer-generated literary, dramatic, musical or artistic work. A database is a form of literary work and, to complete the syllogism, it should be possible to have a computer-generated work in which copyright subsists. Until 1 January 1998, this probably would not have been an issue. However, changes made to the copyright provisions in the Act by the Copyright and Rights in Databases Regulations 1997,[134] suggest that it may no longer be possible to have a copyright database which has been computer-generated.

The test for subsistence of copyright, we have seen, has in the past been quite generous, requiring that the work originated from the author and is the result of a minimum of skill, effort or judgment. This test continues to apply to the original works of copyright, but with the exception of databases which, under s 3A(2), are original for copyright purposes if, and only if, by reason of the selection or arrangement of the contents of the database the database constitutes the *author's own intellectual creation*. This phrase, 'author's own intellectual creation', is new to copyright in the United Kingdom and derives from the European Directive on the legal protection of databases.[135] When one looks at the defenition of computer-generated work in s 178, being a work generated in circumstances such that there is no human author, this strongly suggests that there can be no such thing as a computer-generated database which is, without more, protected by copyright as a database.[136] It could only

**131** ASCII stands for the American Standard Code for Information Interchange. In some cases, a form of encryption is used.

**132** As an example of a digital representation of a letter, the letter 'E' is ASCII code 69 which would be represented as '01000101' using binary notation.

**133** *See Shetland Times Ltd v Dr Jonathon Wills* [1997] FSR 604, correctly forecast by Millard, C. 'Copyright' in Reed, C. (ed) (1996) *Computer Law* (3rd edn) Blackstone Press, pp. 104–53, at p. 115.

**134** SI 1997/3032.

**135** OJ L77, 27.3.96, p. 20. This phrase was also used in relation to computer programs, OJ L122, 17.5.91, p. 42, but was not included in the implementing regulations, the Copyright (Computer Programs) Regulations 1992, SI 1992/3233. *See also* the German Copyright Act s 2(2) which requires a work to be a personal intellectual creation.

**136** Of course, the contents of the database may be protected by copyright, independently.

be a copyright work if the skill and judgment of the computer programmer was taken into account, a form of indirect authorship. But if this is so, then the work cannot be computer-generated, adding fuel to the argument that there can be no such thing as a computer-generated work.[137] A further arguement for computer-generated databases not being works of copyright is the new concept of a database right, discussed later.

137 Computer-generated works are discussed in more detail later in this chapter.

Where a database is created by direct human skill or judgment, it may be a work of copyright even if the constituent parts are commonplace or in the public domain. Decisions as to what to include, what to exclude, what sort of information to collect and how that information will be structured and arranged may require an act of intellectual creation. In this respect, earlier judical statements that compilations can be original even though their constituent parts are not original, such as in *Macmillan & Co Ltd v K & J Cooper*,[138] remain good law.

138 (1923) 40 TLR 186.

In general terms, it can be said that many databases are protected by copyright as literary works. A database containing, for example, selected substantial extracts from works of literature will have protection in a number of ways. Assuming it has not expired and all the other requirements are present, each extract will have its own copyright. The database as a whole will have its copyright provided it is the author's own intellectual creation. Furthermore, if the making of the database required a substantial investment, it will also be protected by the new database right, discussed later.

Before 1 January 1998, databases would fall to be protected as compilations but now, as a result of the changes made to the Act, databases are expressly excluded from compilations and are treated separately. Before looking at the changes made by the Copyright and Rights in Databases Regulations 1997, it will be helpful to look at developments in the United States in comparison to the position in the United Kingdom prior to 1 January 1998. It is highly likely that developments in the United States influenced the mechanism of protection for databases set out in the European Directive.

### Developments in the United States and the United Kingdom approach before 1 January 1998

The subsistence of copyright in a database *qua* database could be questionable where its creation has not required the expenditure of skill or judgment. Some databases are the result of effort alone; once the nature of its contents have been determined, there is no room for skill or judgment in the selection of material to be entered into the database. Hence there can be no copyright in the compilation, and *G A Cramp & Sons Ltd v Frank Smythson Ltd*[139] is good authority for this proposition. An example is where a company decides to make a simple database of the names and addresses of all its clients. The 'sweat of the brow' doctrine, affording copyright protection to works which are the result of labour only, was rejected in the United States Supreme Court in *Feist Publications Inc v Rural Telephone Service Co Inc*,[140] in which it was held that the 'white pages' section in a typical telephone directory was not protected by copyright because of a lack of creativity, not owing its origin to an act of authorship. The court did, however, recognise that a compilation of facts could be the subject of copyright because the author has to choose which facts to include and in what order to place them. Similarly,

139 [1944] AC 329.

140 (1991) 111 S Ct 1282.

141 And the work involved in devising the classification system (a non-literal form of work?). However, in *Bell South Advertising & Publishing Corp v Donnelly Information Publishing Inc*, 2 September 1993, 11th Circuit Court of Appeals, the court held that taking a large amount of data from a yellow pages directory did not infringe copyright.

142 5 December 1994, 2nd Circuit Court of Appeals (unreported).

143 An approach rejected by Jacob J in relation to computer programs in *IBCOS Computers Ltd v Barclays Mercantile Highland Finance Ltd* [1994] FSR 275.

144 [1992] FSR 409. The issue was whether a substantial part had been taken.

145 Bull, G. 'Licensing and Distribution of Market Data' [1994] 10 CLSR 50 at 51. However, in *Powerflex v Data Access Corp* [1997] FCA 490, the Federal Court of Australia rejected the notion that a word in a computer program could itself be a program. Even though a single word in a high-level language program may result in a series of instructions being processed, the word is merely the cipher or trigger for the series of instructions.

146 For analysis and discussion of the new law on databases, *see*, for example, Angel, J. and Quinn, T. 'Database Law' [1998] 14 CLSR 34; Lai, S. 'Database Protection in the UK: The New Deal and its Effects on Software Protection' [1998] EIPR 32 and Chalton S. 'The Effect of the Database Directive on UK Copyright Law in Relation to Databases: A Comparison of Features' [1997] EIPR 278.

147 SI 1997/3032.

148 OJ L77, 27.3.96, p. 20.

149 Recitals 5–12.

the 'yellow pages' section of a telephone directory could be protected because of the presence of original material.[141] In *CCC Information Services Inc v Maclean Hunter Market Reports Inc*[142] the court, in determining whether a compilation of secondhand car values was protected by copyright, considered that *Feist* did not raise a high barrier against copyright subsistence but merely required that there was some originality, although only those 'original' elements would be protected.

There were two major differences between the United States and prior United Kingdom copyright law in that the United Kingdom was probably more generous in terms of originality, and the courts here would be more reluctant to break down a work into its constituent parts and consider whether certain parts were original whilst others were not.[143] However, an opportunity to examine this question was missed in *Waterlow Directories Ltd v Reed Information Services Ltd*[144] which concerned an alleged infringement of copyright in a legal directory containing names and addressess of barristers and firms of solicitors by entering extracts into a word processor.

Bull argues that a single datum, for example, 'Megatron Shares – 120p', could have been protected by copyright in the United Kingdom if available as electronic text in which case it could have been considered to be a computer program.[145] Although 'computer program' is not defined in the Act, it is likely to be required to be some code that is executable by the computer's processor in a way that controls or conditions the operation of a computer. This is not the case where the datum is stored simply in ASCII code, but could be the case where it is encrypted and includes instructions so that the computer can decrypt it. Of course, a relatively small collection of such data could have qualified as a compilation under the Act before 1 January 1998.

## Protection for databases from 1 January 1998[146]

The Copyright and Rights in Databases Regulations 1997[147] (the '1997 Regulations') implemented the European Directive on the legal protection of databases,[148] making some changes to the copyright provisions of the Copyright, Designs and Patents Act 1988 and creating a new 'database right'. Thus, a two-tier approach to the protection of databases is taken, so that those that are the author's own intellectual creation will be protected by copyright, and databases which involve in their making a substantial investment in obtaining, verifying or presenting the contents of a database will be protected by a database right of lesser duration than copyright. The Regulations came into force on 1 January 1998, the date for compliance required in the Directive.

The desire to harmonise the protection of databases throughout the Community was an important feature of the Directive. The rationale for strong and effective protection can be seen in some of the recitals to the Directive. It is recognised that databases are vital to the development of an information market and in other fields and the exponential growth in the amount of information generated and processed in all sectors of commerce and industry requires significant investment in information systems. Identifying a great imbalance in the investment in databases as between member states and in comparison to third countries, the creation of a stable and uniform legal protection for databases is seen as essential to ensuring that substantial investment in modern information systems.[149] The link between legal protection and investment is seen as important, and commercially valuable databases which would otherwise fail to be protected under copyright law are given their own distinct form of protection.

Before looking separately at the changes to the copyright provisions as they apply to databases and the database right, a number of points should be made.

1  The rights provided apply to both electronic and non-electronic databases, reflecting the desire of the Commission to the European Communities not to distinguish between computer databases and paper databases, so that there can be no regulatory advantage for those who do not adopt and make use of information technology.

2  The database right can be seen as a 'quasi-copyright', bearing a number of similarities with copyright. It has been referred to as a *sui generis* right.[150]

3  There is a substantial overlap between copyright and rights in databases. Thus, in most cases, a database subject to copyright may also have a database right. This has some implications, for example the author of a database may be a different person to the maker of a database.

4  Copyright and the right in a database are both without prejudice to any copyright in the contents of a database. Where a database contains individual works of copyright, they will remain to be protected by copyright. Where a person without authorisation takes one of those works, he will infringe the copyright in the work. If he takes more than one work, he will infringe the copyright in the individual works, and may infringe the copyright in the database as a whole and may infringe the database right.

5  Authors of copyright databases have moral rights in the same way as applies to other literary works.[151]

6  The new provisions as to copyright in databases and in relation to the database right do not apply to music compilations on CD-ROM.[152]

### Copyright provisions for databases

The Copyright, Designs and Patents Act 1988 s 3(1) is amended so as to add 'database' to the growing, but clearly non-exhaustive, list of things that are literary works and to exclude databases from compilations. Thus, databases are treated separately from other forms of compilation. Though many of the copyright provisions apply identically to each, there are differences, such as in relation to the permitted act of fair dealing.

A new s 3A is added, defining a 'database' as a collection of independent works, data or other materials which (a) are arranged in a systematic or methodical way, and (b) are individually accessible by electronic or other means.[153] A database is original for copyright purposes if and only if, by reason of the selection or arrangement of its contents, the database constitutes the author's own intellectual creation. Recital 16 to the Directive states that no other criterion should be applied, in particular, no aesthetic or qualitative criterion. This seems bound to narrow the scope of copyright for databases as databases in the United Kingdom with its traditional generous approach to copyright subsistence. However, pre-existing databases are not to be prejudiced. Thus, where a database was created on or before 27 March 1996 (the date the Directive was published) and was protected by copyright immediately before 1 January 1998, that copyright will continue for its full term, notwithstanding that the database would not qualify for copyright under the new test for originality.[154]

150  So described in the Directive; *see* Chapter III of the Directive.

151  Recital 28 states that the moral rights belong to the natural person who created the database though such moral rights are outside the scope of the Directive. No moral rights are granted to makers of databases in relation to the database right.

152  Recital 19 of the Directive. Of course, protection will remain available as musical works, literary works (where there are lyrics), and sound recordings in addition to any rights in performances.

153  'Other means' indicating that the provisions apply equally to non-computer databases, confirmed in recital 14 to the Directive.

154  Recital 60. However, the effect of this derogation is confined to the territory of the member state concerned.

| Last name | First name | Address Line 1 | Address Line 2 | City | Post Code | Credit limit |
|---|---|---|---|---|---|---|
| Lyon | Christopher | The Den | Marine Terrace | Seabrough | F15 6PP | 5000 |
| Raffe | George | 34 Tree Tops Lane | | Windsor | BR1 8HT | 1500 |
| Madiller | Richard | Hermitage Cottage | Carapace Lane | Shelsea | SH4 1EE | 2000 |
| Conder | Anna | 2 Glidewell Square | | Crawley | SS8 9GB | 500 |

*Records*

**Fields**

**Figure 8.4 Structure of a database**

We have seen that copyright protection can extend beyond the literal expression of the literal work to non-literal elements such as, in the case of a computer program, the underlying structure of the work. The same ought to apply to a database and, indeed, recital 15 to the European Directive states that copyright protection should cover the structure of a database. But what is the structure of a database? Conventionally, databases are structured into records and fields. A record is simply a set of data relating to one entry in the database. For example, in the case of a database of customers, a record is all the information in the database relating to a particular customer. A record is broken down into fields. For example, in our customer database, there may be one field containing the last name of the customer, another for the first names, a field for the first line of his address, one for the second line and so on. Figure 8.4 gives an example of a database so structured.

Fields in a database may be of different sizes and types. For example, some fields will contain alphabetic information, some may contain numeric information (integer, decimal or exponential), alphanumeric information, dates etc. In some cases, the size of the field will be dictated by its type, in other cases, such as a field containing information relating to a person's first name, it is a matter of pre-determining the longest likely name and sizing the field accordingly.[155] The work in designing the database in terms of the information it will contain and the structure of that information can be considerable. Where the design of computer software comprising computer programs and databases is concerned, the work involved in the design of the database structure can be the most difficult element in the overall design and require the greatest amount of research and development work. The fact that the Directive recognises this is to be welcomed and it is to be hoped that the courts appreciate the importance of protecting the structure of a database.[156]

With modern developments in computer software technology, the issue of database structure has become more complex. No longer is it appropriate to think of distinct and separate databases as in old COBOL systems. In many cases now, databases are relational, with a number of databases linked together by some common element. For example, one database may contain details of individual clients, including a reference number with another database containing transactions including customer reference numbers. By combining these databases, a list of transactions can be generated, grouped by individual customer, for

155 In some systems, the size of the field does not have to be specified as it is dynamic, that is, the field will grow or shrink to hold precisely the amount of information in the record in question.

156 After a shaky start, the signs are now good. *See* Jacob J in *IBCOS Computers Ltd* v *Barclays Mercantile Highland Finance Ltd* [1994] FSR 275 and his criticism of Judge Paul Baker in this respect in *Total Information Processing Systems Ltd* v *Daman Ltd* [1992] FSR 171, discussed earlier in this chapter.

example, for the purpose of sending out invoices. Further examples of database structure may be found in links in Internet Websites and hypertext links generally. Potentially, all such elements could be the subject of copyright protection.

The restricted act of making an adaption has some definitions specific to particular forms of work, such as in the case of a musical work or computer program. As databases are treated individually, there is need for clarification of this restricted act for databases and, accordingly, a definition of making an adaption of a database is inserted into the Copyright, Designs and Patents Act 1988 s 21, being an arrangement or altered version or a translation of it. Specific provision is required for making an adaptation but not for the other restricted acts in the Directive which are already covered by ss 17–20.

An arrangement of a database could be a new version in which the database has been sorted into a particular order. An altered version could be where a person has taken a partial copy of the database by omitting some of the fields. A translation of a database could occur where a person has taken a database used with a particular type of database software, such as Borland dBase, and imported it into a different type of database software, such as Microsoft Access.

The Directive leaves much to member states as regards the permitted acts under copyright. The United Kingdom approach is to adopt the traditional permitted acts that apply to literary works, with the exception of fair dealing for research and private study for which specific provision is made for databases. There are two differences for databases. First, under s 29(1A), fair dealing for research or private study requires that the source be indicated. Secondly, it is not fair dealing to do anything in relation to a database for a commercial purpose: s 29(5). Neither of these constraints applies in the case of other literary works,[157] and this reflects, perhaps, the commercial significance attached to databases. Fair dealing in other works for commercial purposes is a possibility (although in some cases, it may not be deemed to be fair), but this restriction reflects the language of the Directive. A requirement that the source be indicated is not required for this form of fair dealing for other forms of work, but it is required for other forms of fair dealing, such as fair dealing for criticism or review. Of course, the new fair dealing provision only applies to the copyright in the database *per se* and not to the individual works contained within it. Therefore, it may be fair dealing to make a copy of part of a work contained in a database for commercial research, provided that a substantial part of the database itself is not taken, and provided that there is no infringement of the database right.

A new s 50D is inserted into the Copyright, Designs and Patents Act 1998, being essentially a non-derogation from grant provision for persons having a right to use a database or part of it (whether under a licence to do any of the acts restricted by the copyright in the database or otherwise). It is not an infringement of copyright in a database for such a person to do, in the excersise of that right, anything which is necessary for the purposes of access to and use of the contents of the database or of that part of the database. This provision acknowledges that a person may be restricted to using part only of a database. For example, his use may be restricted to certain records or certain fields. In the case of a database of potential customers in the United Kingdom, a person may be permitted to access and retrieve information about persons living in England, or may be permitted to access and retrieve information about all the persons in the database with the exception of credit information relating to them.

157 Fair dealing is limited in the case of computer programs so as not to allow the act of decompilation, which is provided for separately in s 50B. However, lawful decompilation can be, and often will be, performed for commercial purposes.

This right cannot be prohibited or restricted. New s 296(B) makes void any term or condition in an agreement in so far as it purports to prohibit or restrict the acts permitted under s 50D or any act necessary for the excersise of the rights granted by the agreement.

### The database right

The database right is intended to provide protection to databases which, although they may fail to meet the requirements for copyright protection as a database, are commercially valuable, being the result of a substantial investment. However, the right is not restricted to databases in which copyright does not subsist and many databases subject to copyright should also be subject to the database right. The overlap could be important for the owner of the database because infringement and exceptions to infringement are not identical for both rights. In particular, the repeated and systematic extraction of *insubstantial* parts may infringe the database right in circumstances where the copyright is not infringed.

Subsistence of the database right is unaffected if the database is also a work of copyright or if the works contained in database are themselves copyright works. Thus, a database of photographs which involved in its making the excersise of skill and judgment (or, more properly now, the author's intellectual creativity) and a substantial investment, for example, in presenting its contents will be subject to copyright at two levels (the individual photographs and the database as a whole) and also will be subject to the database right.

The database right is set out in Part III of the Copyright and Rights in Databases Regulations 1997[158] and reg 12 contains some of the main definitions, although it should be noted that 'database' has the same meaning as for copyright.[159] The other definitions are:

- 'extraction', in relation to any contents of a database, means the permanent or temporary transfer of those contents to another medium by any means or in any form;
- 'investment' includes any investment, whether of financial, human or technical resources;
- 'lawful user', in relation to a database, means any person who (whether under a licence to do any of the acts restricted by any database right in the database or otherwise) has a right to use the database;
- 're-utilisation', in relation to any contents of a database, means making those contents available to the public by any means;
- 'substantial', in relation to any investment, extraction or re-utilisation, means substantial in terms of quantity or quality or a combination of both.

Lending a copy of a database (not for direct or indirect commercial advantage) by an establishment accessible to the public does not constitute extraction or re-utilisation of the contents of a database, but this exception does not apply to making available for on-the-spot reference use which could, therefore, fall within extraction or re-utilisation.[160] Exhaustion of rights within the EEA applies to copies sold within the EEA by or with the consent of the owner of the database right to the extent that further sale of such copies does not constitute extraction or re-utilisation of the contents of the database.[161]

158 SI 1997/3032.

159 As given by s 3A(1).

160 Regulation 12(2) and (3). Regulation 12(3) allows the charging of a payment, provided that it does not exceed that necessary to cover the costs of the establishment.

161 Regulation 12(5).

The database right is a property right which subsists in a database if there has been a substantial investment in obtaining, verifying or presenting the contents of the database,[162] subject to qualification requirements. Under reg 18, the latter are satisfied if, at the material time, the maker (or at least one of them where there are joint makers) is:

- a national of an EEA state (or habitually resident in the state);
- a body incorporated in an EEA state, having its central administration or principal place of business in an EEA state or a registered office in the EEA and the body's operations linked on an ongoing basis with the economy of an EEA state; or
- a partnership or other unincorporated body formed under the law of an EEA state, having at that time its central administration or principal place of business within the EEA.

The 'material time' is time when a database is made or, if its making extended over a period, a substantial part of that period. The qualification requirements do not apply in the case of parliamentary database right: reg 18(3). There appears to be a mistake in the Regulations because the exception from the qualification requirements has not been extended to Crown database right.[163]

The 'maker' of a database subject to the database right is defined in reg 14(1) as the person who takes the initiative in obtaining, verifying or presenting the contents of a database and assumes the risk of investing in that obtaining, verification or presentation, such acts constituting the act of making a database. Under reg 15, the maker is the first owner of the database right. There are provisions equivalent to those under copyright law for employees. Thus, where an employee makes a database in the course of his employment, it will be the employer who is the maker of the database, subject to agreement to the contrary. Crown and parliamentary database right are also provided for. Where two or more persons act in collaboration in taking the initiative and assuming the risk of investing, they will be joint makers of the database. Unlike copyright law, there is no requirement that the contribution of each is not distinct.

The term of protection afforded by the database right is set out in reg 17 as 15 years from the end of the calendar year during which the making of the database is completed, although, if it is made available to the public before the end of that period, the right will continue to endure for 15 years from the end of the calendar year during which it was first made available.

A great many commercially exploited databases are subject to modification, either as a continual process or by subsequent releases or updates. The Directive attempted to deal with this by providing for a fresh 15-year term when the changes become substantial, including any substantial change resulting from an accumulation of successive additions, deletions or alterations, provided the database would be considered to be a substantial new investment.[164] The Regulations follow the same formula. Databases made on or after 1 January 1983 in which database right subsists on commencement shall, under reg 29, qualify for 15 years beginning with 1 January 1998.[165]

Infringing acts are defined in reg 16 as the extraction or re-utilisation of all or a part of the contents of the database without the consent of the owner. Bear in mind that substantiality is a question of quantity or quality or both. Accepting that repeatedly taking insubstantial parts can compromise the owner's

162 Regulation 13(1).

163 Both Crown copyright and parliamentary copyright are excluded from the normal qualification requirements: s 153(2).

164 Evaluated qualitively or quantatively, Article 10(3).

165 Regulation 30.

economic rights in a database, reg 16(2) provides that the repeated and systematic extraction or re-utilisation of insubstantial parts of the contents of a database *may* amount to the extraction or re-utilisation of a substantial part of those contents (emphasis added), A person could periodically and at frequent intervals extract valuable information from a very large database by searching for particular entries using keywords. It could be difficult to show that a substantial part of the database has been used. This could be particularly important as more databases will be made available on-line or via the Internet. Presumably Laddie J will not be happy with successive insubstantial taking amounting to infringement.[166]

In terms of 'insubstantial infringement', the Directive further requires that the repeated and systematic extraction or re-utilisation must imply acts conflicting with a normal exploitation of the database or be unreasonably prejudical to the legitimate interests of the maker of the database. The Regulations simply state that such taking *may* amount to the extraction or re-utilisation of a substantial part of the contents of the database. Certainly, prejudice to the owner's commercial exploitation should infringe, but it should be much wider than that. The owner of the database may make it available on a non-profit basis to the members of the public who satisfy certain criteria, such as being members of a club or having certain attributes.

In the event of ligitation, presumably it will be for makers subject to this right to show that the accumulation of insubstantial extractions or re-utilisations has conflicted with their normal exploitation of the database or prejudiced their legitimate interests within the spirit of the Directive.

There are 'non-derogation' provisions in that a lawful user of a database which has been made available to the public has a right to extract or re-utilise insubstantial parts of the database for any purpose, and any term in an agreement, under which the right to use a database or part of a database has been granted, which purports to prevent the person having the right from extracting or re-utilising insubstantial parts of the contents of the database (or part of that database) shall be void.[167]

There is also a fair dealing exception to infringement. Where the database has been made available to the public, fair dealing with a substantial part of the contents is allowed if:

- the part is extracted by a person who is otherwise a lawful user;
- it is extracted for the purposes of illustration for teaching or research (but not for a commercial purpose); and
- the source is indicated.[168]

Further exceptions are set out in Sch 1 to the Regulations and cover parliamentary and judical proceedings, Royal Commissions and statutory inquiries, material open to public inspection or on official register, material communicated to the Crown in the course of public business, public records and acts done under statutory authority. These mirror the equivalent permitted acts for copyright in ss 45 to 50 of the Copyright, Designs and Patents Act 1988. However, apart from these exceptions and those mentioned above, none of the other permitted acts that apply to literary works applies to the database right. In particular, it should be noted that fair dealing for criticism or review or for reporting current events does not apply in relation to the database right. It is

**166** *See* his criticism of *Cate* v *Devon & Exeter Constitutional Newspaper* Co (1889) 40 Ch D 500 on this particular point in *Electronic Techniques (Anglia) Ltd* v *Critchley Components Ltd* [1997] FSR 401 at 409, discussed in Chapter 6.

**167** Regulation 19.

**168** Regulation 20.

questionable whether fair dealing for private study is available. It depends on whether this would fall within the meaning of research.

There is an exception to infringement of the database right which resembles one of the permitted acts for copyright works. The database right is not infringed where it is not possible by reasonable inquiry to ascertain the identity of the maker of the database and it is reasonable to assume that the database right has expired: reg 21.

There are some useful presumptions that apply to the database right, not dissimilar to some of those for copyright works. Under reg 22, where a name purporting to be that of the maker of the database appears on copies of the database as published, it is presumed that that person is the maker and the database was not made in circumstances where the employer would be the first owner or in the case of Crown or parliamentary database right. Where copies of a database as published bear a label or mark stating that a named person was the maker and that it was first published in a specified year, the label or mark shall be admissible as evidence of those facts and presumed correct until the contrary be proved.

The Regulations are silent on the burden of proof as to whether there has been a substantial change resulting in a further 15 years' protection. The recitals to the Directive state that it is the maker of the database who has the burden of proof in this respect and in terms of the date of completion of the making of the database. Nevertheless, the effect under English law is probably the same, where a defendant challenges either aspect. Perhaps it is a pity that there is not an equivalent to the presumption that applies in respect of the design right (and infringing copies of copyright works) to the effect that, if it can be shown that the right subsists or subsisted in the design, then it did not so subsist at the time of the infringement unless the contrary be proved. However, this would conflict with the Directive.

The provisions for dealing, rights and remedies (including those of exclusive licensees) that apply to copyright works are declared under reg 23 to apply also in respect to the database right.

Schedule 2 to the Regulations contains provisions for licensing the database right and deals with licensing schemes and licensing bodies and referral of licensing schemes to the Copyright Tribunal. These are equivalent to the provisions in ss 116–129 and 144 of the Copyright, Designs and Patents Act 1988 that apply to copyright works. The jurisdiction of the Copyright Tribunal is enlarged accordingly.

The Regulations will apply to databases made before or after commencement.[169] Regulation 27 states that agreements made before commencement are unaffected and no act done before commencement or in pursuance of an agreement made before commencement infringes the database right. Regulation 28 provides that if a database was made on or before 27 March 1996 (the date the Directive was published in the Official Journal) and was a copyright database immediately before commencement, that copyright continues for the remainder of its term in accordance with s 12 of the Copyright, Designs and Patents Act 1988, that is, in most cases, life of the author plus 70 years.

169 Regulation 27, subject to regs 28 and 29.

## COMPUTER-GENERATED WORKS

The Copyright, Designs and Patents Act 1988 has a curious provision in that it recognises computer-generated works as a separate species of work with different rules for authorship and duration of copyright. These provisions apply only to literary, dramatic, musical or artistic works.[170] While it is important that works produced using a computer should not be denied the protection of copyright on the basis that the direct human contribution required to make the work is small or negligible, it may be difficult to differentiate between a computer-generated work and other works that have been created with the aid of a computer system.

Section 178 of the Act defines a 'computer-generated work' as being a work that is 'generated by computer in circumstances such that there is no human author'. It is not an easy task to determine the meaning of this definition, nor is it easy to think of examples of such works. All works generated by computer owe their creation to a human being, although the human element may be indirect, such as where a computer program contains all the instructions necessary for the creation of the work and the direct human involvement consists of nothing more than switching on the computer and starting up the program. For example, take the artistic work represented in Figure 8.5. It was produced by the author of this book using a computer program containing formulae to generate fractal geometry based on the work of the French mathematician Dr Mandelbrot. The only skill used by the author was to zoom in on an interesting looking part of the main figure. Is this a computer-generated work, or has the skill used in selecting an area to be enlarged prevented this result? If the work becomes popular and prints are made of it and sold, to whom should the royalties be paid – to the author of this book, to Dr Mandelbrot or to the person who wrote the program?[171]

The question of whether a work created using a programmed computer is or is not a computer-generated work is significant because it affects the determination of the authorship and, consequently, the ownership of the copyright subsisting in the work. Of lesser import is the fact that the copyright subsisting

170 *See* the Copyright, Designs and Patents Act 1988 s 9(3).

171 And what is the position if the author did not zoom in selectively and had simply printed the first diagram produced by the programmed computer?

**Figure 8.5  A computer-generated work?**

in computer-generated works runs from the end of the calendar year in which the work was made and not by reference to the year in which the author dies.[172] For most cases, therefore, the duration of copyright in computer-generated works will be shorter than for other original works.

Indirect human authorship had been recognised by the courts prior to the 1988 Act, even in the case of a programmed computer intended to select random letters for a competition. In *Express Newspapers plc v Liverpool Daily Post & Echo plc*,[173] the defendant claimed that grids of letters produced by computer for a newspaper competition could not be protected by copyright because the grids had no human author.[174] This was rejected by Whitford J, who said that the computer was no more than a tool with which the winning sequences of letters were produced using the instructions of a programmer. He said that the defence submission that there was no human author was as unrealistic as saying that a pen was the author of a work of literature.

There are two possibilities: first that the provisions in the Act concerning computer-generated works are something of a red herring, that there can never be such a thing, or, secondly, that the Act overrules the *Express Newspapers* case because it is inconsistent with the Act.[175] If the idea of human authorship can be reconciled with lists of letters drawn randomly by a programmed computer, there seems to be little possibility of a work being considered to be 'computer-generated' within the meaning of the Act, because it is difficult to think of a work where the direct human contribution is less. On the other hand, if the concept of a computer-generated work within the meaning assigned to it by the Act is accepted then, as regards works produced with the aid of a computer, it still does not help to draw the line between works that are computer-generated and those that are not.[176]

## SATELLITE BROADCASTING

The broadcasting of television, films and the like by satellite raises fundamental issues of copyright, such as where the broadcast is made from. For example, is it made from the earth station or the satellite? This will affect the identity of the national rules of copyright law that will apply. How does the broadcaster control the reception of his broadcast in other countries? According to the 'Bogsch' theory, the broadcaster would need to obtain the necessary right in each of the countries within the area of reception of the broadcast (its 'footprint').[177] Another difficulty is controlling the capture and re-transmission of a broadcast without permission. A further problem relates to the sale of unauthorised decoders used to receive encrypted broadcasts and 'smartcards' for use with decoders.

A satellite broadcast is taken to be made from the place where, under the control and responsibility of the person making the broadcast, the programme-carrying signals are introduced into an uninterrupted chain of communication (including in the case of a satellite transmission, the chain leading to the satellite and down towards the earth).[178] Re-broadcasting or including a broadcast in a cable programme service are restricted acts and will be infringed by anyone doing either without the licence of the copyright owner.[179] There are special provisions for determining the place of making broadcasts in the case of satellite broadcasts originating from a country outside the European Economic Area not providing an adequate level of protection and for determining the maker of such broadcasts.[180]

---

172 Section 12(7).

173 [1985] 1 WLR 1089.

174 A similar example, concerning the making by programmed computer of lists of runners and riders for horse races, is the unreported case of *The Jockey Club v Rahim*, 22 July 1983, Chancery Division.

175 It is open to debate whether the provisions as to construction contained in the Copyright, Designs and Patents Act 1988 s 172 show that there has been a sea change as regards works created by a programmed computer. For an argument that there is no such thing as a computer-generated work, *see* Bainbridge, D. I. 'The Copyright Act: a Legal Red Herring', *Computer Bulletin*, Vol. 1, Pt.8, October 1989, p. 21.

176 Tapper argues that the computer-generated works provisions are ill-conceived and should be abolished. Tapper, C. 'The Software Directive: A UK Perspective' in Lehmann, M. and Tapper, C. (1993) *A Handbook of European Software Law*, Clarendon Press, pp. 143–61, at p. 150.

177 Accepted by the Austrian Supreme Court in *Re Satellite Television Broadcasting* [1995] FSR 73. This case pre-dated Austria's accession to the European Community.

178 Copyright, Designs and Patents Act 1988 s 6(4) as modified by the Copyright and Related Rights Regulations 1996 (SI 1996/2967). These Regulations implemented, *inter alia*, the Council Directive on the coordination of certain rules concerning copyright and rights related to copyright applicable to satellite broadcasting and cable retransmission, OJ L248, 6.10.93, p. 15. Previously the place from which the broadcast was made, in the case of a satellite transmission, was the place from which the signals carrying the broadcast are transmitted to the satellite.

179 Section 20.

180 Section 6A, inserted by the Copyright and Related Rights Regulations 1996, SI 1996/2967, discussed in more detail in Chapter 3.

Some organisations make encrypted broadcasts which require a decoder to view the programme. It is an offence to make, import, sell or let for hire any unauthorised decoder by s 297A.[181] Previously, although the fraudulent reception of transmissions (broadcasts and cable) carried criminal penalties by s 297, there were only civil remedies against any person responsible for making, importing, selling or letting for hire unauthorised decoders and this provision had caused considerable problems of interpretation.

In *BBC Enterprises Ltd v Hi-Tech Xtravision Ltd* [182] the plaintiff provided a satellite television service known as 'BBC TV Europe'. The defendant sold decoders at a price considerably lower than that charged by the distributors authorised by the plaintiff. The offence of fraudulently receiving a programme included in a broadcast or cable programme service in s 297 of the Copyright, Designs and Patents Act 1988, was held to be inapplicable for reasons of jurisdiction. The plaintiff therefore based his claim on s 298 of the Act, which controls apparatus, devices or information to assist persons to receive programmes or other transmissions when they are not entitled to do so. In the Chancery Division, it was held that the unauthorised reception of waves in the ether caused by wireless telegraphic transmission did not represent an interference with property rights at common law and that no one had rights of property in those wireless transmission waves. Scott J suggested that a right to prohibit reception had to be found outside s 298 before it was possible to say that persons were not entitled to receive programmes and it is not an infringement of copyright to receive a broadcast. Therefore, the foreign viewers of 'BBC TV Europe' could not be described as persons who were 'not entitled to do so' within s 298.[183] Scott J was of the opinion that s 298 was inept legislation and that the legislature was under a misapprehension as to the law.

The Court of Appeal reversed the decision in the Chancery Division. While the Court accepted that the right involved was probably not a proprietary right, it was held that the plaintiff's claim disclosed a good cause of action, rejecting the interpretation of s 298 suggested by Scott J.[184] Staughton LJ said that s 298 contained both the right and the remedy. The person who seeks to charge for encrypted transmissions has the right not to have others making apparatus designed for use by persons not authorised by him to receive the programmes.[185] The defendant's appeal was dismissed by the House of Lords, which held that providers of satellite programmes broadcast from the UK are protected by s 298 and are thus entitled to collect charges for the reception of these programmes, and this covered, indirectly, persons receiving the transmissions in other countries that lie within the 'footprint' of the transmissions.[186] As with s 296, it is the copyright owner who has the right and the person responsible is to be treated as infringing copyright. The criminal offence in s 297A carries a maximum penalty of a fine not exceeding level 5, currently £5000. A 'decoder' is defined as any apparatus designed or adapted to enable (on its own or with other apparatus) an encrypted transmission to be decoded. Apparatus is defined widely as including any device, component or electronic data and will, therefore, include decoders that exist in software form only.[187] The transmission must be one from within the UK, though there is a statutory defence if the person charged did not know and had no reasonable ground for knowing that the decoder was unauthorised. A decoder is unauthorised if it enables an encrypted transmission that is paid for to be viewed without payment.

181 Inserted by the Broadcasting Act 1990 s 179.

182 [1990] Ch 609.

183 *The Times*, 28 November 1989.

184 [1990] Ch 609.

185 There is no similar problem with the Copyright, Designs and Patents Act 1988 s 296 as making a copy of a work issued in an electronic form will almost certainly infringe copyright.

186 [1991] 3 WLR1.

187 The Copyright, Designs and Patents Act 1988 s 297A(3) contains definitions.

Some decoders are used with 'smartcards'. These are cards containing an algorithm that allows the decoder to unscramble the encrypted signals. By altering the encryption algorithm and issuing new smartcards containing the new algorithm periodically, the broadcast provider can derive a continuing income from his broadcasts. Human nature being what it is, it was not long before someone started selling unauthorised smartcards.[188] In *British Sky Broadcasting Group Ltd* v *Lyons*[189] the defendant bought in Germany unauthorised smartcards for use with the plaintiff's decoders and sold them in the UK. He was described by Aldous J as a parasite. However, when sued under s 298 of the Act, he raised a number of interesting defences. First, he argued that, as s 298(2)(a) gives rights and remedies against a person only in relation to any apparatus or device designed or adapted to enable or assist persons to receive programmes or other transmission when they are not entitled to do so, the device or apparatus must have some feature specifically designed to enable *unauthorised use*. There was no evidence that the defendant's smartcards were in any way different from those of the plaintiff. Aldous J rejected this submission as untenable, it being sufficient that it enabled persons, who were otherwise not entitled to do so, to receive the programmes.

The defendant also raised a number of 'Euro-defences', claiming that s 298 conflicted with Article 7 (now Article 6 – discrimination of grounds of nationality) and Article 30 (quantitative restrictions on trade between member states). These too were rejected by Aldous J. In particular, s 298 did not offend against Article 7 because the right was given in relation to broadcasts from the UK irrespective of the broadcaster's nationality. In the absence of full harmonisation, it is up to national legislatures to determine the precise conditions and procedures for the protection of industrial property,[190] even though s 298 favoured broadcasters with transmitters in the UK. It should be noted that the definition of 'decoder' in s 297A is wide enough to cover smartcards as well as the equipment into which they are inserted. Thus, a person who makes, imports, sells or lets for hire an unauthorised smartcard will, if he has the requisite *mens rea*, be guilty of an offence.

## COPYING TECHNOLOGY

Improvements in copying technology and reductions in the cost of making copies of all manner of copyright works have seriously challenged the efficacy of copyright law as a means of controlling unauthorised copying. For example, considerable advances have been made in photocopying in terms of both quality and the cost of making copies in real terms. An additional worry for the owners of copyright in printed materials such as books, magazines and sheet music is the much greater availability of photocopying machines. Most employed persons and students have relatively easy access to a photocopier these days. In 1965, the Society of Authors and the Publishers Association made an announcement, concerning the fair dealing provisions for research or private study, indicating the amount of photocopying which authors and publishers would not normally consider to be unfair. Because of subsequent advances in technology and the dramatic increase in the amount of photocopying, this 'allowance' was withdrawn in 1985.[191] The announcement had, of course, no standing in

188 In Ireland, the Irish High Court considered that a smartcard was a computer program: *News Datacom Ltd* v *Satellite Decoding Systems* [1995] FSR 201.

189 [1995] FSR 357.

190 *See Keurkoop* v *Nancy Kean Gifts* [1982] ECR 2853; *Volvo AB* v *Erik Veng (UK) Ltd* [1989] 4 CMLR 122.

191 The British Copyright Council, *Reprographic Copying of Books and Journals*, 1985, p. 5. The Society of Authors and the Publishers Association are members of the British Copyright Council.

law and was merely a guideline, and in any case the fair dealing provisions are not needed unless the amount copied is a substantial part of the work. Another factor rendering the guidelines irrelevant to some extent is the establishment of the Copyright Licensing Agency, which issues blanket licences permitting the copying of substantial parts of works covered by the scheme. This type of arrangement is growing in significance and is likely to continue to do so as a means of obtaining income to be distributed amongst copyright owners, and it is probable that such schemes will be developed in the future for other kinds of works.[192] One major factor that will encourage this is the difficulty of enforcing copyright where the copying is done by private individuals for their own use.

Another technical innovation which has worried the music, film and broadcasting industries is the development of copying devices such as home music centres with twin cassette decks and video recorders. The computer industry itself is extremely vulnerable to copying as many computer programs can be copied very easily. Attempts to restrict or stop the sale of twin cassette music centres failed, as was noted in Chapter 6. It had been argued, and indeed it was suggested in a White Paper, that a levy should be imposed on the sale of blank audio cassette tape as a means of retrieving some of the profit lost as a result of copying.[193] However, this proposal did not survive in the Copyright, Designs and Patents Act 1988.

Copying of broadcasts, cable programmes, films and audio recordings is likely to increase as technology improves. For example, the introduction of digital audio tape (DAT), compact discs and mini-disks permits the making of copies of better quality than was previously possible. In terms of the law, there is little that can be done as regards copying in the home for private purposes, apart from imposing a levy on blank media. The only workable alternative is for anti-copying technology to be developed and applied to recordings that are made available to the public. However, this may have a negative effect in that, for some, the very fact that the recordings can be copied is an important factor in the decision to purchase or hire. For example, a person who buys a compact disc of music to be played at home might also like to make a copy on audio tape to play in his car while driving to and from work, although strictly this infringes copyright.[194]

Attempts to render computer programs difficult to copy have been made for some time. Some consist of a 'dongle', a piece of computer hardware that plugs into a computer. When the computer program is run, it checks to see if the dongle is in place before continuing. Other forms of copy protection involve the scrambling of the program code on the magnetic disk or alterations to the disk directory. Inevitably, it was not long before devices and software designed to overcome these attempts at copy protection appeared on the market. For example, relatively inexpensive computer software could be obtained to make copies of 'protected' programs costing many hundreds of pounds, often sold as having some ostensibly legitimate but unlikely use.

There can be little sympathy for those who make and sell devices deliberately designed to permit the copying of works that are copy-protected. They are now controlled by the Copyright, Designs and Patents Act 1988, s 296, which provides that the making, importation, sale or hire, etc. of devices or means specifically designed or adapted to circumvent copy protection of works issued to the public in electronic form are to be treated as an infringement of

192 An early example is the Performing Right Society. Under the Copyright Act 1956, there was a statutory recording licence. Any person could make records to be sold by retail as long as they paid the copyright owner 6¼ per cent of the ordinary retail selling price. This has been abolished by the Copyright, Designs and Patents Act 1988 Sch 1, para 21. A Public Lending Right Scheme was introduced by the Public Lending Right Act 1979 to distribute an annual sum of money amongst authors of literary works loaned out by public libraries.

193 *Intellectual Property and Innovation*, Cmnd 9712 (HMSO, 1986). The proposed levy did not extend to short tapes used, predominantly, for computer programs, or to video tape. Blank tape levy schemes appear to work effectively in some European countries, especially in Germany.

194 Generally, the use of anti-copying techniques used with computer programs had such a negative effect. Apart from the copying problem, such devices may make the program less convenient to use in practice.

copyright. Furthermore, publishing information to enable or assist the circumvention of copy protection is similarly treated. However, this is actionable only by the copyright owner, and presumably an exclusive licensee of the copyright owner, and the device or means or information must be directed to the form of copy protection employed by the copyright owner.[195] In addition to devices and means intended to prevent or restrict copying, 'copy protection' also includes those that are directed at impairing the quality of copies made from the original. Of course, these provisions are not just aimed at computer programs, but also concern copy protection of audio and visual works that are issued in an electronic form, which is widely defined in the Act by s 178. Some equipment can be used for making copies of sound and video recordings and computer programs legitimately, without infringing copyright, for example twin tape cassette machines, computer disk drives, 'double' video recorders. Even though such equipment can also be used to make unauthorised copies, it will not fall within the scope of s 296 because it is not specifically designed to overcome copy protection. Where equipment or software has lawful uses, it would obviously be unsatisfactory to ban its sale.[196]

## SCIENTIFIC DISCOVERIES, GENETIC SEQUENCES AND FORMULAE

In this increasingly technological world, where the means of production and dissemination are more widely available than ever before, freeing authors from the control of publishers, there may be more emphasis on invention, innovation and original thought than the means of expression and commercial reproduction. An important factor is that copyright has now moved into the technological field and the shift of power from publishers to authors may serve as a catalyst for change in emphasis. Take, for example, a person who devises an original mathematical formula. It can be used to generate valuable information such as the chances of a particular horse winning a race. Or perhaps a scientist has by careful experimentation discovered a new aerodynamic model for turbulent flow of fluid over a surface which can be expressed mathematically. A geneticist determines the genetic sequence of a viral infection. Are such things the subject of copyright protection, and should they be?

We will see in the section on patents that certain things are expressly excluded from the grant of a patent, as such. These include a discovery, scientific theory or mathematical method, a scheme, rule or method for performing a mental act, playing a game, or doing business, or a program for a computer.[197] Practical applications of such things may, however, be patentable. For example, a scientific discovery cannot form the basis of a patent, but a new industrial process based on that theory can be patented. What the patent system cannot protect is the theory itself. Apart from anything else, the protection of theories and the like by patents would give the proprietor far too strong a monopoly position. In the light of this, should copyright protect something that the patent system does not?

Consider the case of a new formula used to calculate the size of a timber beam to support a roof over a building. Variables used by the formula might include the span (s), the horizontal spacing between beams (h), the maximum roof load (including wind and snow loads) (w), the strength timber (t), the slenderness

**195** The Copyright, Designs and Patents Act 1988 s 101 provides that an exclusive licensee has the same rights as if the licence had been an assignment. Section 296 also contains provisions for delivery up and seizure of devices and means.

**196** The music industry failed in its attempt to interfere with the sale of twin cassette music centres, see *CBS Songs Ltd v Amstrad Consumer Electronics plc* [1988] AC 1013. In the USA, an attempt to ban the sale of the Betamax video recorder failed on similar grounds: *Sony v Universal City Studios* (1984) 104 US 774.

**197** Patents Act 1977 s 1(2).

ratio (the ratio of the depth of the beam compared to its height) (r), the factor of safety (F) and so forth. The formula[198] might look something like this:

$$d = F \times \int (f(s) + f(h)) \div f(t) + 0.235 \times F\Sigma\partial w \div r$$

Where $f()$ denotes some function of the variable enclosed in brackets.

The formula is likely to be the result of a significant amount of theoretical work supported by empirical research. Once it has been developed and tested, its application to practical situations will probably be a fairly simple matter, though requiring mathematical skills. Imagine that a person other than the devisor of the equation decides to use the formula in a computer program to design timber beams. The program is used to create a whole set of tables by which a person wishing to determine an appropriate size for timber beams to span a roof can quickly and easily do so.

Several questions fall to be considered. Is the formula a work of copyright in its own right? Is the set of tables a work of copyright? If so, does the deviser of the formula have any rights in the tables? Taking those questions *seriatim*:

1 Is the formula a work of copyright? If it is accepted that skill and judgment have been expended in the creation of the formula, there seems to be no doubt that the formula is a work of copyright, being an original literary work. Aldous J considered that there was no reason why this should not be so in *Bookmakers' Afternoon Greyhound Services Ltd* v *Wilf Gilbert (Staffordshire) Ltd*[199] in the context of a formula for calculating forecast dividends for greyhound races. There are authorities which suggest otherwise. In *Exxon Corp* v *Exxon Insurance Consultants International Ltd*,[200] the single word 'EXXON' was held not to be an original literary work, even though significant market research had been undertaken in deciding a new corporate name. In that case, great reliance was placed on the quote by Davey LJ in *Hollinrake* v *Truswell*[201] to the effect that a literary work should 'afford either information or instruction, or pleasure, in the form of literary enjoyment'. It is submitted that that approach is no longer valid, primarily because of the extention of literary copyright to computer programs. An object code program installed in a silicon chip and invisible to the naked eye would surely fail Davey LJ's test, yet such a program is undoubtedly protected by copyright.[202] The better view, therefore, is that a formula that is a result of skill and judgment is a work of copyright. This accords also with the approach taken by Judge Paul Baker in *Microsense Systems Ltd* v *Control Systems Technology Ltd*[203] where he accepted that there was an arguable case that a list of mnemonics was protected by copyright, at least by virtue of the skill and judgment in devising the functions to be represented by the mnemonics.

2 Is the set of tables a work of copyright? Returning again to the *Bookmakers' Afternoon Greyhound Services* case, the plaintiff submitted that, in determining whether forecasts such as 'BAGS Forecast £2.25' derived using a formula were themselves works of copyright, the skill and judgment in devising the formula should be taken into account. Aldous J did not accept that proposition. He said:

> A person who takes a work, whether it be a formula, a book or a poem, and uses it to produce another work, will only obtain copyright in that other work, if the skill, labour and judgment used to produce that other work are sufficient.[204]

Therefore, the creation of the derivative work must itself require skill and judgment, independent from that of the first work. Making calculations using a formula might require little skill beyond a basic understanding of arithmetic, such as working a percentage of a number, or it may require advanced mathematical skill, for example, requiring proficiency in differential calculus.[205] One problem with this approach is where the formula has been incorporated in a computer program. Here it may be a question of considering the skill and judgment of the person using the program. If he simply enters factual data the resultant output may not be protected by copyright as in the *Bookmakers'* case, *a fortiori* where only a single or small number of calculations are performed.

A table is itself a work of copyright and protected as such, provided that there is skill and judgment in its making. This will be so in deriving a set of tables to design timber beams. The person setting about the task will have to decide on the ranges of parameters, the increments in those parameters, how to design the layout of the tables for ease of use, etc. A table or set of tables could also be viewed as a database, subject to copyright and/or the database right, whether the table resides in software form or is printed out on paper. The database right may be particularly useful as it overcomes the need for skill and judgment by requiring a substantial investment only.[206]

3 Does the deviser of a formula have any rights in the result of using it? If the formula is a work of copyright and the person using it performs any of the restricted acts without the licence of the owner of the copyright in the formula, there will be an infringement of its copyright. This would be so if the formula were expressed in a computer program, and it would seem to be sensible to hold the same if the formula is not directly expressed but is broken down into a number of individual calculations on the basis of non-literal copying. However, if a person simply uses the formula without reproducing it, there can be no infringement. The formula simply is the tool by which the calculated results are obtained in the same way as a pen or paintbrush is used to create a new work. In this respect the situation is analogous to the creation of random numbers by a programmed computer in *Express Newspapers plc* v *Liverpool Daily Post and Echo plc*.[207]

Similar considerations ought to apply to other technical discoveries such as a hithero unknown chemical reaction[208] or a genetic sequence.[209] Provided that there is skill and judgment in their discovery or creation, and they have been expressed in an appropriate manner (for example by being written down), there is no reason why they should not be protected by copyright. Copyright will not, however, prevent the use of such things by others. All that is controlled are the specific acts restricted by copyright. Nor does copyright prevent the independent creation of the same or a similar work. If the discovery or whatever is published, perhaps in an academic journal, a limited amount of copying may be permitted in the course of developing a practical application of the discovery, on the basis of the fair dealing provisions or by virtue of an implied licence. Public interest may also be an issue. Of course, where the discovery has not been published, it may be protected by the law of breach of confidence.

205 Aldous J did not consider the fact that performing the calculations in the bookmaker's case required 'a certain amount of education' meant that the results were protected by copyright.

206 *See* the section on databases, earlier in this chapter.

207 [1985] 1 WLR 1089.

208 Such as in *Merrell Dow Pharmaceuticals Inc* v *H N Norton & Co Ltd* [1996] RPC 76, where a patent for a chemical reaction in the human liver was held invalid.

209 It has been suggested that DNA sequences are protected by copyright provided they are sufficiently long: Laddie *et al* (1995) *The Modern Law of Copyright* (2nd edn) Butterworths, at p. 859.

## COPYRIGHT AND ELECTRONIC PUBLISHING

All forms of work can be stored and transmitted or made available electronically. Literary, dramatic, musical and artistic works can be represented in digital form as can films and sound recordings. It is not surprising that the growth of multimedia and communications networks is now posing considerable challenges to copyright law and the traditional role of copyright. Already there are claims that copyright law is doomed in this arena, quickly to be overtaken by contractual means of controlling the use and dissemination of copyright works.[210] Serious issues have already been raised in relation to the Internet, copyright and freedom of speech apart from concerns in other areas of law.[211] In the United States, copyright infringement action has been taken by the Church of Scientology against an ex-member who placed some of the Church's materials on the Internet,[212] and in *United States* v *LaMacchia*[213] a student from the Massachusetts Institute of Technology who operated a bulletin board encouraged others to use it to exchange commercial software. It was estimated that in excess of $1 million of software was copied.[214] Even the act of digitisation, converting a conventional work into digital form, has wide-ranging implications, as discussed in Chapter 6.[215]

### What is electronic publishing?

The term 'electronic publishing' could include publication or dissemination of information by one of the following methods:

- sale, rental or lending of a physical carrier containing a copy of the work or works in question, for example, CD-ROM, magnetic disk or magnetic tape;
- by means of cable networks, for example, the Internet or on-line facilities; or
- by means of a broadcast, whether or not encrypted – for example, Prestel and CEEFAX.

All these forms of electronic publishing are capable of supporting copyright. The individual works so made available may be subject to copyright and, in some cases, there will be other copyrights, such as that in a broadcast or cable programme, or there may be compilation or database copyrights in addition to the database right.

The fact that the publication is electronic should not, by itself, cause problems because of the wide definitions in the Copyright, Designs and Patents Act 1988. For example, the word 'electronic' has a particularly wide meaning by s 178, being 'actuated by electric, magnetic, electro-magnetic, electro-chemical or electro-mechanical energy' and the term 'in electronic form' means in a form usable only by electronic means. 'Writing' is defined as including any form of notation or code, whether by hand or otherwise and regardless of the method by which, or medium in or on which, it is recorded. However, even such a robust approach to definitions may fail to keep up with technological change. Would the above definitions be appropriate in relation to a liquid DNA computer?[216] Nevertheless, it is clear that these definitions apply to CD-ROM, laser and magnetic disk technology, and this is important as, by s 17(2), copying includes storage in any medium by electronic means.

210 Holderness, M. 'Grateful thanks for an open show', *The Times Higher Educational Supplement,* 18 February 1994, p. 19.

211 For example, in terms of defamation, pornography and electronic commerce.

212 *Religious Technology Center* v *Netcom On-Line Communications Services Inc* 21 November 1995, District Court for the Northern District of California.

213 871 F Supp 535 (D Mass 1994).

214 Because the student had no motive to gain from his activities commercially, a prosecution under the United States Copyright Act was bound to fail. He was prosecuted unsuccessfully under the Computer Fraud and Abuse Act 1986.

215 *See Anacon Corp Ltd* v *Environmental Research Technology Ltd* [1994] FSR 659. *See also,* Cornish, W. R. 'Authors in Law' (1995) 58 MLR 1 at 14.

216 Described in Alexander, G. 'DNA Holds Key to Explosion in Computer Power', *The Sunday Times,* 30 April 1995, p. 29.

## Multimedia

A CD-ROM disc typically may contain a whole range of works. For example, a multimedia product on the topic of heavy metal music may include:

- the music shown in conventional notation and/or waveform,
- the sound of the music played, perhaps by different performers and/or indifferent styles,
- an oral and/or textual description of background material relating to the composers and performers,
- film sequences showing the music being performed in studios or at live concerts,
- photographs or films showing the composers' birthplaces, childhood days, homes and acquaintances, and
- title sequences, trade marks, background music, and so on.

A feature of multimedia is the freedom that the person using it has to move about at will. The information is, therefore, structured and may have hypertext links. In terms of copyright subsistence, all the works above may be subject to copyright in addition to the whole as a database. However, a compilation of music on CD-ROM is excluded from protection as a database (either under copyright law or under the database right), but may qualify for a compilation copyright.[217] Apart from rights in the individual works and rights in the whole as a database or compilation, there may be further copyrights in the non-literal elements relating to structure and cross-referencing of items. A major difficulty for a company producing a multimedia work is making sure that all the necessary permissions have been obtained. This may be made more difficult by the spectre of revived copyright resulting from the extension of the term of copyright to life plus 70 years.[218]

## The Internet

The Internet is made up of interlinked public telecommunications networks to which computers are connected. Anyone can gain access by use of an appropriate modem, usually with an appropriate agreement with an access provider (or internet service provider – ISP), a person who provides a 'gateway' to the Internet. Material can be accessed, viewed, retrieved, printed and downloaded from all over the world and a vast amount of information is available. Virtually any type of work can be made available via the Internet. At the present time, there is no one person who is in overall control of the Internet; it could be described as information technology communications anarchy. The legal implications are immense.[219]

Whilst copyright still subsists in materials on the Internet (individually or collectively, as databases or compilations, or as cable programmes), there is a view held by some that placing material on the Internet is equivalent to placing it in the public domain. Nothing could be further from the truth. Even if the owner of the work does not mind others freely copying the material, that fact does not prejudice the subsistence of copyright. In any case, a person who abandons his economic rights under copyright might feel aggrieved if another later claims he was the author or makes a derogatory treatment of it. Abandonment of the economic rights does not necessarily mean that the moral rights under copyright law have also been waived.[220]

217 Recital 19 of the Directive on the legal protection of databases.

218 For a comprehensive description of some of the practical difficulties associated with publishing on multimedia, *see* Henry, M. (1994) *Publishing and Multimedia Law*, Butterworths.

219 *See* Gringas, C. (1997) *The Laws of the Internet*, Butterworths.

220 However, in the United Kingdom, the right to be identified must be asserted. This may be done by a simple statement such as 'the author hereby asserts his right to be identified as such'.

Apart from any copyright in the individual works and compilations of works, there may be separate copyrights in works as cable programmes included in a cable programme service.[221] Section 7(1) of the Copyright, Designs and Patents Act 1988 defines a cable programme service as a service consisting wholly or mainly in sending visual images, sounds or other information by means of a telecommunications system, otherwise than by wireless telegraphy, for reception:

(a) at two or more places (whether for simultaneous reception or at different times in response to requests by different users), or
(b) for presentation to members of the public.

We have seen from *The Shetland Times* v *Dr Jonathan Wills*[222] that operating a website was considered to be operating a cable programme service within the above meaning and that, although subscribers could send information as well as receive it, the service was not predominantly interactive and, in any event, the interactive feature of the system could be considered to be severable.

There are difficulties with applying cable programme copyright to the Internet. This form of copyright was intended to be the equivalent to the broadcast copyright for providers of cable television. In this sense it works well but, by s 9(2)(c), the author of a cable programme is the person providing the cable programme service in which the programme is included. But who is providing the service? The access provider (ISP) who arranges connection to the Internet does not, in reality, provide the service in which the programmes (or works) are included. Rather, the access provider is a facilitator rather than a provider. The person making the cable programme service is the person controlling the web page. A further implication is that very small individual works may fall to be considered to be cable programmes. A cable programme is any item included in a cable programme service, which is a service which consists wholly or mainly in sending visual images, sounds or other information by means of a telecommunications system, otherwise than by wireless telegraphy. A small amount of data is information[223] and there would not appear to be the problems with the *de minimis* rule that there might be with other works of copyright. To this, some other problems for copyright in 'cyberspace' can be added. For example, it is impossible to control copying and unauthorised use of works (copies can be made on disk virtually instantaneously – much cheaper and quicker than photocopying). Also, the international dimension is a nightmare in terms of policing and acting against infringers. If, eventually, encryption becomes widespread, other issues will arise. For example, if information is available only to subscribers who are prepared to pay for access, what becomes of the permitted acts under copyright law. If access can be controlled, then even gaining access or doing acts in respect of insubstantial parts of works will not be possible.

Until recently, there has been an emphasis on the medium on which a work is stored with too little appreciation of the nature of copyright. For example, a book comprises two separate and distinct property rights. The paper, ink and binding together make an item of tangible property as a 'good'. The work contained within the book and expressed therein is subject to a copyright which is a form of intangible property. There has been insufficient focus on the existence of the intangible right that is copyright, and the advent of the Internet freeing the copyright from its medium, like releasing the genie from the bottle, will have interesting, and probably unexpected, consequences.

**221** Millard, C. 'Copyright' in Reed, C. (ed) *Computer Law* (3rd edn) (1996) Blackstone Press, at p. 115. Millard appears to be the first person to see this possibility.

**222** [1997] FSR 604, discussed in Chapters 3 and 6.

**223** Presumably, all that is required is that the data convey some meaning.

Apart from all the copyrights mentioned above, there may also be copyrights in the overall structure and layout of a website or web pages and, probably also, in respect of hypertext links, HTML versions of works and 'applets' (executable code which runs automatically).

There is a proposal for a Directive on the harmonisation of certain aspects of copyright and related rights in the Information Society[224] following the WIPO Copyright and Performing Rights Treaties to modify the Berne Copyright Convention. The proposal is designed to take more account of works stored or transmitted in digital form, particularly in terms of the Internet. The main provisions include:

- a reproduction right in respect of direct or indirect, temporary or permanent reproduction;
- rights of communication to the public by wire or wireless means (not subject to exhaustion of rights);
- a distribution right;
- controls over the circumvention of technological measures to prevent unauthorised copying;
- legal protection for electronic 'rights management information' (information which identifies the work, the author, the owner of any right in the work, or information about terms and conditions of use). This will extend to the distribution, etc. without consent, of any works, with the express knowledge that such information has been removed or altered (and also extends to the database right);
- date for compliance is 30 June 2000.

Some of these already are catered for in United Kingdom law, but of particular relevance is the protection of electronic rights management information. The justification for this is that material placed on the Internet is especially vulnerable and, if information relating to copyright and what use may be made of the work were removed, many persons accessing the work would think that they could do anything they wished with the work. At least by providing protection for such information anyone accessing the work will know that it is protected, who owns the copyright and what use may be made of the work without infringing copyright. The protection afforded is likely to take the form of both civil remedies and criminal penalties.

### Legal liability of facilitators[225]

Persons who facilitate access to material on the Internet, whether ISPs or employers making web pages available to employees or in any other case, run the risk of being held liable for things done by persons subscribing to or otherwise using the access to place material on the Internet. In some respects, liability is analogous to the liability of a traditional library for infringing acts performed by persons using the library facilities. Particular forms of infringement considered below are:

- secondary infringement by transmission
- authorising infringement
- contributory infringement
- joint infringement.

In the following discussion, 'ISP' is used for any person who allows or facilitates access to the Internet by another or allows another to place material thereto.

### Secondary infringement by transmission

An ISP transmits works from or through his computer to persons accessing those works. That being so, if the work in question has been made available without the licence of the copyright owner, there is a possibility of liability for secondary infringement under the Copyright, Designs and Patents Act 1988 s 24(2). That provision makes it an infringement to transmit a work, without the licence of a copyright owner, by a telecommunications system knowing or having reason to believe that infringing copies will be made by means of the reception of the transmission in the United Kingdom or elsewhere. The identity of the place of reception is of no consequence. However, the definition of 'infringing copy' does provide some territorial constraint on the infringement. In relation to infringing copies made outside the United Kingdom, under s 24(3), the copy must have been imported or is proposed to be imported into the United Kingdom, and its making in the United Kingdom would have constituted an infringement of the copyright in the work in question or a breach of an exclusive licence agreement relating to the work.

At first sight, this provision looks quite wide, subject to the neccessary knowledge, but a severe limitation on this form of infringement is that the transmission must be otherwise than by broadcasting or inclusion in a cable programme service. As noted earlier, in the *Shetland Times* case, it was held that running a website was operating a cable programme service. Apart from any websites, bulletin boards, forums or other services offered by the service provider, most of the information accessed by subscribers will derive from elsewhere. The service provider is merely the channel through which the information flows. Nevertheless, this should not prevent it from being a cable programme service. There will, however, be parts of the Internet service which are outside the definition of cable programme service, such as e-mail which appears to fall within the exclusion in s 7(2), being predominantly interactive. Bulletin boards likewise could be excluded. It is in respect of such services that liability under s 24(2) could occur.

Liability will be possible in respect of parts of the service not deemed to be a cable programme service wherever the information comes from. The language of s 7, dealing with cable programmes, makes it clear that parts of a service may be severable for this purpose, as accepted in the *Shetland Times* case. The infringement requires transmission, but this would be satisfied if the information merely flowed through the ISP's computer on its way to the subscriber. Such information is received by the service provider, and immediately and instantaneously re-transmitted to the subscriber.[226]

Where the information comprises an infringing work of copyright, a person subscribing to the Internet service will infringe copyright by making a copy. No knowledge is required for that.[227] The Internet service provider will infringe under s 24(2) if, and only if, he has the requisite knowledge. Having reason to believe is an objective test. It is a question of whether the reasonable person, having knowledge of the facts known to the defendant, would have reason to believe that, in this case, infringing copies will be made by means of the reception of the transmission.[228]

**226** The *Concise Oxford Dictionary* definition of transmission includes 'allow to pass through' or 'pass or hand on' (1995) 9th edn. This seems to admit that the transmission may be passive. The use of the word 're-transmission' in other parts of the Act supports this interpretation.

**227** Lack of knowledge could affect an award of damages, *see* s 97(1).

**228** *L A Gear Inc v Hi-Tec Sports plc* [1992] FSR 121, at first instance, and *Hutchinson Personal Communications Ltd v Hook Advertising Ltd* [1995] FSR 365.

ISPs need to be aware of this potential infringement. It may be tempered somewhat by the fact that s 24(2) mentions 'infringing copies' rather than a single copy and, as far as reception outside the United Kingdom is concerned, the copies must be imported or intended to be imported into the United Kingdom. Another issue is whether the ISP is likely to have knowledge of facts giving him reason to believe. This may be a question of whether and to what extent the service provider monitors the material being accessed by his subscribers.

This form of secondary infringement will be of much more extensive application if the *Shetland Times* case, which was not a full trial of the issues, is subsequently held to be wrong in respect of classifying websites as cable programme services. There was some argument in that case that the website operator did not 'send' the information, it merely waited passively to be accessed by callers at the website. That was rejected by the judge, but the question is certainly not beyond doubt. Whereas the s 24(2) infringement uses the word 'transmits', s 7(1) defines a cable programme service in terms of 'sending visual images, sound or other information'. If it is subsequently held, contrary to the *Shetland Times* case, that a website does not 'send' information, this will leave secondary infringement by transmitting without the licence of the copyright owner fully intact.[229]

**229** A further possibility is that, under s 7(3), the Secretary of State can amend the exceptions to cable programme services by addition or removal.

### Authorising infringement of copyright

The acts restricted by the copyright in a work are set out in the Copyright, Designs and Patents Act 1988 s 16(1), which states that the owner has the exclusive right to do those acts in the United Kingdom. Section 16(2) goes on to say that copyright in a work is infringed by a person who without the licence of the copyright owner does, *or authorises another to do*, any of the acts restricted by the copyright (emphasis added). It does not state expressly that the act of authorisation itself must be done in the United Kingdom to infringe.

In *ABKCO Music & Records Inc v Music Collection International Ltd*,[230] a Danish company granted a licence to an English company to manufacture and issue to the public recordings of the plaintiff's sound recordings in the United Kingdom and Eire. It was held that it did not matter where the authorisation was given as long as the restricted act was carried out within jurisdiction. The act of authorisation was not limited territorially unlike the restricted acts themselves.

**230** [1995] RPC 657.

Performing a restricted act and authorising its performance are separate torts.[231] However, the authorisation is a tort only if the act authorised is restricted by copyright in the United Kingdom. Thus, if an American ISP authorises persons in England to place infringing material on the Internet, the ISP infringes under s 16(2) and this is within the jurisdiction of the English courts.

**231** *Ash v Hutchinson & Co (Publishers) Ltd* [1936] Ch 489.

If an Australian makes a copy in Australia of a work subject to United Kingdom copyright, that does not infringe the United Kingdom copyright (notwithstanding the effect of the Berne Convention). If that Australian then places a copy of the work on his website and persons in the United Kingdom access it and make copies, then the Australian infringes the United Kingdom copyright by authorisation. The persons accessing the work also infringe copyright by performing a restricted act, bearing in mind that simply accessing the work will produce a transient copy in the computer's memory. There is no need for a hardcopy print to be made or for the work to be saved to a disk.

## What is authorisation?

Earlier cases show that the concept of authorisation is fairly wide, being 'sanction, countenance or approve' in *Evans* v *Houlton*,[232] and turning a blind eye may amount to authorisation. In *PRS* v *Ciryl*[233] it was said that 'indifference, exhibited by acts of commission or omission, may reach a degree from which authorisation or permission may be inferred'. Failing to inform users of a library with photocopying facilities about copyright law and failing properly to supervise the use of the copiers was held to authorise infringement of copyright in the Australian case of *Moorhouse* v *University of New South Wales*.[234]

More recently, in *CBS Songs Ltd* v *Amstrad Consumer Electronics plc*,[235] Lord Templeman agreed with Atkin LJ in *Falcon* v *Famous Players Film Co*[236] where he said that, in the context of copyright, authorisation means '... the grant or purported grant, which may be express or implied, of the right to do the act complained of'. Although *CBS* v *Amstrad* concerned authorisation under the Copyright Act 1956 s 1(2), that meaning should still apply under the 1988 Act. In that particular case, Amstrad was not authorising infringement of copyright by the sale of its twin cassette tape machines, it was merely facilitating unauthorised copying.

It would appear that an ISP could be said to authorise infringement if it fails to inform subscribers of copyright law and the importance of not infringing copyright and, additionally or alternatively, fails to monitor the material made available through its service. *A fortiori*, the same applies to the owner of a website, such as an employer, who allows others to place material on it. Indeed, in such a case, the website owner needs to be particularly vigilant.

As an example consider an employee who has two photographs, but is not the owner of the copyright in either and has no licence to copy. The employee has been informed about copyright law and warned of the dangers of placing infringing material on the website by his employer. He has shown the first photograph to the employer and asked if it is permissible to place it on the site. The employer said it was acceptable to do so. The employee scanned both photographs and placed them on the web pages made available for him by his employer. This is an act of infringement by the employee. In respect of the first photograph, the employer has expressly authorised the infringement of copyright. In the second case, it is less likely that the employer has authorised infringement although, if he rarely or never carries out checks on what is contained in the web pages, it is arguable that he has.

There will be further infringements by persons accessing the relevant web pages, and in respect of these the employer will be liable (providing the persons access the pages in the United Kingdom) for authorising infringement in connection with both photographs.

Wherever the location of the computer containing the infringing material or the place where the service provider is established, it is almost inevitable that at least one person in the United Kingdom will gain access to the material. That being so, if the material includes works subject to United Kingdom copyright, the service provider will be at risk of an action for infringement by authorising someone to carry out a restricted act in the United Kingdom.

232 [1923–1928] MacG CC 51.
233 [1914] KB 1.
234 [1976] RPC 151.
235 [1988] AC 1013.
236 [1926] 2 KB 474.

## Contributory infringement

In the United States a person may be liable on the basis of contributory infringement. In *Religious Technology Center* v *Netcom On-Line Communication Services Inc*[237] it was said that service providers could be liable for contributory infringement if they had knowledge of the infringement but had not taken any steps to put a stop to it.[238] The concept of control was important. An analogy with a building lease was rejected by the court. It had been argued that a lessor of premises later used, for example, to make infringing copies of a work, would not be liable. The court considered that an ISP, unlike a lessor of premises, does retain a measure of control over the use of the system. In the past, Netcom had suspended accounts of subscribers who had used the system to post infringing software.

Contributory infringement can be likened to authorising infringement, but is not so extensive. For example, it would appear that contributory infringement in the United States requires actual knowledge, whereas authorising infringement in the United Kingdom can be inferred, for example, where a person is indifferent as to whether infringing material is involved. Can an ISP be said to be a joint infringer of copyright merely because he has facilitated the infringement? It would appear that two issues are relevant here, being one of control, the other being whether the joint infringers have a common design.

Who controls the service or the website? In *Amstrad Consumer Electronics plc* v *The British Phonograph Industry Ltd*[239] it was held that supplying machines which would be likely to be used unlawfully to copy pre-recorded cassettes subject to copyright protection was insufficient to make the manufacturer or supplier a primary infringer of copyright. Nor could this be seen as authorising infringement of copyright because the supplier had no control over the way the machines were used once sold.

Joint infringers are two or more persons who act in concert pursuant to a common design to infringe.[240] In the case of twin-tape cassette machines, Amstrad had no control, nor was there any common design between Amstrad and purchasers of its machines. ISPs and operators of websites are not in the same position, as they do have some measure of control. They can erase infringing material quickly. They can check that material transmitted through their service or placed on the website does not infringe. ISPs should especially keep an eye on their bulletin boards. In reality, however, monitoring all the material will be impracticable, and it may be that some form of random checking is carried out. Nonetheless, even though there is the potential for control, it will be harder to demonstrate a common design to infringe copyright if the service provider and website operator run the service or site properly, using effective auditing systems. On the other hand, if they encourage, even tacitly, others to place infringing material on the Internet, it could be said that there is a common design, being the dissemination of infringing material. As a joint infringer, the ISP will be likely to be liable additionally for authorising infringement.

### Conclusions

ISPs and website operators must ensure that persons making material available on the Internet through them are aware of the importance of not infringing copyright. This should be backed up by a reasonable amount of monitoring to check that infringing material is not being used. Whilst 'surfing the net' the

237 907 F Supp 1361 (ND Cal 1995).

238 Hails R.I., Jr. 'Liability of On-Line Service Providers Resulting from Copyright Infringement Performed by their Subscribers' [1996] 5 EIPR 304.

239 [1986] FSR 159.

240 *The Koursk* [1924] P 140, *per* Scrutton LJ at 156, approved by Lord Templeman in *CBS* v *Amstrad, above.*

author of this book came across an American website that contained the complete text of all the scripts from the popular TV series the 'X-Files', placed there by someone who readily accepted that what he had done was probably illegal!

Perhaps a useful solution is to require that the person placing the material on the Internet or website provides a warranty (backed by an appropriate indemnity) that the material does not infringe third-party rights, though this also should be backed by at least a degree of monitoring. However, in terms of electronic rights management information, careful monitoring could create onerous obligations to verify, in suspicious cases, that the information has not been removed or modified. Again, an ISP is likely to require a warranty from the subscriber.

If an ISP discovers that a subscriber has placed infringing material on the Internet, he should take immediate steps to remove it, However, it should be reasonable to allow the ISP sufficient time to satisfy himself that the material does indeed infringe a third-party right, otherwise he could be in breach of his contract with the subscriber unless he has an appropriate term in the contract to cover this eventuality. ISPs should develop procedures for dealing with allegations of infringement.

The copyright laws of other countries should be checked to see what the possible exposure to infringement proceedings is. However, the concept of infringing by authorisation should be fairly widespread deriving from the Berne Convention for the Protection of Literary and Artistic Works. For example, Article 9(1) of the Convention gives authors of literary and artistic works the exclusive right of *authorising* their reproduction in any form.

A number of other rights may be infringed including moral rights. Even if a person is happy to allow others to download freely his material, he may still be upset if his moral rights are not respected, such as his right to be identified as the author. A final point is that the copyright owner who gives permission for free use of the work is not always going to be the person who has the moral rights.

# 9

# European and international aspects of copyright

## INTRODUCTION

The freedom to exploit intellectual property rights internationally is vital to the future growth of investment in the creative fields. But even if the prospect of international trade in the work or article concerned is not contemplated, international protection cannot be ignored. For example, a copyright owner might intend to sell a book or recording of music only on the domestic market, but pirate copies could be produced in a foreign country with weak intellectual property laws and imported into the domestic market, seriously damaging the copyright owner's commercial interests.[1]

Of central importance is the state of law in the European Community. The United Kingdom became a member of the European Economic Community at the beginning of 1973, and with the coming of the single market the interaction between UK intellectual property law and the Treaty of Rome is of utmost importance.[2] By Article 3 of the Treaty (as amended) the aims of the Union include the elimination of quantitative restrictions on the import and export of goods and the abolition of obstacles to freedom of movement for persons, services and capital, ensuring that competition in the common market is not distorted. Exploitation of intellectual property may be in conflict with some of these aims, and although one might expect the main problems to result from patents or trade marks, there are several issues involving copyright.

One thing to be borne in mind is that these aims are applicable only as regards trade between member states. Another aim of the Community is the approximation of the laws of the member states to the extent required for the proper functioning of the common market, that is the harmonisation of laws. This is not a wholesale levelling of national differences, or at least has not yet proven to be, although domestic UK intellectual property law has been changed significantly as a result of EC legislation and will be further changed in the near future.

## COPYRIGHT LAW AND THE TREATY OF ROME

By virtue of the European Communities Act 1972, Community law takes precedence over inconsistent domestic law. Section 2(1) of that Act states:

> All such rights, powers, liabilities, obligations and restrictions from time to time created or arising by or under the [Community] Treaties, and all such remedies and procedures from time to time provided for by or under the Treaties, as in accordance

1 Of course, there may be remedies available in the domestic country.

2 This is the European Economic Treaty signed on 25 March 1957, now referred to as the EC Treaty. Also signed in Rome on the same day was the Treaty establishing 'Euratom', the European Atomic Energy Community.

with the Treaties are without further enactment to be given legal effect or used in the United Kingdom shall be recognised and available in law, and be enforced, allowed and followed accordingly ...

Section 2(2) allows amendment of existing law by means of statutory instrument in order to comply with Community obligations. Thus, an Act of Parliament may be modified by a Secretary of State, a fact which seems to run counter to the concept of parliamentary supremacy.[3] There has been some criticism of this process in relation to Directives. By using a different form of words to that in the Directive, the relevant department is applying its own interpretation to Community law, something which is, arguably, the job of the courts.[4] In any case, by introducing another layer of legislation, uncertainty is increased as there are often doubts as to whether a regulation has correctly implemented a Directive.[5]

Any doubts about the supremacy of European Community law over inconsistent domestic law were laid to rest well before the UK's entry on 1 January 1973.[6] Therefore, if national legislation implementing a Community obligation does so imperfectly, it is the meaning in the relevant Community text that takes precedence.

The exercise of intellectual property rights might conflict with several provisions in the Treaty of Rome 1957 (the EC Treaty, as amended). Those provisions are:

- Articles 30–36 which promote the free movement of goods
- Article 85 which prohibits restrictive trade practices
- Article 86 which prevents the abuse of a dominant trading position.

Readers should note that, as a result of the Amsterdam Treaty,[7] Articles 85 and 86 will be renumbered Articles 81 and 82 respectively.

Also, Article 6 of the Treaty[8] provides that any discrimination on the grounds of nationality shall be prohibited. Therefore, one member state may not exclude authors and performing artists from another member state from the rights enjoyed by nationals. German law on copyright and related rights provided that non-German nationals could not rely on the provisions which prohibited the distribution of unauthorised recordings of performances given outside Germany. In *Collins v Imtrat Handelsgesellschaft mbH*,[9] Phil Collins and Cliff Richard argued that this provision offended against Article 6 in an action relating to the distribution in Germany of bootleg recordings of their performances given in the USA and the UK. The German Copyright Act 1965 ss 96(1) and 125(1) granted protection to German nationals in respect of their performances, but this did not extend to foreign artists if the performance was given outside Germany. The German courts referred the matter to the European Court of Justice for a preliminary ruling under Article 177 and the Court confirmed that copyright and related rights fell within the scope of Article 6 and the principle of non-discrimination applied to those rights. This was so even though there was not yet full harmonisation of copyright and related rights throughout the Community: they fell within the Treaty's provisions because of their effect on intra-Community trade in goods and services.

The *Phil Collins case* has some important implications in the field of copyright and neighbouring rights. The European Court of Justice confirmed that, in the absence of Community provisions harmonising national legislation, the determination of the rules and conditions relating to the protection of literary

3 A Minister laying a regulation before Parliament would have to act *intra vires*.

4 *See* Laddie *et al* (1995), *The Modern Law of Copyright* (2nd edn), Butterworths, at p. 14.

5 *See* the discussion on the implementation of the computer program Directive in Chapter 8.

6 *See*, for example, *Costa v ENEL* [1964] ECR 585; *Internationale Handelsgesellschaft Case* [1970] ECR 1125.

7 OJ C 340, 10.11.97, p. 143.

8 Formerly Article 7 of the EC Treaty.

9 [1994] FSR 166.

and artistic property was a matter for member states. Nevertheless, the exercise of that power by member states was conditional upon full compliance with the fundamental principles of the Treaty and relevant international conventions. Thus, copyright (and rights in performances) falls within the application of the Treaty, and the provisions on equal treatment, *inter alia*, may be invoked against national authorities by anyone concerned.[10] It should be noted that the reciprocity provisions of conventions such as the Berne Copyright Convention allow exceptions to the principle of national treatment.[11] Examples relate to the term of copyright and *droit de suite* (the artist's re-sale right)[12] and these must now, within the European Community, be treated with caution.

The exercise of intellectual property rights may entail the control and dividing up of markets by the number and type of licence agreements entered into by the owner and the terms contained in them. For example, a UK company may own the copyright in a sound recording and decide to grant a licence to a Dutch company to make and sell copies in The Netherlands. A similar licence may be granted to a French company, and both licence agreements may purport to prohibit either the Dutch or French company selling the recordings outside their respective countries. This would appear to interfere with the principle of the free movement of goods, especially if the recordings sell at different prices in different countries.

European Community law does recognise intellectual property rights. Article 222 of the Treaty of Rome states that nothing in the Treaty shall prejudice the rules in member states governing the system of property ownership, and intellectual property is undoubtedly a form of property. However, this refers to domestic law in member states, and where the exercise of those rights interferes with the provisions of the Treaty the rights will be compromised. Article 222 has to do with the *existence* of a right, whereas Articles 30–36 are concerned with the *exercise* of that right. If Community legislation requires a reduction in the protection afforded by a member state this would, presumably, conflict with Article 222 and be *ultra vires*. The point is not without some interest, as the new law on databases implies a higher standard of originality for copyright subsistence: *see* Chapter 8.

In principle, because copyright affords a weaker form of protection and does not lock away ideas as such, the possibility for conflict with Community law seems to be less than with patents or trade marks. However, there are a number of cases dealing with copyright licensing, disparity in protection between member states, problems with collecting societies and issues similar to those occurring in the *British Leyland* spare parts case.[13] First, the reconciliation of copyright with the free movement of goods will be considered, followed by the impact of Articles 85 and 86.

### The freedom of movement of goods and copyright

Article 30 of the Treaty states that, 'Quantitative restrictions on imports and all measures having equivalent effect [are] ... prohibited between member states' and Article 34 contains a similar provision as regards exports. Although Article 36 permits such restrictions and measures if they are for the protection of industrial and commercial property, the prohibitions have been held to apply to copyright and neighbouring rights.[14] The purpose of Articles 30 and 36 is to

10 In other words, Article 6 of the EC Treaty has direct effect.

11 The principle of national treatment requires that nationals of other member states must be given treatment no less favourable than that afforded to the member states' own nationals.

12 Articles 7(8) and 14(2) respectively of the Berne Copyright Convention. There is a proposal for a Directive on the artists' re-sale right; *see* post.

13 [1986] 2 WLR 400, discussed in Chapter 6.

14 *Deutsche Grammophon GmbH v Metro-SB-Gröss-markte GmbH & Co* [1971] ECR 487. *See also Collins* v *Imtrat Handelsgesellschaft mbH* [1994] FSR 166.

reconcile the requirements for the free movement of goods with the necessary respect for the legitimate exercise of exclusive rights in 'literary and artistic property'.[15] This has entailed the development of the doctrine of *exhaustion of rights* which is applied where the owner of the rights associated with copies of works that have been lawfully sold or distributed within a member state attempts to use those rights to prevent the subsequent importation of the copies into another member state. The doctrine is used to suppress the exercise of the rights in such circumstances. For example, the owner of a copyright in an artistic work who sells prints of the work to the public cannot use his rights to prevent any subsequent re-sale of those prints.

The principle of exhaustion of rights is not new and has developed in a number of jurisdictions, though in the United Kingdom it had not attained the status of a general principle or doctrine. Specific laws may have had a piecemeal effect in relation to exhaustion. For example, in *Betts* v *Willmott*,[16] the proprietor of a patent for metallic capsules for covering the necks of wine bottles sued to restrain the sale of capsules in England. The proprietor had made capsules in England and France and, although he could show that the capsules in question had not been made by him in England, he could not prove that they had not been made by him in France. Lord Hatherley said:

> When a man has purchased an article he expects to have the control of it, and there must be some clear and explicit agreement to the contrary to justify the vendor in saying that he has not given the purchaser his licence to sell the article, or use it wherever he pleases as against himself.[17]

The *Betts* v *Willmott* principle appears to apply also to copyright.[18] An agreement to the contrary would defeat the presumption that the proprietor's right in respect of re-sale had been exhausted. The doctrine as developed in the European Community is not so fragile.

The European Court of Justice is prepared to recognise that certain activities fall within the normal exploitation of the work even though, at first sight, they may seem to be in conflict with Articles 30–36. For example, in *Bassett* v *Société des Auteurs, Compositeurs et Editeurs de Musique (SACEM)*[19] a royalty of 8.25 per cent was charged by SACEM for playing records in a discotheque in Fréjus in France. The 8.25 per cent was calculated on the basis of a performing right and a mechanical reproduction right. In all other member states, except Belgium, the mechanical reproduction rights were exhausted on an assignment to a manufacturer of phonograms and only a performance royalty had to be paid. The court held that Articles 30–36 did not prohibit the levying of the supplementary mechanical reproduction fee in addition to the usual performance fee, even though the mechanical reproduction fee was not payable in the member state where the recordings were first lawfully put on the market.[20] The extra royalty was seen as being part of the normal exploitation of the copyright and was not, therefore, an 'arbitrary discrimination or disguised restriction' on the trade between member states.

### Parallel imports

Parallel importing occurs when someone, often a third party, attempts to import copyright articles from one country, where they have been lawfully distributed,[21] to another country, usually against the copyright owner's wishes.[22] However,

**15** So it was stated in *EMI Electrola GmbH v Patricia Imund Export Verwaltungsgesellschaft mbH* [1989] 2 CMLR 413. This reconciliation implies that protection should be refused to any abusive exercise of those rights which might tend to maintain or establish artificial boundaries within the Common Market.

**16** (1871) LR 6 Ch App 239.

**17** At 245.

**18** So it was held in High Court, Singapore, in *Aztech Systems Pte Ltd v Creative Technology Ltd* [1996] FSR 54, in which the principle was applied to a computer program lawfully acquired without restriction as to its use.

**19** [1987] ECR 1747. SACEM is a French collecting society which collects and distributes royalties in respect of the performing and mechanical reproduction rights for literary, dramatic and musical works.

**20** The 8.25 per cent was made up of 6.6 per cent performance fee and 1.65 per cent mechanical reproduction fee.

**21** Perhaps under a licence agreement.

**22** This is not restricted to copyright.

any attempt to prevent or interfere with this will, at once, bring into question the applicability of Articles 30–36. In *Musik Vertrieb Membran GmbH v GEMA*,[23] Musik Vertrieb imported sound recordings into Germany from the UK and other member states. The royalty fee paid, under the then statutory licence fee arrangements subsisting in the UK, was 6.25 per cent.[24] There was no statutory licence system in place in Germany at the time, but the normal royalty payable to the German collecting society, GEMA, was 8 per cent. GEMA therefore sued for the difference, 1.75 per cent. The European Court ruled that GEMA could not claim the difference on the basis of Articles 30–36 as the recordings had been put on the market with the consent of the copyright owner. However, the 'consent' in this case was not true consent as such but as a result of statutory licence. Nevertheless, the European Court appeared to accept that, on the facts, the owner had consented and it stated (at 166):

> Articles 30 and 36 ... [preclude] the application of national legislation ... where those sound recordings are distributed on the national market after having been put into circulation in that other member state by or with the consent of the owners of those copyrights ...

This is to treat the notion of consent very widely and, in essence *de jure* consent is looked for rather than *de facto* consent, although the right owner under a statutory licence is unlikely to refuse the royalties accrued in this way. However, it does appear that the Court may have changed its approach since the *Musik Vertrieb* case, as discussed below.

More recently, it has been held that Articles 30–36 did not prevent the working of national legislation to allow a copyright owner to rely on exclusive rights in order to prevent the sale in one member state of copies of a work made in another member state lawfully although without the consent of the copyright owner. So it was held in *EMI Electrola GmbH v Patricia Im-und Export Verwaltungsgesellschaft mbH*[25] in which copies of Cliff Richard recordings were made in Denmark, where exclusive rights under Danish copyright law had expired, and imported into Germany. However, such a restriction could not be justified on the ground of disparity of protection under national copyright laws where it constituted a means of arbitrary discrimination or a disguised restriction on trade between member states. The question of whether an attempted restriction on parallel importing is controlled by Articles 30–36 appears to depend largely upon consent, that is whether the articles have been made available in the other country by the consent of the right owner, and it seems that the European Court is tending to move away from its decision in *Musik Vertrieb* and to require actual rather than illusory consent.[26]

The above cases show the working of the doctrine of exhaustion. The sale or distribution of articles embodying a copyright work (or a patent or design right) in one member state with the consent of the owner is said to exhaust the owner's rights to further control, exclusively, subsequent dealings in those articles.

A useful statement of important points regarding the application of Articles 30–36 to copyright was given in *Warner Bros Inc v Christiansen*,[27] which concerned video rental rights. At the time, there was no rental right in the UK once video films had been made and sold with the owner's consent, but there was such a right in Denmark. Warner Bros. made video films in the UK and granted a licence to a Danish company to make them there. A parallel importer

23 [1981] ECR 147. The court rejected an argument that, because of the existence of moral rights, copyright could not be compared to industrial and commercial property within Article 36.

24 Copyright Act 1956 s 8. The statutory licence fee was abolished by the Copyright, Designs and Patents Act 1988.

25 [1989] 2 CMLR 413.

26 For example, in the patent case of *Pharmon BV v Hoechst AG* [1985] ECR 2281, a drug made under a compulsory licence was not made with the patentee's consent.

27 [1991] FSR 161.

bought videos in the UK and intended to hire them out in Denmark. The court ruled that an injunction against the parallel importer was justified and that the rental rights under Danish law were applicable and were not prohibited by Articles 30–36. The court further stated the principles that apply in terms of film copyright and Articles 30–36, including the following.

1. The inclusion of an exclusive rental right among rights granted to copyright holders under national law constitutes a quantitative restriction under Article 30.
2. The rights of the owner of a copyright work that are not touched by the rules of the Treaty are the exclusive rights of performance and reproduction.[28]
3. Where rental to the public constitutes a significant market and source of revenue for copyright owners and the only way for the latter to secure a share of that revenue is to grant an exclusive right to authorise such hiring out, national copyright laws conferring such an exclusive rental right are justified by Article 36(1).
4. Where the copyright owner chooses to market copies of films in the form of videos in a member state whose copyright law does not grant an exclusive rental right, that does not exhaust his rental right in another member state whose law grants such a right. It is, therefore, permissible under Article 36 for him to enforce his rental right in the latter state, and this also applies to copies imported from the former state.

The above principles should also apply to other works. Surprisingly, there have not been any reported cases on the rental of computer programs. Of course, licence agreements for the acquisition of computer programs usually contain terms prohibiting the subsequent transfer or rental of the program. It is interesting to note that this apparently reluctant acknowledgement of rental rights has been overtaken by the Directive on rental and lending rights with its welcome acceptance of the need to grant control of rental to owners of copyright and related rights.

## Anti-competitive practices, Articles 85 and 86[29]

Articles 85 and 86 are the main provisions to counter anti-competitive practices that may result from a cartel or from an abuse of a dominant position.[30] For example, all the manufacturers of vehicle tyres could get together and agree to raise their prices to a common level rather than try to compete in terms of the price each asks for its tyres. The manufacturer of a motor vehicle might refuse to allow others to make spare parts for his vehicles. Article 85(1) makes agreements between undertakings and decisions by associations of undertakings and concerted practices that may affect trade between member states illegal, if they have as their object or effect the prevention, restriction or distortion of competition within the European Community. Particular agreements, decisions and concerted practices are stated to be those which:

(a) directly or indirectly fix purchase or selling prices or any other trading conditions;
(b) limit or control production, markets, technical development, or investment;
(c) share markets or sources of supply;
(d) apply dissimilar conditions to equivalent transactions with other trading parties, thereby placing them at a competitive disadvantage;

28 There have been changes to the law in these areas.

29 As a result of the Amsterdam Treaty these will be renumbered Articles 81 and 82 respectively.

30 A cartel is an association of independent organisations which have agreed to pursue a course of action which will benefit all of them, such as fixing prices, unfair bidding practices and acceptance of contracts.

(e)  make the conclusion of contracts subject to acceptance by the other parties of supplementary obligations which, by their nature or according to commercial usage, have no connection with the subject of such contracts.

Note that the provision applies where the object of the agreement or decision is the prohibited impact on competition, whether or not it has that impact in practice, or where this is the effect regardless of intention.

Obviously, a licence agreement in relation to the exploitation of a work in which copyright subsists could be caught by Article 85(1). For example, a licence might state that the licensee must restrict his operation to a part of the territory of the European Community, or that the licensee may make only a specified number of copies or that the licensee may not sell or distribute copies of similar works made by organisations that are rivals of the licensor. The European Court has made it clear that it will be prepared to act against exclusive copyright licences if they offend,[31] and although intellectual property rights *per se* do not fall within the meaning of term 'agreement' within Article 85(1), the exercise of an intellectual property right might well do so.[32] Terms within licence agreements, such as export bans, may be susceptible to control. To some extent it is a matter of whether the provision is part of the specific subject matter of the right, and in *Re Ernest Benn Ltd*[33] an export ban was objected to on the basis of Article 85(1). Exemption from the provisions of Article 85(1) is possible, either individually or through block exemption under Article 85(3), and a number of Commission regulations have been passed giving block exemptions, for example in respect of technology transfer agreements.[34] There are, however, no specific block exemptions directed at copyright works.

Reciprocal agreements between collecting societies protecting national interests do not fall foul of Article 85. In *Ministère Public* v *Tournier*[35] it was held that such collecting societies were pursuing legitimate aims where they sought to safeguard the rights and interests of their members, and contracts with users for that purpose could not be regarded as falling within the meaning of Article 85(1). However, this assumed that the practice was not excessive and did not go beyond what was necessary to achieve those legitimate aims.

Article 86 prohibits the abuse of a dominant position within the Common Market. It states:

> Any abuse by one or more undertakings of a dominant position within the common market or in a substantial part of it shall be prohibited as incompatible with the common market in so far as it may affect trade between member states ...

Again, it must be noted that the abuse must affect trade between member states, and if it does not there is no remedy under European Community law no matter how unfair the practice concerned.[36] Four examples of abuse are given in Article 86:

- the imposition of unfair trading conditions or prices
- the limitation of production, markets or technical developments
- discrimination against some trading parties
- the imposition of unconnected supplementary obligations in contracts.

Examples would include the limitation of the supply of music recordings or video films in respect of some member states, probably coupled with high prices. A supplementary obligation that would offend is where a publisher will

31  *Coditel v Ciné Vog Films* [1982] ECR 3381.

32  *Keurkoop v Nancy Kean Gifts BV* [1982] ECR 2853.

33  [1979] 3 CMLR 636.

34  Commission Regulation (EC) No. 240/96, OJ L31, 9.2.96, p. 2, discussed in Chapter 15.

35  [1991] 4 CMLR 248.

36  There may be a remedy under national law. For example, the UK Competition Act 1980 and the soon to be enacted Competition Act 1998.

supply only to retail outlets who agree not to buy from a rival publisher resident in another country.

What constitutes an abuse of a dominant position is not defined as such in Article 86, but in *Hoffmann-La Roche AG v EC Commission*[37] it was described as:

> an objective concept relating to the behaviour of an undertaking in a dominant position which is such as to influence the structure of the market where, as a result of the presence of the undertaking in question, the degree of competition is weakened and which, through recourse to methods different from those which condition normal competition ... has the effect of hindering the maintenance of the degree of competition still existing in the market or the growth of that competition.

Abuse is therefore directed at the use of methods different from normal commercial practices. Refusing to supply further goods until those already supplied have been paid for is outside Article 86.[38] This is a normal business practice.

Merely occupying a dominant position does not automatically bring Article 86 into play. For example, a collecting society occupies a dominant position in its particular country of operation, and in *Bassett v SACEM*[39] the French collecting society SACEM was occupying a dominant position but the exercise of its power was not an abuse as such. The European Court of Justice will not normally interfere unless some plain abuse is present. In *Volvo AB v Erik Veng (UK) Ltd*,[40] Volvo refused to grant licences to spare part manufacturers and the Court held that the proprietor of a protected design has a right to prevent third parties from manufacturing, selling or importing spare parts incorporating the design and that this was the very subject matter of the right. Consequently, the Court would not impose a compulsory licence, because to do so would be to take away the essence of the right even though royalties would be payable. Volvo's decision to refuse to grant a licence was not, therefore, an abuse of its dominant position.[41] Lack of harmonisation in design law was another reason for the Court's reluctance to intervene.

This lack of interference with the exercise of the right to choose whether to grant licence rights is not absolute, and in *RTE & ITP v Commission of the European Communities*,[42] the European Court of Justice dismissed an appeal from a decision of the Commission effectively granting a compulsory licence in respect of listings for forthcoming television programmes even though the television companies concerned were refusing to make them available at all, except to their own publications. Although the Court accepted that mere ownership of copyright did not confer a dominant position on its owner, the fact that the television companies had a *de facto* monopoly in relation to information concerning forthcoming programme schedules meant that they were in a dominant position. The companies could effectively prevent competition from weekly television magazines containing listings of programmes. Exercise of the property right in a work of copyright would not, on the basis of the *Volvo v Veng* decision, normally constitute an abuse of a dominant position. However, by withholding the information, the television companies were preventing others from marketing a competing product for which there was public demand. Such refusal to licence could not be justified on the basis of the companies' broadcasting or publishing activities. The Court confirmed that the requirement that trade between member states be affected was satisfied by showing that the conduct concerned was

37 [1979] ECR 461.

38 *See Leyland Daf Ltd v Automotive Products plc, The Times*, 9 April 1993.

39 [1987] ECR 1747.

40 [1989] 4 CMLR 122.

41 Compare this with *British Leyland Motor Corp Ltd v Armstrong Patents Co Ltd* [1986] 2 WLR 400.

42 [1995] FSR 530. The Commission's decision is reported in OJ L28, 21.12.88, p. 430.

capable of affecting such trade, and it was not necessary to show that trade had in fact been affected.[43]

A distinction can be made between the *RTE* and the *Volvo* cases in that, although it refused to grant licences, Volvo did supply spare parts; whereas in the *RTE* case, the listings were not made available in advance at all. The Broadcasting Act 1990 anticipated the outcome of the *RTE* case, as s 176 imposes a duty to provide advance information about programmes broadcast by the BBC, the ITC and the Welsh Authority.[44]

A defendant sued for an infringement of copyright might, in desperation, advance a 'Euro-defence', for example under Article 86 of the Treaty. If nothing else, such a ploy might lengthen the proceedings, especially if the case is referred to the European Court for a preliminary ruling under Article 177.[45] In *Ransburg-Gema AG v Electrostatic Plant Systems*[46] it was alleged that the defendant had infringed the copyright subsisting in certain drawings. The defendant entered a 'Euro-defence' claiming that the plaintiff was guilty of a breach of Article 86. In striking out the Euro-defences, Aldous J held that there must be a connection between the alleged actions of the plaintiff and the alleged breach under Article 86. The existence of an exclusive right and its exercise were not *per se* a breach of the Treaty of Rome. Further, to show this, the Euro-defence must be sufficiently detailed. In the earlier case of *Imperial Chemical Industries Ltd v Berk Pharmaceuticals Ltd*,[47] Megarry V-C struck out Euro-defences because the defendant had failed to show a sufficient nexus between the alleged breach of Article 86 and the right claimed by the defendant – in that case, to imitate the plaintiff's get-up. Defences under Article 86 are common but rarely, if ever, succeed in the English courts. In *Pitney-Bowes Inc v Francotyp-Postalia GmbH*,[48] Hoffman J said (at 77):

> There is, as far as I know, no English case in which a defence under Article 86 to an action asserting intellectual property rights has actually succeeded.

However, it is clear that Articles 85(1) and 86 can be used in national courts as a sword or a shield. For example, in *Custsforth v Mansfield Inns Ltd*,[49] the plaintiff succeeded in obtaining an injunction in the High Court to prevent the defendant brewery enforcing an obligation to purchase games equipment from nominated suppliers (not including the plaintiff), which was contained in agreements between the brewery and tenants of public houses.

The occasions when the European Court will interfere with the normal exploitation of copyright are quite rare, and the Court seems to have achieved a fine balance between commercial exploitation and misuse of the right. The fact that copyright law is not fully harmonised throughout the Community has the effect of raising the status of, and hence the ability to rely on, national laws. Whether in the course of time, as copyright laws are assimilated within the Common Market or a Community-wide copyright is achieved, the European Court will be more willing to intervene with the exploitation of copyright remains to be seen.

## HARMONISATION

Although significant steps have been taken already, copyright law has not been fully harmonised throughout the Community. All the member states are signa-

43 The Court of First Instance had correctly found that the exclusion of all potential competitors had affected the market comprising Ireland and Northern Ireland.

44 It applies to the BBC's United Kingdom services, the ITC's regulated services, and, in addition, to any national service regulated by the Radio Authority. In the absence of agreement as to the payment, the Copyright Tribunal has the power to fix payments. These provisions came into force on 1 March 1991.

45 This can take about 18 months.

46 [1990] FSR 287.

47 [1981] FSR 1.

48 [1991] FSR 72.

49 [1986] 1 WLR 558.

tories to the Berne Copyright Convention, but there are still differences in copyright law and this is likely to remain so for some considerable time. Up to now there have been five Directives harmonising copyright law,[50] all of which have been implemented in the United Kingdom. Some of the Directives were implemented late which required some complicated savings and transitional provisions.[51] At the time of writing, there are no outstanding Directives to comply with.

**50** Some of these Directives have also harmonised some aspects of rights in performances.

**51** The rental rights and satellite broadcasting Directives were implemented on 1 December 1996 (some 18 months and 12 months late respectively) and the term of copyright Directive was implemented on 1 January 1996, some six months late.

**52** Following a Green Paper, 'Copyright and Related Rights in the Information Society', COM (95) 382, 19 July 1995.

Presently, there are proposals for a Directive on artists' re-sale right, discussed below, and a Directive on copyright in the Information Society[52] which was discussed in Chapter 8. The Commission has also been looking at home copying of sound and audio-visual recordings and moral rights. Table 9.1 summarises the legislative measures taken or proposed by the European Community that affect copyright and neighbouring rights.

### Artists' re-sale right

Some countries, notably France have for some time provided for a right for artists and others to receive a royalty on the subsequent sale of their original works of art. The right is known as *droit de suite* and is an option in the Berne Copyright Convention, Article 14[ter] of which provides for a right to an interest in the re-sale of original works of art and manuscripts. The rationale underlying the right is that contemporary artists are often not able to sell their works for a reasonable price at the time they create them. Later, however, their works may command much higher prices. One only has to think of Van Gogh who was unable to sell his works during his lifetime, yet they now sell for millions of pounds.

In furtherance of greater harmonisation, and especially because some member states do not provide for such a right, the Commission has published a proposal for a European Parliament and Council Directive on the re-sale right for the benefit of the author of an original work of art.[53]

**53** OJ C178, 21.6.96, p. 16, COM (96) 97 Final.

The proposal is to give the author of an original work of art or manuscript an inalienable right to receive a royalty payable by the seller on the price obtained from any subsequent sale of the work except where the sale is a private sale, being between two private individuals. Sales by professional sellers such as salerooms, art galleries and, in general, any dealer in works of art will be subject to the royalty.

The type of works covered will be, by Article 3 of the proposal, manuscripts and works of 'plastic art'[54] such as pictures, collages, paintings, drawings, engravings, prints, lithographs, sculptures, tapestries, ceramics and photographs which have been made by the author or artist himself. Also included are 'copies considered to be original works of art according to professional usage'. This is likely to include limited edition copies where the artist has controlled the production of the copies, for example, limited-edition prints made of an original painting.

**54** The term is not defined in the proposal.

The proposed scale of royalty payment is set out in Article 4 on a sliding scale. For a sale price of between 1000 and 50 000 Ecu, the royalty will be 4 per cent and on a sale price of over 250 000 Ecu, the royalty will be 2 per cent. No royalty will be payable where the sale price is less than 1000 Ecu. It will be net of tax. It is proposed that the royalty should be paid to the author or artist or to his estate. Royalties may be collectively managed and appropriate arrangements

**Table 9.1 EC measures affecting copyright**

| Description | Compliance date | Reference | Comment |
|---|---|---|---|
| *Directives* | | | |
| Legal protection of computer programs | before 1 January 1993 | OJ L122, 17.5.91, p. 42 | Given effect by the Copyright (Computer Programs) Regulations 1992 (*see* Chapter 8). |
| Rental and lending rights and certain rights relating to copyright | not later than 1 July 1994 | OJ L346, 19.11.92, p. 61 | Given effect by the Copyright and Related Rights Regulations 1996 (*see* Chapters 3 and 4). |
| Copyright and neighbouring rights relating to satellite broadcasting and cable retransmission | before 1 January 1995 | OJ L248, 06.10.93, p. 15 | Given effect by the Copyright and Related Rights Regulations 1996 (*see* Chapters 3 and 4). |
| Harmonising the term of protection of copyright and certain related rights | not later than 1 July 1995 | OJ L290, 24.11.93, p. 9 | Given effect by the Duration of Copyright and Rights in Performances Regulations 1995 (*see* Chapter 3). |
| Legal protection of databases | before 1 January 1998 | OJ L77, 27.3.96, p. 20 | Given effect by the Copyright and Rights in Databases Regulations 1997 (*see* Chapter 8). |
| *Proposals for Directives* | | | |
| Resale right for the benefit of the author of an original work of art | before 1 January 1999 | OJ C178, 21.6.96, p. 16 | |
| Harmonisation of certain aspects of copyright and related rights in the Information Society | by 30 June 2000 | COM(97) 628 Final, 10.12.97 | *See* Chapter 8. |

may be made where the author is a national of another member state. Nationals of third countries will have a right to receive the royalty on re-sale if their country affords reciprocal rights to nationals of EC member states.

By Article 8 of the proposal, the right to receive the royalty will endure as long as copyright – that is, life plus 70 years – and it is intended that it will come into effect no later than 1 January 1999. The Commission will review the threshold and royalty rates every five years thereafter.

## INTERNATIONAL CONVENTIONS

The two international copyright conventions lay down minimum standards for copyright protection and provide for reciprocity of protection between those countries that have ratified the conventions. At the present time, each convention has a significant number of members (Berne has well over 100) and many countries, including the UK, have ratified both conventions. The USA, one of the original members of the Universal Copyright Convention, has also joined the Berne Copyright Convention, as has the People's Republic of China. The Berne Copyright Convention is administered by the World Intellectual Property Organization and the Universal Copyright Convention by UNESCO, the United Nations Educational, Scientific and Cultural Organization. The Berne Copyright Convention dates from 1886 and has European origins. It has been and continues to be very successful, but, as a means of encouraging other states to join an international copyright 'club', without requiring the Berne Copyright Convention to be watered down, the Universal Copyright Convention came into existence in 1952. One of the aims of this convention was to narrow the gap between the European concept of *droit d'auteur* and the common law notion of copyright law based firmly on economic rights.[55] (This ignores the fact that the UK seems to have coped quite happily with the Berne Copyright Convention since its ratification in 1887.)

The way in which the United Kingdom extends copyright to other convention countries is by virtue of the Copyright, Designs and Patents Act 1988 s 159, which gives power to Her Majesty in Council to apply the copyright provisions of the Act to citizens of other countries, bodies incorporated under the laws of other countries, in respect of works first published in other countries or to broadcasts or cable programmes made from or sent from other countries. Where the other country is not a convention country or member of the EEC, a condition is that the other country must provide adequate protection to owners of copyright under the 1988 Act.[56]

The Copyright (Application to Other Countries) Order 1993[57] has been made under s 159 and applies the qualification for copyright provisions[58] to:

(a) citizens or subjects of specified countries or domiciled or resident there as those provisions apply to British citizens or persons domiciled or resident in the United Kingdom;
(b) bodies incorporated under the law of the specified countries as they apply to bodies incorporated under the law of part of the United Kingdom; and
(c) works first published in a specific country as they apply to works first published in the United Kingdom.[59]

55 For a history and detailed description of these conventions, *see* Stewart, S.M. (1989) *International Copyright and Neighbouring Rights* (2nd edn) Butterworths, especially Chapters 5 and 6. Details of other international conventions, agreements and treaties are contained in this excellent text.

56 Section 160 permits restriction of protection in relation to countries not providing adequate protection to British works of copyright.

57 SI 1993/942, as amended by the Copyright (Application to Other Countries) (Amendment) Order 1994, SI 1994/263.

58 Sections 153 to 155.

59 Article 2(1).

Over 120 countries are listed in Sch 1 to the Order, as amended.[60] Similar provisions apply to broadcasts. There are also provisions denying protection in some cases, for example, by reference to the author of another country where the work was first published before 1 August 1989.[61] There are also certain modifications, for example, in relation to sound recordings and typefaces. As regards works created before the 1988 Act came into force, the situation is complex in the extreme and outside the scope of this book.[62]

An examination of some of the provisions of the Berne Convention will give a feel for its influence on UK copyright law.[63] Article 1 of the Berne Convention states that:

> The countries to which this Convention applies constitute a Union for the protection of the rights of authors in their literary and artistic works.

However, 'literary and artistic works' are comprehensively defined by Article 2 as including 'every production in the literary, scientific and artistic domain, whatever may be the mode or form of its expression', which then goes on to give a comprehensive and wide list of examples. Protection is afforded also to translations, adaptations, arrangements of music and other alterations of a literary or artistic work (Article 2(3)). Generally, the term of protection is the life of the author and 50 years after his death, but countries in the Union may grant longer terms.[64] The text of the convention contains all the other main provisions, such as the rights of the author in relation to the work, 'permitted' acts and the author's moral rights.[65] The convention can be thought of as a basic statement of principle with the detailed implementation being left to the member countries. Both of the conventions allow ample scope for differences in implementation and many provisions are optional. For example, in the Berne Copyright Convention, *droit de suite*, the artist's re-sale right, is available 'only if legislation in the country to which the author belongs so permits'.[66] United Kingdom copyright law does not provide for this right, and therefore UK artists do not have a right to a payment on the subsequent re-sale of their works.[67]

The Universal Copyright Convention lacks the detail of the Berne Copyright Convention and takes a more 'broad brush' approach. Article I states:

> Each Contracting State undertakes to provide for the adequate and effective protection of the rights of authors and other copyright proprietors in literary, scientific and artistic works, including writings, musical, dramatic and cinematographic works, and paintings, engravings and sculpture.

The minimum term of protection shall not be less than the life of the author and 25 years after his death. One important difference between the conventions is that the Berne Copyright Convention requires no formalities – 'The enjoyment and the exercise of these rights shall not be subject to any formality'[68] – whereas the Universal Copyright Convention permits contracting states to require compliance with formalities, including deposit, registration, and the payment of fees. This has important implications for other countries, for to obtain reciprocal protection in a country having formalities, works must bear the copyright symbol © accompanied by the name of the copyright proprietor and the year of first publication 'placed in such a manner and location so as to give reasonable notice of claim to copyright'.[69] This explains the importance of using such a symbol in order to obtain the greatest possible

60 Schedule 2 contains the list of countries enjoying full protection for sound recordings (over 50 countries) and Sch 3 lists those enjoying protection in respect of broadcasts (around 50 countries).

61 This is a simplification. The Order should be checked for the precise position.

62 *See* Laddie, H. *et al* (1995) *The Modern Law of Copyright*, (2nd edn) Butterworths, Chapter 4.

63 It is instructive to read the conventions, both of which are reproduced in full in Phillips, J. (ed.) (1994) *Butterworths Intellectual Property Law Handbook* (2nd edn) Butterworths.

64 Article 7.

65 Moral rights are provided for in Article 6bis which came about as a result of the Rome Act (an Act modifying the Convention) in 1928. It took the United Kingdom just 60 years to comply.

66 Article 14ter

67 But they may have such a right in France and other countries recognising the right as a result of the *Phil Collins Case, see* supra.

68 Article 5(2).

69 Article III(1).

70 In any case, the use of a notice may help evidentially, for example, as regards the date of origin of the work and whether the infringer knows or has reason to believe that copyright subsisted in the work.

71 The Satellite Convention 1974 and the Phonogram Convention 1971. The United Kingdom has ratified the latter. The Phonogram Convention is the source of the symbol Ⓟ accompanied by the year of the first publication. A 'phonogram' is an 'exclusively aural fixation' and excludes videograms: Article 1(a). Reciprocal rights are given to the producers of phonograms. Another convention is the Rome Convention for the Protection of Performers, Producers of Phonograms and Broadcasting Organizations 1961, which has been ratified by the United Kingdom. *See* Chapter 10 on rights in performances.

72 Administered by the World Trade Organization.

73 Whilst accepting the territorial nature of copyright, doubts are raised in connection with transnational activities, such as the international distribution of broadcasts and cable programmes, *see* Goltz, H. and Pritesche, K. U. 'Cable & Satellite Television – Copyright and Other Issues under German Law' [1988] 9 EIPR 261, at 263.

74 *ABKCO Music & Records Inc v Music Collection International Ltd* [1995] RPC 657.

75 *Tyburn Productions Ltd v Doyle* [1991] Ch 75, applying *Def Lepp Music v Stuart Brown* [1986] RPC 273.

76 [1988] ECR 5565.

international protection with respect to copyright works, even though, in the United Kingdom, there is no requirement for such a notice.[70]

The international conventions have played and will continue to play an important role in the development of copyright law and in laying down minimum standards. In addition to the Berne and the Universal Copyright Conventions, there are other conventions dealing with copyright matters such as satellite broadcasts and phonograms.[71] The GATT TRIPs agreement (Trade-Related Aspects of Intellectual Property Rights) may also be relevant.[72] The reciprocal protection initiated by the conventions has been instrumental in the protection of works of copyright on a much wider and more homogeneous scale than would otherwise have been the case.

## JURISDICTION

Intellectual property rights are territorial and, apart from the implications of international conventions mentioned in the previous section, the English courts might be expected to refuse to hear an action based on the alleged infringement of a United Kingdom right which occurs outside jurisdiction. Because rights under intellectual property are territorial, only acts done within the United Kingdom infringe United Kingdom copyright.[73] An exception is where infringement by authorisation is concerned and in such a case it does not matter where the authorisation was given provided that the restricted act was performed within jurisdiction.[74] As a corollary to the rule that infringements out of jurisdiction will not be entertained in the English courts, neither would they be expected to accept jurisdiction over disputes relating to alleged infringements of foreign patents, copyrights or trade marks.[75]

Things are not that straightforward, however, and it seems that in some cases, the plaintiff in an alleged infringement of a copyright might have a choice of jurisdictions in which to bring his action. Before examining recent developments regarding jurisdiction, it will be useful to look at some of the provisions of the Brussels Convention on Jurisdiction and Enforcement of Judgments, given effect by the Civil Jurisdiction and Judgments Act 1982.

Article 2 of the Brussels Convention states that persons domiciled in a contracting state shall, whatever their nationality, be sued in the courts of that state. This is subject to the other provisions of the Convention and Article 5 allows, *inter alia,* a person who is domiciled in one contracting state to be sued in another contracting state if, in matters relating to tort, delict or quasi-delict, the harmful event occurred in that other state. Infringements of a copyright or patent, for example, is a tort. Article 6(1) allows a person domiciled in a contracting state to be sued in another contracting state if he is one of a number of defendants and one of them is domiciled in that other state. In *Athanasios Kalfelis v Bankhaus Schröder, Münchmeyer, Hengst & Co,*[76] the European Court of Justice interpreted Article 6(1) narrowly, so that there must be a connection between the defendant not domiciled in the contracting state where litigation was to take place and the defendant domiciled in that state, such that it would be expedient to determine the actions together, so as to avoid irreconcilable judgments resulting from separate proceedings.

Article 16(1) gives the courts of a contracting state exclusive jurisdiction, regardless of domicile, in proceedings which have as their object rights *in rem* in immovable property, where that property is situated in that state. Article 16(4) gives the courts of a contracting state exclusive jurisdiction, regardless of domicile, in proceedings concerned with the registration or validity of patents, trade marks, designs, or other similar rights required to be deposited or registered where the contracting state is the one in which the deposit or registration has taken place or has been applied for (or is deemed to have taken place under the terms of an international convention).

Article 16(4) does not apply to copyright, being an informal right. It is not clear whether copyright is a 'movable' (that is, personal)[77] property, but Article 16(1) would apply only where the issue was in relation to the ownership of the copyright.

An important case that signifies an important step in applying the Brussels Convention to intellectual property disputes is *Gareth Pearce* v *Ove Arup Partnership Ltd*.[78] In that case, the plaintiff claimed that he had UK and Dutch copyright in his architectural drawings for a building, originally drawn by the plaintiff for a town hall in London Docklands. He alleged that the second and third defendant copied his plans and used them to construct a building called the Kunsthal in Rotterdam, built by the first defendant. The fourth defendant was the owner if the building. This, the plaintiff claimed, was an infringement of his Dutch copyright. He sued in England on the basis of the Brussels Convention, Article 6(1), in that at least one of the defendants (the building contractor) was domiciled in the United Kingdom. One of the main issues in the case was whether the action was justiciable in the English courts.[79]

On the basis of *The British South Africa Co* v *The Companhia de Moçambique*[80] and *Def Lepp Music* v *Stuart Brown*,[81] a claim made in respect of a breach of a foreign statutory intellectual property right would not be entertained in an English court, such a claim being regarded purely as local. Further, the *Def Lepp* case is also an example of a claim failing because of the double actionability rule. However, the *Moçambique* rule and the double actionability rule were effectively overruled by the Brussels Convention as far as necessary to give effect to that convention. Therefore, the English courts had jurisdiction to hear the claim of infringement of Dutch copyright against the first, English domiciled defendant and, by the operation of Article 6(1) of the convention, also had jurisdiction to hear the action against the other defendants.

Of course, a court in the United Kingdom might properly be wary of hearing an action involving the infringement of a foreign intellectual property right, but courts in the Netherlands and Germany have already shown a willingness to accept jurisdiction in cases involving the infringement of patents in other contracting states of the Brussels Convention.

In the *Gareth Pearce* case, Lloyd J remarked on the possibility of 'forum shopping', where a plaintiff takes into account the procedures and remedies available in different states where he has a choice, and accepted that, in appropriate circumstances, an English court might not be able to refuse jurisdiction to hears cases involving, for example, infringement of the French law of privacy or the artists' *droit de suite* or some other action in foreign law not having an equivalent in English law.[82]

Determination of jurisdiction may be subject to further clarification on the scope and application of some of the provisions of the Brussels Convention as

77 *See* the Copyright, Designs and Patents Act s 90(1) which states that copyright is transmissible as personal or moveable property. 'Moveable property' is the Scots equivalent of personal property. However, this is not conclusive.

78 [1997] FSR 641, approved by the Court of Appeal in *Fort Dodge Animal Health Ltd* v *Akzo Nobel NV* [1998] FSR 222, a patent case.

79 The other main issue was whether the action should be struck out as an abuse of process, being purely speculative. On this point the defendants succeeded.

80 [1893] AC 602, a claim involving foreign land.

81 [1986] RPC 273, followed in *Tyburn Productions Ltd* v *Doyle* [1991] Ch 75.

82 [1997] FSR 641 at 652.

the Court of Appeal recently made a reference for a preliminary ruling to the European Court of Justice on these very matters in a patent case.[83]

Where the defendant is not domiciled in a contracting state, he can be served with process if he is present within the jurisdiction of a part of the United Kingdom, otherwise leave of the court is required. It might be given, for example, in the case where a tort has been committed within jurisdiction and the court considers it proper for service of process out of jurisdiction.

However, even if a court within part of the United Kingdom could entertain a claim against a defendant domiciled out of jurisdiction, where there is a conflict between that part of the United Kingdom and a non-Brussels Convention state, the court here might stay or dismiss the action on the grounds of *forum non conveniens*, that is, that the courts here are less appropriate to hear the case than the courts in that other country. For example, in *Re Harrods (Buenos Aries) Ltd*[84] the English court considered that the Argentinian courts were more appropriate to decide the issues.

83 *Fort Dodge Animal Health Ltd* v *Akzo Nobel NV* [1998] FSR 222.

84 [1992] Ch 72.

# 10

## *Rights in performances*

### INTRODUCTION

A well-known soprano gives a live performance of an operatic aria by Mozart. Unknown to the soprano, a member of the audience makes a recording of the performance on a magnetic tape and then later makes copies which he sells to the public without the singer's permission. Under copyright law, there is nothing that can be done to prevent the sale of the recordings of the performance. The music and lyrics are out of copyright, so there is no infringement of the musical or literary work. Indeed, the only relevance of copyright law is that the person who made the recording without permission owns the copyright in it as a sound recording. Had the singer agreed a recording contract with a publisher, the publisher would be unable to use copyright law to prevent the sale of the unauthorised recordings, which have a separate and independent copyright to the publisher's recording. The authorised and unauthorised master recordings are coterminous, and there is no link between them associated with the acts restricted by the copyright in the publisher's sound recording. There may still be problems even if the music is protected by copyright, because the owner of that copyright may be reluctant to pursue a claim for infringement with respect to one performance.

This state of affairs is clearly untenable and this 'loophole' in copyright law is closed by the law relating to performances. However, this area of law has only recently gained the status of a fully-fledged intellectual property right. The first law on the subject was the Dramatic and Musical Performers' Protection Act 1925, which provided criminal penalties in respect of the making of recordings of dramatic and musical performances without consent. This Act was basically re-enacted in 1958, and by the Performers' Protection Act 1963 the provisions were extended to all the original works of copyright, that is literary, dramatic, musical and artistic works.[1] The Performers' Protection Act 1972 increased the maximum penalties available. However, these Acts appeared to give rise to criminal liability only, and did not seem to give any civil remedies to performers or to those with whom the performers may have had recording contracts. The offences related to recording a live performance, broadcasting it, transmitting it via a cable distribution system or performing it in public without the consent of the original performers. The use of an unauthorised audio or audio-visual recording for the purpose of broadcasting, inclusion in a cable system or public performance, and dealing with such unauthorised recordings were also offences.

The question as to whether the law gave a right to civil actions was considered both in respect of performers and recording companies. In *Rickless* v

1 The purpose of the 1963 Act was to achieve compliance with Convention for the Protection of Performers, Producers of Phonograms and Broadcasting Organizations (the Rome Convention), 26 October 1961.

268

2  [1988] 1 QB 40.

3  Applying the *dictum* of Lord Diplock in *Lonrho Ltd* v *Shell Petroleum Co Ltd* [1982] AC 173.

4  [1983] Ch 135.

5  In this context, a 'bootleg' recording is one made without the permission of either the performer or the authorised recording company, if any.

6  *Intellectual Property and Innovation*, Cmnd. 9712 (HMSO, 1986). The problems had also been discussed earlier in the Whitford Committee Report, *Copyright and Designs Law*, Cmnd. 6732 (HMSO, 1977) and in the Green Paper, *Reform of the Law relating to Copyright, Designs and Performers' Protection*, Cmnd. 8302 (HMSO, 1981).

7  The Copyright, Designs and Patents Act 1988 s 180(3). Unless otherwise stated, in this chapter, statutory references are to the Copyright, Designs and Patents Act 1988.

8  Assuming the making of the copies was not in pursuance of arrangements made before the commencement of the new provisions. A person having an exclusive recording contract with the acrobats in relation to the performance could also sue because his recording rights had been infringed.

9  The Copyright, Designs and Patents Act 1988 s 192.

*United Artists Corp*,[2] the defendant made a new film by using clips and out-takes (discarded excerpts) from previous 'Pink Panther' films starring the late Peter Sellers. The plaintiff, who owned the rights of Peter Sellers' services as an actor, sued for, *inter alia*, breach of the Dramatic and Musical Performers' Protection Act 1958 s 2 because the defendant failed to obtain the permission of the actor's executors. The trial judge awarded damages of US $1m and the defendant appealed to the Court of Appeal, arguing that s 2 did not give rise to a private cause of action. The Court of Appeal dismissed the appeal confirming that s 2 of the Act conferred a right to civil remedies to the performer whose performance had been exploited without written consent in addition to imposing criminal penalties.[3] The basis for this decision was that, by imposing the criminal penalties, the Act imposed an obligation or prohibition for the benefit of a class of persons, in this case performers, and consequently this gave a cause of action to any aggrieved performer. However, in *RCA Corp* v *Pollard*,[4] the Court of Appeal reluctantly found that the Acts did not give civil remedies to recording companies. This highlighted the problem that recording companies were having with 'bootleg' recordings and the regrettable lack of civil remedies under the 1958–1972 Acts.[5] The ease of making good quality bootleg recordings because of technological advances was of particular concern.

These problems were identified in the White Paper preceding the Copyright, Designs and Patents Act 1988.[6] That Act repealed the previous Acts in their entirety and replaced them with new provisions contained in Part II of the Act. In addition to giving a civil right of action to recording companies having an exclusive licence with the performer and confirming civil remedies for performers, the new provisions extend to live performances by a variety of artistes such as jugglers and acrobats, and bring the criminal penalties and powers of search and seizure more in line with those available in copyright law.

## RIGHTS GRANTED BY THE COPYRIGHT, DESIGNS AND PATENTS ACT 1988 AS ENACTED

The Copyright, Designs and Patents Act 1988 Part II came into force on 1 August 1989. This area of law was largely new, rights in performances having been considerably expanded in comparison with previous law. The provisions were retrospective in that live performances that were made prior to the coming into force of the new law were protected, but a right of action did not accrue in respect of acts carried out before that date.[7] In other words, new rights were retrospectively granted, but new liabilities had not been retrospectively imposed. For example, a live performance by a team of acrobats made in 1987 was protected. If a bootleg film was made of the performance, the making of the film did not infringe any intellectual property rights and there could be no legal action in respect of it. However, if the person who made the film decided to make and sell copies to the public, the acrobats could sue for infringement of their performers' right.[8]

Two separate and distinct rights were created by the 1988 Act: a performer's right and a recording right. The nature of the rights was somewhat peculiar as the rights were not transmissible, except that a performer's right would pass on the death of the performer concerned.[9] However, by s 185(2)(b), the benefit of an exclusive recording licence could be assigned, and by s 185(3)(b) a person could assign the benefit of a licence to make recordings for commercial exploitation. Either the person having recording rights, or the person granting the licence had to be a qualifying person. As a result of these limitations on transmissibility, rights in performances were not true property rights. The performer's right, in particular, had some features in common with the author's moral rights under copyright law. However, in other respects, the rights were very similar to copyright. Rights in performances subsist alongside and were independent of copyright, both the economic and moral rights. A fairly complex mosaic of rights could be involved. For example, a live performance might take place of a piece of music by a singer (Cynthia) and orchestra (Harvey and the Syncopators). The music was recently written by Filbert and the lyrics by Hamstein, who have assigned their copyrights to the Palm Beach Music Publishing Company. A television company (SKB TV) may have had an exclusive recording contract with the singer and orchestra. If a person, John Silver, was in the audience and made a bootleg recording with the intention of making copies for sale, then John infringed the following rights:

1 Palm Beach's copyright in the musical and literary work;
2 the performance right belonging to Cynthia and to each and every member of the orchestra;
3 SKB TV's recording right.

In addition, if John made copies that were issued to the public, but which did not mention the fact that the music was written by Filbert and Hamstein, they would have an action against John for infringement of their moral right to be identified as the authors of the music and lyrics. If he sold or rented copies to the public, John would further infringe the copyrights.[10] The situation could be even more complex if the music was subject to an agreement with a collecting society, or if SKB TV had assigned the benefit of the exclusive recording contract to another. John was, therefore, exposed to a veritable battery of civil actions, but he was also liable to be prosecuted for offences under copyright law[11] and for dealing with illicit recordings.[12]

10 He could have had further liabilities arising from rental and lending rights provided for in pursuance of the rental and lending rights Directive.

11 The Copyright, Designs and Patents Act 1988 s 107(1).

12 Ibid s 198(1).

## RIGHTS IN PERFORMANCES EXTENDED AND ENLARGED

Rights in performances have been significantly strengthened as a result of the Copyright and Related Rights Regulations 1996[13] which implemented, *inter alia*, the Directive on rental right and lending right and on certain rights related to copyright in the field of intellectual property.[14] The rights of a person having recording rights are basically unchanged, but the rights of performers have been transformed. As mentioned earlier, performers' rights were analogous to moral rights under copyright law. These rights continue and new ones have been added, but the most dramatic change is that, alongside these, performers are given full property rights which can be exploited and dealt with just as a copyright. A performer now has 'property rights' and 'non-property rights', as indicated in Figure 10.1. It should be noted that, in some cases, there is some relationship between the property rights and the non-property rights. For example, a performer's non-property rights are infringed by a person making without

13 SI 1996/2967. The new provisions came into force on 1 December 1996.

14 OJ L346, 27.11.92, p. 61.

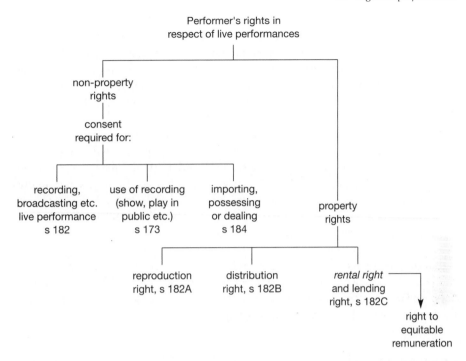

Performer's rights in
respect of live performances

non-property
rights

consent
required for:

recording,
broadcasting etc.
live performance
s 182

use of recording
(show, play in
public etc.)
s 173

importing,
possessing
or dealing
s 184

property
rights

reproduction
right, s 182A

distribution
right, s 182B

*rental right*
and lending
right, s 182C

right to
equitable
remuneration

*Note*: if a performer transfers his rental right in relation to a sound recording or film,
this is replaced by a right to an equitable remuneration for the rental (s 191G(1)).
This right also applies in the case of playing a sound recording in public or including a
sound recording in a broadcast or cable programme service.

**Figure 10.1 Performers' rights**

the performer's consent, other than for that person's private and domestic use, a recording of the whole or any substantial part of a qualifying performance directly from the live performance.[15] If that person then makes copies of the recording, directly or indirectly, that will infringe the performer's property right of reproduction.[16]

Before these important changes, the duration of rights in performances had been modified to bring them more in line with the rules applying to copyright sound recordings. Until 1 January 1996, the duration of rights in performances was simply 50 years from the end of the calendar year during which the performance took place. As a result of the Duration of Copyright and Rights in Performances Regulations 1995,[17] a new s 191 was substituted into the Act.[18] The basic rule on the duration of rights in performances is now as follows:

(a) 50 years from the end of the calendar year in which the performance took place, or

(b) if during that period a recording of the performance is released, 50 years from the end of the calendar year during which it was released.

This is similar to that applying to sound recordings. Where the performer is not a national of a European Economic Area state, the term of protection is as in the country of which the performer is a national provided it is not longer than that available under the new rules.

The definition of 'released' is when the recording is first published, played or shown in public broadcast or included in a cable programme service. As is general in the Act, no account is taken of any unauthorised act.

The 1995 Regulations contain a number of transitional provisions, particularly dealing with extended rights and revived rights. In principle, these are similar to those applying to extended and revived copyright, for which see Chapter 3.

It is possible that a recording made without the performer's consent may be shown in public or broadcast when the performer is still alive, if the performance was more than 50 years ago and it was released soon after. However, the decision in the *Rickless* case may still give rise to a separate civil right of action based on the offences which have no time limit.[19]

In the remainder of this chapter some common ground is covered, then the performers' non-property rights as modified by the 1996 Regulations will be described. This will be followed by the new performers' property rights. The rights of persons having an exclusive recording contract with the performer, or the benefit of such a contract, are then considered, followed by the permitted acts, the transitional provisions and the criminal offences, which remain unchanged by the 1995 and 1996 Regulations.

## COMMON GROUND

The rights are given to performers and persons having recording rights, and their consent is required for the exploitation of the performance or the making of recordings.[20] Rights in performances should not be confused with 'performing rights'. This term is usually used to signify rights under copyright in relation to the acts of performing, showing or playing a work, in which copyright subsists, in public. For example, where a retail store wishes to play background music, it will require the permission of the relevant copyright owners. The copyright performing rights are usually administered by collecting societies such as the Performing Right Society (in the United Kingdom).

A performance is a live performance given by one or more individuals which is a dramatic performance (including dance and mime), a musical performance, a reading or recitation of a literary work, or a variety act or any similar presentation.[21] If a person sings live to a recorded backing track, for example in a 'karaoke bar', the live performance relates to the live singing only.[22] The meaning of 'recording' is important in terms of recording rights and infringement and is defined in s 180(2) as being a film or sound recording made directly from a live performance, or made from a broadcast or cable programme including the performance or made directly or indirectly from another recording of the performance. Therefore, copies made from a master recording that was made during the performance count as being recordings.

For the rights to exist, certain qualification requirements must be satisfied. The performers' rights subsist only if the performance is a qualifying performance which, by s 181, means that it must be given by a qualifying individual or take place in a qualifying country. Section 206 defines a qualifying individual as being a citizen or subject of a qualifying country or a person who is resident

19 *See* De Frietas, D. 'The Copyright, Designs and Patents Act 1988 (4)' (1989) 133 *Solicitors Journal* 734 at 735. Section 180(4) states that the rights conferred are independent of 'any other right or obligation arising otherwise than under this Part.'

20 The performer's consent is required in relation to the performers' rights, but the consent of either the performer or the person having the recording right is required in relation to the recording right.

21 Section 180(2).

22 However, there is also a public performance of the backing track and there will be an infringement of this unless permission to play the track has been obtained or a licence scheme is in operation and covers the playing of the particular backing track in question.

in such a country. 'Qualifying country' means the United Kingdom and any other member state of the European Economic Community and any other country designated by Order in Council under s 208, that is to countries enjoying reciprocal protection.[23] The current order is the Performances (Reciprocal Protection) (Convention Countries) Order 1994.[24]

For the recording right, by s 185, the person having recording rights who is a party to an exclusive recording contract with the performer or the assignee of the benefit of such a contract must be a qualifying person.[25] If not, then the right might still arise where a person who has been licensed to make recordings or to whom the benefit of such a licence has been assigned is a qualifying person. A qualifying person can be a qualifying individual or a body corporate formed under the law of the United Kingdom or of another qualifying country which carries on a substantial business activity in any qualifying country: s 206. It should be noted that the recording right can arise even though the performance is not a qualifying performance, so that an Italian film company having an exclusive recording contract to record the live performance of a juggler from North Korea which takes place in India will have recording rights which are enforceable in the United Kingdom, even though the juggler himself has no rights in relation to his own performance subject to United Kingdom law. The performance is not a qualifying performance because the juggler fails to meet the requirements for a qualifying individual and the performance does not take place in a qualifying country.[26]

### Illicit recording

The meaning of 'illicit recording' is important in terms of some forms of infringement of the rights and for the offences. It is the equivalent of an infringing copy of a work in which copyright subsists, but there are some differences.

By s 197, an illicit recording is:

(a) for performer's rights, a recording of the whole or any substantial part of a performance made, otherwise than for private purposes, without the performer's consent;

(b) for the recording rights, a recording of the whole or any substantial part of a performance subject to an exclusive recording contract made, otherwise than for private purposes, without the consent of either the performer or the person entitled to the recording rights;

(c) a recording which is an illicit recording under the provisions of Sch 2 to the Copyright, Designs and Patents Act 1988 (the permitted acts in relation to performances). This covers recordings, the making of which did not infringe the rights in performances because they were made for a permitted act, but which have been used subsequently outside the terms of the exception. For example, where a recording made for educational purposes has been sold.[27]

The place where the recording was made is immaterial and there is no reason to believe that the question of substantiality will be construed otherwise than it is for copyright purposes.

[23] This includes countries that are members of the Rome Convention for the Protection of Performers, Producers of Phonograms and Broadcasting Organizations, 1961.

[24] SI 1994/264.

[25] An exclusive recording contract is a contract between the performer and another person under which that other person is entitled to the exclusion of all others, including the performer, to make recordings of one or more of his performances with a view to their commercial exploitations: s 185(1).

[26] North Korea and India are not members of the Rome Convention.

[27] *See* Sch 2, para 6(2).

## Consent

The issue of consent is central to the infringement of the rights. There is no requirement for the consent to be in writing and, by s 193(1), consent may relate to a single specific performance, a number of performances or performances generally. Future and past performances are included, so that consent can be given retrospectively. Persons having any of the rights devolved to them are bound by consents given by previous right holders. This is strict and there are no statutory exceptions for 'equity's darling'.

In the absence of express consent, it seems reasonable to suppose that it may be implied, and it will be so implied if it is necessary and reasonable to do so. The same applies to the need to obtain consent if the intended use of a recording of a performance appears to exceed the terms of the original consent. However, consent given in respect of a particular use does not necessarily prohibit, by implication, other uses; something else must be shown, for example, that the new intended use raises an implication that further consent is required. In *Grower v British Broadcasting Corporation*[28] the BBC had made a recording of a performance of 'Hoochie Coochie Man' by the Jimi Hendrix Experience for the immediate purpose of broadcasting on a radio programme hosted by Alexis Korner who had, at the invitation of Hendrix, joined in the performance, playing a guitar. It appeared that Korner had consented to the making of the recording and the broadcasting of that recording. In an agreement made in 1988, the BBC granted a licence to a Californian company in respect of the sound recording. The licence included a term that the Californian company obtain the consent of any artists who had contributed to the recording before exploiting the recording. The plaintiffs, the executors of Korner's estate, sued the BBC (as joint tortfeasor) on the basis that the Californian company had exploited the sound recording without their consent and that this was a breach of the performer's rights under Part II of the Copyright, Designs and Patents Act 1988. It was held, *inter alia*, that the plaintiff would have to establish that there was an implied term that the BBC either obtain the plaintiffs' consent to exploit the sound recording or that the BBC would guarantee that a licensee or assignee of the copyright in the sound recording would obtain the consent of all the performers, and neither implication was necessary nor reasonable in the circumstances.[29]

28 [1990] FSR 595.

29 Of course, the BBC owned the copyright in the sound recording. Nor was the BBC liable as joint tortfeasor as, although the BBC may have facilitated the infringement by the Californian company, it had not participated in it. It was, however, arguable that the making of a back-up copy of the recording was a breach of the Dramatic and Musical Performers' Protection Act 1958, and a breach of the agreement between Korner and the BBC.

### PERFORMERS' NON-PROPERTY RIGHTS

These rights are set out in the Copyright, Designs and Patents Act 1988 s 182 (which has been substituted by the 1996 Regulations) and ss 183 and 184 (which are as before). A performer's rights in a qualifying performance are infringed by any person who, without the performer's consent, does any of the following acts in relation to the whole or any substantial part of a qualifying performance:

(a) makes a recording directly from the live performance, other than for that person's private and domestic use (s 182(1)(a));

(b) broadcasts live, or includes live in a cable programme service (s 182(1)(b));

(c) makes a recording directly from a broadcast of, or cable programme including, the live performance, other than for that person's private and domestic use (s 182(1)(c));

(d) by means of a recording which was, and which that person knows or has reason to believe was, made without the performer's consent, shows, plays in public, broadcasts or includes in a cable programme service (s 183);

(e) imports into the United Kingdom, otherwise than for his own private and domestic purposes, or, in the course of a business, possesses, sells, lets for hire, offers or exposes for sale or hire or distributes an illicit recording, which he knows is or has reason to believe is an illicit recording (s 184).[30]

Infringement is actionable as a breach of statutory duty.[31] For the infringements under s 182, damages are not available as against a defendant who can show that, at the time of the infringement, he had reasonable grounds for believing that consent had been given.

The performers' non-property rights are not assignable or transmissible except as set out in new s 192A.[32] The performer may provide for the rights to pass under his will to a specific person or persons, otherwise, on his death, the rights become exercisable by his personal representatives.[33] Should the performer bequeath his non-property rights to more than one person, the rights are exercisable by each independently of the other or others.

There are provisions for delivery up of illicit recordings following application to the court by the performer or person having the recording rights, as appropriate.[34] Performers and persons having recording rights have a limited right of seizure in respect of illicit recordings. This right is similar to that applying to infringing works of copyright under s 100. It is not to be exercised at permanent or regular places of business and notice must first be given to the police. It is intended to be used, for example, at car boot sales and the like.

## PERFORMERS' PROPERTY RIGHTS

These full property rights are the reproduction right, distribution right and rental right and lending right. If the performer transfers his rental right, this is then replaced by a right to an equitable remuneration in the case of the rental of a sound recording or film containing the performance.

### Reproduction right

This is a right which, under s 182A, is infringed by the making of a copy of a recording of the whole or a substantial part of a qualifying performance without the consent of the performer, otherwise than for the private and domestic use of the person making the copy. It matters not whether the copy is made directly or indirectly. Making the recording in the first place will infringe the performer's non-property right. The right is to authorise or prohibit the making of such copies.

All the three performers' property rights refer to the consent of the performer. As the rights are full property rights and assignable as such, the consent referred to should be that of the owner of the right. The Directive is better as it speaks of the 'rightholder'.

**30** There is a defence to this form of infringement under s 184(2) where the defendant shows that the illicit recording was innocently acquired either by him or a predecessor in title. Innocence in this case means that the person did not know and had no reason to believe that it was an illicit recording: s 184(3). This is not a complete defence but serves to limit damages to a reasonable payment in respect of the act complained of.

**31** Section 194.

**32** These provisions are almost identical to those prior to the 1996 Regulations.

**33** It may be that the performer does not specifically bequeath all his non-property rights, in which case, those not bequeathed are exercisable by his personal representatives.

**34** Section 195. There is a limitation period of six years under s 203, and s 204 contains provisions for court orders for disposal.

### Distribution right

This right is the right to authorise or prohibit the issue of copies of the recording to the public. Under s 182B(1), the right is infringed by a person who issues to the public copies of a recording of the whole or a substantial part of a qualifying performance without the performer's consent. Issuing to the public means putting into circulation copies not previously put into circulation in the European Economic Area (EEA) by or with the consent of the performer, or putting into circulation outside the EEA copies not previously put into circulation in the EEA or elsewhere. However, the doctrine of exhaustion of rights applies and this does not extend to subsequent distribution (without prejudice to the consent required for rental or lending) or subsequent importation into the United Kingdom or another EEA state,[35] except so far as putting into circulation in the EEA by or with the consent of the performer applies to putting into circulation into the EEA copies previously put into circulation outside the EEA.

What this contrived set of rules is probably trying to achieve is that the performer's distribution right will be infringed if a person puts copies into circulation anywhere without the consent of the performer, or imports into an EEA state copies from outside the EEA without the performer's consent, whether or not those copies were put into circulation by or with the consent of the performer. The rental right and lending right Directive is much simpler on this point merely stating that the rightholder's distribution right is exhausted by first sale within the Community made by the rightholder or with his consent.[36] Of course, sale of a copy of a recording does not, by itself, exhaust any rental or lending right.

Issuing copies of a recording also covers the situation where the original recording is issued to the public.

### Rental right and lending right

The right here is to authorise or prohibit rental and lending of copies of the performance to the public. The right is infringed, under s 182C, by a person who, without the performer's consent, rents or lends to the public copies of a recording of the whole or any substantial part of a qualifying performance.

The meanings of 'rental' and 'lending' are equivalent to those for copyright works as set out in s 18A. Thus, rental is making available for use on terms that the copy will or may be returned for direct or indirect economic or commercial advantage. Lending is making available in such a way but otherwise than for direct or indirect economic or commercial advantage through an establishment accessible to the public. There are exceptions which mirror those for copyright works. The provisions apply equally to the original recording as they do to copies.

Under s 182D, a performer is entitled to an equitable remuneration from the owner of the copyright in a commercially published sound recording of the whole or any substantial part of a qualifying performance if it is played in public or included in a broadcast or cable programme service. This right may not be assigned except to a collecting society, though it may pass under a will or by operation of law and, from then on, it may be further assigned or transferred.

The amount payable by way of equitable remuneration is to be agreed, with the possibility of application to the Copyright Tribunal in the absence of agreement.[37]

35 Section 182B(2) and (3).

36 Article 9(2).

37 The powers of the Copyright Tribunal are extended accordingly.

There is also a right to an equitable remuneration in respect of rental of a film and sound recording under s 191G, where the performer has transferred his rental rights in relation to a sound recording or film. Again the Copyright Tribunal has powers in relation to the amount payable. However, unlike s 182D where there is no specific provision of similar effect, this right cannot be excluded or restricted by agreement. 'Collecting society' is also defined (for the purposes of s 191G only) as a society or other organisation having as its main object or one of its main objects, the exercise of the right to equitable remuneration on behalf of more than one performer.

As with the right under s 182D, this right cannot be assigned except to a collecting society but may pass under a will, etc. Section 191F provides for presumed transfer of the rental right, to be replaced by a right to an equitable remuneration, in the case of an agreement concerning film production being concluded between the performer and the film producer. The absence of the signature of the performer or person acting on his behalf does not exclude the operation of s 191C which deals with prospective ownership of performers' property rights.

### Dealing with performers' property rights and infringement

The provisions for assignment, licensing (including exclusive licences) and prospective ownership are similar to those applying to copyright works. Thus, the assignments must be in writing and signed by or on behalf of the assignor and assignments may be partial.[38] Exclusive licensees may sue for infringement and the provisions for the exercise of concurrent rights are equivalent to those for copyright. Remedies are damages, injunctions, accounts or otherwise[39] (as for copyright) and there is also provision for additional damages under s 191J. Also, there is provision, where licences are available as of right, for a defendant to undertake to take such a licence thereby limiting remedies to damages of twice the amount payable under such a licence.[40]

Where a person is entitled under a bequest (general or specific) to any material thing containing an original recording of a performance which was not published before the death of the testator, the bequest shall be construed as including any performers' rights in relation to the recording to which the testator was entitled immediately before his death.[41] This is subject to any contrary intention in the will or a codicil to it. Again, this is similar to the equivalent provision under copyright law.

### RECORDING RIGHTS

Recording rights are given to a person having an exclusive recording contract with a performer, being one under which that person is entitled to the exclusion of all others, including the performer, to make recordings of one or more of his performances with a view to commercial gain.[42] That person must be a party to the contract and have the benefit of the contract, or be a person to whom the benefit of the contract has been assigned. He must also be a qualifying person. Apart from being able to assign the benefit of the contract, under s 192B, the right is not assignable or transmissible.

38 Section 191B.

39 Section 191I.

40 Similar provisions apply to patents and rights in designs.

41 Section 191E

42 Section 185.

If the person who would otherwise be entitled to the right is not a qualifying person, references are instead to a person licensed by such a person to make recordings for commercial exploitation, or to a person to whom the benefit of such a licence has been assigned if that person is a qualifying person. Thus, for example, if an American company having an exclusive recording contract with a performer to record a live performance to take place in the United Kingdom, and grants a licence to an English company actually to make the recording, it will be the English company which is entitled to the recording right.[43]

Making a recording 'with a view to commercial exploitation' simply means, under s 185(4), with a view to recordings being sold or let for hire, shown or played in public. For the last two acts, the statute does not state that the showing or playing must be with the intention to gain.

Infringement of recording rights occurs in similar ways to infringement of performers' rights and is subject to similar requirements for knowledge. However, there is no infringement of the recording right by a live broadcast or live inclusion in a cable programme service. For the 'making a recording' infringement, the consent required is that of either the performer or the person having the recording right, and this also applies to public showing or playing and the broadcast or inclusion in a cable programme service of a recording of the performance. The consent may have been given previously by the person then entitled to the recording rights.

Importing, possessing and dealing with illicit recordings, if done without consent, will infringe the recording rights (as they do the performer's rights), but the consent needed here is that of the performer in the case of a qualifying performance or, otherwise, the consent of the person having the recording right. There is also a defence of innocent acquisition where the defendant shows that the illicit recording was innocently acquired by him or a predecessor in title, in which case damages will be limited to a reasonable payment.[44]

## EXCEPTIONS

The *Rickless* case was criticised in that it gave civil rights in a way that was probably not intended by Parliament and this meant that such civil rights were without the comprehensive exceptions that apply to copyright and moderate its strength.[45] The fine balance usually maintained between the interests of the owners of intellectual property rights and the public was missing. The 1988 provisions remedy this in an extensive manner and a whole range of exceptions are made which, on the whole, are very similar to those available in copyright law. There are many cross-references to the copyright provisions for definitions. The exceptions are contained in Sch 2 to the Copyright, Designs and Patents Act 1988 and, although there is not room to discuss them here in detail, Table 10.1 should give some indication of their scope.[46]

Even though the rights in performances have been considerably extended, it has not been necessary substantially to modify the permitted acts, apart from providing some new ones in respect of lending.

The Copyright Tribunal is, by s 190, given limited powers in respect of performances, and a person who wishes to make a recording of a performance may ask the Tribunal to give consent where the identity or whereabouts of the per-

[43] The United States does not enjoy reciprocal protection as yet: Performances (Reciprocal Protection)(Convention Countries) Order 1994, SI 1994/264.

[44] Section 188(2).

[45] *See* Dworkin, G. and Taylor, R. D. (1989) *Blackstone's Guide to the Copyright, Designs and Patents Act 1988,* Blackstone Press, at p. 127.

[46] For general principles, references should be made to Chapter 7.

**Table 10.1 Exceptions to infringement of rights in performances**

| Exception | Comment |
| --- | --- |
| Criticism, review and reporting current events (para 2) | There is no exception for research and no requirement for a sufficient acknowledgement (but this may be required for copyright) |
| Incidental inclusion (para 3) | As with copyright, deliberate inclusion is outside the exception |
| 'Educational purposes' (paras 4–6) | Similar exceptions to those for copyright but less extensive |
| Copy required as a condition of export, e.g. article of cultural or historical importance (para 7) | The long list of exceptions for libraries and archives for copyright are missing for performances |
| Public administration (paras 8–11) | Similar to copyright exceptions but not as many |
| Transfer of copies in electronic form (para 12) | Allows the making of a back-up copy in some cases |
| *Miscellaneous* (paras 13–21) | These are all very similar to the copyright exceptions |
| Recordings of spoken words Recordings of folk songs Club and society purposes | |
| *Broadcasts/cable programmes* Incidental recording for: Supervision and control Free public showing/playing Reception/retransmission Subtitled copies for hard of hearing, etc. Recording for archival purposes | |
| *Lending of copies by* Educational establishments (para 6A) Libraries or archives (para 6B) Order of the Secretary of State (para 14A) | Inserted by the Copyright and Related Rights Regulations 1996 |

former cannot be ascertained by reasonable enquiry or where the performer unreasonably witholds his consent. This could prove useful in dealing with the problem of the 'Tenth Spear Carrier', that is, where an extra in a film refuses to consent.[47] In exercising this power, the Tribunal shall take into account:

47 Prime, T. (1992) *The Law of Copyright*, Fourmat, at p. 284.

(a) whether the recording from which the new recording is to be made was made with the performer's consent and is lawfully in the possession and control of the person proposing to make the new recording, and

(b) whether the making of the new recording would be consistent with the obligations and purposes of the parties to the arrangements under which the original recording was made.

Where the performer unreasonably withholds consent, the Tribunal may give consent only if satisfied that the performer's reasons do not include the protection of any of his legitimate interests, but it is for the performer to show what his reasons are and, in default, the Tribunal may make any such inference as it thinks fit. Where the Tribunal gives consent to the making of the further recording(s), it may make such order for payment as it thinks fit as being the appropriate consideration for the consent, unless the parties have agreed payment in the meantime. Of course, in most cases, the recording company will have obtained all the necessary consents.

## TRANSITIONAL PROVISIONS AND SAVINGS

The 1996 Regulations apply to performances given before or after commencement (1 December 1996), but no act done prior to commencement will infringe or give rise to a right to equitable remuneration.[48] Further, unless expressly agreed, an agreement made before 19 November 1992 (the date of adoption of the rental right Directive) is not affected, nor is any act done after commencement an infringement of any new right in pursuance of such an agreement.[49]

48 Regulation 26.

49 Regulation 27.

Any new right relating to a qualifying performance may be exercised from commencement and where, before commencement, the owner or prospective owner of one of the performers' rights authorised the making of a copy of a recording of a performance, any new right relating to that copy will vest on commencement in the person so authorised, in the absence of any agreement to the contrary.[50]

50 Regulations 30 and 31.

No right to an equitable remuneration arises in respect of any rental of a film or sound recording before 1 April 1997 nor in respect of any rental after that date but made in pursuance of an agreement entered into before 1 July 1994 unless, before 1 January 1997, the performer or successor in title notifies the person by whom the remuneration would be payable that he intends to exercise that right. Because of the timing of the Regulations, this left just a few short weeks for performers (and relevant copyright authors) to make their notification. The significance of the dates 1 July 1994 and 1 January 1997 is that they are set out in the Directive's provisions in Article 13 (application in time).

## OFFENCES

The criminal offences are similar to those under the previous Acts and are detailed in s 198. A person commits an offence if, without sufficient consent, he:

(a) makes for sale or hire, or
(b) imports into the United Kingdom, otherwise than for his private and domestic use, or
(c) possesses in the course of business with a view to committing an act infringing any of the rights in performances, or
(d) in the course of business –
    (i) sells or lets for hire, or

(ii) offers or exposes for sale or hire, or

(iii) distributes,

a recording which he knows, or has reason to believe, is an illicit recording.

The offences under (a), (b) and (d) (iii) are triable either way, carrying a maximum of two years' imprisonment and/or a fine. The other offences, including those described below, are triable summarily only and carry a maximum penalty of a fine not exceeding level 5 on the standard scale or a term of imprisonment not exceeding six months or both.[51] It is also an offence, without sufficient consent, to cause a recording to be shown or played in public, or to broadcast it or include it in a cable programme service; for the offence to be made out, it is required that the person concerned knows or has reason to believe that any of the rights in performances will be infringed as a result of his actions. None of the above offences is committed if the act comes within any of the exceptions in Sch 2.

The meaning of 'sufficient consent' depends on whether the performance is a qualifying performance.[52] If it is, then it is the consent of the performer. Otherwise, and for the purposes of the 'making' offence, it is the consent of the performer or the person having the recording rights. For all the other offences involving a non-qualifying performance, it is the consent of the person having the recording rights. There are provisions for orders for delivery up in criminal proceedings (s 199) and for search warrants (s 200), and orders may be made for the disposal of illicit recordings (s 204). These provisions are similar to those available in respect of the copyright criminal offences.[53]

Directors, managers, secretaries, and other similar officers of corporate bodies may also be liable where the offence is committed by a corporate body with their consent or connivance.[54] It is an offence for a person falsely to represent that he is authorised by any person to give the necessary consent in relation to a performance unless he believes, on reasonable grounds, that he is so authorised. This offence is triable summarily only and carries a maximum sentence of imprisonment for a period not exceeding six months and/or a fine not exceeding level 5 on the standard scale.

**51** Level 5 is currently £5000.

**52** Section 198(3).

**53** By s 198A, inserted by s 165 of the Criminal Justice and Public Order Act 1994, local weights and measures authorities are given equivalent powers to those under the Trade Descriptions Act 1968 in relation to making test purchases, seizing illicit recordings, etc.

**54** Section 202. Both the officer and the corporate body are criminally liable.

## SUMMARY

The statutory extension of performers' protection to give civil rights not only to performers but also to persons having exclusive recording contracts with those performers is welcome, and is a direct response to the growing problem of bootleg recordings. The subsequent development of performers' property rights is further recognition of the importance of such rights. The inclusion of variety acts, extending the scope beyond performances of the 'original works' category of copyright, is sensible as such performances are no less deserving of protection. The law on rights in performances now makes it all the more important to ascertain the consent of *all* those taking part in a performance before making a recording, and it could hinder the future use of old recordings to make new recordings, for example by making a compilation of old recordings. The spectre of 'bit-part' actors withholding consent and preventing this future exploitation will be ever present in the minds of film and record companies.[55] This could have serious consequences for the British Broadcasting Corporation which has a large number of recordings of television comedy and drama, much of which was broadcast live. However, the Copyright Tribunal is there as a last resort should the performer unreasonably withhold his consent.

Some measure of international protection is afforded through the Rome Convention of 1961 for the Protection of Performers, Producers of Phonograms and Broadcasting Organizations, which has been ratified by over 40 countries, including the United Kingdom.

55 Of course, employment and service contracts should provide for these rights in a way that facilities future exploitation of the work.

# Part Three

# THE LAW OF BREACH OF CONFIDENCE

# 11

## *Law of breach of confidence*

### INTRODUCTION

This area of law is concerned with secrets of all kinds. They may be of a personal, commercial or industrial nature, or concern the state and its administration. State secrets received a great deal of publicity a few years ago as a result of the publication of *Spycatcher*, written by Peter Wright, a former assistant director of MI5, but it is in relation to trade secrets and business information that the law of confidence is of everyday importance. An obligation of confidence may arise in contract or be imposed by equity. The vast majority of persons owe an obligation of confidence to others: all employees have a duty of confidence or fidelity to their employers, consultants owe a duty to their clients, doctors have a duty of confidence in respect of their patients, and solicitors are bound by a duty of confidence to their clients. The law of confidence also covers business transactions and negotiations, and an obligation of confidence will be implied in a great many situations where there is no express agreement as to confidentiality.

1 [1995] FSR 765.

Breach of confidence lies in the domain of equity and is almost entirely based on case law. In *Kitechnology BV v Unicor GmbH Plastmaschinen*[1] it was said that claims for breach of confidence did not arise in tort, were certainly non-contractual but were part of the equitable jurisdiction of the court. However, there is statutory recognition of the law of breach of confidence. For example, the Copyright, Designs and Patents Act 1988 s 171(1) states that:

> Nothing in this Part [the part of the Act dealing with copyright law] affects ... the operation of any rule of equity relating to breaches of trust or confidence.

2 *See Lord Advocate v The Scotsman Publications Ltd* [1990] AC 812 for a discussion of the Official Secrets Act 1989.
3 Section 2 of the 1911 Act became so infamous that juries had become inclined to acquit regardless of the evidence – for example, the trial and acquittal of the senior civil servant Clive Ponting for disclosure of cabinet minutes relating to the sinking of the *General Belgrano*; see *R v Ponting* [1985] Crim LR 318.

The notoriously widely drafted Official Secrets Act 1911 s 2 (now replaced and narrowed by the Official Secrets Act 1989 s 1),[2] provided for a number of offences relating to the disclosure of confidential information to unauthorised persons.[3] Otherwise, disclosure of confidential information lies within the scope of the civil law, and being equitable, the law of confidence has proven to be reasonably flexible and a particularly useful adjunct to other intellectual property rights.

4 An exception is made where the information has been released by a person acting in breach of confidence in the previous six months: Patents Act 1977 s 2(4).

Whereas other rights such as copyright and patents are particularly useful when the subject matter is made public by exploitation by the right owner, the law of breach of confidence gives protection to things not released to the public or part of the public domain. Indeed, this is the whole point of the law of confidence, and its most useful feature is that, in appropriate cases, an injunction can be obtained preventing an anticipated wrongful release or use of the information that is the subject matter of the confidence. In terms of patent law, confidence is vital to the grant of a patent as it is essential that details of the invention do not fall into the public domain before the filing of the patent application, otherwise the patent will be refused.[4] Confidence protects the invention and its detail. In some circumstances the inventor may decide to keep his invention secret in preference to obtaining a patent, as the latter gives a maximum of 20 years' protection only. It depends on whether the information can be kept secret. As regards copyright, it has been seen that, as a matter of principle, copyright does not protect ideas, only the expression of ideas. However, confidence can and does protect ideas, but only until such time as those ideas are published in some way.

There is no fundamental right to privacy at English law. The law of confidence should not be confused with privacy. Invasions of privacy can be dealt with by an action for defamation or malicious falsehood, but this course may not always be satisfactory, as in *Kaye v Robertson*[5] in which a journalist and a photographer gained access to Mr Gordon Kaye's private hospital room and took photographs and conducted an interview when Mr Kaye was in no fit state to be interviewed or to give consent. Mr Kaye, the actor from the television comedy series '*Allo 'Allo* had, while driving, been struck by a piece of wood and suffered severe head and brain injuries. In allowing in part the appeal against an injunction imposed by Potter J, the Court of Appeal judges were unanimous in their call for a legal right to privacy.[6]

The Copyright, Designs and Patents Act 1988 gives a limited right to privacy in respect of certain photographs and films.[7] The law of breach of confidence may indirectly protect privacy if, for example, materials of a private nature have been shown or given to another to whom a duty of confidence attaches. The basic requirement for confidence is the existence of a duty which may be expressed or imputed from the circumstances.

## DEVELOPMENT OF THE LAW OF BREACH OF CONFIDENCE

The law of breach of confidence has had an erratic history. From earlier beginnings, it largely developed in a spurt in the early to middle of the nineteenth century, and then lay relatively dormant until the late 1940s when it was realised that this was an extremely useful area of law. Some of the early cases involved 'patent medicines'. There was obviously a lot of money to be made from these magic cures, bearing in mind that conventional medicine was still fairly primitive at this time and that the public at large was relatively ignorant and uneducated. In *Morison v Moat*,[8] such a medicine was made known as 'Morison's Vegetable Universal Medicine'. There was a dispute between the son of the person who originally devised the recipe and the partner, Thomas Moat, who had improperly told his own son of the recipe. It was held that there was an equity against the defendant. It was a breach of faith and of contract by the partner, Thomas Moat, to tell his son of the secret who, therefore, derived his knowledge under a breach of faith and of contract and could not claim a title to the recipe. Although the term 'breach of confidence' was not used at this stage, it was clear that the breach of faith was actionable *per se* and was not dependent upon the existence of a contract. There was no contractual relationship between the son of the originator of the recipe and the son of the defendant.

Another important case which helped establish this area of law concerned etchings made by Queen Victoria and Prince Albert. The case is *Prince Albert v Strange*.[9] The Queen and Prince Albert made etchings for their own amusement, intended only for their own private entertainment, although they sometimes had

5 [1991] FSR 62.

6 For a discussion of this case and the need for a law of privacy, *see* Markesinis, B. S. I. 'Our Patchy Law of Privacy – Time to do Something about it' (1990) 53 MLR 802; and Prescott, P. '*Kaye v Robertson* – a Reply' (1991) 53 MLR 451. *See also* the Calcutt Committee Report, *On Privacy and Related Matters*, Cm 1102 (HMSO, 1990). For a description of the trend in New Zealand towards recognising a tort of invasion of privacy, *see* Katz, J. 'Sex, Lies, Videotapes and Telephone Conversations: The Common Law of Privacy from a New Zealand Perspective' [1995] 1 EIPR 6.

7 The Copyright, Designs and Patents Act 1988 s 85.

8 (1851) 9 Hare 241.

9 (1849) 1 Mac & G 25.

prints made to give to friends. Some of the etchings were sent to a printer for impressions (prints) to be made from them. While at the printers, someone surreptitiously made some additional prints from the etchings which came into the hands of the defendant who intended to display the prints in an exhibition to which the public could go on payment of an admission charge. The defendant advertised his intention to hold the exhibition and was sued by the Queen's Consort. It was held that relief would be given against the defendant even though he was a third party. The defendant had argued that the prints were not improperly taken, but it was said that his possession must have originated in a breach of trust, a breach of confidence or a breach of contract, and therefore an injunction was granted preventing the exhibition. Again, it was clear that relief was available without having to rely on a contractual relationship.

## THE MODERN LAW OF BREACH OF CONFIDENCE

The law of breach of confidence began its renaissance about 40 or 50 years ago. It became apparent that this area of law was extremely well suited to protecting 'industrial property' during the development stages before other legal rights were able to afford protection.[10] Indeed, some industrialists had come to the conclusion that it was better to keep some details of their processes secret rather than obtain a patent which would mean that, eventually, the idea would fall into the public domain. However, it seems as if the significance of this area of law was not fully appreciated by law reporters. A number of important cases were reported in some series of law reports retrospectively, several years after the disposal of the cases.

The first major case on the law of breach of confidence that laid the foundations for its modern form was *Saltman Engineering Co Ltd* v *Campbell Engineering Co Ltd*.[11] The plaintiff owned the copyright in drawings of tools for use in the manufacture of leather punches. The defendant was given the drawings and instructed to make 5000 of the tools at 3s 6d each. After completing the order, the defendant retained the drawings and made use of them for its own purposes. In finding for the plaintiff, holding that there was an implied condition that the defendant should treat the drawings as confidential, not make other use of them and should deliver the drawings with the tools made pursuant to the agreement,[12] Lord Greene MR described the nature of confidential information thus:

> The information, to be confidential, must, I apprehend, apart from contract, have the necessary quality of confidence about it, namely, it must not be something which is public property and public knowledge. On the other hand, it is perfectly possible to have a confidential document, be it a formula, a plan, a sketch, or something of that kind, which is the result of work done by the maker upon materials which may be available for the use of anybody; but what makes it confidential is the fact that the maker of the document has used his brain and thus produced a result which can only be produced by somebody who goes through the same process.[13]

Lord Greene also emphasised that an obligation of confidence is not limited to cases where the parties are in a contractual relationship; that the law will prevent an abuse of position by the recipient of confidential information. He also indicated that there need be nothing special about the information concerned

**10** 'Industrial property' can be considered to include patents, trade marks and industrial designs.

**11** [1963] 3 All ER 413, also reported in (1948) 65 RPC 203.

**12** There was no contract between the plaintiff and the defendant who had been sub-contracted to make the tools. The defendant was instructed to deliver up the drawings and an inquiry into damages was ordered.

**13** [1963] 3 All ER 413 at 415.

and that others may be able to derive the information for themselves but will need to invest some effort to obtain that information. In other words, the recipient of confidential information will be prevented from making unfair use of the information outside that contemplated by the person giving it. It can be said that a person fixed with a duty of confidence is in an analogous position to that of a trustee; however, in the case of a person fixed with an obligation of confidence, the nature of that duty is always negative, that is he must not use or divulge the information outside the authority given to him by his confidant.

Megarry J further developed the action of breach of confidence and laid down a good working formula for the application of this area of law in the case of *Coco v A N Clark (Engineers) Ltd.*[14] The plaintiff, one Marco Paolo Coco, designed a moped engine and had entered into informal negotiations with the defendant with a view to the latter manufacturing the engine. In the end the negotiations broke down and no contract was executed between the plaintiff and the defendant. The plaintiff suggested that the defendant had deliberately caused the breakdown in negotiations with a view to making the engine without paying the plaintiff. When the defendant decided to manufacture its own engine to a design which closely resembled the plaintiff's design, the plaintiff sought an interlocutory injunction to prevent the defendant using confidential information given by the plaintiff for the purposes of a proposed joint venture.

14 [1969] RPC 41.

Megarry J stated that the doctrine of confidence required three elements as follows:

1 the information must have the necessary quality of confidence about it (using Lord Greene's definition in *Saltman*);
2 the information must have been imparted in circumstances importing an obligation of confidence;
3 there must be an unauthorised use of that information to the detriment of the party communicating it.

However, in the event, the plaintiff was not granted an injunction and had, at best, a weak case. Where information was communicated in the expectation that the plaintiff would be paid, it was doubtful whether an injunction was an appropriate remedy if there was subsequently a dispute. Megarry J ordered that the defendant should give an undertaking to pay a royalty of five shillings per engine made into a special joint bank account on trusts, should he manufacture the engines, pending the full trial. The formula used by Megarry J forms a useful basis for exploring the nature and scope of the law of breach of confidence and is used as a framework for the discussion later.

The equitable nature of the law of breach of confidence was stressed by Ungoed-Thomas J in *Duchess of Argyll v Duke of Argyll*[15] where he said:

15 [1967] Ch 303 at 322.

> These cases [*Prince Albert v Strange*, etc.] in my view indicate (1) that a contract or obligation of confidence need not be expressed but can be implied ... (2) that a breach of confidence or trust or faith can arise independently of any right of property or contract other, of course, than any contract which the imparting of the confidence in the relevant circumstances may itself create; (3) that the court in the exercise of its equitable jurisdiction will restrain a breach of confidence independently of any right at law.

It is clear that an obligation will be implied in many situations but, as Ungoed-Thomas J acknowledges, the obligation may be created expressly by way of a contract (an express contractual obligation may run alongside or replace an obligation that would otherwise be imposed by equity). For example, a contract of employment or service may include terms imposing an obligation of confidence on one or both parties. Further, in some contracts, the subject matter may be the confidential information itself, for example where a designer gives details of his design to a manufacturer in return for royalties.

Being rooted in equity, the law of confidence retains a useful flexibility and it has been developed at an extraordinary rate by the courts over the last three or four decades. Nevertheless, the Law Commission recommended that this area of law be codified and a draft Bill was produced in 1981.[16] A major advantage of the law of breach of confidence has been its flexibility and the way in which it has been developed by the courts, freed from the straightjacket of statutory interpretation. It might be wondered, therefore, what would be gained by codifying this area of law, which works reasonably effectively, to replace it with sterile legislation. The Law Commission must have appreciated this as much of the draft Bill is couched in general terms, and indeed the Law Commission stated:

> … we should emphasize that the legislative framework which we envisage would allow the Courts wide scope in applying its principles to differing situations and changing social circumstances.[17]

If this is the basis upon which the legislation would be founded it is difficult to see what advantage would be gained by its promulgation. Widely drafted legislation might have some unfortunate and unpredictable effects, while the track record of the courts in developing this area of equity has been good and there is no reason to believe that judicial common sense cannot provide for the future satisfactory development of the law of confidence. Such considerations may account for the fact that no moves have been made to codify the law of confidence and it would seem that codification is extremely unlikely in the foreseeable future.[18]

One area the draft Bill addressed that is unclear and in need of development is the position of persons improperly acquiring information, for example by industrial espionage. In many cases, the information concerned has been divulged willingly by the person who 'owns' the information. However, where a person acquires information by eavesdropping, or by other means such as computer hacking or other unauthorised taking or copying of information, it is not certain whether an obligation of confidence exists. Perhaps the difficulty stems from one of the guidelines laid down by Megarry J in *Coco v A N Clark (Engineers) Ltd*,[19] that is that the information must have been imparted in circumstances importing an obligation of confidence. This is an important point as, because of developments and improvements in areas of technology such as telecommunications, it is much easier for determined people to gain access to confidential information on a worldwide basis. In the case of *Prince Albert v Strange*,[20] the court did not know how the prints came into the defendant's possession, only that the prints must have been made surreptitiously. Nevertheless, the court was willing to give relief. It is possible that the principle as associated with this case can be applied to computer hackers and other persons gaining access to confidential material without permission, that is in respect to the improper acquisition of information, and that Megarry J's test is unduly restrictive.

16 The Law Commission, Law Comm. No. 110, *Breach of Confidence*, Cmnd 8388 (HMSO, 1981).

17 *Op cit*, para 6.1.

18 For a brief overview of the Law Commission's draft Bill, *see* Reid, B. C. (1986) *Confidentiality and the Law* (Waterlow) at p. 190.

19 [1969] RPC 41.

20 (1849) 1 Mac & G 25.

Returning to Megarry J's formula for breach of confidence, the nature of this useful area of law is now examined in more detail commencing with the necessary quality of confidence.

## CONFIDENTIAL QUALITY

### Nature of confidential quality

The sort of material protected may be technical, commercial or personal. Often the information will be related to commercial or industrial enterprise such as in the *Coco* case. The value of such information should not be taken for granted and it can be surprising how important some secrets are even though they may seem very mundane. For example, there was a dispute about a cockle bottling secret in which the cockle bottlers' greatest problem was discussed, being to achieve the right acidity level, that is strong enough to preserve the cockles without being too strong so as to be unpleasant to taste.[21] Secrets of a personal nature are also protected, even if relating to sexual conduct of a lurid nature. It was held in *Stephens v Avery*[22] that there was no reason why such information, expressly communicated in confidence, could not be subject to an enforceable duty of confidence. The background to that case was the killing of Mrs Telling by her husband. Details of a sexual relationship between Mrs Stephens, the plaintiff, and Mrs Telling were disclosed in confidence to a friend, Mrs Avery, the defendant, who had published the information in a newspaper. While a court would not protect information of a grossly immoral nature, on the basis of *Glyn v Weston Feature Film Co Ltd*,[23] the difficulty in this instance was identifying what was grossly immoral. A general code of sexual morals accepted by the overwhelming majority of the public no longer existed and there was no common view that sexual conduct between consenting adults, two females in this case, was grossly immoral.[24] After all, the story was not so shocking as to prevent the editor spreading the story across the pages of a major national newspaper for personal profit, and it lay ill in the mouth of the defendant to claim that the law did not protect the confidentiality of information of this sort.

An objective test should be applied to determine whether information is truly confidential. Simply marking a document with the words 'PRIVATE AND CONFIDENTIAL' will not suffice if the contents are commonplace and lie within the public domain, such as a simple, straightforward recipe for bread which contains nothing unusual in terms of the ingredients or the methods to be employed in the mixing and baking of the dough. In *Dalrymple's Application*[25] a manufacturer distributed over 1000 technical bulletins to members of a trade association, marking them 'CONFIDENTIAL' and including a statement on the front of the documents to the effect that the contents were not to be divulged to non-members. The material in the bulletins could not be regarded as confidential. Even distribution of a report marked 'PRIVATE AND CONFIDENTIAL' to only ten out of 350 members of the British Cast Iron Research Association was fatal to confidentiality.[26]

Trade practice may give an indication of whether a form of information will be regarded as confidential by the courts. For example, in *IBCOS Computers Ltd v Barclays Mercantile Highland Finance Ltd*,[27] Jacob J said that source code for a computer program was confidential because it was not usually given

---

21 *The Times*, 24 June 1986. In an earlier dispute which involved the same plaintiff who was a bottler of cockles and mussels, the founder of the plaintiff company had obtained £530 000 in damages in respect of the copying of an onion peeling machine.

22 [1988] 1 Ch 457. Followed in *Michael Barrymore v News Group Newspapers Ltd* [1997] FSR 600.

23 [1916] 1 Ch 261.

24 Because the analogy with copyright law in respect of works of a grossly immoral nature failed to find sympathy, the modern relevance of cases like *Glyn v Weston Feature Film Co Ltd* [1916] 1 Ch 261 must be doubted.

25 [1957] RPC 449.

26 *Young's Patents* (1943) 60 RPC 51.

27 [1994] FSR 275.

to clients by software developers who regarded it as confidential. Even if source code is made available to a client under a licence agreement, the licence will most likely contain terms imposing an obligation of confidence on the licensee in respect of the source code.[28]

**28** Jacob J went on to find that one of the defendants had access to the plaintiff's source code while writing his software and was, consequently, in breach of confidence in addition to infringing copyright.

The information does not have to be particularly special in any way and a compilation of already known information such as a list of customers can, when taken as a whole, be regarded as confidential. What makes such information worth protecting by confidence is the fact that time and effort has been expended in gathering, selecting and arranging the information. In other words, a competitor should not be permitted to take a short-cut by 'stealing' information belonging to someone else – he should have to go through a similar process and discover the information for himself by his own labours.[29]

**29** In *Oxford* v *Moss* (1978) 68 Cr App R 183 it was held that information is not property for the purposes of theft.

**30** [1998] FSR 248.

A combination of information taken together may be confidential even though, taken separately, there is some doubt about this. In *Indata Equipment Supplies Ltd* v *ACL Ltd*,[30] the information disclosed by the plaintiff to the defendant concerned the provision of a fleet of cars to a potential client of the plaintiff, being information relating to the price of cars, full details of the client's requirements, the sums it was prepared to pay, its preferred payment scheme and its time constraints. The defendant used this information to offer the client a lower 'on the road' price for the cars. In finding the profit margin and, to a lesser degree, the invoice price to be confidential information, Otton LJ said (at 259):

> The information for which confidence is claimed must not be considered in isolation but in the context of other information where it is doubtful that any confidence arose.

Simon Brown LJ expressed some doubt about whether the invoiced prices were protected by confidence as he thought it difficult to think of circumstances in which a buyer would need the seller's authority to disclose the price of goods he had bought to another.

**31** [1976] FSR 345.

In *Thomas Marshall (Exports)* v *Guinle*,[31] the defendant was appointed as the managing director of the plaintiff company for ten years. The company's business largely concerned the purchase of clothing from eastern Europe and the Far East and the sale of such clothing to retail outlets. The defendant's service agreement stated that he was not to engage in any other business without the company's consent and that he must not disclose confidential information. Further, after ceasing to be the managing director, he was not to use or disclose confidential information about the suppliers and customers of the plaintiff company. The defendant began to trade on his own account and on behalf of two companies in competition with the plaintiff company. When his service contract had another four-and-a-half years left to run, he purported to resign. It was held that the court would restrain the defendant from committing further breaches of his employment contract and that an interim injunction would be granted in respect of the defendant's breach of the obligations of fidelity and good faith to his employer. Megarry V-C suggested that four elements were important when testing for confidential quality:

1  the information must be such that the owner believes that its release would be injurious to him, or would be advantageous to his rivals or to others;
2  the owner of the information must believe it to be confidential or secret and not already in the public domain;

3 the owner's belief in 1 and 2 above must be reasonable; and
4 the information must be judged in the light of usages and practices of the
   particular trade or industry concerned.

According to this test, a certain amount of subjectivity is allowed on the part of
the owner of the information, but this is restricted by the requirement that the
owner's beliefs must be reasonable. On this basis, it is possible that a duty of
confidence could arise and attract legal remedies even if the information was
actually in the public domain if the owner's contrary belief was reasonable.
This seems to go too far. Surely, the test of whether information is confidential
is objective. In *Lancashire Fires Ltd* v *S A Lyons & Co Ltd*,[32] Carnwath J, at
first instance, noted this subjective emphasis in *Thomas Marshall*, saying that it
does not appear in earlier authorities and explaining its presence by the context
of *Thomas Marshall* which was concerned with the construction of a specific
provision in a contract. Conversely, as an actionable breach of confidence is
based, at least partly, on an equity being fastened on the conscience of the
defendant, the behaviour of the defendant may be a factor.[33]

32 [1996] FSR 629.

33 The behaviour of the
defendant in *Indata Equipment
Supplies Ltd* v *ACL Ltd* [1998]
FSR 248 seemed to colour the
judgment of Simon Brown and
Otton LJJ.

## Trade secret

The term 'trade secret' is often used in relation to confidential information associated with industrial and commercial activity. The classification of some forms
of confidential information as trade secrets is important because the protection
afforded by the law may depend upon it. Unfortunately, there is no satisfactory
legal definition of the term.[34]

In *Herbert Morris Ltd* v *Saxelby*,[35] Lord Atkinson spoke of trade secrets thus
(at 705):

> ... trade secrets, such as prices, &c. or any secret process or things of a nature which
> the man [the defendant] was not entitled to reveal.

34 *See* Coleman, A. (1992)
*The Legal Protection of Trade
Secrets*, Sweet & Maxwell,
Chapter 2 for an exhaustive
discussion of the meaning of
'trade secret'.

35 [1916] 1 AC 688.

In that case, Lord Parker suggested a test based on the detailed nature of the
information. Information that was far too detailed to be carried away in the head
was a trade secret, whereas a general method or scheme that could easily be
remembered could not be regarded as a trade secret. At first instance, in *Faccenda
Chicken Ltd* v *Fowler*,[36] Goulding J defined three classes of information, being:

36 [1985] 1 All ER 724.

1 information which, because of its trivial character or its easy accessibility
   from public sources, cannot be regarded as confidential;
2 information which an employee must treat as confidential, but which, once
   learned, reasonably remains in the employee's head and becomes part of his
   skill and experience; and
3 specific trade secrets so confidential that a continuing duty of confidence
   applies even beyond the termination of employment or the service contract.

This classification provides little guidance as to what precisely distinguishes a
trade secret from information in the second category, but it does show that such
information will be given less protection. In *Lancashire Fires Ltd* v *S A Lyons
& Co Ltd*,[37] Bingham MR said that the distinction between class 2 and class 3
may, on the facts, be very hard to draw but the Court of Appeal did apply
Goulding J's classification. There may be a problem with Goulding J's first cate-

37 [1996] FSR 629.

38 [1997] RPC 289.

gory, and in *Ocular Sciences Ltd* v *Aspect Vision Care Ltd*,[38] Laddie J admitted difficulty with it, arguing that it had little to do with confidence. Perhaps it is more a question of the employee's duty of fidelity to his present employer. This duty would prevent him, whilst still employed, putting his skill and expertise at the disposal of another employer whether or not that involved confidential information. As Laddie J said, '... he is expected to work for his employer not for his employer's competitors'.

39 [1991] 1 WLR 251.

Of trade secrets, in a restraint of trade case, *Lansing Linde Ltd* v *Kerr*,[39] Staughton LJ spoke in terms of information that would be liable to cause real harm if it was disclosed to a competitor, provided it was used in a trade or business and the owner had either limited the dissemination of the information, or at least not encouraged or permitted widespread publication. Butter-Sloss LJ stressed the need to take account of the changing nature of business and the need to take account of '... the wider context of highly confidential information of a non-technical or non-scientific nature ...'.[40]

40 [1991] 1 WLR 251 at 270.

While it is clear that a secret industrial process containing an inventive step is capable of being a trade secret, the position is less predictable in terms of confidential price lists, databases containing customer names and addresses and clients' accounts. The test of what can be remembered by an ex-employee does not help, as many new inventions may easily be remembered. Neither would it be realistic to limit trade secrets to inventions that are potentially patentable. Information relating to clients' credit ratings and the types of goods that they buy may be very valuable and, in the right circumstances, fall to be considered a trade secret. In *PSM International plc* v *Whitehouse & Willenhall Automation Ltd*[41] drawings, quotations, price costing and business strategies were considered to rank as trade secrets.

41 [1992] FSR 489.

## Publication

If the information has been published or disclosed to third parties in the absence of an obligation of confidence, it falls into the public domain and the law of confidence cannot prevent its subsequent use and further disclosure. Unless his conscience is fixed by equity, a person who has received the information in circumstances such that he was not, or could not reasonably have been, aware of the confidential nature is free to make use of that information or to pass it on to others. However, even if the information has fallen into the hands of innocent third parties because of a breach of confidence, there will be remedies available against the person in breach. When a patent is applied for, the specification of the invention is available for public inspection 18 months after the priority date. The protection afforded by the law of confidence is then lost, to be replaced by the patent, once granted.[42] The information is in the public domain even though it may be available only after a search at the Patent Office. In *Mustad & Son* v *Dosen*,[43] a case concerning information about a machine for the manufacture of fish hooks for anglers, it was held that publication through the master by obtaining a patent effectively destroys the servant's duty of confidence in respect of the subject matter of the patent grant. However, this principle has been distinguished as regards a patent obtained by a third party.

42 Once the patent has been granted, the proprietor can sue for infringement in relation to acts done after the date of publication of the patent.

43 [1964] 1 WLR 109. This case was actually decided in 1928.

44 [1965] 1 WLR 1293.

In *Cranleigh Precision Engineering Ltd* v *Bryant*,[44] Bryant was the managing director of the plaintiff company which manufactured above-ground swimming pools invented by Bryant. No patent had been granted in respect of the plaintiff's swimming pools. Patent agents, acting on behalf of the plaintiff, informed Bryant of a patent belonging to a rival company (known as the Bischoff patent) which concerned a similar swimming pool but which lacked two special features which the plaintiff's design incorporated.[45] Bryant did not inform his co-directors of the Bischoff patent. Later, Bryant left and set up his own company and obtained an assignment of the Bischoff patent. He was sued, *inter alia*, for injunctions to restrain him and his company from making use of or disclosing information relating to the plaintiff's swimming pools.

45 The special features were a plastic strip clamping the inner and outer walls together and an overlapping interfit of the metal plates forming the outside wall of the swimming pool.

It was argued on behalf of the defendant that, because knowledge of the Bischoff patent was in the public domain, there could be no breach of confidence. However, although details of the Bischoff patent could be inspected by anyone, it was especially relevant to the plaintiff because of the possible effect of the Bischoff patent on the plaintiff's swimming pools and the possibility of a conflict over rights. Bryant had acted in breach of confidence in making use, as soon as he left the plaintiff's employ, of the information concerning the Bischoff patent and in terms of the *various effects on the plaintiff's position* of that information. The case of *Mustad & Son* v *Dosen* was distinguished on the grounds that, in that case, the patent was granted to the master (employer), that is, publication was by the master of the person alleged to have committed the breach of confidence. In *Cranleigh Precision Engineering Ltd* v *Bryant*, the publication was by another; Bryant's 'master' (the plaintiff) had never published anything, not even the specification for its own swimming pool.

If the information has found its way to the public domain, the person who owed another an obligation of confidence in respect of that information may be prevented from making use of the information himself for a period of time. This is known as the 'springboard' doctrine. The person who was under an obligation of confidence is not allowed to use it as a springboard from which to launch his own project if to do so would be harmful to the person to whom the obligation was owed. In *Terrapin* v *Builders Supply Co (Hayes) Ltd*[46] it was said by Roxburgh J that:

46 [1967] RPC 375, actually decided in 1959.

> ... a person who has obtained information in confidence is not allowed to use it as a springboard for activities detrimental to [the owner] and springboard it remains even when all the features have been published ...[47]

47 [1967] RPC 375 at 392.

However, the springboard effect does not last indefinitely. After all, if the information has been published others are free to use it, so why should the person who originally owed an obligation of confidence be restricted. Of course, one justification is that the information has been published because of a breach of that obligation. In *Roger Bullivant Ltd* v *Ellis*,[48] the plaintiffs specialised in a type of construction work known as underpinning. This is a means of replacing defective foundations. The defendant, who had been an employee of the plaintiffs, with others, set up a rival business. It was discovered that the defendant had taken a copy of a card index of customers which had been compiled by the plaintiffs. The defendant had deliberately made use of the card index and could not complain if the court restrained him from using it, even though his obligation of confidence as an ex-employee was weaker and he would have been free to use information that he simply had remembered. It was said that the spring-

48 [1987] FSR 172.

board doctrine would not normally extend beyond the period for which the unfair advantage gained would reasonably be expected to remain, and the purpose of an injunction in such circumstances was not to punish the defendant but to protect the plaintiff. It was argued that the information was freely available elsewhere but, on the basis of *Robb* v *Green*,[49] it was said that the defendant could not complain if the law was unable to distinguish between the information he was able to use and that which he could not.

Where the information has entered the public domain, it can no longer be regarded as confidential and the obligation of confidence owed by the defendant cannot continue. If everyone else is free to further publish or use the information why should the defendant be prevented from doing so? In such cases, the only justification for the springboard doctrine is to prevent the defendant having a head start over others who are free to use the information because of his breach of confidence. He would be able to enter the market place before any other who is free to use the information. Where this is not so, for example, where the information can be put to use immediately, it would seem that the remedy ought to lie in damages only as the only purpose of the injunction would be to punish the defendant further rather than to protect the interests of the plaintiff.

In *Attorney-General* v *Guardian Newspapers (No. 2)*,[50] one of the *Spycatcher* cases, Lord Goff said that it was difficult to see how a confidant who publishes information to the whole world could be prevented from further disclosing it. This would mean that the confidant could not mention in public what was now common knowledge. Laddie J was attracted to this conclusion in *Ocular Sciences Ltd* v *Aspect Vision Care Ltd*,[51] thereby casting some doubt on the springboard doctrine. He said that the court counters any unfair benefit to the defendant by imposing financial penalties or imposing a constructive trust. However, the *Attorney-General* v *Guardian* case was concerned with publication rather than other forms of use. What, for example, of the situation where the defendant has published the information but can put it to practical use some time before anyone else because of his particular training and experience of using the information? Perhaps the information concerns a new technique that has to be learnt and practised before it can be applied successfully. In such cases, there may yet be a place for the springboard doctrine. Alternatively, it may be technical information relating to a new industrial process and the defendant, because of his knowledge of specialist component manufacturers and potential customers, can realise a commercial reward long before anyone else. On the other hand, if the information can be put to immediate use, for example, if it relates to a planned takeover bid for a company quoted on the stock market, there seems little point in injuncting the defendant.

### Public interest

As with copyright, a defence of public interest is available in an action for breach of confidence. Of course, in many cases where this is relevant, there will be issues of both confidence and copyright, such as where someone publishes a confidential document.[52] The courts will not respect an obligation of confidence if it is in the public interest that the confidential information is made known to the public at large or to a restricted class of the public, such as an official body.

---

49 [1895] 2 QB 315.

50 [1990] 1 AC 109.

51 [1997] RPC 289.

52 For example, *Lion Laboratories Ltd* v *Evans* [1984] 2 All ER 417, discussed in Chapter 7.

Public interest is relevant where it concerns the administration of justice, for example, the law of confidence cannot be used as a means of suppressing information concerning criminal conduct.[53] But it is wider than that and can cover matters about religion,[54] price-fixing[55] and about persons in the public eye. It can extend to 'mug-shots' (photographs taken by the police of persons suspected of having committed a criminal offence) in pursuance of the Police and Criminal Evidence Act 1984. In *Hellewell* v *Chief Constable of Derbyshire*[56] the plaintiff complained that the police had given copies of a photograph of him to local shopkeepers involved in a shop watch scheme and who were concerned at the level of shoplifting. At the time the plaintiff had been charged with theft, though not convicted.[57] The judge said that the police were not free to use the photograph in whatever way they wished and that it might be described as a piece of confidential information. However, the judge, referring to the plaintiff's long list of convictions and the fact that the dissemination of the photograph was limited to shopkeepers and their staff, held that the actions of the police were obviously and unarguably in the public interest. The police had acted in good faith for the prevention or detection of crime.

Three points about public interest are considered below, namely where the proposed publication is potentially defamatory, where there is a conflict in public interests and, finally, as regards the scope and nature of the disclosure.

## Potentially defamatory publication

It is recognised that the public have an interest in the truth. If a person intends to publish material which is clearly untrue and defamatory, there is little doubt that the courts would, if asked, grant an injunction preventing publication unless the defendant pleads justification. However, if a person has obtained information in confidence which might injure the reputation of another, he may be free to publish it if such publication can be said to lie within the public interest. This will apply particularly to information concerning the character of persons in the public lime-light, such as politicians and show-business personalities who actively seek publicity. Of course, public interest can only be realised if the information is true, and the courts will not usually restrain publication if the person intending to publish the information is likely to raise the defences of justification or fair comment if sued for defamation. In this respect, there is something to be said for the 'publish and be damned' attitude of the Duke of Wellington. After all, the aggrieved party has, if the information is untrue, remedies under the tort of defamation which can be quite effective bearing in mind the burden of proof in such an action.

There are two reasons why the courts are reluctant to restrain publication of information even if claimed to be defamatory. First, the defences of justification or fair comment in a defamation action are for a jury to decide, not the court asked for injunctive relief. Secondly, the courts have to take account of freedom of speech.[58] The motive behind the threatened publication may not be particularly relevant to the issue, even if the defendant intended to be paid for his silence. In *Holley* v *Smyth*,[59] the defendant was the sole beneficiary of a trust. He threatened to send press releases to the media alleging fraud on the part of the trustees unless they paid him £200 000, being the amount by which the defendant claimed the trust had been defrauded. The Court of Appeal, by a majority, discharged an injunction restraining publication on the basis that the plaintiffs were not entitled to interlocutory injunctions unless the information was manifestly untrue.

53  *See Gartside* v *Outram* (1857) 26 LJ Ch (NS) 113. However, in *Re Barlow Clowes Gilt Managers Ltd, The Times,* 13 June 1991, it was said that information received by liquidators in confidence for the purposes of liquidation should not be disclosed to defendants in collateral criminal proceedings unless there was a compelling reason to divulge the information such as a court order.

54  For example, in *Hubbard* v *Vosper* [1972] 2 QB 84, it was held, *inter alia,* that it was in the public interest that details about the Church of Scientology be made known to the public.

55  *Initial Services Ltd* v *Putterill* [1968] 1 QB 396.

56  *The Times,* 13 January 1994.

57  He was subsequently convicted.

58  *Bonnard* v *Perryman* [1891] 2 Ch 269.

59  *The Times,* 20 December 1997.

60 [1977] 2 All ER 751.

In *Woodward* v *Hutchins*,[60] the defendant was a public relations officer who worked for the plaintiffs, who were pop singers including Tom Jones, Englebert Humperdinck and Gilbert O'Sullivan. The singers wanted to be presented to the public in the best possible light in order to encourage large audiences to attend their concerts. The defendant went on tour with the singers and saw their 'goings on'. Later, when no longer engaged by the plaintiffs, he wrote a series of articles about the plaintiffs' discreditable conduct, including a case of adultery; it was a typical 'Sunday paper' story with headings such as 'Why Mrs Tom Jones threw her jewellery from a car window and Tom got high in a jumbo jet' and 'Tom Jones is Superstud'. The first article was published and the singers applied for an injunction to prevent further articles being published on the grounds that they were defamatory and had been written in breach of confidence. Lord Denning MR said that the public interest in the truth outweighed the public interest in protecting confidential information in this case. The remaining articles could be published, leaving the plaintiffs free to pursue a claim for damages in libel. The defendant had made it clear that he would plead justification if sued for defamation. An important factor in the decision is that the plaintiffs had sought publicity which was favourable to them, and they could not therefore complain if the public were given true information showing them in a less favourable light.

This case can be seen as a considerable extension of the public interest defence to breach of confidence, but it should be treated with care considering its particular facts. For example, public interest would not apply if the person to whom the information related had not previously sought publicity. One way of looking at *Woodward* v *Hutchins* is to say that it is really an instance of the public being disabused of a misrepresentation previously made to it by or on behalf of the plaintiffs.

### Conflict of differing public interests

There may be more than one type of public interest involved where confidential information is concerned. Public interest can be served by the disclosure of certain types of information to a limited section of the public or to the public at large, depending on the nature of the information. However, the public interest can be best served by maintaining confidences generally, that is by discouraging potential breaches of confidences by a strong and certain law. For example, the public interest in maintaining confidences between doctors and their patients is extremely high. Sometimes there will be a conflict between these forms of public interest, and the court must balance one against the other in coming to its decision.

61 [1990] Ch 359.

62 Now the Mental Health Act 1983 ss 37 and 41.

In *W* v *Edgell*,[61] W had killed five people and had been diagnosed as suffering from paranoid schizophrenia. At his trial, his plea of diminished responsibility was accepted and he was detained without time limit under the Mental Health Act 1959 ss 60 and 65.[62] Later, W's condition improved and his doctor recommended transfer to a regional secure unit. The doctor said that the illness was under control and W was no longer a danger provided he stayed on medication. The Home Secretary refused his consent to the transfer. W applied to a mental health review tribunal for discharge or transfer. Dr E was instructed to examine W and make out a report. The report was unfavourable to W and Dr E sent a copy to W's solicitor in the belief that it would be placed before the tribunal, but W's solicitor withdrew the application. Dr E heard of this and realised that there would not be a copy of his report on W's file for future reference. Being concerned at this, Dr E sent a copy of his report to the Home Secretary. W complained that this was a breach of the confidential relationship between a patient and a doctor.

In the High Court, it was said that Dr E owed a duty of confidence to W which was created and circumscribed by the particular circumstances of the case. Dr E considered that W had a psychopathic personality and thought that W's solicitors intended to suppress the report. Because of this, Scott J considered that Dr E also owed a duty to the public which required him to place before the proper authorities the results of his examination of W who was not an ordinary member of the public. W unsuccessfully appealed to the Court of Appeal. It was held that although W had a personal interest to see that the confidence he had reposed in Dr E was not breached, the maintenance of a duty of confidence by a doctor to his patient was not a matter of private but of public interest. The public interest in maintaining confidence had to be balanced against the public interest in protecting others from possible violence. In this case, the public interest in restrictive disclosure outweighed the public interest that a patient's confidences should be respected. Bingham LJ said:

> Only the most compelling circumstances could justify a doctor in acting in a way which would injure the immediate interests of his patient, as the patient perceived them, without obtaining his consent.[63]

63 [1990] Ch 359 at 423.

On the facts Dr E acted very responsibly and, it would appear, under a sense of public duty. It is clear that breach of confidence in a relationship as sensitive as doctor and patient would be legally permissible only under the most compelling and narrow circumstances.

## Scope and nature of the disclosure

It is clear that, in some circumstances, whether the public interest defence applies depends on the scope and nature of the disclosure. Sometimes, a very restrictive disclosure will be appropriate such as in W v *Edgell*, but had that particular disclosure been made to a newspaper, the defendant probably would not have been successful in his public interest defence. If there is a public interest in the disclosure, the judges will take into account the persons to whom the confidential information is communicated. For example, the public interest might be best served by disclosure to a responsible body rather than to the media.[64] Another, often related, factor might be whether the disclosure was done for gain or reward, although this is not decisive.[65]

Simply because the confidentiality of information is breached for one particular purpose does not mean that it can be used for other purposes. Certain documents were seized legally by the police investigating a fraud case in *Marcel v Commissioner of Police of the Metropolis*.[66] It was held that the police were not entitled to disclose those documents to a third party to use in civil proceedings, because the public interest in ensuring that the documents were used solely for public purposes appropriate to the powers of seizure conferred on the police outweighed the public interest in ensuring that all relevant information was available in civil proceedings. The police had a duty not to disclose such documents to third parties except by the order of the court. This case also provides another example of a conflict between two competing public interests.

64 This was identified as a factor in *Lion Laboratories Ltd v Evans* [1984] 2 All ER 417.

65 Profit was obviously a motive for publication in *Woodward v Hutchins*, supra.

66 [1991] 1 All ER 845. The documents were seized under the provisions in the Police and Criminal Evidence Act 1984 Part II.

## OBLIGATION OF CONFIDENCE

The second requirement for an action in breach of confidence is that there must be an obligation of confidence which arises from the circumstances in which the information was imparted.[67] This obligation may arise by express agreement or prior notice, or it may be implied by law, for example, in a fiduciary relationship or by general equitable principles. Commonly, an obligation of confidence will be established and delineated by a contract which has express terms dealing with confidence or, in the absence of such express terms, by implied terms depending on the nature of the contract. The obligation of confidence may extend beyond the termination of the contract. However, a contract is not essential and frequently the obligation will arise in preliminary negotiations for a contract, even though the contract is never executed. It is axiomatic that an obligation of confidence will apply where there is a duty of good faith, for example between doctor and patient or between solicitor and client. Nevertheless, the circumstances where the obligation will be appropriate are much wider than this and include business transactions, commercial negotiations, the relationship between husband and wife and, sometimes, disclosures to third parties.

68 [1996] FSR 424.

There are limits to the occasions when a duty of confidence will be implied. The defendant in *Carflow Products (UK) Ltd* v *Linwood Securities (Birmingham) Ltd*[68] was sued for infringement of a registered design and an unregistered design right in respect of a design for a steering wheel lock for cars. The defendant had made a prototype steering wheel lock of its own and Jacob J held that there was no evidence of copying and, as a result, the unregistered design right claim failed. As regards the registered design claim, the defendant argued that, as the prototype had been shown to a potential buyer before the filing date of the registered design, that buyer was not under a duty of confidence, being free in equity and law to use or disclose it. If that was the case, then the registered design would be invalid for lack of novelty.[69]

69 Alternatively, the defendant's lock was outside the scope of the registration.

In deciding whether the disclosure was in confidence, Jacob J said there were two approaches, a subjective one (what the parties thought they were doing by way of imposing or accepting obligations of confidence) and an objective approach. As to the former, on the evidence Jacob J held that neither party thought an obligation of confidence was being imposed or accepted. As to the objective approach, the reasonable man (officious bystander)[70] would know that what was being shown was a prototype and that the law provides a number of ways in which it could be protected, for example, by registration as a design, by application for a patent or by the unregistered design right. Therefore, he would not expect that an obligation of confidence arose merely by showing a prototype for something which was being offered for sale. Obviously, in circumstances where there is any doubt as to whether an obligation of confidence will be imposed by the courts, it would be better to impose an express duty.

70 The reasonable man must be someone with some knowledge of the industry and the importance of securing protection of some form. The man on the Clapham omnibus knows little of intellectual property rights.

Four particular issues are considered below: express contractual terms imposing a duty of confidence, the employer/employee relationship, covenants in restraint of trade, and the position of third-party recipients.

### Express contractual term

It is quite common for formal contracts to contain terms dealing with matters of confidence and imposing a duty on one or both parties not to use or disclose certain types of information. A computer software company engaged to write and install computer programs for a client will be expected not to divulge any details of the client's business to competitors. An advertising agency asked by a drinks manufacturer to mount an advertising campaign for a new brand of lager will be under a duty not to disclose information about the new product until after its launch. A duty of confidence will exist between two companies submitting a joint tender for a contract where preparation of the tender involves an exchange of confidential information.[71] Of course there will be an equitable duty, but expressly providing for the duty in a contract means that it can be more stringent and focused in its scope. Breach of confidence will then constitute a breach of contract, giving contractual remedies to the aggrieved party. Terms dealing with confidence, often imposing a reciprocal duty, are common in contracts between business organisations, between consultants and businesses engaging them, and between employers and their employees, as discussed later.

As with any contractual term, care must be taken in the drafting. The courts will not impose a duty of confidence to benefit a person other than the person intended. In *Fraser v Evans*,[72] the plaintiff was a public relations consultant who had been engaged by the Greek government to prepare a report. The contract included an express term stating that the plaintiff must not divulge any of the information contained in the report during or after the currency of the contract. A copy of the report had been surreptitiously obtained and came into the hands of the *Sunday Times*. The plaintiff was granted an *ex parte* order restraining publication of the report or parts of it in the newspaper on the grounds that it would be defamatory and would be a breach of confidence. The plaintiff considered that an article based on the report would show him in a bad light. On the defendant's appeal, it was held that the plaintiff was not entitled to an injunction. Although the plaintiff owed a duty to the Greek government, no reciprocal duty was imposed by the contract, neither could such a duty be implied. The courts can give effect to an obligation of confidence only at the instance of the party to whom such obligation is owed. It was also held, *obiter*, that although the plaintiff owned the copyright in the report, this did not extend to preventing the use of the information contained within it, once again illustrating the distinction between idea and expression in copyright.

When items are distributed to the public or to a limited section of the public, it can be assumed that confidential information embodied within those items will automatically lose its confidential quality and a person obtaining one of the items will not owe an obligation of confidence to its manufacturer. Other branches of intellectual property law are more appropriate, such as patent law and copyright law. However, if the distribution occurs by way of a contract, the contract may include terms attempting to impose a continuing duty of confidence, for example by prohibiting dismantling or reverse engineering. In *K S Paul (Printing Machinery) Ltd v Southern Instruments Ltd*,[73] there were two defendants. The second defendant hired from the plaintiff a telephone answering machine which was enclosed in a box which concealed the workings of the machine. The contract of hire included a condition that the machine should not be removed from its installation position or interfered with. The machines were not available except under such conditions. The second defendant allowed the first defendant to remove the machine, dismantle it and examine it. Access to the confidential information concerning the workings of the machine was thus obtained. An injunction was granted to the plaintiff restraining the use of con-

71 An interlocutory injunction was granted to enforce or restrain derogation from agreed terms in relation to a defence contract in *Simtech Advanced Training & Simulation Systems Ltd v Jasmin Simtec Ltd* [1995] FSR 475.

72 [1969] 1 QB 349.

73 [1964] RPC 118.

fidential information obtained from the 'machines of the type hired by the plaintiffs … from any unlawful inspection of any such machines'. The contract of hire had effectively prolonged the effectiveness of confidence and applied to a third party who had been allowed by the hirer to dismantle the machine.

It is arguable that sales to the general public may not destroy the application of the law of breach of confidence if, by the very nature of the product, the secret information is not accessible or is accessible only after doing something which infringes some right or duty.[74] For example, if a computer program is licensed in object code form, the licensee, or any other person for that matter, will not be able to gain access to the ideas locked away in the program without carrying out reverse analysis of the program, an operation that will normally infringe the copyright subsisting in the program, unless falling within the scope of the permitted acts under copyright law. However, by the Copyright, Designs and Patents Act 1988 s 296A, any term or condition in an agreement relating to the use of a computer program shall be void in so far as it purports to prohibit or restrict, *inter alia*, the use of any device or means to observe, study or test the functioning of the program in order to understand the ideas and principles which underlie any element of the program.

## Employer/employee relationship

An employee owes a duty of confidence to his employer and this duty may be expressly stated in the contract of employment, and in any case will be implied by law. It can be said that an employee always has a duty to act in his employer's best interests together with a duty of good faith, and this will obviously include a duty not to divulge confidential information about his employer's business to others without the consent of the employer. The sort of information concerned may be rather special, a 'trade secret' such as details of a technique to improve the strength or durability of a type of plastic, or it may be ordinary and mundane, such as details of the customers of the employer. There may be exceptions to this duty, for example, if the information pertains to a criminal offence, or if it is in the public interest that the information is disclosed.

There is seldom any doubt about the duty owed by a present employee. Although the law will be quick to imply a duty of fidelity, inclusion of terms dealing with this in a contract of employment at least have the effect of focusing the employee's attention on the importance of not misusing confidential information. If there are express terms in the contract of employment which attempt to strengthen this duty they must, of course, be clear and unambiguous.

Where the information would be likely to be regarded by employees as a trade secret, it is not essential that the employer specifically points this out. In *Lancashire Fires Ltd* v *S A Lyons & Co Ltd*,[75] Bingham MR said (at 674):

> We do not accept that it is incumbent on an employer to point out to his employee the precise limits of that which he seeks to protect as confidential, particularly where, as here, what is new is an integral part of a process.

For the avoidance of doubt, however, an employer would be advised to make explicit the extent of the confidential material. This is an important factor in determining whether information should be protected as set out in *Faccenda Chicken* v *Fowler*, discussed later.

**74** For an American view of this possibility, *see* Davidson, D. M. 'Protecting Computer Software: A Comprehensive Analysis' (1983) 23(4) *Jurimetrics Journal*, 337 at 358.

75 [1996] FSR 629.

## Ex-employees

Many problems arise through the use or disclosure of confidential information by ex-employees, and here the law is faced with a dilemma, for not only does the employer have an interest in maintaining confidence, but the employee also has a competing interest in that he should be free to use his skill and knowledge to earn a living elsewhere.

After confirming that the law will restrain unauthorised disclosure or use of information which is confidential in the *Coco* v *Clark* sense, Laddie J discussed the public policy in respect of the employee's skill and knowledge in *Ocular Sciences Ltd* v *Aspect Vision Care Ltd*.[76] He said (at 370), presumably in the context of information within Goulding J's second category in *Faccenda Chicken*:

> On the other hand, for public policy reasons, an employee is entitled to use and put at the disposal of new employers all his acquired skill and knowledge. That is so, no matter where he acquired that skill and knowledge and whether it is secret or was so at the time he acquired it. Where an employer's right to restrain misuse of his confidential information collides with the public policy, it is the latter which prevails.

This goes further than other cases, and probably further than Laddie J intended, as he then went on to say the difficulty was in distinguishing between information in Goulding J's second and third categories. Certainly public policy should require that an ex-employee should be able to make use of his learned skill and knowledge as a general principle. This should not, however, extend to information in Goulding J's third category, specific trade secrets so confidential that there is a continuing duty of confidence after employment. In *Printers & Finishers Ltd* v *Holloway*,[77] Cross J referred to information regarded as a separate part of the employee's stock of knowledge which '... a man of ordinary honesty and intelligence would recognise to be the property of his old employer, and not his to do as he likes with ...', adding that the court would restrain the use of such information by injunction.

Much of the attractiveness of a potential employee to other employers will be the fact that he has built up skill and experience in his previous employments, and it may be difficult to separate this from a previous employer's confidential information. As a further complication, in some cases the employment contract may contain terms trying to restrict an employee's use of confidential materials after the termination of employment. When there are no express terms, the employer will not be protected to any great extent. For example, if an ex-employee simply remembers some information about a few of his previous employer's customers there will be nothing to prevent the ex-employee using this information himself or putting it at the disposal of his new employer. Of course, it would be different if he deliberately memorised the customers' names or made a copy of them.[78] In the absence of an express term in the contract of employment dealing with confidentiality, it was said in *Printers and Finishers Ltd* v *Holloway*[79] that there would be nothing improper in the employee putting his memory of particular features of his previous employer's plant at the disposal of his new employer. Even if there was an express term, the previous employer would have to show that the information was over and above the employee's normal skill in the job and amounted to a trade secret.

In *Northern Office Microcomputer (Pty) Ltd* v *Rosenstein*,[80] a case from the Supreme Court of South Africa involving the laws of copyright and trade

76 [1997] RPC 289.

77 [1965] RPC 239.

78 *Robb* v *Green* [1985] 2 QB 315. Making a copy of a list of customers would also be an infringement of copyright provided the list was original in copyright terms.

79 [1965] RPC 239.

80 [1982] FSR 124.

secrets relating to computer programs, the problem of where to draw the line between the conflicting interests of an employee and his previous employer was considered. It was conceded by Marais J that:

> ... the dividing line between the use by an employee of his own skill knowledge and experience and the use by him of his employer's trade secrets is notoriously difficult to draw.[81]

81 [1982] FSR 124 at 138.

In recognising that computer programs that were not commonplace should be eligible for protection as trade secrets, Marais J said that the protection given by the law of trade secrets in the context of ex-employees should be of a limited nature only and that all that should be protected was the employer's 'lead-time', the time to develop the program. That is, the advantage the employer has in getting his product to the market place first should be protected and nothing more. He went on to say that, in many cases, the employer's trade secrets were no more than the result of the application by an employee of his own skill and judgment, but if the employee was engaged specifically to produce that information then it could still amount to a trade secret. However, if the material was commonplace, there would be nothing to stop the ex-employee deriving the same or similar material again as long as he did not simply copy his employer's material. The employee would not have to 'wipe the slate of his mind clean' on the termination of his employment.

## A test for employees' and ex-employees' obligation of confidence

82 [1986] 1 All ER 617.

An important case which clarified the principles to apply in the employer/employee relationship is *Faccenda Chicken Ltd v Fowler*.[82] This was about the alleged wrongful use by the defendant ex-employee (with a wonderfully appropriate surname) of his employer's sales information. This comprised customers' names and addresses, the most convenient routes to customers, the most suitable times for delivery, prices charged and details of customers' usual orders – information which was, by its very nature, fairly mundane and ordinary, but which was nevertheless still within the scope of the law of breach of confidence. The employer's business was supplying fresh chickens from itinerant refrigerated vans to retailers and caterers. The defendant was engaged by the plaintiff as a sales manager and left the plaintiff company to set up in business on his own account, taking eight of the plaintiff's employees with him. He started selling fresh chickens from refrigerated vans in the same area in which the plaintiff operated. The employer's action for breach of confidence failed because the information was not of the type which an employee was bound, by an implied term in his contract of employment, not to use or disclose subsequent to the termination of employment. Neill LJ, delivering the judgment of the court, stated the Court of Appeal's views on the relevant principles to apply in cases involving confidentiality between master and servant.

1 If there was a contract of employment the employee's obligations were to be determined from that contract.
2 In the absence of any express terms, the employee's obligations would be implied.
3 While still in employment, there was an implied term imposing a duty of good faith or fidelity on the employee. This duty might vary according to the nature of the contract, but would be broken if the employee copied or deliberately memorised a list of customers.

4  The implied term imposing an obligation on the employee after the termination of his employment was more restricted than that imposed by the duty of fidelity. It might cover secret processes of manufacture or designs, or special methods of construction or other information of a sufficiently high degree of confidentiality so as to be classed as a trade secret.

5  Whether information fell within this implied term to prevent its use or disclosure by an ex-employee depended on the circumstances, and attention should be given to the following:

(a) the nature of employment – a higher obligation might be imposed where the employee regularly handled confidential material;

(b) the nature of information – it should be an authentic trade secret, or at least highly confidential;

(c) whether the employer stressed the confidential nature of the material; and

(d) whether the information could be easily isolated from other material the employee was free to use, this being useful evidentially rather than being a conclusive test.

On the last point, separability of information would tend to suggest that it was more likely that the information could be classed as confidential. The Court left open the question of whether it would make any difference if the ex-employee used the information himself or if he simply sold it to another. Although the decision in this case seems a trifle unfair in that the ex-employee calculatingly and deliberately took advantage of his employer's business and reputation, it can be argued that the employer should have considered using a restrictive covenant which might have prevented the employee from competing in the area for at least a year or two. However, Mr Fowler was walking a thin line, for in *Normalec v Britton*[83] the defendant decided to sell the same goods as his employer (electric bulbs and fittings) to the same customers he had been seeing on behalf of his employer. Worse still, the defendant did this while he was still in the employ of the plaintiff. The defendant was held to have a fiduciary duty to his employer who was entitled to the profits made by the defendant, and the court also granted an injunction preventing the defendant from selling to the plaintiff's customers even after the termination of his employment.[84] The one major difference between this case and the *Faccenda Chicken* case is that here the activity was commenced while the defendant was still employed and while he still was under a duty of good faith or fidelity to his employer.[85]

## Employer's obligation

The obligation of confidence arising from a contract of employment is not all one way. In many cases, the employer will owe a duty of confidence to his employees. An employer will hold information concerning the employee, such as marital status, salary and career details. This information should not be divulged to others without the employee's permission except in circumstances where disclosure is permitted by express provision (for example, in pursuance of an attachment of earnings order)[86] or is implied (for example, where salaries are calculated and paid by a third party). If the employee's details are stored on a computer, there will usually be restrictions on disclosure by virtue of the Data Protection Act 1984 s 5(2).[87] Prospective employers also owe a duty of confidence in respect of *curricula vitae* submitted by job applicants.

83  [1938] FSR 318.

84  In *Balston Ltd v Headline Filters Ltd* [1990] FSR 385, an intention to set up in business in competition with the company of which he was a director was held not to conflict with the director's fiduciary duty to the company even though preliminary steps had been taken while he remained a director.

85  For an interesting description of this case and other dramatic intellectual property cases, *see* Pearson, H. and Miller, C. (1990), *Commercial Exploitation of Intellectual Property*, Blackstone Press, at pp. 3–5.

86  Attachment of Earnings Act 1971.

87  *See Rowley v Liverpool City Council* (unreported) 24 October 1989. In this case disclosure was lawful under the Data Protection Act 1984 s 34(5), being required in the course of legal proceedings. The 1984 Act will soon be replaced by the Data Protection Act 1998.

Some employers operate employee suggestions schemes, usually with the possibility of rewards for suggestions having merit that will be used by the employer. By taking part in the scheme, an employee can be said to have waived his rights, if any, in the information he has disclosed in this way if his employer uses the information.[88] However, if the employer does not make use of the information it seems that a duty of confidence will arise. In *Prout* v *British Gas plc*[89] the plaintiff, while employed by the defendant, submitted an idea for a new design of bracket for warning lamps placed around excavations. The bracket was supposed to be vandal-proof. The plaintiff was given an award by the defendant on the basis of its suggestions scheme, but later the defendant said that it had no interest and agreed to allow the plaintiff to pursue a patent application on his own behalf. On the issue of confidence, it was held that there was a contractual or equitable duty of confidence imposed on the defendant, the employer. Although this duty would normally end once the idea was used in public for the first time without any objection from the employee, a fresh duty could arise if the employee gave notice of his intention to apply for a patent and would continue until the filing date of the application. In this particular case it was held that the employer was in breach of confidence by its subsequent use of the lamps. This extension of duty beyond the first consensual public use could apply only where long-term trade or commercial secrecy was possible, or where an application for legal protection requiring novelty was envisaged. However, public use could easily destroy novelty and would do so in many cases.

## Covenants in restraint of trade

An employer must be careful not to draft terms which are too wide in a contract of employment imposing a continuing duty of confidence after the employment has been terminated.[90] Terms that are too wide are in danger of being struck out by a court as being in restraint of trade. On appointment, an employee may agree to sign a contract restricting his use or disclosure of information concerning his employer's business, or agreeing not to work for a competitor after the termination of the contract of employment.[91] Generally, such agreements will be enforced by the courts only if they are reasonable between the parties and not against the public interest. In particular, an employer cannot use the law of confidence to protect himself against future competition *per se*. If a term in the contract of employment is a clear attempt to prevent future competition rather than a legitimate means of protecting the employer's business interests, it will not be enforced by the courts.[92]

Restrictive terms are usually referred to as covenants in restraint of trade and are frequently expressed in terms of preventing the employee working for a competitor or setting up a business in competition within a given area and for a given period of time.[93] These two factors, time and area, define the extent of the restraint. If the covenant is too wide in terms of either factor, the courts are unlikely to enforce it, and it is clear that the two factors must be considered together. In *Fitch* v *Dewes*,[94] a solicitor's clerk was prohibited from entering into the employment of another solicitor within a seven-mile radius of Tamworth Town Hall. The restriction was indefinite in terms of time, but nevertheless, because the geographic area was small, it was held to be valid. However, in *Herbert Morris Ltd* v *Saxelby*,[95] a restriction that an engineer

88 In some cases, the information will be treated as belonging to the employer by virtue of the contract of employment.

89 [1992] FSR 478.

90 The same applies to independent consultants and the like engaged to perform some work.

91 Alternatively, such a promise might be extracted from the employee on payment of a settlement at the end of the contract of employment.

92 *Berkeley Administration Inc* v *McClelland* [1990] FSR 505; *Roberts* v *Northwest Fixings* [1993] FSR 281. The courts will not lend their aid to a determined attempt to stop competition.

93 It should be noted that such covenants are not always concerned with confidential information.

94 [1921] AC 158.

95 [1916] 1 AC 688.

could not work for a competitor anywhere as an engineer for seven years was held to be void.[96] In any case, a restrictive covenant will not be enforced:

> unless the protection sought was reasonably necessary to protect a trade secret or to prevent some personal influence over customers being abused in order to entice them away.[97]

Geographical area will not be particularly relevant if the employer's business is carried out over the telephone or by facsimile transmission. A covenant prohibiting the former employee from carrying on a business as an employment agent within a 3000-metre radius (about 1.2 miles) of the employer's place of business for a period of six months was held to be too wide in *Office Angels Ltd v Rainer-Thomas*.[98] It was said that, as clients' orders were placed over the telephone, the location of the business was of no concern to them. Therefore, the area restriction was inappropriate.[99] However, even a small area restriction could be unduly restrictive if the area was one where most of the relevant business was undertaken.

Covenants in restraint of trade often include non-solicitation clauses. That is, the ex-employee may not approach or do business with the employer's customers or clients. The scope of such covenants needs careful thought. In *G W Plowman & Sons Ltd v Ash*[100] a sales representative for the plaintiff, who was a corn and agricultural merchant and animal feeding stuffs manufacturer, had a service agreement which contained a covenant not to carry on a business in the same field for two years within 20 miles of Spalding after termination of employment. It also contained a non-solicitation clause as regards persons who had been customers of the plaintiff during the period of employment. The fact that this was not limited to customers of whom the defendant had personal experience was not fatal to the clause. It was held valid by the Court of Appeal because, in the words of Russell LJ, the salesman would be likely to 'acquire special influence over or knowledge of the requirements of any of the employer's customers' whether or not he dealt directly with them. This was because of the nature of the employer's business and because the defendant would be well-known to all the customers as representing the plaintiff.

There are limits to non-solicitation clauses and the above case was distinguished in *Austin Knight (UK) Ltd v Hinds*[101] in which the defendant, who worked for a recruitment consultancy, dealt with about one-third of the consultancy's customers. She was made redundant and her contract of employment contained a covenant preventing her from soliciting or endeavouring to entice away any person who had been a customer of the plaintiff during her employment. This was held to be unreasonably wide because it purported to prevent the defendant from approaching all the former customers even though she dealt with only one-third of them. Unlike the *Plowman* case, there were no grounds to infer that she was known to the two-thirds she did not deal with. Nor was there anything to suggest that she had misused any confidential information belonging to the plaintiff. On this last issue it was said by Vinelott J that there was no evidence that the defendant had taken with her or misused any database or confidential documents.

If a covenant in restraint of trade is drafted too widely it will be void. The courts will not narrow it down to an acceptable level and apply that instead. In *J A Mont (UK) Ltd v Mills*,[102] Simon Brown LJ said:

---

**96** For more on covenants in restraint of trade involving employees, *see* Selwyn, N. (1996) *Law of Employment* (9th edn) Butterworths.

**97** *Per* Neill LJ in *Faccenda Chicken Ltd v Fowler* [1986] 1 All ER 617 at 626.

**98** [1991] IRLR 214.

**99** The covenant was too wide because it went beyond that necessary to protect the employer's interest.

**100** [1964] 1 WLR 568.

**101** [1994] FSR 52.

**102** *Independent*, 7 January 1993.

... as a matter of policy, it seems to me similarly that the court should not too urgently strive to find within restrictive covenants *ex facie* too wide, implicit limitations such as alone could justify their imposition.

To construe covenants otherwise would encourage employers to draft their covenants deliberately in wide terms.[103] However, in *Littlewoods Organisation Ltd v Harris*[104] Lord Denning MR adopted a much more relaxed approach to construction, and a covenant that an employee '... shall not at any time within twelve months ... enter into a contract of service or other agreement of a like nature with GUS or any subsidiary thereto' was interpreted as being limited to the mail order side of those parts of the GUS organisation that operated in the United Kingdom. The distinction is that in this case there had been an attempt to draw up a reasonable covenant.

### Subject matter of covenants

There is some judicial confusion about the proper subject matter of a covenant in restraint of trade in terms of confidential information. In *Faccenda Chicken*, Neill LJ suggested that only trade secrets or their equivalent could be protected by a restrictive covenant and that more mundane information could not. However, this was *obiter* (there was not a restrictive covenant imposed on the defendant) and it conflicts with Neill LJ's own description of the implied term imposed after termination of employment. The implied term protects trade secrets, and consequently there is no need for a restrictive covenant in respect of them. In *Balston Ltd v Headline Filters Ltd*.[105] Scott J declined to follow that part of Neill LJ's judgment to the effect that confidential information that could not be protected by an implied term *ipso facto* could not be protected by a suitably limited express covenant.[106] This accords with common sense as most business organisations possess information that would harm them or benefit others if divulged, even though that information is not a trade secret or associated with one. By limiting the restriction the courts are seeking to arrive at an equitable balance between the interests of employer and employee alike.

### Garden leave

Employers are often worried about the harm that can be caused to them by an employee working his notice. The employee might attempt to influence clients or remove confidential materials. It is not unknown for employees who have been given notice of termination of their employment to be told to stay at home and 'enjoy the garden' during their period of notice. This 'garden leave' may last for some time if the employee is in a senior position subject to lengthy period of notice. If the employee attempts to work for another employer during his garden leave, the courts may act to restrain him by granting an injunction.

A 'high-flying' professional may be anxious to start work for another organisation as quickly as possible and challenge the period of notice. In *GFI Group Inc v Eaglestone*[107] a highly paid financial services broker challenged his 20-week period of notice. The court was tempted to hold him to this because, in his line of work, his word was his bond. However, the period was reduced to three months because of some exceptional circumstances, one of which was that some other brokers were only on four weeks' notice.

**103** *See also Mason v Provident Clothing and Supply Company Ltd* [1913] AC 724.

**104** [1978] 1 All ER 1026.

**105** [1987] FSR 330, an interlocutory hearing.

**106** At first instance, in *Faccenda Chicken Ltd v Fowler* [1985] 1 All ER 724, Goulding J classified information available to employees in three categories. The second category, confidential information falling short of a trade secret, was, he suggested, capable of being protected by a restrictive covenant. In the Court of Appeal, Neill LJ disagreed with this proposition.

**107** [1994] FSR 535.

Factors that may be relevant to the grant of an injunction include the amount and nature of confidential information the employee had access to and the seniority of the employee. However, in *Provident Financial Group* v *Hayward*[108] the Court of Appeal refused to grant an injunction against an employee on garden leave because little of the period of notice remained, there was no evidence of a serious prospect that the employer's interests would be harmed and the employee worked in an administrative capacity, having access to very little confidential information. It could also be argued that enforced garden leave is a breach of the contract of employment, as an implied term is that the employer provides suitable work, if available.

108 [1989] 3 All ER 298.

Where there is a restrictive covenant for a period of time, the time during which the employee is 'enjoying' his garden leave is not, in the normal case, deducted from the time limit in the covenant. In *Credit Suisse Asset Management Ltd* v *Armstrong*,[109] Neill LJ declined to set off the time on garden leave. In that case, the duration of the garden leave was six months and the period in the covenant was 12 months. Neill LJ did, however, add a caveat on the basis of public policy, saying that a court might decline to enforce the covenant where, for example, the length of garden leave was exceptional.

109 *The Times*, 3 June 1996.

## Third-party recipients

The general rule is that a third party who comes by the information without knowing it to be confidential, or in circumstances where an obligation of confidence cannot be imposed, is free to use the information or to disclose it as he sees fit, especially if it entered the public domain. This is the one fundamental weakness of the law of breach of confidence – innocent third parties are largely unaffected by this area of law. They may, however, be subject to other rights, duties or liabilities. For example, the information may be in the form of a literary work and a question of infringement of copyright might be raised. Alternatively, use of the information may result in an action for passing off, or its publication may be defamatory.

The position of the person who is not aware of the confidential nature of the information at the time it is disclosed to him but subsequently becomes so aware is less clear. In *Fraser* v *Evans*[110] Lord Denning MR said (at 361):

110 [1969] 1 QB 349.

> No person is permitted to divulge to the world information he has received in confidence, unless he has just cause or excuse for doing so. Even if he comes by it innocently, nevertheless once he gets to know that it was originally given in confidence, he can be restrained from breaking that confidence.

There are dicta in *Prince Albert* v *Strange*,[111] *Union Carbide Corp* v *Naturin Ltd*[112] and other cases which suggest that the power of the court to restrain use or further disclosure of confidential information could extend to cases where a person obtains information without notice of the breach. In *Lancashire Fires Ltd* v *S A Lyons & Co Ltd*,[113] the third defendant, who had been employed by the plaintiff as a financial manager, was given information relating to a new process for making artificial coal and logs for gas fires by the second defendant (who had also been employed by the plaintiff) in breach of confidence. The second and third defendants set up a company to exploit the confidential technology and the Court of Appeal confirmed that the third defendant could also be restrained from using the information. A particular factor was the public interest in the maintenance of confidences.

111 (1849) 1 Mac & G 25.
112 [1987] FSR 538.

113 [1996] FSR 629.

It can be said that an equity fastens on the person's conscience once he discovers the confidential nature of the information. However, equitable remedies are discretionary and injunctive relief may not be given where it could cause hardship to the parties. The person to whom the information has been given might have performed work or made contracts with other persons in reliance on that information. This factor did not, however, prevent an Australian judge imposing injunctions on all the defendants (most of whom had unwittingly paid for the information).[114]

There will be circumstances where a third party will be bound by an obligation of confidence even though the owner of the information did not impart the information to the third party directly. The third party may receive confidential information knowing it to be confidential, or in circumstances in which a reasonable man would have suspected that it was confidential. In other cases, he may discover the confidential nature of the information subsequently. It appears that only when the recipient actually knows of the confidential nature will he be under an obligation not to use or divulge the information further. In *Fraser* v *Thames TV Ltd*,[115] three actresses formed a rock group with the assistance of a manager and developed an idea for a TV series known as *The Rock Follies*. They discussed the idea orally with Thames TV in confidence, and it was agreed that the actresses were to have first refusal should the series proceed. When Thames TV decided to proceed, one of the actresses could not get a release from another part and Thames TV replaced her with another actress. It was held that the court would prevent a person disclosing an idea in written or oral form until it became general public knowledge, provided that:

1 the circumstances imputed an obligation of confidence, and
2 the content was clearly identifiable, potentially attractive in a commercial sense and capable of being brought to fruition.

For a third party to be fixed with an obligation of confidence, he must know that the information was confidential and had been imparted in confidence. Even though it was disclosed to several people, it was disclosed to each and all of them in confidence. An argument by counsel for the defence that the idea lost its confidentiality when it was disclosed to others was rejected by Hirst J, who said that the disclosure to others was plainly also in confidence and, therefore, confidence remained intact.[116] The actress who had been replaced was awarded very substantial damages.

The issue of the innocent third-party recipient was considered again in *Valeo Vision SA* v *Flexible Lamps Ltd*.[117] The plaintiff gave some drawings and other confidential information relating to rear light clusters for vehicles to a third party, the German truck manufacturer MAN. The third party later disclosed these to the defendant who took them in good faith, believing that the third party had the right to disclose them. Aldous J said that the equitable rule, that a person who is a *bona fide* purchaser for value without notice of confidential information will escape the arm of equity, was too narrow. However, it was settled law that equity would provide relief by way of damages only where a person had his conscience fixed by equity, objectively or subjectively. Nevertheless, the court would still, in appropriate cases, grant an injunction restraining further misuse of the information.

The granting of an injunction would be ineffective once the information has entered the public domain and is readily available. It could also be very unfair on the innocent recipient against whom action is taken. In the above case, an

**114** *Wheatley* v *Bell* [1984] FSR 16.

**115** [1984] 1 QB 44.

**116** *See also Franchi* v *Franchi* [1967] RPC 149.

**117** [1995] RPC 205.

injunction was held to be inappropriate as the information had already entered the public domain. Contrary to some earlier judicial statements as regards the knowledge required to bind the conscience of the third party so as to give rise to damages,[118] Aldous J in *Valeo Vision* made it clear that constructive knowledge will suffice. That is where the third party was in the possession of such facts that would make the reasonable man suspect that the information was subject to an obligation of confidence.

A discussion of third-party recipients is not complete without consideration of the position of a person who obtains the information surreptitiously, for example in circumstances involving industrial espionage. Can such a person be fixed with an obligation of confidence? At first sight it appears not, especially when the formula used in the *Coco* case is examined, as it seems to suggest that the information is given voluntarily by its owner. There is very little case law on this point, but in *Malone* v *Commissioner of Police*[119] Megarry V-C was of the view that an eavesdropper would not owe a duty of confidence. *Malone* involved telephone-tapping, an activity which is now illegal under the Interception of Communications Act 1985 s 1 which makes it an offence intentionally to intercept a communication during its transmission through a public telecommunications system.

In *Malone* the telephone tap was lawful, but Megarry V-C spoke of unknown hearers and said that a person using a telephone to disclose confidential information must accept the risk of being overheard as that risk is inherent in the mode of communication. This case was distinguished in *Francome* v *Mirror Group Newspapers Ltd*,[120] where it was held that there was a serious issue to be tried on the basis of breach of confidence concerning information obtained by way of an illegal telephone tap. Although a person using a telephone takes the risk of being overheard because of imperfections or accidents, he does not willingly take the risk of an illegal tap. The same principle should apply to facsimile transmission. The sender takes the risk of the information being seen by persons other than those for whom it is intended, who have access to the room where the receiving machine is installed. Even the risk of misdirection must be accepted. It must be questionable whether confidentiality can remain intact if a number of persons, other than those directly associated with the addressee such as secretarial staff, have an opportunity to read the contents of a facsimile transmission. Likewise, the status of a notice on the transmitted material to the effect that it is confidential and must not be read by anyone other than the addressee is doubtful. It should be noted that in the case of *Prince Albert* v *Strange*,[121] the court found for the plaintiff even though it was not known how the defendant had gained possession of the subject matter, only that it must have been done surreptitiously. If the information in question contains personal data and is subsequently stored in a computer by the eavesdropper or spy, there may be an offence under data protection law.

## UNAUTHORISED USE

The final ingredient for an action for breach of confidence is an unauthorised use of the information to the detriment of the party communicating it. It will usually be fairly obvious when there has been an unauthorised use of confidential material. The use or disclosure complained of must be related to the nature of the

118  For example, Hirst J in *Fraser* v *Thames Television Ltd* [1984] 1 QB 44 at 65.

119  [1979] 2 All ER 620.

120  [1984] 2 All ER 408.

121  (1849) 1 Mac & G 25.

obligation of confidence. For example, in an agreement between the owner of confidential information and a manufacturing company which is going to exploit it commercially on the basis of agreed royalty payments, the company will be permitted to use the information for the purposes detailed in the agreement. In addition, other use and subsequent disclosure may be implied. For example, the company may be able to divulge the information to sub-contractors while stressing its confidentiality, and to the company's own employees and to sister companies if part of a group. It is really a matter of construing the agreement.

Liability for unauthorised use may be joint, but is not restricted to cases where all joint tortfeasors have played an active role in the breach of confidence. Thus, a person embarked upon a common design with another who is solely responsible for the breach of confidence may also be injuncted.[122] However, where the confidential information is jointly owned, it appears that one joint owner cannot prevent the other joint owners making use of the information without him, in the absence of any contractual agreement to the contrary. In *Murray v Yorkshire Fund Managers Ltd*,[123] a team of six persons put together a package of information relating to the purchase of a company. The information was communicated to a third party by the team and the third party started to use the information with the blessing of the team bar one, the plaintiff, who objected and commenced proceedings to restrain the third party from using the information. Although the first two elements in *Coco v Clark* were present, the last, an unauthorised use, was not. There was no binding agreement that all the members of the team would continue to be involved and any of them could withdraw at any time. If this was so, then some of the members of the team could decide to go ahead without one of their number, either on their own or jointly, with others. Although the information initially belonged to all the members of the team, if one could be excluded, then he could not after exclusion prevent the use of the information by the others.

If the information is a mixture of public and private materials then the recipient must be especially careful to use only that which is public, unless he has permission to use the private information. In *Seager v Copydex (No. 1)*[124] the defendant designed a carpet grip using details from the public domain, but also incorporating some ideas it had discussed with the plaintiff some years before. The defendant claimed it had forgotten about the latter so it was effectively a case of subconscious copying. Nevertheless, and notwithstanding the apparent innocence of the defendant's actions, Lord Denning MR found for the plaintiff. It would appear, therefore, that the state of the mind of the person using the information in breach of confidence does not affect liability, although it could be relevant when it comes to determining damages.

That there should be some detriment to the party communicating the information is doubtful.[125] In many cases, the justification for protecting confidences is that they are tied up with commercial activity, investment and marketing and industrial manufacture. In other words, confidence has an economic value to its owner who will have a vested interest to see that his competitors do not have access to the information, at least not without paying for it. But the law of breach of confidence has a tremendously wide scope, and in some cases economic considerations are largely irrelevant, for example where the disclosure of the information is likely to harm a person's public standing.

**122** *Lancashire Fires Ltd v S A Lyons & Co Ltd* [1996] FSR 629, applying *Unilever plc v Gillette (UK) Ltd* [1989] RPC 583, a patent case.

**123** *The Times*, 8 December 1997.

**124** [1967] 2 All ER 415.

**125** For a discussion on this point, *see* Cornish, W.R. (1989) *Intellectual Property: Patents, Copyright, Trade Marks and Allied Rights* (2nd edn) Sweet & Maxwell, at pp. 235–6.

Where the information has economic value, it is easily understandable why the owner of the information would not want to see his competitors have some advantage from it. In *R v Licensing Authority, ex p Smith Kline & French Laboratories Ltd*,[126] SKF[127] originated a drug (Cimetidine) to control gastric acid secretion and heal peptic ulcers. SKF marketed the drug under the name 'Tagamet' and obtained patents in respect of it in 1972, which were extended to 1992 on the basis that during the last four years the patents would be endorsed 'licences of right'.[128] SKF and others wishing to sell the drug had to obtain a product licence from the licensing authority. SKF objected to the licensing authority using confidential information submitted by SKF in support of its own application in order to consider other companies' applications for product licences. The High Court held that this was a breach of confidence, but this was reversed in the Court of Appeal. The House of Lords upheld the Court of Appeal saying that the licensing authority, at its discretion and in the performance of its duties under the Medicines Act 1968 and Community law, had a right to make use of all the information provided by applicants for product licences in determining whether to grant other applications.[129] Two important factors were the protection of public health and the harmonisation of the national laws throughout member states.

Of course, this case has tremendous significance for originators of medicines and generic manufacturers. The originator has all the expense of research, development and, in particular, testing new drugs and medicines. If the drug or medicine was covered by patents then, theoretically, all the competitor would have to do would be to look up the patent specifications (being documents available for public inspection) and then, at the appropriate time, apply for a compulsory licence in respect of the patents or to have the patents endorsed 'licences of right'. However, the patent owner's monopoly will not be easily disturbed unless there is some evidence that the patent is not being worked or is being unfairly exploited in some way.[130] This reluctance to interfere with the monopoly provided by patents is justifiable in the context of something like a drug, where a potential competitor could seriously undercut the originator because the former has not spent large sums of money on research and development.

## REMEDIES

The whole rationale and justification for the law of breach of confidence is that it can and should be used to preserve secrets and confidences. Because of this the most appropriate remedy is the *quia timet* injunction, which will be granted to prevent general publication or other disclosure of the subject matter of the confidence. However, as previously noted, an injunction will not normally be granted if the aggrieved party complains that publication would be defamatory and the defendant is likely to raise a defence of justification or fair comment. In such a case, the courts will usually allow the defendant to publish and take the risk of paying damages, which could be considerable, should his defence in a defamation action fail. In some cases, an injunction may be granted to prevent the defendant making use of the information himself, even though innocent third parties may be free to use it (the so-called springboard doctrine discussed earlier in this chapter). However, normally, once the information has fallen into the public domain, an

126 [1989] 1 All ER 175.

127 Smith Kline and French Laboratories Ltd.

128 The extension was by virtue of the Patents Act 1977 Sch 1. Under the Patents Act 1949 the maximum duration of a patent was 16 years.

129 Article 3 of EEC Directive 65/65 stated that no proprietary medical product could be marketed in a member state unless authorised by a competent body of that state. A product licence was required under the Medicines Act 1968 s 7(2), (3) and the applicant had to supply a great deal of scientific material. Section 20(1)(b) was amended to take account of the streamlined procedure introduced by Directive 87/21/EEC which made it easier for generic applicants to obtain product licences. For example, results of tests were not required if the originator consented to the use of confidential information. The question basically was whether applicants for product licences could avoid supplying all the material required on the basis that the licensing authority could use the information supplied by SKF in their application.

130 *See* Chapter 13 for licences of right and compulsory licences.

injunction will not be granted because it is ineffective, for example as in one of the *Spycatcher* cases, *Attorney-General* v *The Observer Ltd.*[131] In the House of Lords it was held that injunctions would not be granted against the *Observer* and the *Guardian* preventing them from reporting on the contents of *Spycatcher* because publication abroad had effectively destroyed the secrecy of the book's contents.[132]

Being equitable, injunctions are discretionary, and the decision to grant an injunction will be influenced by factors such as the innocence of the defendant – for example, in the case of non-deliberate use of information as in *Seager* v *Copydex (No. 1)*,[133] and whether an injunction is really necessary. In *Coco* v *A N Clark (Engineers) Ltd*,[134] the court decided that payment of damages in the form of royalties would be an appropriate alternative pending full trial. Other considerations might be whether the plaintiff delayed in taking legal action (the doctrine of laches applies), whether he was careless with the information or whether he should have sought other legal means of protecting the information, for example by obtaining a patent.

In terms of confidential information, an injunction may be for either or both of two purposes. The first is to restrain the continued use of the information and the second is to restrain publication. The latter will not normally be appropriate where the information has already entered the public domain, subject to what has been said earlier in this chapter in relation to the springboard doctrine. In *Ocular Sciences Ltd* v *Aspect Vision Care Ltd*,[135] Laddie J clearly identifies between the two purposes and when they are appropriate. In that case, he applied the guidelines in *Shelfer* v *City of London Electric Lighting Co*[136] to the effect that the court should grant damages in substitution for an injunction where the injury to the plaintiff's legal rights is small, is capable of being estimated in money, is adequately compensated by a small money payment and the case is such that it would be oppressive to the defendant to grant the injunction. On the facts, the information relating to contact lenses was not substantial, the damage to the plaintiffs, if any, was small and the granting of an injunction would be oppressive. The plaintiffs' proceedings had been vexatious in a number of respects and some reckless claims to confidentiality had been put forward. Therefore, Laddie J refused to grant this form of injunction.

If the information has been disclosed or used in some way in breach of confidence then it will usually be too late for an injunction, but damages may be available. Damages may be calculated on the basis of conversion, breach of confidence being in the nature of an equitable tort. The most thorough and comprehensive discussion of the relevant principles is to be found in *Seager* v *Copydex Ltd (No. 2)*,[137] where it was said that the value of confidential information depends upon its nature, and one of the following two formulae would be appropriate:

1 if there is nothing very special about the information, and it could have been obtained by employing a competent consultant, then the value (for the purpose of damages) is the fee that consultant would charge;
2 if the information is something special involving an inventive step, then the value is the price a willing buyer would pay for it.

If the information is commercial in nature and used in the manufacture of an object which is sold or hired, then it would seem that damages should be assessed on the basis of the fee the owner of the information reasonably might have expected had the information been used with his licence. Assessing dam-

131 [1989] AC 109.

132 The *Sunday Times* was in breach of confidence when it published an extract before copies of the book had become readily available in the United Kingdom and the newspaper was liable to account for the resulting profits. However, the *Sunday Times* could now continue with its further serialisation of *Spycatcher*.

133 [1967] 2 All ER 415.

134 [1969] RPC 41.

135 [1997] RPC 289.

136 [1895] 1 Ch 287.

137 [1969] RPC 250.

ages for future infringement would be difficult using the second formula in *Seager*, above. One might also question why a patent had not been applied for if there was an inventive step. A better approach would be that used in the *Coco* case, where an order was granted to the effect that the defendant should pay into a trust account a royalty on engines made in the future.

As regards innocent third parties, damages will be available, as a general rule, only if the third party's conscience is fixed by equity, that is if they knew or ought to have known that the information was subject to an obligation of confidence. Injunctions may be available, if appropriate, notwithstanding the innocence or *bona fides* of the third party. Each case must be treated on its own merits and it is, effectively, a matter of satisfying the equity raised by the third party's intentions in relation to the information. Basic equitable principles should guide the courts in the exercise of their discretion in such matters and the interests of a third-party purchaser without knowledge, actual or constructive, should be paramount.

If the information has been exploited commercially in breach of confidence, an account of profits may be more beneficial to the plaintiff. An account is an alternative to damages, and being an equitable remedy is discretionary. In *Peter Pan Manufacturing Corp* v *Corsets Silhouette Ltd*[138] a manufacturer of brassières made use of confidential information under a licence agreement. After the expiry of a licence agreement, the manufacturer continued to use the information, clearly in breach of confidence. In an action for breach of confidence, the plaintiff asked for an account of profits based on the whole of the profits accruing from the brassières, but the defendant claimed that the account of profits should be based only on the profit resulting from the wrongful use of the confidential information, that is the profit relating to the parts of the brassières incorporating the confidential information. The difference between the two sums was substantial and the plaintiff was awarded the higher sum because it was accepted by the court that the defendant would not have been able to make the brassières at all without the use of the confidential information.

Finally, another equitable remedy which might be available, depending upon the circumstances, is an order for the destruction of articles that have been made by using the confidential information, or which incorporate the tangible expression of such information. For example, an order for destruction of any of the brassières still held in stock by the defendant in the above case might have been appropriate. Such an order would not be granted as regards articles lawfully in the possession of third parties, unless somehow implicated in the breach of confidence.

138 [1963] RPC 45.

*Part Four*

# PATENT LAW

# 12

## *Patent law – background, basic principles and practical aspects*

### INTRODUCTION

Patent law concerns new, industrially applicable inventions. It is perhaps fitting that intellectual property law reserves a very special and powerful mode of protection for inventions that meet exacting standards. The grant of a patent effectively gives the inventor, or more commonly his employer, a monopoly to work the invention to the exclusion of others for a period of time, not exceeding 20 years. However, the monopoly is not absolute and there are a number of checks and balances to curb its abuse. The invention might concern a new or an improved product, for example, a new type of window lock or an improvement to the design of scaffolding clamps. Alternatively, the invention may concern some industrial process, such as a new method of rustproofing motor car bodies or an improved method of making printed circuit boards for electronic equipment. Because of the strength of this form of property right, high standards are required – the invention must be new and it must involve an inventive step, that is it must be more than merely an obvious application of technology. Furthermore, the invention must be capable of industrial application and must not fall within certain stated exclusions. These requirements are explored in detail in the next chapter; suffice it to say for now that patents are not granted lightly and an application is subjected to a thorough examination process.

In common with other intellectual property rights, a patent is a form of personal property that may be assigned, licensed or charged by way of a mortgage. However, it is declared by the Patents Act 1977 s 30(1) that a patent is not a thing in action, though why this should be so is incomprehensible.[1] Patent law grants a monopoly for a limited period of time in respect of an invention in return for disclosure of the details concerning the invention. These details are available for public inspection and are sufficiently comprehensive so that a person skilled in the particular art would be able to make practical use of the invention, in other words, he would be able to work the invention.[2] Disclosure is a central prerequisite for the grant of a patent and it must be total, with nothing of substance withheld, otherwise it might be difficult for others to make use of the invention once the patent has expired.[3] In *Young* v *Rosenthal*,[4] Grove J said (at 31):

> Then he [the applicant] is bound so to describe it in his specification as that any workman acquainted with the subject ... would know how to make it; and the reason of that is this, that if he did not do so, when the patent expired he might have some trade mystery which people would not be able actually to use in accordance with his invention (although they had a right to use it after his invention had expired), because they would not know how to make it.

1 On the other hand, copyright is a chose in action. The difference is of no consequence as assignment of patents is provided for by the Patents Act 1977.

2 Patent legislation uses the term 'a person skilled in the art'. This means a person (or team of persons) having knowledge and experience of the science or technology concerned.

3 An early example of a patent being declared invalid because of a failure to fully disclose how to work it is *The King* v *Arkwright* (1785) 1 WPC 64.

4 (1884) 1 RPC 29.

The holding back of part of the invention runs counter to the whole rationale of patent law and such applications will be rejected, or the applicant will be asked to modify and enlarge his disclosure accordingly.

After the expiry of the patent, the invention falls into the public domain and anyone is free to make use of it. One might wonder what the state or the general public get in return for this grant of privilege. The fact that the details of the invention are published means that competitors, researchers and the like have immediate access to this information which they may study and use subject to the scope of the infringing acts. The system benefits everyone by this because the wider availability of such information helps to spread and widen technical knowledge and, importantly, because investment is encouraged, wealth and employment are created and maintained. The whole patent transaction can be thought of as a bargain or contract between the inventor (or his employer) and the state, both parties bringing consideration to that contract[5] (*see* Table 12.1).

5 The person applying for the patent brings consideration in terms of fees and by adding his invention to the store of public information, ultimately giving his invention to the state or even the world at large.

**Table 12.1 Patent consideration**

| Patent – concept of contract – consideration | |
|---|---|
| *Patentee's consideration* | *State's consideration* |
| 1. Details available for public inspection. | 1. Examination and search by Patent Office may assist in the drawing up or amendment of the application. |
| 2. Invention falls into the public domain on expiry. | 2. Wealth of information available at Patent Office will help in the framing of patent application. |
| 3. Some things can be done during the life of the patent (non-infringing acts) by others. | 3. The granting of a limited monopoly. |
| 4. The invention may be vulnerable to a compulsory licence. | 4. A priority date will be given assisting in applications in other countries. |
| 5. Competition law may impose restrictions on the exploration of the patent. | 5. Useful evidential materials available, presumptions. |
| 6. Fees have to be paid. | |
| 7. The risk that the invention may be appropriated by the Crown (although payment may be made). | |

Without a patent system, inventors and their employers would attempt to keep the details of the invention secret, relying on the law of confidence for protection. In some cases, it would be impossible to keep the details of the invention secret. For example, if it concerned a new type of gearing arrangement for a bicycle, anyone purchasing a bicycle with the new system fitted would be able to discover the inventive step by an examination of the gears, perhaps after dismantling them. However, if the invention concerned some new industrial process used for making bicycle gears, it might be possible to maintain secrecy because an inspection of the finished product would not necessarily disclose the manufacturing process. In the first case, obtaining a patent is the most effective way of protecting the invention and the investment incurred in developing it. Other ways do exist but are not usually as attractive. For example, the inventor will be first to the marketplace with his gear system, and it could be several months or years before competitors can equip their factories and organise their production and marketing of a similar system. The duration of this lead-time is often proportional to the complexity of the technology required to put the invention into practice, although this lead-time might be dramatically reduced where the first product has to undergo rigorous safety testing and the competitor's product can largely avoid this by reliance on the testing of the first product. For example, in *R* v *Licensing Authority, ex p Smith Kline & French Laboratories Ltd* [6] information given by a drug manufacturer to a licensing authority, in order to obtain a product licence in respect of a drug, was used by the authority in determining whether to grant a product licence to a second manufacturer.

**6** [1989] 1 All ER 175. For a fuller discussion of this case in terms of the law of confidence *see* Chapter 11.

In the second case, where the invention relates to a process, the owner might be well advised to seek patent protection because of the uncertainty of the law of confidence. This flawed form of legal protection is little better than useless if details of the invention fall into the hands of third parties who have acquired the information in good faith. Depending on how tight security measures can be made, a patent will usually be an attractive alternative to the law of breach of confidence. However, where secrecy can be assured, there is no need to obtain a patent, and indeed the grant of a patent is a poor alternative as competitors will be able to find out about the process and gain a valuable insight into the way the patentee's business is likely to develop in the future. The invention will be available for anyone to use after expiry of the patent and compulsory licences might be available during its existence. If the secret can be maintained indefinitely, this will be preferable on all counts.

If the invention relates to a product rather than to a process, it may be possible to register some aspects of the shape of the product as a design or it may fall within the unregistered design right. Additionally, there will be copyright in the drawings and written descriptions of the invention. However, copyright protection is a poor substitute for a patent as, in principle, copyright protects only the expression of an idea, whereas a patent can protect from exploitation by others the idea that is encapsulated in the invention. The nature of patent protection was described by Buckley LJ in *Hickton's Patent Syndicate* v *Patents and Machine Improvements Co Ltd* [7] in the following terms:

**7** (1909) 26 RPC 339 at 348.

> Every invention to support a patent must ... either suggest a new way of making something ... or it may mean the way of producing a new article altogether; but I think you are losing the grasp of the substance and seizing the shadow when you say that the invention is the manufacture as distinguished from the idea. It is much more true to say that the patent is for the idea as distinguished from the thing manufactured. No doubt you cannot patent an idea, which you have simply conceived, and have suggested no way of carrying out, but the invention consists in thinking of or conceiving something and suggesting a way of doing it.

The strength of protection afforded to inventions through the patent system is one reason why patent protection is of a shorter duration than that available for works of copyright.

## BRIEF HISTORICAL PERSPECTIVE

As with the origins and development of other intellectual property rights, Eng-land has a prime place in world history and has set the mould for patent rights internationally. It is no coincidence that England was the country where the first major steps towards an industrial society were taken. Whether this was a direct result of the patent system is arguable, but it is without doubt that patents had an important role to play in the Industrial Revolution. Before this, the origins of patent law can be seen emerging in medieval times. *Letters patent* were open letters with the King's Great Seal on the bottom granting rights, often to foreign weavers and other craftsmen, allowing them to practise their trade and overcoming guild regulations which suppressed competition. The first such letters patent were granted in 1311 to John Kempe, a Flemish weaver who wanted to practise his trade in England, one of the earliest recorded instances of a patent.[8] The regulation of trade was deemed to fall within the provenance of the Crown and letters patent proved to be a useful method of encouraging the establishment of new forms of industry and commerce, giving the Crown pow-erful control over trade. In this early form, there was no need for anything inventive, it had more to do with the practice of a trade and the granting of favours by the Crown. However, some letters patent were granted for inven-tions; for example, a patent was granted to John of Utyman in 1449 for his new method of making stained glass. Eventually, there was a strong need for an effective system that prevented unfair competition where, for example, one person had made some novel invention and wanted to stop others from simply copying it. A monopoly system developed in the reign of Elizabeth I and many letters patent were granted.

Monopolies are controversial. There are many dangers associated with monopolies, such as overcharging, manipulation of markets or a refusal to make the product available. In particular, the Tudor monarchs saw the system of monopolies as a good way of raising revenue. However, unease was growing at how the system was open to abuse and the law began to curb such excesses. *Darcy* v *Allin*[9] is an example of an early patent case which involved a monopoly for the making, importation and selling of playing cards. The patent was held to be invalid as being, *inter alia*, a common law monopoly. James I issued a number of proclamations against monopolies, including the 'Book of Bounty' which gen-erally prohibited monopolies but excepted inventions provided they were not contrary to law, hurtful to the state or trade, or generally inconvenient.[10] In the slightly later *Clothworkers of Ipswich Case*[11] patents of a limited duration were recognised by the courts. The Statute of Monopolies, 1623 s 6[12] gave recognition to patents as an exception to the general rule against monopolies:

> Provided ... that any declaration before mentioned shall not extend to any letters patent and grants of privilege for the term of fourteen years or under ... of the sole working or making of any manner of new manufactures within this Realme, to the true and first inventor and inventors of such manufactures which others at the time of making such letters patent and grants shall not use, so as also they be not contrary to the law, or mischievous to the State, by raising prices of commodities at home, or hurt of trade, or generally inconvenient ...

So, the true and first inventor was given 14 years in which he could exploit his invention to the exclusion of others. The section also makes it clear that the

8  For an early historical perspective, *see* Davenport, N. (1979) *The United Kingdom Patent System*, Mason; and Young, D. *et al* (1994) *Terrell on the Law of Patents* (14th edn) Sweet & Maxwell.

9  (1602) Co Rep 84b.

10  Young, D. *op cit*, at p. 3.

11  (1614) Godbolt 252.

12  21 Jac 1 c.3. It seems that the world's first patents statute was passed in Venice in 1474, *see* Reid, B. C. (1993) *A Practical Guide to Patent Law* (2nd edn) Sweet & Maxwell, at p. 1.

monopoly granted is not to be abused. Although there was a long way to go, the seeds of the modern patent system were sown. The basis of the 14-year period was that the duration of apprenticeship was seven years and, at the end of the first seven years, the proprietor was expected to take on an apprentice and teach him how to work the invention. Thus, at the end of 14 years, there would be at least one other person who was free in law to work the invention.[13] In some cases, a longer term was granted. In *Lairdet's Patent*[14] a patent was granted for 18 years by private Act because it was accepted that a longer term was needed to allow the proprietor to receive adequate recompense and to encourage him to make it available to the public. However, the proprietor was constrained as to the price he could charge for his cement.

Initially there was no requirement for a written description of the invention to be provided by the applicant, but this gradually became common practice. At first, however, descriptions were not made publicly available. They became known, as they still are, as specifications.[15] By 1718, the provision of a specification was often a requirement. The drafting of them could be quite important, as Arkwright discovered to his chagrin when his main patent for a water powered spinning machine was held to be invalid through want of detail in 1785.[16] Applications were still made to the Monarch, or later to the law officers of the Crown, and the system became difficult, long-winded and expensive. James Watt was critical of the system and submitted proposals for reform in 1790. Charles Dickens wrote a critical exposé of it[17] and the system was overhauled by the Patent Law Amendment Act 1852. This saw the beginnings of the Patent Office and the opening of the Patent Office Library soon followed,[18] as did a system for classifying patents.[19] The Patents, Designs and Trade Marks Act 1883 gave effect to the provisions in the Paris Convention for the Protection of Industrial Property 1883. The 1883 Act also substituted the Seal of the Patent Office for the Monarch's Great Seal.

Until the early part of the twentieth century, patent applications were not searched for novelty. It was basically a deposit system, with applications simply being checked for satisfactory completion. However, as a result of the Patents Act 1902, novelty searches were commenced and the granting of patents became a much more exacting process. There were other Acts, culminating in the Patents Act 1949, all of which can be seen as being developments based on the same traditions. However, the current Act, the Patents Act 1977, is different in that it was designed to take account of the European Patent Convention, which established the European Patent Office, and the imminent Community patent system. Since the coming into force of the 1977 Act, letters patent are no longer issued, but instead a certificate from the Comptroller-General of Patents Designs and Trade Marks is provided. The maximum term of a patent has been extended from 16 years to 20 years.

## JUSTIFICATION FOR PATENT RIGHTS

An inventor owns a property right in his invention. This is a natural right and accords with the views on property rights of philosophers such as Locke. Furthermore, there is no substantial principle of classic jurisprudence that requires that property rights be limited temporarily. Neither need they be so limited if

13 For example, *Buck's Invention* (1651) 1 WPC 35.

14 (1773) 1 WPC 52.

15 Between 1853 and 1857, nearly all the patents granted since 1671 were published; *see* Davenport, N. (1979) *The United Kingdom Patent System*, Mason, at p. 53.

16 *The King* v *Arkwright* (1785) 1 WPC 64. Arkwright was a barber from Bolton who left his business and nagging wife to pursue his interest in inventing.

17 Dickens, C. *A Poor Man's Tale of a Patent*, reprinted in Phillips, J. (1984) *Charles Dickens and the 'Poor Man's Tale of a Patent'* ESC Publishing. In a plea to end the considerable bureaucracy involved, the closing sentence ends with the sentiment '… England has been chaffed and waxed sufficient'. (One of the officials involved in the process was the Deputy Chaff-wax who appears to have been responsible for preparing the wax for the Sealer.)

18 In 1855. Now known as the Science Reference and Information Service.

19 For a description of the period leading up to the 1852 Act, *see* Dutton, H. I. (1984) *The Patent System and Inventive Activity during the Industrial Revolution, 1750–1852*, Manchester University Press.

the inventor and his successors in title choose to keep secret details of the invention or how it works. However, such a property right, protected only by the law of confidence, is very vulnerable. Details of the invention might be disclosed in breach of confidence and eventually there may be those who, having acquired the details in good faith unaware of their confidential nature, are free in law and equity to put the invention to work.

What the patent system does is to guarantee a limited term of protection in return for the inventor's agreement to disclose details of his invention and, ultimately, to abandon his property right in it. This accords with the contract view of patents discussed earlier. Inventors are offered a stronger and more effective property right than under their natural right on condition that they will lose all rights in the invention when the patent expires.

The conventional justification for a patent system is that inventors and investors are rewarded for their time, work and risk of capital by the grant of a limited, though strong, monopoly. This benefits society by stimulating investment and employment and because details of the invention are added to the store of available knowledge. Eventually, after a period of time, depending on how long the patent is renewed (subject to a maximum of 20 years),[20] anyone will be free to put the invention to use. This utilitarian approach found favour with great English philosophers such as Jeremy Bentham, who argued that, because an invention involved a great deal of time, money and effort and also included a large element of risk, the exclusive use of the invention must be reserved for a period of time so that it could be exploited and thereafter used for the general increase of knowledge and wealth. He said that such exclusive use cannot:

> ... otherwise be put upon any body but by the head of law: and hence the necessity and the use of the interposition of law to *secure* to an inventor the benefit of his invention.[21]

Of course, the proprietor of a patent is likely to use this economic privilege to his advantage and the resulting product will be priced accordingly, subject to market forces. The mere fact that competition can be restrained by way of injunction will tend to maintain prices. However, that does not, by itself, indicate that patents are against the public interest. Indeed, it is in the public interest that patent monopolies are enforced.[22] The proprietor may demand a high price reflecting two factors, the cost of research and development required to bring the invention to fruition and the natural commercial desire to obtain a large profit. Another factor is the marketing effort required to establish a demand for the product or process. However, the owner of the patent (the proprietor) does not have *carte blanche* in fixing his prices for the following reasons:

1 consumers have managed thus far without the invention and may continue to do so by refusing to pay high prices;
2 the equation between volume of sales and profit margin must be considered. Sometimes a cheaper price will make more money for the owner of the patent by increasing sales disproportionately;
3 the consuming public may not have a need for the invention and it may be difficult to attract sales at any price. The sad fact is that a great many inventions fail to be commercially viable; and
4 there are various safeguards and controls to prevent abuse of patents both in terms of domestic law (that is, UK law) and European Community law.

20 Pharmaceutical patents can now be renewed up to a maximum of 25 years, Supplementary Protection Certificate for Pharmaceutical Products, EC Regulation No. 1768/92, OJ L182, 2.7.92, p. 1 and Patents (Supplementary Protection Certificates) Rules 1997, SI 1997/64.

21 Bentham, J. *Manual of Political Economy*, reprinted in Stark, W. (ed) (1952), *Jeremy Bentham's Economic Writings*, Vol. 1, Allen & Unwin, at p. 263.

22 *Per* Aldous J in *Chiron Corporation v Organon Teknika Ltd (No. 10)* [1995] FSR 325 at 333.

On the first point, John Stuart Mill, who strongly supported the patent system, was considered by Smit to have:

> ... adopted the rhetoric of the free market economy by suggesting that the reward depended on the invention proving to have economic value and that, in any event, only the users of the commodity created were paying for the increased price caused by the patent monopoly.[23]

A patent, therefore, is not necessarily a licence to print money, and a great deal of market research and economic judgment is essential before embarking upon the development of inventions. Bearing in mind that most important patents are granted to corporate organisations, this is a highly significant factor. The days of eccentric inventors are by no means gone, and simple and easily developed inventions are still a possibility, such as the Biro ball point pen or reflecting roadstuds ('cats' eyes'). But in most cases the advent of technology and its increasing complexity have necessitated substantial capital investment. The pharmaceutical industry is a good example of this; the cost of developing and testing new drugs requires large and long-term investment well before any rewards can be secured. Cursorily examined, the price charged for the finished product may seem exorbitant but could be the result of all sorts of preliminary and hidden costs associated with the invention. Speaking of the once popular exaggeration that drugs cost 'twopence a bucket to make and sell at £10 per pill', Walton points out that:

> What at first sight looks like profiteering, on examination turns out to be not so. What the drug houses sell is not a substance (whose manufacturing cost is commonly negligible) but a service. The cost of research – including the cost of all the abortive investigations – the clinical trials – the creation and maintenance of the market by initial and continuing promotion – the back-up servicing by the originating drug house which has at all times to deal with any slow to emerge problems caused by use of the drug – all this has to be paid for.[24]

These costs, which can be disproportionately large in comparison with the cost of manufacturing, will be incurred only by companies and organisations that can foresee a profitable return on them, and the only way this can be guaranteed is to secure some form of legal protection that will ensure that this is a practical possibility. Without such protection another manufacturer would be able to come along, steal the idea and sell the product for far less than the originator could ever hope to. The other manufacturer would have the considerable advantage of not having to pay any of the costs identified by Walton, except, perhaps, some minimal marketing costs.

The Industrial Revolution brought a great many pressures upon the patent system, eventually leading to major reforms starting with the Patent Law Amendment Act 1852. During the preceding period there had been much debate about whether inventions should be afforded legal protection by the grant of patents, and indeed in Switzerland and The Netherlands patent law was dismantled to be reintroduced later in the nineteenth century. The fact that this could happen and that the whole rationale for the granting of patents could be challenged in England now seems incredible. Nevertheless, the demise of the patent system was anticipated in the press, including *The Times* and *The Economist*.[25] Arguments for the abolition of the system centred around the detrimental effect of patents on competition and free trade.[26] Some commentators considered that

23 Smit, D. van Zyl, *The Social Creation of A Legal Reality: A Study of the Emergence and Acceptance of the British Patent System as a Legal Instrument for the Control of New Technology*, unpublished PhD thesis, University of Edinburgh, 1980.

24 Walton, A. 'The Copyright, Designs and Patents Act 1988 (1)', (1989) 133 *Solicitors Journal* 646 at 650. Walton's comment was made in the context of compulsory licences, discussed in Chapter 13.

25 *The Times*, 29 May 1869; *The Economist*, 5 June 1869.

26 For a comprehensive description of the arguments for and against a patent system that were raging in the mid-nineteenth century, *see* Dutton, H. I. (1984) *The Patent System and Inventive Activity during the Industrial Revolution, 1750–1852*, Manchester University Press, Chapter 1.

patents had served their purpose and were no longer needed in a developed industrial society, while others saw patents as insidious and positively harmful, *The Economist* in 1851 noting that the granting of patents:

> ... inflames cupidity, excites fraud ... begets disputes and quarrels betwixt inventors, provokes endless lawsuits, makes men ruin themselves for the sake of getting the privilege of a patent, which merely fosters a delusion of greediness.[27]

27 *The Economist,* 26 July 1851.

Convincing arguments had to be developed by those keen to see the patent system retained and improved. As Dutton suggests, those arguments are still valid today and include:[28]

28 Dutton, H. I., *op cit.*

1 *The contract theory.* Temporary protection granted in reward for knowledge of new inventions.
2 *The reward theory.* Inventors should be rewarded for making useful inventions and the law must be used to guarantee this reward so that inventors can receive sufficient recompense for their ingenuity.
3 *The incentive theory.* By constructing a framework whereby invention is rewarded, this will act as an incentive to make new inventions and to invest the necessary time and capital. This is a forward-looking approach contrasted to the latter which is retrospective.
4 *The natural law/moral rights theory.* Individuals have a right of property in their own ideas and this right should be protected from being usurped or stolen by others. (This is similar to moral rights in copyright law and accords with the rationale of French law, though until recently of little import in the UK where the emphasis has been on economic rights rather than on moral rights.)

In *Chiron Corporation v Organon Teknika Ltd (No. 10)*[29] Aldous J put the justification for the patent system in very pragmatic terms, saying that nearly every country had chosen to adopt a patent system because:

29 [1995] FSR 325.

> ... it is generally accepted that the opportunity of acquiring monopoly rights in an invention stimulates technical progress in at least four ways. First it encourages research and invention; secondly, it induces an inventor to disclose his discoveries instead of keeping them a secret; thirdly, it offers a reward for the expense of developing inventions to the state at which they are commercially practical and, fourthly, it provides an inducement to invest capital in new lines of production which might not appear profitable if many competing producers embarked on them simultaneously ... It is inherent in any patent system that a patentee will acquire a monopoly giving him a right to restrict competition and also enabling him to put up or at least maintain prices. That affects the public and is contrary to the public interest, but it is the recognised price that has been accepted to be necessary to secure the advantages to which I have referred.[30]

30 At 332.

Encouragement, inducement and reward are the main factors underlying the patent system. The public interest, although apparently jeopardised by the grant of a monopoly, is secured by increased industrial activity, developing new technologies and disclosure of new and useful inventions. Furthermore, patent law contains a number of safeguards, such as compulsory licensing and Crown use, to curb any significant abuse of the patent monopoly.

Much of the dissatisfaction with the patent system until the middle of the nineteenth century could be explained by the parlous state of patent law at the time. It was clear that something had to be done – either the patent system should be abandoned, or it should be reformed and streamlined to meet the needs of a heavily industrialised society that depended on invention and innovation for future growth and prosperity. The arguments of the supporters of a strong patent system won the day and the latter course was taken. However, it should be appreciated that having a strong system of patent law is not a foregone conclusion and that there are some good reasons to the contrary. If patent law were to be abolished tomorrow, inventive activity would not cease altogether – other factors would come to the fore, such as the inventor's lead-time, that halcyon period before competitors can equip their factories and commence manufacture, when he has no competition. Depending upon the nature of the invention, that period may be long enough to justify the initial expense associated with putting the invention to use. However, in many cases, the lead-time would be insufficient and the inventor would have to look to factors such as quality and value for money as a way of making the whole undertaking profitable and worthwhile. Trade marks and business goodwill are other ways in which the invention could be successfully exploited by the inventor or the owner of the patent. In spite of the arguments for and against patents, it is now unthinkable that the patent system would be abolished. Over the last 100 or so years, patents have become established on a worldwide basis, with almost all the countries with developed industries having some form of patent protection for inventions.[31] Some industries, such as pharmaceuticals and electronics, would become stagnant without patent protection through lack of investment.

As noted above, the presence of a strong and effective patent system may bring numerous benefits such as the dissemination of information and providing an incentive to invest in the development of new products and processes which will eventually fall into the public domain. However, the patent system does not always stand up well to close scrutiny as many inventors who have had to deal with the system will testify. Obtaining a patent is expensive and takes a long time. It may be several years before action can be taken against an infringer. It could be said that the system favours large wealthy corporations which have the deep pockets required to acquire patents and defend them on a global scale. Unless the sole inventor can find a 'product champion', that is, an investor prepared to put up substantial funds, he will be seriously disadvantaged. One critic of the system is James Dyson, the inventor of the wheelbarrow with a ball for a wheel and the bagless vacuum cleaner. Recently, he brought a case before the European Court of Human Rights, arguing that patent renewal fees are illegal as the inventor gets nothing in return,[32] although proponents of the patent system would disagree, pointing to the continued protection afforded by payment of the renewal fees.

Another, perhaps more worrying, concern is that a system which was designed around technology from a simpler era, is unable to provide an appropriate level of protection, taking account of all the checks and balances, in the context of new and emerging technologies. Information technology and genetic engineering are two important examples. We will see the difficulty patent law has in addressing the protection of software inventions in the following chapter. Consider the situation whereby a commercial organisation has economic rights in genetic material, rights which can last for up to 20 years. Thurow

**31** Even the former USSR had patent laws: Mamiofa, I. E. 'The Draft of a New Soviet Patent Law' [1990] 1 EIPR 21.

**32** *The Sunday Times*, 1 March 1998.

claims that tweaking the existing system will not provide a solution, and he argues for a new system which strikes a balance between the production and distribution of new ideas.[33] He is also critical of judge-made law in this area saying that judges do not consider what is appropriate in terms of accelerating technological and economic progress. Rather, they are concerned with how to fit new technology into the existing legal framework with minimum disruption to established principles. In particular, Thurow suggests an optimal patent system would differentiate between different industries, types of knowledge and types of inventors. For example, the electronics industry wants speed and short-term protection, whilst the pharmaceutical industry wants long-term protection because it takes a number of years before a new drug can be sold to the public. For the most part, in the latter case the companies involved can well afford the expense of acquiring, maintaining and defending their intellectual property rights. Small, innovative electronics companies are less able to afford this expense, or even to understand such a complex system.

33 Thurow, L.C. 'Needed: a New System of Intellectual Property Rights', *Harvard Business Review*, September–October 1997, p. 95.

## Patent strategy

Intellectual property rights are considered to be of the utmost importance in Japan and companies there have developed efficient strategies for exploiting their patents to the fullest extent.[34] An 'attacking' strategy is at the foremost, an important goal being to use the patents in a way which excludes competitors and secures a large a market for the proprietor. Licences are often subject to an obligation to grant back, for no fee, rights in improvements on the original invention. Of course, in the context of Europe this may well offend against competition law.

34 Guntram Rahn 'Japanese Patent Strategy', in The European Patent Office, *Annual Report 1995*, at p. 9.

An ideal outcome is where the invention for which the patent has been granted is combined with an industry standard, for example, the Japan Victor Company's VHS technology which became the industry standard for video recorders.

The Japanese also widely use patents defensively to avoid needless conflicts and litigation by 'blanketing' the invention with a close network of patent filings, trying to predict future applications and improvements on the basic invention for the purpose of pre-empting competitors and covering any possible future applications. If successful, this ties a competitor's hands together and deprives him of technical mobility and flexibility. This approach is also known as 'ring-fencing' the invention.

An important source of inventions is the employee. In many organisations employees, who are not directly employed in the search for new inventions, are encouraged to submit ideas through a company suggestions scheme. However, in the United Kingdom it is a sad fact that many suggestions, whether made as a result of a formal scheme or otherwise, are not taken up. In any case, if an employee has an idea for a new invention in a situation where he may be entitled to be the proprietor of the invention, he would be well advised to seek professional advice rather than to submit it to his employer. The rewards offered by employers for useful suggestions are likely to be minuscule compared with the income which may be derived from a successful patent.

Nevertheless, the Japanese approach is to provide an incentive to employees to be patent-minded, thinking of new inventions and ways to improve or create policies in respect of patents within the company. This is known as the 'motivation' strategy. If handled properly, it can encourage suggestions from a company's human resources at all levels, even from the humblest shop-floor worker. This in turn should engender a feeling of worth, motivation and loyalty from amongst employees.

A desideratum for many Japanese companies is to build a strong patent portfolio. This will enhance a company's technological reputation and in the area of research and development generally. This can improve investors' confidence in the company and facilitate the raising of new capital. Coupled with effective and well-known trade marks, this will be a powerful combination and will encourage other companies to seek licences to work the company's technology. A strong portfolio of intellectual property rights is central to a 'patent licensing' strategy.

With strategies such as those outline above, Japanese companies have been extremely successful in the protection and exploitation of intellectual property. Over 80 per cent of the world's patents are granted by the European Patent Office, the United States Patent and Trademark Office and the Japanese Patent Office. Japanese companies are amongst the world's most vigorous patent applicants, especially in the USA and Europe. As the Japanese economy is largely based on high-tech industry, this leads to reliance on intellectual property rights. It is widely recognised in Japan that, if it intends to keep its place as a very effective and successful high-technology industrial country, it must take intellectual property rights very seriously as the key to protecting and exploiting intellectual property.

## PRACTICAL CONSIDERATIONS

Three possibilities present themselves to an inventor who is resolved on securing a patent for his invention. An application may be made for a UK patent, for a 'European' patent designating a number of member states of the European Patent Convention (EPC) or under the Patent Cooperation Treaty (PCT) designating some or all of the contracting states. In all cases, applications can be handled by the Patent Office in London. However, a European application can instead be filed direct with the European Patent Office, in which case permission must first be obtained from the UK Patent Office which checks to see whether the application compromises national security.[35] The procedure for obtaining a United Kingdom patent will be described below, but first some definitions are given relating to the terms used and documents submitted.[36]

### Filing date

This is the date when the application is received by the Patent Office. The application must contain a request for a patent, full identification of the applicant, a full description of the invention and the filing fee.[37] All these things must be received before the application can be given a filing date. The claims and search fee must be submitted within 12 months of the filing date (or earlier priority date) if the patent application is to proceed. The filing date is important because it is the date used to determine the duration of the patent. That is, the 20 years maximum period available starts to run from the filing date.

35 The Patents Act 1977 s 23. Unless otherwise stated, in this chapter statutory references are to this Act.

36 The procedure for a patent under the European Patent Convention is broadly similar. Patent Cooperation Treaty patents are somewhat different in that, after search and publication, applications must be made to the individual countries; this is known as entering the national phase and can be quite complex. The procedure for a United Kingdom patent is laid out in detail in the Patents Act 1977 and the Patents Rules 1995, SI 1995/2093.

37 The Patents Act 1977 s 15(1).

## Priority date

Section 5(2) of the Patents Act 1977 allows an invention to claim the priority of an earlier application filed within the preceding 12 months if the later application is supported by matter disclosed in the earlier application. For example, an inventor may apply for a United Kingdom patent for his invention and then, within 12 months, apply to the European Patent Office, designating a number of member states, and the priority date of the resulting European patents will be that of the original United Kingdom patent, assuming that it supports the invention as claimed in the application to the European Patent Office. The consequences of a failure to support the later application can be severe. In *Biogen Inc v Medeva plc*[38] the House of Lords confirmed the Court of Appeal decision that the patent in suit was invalid. It relied on the priority of an earlier application. The problem was that, contrary to s 5(2), the invention claimed in the latter application was not supported by matter disclosed in the earlier application. The technology in the relevant field (genetic engineering) had moved very rapidly and, without being able to rely on the priority of earlier application, it was conceded that the second application was obvious.

The priority date is important because it is the state of the art at that date that is considered when judging the invention for novelty. It is also relevant in terms of infringement in that persons who in good faith, before the priority date, either have done an act that would constitute infringement or have made effective and serious preparations for such an act may continue to do so after the grant of the patent.[39]

## Specification

This is a very important document, probably the most important thing submitted by the applicant. The specification must contain a description of the invention, one or more claims together with any drawings required to illustrate the invention. The specification should fully describe the invention – anything omitted at this stage could have the effect of jeopardising the application or cutting down the usefulness and scope of the patent should it be granted. The specification should also be sufficiently detailed so that a person skilled in the art can understand and work the invention. For example, if the invention concerns a new type of tow bar for a vehicle, the specification should be such that a skilled vehicle engineer would be able to make it, fit it and use it.

Specifications usually contain a number of drawings. Judges by their training are better equipped to interpret the written word than drawings. In *Van der Lely NV v Bamfords Ltd*,[40] Lord Reid said that judges were not expert at interpreting visual evidence (photographs in this case) and the question to be asked is what the eye of a person with appropriate skill and experience would see in the photograph. Where the evidence was contradictory, the judge must decide which interpretation to accept, not by reading or construing the photograph, but by looking at it to see which explanation is the most plausible.

38 [1997] RPC 1.

39 Patents Act 1977 s 64.

40 [1963] RPC 61.

An example of a patent specification is given at the end of this chapter and should be referred to. It contains on the front page, the application number, date of filing,[41] the name and address of the applicant, inventors, agent and address for service, the classifications for the invention, a document cited by the examiner which may have a bearing on the novelty of the invention, field of search, title, abstract and, usually as here, a drawing. The little numbers in brackets alongside the entries are known as INID numbers and are used to standardise the layout of the page to help with processing of the information contained on the page.[42] For example, on the front page of the sample application at the end of this chapter, (71) is the name of the applicant, (54) is the title of the invention, (57) is the abstract and (51) is the International Patent Classification. The remainder of the specification contains a detailed description of the invention and the claims. Sometimes there will be further drawings and there may amendments to the claims.

## Claims

The application will include a statement of the claims defining the invention for which protection is required. There will usually be several claims, some of which may be alternatives. The purpose of the claims is to define the limit of the monopoly and, therefore, they must be very carefully drawn up. According to Lord Russell in *Electric & Musical Industries Ltd* v *Lissen Ltd*,[43] the function of the claims is to define clearly and with precision the monopoly claimed so that others may know the exact boundaries of the area in which, if they venture therein, they will be trespassers. The ideal situation from the applicant's point of view is a set of valid claims which give the widest scope to the invention. The claims in the example should be carefully studied with this in mind. They provide a good example of the care and thoroughness that a patent agent employs in the drafting of claims.

Under the Patents Act 1977 s 14(5), the claims shall:

(a) define the matter for which the applicant seeks protection;
(b) be clear and concise;
(c) be supported by the description; and
(d) relate to one invention or to a group of inventions which are so linked as to form a single inventive concept.

Claims (and the same applies to amended claims) are required to be clear and concise: s 14(5). In *Strix Ltd* v *Otter Controls Ltd*,[44] a case involving a patent for a back-up control to switch off an electric kettle where there had been a failure of the kettle's 'dry-boil' protector, it was accepted that, although something clearer and more concise could have been drafted, the test was whether a person skilled in the art would have difficulty in understanding the language used in the claim.

The example at the end of the chapter is a good example of a group of inventions forming a single inventive concept. Claims 1, 20 and 39 relate to three different aspects – a beverage package, a method of packaging a beverage, and a beverage when so packaged. Rule 22 of the Patent Rules 1995[45] states that where two or more inventions are claimed (whether in a single claim or in separate claims), and there exists between or among those inventions a technical relation-

---

**41** This particular example does not have a priority date. Where the priority of an earlier application is claimed, a reference to the date and country of the earlier application will all be noted on the front page.

**42** This system was devised by ICIREPAT, the International Committee for Information Retrieval by Examining Patent Offices.

**43** (1939) 56 RPC 23; *see also Glaverbel SA* v *British Coal Corp* [1995] RPC 255.

**44** [1995] RPC 607.

**45** Patent Rules 1995, SI 1995/2093.

ship which involves one or more of the same or corresponding special technical features, then those inventions shall be treated as being so linked as to form a single inventive concept for the purposes of the Act. 'Special technical features' are defined as those technical features which define a contribution which each of the claimed inventions, considered as a whole, makes over the prior art.

Sometimes, an omnibus claim will be included, usually as the final claim, for example:

> the widget as substantially described hereinbefore with reference to the accompanying drawings.

The way claims are interpreted is important. By s 125(1) of the 1977 Act, the invention shall be taken to be that specified in a claim as interpreted by the description and any drawings contained in the specification. The extent of protection afforded by the grant of the patent is to be determined accordingly. But interpretation of claims can be wider than this and a purposive approach to interpretation is taken, rather than a strict literal approach, in accordance with the European Patent Convention. This feature is discussed in depth in Chapter 14.

Patent agents use language designed to maximise the protection afforded by the patent when granted. It can, at first sight, seem curious. For example, if a person invents something that has three components, such as three legs, a patent agent will draft the claim in terms of a 'plurality' of components where it might be possible to use two or four components. However, using this term excludes the singular.[46] If the invention can be worked with one or more components, a better expression would be 'a single or plurality of ...' or 'one or more ...'.

Often claims will contain numeric data. For example, where a range of numbers is claimed, it was held in *Auchincloss* v *Agricultural & Veterinary Supplies Ltd*,[47] that anything outside that range is outside the monopoly and is not a variant in the sense used in *Catnic*.[48] In *Hoechst Celanese Corp* v *BP Chemicals Ltd*,[49] a reference in a claim to '50 per cent of its dry physical dimension' was held to be a reference to a linear dimension (radius) of the particle concerned rather than the volume, as the defendant contended.

Sometimes, patent agents and others drafting patent claims may come down with a sad case of 'parametritis'. This term has been used by judges in relation to an attempt to repatent the prior art by placing new limits on claims by using a series of parameters which were not mentioned in the prior art, for example, because the equipment to measure them did not exist at the time. Another practice is to draft claims in an unnecessarily complicated manner. As the claims of a granted patent are prima facie valid, this may make it difficult for an opponent to challenge the claim. However, using obscure, difficult or complex language is not, by itself, a ground for invalidity and, within wide limits and notwithstanding the requirement that the claims must be clear and concise, an applicant for a patent can use what language he wishes to define the scope of his invention. Of course, the court must be on guard not to be impressed with obfuscatory language.[50]

In the next chapter, we will see that patents are available for second uses of known substances or compositions for medicinal use. However, great care must be taken to draft the claims in such cases, and a certain form of claim has become

46 *Mabuchi Motor KK's Patents* [1996] RPC 387.

47 [1997] RPC 649.

48 *Catnic Components Ltd* v *Hill & Smith Ltd* [1982] RPC 183, discussed in detail in Chapter 14. For a description of the approach of the European Patent Office in terms of ranges of numbers *see* Ashley, G. and Björk, P. 'Patentability of Alloys at the European Patent Office' (1997) 2 (3) *Intellectual Property*, CLT Professional Publishing at p. 3.

49 [1997] FSR 547.

50 *Raychem Corp's Patents* [1998] RPC 31, *per* Laddie J.

51 [1985] OJ EPO 64.

widely acceptable, known as a 'Swiss type claim'. In *Eisai*,[51] the enlarged board of appeal of the European Patent Office approved such a type of claim, which normally takes the form:

> Use of a substance or composition X for the manufacture of a medicament for a specified new and inventive therapeutic application.

A typical claim for a first medical use of a known product might take the form:

> Substance or composition X ...
> > ... for use as a medicament
> > ... for use as an antibiotic; or
> > ... for use in treating disease Y.

52 [1996] RPC 341.

In *Hoerrmann's Application*,[52] the court held that, when making a claim to a further medical use, the claims must be supported by the description (as *per* s 14(5)) and in such a case, this would require a clear indication that the treatment had been tried and tested – it must come over as a reality and not merely a possibility.

## Abstract

53 SI 1995/2093, r 19.

The abstract is simply a concise summary of the matter contained in the specification, normally not exceeding 150 words.[53] The abstract must indicate the technical field to which the invention belongs and it should be clear about the technical problem and give some idea of the solution to that problem and the principal use or uses of the invention. Where appropriate it will include the chemical formula best characterising the invention. The abstract provides useful information to help in the searching process, for example when searching for anticipatory materials. Indeed it is a requirement that the abstract be drafted accordingly. By reading the abstract, it should be possible to determine whether it is necessary to consult the specification itself. Abstracts are included with other information in on-line and printed searching services.

54 The Patent Office produce some free literature on intellectual property. It is of excellent quality and of interest: *Patent Protection* and *How to Prepare a UK Patent Application*. These and others are available from The Patent Office, Marketing and Information Directorate, Cardiff Road, Newport, Gwent NP9 1RH.

## Procedure for a United Kingdom patent[54]

The procedure described below applies where there has not been a declaration of priority from an earlier application. If there has been such a declaration, step 2 is different in that the claims and abstract must be filed within 12 months of the earliest priority date or within one month of the date of filing the application whichever is the later, but the form and search fee must be submitted within 12 months of the earliest declared priority date.

In simple terms, the application procedure is as follows.

1 *File application*: submit application including a request for a patent, identification of the applicant (full name and address), description of the patent and the filing fee.
2 *File claims, etc.*: within 12 months, file the claims, abstract, form requesting preliminary examination and search together with the search fee.
3 *Preliminary examination and search*: the application will then be checked to ensure all necessary documents and forms have been filed and fees paid. The

application will then go to a Patent Office examiner who will make a search, mainly amongst patent specifications to check for novelty and obviousness. After this a search report will be issued. This report helps the applicant to decide whether his invention is new and not obvious. In some cases, amendments may have to be made to the claims or description. Any amendment to the claims must not cover something not already disclosed in the specification as first filed. In the light of materials identified by the search, or for other reasons, the applicant might decide to withdraw the application before early publication thereby keeping his invention secret, in as much as it is not anticipated by the prior art.

4 *Early publication*: the application will be published together with the search report and any amended claims received before date of publication. Normally, this takes place 18 months after the priority date.[55] The contents of the specification are no longer confidential and become part of the state of the art. The date of early publication is important because it is the date from which damages for infringement ultimately can be claimed. For example, if there is an infringement of the patent between the early publication and grant, assuming it is finally granted, an action in respect of that infringement can be commenced *after* the patent has been granted. Early publication is known as 'A' publication. The example at the end of the chapter is an 'A' publication.

5 *Substantive examination*: this is the final stage before the grant of the patent. Within six months of the date of early publication, yet another form and fee has to be submitted to the Patent Office. The application will lapse if the form and fee are not received within those six months.[56] Once the patent application has been published and before grant any person may make written observations on the patentability of the invention. Reasons for the observations must be given and the Comptroller must consider the observations.[57] The specification is examined to see whether it complies with the requirements of the Patents Act 1977, especially whether the invention claimed is new and non-obvious, whether the description is adequate so that it can be carried out by a person skilled in the art concerned and whether the claims are clear and consistent with the description. It is common for the specification or claims or both to require amendment in the light of objections raised by the examiner. Once all the examiner's objections have been met, assuming they can be, the patent is granted. The patent as granted is published. This is known as 'B' publication.

Figure 12.1 illustrates a simplified flowchart for the UK patent application process. The period allowed for putting an application in order so that it complies with the Act is four-and-a-half years or 12 months from the date of the first report under the substantive examination provisions, whichever expires the later.[58] Under the usual procedure, it can be seen that the shortest period is theoretically a little over 18 months, but a period of between two and three years is more realistic. However, the Patent Office will consider shortening the publication period and the time between publication and full examination if the applicant can make out a good case. The initial grant is for four years. Thereafter the patent may be renewed annually up to a maximum of 20 years from the date of filing.

55 If there is no declared priority date, early publication takes place 18 months from the date of filing the application, the Patent Rules 1995, SI 1995/2093, r 27.

56 It is possible to obtain a one month extension.

57 The person making the observations does not, as a result, become a party in any proceedings under the Act before the Comptroller, the Patents Act 1977 s 21. Under this provision, a person may claim that the invention is not new because he was working the invention before the priority date.

58 Section 18 and r 34, the Patent Rules 1995, SI 1995/2093.

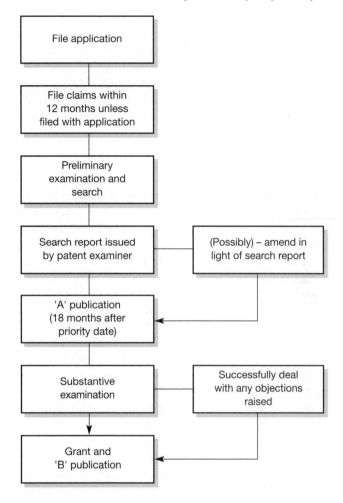

**Figure 12.1 Flowchart of a UK patent application (simplified)**

On account of the difficulties faced by small and medium-sized undertakings which may need to exercise their rights much sooner than the traditional period of two to three years, bearing in mind that a patent cannot be enforced until it has been granted, the Patent Office now offers a speedier service. Patent procedure is accelerated by combining the search and examination stages and, by so doing, the time taken to obtain the grant of a patent may be as little as one year.[59]

The new procedure, which is an alternative to the traditional procedure, is initiated by filing a request for search together with a request for examination at the same time. A request for early publication and early grant must also be made by the applicant. Combined search and examination is not likely to be appropriate in all cases. The applicant may have insufficient time fully to assess the prior art and make modifications to his application and, by the time the patent has been granted, the search and examination may not be complete. It would be likely to be useful, however, where the invention is 'clear cut' in terms

**59** The Patent Office has published a fact sheet entitled *Combined Search and Examination*, March 1995.

of the requirements of the Act. For example, where it is clear that the invention is new, involves an inventive step, is capable of industrial application and not excepted. The new procedure, which was available from 3 July 1995, is unlikely to be appropriate where the distinction between the invention and the prior art is imprecise, or where there is an issue concerning the exceptions or where the technology involved is particularly complex. Nevertheless, the fact that the Patent Office has gone some way to meeting the wishes of users of the patent system is to be welcomed.

## Patents after grant

After four years a patent must be renewed annually by submission of the appropriate form and renewal fee within the three months preceding the anniversary of the date of filing.[60] There is provision for restoration of a patent which has ceased to have effect because of a failure to pay the renewal fee.[61] The restoration period is set down in the Patent Rules 1995 r 41(1) as 19 months beginning with the day the patent ceased to have effect. However, under s 28(3) the Comptroller shall restore the patent on payment of any outstanding renewal fees and a restoration fee only if he is satisfied that the proprietor had taken reasonable care to see that any renewal fee was paid on time or that the renewal fee and any additional restoration fee were paid within six months from the end of the time when the renewal fee should have been paid.

In *Atlas Powder Co's Patent*,[62] Atlas was taken over by ICI and decided not to renew its United Kingdom patent. An unforeseen consequence was that a Malaysian patent belonging to Atlas in respect of the same invention lapsed because the United Kingdom patent ceased to have effect. In terms of what is required by the first limb of s 28(3) (reasonable care to see that the renewal fee is paid), the Court of Appeal decided that this requires an intention to ensure that the fee was paid, or at least that the proprietor had taken some steps towards that. A deliberate decision not to renew is not consistent with the statutory requirement and restoration was not permitted.

After a patent has been granted it may still be amended under s 27 subject to s 76. Any such amendment is treated as having effect from the date of grant and there is provision for opposition. A failure to respond to any opposition will result in the application for amendment being treated as withdrawn.[63] The Comptroller may amend a specification on his own initiative to recognise a registered trade mark. Amendment under s 27 is not permitted where proceedings in which the validity of the patent has been put in issue are pending.[64]

Section 76[65] deals with amendment generally. The basic rule is that additional matter must not be disclosed. In terms of amendment after grant, s 76(3) requires that any amendment does not result in additional matter being disclosed in the specification or which extends the protection conferred by the patent.[66] In *Mabuchi Motor KK's Patent*,[67] it was held that an amendment to cut down the claims in a patent specification does not offend s 76. Under s 75, amendment may be allowed in revocation proceedings, subject to s 76, but this is discretionary. In *Mabuchi*, in relation to amendment under s 75, the Patents Court held that an amendment should be refused only on very compelling grounds. The proprietor's requested amendment was designed to catch infringe-

60 Rule 39, the Patent Rules 1995, SI 1995/2093. The date of filing is determined in accordance with s 15.

61 Section 28.

62 [1995] RPC 666.

63 *Norsk Hydro AS's Patent* [1997] RPC 89.
64 However, s 75 does permit amendment where the validity of the patent is in issue in live proceedings.

65 Subsituted by the Copyright, Designs and Patents Act 1988, s 295 and Sch 5 para 20.

66 Amendment under s 37(4), where an application for revocation is made in a case where the person registered as proprietor was not entitled to the patent but the person who was entitled makes a new application, is subject to not disclosing additional matter only.

67 [1996] RPC 387.

ment and to avoid the prior art, but it was accepted by the court that this was not to be equated with acting in a blameworthy manner. Although the amendment was allowed, the defendant's '*Gillette*' defence succeeded.[68]

**68** The '*Gillette*' defence is discussed in Chapter 14.

## Cost of applying for a patent

The cost of applying for a patent can be quite high; apart from paying the appropriate fees to the Patent Office, the drawing up of the necessary documents and drafting of claims will usually take a considerable amount of time. Additionally, in most cases, the services of a patent agent will be required. Some of the main fees payable to the Patent Office in respect of a UK patent, as from 11 May 1992[69] are as follows:

**69** Patents (Fees) Rules 1996, SI 1996/2972. The fee for substantive examination has been reduced from £130.

| | | |
|---|---|---|
| Filing fee | (Form 1/77) | £25 |
| Request for preliminary examination and search | (Form 9/77) | £130 |
| Request for substantive examination | (Form 10/77) | £70 |

Renewal fees – on a sliding scale varying from £110 for fifth year to £450 for twentieth and final year.

There is a whole range of other fees and forms for various purposes, for example, for amendments, assignments, restoration, etc.

## Classification system

Current and old patents have to be consulted for several reasons, the obvious one being to determine whether a 'new' invention has been anticipated and is, therefore, likely to be refused a patent on the ground of lack of novelty. Other reasons relate to patent documents as a valuable source of information in terms of gaining information about competitors and a particular field of technology, seeing how certain problems have been tackled in the past, as a way of gaining inspiration and as a research tool. The Patent Office presently holds specifications and abstracts for every British patent dating from 1617, comprising over 2 million inventions, in addition to over 23 million patent publications from overseas. It will come as no surprise that some sort of classification scheme is needed to assist in searching for relevant documents. Patent abstracts and specifications are classified and indexed to make the task of searching easier. For example, for specifications, the system used is based on three elements: a section, a division, and a heading. There are eight sections lettered from A to H as follows:

A    Human necessities
B    Performing operations
C    Chemistry and metallurgy
D    Textiles and paper
E    Civil engineering and building accessories

F    Mechanics, heating and lighting
G    Instrumentation
H    Electricity

In addition there is a 'division not specified'. Each section is divided into between two and eight divisions, which are further divided into between two and 24 headings. As an example, the classification for toys is A6S (A6 being entertainments). Further subdivisions are used below the headings level and are known as 'terms', which are developed and expanded pragmatically in response to volume of applications.

There is also a Universal Indexing Schedule and an International Patent Classification (IPC), the latter being used by the European Patent Office. The IPC is arranged in eight sections in a way similar to the UK classification. In practice, UK patent specifications will carry all three classifications. The Patent Office and the Science Reference and Information Service have access to several computer databases. Well over 30 million patents have been published worldwide and that figure is being increased by around 1 million each year.

## Patent agents

Persons wishing to apply for a patent normally use the services of a patent agent because of the complexity and technicality associated with patent applications and the importance of correctly defining the scope of the patent and extent of the claims. Although anyone can act for another in an agency capacity in respect of a patent application,[70] under the Copyright, Designs and Patents Act 1988 s 276, only registered patent agents may describe themselves as patent agents or patent attorneys.[71] Communications between a client and his patent agent are privileged provided the agent is registered.[72] There is a professional body for patent agents, the Chartered Institute of Patent Agents. Chartered patent agents now have a right of audience in the Patents County Court.

## Some statistics concerning UK patents

A patent is initially granted for four years, after which the patent may be renewed annually. There are a large number of patent applications made each year for the UK alone, over 27 000 with around 180 000 renewals.[73] The number of patents renewed in 1996 ranged from 21 151 in the fifth year down to 3196 which were renewed for their twentieth and final year. The total income from patent fees for the year ending 31 March 1997 received by the Patent Office was £37 million. These figures indicate the importance of the patent system as perceived by inventors and their employers. While UK-based applicants account for over two-thirds of applications for UK patents, other countries such as the USA (9.6 per cent), Japan (5.7 per cent) and Germany (3.3 per cent) are also significant sources of applications.

Over one-third of applications are based on a claim to a priority in relation to an earlier application elsewhere. In 1996, a total of 4212 patents were marked to the effect that licences were available as of right.[74] No compulsory licences were granted under s 48(1) and there were no awards of compensation for employees making inventions of outstanding benefit to their employers

70 Subject to restrictions under the European Patent Convention in relation to European patents, the Copyright, Designs and Patents Act 1988 s 274.

71 Solicitors may also use the description patent attorney.

72 The Copyright, Designs and Patents Act 1988 s 280.

73 The Patent Office, *Annual Report and Accounts 1996-1997* (The Stationery Office, 1997).

74 Under the Patents Act 1977 s 46(1).

under s 40 of the Act, although one claim was lodged. A total of 96 patents were revoked, mainly by the Comptroller.

Success rates for patent applications cannot be directly obtained from the Patent Office's Annual Report. Because of the time lag in the grant of a patent, which may be as much as three to four years, it is not an easy task to determine what percentage of applications are successful. However, in 1996, 7132 patents were granted in the UK. This should be compared with 27 143 applications made and 11 452 applications published in the same year, bearing in mind that the grant will relate to applications made prior to 1996. At least these figures do give a rough comparison.

### Example patent application and specification

There follows a reproduction of a patent application made to the United Kingdom Patent Office (No. GB 2183592A). This is reproduced by permission of Guinness Brewing Worldwide Ltd and their patent attorneys, Urquhart-Dykes & Lord. The application should be studied in the light of the description of the constituent parts of a patent specification given earlier in this chapter. The format of the specification and the high standard of draftsmanship particularly should be noted.

## (12) **UK Patent Application** (19) **GB** (11) **2 183 592** (13) **A**

(43) Application published **10 Jun 1987**

(21) Application No **8529441**

(22) Date of filing **29 Nov 1985**

(71) Applicant
**Arthur Guinness Son & Company (Dublin) Limited,**

**(Incorporated in Irish Republic),**

**St. James's Gate, Dublin 8, Republic of Ireland**

(72) Inventors
**Alan James Forage,**
**William John Byrne**

(74) Agent and/or Address for Service
**Urquhart-Dykes & Lord, 47 Marylebone Lane, London W1M 6DL**

(51) INT CL⁴
**B65D 25/00 5/40**

(52) Domestic classification (Edition I)
**B8D** 12 13 19 7C 7G 7M 7P1 7PY SC1
**B8P** AX
**U1S** 1106 1110 1111 B8D B8P

(56) Documents cited
**GB 1266351**

(58) Field of search
**B8D**
**B8P**
**Selected US specifications from IPC sub-class B65D**

(54) **Carbonated beverage container**

(57) A container for a beverage having gas (preferably at least one of carbon dioxide and inert (nitrogen) gases) in solution consists of a non-resealable container 1 within which is located a hollow secondary chamber 4, eg a polypropylene envelope, having a restricted aperture 7 in a side wall. The container is charged with the beverage 8 and sealed. Beverage from the main chamber of the container enters the chamber 4 (shown at 8*a*) by way of the aperture 7 to provide headspaces 1*a* in the container and 4*a* in the pod 4. Gas within the headspaces 1*a* and 4*a* is at greater than atmospheric pressure. Preferably the beverage is drawn into the chamber 4 by subjecting the package to a heating and cooling cycle. Upon opening the container 1, eg by draw ring/region 13, the headspace 1*a* is vented to atmosphere and the pressure differential resulting from the pressure in the chamber headspace 4*a* causes gas/beverage to be ejected from the chamber 4 (by way of the aperture 7) into the beverage 8. Said ejection causes gas to be evolved from solution in the beverage in the main container chamber to form a head of froth on the beverage. The chamber 4 is preferably formed by blow moulding and located below beverage level by weighting it or as a press fit within the container 1 by lugs 6 engaging the container walls, the container being preferably a can, carton or bottle. The chamber 4 may initially be filled with gas, eg nitrogen, at or slightly above atmospheric pressure, the orifice being formed by laser boring, drilling or punching immediately prior to locating the chamber 4 in the container 1.

The drawings originally filed were informal and the print here reproduced is taken from a later filed formal copy.

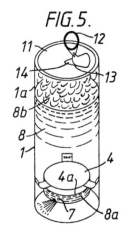

FIG. 5.

Reference to UK Patent Application 2,183,592A is made with kind permission of Guinness Brewing Worldwide Limited and their Patent Attorneys, Urquhart-Dykes & Lord.

29 NOV 8529441

1/2                                    2183592

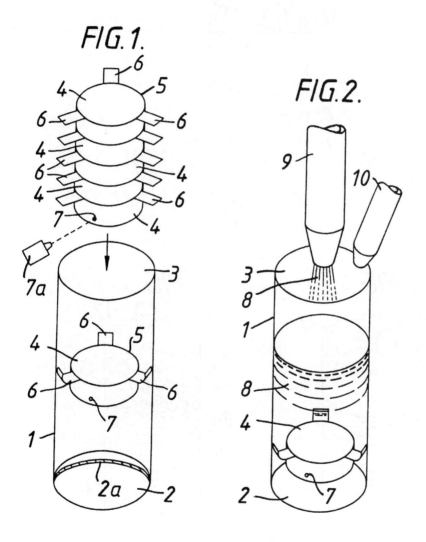

FIG. 1.

FIG. 2.

29   Nov 85 29441

2/2                              2183592

## FIG. 3.

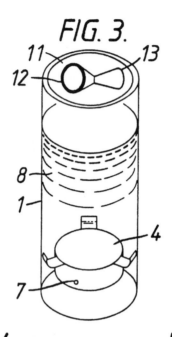

## FIG. 4.                    FIG. 5.

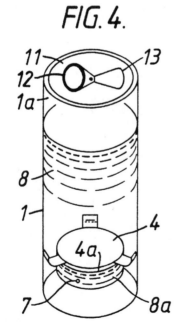      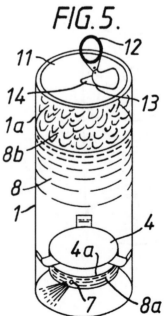

SPECIFICATION

## A beverage package and a method of packaging a beverage containing gas in solution

*Technical field and background art*

This invention relates to a beverage package and a method of packaging a beverage containing gas in solution. The invention more particularly concerns beverages containing gas in solution and packaged in a sealed, non-resealable, container which, when opened for dispensing or consumption, permits gas to be evolved or liberated from the beverage to form, or assist in the formation of, a head or froth on the beverage. The beverages to which the invention relates may be alcoholic or non-alcoholic; primarily the invention was developed for fermented beverages such as beer, stout, ale, lager and cider but may be applied with advantage to so-called soft drinks and beverages (for example fruit juices, squashes, colas, lemonades, milk and milk based drinks and similar type drinks) and to alcoholic drinks (for example spirits, liquers, wine or wine based drinks and similar).

It is recognised in the beverage dispensing and packaging art that the characteristics of the head of froth which is provided on the beverage by the liberation of gas from the beverage immediately prior to consumption are an important consideration to the consumers enjoyment of the product and are therefore of commercial importance. Conventionally beverages of the type discussed above containing gas in solution and packaged in a non-resealable container (such as a can, bottle or carton) provide a headspace in the container within which gas is maintained under pressure. Upon opening of the package, the headspace gas is vented to atmosphere and the beverage is usually poured into a drinking vessel. During such dispensing of the beverage it is usual for gas in solution to be liberated to create the froth or head. It is generally recognised that when dispensing a beverage as aforementioned, the gas is liberated as a result of the movement of the beverage over a surface having so-called gas nucleation or active sites which may be the wall of the drinking vessel into which the beverage is poured. There is therefore a distinct possibility with conventional beverage packages that upon opening of the container after storage and until the beverage is poured therefrom, the beverage will have little or no froth or head - such a headless beverage is usually regarded by the consumer as somewhat unattractive and unappealing especially where the beverage is to be drunk directly from the container. Admittedly it may be possible to develop a head or froth within the container by agitating or shaking the package (so that the movement of the beverage over the interior surface of the container causes the liberation of the gas in solution) but this is clearly inconvenient once the container is opened and is inadvisable if the package is shaken immediately prior to opening as the contents tend to spray or spurt on opening.

There is therefore a need for a beverage package and a method of packaging a beverage containing gas in solution by which the beverage is packaged in a non-resealable container so that when the container is opened gas is liberated from the beverage to form or assist in the formation of a head or froth without the necessity of an external influence being applied to the package; it is an object of the present invention to satisfy this need in a simple, economic and commercially viable manner.

*Statements of invention and advantages*

According to the present invention there is provided a beverage package comprising a sealed, non-resealable, container having a primary chamber containing beverage having gas in solution therewith and forming a primary headspace comprising gas at a pressure greater than atmospheric; a secondary chamber having a volume less than said primary chamber and which communicates with the beverage in said primary chamber through a restricted orifice, said secondary chamber containing beverage derived from the primary chamber and having a secondary headspace therein comprising gas at a pressure greater than atmospheric so that the pressures within the primary and secondary chambers are substantially at equilibrium, and wherein said package is openable, to open the primary headspace to atmospheric pressure and the secondary chamber is arranged so that on said opening the pressure differential caused by the decrease in pressure at the primary headspace causes at least one of the beverage and gas in the secondary chamber to be ejected by way of the restricted orifice into the beverage of the primary chamber and said ejection causes gas in the solution to be evolved and form, or assist in the formation of, a head of froth on the beverage.

Further according to the present invention there is provided a method of packaging a beverage having gas in solution therewith which comprises providing a container with a primary chamber and a secondary chamber of which the volume of the secondary chamber is less than that of the primary chamber and with a restricted orifice through which the secondary chamber communicates with the primary chamber, and charging and sealing the primary chamber with the beverage to contain the gas in solution and to form a primary headspace in the primary chamber, and charging the secondary chamber with beverage derived from the primary chamber by way of said restricted orifice to form a secondary headspace in the secondary chamber whereby the pressures in both the primary and secondary chambers are at equilibrium and gaseous pressures in both the primary and secondary headspaces are at a pressure greater than atmospheric so that, when the container is broached to open the primary headspace to atmospheric pressure, the pressure differential caused by the decrease in pressure at the primary headspace causes at least one of the beverage and gas in the secondary chamber to be ejected into the beverage of the primary chamber by way of said restricted orifice and the said ejection causes gas to be evolved from solution in the beverage in the primary chamber to form, or assist in the formation of, a head of froth on the beverage.

The present invention is applicable to a wide range of beverages of the type as previously discussed and where those beverages contain gas in solution which gas is intended to be liberated to form or assist in the formation of the head or froth on the beverage. Understandably the gas in solution must not detract

5 from, and should preferably enhance the characteristics required of the beverage and be acceptable for use with food products; preferably therefore the gas is at least one of carbon dioxide and inert gases (by which latter term is included nitrogen)

10 although it is to be realised that other gases may be appropriate.

The present invention was primarily developed for the packaging of fermented beverages such as beer, ale, stout, lager and cider where among the desirable

15 qualities sought in a head are a consistent and regular, relatively fine, bubble size; a bubble structure which is substantially homogeneous so that the head is not formed with large irregularly shaped and random gaps; the ability for the head or bubble

20 structure to endure during a reasonable period over which it is likely to be consumed, and a so-called "mouth-feel" and flavour whcih may improve the enjoyment of the beverage during consumption and not detract from the desirable flavour characteristics

25 required of the beverage. These desirable qualities are of course equally applicable to non-fermented beverages, for example with so-called soft drinks. Conventionally, beverages of the type to which the invention relates are packaged in a non-resealable

30 container which when opened totally vents the headspace to atmosphere, contain carbon dioxide in solution and it is the liberation of the carbon dioxide on opening of the package and dispensing of the beverage into a drinking vessel which creates the froth or

35 head; however, the head so formed has very few of the aforementioned desirable qualities - in particular it is usually irregular, lacks homogeneity and has very little endurance so that there is a tendency for it to collapse after a short period. It has been known for

40 approximately 25 years and as discussed in our G.B. Patent No. 876,628, that beverages having in solution a mixture of carbon dioxide gas and inert gas (such as nitrogen or argon) will, when dispensed in a manner whereby the mixed gases are caused to

45 evolve to develop the head or foam from small bubbles containing the mixture of carbon dioxide and, say, nitrogen gases, provide the desirable qualities for the head as previously discussed. Commericially the formation of the head by the use of mixed

50 gases as aforementioned has been widely employed in the dispensing of beverage in a draught system and on demand from a bulk container (such as a keg or barrel) where the gases are caused to evolve by subjecting the beverage to intense shear forces in

55 passing it under pressure through a set of small holes. Beverages, particularly stout, having a mixture of carbon dioxide and nitrogen gases in solution and dispensed in draught using the aforementioned technique have met with considerable commercial

60 success and it was soon realised that there was a need to make available for consumption a similar beverage derived from a small non-resealable container suitable for shelf storage and retail purposes.

Research has indicated that to achieve the initia-

65 tion of a head on a beverage containing carbon

dioxide and inert gas such as nitrogen in solution it is necessary to provide so-called "active sites" which are regions where the beverage is subjected to a high local strain (such a strain being higher than the

70 cohesive force of the beverage). In these conditions the beverage prefers to generate a bubble of mixed gases instead of "bending around" the active site. It was found that an active site could be solid, liquid or gas such as granules, restrictor holes, rapid streams

75 of liquid or bubbles and the like. It was also found that ultrasonics could produce a "ghost" active site by the formation of extreme pressure gradients. There has however been a problem in providing an "active site" in a beverage packaged in a non-

80 resealable small container in a manner which is commercially and economically acceptable. During the past 25 years considerable expenditure has been devoted to research and development in an attempt to overcome the aforementioned problem. For ex-

85 ample, our G.B. Patent No. 1,588,624 proposes initiating the evolution of mixed carbon dioxide and nitrogen gases from a beverage by subjecting the beverage to ultrasonic excitement, by injecting a gas, liquid and/or foam into the beverage by use of a

90 syringe-type device, or by pouring the beverage over an excitation surface such as polystyrene granules. Although these latter proposals were successful in achieving the desired head formation, the necessity to use ancilliary apparatus had commercial dis-

95 advantages (for example, it is unreasonable to expect a retail customer to have available an ultrasonic signal generator; also the steps required to effect initiation of the head following opening of the beverage package involved an inconvenient discipline and

100 time factor). In a further example our G.B. Patent No. 1,266,351 relates to a non-resealable package containing beverage having mixed carbon dioxide and inert gases in solution; in this disclosure a can or bottle has two chambers of which a larger chamber

105 contains the beverage while the smaller chamber is charged under pressure with the mixed gases. On opening of the can or bottle to expose the larger chamber to atmosphere, its internal pressure falls to atmospheric permitting the pressurised gas in the

110 small chamber to jet into the beverage by way of a small orifice between the two chambers. This jet of gas provides sufficient energy to initiate the formation of minute bubbles and thereby the head from the evolution of the mixed gases in the beverage

115 coming out of solution. By this proposal the small gas chamber is initially pressurised with the mixed gases to a pressure greater than atmospheric and from a source remote from the beverage; as a consequence it was found necessary, particularly in the

120 case of cans, to provide a special design of two chambered container and an appropriate means for sealing the smaller chamber following the charging of that chamber with the mixed gases (such charging usually being effected, in the case of cans, by injec-

125 ting the mixed gases into the small chamber through a wall of the can which then had to be sealed). Because of the inconvenience and high costs involved in the development of an appropriate two chambered container and the special facilities required for

130 charging the mixed gases and sealing the container,

the proposal proved commercially unacceptable.

The container employed in the present invention will usually be in the form of a can, bottle or carton capable of withstanding the internal pressures of the
5 primary and secondary chambers and of a size suitable for conventional shelf storage by the retail trade so that, the overall volume of the container may be, typically, 0.5 litres but is unlikely to be greater than 3 litres.

10 By the present invention a two chambered container is employed as broadly proposed in G.B. Patent No. 1,266,351; however, unlike the prior proposal the secondary chamber is partly filled with beverage containing gases in solution and the bever-
15 age in the secondary chamber is derived wholly from the beverage in the primary chamber so that when the contents of the primary and secondary chambers are in equilibrium (and the primary and secondary headspaces are at a pressure greater than atmosphe-
20 ric) immediately prior to broaching the container to open the primary headspace to atmosphere, the pressure differential between that in the secondary headspace and atmospheric pressure causes at least one of the beverage and the headspace gas in the
25 secondary chamber to be ejected by way of the restricted orifice into the beverage in the primary chamber to promote the formation of the head of froth without the necessity of any external influence being applied to the package. The pressurisation of
30 the headspace gas in the secondary chamber is intended to result from the evolution of gas in the sealed container as the contents of the container come into equilibrium at ambient or dispensing temperature (which should be greater than the tem-
35 perature at which the container is charged and sealed). Consequently the present invention alleviates the necessity for pressurising the secondary chamber from a source externally of the container so that the secondary chamber can be formed as a
40 simple envelope or hollow pod of any convenient shape (such as cylindrical or spherical) which is located as a discrete insert within a conventional form of can, bottle or carton (thereby alleviating the requirement for a special structure of can or bottle as
45 envisaged in G.B. Patent No. 1,266,351).

Although the head or froth formed by pouring wholly carbonated beverages tends to lack many of the desirable qualities required of a head as previously discussed; our tests have indicated that by
50 use of the present invention with wholly carbonated beverages (where the head is formed by injection of gas or beverage from the secondary chamber into the primary chamber) the resultant head is considerably tighter or denser than that achieved solely by
55 pouring and as such will normally have a greater life expectancy.

The beverage is preferably saturated or supersaturated with the gas (especially if mixed carbon dioxide and inert gases are employed) and the
60 primary chamber charged with the beverage under a counterpressure and at a low temperature (to alleviate gas losses and, say, at a slightly higher temperature than that at which the beverage freezes) so that when the container is sealed (which may be
65 achieved under atmospheric pressure using con-

ventional systems such as a canning or bottling line), the pressurisation of the primary and secondary headspaces is achieved by the evolution of gas from the beverage within the primary and secondary
70 chambers as the package is handled or stored at an ambient or dispensing temperature (greater than the charging temperature) and the contents of the container adopt a state of equilibrium. As an optional but preferred feature of the present invention, following
75 the sealing of the container, the package may be subjected to a heating and cooling cycle, conveniently during pasteurisation of the beverage. During such a cycle the gas within the secondary chamber is caused to expand and eject into the primary
80 chamber; during subsequent cooling of the package, the gas in the secondary chamber contracts and creates a low pressure or vacuum effect relative to the pressure in the primary chamber so that beverage from the primary chamber is drawn into the sec-
85 ondary chamber by way of the restricted orifice. By use of this preferred technique it is possible to ensure that the secondary chamber is efficiently and adequately charged with beverage and has the desired secondary headspace.

90 The restricted orifice through which the primary and secondary chambers communicate is conveniently formed by a single aperture in a side wall of the secondary chamber and such an aperture should have a size which is sufficiently great to alleviate
95 "clogging" or its obturation by particles which may normally be expected to occur within the beverage and yet be restricted in its dimensions to ensure that there is an adequate jetting effect in the ejection of the gas and/or beverage therethrough from the sec-
100 ondary chamber into the primary chamber to promote the head formation upon opening of the container. The restricted orifice may be of any profile (such as a slit or a star shape) but will usually be circular; experiments have indicated that a restricted
105 orifice having a diameter in the range of 0.02 to 0.25 centimeters is likely to be appropriate for fermented beverages (the preferred diameter being 0.061 centimetres). It is also preferred that when the package is positioned in an upstanding condition in which it is
110 likely to be transported, shelf stored or opened, the restricted orifice is located in an upwardly extending side wall or in a bottom wall of the secondary chamber and preferably at a position slightly spaced from the bottom of the primary chamber. It is also
115 preferred, particularly for fermented beverages, that when the contents of the sealed package are in equilibrium and the package is in an upstanding condition as aforementioned, the restricted orifice is located below the depth of the beverage in the
120 secondary chamber so that on opening of the container the pressure of gas in the secondary headspace initially ejects beverage from that chamber into the beverage in the primary chamber to promote the head formation. It is believed that such ejection
125 of beverage through the restricted orifice is likely to provide a greater efficiency in the development of the head in a liquid supersaturated with gas than will the ejection of gas alone through the restricted orifice; the reason for this is that the restricted orifice
130 provides a very active site which causes the bever-

age to "rip itself apart" generating extremely minute bubbles which themselves act as active sites for the beverage in the primary chamber, these extremely minute bubbles leave "vapour trails" of larger initia-
5 ted bubbles which in turn produce the head. Since the extremely minute bubbles are travelling at relatively high speed during their injection into the beverage in the primary chamber, they not only generate shear forces on the beverage in that chamber
10 but the effect of each such bubble is distributed over a volume of beverage much larger than the immediate surroundings of an otherwise stationary bubble.

A particular advantage of the present invention is
15 that prior to the container being charged with beverage both the primary and secondary chambers can be at atmospheric pressure and indeed may contain air. However, it is recognised that for many beverages, particularly a fermented beverage, prolonged
20 storage of the beverage in contact with air, especially oxygen, is undesirable as adversely affecting the characteristics of the beverage. To alleviate this possibility the secondary chamber may initially be filled with a "non-contaminant" gas such as nitrogen (or
25 other inert gas or carbon dioxide) which does not adversely affect the characteristics of the beverage during prolonged contact therewith. The secondary chamber may be filled with the non-contaminant gas at atmospheric pressure or slightly greater (to allev-
30 iate the inadvertent intake of air) so that when the container is charged with the beverage, the non-contaminant gas will form part of the pressurised headspace in the secondary chamber. As previously mentioned, the secondary chamber may be formed
35 by an envelope or hollow pod which is located as a discrete insert within a conventional form of can, bottle or carton and such a discrete insert permits the secondary chamber to be filled with the non-contaminant gas prior to the envelope or pod being
40 located within the can, bottle or carton. A convenient means of achieving this latter effect is by blow moulding the envelope or pod in a food grade plastics material using the non-contaminant gas as the blowing medium and thereafter sealing the envelope
45 or pod to retain the non-contaminant gas therein; immediately prior to the pod or envelope being inserted into the can, bottle or carton, the restricted orifice can be formed in a side wall of the pod or envelope (for example, by laser boring). Immediately
50 prior to the container being sealed it is also preferable to remove air from the primary headspace and this may be achieved using conventional techniques such as filling the headspace with froth or fob developed from a source remote from the container and
55 having characteristics similar to those of the head which is to be formed from the beverage in the container; charging the primary chamber with the beverage in a nitrogen or other inert gas atmosphere so that the headspace is filled with that inert gas or nit-
60 rogen; dosing the headspace with liquid nitrogen so that the gas evolved therefrom expels the air from the headspace, or by use of undercover gassing or water jetting techniques to exclude air.

Although the secondary chamber may be con-
65 structed as an integral part of the container, for the

reasons discussed above and also convenience of manufacture, it is preferred that the secondary chamber is formed as a discrete insert which is simply deposited or pushed into a conventional form
70 of can, bottle or carton. With cans or cartons such an insert will not be visible to the end user and many bottled beverages are traditionally marketed in dark coloured glass or plastics so that the insert is unlikely to adversely affect the aesthetics of the package. The
75 discrete insert may be suspended or float in the beverage in the primary chamber provided that the restricted orifice is maintained below the surface of the beverage in the primary chamber on opening of the container; for example the insert may be loaded or
80 weighted to appropriately orientate the position of the restricted orifice. Desirably however the insert is restrained from displacement within the outer container of the package and may be retained in position, for example at the bottom of the outer con-
85 tainer, by an appropriate adhesive or by mechanical means such as projections on the package which may flex to abut and grip a side wall of the outer container or which may engage beneath an internal abutment on the side wall of the outer container.
90

## Drawings

One embodiment of the present invention as applied to the packaging of a fermented beverage such as stout in a can will now be described, by way of
95 example only, with reference to the accompanying illustrative drawings, in which:-

*Figures 1 to 4* diagrammatically illustrate the progressive stages in the formation of the beverage package in a canning line, and
100 *Figure 5* diagrammatically illustrates the effect on opening the beverage package prior to consumption of the beverage and the development of the head of froth on the beverage.

105 ## Detailed description of drawings

The present embodiment will be considered in relation to the preparation of a sealed can containing stout having in solution a mixture of nitrogen and carbon dioxide gases, the former preferably being
110 present to the extent of at least 1.5% vols/vol and typically in the range 1.5% to 3.5% vols/vol and the carbon dioxide being present at a considerably lower level than the amount of carbon dioxide which would normally be present in conventional, wholly car-
115 bonated, bottled or canned stout and typically in the range 0.8 to 1.8 vols/vol (1.46 to 3.29 grams/litre). For the avoidance of doubt, a definition of the term "vols/vol" is to be found in our G.B. Patent No. 1,588,624.

The stout is to be packaged in a conventional form
120 of cylindrical can (typically of aluminium alloy) which, in the present example, will be regarded as having a capacity of 500 millilitres and by use of a conventional form of filling and canning line appropriately modified as will hereinafter be described.
125 A cylindrical shell for the can 1 having a sealed base 2 and an open top 3 is passed in an upstanding condition along the line to a station shown in Figure 1 to present its open top beneath a stack of hollow pods 4. Each pod 4 is moulded in a food grade plastics
130 material such as polypropylene to have a short (say 5

millimetres) hollow cylindrical housing part 5 and a circumferentially spaced array of radially outwardly extending flexible tabs or lugs 6. The pods 4 are placed in the stack with the chamber formed by the
5  housing part 5 sealed and containing nitrogen gas at atmospheric pressure (or at pressure slightly above atmospheric); conveniently this is achieved by blow moulding the housing part 5 using nitrogen gas. The volume within the housing part 5 is approximately 15
10  millilitres. At the station shown in Figure 1 the bottom pod 4 of the stack is displaced by suitable means (not shown) into the open topped can 1 as shown. However, immediately prior to the pod 4 being moved into the can 1 a small (restricted) hole 7
15  is bored in the cylindrical side wall of the housing part 5. In the present example, the hole 7 has a diameter in the order of 0.61 millimetres and is conveniently bored by a laser beam generated by device 7a (although the hole could be formed by punching or
20  drilling). The hole 7 is located towards the bottom of the cylindrical chamber within the housing part 5. Since the hollow pod 4 contains nitrogen gas at atmospheric pressure (or slightly higher) it is unlikely that air will enter the hollow pod through the
25  hole 7 during the period between boring the hole 7 and charging of the can 1 with stout (thereby alleviating contamination of the stout by an oxygen content within the hollow pod 4).
    The hollow pod 4 is pressed into the can 1 to be
30  seated on the base 2. Conventional cans 1 have a domed base 2 (shown by the section 2a) which presents a convex internal face so that when the pod 4 abuts this face a clearance is provided between the hole 7 and the underlying bottom of the chamber
35  within the can 1. It will be seen from Figure 1 that the diameter of the housing part 5 of the pod 4 is less than the internal diameter of the can 1 while the diameter of the outermost edges of the lugs 6 is greater than the diameter of the can 1 so that as the pod 4 is
40  pressed downwardly into the can, the lugs 6 abut the side wall of the can and flex upwardly as shown to grip the can side wall and thereby restrain the hollow pod from displacement away from the base 2.
    The open topped can with its pod 4 is now displa-
45  ced along the canning line to the station shown in Figure 2 where the can is charged with approximately 440 millilitres of stout 8 from an appropriate source 9. The stout 8 is supersaturated with the mixed carbon dioxide and nitrogen gases, typic-
50  ally the carbon dioxide gas being present at 1.5 vols/vol (2.74 grams/litre) and the nitrogen gas being present at 2% vols/vol. The charging of the can 1 with the stout may be achieved in conventional manner, that is under a counterpressure and at a temperature of
55  approximately 0°C. When the can 1 is charged with the appropriate quantity of stout 8, the headspace above the stout is purged of air, for example by use of liquid nitrogen dosing or with nitrogen gas delivered by means indicated at 10 to alleviate contamina-
60  tion of the stout from oxygen in the headspace.
    Following charging of the can 1 with stout and purging of the headspace, the can moves to the station shown in Figure 3 where the can is closed and sealed under atmospheric pressure and in conventional manner
65  by a lid 11 seamed to the cylindrical side wall of the

can. The lid 11 has a pull-ring 12 attached to a weakened tear-out region 13 by which the can is intended to be broached in conventional manner for dispensing of the contents.
70      Following sealing, the packaged stout is subjected to a pasteurisation process whereby the package is heated to approximately 60°C for 15-20 minutes and is thereafter cooled to ambient temperature. During this process the nitrogen gas in the hollow pod 4a
75  initially expands and a proportion of that gas passes by way of the hole 7 into the stout 8 in the main chamber of the can. During cooling of the package in the pasteurisation cycle, the nitrogen gas in the hollow pod 4 contracts to create a vacuum effect
80  within the hollow pod causing stout 8 to be drawn, by way of the hole 7, from the chamber of the can into the chamber of the pod so that when the package is at ambient temperature the hole 7 is located below the depth of stout 8a within the hollow
85  pod 4.
    Following the pasteurisation process the contents of the can 1 will stabilise in a condition of equilibrium with a headspace 1a over the stout 8 in the primary chamber of the can and a headspace 4a over the
90  stout 8a in the secondary chamber formed by the hollow pod 4 and in the equilibrium condition. With the sealed can at ambient temperature (or a typical storage or dispensing temperature which may be, say, 8°C) the pressure of mixed gases carbon dioxide
95  and nitrogen (which largely results from the evolution of such gases from the stout) is substantially the same in the headspaces 1a and 4a and this pressure will be greater than atmospheric pressure, typically in the order of 25lbs per square inch (1.72
100  bars).
    The package in the condition shown in Figure 4 is typically that which would be made available for storage and retail purposes. During handling it is realised that the package may be tipped from its up-
105  right condition; in practice however this is unlikely to adversely affect the contents of the hollow pod 4 because of the condition of equilibrium within the can.
    When the stout is to be made available for consumption, the can 1 is opened by ripping out the re-
110  gion 13 with the pull-ring 12. On broaching the lid 11 as indicated at 14 the headspace 1a rapidly depressurises to atmospheric pressure. As a consequence the pressure within the headspace 4a of the secondary chamber in the pod 4 exceeds that in the
115  headspace 1a and causes stout 8a in the hollow pod to be ejected by way of the hole 7 into the stout 8 in the primary chamber of the can. The restrictor hole 7 acts as a very "active site" to the supersaturated stout 8a which passes therethrough to be injected
120  into the stout 8 and that stout is effectively "ripped apart" to generate extremely minute bubbles which themselves act as active sites for the stout 8 into which they are injected. These minute bubbles leave "vapour trails" of larger initiated bubbles which dev-
125  elop within the headspace 1a a head 8b having the previously discussed desirable characteristics.
    It is appreciated that the headspace 1a occupies a larger proportion of the volume of the can 1 than that which would normally be expected in a 500 millilitre
130  capacity can; the reason for this is to ensure that

there is adequate volume in the headspace 1a for the head of froth 8b to develop efficiently in the event, for example, that the stout is to be consumed directly from the can when the tear-out region 13 is removed.
5  Normally however the stout 8 will first be poured from the can into an open topped drinking vessel prior to consumption but this pouring should not adversely affect the desirable characteristics of the head of froth which will eventually be presented in
10  the drinking vessel.

In the aforegoing embodiment the can 1 is charged with stout 8 (from the source 9) having in solution the required respective volumes of the carbon dioxide and the nitrogen gases. In a modification the can 1 is
15  charged with stout (from source 9) having the carbon dioxide gas only in solution to the required volume; the 2% vols/vol nitrogen gas necessary to achieve the required solution of mixed gas in the packaged stout is derived from the liquid nitrogen dosing of
20  the headspace in the can.

CLAIMS

1.  A beverage package comprising a sealed, non-
25  resealable, container having a primary chamber containing beverage having gas in solution therewith and forming a primary headspace comprising gas at a pressure greater than atmospheric; a secondary chamber having a volume less than said primary
30  chamber and which communicates with the beverage in said primary chamber through a restricted orifice, said secondary chamber containing beverage derived from the primary chamber and having a secondary headspace therein comprising gas at a pres-
35  sure greater than atmospheric so that the pressure within the primary and secondary chambers are substantially at equilibrium, and wherein said package is openable, to open the primary headspace to atmospheric pressure and the secondary chamber is arran-
40  ged so that on said opening the pressure differential caused by the decrease in pressure at the primary headspace causes at least one of the beverage and gas in the secondary chamber to be ejected by way of the restricted orifice into the beverage of the primary
45  chamber and said ejection causes gas in the solution to be evolved and form, or assist in the formation of, a head of froth on the beverage.

2.  A package as claimed in claim 1 in which the container has a normal upstanding condition with an
50  openable top and said secondary chamber has an upwardly extending side wall or a bottom wall within which said restricted orifice is located.

3.  A packaged as claimed in either claim 1 or claim 2 in which with the pressures within the
55  primary and secondary chambers substantially at equilibrium the restricted orifice is located below the depth of the beverage within the secondary chamber.

4.  A package as claimed in any one of the preced-
60  ing claims wherein the secondary chamber comprises a hollow and discrete insert within the container.

5.  A package as claimed in claim 4 in which the insert floats or is suspended in the beverage in the
65  primary chamber and means is provided for locating the restricted orifice below the surface of the beverage in the primary chamber.

6.  A package as claimed in claim 5 in which the insert is weighted or loaded to locate the restricted
70  orifice below the surface of the beverage in the primary chamber.

7.  A package as claimed in claim 4 wherein means is provided for retaining the insert at a predetermined position within the container.
75  8.  A package as claimed in claim 7 wherein the container has a normal upstanding condition with an openable top and said insert is located at or towards the bottom of said container.

9.  A package as claimed in either claim 7 or claim
80  8 wherein the insert comprises a hollow pod or envelope having means thereon for retaining it in position within the container.

10.  A package as claimed in claim 9 wherein the retaining means comprise flexible tab means which
85  engage a side wall of the container to retain the insert.

11.  A package as claimed in any one of claims 4 to 10 wherein the insert comprises a hollow moulding.

12.  A package as claimed in claim 11 when
90  appendant to claim 10 in which the container has a side wall and the moulding is substantially cylindrical with radially extending tabs engaging the wall of the container.

13.  A package as claimed in any one of claims 4 to
95  12 in which the container has a base on which the insert is located and said restricted orifice is located in an upwardly extending side wall of the insert spaced from said base.

14.  A package as claimed in any one of the pre-
100  ceding claims in which the beverage has in solution therewith at least one of carbon dioxide gas and inert gas (which latter term includes nitrogen).

15.  A package as claimed in claim 14 in which the beverage is saturated or supersaturated with said
105  gas or gases.

16.  A package as claimed in any one of the preceding claims in which the container is in the form of a can, bottle or carton.

17.  A package as claimed in any one of the pre-
110  ceding claims in which the restricted orifice comprises a circular aperture having a diameter in the range of 0.02 to 0.25 centimetres.

18.  A package as claimed in any one of the preceding claims and comprising a fermented beverage
115  having in solution therewith carbon dioxide in the range 0.8 to 1.8 vols/vol (1.46 to 3.29 grams/litre) and nitrogen in the range 1.5% to 3.5% vols/vol.

19.  A beverage package substantially as herein described with reference to the accompanying illust-
120  rative drawings.

20.  A method of packaging a beverage having gas in solution therewith which comprises providing a container with a primary chamber and a secondary chamber of which the volume of the secondary
125  chamber is less than that of the primary chamber and with a restricted orifice through which the secondary chamber communicates with the primary chamber, and charging and sealing the primary chamber with the beverage to contain the gas in solution and to
130  form a primary headspace in the primary chamber,

and charging the secondary chamber with beverage derived from the primary chamber by way of said restricted orifice to form a secondary headspace in the secondary chamber whereby the pressures in both
5 the primary and secondary chambers are at equilibrium and gaseous pressures in both the primary and secondary headspaces are at a pressure greater than atmospheric so that, when the container is broached to open the primary headspace to atmos-
10 pheric pressure, the pressure differential caused by the decrease in pressure at the primary headspace causes at least one of the beverage and gas in the secondary chamber to be ejected into the beverage of the primary chamber by way of said restricted ori-
15 fice and the said ejection causes gas to be evolved from solution in the beverage in the primary chamber to form, or assist in the formation of, a head of froth on the beverage.

21. A method as claimed in claim 20 which com-
20 prises subjecting the sealed container to a heating and cooling cycle whereby gas within the secondary chamber is caused to expand and eject by way of the restricted orifice into the primary chamber and subsequently to contract and create a low pressure ef-
25 fect in the secondary chamber relative to the primary chamber to draw beverage from the primary chamber into the secondary chamber by way of said restricted orifice.

22. A method as claimed in claim 21 in which the
30 heating and cooling cycle comprises pasteurisation of the beverage.

23. A method as claimed in any one of claims 20 to 22 in which the container has an upstanding condition with an openable top and which comprises
35 locating the restricted orifice within an upwardly extending side wall or bottom wall of the secondary chamber.

24. A method as claimed in any one of claims 20 to 23 which comprises charging the secondary
40 chamber with beverage from the primary chamber to the extent that the restricted orifice is located below the depth of beverage in the secondary chamber.

25. A method as claimed in any one of claims 20
45 to 23 which comprises forming the secondary chamber by a discrete hollow insert located within the primary chamber of the container.

26. A method as claimed in claim 25 in which the hollow insert is to float or be suspended in the bever-
50 age in the primary chamber and which comprises loading or weighting the insert to locate the restricted orifice below the surface of the beverage in the primary chamber.

27. A method as claimed in claim 25 which com-
55 prises retaining the insert at a predetermined position within the container.

28. A method as claimed in any one of claims 25 to 27 which comprises forming the hollow insert having the restricted orifice in a wall thereof and loc-
60 ating the insert within the primary chamber prior to the charging and sealing of the primary chamber.

29. A method as claimed in any one of claims 25 to 28 which comprises forming the hollow insert by blow moulding.
65 30. A method as claimed in claim 29 which com-

prises blow moulding the hollow insert with gas for dissolution in the beverage so that said gas is sealed within the secondary chamber, and forming said restricted orifice in the wall of the insert immediately
70 prior to locating the insert in the primary chamber.

31. A method as claimed in claim 30 which comprises sealing said gas in the secondary chamber at atmospheric pressure or at a pressure slightly greater than atmospheric.
75 32. A method as claimed in any one of claims 25 to 31 which comprises forming the restricted orifice in the hollow insert by laser boring, drilling or punching.

33. A method as claimed in any one of claims 25
80 to 32 in which, prior to it being sealed, the container has an upstanding condition with an open top through which the primary chamber is charged with beverage and which comprises locating the insert through said open top to provide the secondary
85 chamber within the container.

34. A method as claimed in claim 33 when appendant to claim 27 which comprises press fitting the insert within the container so that during its location the insert engages with a side wall of the container to
90 be retained in position.

35. A method as claimed in any one of claims 20 to 34 which comprises, prior to sealing the primary chamber, purging the primary head space to exclude air.
95 36. A method as claimed in any one of claims 20 to 35 in which the gas comprises at least one of carbon dioxide gas and inert gas (which latter term includes nitrogen).

37. A method as claimed in claim 36 in which the
100 beverage is fermented and has in solution carbon dioxide in the range 0.8 to 1.8 vols/vol (1.46 to 3.29 grams/litre) and nitrogen in the range 1.5% to 3.5% vols/vol.

38. A method of packaging a beverage as
105 claimed in claim 20 and substantially as herein described.

39. A beverage when packaged by the method as claimed in any one of claims 20 to 38.

110 _____

Printed for Her Majesty's Stationery Office by
Croydon Printing Company (UK) Ltd, 4/87, D8991685.
Published by The Patent Office, 25 Southampton Buildings, London, WC2A 1AY,
from which copies may be obtained.

# 13

## Requirements for patentability and ownership of patents

### INTRODUCTION

The long title to the Patents Act 1977 includes the aim of giving effect to certain international conventions on patents. The influence of the European Patent Convention, signed in Munich in 1973, is evident in the basic requirement for patentability. Article 52(1) of the European Patent Convention states that:

> European patents shall be granted for any new inventions which are susceptible of industrial application, which are new and which involve an inventive step.

The Patents Act 1977 s 1(1) requires the following conditions to be satisfied for a patent to be granted for an invention:

(a)  the invention is new;
(b)  it involves an inventive step;
(c)  it is capable of industrial application; and
(d)  the grant of a patent for it is not excluded by subsections (2) and (3) below.

The similarities are even more pronounced when the exceptions in s 1(2) and (3) are compared to the equivalent provisions in the European Patent Convention. Because of the influence of the European Patent Convention on United Kingdom patent law, where appropriate, references will be made to the Convention and to judgments of the boards of appeal of the European Patent Office in Munich. The judgments are of persuasive authority and will normally be followed by UK judges.[1] Congruity in the international development of patent law is seen as being of great importance. Indeed, the Patents Act 1977 s 130(7) states that a number of important provisions of the Act are declared to have, as nearly as practicable, the same effect in the UK as the corresponding provisions of the European Patent Convention, the Community Patent Convention and the Patent Co-operation Treaty.[2] In a case prior to the 1977 Act, Lord Parker LCJ said, in terms of Australian and New Zealand decisions:

> Finally one cannot shut from one's mind the desirability of having a homogeneous development of the law in all countries which have adopted our system of patent legislation. That desirability must result in a tendency of our Court to follow those decisions if it is possible to do so.[3]

In the light of the UK's membership of the European Patent Convention, the same sentiments must now hold in respect of decisions of the European Patent Office. The same holds true as regards the Patent Co-operation Treaty.

1 And sometimes distinguished!

2 Those provisions deal with, *inter alia*, patentability, infringement, burdens of proof and extent of invention.

3 *Swift's Application* [1962] RPC 37.

## BASIC REQUIREMENTS

The basic statement of the requirements for patentability, that is novelty, inventive step and industrial application, followed by the exclusions from patentability, provides a good framework in which to explore the legal consequences and meaning of these words and phrases. The first point which must be made, however, is that the Patents Act 1977 contains no definition of what an invention is. Either this is because those responsible for drafting the Act felt that the task was too daunting, or that a definition might be later seen as sterile and a fetter on the development of the law in tune with technological development. Another explanation was that they did not really know with any certainty. Many other common words from the world of technology cause similar problems, for example, 'computer' or 'computer program'. A dictionary definition of 'invention' might talk in terms of an imaginative design, or product or innovation or something produced for the first time. Schmookler gives a more rigorous definition and sub-divides inventions into process inventions and product inventions.[4] The former are new ways of producing something old and the latter are old ways of producing something new. Every invention can thus be considered to be a 'new combination of pre-existing knowledge which satisfies some want'.[5] On the other hand, innovation can be said to be the first use of an invention.[6] In practice, the lack of definition causes few problems because the basic requirements of novelty, inventive step and industrial application, as defined in the statute and as interpreted by the courts, in most cases produces an effective and practical explanation of 'invention' for the purposes of patent law. Nevertheless, there may be a number of occasions when the meaning of 'invention' may be important.

The word 'invention' may be equated, to some extent, with the requirement for industrial application. In *IBM/Card Reader*[7] the applicant had claimed a method of allowing any machine readable bank card or credit card to be used by any card-reading machine to carry out any transactions. The technical board of appeal of the European Patent Office held that the method was not patentable as the use of the word 'inventions' in Article 52 of the European Patent Convention required that the claimed subject matter had a technical character and, in principle, was industrially applicable. The card was, in effect, equivalent to an application form, and the method involved (the user presenting the card to the machine) was part of a business operation as such. The board further confirmed that the presence of technical means to carry out a business activity does not mean that the business activity has a technical character and therefore is an invention.

The scope and nature of the invention as claimed must be determined from the claims as interpreted by the description. This is made clear by s 125(1) and the protocol on Article 69 of the European Patent Convention (which concerns the interpretation of patent claims).[8]

Section 1 of the Act requires that there must be an invention, and the exclusions to patentability in s 1(2) and 1(3) of the Act do not limit things that are not inventions to the particular exclusions specified.[9] In *Genentech Inc's Patent*[10] Mustill LJ said (at 262):

> ... the question whether the claim discloses anything which can be described as an invention must be answered in the affirmative before compliance with paragraphs (a)–(d) becomes relevant [s 1(1)(a)–(d)].

4 This is, indeed, the approach taken by the Patents Act 1977. The distinction is quite clearly seen in s 60, on infringement. Unless otherwise stated, in this chapter, statutory references are to the Patents Act 1977.

5 Schmookler, J. (1986) *Invention and Economic Growth*, Harvard University Press, Chapter 1.

6 Dutton, H. I. (1984) *The Patent System and Inventive Activity During the Industrial Revolution 1750–1852*, Manchester University Press, at p. 9.

7 [1994] EPOR 89.

8 *Per* Hobhouse LJ in *Biogen Inc v Medeva plc* [1995] RPC 25 at 87, disapproving the suggestion of Aldous J that the invention was to be determined by the wording of the claim independently of the description in *Chiron Corp v Organon Teknika Ltd (No. 3)* [1994] FSR 202.

9 *See Lux Traffic Controls Ltd v Pike Signals Ltd* [1993] RPC 107, where it was held, *inter alia*, that the Patents Act 1977 s 1(2) comprised a non-exhaustive list of non-patentable things and a method of controlling traffic as such was not patentable.

10 [1989] RPC 147.

He went on to confirm that there will often be a substantial overlap between an objection on the basis that the thing claimed is not an invention and other objections, being lack of novelty, lack of inventive step, being incapable of industrial applications or excluded by s 1(2) and 1(3).

It is possible to apply for a single patent in relation to more than one invention if they are so linked as to form a single inventive concept.[11] This might be particularly relevant where the inventions concern a process and the product which results from putting the process into effect. In practice, this would normally cause little difficulty. However, if a claim is to a class of products, the claim might be invalid if some of the products cannot be made. In *May & Baker Ltd* v *Boots Pure Drug Co Ltd*[12] a claim to a class of 'sulpha-thiazole' products was amended to cover two specific products only as it was unlikely that all the class would have had the therapeutic properties claimed.

In *Biogen Inc* v *Medeva plc*[13] patents were granted in the European Patent Office (designating the UK and other countries) concerning a vaccine for Hepatitis B which had been genetically engineered. In an action for infringement, the defendant counterclaimed successfully for revocation on a number of grounds. The problem facing an applicant for a patent in respect of a range of products rather than a process was well stated by Hobhouse LJ (at 94):

> ... [the plaintiffs] could not make any claim to a process ... if they had invented a process, they could also have claimed a monopoly over anything produced by that process. But they could not do this and had simply to claim the invention of products independently of the process by which they were produced. They wished to make the claim as wide as possible.[14]

However, the difficulty for the applicant is to take care not to claim more products than would actually display the claimed properties. It is no use claiming a vast range of products hoping to be able to show, later, that some or all of them conform. The applicant has a choice and if he wishes to claim a wide range of products of a class he must make a sufficiently wide disclosure. If he cannot make the appropriate disclosure, he is trying to claim more than he is entitled to.

## Novelty

The invention must be new. It must not already have been available to the public. The question of novelty (whether the invention is new) has a special meaning assigned to it under the Patents Act 1977 s 2(1), which states that an invention is new if it 'does not form part of the state of the art'. Section 2(2) continues and describes the 'state of the art' as comprising all matter[15] made available to the public before the priority date of the invention whether by written or oral description, by use or in any other way.[16] This includes matter contained in other patent applications having an earlier priority date. Therefore, novelty is really a question of whether the invention has been 'anticipated', for example by a previous patent, or by publication or use. The anticipating patent, or publication could have occurred anywhere in the world as s 2(2) of the Act refers to public availability in 'the United Kingdom or elsewhere'. Whether publication in a limited circulation journal published in a remote part of South America would count is a moot point. Some sense of realism must be preserved and, under the 1949 Act, anticipatory matter did not include that which would not have been discovered during the course of a diligent search.[17]

---

11 The Patents Act 1977 s 14(5).

12 (1950) 67 RPC 23.

13 [1995] RPC 25.

14 For a criticism of this case and its apparent contradiction of the decision of the European Patent Office which found the patent valid, *see* Reid, B. C. 'Biogen in the EPO: The Advantage of Scientific Understanding' [1995] 2 EIPR 98. The House of Lords confirmed the Court of Appeal decision that the patent was invalid: [1997] RPC 1, discussed later in this chapter.

15 Whether a product, a process, information about either, or anything else (in other words, anything!).

16 The phrase 'made available to the public' was used in the definition of 'published' in the Patents Act 1949 s 101 and should be given the same meaning, *PLG Research Ltd* v *Ardon International Ltd* [1993] FSR 197. At least one member of the public should be free in law and equity to use it.

17 *General Tire & Rubber Co* v *Firestone Tyre & Rubber Co Ltd* [1972] RPC 457, *per* Sachs LJ. Section 130(1) defines 'published' as being made available to the public (in the UK or elsewhere) and a document shall be taken to be published if it can be inspected as of right at any place in the UK by members of the public, whether on payment of a fee or not.

The act or series of acts that make the invention available to the public do not have to be on a particularly wide scale. Using an invention in public in one locality only will suffice to anticipate a patent. In *Windsurfing International Inc v Tabur Marine (Great Britain) Ltd*,[18] the Court of Appeal held that a 12-year-old boy, who built a sailboard and used it in public for a few weekends at a caravan site at Hayling Island in Hampshire, had effectively anticipated a later patent for a sailboard which was declared invalid for want of novelty (and also because it lacked an inventive step).

Under s 2(3), the state of the art includes matter in other patent applications published on or after the priority date of the invention being tested against the state of the art, provided the priority dates of those other applications are earlier. Patent applications are published 18 months after their priority dates, unless withdrawn, and this provision simply includes in the state of the art all those unpublished applications that have an earlier priority date. Thus, it is possible for a patent application to be pre-empted by material that cannot, at the time of making the application, be discovered or inspected by the applicant.

Inventors may wish to demonstrate their invention to others, for example, to secure investment or to show to potential licensees. If such demonstrations are held before the priority date the inventor runs a grave risk of jeopardising his application by compromising the novelty of his invention. The inventor must be very careful not to disclose details of the invention, but it may be safe to allow third parties to see a demonstration if this is held in private and the confidentiality of the event is stressed. In *Pall Corp v Commercial Hydraulics (Bedford) Ltd*,[19] the plaintiff sent samples of his claimed product (hydrophilic microporous membranes) to a potential customer for testing in comparison with other membranes. Other suppliers were present at the test which had been arranged. However, details of the nature and construction of the membrane were not disclosed and it was not possible to determine these details from a visual inspection of the membrane. After the patent had been granted, it was challenged on the basis that it had been made available to the public before the priority date. It was held, *inter alia*, that delivering samples in confidence to persons who knew that they were experimental and secret did not make the invention available to the public for the purposes of s 2(1) of the Act and did not, therefore, prejudice the novelty of the invention.[20]

It should be mentioned that, on the issue of novelty, cases under the Patents Act 1949 must be treated with caution as, under that Act, reasons for invalidity on the grounds of lack of novelty were somewhat different and prior secret use could invalidate a patent or be a reason for rejecting an application for a patent. In the 1949 Act a patent would be invalid if the invention was 'used in the United Kingdom before the priority date of the claim',[21] or if the invention 'is not new having regard to what was known or used before the priority date of the claim, in the United Kingdom'.[22] In *Quantel Ltd v Spaceward Microsystems Ltd*,[23] Falconer J made the point (at 108):

> [under the 1949 Act] there was no requirement that the prior dated use had to make the invention available to the public. Accordingly, cases of prior use decided under the 1949 Act *not* decided upon the criterion of whether the prior use made the patented invention available to the public, may no longer be good law.
>
> [original emphasis]

18 [1985] RPC 59.

19 [1990] FSR 329.

20 *See also Vax Appliances Ltd v Hoover plc* [1991] FSR 307, decided along similar lines on the issue of prior use under the Patents Act 1949 s 32.

21 Section 14(1)(d).

22 Section 32(1)(e).

23 [1990] RPC 83.

Now, under the 1977 Act, secret prior use, for example of a new industrial process by an employer whose employees are subject to a duty of confidence, cannot anticipate the patent because it is not made available to the public. However, this runs counter to the basic notion, underlying the Statute of Monopolies 1623, that monopolies ought to be limited in time.

Until recently, there was a general lack of authority on the meaning of prior experimental use in the context of anticipation. Under the 1949 Act, even secret experimental use would constitute disclosure to the public unless it was reasonably necessary, by or with the consent of the proprietor, and took place within one year before the priority date.[24] There is no equivalent provision in the 1977 Act, and in *Prout v British Gas plc*[25] it was argued that a patent for an anti-vandal mounting bracket for a warning lamp was invalid because it had been used experimentally at a location on a public highway notorious for vandalism. However, Judge Ford held that the patent was valid none the less. There was some persuasive German authority that anticipatory use had to be more than mere trials in public and that the use of the finished invention was required. He also accepted that the repeal of the 1949 Act, particularly s 51(3) on trial use, revived the previous common law on the subject to the effect that experimental use to test the invention does not destroy the invention's novelty.

Field trials of a traffic light control system were carried out before the relevant filing in *Lux Traffic Controls Ltd v Pike Signals Ltd*.[26] The defendant argued that the invention had been made available to the public because a prototype had been used in public and it did not matter whether anyone, in fact, observed the particular feature claimed by the patentee. Aldous J confirmed that anticipation of a patent required an enabling disclosure such that the public were enabled to make or obtain the invention. He went on (at 133):

> Further it is settled law that there is no need to prove that anybody actually saw the disclosure provided the relevant disclosure was in public. Thus an anticipating description in a book will invalidate a patent if the book is on the shelf of a library open to the public, whether or not anybody read the book and whether or not it was situated in a dark and dusty corner of the library.

In the present case a prototype controller was made available to a contractor and, had a skilled man examined it, he would have seen how it worked. Whether such a person did examine it was of no consequence. The fact remained that the contractor was free in law and equity to examine the controller. The relevant claim in the patent was held to be invalid on the ground of lack of novelty.[27]

On the issue of prior experimental use *Lux v Pike* is difficult to reconcile with *Prout v British Gas*, and although the latter was not mentioned by Aldous J in the former case, both judges referred to the lack of English authority. In *Lux v Pike*, Aldous J cited three cases heard in the European Patent Office.[28] The upshot of these three cases appears to be that if the public have an opportunity to discover the relevant features of the invention without being under any obligation of confidence then the invention is made available to the public for the purposes of determining the state of the art. Of course, in *Lux v Pike* independent contractors had been given the controllers, whereas in *Prout v British Gas* the prior use was by employees. However, in the latter case any member of the public, including vandals, might have taken the opportunity to examine the

24 Sections 32(2) and 51(3).

25 [1992] FSR 478.

26 [1993] RPC 107.

27 Arguments based on obviousness and not being an invention failed. A second patent for another controller was held valid and infringed by the defendant.

28 *Luchtenbenberg* T84/83 [1979–85] EPOR 796, *Telemacanique* T482/89 and *Union Carbide* T245/88 [1991] EPOR 373.

product to discover how it worked, though presumably, as this would probably have amounted to trespass to goods, they would not have been free in law to do so. The advice to anyone contemplating field trials in respect of a new invention must be, in the light of the uncertainty still surrounding this aspect of prior use, file the patent application first.

The enlarged board of appeal of the European Patent Office addressed the question of whether something has been made available to the public in the context of the chemical composition of a substance in *Availability to the Public*.[29] The President of the European Patent Office referred the following points to the enlarged board of appeal for its determination.

29 [1993] EPOR 241.

1  Is the chemical composition of a product made available to the public by virtue of the availability to the public of that product irrespective of whether particular reasons can be identified to cause the skilled person to analyse the composition?  And, if the answer to this is in the affirmative.
2  Does the principle extend to the more general case whereby all information which can be obtained from a product is made available to the public by virtue of the availability of that product irrespective of whether particular reasons exist to cause the skilled person to search for that information?

The board responded by saying that the chemical composition of a substance is part of the state of the art when the substance as such is available to the public and can be analysed and reproduced by the skilled person, irrespective of whether or not particular reasons can be identified for analysing the composition. The same principles apply *mutatis mutandis* to any other product. Article 54(2) of the European Patent Convention makes no distinction between the different means by which any information is made available to the public. Where it is possible for the skilled person to discover the composition of a substance or the internal structure of the product and to reproduce it *without undue burden*, then both the product and the composition or internal structure become part of the state of the art.

30 [1996] FSR 292.

In *Milliken Denmark AS v Walk Off Mats Ltd*,[30] the patent for washable floor mats with a rubber or plastic backing having perforations so as to allow machine washing without the risk of the backing bursting was ordered to be revoked. There had been non-confidential prior use by an American company which was a part owner of the defendant company. The United States company had previously supplied customers with mats with perforations and mere knowledge of the perforations would enable the skilled man to work the invention and the fact that he might not realise the advantage of having perforations was irrelevant. Jacob J, referring to the approach in *Lux* and *Availability to the Public*, to the effect that an invention will become part of the state of the art if the product is made available to the public even if no person in fact examines or inspects it to acquire knowledge of the invention, said (at 311):

> The rule ... seems harsh when prior use is by the patentee. Likewise it seems harsh when the publication is in written form but is in an obscure language and a document placed in an obscure library: a leaf in a forest is available to the public even if the wise man hid it there. But the rule provides a 'brightline' test – avoiding subjectivity and most questions of degree ('undue burden' remains). Nor does it seem harsh when one considers that the patentee can protect himself by applying for a patent before making the product available to the third parties ...

In speaking of 'undue burden', Jacob J was referring to the enlarged board of appeal's requirement that the skilled man must be able to discover the composition or internal structure and reproduce it without undue burden. It is clear from these cases that anticipation may occur even if the skilled person would not have appreciated the benefit or purpose of the invention. Obviously the safest course is to file the patent application first, before allowing persons not under a duty of confidence the potential of access to the invention.

It is only one short step from the position that an invention is made available to the public if it is made available to a person who does not in fact examine it, though he is free to do so, to the proposition that an invention is made available to the public even though the public do not know and cannot know it has been made so available. In *Merrell Dow Pharmaceuticals Inc v H N Norton & Co Ltd*[31] the plaintiff had a patent for a drug 'terfenadine' which had expired. The drug was used as an antihistamine treatment and, unknown at the time, its use caused an acid metabolite to be made in the human liver. The plaintiff, upon discovering this, applied for a patent in respect of the acid metabolite. The defendant started selling terfenadine after the first patent had expired and was sued for infringement of the second patent on the ground that the defendant was supplying the means to put the invention into effect.[32] The second patent was revoked in the Patents Court and the Court of Appeal dismissed the appeal of the plaintiff. It was held that the disclosure of a process made available to the public made available everything which inevitably took place as part of that process, whether appreciated or not. Nicholls V-C said (at 238):

> Any other conclusion would run counter to one of the golden threads of jurisprudence relating to patents. Patents exist today to reward and thereby encourage inventors; they are not intended to make it possible to take out of public use processes or products already made available to the public.

The House of Lords confirmed that the patent was invalid for want of novelty.[33] The invention had been made available to the public by virtue of the specification for the terfenadine patent which included in the description of the invention the phrase '... a part of the chemical reaction in the human body produced by the ingestion of terfenadine and having an anti-histamine effect'. The invention was being worked before the priority date because the public were able to take terfenadine and, by doing so, necessarily they were working the invention disclosed in the second patent. The chemical reaction described was taking place in their livers even though they did not know. Lord Hoffman said (at 90):

> It enabled the public to work the invention by making the acid metabolite in their livers. The fact that they would not have been able to describe the chemical reaction in these terms does [not] mean that they were not working the invention. Whether or not a person is working a product invention is an objective fact independent of what he knows or thinks about what he is doing.

In particular, Lord Hoffman cited two decisions of the European Patent Office boards of appeal: *BAYER/Diastereomers Decision*,[34] and *CPC/Flavour Concentrates Decision*.[35] The latter concerned an application for a patent in respect of a process for making flavour concentrates from vegetable or animal substances by extraction with fat solvents in pressure cookers. Pre-existing recipes for pressure-frying chickens disclosed processes having the same effect although they were couched in non-technical language. The Technical Board of Appeal stated (at 98):

31 [1995] RPC 233. Affirmed in the House of Lords, [1996] RPC 76.

32 An infringement under the Patents Act 1977 s 60(2).

33 *Merrell Dow Pharmaceuticals Inc v H N Norton & Co Ltd* [1996] RPC 76.

34 [1979–1981] EPOR 308.
35 [1989] 2 EPOR 95.

It is sufficient to destroy the novelty of the claimed process that this process and the claimed process are identical with respect to starting material and reaction conditions since processes identical in these features must inevitably yield identical products.

The House of Lords' avoidance of the unfortunate consequence of allowing what was, essentially, continuing protection for an expired patent accords with common sense and the views of the European Patent Office that the effect of Article 54 (the equivalent to s 2 of the Act) is to prevent the state of the art being patented again.[36] Perhaps, however, the manner in which the Patents Court and the Court of Appeal dealt with the problem is to be preferred. Had the second 'invention' not been disclosed in the specification for the first patent, the outcome in the House of Lords might well have different. Although if there had not been disclosure in the specification of the first patent, that could have been invalid for lack of sufficiency. Whilst there are good policy reasons for not granting protection beyond the normal 20-year period the more technical approach of the House of Lords conforms better with patent law as it has developed. The fact that persons taking terfenadine were producing the acid metabolite should not, on the basis of *Lux* and *Availability to the Public*, be a sufficient ground without more for adding the acid metabolite to the state of the art. It could, after all, probably require an 'undue burden' to discover the composition of the metabolite. Would even the skilled man realise that it was being produced in the human liver if there was no mention of the chemical reaction in the specification for terfenadine?

In the United States and in Germany, the equivalent patents for the acid metabolite produced by taking terfenadine were held not to be infringed by a defendant selling the drug after expiry of the patents. In each case, the court held that the second patent would be limited to the production of the acid metabolite *outside* the human body.[37]

If published material does not adequately describe what is claimed there can be no loss of novelty. If someone else thought of the idea underlying the invention before the priority date, that alone would not be sufficient to invalidate the patent unless it was made available to the public. For example, in *Catnic Components Ltd v C Evans & Co (Builders Merchants) Ltd*[38] a challenge on the ground of lack of novelty by way of another person having a similar idea and making a model of a lintel failed even though the model had been shown to a number of people. The model was not the lintel (it was in fact too short to be used as a lintel) and therefore the plaintiff's patent for a new lintel was valid.

A prior publication which deals with a different problem to the one dealt with in the patent application could still amount to anticipation under old UK law. In *Molins v Industrial Machinery Co Ltd*,[39] an application was made in respect of a method of distributing tobacco evenly in the manufacture of cigarettes on a high-speed machine. The method involved pushing the tobacco in the same direction as the paper in which it would be wrapped. But this was held to have been anticipated by an earlier patent which used the same movement but in a slow-speed machine. This was so even though the movement in the older machine was not intended to cure the problem of uneven tobacco distribution. However, a carefully drafted application that is directed to a new purpose, not previously disclosed, might now succeed.[40] It has been accepted that the nature of novelty has been changed under Article 54 of the European Patent Convention and new purposes may be patentable and not anticipated by inherent prior disclosure.[41]

36 *BAYER/Diastereomers Decision* [1979–81] EPOR 308.

37 *Terfenadin* [1998] FSR 145 and *Marion Merrell Dow Inc v Baker Norton Pharmaceuticals Inc* [1998] FSR 158.

38 [1983] FSR 401.

39 (1938) 55 RPC 31.

40 *See* the European Patent Office case of *Mobil Oil* [1990] OJ EPO 93, discussed later.

41 Falconer J recognised the changed nature of novelty in *Quantel Ltd v Spaceward Microsystems Ltd* [1990] RPC 83 at 108.

Anticipation is judged by considering how a prior publication, for example, would be construed by a person skilled in the art. This extension of the reasonable man test is essential as many technical publications are incomprehensible to the layperson. It is acknowledged that if the art is in a highly developed technology, it might be a matter of how it can be construed by a team of persons skilled in the particular art. This was accepted in *General Tire & Rubber Co v Firestone Tyre & Rubber Co Ltd*,[42] in which the validity of Firestone's patent for making oil-extended rubber for tyres was challenged by an alleged infringer. Attacks on the validity of patents frequently come from defendants in infringement actions, where it is often the best form of defence and certainly puts the plaintiff to a great deal of additional trouble. As regards the rubber patent and the issue of anticipation, there had been a prior publication, but whether it related to Firestone's patent was ambiguous. It was said that if a prior publication contained a direction that was capable of being carried out in a manner which would infringe but would be at least as likely to be carried out in a way that would not do so, the patentee's claim would not be judged to be anticipated.[43] To anticipate the claim, the prior publication must contain a clear and unmistakable direction to do what the patentee claimed to have invented.

*General Tire* has been used on numerous occasions as authority for the 'clear and unmistakable direction' approach to anticipatory material. A recent example, which adds something of a gloss to this principle, is *Union Carbide Corp v BP Chemicals Ltd*[44] in which Jacob J in the Patents Court said that a direction in a prior publication not to do something because it would have adverse consequences was not a direction to do that same thing because it had beneficial consequences. In such a case, the invention lies in finding that those in the art at the time of the prior publication had been wrong. Jacob J also confirmed that disclosure of a range of value, for example, 15 to 70 per cent, discloses each and every part of the range. However, there may still be room for invention if a part of the range is claimed later if there is something special (that is, inventive) about that later claimed range.

Matter that has been obtained unlawfully or in breach of confidence, or which has been divulged in breach of confidence is to be disregarded when considering the novelty of an invention.[45] In the case of a patent application, this covers the period of six months preceding the date of filing of the patent so that, effectively, if there has been a disclosure of the invention because of a breach of confidence, for example, by a potential manufacturer of products made in accordance with the invention who has been in negotiations with the inventor, there is a six-month time limit during which that disclosure will be ignored in the determination of novelty. There is provision for the inventor to display the invention at an international exhibition without this destroying the novelty of the invention, subject to the inventor making a declaration and filing written evidence. The six-month time limit applies and the patent application must be filed within six months of the act of displaying the invention at the exhibition.[46]

One thing an inventor must be careful to avoid is anticipating his own invention, for example, by publishing details of it in an academic or trade journal before the priority date (normally the date of filing the application). However, to anticipate the invention, the publication must clearly describe the invention as claimed.[47] Tempting as it might be to publicise his ingenuity, the inventor would

42 [1972] RPC 457.

43 It might, however, fail on the grounds of obviousness.

44 [1998] RPC 1.

45 The Patents Act 1977 s 2(4). Unlawfully obtained matter would include, for example a stolen model of something incorporating the invention or manufactured using the invention. Whether it applies to stolen information is less clear because of the difficulty with respect to theft of information, for example, *Oxford v Moss* (1978) 68 Cr App R 183. However, details of the invention stored on a computer would be covered, as to gain access to them without authorisation will usually be an offence under the Computer Misuse Act 1990 s 1. Of course, 'unlawfully' includes civil wrongs as well as criminal offences and could cover trespass (to land and goods) and conversion.

46 The Patents Act 1977 s 2(4). The Patents Rules 1995, SI 1995/2093 r 5 sets out the detailed provisions.

47 *Lux Traffic Controls Ltd v Pike Signals Ltd* [1993] RPC 107. In that case a published paper did not describe the invention sufficiently clearly so as to make it known to the public.

be advised to restrain his ego and keep the details of his invention secret, and in any dealings with advisers, potential manufacturers, assignees or licensees, to make it clear that discussion of the invention is in the strictest confidence.

## New uses for old inventions

Old inventions may be patentable if the claims are directed to a new use. If sufficiently different, the new use will not be considered to be part of the state of the art. For inventions other than drugs for the treatment of humans and animals, new uses for old inventions may be patentable up to a point if there is some new technical effect, for example, by combining two previous inventions in a new and non-obvious way.[48] However, in the case of drugs for the treatment of humans or animals, it appears that only the first use is patentable, although at first reading s 2(6) gives the opposite impression. It states that the fact that the drug (substance or composition) already forms part of the state of the art does not prevent the new method of use from being patentable if 'the use of the substance or composition *in any such method* does not form part of the state of the art' (emphasis added). The key words are 'any such method', which seems to include the first use, at least on a strict literal interpretation. The omission of the word 'any' would clearly permit 'second use patents', and the only conclusion that can be reached is that the inclusion of the word 'any' was quite deliberate.[49]

The literal approach, denying second use patents for drugs, found some support in the English case of *John Wyeth's & Brothers Ltd's Application: Schering AG's Application*,[50] although the court decided to follow the enlarged board of appeal of the European Patent Office[51] which held that second and subsequent new uses of known substances or compounds were patentable. Either interpretation was possible but it was important to achieve conformity with the European Patent Convention. In *Eisai*,[52] the enlarged board of appeal held that:

1 claims directed to the use of a product for the treatment of an illness in a human or animal body (when such use was the second or subsequent medical use) were equivalent to claims for a method of treatment of the human or animal body and therefore excluded from patentability,[53]
2 claims directed to the use of a product for the manufacture of a medicament for a specified new therapeutic use were not lacking in novelty.[54]

This is a fairly restrictive interpretation which does not apply to 'non-medical' inventions, that is, those falling outside the scope of s 2(6) where the question of novelty depends on whether the new use for a new purpose had previously been made available to the public. Secret or hidden uses will not be considered to be grounds of objection.[55] In *Mobil Oil*, which concerned a claim based on the discovery that an existing compound used for preventing rust was also effective as a lubricant, the example of a compound that had been previously known and used as a plant growth regulator was discussed. Imagine that it was later discovered that this same compound was effective also as a fungicide and the patent claim is for the use of the compound as a fungicide. The method of use is the same for both purposes, that is application to plants, and so the only novelty that can be claimed is in the use of the compound as a fungicide rather than as a growth regulator, that is in *the purpose of the use*. In such a case, the question of novelty has to be determined along basic principles, that is has that functional technical feature previously been made available to the public?

48 *See* the discussion later on *Parks-Cramer Co v G W Thornton & Sons Ltd* [1966] RPC 407. Prior to the 1977 Act, there had to be novelty in the mode of using the old product as distinguished from novelty of purpose, *Lane-Fox v The Kensington and Knightbridge Electric Lighting Co Ltd* (1892) 9 RPC 413.

49 In fact, Article 54(5) of the European Patent Convention, the equivalent provision to the Patents Act 1977 s 2(6), also includes the word 'any'.

50 [1985] RPC 545.

51 *Eisai* [1985] OJ EPO 64. *See* Paterson, G.D. 'The Patentability of Furthur Uses of a Known Product under the European Patent Convention' [1991] 1 EIPR 16.

52 [1985] OJ EPO 64.

53 Article 52(4) of the European Patent Convention – *see* also the Patents Act 1977 s 4(2) which denies patentability to methods of treatment of the human or animal body by surgery or therapy or of diagnosis practiced on the human or animal body.

54 Article 54 of the European Patent Convention, the Patents Act 1977 s 2.

55 *Mobil Oil* [1990] OJ EPO 93.

In *Mobil*, the enlarged board of appeal in the European Patent Office suggested that a new use of a known compound may reflect a newly discovered technical effect which could be considered as a functional technical feature of the relevant claim. If that technical feature had not previously been made available to the public the claim would be novel even though it had inherently taken place in the course of carrying out what previously had been made available to the public. However, this contradicts the view on novelty taken in *Merrell Dow Pharmaceuticals Inc v H N Norton & Co Ltd*[56] and was seriously doubted as being correct in the Patents Court hearing of that same case by Aldous J.[57]

In the appeal to the House of Lords in *Merrell Dow*,[58] Lord Hoffman also cast some doubt on the decision in *Mobil Oil* as regards second or subsequent uses of known compositions of substances for non-medical uses. He stressed the English emphasis on infringement and said it would be difficult to tell, for a second invention such as that in *Mobil Oil*, whether the alleged infringer was using it for the forbidden purpose. That is, how can you tell whether a person is using the oil additive as a lubricant (lawful after the expiry of the first patent) or to reduce friction (which would infringe the second patent)? However, whichever purpose the person alleged to have infringed had in mind is irrelevant to the existence of infringement. It may, at best, reduce the exposure to damages. If a person used the additive for the purpose of lubrication, it would also reduce friction, whether or not he knew this. The danger, similar to that perceived in the Court of Appeal in *Merrell Dow*, discussed earlier, is that the patent monopoly can be extended beyond its normal life if a new hitherto unknown effect can be discovered by the patentee. This might be acceptable if it involves a *new use*, but not if it involves a *known use* but for a *new purpose*. Although the view of the House of Lords, as that in the Patents Court and Court of Appeal, is strictly *obiter*, it throws serious doubt on the correctness of the enlarged board of appeal of the European Patent Office.

[56] [1995] RPC 233.
[57] [1994] RPC 1 at 12.
[58] [1996] RPC 76.

## Inventive step

The Patents Act 1977 does not define the term 'invention', but Lord Hoffman usefully described different forms of invention in *Biogen Inc v Medeva plc*.[59] He said that it is the addition of a new idea to the existing stock of knowledge and that (at 34):

[59] [1997] RPC 1.

> Sometimes, it is the idea of using established techniques to do something which no one had previously thought of doing. In that case, the inventive step will be doing the new thing. Sometimes, it is finding a way of doing something which people had wanted to do but could not think how. The inventive idea would be the way of achieving the goal. In yet other cases, many people may have a general idea of how they might achieve a goal but not know how to solve a particular problem which stands in their way. If someone devises a way of solving the problem, his inventive step will be that solution but not the goal itself or the general method of achieving it.

These three forms of invention can be classified as (a) the goal itself, (b) the general method of achieving the goal, and (c) the solution to a problem. The last two forms of invention, in their different ways, can be thought of fulfilling a 'long felt want', a phrase often used in patent law. Its presence is sometimes useful in determining whether an inventive step is present. It is not, of course, conclusive.

The invention must involve an inventive step. Under s 3, this applies when the invention is not obvious to a person skilled in the art having regard to all matter forming part of the state of the art, but not including matter from patent applications with earlier priority dates which is published later than the priority date of the invention. This is different to the position concerning novelty as, normally, matter in earlier applications that has not yet been published is taken to be a part of the state of the art.[60] This material is used to test for novelty but not for inventive step.

The word 'obvious' does not have any special legal meaning and it has been said that it is not necessary to go beyond the dictionary definition but to take it to mean 'very plain'.[61] It is manifestly evident that the notional skilled worker cannot be endowed with inventive faculties himself, however technical the art, otherwise all inventions could be considered to be obvious. The person skilled in the art is simply someone with a wide knowledge of the technology within which the invention lies (or a team of persons so skilled). The question becomes, would the invention be obvious to such a person or persons?[62] In some fields, a person skilled in the art who does not possess inventive faculties may be a contradiction, for example, in the engineering professions where engineers are trained in problem-solving by the application of ingenuity, the very word 'engineer' sharing a common origin with the word 'ingenuity'.

The notional skilled worker does not have inventive ability, but he does have knowledge common to the particular art. That is known as common general knowledge and is the basis for determining whether, in the light of that knowledge, an invention is obvious. Common general knowledge does not include every published patent specification in a particular art, but is restricted to those which are generally known to those who engaged in that particular art.[63] In *Beloit Technologies Inc v Valmet Paper Machinery Inc*,[64] Aldous LJ accepted that the notional skilled man may not have the advantage of the facilities available in some large corporations with extensive library facilities and patent departments. He said (at 494):

> The notional skilled addressee is the ordinary man who may not have the advantages that some employees of large companies may have.

Therefore, the person skilled in the art does not know everything. He simply knows that which is known to a large proportion of those working in the relevant art. Knowledge which is known by some, perhaps a few only, can be described as public knowledge and this must be distinguished from common general knowledge.[65]

Invention requires something more than simply showing that something can be done. It must show how it can be done – a particular way in which the underlying idea can be translated into a practical method of implementation. Otherwise, the patent could extend to all possible ways of achieving the end result. A patent must be for more than an end result and must relate to the means utilised to realise that end. In *Biogen Inc v Medeva plc*[66] a patent in respect of a vaccine for Hepatitis B which had been genetically engineered was declared invalid. Lord Hoffman said (at 52):

> It is said that what Professor Murray showed by his invention was that it could be done ... Those who followed, even by different routes, could have greater confidence by reason of his success. I do not think that this is enough to justify a monopoly in the whole field ... The Wright Brothers showed that heavier-than-air flight was possible, but that did not entitle them to a monopoly in heavier-than-air flying machines ... care is needed not to stifle further research and healthy competition by allowing the first person who has found a way of achieving an obviously desirable goal to monopolise every other way of doing so.

60 *See* the Patents Act 1977 s 2(3).

61 *General Tire & Rubber Co v Firestone Tyre & Rubber Co Ltd* [1972] RPC 457.

62 Conversely, if the invention is not obvious to skilled and inventive persons it must involve an inventive step, *Intalife International NV v Cellular Ceilings Ltd (No. 2)* [1987] RPC 537.

63 *British Acoustic Films Ltd v Nettlefold Productions Ltd* (1936) 53 RPC 221, *per* Luxmore J at 250, approved by the Court of Appeal in *General Tire & Rubber Co v Firestone Tyre & Rubber Co Ltd* [1972] RPC 457.

64 [1997] RPC 489.

65 *Richardson-Vicks Inc's Patent* [1997] RPC 888, where it was said that a person skilled in the art of obtaining regulatory approval for new drugs was not a person skilled in the art of producing new combination drugs.

66 [1997] RPC 1.

Obviousness is judged by looking at the invention as a whole and considering the entire state of the art at the relevant time. A process known as 'mosaicing' has occasionally been used to attack the validity of a patent by showing that it is obvious. This process consists of piecing together several unrelated bits of information in different documents which, when combined, are capable of showing obviousness. But the use of such a technique is theoretically very unsound because, if this is the first time the mosaic has been constructed, that in itself is indicative of non-obviousness. If it were otherwise someone else would have pieced the bits together previously. In practice, mosaicing is unlikely to find favour in the courts, although there are exceptions – for example, where it would be reasonable for the notional uninventive skilled worker to fit the pieces together, an unlikely phenomenon as the very act of mosaicing implies both detective and inventive skills. Accepting that the skilled man has no inventive faculties ('incapable of a scintilla of invention'), Lord Reid said of mosaicing:

> When dealing with obviousness, unlike novelty, it is permissible to make a 'mosaic' out of the relevant documents, but it must be a mosaic which can be put together by an unimaginative man with no inventive capacity.[67]

Whether the invention is obvious is a question of fact. For example, in *Lux Traffic Controls Ltd* v *Pike Signals Ltd*,[68] the defendant claimed that the plaintiff's two patents in relation to traffic signal control systems were invalid on a number of grounds. The second patent was for a means of varying the 'intergreen' period, the safety period between the lights in one direction changing to red and before the lights in the other direction changed to green. It was argued that it was obvious. However, being unsupported by evidence, the court expressed surprise that the invention had not been proposed before if that was the case. The invention may have been simple, but it represented an advance and a technical contribution to the art.[69]

When obviousness has to be determined retrospectively, for example where the validity of a patent is in issue, commercial success is an important and telling factor that can be taken into account. If the invention fulfils a 'long-felt want', this is good evidence of non-obviousness, even if the prior art is old. Indeed, contrary to first impression this may indicate that the invention is not obvious on the basis of 'long-felt want'.[70] However, if commercial success is taken as a yardstick of non-obviousness, consideration must also be given to market forces. In *Technograph Printed Circuits Ltd* v *Mills & Rockley (Electronics) Ltd*,[71] the defendant alleged that the plaintiff's method of making printed circuit boards using a silk screen printing method was invalid because of obviousness and lack of novelty, relying on a prior US patent relating to the manufacture of electrostatic shields and aerials. It was held that the plaintiff's patent was valid because the adaptation of the method described in the US patent, where it was used in relation to three-dimensional objects, to printing a pattern on a flat circuit board was not an obvious step. Although the invention turned out to be an enormous commercial success, this was some years later and the invention was not widely used for some years. At first instance, Harman J said:

> It was objected that in fact it was not until ten years after the invention was published that it was commercially adopted ... and it was argued from this that it was not a case of filling a long felt want. I do not accept this argument. In the years immediately following the war, manufacturers could sell all the machines they wanted using the old point-to-point wiring and had no need to trouble themselves with anything better.[72]

67 *Technograph Printed Circuits Ltd* v *Mills & Rockley (Electronics) Ltd* [1972] RPC 346 at 355.

68 [1993] RPC 107.

69 The first patent was held to be invalid through lack of novelty because prototypes had been made available to contractors who were able to examine them, and such examination would have been sufficient to disclose the invention.

70 *Brugger* v *Medic-Aid Ltd* [1996] RPC 635.

71 [1969] RPC 395.

72 The House of Lords confirmed that the invention was non-obvious in [1972] RPC 346.

Therefore, commercial success as an indicator of obviousness must be treated cautiously. Lack of immediate commercial success, as in the above case, might be explained by factors that have nothing to do with the obviousness of the invention. The correlation that the proprietor hopes will be confirmed by commercial success is that the invention cannot have been obvious because it clearly satisfies a demand, and that demand would have been long since satisfied had the invention been obvious. While this might be a reasonable assumption, the opposite is not tenable: lack of success does not necessarily directly equate to obviousness. Something might be highly inventive but fail to sell because, put simply, consumers have no desire for it. That commercial success as a measure of non-obviousness should be treated cautiously was confirmed by Mummery J in the Patents Court in *Mölnlycke AB v Proctor & Gamble Ltd (No. 3)*,[73] a case involving a patent for disposable nappies, where he said that whether an invention was obvious was something which must be considered technically or practically rather than commercially. Commercial success might be relevant if it was due to the precise improvement which satisfied the long-felt want, but not if it was due to things such as appearance, get-up, price, marketing strategies or advertising campaigns. This was confirmed by Nicholls V-C in *Mölnlycke AB v Proctor & Gamble (No. 5)*,[74] where he said that secondary evidence such as that relating to commercial success had a place, but its importance or weight would vary from case to case. The complexity and routine of such evidence must not allow it to obscure that fact that it is no more than an aid in assessing the primary evidence.

Laddie J cast further doubt on the utility of commercial success being used to suggest inventiveness in *Raychem Corp's Patents*[75] in which he said that commercial success was rarely an indicator of non-obviousness. It would, in many cases, be very difficult to demonstrate the necessary causal link and it may be the result of other factors such as improved marketing. He then criticised the practice of pleading commercial success saying that normally it only adds time and expenses to the proceedings and serves no useful purpose. However, in that case, the evidence that commercial success resulted from non-obviousness was very weak. Of course, the court should always be wary of being seduced by evidence that the invention has been very successful but it can be useful if it is accompanied by evidence of a long-felt want.[76] But, even then, other factors such as marketing effort must also be considered. Nevertheless, if a patentee, whose patent is under attack for lack of inventive step, is confident that he can show at least an arguable case that commercial success is the result of the invention being non-obvious, he would be foolish not to put in such evidence. As the consequences of a finding of invalidity can be dire for the patentee, the court should be slow to criticise a patentee for doing what he can to protect his patent from attack.

The fact that it would be relatively inexpensive to experiment and to make prototypes is another point in favour of a finding of non-obviousness, especially when the problem that the invention sought to solve had existed for some time. So it was held in *Mölnlycke AB v Proctor & Gamble Ltd*.[77] It was argued that the plaintiff's dedicated fastening surface used for refastenable disposable nappies was obvious. The court disagreed because there had been an increasing need for multiple taping over a number of years and, had the idea been obvious, it would have occurred to someone much sooner, especially as it would cost very little to make prototypes. The invention was not obvious even though some of the defendant's employees had the same idea before or at around the same time. The fact that a competitor has had the same idea does not affect the state of the art unless the competitor makes it available to the public or files a patent application in respect of it.

73 [1990] RPC 498.

74 [1994] RPC 49.

75 [1998] RPC 31.

76 Where the prior art is available only a short time before the priority date of the patent, commercial success is not applicable, *BSH Industries Ltd's Patents* [1995] RPC 183. Presumably, this is because of an absence in such circumstances of a long-felt want.

77 [1992] FSR 549; appeal dismissed, *see* [1994] RPC 49.

If an invention takes a long time to conceive, that itself suggests that it is non-obvious.[78] Again, however, evidence of the length of time to find a solution can never be conclusive because researchers may work for years and still miss the obvious.[79] Neither does taking a commercial decision to pursue a series of experiments in the hope of finding a solution to a problem constitute an inventive step. In *Biogen Inc* v *Medeva plc*[80] the plaintiff embarked upon a series of experiments using known methods to find recombinant DNA molecules. Others knew that this approach might have worked, but had dismissed it as too unlikely to succeed to have been worthwhile. Hobhouse LJ made a useful analogy with placing a bet on a horse that appears to most to have little chance of winning a race. If the horse then wins, the gambler cannot be said to have invented a way of picking winners.[81]

The invention may be the application of well-known technology to a particular problem, usually a new problem or an old one that has escaped attempts to solve it. Although novelty may be in issue, a second use of existing technology for a new purpose may still be acceptable on this point; but more importantly the question of obviousness will be raised. Consideration of the magnitude of the problem and whether there have been many attempts to find a solution in the past, all of which have proved to be unsuccessful, will provide a useful rule of thumb. If such is the case, it can be presumed that the invention is not obvious, and again the commercial success of the invention can prove to be a helpful factor in deciding obviousness. In *Parks-Cramer Co* v *G W Thornton & Sons Ltd*,[82] the invention was for a method of cleaning floors between rows of textile machines. There had been many attempts to find a satisfactory solution but none of them, unlike the present invention, actually worked. All the invention consisted of was an overhead vacuum cleaner which moved automatically up and down the rows between the machines. But attached to the cleaners were long vertical tubes, reaching almost to the floor. In the High Court, the trial judge considered that the patent was invalid because it was obvious. He said that it was common knowledge to every competent housewife that dust could be removed from a floor by the passage of a vacuum cleaner.[83] However, the Court of Appeal held that the patent was valid. The many unsuccessful attempts by inventors to find a solution and the immediate commercial success of the invention denied the possibility of a finding of obviousness. Diplock LJ said:

> As in all other cases of obviousness, the question is one of degree. There may be an inventive step in recognising that a problem exists at all; but given a problem which is known to exist which it is the object of the invention to solve, the question always is: 'Is the solution claimed by the patentee one which would have occurred to everyone of ordinary intelligence and acquaintance with the subject matter of the patent who gave his mind to the problem?'[84]

The plaintiff was granted an injunction and an order was made for the delivery up or destruction of the infringing articles.

The courts have to draw a line somewhere when it comes to new uses of old technology and the question of obviousness. There must be a sufficient inventive step. Merely taking two older inventions and sticking them together will not necessarily be regarded as an inventive step. It is all a question of degree, and it is difficult to lay down hard and fast rules. For example, in *Williams* v *Nye*,[85] Williams took out a patent for an improved mincing machine made up from a combination of two old machines, a mincing machine and a filling machine. What he did was to take the cutter from one machine and simply replace it with the cutter from the other machine. When the plaintiff sued the defendant for

78 Despite *dicta* suggesting the contrary *per* Tomlin J in *Samuel Parks & Co Ltd* v *Cocker Brothers Ltd* (1929) 46 RPC 24 at 248.

79 *Per* Aldous J in *Chiron Corp* v *Organon Teknika Ltd (No. 3)* [1994] FSR 202 at 224.

80 [1995] RPC 25.

81 The House of Lords found the claimed invention to be too broad and to be invalid for insufficiency, *Biogen Inc* v *Medeva plc* [1997] RPC 1.

82 [1966] RPC 407.

83 Perhaps the judge should have used the term 'houseperson' instead.

84 [1966] RPC 407 at 418.

85 (1890) 7 RPC 62.

infringement of the patent, the defendant claimed that the patent was invalid, and this claim was successful because it was held that there was insufficient invention. However, the court accepted that a slight alteration might produce important results and be the result of great ingenuity. Cotton LJ said:

> ... in order to maintain a patent there must be a substantial exercise of the inventive power or inventive faculty. Sometimes very slight alterations will produce very important results, and there may be in those very slight alterations very great ingenuity exercised or shown to be exercised by the Patentee.

Therefore, there seems to be a fine line drawn between what does and what does not constitute an inventive step. Even if the inventiveness appears at first sight trivial, the utility of the new invention and whether it is a significant improvement in the state of the art should be considered. Also one has to ask the obvious question: Why did nobody else do it before? After all, many of the most successful inventions seem, in retrospect, to be very simple, but simplicity should not be confused with obviousness.

It may be well known that you could combine two things, but nobody has thought to do it, perhaps because of technical prejudice. In *Petra Fischer's Application*,[86] the alleged invention was putting a diesel engine into a cabriolet car. The fact that those skilled in the art have been prejudiced against doing that does not mean that it is inventive. The alleged invention taught nothing new as the skilled man knew it was possible to put a diesel engine into a cabriolet car even though he did not think it was worth doing, for example, because of the problem of vibration of such an engine in a less rigid body shell or because he did not think it would sell. Reasons such as these were why it had not been done before – it had nothing to do with inventiveness.

### Tests for inventive step

Oliver LJ postulated a test for obviousness in *Windsurfing International Inc v Tabur Marine (Great Britain) Ltd*,[87] being:

1 identify the inventive concept embodied in the patent in suit;
2 the court then assumes the mantle of the normally skilled but unimaginative addressee in the art at the priority date, imputing to him what was, at that date, common general knowledge in the art in question;
3 identify what, if any, differences exist between the matter cited as being 'known and used' and the alleged invention;
4 the court then asks itself the question whether, viewed without any knowledge of the alleged invention, those differences constitute steps which would have been obvious to the skilled man or whether they require any degree of invention.

Although *Windsurfing* involved a patent under the 1949 Act, the above test has been approved and applied on numerous occasions ever since.[88] It does not, however, alter or supplement the statutory provision, it merely affords a structured way of assessing whether the requirement of inventive step has been satisfied. In *PLG Research Ltd v Ardon International Ltd*[89] the Court of Appeal confirmed that patents for heavy-duty plastic netting made by stretching sheets of perforated plastic were non-obvious, reversing the decision of Aldous J in the Patents Court on this point. Millett LJ neatly summarised the principles to be adopted in terms of obviousness:[90]

86 [1997] RPC 899.

87 [1985] RPC 59 at 73.

88 See *Mölnlycke AB v Procter & Gamble Ltd (No. 5)* [1994] RPC 49. For a good example of the test in use, *see* Balcombe LJ in *Optical Coating Laboratories Inc v Pilkington P E Ltd* [1995] RPC 145 at 163.

89 [1995] RPC 287. *See also* [1995] FSR 116 in which the judgment of the court is reported as being given by Neill LJ rather than Millet LJ.

90 The principles were first enunciated in *Mölnlycke AB v Procter & Gamble Ltd (No. 5)* [1994] RPC 49, but Millett's description is clearer.

1 the criterion for determining whether the claimed invention involves an inventive step is wholly objective and is defined in s 3 of the Act;

2 the test is qualitative, not quantitative, and paraphrasing the statutory test in other cases does not assist;[91]

3 the court must make findings of fact as to the state of the art at the priority date and, in the light of that, decide whether the invention was obvious to the skilled person;

4 assessment of obviousness with hindsight must be avoided;

5 where the validity of a patent is being attacked on the basis of lack of inventive step the burden of proof lies on the person making the attack to show that the invention did not involve an inventive step;

6 the *Windsurfing* test continues to be of assistance.

Millett LJ went on (at 313):

> The value of [the *Windsurfing*] analysis is not that it alters the critical question; it remains the question posed by the Act. But it enables the fact-finding tribunal to approach the question in a structured way.

Almost invariably, a court faced with the task of deciding whether an invention involves an inventive step, will adopt the *Windsurfing* test. However, it is arguable whether it ought to be used at all. The statutory provision is straightforward and requires a one-step test only, that is, whether the invention is not obvious to a person skilled in the art.[92] There is a danger, in breaking this down, that artificiality will be introduced which might distort the test. A simpler formulation is to ask whether, from the point of view of a person who had total knowledge of the state of the art, the invention was obvious at its priority date. It goes without saying that the person concerned cannot be endowed with inventive faculties, otherwise not a single patent would ever be granted again. It is important also to bear in mind the philosophy behind the doctrine of obviousness, which is, according to Millett LJ in *PLG Research* (at 313):

> ... that the public should not be prevented from doing anything which was merely an obvious extension or workshop variation of what was already known at the priority date.

Simple variants of existing inventions will be unlikely to be patentable. Something else is needed, and this could be described as the inventor's genius in thinking of something which others have not yet been able to conceptualise.

## Industrial application

Another requirement is that the invention is capable of industrial application. This requirement demonstrates the practical nature of patent law, which requires that the invention should be something which can be made industrially or relate to an industrial process.[93] An application for a patent that depends upon the use of hitherto undiscovered materials in its manufacture would be refused.[94] The invention has to be something that can be worked industrially, and to some extent this requirement distinguishes patents from other forms of intellectual property such as original works of copyright. It confirms the difference between 'industrial property' and copyright.

Under s 4(1) an invention is capable of industrial application if it can be made or used in any kind of industry, including agriculture. However, this does

---

**91** Excluding the *Windsurfing* test, presumably.

**92** The Patents Act 1977 s 3 goes on to define what matter is to be taken as part of the state of the art.

**93** Under ibid s 4(1) 'industry' includes agriculture.

**94** Under the Patents Act 1949, a patent could be invalidated on the grounds of inutility: s 32(1)(g).

95 The Patents Act 1977 s 4(2). The reason is to ensure that medical practitioners (and veterinary surgeons) are not subjected to restraint by a patent when tending patients, *John Wyeth & Brother Ltd's Application: Schering AG's Application* [1985] RPC 545.

96 Section 4(3).

97 *See Schering AG's Application* [1971] RPC 337, where a patent was granted to a method of contraception involving doses of gestagen. However, in 1936, an application in respect of 'improvements in pessaries' (contraceptive devices) was refused by exercise of the Royal Prerogative, *Riddlesbarger's Application* (1936) 53 RPC 57.

98 *Stafford-Miller's Application* [1984] FSR 258.

99 However, this does not prevent the surgeon from keeping his new technique secret, which he may want to do if he works in the private sector and has built up a high reputation because of the effectiveness of his methods.

100 For example, the Patents Act 1949 s 101(1).

101 However, the exception of surgery, therapy and diagnosis from industrial application is important.

102 The Patents Act 1949 s 32(1)(g).

103 For a recent example, where it was argued, unsuccessfully, that not all the products claimed had a use, *see Chiron Corp.* v *Organon Teknika Ltd (No. 3)* [1994] FSR 202. The defendant also raised a number of other defences, including the s 44 defence which was successful.

104 [1969] RPC 267.

not cover methods of treatment of human or animal bodies by surgery or therapy, or of diagnosis practised on human or animal bodies,[95] but this exclusion does not extend to products consisting of substances or compositions used in any such methods.[96] Therefore, drugs are capable of industrial application and are patentable in principle. The words 'treatment' and 'diagnosis' imply an illness or disease of some kind which does not include conception or pregnancy, neither of which is considered to be an illness.[97] Further, as treatment of the human or animal body is excluded, treatment to rid a person or animal of, for example, an infestation of lice, may be patentable if it is accepted that such treatment is directed towards ridding the human of lice and not the human or animal body as such.[98]

The reason for the exclusion of surgery, therapy or diagnosis is probably a policy decision to prevent restrictions on the spread and adoption of new and improved methods of treatment. For example, if a surgeon develops a new and improved way to perform back surgery, it is in the public interest that such a method be available to all surgeons.[99] Nevertheless, this does not sit comfortably with the fact that drugs can be, and often are, patented. One difference between the surgeon and the drug company is that the former is in a profession where he is expected to pass on his knowledge to others (he will probably be very keen to publish his new technique) and will not expect financial recompense for his idea but will hope for kudos and the respect of colleagues; whereas the drug company, operating in a competitive industry, needs a patent to justify investment in research and development.

Before the 1977 Act, the requirement equivalent to industrial application came from the phrase 'manner of new manufacture',[100] but it is no easy task to tell whether the change in phraseology makes any difference when it can strongly be argued that the requirement that the invention is capable of industrial application is totally unnecessary, especially when the exceptions contained in s 1(2) (discussed later) are considered, as these exceptions probably account for anything which might not have industrial application.[101] Otherwise, lack of industrial application may be relevant if the invention as claimed simply does not work. This may be analogous to the provisions relating to inutility in the 1949 Act.[102]

There have been relatively few cases where the question of industrial application was at issue.[103] One example under the 1949 Act, where the phrase used was 'manner of manufacture', was *Hiller's Application*.[104] An application for a patent for an improved plan for underground service distribution schemes for housing estates was turned down. The scheme involved the location of gas and water mains, electricity cables and storm and foul water drains. The alleged novelty lay in the idea of locating the main supply route alongside the road rather than underneath it, with branches passing under the road at intervals serving adjacent houses. The appeal to the Patent Appeal Tribunal was turned down by Lloyd-Jacob J who said that the scheme could not constitute a 'manner of manufacture'. He did not need to trouble himself to go on to consider another possibly fatal objection to the application on the ground of lack of novelty. There were other good grounds why the application should have been refused which were not really considered in the judgment, not the least being that it would give a disproportionate monopoly which would be certain to restrict the freedom of providers of public utilities. Finally, the scheme lacked an inventive step, being obvious and representing no more than good practice in the construction industry.

Another example of a refusal because the invention did not represent a new manner of manufacture was *C's Application*,[105] in which an application in respect of an invention comprising a musical notation, in which sharps and flats were printed in different colours and sizes compared to natural notes, was refused. However, in *Pitman's Application*,[106] an application for a patent for an improved method of teaching pronunciation was allowed. The method involved visually conveying inflection and stress by using upper and lower case print and by the vertical displacement of the letters in relation to a median line. The arrangement was in the form of a printed sheet, but the patent specification referred to the use of the sheet in conjunction with a reading machine. The invention possessed a definite mechanical purpose when considered together with the reading machine and was not simply a literary or intellectual arrangement of matter. In this way, the case is distinguishable from *C's Application*.

Industrial application may be in issue where a range of substances is claimed and it is argued that some do not do what is claimed. In *Chiron Corp v Murex Diagnostics Ltd*,[107] a range of polypeptides encoded by a genome of Hepatitis C virus was claimed. The defendant in an infringement action challenged the validity of the patent on the basis, *inter alia*, that the invention was not capable of industrial application because the claim included polypeptides unconnected with Hepatitis C virus. These polypeptides had no conceivable use. At first instance, Aldous J held that the patent was capable of industrial application. He said (at 575):

> Although the range of polypeptides falling within the claims ... may be large, there is no evidence to suggest that once the sequence is known they could not be made by industry.

The defendant appealed, claiming that Aldous J was wrong to substitute the word 'by' for 'in', arguing that the correct question was whether the invention could be made or used *in* industry not *by* industry. The defendant submitted that there was no industry in making the useless. The plaintiff argued that the defendant's objection was merely 'a puzzle at the edge of the claim'.[108] Whilst what was claimed must have some practical use, a claim in respect of practical things is not invalidated by the inclusion at the edge of the claim of something for which there is no present or foreseeable use. The Court of Appeal was unimpressed by that argument and Morritt LJ said (at 607):

> We accept that the polypeptides claimed ... can be made ... [but it is required] that the invention can be made or used 'in any kind of industry' so as to be 'capable' or 'susceptible of industrial application' ... the manifest intention of the Patents Act 1977 and the European Patent Convention [is] that monopoly rights should be confined to that which has some useful purpose. ... the judge fell into error by giving the sections too literal a construction and in considering what can be made and used by industry rather than what can be made and used in any kind of industry.[109]

As a result, the court held that part of the relevant claim was invalid. Of course, in such a case where a range or class of products is claimed, it may be possible to amend the specification to eliminate those incapable of being made or not having the claimed effect.[110]

Industrial application can be equated with *technical effect*,[111] and if there is some technical effect, that is if the use or working of the invention produces some tangible and physical consequences or if the invention is itself a physical

105  (1920) 37 RPC 247.

106  [1969] RPC 646.

107  [1996] RPC 535.

108  A phrase used by Lord Shaw of Dunfermline in *British Thompson-Houston Co Ltd v Corona Lamp Works Ltd* (1922) 39 RPC 49 at 89.

109  However, Morritt LJ used the phrase 'made *and* used in any kind of industry' when the statutory test uses the phrase ' made *or* used in any kind of industry' (emphasis added).

110  *See*, for example, *May & Baker Ltd v Boots Pure Drug Co Ltd* (1950) 67 RPC 23.

111  The phrase 'technical effect' derives from case law; it is not taken from the Patents Act 1977.

entity (as opposed to information), then the requirement should be met. Technical effect is important when considering the scope of the exceptions to patent protection contained in s 1(2) of the Act which is discussed below.

## EXCLUSIONS FROM PATENTABILITY

One form of exclusion has already been described. The treatment or diagnosis in relation to human and animal bodies is excluded because this is not considered to be capable of an industrial application. Section 1(2) and 1(3) of the Act contain a range of things that are excluded from patentability. While in many cases these exclusions can be justified on the ground of lack of technical effect, in some cases the exclusions are more controversial. For example, computer programs are excluded. The exclusions in s 1(2) can be classified as those necessary because of the nature of the subject matter, either being information orientated, and therefore more appropriately protected by copyright, or because they are too abstract and removed from immediate industrial application or manufacture. The exclusions in s 1(3) are based on policy considerations relating to social welfare, morality and ethics.

### Exclusions in s 1(2)

The Patents Act 1977 s 1(2) states that anything which consists of the following (amongst other things – the list is not exhaustive) are not inventions for the purposes of the Act:

(a) a discovery, scientific theory or mathematical method;
(b) a literary, dramatic, musical or artistic work, or any other aesthetic creation whatsoever;
(c) a scheme, rule or method for performing any mental act, playing a game or doing business, or a program for a computer;
(d) the presentation of information.[112]

However, the section goes on to say that 'the foregoing provision shall prevent anything from being treated as an invention … only to the extent that a patent or application for a patent relates to that thing *as such*' (emphasis added). Herein lies the problem: things in the list are not excluded totally and unequivocally, but only if the patent application is directed towards the excluded thing itself.[113] This has caused some judicial differences in the way s 1(2) has been interpreted, especially in the context of computer programs. Before this is examined in detail, the nature of the other exclusions will be discussed briefly.[114]

That the list of excluded things is not exhaustive does not mean that a whole range of other things can be excluded by adding copiously to the list.[115] It is likely that any additions to the list will be, at least, analogous to those specified in the Act. One example of something added to the list was a method of controlling traffic in *Lux Traffic Controls Ltd v Pike Signals Ltd*.[116]

**112** These exclusions are derived from the European Patent Convention, but the position is not far removed from earlier UK law because of the requirement that the invention was a 'manner of manufacture'. This would automatically exclude most of these things anyway.

**113** Thus, theoretically it should be possible to obtain a patent on an industrial application of a scientific theory though not for the theory itself.

**114** The basic principles which have been developed in respect of the patentability of computer programs should also apply to the other excluded materials mentioned in the Patents Act 1977 s 1(2).

**115** *Chiron Corp v Murex Diagnostics Ltd* [1996] RPC 535.

**116** [1993] RPC 107.

## A discovery, scientific theory or mathematical method

The things excepted in this category are the raw materials which are part of the stock-in-trade of scientists, and if previously unknown ones are discovered they should be available to all. But there is another reason why they cannot be patented and that is that, by themselves, they have no technical effect. They have to be applied before there can be a technical effect and therefore an industrial application. But in common with the other exclusions in s 1(2), these exclusions relate to patent applications for the stated things as such. If a mathematical formula is embodied into a measuring device then that device itself may well be patentable.

In *Chiron Corp v Organon Teknika Ltd (No. 3)*[117] the defendant argued that the plaintiff's patent sought to monopolise methods of testing blood, based on its discovery of the sequence of Hepatitis C virus. However, this was rejected by Aldous J, who confirmed that a claim directed to the technical effect of a discovery may well be patentable. He said (at 239):

> Many inventions that are patented arise out of a discovery. However, the section [s 1(2) of the Act] makes it clear that something further is needed to make that discovery patentable ... In the present case, the claims are concerned with a technical aspect of the discovery. They are limited to products, kits, methods of testing, vaccines and cell cultures.

The fact that mathematical theories cannot be patented is not new. In *Young v Rosenthal*,[118] there was an alleged infringement of a patent for improvements in the manufacture of corsets using seams arranged in diagonal patterns in accordance with a mathematical formula. In addressing the jury, Grove J said (at 31):

> An invention of an idea or mathematical principle alone, mathematical formula or anything of that sort could not be the subject of a patent. It must be a manufacture, and it must be a manufacture which is new in this realm.

The jury found that the plaintiff's invention had been copied by the defendant, but that the patent was invalid because it was neither novel nor useful. However, it is arguable that there is a technical effect.[119] The quote from Grove J confirms the view that there is a large overlap between s 1(2) and s 1(1)(c) (the industrial application requirement) and that one or other is unnecessary. This category is discussed further in the section devoted to computer programs.

The practical application of a discovery might be perfectly obvious once the discovery has been made yet it might still be patentable. In *Genentech's Patent*,[120] involving recombinant DNA technology, Whitford J said at first instance (at 566):

> It is trite law that you cannot patent a discovery, but if on the basis of that discovery you can tell people how it can be usefully employed then a patent of invention may result. This in my view would be the case even though once you have made the discovery the way in which it can be usefully employed is obvious enough ... The language of section 1(2) ... is apt as an embodiment of this principle of United Kingdom patent law.

In the subsequent appeal, the Court of Appeal agreed with Whitford J.[121] Dillon LJ said (at 240):

> In so far as a patent claims as an invention the practical application of a discovery, the patent does not, in my judgment, relate only to the discovery as such, even if the practical application may be obvious once the discovery has been made, even though unachievable in the absence of discovery.[122]

117 [1994] FSR 202.

118 (1884) 1 RPC 29.

119 Of course, this case long pre-dates the specific exception in the Patents Act 1977 s 1(2).

120 [1987] RPC 553.

121 [1989] RPC 147.

122 The Court of Appeal again confirmed this approach as being correct in *Gale's Application* [1991] RPC 305.

Proprietors of patents do not engage in research aimed at making discoveries simply for the acclaim resulting from their discovery. They do so with a view to developing a practical application of the discovery so that they may exploit it commercially. The scope of the exclusion of discoveries as such from the grant of a patent was reviewed again in *Chiron Corp v Murex Diagnostics Ltd.*[123] The Court of Appeal accepted that *Genentech* and *Gale* represented good law in this respect and yet again approved Whitford J's statement above. The above principles relating to the patentability of discoveries are very important in the context of genetic engineering where much research is undertaken to discover and isolate genetic sequences and to discover genetic defects causing diseases. As mentioned earlier, the rationale for allowing patents in such areas is to encourage investment in such research and reward the achievement of being able to make something useful that could not be made before.

**123** [1996] RPC 535.

### A literary, dramatic, musical or artistic work, or any other aesthetic creation whatsoever

These works and creations are plainly the subject matter of copyright law or design law, hence the exclusion. In most cases, these works will not be capable of industrial application and are thus excluded twice over. Copyright law is more suited to these types of works because a patent would give a protection that is too strong. Copyright does not provide a monopoly and the independent creation of similar works is permissible.[124] However, such works could be indirectly patented if they were part of some machine or process, for example in *Pitman's Application* discussed above.

**124** But a registered design enjoys a monopoly during its life.

### A scheme, rule or method for performing any mental act, playing a game or doing business, or a program for a computer

(Computer programs are discussed separately later in this chapter.) It is not possible to stop people thinking or doing mental arithmetic. If a patent were to be granted, say, for a method of mental arithmetic, it would be unenforceable anyway. As far as methods of playing games and doing business are concerned, this means that it is not possible to patent, for example, a new chess opening or a new method of assessing bids for large construction schemes.[125] However, copyright law may protect the expression of the scheme, rule or method and, depending upon the circumstances, the law of confidence could give some protection. Some of the things under this heading will not be capable of industrial application anyway (in a direct sense). Unlike most of the other items in this sub-category, computer programs are capable of being applied industrially and are often so used, for example, in controlling an industrial process such as an electronically controlled furnace, or in robotics.

**125** On arithmetic, *see Re Gale's Patent Application* [1991] RPC 305, and on methods of doing business *see Re Merrill Lynch, Pierce Fenner and Smith Inc's Application* [1988] RPC 1 and [1989] RPC 561. Both of these cases are discussed in the section on computer programs below.

### The presentation of information

This is another exception that can be best explained on the ground that this is properly within the scope of copyright. If the information is presented in textual form, it will be a literary work; if it is represented as a flowchart then it will be an artistic work. Other ways of presenting information may give rise to other forms of copyright, such as a film, sound recording or broadcast. If the information is presented orally without previously being recorded, then it will not be protected by copyright until it is so recorded. The law of confidence may also apply to the information presented. One example under this category that might otherwise have met the requirements for patentability was the old 'Swingometer' which was brought out on election days by the BBC. The original device was mechanical and used extensively by that likeable political broadcaster the late Bob MacKenzie to indicate predictions of the likely overall distribution of election successes between the two major parties.[126]

## Computer programs

The exclusion from patentability of computer programs as such is in line with international trends as regards the legal protection of computer programs. Copyright is seen as the proper vehicle for the protection of computer programs, although when the Patents Act 1977 was being drafted it was far from clear whether copyright did protect computer programs. Even before the 1977 Act, computer programs were not generally patentable *per se* because they did not equate to a 'manner of manufacture', but there have been cases, both in the UK and in the USA, where computer programs have been involved in applications for patents, usually as being part of a piece of machinery or an industrial process. Attempts to obtain a patent directly or indirectly for a computer program are a reflection of the perceived attractiveness of patents in terms of the relative strength of protection granted in comparison with copyright law, in spite of the shorter period of protection.

As with the other exclusions, computer programs are not patentable as such. If they are applied in some practical or technical manner, they may be patentable if the claims are directed to that practical or technical feature, although there are other problems to surmount such as if the program is primarily concerned with one of the other exclusions. Nevertheless, there are those who claim that patents are available for software inventions on a much larger scale than is commonly considered to be the case.[127] Much may rest on the manner in which the patent specification and the claims are drafted.

In *Fujitsu Ltd's Application*,[128] the Court of Appeal confirmed that software used to generate and manipulate images of crystal structures of inorganic material was not patentable. The images were simply substitutes of manually assembled plastic models previously used and the software did not provide a technical advantage and was, therefore, excluded under s 1(2)(c) as being a program for a computer. It could also be deemed to be a method of performing a mental act, as discussed later, and this provides yet another trap for the applicant for a patent in respect of a software invention.

Some commentators have argued for the direct protection of computer programs by the law of patents.[129] There are, however, a number of features of the patent system that could hinder the widespread use of patents for computer programs. There may be difficulties in determining the prior act, disclosure of source code might be required, infringement could be difficult to test for and, perhaps worst of all, the length of time to obtain a patent (typically around two or three years) makes the system inappropriate for many software developers.[130]

---

126 The latest computerised version as operated by Peter Snow somehow lacks the charm of its progenitor.

127 For example, *see* Beresford, K. 'The Patenting of Software in Europe and the UK', *Patent World*, April 1997, Issue 91, p. 14.

128 [1997] RPC 608.

129 *See*, for example Bender, D. 'Computer Programs: Should They Be Patentable?' (1968) 68 *Columbia Law Review* 241.

130 For answers to these criticisms, *see* Hart, R. 'Software Patentablility' [1994] 10 CLSR 296 at 302. Another discussion on the appropriateness of the patent system for software is McQuaker, R. 'Software Patents' [1995] 11 CLSR 259.

In the USA, under the 'mental steps' doctrine, a patent cannot be granted for an invention consisting primarily of a mental activity or a mathematical algorithm.[131] In the leading case of *Diamond* v *Diehr*,[132] the United States Supreme Court eased the availability of patents for computer programs by developing a two-stage test:

1 determine whether the mathematical algorithm is either directly or indirectly recited by the claim;
2 determine whether the claim, taken as a whole, merely recites a mathematical algorithm.

This latter test requires the resolution of two ensuing questions:

(a) Does the claim apply the mathematical formula in a structure or process which, considered as a whole, comprises a form of post-solution activity that fulfils a function of the patent laws?
(b) Is the post-solution activity significant? In other words, is the end-product merely a pure number as in *Benson* or *Flook*, or an applied solution that directly affects physical elements or controls process steps?[133]

In *Diamond* v *Diehr* the applicant was seeking to patent a process for curing synthetic rubber employing a mathematical formula used in a programmed digital computer. He was not seeking to patent a mathematical formula and the process was held to be patentable.[134] However, Webber argues that United States law and Australian patent practice have gone further, and that eventually the patenting of computer programs as such will be allowed in those countries.[135]

Webber quotes the US case of *Arrhythmia Research Technology Inc* v *Corazonix Corp*,[136] where, on appeal, it was held that a machine incorporating a process for analysing electro-cardiographic signals was patentable. A new test adopted by the Australian Patent Office is framed in terms of the production of some commercially useful effect. This seems wider than the current situation applying in the UK as neither the *Arrhythmia* case nor the Australian guideline reject an effect that is not external to a computer, that is a process that is entirely software based. In *IBM* v *Commissioner of Patents*[137] a claim to a method of producing a visual representation of a curve comprising a series of computations was allowed on appeal even though there was no specific application or physical steps within the claim.[138]

The rationale for the law as expressed in *Diamond* v *Diehr* is that a patent should not pre-empt or monopolise something, such as an algorithm or mathematical method, that is traditionally not patentable. Nevertheless, allowing software-based processes does not necessarily restrict algorithms, and is not the same as granting patents for computer programs *as such*. It is just an alternative view of what constitutes a patentable technical effect. The position in the USA and Australia is not dissimilar to that subscribed to by the UK and the European Patent Office. However, it seems that the application of apparently similar law in the USA results in a more generous approach to software patents there. The electronic securities trading system in the *Merrill Lynch* case, discussed below, was held unpatentable in the UK even though it was patented in the USA.[139] Perhaps it is really a question of the interpretation of what constitutes a technical effect. Two aspects concerning the patentability of computer programs which are of particular interest are the form of storage and the technical effect produced by running the program.

131 The UK courts have also applied the mental steps doctrine to computer programs. For a comparative description of patent protection in the USA, Germany, France, Japan and Canada, *see* Hoffman, G., Grossman, J. Keane, P. and Westby, J. 'Protection for Computer Software: An International Overview: Part 2' [1989] 1 EIPR 7.

132 (1981) 450 US 175.

133 *Gottschalk* v *Benson* (1972) 409 US 63, *Parker* v *Flook* (1978) 437 US 584.

134 This case has been followed subsequently in the USA on a number of occasions.

135 Webber, D. 'Software Patents: A New Era in Australia and the United States?' [1993] 5 EIPR 181. *See also* Hoptroff, C. 'Wider International Patentability' (1994) in The Patent Office, *Legal Protection for Software Related Innovation*, The Patent Office, at p. 41.

136 (1990) 22 USPQ 2d 1033.

137 (1992) AIPC 90-853.

138 Hoptroff, C., *op cit*, at 45.

139 Hoptroff, C., *op cit*, at 43.

## Mode of storage

In the UK, there were some patent applications involving computer programs prior to the 1977 Act where the important issue was whether the invention related to a manner of manufacture. For example, in *Gever's Application*,[140] data processing apparatus was arranged to work in a certain way by the use of punched cards. The purpose of the apparatus was to file world trade marks in such a way that they could be easily searched for similarity and prior registration. The patent application, concerning a piece of machinery which functioned in a certain way because of the punched cards, was allowed to proceed. The cards were described by Graham J as a 'manner of manufacture' because he considered that a punched card was analogous to a cam for controlling the cutting path of a lathe. This was distinguished from a card that merely had written or printed material on it, intended to convey information to the human eye or mind and not meant to be ancillary to some machine by being specially shaped for that purpose. However, this approach is at odds with technical reality because, essentially, the form of storage of the computer program should not be relevant to the question of its patentability. Nevertheless, in another case, *Burrough's Corporation (Perkin's) Application*,[141] computer programs which controlled the transmission of data to terminals from a central computer (a communications system) were held to be the proper subject matter of a patent because the programs were embodied in physical form. They were 'hard-wired', that is to say permanently embedded in the electronic circuits of the equipment. A more recent example of this artificial distinction between forms of storage of computer programs is the decision of Aldous J in *Re Gale's Patent Application*[142] where he suggested that a programmed ROM (read only memory) chip was patentable but the same program on a magnetic disk would not have been patentable. This inconsistent approach was remedied in the Court of Appeal where the operation of the program was seen to be all-important and the mode of storage to be irrelevant. The applicant had developed a computer program to calculate square roots which was incorporated in read only memory (ROM) circuitry and which did not produce any technical effect whatsoever. Nicholls LJ felt obliged to part company with Aldous J on the distinction between a claim relating to a magnetic disk containing a computer program and a ROM with particular circuitry. To hold otherwise would mean that any computer program would be patentable simply by installing it on a computer chip even if it produced no technical, physical or tangible effect. Such an approach would drive a coach and horses through s 1(2) as regards computer programs.

## Technical effect

Two alternative approaches have been made to the question of the patent protection of inventions that include a computer program and the effect of the words 'as such' at the end of s 1(2). The first is that the patent application should be considered without the contribution of the excepted thing. For example, if a machine includes a computer program[143] it is then a question of whether the machine, without taking the computer program into account, adds anything to the state of the art. Does the machine, ignoring the computer program, meet the requirements for patentability? If the only novel and inventive step comes from or resides in the computer program itself, then the machine as a whole is not

140 [1970] RPC 91.

141 [1974] RPC 147.

142 [1991] RPC 305.

143 Or if the invention incorporates a programmed computer.

patentable. The judgment of Falconer J in the case of *Re Merrill Lynch, Pierce Fenner & Smith Inc's Application*[144] at first instance illustrates this approach.[145] The invention related to an improved data processing system for implementing an automatic trading market for securities. The system received and stored the best current bids, qualified customer buy and sell orders, executed orders, produced reports of trade particulars for customers and national stock reporting systems in addition to monitoring stock inventory and profit. The Principal Examiner of the Patent Office rejected the application for a patent and the appeal against his decision to the Patents Court was dismissed. It was held that where an invention involves any of the excluded materials in s 1(2), then the proper construction of the qualification in that subsection requires that the Patent Office enquires into whether the inventive step resides in the contribution of the excluded matter alone. If the inventive step comes only from the excluded material, then the invention is not patentable because of s 1(2). However, in a somewhat contradictory statement, Falconer J said:

> If some practical (i.e. technical) effect is achieved by the computer or machine operating according to the instructions contained in the program, and such effect is novel and inventive (i.e. not obvious), a claim directed to that practical effect will be patentable, notwithstanding it is defined by that computer program.

The application failed because there was no practical or technical effect – the operation was entirely software based. However, the Technical Board of Appeal in the European Patent Office had previously taken a different approach, although Falconer J considered that this was not inconsistent with his decision. He was later to be proved wrong.[146]

In *Vicom Systems Inc's Patent Application*,[147] a different approach was taken. This case concerned an application to the European Patent Office and the invention related to digital image processing, the process steps being expressed mathematically in the form of an algorithm. It was held by the Technical Board of Appeal that this claim was allowable after amendment to stress the technical effect. It was said that:

> ... a claim directed to a technical process which process is carried out under the control of a program (be this implemented in hardware or in software), cannot be regarded as relating to a computer program as such within the meaning of Article 52(3) EPC, as it is the application of the program for determining the sequence of steps in the process and it is the process for which in effect protection is sought. Consequently, such a claim is allowable under Article 52(2)(c) and (3) EPC.[148]

Thus, in an application such as this, where the subject matter of the invention is the technical effect produced by the operation of a computer program, the technical effect should be patentable, provided the other requirements are present, that is novelty, inventive step and industrial application. The patent is granted in relation to the technical effect and not the computer program as such, and it should make no difference whether or not the inventive step resides in the computer program itself. This decision is entirely consistent with the Patents Act 1977 and the European Patent Convention and, on a purely logical basis, the method of implementing the invention should make not one iota of difference. Otherwise, a new and inventive technical effect would be patentable if it was implemented by mechanical means (for example, by using a diesel engine to power rods, cams and levers), but not if advantage was taken of modern

**144** [1988] RPC 1.

**145** There was a further unsuccessful appeal to the Court of Appeal, *Re Merrill Lynch, Pierce Fenner & Smith Inc* [1989] RPC 561.

**146** The then current differences in interpretation of the scope of the exclusions from patent between the United Kingdom and the European Patent Office are described in Hart, R. J. 'Applications of Patents to Computer Technology – UK and the EPO Harmonisation?' [1989] 2 EIPR 42.

**147** [1987] 2 EPOR 74, [1987] 1 OJ EPO 14.

**148** Article 52(2) and (3) of the European Patent Convention corresponds to the Patents Act 1977 s 1(2).

technology by implementing the invention electronically using a programmed computer. Such a result would be absurd. It would provide a disincentive to apply robotics and computer control systems industrially. The *Vicom* case also confirms that there should be no distinction between different modes of storage (hardware or software) as regards patentability.

The apparent inconsistency between the UK approach and the European Patent Office approach was resolved and the European Patent Office's interpretation of the effect of the exclusions was approved of in *Genentech Inc's Patent* discussed earlier.[149]

One issue that had not been fully resolved was the extent of the patentability of computer programs when installed or used in a conventional computer, for example, if an item of computer hardware contains some computer software but the former is orthodox and the latter is new and contains an inventive step, but the two together do not produce any external technical effect. In *Genentech Inc's Patent*,[150] Dillon LJ said (at 240):

> It would be nonsense for the [Patents Act 1977] to forbid the patenting of a computer program, and yet permit the patenting of a floppy disk containing the computer program, or an ordinary computer when programmed with the program; it can well be said, as it seems to me, that a patent for a computer when programmed or for the disk containing the program is no more than a patent for the program as such.

This approach was approved of in the Court of Appeal in *Re Merrill Lynch, Pierce Fenner & Smith Inc's Application*,[151] where Fox LJ said that '... it cannot be permissible to patent an item excluded by s 1(2) under the guise of an article which contains that item' and, more recently, in *Re Gale's Patent Application*.[152] To hold otherwise would be to totally undermine the effect of s 1(2) and there must, therefore, be some technical effect that is novel and non-obvious which results from the use of the computer program and which is not limited to the mere device in which the program is contained or executed. If the only conceivable use of the computer program is running it in a computer there can be no patent. The European Patent Office has also adopted this stratagem in *IBM/Document Abstracting and Retrieving*,[153] where an application for a patent for a method of automatically abstracting, storing and retrieving documents in an information storage and retrieval system was rejected by the Technical Board of Appeal. One crude but effective way of distinguishing between patentable and non-patentable computer programs (and other excluded materials) is to differentiate between intellectual and industrial uses of computer technology and to accept, as a rule of thumb, that intellectual effects are not patentable whereas industrial effects are.

Subsequent cases have confirmed the above approach. An application for a patent for an expert system shell[154] was refused in *Re Wang Laboratories Inc's Application*[155] because it was for nothing more than a computer program. When the system had been developed it did not form with the computer a new machine. Similarly, a claim in relation to a compiler program[156] was no more than a claim for the compiler program itself.[157] In Germany it has been confirmed that a similar approach applies, and in *Re The Computer Generation of Chinese Characters*[158] a word processing program using Chinese characters was not patentable because it did not solve a technical problem by a technical method and did not make a technical contribution to the state of the art. It was mainly intellectual in nature and did not make use of methods beyond human intellectual activity.

149 [1989] RPC 147.

150 [1989] RPC 147.

151 [1989] RPC 561. *See also Re Wang Laboratories Inc's Application* [1991] RPC 463.

152 [1991] RPC 305.

153 [1990] EPOR 98.

154 An expert system shell is a program or suite of programs that allow a system developer to enter rules and facts to form an expert system directed towards providing solutions in particular knowledge domains. For example, a computer system that gives medical advice on stomach pains.

155 [1991] RPC 463.

156 A program used to create an object code version of a source code program.

157 *Re Hitachi Ltd's Application* [1991] RPC 415.

158 [1993] FSR 315.

## Mental steps doctrine

Many computer programs perform operations that were or could have been performed by the human mind. As such, methods of performing mental acts are excluded by s 1(2). However, even if such a method is incorporated in a computer in a way which is different to the way a human would perform the mental act, this does not make the invention patentable. In *Wang*, Aldous J said (at 472):

> The fact that the scheme, rule or method is part of a computer program and is therefore converted into steps which are suitable for use by a person operating the computer does not matter ... The method remains a method for performing a mental act, whether a computer is used or not ... The method may well be different when a computer is used, but to my mind it still remains a method for performing a mental act, whether or not the computer adopts steps that would not ordinarily be used by the human mind.

**159** [1993] RPC 427.

In *Raytheon Co's Application*,[159] the invention was an automated process for identifying ships from a silhouette which was then matched against a database of known silhouettes. The deputy judge rejected the application on the basis that it was a method of performing a mental act. The exception is far-ranging if this is right, and in the light of this case and *Wang*, automation by technical means of operations that could in principle, even if not in practice, be carried out in the human mind is caught by the exception no matter how unrealistic (or even impossible) it would be for a human being to carry out the act. Taken to its extreme, this approach could prevent the patenting of all software-related inventions. Once more the UK seems to be at odds with the approach of the European Patent Office. Haselden argues that the latter is likely to accept applications involving the automation of a mental act which include a sufficient technical contribution.[160]

**160** Haselden, D. 'UK and European Patentability' (1994) in The Patent Office, *Legal Protection for Software Related Innovation*, The Patent Office, 30 at 39.

**161** [1997] RPC 608.

In *Fujitsu Ltd's Application*,[161] the applicant developed software to produce computer-generated images of any two chosen crystal structures of inorganic material, parts of which could be selected. This data was then converted into data containing a combination of the two chosen crystal structures producing an image of the resulting combined structure for the purpose of research. The intention was to replace the traditional, manual method of constructing a crystal structure by assembling three-dimensional plastic models. The Patent Office rejected the application objecting that it was the performing of a mental act under s 1(2)(c). Laddie J in the Patents Court agreed.[162] The Court of Appeal confirmed that the application was caught by s 1(2)(c), being either an application for a computer program as such or a method of performing a mental act as such.

**162** *Fujitsu Ltd's Application* [1996] RPC 511. Laddie J set out the principles to apply in a useful manner.

As the operation relied on the operator's selection of data and exercise of skill and judgment, the application was in substance for a scheme or method for performing a mental act. Originally, the traditional method was to assemble a plastic models by hand and all the computer program did was to automate this operation. The images were simply substitutes of a manually assembled plastic model previously produced which did not provide a technical advantage and therefore were excluded by s 1(2)(c) as being a program for a computer. Aldous LJ rejected the appellant's argument that that exclusion should be construed narrowly, requiring that the mental act should be as performed in the human mind. He said that the question should be determined without recourse to evidence as to how the human mind actually works. Nor was there any room for reading into the test that the act had to be one that had previously been performed by the human mind.

The difficulty for the applicant was that the practical application or technical effect produced by means of the computer program was, itself, excluded material, being a scheme or method of performing a mental act. The result of all the case law in relation to s 1(2) would appear to be that a practical application of any of the things listed in the subsection is patentable in principle, provided it is not itself within the list.[163] Thus, a new software driven process for making metal castings should be patentable, but not a new computer program to present information in a new manner even though it could be argued that such an application is neither for a computer program *as such* nor for the presentation of information *as such*.

It is noteworthy that the equivalent application by Fujitsu in Japan was granted and that the World Trade Organization TRIPs (Trade Related Aspects of Intellectual Property Rights) Agreement contains no express exclusion for computer programs. The debate over the desirability of granting patents to software inventions is sure to continue. The software industry is itself split over the issue. Many small software companies are concerned that the big companies will monopolise whole areas of software technology. This fear disregards the basic fact that few software inventions will be patentable for other reasons.

Many newly written computer programs will lack novelty, for example, where the program simply automates a known process. Alternatively, it could be regarded as obvious to the skilled man to apply computer technology to an existing manual process. Surely, a better approach to the *Fujitsu* application would have been to reject the application on either of these grounds. However, where a computer program performs some completely new and inventive process or procedure, there is little justification for denying patent protection simply because that process or procedure is within the excluded material. Would it be right to deny a patent for a computer-controlled method of operating traffic signals at a busy intersection which was based on an entirely new theory or algorithm of traffic control? It would be patentable if that same theory or algorithm could be put into operation by means of conventional electrical circuitry which does not include any computer programs. That is a very unsatisfactory and illogical conclusion.

### Exclusions in s 1(3)

Further exclusions are contained in the Patents Act 1977 s 1(3) and the things excluded can be considered to be so excluded mainly on policy grounds. For example, s 1(3)(a) excludes inventions, the publication or exploitation of which would generally be expected to encourage offensive, immoral or anti-social behaviour. Section 1(4) states that behaviour shall not be regarded as offensive, immoral or anti-social only because it is prohibited by law; something more than mere illegality is required. It may be possible to obtain a patent for an invention which can be used in two ways, one of which is illegal. For example, an invention might relate to a radio transmitter/receiver that can be used lawfully by licensed radio amateur operators (radio 'hams'), but other persons might use it to listen to or interfere with police transmissions or to broadcast without a licence. The fact that the radio set may have an unlawful use does not automatically debar it from patentability. To some extent, there is some discretion in the decision to accept the patent application, subject to appeal. It depends on whether the invention is expected to encourage the sort of behav-

163 Assuming that all the other requirements such as novelty and inventive step are present.

**164** For example, in *Schering AG's Application* [1971] RPC 337, a contraceptive method was not rejected, but in *Riddlesbarger's Application* (1936) 53 RPC 57 the Royal Prerogative was exercised to refuse a patent for a contraceptive device. Prior to the 1977 Act, there was no direct equivalent to s 1(3).

**165** Louis Pasteur obtained a patent for purified brewer's yeast in the United States of America in 1873. Eisenschitz, T. S. (1987), *Patents, Trade Marks and Designs in Information Work,* Croom Helm, at p. 54. In *American Cyanamid Co (Dann's) Patent* [1971] RPC 425, a method of producing antibiotics using micro-organisms was held to be patentable.

**166** Amended by the Plant Varieties Act 1983. From 27 May 1995 there has been a Community Plant Variety Rights Regulation (Council Regulation 2100/94) OJ L227, 1.9.94, p. 1.

**167** The Plant Varieties and Seeds Act 1964 s 3. For trees and grapevines, the minimum period of protection is 25 years and for other plant varieties it is 20 years.

**168** Ibid s 4.

**169** Eisenschitz, T. S., *op cit,* at p. 53.

**170** For example, in *Genentech Inc's Patent* [1989] RPC 147. See Reid, B. C. (1993) *A Practical Guide to Patent Law* (2nd edn) Sweet & Maxwell, at pp. 23–4.

**171** *Onco-Mouse/Harvard* [1990] EPOR 4 and [1990] EPOR 501.

**172** OJ C 286, 22.9.97, p. 87.

**173** The *Official Journal* reference of the common position text is OJ C 100, 8.4.98, p. 17.

iour described. Contraceptive devices no longer are considered to encourage immoral behaviour in the UK, although they might be so considered in other countries that are parties to the European Patent Convention and which are predominantly Roman Catholic.[164] Examples of inventions which might be rejected as being expected to encourage offensive, immoral or anti-social behaviour might be a booby-trap bomb or a 'do-it-yourself' abortion kit. An invention that some might argue should have been excluded on the ground of encouraging anti-social behaviour is the Sony 'Walkman'! However, bearing in mind the present social climate and degree of tolerance, it is unlikely that s 1(3)(a) will be used very often.

Section 1(3)(b) excludes from patentability varieties of animals or plants, or any essentially biological process for the production of animals or plants. This does not extend to micro-biological processes or the products of such processes, for example brewer's yeast.[165] Plants may be protected under the Plant Varieties and Seeds Act 1964.[166] Under this Act, proprietary rights are granted to the breeders or discoverers of distinctive, uniform and stable plant varieties for a period not exceeding 30 years.[167] The rights are monopolistic in nature and are to produce and sell (or offer to sell) reproductive material of the plant variety.[168] The scheme is administered by the Plant Variety Rights Office under the control of the Controller of Plant Variety Rights.

One problem with s 1(3)(b) is how to differentiate between biological and micro-biological processes. The distinction is of primary importance because the former are not patentable under any circumstances, while the latter may qualify if the other requirements are satisfied. Micro-organisms can be considered to be very small, independent units invisible to the naked eye, and to be patentable some form of human intervention is required.[169] Genetic engineering processes and techniques are patentable and are likely to become of some importance. Patents have been granted in the United Kingdom in relation to DNA.[170]

## Genetic engineering

It is possible to obtain a patent in some countries for a new breed of animal, for example in the United States, but the scope of the exclusion in s 1(3)(b), and the corresponding provision of the European Patent Convention, Article 53(b), is unclear. The Board of Appeal of the European Patent Office granted a patent for a laboratory mouse that had been genetically altered (a transgenic animal) so as to be more likely to develop cancerous cells in a short period of time.[171] It was accepted that this mouse was not a new variety of animal and, as a result, not excepted from the grant of a patent. Obviously, this is a very sensitive, ethical issue and decisions in this area require careful consideration of animal rights and the potential benefits to man and animal alike.

For some time, there have been moves to adopt a Directive on the legal protection of biotechnological inventions. After first rejecting a proposal on 1 March 1995, the European Parliament rejected the amended proposed Directive on 16 July 1997.[172] However, it was still accepted that this was an area in need of clarification and a further revised proposal was prepared by the Commission and was adopted by the Council on 26 February 1998. Following this, on 12 May 1998, the European Parliament voted to accept the common position text of the Directive on the legal protection of biotechnological inventions.[173] The following description is based on the common position text.

The recitals to the Directive give important information as to its *raison d'être*. It is seen as important because of the increasing role in a broad range of industries being played by biotechnology and genetic engineering. This is a matter of some importance in the future industrial development of the Community. Adequate legal protection is needed to encourage the high-risk investment involved in research and development in biotechnology, in particular in genetic engineering. Advantages of protecting biotechnology and genetic engineering identified in the recitals include the development of less polluting and more economical methods of cultivation and improvements in combating major epidemics, endemic diseases and hunger in the world. It is noted that the Agreement on the Trade Related Aspects of Intellectual Property Rights (TRIPs Agreement) requires that patent protection must be provided for products and processes in all areas of technology.

Of course, genetic engineering is a sensitive subject raising numerous moral and legal issues. Something of a complex balancing act must be achieved incorporating safeguards in respect of the fundamental dignity and integrity of the person. Indeed, if an invention is based on or uses biological material of human origin, the person from whom the material has been taken must give free and informed consent to the filing of the patent application.[174]

174 Recital 26.

The Directive is to be without prejudice to existing national exclusions from patentability of processes for treatment of the human or animal body by surgery or therapy and diagnostic methods practised on the human or animal body. Other things are excluded including a list of specific things contrary to the *ordre public* or morality. The list is not exhaustive but does provide national patent offices a guide to what else should be excluded under this head.[175] Unlike the list of exclusions in s 1(2) of the Patents Act 1977, this list is likely to grow significantly with time.

175 Recital 38.

Article 1 of the Directive states that biotechnological inventions shall be protected under national patent law and that national patent laws shall be adjusted accordingly; presumably, this will filter down through changes to the European Patent Convention. The Directive is to be without prejudice to member states' international obligations, particularly under the TRIPs Agreement and the Convention on Biological Diversity.[176]

176 Third Conference of the Parties to the Biodiversity Convention, November 1996.

Article 2 gives important definitions. Thus, 'biological material' means any material containing genetic information and capable of reproducing itself or being reproduced in a biological system, and 'microbiological process' means any process involving or performed upon or resulting in microbiological material. A process for the production of plants or animals is deemed to be essentially biological if it consists entirely of natural phenomena, such as crossing or selection.

The basic statement of what is patentable is given in Article 3 as inventions which are new, involve an inventive step and are capable of industrial application. This is so even if they concern a product consisting of or containing biological material or a process by means of which biological material is produced, processed or used. The fact that the material previously occurred in nature does not prevent it being patented if it is isolated from its natural environment or produced by means of a technical process.

There are a number of exclusions from patentability under Articles 4 to 6.

● Article 4 excludes plant and animal varieties and any essentially biological process (though not microbiological processes or technical process or products derived from such processes), much the same as under the present version of the European Patent Convention and the Patents Act 1977. However, inventions which concern plants or animals may be patentable if the technical feasibility of the invention is not confined to a particular plant or animal variety.

- The human body (at various stages) and the simple discovery of one of its elements such as the sequence or partial sequence of a gene is not patentable under Article 5. However, an element isolated from the human body or otherwise produced by a technical process including genetic sequences may be patentable even if the structure of that element is identical to that of the natural element. This bears some relation to the approach in *Genentech*, discussed earlier. For patents involving genetic sequences, the industrial application must be disclosed in the patent application.

- The *ordre public* and morality exception in Article 6 mirrors the exception in Article 53(a) of the European Patent Convention and states that the following, in particular, are to be considered unpatentable:
  (a) processes for cloning human beings;
  (b) processes for modifying the germ line genetic identity of human beings;
  (c) uses of human embryos for industrial or commercial purposes;
  (d) processes for modifying the genetic identity of animals which are likely to cause them suffering without any substantial medical benefit to man or animal, and also animals resulting from such processes.

The scope of protection afforded is defined in Articles 8 to 11. Basically, the protection of biological material or processes to produce biological material possessing specific characteristics extends to derived material possessing those same characteristics: Article 8. Where the patented product contains or consists of genetic information, the protection extends to all material in which the product is incorporated and in which the genetic information is contained and performs its function: Article 9. However, this is without prejudice to the exclusion in Article 5(1), being the human body (at various stages) and the simple discovery of one of its elements such as the sequence or partial sequence of a gene.

Article 10 contains what can best be described as an exhaustion of rights principle. The protection does not extend to biological material obtained by propagating or multiplying biological material placed on the market within the Community by the patent holder or with his consent where such propagation or multiplication necessarily results from the application for which the material was marketed. Such derived material must not, however, be subsequently used for other propagation or multiplication. Article 11 allows derogation from Articles 8 and 9 in the context of the sale or other commercialisation of plant propagating material, or breeding stock or animal reproductive material to a farmer. For example, sale of the relevant material to a farmer carries an implied authorisation to the farmer to use the product of his harvest material for propagation or multiplication by him on his own farm as permitted under Council Regulation No. 2100/94 on Community plant variety rights.[177] In respect of breeding stock or animal reproductive material, the implied authorisation is for use for agricultural purposes including making the animal or animal reproductive material available for the purposes of pursuing the farmer's agricultural activity, though not including sale within the framework or for the purpose of a commercial reproduction activity. The extent and conditions of this latter derogation shall be determined by national law, regulations and practices.

177 OJ L 227, 1.9.94, p. 1 as amended by Regulation No. 2506/95 OJ L 258, 28.10.95, p. 3.

There are special provisions for compulsory licensing, including cross-licensing in relation to plant varieties under Article 12 and provisions for the deposit and access to biological material which cannot be described in a patent application so as to enable the invention to be reproduced by a person skilled in the art: Articles 13 and 14.[178]

178 There are equivalent provisions in the Patent Rules 1995, SI 1995/2093, Sch 2 in respect of the deposit of micro-organisms.

The Commission's European Group on Ethics in Science and New Technologies is charged with evaluating all ethical aspects of biotechnology under Article 7. The Commission is required under Article 16 to submit the following reports to the European Parliament and the Council:

(a) every five years, a report shall be submitted stating any problems encountered with regard to the relationship between the Directive and international agreements on the protection of human rights to which member states have acceded;
(b) every two years a report assessing the implications for basic genetic engineering research of failure to publish, or late publication of, papers on subjects which could be patentable – this is because one of the impacts of granting patents is that dissemination of information relating to new inventions is delayed usually either until the application has a priority date or until the patent specification is published; there may also be problems in that only the minimum information required for disclosure under patent law is made available;
(c) every year, a report on the development and implications of patent law in the field of biotechnology and genetic engineering.

Compliance with the Directive is required two years after the date of its publication in the *Official Journal* of the European Communities. In terms of microbiology, the European Patent Convention already appears to comply with much of the Directive. However, it is difficult to gauge the precise limits of that compliance and the Directive gives welcome clarification and brings much wanted detail to this area of patent law. As far as biological material is concerned, the Directive marks a step forward. Although the general rule is that plant or animal varieties or biological processes for the production of plants or animals are still excluded from patentability, the latter may be patentable if they are applicable to more than one variety of plant or animal – cross-variety applications may be patentable.

The introduction of further safeguards is welcome, but how well they will work in practice remains to be seen. It seems that the Commission, European Parliament and Council also have reservations, which are reflected in the need for monitoring and reporting imposed on the Commission. We could see some strange or bizarre subject matter in patent applications in the future. It is interesting to note that, whilst processes for cloning of humans are unpatentable, there is no such exclusion for animals. Dolly the sheep may soon be joined by many other animal clones. A further difficulty might be that the safeguards in terms of animals seem weak. Processes for modifying the genetic identity of animals likely to cause them suffering may be patentable if that suffering is outweighed by the medical benefits. In many cases such benefits will only be perceived benefits at the time the patent is applied for and not certain to be attained.

## OWNERSHIP AND DEALINGS IN PATENTS

The Patents Act 1977 contains a large number of provisions concerning the ownership of patents (the owner of a patent is referred to as its proprietor), dealings with patents (assignment, licensing, mortgaging), Crown use, compulsory licences and licences as of right. The provisions are generally lengthy and complex. At the outset, a distinction has to be made between the inventor and the proprietor of a patent, although in some cases the inventor will be the proprietor of the patent. The inventor of an invention is, by s 7(3), the actual devisor of the invention. Where the invention is the result of the combined efforts of two or more persons, they are the joint inventors of the invention. Where there are joint inventors, it is inappropriate to divide up the claims to see which has contributed which element.[179] It is important to identify who in substance was responsible for the invention, and if that is two or more persons then they are the joint inventors.

The proprietor is the person to whom the patent is granted and who, therefore, has the right to work the patent. If the inventor is not the proprietor of the patent, he has a right to be mentioned as being the inventor in any patent granted and in any published application.[180] Failure to identify the inventor will prevent an application from proceeding. A patent is a form of personal property,[181] but not a thing in action, and may be transferred, created or granted only in accordance with s 30(2)–(7) inclusive. The availability of compulsory licences in certain circumstances prevents the abuse of the monopoly granted to the proprietor of the patent.

### Proprietorship

While any person can apply for a patent either on his own or jointly, it will be granted only to certain persons identified in s 7. Primarily, it will be granted to the inventor, or joint inventors, except where someone else has a better entitlement to it. This may arise through any enactment or rule of law, any foreign law or treaty or international convention, or by any enforceable term in an agreement with the inventor that was entered into prior to the making of the invention. An example might be where an inventor is commissioned to produce an invention to overcome a particular problem. Equitable interests are not effective to make any other person entitled to the patent as far as the Act is concerned. The patent will be granted to the legal owner only, although any equitable owner may have a claim to the benefit accruing from the patent under a trust. Additionally, an invention made by an employee shall be taken to belong to his employer.[182] This situation might, in any case, be covered expressly by the contract of employment. Section 7(2)(c) also provides for the grant of a patent to a successor in title to the person who would otherwise have been entitled to the patent.

To facilitate patent applications there is a rebuttable presumption that the person making the application is entitled to the grant of the patent.

At any time before a patent has been granted a reference may be made under s 8(1) to the Comptroller to determine whether the person making the reference (alone or with any other persons) is entitled to be granted the patent, or has or would have any right in or under the patent or application for the patent. A

179 *Henry Brothers (Magherafelt) Ltd* v *The Ministry of Defence and Northern Ireland Office* [1997] RPC 693.

180 The Patents Act 1977 s 13(1).

181 Ibid s 30(1).

182 Ibid s 39.

reference may also be brought by any of two or more co-proprietors of an application to determine whether any right in or under the application should be transferred or granted to any other person. Where the Comptroller considers the question arising would be more properly dealt with by the court, he may decline to deal with it, effectively handing it over to the court. The Comptroller (or court) may order, *inter alia*, that the application may proceed in the name of the person making the reference, solely or jointly with any other applicant, or refuse to grant the patent, or order the application be amended so as to exclude matter in respect of which the question was referred or order the transfer or grant of any licence or other right in or under the application and give direction to any person for carrying out the provisions of the order.

In *Goddin and Rennies Application*,[183] Rennie made contributions to Goddin's design for covers for circular fish tanks. Rennie had visited the site at which Goddin had erected a tank under an obligation of confidence, and later it was agreed that Rennie would make the net covers for the tank to be fixed to the frame of the cover. The patent was applied for in the name of Goddin's company, Woodwick Fish Farms Ltd, and mentioned both Goddin and Rennie as inventors. Later, Goddin made an application under s 8(1). The patent application had been assigned to Goddin.

The Court of Session, Outer House in Scotland held that there was an implied term in the agreement between Rennie and Goddin to the effect that any improvement thought of by Rennie would belong to Goddin's company. However, Rennie had made a suggestion for an elliptical frame before the contractual arrangement and separate from it. He was, therefore, entitled to the benefit of the relevant parts of the claims involving that suggestion. The patent was granted in Goddin's name only, subject to Rennie having an irrevocable exclusive licence in respect of those parts of the claims relating to the feature of the elliptical frame with a power to sub-licence. The royalty was set at $2\frac{1}{2}$ per cent of the ex-works sale price of products made under those claims and Goddin was to be solely responsible for the cost of maintaining the patent.

Under s 12, provisions not unlike those in s 8 apply in relation to an application made under the law of a country other than the United Kingdom or under any treaty or in a convention country.[184] This is subject to provisions concerning jurisdiction and stays under s 82, for example, where proceedings are before the competent authority in respect of the foreign, treaty or convention application.

Where there are two or more proprietors of a patent, their ownership is equivalent to ownership as tenants in common, that is they are each entitled to an undivided share in the patent,[185] and if one of the owners dies his share passes under his will or by intestacy and does not automatically pass to the remaining owners.

Under s 36(2) where two or more persons are proprietors, each may 'by himself or his agents' do for his own benefit without the consent of the other or others any act which would otherwise infringe the patent. The term 'agent' is used in a loose sense and would cover, for example, an independent contractor working the invention for the benefit of the joint proprietor. The question is whether the act is, in substance, an act under a licence or use by the proprietor. In *Henry Brothers (Margerafelt) Ltd* v *The Ministry of Defence and Northern Ireland Office*,[186] the Crown, being a joint proprietor, engaged an independent contractor to construct a building incorporating the invention. It was held that

183 [1996] RPC 141.

184 An example is *Ladney and Hendry's International Application* [1998] RPC 319 where a reference was made in respect of an application under the Patent Cooperation Treaty. The Court of Appeal reinstated the hearing officer's decision that the reference failed.

185 The Patents Act 1977 s 36(1).

186 [1997] RPC 693.

this was use by the Crown, the contractor was the means by which the Crown obtained construction of its building. There are, however, some limits to what a joint proprietor can do without the consent of the other or others. Under s 36(3) the consent of the others is required to grant a licence under the patent, or to assign or mortgage a share in the patent.

An agreement between joint owners to the effect that one will forfeit his rights under certain circumstances, for example, after failing to pay a share in the expenses related to renewing the patent, will not necessarily be considered to be void as a penalty clause. However, the court has an equitable jurisdiction to grant relief against forfeiture. It was held thus in *BICC plc v Burndy Corp*,[187] where the court granted an extension of time for payment of the agreed expenses associated with the upkeep of the patent.

187 [1985] RPC 273.

### Employee inventors

The Act deals with employee inventors in far more detail than is the case, for example, in copyright law. The relevant provisions are of great import because a very large number of applications for the grant of a patent will concern inventions made by employees. 'Employee' is defined in s 130(1) as being a person who works or worked under a contract of employment, or in employment under or for the purposes of a government department or a person who serves or who has served in the naval, military or air forces of the Crown. By s 39, an employee invention belongs to the employer in either of the following circumstances:

1 the invention was made in the course of the employee's normal duties as an employee or, if not, in the course of duties specifically assigned to the employee, provided that, in both cases, the circumstances are such that the invention might reasonably be expected to result from the carrying out of those duties (s 39(1)(a));
2 the invention was made in the course of the employee's duties which, at the time of making the invention, were such that the employee had a special obligation to further the interests of the employer's undertaking (s 39(1)(b)).

In all other circumstances, the invention belongs to the employee rather than to the employer.

These provisions apply as between the employee and the employer and would not, for example, affect any third-party rights. They will apply where an employee's duties include making inventions in the normal course of his duties, for example, where an employee is engaged in a research and development capacity. They would also apply where a workshop manager was given the task of trying to solve a particular problem with the employer's equipment or using his employer's working practices, and the manager makes the invention in the course of carrying out that task. They would not normally apply where, say, a clerical worker working for a manufacturing company devised an invention which improved his employer's assembly line and which had nothing to do with the employee's normal duties and in respect of which he had not been assigned any relevant specific duties.

The terms of the contract of employment, express or implied, will assist the court in determining whether the circumstances in which the invention was made fall into either of the above two categories. In *Electrolux Ltd* v

*Hudson*,[188] an employee of the plaintiff (a company making electrical appliances) invented, with his wife at home one evening, an adapter for a vacuum cleaner that would allow the use of any type of disposable bag in any make of vacuum cleaner taking disposable bags. At the time the defendant was employed as a senior storekeeper. The plaintiff claimed entitlement to the patent for the invention on the basis of the defendant's contract of employment. However, it was held that the relevant term in the contract was too wide (it was probably too wide even for a person employed in a research capacity) and the court refused to imply an appropriate term because the employee was not employed to invent; he was employed as a storekeeper.

188 [1977] FSR 312.

A reference under s 37 (determination of the right to a patent after grant) was made in *Greater Glasgow Health Board's Application*[189] to see whether an employed hospital doctor was entitled to be the proprietor of a patent for the invention of a spacing device for an opthalmoscope. The doctor, a registrar, had a very wide job description which referred to research facilities which the doctor was encouraged to avail himself of for basic clinical research. The contract did not, however, express this as a duty and the court held that his duty to treat patients did not extend to devising new ways of diagnosing and treating patients. The doctor was entitled to be the proprietor of the patent. He had made the invention in his own time, during a period when he was working over 80 hours a week.

189 [1996] RPC 207.

Some further indication of the circumstances in which an employee invention will or will not belong to the employer was given in the Patents Court in *Harris' Patent*.[190] The invention was for a slide valve for controlling the flow of material such as coal dust and was an improvement over the 'Wey' valve. Harris made the invention while he was a manager of the Wey valve department of R company, who were licensees of S, a Swiss company. Harris made the invention during the period after he was informed that he was to be made redundant and before he left the employ of R company. The patent was granted and the question of who was entitled to the patent was referred to the Comptroller under s 37. Harris's primary duty had been to sell Wey valves, and R company had no research facilities and did not undertake any creative design. Major problems were referred to the Swiss company. It was held that the rights between an employee and employer were governed only by s 39. The employee's normal duties were the actual duties he was employed to perform. Any duty of fidelity owed to the employer did not assist in formulating those normal duties. Because R company never solved design problems it could not have been part of Harris's duties to provide solutions to problems and his duty in respect of problems was to report them for transmission to the Swiss company. Neither was the invention made in circumstances such that an invention might reasonably be expected to have resulted from the carrying out of the employee's normal duties. The invention did not fall within s 39(1)(b) – the employee's obligation was to sell Wey valves.

190 [1985] RPC 19.

*Staeng Ltd's Patents*[191] is a good example of factors that favour the employer. Staeng Ltd was the proprietor of the patents in suit and Mr Robertson, an employee of Staeng, was named as inventor. There was no dispute between Staeng and Mr Robertson. Mr Neely was employed by another company, Hellerman, which had cooperated with Staeng in the development of electrical connector kits, and there had been a number of meetings between Mr Robertson and Mr Neely. At one of these meetings, Mr Neely, after being asked by

191 [1996] RPC 183.

Mr Robertson whether he could think of an alternative way of holding the cable screen, suggested a constant tension spring which turned out to be an important aspect of the patents. Mr Neely later claimed that he was entitled to be named as inventor under s 13(3), and that he was also entitled to be the proprietor of the patents on the basis that his duties did not require him to invent. Nor was he under a special obligation to further his employer's interests.

The Patent Office held that Mr Neely failed to show that he was the sole inventor. He was not skilled in the relevant art and only came up with the idea after prompting by Mr Robertson. Both Mr Neely and Mr Robertson were joint inventors. On the question of Mr Neeley's employer's entitlement, as between Mr Neely and his employer, it was held that the employer was entitled. Mr Neely made the invention in the course of his normal duties in circumstances such that invention could reasonably be expected to result. Although his role was primarily one of marketing, he had a wide-ranging brief to generate new ideas for new products. Furthermore, Mr Neely was a senior executive. He knew that his employer was contemplating acquiring Staeng Ltd, and that being so, the invention might be of advantage to his employer. Therefore, he was under a special obligation to further the interests of his employer's undertaking.

An employee might devise an invention which is of outstanding benefit to his employer in circumstances such that the employer will be taken as being entitled to the patent. This might seem unfair because the benefit of the invention may far exceed the employee's salary for the period of time he has been involved with the invention. However, the employee has been given consideration for his work, that is his salary, and the employer may have been prepared to pay the employee his salary even if no useful invention resulted, simply as a speculative investment in the hope that a valuable invention would result. Even so, the employee may apply for compensation under s 40, which allows the Comptroller or a court to award compensation where the invention is of outstanding benefit to the employer and it is just to do so. Although there is little case law on the provisions, it is clear that the benefit must be extraordinary and not such as might be expected to result from the employee's normal duties.[192] In fact the use of the word 'outstanding' suggests that compensation will be awarded under these provisions only in exceptional circumstances.[193]

Section 41 lays down the basic principles for the calculation of the amount of the compensation, being an award that gives the employee a fair share in the benefit derived or expected to be derived. These provisions also apply where the invention initially belonged to the employee and he has subsequently assigned it to the employer or granted an exclusive licence to him. This might apply where, because of the employee/employer relationship, the employer is able to bring pressure to bear upon the employee. Of course, one way that the employer can avoid the compensation provisions where the employer is the person entitled to the patent is not to apply for a patent and to rely on the law of confidence. There are very few applications for compensation under s 40.[194]

It is conceivable that in some circumstances where the patent initially belongs to the employee, the equitable doctrine of undue influence might apply, for instance where an employee has been pressurised by his employer to assign the patent to his employer or to grant an exclusive licence in favour of his employer, and where the terms of the agreement are grossly unfavourable to the employee. However, the employee/employer relationship does not automatically

**192** *GEC Avionics Patent* [1992] RPC 107.

**193** *British Steel's Patent* [1992] RPC 117.

**194** Only four were lodged in the years 1994–96. None was allowed.

give rise to a presumption of undue influence and the employee would have to prove the nature of the pressure. If the doctrine of undue influence does apply, the effect is to make the agreement voidable. Section 42 has a similar effect as it makes terms in contracts between an employee and his employer (or some other person at the request of the employer or through the employee's contract of employment) unenforceable if and to the extent that those terms attempt to diminish the employee's rights in inventions.

### Dealing in patents

As with other forms of intellectual property, patents may be dealt with by way of assignment or licensing, either exclusive or otherwise. They may also be mortgaged or vest by operation of law as other personal property. For example, if the proprietor dies the patent will vest in the proprietor's personal representatives. Patent applications may also be dealt with, which is understandable considering the length of time that may pass before the patent is finally granted. Where there are two or more proprietors of a patent or application for a patent, the consent of all of them is required for a licence, assignment or mortgage.[195] Under s 30(6), any purported assignment or mortgage of a patent or patent application is void unless it is in writing and signed by or on behalf of the parties to the transaction. An assent by a personal representative must be signed by or on behalf of the personal representative.

If the requisite formalities are not complied with, for example, if the assignment is signed by one party only, this is likely to operate as an agreement to assign in equity. The assignee will be the beneficial owner and the assignor will remain the legal owner of the patent. The beneficial owner will be able to sue for infringement of the patent provided at some stage the legal owner is made a party to the proceedings. An example is *Baxter International Inc v Nederlands Produktielaboratorium voor Bloedtransfusiapparatuur BV*,[196] where the defendant applied to strike out the plaintiff's action on the ground that the assignments in question had been signed only by the assignor. In that case, both assignments contained a covenant of further assurance common in agreements to assign. It stated:

> We agree to execute all documents required in connection with the patent applications and patents and to execute all further documents necessary to vest title in said patents and applications to the Assignee.

Agreements to assign are very common especially where the patents are part of a much larger transaction involving other forms of property rights. It is common for a short form assignment to follow an agreement to assign.[197] Transactions creating equitable interests are not registrable transactions under s 33 (see below) and are not, therefore, subject to the limitation of the availability of damages or accounts for a failure to register the transaction under s 68.

In *Insituform Technical Services Ltd v Inliner UK Plc*[198] it was held that an assignment of an exclusive licence was not a right *in* a patent but a right *under* a patent and therefore was not caught by s 30(6). The defendant had argued that the second plaintiff, an exclusive licensee, was not entitled to relief on the basis of s 30(6).[199]

A licence for the working of the invention may be granted under a patent or application for a patent by s 30(4). The licence may permit the making of sub-

195 The Patents Act 1977 s 36(3).

196 [1998] RPC 250.

197 *See*, for example, *Coflexip Stena Offshore Ltd's Patent* [1997] RPC 179.

198 [1992] RPC 83.

199 In the event, the relevant patent, relating to the coating of a fibrous sheet used for lining pipes, was held to be invalid for lack of inventive step.

licences and, unless the licence or sub-licence provides otherwise, a licence or sub-licence may be assigned or mortgaged. An exclusive licence is one conferring, to the exclusion of all others (including the proprietor or applicant), any right in respect of the invention to which the patent or the application relates.[200] An exclusive licensee has the same right as the proprietor to bring proceedings in respect of any infringement of the patent after the date of the licence agreement.[201]

Certain types of transaction must be registered. They are listed in s 33(3) and are:

(a) an assignment of the patent or application for a patent;

(b) a mortgage of the patent or application or the grant of a security over it;

(c) the grant or assignment of a licence or sub-licence or mortgage of a licence or sub-licence, under the patent or application;

(d) the death of the proprietor or one of the proprietors of the patent or application or any person having a right in or under the patent or application and the vesting by an assent of personal representatives of a patent or application or any such right;

(e) any order or directions of a court or other competent authority transferring a patent or application or any right in or under it to any person, or that an application should proceed in the name of any person together with registration of the event under which the court or authority had the power to make the order or give the directions.

It is essential that such transactions are registered for two reasons: first, the result of s 33 is that registration of acquisition of property in a patent or an application defeats earlier transactions, instruments or events that have not been registered (registration effectively gives proof of title); and secondly, the subsequent proprietor of the patent or an exclusive licensee may be unable to obtain damages or an account of profits for any infringement of the patent.[202]

## Licences as of right

The proprietor may, at any time after the grant of the patent, apply to the Comptroller to indicate that licences as of right are available in respect of the patent.[203] This provision might be used by a proprietor who has been unable to exploit his patent to good effect. Whether making an entry in the register that licences are available as of right makes any difference is doubtful, because if the invention was commercially attractive in the first place, the proprietor should have had no difficulty in finding an organisation willing to exploit the patent under an assignment or exclusive licence. However, apart from this form of free advertising, there is an added bonus for the proprietor because subsequent renewal fees are reduced by one half. If any person desires to take up the offer, the licence terms shall be as agreed between the parties, or failing agreement upon such terms as may be settled by the Comptroller on the application of either party. The entry on the register to the effect that licences are available as of right may be later cancelled by application of the proprietor (s 47).

Supplementary protection certificates (SPCs) are available for medicinal products by virtue of Council Regulation (EEC) 1768/92. SPCs give an additional five years' protection following expiry of the basic patent. Article 5 of the Regulation confirms that the SPC confers the same rights and is subject to the

**200** The Patents Act 1977 s 130, the interpretation section.

**201** Ibid s 67. The proprietor shall be made a party to the proceedings.

**202** Ibid s 68.

**203** Ibid s 46. There were 387 applications in 1996.

same limitations and obligations as those conferred or existing under the basic patent. Thus, if licences as of right were available at the expiry of the basic patent, they will remain available under the SPC.[204] In the Patents Court, Aldous J said that an SPC gives no more or less rights than those that existed under the basic patent. An argument that s 46(3)(a), entitling any person as of right to a licence where an entry is made by the proprietor that licences are available as of right, allowed a person to have only one licence (that is, that under the basic patent) was rejected. Aldous J said (at 674):

> I cannot accept that submission. A person may only have one licence at a time, but a person can apply at any time for a licence providing he is not a licensee at the time his application is made.

Therefore, if the licence of right expires at the time of the basic patent, a new right to licence accrues with the grant of the SPC and, consequently, the Comptroller has the jurisdiction to grant such licence in appropriate terms.

An entry on the register in respect of licences as of right may also come about from the operation of s 51, which concerns references to the Monopolies and Mergers Commission. This is an option open to the Comptroller where matters specified in the Commission's report operate, have operated or are likely to operate against the public interest.

In settling the terms of a licence of right (and a compulsory licence), the Comptroller must have regard to EC competition law. It had been the practice in the UK to allow a licensee of right to import the patented product from outside the European Community if the proprietor of the patent worked the patent by importing the product to the UK. However, if the proprietor manufactured the product within the UK, the licence of right would not allow the licensee to import the product from outside the European Community.[205] This was held by the European Court of Justice, in *Generics (UK) Ltd* v *Smith Kline and French Laboratories Ltd*,[206] to be discriminatory because it encouraged proprietors of patents to manufacture the patented product in their national territory rather than importing the product from other member states.

Under the Patents Act 1949, the maximum term of a patent was 16 years, but existing patents that were less than 11 years old when the 1977 Act came into force (on 1 June 1978) were extended to a maximum of 20 years subject to their being treated as endorsed 'licences of right' for the last four years of their life. However, because of the special problems with pharmaceutical products, where the exploitation period is reduced because of the time taken to test and obtain a licence under the Medicines Act 1968, the proprietor of a patent for a product is allowed to file a declaration preventing licences as of right extending to pharmaceutical use.[207]

## Compulsory licences

There has always been a danger that the proprietor of a patent will abuse the monopoly granted to him. For example, an inventor, Mary, develops an everlasting light bulb and obtains a patent for it. Brightlight Ltd, a manufacturer of conventional light bulbs, offers a large sum of money to Mary for an assignment of the patent, to which she agrees. Brightlight then suppresses the invention and does not put it to use, preferring to continue making conventional light

204 *Research Corp's Supplementary Protection Certificate* [1994] RPC 387 (Patent Office) and [1994] RPC 667 (Patents Court).

205 This was the Comptroller's view of the provisions in the Patents Act 1977 ss 48(3) and 50(1) when the patent was not being worked in the UK. However, in *EC Commission v United Kingdom* [1993] FSR 1, it was held that s 48 offends against Article 30 of the Treaty of Rome, *see* post.

206 [1993] 1 CMLR 89.

207 The Patents Act 1977 Sch 1, para 4A inserted by the Copyright, Designs and Patents Act 1988 s 293. Patents for medicinal products may now be extended to a maximum of 25 years, Patents (Supplementary Protection Certificates) Rules 1997, SI 1997/64.

bulbs. This state of affairs cannot exist as far as a patented invention is concerned because of the availability of compulsory licences under which others may work the invention against the wishes of the proprietor of the patent. Compulsory licences not only cover situations where a patent is not being worked, but also are available in other circumstances such as where demand for a product is not being met on reasonable terms.

Compulsory licences cannot be granted until after three years from the date of the grant of the patent, after which any person may apply for a licence under the patent and/or for an entry to be made on the register to the effect that licences are available as of right.[208] The grounds on which such application may be made are listed in s 48(3) and are:

(a) the invention is not being worked in the UK to the fullest extent that is reasonably practicable (assuming it is capable of being commercially worked in the UK);

(b) in the case of an invention which is a product, demand for it in the UK is not being met on reasonable terms or is being met substantially by importation;

(c) where the invention is capable of being commercially worked in the UK and it is being prevented or hindered from being so worked by the importation of the product (in the case of a product invention), or by the importation of a product obtained directly by means of the process or to which the process has been applied (for a process invention);

(d) the proprietor refuses to grant a licence or licences on reasonable terms with the result that:

   (i) a market for the export of any patented product made in the UK is not being supplied; or

   (ii) the working or efficient working in the UK of any other patented invention which makes a substantial contribution to the art is prevented or hindered; or

   (iii) the establishment or development of commercial or industrial activities in the UK is being unfairly prejudiced;

(e) because of conditions imposed by the proprietor on the grant of licences, or on the disposal or use of the patented product or on the use of the patented process, the manufacture, use or disposal of materials not protected by the patent, or the establishment or development of commercial or industrial activities in the UK is unfairly prejudiced.

It can be seen that the grounds are fairly wide and do not necessarily equate with the notion of abuse, for example where demand is being met by importation. Anyone can apply, even an existing licensee of the patent, who shall not be estopped from applying for a compulsory licence because of any admission made by him, whether in such a licence or otherwise, or because he has accepted a licence in the first place.[209]

The grounds stated in s 48 are expressed in terms that focus upon the UK, and therefore the proprietor of a patent can reduce the likelihood of a compulsory licence being granted if he manufacturers the product, if there is one, in the UK rather than manufacturing elsewhere and importing into the UK. The proprietor is encouraged to work his invention in the UK and this could easily fall foul of the free movement of goods principle enshrined in Article 30 of the Treaty of Rome. In particular, s 48(3)(b)(ii), which provides for compulsory

208 Section 48(1). Note, it is three years from the date of grant, not the priority date.

209 Ibid s 48(8).

licences where demand for a patented product is being met to a substantial extent by importation, can discriminate against imports from other member states. This was held to offend against Article 30 in *EC Commission* v *United Kingdom*[210] and was not considered necessary to protect the specific subject matter of the patent.[211] The other provisions in s 48(3) must be regarded as being subject to Article 30 of the Treaty of Rome. This also applies to the guidelines contained in s 50(1) on the Comptroller's exercise of his powers under s 48, discussed next. Appropriate amendments to the Patents Act 1977 are long overdue.

Guidelines for the exercise of the Comptroller's powers with respect to applications under s 48 are contained in s 50. The Comptroller shall take into account the following general purposes by s 50(1):

(a) the working of the invention to the fullest extent that is reasonably practicable in the UK without undue delay if it is in the public interest for the invention to be worked on a commercial scale;
(b) having regard to the nature of the invention, the inventor or other person entitled to the patent shall receive a reasonable remuneration;
(c) the interests of any person currently working or developing a patented invention in the UK shall not be unfairly prejudiced.

Subject to s 50(1), in determining whether to order a compulsory licence the Comptroller must take account of a number of factors contained in s 50(2), being:

(a) the nature of the invention, the time since publication of the grant of the patent and measures taken by the proprietor or any licensee to make full use of the invention;
(b) the ability of any person to whom the licence would be granted to work the invention to the public advantage; and
(c) the risks to be undertaken by that person in providing capital and working the invention if the order is granted.

No account is taken of matters occurring subsequent to the application for a compulsory licence. The fact that one of the grounds for a compulsory licence is present is not sufficient, *per se*, for the grant of the licence. In *Therma-Tru Corp's Patent*,[212] the Patents Court said that there was no reason why a compulsory licence could not include a right to sub-licence but this would be exceptional. The application was refused because both the applicant and its proposed sub-licensee were financially stretched and there was a substantial risk that the sub-licensee would not be able to work the invention.

If the patent is being worked in the UK, it was held in *Research Corporation's (Carboplatin) Patent*[213] that it would normally run counter to policy to grant a licence of right (or compulsory licence) which permitted importation. Furthermore, if the price of the product was reasonable and demand at that price was being fully met, it was irrelevant to say that demand would be greater if the price was lower. The question is whether, in all the circumstances, the price being charged was reasonable.

The applicant for a compulsory licence must establish a *prima facie* case that the grounds relied upon apply. A mere suspicion will not be sufficient and an order for discovery will not be granted unless a *prima facie* case is raised by the applicant. In *Richco Plastic Co's Patent*[214] the only evidence that the applicant

210 [1993] FSR 1.

211 Articles 36 and 222 discussed in Chapter 15.

212 [1997] RPC 777.

213 [1990] RPC 663. But this decision is now very questionable in the light of *EC Commission* v *United Kingdom* [1993] FSR 1, discussed above.

214 [1989] RPC 722.

had was that the patentee had an associated company in the United Kingdom and an investigation at the UK Companies Registry which showed an entry for the company which did not refer to manufacturing costs but only to the costs of purchasing and importing. The application was dismissed as being an abuse of process. In practice, applications for compulsory licences are very rare.[215]

## Terms of licence as of right or compulsory licence

If the Comptroller has to settle the terms for a licence as of right or a compulsory licence he should do so with a view to securing, *inter alia*, that the proprietor of the patent receives a reasonable remuneration having regard to the nature of the invention. This can be done only by considering what a willing licensor and a willing licensee would have agreed upon as a reasonable royalty to be paid for the rights granted under the licence as of right. So it was held in the Court of Appeal in *Allen & Hanburys Ltd's (Salbutamol) Patent*.[216] This would include taking account of the research and development costs and promotional costs incurred in creating and maintaining a market for the product. Regard should also be had for the reward deserved by the proprietor for his contribution to the art, secured by an appropriate measure of profit upon the capital invested. It was suggested that this position is not unlike that pertaining under the compulsory licensing provisions in the Patents Act 1949 s 41 which caused much concern in the drug industry.[217] The s 41 approach did not altogether die with the revocation of the 1949 Act.[218] It was held in *Geigy SA's Patent*[219] that three elements should be taken into account in calculating the licence fee: an allowance for research and development costs, an allowance for promotional costs and an appropriate uplift. The first two are the compensation element and the third is the reward element. However, the applicability of this test now seems in doubt, as discussed below.

The best way of determining what willing parties would agree upon is to look at comparable licences where these exist. Though even here consideration must be given to the scope of the licence and the other terms in the agreement.[220] In *Smith Kline & French Laboratories Ltd's (Cimetidine) Patents*,[221] Lloyd LJ said (at 236):

> For my part I have no doubt that where close comparables exist, they provide by far the best and surest approach. There is no better guide to what a willing licensor and a willing licensee would agree than what other licensors and licensees have in fact agreed in comparable cases.

The presumption of willing parties to a licence could be extended to contemplate that they had a common understanding about future pricing policy, and if price cutting was likely to ensue the court should decide where the floor should be and what profits should be available calculated on that basis.[222]

Another possible method of calculating the terms is the 'profits available' approach in which the exercise is to determine what the available profits are and to divide these between the licensor and licensee. However, this is difficult to apply in practice and should be considered to be a last resort where there is nothing else to go on. It is accepted by the court that there are particular 'going rates' in specific industries. For example, in *Shiley Inc's Patent*,[223] which involved the settlement of terms for a licence of right in relation to a heart valve

**215** There were no applications from 1991 to 1994. There were three in 1995 and three in 1996.

**216** [1987] RPC 327.

**217** The Patents Act 1949 s 41 allowed the Comptroller to grant compulsory licences, *inter alia*, for medical patents. He was obliged to secure that medicines would be available to the public at the lowest prices consistent with the patentee deriving a reasonable advantage for his patent rights. For a discussion of the effects of s 41 of the Patents 1949 and its demise in respect of pharmaceutical products, *see* Walton, A. 'The Copyright, Designs and Patents Act 1988 (1)' (1989) 133 *Solicitors Journal* 646 at 650–851.

**218** Although many of the provisions of the 1949 Act continue to apply to patents and applications existing on 1 June 1978 by virtue of the transitional provisions, s 41 does not. However, the courts still seek guidance from s 41, *see Shiley Inc's Patent* [1988] RPC 97.

**219** [1964] RPC 391, approved by the Court of Appeal in *Allen & Hanburys Ltd's (Salbutamol) Patent* [1987] RPC 327.

**220** *Knutsson's and Bjork's Patents* [1996] RPC 461.

**221** [1990] RPC 203.

**222** *Research Corporation's (Carboplatin) Patent* [1990] RPC 663.

**223** [1988] RPC 97.

prosthesis, it was said the range of royalty in the mechanical engineering field was 5 to 7 per cent, but the norm in the pharmaceutical industry was between 25 and 30 per cent. However, even though the patent was in the mechanical engineering field, being a mechanical surgical device, the royalty payable was set at 15 per cent because of factors such as the proprietor's pioneering work and the high profit margins in the particular technology.

The difference between the comparable licence and the s 41 approach can be quite large. In *American Cyanamid Co's (Fenbufen) Patent*,[224] Aldous J applied both of the methods (he considered the profits available method of no assistance because there was no clear evidence of how the profits should be split). He calculated that the royalty to produce a reasonable remuneration based on comparable licences was 27 per cent, but that the application of the s 41 test gave between 45 and 54 per cent. He said that the s 41 royalty was not correct and the final figure awarded was 27 per cent uplifted to 32 per cent to take account of exceptional promotional costs.

224 [1990] RPC 309.

The calculation of royalties in respect of compulsory licences and licences of right will continue to be a source of difficulty. It is not possible to lay down a strict percentage to be applied universally because of variations in development and promotional costs, and there is a danger that the patentee will be robbed of his reward if the rate is set too low. While it is essential that the incentive to invent is maintained, it is important that certain inventions, especially those related to drugs, are readily available at reasonable prices. The willing parties approach is by far the most satisfactory, but sometimes there will be nothing to compare the licence with. In such circumstances, the old s 41 approach may still be of some assistance as the profits available approach is deeply flawed. For example, what happens if there are subsequent applications for licences of right? The patentee's remaining share of the available profit will be diluted still further.

## CROWN USE

A patent is a right granted by the Crown and there are detailed provisions in the Act for Crown use. The forms of use covered are listed in s 55 and are declared not to be an infringement of the patent.[225] They are:

225 *See also* the Patents Act 1977 s 56 which expands upon the meaning of some of the provisions and terms.

1 *Product inventions.* To make, use, import, keep or sell or offer to sell it. Sale and offers to sell must be incidental or ancillary to the previously mentioned activities. To sell or offer to sell it for foreign defence purposes. For the production or supply of specified drugs and medicines, to dispose or offer to dispose of it otherwise than by selling it for any purposes.
2 *Process inventions.* To use it or to do any of the above in relation to a product obtained directly by means of the process.
3 *Specified drugs or medicines* (product inventions or the product of a process invention). To sell or offer to sell the drug or medicine.
4 *Any type of invention.* To supply or offer to supply to any person the means, relating to an essential element of the invention, for putting the invention into effect. To dispose or offer to dispose of anything made, used, imported or kept which is no longer required for that purpose.

**226** 'Relevant communication' means, by s 55(9), a direct or indirect communication of the invention by the proprietor of the patent or any person from whom he derives title.

**227** [1991] FSR 221.

Crown use is subject to a royalty being paid to the proprietor of the patent, but not in relation to things done before the priority date unless done as a result of a confidential relevant communication.[226] The use must be for the services of the Crown and by any government department or any person authorised in writing by a government department. A health authority is, for the purposes of s 55, a government department. In *Dory* v *Sheffield Health Authority*,[227] the proprietor of a patent for machines for treating kidney stones sued the health authority for patent infringement. It was held that the use of the machines by the health authority was Crown use and that the authority exercised the functions of the Secretary of State which were devolved to the authority by the National Health Service Act 1977 and regulations made under that Act.

Section 57 deals with the rights of third parties that are affected by the Crown use and fundamentally prevents third-party rights interfering with the Crown use and apportions certain expenditure and royalty payments between the then proprietor and an assignee of the patent, or between the proprietor and an exclusive licensee. If the proprietor of the patent or an exclusive licensee suffers loss from not being awarded a contract in relation to the invention where the invention is used for the services of the Crown, the government department concerned is under a duty to pay compensation.[228] Compensation is payable only to the extent that the contract could have been fulfilled from existing capacity, and factors relevant to determining the loss are the profit that would have resulted from the contract and the extent to which manufacturing or other capacity was under-used.[229] The compensation is calculable on the contract lost as a result of the Crown use only and not for other contracts. The amount payable by way of royalties in respect of Crown use or the amount of compensation is to be agreed between the relevant government department and the proprietor with the approval of the Treasury, but in the absence of agreement may be referred to the High Court[230] as may other disputes regarding Crown use, under s 58.

**228** The Patents Act 1977 s 57A (added by the Copyright, Designs and Patents Act 1988, Sch 5, para 16(1)).

**229** The Patents Act 1977 s 57A(2) and (3).

There are extended provisions for Crown use during a period of emergency, which is a period declared to be so by Order in Council.[231] During a period of emergency, the powers exercisable by any government department or person authorised by a government department include the power to use the invention for any purpose that appears to the department to be necessary or expedient for one or more stated reasons, including the efficient prosecution of any war in which Her Majesty may be engaged, the maintenance of supplies and services essential to the life or well-being of the community and for assisting in the relief of suffering in any country outside the UK that is in grave distress as a result of war. However, to these are added some reasons which extend the meaning of 'emergency' somewhat, for example promoting the productivity of industry, commerce and agriculture and also for redressing the balance of trade, that is increasing exports and reducing imports.

**230** In Scotland, the Court of Session and, in Northern Ireland, the High Court in Northern Ireland: ibid s 130.

**231** Ibid s 59.

Crown use may be involved where the invention concerns the country's defence, and an order may have been given under s 22 prohibiting or restricting the publication or communication of information contained in the patent application. Failure to comply with such directions is an offence triable either way.[232] The wide powers under s 22 apply where the information is prejudicial to the defence of the realm or to the safety of the public. It could mean that an invention is kept secret and the exploitation of it by the proprietor is hindered

**232** The maximum penalty on indictment is imprisonment for a period not exceeding two years and /or a fine. On summary conviction, the maximum penalty is a fine of £1000: s 22(9).

or even prevented, although the Secretary of State must keep the position under review from time to time (at least once a year). For example, in the early 1980s, an inventor devised a method of cryptography that was intended to be used for combating piracy of audio and video tapes and computer programs. However, and unfortunately for the inventor, it also had military uses and was subject to a s 22 direction.[233] As the apparent intention of the Ministry of Defence was not to use the invention but to keep it secret and prevent others from being able to use it, the unlucky inventor may not receive any income from his invention[234] unless some *ex gratia* payment is made. Had the inventor not tried to patent his invention he might have been able to exploit it relying on the law of confidence to protect his ideas.

[233] *The Times*, 17 February 1984.

[234] If it is used then, under the Patents Act 1977 s 55, royalties will be payable.

# 14

## *Patents – infringement, defences and remedies*

### INTRODUCTION

The strength of the rights granted by patent law is such that infringement of the patent and defences to infringement actions have to be carefully drawn out. Patent infringement is not measured in terms of whether a substantial part has been taken, as is infringement of a work of copyright, but there are difficulties where the invention has not been taken in its entirety by an alleged infringer, or where some feature of the invention has been changed. Where the alleged infringement is not a direct copy but a variant, the courts may have some difficulty in determining whether the variant does indeed infringe the patent. It is in the light of subsequent variants of an invention that the value of a precise and appropriate specification can be seen; not too wide as to cause rejection of the application and not so narrow as to permit slight variations being made lawfully.

The scope of the infringing acts and the stated exceptions to infringement strive to achieve a balance between the interests of the proprietor and those of others, including his competitors. Reverse engineering[1] is permitted *per se*, but is hardly necessary as a study of the patent specification, a document available to the public, should be sufficient to determine how the invention works and what it does. Patent actions often involve challenges to the validity of the patent concerned and proprietors (or exclusive licensees) must be prepared to defend their patent. Commonly, challenges will be made on the grounds of anticipation or lack of inventive step. Partly because of this, but mainly as a result of the technical nature of patents, litigation in this field tends to be expensive and time-consuming. Trials lasting several weeks and costs running to millions of pounds are not unheard of. In *Chiron Corp v Organon Teknika Ltd (No. 3)*[2] the defendant argued that the patent in suit was obvious, that it was invalid for insufficiency, that it was a patent for a discovery as such, that it was not capable of industrial application and that some claims were invalid, being methods of treatment. The defendant further claimed, successfully, that it could rely on the s 44 defence.

As with other statute-based forms of intellectual property rights, with the single exception of registered trade marks, the culpability of the infringer is relevant in determining whether damages are available in a particular case. In some cases the defendant's knowledge is also the key to the question of infringement. Like design law and the new trade mark law, there is a remedy for groundless threats of infringement proceedings and, as is the case with registered designs and registered trade marks, certificates of contested validity are available. There are also some criminal penalties associated with patents.

[1] Sometimes referred to as reverse analysis. This occurs when the invention or the ideas underlying it are discovered by dismantling and inspecting components of articles made to the invention.

[2] [1994] FSR 202.

## CHOICE OF COURT

Before looking in detail at infringement, defences and remedies, a brief word or two should be given on the choice of court for the hearing of a patent action.[3] In the past litigants were faced with little option but the inevitable expense associated with an action in the Patents Court, part of the Chancery Division of the High Court. Average costs in that court have been estimated at £500 000.[4] The Patent Office itself has limited jurisdiction to hear certain matters, as governed by the 1977 Act, for example to grant compulsory licences and settle the terms of licences of right, to revoke patents, to award compensation to employees in respect of inventions of outstanding benefit to their employers, etc. Under s 61(3), with the agreement of the parties the Comptroller may hear infringement actions. The Patent Rules 1995 lay down the procedural aspects.[5]

Following some speculation that the Patent Office should be given wider powers and a subsequent recommendation that a special county court to hear patents cases be set up,[6] the Patents County Court was established by virtue of the Copyright, Designs and Patents Act 1988 Part VI.[7] The procedure is governed by normal county court procedures with some modification.[8]

The subject matter of the jurisdiction of the Patents County Court is to hear proceedings relating to patents or designs and ancillary matters. The normal county court limits as to the damages that can be awarded do not apply and parties can be represented by a patent agent. Registered patent agents now have a right of audience in the Patents County Court.[9] The Patents County Court should result in speedier, less expensive hearings – and as might be expected has been the target of brickbats and bouquets. In *Prout* v *British Gas plc*,[10] Sir Thomas Bingham MR said:

> [the Patents County Court] has not been in operation for very long and during the period that it has been in operation it has been conspicuously successful. Part of the source of that success has been that it has set out to be as economical of time and expense and as innovative in terms of procedure as possible, consistent always of course with the requirements of justice and the entitlement of the parties to a fair hearing.[11]

A number of criticisms have been levelled at the court and its judge, Peter Ford, and reported by Conn.[12] They include indecision and lack of firmness on the part of the judge. However, much of the trouble seems to stem from procedural difficulties to which Judge Ford has addressed himself, strengthening the court's *raison d'être* of providing easy access to litigation for persons and companies without large resources.

In relation to transfers of proceedings to or from the High Court, the Patents County Court has a discretion under s 289(2) of the Copyright, Designs and Patents Act 1988 which states that the court shall 'have regard to the financial position of the parties and may order the transfer to a patents county court or, as the case may be, refrain from ordering their transfer to the High Court notwithstanding that the proceedings are likely to raise an important question of fact or law'. In *Chaplin Patents Co. plc* v *Group Lotus plc*,[13] the Court of Appeal accepted the existence of that discretion, although the Master of the Rolls said that he would have ordered transfer had it been up to him, in view of the substantial nature of the action in that case.

Subsequently, in *Pavel* v *Sony Corporation*,[14] the Court of Appeal cast doubt on whether the present provisions relating to transfer of trial are satisfactory.

3 For a fuller description, *see* Reid, B. C. (1993) *A Practical Guide to Patent Law* (2nd edn) Sweet & Maxwell, Chapters 7, 8 and 11.
4 Conn, D. 'Cut-price Court in Spin', *The Times*, 23 November 1993.
5 The procedure for the Patents Act 1977 s 61(3) reference is stated in SI 1995/2093 rules 72 and 73.
6 *Intellectual Property and Innovation*, Cmnd 9712 (1986), HMSO and the Oulton Committee Report (1987).
7 *See also* the Patents County Court (Designation and Jurisdiction) Order 1990, SI 1990/1946.
8 For example, the Patents County Court may grant *Anton Piller* orders and *Mareva* injunctions, the County Court Remedies Regulations 1991 regs 2 and 3, SI 1991/1222.
9 The Copyright, Designs and Patents Act 1988 s 292.

10 (Unreported) 4 May 1993 (Court of Appeal).

11 This case was an appeal from the judgment of Judge Ford in the Patents County Court, [1992] FSR 478, on the question of costs.
12 Conn, D., *op cit.*

13 *The Times*, 12 January 1994.

14 *The Times*, 22 March 1996.

The parties in that case were criticised for over-elaboration of the issues in what should have been a relatively simple case. The specification of the patent in issue ran to two and a half pages and should have been easily understood without the need for scientific help. Altogether, there were nearly eight days of interlocutory hearings and the trial lasted nearly four weeks, resulting in costs in the order of £2.2m with the plaintiff ending up on legal aid.[15] Aldous LJ said:

> ... whether the fault for those lamentable events was that of the procedure or something else was not for his Lordship to decide. However, some alteration was necessary if the purposes of the Patents County Court were to be achieved.

The manner in which some litigants behave in the Patents County Court compromises its fundamental purpose of providing fast and inexpensive relief for patent proprietors who do not have deep pockets where the nature of the case is relatively straightforward. The difficulty of fixing a ceiling of, say £50 000, is that often larger sums are at stake, even in relatively simple cases.

Inevitably, any new court must undergo its teething problems. It is reputed that the first seven decisions of the Patents County Court, tested in the Court of Appeal, were overturned.[16] The need for an inexpensive forum to hear patent disputes is, however, unquestionable, and in time the Patents County Court should develop into a worthwhile and valued alternative to the Patents Court in the Chancery Division.

## INFRINGEMENT

A patent may relate to a product or a process. If the invention is a process, it may be used to make a product. An example of a product invention is a new type of golf ball, and an example of a process invention is a new process for making ordinary golf balls. Under s 130, a patented product is a product which is a patented invention or, in relation to a patented process, a product obtained directly by means of the process or to which the process has been applied.

Section 60[17] defines an infringement of a patent as the doing of any of the following things in the United Kingdom in relation to the invention without the proprietor's consent.

1 *Product invention* – to make, dispose of, offer to dispose of, to use or import the product or to keep it, whether for disposal or otherwise (s 60(1)(a)).
2 *Process invention* – to use the process or offer it for use in the United Kingdom when the person concerned does so knowing, or where in the circumstances it would be obvious to a reasonable man, that such use would be without the consent of the proprietor and would be an infringement of the patent (s 60(1)(b)).
3 *Process invention* – to dispose of or offer to dispose of, to use or import or to keep (whether for disposal or otherwise) any product obtained directly by means of the process (s 60(1)(c)).
4 *All inventions* – to supply or offer to supply in the United Kingdom a person (other than a licensee or other person entitled to work the invention) with any of the means, relating to an essential element of the invention, for putting the invention into effect (s 60(2)). The alleged infringer must know, or it must be obvious to a reasonable man in the circumstances, that those means are suitable for putting, and are intended to put, the invention into effect in the UK.[18]

15 *The Times*, 22 April 1996, p. 37.

16 Conn, D., *op cit.*

17 Unless otherwise stated, in this chapter, statutory references are to the Patents Act 1977.

18 This provision does not apply to the proprietor of the patent. So, for example, if the proprietor grants an exclusive licence to one person he does not infringe by supplying the means suitable for putting the invention into effect to another person. The proprietor will probably be in breach of his licence agreement with the first person and the second person will infringe the patent if he works the invention.

In relation to the s 60(1)(a) infringement, it has been held that negotiating with a customer, during the currency of a patent, to supply a product after the relevant patent had expired did not infringe.[19] A product obtained directly from a patented process must be obtained directly without any intermediate steps to be within s 60(1)(c). In *Pioneer Electronics Capital Inc v Warner Manufacturing Europe GmbH*[20] the plaintiff had a patent for a process for making optical discs. There were some intermediate steps, including making stampers from which the discs could be mass-produced. It was held that the defendant had not infringed the patent because none of his discs was a direct product of the patented process and that a causal link, however important, was not sufficient. Aldous J looked at the German and French versions of the European Patent Convention,[21] because, under s 130(7), a number of provisions of the Patents Act 1977, including s 60, are framed to have, as nearly as practicable, the same effects in the United Kingdom as the corresponding provisions of the European Patent Convention and the Community Patent Convention. In particular, the German word *unmittelbar* suggested that no intermediate points would be allowed between the process and the product. The Court of Appeal dismissed the plaintiff's appeal, agreeing with Aldous J's views on the meaning of *unmittelbar*.[22] The Court also held that the product in question did not cease to be the product if it was subjected to further processing, provided that it did not lose its identity and that it retained its essential characteristics. Whether this was so was a question of fact and degree, a test which would often be difficult to apply. However, in the present case, the finished disc was not an identical copy of the master disc and different in a material way from it as a result of three further stages of production. For example, the master was not capable of being played in a compact disc player.

The final type of infringement ('supplying the means') could occur where one person supplies another with a kit of parts for the latter to assemble. This was not an infringement before the 1977 Act came into force.[23] However, this infringement does not apply to the supply, or offer to supply, of a staple commercial product unless made with the purpose of inducing an act that is an infringement under any of the first three infringing acts above by the person supplied (or the person to whom the offer was made).[24]

The infringing acts under s 60 must be done in the United Kingdom to infringe. This reflects the territorial nature of a patent. In *Lacroix Duarib SA v Kwikform (UK) Ltd*,[25] the plaintiff claimed that the defendant had infringed his patent for scaffolding to be used inside large hollow structures, such as the hulls of large ships during their construction. The defendant made its scaffolding in 'collapsed' form and it was to be assembled or erected in Korea by Daewoo in its shipbuilding operations. The defendant's argument was that, since its scaffolding was only in collapsed form in the United Kingdom, there was no infringement of the patent as claim 1 of the specification referred to the complete assembly only.

As to whether infringement by a 'kit of parts' was possible, Laddie J was referred to the judgment of Graham J in *Rotocrop International Ltd v Genbourne Ltd*[26] where it was held that there was direct infringement by a kit of parts for a bin for making compost of a patent which claimed a fully assembled bin. Graham J considered the kit, in the circumstances, to be the 'bin'. Laddie J thought it inappropriate to depart from that decision.[27]

**19** *Gerber Garment Technology Inc v Lectra Systems Ltd* [1995] RPC 383, appeal against damages allowed in part in the Court of Appeal, [1997] RPC 443.

**20** [1995] RPC 487.

**21** Article 24(2).

**22** *Pioneer Electronics Capital Inc v Warner Music Manufacturing Europe GmbH* [1997] RPC 757.

**23** The Patents Act 1977 came into force on 1 June 1978.

**24** Ibid s 60(3).

**25** (Unreported) 9 December 1997, Patents Court.

**26** [1982] FSR 241.
**27** Laddie J considered that, if the narrower construction of s 60(1)(a) advanced by the defendant was to be taken, it would be better left to a higher court, especially as there was no authority on this issue.

Cases prior to the 1977 Act and Canadian authorities indicating infringement by a kit of parts were discounted by Laddie J who said that the 1977 Act marked a sea change in patent law. Terrell suggests that a kit of parts might infringe as it could amount to the completed article. Also, unless the kit is made for export, liability for indirect infringement is also likely to arise by virtue of s 60(2). The manufacturer of a kit of parts may also be considered to be a joint tortfeasor with the person who assembles the parts.[28] Nevertheless, doubt remains as to whether making a kit of parts for assembly outside jurisdiction infringes a patent which claims the assembled product. It is surprising that this point has not been litigated more often, and even more surprising that the 1977 Act does not directly deal with it as the Registered Designs Act 1949 does.[29]

Under the 1949 Act there was no definition of 'infringement' in the Act. The letters patent commanded the public not to make use of the patent directly or indirectly, or put it into practice or in any way imitate the same. Thus, the 1977 Act appears to afford a more limited monopoly as regards the scope of infringement.

There are various exceptions to the above infringements and these will be discussed in the section on defences. In the meantime, infringement will be considered further. The patent is granted on the basis of the specification and the claims included in the application, perhaps after amendment. It is to these documents that a court must turn to determine whether the patent has been infringed. This is confirmed by s 125(1) which states that a patent shall, unless the context otherwise requires, be taken to be that specified in a claim of the specification as interpreted by the description and any drawings in the specification. The extent of the protection conferred by the patent is to be determined accordingly. Hence the importance of the claims.

If the alleged infringer has simply duplicated the product or process patented as described in the specification then, subject to the defences or a challenge on the validity of the patent, there should be no hesitation in finding that an infringement has occurred. But what if the alleged infringer has not simply duplicated the invention but has introduced some changes, producing a variant? If this has happened, it is then a matter of construing the patent specification and claims to find out whether the grant extends to the variant. The alleged infringer is likely to suggest that his variant lies outside the invention claimed by the patent, while the proprietor will argue that the variant falls within the patent as granted. If the former is true, then no matter how close to that dividing line the variant lies, there is no infringement of the patent.

## Interpretation of claims

A literal interpretation of the specification and claims is always a possibility, given the predilection that lawyers have for this approach. Nevertheless, a literal approach to interpretation does not sit comfortably with the knowledge that patent specifications are written for scientists, engineers and technologists rather than for lawyers. Lord Reid disapproved a strict literal approach to the construction of a patent specification in *Rodi & Wienenberger AG v Henry Showell Ltd*,[30] where he said (at 378):

> ... claims are not addressed to conveyancers: they are addressed to practical men skilled in the prior art, and I do not think that they ought to be construed with that meticulousness which was once thought appropriate for conveyancing documents.

**28** Young, D. *et al* (1994) *Terrell on the Law of Patents*, (14th edn) Sweet & Maxwell, at p. 176.

**29** Section 7(4) Registered Designs Act 1949.

**30** [1969] RPC 367.

Another way to resolve the question of infringement by a variant is to consider whether the differences between the variant and the patented invention are material, that is, do they differ in essential or inessential respects. The invention claimed can be considered as comprising essential and non-essential integers (components), those that are fundamental to the invention and those that are not. If the alleged infringer has taken all of the essential integers then there is an infringement even if there are substantial differences in respect of the non-essential integers. This has been described by various judges as taking the 'pith and marrow' of the invention. However, when applying this principle, the scope of the patent claims is vital. Viscount Radcliffe said in *Van der Lely NV v Bamfords Ltd*[31] (at 78):

31 [1963] RPC 61.

> When, therefore, one speaks of theft or piracy of another's invention ... and this 'pith and marrow' principle is invoked to support the accusation, I think that one must be very careful to see that the inventor has not by the actual form of his claim left open to the world the appropriation of just that property that he says has been filched from him ...

In other words, the inventor must be very careful when drafting his claims to make sure that they are not framed too narrowly that some slight and insignificant modification can be effected without infringing the patent. The essential integers claimed must be those very parts which the proprietor wishes to protect.

The 'pith and marrow' test still leaves the problem of interpretation, and the question of construction of patent claims in the context of variants came to a head in the case of *Catnic Components Ltd v Hill & Smith Ltd*[32] which involved several variants of steel lintels.[33] The plaintiff was a proprietor of a patent for steel lintels that had a rear support member which was vertical and so described in claim 1 of the specification by the phrase 'second rigid support member extending *vertically* from or from near the rear edge of the first horizontal plate or part adjacent its rear edge' (emphasis added).[34] The defendant made a similar lintel, but with the rear support member inclined between 6–8 degrees (depending on the particular model of lintel) from the vertical. Figure 14.1 gives an approximate representation in cross-section of one of the plaintiff's lintels and one of the defendant's lintels.

32 [1982] RPC 183. This case concerned a patent granted under the 1949 Act, but it has been accepted as being applicable to 1977 Act patents.

33 A lintel is a beam used to support some load, such as a wall, above an opening. For example, lintels are used above windows and doors to support the wall above and any transmitted loads.

34 Patent Specification No. 1298798 (GB).

35 For a six-degree inclination from the vertical the reduction was only 0.6 per cent and for an eight-degree inclination the reduction was 1.2 per cent.

The strength of a steel lintel in this form of construction derives to some extent from the verticality of the rear member, and the defendant's lintel had a reduced load-bearing capacity compared to the plaintiff's lintel, but because of the small inclination from the vertical this reduction was small.[35] The House of

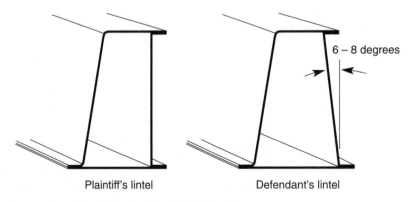

Plaintiff's lintel    Defendant's lintel    6 – 8 degrees

**Figure 14.1  Steel lintels in *Catnic* v *Hill & Smith***

Lords found that the plaintiff's patent had been infringed and the defendant's argument that the verticality of the plaintiff's lintel was essential to its function and that, therefore, there was no 'pith and marrow' infringement was rejected. It was confirmed that a purposive approach[36] should be adopted in the construction of patent specifications, Lord Diplock saying (at 243):

36 This is a modern equivalent of the 'mischief rule', that is the rule in *Heydon's Case* (1584) 3 Co Rep 7a. In other words, the word 'vertically' did not mean 'vertically' but 'vertically or nearly so'.

> A patent specification should be given a purposive construction rather than a purely literal one derived from applying to it the kind of meticulous verbal analysis in which lawyers are too often tempted by their training to indulge.

Lord Diplock identified the real crux of the matter as being whether practical persons, skilled in the art, would understand that strict compliance with a particular word or phrase was intended by the patentee to be an essential requirement of the invention. If so, any variant that did not comply would fall outside the claim regardless of whether it had any effect. If the variant did have a material effect, there would be no infringement. Lord Diplock went on to suggest (and apply) a test that has become that favoured for deciding whether variants infringe.[37] The test, as usefully reformulated into a three-part test by Hoffman J in *Improver Corp* v *Remington Consumer Products Ltd*,[38] is as follows.

37 *See*, for example, *A C Edwards Ltd* v *Acme Signs & Displays Ltd* [1990] RPC 621, concerning apparatus for displaying prices at petrol filling station forecourts, *Southco Inc* v *Dzeus Fastener Europe Ltd* [1990] RPC 587, which involved a lift and turn latch for a cabinet door and *Improver Corp* v *Raymond Industries Ltd* [1991] FSR 223, discussed later.

38 [1990] FSR 181.

1 Does the variant have, in fact, a material effect on the way the invention worked? If the answer is 'yes', the variant falls outside the claim and does not infringe. If the answer is 'no', the second question is asked.
2 Would it have been obvious, at the date of publication of the patent specification, to the informed reader (presumably a person skilled in the art) that the variant had no material effect? If the answer to this is 'no' then the variant falls outside the claim, but if the answer is 'yes' the final question must be asked.
3 Is it apparent to any reader skilled in the art that a particular descriptive word or phrase used in a claim cannot have been intended to exclude minor variants which would have no material effect upon the way in which the invention worked? If the answer to this is 'no' then the variant lies outside the claim, but if 'yes' the variant infringes the patent.

Another way of expressing the third question is whether the skilled reader would understand from the language of the claim that strict compliance with the primary meaning of the claim was intended.[39] Figure 14.2 shows a flow-chart approach to the test.

39 *See* the restatement of these questions by Hoffman J in *Improver Corp* v *Remington Consumer Products Ltd* [1990] FSR 181, approved in *Sundstrand Corp* v *Safe Flight Instrument Corp* [1994] FSR 599.

The purposive approach and the *Catnic* test have become the basic method of determining whether variants infringe. This can be criticised because it can lead to uncertainty. If a strict literal approach were to be adopted then a potential competitor wishing to make a non-infringing variant should be able to determine just how far he can go without infringing. It would also encourage persons drafting patent claims to use greater precision which would further reduce uncertainty, or to use appropriate language such as 'generally cylindrical'.[40] Although the *Catnic* approach has been readily accepted under the 1977 Act,[41] it has been challenged in the Court of Appeal. Article 69 of the European Patent Convention states that the extent of protection conferred by a European patent shall be determined from the claims, using the description and drawings to interpret the claims. The Protocol on the interpretation of Article 69 emphasises that a strict literal approach should not be used nor should the claims serve only as a guideline. Article 69 is to be '... interpreted as defining a position between these extremes which combines a fair protection for the patentee with a reasonable degree of certainty for third parties'.

40 *Conoco Speciality Products (Inc)* v *Merpro Montassa Ltd* [1994] FSR 99.

41 For example, in *Anchor Building Products Ltd* v *Redland Roof Tiles Ltd* [1990] RPC 283, it was held that the *Catnic* test was the same as that in the 1977 Act and the Protocol.

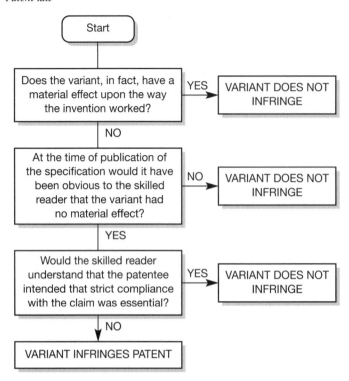

**Figure 14.2 Flowchart – whether variant infringes patent**

Section 125(3) provides that the Protocol shall apply for the purpose of s 125(1) which is the equivalent to Article 69(1), requiring the extent of the protection to be determined from the claims as interpreted by the description and any drawings contained in the specification. As *Catnic* was decided under the 1949 Act, the question is whether it truly accords with s 125(1) and the Protocol.[42] In *PLG Research Ltd* v *Ardon International Ltd*,[43] in an infringement action in respect of patents for making plastic nets used in civil engineering, Neill LJ seriously doubted the relevance of the *Catnic* test to the 1977 Act, confirming that claims should be construed in accordance with the Protocol on Article 69. He said (at 133):

> ... The expression to be construed is 'substantially uniplanar.' The word 'substantially' imports a degree of flexibility which precludes an exact and literal construction, and makes it unnecessary to consider whether Lord Diplock's purposive construction was an accurate if proleptic application of the Protocol ... [the precise meaning of Lord Diplock's words are] a matter which should now be left to legal historians.

This extreme attack on *Catnic* left patent lawyers reeling. Neill LJ suggested that if the two tests were the same, reference to *Catnic* was unnecessary; while if they were different *Catnic* should not be used in any case.[44] However, Neill LJ's comments as to the *Catnic* test were, as he admitted, *obiter*. Aldous J noted this in *Assidoman Multipack Ltd* v *The Mead Corp*[45] where he distinguished *PLG Research* and, after reviewing the history and background of the construction of patent claims, held that the *Catnic* test was still relevant and was entirely consistent with the Protocol. Aldous J said (at 236):

42 For a description of the impact of the Protocol, *see* Sherman, B. 'Patent Claim Interpretation: The Impact of the Protocol on Interpretation' (1991) 54 MLR 499.

43 [1995] FSR 116. This case is also reported at [1995] RPC 287 where the judgment is stated to have been handed down by Millett LJ.

44 For a discussion of *PLG Research* v *Ardon*, see Cole, P. 'Purposive Construction and Inventive Step' [1995] 3 EIPR 147.

45 [1995] FSR 225.

I would be loathe to discard 14 years of case law ... The middle ground referred to in the Protocol is not clearly defined and every court within the Community has adopted a method of interpretation which it believes to be consistent with the Protocol ... I have been unable to think of any better guidance [than the *Catnic* test] which hopefully will result in consistent decisions between the courts of this country and those of other parties to the Convention.

Aldous (by now LJ) had the opportunity soon after to reinforce his views in the Court of Appeal in *Kastner v Rizla Ltd*,[46] approving the *Assidoman* decision and confirming the continuing value of the *Catnic* test as representing the *via media* called for by the Protocol. It has also been followed by Jacob J in *Beloit Technologies Inc v Valmet Paper Machinery Inc*[47] and is sure to remain a useful way of applying the spirit of the Protocol.

Where there is a range of numbers with an upper and lower limit, a departure from that range is not a variant in the *Catnic* sense. If the alleged infringement is just outside the claimed range, it does not help the proprietor to say that the departure is just a little one. So it was held in *Auchincloss v Agricultural & Veterinary Supplies Ltd*[48] where a patent for compositions for destroying viruses and other micro-organisms claimed ingredients within numeric ranges, for example '25 to 60 parts by weight of an oxidising agent'.

## Equivalents

Sometimes the alleged infringement may contain mechanical equivalents, an alternative that works equivalently. A mechanical equivalent may be more than a mere variant as in the *Catnic* case. It is then a question of deciding which are the essential integers of the claim in the 'pith and marrow' approach to interpretation discussed above. For example, in *Rodi & Wienenberger AG v Henry Showell Ltd*[49] it was held that replacing two 'U-shaped' bows in a flexible watch strap with a single large 'C-shaped' bow was not an infringement because the 'U-shaped' bow was an essential integer. Conversely, in *Marconi v British Radio Telegraph & Telephone*[50] the replacement of an auto-transformer with a two-coil transformer did not prevent a finding of infringement because the auto-transformer was not an essential integer.

The Court of Appeal in Hong Kong had to deal with a mechanical equivalent in *Improver Corp v Raymond Industries Ltd*.[51] The plaintiff's patent was for a device, called the 'Epilady', for removing hair from arms and legs. The defendant imported and distributed a device which performed the same function and was called 'Smooth & Silky'.[52] It was held, applying the Diplock test in *Catnic*, that the first and second questions are questions of fact and the answers to them are not conclusive to the third question, which was one of construction. Even a purposive construction might produce the conclusion that the patentee was confining his claim to the primary meaning and excluding the variant, even though the variant might make no material difference – and this would have been obvious at the time. On the evidence, there was no material difference – both devices trapped and plucked hair from the skin, and it was obvious that both worked in the same way. The answer to the first two questions in the flowchart were therefore 'no' and 'yes' respectively, and the third question fell to be determined. It was held that it was important to look at all the essential integers in the patent specifica-

46 [1995] RPC 585.

47 [1995] RPC 705. *See also* the Court of Appeal decision, [1997] RPC 489. The test has also been approved by the Federal Court of Canada in *Eli Lilly & Co v Novopharm Ltd* [1996] RPC 1.

48 [1997] RPC 649.

49 [1969] RPC 367.

50 (1911) 28 RPC 181.

51 [1991] FSR 223.

52 The case was decided under the Patents Act 1977, which was in force in Hong Kong.

tion and claim to see if all those essential integers were present in the alleged infringement.[53] The alleged infringing device could perform the same task as long as it did so differently as regards at least one essential integer, and this is so even if the difference had no material effect upon the way the invention worked.

The specification and relevant claim, therefore, must be construed to determine what the essential integers are and these compared to the alleged infringing product or process. In the above case, the specification and claim referred to a helical spring that was rotated to pluck out hairs. It was held that this was an essential integer, and the fact the defendant used an elastomeric (rubber) rod instead (even though this had no material effect on how the invention worked) indicated that the defendant's device did not infringe the patent. The skilled man, reading the patent specification and claim, would have considered that the patentee had not intended to include such a variant. As the helical spring was rotated, its windings opened and closed up trapping and plucking out hairs. The defendant's device did the same thing but by using a rubber rod with slits in it. In a claim in the Patents Court involving the same devices, Hoffman J applied the *Catnic* test and his answers were 'no', 'yes' and 'yes', and therefore, in his opinion, the 'Smooth & Silky' hair remover did not infringe.[54]

The 'Epilady' case is also interesting because it shows differences of approach to infringement and the effect of the Protocol on the interpretation of Article 69. In Germany, in a parallel action involving the same parties and patent, it was held, eventually, that the defendant's rubber rod with slits in it infringed the 'Epilady' patent.[55] Jacob suggests that there is an approach to infringement in Germany whereby a mechanical equivalent that is obvious will infringe even though the integer it replaces is an essential one.[56] Although the law on infringement by variants and mechanical equivalents is not settled, it is suggested that the following tests should be used:

1 where the critical aspect of the alleged infringement is a minor variant, that is, it does the same thing in the same way (as in the *Catnic* case), it should not escape an infringement action merely because of an inappropriately narrow or restrictive choice of words;

2 where the aspect of the alleged infringement under consideration is a mechanical equivalent, that is it performs the same function but by different means (as in the *Improver* case) then the issue is whether, interpreting the last *Catnic* question, the patentee intended strict compliance with the primary meaning of the language of the claim or whether he used the word or phrase under consideration as having a figurative meaning, denoting a class of things which include the variant and the literal meaning, the latter being perhaps the most perfect or best known example of the class.[57]

The application of the purposive approach may operate harshly on a defendant, because in an interlocutory hearing it is likely to be used even more generously. The slightest hint of infringement might be sufficient to convince a judge that there is a serious issue to be tried. In *Beecham Group plc v J & W Sanderson Ltd*, Aldous J said:

> Patent claims are difficult to construe after a trial, and are even more difficult on motion without proper education as to the background and the technical effect of differences. This case is no exception, and I conclude that there is a serious issue to be tried as to whether the defendant's toothbrushes infringe claim 1.[58]

53 The word 'integer' is used to describe an element of an invention, assuming that it can be broken down into elements. The number of integers can be increased by adding to the claims by use of alternatives. For example, 'an offset eccentrically mounted widget which is attached to the mounting by magnetic means (claim 1) and a widget as in claim 1 which is attached to its mounting by plastic friction clips (claim 2)'.

54 *Improver Corp v Remington Consumer Products Ltd* [1990] FSR 181.

55 [1991] RPC 597.

56 Jacob, R. 'The Herchel Smith Lecture 1993' [1993] 9 EIPR 312 at 313. According to Jacob J in *Beloit Technologies Inc v Valmet Paper Machinery Inc* [1995] RPC 705, the Epilady cases make 'an excellent discussion basis for law students'.

57 *Per* Hoffman J in *Improver Corp v Remington Consumer Products Ltd* [1990] FSR 181. He described the figure in the figurative meaning being a form of synecdoche (where a part is made to represent the whole) or metonymy (substitution of the name of an attribute or adjunct for that of the thing meant).

58 (Unreported) 18 June 1993.

Could it be that plaintiffs are given the benefit of doubt because of the purposive approach? This particular case concerned a patent for a toothbrush having a flexible handle by virtue of 'V-shaped' folds transverse to the handle. The defendant's toothbrush achieved flexibility by means of a helical spring or auger construction, having coils connected to a central core. However, although Aldous J decided there was a serious issue to be tried, he refused an injunction after consideration of the balance of convenience, although he did order the defendant to pay 15 pence into a joint bank account for each toothbrush it sold.

### Evidence

Of course, in a patent infringement action, the plaintiff carries the burden of proof. He has to adduce evidence of the infringement and convince the court, on a balance of probabilities, that the defendant has infringed his patent. However, and in exceptional cases, a judge may come to a conclusion that he just does not know which side of the line the decision ought to be (in which case, the plaintiff has failed to discharge his legal burden of proof). In *Morris* v *London Iron & Steel Co*[59] May LJ accepted that this could happen. He said (at 501):

> In the exceptional case, however, a judge conscientiously seeking to decide the matter before him may be forced to say, 'I just do not know'; indeed to say anything else might be in breach of his judicial duty.

Such indecision might be caused by a real and irreconcilable conflict between rival scientific theories. It does not, however, allow the plaintiff the opportunity to adduce fresh evidence in the hope of tipping the balance in his favour. Fresh evidence will be admitted only if all the conditions in *Ladd* v *Marshall*[60] are satisfied. They are:

1 if it is shown that the evidence could not have been obtained with reasonable diligence for use at the trial;
2 if the further evidence is such that, if given, it would probably have an important influence on the result of the case, though it need not be decisive; and
3 if the evidence is such as presumably to be believed in.

In *Imperial Chemical Industries* v *Montedison (UK) Ltd*,[61] the plaintiff failed to meet condition 1. Stuart-Smith LJ said (at 468):

> It is incumbent upon a party to adduce such evidence as he considers relevant and persuasive relating to the findings of fact which the judge may make. He cannot wait for the findings and then say 'Oh well, I could have called more evidence on that point'.

There is no exception to the rule in *Ladd* v *Marshall* should the judge fail to find the burden of proof discharged. The trial judge failed to make a positive finding in the *ICI* case and considered that he did not have to decide between the conflicting theories. Essentially, what he was saying was that the case was not proved to his satisfaction beyond the balance of probability.

### Title to sue for infringement

The proprietor or exclusive licensee has title to sue for infringement of a patent. However, if the relevant interest has not been registered under s 32 the owner of the interest will not be entitled to damages or an account of profits in respect

59 [1987] 2 All ER 496.

60 [1954] 1 WLR 1489.

61 [1995] RPC 449.

of infringements occurring before registration, unless registration takes place within six months (s 68). The court (or Comptroller) has a discretion to extend that period if satisfied that the interest was registered as soon as possible after, provided it was not practicable to register sooner. If a party to proceedings is found not to have title to sue he will be struck from the action, as in *Bondax Carpets Ltd* v *Advance Carpet Tiles*[62] where the third plaintiff was struck from the action. His contract with the second plaintiff had nothing to do with the rights under the patent.

One or more joint proprietors of a patent may bring an action for infringement without the concurrence of the others, but they must be made parties to the proceedings.[63] The infringing acts are to be construed in the context of one or more joint proprietors of the patent subject to s 36. This means that the consent of the proprietor referred to in s 60 will usually require the consent of each and every one of the proprietors of the patent. Under s 67, the exclusive licensee of a patent has the same rights as the proprietor to bring an action for infringement committed after the date of the licence. In any action by an exclusive licensee, the proprietor shall be made a party to the proceedings.

## DEFENCES

A person sued for an alleged infringement of a patent has several and varied escape routes. He might challenge the validity of the patent, claiming that it should be revoked because it has been anticipated or that it is obvious. Section 74 permits the defendant to put the validity of the patent in issue. Once the validity of a patent has been put in issue and evidence has been given in court, the court must rule on it even if the parties are no longer interested. The reason is that third parties may be affected.[64] Putting validity in issue may also be done under certain other circumstances.[65] The defendant may claim that the patent has lapsed or expired, or he may challenge the plaintiff's title to it or his right to sue. On the other hand, the defendant might be able to reduce his liability by showing that the patent is only partially valid. If the patent is only partially valid, the defendant will escape damages and costs in respect of the invalid part. Under s 63, the plaintiff must show that the specification was framed in good faith and with reasonable skill and knowledge; but even if he does, the court or Comptroller still has a discretion as to the date from which damages should be calculated and in respect of costs and expenses. This is an unfettered discretion though the conduct of the parties and the position of the general public may be influential.[66] Under the previous law, the presence of an invalid claim rendered the whole patent invalid. Section 63(2) had swept that rule away. However, the discretion conferred by s 63(2) arises only if the defendant infringes a valid claim and the plaintiff has maintained an invalid claim on the register.

Section 46 concerns licences of right. Where a patent has such an entry against it, in infringement proceedings (except where it relates to the importation of any article from a country outside the European Community), if the defendant undertakes to take a licence on terms to be agreed (or, failing agreement, to be settled by the Comptroller) then no injunction will be granted against him and the maximum award of damages against him is double the amount payable under the licence had the licence, on those terms, been granted

62 [1993] FSR 162.

63 The Patents Act 1977 s 66(2).

64 *Ocular Sciences Ltd* v *Aspect Vision Care Ltd* [1997] RPC 289.

65 For example, on the application by any person that the invention is not a patentable invention, or the person to whom the patent was granted was not entitled to it or that the specification does not disclose the invention clearly and completely enough, etc. (s 72), in proceedings in connection with alleged groundless threats of infringement proceedings (s 70), proceedings in respect of a declaration under s 71 and in disputes relating to Crown use (s 58). The Patents Act 1949 contained some other specific grounds, for example, false suggestion under s 32(1)(j), *see Intalite International NV* v *Cellular Ceilings Ltd (No. 2)* [1987] RPC 537.

66 *Gerber Garment Technology Inc* v *Lectra Systems Ltd* [1995] FSR 492 at first instance.

before the earliest infringement. This provision could be seen as encouraging infringement of patents endorsed licences of right as, if sued, all the defendant has to do is to make the necessary undertaking. If he does this, the most he risks is twice what he would have paid under the licence.

Apart from these points, other defences to an infringement action are:

1  The act was done privately and not for commercial purposes: s 60(5)(a) – note the use of the conjunctive, the act must be both private and non-commercial.

2  The act was done for experimental purposes relating to the subject matter of the invention: s 60(5)(b) – this might permit making the subject matter of the invention to see more clearly how it works. However, making or experimenting with a patented product for the purposes of obtaining official approval from the Ministry of Agriculture, Fisheries and Food was held not to be within s 60(5)(b) in *Auchincloss* v *Agricultural & Veterinary Supplies Ltd.* [67]

3  The act consists of the extemporaneous preparation in a pharmacy of a medicine for an individual in accordance with a registered medical or dental practitioner's prescription, or consists of dealing with a medicine so prepared: s 60(5)(c).

4  Use in relation to certain ships, aircraft or vehicles temporarily or accidentally in the UK or crossing the UK: s 60(5)(d)–(f).[68]

5  The act was done in good faith by the defendant before the priority date of the invention, or he made in good faith effective and serious preparations to do such an act and the defendant claims under s 64 that he has the right to do the act or to continue to do the act. Alternatively the defendant may claim that he has obtained this right as being a partner of such a person, or that he has acquired it with the relevant part of that person's business. Under s 28A similar provisions apply in respect of acts and preparations in relation to a patent after expiry of the renewal period and before publication of an application for restoration (assuming, of course, that the application for restoration is successful).

6  The act complained of is not an infringing act, it does not fall within the meaning of infringement in s 60.

7  The alleged infringing product or process lacks novelty or is obvious. Therefore, the patent claims are invalid if they cover the alleged infringement or, if valid, they cannot cover the alleged infringement. This is the 'Gillette' defence, from *Gillette Safety Razor Co* v *Anglo-American Trading Co Ltd.*[69] However, Terrell suggests that a defence drafted in such terms would fail to comply with the Rules of the Supreme Court.[70] Nevertheless, the defence is frequently used. A recent successful example can be found in *Mabuchi Motor KK's Patents*[71] where the patent was held to be valid but not infringed.

8  At the time of the infringement there was in force a contract or licence containing a condition or term void by virtue of s 44. This covers terms requiring the other party to purchase anything other than the patented product, or prohibiting the acquisition of anything other than the patented product from a specified third party.

9  The plaintiff's rights have been exhausted under European Community law. This might apply in terms of parallel importing, discussed in Chapter 15.

10  A 'Euro-defence', based on Articles 30, 85 or 86 of the Treaty of Rome, discussed in Chapter 15.

67 [1997] RPC 649, following *Monsanto Co v Stauffer Chemical Co* [1985] RPC 515.

68 Including air space, internal and territorial waters. These exceptions apply to 'relevant' ships, aircraft, hovercraft and vehicles registered in or belonging to Paris Convention countries other that the UK. The provisions also apply to exempted aircraft under the Civil Aviation Act 1982 s 89.

69 (1913) 30 465.

70 Ord. 104, r 6. Young, D. *et al* (1994) *Terrell on the Law of Patents* (14th edn) Sweet & Maxwell, at p. 303.

71 [1996] RPC 387.

11  The defendant has an implied licence, for example, to repair a product to which the patent relates.[72] The principle of non-derogation from grant should also be available in some circumstances.

12  The doctrines of estoppel and laches should apply. However, estoppel does not place a positive duty on a proprietor of a patent to publicise the patent or make enquiries: *Lux Traffic Controls Ltd v Pike Signals Ltd*.[73] Inactivity on the part of the proprietor or exclusive licensee may bar him from the equitable remedies, in particular an interlocutory injunction. A warning may suffice to prevent the plaintiff's claim being barred by laches: *T J Smith & Nephew Ltd v 3M United Kingdom plc*.[74]

The claims may be central to the issue of infringement and validity. Where there is an application to revoke a patent under s 72(1) on the grounds of alleged invalidity, it would seem, in as much as the challenge concerns the claims, that the *Catnic* test is equally valid as in infringement proceedings.[75] On the one hand, the defendant will want to show that the claims are narrow and do not extend to the alleged infringement. On the other hand, the defendant will argue that the claims are too wide, and hence the patent is invalid, or only partially valid, because the claims embrace some material that lacks novelty or is obvious to the notional skilled worker. This may be particularly relevant in terms of the *Gillette* defence mentioned above, where the defendant argues that his product lacks either novelty or an inventive step or, better still, both.

The s 44 defence may seem draconian from the proprietor's point of view (it is a complete defence), but its purpose is to discourage abuse of the patent monopoly. Section 44 makes void conditions or terms requiring the other party (for example, a licensee or purchaser of patented products) to acquire other products, or prohibiting him from acquiring or using other products from third parties or using a patented process belonging to a third party. For example, the proprietor of a patent for grease guns might insist that a purchaser buy grease cartridges for the gun from him and no one else. This severely limits the proprietor's ability to impose 'tying-in' clauses, for example, where the proprietor grants a licence to work a patented process but insists that the licensee also acquires raw materials from the licensor and no one else. Section 44(3) states that it is a defence to prove that a contract or licence containing a condition or term void under s 44 was in force at the time of the alleged infringement. The defendant to the action does not have to be a party to the contract or licence and may have no relationship whatsoever with the proprietor or his exclusive licensee.[76]

The fact that a contract is not subject to law in the UK does not prevent the operation of s 44 provided the contract in question concerns a UK patent. In *Chiron Corp v Organon Teknika Ltd*[77] one of the plaintiffs had a patent valid in the UK relating to Hepatitis C virus. It granted a licence to a co-plaintiff and a third party which contained a term requiring that the licensees purchase materials not covered by the patent claims. The licences were subject to the law of New Jersey in the USA. It was held that, as far as the applicability of s 44 was concerned, it was irrelevant that the contract or agreement was governed by foreign law, and it was also irrelevant that the foreign law in question did not include a provision having equivalent effect to s 44. United Kingdom patents were the concern of s 44 as were contracts affecting UK patents, whatever the law applicable to those contracts was. In the hearing in the Patents Court,[78] Aldous J described s 44 as being penal, though the Court of Appeal disagreed with this description of the section. Strong measures are required to counter strong abuses.

72 *Solar Thomson Engineering Co Ltd v Barton* [1997] RPC 537.

73 [1993] RPC 107.

74 [1983] RPC 92. Otherwise the normal limitation period of six years applies under the Limitation Act 1980.

75 *Conoco Speciality Products (Inc) v Merpo Montassa Ltd* [1994] FSR 99.

76 There are some limitations, for example where the supplier or licensor was willing to supply the product or grant the licence on reasonable terms without the offending term or condition: the Patents Act 1977 s 44(4).

77 (Unreported) 25 February 1993.

78 [1993] FSR 324. *See also Chiron Corp v Organon Teknika Ltd (No. 3)* [1994] FSR 262.

Section 44(1)(c) makes void conditions or terms in a contract for the supply of a patented product or of a licence to work the patented invention which prohibit the person supplied or the licensee, as the case may be, from using articles (whether patented products or not) which are not supplied by the supplier under the contract or from using any patented process not belonging to the licensor (or, in either case, a nominee of such a person). This extends to restrictions on the use of such articles or processes. In *Chiron Corp* v *Murex Diagnostics Ltd*[79] the Court of Appeal held that the term 'patented products' in the phrase 'whether a patented product or not' referred to patents other than the patent subject to the relevant contract of supply or licence. Therefore, there was no breach of s 44(1) until an actual product could be identified which was not within the patent.[80] The court approved the *dicta* of Dunn LJ in *Fichera* v *Flogates Ltd*,[81] where he said (at 289):

> The mischief to which the section was directed was to prevent a patentee from abusing his monopoly by placing restrictions on the acquisition and use of products other than the patented products.

Other interesting observations on the operation of s 44 were made in *Chiron* v *Murex*. For example, s 44(1) also operates as regards an invention in respect of which the patent has not been granted at the time of the agreement. Once the patent is granted, s 44(1) makes the restriction void. Further relevant restrictions that prevent a licensee doing things outside the United Kingdom only will be caught. In the particular case, the restriction prevented export even though export is not an infringing act.

An English company, Ortho Ltd, had an exclusive licence from the plaintiff under the United Kingdom patent to offer for sale and sell the patented product. There was no term in the licence which offended against s 44, although there was such a term in another agreement to which the proprietor was a party. It was argued that an exclusive licensee must be caught by s 44 if the proprietor is caught, meaning that the exclusive licensee cannot have a right to sue. This was accepted at first instance by Aldous J, but the Court of Appeal rejected that proposition. The Court referred to s 101(3) of the Copyright, Designs and Patents Act 1988, which specifically provides that in an action brought by an exclusive licensee, a defendant may avail himself of any defence which would have been available to him had the action been brought by the owner of the copyright.

The Court of Appeal said that the absence of provision for such a defence in the Patents Act 1977 showed that Parliament did not intend to make it available for an exclusive licensee of a patent. As the exclusive licensee was not a party to the contract containing the offending restriction and as it had not consented to it, the s 44 defence was not available as against the English exclusive licensee.

The s 64 defence (acts done in good faith before the priority date) is an important one as, in a particular industry, many organisations may be working towards the same goal at the same time. Some important points to note about s 64 are as follows.

1 The Act must be such as would be an infringement of the patent were it in force. If the prior act was not an infringement (for example, if it fell within one of the defences in s 60(5)), s 64 does not apply.

79 [1996] RPC 535.

80 Following Lord Reid in *Tool Metal Manufacturing Co Ltd* v *Tungsten Electric Co Ltd* (1955) 72 RPC 209.

81 [1984] RPC 257.

2 'Continue to do the act' means 'that act'. This would appear to cover the continuance of a single infringing act carried on over a period of time (for example, building an infringing radio mast). However, it would seem to allow repeating a single infringing act such as continuing to make infringing products.[82]

3 It is difficult to determine whether there are any qualitative restrictions. That is, can the person relying on s 64 in respect of an act falling within one claim work any of the other claims, including the most favoured embodiment. For example, can a prior user who made brass widgets now make plastic widgets which are covered by another claim? There were two contradictory cases on this point[83] but the better view, which has been reinforced by the most recent case to decide the issue,[84] is that s 64 does not give a general licence to other infringing acts beyond those done before the priority date or in respect of which serious and effective preparations were made before the priority date.

4 The proprietor will find that his monopoly has turned into a duopoly. However, this is not as bad as it might seem. No one else except the prior user or his assignee can do the act, and he may not be allowed to use the best embodiment unless his prior user extended to that.

5 The prior user may assign his right to continue to do the act. (Note it is a right and not just a defence.) However, he is not allowed to grant licences.

6 If the patent relates to a product, there may be other rights, such as a design right. Would the right under s 64 overrule these other rights?

There is a period of limbo that can apply where the prior act, or preparations for the act, comes between the priority date and the date of publication of the specification. This may be relevant where a person suspects that a patent application has been filed that may cover the act by its claims. Although no damages can be awarded for acts done before publication, they may be awarded if continued thereafter.[85] The person applying for the patent is unlikely to volunteer information concerning his patent at this stage, and the person intending to do the act has either to take a chance or wait until publication. This may be unsatisfactory, particularly where some considerable initial expense is involved such as constructing a new factory or installing a new production line.

To take an example, say that Deuce Developments Ltd commenced making and selling extendible pruning shears for reaching high branches of fruit trees in November 1993. The shears incorporated a novel design of hinge, but Deuce did not apply for a patent in respect of it. During April 1993, Metal Modes Ltd filed an application for a patent in relation to a hinge. Deuce was not aware of this and Deuce did not start making serious and effective preparations to produce its shears until June 1993. When the patent specification was published, Deuce decided to change the design of its hinge so as not to infringe the patent, should it be granted. When the patent is granted to Metal Modes, it can do nothing about Deuce having made the shears prior to publication (it could have sued for damages as from the publication date had Deuce continued to make shears with the hinge as covered in the claims) but it can take action against persons who acquired the early shears with the infringing hinge if those persons are using them. This is an infringement under s 60. However, those persons will be able to sue Deuce on the basis of a breach of the Sale of Goods Act 1979 s 12(2), the implied warranty of quiet possession of goods. The case of *Microbeads AC v Vinhurst Road Markings Ltd*[86] gives an excellent example of the consequences of acts done between filing and

82 *See* Young, D. *et al* (1994) *Terrell on the Law of Patents* (14th edn) Sweet & Maxwell, at p. 210.

83 *Helitune v Stewart Hughes* [1991] RPC 78, taking a wide view and *Lubrizol Corp v Exxon* [1992] RPC 281, taking a narrow view. Both of these cases were in the Patents Court.

84 *Lubrizol Corp v Esso Petroleum Co Ltd* [1997] RPC 195.

85 The Patents Act 1977 s 69. Proceedings may not be brought until after the patent has been granted.

86 [1975] 1 All ER 529.

publication of a patent that infringe, which, as they were not a continuance of acts or the result of serious and effective preparations done before the priority date are not saved by s 64. In the *Microbeads* case road-marking machines were made and sold after the priority date of the patent application made by a third party who later obtained a patent in respect of the machines.

Other points may be relevant, for example whether there is an express licence and, if so, whether it permits the acts complained of. Another way to escape liability is for the defendant to show that the plaintiff, if he claims to be an exclusive licensee, is indeed not an exclusive licensee, or even if he is that the acts complained of were performed before the licence took effect.[87] There is a presumption in favour of the proprietor under s 100 which states that if the patent in question has been granted for a process for obtaining a new product, the same product produced by anyone other than the proprietor or his licensee shall be taken to have been obtained by means of that patented process. This presumption is rebuttable on proof to the contrary and is relevant to infringement actions under s 60(1)(c), that is infringement of a process patent by disposing of, offering to dispose of, using, importing or keeping any product obtained directly by means of the process.

### Groundless threats of infringement proceedings

There is a remedy for groundless threats of infringement proceedings and any person aggrieved can bring an action for a declaration that the threats are unjustifiable, for an injunction against the continuation of those threats and for damages for any losses sustained as a result of the threats.[88] The threats may be made by 'circulars, advertising or otherwise' and need not be directed against the person aggrieved.

The statutory provisions on groundless threats actions seem fairly straightforward at first sight, though they have generated some case law. Particular issues are: what constitutes an actionable threat, who can be a person aggrieved and what is the scope of the defences in s 70(2) and 70(4). A series of recent cases (*Brain v Ingledew* and others) has been very instructive. The issues are examined in turn below.

Notification of the existence of the patent, *per se*, does not constitute a threat of proceedings under s 70(5). Therefore, a timely letter pointing out that a certain invention is subject to a patent is not a threat. However, if the letter is ambiguous the benefit of the doubt will not be given to the author. A threatening letter should be read through the eyes of the reasonable and normal person and any vagueness should be construed against the threatener. Jacob J suggested so in *Patrick John Brain v Ingledew Brown Bennison and Garret*[89] in which he said, in relation to the s 70(4) defence, discussed later (at 597):

> ... to read the letter narrowly would be to give the benefit of the doubt to the threatener because he had written a woolly but ferocious letter. That cannot be right.

That case, the first in the series, *Brain v Ingledew*, involved an application under RSC Ord 14A which allows a judge to determine questions of law or of the construction of a document. In finding that a threats action could be brought in respect of threats issued before a patent is granted, in respect of rights under s 69 (the right to sue for infringement between the date of publica-

87 The Patents Act 1977 s 130(1) defines 'exclusive licence' as a licence from the proprietor (or applicant for a patent) conferring on the licensee (including persons authorised by the licensee) and to the exclusion of all others (including the proprietor or applicant) any right in respect of the invention to which the patent or application relates.

88 Ibid s 70.

89 [1995] FSR 552.

tion and date of grant of the patent, subject to proceedings not being brought until after grant), Jacob J went further and made further declarations. He said that the letter did amount to a threat of proceedings within s 70; that the plaintiff (who had set up and managed the company threatened) was a person aggrieved and that the threats in the letter sent by the defendant went further than simply threatening to bring proceedings in respect of using a process.[90]

The Court of Appeal allowed the defendant's appeal as far as these further declarations.[91] The Court held that these were matters of fact and it was not open to the judge to decide such matters under RSC Ord 14A. However, the first declaration to the effect that a threats actions could be brought in respect of threats made before the patent was granted was accepted as being correct in principle. This provides the court with quite a dilemma. How does the court determine whether the act complained of infringes a patent which has not yet been granted?[92]

'Any person aggrieved' may bring a threats action. The defence to an action in s 70(4), that is, that proceedings may not be brought if the threat relates to the making or importing of a product for disposal or the use of a process, suggests that the remedy is designed to protect secondary infringers such as retailers or distributors. However, this is not so as the question of whether proceedings may be brought depends on whether the threats relate to certain types of acts rather than on the type of person involved.[93] In *Bowden Controls Ltd* v *Acco Cable Controls Ltd*[94] and in *Dimplex (UK) Ltd* v *De'Longhi Ltd*,[95] the plaintiff brought an action in respect of threats made to its customers.

To bring an action, the plaintiff will have to show that he has been caused damage by the threats, or that it is likely that he will be damaged by them. In *Reymes-Cole* v *Elite Hosiery Co Ltd*,[96] it was held that the person aggrieved must establish that the threats have caused or are likely to cause damage which is more than minimal. However, customers (e.g. retailers) who have been threatened with infringement proceedings may simply not want to get involved and prefer to leave it to the person supplying them to fight the threatener. That being so, it may be difficult to obtain evidence of damage. In *Dimplex (UK) Ltd* v *De'Longhi Ltd*,[97] there was no evidence from customers in the United Kingdom but a French customer, who had also received a letter from the defendant threatening proceedings for infringement of its patent, sought an indemnity from the plaintiff otherwise it would no longer sell the plaintiff's product. The court was prepared to accept this as evidence of how the English customers were likely to react; the fact that the customer seeking the indemnity was in France did not matter. The plaintiff was likely to suffer damage which was more than minimal.

The need to prove damage has been put into some doubt recently by Laddie J in *Brain* v *Ingledew Brown Bennison & Garrett (No. 3)*[98] where he suggested that whether a person had been threatened directly or indirectly, he did not need to prove damage. However, he then made it clear that there must be a recognisable grievance. He said that the fact that a trader bringing the action is able to assuage the fears of potential customers who had been threatened so that the threats did not cause a recoverable loss did not mean that he was not a person aggrieved. He was a person with a real commercial interest which had been interfered with by the defendant and, consequently, his was a grievance which the court recognised.

90 This particular form of threat is within the defence to a threats action in s 70(4), *see* later.

91 *Patrick John Brain* v *Ingledew Brown Bennison & Garrett* [1996] FSR 341.

92 Section 70(2) provides that relief is not available to the person aggrieved by the threats if the defendant proves the alleged infringing acts are infringing or would infringe the patent. This is discussed below.

93 *Cavity Trays Ltd* v *RMC Panel Products Ltd* [1996] RPC 361.

94 [1990] RPC 427.

95 [1996] FSR 622.

96 [1965] RPC 102.

97 [1996] FSR 622.

98 [1997] FSR 511.

It has been noted that the person bringing the proceedings for a threats action need not be the person threatened and the provisions may, depending on the circumstances, extend to persons having an interest in the person actually threatened. For example, in *Brain v Ingledew Brown Bennison & Garrett (No. 3)*,[99] the plaintiff had set up and was managing the company which had been threatened. The court held that a director, executive or shareholder of a company threatened could be a person aggrieved. It would be a matter of looking at the circumstances. For example, if the threats were such as to severely disrupt the sales of products made by a company so as to jeopardise the company's future viability, this could in turn have a serious impact on shareholders and directors sufficient to give them a cause of action in relation to the threats.

Section 70(2) is to the effect that the person bringing a threats action will not be entitled to relief if the person making the threat can prove that acts complained of constitute or, if done, would constitute an infringement of the patent which has not been shown by the plaintiff to be invalid in a relevant respect. Proving infringement is no more difficult than in respect of a normal infringement action, except where the acts have not yet been done, where there may be some uncertainty as to their precise nature. Whether a patentee would want to be put to such proof as a result of a carelessly drafted letter is another matter. Furthermore, the patentee may have to defend his patent from an attack on its validity.

A real difficulty for the patentee is where the patent has not been granted. The threats are issued in that period between publication and grant. The specification, including the claims of the patent, may be amended before grant. Indeed, the patent may not be granted at all, for example, where the applicant is unable to deal with objections raised during examination. There was some judicial diversity of opinion over this point in the Court of Appeal in *Patrick John Brain v Ingledew Brown Bennison & Garrett*.[100] Aldous LJ said that it would be desirable for the patent to be granted before trial of the threats action, but if there was an 'extraordinary delay' in grant the court could look at the published specification and decide on a balance of probabilities whether the acts complained of would infringe the patent when granted. Hobhouse LJ was unsure of this approach, saying that he would want further evidence before concluding that the matter could be decided on a balance of probabilities. Unfortunately, the third judge, Beldam LJ, agreed with both judgments! However, in *Brain v Ingledew Brown Bennison & Garrett (No. 2)*,[101] Laddie J said that, absent a granted patent at the time of the trial, the s 70(2) defence to a threats action could not be determined and the patentee who had issued the threats had to take the risk that the patent might not be granted by the time of trial.

Where the grant is likely to be made in the near future at the time of the trial, it may be that the court will grant a short stay in the threats proceedings. Otherwise, the applicant for a patent would be very foolish to issue threats not saved by s 70(4) until his patent is granted. The wording of s 70(2) reinforces the view of Laddie J which is to be preferred. It states that the acts complained of must constitute or, if done, would constitute an *infringement of the patent*.

There are some forms of infringement in respect of which a patentee can threaten to bring an action without risking falling foul of a threats action. They are indicated in Figure 14.3 alongside the various possible forms of infringement of a patent. Of course, the patentee must be very careful to ensure that his 'threat' does not extend outside the bounds of 'permitted' allegations. Under s 70(4), the right to bring proceedings for groundless threats of infringement proceedings does

99 [1997] FSR 511.

100 [1996] FSR 341.

101 [1997] FSR 271.

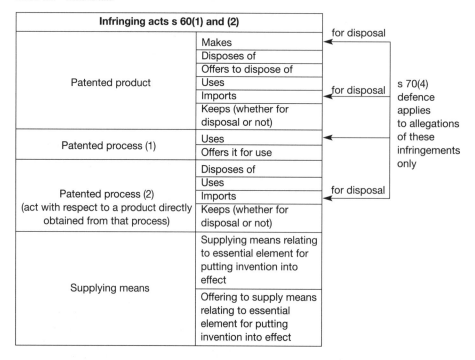

| Infringing acts s 60(1) and (2) | | |
|---|---|---|
| Patented product | Makes | |
| | Disposes of | |
| | Offers to dispose of | |
| | Uses | |
| | Imports | |
| | Keeps (whether for disposal or not) | |
| Patented process (1) | Uses | |
| | Offers it for use | |
| Patented process (2) (act with respect to a product directly obtained from that process) | Disposes of | |
| | Uses | |
| | Imports | |
| | Keeps (whether for disposal or not) | |
| Supplying means | Supplying means relating to essential element for putting invention into effect | |
| | Offering to supply means relating to essential element for putting invention into effect | |

*Note*: it is assumed that the product referred to in s 70(4) is either the patented product or a product directly obtained by means of that process.

**Figure 14.3  Scope of s 70(4) defence**

not arise where the allegation consists of making or importing a product for disposal or of using a process. In *Therm-A-Stor Ltd* v *Weathershield Windows Ltd*,[102] the Court of Appeal held that this extended to the 'supplying the means' infringement under s 60(2). This would require a purposive construction of the subsection which the Court of Appeal later in *Cavity Trays Ltd* v *RMC Panel Products Ltd*[103] was unable to accept in view of its clear and unambiguous wording. In that case, there was some discussion of *Therm-A-Stor* in which the judgment was regarded as difficult to follow in places and which was not taken to require a court to depart from the clear and express words of the statute.

Laddie J, in *Brain* v *Ingledew Brown Bennison & Garrett (No. 3)*,[104] admitted some difficulty in understanding the legislative philosophy underlying the exceptions in s 70(4). He considered that s 70(4) did not permit threats in respect of offering a process for use. This is a separate form of infringement and only using a process is included in the subsection.

The threats must relate to the patent and, in *Easycare Inc* v *Bryan Lawrence & Co*,[105] although a patent for a hoof protector for horses was mentioned by the threatener who was the proprietor of the patent, the threats were clearly stated as being to protect the 'name and reputation' of the threatener. Accordingly, an application for interlocutory relief was refused as, *inter alia*, there was no serious issue to be tried as regards the threats.

Under s 71, any person may apply to the court for a declaration that a certain act does not constitute an infringement of the patent, provided that a written application has been submitted to the proprietor accompanied by full

102 [1981] FSR 579.

103 [1996] RPC 361.

104 [1997] FSR 511.

105 [1995] FSR 597.

details and the proprietor has refused or failed to give the acknowledgement requested. This enables a person to seek clarification as to whether his intended actions will infringe where the proprietor has been unhelpful on this question. It does not, however, apply to patent applications.

## REMEDIES

The remedies available for infringement of a patent are an injunction, damages, an account of profits, an order for delivery up or destruction and a declaration that the patent is valid and has been infringed by the defendant.[106] However, damages and an account of profits are alternatives and may not, by s 61(2), both be awarded or ordered in respect of the same infringement. The question of infringement may be referred to the Comptroller if both parties (the proprietor and any other person who has allegedly infringed the patent) are willing in which case remedies are limited to damages and/or a declaration.[107] Assessment of damages is discussed later.

The remedies in the Patents Act 1977 are not necessarily exhaustive. In *Crossley* v *The Derby Gas Light Co*,[108] the Lord Chancellor accepted that the court could grant an injunction to prevent a person selling, after expiry of a patent, an article made during the subsistence of the patent.[109] However, there are limits and, in *Union Carbide Corp* v *BP Chemicals Ltd*,[110] it was held that the law of restitution did not apply so as to give a cause of action of unjust enrichment.

The purpose of an account of profits is not to punish the defendant but to prevent his unjust enrichment. An account is limited to the profits actually made and attributable to the infringement and the plaintiff must take the defendant's business as it is.[111] The fact that the defendant could have made more profit if he had been more efficient is of no consequence. Accounts are rarely asked for in patent cases because of their complexity.

'Innocent' infringers may escape some of the remedies. Under s 62(1), neither damages nor an account of profits is available if the defendant can prove that, at the time of the infringement, he was not aware and had no reasonable grounds for supposing that the patent existed, the latter being a form of constructive notice. The application of the word 'patent' or 'patented' or words expressing or implying that a patent has been obtained for the product does not necessarily fix the defendant with constructive notice unless accompanied by the number of the patent or application. It would, however, be difficult for a defendant to prove to the court that he did not know of the existence of the patent if he copied a product to which the word 'Patented' was applied. The burden of proof in this matter lies with the defendant.

Under s 25(4) there is, in effect, a period of six months' grace for payment of a renewal fee for a patent, but by s 62(2), in respect of any infringement done during this period, the court or the Comptroller has a discretion as to whether to award damages or make an order for an account of profits. Another provision relates to the situation where the infringement occurred before an amendment to the specification was allowed. In this case, damages are not available unless the court or the Comptroller is satisfied that the specification as published was framed in good faith and with reasonable skill and knowledge.[112]

**106** The Patents Act 1977 s 61.

**107** Ibid s 61(3).

**108** (1834) 4 LT Ch 25.

**109** The European Court of Justice upheld a decision of a Dutch court to impose a temporary injunction of 14 months after expiry of a patent. This period was the average time taken to obtain marketing approval. A third party had applied for authorisation and included a sample of the patented drug before the patent had expired. *Generics BV v Smith Kline & French Laboratories Ltd* [1997] RPC 801.

**110** [1998] FSR 1.

**111** *Potton Ltd v Yorkclose Ltd* [1994] FSR 567.

**112** The Patents Act 1977 s 62(3).

The meaning of the phrase 'framed in good faith and with reasonable skill and knowledge' was considered in *Hoechst Celanese Corp v BP Chemicals Ltd*.[113] Following Aldous J in *Hallen Co v Brabantia (UK) Ltd*,[114] Laddie J said that the test for 'good faith' was one of honesty, based on what the proprietor or his agent actually knew. That is a subjective test. As for 'reasonable skill and knowledge', Laddie J said that it was whether, in the circumstances pertaining at the time, including what was known of the prior art, a competent patentee (or, in many cases, the patent agent drafting the specification) would or could have been expected to frame the specification in the way it was framed. That is an objective test. In the present case, although the patentee had not bothered to examine the documents cited in the search report, it was held that the specification was framed in good faith and with reasonable skill and knowledge.[115]

By s 69, the applicant for a patent is able to sue for infringements which occurred between the publication of the application and the grant of the patent. It is also required that the act, if the patent had been granted at the date of publication, would have infringed the patent and the claims as published. The claims have to be interpreted by reference to the description and any drawings referred to in the description or claims.[116]

Damages may not be available or may be limited if the patent is found to be partially valid only by s 63. Damage and costs will not be available at all unless the court (or Comptroller as the case may be) is satisfied that the plaintiff has proved that the specification was framed in good faith and with reasonable skill and knowledge. Even then, the court or Comptroller has a discretion as to costs and as to the date from which damages should be calculated.

If the validity of a patent is challenged and it is found to be wholly or partially valid, the court (or Comptroller if the hearing is before him) may certify the finding and the fact that the validity was so contested (s 65(2)). In any subsequent proceedings, including proceedings in the same action,[117] the proprietor can obtain his costs of the further proceedings on an indemnity basis if the judgment is made in his favour. A further certificate of contested validity may be granted.

There is a limitation on the availability of damages or an account of profits if a transaction, instrument or event by which a subsequent proprietor (or co-proprietor) or exclusive licensee acquired his rights in the patent has not been registered promptly. Section 68 so provides where the transaction, instrument or event was not registered within six months or, if it was not practicable to register in that time, it was not registered as soon as practicable after that six-month period. A number of transactions, instruments and events are registrable under s 33 including assignments, mortgages, licences and sub-licences,[118] the death of a proprietor and orders of the court or competent authority transferring the patent or application or any right in or under it to any person. But, as only the proprietor or exclusive licensee has a right to sue, the limitation on remedies only applies to these persons. A further incentive for registration of these and other registrable transactions, instruments and events is that, failing registration, they may be vulnerable to a subsequent change in proprietorship of the patent or application.[119] The purpose of these provisions is to ensure that the register reflects accurately the fact of proprietorship and subsisting rights in respect of a patent or an application for a patent rather than to provide a fortuitous defence.[120]

---

113 [1997] FSR 547.

114 [1990] FSR 134.

115 Although the documents had been cited by the European Patent Office, in the end the application was accepted and the documents ignored in examination. The patentee later amended his patent to take account of the prior art.

116 Section 62(2) and (3) do not apply (discretion to refuse damages or an account of profits in relation to the further period for renewal or with respect to an amendment to the specification). There is, however, some discretion left to reduce damages if it would have been reasonable to expect that the patent would not have been granted or the act would not have infringed (s 69(3)). This defence was first raised in *Unilever plc v Chefaro Proprietaries Ltd* [1994] 8 EIPR D–206, where it was held to require an objective test and to be of very limited scope.

117 *Mölnlycke AB v Procter & Gamble Ltd* [1992] FSR 549.

118 Assignments of mortgages, licences and sub-licences must also be registered.

119 Section 33(1).

120 *Coflexip Stena Offshore Ltd's Patent* [1997] RPC 179, *per* Jacob J.

Exceptionally, a court may refuse an injunction to restrain the defendant from further infringement. Aldous J refused an injunction in *Biogen Inc v Medeva plc.*[121] The defendant claimed that the grant of an injunction would lead to loss of human life and/or avoidable damage to human health. The patent related to a vaccine for Hepatitis B. However, the background facts were likely to change – the defendant's own vaccine might soon be approved or it might obtain a compulsory licence for the plaintiff's patent. In a previous case, Graham J said:

> A life-saving drug is in an exceptional position ... it is at the least very doubtful if the court in its discretion even ought to grant an injunction ...[122]

Of course, it must be recalled that, as an equitable remedy, the grant of an injunction is always discretionary. That is not to say that damages would not be appropriate in such cases.

By s 50 of the Supreme Court Act 1981, the court has a discretion to award damages in lieu of an injunction. In *Chiron Corp v Organon Teknika Ltd (No. 10)*[123] the defendant argued that an injunction would be contrary to the public interest. The patent in question related to test kits for the Hepatitis C virus, and the defendant claimed that an injunction would prevent the public having access to the kits and would hinder research and development. Aldous J said that the test in *Shelfer v City of London Electric Lighting Co*[124] laid down by Smith LJ was still appropriate. The test (or rather, working rule) is:

1  if the injury to the plaintiff's legal rights is small; and
2  is one which is capable of being estimated in money; and
3  is one which can adequately be compensated by a small money payment; and
4  the case is one in which it would be oppressive to the defendant to grant an injunction;

then damages in substitution for an injunction may be given. However, that is a 'good working rule' and the court's discretion under the section is not limited and the interests of third parties or the public can be taken into account. Considering the general nature of the patent monopoly and controls over abuses, Aldous J refused to limit the injunctions sought. He also refused a stay of the injunctions pending appeal.

However, where the loss claimed is not itself recoverable, for example, for being too remote under tortious principles, an injunction will not be granted to protect the proprietor or exclusive licensee from such loss. This was said by Goff LJ in *Polaroid Corp v Eastman Kodak Co*[125] and, in *Peaudouce SA v Kimberley-Clark Ltd*,[126] the court held that it was wrong in principle to grant an injunction to protect against an irrecoverable loss, in that case, being a loss to other members of the plaintiff's group of companies.

Where a case has been determined on its merits and there is an appeal, the court may decide to grant a stay of any injunction. However, in such cases, the *American Cyanamid*[127] principles are less relevant: they apply to interlocutory hearings. Where there is an appeal against a decision taken at full trial, an application for a stay should be decided in accordance with the approach set out by Buckley LJ in *Minnesota Mining and Manufacturing Co v Johnson & Johnson Ltd.*[128] A major factor is that the plaintiff's patent has been held to be valid and infringed, and in *Minnesota Mining*, Buckley LJ said (at 676):

121 [1995] RPC 25. The patent was found to be invalid in the Court of Appeal and this was confirmed in the House of Lords, *see* [1997] RPC 1.

122 *Roussel-Uclaf v G D Searle & Co Ltd* [1977] FSR 125 at 131.

123 [1995] FSR 325.

124 [1895] 1 Ch 287.

125 [1977] RPC 379.
126 [1996] FSR 680.

127 *American Cyanamid Co v Ethicon Ltd* [1975] AC 396.

128 [1976] RPC 672.

The object ... must surely be so to arrange matters that, when the appeal comes to be heard, the appellate court may be able to do justice between the parties, whatever the outcome of the appeal may be.

Important factors are whether the appeal is to be made in good faith and whether there is a genuine chance of the appeal being successful, damage caused to the parties either way and, of course, the particular facts of the case.

Where there is an entry on the register to the effect that licences of right are available in respect of the patent and the defendant undertakes to take a licence, an injunction will not be granted against him. Also, the amount recoverable against him is limited to a maximum of double the amount that he would have paid had the infringing acts all been done under the licence.[129] It therefore makes sense for a person who is about to be sued for infringement to check whether licences of right are available for the patent concerned where there is any likelihood that damages will be assessed otherwise than on the basis of lost royalties and will be substantially more than the royalty payments under the licence of right. However, if the infringer did not have a licence and failed to undertake to apply for a licence of right an injunction could be imposed and damages would not be limited: they would be assessed at the damage actually caused to the plaintiff.[130]

**129** The Patents Act 1977 s 46(3)(c). The defendant's undertaking can be made at any time before the final order in the proceedings without admission of liability: s 46(3A).

**130** *Gerber Garment Technology Ltd v Lectra Systems Ltd* [1995] RPC 383.

### Assessment of damages

The calculation of damages can give rise to complex considerations. The basic principle was stated by Lord Wilberforce in *General Tire & Rubber Co v Firestone Tyre & Rubber Co Ltd*[131] in the following terms (at 185):

**131** [1975] 2 All ER 173.

> As in the case of any other tort ... the object of damages is to compensate for loss or injury. The general rule at any rate in relation to 'economic' torts is that the measure of damages is to be, so far as possible, that sum of money which will put the injured party in the same position as he would have been in if he had not sustained the wrong.

If the proprietor has been exploiting the patent by granting licences to others in return for royalties, then his loss is the capitalised value of the royalties that the infringer would have paid had he taken a licence. For example, if the infringer had made 500 articles that were covered by the patent and the proprietor had granted others a licence to make such articles in return for a royalty of £30 per article, then the damages should be assessed at £15 000. (This convenient method becomes less easy to use if the proprietor has granted licences in respect of the patent to different persons at different royalty rates.) Alternatively, the royalty may be calculated as a percentage of the net sale price of the articles where the infringer has been selling them at a lower price than legitimate licensees.

The royalty method of calculation falls down altogether if the proprietor does not grant licences but works the patent himself. In this case it is a question of the profits lost as a result of the infringer's activities. Here, many factors may be relevant, including the effect on the market place of the infringement. Particular issues include:

● whether every sale of an infringing article represents a lost sale for the proprietor;
● whether the proprietor would have sold other articles along with those lost sales (for example, the buyer may have also purchased non-patented articles in addition to the patented article) – these damages are often referred to as parasitic damages;

- whether the infringer had generated additional interest in the patented article through his marketing efforts;
- what the effect on the market was by changing a monopoly into a duopoly (for example, did the proprietor have to reduce his prices to compete with the infringer);
- typical profit margins for the category of article concerned;
- whether the infringer had deliberately undercut the proprietor's sale price.

An instructive case on the issue of damages where the proprietor had no intention of licensing the patent is *Catnic Components Ltd* v *Hill & Smith Ltd,*[132] which was a follow-up to the House of Lords case on infringement of lintels by a variant.[133] The plaintiff's claim for damages was under the following heads.

132 [1983] FSR 512.

133 [1982] RPC 183.

1 Loss of profits on each sale made by the defendant of infringing lintels – on the basis that every sale of the defendant's represented a lost sale to the plaintiff.
2 Loss of profits on the sale of non-patented lintels that the plaintiff would have sold alongside the patented lintels – parasitic damages.
3 A notional royalty of 20 per cent for any infringing lintels not subject to an award under 1 and 2 above.
4 Compound interest at 2 per cent above clearing bank base rate.
5 Exemplary damages on the sale at a large discount of infringing lintels by the defendant between the hearing in the House of Lords in the main action and the delivery of the judgment.

The defendant disputed these claims arguing that the plaintiff's lost sales, if any, were less than the defendant's sales of infringing lintels; that the plaintiff was not, in law, entitled to parasitic damages or exemplary damages and that interest payable should be simple interest at clearing bank rate *less* 2 per cent. The defendant conceded that the plaintiff was entitled to a royalty of 2 per cent on gross sales values.

It was held that it was proper to assume that each sale made by the defendant represented a lost sale unless the defendant could prove otherwise. A proper notional royalty rate was that which a potential licensee who had not yet entered the market would pay. No regard would be had to the fact that such a person could, instead, sell non-infringing lintels. On that basis, the appropriate royalty rate was 7 per cent net of tax. Parasitic sales were not allowable as not being a direct and natural consequence of the infringement. Although the defendant's discounted sales made shortly before the House of Lords judgment fell within the second category of acts for which exemplary damages might be awarded (benefit to defendant far outweighed the potential loss) in *Rookes* v *Barnard*,[134] they could not be awarded because there was no authority for it.[135] Neither was there any authority for compound interest, and the plaintiff was entitled only to simple interest calculated at clearing bank base rate plus 2 per cent.

134 [1964] AC 1129.

135 *Broome* v *Cassell & Co* [1972] AC 1027.

Recently, in the Patents Court, Jacob J chose not to follow *Catnic* v *Hill & Smith* as regards 'parasitic damages'. In *Gerber Garment Technology Inc* v *Lectra Systems Ltd*[136] it was held that patent infringement is a matter where secondary loss, provided it was reasonably foreseeable, should be recoverable on basic tortious principles. Such secondary loss may consist of the sale of unpatented articles which go with the patented article as a commercial matter (in the present case, the sale of machines to be used with the patented machines, servicing the machines

136 [1995] RPC 383.

and the sale of spare parts). The secondary loss would even extend to loss caused by the infringer establishing a 'bridgehead' or 'springboard' (for example, by negotiating with clients) before the expiry of the relevant patents.[137]

A further head of damages was for price depression. More controversially, part of the overall award of $5.9m included losses suffered by subsidiary companies. The plaintiff held all the shares in a number of subsidiaries and the resulting losses to these companies were taken into account on the basis that every dollar lost by a wholly-owned subsidiary was a dollar lost to the parent company.[138]

In the appeal from Jacob J's award of damages, the Court of Appeal accepted that where a shareholder in a company had a cause of action but the company had none, the shareholder could, in principle, sue in respect of loss caused to the company.[139] However, in the present case, the plaintiff had failed to prove he had both a personal cause of action and a personal loss.[140] In this case, the companies, including the plaintiff and its subsidiaries, were all part of a larger group. The plaintiff was not the holding company but an intermediate company. Hobhouse LJ said of the 'one dollar lost' rule (at 479):

> The position of parent companies and their subsidiaries vary widely ... there is no 'self-evident' truth. It all depends on the circumstances. Where, as here, the relevant companies are carrying on business in different countries, the starting point must be that an income loss suffered by one company will normally not translate directly into an equal monetary loss to the other company.

Hobhouse LJ compared simple groups of companies operating in the same country with groups with subsidiaries operating in different countries which may be subject to different tax regimes and exchange controls and an inflating local currency.

As an infringement of a patent is a statutory tort, it can be expected that normal tortious rules concerning damages apply as they apply to other torts. The basic rule is that the injured party should be restored to the position he would have been in had the tort not been committed. Recoverable losses are those that are foreseeable, caused by the tort and not excluded by public or social policy. In *South Australia Asset Management Corp v York Montague Ltd*,[141] Lord Hoffman said that liability is normally limited to consequences which are attributable to that which made the act wrongful. Staughton LJ in *Gerber Garment* said (at 453):

> ... at first impression the Patents Act is aimed at protecting patentees from commercial loss resulting from the wrongful infringement of their rights. That is only a slight gloss upon the wording of the statute itself. In my judgment, again as a matter of first impression, it does not distinguish between profit on the sale of patented articles and profit on the sale of convoyed goods [meaning goods sold alongside the patented articles].[142]

*Gerber Garment* is not inconsistent with *Catnic v Hill & Smith* as, in that case, it was held that the loss of sales of lintels other than those subject to the patent was not a natural and direct consequence of the acts of infringement. As a principle, losses of sales of non-patented goods sold alongside the patented goods are recoverable provided the basic test for recoverability in tort is satisfied. The same applies to the sale of spare parts and the work of servicing the patented goods. It is arguable that this basic principle goes further than now appears to be the case in the United States where, in *Rite-Hite Corp v Kelly Co Inc*,[143] it was held that for recovery for lost sales of unpatented goods sold with patented

---

**137** Jacob J claimed that the provisional opinions in *Polaroid Corp v Eastman Kodak Co* [1977] RPC 379 were adopted by Falconer J in *Catnic Components Ltd v Hill & Smith Ltd* [1983] FSR 512 as part of the *ratio* of the case. Jacob J held that he was wrong to do so!

**138** This was accepted in *George Fischer (Great Britain) Ltd v Multi-Construction Ltd* [1995] 1 BCLC 260. In that case, the group of companies were all operating in the same country under the same tax system.

**139** *Gerber Garment Technology Inc v Lectra Systems Ltd* [1997] RPC 443.

**140** Staughton LJ dissenting on this point.

**141** [1996] 3 WLR 87.

**142** After reviewing the case law, Staughton LJ concluded that there was no rule of law contradicting his first impression.

**143** [1996] FSR 469.

goods, they must function together so as to produce a desired end product or result, for example, as being components of a single assembly or which operate as a functional unit. Damages in respect of goods sold alongside the infringing goods and bought only as a matter of 'convenience or business advantage' are not recoverable. If that is so, this case is not irreconcilable with the English cases and can be said simply to point to a lack of causation in respect of such losses. In *Catnic v Hill & Smith*, it was accepted that, as a common practice, builders obtain from one supplier all their requirements for lintels for the erection of a particular building, and in *Gerber Garment* the articles sold with the patented articles (automated fabric cutting machines) were computer-aided design machines for designing cutting patterns.

## CRIMINAL OFFENCES

Infringements of patents associated with selling, distributing and importing products that are subject to a patent are dealt with as civil wrongs and there are no criminal penalties for such dealings, although, depending on the circumstances, trade description, forgery or trade mark offences may be committed. There are a number of offences provided for by the Patents Act 1977, but these do not directly relate to unauthorised dealing. Section 109 makes it an offence, triable either way, to make, or cause to be made, a false entry on the patents register. This also extends to writings purporting to be copies of such entries and to the use of such writings in evidence. The maximum penalty on indictment is imprisonment for a term not exceeding two years and/or a fine. On summary conviction, the maximum penalty is a fine not exceeding £1000.

Two offences deal with unauthorised claims with respect to patents. The first, under s 110, covers false representations that anything disposed of for value is a patented product, for example where the product has the words 'patented in the United Kingdom' or just simply the word 'patent' applied to it and there is no such patent. The second offence, under s 111, covers representations that a patent has been applied for in respect of any article disposed of for value when this is not true, or if the patent application has been withdrawn or refused. For both offences, a reasonable period of grace is allowed after the expiry or revocation of a patent, or the refusal or withdrawal of an application, to allow sufficient time to prevent the making or continuance of the representation. An example that would probably be deemed to fall within this period of grace is where an article to which a patent relates is being manufactured and has the word 'patented' embossed on it. Later, the patent is revoked. It would be expected that the person concerned would take immediate steps to prevent continuing application of the word 'patented' to new articles and that he would remove the word from his existing stock (if this is practicable), but he would not be expected to take action to remove the word from articles that he has sold to retailers. A further defence to these two offences is that the accused person had used due diligence to prevent the commission of the offence. The penalty for an offence under ss 110 or 111 is a fine not exceeding level 4 on the standard scale (currently £2500). These offences are triable summarily only.

Any person who uses on his place of business or on any document the words 'Patent Office' or any other words suggesting a connection between his place of business and the Patent Office, or indeed that his place of business is the Patent Office, is guilty of an offence and will be liable on summary conviction to a fine not exceeding level 5 on the standard scale (currently £5000).[144] An appropriate officer of a body corporate who consents or connives in the commission of any offence under the Act by that body corporate is also guilty of the relevant offence.[145] This also applies in the case of offences attributable to the neglect of the officer.[146] Appropriate officers are directors, managers, secretaries or other similar officers, or any person purporting to act in such a capacity. Where the affairs of the corporation are managed by its members, then those members may be liable as if they were directors.

Finally, a person who is not a registered patent agent commits an offence by carrying on a business (otherwise than in partnership) under a name or description containing the words 'patent agent' or 'patent attorney', or if in the course of business he otherwise describes himself or permits himself to be described as a 'patent agent' or 'patent attorney.[147] There are equivalent restrictions for partnerships and corporations. The maximum penalty is a fine not exceeding level 5 on the standard scale.

**144** The Patents Act 1977 s 112.

**145** Ibid s 113(1).

**146** Notice the difference between this provision and the equivalent provision for registered designs, where only consent and connivance bring criminal liability on the shoulders of the officer, mere negligence being insufficient (Registered Designs Act 1949 s 35A). Neither is neglect sufficient for criminal liability of officers of corporations in respect of the offence of fraudulent application of a trade mark under the Trade Marks Act 1994.

**147** The Copyright, Designs and Patents Act 1988 s 276.

# 15

## *Patents in Europe*

### INTRODUCTION

More than with any other form of intellectual property right, it is difficult to reconcile patents with the provisions of the Treaty of Rome promoting the free movement of goods, controlling restrictive trade agreements and preventing the abuse of dominant trading positions. However, even here, the general principle is that patent rights are to be recognised and are not to be compromised lightly. For example, one of the block exemptions from Article 85(1) permitted under Article 85(3), the 'Technology Transfer' Regulation,[1] concerns patent licensing and know-how licensing agreements or mixed patent and know-how licence agreements. The Regulation permits the inclusion of certain categories of terms in those agreements and is discussed later in this chapter. Provided the licence agreement is drawn up carefully, taking full account of the Regulation, it will not offend against Article 85(1). However, the exemption does not extend to all forms of agreements, for example pooling agreements and licences in the context of joint ventures. For such agreements, individual exemption must be sought. Also, there may be issues concerning whether a particular term in a licence drafted to accord with a specific exemption in the Regulation does indeed conform or whether there are any additional terms outside the scope of the Regulation which offend against Article 85(1).

Harmonisation of patent law is not the issue it might once have been, thanks to the European Patent Convention. All the member states of the European Community now belong to this Convention, and some non-Community countries such as Switzerland and Liechtenstein are full members of the Convention. The latest addition is Cyprus. It must be noted that the European Patent Office is not a Community organisation, although when the Community patent system comes into force it will be administered by the European Patent Office.

This chapter is concerned primarily with the impact of the Treaty of Rome (as amended) on the exercise of patent rights, followed by a discussion of the implications of the proposed Community patent system. As regards the relevant Treaty provisions, reference should be made to Chapter 9 for a detailed description of them.

### PATENTS AND THE TREATY OF ROME

Points of conflict between patent law and the Treaty provisions as identified and set out in Chapter 9 are discussed here within the same overall structure. Reference should be made to that chapter for the basic principles which are generally also applicable to patent law. First, we will consider the effects of

1 Commission Regulation (EC) No. 240/96 of 31 January 1996 on the application of Article 85(3) of the Treaty to certain categories of technology transfer agreements, OJ L31, 9.2.96, p. 2, replacing the 'patent licensing Regulation' (EEC) No. 2349/84, OJ L219, 16.8.84, p. 15 and the 'know-how licensing Regulation' (EEC) No. 556/89, OJ L61, 4.3.89, p. 1.

Articles 30–36, promoting the free movement of goods, followed by Article 85, prohibiting restrictive trade practices, and finally Article 86, preventing the abuse of a dominant trading position.

It should be noted that there is a *de minimis* doctrine that applies in relation to Articles 85 and 86. Article 85 will not apply where the effect on the market is insignificant: see *Völk* v *Vervaecke*.[2] The Commission has also issued notices giving guidance, the latest dating from 1997 and which provides quantitative guidance that the goods or services covered by the agreement under consideration do not represent more than 5 per cent of the total market for such goods or services, and the aggregate annual turnover of the participating undertakings is not more than 300 million Ecu.[3] The criteria are for guidance only, however, and are not conclusive.

2 [1969] ECR 295.

3 Notice on Agreements of Minor Importance, OJ C372, 9.12.97, p. 13.

## Role of national courts

National courts frequently are faced with cases in which issues under European Community law fall to be determined. For example, a defendant in a patent infringement action in the United Kingdom may plead a 'Euro-defence' based on Articles 30, 85 or 86.[4] Article 177 gives a discretion to national courts to refer questions of Community law to the European Court of Justice. It states:

4 For example, Article 30 was pleaded in *The Wellcome Foundation Ltd* v *Dispcharm Ltd* [1993] FSR 433 and Article 86 was pleaded in *Chiron Corp* v *Organon Teknika Ltd (No. 2)* [1993] FSR 324 and in *Pitney Bowes Inc* v *Francotyp-Postalia GmbH* [1991] FSR 72.

The Court of Justice shall have jurisdiction to give preliminary rulings concerning:

(a)  the interpretation of this Treaty;

(b)  the validity and interpretation of acts of the institutions of the Community;

(c)  the interpretation of the statutes of bodies established by an act of the Council, where those statutes so provide. Where such a question is raised before any court or tribunal of a Member State, that court or tribunal may, if it considers that a decision on the question is necessary to enable it to give judgment, request the Court of Justice to give a ruling thereon.

   Where any such question is raised in a case pending before a court or tribunal of a Member State, against whose decisions there is no judicial remedy under national law, that court of tribunal shall bring the matter before the Court of Justice.

The last part of Article 177 is expressed in the imperative and applies to the 'court of last resort', that is the court from which there is no appeal. Thus, in a hearing in the House of Lords, the House must refer a matter concerning doubts as to the validity or interpretation of Community law to the Court of Justice.[5]

The question of referral under Article 177 is less clear when a case has been heard in a lower court but leave to appeal has been refused. Does that lower court then become the court of last resort? In *Chiron Corp* v *Murex Diagnostics Ltd (No. 8)*[6] the defendant in a patent infringement action set up a defence under Article 86. The plaintiff applied to the Patents Court to strike out the relevant paragraph of the defence and was refused leave to amend. The defendant's appeal to the Court of Appeal was unsuccessful and the Court of Appeal refused leave to appeal to the House of Lords. The defendant then applied for an Article 177 reference which was adjourned pending a petition to the House of Lords for leave to appeal, which was refused. The defendant made a new application to the Court of Appeal for an Article 177 reference. It was held that:

5 Note that Article 177 references still go to the European Court of Justice and not to the Court of First Instance.

6 [1995] FSR 309.

1 When considering whether to grant or refuse leave to appeal, the House of Lords is acting in a judicial rather than in an administrative capacity, and therefore granting leave to appeal is a judicial remedy. Thus, in such cases, the House of Lords is the court of last resort.

2 Where an appeal lies to a higher court with the leave of either the lower or higher court, only the higher court can be obliged to make an Article 177 reference.

3 When a court has given judgment, it may not later make an Article 177 reference as such references are for *preliminary* rulings only.

In the present case, the House of Lords, by its refusal to grant leave to appeal, could be taken to indicate that it did not consider a reference under Article 177 to be necessary. Had the House of Lords considered that it was or might be necessary, it could have granted leave and either made an immediate reference or heard argument and then adjourned pending the decision of the European Court of Justice. The Court of Appeal will be the court of last resort only in rare cases where there is no right to apply to the House of Lords for leave to appeal, or where the Court of Appeal refuses leave to apply for judicial review. Article 177 allows any court or tribunal to refer matters within its scope. Thus, where a court is not the court of last resort, it may refer the matter for a preliminary ruling if it wishes. In *Research Corp's Supplementary Protection Certificate*[7] it was accepted that the Comptroller of Patents could request a preliminary ruling under Article 177 when acting in a judicial or quasi-judicial capacity. In the present case, he refused to do so because he considered the construction of Article 5 of Council Regulation (EEC) No. 1768/92 to be beyond doubt.[8]

Article 177 references can take some time, typically 18 months. Lord Denning spoke of the delay in *H P Bulmer Ltd* v *Bollinger SA*[9] as being an important factor to be taken into account by a judge in deciding whether to refer a case to the Court of Justice. He went on to say that English judges should apply the Treaty of Rome themselves in most cases, using the European style of interpretation.

The Commission to the European Community is not opposed to a greater role being taken by national courts. Indeed, during 1993 it issued a notice on the co-operation between national courts and the Commission setting out their respective functions.[10] The main points are:

1 The Commission has sole power to exempt certain types of agreement from Article 85(1).

2 The simultaneous application of national competition law is compatible with the application of European Community law provided that it does not affect the effectiveness and uniformity of the latter.

3 The Commission will concentrate on notifications, complaints and own-initiative proceedings of particular political, economic or legal significance. In the absence of any such criteria, notifications will normally be dealt with by comfort letters[11] and complaints should, as a rule, be dealt with by national courts.

4 If the national courts can provide sufficient protection for the plaintiff, there will not normally be sufficient European Community interest to justify investigation. Of particular importance is the fact that national courts, in the enforcement of European Community competition law, can grant interim relief and award damages and costs.

7 [1994] RPC 387.

8 The doctrine of 'acte clair'; *see* Kerr LJ in *R v Pharmaceutical Society of Great Britain, ex parte Association of Pharmaceutical Importers* [1987] 3 CMLR 951 at 956.

9 [1974] 2 All ER 1226.

10 OJ C39, 13.2.93, p. 6.

11 *See* post.

5 Nevertheless, national courts should avoid decisions that conflict with those taken or envisaged by the Commission. If the Commission has not ruled on a particular point, case law of the European Court of Justice and previous decisions of the Commission will provide guidance.

This reinforces the principle of subsidiarity, leaving more decision making to the member states, although this can result in an uneven application of legal rules which may, in turn, cause conflicts with the Treaty of Rome.

## Patent law and the freedom of movement of goods

Article 30 prohibits quantitative restrictions on imports and all measures having equivalent effect between member states. There is a derogation in Article 36 allowing prohibitions and restrictions on imports, exports or goods in transit that are justified on the grounds of protecting industrial and commercial property. However, such prohibitions and restrictions must not constitute a means of arbitrary discrimination or a disguised restriction on the free movement of goods. Although the doctrine of exhaustion of rights is clearly a result of Article 30, the prohibition therein applies to other situations also.

The doctrine of freedom of movement of goods existed to some extent in the United Kingdom prior to its membership of the European Community. In some cases, the courts were prepared to imply a licence allowing the purchaser of an article to resell it. For example, in *Betts v Willmott*,[12] an old patent case, the plaintiff sold metal capsules to the defendant in France. The plaintiff, who had factories in England and France, tried to prevent the capsules being resold in England. Lord Hatherley said (at 245):

> When a man has purchased an article he expects to have control of it, and there must be some clear and explicit agreement to the contrary to justify the vendor in saying that he has not given the purchaser his licence to sell the article, or use it wherever he pleases as against himself.

Of course, under traditional English law, such freedom to resell (and presumably also to import) was entirely vulnerable to the principle of freedom of contract. The European model is much stronger and of far greater application. Another area of English law which could apply to ensure freedom of movement in limited circumstances is the doctrine of non-derogation from grant.

The manner in which compulsory licences are granted has conflicted with Article 30. In *EC Commission v United Kingdom*[13] it was held that a provision of national law (in this case the Patents Act 1977 s 48) that equated a position where demand was being substantially met by importation from other member states with insufficient exploitation of a patent giving rise to the grant of a compulsory licence, offended against Article 30. It was not saved by Article 36 which protects the specific subject matter of industrial property. The definition of what constitutes the specific subject matter of a patent given in *Centrafarm BV v Sterling Drug Inc*[14] was affirmed.

It is essential that trade between member states is affected or likely to be affected by the restrictions or measure in question. The grant of a compulsory licence to work a patent subject to a prohibition on importation from outside the European Community did not affect trade between member states in *Generics (UK) Ltd v Smith Kline and French Laboratories (UK) Ltd.*[15] The imposition of excessive prices in the UK did not, *per se*, affect trade between member states.[16]

12 (1871) LC 6 Ch App 239.

13 [1993] FSR 1.

14 [1974] ECR 1147, *see* post.

15 [1993] 1 CMLR 89. However, the criteria could be applied in such a way as to affect trade between member states.

16 *Chiron Corp v Organon Teknika Ltd (No. 2)* [1993] FSR 324.

The doctrine of exhaustion of rights applies to patents as it does to trade marks, copyright and allied rights. The doctrine is that the owner or proprietor of an intellectual property right who consents to the marketing of his goods or articles in one member state cannot use that right to prevent the importation of the goods or articles into another member state or their subsequent sale. To this extent, the right is said to be exhausted by the first consensual marketing.[17] This leaves the proprietor of a patent with the dilemma of whether or not to exploit the patent in more than one member state. Of course, this doctrine does not affect other patent rights, such as the right to prevent the making of the product, or the use of the process that is the subject matter of the patent. It is the right to prevent subsequent dealing, and particularly importation of the product, which is touched by Article 30.

The effect of Article 30 on the exercise of a patent right is often brought into question in cases involving parallel importing. For example, in *Centrafarm BV v Sterling Drug Inc*,[18] Sterling Drug was the proprietor of patents in the UK and The Netherlands in respect of a drug. It had UK and Dutch subsidiary companies and granted licences to both of them in respect of the drug. Due to government regulations in the UK, the drug there cost approximately half the cost in The Netherlands. The UK company exported large quantities of the drug to The Netherlands, undercutting the Dutch company. It was held that this was permissible because the drug had been put on the market with the parent company's consent, thereby exhausting its rights under the patent. The Dutch subsidiary had wanted the parent company to exercise its patent rights to prevent the importation into The Netherlands of the drug made in the UK. Therefore, it is difficult for a proprietor of patents in respect of the same invention in different member states to maintain price differentials between those member states. Purely economic considerations affecting the marketing of a product may be distorted and it could mean that a decision is taken not to market a product in a country where a low price would be appropriate or necessary.[19] However, for the exhaustion doctrine to apply, the marketing must have been with the consent of the patentee, and in *Parke, Davis & Co v Probel*[20] the doctrine did not apply and the proprietor of a Dutch patent was able to prevent a drug's importation into The Netherlands from Italy where the drug had been made without the consent of the patentee.[21]

There have been problems in applying the doctrine of exhaustion of rights to situations where patents are available for a particular category of product in some member states but not others. At one time, some countries such as Italy, Portugal and Spain did not provide for the patenting of pharmaceutical products. In *Merck & Co Inc v Stephar BV*,[22] the proprietor of a Dutch patent for a drug consented to the marketing of the drug in Italy. It was held by the European Court of Justice that the rights had been exhausted even though, in Italy, the proprietor of the Dutch patent was not in a monopoly position and could not make the usual profits flowing from a patent monopoly. In turn, he might have to sell his drugs more cheaply in Italy to compete with others who could lawfully manufacture the drug there and face the prospect of damage to the profitability of his Dutch operation caused by a parallel importer. The crucial test was, however, that the drugs had been put on the market in Italy by or with the consent of the proprietor of the Dutch patent.

17 The doctrine was first formulated in *Consten and Grundig v Commission* [1966] ECR 299, a case concerning the scope of Article 85(1).

18 [1974] ECR 1147.

19 *See* Whish, R. (1992) *Competition Law* (3rd edn) Butterworths, Chapter 19 for a discussion of this case and its implications in addition to a detailed discussion of the effect of UK and European Community law on anti competitive practices.

20 [1968] ECR 55.

21 The availability of a licence in one member state may also defeat the right to prevent imports made in another country without consent, *Allen and Hanbury v Generics(UK)* [1986] RPC 203.

22 [1981] ECR 2063.

The correctness of this decision was doubted in *Merck & Co Inc v Prime-crown Ltd*.[23] Before Spain and Portugal joined the European Community, patents for pharmaceutical products were not available. However, under the Acts of Accession to the Community, Spain and Portugal were required to grant patents for pharmaceutical products. However, the Acts of Accession provided that, in effect, the exhaustion of rights principle was not to apply for three years until after pharmaceutical products became patentable in Spain and Portugal. Two issues required to be resolved by the European Court of Justice. The first was to determine precisely when the three-year period postponing the application of exhaustion of rights to pharmaceutical products ended. Was it three years after such products became patentable, or three years from the end of the calendar year during which they became patentable? The second question for the court was whether the rule in *Merck* v *Stephar* needed reconsidering.

The court held that the three-year period expired three years from the precise time at which drugs became patentable in Spain and Portugal and not three years from the end of the calendar year during which they so became patentable. The Acts of Accession were ambiguous on this point but, because the three-year period was a derogation from the normal working of the EC Treaty, the court said that it must be construed so as to cause the earliest application of Articles 30 and 36.

Of the rule in *Merck* v *Stephar*, the court held that it still applied. The plaintiff submitted a number of reasons for modifying the rule, including state controls on prices and ethical or moral obligations to supply drugs in a member state even though they were not patentable there. However, the plaintiffs in the infringement actions which led to the Article 177 reference had freely sold their drugs in Spain and Portugal.[24] They had not been compelled to do so by any rule of law. Simply being under an ethical or moral obligation was not a reason to depart from the rule. Neither was the imposition of price controls by a member state a reason to depart from the rule. The distortion caused by price controls was a matter to be dealt with by measures taken by the European Community rather than by providing a special derogation from the principle of freedom of movement.

The European Court of Justice accepted that where a proprietor of a patent was compelled by law to sell his products in a member state, he did not consent to the sale in any real sense and could use his rights to prevent imports. That had not been the case here. Thus, the rule in *Merck* v *Stephar* has been qualified to that limited extent only.

The existence/exercise distinction is used by the European Court of Justice and it is only the exercise of the right that is controlled. It will be so controlled if it does not relate to the 'specific subject matter' of the right, which was defined in the *Centrafarm* v *Sterling Drug* case as being:

> ... the guarantee that the patentee, to reward the creative effort of the inventor, has the exclusive right to use an invention with a view to manufacturing industrial products and putting them into circulation for the first time, either directly or by the grant of licences to third parties, as well as the right to oppose infringements.

Often, there will be a tension between Article 30 and Article 36. In *Generics BV v Smith Kline & French Laboratories Ltd*,[25] SKF had a Dutch patent for the drug cimetidine. Before the patent expired, a third party filed applications for market-

**23** [1997] FSR 237. The defendant in the original infringement action had bought the drugs in Spain and Portugal and imported them into the UK.

**24** The case was referred to the European Court of Justice by Jacob J, *see Merck & Co Inc v Primetown Ltd* [1995] FSR 909.

**25** [1997] RPC 801.

ing authorisation in respect of the drug to the Dutch assessment board for medicinal products, submitting samples of the drug as required. The authorisations were granted and were assigned to Generics shortly before the patent expired. SKF applied for and was granted a temporary injunction to take effect immediately upon the expiry of the patent, restraining Generics from offering for sale or supplying the drug. The injunction was to last 14 months after the patent expired, this being the average time it took to obtain marketing authorisation.

The European Court of Justice accepted that the consequence of Dutch law was that a person other than the proprietor of the patent could not sell cimetidine as soon as the patent had expired. This was a measure having equivalent effect to a quantitative restriction on importation within Article 30. The drugs were lawfully on the market in other member states, but the effect of the approach of the Dutch court was to prevent anyone importing them from another member state and offering them for sale in The Netherlands.[26] However, the European Court of Justice also held that such a restriction was justified under Article 36 and confirmed that the use of samples to obtain marketing authorisation was within the specific subject matter of a patent.

The outcome of the case was to place the proprietor of the patent in the same position he would have been in had his patent rights been respected whilst the patent was still in force. However, neither the Patents Act 1977 nor the European Patent Convention extend infringement to obtaining authorisation.[27] The applicant for authorisation would only infringe if he made the product whilst the patent was still in force.[28] What if the third party lawfully purchased a quantity of the drug made by the proprietor of the patent and submitted that for marketing authorisation? In the present case, the samples submitted by Generics had not been put on the market by or with the consent of SKF.

Of course, the proprietor or his licensee might attempt to use contractual methods to prevent the subsequent resale of the products, and if it affects trade between member states this also will be controlled. The fact of the matter is that, in the European context, the use of patents (or other intellectual property rights) to divide the market and maintain territorial boundaries is vulnerable to challenge and control. This may be a good thing; for example, where a manufacturer is deliberately operating price differentials for no other reason than to make unreasonable profit margins, a parallel importer may soon put an end to this practice. However, there may be other good reasons for price differentials, such as differing legal measures, but such justifiable reasons may disappear or become less numerous as the single market is consolidated.

## Anti-competitive practices and patents

Article 85 of the Treaty of Rome prohibits anti-competitive agreements and the like which have, as their object or effect, the distortion of competition within the Common Market. Two forms of agreement are relevant to the discussion: those which involve cross-licensing and agreements to pool intellectual property rights. For example, two companies based in different member states holding different patents in respect of a similar process (for example, the manufacture of engine castings) may agree to share the exploitation of their patents, dividing up the market between them. Another example might be where the patents pooled are complementary, for example, where one relates to the casting of a

26 The rule in *Procureur du Roi* v *Dassonville* [1974] ECR 837 applies Article 30 where the law in question is capable of hindering directly or indirectly, actually or potentially, intra-Community trade.

27 The defence of doing an act for experimental purposes would not seem to apply. Dutch patent law allows examination of the patented product, but has been held not to apply to the submision of samples of medicinal products.

28 Or performed any of the other infringing acts unless the proprietor's rights had been exhausted.

part for an engine and the other relates to the finishing of the cast part and removal of the casting 'fins'. (An example of a case where the Commission has taken action against a patent pooling agreement is *Re Video Cassette Recorders Agreement*.[29]) The Technology Transfer Regulation allows block exemption in respect of the licensing of patents and/or know-how under certain circumstances, but this does not apply to pooled patents, joint venture patent agreements and cross-licensing, that is reciprocal patent licences.[30] It is, however, possible for an organisation to apply to the Commission for individual exemption if the activity concerned does not fall within a block exemption. The block exemption is discussed later.

In *Re Alcatel Espace and ANT Nachrichtentechnik*[31] there was an application to the Commission for a negative clearance or individual exemption in respect of an agreement between a French Company and a German company, both involved in the manufacture of communication equipment, for the purposes of joint research and development, production and marketing activities. The agreement included a term to the effect that the relevant patents owned by each party (or to which each party was entitled) would be communicated to the other party and the parties would be free to work each other's patents on a royalty-free, non-exclusive licence basis. First of all, the Commission held that the agreement offended against Article 85(1) because it would allocate research and development so that only one party would carry this out, that the agreement provided for the procurement by one party of equipment made by the other and that decision-making processes were to be allocated to common committees. The Commission considered all of these would restrict competition. The block exemption relating to research and development agreements was not applicable as the agreement went beyond its scope.[32] However, the Commission granted an individual exemption under Article 85(3) for a period of ten years, subject to notification of changes in the agreement. The reasons given by the Commission are instructive:

1  the planned co-operation would lead to improved technical solutions which would be discovered more rapidly and would contribute to technical progress which would benefit customers;
2  the agreement only imposed restrictions necessary to the above objective. The fact that the agreement did not prohibit either party from engaging in other activities outside the scope of the agreement was an important factor;
3  the nature of the market implied that separate marketing was not practicable;
4  the parties' market share was not high.

Agreements of the type mentioned above are sometimes described as 'horizontal agreements' because they reflect mutuality of restrictions. On the other hand, a vertical agreement is simply one between licensor and licensee, for example where the proprietor of a patent grants an exclusive licence to a manufacturing company permitting that company to make, export and sell the product. Figure 15.1 shows an arrangement where two companies, Acme Ltd and Azimuth plc, have pooled their patents and Acme has subsequently granted an exclusive licence to Zenith SA to make and sell the product in France (the patent pooling agreement allows either party to grant such licences in respect of their own patents).

Both types of agreements could be invalid if challenged if they affect trade between member states. The types of terms that are likely to cause problems are

29  [1978] CMLR 160. Upon leaving the 'pool' any member had to surrender its rights under the agreement, but also had to allow the remaining members to continue to use its rights.

30  Commission Regulation (EC) No. 240/96 on the application of Article 85(3) of the Treaty to certain categories of technology transfer agreements.

31  [1991] 4 CMLR 208.

32  Commission Regulation (EEC) No. 418/85 of 19 December 1984 (as amended).

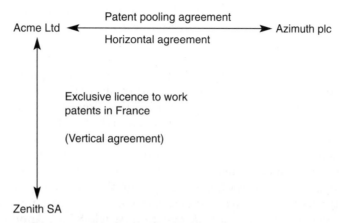

Acme Ltd ← Patent pooling agreement → Azimuth plc

Horizontal agreement

Exclusive licence to work
patents in France

(Vertical agreement)

Zenith SA

**Figure 15.1 Horizontal and vertical agreements**

those that attempt to extend the agreement or any part of it beyond the term of the patent, those which tie the licensee to the licensor, for example where the licensee agrees to purchase goods from the licensor that are unconnected with the patent in question, and terms which state that the licensor is not to work the patent in countries other than those included in the licence agreement.[33] It is certainly the case that any licence which includes some sort of exclusive right should be drawn up very carefully and specialist advice taken where there is any possibility of exploitation in more than one member state, or where the product is likely to be exported, with or without the consent of the parties to the agreement. However, some terms have been declared to be permissible, such as minimum royalty clauses and terms requiring minimum quantities of the product to be made by the licensee, as they are properly within the normal exploitation of the patent and go to the specific subject matter of the patent. Terms which purport to prevent the licensee from challenging the validity of the patent, or which require him to refrain from competing with the licensor, are likely to be struck out by the Commission or European Court if they could affect inter-state trade.

A whole list of provisions in a licence agreement in respect of a patent and a trade mark were, according to the Commission in the case of *Velcro SA* v *Aplix SA*,[34] caught by Article 85(1), including:

1 exclusivity preventing the licensor exploiting the patents and trade mark in the licensed territory, or granting further licences there when the basic patents expired;
2 an export ban preventing the licensee selling outside the licensed territory;
3 the automatic extension of certain terms on the expiry of basic patents on the basis of improvement patents;
4 an obligation to obtain manufacturing equipment exclusively from a named manufacturer;
5 an obligation not to use specialised manufacturing machinery outside the licensed territory;
6 an obligation on the parties not to compete with each other;
7 an obligation to allow the licensor to acquire title to improvement patents in other member states for improvements discovered by the licensee; and
8 a provision for the unilateral extension of the patent licence.

33 The case of *AIOP* v *Beyrard* [1976] 1 CMLR D14 concerned a provision which purported to allow the unilateral extension of the licence by the licensor. *See also Kai Ottung v Klee & Weilbach* [1990] 4 CMLR 915, about an obligation to pay royalties after the expiry of a patent. The European Court considered that whether an agreement affected inter-state trade and thus offended against Article 85(1), was a matter for a national court to decide from the economic and legal context in which the agreement was concluded.

34 [1989] 4 CMLR 157.

It cannot be disputed that the agreement in this case contained a great many provisions that were capable of affecting trade between member states (the above list is not complete – there were other reasons why the agreement was caught by Article 85(1)). However, it is natural for commercial organisations to have their own interests at heart when drawing up licensing agreements, and too much interference by the European Court can be criticised as being counter-productive and likely to restrict trade, the flow of information and collaboration by destroying the commercial viability of licences and other agreements. A comparison of the *Velcro* and *Alcatel Espace* cases indicates that the 'look and feel' of an agreement is very important – whether it prohibits certain activities, or merely discourages them. For example, a collateral term insisting that equipment is obtained only from the other party will be struck down, but a term stating that equipment should or may be obtained from the other party may survive an attack based on Article 85(1). Another factor is that, in some cases, the complaint has not come from a third party whose trade has been affected adversely by the operation of the agreement, but from one of the parties to the agreement itself, who is now trying to free himself of terms to which he had earlier expressly agreed.

## Exemption from Article 85(1)

The fact that exemption from Article 85(1) is available or can be obtained has already been mentioned. The effects of Article 85(3), which allows derogations from Article 85(1), will now be looked at in more detail. Article 85(3) permits the provisions of Article 85(1) to be declared inapplicable in the case of agreements that contribute to the improvement of the production or distribution of goods, or to promoting technical or economic progress. Consumers must be allowed a fair share of the resulting benefit and such derogation from the force of Article 85(1) does not apply to agreements, decisions or concerted practices that:

1 impose on the undertakings concerned restrictions which are not indispensable to the attainment of the above objectives;
2 afford such undertakings the possibility of eliminating competition in respect of a substantial part of the products in question.

The Commission is empowered to provide for block exemption for certain categories of agreements and concerted practices which fall within the scope of Article 85(1). It may also grant individual exemption. The first block exemption for patent licences came into force in 1984 and was intended to last for ten years.[35] There was also a block exemption for certain categories of know-how licensing agreements.[36] As know-how (generally confidential information relating to the use or application of industrial processes) is often licensed along with patents, it was considered desirable, in the interests of simplification and encouraging the dissemination of technical knowledge, to combine the two block exemptions into a single Regulation. The 1984 Regulation on patent licensing was extended beyond its normal ten years pending the new Commission Regulation (EC) No. 240/96 on the application of Article 85(3) of the Treaty to certain categories of technology transfer agreements, often referred to as the Technology Transfer Regulation.[37] This Regulation came into force on 1 April 1996 and is declared to apply until 31 March 2006. Pre-existing

35 Commission Regulation (EEC) No. 2349/84 on the application of Article 85(3) of the Treaty to certain categories of patent licensing agreements, OJ L219, 16.8.84, p. 15.

36 OJ L61, 4.3.89, p. 1.

37 OJ L31, 9.2.96, p. 2.

agreements in force at 31 March 1996 which fulfilled the requirements of the previous two Regulations are unaffected by the prohibition in Article 85(1).

The Technology Transfer Regulation applies to the licensing of member states' own patents, to European patents (within the European Patent Convention) and Community patents (when underway). 'Know-how' is defined in Article 10 as a body of technical information that is secret, substantial and identified in any appropriate form.[38] The Regulation applies to patent licences, know-how licences and mixed licences, that is, licences including patents and know-how. It does not apply the 'pooling' of technology, to licensing in a joint venture situation,[39] cross-licensing between competitors or to licences including other intellectual property rights which are not ancillary to the exploitation of the know-how or patents.

The new Regulation takes a similar approach to the old patent licensing Regulation, that is, it provides formal exceptions from Article 85(1) prohibiting restrictive trade agreements, a 'white list' being clauses not generally restrictive of competition and a 'black list' being clauses outside the protection afforded by the Regulation.

The approach taken by the Regulation is to:

- disapply Article 85(1) of the Treaty in respect of agreements between two undertakings only which include one or more of a list of obligations conforming to Article 1;
- allow the inclusion of further clauses (set out in Article 2(1)) which are generally not restrictive of competition without prejudice to the application of Article 1 – under Article 2(2) such clauses are also exempted even if they fall within the scope of Article 85(1) of the Treaty and even if they are not accompanied by any of the obligations exempted by Article 1 – this also applies if the clauses in question are of more limited scope than is permitted in Article 2(1);
- disapply the exemptions in Articles 1 and Article 2(2) if the agreement contains prohibitions, restrictions or obligations set out in Article 3 – therefore, advantage cannot be taken of the exemptions in Articles 1 and 2(2) if any term within Article 3 is present – such terms, therefore, are to be avoided at all costs;
- where an agreement contains obligations which are restrictive of competition and are not covered by Articles 1 or 2 and which are not within the scope of Article 3, exemption may be obtained by notifying the agreement to the Commission if the Commission does not oppose the exemption within a period of four months.

Therefore, a person drafting a licence agreement in respect of a patent or patents and/or know-how can include any of the obligations contained in Articles 1 and 2(1), but must steer clear of the terms in Article 3. If the agreement contains other terms which are restrictive of competition, the Commission must be notified. The provisions of the Regulation are described below in overview with examples of some of the terms within Articles 1 to 3.

Article 1 applies to pure patent licences or know-how licences and to mixed patent and know-how licences, including agreements containing ancillary provisions relating to intellectual property rights other than patents. Examples of the obligations within Article 1(1) are:

**38** Article 10 also contains a number of other definitions, including 'secret', 'substantial', and 'identified'.

**39** There is an exception to this where a parent undertaking grants the joint venture a patent or know-how licence in relation to products which are interchangeable or substitutable for goods or services of the joint venture undertakings representing not more than 20 per cent of those goods or services or, in the case of production and distribution, not more than 10 per cent.

- territorial restrictions, for example:
  - obligations on the licensor not to exploit the licensed technology in the licensed territory nor to grant licences to other undertakings to exploit therein;
  - obligations on the licensee not to exploit the licensed technology in the licensor's territory within the common market and not to manufacture or use the licensed product, or use the licensed process in territories within the common market which are licensed to other licensees;
  - obligations on the licensee not to pursue an active policy of putting the licensed product on the market in the territories within the common market which are reserved for other licensees and not to put the licensed product on the market in the territories licensed to other licensees within the common market in response to unsolicited orders;
- other obligations, for example, that the licensee must use the licensor's trade mark or get up provided that the licensee is not prevented from identifying himself as manufacturer, and obligations in respect of limiting production of the licensed product to the quantities the licensee requires for manufacturing his own products.

Generally, the exemptions apply during the life of the relevant agreement only to the extent that the relevant patents are in force and/or the relevant know-how remains secret and substantial. There are limitations on the territorial restrictions, for example, the obligation not to respond to unsolicited orders is limited to no more than five years from the time the licensed product is first put on the market within the common market by one of the licensees. In the case of pure patent licence agreements, the other territorial restrictions apply only as long as parallel patents[40] are in force[41] (in the territories of the licensor, licensee or other licensees, as appropriate). Where the agreement is a pure know-how licensing agreement, the other territorial restrictions may not endure for more than ten years from the date the product is first put on the market within the common market by one of the licensees. There are further limitations.

Perhaps for the avoidance of doubt, although it does seem to state the obvious, the exemption in Article 1 also applies where the obligations are of more limited scope than is permitted by paragraph 1 of that Article.

Article 2(1) contains a list of 18 types of obligations. These are exempt from Article 85(1) of the Treaty whether or not there are also any of the obligations in the agreement falling within Article 1. Examples of the obligations include:

- an obligation on the licensee not to divulge the know-how – the licensee may be made subject to this obligation after the agreement has expired;
- an obligation on the licensee not to grant sublicences or assign the licence;
- an obligation on the licensee not to exploit the know-how or patents after termination of the agreement in so far and as long as the know-how remains secret or the patents are still in force;
- an obligation on the licensee to grant to the licensor a licence in respect of his own improvements to or his new applications of the licensed technology – this is subject to conditions including, where the improvement is severable, that the licence is not exclusive and that there is an obligation on the licensor to grant an exclusive or non-exclusive licence of his own improvements to the licensee;

40 'Parallel patents' are patents protecting the same invention in various member states.

41 Under the Patents Act 1977 s 45, the licensee can give three months' notice to terminate the licence following the expiry of the patent.

- obligations on the licensee to inform the licensor of misappropriation of the know-how or of infringements of the licensed patents, or to take or assist the licensor in taking legal action against such misappropriation or infringements;
- an obligation on the licensee to pay a minimum royalty or to produce a minimum quantity of the licensed product or to carry out a minimum number of operations exploiting the licensed technology;
- an obligation on the licensee to mark the licensed product with an indication of the licensor's name or of the licensed patent;
- a reservation by the licensor of the right to terminate the agreement if the licensee contests the secret or substantial nature of the licensed know-how or challenges the validity of the licensed patents within the common market belonging to the licensor or undertakings connected with him;
- an obligation on the licensee to use his best endeavours to manufacture and market the licensed product.

Article 3 contains what can best be described as a 'black list'. Examples of prohibitions, restrictions or obligations caught by Article 3 are:

- restrictions in the determination of prices, components of prices or discounts for the licensed products;
- requirements imposed on one or both parties, without any objectively justified reason, to refuse to meet orders from users or resellers in their respective territories who would market products in other territories within the common market or placing other barriers hindering resellers (this provision is designed to reinforce the doctrine of exhaustion of rights);
- an obligation on the licensee to assign in whole or in part to the licensor rights to improvements to or new applications of the licensed technology, often referred to as 'grant back' (non-exclusive licences are, however, generally permissible under Article 2).

Where an agreement has been notified in accordance with Article 4, exemption is, effectively, automatic if the Commission does not oppose within four months. The Commission may oppose the notification of its own volition but if it receives a request to do so from a member state, it shall oppose within two months of the member state being informed of the notification. The request must be justified on the basis of the competition rules in the Treaty. Opposition may be withdrawn by the Commission at any time.[42] This may occur, typically, where the parties to the agreement have amended it so as to comply with the conditions in Article 85(3).

In particular, the provisions for exemption through notification apply where a licensee is obliged, at the time the agreement is entered into, to accept quality specifications, further licences or procure goods or services not necessary for the technically satisfactory exploitation of the licensed technology or for ensuring that the licensee conforms to quality standards respected by the licensor and other licensees.[43] Likewise, prohibitions on challenges to the secrecy or substantiality of the know-how or to the validity of patents belonging to the licensor or undertakings connected with him should be notified under Article 4.[44] Note that Article 2 allows terms which give the licensor a right to terminate the agreement in the face of a challenge to the know-how or patents, it does not extend to a prohibition of such challenges.

42 Where the opposition was in response to a request by a member state, the opposition may be withdrawn only after consultation with the Advisory Committee on Restrictive Practices and Dominant Positions.

43 Some of these obligations could offend against the Patents Act 1977 s 44.

44 'Connected undertakings' are defined in Article 10. They include those having more than half of the capital, business assets or voting rights or the power to appoint more than half the board of directors or the right to manage the affairs of the other undertaking.

The Regulation applies also to agreements where the licensor is not the holder of the know-how or patent but is authorised to grant the licence, for example, where a licensee of a patent grants a sub-licence, assignments where the risk of exploitation remains with the assignor, for example, where payment to the assignor is a royalty based on sales of a patented product made by the assignee, and to licences in which the rights and obligations of the licensor and licensee are assumed by undertakings connected with them.

Even though the agreement conforms with the Regulation in all other respects, under Article 7, the Commission reserves the right to withdraw the benefit of the Regulation in particular cases where the agreement has certain effects incompatible with the conditions laid down in Article 85(3). Some particular examples are set out in the Article, for example where the licensed product is prevented from being exposed to effective competition with identical goods or services or interchangeable or substitutable goods or services, particularly where the licensee's market share exceeds 40 per cent. Another example is where orders from resellers are refused.

Agreements that fall outside the block exemption may be individually exempted following notification to the Commission. The Commission may also give a negative clearance (or comfort letter). A comfort letter may mean that the Commission does not consider that the agreement is caught by Article 85(1), or that it is but saved by Article 85(3). This means that the Commission can see no reason to intervene in the light of information available to the Commission at the time. An individual exemption under Article 85(3) is granted for a specific period of time which may be extended, an example being the *Re Alcatel Espace* case where an individual exemption was granted for ten years.[45] The advantage of an Article 85(3) exemption over a negative clearance is that the former carries an immunity against fines imposed by the Commission while the latter does not.

45 [1991] 4 CMLR 208.

## Abuse of a dominant trading position

The exploitation of a patent may offend Article 86, and the discussion in Chapter 9 on the refusal to grant licences in respect of copyright materials applies equally to patents. In *Chiron Corp* v *Organon Teknika Ltd (No. 2)*[46] Aldous J restated that a refusal to grant a licence to work an intellectual property right could not, *per se*, be an abuse of a dominant position. Therefore, refusal to grant a licence except on unfair or unreasonable terms also was not an abuse.[47] However, this must now be viewed in the light of *RTE & ITP* v *Commission*,[48] in which the European Court of Justice held that the television organisations were abusing their dominant position under Article 86 by refusing to grant licences in respect of information concerning forthcoming television programmes. An important feature of this case was that the information was not available elsewhere. Therefore, at least where there are comparable or equivalent products on the market, refusal to grant a licence should not, *per se*, be an abuse of a dominant position. The issue is more unpredictable when there are not similar or equivalent products available, although in *RTE* a significant factor was that, by denying access to the information to others, the television organisations were reserving for themselves the secondary market of publishing details of forthcoming television programmes.

The basic ingredients for an infringement of Article 86 were laid down in *Parke, Davis & Co* v *Probel*[49] as:

46 [1993] FSR 324.

47 Following Hoffman J in *Pitney Bowes Inc* v *Francotyp-Postalia GmbH* [1991] FSR 72, who in turn followed the European Court of Justice in *Volvo AB* v *Erik Veng (UK) Ltd* [1989] 4 CMLR 122.

48 [1995] FSR 530.

49 [1968] FSR 393.

1  the existence of a dominant position;
2  an improper exploitation of it; and
3  the possibility that, as a result, trade between member states may be affected;

confirming that being in a dominant position is not sufficient by itself to bring Article 86 into play – something further is needed. An important factor indicating dominance is the ownership of intellectual property rights. In particular, ownership of a patent might constitute a considerable barrier to entry into the relevant market by third parties. Adopting commercial strategies to establish barriers to competitors entering the market was held to be an abuse.[50]

In *Tetra Pak Rausing SA v EC Commission*,[51] Tetra Pak, the world leaders in cartons and filling machines for liquid foods, especially aseptic packaging for *UHT* milk, through the acquisition of another company obtained the exclusivity of a patent licence for an alternative process of sterilisation.[52] Tetra Pak argued that Article 86 was inapplicable because a block exemption applied to the licence.[53] The European Court considered the implications of Article 86 and the relationship between Articles 85(1) and 86, and the effect of an exemption under Article 85(3) on the operation of Article 86. It was held that Articles 85 and 86 were complementary in as much as they have a common objective in accordance with Article 3(f) (the institution of a system ensuring that competition in the Common Market is not distorted), but the Articles constitute two independent provisions addressing different situations. Therefore, an exemption under Article 85(3) cannot be such as to render Article 86 inapplicable. The fact that a company in a dominant position becomes more dominant through the acquisition of a patent licence does not *per se* constitute an abuse within Article 86. Account must be taken of the circumstances surrounding the acquisition, such as the effect on competition within the relevant market. The European Court upheld the Commission's finding that there had been an abuse of a dominant position. In a subsequent case, *Elopak Italia Srl v Tetra Pak (No. 2)*[54] it was held that Tetra Pak had been pursuing a policy of eliminating competition and the company was fined 75 million Ecu.

A tying clause is one that requires a buyer of goods or a licensee under a patent to obtain other goods or services or raw materials from the seller or licensor. For example, a company selling patented toothbrushes to retail outlets might insist that the company's toothpaste is also purchased by the outlets. The Patents Act 1977 can make such tying clauses void under certain circumstances, and the existence of contracts or licences containing them could provide a complete defence to an infringement action.[55] European Community law can also control such tying clauses if they conflict with Article 86. For example, in *Eurofix-Bauco v Hilti AG*[56] users of Hilti nail-guns, used to fire nails into walls, were required to buy nails from Hilti when they bought cartridges for the guns. Other manufacturers made suitable nails. Hilti was fined 6 million Ecu for this infraction of Article 86. The tying of the purchase of sailboards and rigs was also held to be an abuse of a dominant position in *Windsurfing International Inc v EC Commission*.[57]

Compulsory licences may not be liked by proprietors of patents, but if they are unco-operative in settling the terms of such licences that might be viewed as an abuse under Article 86 if the purpose is to delay the evil day when the licence is available. Hilti were held needlessly to have protracted proceedings for the

50  *Masterfoods Ltd v H B Ice Cream Ltd* [1994] FSR 1, High Court of Ireland.
51  [1991] 4 CMLR 334.
52  Tetra Pak had 92 per cent of the European Union market in aseptic filling machines, and 89 per cent of the market for cartons.
53  Under Commission Regulations (EEC) No. 2349/84 of 23 July 1984 (exemption from Article 85(1)).
54  [1992] 4 CMLR 551.
55  The Patents Act 1977 s 44.
56  [1989] 4 CMLR 677.
57  [1986] ECR 611.

grant of a licence of right in *Hilti AG* v *EC Commission*.[58] The company had demanded a royalty six times that finally adopted by the Comptroller of Patents. The patent had originally been granted under the Patents Act 1949 and an additional four years were allowed subject to licences being available as of right.[59]

## THE COMMUNITY PATENT

The European Patent Convention has operated very successfully for a number of years and gives a patent that takes effect in those member states specified by the proprietor. This Convention does not, however, provide a unitary Community-wide patent system where a single grant automatically takes effect throughout the Community. The European Patent Convention can be seen as an important stepping stone towards the Community-wide patent. Plans have been around for some 20 years now and the Convention for a European Patent for the Common Market dates from 1975.[60] The latest version was published in 1989 and contains the procedures for bringing the patent system into operation.[61] It is expected that the Community-wide patent will become popular once it is in place. The growth of business at the European Patent Office since its establishment gives a taste of what is to come.[62] The Community patent will grant a patent that has effect throughout the Community and, in the context of the breaking down of trade barriers and the single market, is of the utmost importance. The Community Patent Convention takes account of the developments in European Community law relating to the freedom of movement of goods and anti-competitive practices. For example, it expressly deals with the doctrine of exhaustion of rights. The Patents Act 1977 explicitly takes account of the Community Patent Convention, giving direct legal effect to the Convention and decisions and cases under it.[63] By the 1989 Agreement (Article 10), before it can come into force the Agreement must be ratified by all 15 signatory states. It will then become a reality three months after the last state ratifies.

The Community patent will not replace national patents, or, during a transitional period, the European patent. All three systems will coexist. The pricing structures of the systems are likely to be such that it will not be economical to apply for anything other than a national patent if it is intended to exploit the invention in one country only. Alternatively, a European patent designating three or more member states might be acceptable in some cases. There are now 19 member states to the European Patent Convention, being the member states of the European Community together with Liechtenstein, Monaco, Switzerland and, most recently, Cyprus. There are also some extension states (to which patents can be extended) including Albania, Lithuania, Latvia and Slovenia. However, for proprietors wishing to obtain full protection throughout the Community, the Community patent will be the most attractive, and eventually the only real, option where a patent is required in more than one member state.

A Green Paper on the Community Patent was adopted by the Commission on 24 June 1997.[64] It sought views on many aspects of the proposed system from interested parties including industry, patent agents and individual inventors. It should not be very long before the Commission makes it clear what the timetable will be for the introduction of the Community patent.

58 [1992] 4 CMLR 16.

59 The Patents Act 1977 Sch 1, para 4.

60 OJ L401, 30.12.89, p. 1. One problem that will have to be faced is that there are differences in membership of the European Community and the European Patent Convention. It is possible that the Community-wide patent might extend beyond the boundaries of the European Community. The reader must be careful to distinguish between the European Patent Convention, currently in operation, and the Community Patent Conversion, to be implemented in the future.

61 Community Patent Agreement (89/695/EEC), 15 December 1989, OJ L401, 30.12.89, p. 1.

62 The Community-wide patent will also be administered by the European Patent Office.

63 The Patents Act 1977 s 86 and 87.

64 COM (97) 314.

Developments in eastern Europe have important implications for the Community patent and the European patent. If more countries join the European Community, the geographical reach of the two Conventions may change. This could take some time, as patent law in countries wishing to join either Convention must be compatible with that laid down in the appropriate Convention. The fact that European Patent Convention countries include some non-European Community countries brings into question the availability of the Community patent to such countries. The 1989 agreement allows non-European Community countries to join the Community Patent Convention by invitation on the basis of a special agreement. However, the administration of the Community patent may become a problem, with different arrangements being established for different countries, perhaps with several grades of membership. Already, more countries wish to join the European Patent Convention, for example Finland and Slovenia, and closer relations are being forged between the European Patent Office and patent authorities in the Czech Republic, Poland and other European countries.

## THE UTILITY MODEL

65 COM (97) 691 Final 12 December 1997.

The Commission to the European Communities has submitted a proposal for a Directive for the protection of inventions by a utility model.[65] Although the proposal is primarily to harmonise the utility model form of protection for inventions throughout the Community, it will create a new intellectual property right in the United Kingdom which is proposed to take effect by 31 December 1999.[66] The utility model form of protection has much in common with a patent but should be much less expensive and quicker to obtain. A harmonised utility model is seen by the Commission as a means to encourage the freedom of movement of goods protected by the right. It is perceived as being particularly important for small and medium-sized enterprises (SMEs) which are unable to make full use of the patent system,[67] particularly in relation to improvements to existing technology. Industries for which this form of legal protection is deemed to be most appropriate include toy manufacturing, clock and watch making, optics, microtechnology and micromechanics. The basic nature of the proposed utility model is described below.

66 The only member states presently without a utility model form of protection are Luxembourg, Sweden and the United Kingdom.

67 For example, because of a lack of resources or expertise.

### Basic requirements

The utility model is described as 'a registered right conferring exclusive protection for a technical invention'. Article 3 states the basic requirements for protection, being that the subject matter is an invention, susceptible of industrial application, which is new and involves an inventive step, mirroring the basic requirements for a patent. Certain things are not regarded as inventions for these purposes under Article 3(2) and further exceptions are contained in Article 4. In general terms, the exceptions are broadly similar to those applying to patents. Article 3(2) is equivalent to the exceptions in the Patents Act 1977 s 1(2), although computer programs are excepted under Article 4. However, the proviso in s 1(2) that the exception applies only if the application relates to the excepted matter *as such*, is missing. Other things excepted under Article 4 are inventions, the exploitation of which would be contrary to public policy or morality, inventions relating to biological material and chemical or pharmaceutical substances or processes.

The explanatory memorandum to the proposal justifies some of the exceptions. Biological, chemical and pharmaceutical inventions undergo lengthy preparation and testing before being marketed and are more suited to the patent system which gives longer protection. Software inventions, to the extent that they include a technical contribution, are patentable and computer programs as such are protected by copyright.

Articles 5, 6 and 7 deal with novelty, inventive step and industrial application. They closely resemble the equivalent definitions for patents with the exception of inventive step which is defined in terms of the application clearly and convincingly indicating that, compared to the state of the art, the invention exhibits either:

(a) particular effectiveness in terms of, for example, ease of application or use, or
(b) a practical or industrial advantage.

To some extent, this follows existing practice in utility models and is a lesser requirement than that applying to patents. The definition lacks precision and would, in that form, be difficult to apply in practice.

As with patents, novelty is based on the international state of the art. Some existing forms of utility models are based on the domestic state of the art, such as the Spanish model, whilst others, such as those in Germany and Portugal, use the international state of the art.

### Formalities

There are numerous similarities with the formalities for the grant of a patent. An application for a utility model must contain a request for grant, a description of the invention, one or more claims, any drawings referred to in the description or claims, an abstract and the filing fee: Article 8. If he so wishes, the applicant can ask for a search, in which case a search fee must also be tendered. Member states may insist on a search report in the event of legal proceedings concerning the utility model. The owner of the right would be wise to obtain a search report before going to court as it may show that it is unlikely to withstand a challenge to its validity.

The date of filing is that when the applicant files documents indicating that a utility model is sought, identifying the applicant and including a description and one or more claims. Under Article 17 a priority system will operate where a filing has been made elsewhere in a Paris Convention country with the 12-month period, as applies for patents. Priority can be claimed in respect of an earlier application for either a utility model or a patent. 'Internal priority' is also possible under Article 18. Where a person has filed a patent application (without a claim to priority from an earlier patent application), he has 12 months to file an application for a utility model. One possibility is that, during the 12-month period, the applicant may file an application for a utility model and then abandon the patent application. Alternatively, he may want both. However, this does not work the other way round. It will not be possible to file an application for a utility model and then use that filing as priority in respect of a patent application.

The advantage of dual protection by a utility model and a patent is that the utility model is likely to be the first granted and give the right to bring an action for infringement before it would be possible to do so in respect of the patent. However, member states may provide that the utility model is ineffective once the patent has been granted and published. If member states do not so provide, they must prevent the bringing of successive actions in relation to the patent and the utility model.

The inventor must be designated, and if the applicant is not the inventor or sole inventor the designation must include a statement indicating the origin of the applicant's right to the utility model: Article 10. Further aspects of the utility model also resemble the equivalent provisions for a patent. For example, under Article 11, the application must relate to a single invention or to a group of inventions so linked as to form a single inventive concept and there is a requirement for sufficiency in Article 12, that is, that the invention must be fully disclosed so that it can be carried out by a person skilled in the art. The claims must be clear and concise and supported by the description although the number of claims must be limited to that strictly necessary having regard to the nature of the invention: Article 13. Limiting the claims is intended to compensate for the lack of any preliminary examination. The abstract is merely to provide technical information and is not to be used for other purposes such as interpreting the scope of the protection sought.

Examination involves checking that the application satisfies the formal requirements as to the information and documents to be submitted, but there is no examination to check whether the requirements as to novelty, inventive step or industrial application are met: Article 15.[68]

**68** At present some countries carry out a preliminary examination, for example, France, whilst others do not.

**69** Under the existing systems, the duration varies considerably. It is six years in Belgium and France, seven years in Greece, eight years in Finland, ten years in Austria, Denmark and Germany. In Portugal it is infinitely renewable.

## Duration

The utility model will have a maximum life of half that for a patent. Article 19 sets out that the duration of the utility model and the initial grant will be for six years, and thereafter it will be renewable for two further periods of two years, giving a maximum term of protection of ten years from the date of filing.[69] There are provisions for lapse of the right and a utility model may be revoked following an application for revocation on one or more specified grounds, including that the subject matter is not protectable under Articles 3 to 7. Lapse and revocation follow the relevant provisions of the Community Patent Convention.

## Rights of proprietor

Article 20 contains details of the rights of the owner, being based on Article 28(1) of the Agreement on the Trade Related Aspects of Intellectual Property Rights ('TRIPs'), administered by the World Trade Organization. The rights differ depending upon whether the invention is in respect of a product or a process. In the former case, the right is to prevent third parties, not having the consent of the proprietor, making, using, offering for sale, selling, or importing for those purposes that product. For a process, the right is to prevent others using the process or using, offering for sale, selling or importing for these purposes at least the product obtained directly from the process without the consent of the proprietor.

There are exceptions, being acts done privately and for non-commercial purposes and acts done for experimental purposes relating to the subject matter of the protected invention. Further exceptions may be provided by member states as long as they do not unreasonably conflict with a normal exploitation of the utility model and do not unreasonably prejudice the legitimate interests of the proprietor, taking into account the interests of third parties. Member states may provide similar provisions as to government use as apply to patents.

In accordance with Article 28(2) of the TRIPs Agreement, the utility model is assignable or transmissible by succession and licences may be granted in respect of it. In line with usual practice, the doctrine of exhaustion of rights applies as regards products put on the market in the Community by or with the consent of the owner. However, this does not extend to products put on the market outside the Community by or with the consent of the owner.

There are no plans to introduce a Community-wide utility model, nor for reciprocity of protection. The Commission claim that neither possibility has aroused much interest. This view may change if the harmonised utility model becomes better used. National enthusiasm for the right varies between those member states that already provide for such a right. Because of its territorial limitations, it is questionable whether much use will be made of the utility model in the United Kingdom. To obtain protection throughout the Community, 15 separate applications will be required, although it is possible that national authorities, such as the Patent Office in the United Kingdom, will act as receiving offices. Another possibility is the future development of a single deposit and search procedure through the European Patent Office though there are no plans for this. The attractiveness of a single application for utility model protection in some or all member states submitted in one of the official languages of the European Patent Office (English, French or German) must surely commend itself to the Commission or European Patent Office or both. Provided the twin goals of speed and low cost are achieved, such an approach will establish the utility model as an effective and useful intellectual property right.

## JURISDICTION[70]

The position as regards jurisdiction in the case of copyright has already been alluded to in Chapter 9. Although similar considerations apply in the case of patents, there are some differences as patents are formal and subject to registration.[71] Again, because patents are territorial in nature and should be expected to have effect only in the territory for which they have been granted, the basic rule is that patents should be litigated in the courts in the country of registration and that 'infringements' occurring outside that country have no remedy, either in the country of registration or the country where the alleged infringement took place. That basic rule has, however, been radically altered by the Brussels Convention on jurisdiction and enforcement of judgments in civil and commercial matters, 1968. This became part of domestic law as a result of the Civil Jurisdiction and Judgments Act 1982 s 2(1), but it is only recently that the full impact of the Convention is starting to be realised.

Previous law included the *Moçambique* rule[72] to the effect that the English courts did not have jurisdiction over disputes concerning foreign land, a rule

70 *See* Duston, S. 'Actions for Infringement of a Foreign Intellectual Property Right in an English Court' (1997) 46 *The International and Comparative Law Quarterly* 918.

71 There are no equivalent provisions for patents to extend United Kingdom patent law to other countries as applies to copyright.

72 *The British South Africa Company v The Companhia de Moçambique* [1983] AC 602.

which was later applied to intellectual property on the basis that it too was an 'immovable', and subsequently modified by the Civil Jurisdiction and Judgments Act 1982 s 30. It was held by Laddie J not to apply to intellectual property in *Coin Controls Ltd* v *Suzo International (UK) Ltd*.[73] He said that patents and other intellectual property right are not accurately described as immovable. Indeed, a patent is described in the Patents Act 1977 as personal property or, in Scotland, as incorporeal moveable property.[74]

A further rule was that of double actionability. In *Boys* v *Chaplin*[75] it was said that for an act done in a foreign country to be actionable in England, it must first of all be actionable as a tort according to English law (it would be a tort if committed in England) and, secondly, it must be actionable as a tort according to the law of the foreign country in which the act was done. However, it was pointed out in *Def Lepp Music* v *Stuart Brown*[76] that an English intellectual property right could never be infringed by an activity taking place out of jurisdiction and could not, therefore, be treated as if it had been done in England. The double actionability rule has been abolished as far as it applies to a claim in tort (or delict in Scotland) by the Private International Law (Miscellaneous Provisions) Act 1995 s 10.

### The Brussels Convention – relevant provisions

The basic rule is that a defendant should be sued 'at home'. Article 2 of the Convention states:

> Subject to the provisions of this Convention, persons domiciled in a Contracting State shall, whatever their nationality, be sued in the courts of that State.

There then follow some exceptions to this general rule, in particular, Article 5(3) allows a person domiciled in a contracting state to be sued in another contracting state:

> In matters relating to tort, delict or quasi-delict, in the courts for the place where the harmful event occurred.

The act of infringing a patent is, of course a tort. A similar provision also applies in respect of a breach of contract where the defendant may be sued in the state in which the contract was to be performed. This could apply, for example, to a breach of a licence agreement in relation to a patent.

Article 6(1) covers the situation where there are a number of defendants not all domiciled in the same contracting state, and a person domiciled in a contracting state may also be sued:

> Where he is one of a number of defendants in the courts for the place where any one of them is domiciled.

In *Athanasios Kalfelis* v *Bankhaus Schröder, Münchmeyer, Hengst & Co*,[77] the European Court of Justice said that Article 6(1) applies where the actions brought against the defendants are related such that it is expedient to hear and determine them together in order to avoid the risk of irreconcilable judgments resulting from separate proceedings. This must be taken with Article 22 which states:

> Where related actions are brought in the courts of different Contracting States, any court other than the court first seised may, while the actions are pending, stay its proceedings.[78]

73 [1997] FSR 660.

74 Sections 30(1) and 31(1), respectively.

75 [1971] AC 356.

76 [1986] RPC 273.

77 [1988] ECR 5565.

78 Article 21 applies in relation to the *same cause of action*. Here any court other than the one first seised must decline jurisdiction.

An example of a situation where Article 6(1) could apply is where there are three defendants, say one domiciled in England, one in Germany and one in France. The English and German defendants are alleged to be joint tortfeasors in relation to an infringing act performed in England in relation to a United Kingdom patent.[79] The French defendant is alleged to have supplied to the other two defendants the means, relating to an essential element of the invention, for putting the invention to effect. Assume validity of the patent is not in issue.

It would appear that the plaintiff could bring an action in England, Germany or France. If the plaintiff commences the action in England, Article 6(1) allows him to join the German and French defendants in the action. If the plaintiff decides to sue in Germany, he may join the other two defendants there also. However, if the plaintiff commences action in the Patents Court in England first and then later brings an equivalent action in a German court, that German court must decline jurisdiction.[80] Alternatively, if he later commences an action in a French court, that court may stay proceedings pending the outcome of the English case.[81] The distinction is that, as between the English and German defendants, the cause of action is the same (infringement under the Patents Act 1977 s 60(1)), whereas, as between the English (or German) and French defendants, the cause of action is related. The French defendant would infringe under s 60(2) but the relationship would be that all defendants were involved, in some way, with the infringing act.

If, instead, the claims against the defendants related to alleged infringements of United Kingdom, German and French patents for the same invention by defendants in England, Germany and France respectively, these would not be related actions and it would not be expedient to try them together because there would be no risk of irreconcilable judgments as three different national rights were concerned, albeit for the same invention. In *Fort Dodge Animal Health Ltd* v *Akzo Nobel NV*,[82] Lord Woolf MR said (at 243) of actions involving a United Kingdom patent and a Dutch patent:

> They are actions relating to two different national rights. True they stem from the same patent application [before the European Patent Office] and similar rules of construction will be applicable, but the rights given by those patents are national rights limited in territory to the State in which they are registered and the ambit of the monopolies will not necessarily be the same as amendment is possible. ... a judgment on infringement in the United Kingdom will depend upon a national right having effect only in the United Kingdom. The same applies to a judgment on the Dutch patent.

It is important to note that even though patents may go the through European Patent Office, once the national stage is reached different rules of procedure and amendment apply in different countries. It is possible for two national patents based on the same invention to end with differing claims because of amendment. In *Coin Controls Ltd* v *Suzo International (UK) Ltd*,[83] Laddie J considered that, for Article 6(1) to apply where two or more national patents are involved, it is crucial that the patents are identical. In *Fort Dodge*, Lord Woolf MR seems to suggest that Article 6(1) would not apply even where the patents are identical in all respects.

What Lord Woolf MR is not saying, however, is that an action for infringement of a foreign patent cannot be heard before an English court. His comments are in relation to Article 6(1) and must be restricted to that provi-

---

79 For example, where there is a common design to infringe in England (over and above financial and voting control of one defendant by the other); *Unilever plc v Chefaro Proprietaries Ltd* [1994] FSR 135 and *The Mead Corp v Riverwood Multiple Packaging* [1997] FSR 484.

80 Article 21.

81 Article 22.

82 [1998] FSR 222.

83 [1997] FSR 660.

84 [1997] FSR 641.
85 [1997] FSR 660.

sion. *Gareth Pearce v Ove Arup Partnership Ltd*[84] and *Coin Controls Ltd v Suzo International (UK) Ltd*[85] are authorities for the proposition that the Brussels Convention can force the courts in a contracting state to hear and determine foreign infringement proceedings, and both were approved by Lord Woolf MR on this point in *Fort Dodge*. The major exception is where there is an issue concerning the validity of the patent or some aspect of its registration, as discussed below.

Article 16(4) grants the following courts exclusive jurisdiction regardless of domicile:

> In proceedings concerned with the registration or validity of patents, trade marks, designs, or other similar rights required to be deposited or registered, the courts of the Contracting State in which the deposit or registration has been applied for, has taken place or is under the terms of an international convention deemed to have taken place.

In such a case, under Article 19 a court in any other state seised of a claim which is *principally concerned* with a matter in Article 16 must declare by its own motion that it has no jurisdiction. Validity is often put at issue by a defendant and the Patents Act 1977 s 74(1)(a) expressly states that validity may be put in issue as a defence in infringement proceedings. As Laddie J said in *Coin Controls*, 'we have always taken the view that you cannot infringe an invalid patent'. The '*Gillette*' defence is quite common. The defendant submits that the patent is invalid if the alleged infringing act falls within its claims, for example, because what the defendant did was not novel or inventive at the priority date of the patent or that the defendant's acts fall outside the scope of the patent claims.

86 One of two reports, named after their authors, on the Brussels Convention and which may be referred to in determining the meaning of the provisions of the Convention: s 3(3) Civil Jurisdiction and Judgments Act 1982. The other report is the Schlosser report.

There does not appear to be any authority on the meaning of 'principally concerned', but the Jenard Report[86] suggests that preliminary or incidental matter is ignored. As Laddie J said in *Coin Controls* (at 676):

> Something which is a major feature of the litigation is not incidental and is therefore a matter with which the action is primarily concerned.

Therefore, validity or registration does not have to be the prime issue provided it is a major issue for Articles 16(4) and 19 to apply, giving exclusive jurisdiction in the state where the patent has been applied for or granted. Of course, it is possible to have an action, for infringement or otherwise, where validity is not in issue. In such a case, Articles 16(4) and 19 do not apply and exclusive jurisdiction is not granted, by virtue of these provisions, to the state in which the patent is in force or has been applied for. This was so in *Plastus Kreativ AB v Minnesota Mining and Manufacturing Co*[87] where Aldous J struck out claims relating to French and German patents, though not for reasons associated with the Brussels Convention.[88]

87 [1995] RPC 438.

88 The plaintiff sought a declaration of non-infringement in respect of United Kingdom, French and German patents, but the defendant (proprietor of the patents) had made no claim in respect of the French and German patents.

89 [1998] FSR 199.

90 A stent is a tubular prosthesis to be inserted into a hollow structure such as a blood vessel.

91 The District Court of the Hague.

Where an action has been commenced in a country other than that in which the patent has been registered and validity has later been put in issue, the court first seised of the action does not necessarily have to decline jurisdiction. The Dutch courts have taken a less cautious approach on this point. *Julio Cesar Palmaz v Boston Scientific BV*[89] concerned an action for infringement of European patents for stents.[90] Of the defendants, all of which were interconnected companies, there were two Dutch, one Belgian, one English, one Swiss, one Norwegian, one French, one Spanish and one Italian. Interim injunctions were sought by the plaintiff in respect of all the countries with the exception of England and Germany. The Dutch court[91] accepted that it had jurisdiction on the basis of Articles 2 and 6(1).

The claims in *Julio Cesar Palmaz* concerned the same European patents. The Dutch court remarked that Article 49 of the European Patent Convention required that they should be interpreted in the same manner and, so as to avoid conflicting decisions, it was expedient that the Dutch court determine the claims. The question of infringement could not be determined without taking a decision on the validity of a patent, this produced a dilemma in respect of Article 16. There were two possibilities. First, the court first seised should divest itself of jurisdiction immediately validity of a foreign patent is put in issue, as in *Coin Controls*. The second possibility is for the court first seised to stay proceedings until the question of validity has been determined in the other jurisdiction. The second alternative was preferred by the Dutch court as being the more satisfactory. The jurisdiction of the court was based on Articles 2 and 6 of the Brussels Convention and the court had jurisdiction to grant cross-border injunctions.[92] The first option was deemed to be unacceptable because jurisdiction would not be established until after the defence had been pleaded and this was said to be contrary to the objects of the Brussels and Lugano Conventions. Furthermore, Article 16 was a derogation from the main rule on jurisdiction and, as such, should be interpreted restrictively.

A consequence of the decision of the Dutch court in *Julio Cesar Palmaz*, where the validity of a patent registered in another state is put in issue, is that a court having jurisdiction under Articles 2 and 6(1) can stay proceedings pending determination of the validity of the patent in the courts of that other state. In the meantime, the court first seised can grant interlocutory relief. Following the determination of validity, the court first seised may then apply that finding to the question of infringement before it.

Two points can be made. First, it is not clear whether the same principles would apply in respect of a court having jurisdiction under Articles 5 and 6(1). The main rule, to which Article 16 is a derogation, is that in Article 2 defendants shall be sued in the courts of the state in which they are domiciled. Article 5 could, itself, be seen as a derogation from Article 2. The second point is that Article 19 uses the phrase 'principally concerned' and this gives the clue that there may be other issues involved. Nevertheless, Article 19 clearly states that the court seised of a claim in respect of which the courts of another contracting state have exclusive jurisdiction by virtue of Article 16 shall declare of its own motion that it has no jurisdiction. There is no discretion in Article 19. It does not say that the court first seised shall stay proceedings until the determination of the validity of the patent or other registered right by the court in that other contracting state. It is submitted that the decision of the Dutch court was wrong, although the court did highlight ambiguities in the Jenard report and concluded that neither that report nor the Brussels Convention foresaw that issues of infringement and validity are, in patent cases, almost inseparable.

Of the approaches taken in *Coin Controls* and *Julio Cesar Palmaz*, neither is satisfactory. If the court first seised divests itself of jurisdiction this will lead to delay. It may also encourage defendants to plead invalidity (although the English courts appear to treat infringement and invalidity as a single issue). It also means that interlocutory relief is not available until the action brought before the court in the state in which the patent is registered. The possibility of staying the action pending a decision as to validity can also be criticised as

92 In the event, the Dutch court came to a provisional conclusion that the patents had not been infringed.

causing delay and the inconvenience of hearings before two different courts in different contracting states. An amendment to the Brussels and Lugano Conventions to widen the scope of Article 16 to include infringement actions would be most welcome.

The rules relating to jurisdiction in intellectual property cases are set out in Figure 15.2. They ignore the effect of *Julio Cesar Palmaz*. The figure assumes a straightforward issue not involving more than one form of intellectual property right. Use the figure to collect one or more contracting states in which jurisdiction is possible.

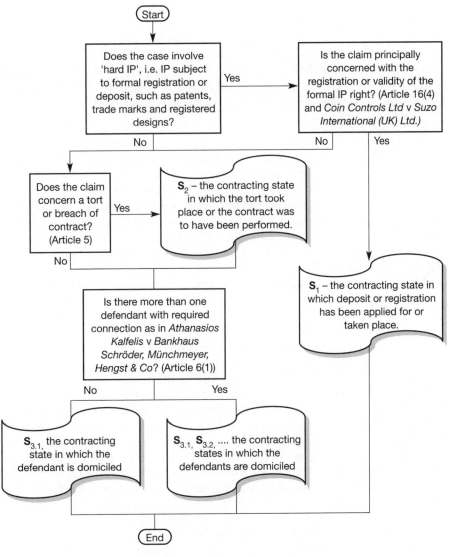

To use flowchart, travel through it according to your particular case, collecting contracting states as you go. The forum(s) you can use is that state or those states 'collected'.

*Note:* Infringing an intellectual property right is a tort. A breach of contract could concern, for example a patent licence agreement.

**Figure 15.2 Forum shopping and intellectual property**

As a further example, consider a Scottish company which is the proprietor of a Spanish patent and the following scenario.

1 The patent is infringed in Spain by a Spanish company. The Scottish company can sue in Spain on the basis of Article 2 (basic rule – defendants play at home). Of course, this was so before the Brussels Convention.[93]

2 The patent is infringed in Spain by a French company. The Scottish company can sue in France on the basis of Article 2 or Spain on the basis of Article 5(3) (the place where the tort occurred).

3 The patent is infringed in Spain by a French company and an English company, as joint tortfeasors. The Scottish company can sue in either France or England by virtue of Article 2 and Article 6(1) (the defendant is one of a number of defendants who can be sued in the courts for the place where any one is domiciled where actions are related).

4 As 3 above but the defendants claim that the patent is invalid. The Scottish company may only sue in Spain on the basis of Article 16(4) and Article 19 (exclusive jurisdiction where the case is principally concerned with validity).

93 As a result of Article 2 of the Paris Convention for the Protection of Industrial Property 1883.

In the third example, the plaintiff is spoilt for choice. He can go 'forum shopping' and choose the country which suits him best. It is likely that factors such as the availability of interim relief, cost, time to come to trial and interpretation of the scope of infringement will strongly influence him. If he selects England or France in which to commence legal action, the courts there may not be keen to apply foreign law, even though there is some common origin in the European Patent Convention but that is the effect of the Brussels Convention. Of course, from a defendant's point of view, he could counterclaim for revocation of the patent on the grounds of invalidity, thus taking away the plaintiff's choice, leaving the country in which the patent has been granted as the only forum.

Where there are several discrete issues before a court where validity is raised, it may be possible to sever the issues and try some of them. However, as Laddie J pointed out in *Coin Controls*, infringement and validity are so interwoven that they should be tried together in the same court. It would be undesirable to split the issues of infringement and validity, and to do so could only result in a proliferation of court actions.

That courts in England and other parts of the United Kingdom could be forced to hear proceedings involving foreign patents is not something judges are likely to view with relish. In *Plastus Kreativ AB v Minnesota Mining and Manufacturing Co*,[94] Aldous J expressed his concern at the prospect, especially as a decision could affect the prices the public have to pay for a product in another country. For example, if an English court decided that a German company was infringing a German patent belonging to the English company, that could drive up prices in Germany for the product. Aldous J suggested such decisions would carry the respect of the public better if tried in the local courts.

94 [1995] RPC 438.

Nor was Laddie J happy with the impact of the Brussels Convention on intellectual property disputes. Registered and unregistered rights may be subject to different regimes. This could be particularly so in relation to passing off and registered trade marks. Actions for these two rights often go hand in hand. An English court could hear an action for passing off by an activity taking place in Germany which also results in a challenge to the validity of a German trade mark, meaning that the trade mark issue must be heard in Germany. Laddie J gives a wonderful example of the potential for complexity and confusion in *Coin Controls*. He stated (at 678):

... an English company might be sued in England for unfair competition in Holland or Germany by alleged use of an unregistered trade name. The court here will not only have to decide questions of Dutch and German law but also factual issues relating to the pronunciation and meaning of similar words spoken in Dutch or German ... Similarly, the fact that what are likely to be essentially the same issues of patent validity may have to be litigated in a number of countries simultaneously is unlikely to impress the user of the EPC system, but this appears to be an inevitable consequence of Article 16(4) of the Convention.

However, the potential difficulties arising from courts ruling on foreign law should not be a reason to decline jurisdiction. So the Schlosser report stated adding that 'where the courts of several States have jurisdiction, the plaintiff has deliberately been given a right of choice, which should not be weakened by application of the doctrine of *forum conveniens*'.

# Part Five

# DESIGN LAW

# 16

## *What is a design?*

### INTRODUCTION

1 Hereinafter referred to as the 'design right'.
2 *Clarke's Design* (1896) 13 RPC 351, *per* Lindley LJ.

There are two forms of designs recognised by the law. One is the registered design provided for by the Registered Designs Act 1949, as amended, and the other is the design right provided for, along principles broadly analogous to copyright law, by the Copyright, Designs and Patents Act 1988 Part III.[1] A 'design' is aspects of or features applied to an article; it is not the article itself[2] and it should be noted that, in intellectual property law, the word 'design' has a restricted meaning. In normal usage the word 'design' can be taken to mean a plan or a scheme, which may be written or drawn, showing how something is to be constructed, or how the elements of an item or article are arranged. Alternatively, a design may be a decorative pattern. In legal terms, a design is defined by reference to the provisions applicable to either the registered design or the design right, as appropriate.

3 Many functional articles also have eye-appeal. They have been so designed to make them more attractive to potential purchasers and may be registrable as designs as a consequence.

Designs may be for functional articles, such as a can opener, a tool box, a container for frozen food or an exhaust pipe for a car. Articles which are functional in nature are generally, but not exclusively, in the province of the design right.[3] Alternatively, a design may relate to decorative articles or decorative features such as an attractive table lamp, an item of mass-produced furniture or a pattern applied to porcelain or pottery. Visually attractive designs which are intended to appeal to the eye fall within the scope of registered designs. However, as will be seen, there is considerable overlap between the two rights. While a purely functional object cannot be registered as a design (eye-appeal being a fundamental requirement), many registered designs also meet the requirements for the design right.

Design law is far from straightforward because of the overlap between the rights which apply, and the extent of this overlap is not altogether clear. The complexity of design law is compounded by the transitional provisions. In a few cases a design may be patentable if, for example, it relates to a function which has novelty, contains an inventive step, has industrial application and is not otherwise excluded from the grant of a patent. Usually, however, one of these requirements will be lacking and protection must be sought through registration of the design or by way of the design right, as appropriate. Occasionally, copyright may provide protection. This part of the book concentrates on registered designs and the design right. Copyright issues also will be discussed where they affect designs. If a design for an article meets the stringent requirements for patentability, it is obviously more fitting that a patent is obtained rather than relying solely on design law, and in some cases an article may be protected by both patent and design law.

4 27 Geo III c 38.

The law of designs has a reasonably long history dating back to the latter part of the eighteenth century. In 1787, the first Designs Act protecting designs was passed[4] which gave a two-month protection to designs applied to linens, cotton, calicoes and muslins. The origins of design law spring from this area. The Copyright in Designs Act 1839[5] set up a system of registration and also extended design laws to designs applied to articles, either as 'surface design' or 'shape designs'.[6] Several other Acts were passed over the next few years and, eventually, these were repealed and replace by the Patents, Designs and Trade Marks Act 1883. A previous distinction between ornamental and useful designs was removed and the duration of protection was set at five years. The Patents and Designs Act 1907 increased the maximum term of protection to 15 years, a remedy for groundless threats of infringement proceedings was introduced and provisions requiring articles to be marked was relaxed. Following further Acts in 1919 and 1932, the current statute, the Registered Designs Act 1949 was enacted. A major step was that a classification system for goods was abolished. Previously, applicants had to specify the class or classes of goods against which they wanted the registration.

With the development of artistic copyright came problems of duplication of rights and the Copyright Act 1911, followed by the Copyright Act 1956, attempted to remove the overlap between a registrable design and artistic copyright. This was modified by the Design Copyright Act 1968 which permitted dual protection to a design both as a registered design and under artistic copyright, but reduced the term of copyright to 15 years.[7] If this was not bad enough, following the distinction between registrable and unregistrable designs highlighted in *Dorling* v *Honnor Marine Ltd*[8] a regrettable state of affairs arose.

The plaintiff in *Dorling* v *Honnor Marine* designed a sailing dinghy and granted a licence to the second defendant to build dinghies to the design and to make kits of parts on his behalf, all in accordance with the plaintiff's drawings. The relationship between the plaintiff and the second defendant broke down and the latter formed a limited company, the first defendant, to which he purported to assign his licence to build the dinghies. The design of the dinghy as a whole was registrable under the Registered Designs Act 1949, but it had not been registered. The individual parts, being purely functional, were not registrable.[9] By making a three-dimensional representation of the drawings in the form of parts for a boat, the defendants had infringed the copyright in the drawings. A defence based on the Copyright Act 1956 s 10, which removed copyright protection from designs registrable under the Registered Designs Act 1949, failed because the parts, as opposed to the dinghy as an entirety, were not registrable. Thus, the outcome of the case was that if a design was aesthetic it was, subject to some other requirements, registrable under the Registered Designs Act 1949 and could be protected for 15 years.[10] If the design was purely functional it was not registrable but could attract artistic copyright through its drawings, which would last for the remainder of the life of the author plus 50 years. Functional designs appeared to be far better protected than aesthetic designs (not being works of copyright), an extremely anomalous situation.

The above unsatisfactory position can partly explain the House of Lords decision in *British Leyland Motor Corp Ltd* v *Armstrong Patents Co Ltd*[11] concerning the reverse engineering of exhaust pipes which infringed indirectly the copyright in the drawings of the exhaust pipes. Their Lordships took the opportunity partly to redress the apparent imbalance between the protection for articles with eye-appeal and purely functional articles by using the principle of non-derogation from grant. Even if a design was registrable there was little incentive for registration as copyright in the drawings could still be enjoyed for 15 years, free of charge. In 1988, the last full year before the main provisions of the Copyright, Designs and Patents Act 1988 came into force, there were only 8748 applications for registered designs received by the Design Registry.[12]

5  2 Vict c 13.

6  *See* Laddie, H., *et al* (1995) *The Modern Law of Copyright and Designs* (2nd edn) Butterworths, paras 29.7–29.40.

7  The Design Copyright Act 1968 and the Copyright Act 1956 were repealed in their entirety by the Copyright, Designs and Patents Act 1988.

8  [1965] Ch 1.

9  The Registered Designs Act requires that a registered design has eye-appeal.

10  This has now been extended to 25 years.

11  [1986] 2 WLR 400.

12  This compares with 30 471 patent applications received by the Patent Office in 1988 and 38 006 trade and service mark applications received by the Trade Marks Registry in the same year. *Patents, Designs and Trade Marks 1990*, 108th Annual Report of the Comptroller-General of Patents, Designs and Trade Marks (HMSO, 1990).

The law of designs has been radically affected by the Copyright, Designs and Patents Act 1988. It has not, however, been simplified, although arguably it is more rational. The law prior to the coming into force of this Act will remain relevant for designs which where created or recorded before 1 August 1989. However, it must be stressed that there was no design right before this date, it being an invention of the 1988 Act. Designs that were created or recorded before 1 August 1989 and which were not registrable under the Registered Designs Act 1949 continue to rely on copyright for protection although only effectively until 1 August 1999[13] (unless the copyright would have expired earlier in any case). Indeed, in *Valeo Vision SA* v *Flexible Lamps Ltd*,[14] the plaintiff successfully relied on copyright protection through its drawings of rear lamp clusters for vehicles even though its registered designs were held to be invalid through want of novelty.

The law of registered designs remains, but with some changes made by the 1988 Act. Because of the complexity of this area of law, the remainder of this chapter is devoted to looking at and comparing the basic elements and definitions of registered designs and the design right, with consideration of artistic copyright where appropriate. First, a brief description of the legal nature of the registered designs and design right is called for.

Some of the statutory terminology used for the registered design is also used for the design right.[15] However, it is important to realise that, whilst there are inevitably some similarities between the rights, they are different and have different legislative origins. The registered design has much in common with a patent and the design right is more like a copyright.[16] Therefore, the meaning of a word or phrase used for both rights will not necessarily be the same for both.

## REGISTERED DESIGNS

The distinguishing feature for registered designs is that of eye-appeal. Although eye-appeal does not automatically bar a design from the design right, it is a specific requirement for a registered design. Whereas the design right applies mainly, but not exclusively, to functional designs, the law of registered designs applies to aesthetic articles. The word 'aesthetic' is chosen carefully to distinguish registered designs from artistic works of copyright. One problem that will be discussed later is ascertaining the boundaries of the description 'aesthetic', and in particular the relationship between 'artistic' and 'aesthetic'. One thing to notice at the outset is that although eye-appeal is a fundamental requirement for a design to be registered, it does not mean that the article to which the design applies cannot also be functional. An example is provided by telephone handsets or food containers which are designed to be attractive and yet are essentially functional articles. The Registered Designs Act 1949 does not require that aesthetic considerations are foremost, only that they are *material*.

For the purposes of the Registered Designs Act 1949, a 'design' means, by s 1(1):

... features of shape, configuration, pattern or ornament applied to any article by an industrial process, being features which in the finished article appeal to and are judged by the eye ...

The design, to be registrable, must be 'new', and this means that it has not previously been registered or published in the United Kingdom prior to the date

13 Copyright, Designs and Patents Act 1988, Sch 1 para 19(1) prevents the operation of s 51 of that Act for ten years from commencement. Section 51 states that making an article or copying an article represented in a design document or model does not infringe the copyright in the design document or model except where the design is for an artistic work or typeface.

14 [1995] RPC 205.

15 *See*, for example, the Registered Designs Act 1949 s 1(1) and the Copyright, Designs and Patents Act 1988 s 213(1)–(3).

16 The design right owes its origins to the European Council Directive on the legal protection of topographies of semiconductor products, OJ L24, 27.1.87, p. 36. *See* Laddie J in *Ocular Sciences Ltd* v *Aspect Vision Care Ltd* [1997] RPC 289 at 421.

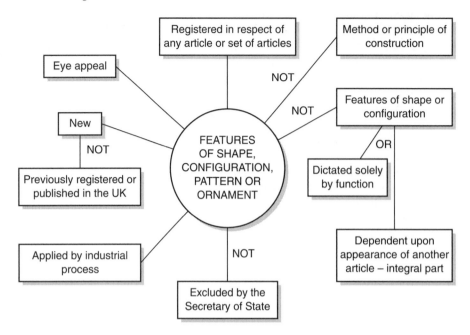

**Figure 16.1  Registered designs**

of application for registration. The creator of a registered design is, as with copyright, known as its author. Unlike copyright and the design right, there are no qualification requirements, but there are some exceptions which are, in part, similar to those for the design right.[17] Figure 16.1 shows a representation of the right, the conditions and the exceptions.

17 Some of the exceptions are identically worded for both rights.

## DESIGN RIGHT

A design right is declared by the Copyright, Designs and Patents Act 1988 s 213(1) to be a property right which subsists in an original design. Section 213(2) defines a 'design' as 'the design of any aspect of the shape or configuration (whether internal or external) of the whole or part of an article'. The remainder of s 213 describes the requirements for a design. There are several similarities between the design right and copyright and, like copyright, the design right is automatic and does not depend on registration but requires some form of tangible expression. There are qualification requirements and the design must be 'original' for the right to subsist. Needless to say, there are differences. A design is not original if it is commonplace in the design field in question at the time of its creation. This is probably a more stringent test than is the case with copyright. Figure 16.2 shows, in the form of a semantic net, the basic requirements for the design right.

Note that the design right applies to any aspect of the shape or configuration of the whole or part of an article, it does not apply to the article itself. Basically, for the design right to apply to a shape or configuration, it must be original (not commonplace) and it must be in some tangible form, that is recorded in a

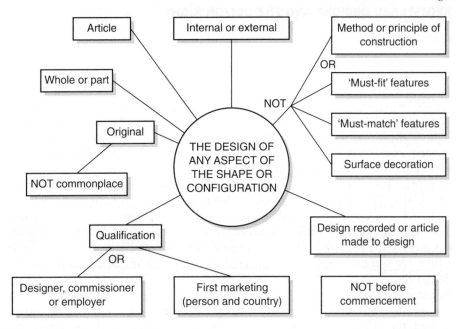

**Figure 16.2 The design right**

design document (alternatively, an article must have been made to the design), and the qualification requirements must be satisfied. The exceptions are similar to, but not identical with, those that apply to registered designs and can be justified on the basis that they prevent the right from becoming too strong or from working to the disadvantage of consumers requiring spare parts. A further exception is surface decoration, which lies firmly within the scope of registered designs. The qualification requirements may be satisfied in one of three ways:

18 The term 'designer' is used here rather than 'authors'; basically, the two terms are equivalent.

1 by reference to the designer;[18] or
2 if the design is created under a commission or in the course of employment, by reference to the commissioner or employer; and
3 by reference to the person by whom and country in which articles made to the design are first marketed.

The design right is a new departure for intellectual property law in the United Kingdom and there was no equivalent right before the 1988 Act, although certain features of shape and configuration may have had copyright protection. For example, a drawing of an article of a particular shape or configuration would have been an artistic work for copyright purposes. The design right provisions are not, however, retrospective; and anything which would have qualified and which was recorded in a design document, or if an article had been made to the design, before the commencement of the design right provisions[19] is excluded. That does not prevent the design right applying to a design that was conceived before 1 August 1989 but which was not recorded until after that date provided no articles were made to the design in the meantime.

19 1 August 1989.

## REGISTERED DESIGNS AND THE DESIGN RIGHT

Design right is often described as applying to functional designs. However, that is not necessarily the sole domain of the design right. There is no reason why a new and attractive design cannot be subject to the design right if it relates to the shape or configuration of some article, even though it would be expected that it should be registered as a design. An example might be a design for a drinking tankard which is a new shape or which has a new shape of handle, made by an industrial process[20] and which, its maker hopes, people will buy for the visual attractiveness of its shape. This should qualify for both rights. One advantage of seeking registration under the Registered Designs Act 1949 is that the period of protection is potentially longer.[21] The protection afforded by registration also is stronger. However, the overlap between the design right and registered designs is not complete. The design right cannot apply to surface decoration, although this is clearly within the scope of registered designs. Because registered designs have a requirement of eye-appeal, features of shape or configuration which are internal cannot be registered as designs, but can be subject to the design right[22]. Nevertheless, in many cases a design will be registrable under the Registered Designs Act 1949 and yet still be subject to the design right. There are no provisions for abrogating one of these rights in favour of the other. Indeed, the Copyright, Designs and Patents Act 1988 explicitly recognises the dual existence of the rights, s 224 raising a presumption that an assignment of the registered design automatically carries with it an assignment of the design right where the proprietor of the registered design and the owner of the design right are one and the same person.[23]

One final point is that the requirement for eye-appeal for registration of a design has been modified. Now aesthetic considerations must be taken into account to a material extent by persons acquiring or using articles to which the design has been applied. Before, the features had to appeal *solely* to the eye. It is difficult to assess to what extent the eye-appeal requirement has changed, though in practice the Design Registry continues to take a liberal view of what constitutes eye-appeal.

## DESIGN RIGHT AND COPYRIGHT

Design law may overlap with copyright protection. Between 1969 and 1 August 1989, an extremely powerful and wide-ranging form of protection for functional designs was to have a drawing from which the article was made. If a person copied the article, he would infringe the copyright in the drawing even though he had never seen it, no matter how mundane the article was.[24] The only provisos were that the drawing should meet the originality requirements for copyright (not an onerous standard by any means) and that a person who was not an expert in that field could recognise the article as being reproduced from the drawing.[25] Even the mass-produced – and, in the judges' opinions, vulgar – furniture in *George Hensher Ltd v Restawhile Upholstery (Lancs) Ltd*[26] would have been protected by copyright, indirectly, had some drawings been made which bore a two-dimensional resemblance to the furniture. Additionally, a design may overlap with other forms of copyright works such as

20 The requirement for industrial process does not appear to be a limiting factor and there is no reason why designs applied to hand-crafted articles should be denied registration on that ground alone.

21 A maximum of 25 years' protection is available for a registered design, whereas the maximum duration of the design right is 15 years, or ten years during which it is exploited commercially.

22 If the outer surface of the article is transparent and the feature can be seen, the design may be registable after all.

23 There is a reciprocal presumption in the Registered Design Act 1949 s 19(3B). Further, s 19(3A) of that Act requires that the registration of an interest under a registered design will not be made unless the registrar is satisfied that the person entitled to the interest is also entitled to the corresponding interest in the design right, if it subsists.

24 For example, *see L B (Plastics) Ltd v Swish Products Ltd* [1979] RPC 551 and, of course, *British Leyland Motor Corp Ltd v Armstrong Patents Co Ltd* [1986] 2 WLR 400.

25 The so-called lay recognition test provided for by the Copyright Act 1956 s 9(8).

26 [1976] AC 64.

sculptures and works of artistic craftsmanship. The design may be recorded in a document in which copyright subsists as a literary work, including computer data, or the design document may be a photograph.

To reduce this overlap, the Copyright, Designs and Patents Act 1988 contains two provisions, ss 236 and 51(1), respectively. The first is that where a work consisting of or including a design is itself protected by copyright, the design right is suppressed in favour of the copyright.[27] If what is done is an infringement of the copyright in the work, then an action lies under copyright law and not for infringement of the design right. That is, if the articles made to the design are themselves works of copyright, they will be protected by copyright rather than by the design right. This could be so if the articles were works of artistic craftsmanship, for example a hand-made wooden toy or an item of jewellery.[28] The second exception applies to cancel out the possibility of indirect copyright infringement by copying the article embodying the design. If an article is made to the design or a copy of such an article is made, this does not infringe the copyright in a design document or model recording or embodying the design.[29] A design document is any record of the design and includes drawings, written descriptions, photographs and computer data.[30] Therefore, if the design is recorded in a drawing and a person makes an article using that drawing, he does not infringe the copyright in the drawing although he does, of course, infringe the design right. However, if the person makes a photocopy of the drawing instead, then the copyright in the drawing will be infringed in that instance, but any subsequent making of articles from the copy of the drawing will infringe the design right only.

As another example, consider a design recorded as computer data, for example as a series of numbers describing the three-dimensional co-ordinates of the design. Without permission, a person copies the computer data onto a magnetic disk and takes the copy away. Later, he prints out the computer data and uses the information to make articles, or he may, for example, enter the computer data into a computer-controlled lathe so that it can be used to make articles to the design. There are two infringements here. First, the copyright in the computer data (as a literary work, being a table or compilation or, possibly, a database) has been infringed by making a copy of it. This infringement is not suppressed by the design right. Second, by making articles, the design right is infringed. In this case, the copyright in the computer data is not infringed because it is not an infringement of a literary work to make three-dimensional work of it;[31] but even if the copyright had been infringed, say in the case of a drawing, the Copyright, Designs and Patents Act 1988 s 51 would operate to suppress that copyright. The effect of s 51 can be seen diagrammatically in Figure 16.3.

In Figure 16.3, a design is recorded in a drawing. Articles have been made to the design. It is assumed that copyright does not subsist in the articles *per se*, for example as works of artistic craftsmanship. A person obtains a drawing and one original article and does one of the following things without the permission of the rights owner:

(a) copies the drawing (directly);
(b) makes articles from the drawings;
(c) makes articles from the original article; or
(d) makes a drawing from the original article.

27 The Copyright, Designs and Patents Act 1988 s 236.

28 Ibid s 52 might apply, reducing the term of copyright to 25 years if the articles are not hand-made or more than 50 are made, *see* Copyright (Industrial Processes and Excluded Articles)(No. 2) Order 1989, SI 1989/1070. Such a design could also be registrable.

29 The Copyright, Designs and Patents Act 1988 s 51.

30 Ibid s 263.

31 *Brigid Foley Ltd* v *Ellot* [1982] RPC 433. But see *Anacon Corp Ltd* v *Environmental Research Technology Ltd* [1994] FSR 659, discussed in Chapter 6.

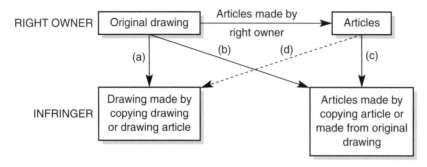

**Figure 16.3 Design right and copyright**

By doing act (a) the person will infringe the copyright in the drawing.[32] Both acts (b) and (c) will infringe the design right, and act (d) may infringe the copyright or the design right (this is discussed below).

An exercise in mental gymnastics may be indulged in by considering the interaction between the Copyright, Designs and Patents Act 1988 ss 51(1), 226(1)(b) and 236. Add to this the question: does making a copy of an article made to a design (as stated in s 51(1)) include making a copy in two dimensions? If the answer to this question is in the affirmative, there is only an action for infringement of design right based on s 226(1)(b), which gives the design right owner the exclusive right to make a design document for the purposes of enabling articles to be made to the design. However, if the answer to the question is 'no', there potentially is an infringement of copyright and the design right because s 51(1) fails to operate, and by s 236 an action will lie in copyright only under s 17 (copying). One speculative consideration is that if s 51(1) does apply to a two-dimensional representation of a design, for example a drawing, and the drawing is copied for purposes other than making articles to the design, for example to study the technology used in the manufacture of the articles, then copying the drawing may escape both copyright and design right liability. Section 51(1) removes copyright protection from the drawing and s 226(1) does not extend to making a design document for other purposes.[33]

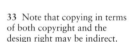

## ARTISTIC, AESTHETIC OR FUNCTIONAL

Contemplating the Copyright, Designs and Patents Act 1988 and the Registered Designs Act 1949 might lead one to think that a design (in a wide sense) can be classified as being artistic, aesthetic or functional. This classification, as sensible as it might at first sight appear, is not without difficulties. It is tempting to try to place an article into one of these categories because of the rational, but false, assumption that each category directly relates to a particular legal right. For example, an article that is artistic should be protected by copyright, an article that has aesthetic qualities should be registered as a design, and a functional article should fall under the wing of the design right. If only things were that simple. We have already seen that there is an overlap between these various rights; this is recognised statutorily by the Copyright, Designs and Patents Act 1988 ss 51(1), 224 and 236 and the Registered Designs Act 1949 s 19(3A) and (3B). We have also seen how the issue of dual concurrent protection is dealt with.

32 Such an infringement was found in respect of drawings showing designs for rear lamps for vehicles: *see Valeo Vision SA v Flexible Lamps Ltd* [1995] RPC 205.

33 Note that copying in terms of both copyright and the design right may be indirect.

There are two difficulties which make a one-for-one correlation between the classification of a work and the form of legal protection troublesome. The first has to do with the fact that the legal meaning of words such as artistic, aesthetic and functional does not necessarily equate with their everyday meaning, as Table 16.1 indicates.

The word 'artistic' can thus have an extensive legal meaning, much wider than its normal sense, and can apply to something that could be described as utilitarian, for example an engineering drawing which represents an article that is purely functional. The second problem stems from the fact that there is an overlap, even in the everyday meaning of these words, in the way in which certain articles may be described. For example, a piece of art deco pottery, such as that designed by Clarice Clift, can be said certainly to be aesthetic – some might argue that it is artistic. But whether it be a teapot or a milk jug, it also has a functional purpose. The same applies to many items which can be described as both functional and aesthetic for, being functional, an item does not cease to be aesthetic – the two descriptions are not mutually exclusive. Many people see beauty in articles which have been designed purely and intrinsically for their functional character. A good example is the steam engine. An train engine like the 'Mallard' was designed primarily for functionality, its streamlined appearance being the result of a desire to reduce wind resistance, yet few would deny that it has beauty.[34]

**34** However, in *Dorling* v *Honnor Marine Ltd* [1965] Ch 1, Danckwerts LJ doubted whether the shape of a boat fell within the meaning of a registered design, it being necessarily functional in his opinion.

### Table 16.1 Everyday and legal meanings of words

| Word | Everyday meaning | Legal meaning |
|---|---|---|
| **Artistic** | Pertaining to art or artists. Having some special quality, the result of imaginative skill. | Depends on type of works, e.g. graphic work, photograph, sculpture or collage – no artistic quality required at all. Other works, e.g. works of artistic craftsmanship, some indefinable quality required. CDPA 1988 s 4.* |
| **Aesthetic** | Attractive, artistic, some sense of beauty which appeals to the eye. Often taken to mean something less than artistic. Something made by a craftsman. | Features of shape, configuration, pattern or ornament which appeal to and are judged by the eye. RDA 1949 s 1. |
| **Functional** | Having a practical use irrespective of visual appearance. | Not defined even indirectly. The design right applies to any aspect of the shape or configuration of an article. CDPA 1988 s 213. |

* See *George Hensher Ltd* v *Restawhile Upholstery (Lancs) Ltd* [1976] AC 64 and *Merlet* v *Mothercare plc* [1986] RPC 115.

CDPA 1988 – Copyright, Designs and Patents Act 1988
RDA 1949 – Registered Designs Act 1949

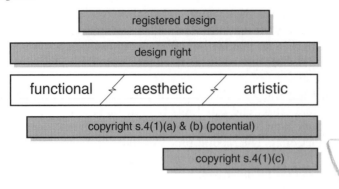

**Figure 16.4 Potential scope of rights in designs**

Figure 16.4 gives an indication of the scope of rights in relation to objects which are artistic, aesthetic or functional. The boundaries between artistic and aesthetic and between aesthetic and functional are not precise. The shaded bars indicate the various rights and their potential extent in relation to the description of an article as being artistic, aesthetic or functional. It can be seen that the design right and artistic copyright under s 4(1)(a) and (b) could apply over the whole spectrum while registered designs and artistic craftsmanship copyright are less extensive in their potential. A particular difficulty is in matching rights to specific articles where they lie in or near the boundaries between the descriptions of objects.

Of course this is an oversimplification, and many other requirements and exceptions apply. For instance, a design right can apply only to aspects of shape or configuration, whereas some artistic works and some registrable designs are two-dimensional, some three-dimensional. Dual protection is partly, but not completely, curtailed.

One of the dilemmas facing the owner of a design that has some sort of eye-appeal is whether or not to attempt to seek registration of the design.[35] Registration, if the design is accepted, is preferable because of a potentially longer period of protection and the stronger form of protection afforded. Registration is not particularly expensive. But failure to register on the basis that the design is probably protected by the design right is dangerous as there is often no way of knowing whether the design right applies to a design short of litigation. Although registration of a design is not conclusive proof that the design meets all the requirements for registration, at least it indicates that the design in all probability does so. The advice has to be: if in doubt, apply for registration. Another reason in favour of registration is that it demonstrates that the owner of the design takes his legal rights seriously, especially if the fact of registration and the registration number is affixed to articles made to the design.

35 This was even more crucial under the Copyright Act 1956 which, under s 10(1), excluded copyright protection from a design which was fundamentally registrable under the Registered Designs Act 1949. The Design Copyright Act 1968 changed this.

## PARTICULAR EXAMPLES

The following articles are considered in the light of the different rights (registered design, design right and artistic copyright) that might apply to the design of the article. The purpose of the examples is to highlight the differences between the rights, their synthesis and interrelationship. Where referred to, statutes are abbreviated thus: Copyright, Designs and Patents Act 1988 (CPDA); Registered Designs Act 1949 (RDA).

## Porcelain figurine

*Artistic copyright*: The figurine could be considered to be a sculpture. The original model and the cast (mould) could also be sculptures (CDPA s 4(2)) as long as they are 'original' (CDPA s 1(1)(a)), irrespective of artistic quality (CDPA s 4(1)). Drawings and preliminary sketches could also be protected by copyright.[36]

*Registered design*: If the shape or configuration (or any surface decoration applied to the figurines) is 'new' (RDA s 1(2)) then the design of the figurine can be registered.[37] A figurine is unquestionably designed to appeal to the eye.

*Design right*: If the shape or configuration is 'original' (CDPA s 213(1)), that is not commonplace, then the design right applies.

It appears that all three rights apply. Copyright is not suppressed because the article is an artistic work (CDPA s 51(1)). An advantage of registering the design is that no causal link is required for infringement to be proved (RDA s 7).[38] However, copyright is wider in terms of the types of infringement, for example if a figurine is shown in television broadcast.[39] But copyright does not prevent similar works being created by independent effort. The existence of the design right is illusory, because if the act complained of infringes copyright the design right is suppressed (CDPA s 236). Finally, it should be noted that the rights could be owned by different persons. For example, if a self-employed sculptor is commissioned to make the original model, he will own the copyright but the commissioner will, provided he has paid money or money's worth, be entitled to register the design on his own behalf.

## Mass-produced furniture

*Artistic copyright*: It is unlikely that the furniture itself will be a work of artistic craftsmanship.[40] In principle, any drawings may be protected, as will be other materials such as computer data defining the three-dimensional shape of the furniture. But this protection will be limited by the CDPA s 51 to direct copying only, for example photocopying the original drawing. Copyright might subsist in any document, such as a drawing, recording the design of a pattern to be applied to the covers to be fitted to the furniture.

*Registered design*: If the shape or configuration is 'new' and has eye-appeal (RDA s 1(2)), then the design may be registered. If the furniture has patterned covers or an embossed surface, this too may be registrable separately. This might be useful if a particular line of furniture is produced with a choice from several different designs of covers, each of which is new and has eye-appeal. However, any aspects of the shape or configuration which relate to a method or principle of construction, or which are related to the function the furniture has to perform are excluded. Therefore, if the furniture has a distinctive shape that results only from the way it is made or the fact that it is designed for sitting upon, the design is not registrable. Obviously, in deciding whether to buy a particular suite of furniture, the appearance is a material factor.

36 Under the Copyright, Designs and Patents Act 1988 s 52 and pursuant regulations, if more than 50 figurines are made by an industrial process and marketed, the term of copyright is reduced to 25 years. It would appear from the wording of s 52 that this would apply to the original model, the cast(s) and any drawings, the figurines being three-dimensional copies of the drawings.

37 Works of sculpture are excluded from registration by the Registration Designs Rules 1995 (SI 1995/2912) reg 26, but only in as much as they are not 'casts or models' used or intended to be used as models or patterns to be multiplied by any industrial process'. A model from which a cast will be made so that the figurines can be mass-produced is, therefore, registrable.

38 For example, in copyright, for infringement by copying, the original thing (or copy of it) must have been copied from directly or indirectly. However, damages are not available against innocent infringers, the Registered Designs Act 1949 s 9.

39 But the number of restricted acts is less for artistic works than it is for other original works. For example, by the Copyright, Designs and Patents Act 1988, the making of an adaptation is not an act restricted by the copyright in an artistic work (s 21), neither is it an infringement to show an artistic work in public (s 19).

40 *See George Hensher Ltd v Restawhile Upholstery (Lancs) Ltd* [1976] AC 64. In some cases, where the furniture has some particular artistic quality, it may be the subject of artisitic copyright as a work of artistic craftmanship. Past examples would include art deco or art nouveau furniture. It might also apply to hand-crafted furniture.

*Design right*: This will apply if the shape or configuration applied to the furniture is 'original' (CDPA s 213(1)). Because the furniture is not itself an artistic work, the design right is not suppressed and runs alongside any registrations in respect of the design. Patterned covers and the like will not, however, be subject to the design right as these are features of surface decoration.

Some of the differences between registered designs and the design right may be important in this case. For example, duration is potentially longer for a registered design. Also, the exceptions are not quite the same. For the design right, features of shape and configuration which relate to the function of the article may be protected if not covered by the 'must-fit' and 'must-match' exceptions, whereas for a registered design functional features are totally excluded. Methods and principles of construction are excepted from both rights. There are also slight differences in the ownership provisions for the two rights.

Copyright in any drawing or painting showing the design of the surface decoration could run alongside a design registration. At first sight, the advantage of registering a design can be doubted. However, there are important differences in terms of infringement and ownership which can make registration as a design a more attractive proposition.

### Can opener

*Artistic copyright*: It is unlikely that this could be considered to be a sculpture even if the handle and casing were injection moulded. Copyright, in principle, again will subsist in any drawings subject to the CDPA s 51(1).

*Registered design*: If the design has not previously been registered or published and has eye-appeal and is not governed by function then the design may be registrable. Many such articles which are essentially functional may be designed also for eye-appeal. Some people are more willing to buy or to pay more for functional articles if they look attractive. Even a container for toilet disinfectant with a neck in the shape of a duck's neck has been registered as a design, as has a container for false teeth.

*Design right*: If the shape of the can opener is not commonplace, the design right may apply in so far as the design does not encompass a method or principle of construction, or is not dictated by the shape of the cans it has to be placed against so that it may be used to open them.

Design right and the rights under design registration can subsist concurrently in the design, but copyright is not relevant. However, design right could apply also to the shape or configuration of any internal mechanism of the can opener if original. If the casing has a pretty pattern printed or embossed on it, that pattern could be the subject of a separate design registration.

### Moulded plastic tray for processed food

*Artistic copyright*: Although the moulded tray has shape, it is unlikely that it would be considered to be a sculpture.[41] However, sculptures are protected irrespective of artistic quality, and it could be possible to consider the original model, from which the trays were made, to be a sculpture. Any copyright in drawings for the tray is likely to be suppressed by the CDPA s 51(1).

41 However, in the New Zealand case of *Wham-O Manufacturing Co v Lincoln Industries Ltd* [1985] RPC 127, it was held that a wooden model from which the moulds for 'Frisbees' were made was a sculpture and the moulds and Frisbees were engravings. Copying a finished Frisbee infringed all these copyrights and the copyright in the working drawings.

*Registered design*: If new, the shape may be registrable. The eye-appeal requirement can be satisfied in two ways: first, from the point of view of the food processor who wants to make his chicken breasts (or whatever) look as attractive as possible to potential customers; second, the customers themselves will be influenced in their purchasing decision by the appearance of the product. The amount of money expended on packaging is ample proof of the importance of attractive containers for food. Although largely irrelevant as to reasons associated with use from the customers' point of view, aesthetic considerations are important in the context of acquisition from the food processor's viewpoint.

*Design right*: If original, the shape of the tray will be protected by the design right.

Registration of the design of food containers is very common and rewards the effort expended in the creation of designs intended to show off the food to best commercial effect.

## OWNERSHIP – DIFFERENCES BETWEEN RIGHTS

The differences in the ownership provisions between artistic copyright, registered designs and the design right have already been alluded to. Before proceeding over the next two chapters to consider the registered design and the design right in more detail, it will be useful to look briefly at these provisions comparatively. The fact that there are differences could be very inconvenient where a particular design attracts two forms of protection. The special provisions that apply, for example, in respect of Crown copyright are omitted for the sake of clarity. There are some differences in terminology. The person creating a work of copyright or a registered design is known as the 'author', whereas the creator of a design in which the design right subsists is called a 'designer'.[42] A copyright and a design right is owned by its 'owner', but for a registered design he is known as the 'proprietor'.

*Artistic copyright*: The author is the first owner of an artistic copyright unless he is an employee creating the work in the course of his employment, in which case his employer is the first owner (the CDPA s 11(1) and (2)).

*Registered design*: The author is the original proprietor of the design subject to two exceptions. The first is equivalent to the copyright provision for employees. The second exception is where the design is created under a commission, in which case the commissioner is entitled to be the original proprietor provided the commission is for money or money's worth.

*Design right*: The designer is the first owner, subject to exceptions relating to employees and commissioned designs. A 'commission' means a commission for money or money's worth.[43] A further provision applies to designs which qualify for the right by reference to the first marketing of articles made to the design. In this case, the person marketing the articles is the first owner of the right.

Table 16.2 shows the identity of potential first owners of the three rights. Which one it is will depend on the circumstances. For example, the first owner of a design right might be the designer, his employer or commissioner, or the person responsible for the first marketing. For artistic copyright, the first owner can only be either the author or his employer.[44] Of course, the first owner may assign the right to another immediately upon its coming into existence, or may agree to do so in respect of a future copyright or design.

42 Statutory recognition is given to the fact that all these rights can be brought about by computer generation and the provisions are equivalent for each of the rights.

43 The Copyright, Designs and Patents Act 1988 s 263(1).

44 Ignoring the Copyright, Designs and Patents Act 1988 s 11(3) which caters for Crown and parliamentary copyright and copyright belonging to certain international organisations.

**Table 16.2 Potential first owners of rights in designs**

| Type of right | Creator of right known as | Owner of right known as | Potential identity of first owner from amongst | | | |
|---|---|---|---|---|---|---|
| | | | Creator | Employer | Commissioner | Marketer |
| Artistic Copyright | Author | Owner | YES | YES | no | no |
| Registered Design | Author | Proprietor | YES | YES | YES* | no |
| Design Right | Designer | Owner | YES | YES | YES* | YES |

\* only if the commission is undertaken for money or money's worth.

## INTERNATIONAL ASPECTS

Unfortunately, the international protection of designs is far from satisfactory.[45] Although the World Intellectual Property Organization includes designs within its brief and there have been moves towards international protection, it has to be said that little has been achieved compared to the co-operation realised as regards copyright and patents. One reason for this is that design protection is effected in many different ways in different states. However, over 20 states belong to the Hague Agreement 1925 (not including the UK) which does go some way towards a unified system for registering designs by deposit without search.[46] Application for registration is made in Geneva, but individual member states can refuse within a certain period of time. However, registration in the UK is subject to a search to ensure that the design is new, whereas some other countries operate a simple deposit system. The design right is, at the present time, unique to the UK, although designs that are subject to this right might fall within the sphere of other rights in different countries; for example, under copyright law or as a 'petty patent' or utility model.

International protection of UK registered designs is automatically afforded in some countries (mainly Commonwealth countries), such as Bermuda, Botswana, Cyprus, Gibraltar, Malaysia, Singapore, and Uganda. Others extend protection by local re-registration of a UK design; these are Guernsey, Jersey, Malta, Montserrat, Tanzania and Trinidad and Tobago. Otherwise, if international protection is required for a design, it must be obtained by application to the appropriate states under their registered designs or petty patents systems.[47] There is at least the advantage of a six-month priority arrangement for designs under the Paris Convention for the Protection of Industrial Property 1883. Some countries operate a law of unfair competition which could be useful in some cases. Of course, because of the much better international copyright position, it may be possible to pursue actions for infringement of copyright in drawings in foreign states.

45 For an excellent description of the international scene as regards designs, *see* Johnston, D. (1989) *Design Protection* (3rd edn), The Design Council, especially Chapter 10 and Appendix A.

46 States which are signatories to the Hague Agreement include France, Germany, the Benelux countries, Italy and Spain.

47 A petty patent (called utility models in some countries) is a weaker variety of patent which is used in countries such as Germany, Italy, Spain and Malaysia. There is a proposal for a harmonising Directive on utility models which would require the United Kingdom to introduce such a right. This proposal is discussed in Chapter 15.

## REFORM OF DESIGN LAW

48 Jehoram, H.C 'The EC Green Paper on the Legal Protection of Industrial Design. Half Way down the Right Track - A View from the Benelux' [1992] 3 EIPR 75.

49 [1989] 4 CMLR 122.

50 Brussels, June 1991. 111/F/5131/91-EN. The Green Paper was not formally published but was circulated to interested parties. For a detailed description of the Green Paper's proposals, *see* Horton, A. A. 'Industrial Design Law: The Future for Europe' [1991] 12 EIPR 442.

51 OJ C 142, 14.5.96, p. 7; common position text OJ C237, 4.8.97, p. 1.

52 OJ C29, 31.1.94, p. 20.

Jehoram remarks that there is 'abundant evidence ... that different national laws on intellectual property can restrict the free movement of goods within the Community'.[48] Indeed, the judgments in the case of *Volvo AB v Erik Veng (UK) Ltd*[49] clearly indicate how lack of harmonisation can emasculate European Community competition law. However, the disparate national treatment afforded to designs is unlikely to survive for much longer. The Commission to the European Community produced a Green Paper in June 1991 on the legal protection of industrial design.[50] This was influenced by a draft for European design law produced by the Max Planck Institute in Munich. There were two main thrusts in the Green Paper: first, a process of limited harmonisation of design laws in member states; second, the implementation of a fully integrated Community system of design rights.

Subsequently, there has been a proposal for a European Parliament and Council Directive on the legal protection of designs[51] which would harmonise on the basis of a registered design system, and a proposal for a European Parliament and Council Regulation on Community design[52] which proposes a two-tier Community design system. The former proposal is discussed towards the end of the following chapter on registered designs.

## COMMUNITY DESIGN

The proposed Community design will apply throughout the Community and will have a unitary nature. A two-tier system is proposed:

- a registered design (not dissimilar to the present UK system), and
- a shorter-term unregistered design right.

53 Discussed in Chapter 17.

The registered Community design is very similar to that suggested in the proposed harmonisation Directive[53] and will last, potentially, for 25 years based on five-year periods. The unregistered design right will last for three years only from the date on which products incorporating the design or made to the design were first made available to the public.

The unregistered right will be particularly useful for those designs that have a relatively short period of time during which they are commercially viable, for example in the case of fashion clothing. It will be unnecessary to register such designs, the unregistered right giving all the protection required. For designs that may have a longer lifespan, registration can be delayed for up to one year allowing

54 By Article 8 such disclosure being deemed non-prejudicial.

for test marketing without destroying the novelty of the design.[54] Therefore, the owner of a design will be able to put articles made to the design on the market before deciding whether it is worthwhile going to the expense and trouble of registration. If the design is not particularly successful, the owner may decide not to bother registering the design (relying on the unregistered right for any copying that takes place). However, if the design is successful and it appears that this success will continue for some years to come, the owner can then apply for registration.

55 Apart, of course, from the registration formalities.

The basic requirements for the rights, whether registered or not, are the same.[55] 'Design', by Article 3(a), means:

> ... the appearance of the whole or any part of a product resulting from the specific features of the lines, contours, colours, shape and/or materials of the product itself and/or its ornamentation.

A 'product' is, by Article 3(b) any:

> ... industrial or handicraft item, including parts intended to be assembled into a complex item, sets or compositions of items, packaging, get-ups, graphic symbols and typographic typefaces, but excluding a computer program or a semiconductor product.

Thus, typefaces will be within the scope of the Community design. At present, these are protected by copyright as artistic works. It would seem, because of this and the inclusion of 'graphic symbols', that 'product' could apply to software items, notwithstanding the exclusion of computer programs. A general requirement is that the design must be novel and have an individual character (Article 4).

A design has an individual character if 'the overall impression it produces on the informed user differs significantly from the overall impression produced on such a user by any previously commercialised or published design' (Article 6). Internal aspects will not be protected unless they can be perceived by the human eye, as 'design' is defined in terms of appearance. Designs that are dictated solely by technical function are excluded; that is, where there is no freedom as regards arbitrary features of appearance (Article 9(1)). However, contrary to the United Kingdom requirement for eye-appeal for registered designs, there will be no specific requirement that the appearance should be a material factor for either the registered or the informal right.

The proposed Regulation, by Article 9(2), contains an exception based on interconnections, that is, 'those features of the appearance of a product which must necessarily be reproduced in their exact form and dimensions in order to permit the product to which the design is applied to be assembled or connected with another product'. This exception does not, however, apply to identical or mutually interchangeable products within a modular system (Article 9(3)).

Some features of the proposed two-tier system of particular note are as follows.

- the unitary nature of the Community design means that it cannot be registered, transferred or surrendered except in respect of the whole Union (Article 1(3)). Ownership may not be split, but of course territorially limited licences may be granted (Articles 30 and 34);
- registration at the Community Design Office will not be subject to substantive examination, thereby saving time and expense, but will be subject to certain formalities (Articles 39, 40, and 48). Priority may be claimed in respect of applications in other states party to the Paris Convention (for up to six months);
- applications may be filed at the Community Design Office or, where the law of member states so permits, at a central national office or the Benelux Design Office (Article 37). In either of the last two cases, the application will be forwarded to the Community Design Office (Article 38);
- the Community Design Office will be entitled to hear direct actions raised by the Commission, member states or third parties against validity, and a Board of Appeal will be set up with ultimate appeal to the Court of Justice of the European Communities (recitals 22 and 24);
- member states may designate certain courts as Community Design Courts having specialist judges (recital 28 and Articles 87 to 98);
- the unregistered design right, while based on the same subsistence requirements as the registered design, will give a right to prevent copying only (Articles 20 and 21).

There is no date for compliance by member states with the proposed regulation. Because of changes to the proposed Directive on the legal protection of designs, the Community design will need to be further modified.

# 17

## *Registered designs*

### INTRODUCTION

A system of registration for designs has been around since the early part of the nineteenth century. The initial demand for a system of registration came from the textile industry, but now all manner of designs are registered, the most common kinds of designs being for toys, games and electrical goods. Initially dealt with separately, for example by the Copyright in Designs Act 1839, registered designs were for some time governed by the same statute as patents and, for a time, trade marks.[1] Eventually, in 1949, patents and designs legislation were separated and the present statute dealing with registered designs is the Registered Designs Act 1949 which was amended by the Copyright, Designs and Patents Act 1988.[2] The 1988 Act includes a copy of the Registered Designs Act 1949 (as amended, in Sch 4 – a very useful and helpful step). The amended version of the 1949 Act came into force on 1 August 1989.

### REQUIREMENTS FOR REGISTRATION

A design may be registered in respect of any article or set of articles. A design means features of:

- shape
- configuration
- pattern or
- ornament

which are applied to an article by any industrial process, being features which in the finished article appeal to and are judged by the eye.[3] A design is thus not restricted to three dimensions and surface decoration can come within the scope of registered designs, as can designs applied to textiles or garments, for example, a new and attractive motif applied to material for making dresses. The additional requirement for the appearance to be material in the acquisition or use of articles to which the design has been applied is discussed below. It remains to be seen to what extent this has changed the requirement for eye-appeal, if indeed it has changed it. Eye-appeal was construed fairly liberally in the recent past.

A design may be registered for a set of articles. A set of articles is, by s 44:

> ... a number of articles of the same general character ordinarily on sale or intended to be used together, to each of which the same design, or the same design with modifications or variations not sufficient to alter the character or substantially to affect the identity thereof, is applied.

An example would be a design applied to cutlery with slight differences depending on the item concerned, whether the particular article is a knife or a fork. A suite of furniture where the same design is applied to a chair and a sofa would qualify as a set of articles. A chess set would not, as the intention of the designer is to produce pieces that can be distinguished from one another; the design of individual pieces such as the queen, rook and bishop will be different; the first part of the definition in s 44 applies, but not the latter. The same principle applies to a typeface design. Each chess piece or each letter or numeral in a typeface could be separately registered, though, in most cases, that would be prohibitively expensive. In any case, typefaces are usually in software form nowadays and are not, therefore, applied to articles.

Whereas a single application for registration is acceptable for a set of articles, multiple applications must be made in the case of a design intended to be applied to more than one article not being part of a set of articles.[4] Thus, if the same design is to be applied to a vase and a table lamp, two separate applications must be made and two fees must be paid.

4 The Registered Design Rules 1995, SI 1995/2912, r 13.

### Applied to an article by any industrial process

The design must be applied to an article (or be intended to be so applied). This might seem a simple and untroublesome prerequisite, but 'article' is defined in s 44(1) as 'any article of manufacture and includes any part of an article if that part is made and sold separately'. It is in respect of parts of an article that difficulty can be met. In *Sifam Electrical Instrument Co Ltd v Sangamo Weston Ltd*[5] it was held that the design of the front of an electric meter was not a part of an article under s 44(1) because it was not intended to be sold separately by the proprietor of the design. Graham J said (at 914):

5 [1973] RPC 899.

> ... on the whole I think the intention must be to grant registration only for such articles as are intended by the proprietor of the design to be put on the market and sold separately, such as for example a hammer handle, or the bit of a bradawl.

The Ford Motor Company applied to register the design of many of the components of its vehicles, such as door panels, steering wheels, seats, bonnets and wheel covers. All the registrations were rejected on the basis of the 'must-match' exception.[6] In the subsequent appeals to the Divisional Court of the Queen's Bench Division, the Court of Appeal and the House of Lords, a different approach was taken.[7] All these appeals were dismissed, but on a different basis. The House of Lords, approved *Sifam v Sangamo*, stressing that the definition of 'article' in s 44(1) should be read as meaning '... if that part is *to be* made and sold separately' (inserted words emphasised).[8] Otherwise, if the phrase 'made and sold separately' is taken literally, this would allow registration of all manner of component parts. Lord Mustill said (at 177):

6 *Ford Motor Co Ltd & Iveco Fiat SpA's Design Application* [1993] RPC 399, although eventually it was accepted that some were registrable (*see* post).

7 There had also been an appeal to the Registered Design Appeal Tribunal: *see Ford Motor Co Ltd's Design Applications* [1994] RPC 545, which was primarily concerned with the must-match exception.

8 [1995] RPC 167.

> In relation to a spare part one asks whether it is made separately, and finds that it is; for its fabrication is not part of the manufacture of an entire vehicle. Equally, the part is sold separately; for the customer buys it without at the same time buying the rest of the car. The article thus satisfies both tests.

Spare parts, being components, are made separately, often by sub-contractors or specialised parts manufacturers, to be supplied to the vehicle manufacturer. They are indeed sold separately as replacements for damaged or worn out parts. But that is a secondary use. The main object is to use the parts to make an entire vehicle, and in this respect the view of McCowan LJ in the Court of Appeal, which was approved in the House of Lords, is faultless. He suggested that to qualify as an article, a spare part must have an independent life as an article of commerce and not be merely an adjunct of some larger article of which it forms part. Although completely in tune with parliamentary intention to deprive many spare parts of protection under the Registered Designs Act 1949, the reading of additional words into s 44(1) is unsatisfactory and has deprived the must-match exception of any real effect. Nevertheless, some spare parts may be registrable where they are obtained to enhance the appearance of the article of which they form part rather than being simple replacements. Examples are sports seats and steering wheels, fancy alloy wheels and wing mirrors. However, the Act does not distinguish between replacement parts and accessories in the definition of 'article'. The House of Lords declined to consider other objections raised by the Registrar which had been added. Lord Mustill said (at 181):

> The purpose of the 'exercise' as it is called [that is, the appeal] is not to provide the occasion for a ramble through the statute, with a pause for your Lordships to express an opinion on every point of interest, and less still for discussion into minor issues on which there is not any great difference between the parties ...

Of course, our adversarial procedure restricts the court from exploratory meanderings through legislation unconnected with the disputed facts of a case, but it is a pity that the opportunity was not taken by the House to examine the must-match exception which was, after all, the original basis for rejecting the designs.

The design must be applied by any industrial process. A definition of 'applied industrially' is given in the Registered Design Rules 1995,[9] but this definition is made for the purposes of the Registered Designs Act 1949 s 6, dealing with the industrial application in terms of corresponding designs relating to artistic works. It is not necessarily of universal application to the remainder of the Act, and in any case relates only to quantity.

There is no justification for limiting the meaning of 'industrial process' beyond an intention merely to apply the design to a number of articles whether by machine or by hand or by a combination of both, nor is there any precedent to suggest such a limitation. The law of registered designs is aimed at industrial designs being designs applied to manufactured articles which are mass produced. Although the regulations define industrial application in terms of, *inter alia*, application to more than 50 articles, it is unlikely that that number has any significance as regards registrability of a design.

Modern technology may stretch the meaning of 'industrial application' to its limits. For example, a typeface design would, in the past, be registrable. Individual characters would be registrable, as would a common design aspect such as a new design of serif. A typeface used to be applied to articles, metal type ('hot metal'). However, most typefaces nowadays are stored as computer data in the form of software fonts. There are no articles to which the typeface design is applied industrially. Copyright protection remains for software typefaces which fall within the scope of artistic copyright.[10] Needless to say, all other forms of design that exist only in software (for example, for an object to be displayed on a computer screen) are not applied to an article and fall outside the realms of registered designs. It is unlikely that, by any stretch of the imagination, the storage of data representing such a design on a magnetic disk could be perceived as

9 The Registered Design Rules 1995, SI 1995/2912, r 35.

10 Although not listed as a specific form of artistic work in the Copyright, Designs and Patents Act 1988 s 4; ss 54 and 55 refer to the copyright in an artistic work consisting of the design of a typeface.

being equivalent to the industrial application of a design to an article. Although such designs fail to be protected directly by copyright, this is inferior to the monopoly rights granted by design registration.

## Novelty

A further requirement is that the design must be new. It will not be considered to be 'new' if it is the same as a design registered in a prior application, regardless of the nature of the article to which it was intended to be applied, or if the design has been published in the United Kingdom prior to the date of application. This also applies to a design which differs only in immaterial details from such designs or in features that are variants commonly used in the trade.[11]

This does not mean to say that a design must be unlike any previous design to be registrable. There may be some similarities, for example, with other articles used to perform the same function. Some of the similarities may be due to the manner in which the function is performed. In *Household Articles Ltd's Registered Design*,[12] the parties made coffee pots of the piston type for making filter coffee. Both coffee pots had glass containers, and similar push rods, giving them a family resemblance. However, where there was design freedom there were notable differences between the coffee pots. Laddie J said that two questions should be asked. First, are any of the remaining features (those not similar) excluded as being immaterial differences or variants common in the trade? Secondly, is the visual impact of those features not excluded sufficiently different from prior art? He went on to confirm that a registered design does not have to exhibit 'novelty of a startling or groundbreaking variety to be valid'.

If a design is registered in respect of a particular article and the proprietor later wishes to register the same design in respect of other articles, the prior registration or publication of the design is ignored when considering whether the design is new.[13] Publication in breach of confidence or contrary to good faith is ignored in determining whether the design has been published.[14] If the design is applied to an article and that article is a copy of an artistic work it is known as a 'corresponding design', and previous use of the artistic work does not prevent the design being new provided that the prior use does not include commercial exploitation of articles to which the design has been applied industrially.[15] Novelty for this purpose is not prejudiced by use outside the United Kingdom. Registration of a corresponding design was allowed in *Bissell AG's Design*[16] notwithstanding the publication in the United Kingdom of an illustration of an article made to the design outside the United Kingdom. The publication was a mere previous use of an artistic work within s 6(4).

Prior to the amendments made by the Copyright, Designs and Patents Act 1988, the design had to be 'new or original', and as this was qualified in similar terms to the present requirement that a design should be 'new', it is unlikely that there has been any significant shift. That is, the design, or a design substantially like it, as before, should not have been previously registered or published in the UK. In any case, the meaning of 'original' did not trouble the courts and the basic test was one of novelty; although, in an extraordinary display of statutory interpretation, it was held by the Registered Designs Appeal Tribunal in *Aspro-Nicholas Ltd's Design Application*[17] that the 'or' in the phrase 'new or original' was not used in a disjunctive sense and

11 This was a ground for invalidity in relation to registered designs for rear lamps for vehicles in *Valeo Vision SA v Flexible Lamps Ltd* [1995] RPC 205.

12 (Unreported) 14 January 1998, Patents Court.

13 The Registered Designs Act 1949 s 4(1). This also applies to slight alterations.

14 *See* ibid s 6. There are other provisions, for example with respect to the first and confidential order placed for an original textile design, exhibitions and disclosure to government departments.

15 Ibid s 6(4), (5). This also applies to designs which differ only in immaterial details or in features which are variants commonly used in the trade. 'Applied industrially' is defined by the Registered Design Rules 1995, SI 1995/2912 r 35, as having the same meaning as for artistic works.

16 [1964] RPC 125.

17 [1974] RPC 645. Another example where a judge interpreted an 'or' in a statute as 'and' is *Stock v Frank Jones (Tipton) Ltd* [1978] 1 All ER 948.

therefore a design must be both new and original to qualify for registration. The courts have frequently had to deal with the question of novelty. In essence it is a matter of whether a design has been anticipated along patent lines. In *Rosedale Associated Manufacturers Ltd v Airfix Products Ltd*[18] it was held that the rules that apply to anticipation of patents also apply to registered designs. It has been observed that the contribution of the design to the store of human knowledge or experience might be another factor in determining novelty, and where the contribution was slight it would be unlikely that the court would find that the design was new.[19]

### Eye-appeal

Before the changes made by the Copyright, Designs and Patents Act 1988, eye-appeal was the fundamental test for which features of a design could be registered, that is, features 'which in the finished article appeal to and are judged solely by the eye'.[20] In *Amp Incorporated v Utilux Pty Ltd*,[21] it was said that there was no requirement for aesthetic or artistic appeal and that it was sufficient if the features in question were capable of being appreciated so as to make an impact on the eye. However, in the House of Lords, Lord Reid said:[22]

> ... 'judged solely by the eye' must be intended to exclude cases where a customer might choose an article of that shape, not because of its appearance but because he thought that the shape made it more useful to him.

In determining whether the features in question have eye-appeal, the court adopts the mantle of the prospective purchaser of the article to which the design has been applied. The design is not viewed through the eyes of an expert in the field.[23] This well-established approach to eye-appeal would appear to exclude any intermediate purchaser, such as a retailer or supplier buying packaging for goods he intends to sell. However, a retailer or supplier may buy attractive packaging or containers because he thinks that they will appeal to the eye of the ultimate purchaser.

In *Lamson Industries Ltd's Application*,[24] Whitford J decided that a design for computer print-out paper having alternative coloured bands upon it was not registrable because the reason customers would buy the paper was that it would be easier to read, and because information could be printed out on the paper more closely spaced. Customers would buy the paper because of its utility and not because of its appearance.

These cases demonstrated a fairly rigorous approach to eye-appeal. However, a more generous attitude was in evidence in the intervening years up to the changes to design law introduced by the Copyright, Designs and Patents Act 1988. An extremely generous example is given in *Gardex Ltd v Sorata Ltd*,[25] which concerned an alleged infringement of the design of a shower tray. The defendant challenged, *inter alia*, the registration of a shower tray including its underside as a design, claiming that the shape of the underside was dictated solely by function. However, it was held that the under surface was intended to have aesthetic appeal and did not solely relate to a method or principle of construction, and therefore the design was validly registered. This seems to be stretching eye-appeal to its limits as, once the shower tray had been installed, the underside would never be seen again. The plaintiff claimed that when he

18 [1957] RPC 239.

19 *Aspro-Nicholas Ltd's Design Application* [1974] RPC 645.

20 The Registered Designs Act 1949 s 1(3) before amendment by the Copyright, Designs and Patents Act 1988.

21 [1970] RPC 397.

22 *Amp Incorporated v Utilux Pty Ltd* [1972] RPC 103 at 108.

23 *Valeo Vision SA v Flexible Lamps Ltd* [1995] RPC 205, *per* Aldous J at 215.

24 [1978] RPC 1.

25 [1986] RPC 623.

had created the design for the underside of the tray it had pleased him so much that he thought it worthy of design registration. This extraordinary claim seemed to find sympathy with the judge.

The test now seems to be more rigorous in that eye-appeal is still required but, in addition, the appearance of the article must be material. Whether the appearance is material involves a curious two-stage test. Section 1(3) states:

> A design shall not be registered in respect of an article if the appearance of the article is not material, that is, if aesthetic considerations are not normally taken into account to a material extent by persons acquiring or using articles of that description, and would not be so taken into account if the design were to be applied to the article.

The presence of so many negatives in s 1(3) makes it difficult to follow. Does it mean that, to be registrable, aesthetic considerations are material in respect of the type of article generally and the particular article? Removing the negatives gives the following test.

1 With respect to articles of the same type as the particular article under scrutiny, are aesthetic considerations normally taken into account to a material extent by persons acquiring or using such articles? If the answer to this question is 'yes' then the appearance is material, but if the answer is 'no' then the second stage of the test is invoked.
2 Would aesthetic considerations be taken into account to a material extent by persons acquiring or using articles to which the design in question has been applied? If the answer is 'yes' then the appearance is material despite the fact that it might not be material generally in respect of similar articles.

For example, a new shape of container may be designed for a liquid disinfectant. Theoretically, persons buying disinfectant should not and do not decide upon which brand to buy on the basis of aesthetic considerations. However, if a particular container has been designed to look attractive while standing on a bathroom shelf, the design may be registrable. Because of the change in emphasis in aesthetic characteristics, it is inevitable that some previously registered designs would not meet the new standards for registration.[26] To deal with this problem, and other changes to the requirements for registrability, for designs which were registered in pursuance of an application made after 12 January 1988 and before 1 August 1989 but which would not be registrable under the new requirements, the design registration is limited to a maximum of ten years after 1 August 1989 provided it does not expire earlier in any event.[27]

The effects of this requirement of 'material appearance' are difficult to predict as it can be argued that even with the most functional of household objects appearance is a factor, especially in terms of their acquisition.[28] Goods have to vie with each other on supermarket shelves and an attractively shaped (and coloured) container or a functional article with an unusual design must have some impact upon buying decisions. The buying public have come to expect care and trouble to have been taken in the design of the outward appearance of articles and containers. The question is whether a particular make of article is preferred to another make because of appearance, and one way of resolving this question might be to look at the relative price of 'designer' articles compared with plain unadorned articles that are purchased for the same function and which can perform that function just as efficiently. In other words, just how much money are people prepared to pay for the design?

26 This situation may also arise because of changes to the exceptions to registrability.

27 The Copyright, Designs and Patents Act 1988 s 266(1). In addition, licences as of right are available for such designs.

28 Another change is that the phrase 'appeal to and are judged solely by the eye' has been changed to 'appeal to and are judged by the eye': s 1(1). This might make it easier for 'designer' functional articles to gain registration, such as a bottle opener in the shape of a hand.

Instead of considering the reasons for acquisition of articles, appearance may be a material factor in terms of usage. In most cases, if appearance is an important factor in the use of the article, it will also be a material factor in its acquisition. A great number of designs fall into this category, for example, a set of dinner plates bearing an attractive pattern, cutlery, a table lamp, household ornaments and *objects d'art*, toys, curtain material, wallpaper and furniture. With respect to these types of articles it is plain that provided the other requirements are satisfied they should qualify for registration. The difficulty lies in determining the position of articles which are normally acquired for their function but which have had, nevertheless, an attractive design applied to them, perhaps in an effort to achieve a competitive edge or as a way of targeting a more discerning buyer who is prepared to pay a premium.

## Exceptions

Even though a design is new it might not qualify for registration because the Registered Designs Act 1949 s 1 contains some exceptions and others are provided for by statutory instrument. Additionally, the Registrar has a discretion to refuse an application generally, or on the grounds that use of the design would be contrary to law or morality.[29] Designs which are expressly excluded by s 1(1) are:

(a) methods or principles of construction; or
(b) features of shape or configuration which are:
    (i) dictated solely by the article's function, or
    (ii) dependent upon the appearance of another article of which the article is intended by the design's author (creator) to form an integral part.

These exclusions serve two main purposes. First, they prevent the right from being too strong and hindering the development of new designs for similar articles or articles of a similar construction. Second, they allow, somewhat controversially and subject to what has been said earlier in respect of the meaning of 'article', the manufacture of matching spare parts by others. This is the 'must-match' exception and is identically worded to the equivalent exception for the design right.[30] In *Cow (PB) & Co Ltd* v *Cannon Rubber Manufacturers Ltd*[31] the plaintiff had a registered design for rubber hot-water bottles having a series of diagonally arranged ribs front and back. The claim to novelty lay in the shape or configuration of the bottle as shown in drawings. The defendant was sued for infringing the design and claimed that the registration was defective because it included a method or principle of construction and included features of shape and configuration dictated by function. Lloyd-Jacob J found for the plaintiff, confirming the validity of the design. The features claimed would not prevent the development of other designs for hot-water bottles, for example by using horizontal, vertical or criss-cross ribs.

Like patent law, registered design law gives rise to a monopoly, and it is important that the protection offered does not extend too far. The equivalent to methods or principles of construction in patent law is discoveries, scientific theories and mathematical methods. One way of looking at methods or principles of construction and functions is to ask the question: Is there any other way such articles could be made; does the right prevent the making of similar articles to other designs? *Amp Incorporated* v *Utilux Pty Ltd*[32] concerned registrations for

29 The Registrar's full title is the Comptroller-General of Patents, Designs and the Trade Marks.

30 Apart from the use of the word 'designer' rather than 'author' (*see* the Copyright, Designs and Patents Act 1988 s 213(3)(b)(ii)).

31 [1959] RPC 240.

32 [1970] RPC 397.

small electrical terminals as used in washing machines and vehicles. They are called 'flag terminals' and a wire is fastened into the terminal by crimping metal ears over it, the terminal then being pushed over a metal tab which is held by channels in the terminal to make the connection. An alleged infringer claimed that the registrations were invalid because the designs were dictated by function. The House of Lords held that the designs were invalid. Although it was argued that the shape of the terminals was not dictated by their function because slight changes could be accommodated, Lord Reid said that this would reduce the exception almost to vanishing point. The argument that a shape is dictated by function only if it is necessary to use that precise shape and no other in order to perform the function was firmly rejected.

Many articles have a number of design features, some of which are related to function, some of which are not. The question with such designs is whether they are registrable and, if so, what the scope of protection is. The position was considered by Lord Oliver in *Interlego AG v Tyco Industries Inc.*[33] He suggested that, where a design includes features dictated by the function to be performed by the relevant article, there are three possibilities (at 242):

33 [1989] AC 217.

- the registrable elements are limited to those parts having eye-appeal
- the design is excluded from registration altogether because of the presence of functional features, or
- the design is excluded only if every feature is dictated by function.

He went on to confirm that the last construction is the correct one.[34] As registration of a design relates to an article as a whole, then notwithstanding that some elements are dictated by function, protection is afforded to the shape *as a whole*. Therefore, questions of novelty and infringement must be answered by looking at the totality of the design.[35] To be excluded from registration on the basis of the functional exclusion, all the novel features must be functional. An example might be the hull of a boat, or the general shape of a sailing dinghy. In *Dorling v Honnor Marine Ltd*[36] the question arose as to whether the shape of a completed sailing dinghy was registrable. Danckwerts LJ said (at 19):

34 Laddie *et al* consider Lord Oliver's judgment wrong on this point; Laddie, H. *et al* (1995) *The Modern Law of Copyright and Designs* (2nd edn), Butterworths, para 30.64.

35 *Per* Aldous J in *Valeo Vision SA v Flexible Lamps Ltd* [1995] RPC 205 at 215.

36 [1965] Ch 1. This case is notable in that it recognised indirect copyright infringement of drawings. An important aspect of the case was whether the shape of the boat was registrable because of the exception from copyright subsistence of anything which could have been registered as a design: Copyright Act 1956 s 10(1) (now repealed).

> It was suggested that the one thing which was registrable was the shape of the completed dinghy ... I feel the greatest doubt whether this was correct. I should have thought that the shape of the boat was necessarily functional.

Would this be true of a new shape of hull designed for performance and appearance or a new shape of sail which was both functional and attractive? Of course, the shape of a boat hull is dictated to some extent by its function – it has to comply with certain rules of hydrodynamics and physics so that it can perform its function efficiently – but a number of alternatives are feasible, as evidenced by the large variety of shapes and profiles made, although many are the result of attempts to achieve the most efficient shape for the particular type of craft concerned. It is undeniable that, in the case of small vessels purchased for pleasure, eye-appeal is a factor in the design equation.

### 'Must-match' exception

The importance of a right to a free market in spare parts was stressed in the *British Leyland* case.[37] The full application of design law to spare parts would

37 *British Leyland Motor Corp Ltd v Armstrong Patents Co Ltd* [1986] 2 WLR 400.

work against such a free market. For example, if a vehicle manufacturer was allowed to register the shape of the body panels of his cars then he could charge exorbitant prices for replacement panels and refuse to grant licences to third-party parts manufacturers, or grant licences only in return for a hefty royalty. In the White Paper that preceded the Copyright, Designs and Patents Act 1988,[38] the Government spelt out its plans to exclude spare parts from the protection of the design right. Because some spare parts would be registrable as designs, the government also stated its intention to extend the exclusion to the Registered Designs Act 1949.[39]

The must-match exception is fairly narrow and applies only if the design features are dependent upon the appearance of another article and it is the author's intention that his articles form an integral part of the other article.[40] An example is a door panel for a car. This obviously forms an integral part of the car. But the question is not so simple in relation to some spare parts. The question of registrability of spare parts for motor vehicles was considered in *Ford Motor Co Ltd & Iveco Fiat SpA's Design Applications*.[41] The judge classified spare parts in two groups. The first group, which the judge decided were excluded by s 1(1)(b)(ii) from registration, covered main body panels, doors, bonnet lids, boot lids and windscreens.[42] He gave an example of a door panel as being an article which is intended by the author of the design to form an integral part of another article, being the vehicle. The second group of components, such as wing mirrors, wheels, seats and steering wheels, can be made in a variety of designs to fit a particular vehicle as substitutions for the original parts while leaving the shape and general appearance of the vehicle unaffected. For example, the owner of a car might buy differently designed parts to give his car a sportier appearance. Such parts are registrable as designs provided the other requirements (for example, novelty) are satisfied. However, the House of Lords concentrated on whether the component was an 'article' within s 44(1) of the Act rather than basing exception from registrability on 'must-match'.[43]

The fact that the main body panels of a vehicle are unlikely to be registrable as designs does not prevent the shape of the entire vehicle being registered. However, the degree of similarity in vehicle design must be taken into account and much of the overall shape of a vehicle will not be new. This is especially important when it comes to considering infringement, and it may be that a comparison between the registered design and an alleged infringement will concentrate on details rather than the overall shape.

### Works primarily of a literary or artistic nature

Other exceptions have been provided for by statutory instrument, under the Registered Designs Rules 1995.[44] These excluded designs fall mainly within the scope of copyright and are:

(a) works of sculpture (but not casts or models for multiple articles made by any industrial process);

(b) wall plaques, medals and medallions;

(c) printed matter primarily of a literary or artistic character, including book jackets, calendars, certificates, coupons, dress-making patterns, greeting cards, labels, leaflets, maps, plans, playing cards, postcards, stamps, trade advertisements, trade forms and cards, transfers and similar articles. Such items are left within the scope of full copyright protection only.

---

**38** 'Intellectual Property and Innovation', Cmnd 9712 (HMSO, 1986).

**39** For example, 'protection would be available only for truly aesthetic, stand alone designs where competitors do not need to be able to copy such designs in order to compete effectively', *per* Lord Young of Graftham, HL Deb 12 November 1987, col. 1479.

**40** All the features must be dependent upon the appearance of the other article: *Valeo Vision SA* v *Flexible Lamps Ltd* [1995] RPC 205. It matters not which article was made or designed first.

**41** [1993] RPC 399. *See* the discussion of the House of Lords decision supra.

**42** The judge also decided that these parts were not articles within the meaning in the Registered Designs Act 1949 s 44 and unregistrable on this count also. The case is notable in that the judge considered the policy behind the changes to the Registered Designs Act 1949 and he considered some of the Parlimentary Debates, in accordance with the decision in *Pepper (Inspector of Taxes)* v *Hart* [1993] All ER 42.

**43** The effect of this approach is that the must-match exception, which exercised so many minds in the period leading up to amendments made to registered design law by the Copyright, Designs and Patents Act 1988, is probably redundant.

**44** The Registered Design Rules 1995, SI 1995/2912 r 26.

An identical list of items is excluded from the operation of s 52 of the Copyright, Designs and Patents Act 1988, which restricts copyright to 25 years for certain exploited artistic works.[45] In *Lamson Industries Ltd's Application*[46] it was held that computer print-out paper having alternating coloured bands on it was not an article consisting of printed matter primarily of a literary character.

## Other exceptions

The Registered Designs Rules also allow the Registrar to insist on consent in respect of the use of portraits of Her Majesty or any member of the royal family, armorial bearings, flags of any country, insignia, etc,[47] the consent being that of any official or other person as appears to the Registrar to be entitled to give such consent. If the design includes the portrait of a living or recently dead person then the Registrar may seek the consent of the person, if living, or of the personal representative before proceeding with the registration.[48] The rules do not define 'recently dead' – presumably this lies within the Registrar's discretion.

Further exceptions lie within the Registrar's discretion. Under the Registered Designs Act 1949 s 3(3), the Registrar may refuse an application or accept it subject to modifications as he thinks fit. Additionally, under s 43(1), the Registrar will not register a design which, in his opinion, would be contrary to law or morality. In *Re Masterman's Application*[49] the Registrar had refused an application for registration of a design in respect of a Scots doll with a kilt which when lifted exposed mimic male genitalia. The Registrar had objected on the basis of both ss 3(3) and 43(1), and because of the judgment of Evershed J in *La Marquise Footwear's Application*[50] disapproving of registration of designs showing representations of genitalia. It was held that the Registrar's decision should be exercised judicially, not administratively. A design which would offend the moral principles of right thinking members of society should not be registered, but in the present case the worst that could be said about the design was that some people might find it distasteful, and that would not be a good enough reason to deprive the applicant of protection against infringement of her design.

## OWNERSHIP OF REGISTERED DESIGN

The person creating a design is known as the author of that design and the basic rule is that the author is entitled to be the original proprietor of the design.[51] There are exceptions to this basic rule, and if the design is commissioned for money or money's worth, the person commissioning the design is, under the Registered Designs Act 1949 s 2(1A), the original proprietor.[52] Otherwise, under s 2(1B), if the design is created by an employee in the course of employment, the employer is treated as the original proprietor. The person by whom the arrangements necessary for the creation of a computer-generated design are made is taken to be the author of the design. A computer-generated design (as with original works of copyright) is one which is generated by computer in circumstances such that there is no human author. What has already been said in relation to computer-generated copyright works also applies here (*see* Chapter 8).

There is a difference as regards first ownership between registered designs and copyright in that the commissioners of designs are automatically given the

**45** Copyright (Industrial Processes and Excluded Articles) (No. 2) Order 1989, SI 1989/1070 reg 2.

**46** [1978] RPC 1.

**47** The Registered Designs Rules 1995, SI 1995/2912 r 24.

**48** Ibid r 25.

**49** [1991] RPC 89.

**50** (1947) 64 RPC 27.

**51** Registered Designs Act 1949 s 2. Proprietorship is equivalent to ownership in copyright law.

**52** Importers, retailers and licensees of the owner of a design are not entitled to be the proprietor: *Lazarus v Charles* (1873) 16 Eq 117; *Re Guitermans Registered Design* (1886) 55 LJ ChD 309.

right of ownership of a registrable design. This little inconvenience is exaggerated when the ownership of the design right is considered, because s 3(2) requires that a person making an application to register a design must also be the owner of the design right where it subsists concurrently in the design.[53] Usually, a person commissioning a design will be the proprietor of the registered design and also will be the owner of the design right. In some cases, however, a design right will be owned by the person first marketing articles made to the design in the UK, and this could be a different person to the intending proprietor of the registrable design. This is unlikely because the qualification requirements for the design right extend to member states of the European Community and certain other designated countries. An example is, in relation to a design which is registrable and in which the design right is capable of subsisting, where a Chinese national resident in China is commissioned by a Saudi Arabian company to create the design. Articles made to the design are then marketed in the European Community by an Italian company. The Saudi Arabian company would be entitled to register the design but for the fact that the Italian company is the owner of the design right. On the basis of s 3(2), an application for registration of the design in the UK must be refused.[54] This ludicrous situation should not come about by assignment because, under s 19(3B), an assignment of the design right automatically includes an assignment of the registered design if their respective owners are one and the same and a contrary intention does not appear. Similarly, an assignment of a registered design automatically carries with it an assignment of the design right, unless the latter is owned by someone other than the proprietor of the registered design.[55] If the design right is later assigned without an assignment of the registered design, the court has the power to order rectification of the register on the application of any person aggrieved (s 20(1)).[56]

The Registered Designs Act 1949 s 2(2) envisages the situation where the design or the right to apply the design to any article is assigned, or is otherwise transmitted to another person. The transferee becomes the proprietor. Joint proprietorship is expressly provided for where one of the proprietors is the original proprietor, and both are treated as being 'the proprietor'. No mention is made of other forms of joint proprietorship such as where a registered design is assigned to two third parties, but this is implicit in the language of s 19. It is possible that transmission is limited to the application of the design in relation to specific articles only. There are provisions for registration of assignments of a registered design by s 19. This section confirms that a registered design can be dealt with in other ways, for example, by a mortgage or licence. Equitable rights are not abrogated by the registration of a design. Proprietors, co-proprietors and persons with legal and equitable interests in a registered design may apply for registration of title or interest, which will be done on proof of the same. A person having an interest must also show a corresponding interest in the design right where such right subsists in the design.[57] There are no requirements in the Act as to the form of any assignment, licence or other transaction. However, in the vast majority of cases, there will be some formal document effecting or recording the transaction. Particulars of the instrument or event by which a person becomes entitled to the registered design or a share in it or other interest in the registered design shall, under s 19(3), be entered in the register. Where the transaction is an assignment and the threshold for stamp duty is reached, the registrar should not enter the details unless the

**53** Indeed, Designs Form 2A, the application form for design registration, contains a declaration to the effect that the applicant claims to own any design right subsisting in the design.

**54** Of course, the Italian company could assign its design right to the Saudi Arabian company to overcome this problem.

**55** The Copyright, Designs and Patents Act 1988 s 224.

**56** The Registrar may also cancel the registration under the Registered Designs Act 1949 s 11(2).

**57** Ibid s 19(3A).

document is stamped. The person entitled under the transaction is responsible for applying for registration,[58] though the person from whom he derived his title or interest may apply to register the transaction if he wishes to.[59]

It is essential that assignments and interests such as licences and mortgages are entered on the register in a timely manner as, under s 19(5), the document evidencing the transaction will not be admissible in court as evidence of title or other interest unless the court otherwise directs. Therefore, if a registered design has been assigned and the assignment has not been registered there are two problems for the assignee. First, he may be vulnerable to later transactions that are registered and, secondly, he may be prevented from suing for infringement. The court does, however, have a discretion and may nevertheless admit the document for evidence, for example, where an assignee or licensee has been the victim of some fraud perpetrated by the assignor or licensor in collusion with a third party infringer. Another example is where there is a contractual dispute between the assignor or licensor and the assignee or licensee.

## RIGHTS GIVEN BY REGISTRATION AND INFRINGEMENT

The Registered Designs Act 1949 s 7 deals with the rights attendant upon registration of a design and also defines infringement of those rights. Registration of a design gives the registered proprietor certain exclusive rights in relation to an article embodying the design, that is an article in respect of which the design is registered and to which the design or one not substantially different has been applied. Those rights are:

(a) to make or import for sale or hire or for use for the purposes of a trade or business;
(b) to sell, hire or offer or expose for sale or hire.[60]

Any person who does any of the above acts without the licence of the registered proprietor infringes the right in the registered design. As with copyright law, the issue of substantiality is central to the question of infringement; however, for registered designs, the question appears to be one of comparing the differences between the two designs. For example, in *Matthew Swain Ltd v Thomas Barker & Sons Ltd*[61] a baking tray having right-angled, goal-post shaped separating wires was held not to infringe a baking tray having semi-circular separating wires. The novel features of the design related to the separating wires. In *Benchairs Ltd v Chair Centre Ltd*,[62] concerning an alleged infringement of a design for a chair, it was said that the court should look at and compare the chairs made by the plaintiff and the defendant, separately and together, and observe the similarities and differences. Whether the defendant's design was substantially different from the plaintiff's design was a matter of comparing the designs as a whole and the supposed views on this matter of people buying or using articles made to the design was a relevant factor in making the comparison.

It is clear that what must be compared is not the articles as a whole, but only those features which are the subject matter of the design registration. Where the design consists of more than one feature the summation of the features should be used to determine whether infringement has occurred, and it is insufficient if there is a resemblance in one of the features if the summation of the designs

58 Section 19(1).

59 Section 19(4).

60 Ibid s 7(1).

61 [1967] RPC 23.

62 [1974] RPC 429.

being compared is substantially different. In *Best Products Ltd* v *F W Wool-worth & Co Ltd*,[63] the plaintiff's design had been applied to a whistling kettle. The design comprised three features: the shape of the body, the shape of the handle, and the shape of the spout. The defendant's kettle was held not to infringe because the spout on his kettle was substantially different to that on the plaintiff's kettle. The spout was an important and prominent feature of the design as a whole.

Novelty statements for registered designs are usually brief and not particularly specific. A common formula is 'the novelty of the design resides in the shape and/or configuration of the article shown in the representation'.[64] Sometimes, already-known features may be excluded (and coloured blue on the representation of the design) and there may be a disclaimer as to any words or numerals that appear in the design. The overall result is that the novelty statement is not usually particularly helpful in testing for infringement and it is the representation of the design that is more important, that is, its visual significance.

Some designs are a totally new departure from what was already known, whereas others differ only by details from what was known before. In the former case comparison between the registered design and the alleged infringement should concentrate on the general form of the new design (where novelty is based on shape and configuration). However, where the novel features are restricted only to details, the comparison should concentrate on such details when testing for infringement. So it was held in *Gaskell & Chambers Ltd* v *Measure Master Ltd*[65] by Aldous J, who decided that the plaintiff's registered design for a spirits dispenser as used in public houses was not infringed by the defendant's spirit measure. The plaintiff's dispenser was a substantial departure from the prior art, and although the defendant's design bore a family resemblance to the plaintiff's design, it was substantially different when judged as a whole.

The details of the defendant's spirit measure were different to the equivalent features of the plaintiff's spirit measure. Although the generality of the two designs was similar, to give protection to such generality could result in an undesirably strong right. The plaintiff's spirit measure used a clear round convex lens at the front with a round bezel and flange for a label and having a downward pointing lever against which a glass could be pushed in order to dispense the drink. There were differences in all these features between the two designs. To extend the protection afforded by the plaintiff's registered design to the defendant's design would prevent anyone making spirit measures that had those simple features. That would give a very strong monopoly approaching that given by a patent.

If the design is not a totally new departure from existing designs and differs only in minor respects, then minor differences between the registered design and the alleged infringement might be quite influential. In *Simmons* v *Mathieson & Co*[66] Fletcher Moulton LJ said (at 490):

> ... if very small differences are to make a thing new or original [the phrase 'new or original' was the basic novelty requirement], very small differences must take you out of the ambit of the registration ...

The reason being that, were it otherwise, infringement would be founded largely on the prior article.

The decision as to whether another design infringes a registered design is based on a comparison of those features that appeal to and are judged by the

63 [1964] RPC 226.

64 If the design relates to surface decoration, the words 'pattern and/or ornament' may be used instead.

65 [1993] RPC 76.

66 (1911) 28 RPC 486.

eye. The relevant 'eye' is that of the interested customer, who should be considered as looking at the two designs side by side. He should then go away and come back later to the alleged infringement. In this way, the court may conclude which design features would strike the eye and be remembered when deciding whether the designs are or are not substantially different.[67]

In some circumstances, the concept of 'imperfect recollection' may be used to test for substantial difference. Infringement may be evaluated not just on the basis of a side by side comparison but by seeing the registered design and, having gone away and come back, deciding whether the other article had the same design applied to it.[68] Would an informed customer or potential customer, having an imperfect recollection, be likely to confuse the registered design with the alleged infringing design? The court will compare the design by looking through the eyes of this hypothetical customer on the basis that he would be interested in the particular design and not merely interested in obtaining an article of the particular type without caring about its design. In view of the 'aesthetic considerations' requirements[69] this test should be relevant in all cases, otherwise the design would have been refused registration. An example of the application of this test is given by the case of *Sommer Allibert (UK) Ltd* v *Flair Plastics Ltd*[70] The plaintiff registered a design to be applied to plastic garden chairs. The backrest had vertical grooves and the seat had grooves running from front to back. The defendant imported a plastic garden chair having horizontal grooves on the backrest and sideways grooves on the seats. After surviving an attack on the validity of the registration,[71] it was held in the Court of Appeal that the defendant's chairs did not infringe the design because no informed customer, even having imperfect recollection, would be likely to confuse the defendant's chair with the plaintiff's chair.

Infringement may also come about in other ways if done without the licence of the registered proprietor:

1 making anything for enabling *any such article* to be made anywhere;[72]
2 doing anything in relation to a kit which would infringe if done to the assembled article;
3 making anything for enabling a kit to be made or assembled anywhere if the assembled article embodies the design.

A 'kit' means a complete or substantially complete set of components intended to be assembled into an article (s 7(4)). However, there can be no infringement in respect of things done before the date that a certificate of registration was granted. Furthermore, there is no infringement of those features of shape or configuration of an article which are excluded by virtue of s 1(1)(b), if any. Reverse analysis of an article made to a design does not infringe *per se*, but there might be an infringement depending upon how the knowledge thus gained is utilised.[73]

A would-be copier is defeated in attempting to overcome the right by making the article in a kit of parts. However, the protection does not extend to details which would not be registrable in their own right, for example, the right does not cover fastening devices used to assemble the parts. In *Dorling* v *Honnor Marine Ltd*[74] Harman LJ said:

> ... I do not think that kits of parts are 'things made for enabling any such article to be made'. It is true that they may be parts of the article but they are not made in order to enable it to be made. If it were otherwise I do not see where one can stop: the words in their widest significance would include the screws and glue used to fasten the parts together.

67 *Gaskell & Chambers Ltd* v *Measures Master Ltd* [1993] RPC 76.

68 *Valor Heating Co Ltd* v *Main Gas Appliances Ltd* [1973] RPC 871.

69 The Registered Designs Act 1949 (amended by the Copyright, Designs and Patents Act 1988).

70 [1987] RPC 599.

71 It had been claimed that the grooves were pattern or ornament and the registration was defective because it relied only upon features of shape and configuration. It was held that the grooves, being three-dimensional, were features of shape and configuration, regardless of the intention of applying them to the chairs. Other objections, raised on the basis that the design was similar to a prior registration and had been published prior to registration, also failed.

72 The Registered Designs Act 1949 s 7(3) – the phrase used is 'in the United Kingdom or elsewhere'. 'Any such article' means any article in respect of which the design is registered and to which that design or one not substantially different has been applied.

73 Reverse analysis, in this context, means taking an article apart and examining its component parts in order to determine the design attributes.

74 [1965] Ch 1.

## DEFENCES TO INFRINGEMENT ACTIONS

Defences to an action for infringement of a registered design will, as is often the case with patent lawsuits, include an attack on the validity of the registration. For example, the defendant may choose to claim that:

1 the design was not new when registered;[75]
2 the registration has expired – this includes expiry by s 8(5) where a design was, at the time it was registered, a 'corresponding design' and the copyright has expired;[76]
3 the design is primarily of a literary or artistic nature and excluded by the Registered Designs Rules 1995;[77]
4 the design is contrary to law or morality and should not have been accepted for registration by the Registrar, or he has otherwise exercised his discretion as to registration incorrectly (a judicial test).

The defence may be in the form of the *Gillette* defence,[78] favoured by defendants in patent actions. In this context, the defence is that either the alleged infringing design is not within the registered design or the registered design is invalid for lack of novelty because the alleged infringing design was not novel at the time of filing the registration. A recent example of this defence being raised in a registered design case is *Carflow Products (UK) Ltd* v *Linwood Securities (Birmingham) Ltd*.[79] The court dismissed the plaintiff's action and gave the defendant leave to discontinue its counterclaim, leaving undecided whether the registered design was, in fact, invalid.

In attacking the validity of a registered design it is acceptable, within reason, for the defendant to plead all close prior art to show lack of novelty.[80] This is unlike the situation with patents where the cited prior art must be kept within realistic boundaries. The reason for the difference of approach is that comparing prior patent specifications is a difficult and time-consuming operation, whereas with registered designs, where visual significance only is important, it is much easier to compare numerous examples of prior art.

In any proceedings where the validity of a registered design is contested and the court holds that the registration is valid, it may certify that the validity of the registration was so contested (s 25 of the Registered Designs Act 1949). The effect of this is that, in future actions involving infringement of the design or its validity, the plaintiff is automatically entitled to his legal costs should the final award or order be made in his favour.

If there is no doubt about the validity of the registration, other defences that might be raised include:

1 the plaintiff does not have *locus standi*, for example, he is not the proprietor of the design;[81]
2 the alleged infringement does not relate to those details of the design claimed in the registration;
3 the defendant's design is substantially different from that of the plaintiff;
4 the alleged infringement occurred before registration (but the design right, if it also subsists in the design, could be infringed);[82]
5 the alleged infringement concerns only those features left out of account when determining whether the plaintiff's design was registrable;[83]

75 The Registered Designs Act 1949 s 11 contains provisions concerning applications for cancellation of registration.

76 A 'corresponding design' is one which, in relation to an artistic work, if applied to an article would produce something which would be a copy of the artistic work: the Registered Design Act 1949 s 44.

77 SI 1995/2912.

78 Named after *Gillette Safety Razor Co v Anglo-American Trading Co Ltd* (1913) 30 RPC 465.

79 [1996] FSR 424.

80 *Lone Star Toys Ltd* v *J M Enterprises of Wetherby Ltd* [1996] FSR 857. Laddie J said that he had no great difficulty in comparing some ten or 15 lanterns which looked like pumpkins cut out as Halloween masks.

81 Or the document evidencing the plaintiff's right or interest in the registered design has not been registered and is not, under s 19(5), admissible in evidence, unless the court otherwise directs.

82 The Registered Designs Act 1949 s 7(5).

83 Ibid s 7(6).

6 the act constituting the alleged infringement was done in good faith or seriously prepared for in good faith after expiry of the registration and before publication of an application for restoration of the right.[84]

A further possibility exists for an infringer when licences are available as of right in respect of the design. Under s 11B, the defendant can undertake to take a licence on terms to be agreed or, failing agreement, on terms to be fixed by the Registrar. If the defendant makes such an undertaking, an injunction will not be granted against him and the amount recoverable in damages or by way of an account of profits shall not exceed double the amount that he would have paid had he obtained a licence on those terms before the earliest infringement. However, unlike the design right, few registered designs will be subject to licences as of right.

There is provision in the Registered Designs Act 1949 for a remedy against groundless threats of infringement proceedings, whether by circulars, advertisement or otherwise.[85] The remedies for groundless threats of infringement proceedings are:

(a) a declaration to the effect that the threats are unjustifiable;
(b) an injunction against the continuation of the threats;
(c) damages, if any have been sustained – for example, the aggrieved party's business may have been detrimentally affected by the threats, or his sales of the articles concerned may have been adversely affected.

It would seem that this provision extends to the situation where a person publicises his views that another design infringes his registration and that he will take legal action for infringement. The burden of proof remains with the person making the threats, that is that the acts (or contemplated acts) complained of infringe the right in the registered design, although the plaintiff would have to show that the registration is valid. Because of this, there is little, if anything, to be gained by making such threats; and if they are without substance, the person making them could find himself liable for any harm caused to the other's business as a result of the threats. Another point is that suing for such groundless threats may precipitate an infringement action.[86]

## REMEDIES

The Registered Designs Act 1949 does not specifically state what remedies are available, although s 9 makes it clear that injunctions and damages are possible remedies: s 11B also mentions an account of profits. An award of damages is not available if the defendant can show that, at the time of infringement, he was not aware and had not reasonable grounds for supposing that the design was registered.[87] It makes good sense, therefore, for a notice to be placed upon articles incorporating the design. However, to be effective, such a notice would have to include the registration number in addition to the word 'registered' or some abbreviation thereof. Merely affixing the words 'Registered Design' would, under s 9(1), appear to be insufficient, but how in such a case a defendant could argue that he had no reasonable grounds for supposing that the design incorporated in the article was not a registered design is hard to imagine. An official form of notice was used in Victorian times to indicate registration, as shown in Figure 17.1.

84 Ibid s 8B(4). In this situation, the person doing what would otherwise be an infringement may continue to do so even after restoration.

85 Ibid s 26. The scope of 'otherwise' could give rise to problems, for example, would it extend to threats made over the telephone?

86 *Rosedale Associated Manufacturers Ltd v Airfix Products Ltd* [1957] RPC 239.

87 The Registered Designs Act 1949 s 9(1).

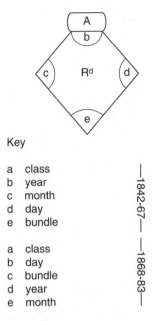

**Figure 17.1 Notice of design registration applied to articles**

(Kindly supplied by the Design Registry.)

Even if damages are not available because of lack of actual or constructive awareness of the right, s 9(2) makes it clear that an injunction still may be granted. An account of profits may also be available regardless of the defendant's lack of knowledge. Orders also may be granted for the destruction of or for the delivery up of infringing articles.[88]

## LICENCES – COMPULSORY AND AS OF RIGHT

Any person may apply to the Registrar for a compulsory licence in respect of a design which is not being applied to the articles for which it is registered to a reasonable extent.[89] This prevents an abuse of the registration by a proprietor who is happy to sit on the design and not exploit it for the time being. The Registrar may make any order he thinks fit. This will include the fixing of royalty payments due under the compulsory licence. Under s 10(2), an order for the grant of a compulsory licence shall take effect as if it were an executed deed. Licences available as of right in respect of a design may be provided for by the Registrar by making an entry on the register to that effect following application to the Registrar by the appropriate Minister or Ministers after a report by the Monopolies and Mergers Commission.[90] The report must contain conclusions that one of the following situations exists which operates or may operate against the public interest:

(a) a monopoly situation
(b) a merger situation which qualifies for investigation
(c) a person engaged in an anti-competitive practice
(d) a person pursuing a course of conduct covered by the Competition Act 1980 s 11 (abuses of monopolies by nationalised industries).

88 *See*, for example, *P B Cow & Co Ltd v Cannon Rubber Manufacturers Ltd* [1959] RPC 240.

89 The Registered Designs Act 1949 s 10.

90 Ibid s 11(A).

Apart from declaring licences available as of right, the Registrar may cancel or modify any conditions in licences granted by the proprietor in respect of the registered design. Failing agreement as to the terms of a licence as of right, the Registrar has the power to fix those terms. There is an appeal procedure to an Appeal Tribunal constituted under the Registered Designs Act 1949 s 28.

If a person has obtained the right to do an act which would have been an infringement by means of the time lag between expiry of the registration and notice of application for restoration of the right, that person may not grant a licence to another person to do that act; although if the act or the preparation for the act was done in the course of business he may assign that right, or it may transmit on his death to any person acquiring the relevant part of the business. He may also authorise any business partners for the time being to perform the act.

## OFFENCES

There are three offences directly associated with registered designs; and if such an offence is committed by a body corporate with the consent or connivance of an officer of the body, such as a director, manager or secretary, that person in addition to the corporate body is guilty of the offence.[91] This also applies to persons purporting to act in such a capacity.

Under s 35, it is an offence for a person falsely to represent that a design applied to any article sold by him is registered in respect of that article. 'Represented' has a restricted meaning in that the offender must have affixed the word 'registered', or any other word(s) to the effect that the design is registered, to the article, for example by stamping, engraving or impressing such word(s). Word of mouth is not sufficient. The liability appears to be strict, albeit in a very narrow sense. For example, it is committed by a person selling the article who has impressed the word 'registered' believing that the design is subject to a valid registration and that he has the right to so mark the article.[92] This offence is triable summarily only and carries a fine not exceeding level 3 on the standard scale (currently £1000). It is also an offence to mark articles in a like fashion after expiry of the right in a registered design. This offence could easily be committed by the proprietor of a recently expired design. However, selling articles to which a design relates after expiry of the design registration is not an offence provided the articles were marked before the expiry of the right.

Section 34 deals with the falsification of the register of designs. It is an offence, triable either way, to make or cause to be made either a false entry on the register or a counterfeit copy of a register entry. The falsification offence extends to producing, tendering or causing to be produced or tendered in evidence a counterfeit copy of an entry in the register. *Mens rea* is required for this offence, that is the person involved must know that the entry or written copy is false. Constructive knowledge is not sufficient. If tried on indictment, the maximum punishment is a term of imprisonment not exceeding two years, or a fine or both. On summary conviction a person may be sentenced to imprisonment for a term not exceeding six months, or a fine not exceeding the statutory maximum (currently £5000) or both. Because the offence is worded 'makes or causes to be made', it could apply to the Registrar and his staff in addition to others.

91 Ibid s 35(A).

92 Ibid s 35(2). Liability is strict in a narrow sense because it will not apply, for example, where the person is a dealer who sells such articles which were already marked when he obtained them. The person has to do the marking himself. However, other offences might be committed, such as obtaining by deception: the Theft Act 1968 s 15.

The Registered Designs Act 1949 s 5 concerns requirements for secrecy in respect of designs which are relevant for defence purposes and allows the Registrar, subject to notification by the Secretary of State, to issue instructions prohibiting or restricting the publication or communication of information pertaining to such a design. Written permission may also be required by a person resident in the UK before an application can be made outside the UK for the registration of a design of a prescribed class. Any person who fails to comply with such instructions, or who makes or causes to be made such an application, commits an offence under s 33. The offence is triable either way and carries the same penalties as an offence under s 34.

## REGISTRATION

The procedures for registration are comprehensively provided for by the Registered Designs Act 1949 and the Registered Designs Rules 1995, and reference to the relevant sections and rules should be made for the fine detail. Applications for registration are handled by the Designs Registry which is a branch of the Patent Office, which publishes a document 'Design Registration' which outlines the procedures for registration.[93] There is no requirement that the proprietor is either a citizen of or resident in the UK, but under the Registered Designs Rules (r 8) he must have an address in the UK for service and this address will be entered on the register. The current fee for registering a design is £60.[94] There will be other expenses, such as those incurred in the preparation of drawings or photographs, and many proprietors use the services of an agent. Other fees are payable if, for example, a clerical error in the application has to be corrected. Following application, an examination and search is carried out at the Designs Registry and, if the Registrar does not object to the application, a certificate of registration will be issued. In straightforward cases, registration should be completed within about three to four months. Articles incorporating the design may be made or sold immediately following filing of the application, although it should be noted that there can be no action for any infringement occurring before the date of grant of the certificate. Of course, if the design right also subsists in the design, an action may be based on this for such infringement.

It was anticipated that changes to design law, especially the removal of copyright protection of designs through their drawings, would produce a rush of applications, especially after 1 August 1989 when the new provisions came into force. There was a slight increase in 1989, but the number of applications has fallen back and remains disappointing. The transitional arrangements may account for this as designs existing prior to 1 August 1989 can still enjoy copyright protection for their design documents until 1999.[95] For many designs created on or after 1 August 1989, the owner may hope to rely on the design right – although it does not give a monopoly right like the registered design.

Table 17.1 shows the numbers of applications and registrations for designs since 1987.[96] The proportion of foreign applicants is notable (a UK registration is accepted in a number of other countries with or without local re-registration). It should also be noted that the volume of registrations was much higher during Victorian times, often being in excess of 20 000 per annum.

93 July 1993. This publication includes a specimen application.

94 Registered Designs (Fees) (No.2) Rules 1995, SI 1995/2913. The fee for designs applied to lace or designs consisting mainly of stripes and checks applied to textiles is £35. The fee for a design applied to a set of articles is £90.

95 Copyright, Designs and Patents Act 1988 s 237, Sch 1 para 19(1). However, licences are available as of right in the last five years: para 19(2).

96 The Patent Office, *Annual Report and Accounts* 1996–1997 (The Stationery Office, 1997).

## Table 17.1  Registered design activity

| Year | Applications | Proportion from foreign applicants % | Designs registered |
|------|-------------|--------------------------------------|--------------------|
| 1987 | 8646 | 51.9 | 7140 |
| 1988 | 8748 | 55.5 | 8049 |
| 1989 | 9317 | 58.9 | 8945 |
| 1990 | 8566 | 55.1 | 9171 |
| 1991 | 8074 | 61.4 | 6271 |
| 1992 | 8267 | 66.8 | 8175 |
| 1993 | 8179 | 68.6 | 8301 |
| 1994 | 8523 | 68.5 | 8261 |
| 1995 | 9246 | 67.6 | 8380 |
| 1996 | 9293 | 67.6 | 8970 |

Because of the time lag between application and grant, the annual totals for designs registered do not necessarily apply to applications made in the same calendar year. There is a priority system and the priority of an earlier application elsewhere may be claimed for up to six months.

### Duration, renewal and restoration of lapsed registration

The initial registration period is five years from the date as of which the design is registered. Registration may be renewed for a second, third, fourth and fifth period of five years. Most designs have a limited commercial life and it is unlikely that many will be renewed for a fourth or fifth period. In 1996, a total of 3322 designs were renewed for a second period and only 1512 were renewed for a third period. It will be the year 2004 before any designs will be renewable for a fourth period as designs registered before 1 August 1989 can be registered for a maximum of 15 years only. There is effectively a period of six months' grace, during which time the registration can be renewed without affecting its validity. If the design was first registered prior to 1 August 1989, the renewal must be made within that six-month period otherwise the right is lost forever.[97] However, in relation to designs first registered on or after 1 August 1989, there is a further six-months period during which the right can be restored.[98] The Registrar publishes notices of applications for restoration, but it is not an automatic right, the Registrar has a discretion and must be satisfied that the proprietor took reasonable care to see that the period of registration was extended in accordance with either ss 8(2) or 8(4). If restoration is applied for and granted there are some effects as regards infringement of the right. Figure 17.2 applies to a design first registered on or after 1 August 1989.

Referring to Figure 17.2, during the period **A** to **B** the right may be renewed (provided it has not previously been renewed for a fifth period of five years) on payment of the appropriate renewal fee plus an additional fee of £18 per month. Under s 8(4), the design is treated as if it had never expired. For the sake of argument, imagine that an application to restore the right is made at time **C**. Then, even if the restoration is permitted, a person may acquire rights in respect of the design if, during the period **B** to **C**, he began an act in good

97 Designs first registered prior to 1 August 1989 cannot be renewed beyond a third five-year period.

98 The Registered Designs Act 1949 s 8A refers to a prescribed period during which the right can be restored. By the Registered Designs Rules 1995, SI 1995/2912 r 41, the prescribed period is 12 months from the date on which the right expired.

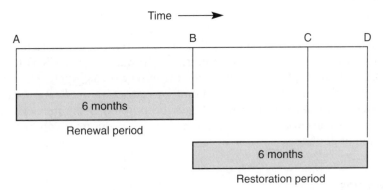

Time ⟶

A                       B          C          D

6 months
Renewal period

6 months
Restoration period

A is the date of expiry of the registration
B is the last date for renewal of the registration
C is the actual date of an application for restoration
D is the last date for application of renewal

Note that the restoration period applies only to designs registered on or after 1 August 1989.

**Figure 17.2  Renewal and restoration of registered design**

99 The right is to do the act or to continue to do the act: the Registered Designs Act 1949 s 8A(4). Section 8A(5) allows business partners and acquirers of the person's business to do the acts.

100 Ibid s 8A(3).

101 Registered Designs (Fees) (No. 2) Rules 1995, SI 1995/2913. The fees for renewal for the fourth and fifth terms have not yet been set. It will be some time before any of the designs will reach this stage.

faith or made effective and serious preparations to do such an act.[99] If the registration is restored, acts which would normally have infringed the design which were done during the period **A** to **B** are treated as infringing acts, as are continuations or repetitions of earlier infringing acts. However, an act which would have infringed which was carried out during the period **B** to **C** gives the proprietor no remedy unless it was a repeat of an earlier infringing act.[100] Fees for renewal are £130 for a second term and £210 for a third term. Restoration fees amount to £240 plus the renewal fee.[101]

## INTERNATIONAL PROTECTION

Some countries, mainly belonging to the Commonwealth, recognise registration in the UK as being equivalent to registration in the country concerned. A large number of these countries (over 30) extend protection to UK registered designs without the need for local registration. These countries include Antigua, Bermuda, Botswana, Cyprus, Fiji, Ghana, Gibraltar, Kenya, Malaysia, Sierre Leone, Uganda, and the Yeminite Arab Republic. Persons and organisations in these countries desiring protection for their designs normally register them at the UK Designs Registry through an agent based in the United Kingdom.

Other countries and territories, such as Guernsey, Jersey, Malta and Tanzania, extend protection to UK registered designs, subject to local re-registration of the design.

If protection is required in another country, apart from those that recognise a UK registration, application must be made in each country for which protection is sought. The Paris Convention for Industrial Property 1883 has been ratified by most of the industrialised countries in the world and a person who has applied for registration of a design in any of the Convention countries is effectively given a priority with respect to applications to other Convention countries made within six months following the first application.[102] The Designs (Convention Countries) Order 1993 has extended these provisions to a number of 'new' countries, such as Belarus, Croatia, the Czech Republic, and the Russian Federation, amongst others.[103] A resident of the UK is forbidden to make such an application until after the expiry of six weeks from the UK application,[104] or if directions prohibiting or restricting publication, etc. have been given by the Registrar. It has already been noted in the previous chapter that there is some variation in legal methods used by different countries for the protection of designs.

## CROWN USE

In common with patents and the design right, the Crown can make use of the subject matter of the right. As regards registered designs, the Registered Designs Act 1949 Sch 1 contains the necessary provisions. Under para 1(1), any government department may use, or authorise the use of, any registered design for the services of the Crown. Terms must be agreed, either before or after use, between the government department concerned and the registered proprietor with the approval of the Treasury. If agreement cannot be reached, the terms are to be determined by reference to the High Court. 'The services of the Crown' are defined in para 1(6) and include:

(a) the supply to the government of a country outside the UK of articles required for the defence of that country or of any other country, subject to an agreement or arrangement involving Her Majesty's Government;
(b) the supply to the UN or any country belonging to the UN of articles required for any armed forces operating in pursuance of a UN resolution, subject to an agreement or arrangement involving Her Majesty's Government.

This is not an exhaustive definition, it merely indicates that the above situations fall within the meaning of 'Crown use'. It would also extend to use for the armed forces of the UK. Given the aesthetic nature of registered designs, it is unlikely that these provisions will be used to any great extent. An example could be where the design relates to an item of clothing or kit which could be used by soldiers. The only time payment will not be made is when the design has been recorded or applied by or on behalf of a government department prior to the date of registration.[105] This does not apply in respect of direct or indirect communications by the registered proprietor or any person through whom he derives title. The effect of this very limited provision is to allow free Crown use of a design independently and concurrently developed by a Government department.

## TRANSITIONAL PROVISIONS

The transitional arrangements were necessary because of the changes in the law relating to registered designs. For designs registered in pursuance of an application filed on or after 1 August 1989, the maximum period for the registration is 25 years. For designs registered in pursuance of an application

102 The Registered Designs Act 1949 s 14(1). The applicant has to complete a declaration concerning the first application.

103 SI 1993/1257, made under the Registered Designs Act 1949 s 13(1).

104 This is a result of ibid s 5 which contains provisions for secrecy of certain designs. The Registrar has powers under this section to prohibit or restrict publication or the communication of information in respect of designs of a class notified by the Secretary of State as being relevant for defence purposes. The Secretary of State may then consider whether publication of the design would be prejudicial to the defence of the realm.

105 Ibid, Sch 1 para 1(2).

made before 1 August 1989, the normal maximum period is 15 years. However, if a design was registered in pursuance of an application made after 12 January 1988 and before 1 August 1989 *and* that design would not now be registrable under s 1 of the Registered Designs Act 1949 as amended, the design registration must expire on 1 August 1999 unless it expires earlier in any event.[106] For such designs, licences were available as of right since 1 August 1994 and a number of applications for such licences have been received at the Designs Registry.

For designs that were created before 1 August 1989, the exclusion of copyright protection for design documents recording the design (or models embodying the design) does not operate for ten years after that date. Although directed at the design right this provision will also affect many registrable designs.[107] However, under the Copyright, Designs and Patents Act 1988, Sch 1 para 6(1), copyright does not subsist in drawings of designs made before 1 June 1957.

The flowchart in Figure 17.3 shows these transitional provisions in relation to a design which existed prior to 1 August 1989.

**106** The Copyright, Designs and Patents Act 1988 s 266(1). Examples might be designs now excluded by the 'must-match' exception which was introduced by the Copyright, Designs and Patents Act 1988, or that would fail to comply with the modified 'eye-appeal' requirements.

**107** The Copyright, Designs and Patents Act 1988, Sch 1 para 19.

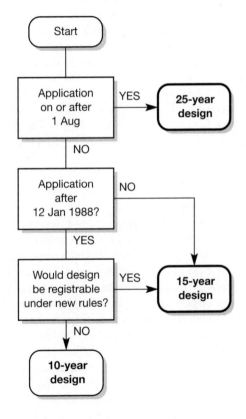

Notes: The periods relate to the maximum available subject to renewal.
The '10-year' designs expire not later than 1 August 1999.

**Figure 17.3 Transitional provisions in relation to registrable designs**

## PROPOSED EC DIRECTIVE TO HARMONISE DESIGN PROTECTION

The proposal for a Council Directive on the legal protection of designs is intended to harmonise design law.[108] It applies to the registered design system only – the unregistered design right and copyright are unaffected. There are some similarities to present United Kingdom registered design law. However, it must be noted that the proposal does not have a specific requirement for eye-appeal but the definition of 'design', being '... the *outwardly visible appearance* of the whole or part of a product resulting from the specific features of, in particular, the lines, contours, colours, shape and/or its ornamentation'[109] (emphasis added) shows that visual significance will still be a factor.

The proposal uses the term 'product' rather than 'article' and a 'product' is '... any industrial or handicraft item, including parts intended to be assembled into a complex product, packaging, get-ups, graphic symbols and typographic typefaces, but excluding a computer program': Article 1(b).

Under Article 3, designs must be new and have individual character. Parts of complex products can only be considered to have a new and individual character if remaining visible during the normal use of the complex product and the visible features themselves are new and have an individual character. This is intended to exclude 'under the bonnet' spare parts from protection. Normal use is use by the end user and not by a person maintaining, repairing or servicing the complex product.

Novelty is judged by whether an identical design has been made available to the public by way of publication, exhibition, use in trade or otherwise (not including disclosure by breach of confidence) before the filing date (or priority date, where applicable): Article 4(1). Designs are considered to be identical if their features differ only in immaterial details.

A design has an individual character, under Article 5, if the overall impression it produces on informed users differs from the overall impression produced on such a user by a design which has been made available to the public before the date of filing (or priority date). The degree of design freedom is to be taken into account in assessing whether a design has an individual character.

As far as making available to the public is concerned, there is a curious 'safeguard clause'. Under Article 6(1), where the events relied on to show the design has been made available to the public could not reasonably have become known in the normal course of business to the circles specialised in the sector concerned, then they are ignored. This restriction on anticipation is to prevent defendants attacking the validity of a registered design on the basis of prior art in remote places or distant museums. This will be very difficult to apply in practice.

Article 7 contains exclusions based on technical function and the equivalent of a 'must-fit' exception which resembles that in the Registered Designs Act 1949. This latter exception does not, however, apply to a modular system such as interlocking units, which may still be registrable. Designs contrary to public policy or accepted principles of morality are also excluded.

Protection extends to any design which does not produce on the informed user a different overall impression, again design freedom being a factor: Article 9. Under Article 10, initial registration will be for five years renewable in five-year periods up to a maximum of 25 years.

108  OJ C345, 23.12.93, p. 14. It was amended significantly in 1996; amended proposal OJ C142, 14.5.96, p. 7.

109  Article 1(a).

A design is not registrable, or if registered may be declared invalid, only in the following cases, by Article 11:

- the design does not fall within the definition of design
- the design is not new or does not have an individual character
- the design relates to technical function or interconnecting features
- the design is contrary to public policy or accepted principles of morality
- the applicant or holder is not entitled to it under the law of the member state
- where the design conflicts with some other right such as a registered trade mark or copyright.

The holder of a registered design shall have the exclusive right to use it, to prevent any third party copying or using it without consent. Use shall cover, in particular, making, offering, putting on the market or using a product in which such a design is incorporated or to which it is applied, or importing, exporting or stocking such a product for those purposes: Article 12.

There are a number of exceptions to infringement by Article 13:

- acts done for private and non-commercial purposes
- acts done for experimental purposes
- reproduction for citation or teaching purposes (but must be compatible with fair trade practice and so as not unduly to prejudice the normal exploitation of the design)
- the rights conferred do not extend to equipment on ships and aircraft registered in another country which are temporarily in the member state and this extends to importation of spare parts and accessories for vessels and their repair.

Originally, Article 14 had a 'must-match' exception where the purpose was to restore the original appearance of a complex product where appearance of the part was dependent upon the whole and the public were not misled as to the origin of the product used to effect the repair. However, this exception would not have applied until three years after the product incorporating the design was put on the market. Effectively original manufacturers of complex products were given a three-year period of protection in respect of 'must-match' spare parts.

The protection of spare parts is an area of some controversy. We have seen that, to be protected in the United Kingdom, a central issue is whether the part to which the design is applied qualifies as an 'article'. If it does not, or is otherwise excluded, for example as falling within the must-fit exception, then there is no protection under registered design law.

The amended proposal replaced the three-year protection with licence of right provisions for 'must-match' spare parts. A third party manufacturer could make such spare parts subject to clearly and indelibly marking the spares with the origin of the parts and after notifying the right-holder and offering a fair and reasonable remuneration for that use and offering to provide information as to the scale of use in a regular and reliable manner. The duration of the right would not be prejudiced.

However, following intense lobbying from car manufacturers, the Council of European Union rejected the licence of right provisions for spare parts, leaving the position as regards spare parts in a confused state. In some member states such as France car manufacturers have a monopoly in spare body parts and it seems that the Directive when adopted will follow this lead. This will result in a significant change in United Kingdom registered design law and could have serious implications for the spare parts industry and directly conflicts with the doctrine of non-derogation from grant. The only check on proprietors of such designs will be the competition provisions in Articles 85(1) and 86 of the EC Treaty. For example, if a major car manufacturer refuses to allow others to manufacture and sell replacement body panels for its cars, that is likely to be construed as an abuse of a dominant position, particularly if the prices charged for replacement parts are excessive.

As is now usual, the doctrine of exhaustion of rights applies to products put on the market by the holder of the registered design or with his consent.

Member states may also choose to protect designs by copyright in addition to registered designs, pending further harmonisation. The date for implementation was stated in the amended proposal to be 1 January 1998.[110] A new date will have to be set when the Directive is adopted.

110 The date in the original proposal was 31 October 1996.

## EXAMPLE REGISTRATION

There follows an example of a registered design for the shape or configuration of a typist's chair, including details from the certificate of registration.[111] Note the date of filing, date of grant and the priority date from an earlier application. There is a description of the article to which the design will be applied, the name and address of the proprietor and, in this case, an address for service in the UK (which is the agent's address). The novelty statement appears on the representation of the design. The design is reproduced with the permission of Fehlbaum & Co and their agents Frank B Dehn & Co.

111 Not all the representations are reproduced here.

## POSTSCRIPT

The Directive on the legal protection of designs was adopted on 13 October 1998, OJ L289, 28.10.98, p. 28. Implementation is due by 28 October 2001. As adopted, the Directive is largely as described above. However, until the Directive is revised, member states are to maintain their existing legal provisions as regards spare parts and may only amend them if the purpose is to liberate the market for such parts.

DATE        13/ 9/1993                                    PAGE        1

       REGISTER ENTRY FOR DESIGN NUMBER    2029805

Date of Application. 16th March 1993

Date Application Treated as having been made under Section 14(2) of the Registered Designs Act 1949 as amended by the Copyright, Designs and Patents Act 1988 28th September 1992

Date as of which design registered 28th September 1992

Certificate of registration granted 19th July 1993

Article in respect of which design registered:
      'Chair                                                '

Name(s) and Address(es) of Proprietor(s):
      Fehlbaum & Co
      Kappeligasse 22
      CH-4125 Riehen
      SWITZERLAND

Address for Service
      Frank B Dehn & Co
      Imperial House
      15-19 Kingsway
      London
      WC2B 6UZ

FEHLBAUM & CO                                                          1/8

292590

The features of the design for
which novelty is claimed are the
shape and configuration of the
article shown in the representations.

Perspective view from
front and right side

_M & CO

Front elevation

# 18

## *Design right*

### INTRODUCTION

The introduction of the design right must be seen in the context of the history of design law prior to the enactment of the right.[1] Until the Design Copyright Act 1968, there was a gap in protection for designs which were primarily functional in nature. Copyright protected artistic works, patents were available for new inventions, and designs having eye-appeal could be protected by registration. However, a design having no eye-appeal, for example an overflow pipe for a washing machine, had no form of protection *per se*.[2] The effect of the Design Copyright Act 1968 was to extend copyright protection to designs applied industrially for a period of 15 years from the end of the calendar year during which the relevant articles were first marketed. Eventually, by way of unanticipated judicial creativity, copyright was recognised as providing protection for functional designs through the medium of drawings for 50 years after the author's death.[3] Thus, unregistrable designs were given much longer protection than the 15 years maximum then available for registered designs.[4] Later, attempts were made to redress this inequality, as in *British Leyland Motor Corp Ltd* v *Armstrong Patents Co Ltd*.[5] It was seen to be important that persons buying articles that would need repairing during their life should be able to have access to a free market in spare parts, and that if a right in functional designs were to be established, some balance would have to be taken into account. Several options faced Parliament:

1  it could introduce a petty patent (utility model) system similar to that existing in some countries;
2  it could extend registered design law to include functional designs; or
3  it could leave protection to be gained via the medium of drawings.

The White Paper that preceded the Copyright, Designs and Patents Act 1988[6] rejected all other solutions and suggested a new right that would apply, automatically, to original designs for three-dimensional articles broadly along copyright principles. However, this was not to be an unfettered quasi-copyright. The design right is an emasculated form of artistic copyright as it applied to industrial designs.[7] A contrast can be made at once with registered designs, for which protection is along lines analogous to patent law.

The Patent Office describe the design right as:

> a new intellectual property right which applies to original, non-commonplace designs of the shape or configuration of articles. ... [It] is not a monopoly right but a right to prevent copying.[8]

Like copyright, the design right is a property right that is subject to qualification requirements. No formalities are required. However, the duration of the

---

1 For a comprehensive and lively description of the background to the design right, *see* Walton, A. 'The Copyright, Designs and Patents Act 1988 (1)' (1989) 133 *Solicitors Journal* 646.

2 Other rights could subsist such as trade marks and goodwill depending on the nature of the article.

3 Graham J in *Sifam Electrical Instrument Co Ltd* v *Sangamo Weston Ltd* [1973] RPC 899 applying *Dorling* v *Honnor Marine Ltd* [1965] Ch 1.

4 The Copyright Act 1956 s 10 effectively removed dual protection for registrable designs. The Design Copyright Act 1968 reinstated artistic copyright protection but limited it to 15 years for registrable designs.

5 [1986] 2 WLR 400.

6 *Intellectual Property and Innovation* Cmnd 9712 (HMSO, 1986).

7 Turner, B. 'A True Design Right: *C & H Engineering* v *Klucznik & Sons*' [1993] 1 EIPR 24.

8 The Patents Office, *Designs: Basic Facts* (The Patent Office, 1992) at p. 6.

right is much less, being effectively no more than ten years. The right applies only to designs for three dimensional articles and there are some controversial exceptions which allow the making of spare parts by others. There is an overlap between this right and the right in a registered design, and some designs that are subject to the design right may also be registered. However, there are different requirements for the two rights and this overlap is not, therefore, absolute. Some functional designs cannot be registered and some registered designs, fall outside the design right provisions. Examples of designs in which a design right is capable of subsisting are exhaust pipes and other parts for motor vehicles, tools, kitchen utensils, office equipment, packaging. Design right is limited so that it will not usually extend to features that must be the shape they are so that they can fit or match another article. The design right is comparatively weak as it is not a monopoly right and it is of short duration. Furthermore, in the last five years of the right, licences are available as of right.

The design right came into existence on 1 August 1989 and is contained in the Copyright, Designs and Patents Act 1988 Pt III. The provisions are not retrospective and designs that were expressed in a tangible form[9] prior to this date are not protected by the design right. Such designs may be protected through their preparatory drawings as s 51 of the 1988 Act does not apply for ten years to such designs, that is until 1 August 1999.[10] The design right provisions apply to England and Wales, Scotland and Northern Ireland. This may be extended to the Channel Islands, the Isle of Man or to any colony by Her Majesty's Order in Council.[11]

As a result of compliance with a European Community Directive, the United Kingdom afforded specific protection to the topographies of semiconductor products. Eventually, this was done by means of the design right and the design right provisions of the Copyright, Designs and Patents Act 1988 were adapted to provide the required degree of protection. This special form of the design right is dealt with towards the end of this chapter.

The Directive on the protection of semiconductor topographies can be seen as providing the model for the design right. Thus, the design right has different origins to the registered design and even though some of the terminology used for both rights is the same or similar, caution must be exercised and meanings applicable to one right are not necessarily directly transferable to the other right.[12]

## SUBSISTENCE OF RIGHT

Under the Copyright, Designs and Patents Act 1988 s 213(1), for the design right to subsist in a design it must be an original design. Furthermore, there is a requirement for qualification which must be satisfied and the design must be fixed in some tangible form by recording it in a design document or by making an article to the design. Computer-generated designs are defined in s 263(1) as designs generated by computer in circumstances such that there is no human designer. What has been said about computer-generated original works of copyright applies equally here and one can question whether there can ever be such a thing as a computer-generated design.[13] 'Design' means the 'design of any aspect of the shape or configuration (whether external or internal) of the whole or part of an article'.[14]

9 Being recorded in a design document or by having an article made to the design.

10 The Copyright, Designs and Patents Act 1988, Sch 1 para 19. For an example, *see Valeo Vision SA v Flexible Lamps Ltd* [1995] RPC 205. Unless otherwise stated, in this chapter statutory references are to the Copyright, Designs and Patents Act 1988.

11 Ibid s 255.

12 *See* Laddie J in *Ocular Sciences Ltd v Aspect Vision Care Ltd* [1997] RPC 289 at 421.

13 *See* Chapter 8.

14 The Copyright, Designs and Patents Act 1988 s 213(2).

There is no requirement for eye-appeal for the design right and, as a result, the right should be capable of subsisting in details which are not readily discernible or distinguishable by the naked eye. The subsistence of the design right in contact lenses was considered by Laddie J in *Ocular Sciences Ltd v Aspect Vision Care Ltd*.[15] After some initial doubt, he accepted that, as the right was intended for functional designs, the right could subsist in respect of detailed relative dimensions because the value of such designs over similar designs may be due to these tiny differences.[16] However, as we shall see, this does not square up with the test for infringement which relies on looking at the whole of the articles to which the design is applied through the eye of the interested person. In *Ocular Sciences*, Laddie J also noted that, as the design can be applied to the whole of any part of an article, a plaintiff can trim his claims accordingly, focusing on those aspects of the defendant's design which most closely match his. Again this is not consistent with the test for infringement given in the statute and as interpreted by the courts.

The design right provisions also apply to articles made in a kit of parts being a complete or substantially complete set of components intended to be assembled into an article, and it is possible that a design right subsists in a component as distinct from the design right in the assembled article.[17] However, as will be seen later, those features of components in the kit of parts which are shaped or configured specifically to match or fit other components are barred from design right protection.

In some respects the design right applies to a broader type of design than is the case with registrable designs. For example, the aspects of shape or configuration can be internal and may apply to part of an article. For a registered design, the requirement for eye-appeal means that the features must be external unless the outside surface of the article is transparent. However, registered designs can also relate to parts of articles – for example, a new design of spout for a teapot will not be rejected simply because it relates only to a part of the teapot and not to the whole pot.[18]

## Exceptions

The design right is declared under s 213(3) not to subsist in:

(a) methods or principles of construction;
(b) features of shape or configuration which:
  (i) enable the article to be connected to, placed in, around or against another article so that either article may perform its function (the 'must-fit' exception), or
  (ii) are dependent upon the appearance of another article of which the article is intended by the designer (creator of the design) to form an integral part (the 'must-match' exception);
(c) surface decoration.

The first exception and the must-match exception are identical to those for registered designs but the surface decoration exception distinguishes the two rights. The must-fit exception is differently worded and is narrower than the equivalent exception for registered designs.[19] Registered designs can be applied to two dimensional articles, such as a textile design, whereas a design to which the

15 [1997] RPC 289.

16 [1997] RPC 289 at 422.

17 The Copyright, Designs and Patents Act 1988 s 260.

18 In such a case, there may be a disclaimer as to the rest of the article which may be coloured blue on the representation and excluded from the novelty statement.

19 A point noted in *Ford Motor Co Ltd's Design Applications* [1994] RPC 545.

design right applies must relate to shape or configuration. This could, as in the registered design case of *Sommer Allibert (UK) Ltd v Flair Plastics Ltd*,[20] apply to a raised surface pattern such as a relief or embossed pattern because that has three dimensions. In that case, it was confirmed that grooves in a garden chair were features of shape and configuration.

The article in the must-fit exception does not have to be an inanimate object. Laddie J refused to construe the exception narrowly to exclude the human eye in *Ocular Sciences Ltd v Aspect Vision Care Ltd*[21] in finding that some features of the design of contact lenses were caught by this exception as they adopted a particular shape to fit the human eye, so that the eye and the lens could perform their respective functions.[22] It was from the viewpoint of these functions that the features were evaluated in terms of the exception.

The must-fit and must-match exceptions have significant implications for the manufacturers of replacement parts. These exceptions are also relevant to manufacturers of accessory parts, for example a lamp to fit on a bicycle mounting, or a dust cover for a typewriter. Because of the must-fit exception, the features that accordingly must be a certain shape or configuration can be made without infringing the design right. In the examples quoted this would extend to the connecting features of the lamp enabling it to be connected to the mounting bracket on the bicycle and the shape of the dust cover in as much as it had to be that shape to fit over the typewriter for which it was designed. Two points must be noted with respect to these exceptions:

1   The exceptions do not extend to other features. For example, in the case of an exhaust system for a motor car, only those parts of the design that relate to the fixing of the exhaust system to the mounting brackets on the car and to the outlet at the engine manifold are excepted from the design right. These features of shape or configuration enable the exhaust to be fitted to the car body and to the engine so that the exhaust system can perform its function, that is the control of noise and engine emissions. Other features of the shape or configuration of the exhaust system may be subject to the right, for example if an unusual shape is selected for a silencer box (perhaps elliptical in cross-section rather than circular) that has nothing to do with the connection of the system to the car. A spare part manufacturer may copy the 'connecting' or interface details but nothing else, unless the other features are commonplace or any design right in them has expired. This seems to be less generous than the 'licence to copy' replacement parts granted by the House of Lords in *British Leyland Motor Corp Ltd v Armstrong Patents Co Ltd*.[23]

2   The other article referred to in s 213(3) could be made by the same person who makes the article we are interested in. For example, if a person manufactures something comprising two articles (or an article that can be taken apart), then the connection between the articles will not be protected by the design right irrespective of the amount of research and development which may have been expended in the design of the connection.[24] The only time this exception cannot operate is if the connection is not relevant to the performance of function by either article. However, this would be highly unlikely.

Another example of the must-fit exception is where a manufacturer makes a television set and sells it together with a stand on which the set can be supported and swivelled around. The connection between the stand and the base of the televi-

---

**20** [1987] RPC 599.

**21** [1997] RPC 289 at 425.

**22** Laddie J considered the presumed legislative intent was to exclude all interfaces.

**23** [1986] 2 WLR 400.

**24** 'Connection' is taken in a wide sense here, covering all the situations described in the Copyright, Designs and Patents Act 1988 s 213(3)(b).

sion set (the mechanical interface) is not protected by the design right. All other features of the shape or configuration of both the television set and the stand are in principle (subject to the other requirements such as originality) capable of design right protection. Another manufacturer can make replacement stands for the television sets copying details of the interface but no other details, unless they are commonplace or if the design right in relation to them has expired.

The basic principles are the same as for the must-match exception. Again, the motor car can provide a good example. Consider replacement doors for a car. They obviously have to be a certain profile on the outside to match the sweep of the bodywork and would look extremely odd if they did not have this profile. The replacement doors also have to be a certain shape to fit the gap left for the door in the car body. All these features are excepted from the design right. However, most car doors have an inner skin which is hidden from view by upholstery (usually plastic). The inner skin often has holes for lightness and ribs for strength. The position and size of the holes and configuration of the ribs are irrelevant as regards appearance and, if their design is original, they may be protected by the design right and do not fall within the scope of the exception. Spare parts manufacturers must be aware of this and be careful not to copy those aspects of shape or configuration in which a design right might subsist and only to copy those elements falling within the exceptions. It must not be forgotten that a design in which the design right subsists may relate to a part of an article and that that part may be internal. It may be difficult, in many cases, to determine where the design right does and does not apply. Also, whether a particular right has expired could be extremely difficult to ascertain as there is not the benefit of a registration system and register that can be consulted to resolve such questions.

We have seen that a raised embossed or ribbed surface may be held to be features of shape or configuration. But is the converse true and what are the limits on surface decoration? Does it extend beyond decoration which is flat or planar? It would seem sensible to assume that the intention was the exclusion from design right protection of *decoration applied to the surface* of an article. That decoration may take many forms. It could be painted decoration or it could be a raised or embossed pattern. It could be like the dimples on a golf ball or plaster mouldings fixed to a fireplace surround or item of furniture. *Mark Wilkinson Furniture Ltd* v *Woodcraft Designs (Radcliffe) Ltd*[25] concerned an alleged infringement of design right subsisting in furniture for fitted kitchens. Noting that the Act gave no assistance, Parker J said (at 73) that 'surface decoration' includes:

> both decoration lying on the surface of the article (for example, a painted finish) and decorative features of the surface itself (for example, beading or engraving).

Parker J decided that the painted surface, the cockbeading (a chamfered edge to the line around a recess) and v-grooves (vertical grooves accentuating the curved corners of the units) were surface decoration, but not the cornice nor the recessed panels in the doors which formed part of the overall shape and configuration of the units and were themselves subject to surface decoration.[26] This latter explanation, that features are not likely to be surface decoration if they themselves are subject to surface decoration, appears attractive at first sight. However, it can be of little assistance in practice if simply applying paint is surface decoration. If a carved shallow wooden relief moulding is applied to the surface of a wooden fire

25 [1998] FSR 63.

26 Otherwise, the design right applied to other features and was held to be infringed.

surround, for example, does it cease to be surface decoration if it is painted, varnished, sandblasted or subjected to further detailed carving?

In *Mark Wilkinson*, Parker J rejected a claim by the defendant that the must-match exception applied as the appearance of each unit was dependent upon the appearance of another article with which it was intended to form an integral part, that other article being the whole fitted kitchen. It was held that the fitted kitchen was made up of a number of matching units, none of which formed an integral part of another.

## Originality

For a design right to subsist in a design it must be original. This is defined in the negative in s 213(4), which states that a design is not original if it is 'commonplace in the design field at the time of its creation'. What, then, does originality mean in the context of the design right? It is clear that it is not as high a standard as required for a registered design, yet it appears to be more stringent than is usually the case in copyright which has been interpreted by judges to require simply that the work has originated from the author and has not merely been copied.[27] For a design to be registered it must be new, having not been previously registered or published in the UK in relation to the article to which the design is to be applied or any other article. This is a fairly high standard of originality. However, for the design right to apply to a design it must not be commonplace in the design field in question. In *C & H Engineering v F Klucznik & Sons Ltd*[28] Aldous J said that the word 'original' should be given the same meaning as in respect of copyright, that is, not copied but the independent work of the designer. He went on to say that this should be contrasted with the novelty requirement for registered designs. However, Aldous J continued (at 428):

> The word 'commonplace' is not defined, but [section 213(4)] appears to introduce a consideration akin to novelty. For the design to be original it must be the work of the creator and that work must result in a design which is not commonplace in the relevant field.

Aldous J seems to put the test of originality the wrong way round. First, he suggests, the design must be original in the copyright sense and, secondly, if it is original in that sense, it must not be commonplace in the design field in question. What the statute requires is that the design is original, adding that it cannot be original if it is commonplace. The test should be: first, is the design commonplace? If it is not, then is it original in the copyright sense?

The meaning of 'commonplace' is important as defendants are likely to argue that the plaintiff's design was commonplace in the design field in question at the time of its creation. This could be taken as meaning that, although some examples of the design may exist, they are not well known or commercialised. Alternatively, it may mean that the design must differ from the existing art, though not by a significant amount. In *Ocular Sciences Ltd v Aspect Vision Care Ltd*,[29] Laddie J remarked that the word 'commonplace' derives from the Directive on the protection of semiconductor topographies which imposed a test of intellectual creation and not being commonplace in the semiconductor industry. Although he said that it was undesirable 'to replace one ambiguous expression by another', he went on to approve counsel's submission that:

27 For example, *see* the judgment of Lord Pearce in *Ladbroke (Football) Ltd v William Hill (Football) Ltd* [1964] 1 WLR 273.

28 [1992] FSR 421.

29 [1997] RPC 289.

Any design which is trite, common-or-garden, hackneyed or of the type which would excite no peculiar attention in those in the relevant art is likely to be commonplace.[30]

A design which is made up of commonplace elements may yet qualify for protection by virtue of the combination of elements provided the combination itself is not commonplace.

As far as the design field in question is concerned, there is no reason to give this a wide meaning especially as infringement is not so limited and will serve to curtail the use of the same design in related fields. Thus, if a design is commonplace in the design field of furniture generally but not in the field of office furniture, a person who makes office furniture to that design without the licence of the owner of the design right, will inevitably infringe. In *Mark Wilkinson Furniture Ltd* v *Woodcraft Designs (Radcliffe) Ltd*,[31] it was held that the design field in question was 'fitted kitchen furniture' not 'cabinetry generally', because the former was a discrete design field with its own particular problems and characteristics. In this respect, subsistence and infringement may not mirror each other. A design right might subsist in an infringing design just as a copyright might subsist in an arrangement of music which is itself an infringement as an adaptation of the original music.

If the meaning of commonplace is simply that the design has been made available to the public, but not on a scale to have become well known, all manner of difficulties could arise. There would be more than one design right subsisting in the same design and the test of whether a design is commonplace would be almost impossible to apply, being very qualitative and subjective. For example, consider the following situations involving two designs which are similar and have been created by two designers, Alice and Bernard. The designs, intended to be applied to a locking mechanism for sliding doors, have been created independently.

1 Alice and Bernard create their designs and record them at around the same point in time.

2 Alice and Bernard create their designs and record them at around the same point in time, but there is a time difference in the marketing of articles made to the designs. Articles to which Alice's design has been applied reach the market place in advance of articles made to Bernard's design. In the meantime, articles to Alice's design do not sell in large numbers.

3 Again, Alice and Bernard create and record their designs at the same time and articles made to Alice's design reach the market place first, but this time large numbers of articles to Alice's design are sold before the appearance of articles made to Bernard's design.

4 Bernard does not create and record his design until after small numbers of articles made to Alice's design have been marketed or sold. (Bernard has not seen the articles.)

5 Bernard creates and records his design after large numbers of articles made to Alice's design have been marketed and sold. (Again, Bernard does not see any of the articles to Alice's design.)

6 Several other similar designs have been recorded and articles made to the designs have been marketed and sold before Bernard, in ignorance of these, creates his similar design.

In 1, 2 and 3 above, both Alice and Bernard have created designs in which the design right is capable of subsisting. The design was not commonplace at the time of its creation by Alice and by Bernard because the creation of the designs was coincident in

30 [1997] RPC 289 at 429, followed by Englehart QC in *Philip Parker* v *Stephen Tidball* [1997] FSR 680.

31 [1998] FSR 63.

time, or nearly so.[32] The fact that numbers of articles have been sold is irrelevant to the subsistence of the design rights and reference must be made to the time when the designs were created, at which time the design or variants of it were not commonplace. Situation 6 is easily dealt with – it is clear that at the time Bernard creates his design the design has become commonplace in the design field. Situations 4 and 5 are less easy to distinguish, but it is clear that the test will be applied objectively, probably through the eyes of an interested person, for example, someone working in or knowledgeable about the design field in question. It is suggested that if only small numbers of articles made to Alice's design have been sold, there is a possibility that Bernard's design can still attract the design right. This prompts another question as to whether it is sufficient that only one other example of a similar design has been created and applied to articles, or whether the design, or variants of the design, are commonly used by a majority of designers in the particular design field. Incidentally, in none of the examples above does Bernard infringe Alice's design right.

### Tangible form requirement

The design right springs into force when the design is recorded in a design document, or alternatively when an article has been made to the design, whichever happens first.[33] 'Design document' is defined by s 263, which contains minor definitions, as 'any record of a design, whether in the form of a drawing, a written description, a photograph, data stored in a computer or otherwise'.[34] This would appear to cover virtually any form of recording and would be likely to include data stored on a compact disc, magnetic tape or a computer disk, depending on the meaning of 'or otherwise'. Bearing in mind the wide variety of forms of storage mentioned specifically, it is certain that this will be construed very widely. The only difficulty could be with temporary storage; and on the basis of the House of Lords judgment in *R v Gold*,[35] temporary storage in a computer's volatile memory may not be sufficient, although as soon as the relevant data is copied onto a computer disk this will be deemed to be recorded. One question which arises is whether storage on a removable computer disk is storage in a computer. However, this should be caught by the scope of the phrase 'or otherwise'.

Old designs cannot be resurrected by the design right because s 213(7) declares that the right does not subsist in designs which were recorded in a design document or which have been applied to an article prior to the commencement of the Copyright, Designs and Patents Act 1988 Pt III.[36]

### Qualification

As with copyright law, some qualification requirements must be satisfied for the right to subsist in a design. These may be fulfilled by reference to the designer, or, where relevant, the designer's employer or the commissioner of the design. A further route to satisfying the qualification requirements is through the first person who markets articles made to the design and the country in which that first marketing took place. There are, therefore, four possible routes to qualification. However, before the provisions can be understood, three terms used have to be defined: they are 'qualifying country', 'qualifying individual' and 'qualifying person'.[37]

'Qualifying country' means the UK and other member states of the European Community. Other countries may be added by Order in Council, either under ss 255

---

32 The time of the creation of a design may be of crucial importance in a case like this and the need for independent evidence as to the date of the creation of a design is a matter which should not be overlooked by designers, their employers and commissioners.

33 The Copyright, Designs and Patents Act 1988 s 213(6).

34 It should be noted that it is the design that is protected, not the design document.

35 [1988] 2 WLR 984.

36 The commencement date is 1 August 1989.

37 Defined in the Copyright, Designs and Patents Act 1988 s 217.

or 256, the latter applying where the other country has reciprocal provisions for design rights. New Zealand, the Channel Islands, the Isle of Man and Bermuda, amongst others, have been added to the list of qualifying countries by Order under s 256.[38]

'Qualifying individual' is a citizen, subject or person habitually resident in a qualifying country.[39]

'Qualifying person' means a qualifying individual or a body having legal personality, including a body corporate which has been formed under the law of a qualifying country and which has, in any qualifying country, a place of business at which substantial business activity is carried out. In determining whether substantial business is carried out, no account is to be taken of dealings with goods which are, at all material times, outside the qualifying country. Under s 263(1) 'business' includes a trade or profession.

The routes to qualification are by reference to:

1 The designer, being the person who creates the design. If the design is computer-generated, the designer is taken to be the person by whom the arrangements necessary for the creation of the work are undertaken.[40] Under s 218(2), a design qualifies for protection if the designer is a qualifying *individual*, or if the design is computer-generated the designer is a qualifying person. A joint design is the result of collaboration between two or more designers such that their individual contributions are indistinct from one another.[41] A joint design qualifies if any of the designers is a qualifying individual (or a qualifying person for a computer-generated joint design). These provisions do not apply, however, if the design is created in the pursuance of a commission or in the course of employment.[42]

2 The commissioner, if the design is commissioned and the commissioner is a qualifying *person* (s 219(1)). A commissioned design is one commissioned for money or money's worth.[43]

3 The employer, if the design is created by the designer in the course of employment and the employer is a qualifying *person* (s 219(1)). Section 263(1) states that 'employee', 'employment' and 'employer' refer to employment under a contract of service or of apprenticeship. This definition is identical to that applying to copyright works.

4 The first marketing of articles made to the design.[44] This can apply only if the other qualification requirements do not. In this case, the requirement is that the first marketing is done by a qualifying *person* exclusively authorised to put such articles on the market in the UK and it takes place in the UK, any other member state of the European Community or other country to which Pt III of the Act has been extended by Order under s 255, but not to countries affording reciprocal protection included by Order under s 256. 'Exclusively authorised' refers (a) to authorisation by the person who would have been the first owner of the right as designer, commissioner or employer had he (or it) been a qualifying person, including a person lawfully claiming under him, and (b) to exclusivity capable of legal enforcement in the UK.

In the case of a joint commission, or a joint employment or joint marketing, the design qualifies if any of the commissioners, employers or marketers is a qualifying person. A design which would not otherwise qualify may so qualify for protection subject to specified requirements in an Order in Council so that an international obligation of the UK is fulfilled.[45] The flowchart in Figure 18.1 sets out the various routes to qualification and their relationship.

38 Design Right (Reciprocal Protection) (No. 2) Order 1989, SI 1989/1294. Regulation 2 gives a full list of countries designated as enjoying reciprocal protection.

39 In respect of the UK, a citizen is a living person who is a British citizen or, in relation to a colony of the UK, a British Dependent Territories citizen in connection with that colony.

40 The Copyright, Designs and Patents Act 1988 s 214.

41 Ibid s 259(1).

42 Ibid s 218(1).

43 Ibid s 263(1).

44 Ibid s 220.

45 Ibid s 221.

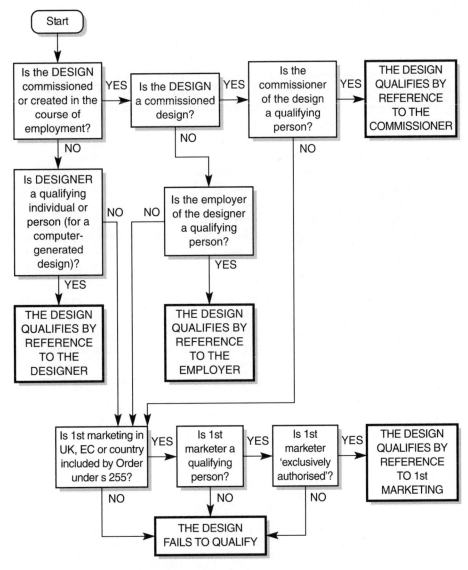

**Figure 18.1 Qualification for the design right**

### Duration of design right

An important date in measuring the duration of a design right is the end of the calendar year during which the design was first either recorded in a design document or an article was made to the design. In other words, this is the end of the calendar year during which the right came into existence. In the discussion below, this date is referred to as the 'end of the creation year'. The generosity of the law with regard to the duration of protection for functional designs through their drawings has been severely curtailed and now the maximum length of protection for a functional design by way of the design right is 15 years from the end of the creation year. In many cases, where the design has been commercially exploited, the period will be less than that. If articles made to the design have been made available for sale or hire anywhere in the world by or with the licence of the owner of the right within five years from the end of the creation year then, by s 216(1)(b), the design right expires ten years from the end of the calendar year during which that happened (the end of the first exploitation year).

The owner of the design right is given, effectively, ten years to exploit his design. However, during the last five years licences are available as of right.[46] The possible reduction in the term of protection from 15 years will not occur if articles made to the design have been offered for sale or hire by a person without the permission of the owner of the right, for example in the case of counterfeit articles, or if articles made to the design are placed in a public exhibition. However, if the owner of the design delays beyond the first five years, that will eat into the time he has in which to exploit the work. Figure 18.2 shows how the duration rules work, assuming that, at some time, articles made to the design are made available for sale or hire.

If period $x$ is less than five years, then the total duration of the right, $d$, is $w + x + y + 10$ years, that is, $z = 10$ years (Date E + 10 years). However, if period $x$ is more than five years, the total duration of the right, $d$, is $w + 15$ years, (Date C + 15 years) and the period $z$ is reduced accordingly. For example, if the design was created (and put in a tangible form) in April 1990, but articles made to the design were not made available for sale or hire until July 1997, the right expires at the end of year 2005. It is, therefore, important to exploit the design commercially within the first five years for maximum duration of commercial protection.

Design rights will always expire at the end of a calendar year irrespective of the actual dates of creation or first exploitation. In Figure 18.2, time interval A

46 Copyists must still beware of other areas of law which might apply to the articles such as registered design or passing-off. In practice the owner will have little more than ten years depending on the time of year he commences offering articles for sale or hire.

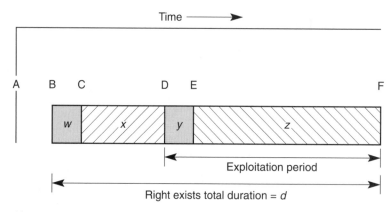

Key:
A – Designer has idea for a design
B – Design recorded in a design document or article made to design (creation)
C – End of calendar year during which creation happens (end of creation year)
D – Articles made to the design are made available for sale or hire (first exploitation)
E – End of calendar year during which articles to design are made available for sale or hire (end of first exploitation year)
F – Right expires.

**Figure 18.2 Duration of design right**

to B is of no relevance as regards the design right. Of course, during this period, the design right has not yet been born and there is no remedy in design law if it is reproduced, say from an oral description, although there may be a remedy under the law of breach of confidence. If the oral description is recorded on magnetic tape, with or without the permission of the designer, the right is born because the design has been recorded in a design document, and the definition of 'design document' in s 263(1) should be wide enough to include this form of storage. The person recording the design will have no design right in it by reason of having recorded it because rights are allocated by reference to the designer who is the person who creates the design. The designer need not be the person recording the design.[47] However, a person who records an oral description of a design will have rights under copyright law in the sound recording thus created.

**47** This point was made by Aldous J in *C & H Engineering* v *F Klucznik & Sons Ltd* [1992] FSR 421.

## OWNERSHIP

The rules for first ownership of the design right are fairly straightforward and the situation is more satisfactory than is the case with works of copyright where the concepts of an implied licence or of beneficial ownership may be called upon to do justice in the case of commissioned works where no provision has been made for ownership. Of course, first ownership is conditioned by the route to qualification and four possibilities exist, there being a one-to-one correlation between the qualifying individual or person and the first owner.

1 *Qualification by reference to the designer*, that is, in respect of a design not created either in the course of employment or in pursuance of a commission. In this case, the designer is the first owner of the design right.[48]
2 *Qualification by reference to the commissioner*. The commissioner is the first owner of the design right.
3 *Qualification by reference to the employer* (not being a design created in the pursuance of a commission). The employer is the first owner of the design right.
4 *Qualification by reference to the first marketing of articles made to the design.* The person so marketing the articles is the first owner of the design right.

**48** The basic statements of first ownership are contained in the Copyright, Designs and Patents Act 1988 s 215.

Joint first owners are possible where there is a joint design, being one created by two or more designers where the contribution of each is not distinct from the other(s). A joint owner's contribution need not be in respect of recording the design but it has to be in relation to the design itself and it is not sufficient if it only relates to the manufacture of articles made to the design. For example, in *Philip Parker* v *Stephen Tidball*,[49] one of the defendants was responsible for stitching together leather cases for mobile telephones. He made suggestions and contributions but they related to the construction of the cases and not to their design. Consequently, he was not a joint owner of the designs in issue.

A joint design will satisfy the qualification requirements if only one individual or person meets those requirements.[50] This leaves the problem of what rights the other joint designers, commissioners, etc. have in terms of ownership, and the approach taken by the Act is that they have absolutely none; only those individuals or persons who meet the qualification requirements are entitled to the design right.[51] For example, if a design is created by three self-employed designers, one being a British citizen, one being a citizen of France and the third

**49** [1997] FSR 680.

**50** If the designers' contributions are distinct then each will be regarded as the sole designer in respect of his own efforts: the Copyright, Designs and Patents Act 1988 s 259(1). The design is thus divisible and can be regarded as a combination of separate designs which can be owned by different persons.

**51** *See* ss 218(4), 219(3) and 220(3).

being a Taiwanese citizen, as far as UK law is concerned, assuming the design was not created in pursuance of a commission, the joint first owners of the design will be the British citizen and the French citizen; the Taiwanese citizen will not be entitled to any ownership rights unless he qualifies by virtue of being habitually resident in a qualifying country. However, the ownership provisions are relatively generous in the scope of their reach and protection is afforded, for example, to citizens of member states of the European Community without there being any equivalent and reciprocal provisions for protection of functional designs created by British citizens. In all cases, the place where the design was created is irrelevant.

## Assignment and licensing

Design rights can be assigned but, under s 222(3), this must be done in writing and signed by or on behalf of the assignor. The right can also pass by testamentary disposition or by operation of law.[52] An assignment may be partial, limited to apply to not all the exclusive rights of the owner, or limited in terms of duration. Licences may be granted by the owner and may be exclusive or otherwise. An exclusive licence, under s 225, must be in writing signed by or on behalf of the design right owner and an exclusive licensee has the same rights and remedies, except against the owner, as if the licence had been an assignment.[53] The Act contains provisions for the exercise of concurrent rights by the owner and an exclusive licensee.[54] Although there is little practical difference between an assignment and a licence, the latter is vulnerable if the design right is assigned to a purchaser in good faith for valuable consideration and without actual or constructive notice of the licence. This also applies to persons taking the right through a bona fide purchaser, even if such other persons have knowledge of the licence or are made a gift of the design right. A future design right, one that will or may come into existence, can be dealt with by assignment or licence just as an existing design right.[55]

In the case of a design where there is an overlap between design right and a registered design, that is when both rights apply to a design, an assignment of the registered design right[56] serves also to assign the design right if the proprietor of the registered design is also the person who owns the design right and vice versa unless a contrary intention appears.[57] However, although it will be unusual, it is possible for the two rights to become separated, for example by an express term to the contrary in the document containing an assignment of either right. The automatic transfer of the other right is a presumption only. Of course, in such circumstances the person obtaining the one right will clearly know that the other right is not to be assigned to him and will be able to predict what he can and cannot do in relation to the design. If there is some doubt, for example if the words expressing the contrary intention are not clear, the *contra proferentum*[58] rule of construction might be applied by the court, or a licence might be implied. At first sight, it might appear that the qualification requirements could frequently lead to separate ownership of the rights. However, under s 3 of the Registered Designs Act 1949, the Registrar will not entertain an application for registration of a design unless it is made by the person claiming to be the design right owner.[59]

52 An example of the latter would be in the case of the liquidation of a company that owns a design right.

53 The Copyright, Designs and Patents Act 1988 s 234(1).

54 Ibid s 235.

55 Ibid s 223.

56 Ibid s 224.

57 The Registered Designs Act 1949 s 19(3B).

58 This rule is used particularly in the context of exclusion clauses where a term that one person relies on to exclude or limit his liability (for example, under a contract where one party seeks to exclude his liability for breach of contract) is ambiguous. The court will usually take the meaning which is least favourable to the party seeking to rely on the term.

59 The Registered Designs Act 1949 s 19(3A) imposes similar requirements in respect of registration of an interest in a registered design. The applicant for registration has to sign a declaration to this effect.

Licences are available as of right in relation to the design right during the last five years of the subsistence of the right, under s 237. If the parties are unable to agree terms they will be settled by the Comptroller-General of Patents, Designs and Trade Marks. This provision significantly weakens the design right. It could be argued that, because the design right is not a monopoly right and because it is further constrained by wide-ranging exceptions, there is no need for this provision.

The would-be licensee under a licence as of right may be faced with one problem stemming from the lack formalities for the right. That problem is how to determine the date at which the design has five years left to run. It may be difficult to determine when the design was created or first commercially exploited. In the circumstances, the owner of the right is unlikely to be particularly helpful about dates. Another difficulty for the potential licensee is that other rights may apply, such as the registered design, and licences are unlikely to be available for such other rights.

## RIGHTS OF OWNER AND INFRINGEMENT

60 The Copyright, Designs and Patents Act 1988 s 263(3).

Under s 226(1), the owner of a design right subsisting in a design has the exclusive right to reproduce the design for commercial purposes by making articles to the design, or by making a design document recording the design for the purpose of enabling such articles to be made. 'Commercial purposes' refers to things done with a view to the article in question being sold or hired in the course of business.[60] As the definition in s 226(2) of 'reproduction' in relation to making articles to the design uses the word 'copying', the design right will not be infringed by a person who independently produces an article made to the same design. Copying a design by making articles exactly or substantially to the design is reproduction by making articles to the design, but substantiality appears to be construed differently to its qualitative meaning in copyright law. Apart from that, it seems the same general principles apply as for infringement of copyright by copying in that there must be a causal connection. That is, the infringing design must have been copied, directly or indirectly, from the first design.[61]

61 *Mark Wilkinson Furniture Ltd* v *Woodcraft Designs (Radcliffe) Ltd* [1998] FSR 63, per Parker J at 74.

### Primary infringement

62 [1992] FSR 421.

63 A pig fender is a device placed around the entrance to a pig shelter to allow the sow to step out into the field while retaining the piglets.

The design right is infringed by any person who does anything without the licence of the right owner which is by virtue of s 226 the exclusive right of the owner. In *C & H Engineering* v *F Klucznik & Sons Ltd*,[62] in an action brought by the plaintiff who claimed infringement of copyright in his drawings of lamb creep feeders, the defendant counterclaimed that the plaintiff had infringed his design right in pig fenders.[63] The pig fender in question had a round tube attached to the top edge. Apart from this tube, the design of the pig fender was commonplace. It was held that s 226 required the owner of the design right to show copying before infringement could be proved, and in this respect the design right is similar to copyright. However, the test for infringement is different, requiring the alleged infringing article to be compared with the design document or model embodying the design to discover whether the alleged infringing article is made exactly to the design or substantially to that design.

This requires an objective test, through the eyes of the person to whom the design is directed (in this case, a pig farmer), looking at the differences and similarities between the designs.[64] In this particular case, Aldous J held that there was no infringement – the plaintiff's pig fender was not made to the defendant's design or made substantially to that design. The objective pig farmer would consider the two designs to be different but with a similar design feature, that is a round bar or tube around the top.

It has already been noted that the design right can apply to a part of an article, but in his interpretation of the test for infringement Aldous J compared the design of the whole articles. This view is supported by the language of s 226(2), which speaks of reproduction in terms of producing articles (not parts of articles) exactly or substantially to the design.[65] This weakens the right where it is applied or limited to a part of an article only and, as in the *C & H Engineering* case, a significant design improvement may accordingly go unprotected. Turner suggests the judge was wrong to look at the whole of the article in testing for infringement.[66]

By using the test of the eye of the interested person, Aldous J applied a test not dissimilar to that used for testing for infringement of registered designs. However, the design right can apply to an internal part of an article that may be concealed from view. Comparison of whole articles does not make sense in relation to internal designs and can be undertaken only when the alleged infringing article has been dismantled and the relevant part considered and compared with the equivalent part of the design document or article made to the design.

It was accepted in *Ocular Sciences Ltd v Aspect Vision Care Ltd*[67] that the design right can subsist in detailed dimensions, for example, applied to a range of articles which differ only slightly from one another, even if those differences are not readily distinguishable by the naked eye. However, where the design right subsists in relation to such detailed dimensions, for infringement to be made out the defendant's designs must be extremely close to those of the plaintiff. In this case, the designs were for a range of contact lenses (220 designs in total) and Laddie J found that some of the defendant's designs were extremely close to those of the plaintiff. However, he accepted that there had been no act of copying the plaintiff's designs and, consequently, there could be no infringement.

Indirect reproduction also infringes, and it is immaterial whether any intervening acts themselves infringe. Therefore, if reproduction is preceded by taking apart an article made to the design it will still be an infringement. However, if such 'reverse engineering' is done so that only non-protected elements can be copied – for example, features, that fall within the must-fit or must-match exceptions – then there will be no infringement of the design. Making a drawing of an article made to the design will infringe only if it is done for the purpose of enabling such articles to be made, so that making a drawing to be displayed in an exhibition of drawings will not infringe. However, giving or selling the drawing to a manufacturer who intends to make the article would infringe if that was the purpose of making the drawing because it enables articles to be made to the design. It would appear from the language of s 226(1) that the 'purpose of enabling' should be present at the time the drawing, or other design document, was made.

64 In *Mark Wilkinson Furniture Ltd v Woodcraft Designs (Radcliffe) Ltd* [1998] FSR 63 it was accepted that infringement should be looked at through the eyes of a person to whom the design was directed, for example, a person interested in buying articles made to the design.

65 This approach was followed in *Philip Parker v Stephen Tidball* [1997] FSR 680.

66 Turner, B., *op cit*, at 25.

67 [1997] RPC 289.

Examples of litigation concerning the design right are still rare. In the Scottish case of *Squirewood Ltd* v *H Morris & Co Ltd*[68] the Court of Session granted an interim interdict[69] to restrain an alleged infringement of the design right subsisting in office furniture. Together with the *Mark Wilkinson* case, in which kitchen units were held to be protected, this case shows that the design right is not restricted to purely functional articles, but also applies to articles for which appearance is important in the eye of the person acquiring articles made to the design.

### Secondary infringement

Another similarity with copyright law is the provision for secondary infringement which approximates to commercial dealing with infringing articles, but there are no equivalent criminal penalties for infringement of the design right. An infringing article is one the making of which to a particular design was an infringement of the design right subsisting in that design.[70] The definition of 'infringing article' extends to articles which have been or are to be imported into the UK if their making in the UK would have been an infringement or a breach of an exclusive licence in respect of the design. A design document, however, is not an infringing article. Secondary infringement occurs when a person, without the licence of the design right owner, does any of the following acts in relation to an article which is an infringing article and the person knows this or has reason to believe it to be so:

(a) imports into the UK for commercial purposes
(b) has in his possession for commercial purposes
(c) sells, hires or offers or exposes for sale or hire, in the course of a business.

It would seem that the knowledge requirement is the same as that for secondary infringement of copyright.[71] Under s 228(4), there is a useful presumption in favour of the plaintiff that when an article was made to the design in which the design right subsists or has subsisted, it was made at a time when the right subsisted unless the contrary can be proved. Bearing in mind that the plaintiff may be the only person with proof of the time the design right first arose, this is very favourable for the plaintiff.

## EXCEPTIONS TO INFRINGEMENT

By s 236, if copyright subsists in a work which consists of or includes a design in which design right subsists, it is not an infringement of the design right to do anything which is an infringement of the copyright in the work. The overlap of actions between the design right and copyright is removed, leaving an action in copyright only. During the last five years of a design right, licences are available as of right[72] on terms to be fixed by the Comptroller-General of Patents, Designs and Trade Marks in the absence of agreement. The Secretary of State has the power to exclude by statutory instrument certain designs from the licence as of right provisions in order to comply with an international obligation, or for purposes relating to reciprocal protection for British designs in other countries. Under s 245, the Secretary of State also has the power on the same basis to provide that certain acts do not infringe design right. In effect,

**68** (Unreported) 1 April 1993, Outer House. For a description and discussion, *see* MacQueen, H.L. 'A Scottish Case on Unregistered Designs' [1994] 2 EIPR 86.

**69** Equivalent to an interlocutory injunction in England and Wales.

**70** The Copyright, Designs and Patents Act 1988 s 228.

**71** *See* the discussion of *LA Gear Inc* v *Hi-Tec Sports plc* [1992] FSR 121 in Chapter 6.

**72** This does not apply to the topography right, described later.

this permits a reduction in the protection offered in respect of a foreign country if that country does not give full reciprocal protection to British designs.

If the owner of a design right imposes restrictive conditions in a licence or refuses to grant licences, and in the opinion of the Monopolies and Mergers Commission this operates, has operated or is likely to operate against the public interest, the terms of such a licence may be varied or licences be declared as being available as of right by means of powers under the Fair Trading Act 1973.[73]

There are similar provisions for Crown use of designs subject to the design right as there are for registered designs. These extend to 'health service purposes', that is the supply of articles for the purpose of providing pharmaceutical, general medical or general dental services. There are provisions for the settlement of terms and the award of compensation if the owner of the right or an exclusive licensee has suffered any loss as a result of not being awarded a contract because of Crown use.[74] It could be argued that the provisions for Crown use are inappropriate here since design right does not give rise to monopolies. However, the provisions may be important if the design is also registered. It would be a nonsense if Crown use applied to one right and not the other if both rights subsisted in the same design.

## DEFENCES TO INFRINGEMENT ACTIONS

A person who has allegedly infringed a design right may plead several defences. Again, the best form of defence often is to attack the validity of the right. For example, a defendant might plead that:

1 the right is not valid because the features copied fall within the exceptions, for example, they relate to a method or principle of construction;[75]
2 the plaintiff's design is commonplace and therefore not original;[76]
3 the qualification requirements are not satisfied in respect of the plaintiff's design;[77]
4 the design right has expired;
5 the design was recorded prior to 1 August 1989.

Assuming that the design is valid, other defences which might be raised by the defendant include:

(a) the plaintiff does not have *locus standi*,[78] for example, he is neither the owner nor the exclusive licensee;
(b) that the act does not fall within the scope of primary or secondary infringement;
(c) the defendant's articles are neither exactly nor substantially made to the plaintiff's design;
(d) the alleged infringement occurred before the right existed or after the right expired (but here the defendant has the burden of proof);
(e) in the case of an alleged secondary infringement, that the defendant did not know and had no reason to believe that the article was an infringing article;
(f) that the act complained of falls within one of the exceptions to infringement.

A further possibility exists for an infringer when licences are available as of right in respect of the design, as they are during the last five years of the right.[79] Under s 239, the defendant can undertake to take a licence on terms to be

73 The Copyright, Designs and Patents Act 1988 s 238.

74 *See* ibid ss 240–244.

75 Ibid s 213(3).

76 Ibid s 213(4).

77 Ibid s 213(5) and ss 218–221.

78 The right to bring a legal action.

79 The Copyright, Designs and Patents Act 1988 s 237.

agreed or, failing agreement, on terms to be fixed by the Comptroller. If the defendant makes such an undertaking, an injunction will not be granted against him, no order for delivery up will be made and the amount recoverable in damages or by way of an account of profits shall not exceed double the amount which he would have paid had he obtained a licence on the terms that would have been agreed or fixed by the Comptroller before the earliest infringement.

As with registered designs, there is provision for a remedy against groundless threats of infringement proceedings. The remedies for groundless threats of infringement proceedings are:

(a) a declaration to the effect that the threats are unjustifiable
(b) an injunction against the continuation of the threats
(c) damages, if any have been sustained as a result of the threats.

The burden of proof is on the person making the threats to show that the acts to which the threats relate to do, indeed, infringe or will infringe his design right.

## REMEDIES

An infringement is actionable by the design right owner, but under s 234 an exclusive licensee has, except against the design right owner, the same rights and remedies as if he were the owner of the right. Damages, injunctions, accounts or otherwise are available to the plaintiff as they are in respect to the infringement of any other property right.[80] However, an award of damages is not available in the case of a primary infringement, without prejudice to other remedies, if it is shown that, at the time of the infringement, the defendant did not know and had no reason to believe that the design right subsisted in the design.[81] In the case of a secondary infringement, a defendant who shows that the infringing article was acquired innocently by him or his predecessor in title will be liable only to pay damages not exceeding a reasonable royalty.[82]

The court has a discretion to award additional damages which are provided for under s 229(3) using an identical formula to that used for copyright under s 97(2). It is unlikely that additional damages will be awarded frequently as, usually, normal damages or an account of profits will be satisfactory.

Orders for delivery up, forfeiture or destruction of infringing articles are possible and proceedings can be brought for these forms of relief in county courts in England and Wales and Northern Ireland subject to the county court limit for actions in tort.[83]

## SEMICONDUCTOR TOPOGRAPHY DESIGN RIGHT

Integrated circuits are commonly known as 'silicon chips' or, quite simply, 'chips'. They are usually made from layers of materials by a process which includes etching, using various 'masks' (templates) which are made photographically. The simplest integrated circuit consists of three layers, one of which is made from semiconductor material. A semiconducting material, in terms of its ability to conduct electricity, is one which lies between a conductor, such as copper, and an insulator, such as rubber. Examples of semiconducting mate-

80 Ibid s 229.

81 Ibid s 233(1).

82 Ibid s 233(2). The meaning of 'innocently acquired' is given in s 233(3), being where the person did not know and had no reason to believe that the article was an infringing article.

83 Ibid ss 230–232.

515

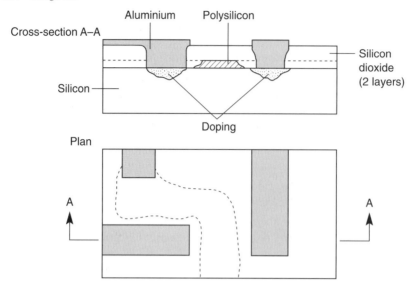

**Figure 18.3 Representation of part of an integrated circuit**

rials include silicon, germanium, selenium and gallium arsenide. A wafer of semi-conductor material is coated with a layer of silicon oxide (an insulator) and the electronic components (for example, transistors) are formed by a process of diffusion (chemically doping the semiconductor material with impurities through holes etched through the oxide). Finally, an aluminium coating is applied which is partly evaporated using a mask, leaving behind the interconnections between components formed in the semiconductor layer. Figure 18.3 shows, diagrammatically, a plan view and cross-section of a tiny part of an integrated circuit.

The patterns formed by the processes of etching the layers and evaporation of the conductor make the electrical circuitry of the integrated circuit. These patterns represent the circuit design. The processes involved in the making of integrated circuits fall within the province of patent law, and the first patents for integrated circuits were filed in the late 1950s. Licences were readily available and in 1961 the first chips were available commercially. Now that the early patents have expired and much of the know-how associated with making integrated circuits lies in the public domain, it is essential that the considerable effort that goes into the design and development of new integrated circuits is protected. The feature of an integrated circuit which is specifically protected in its own right is its topography.

### History

The protection of semiconductor topographies has a fairly short history, as might be expected. Before legislation was introduced, it was possible that integrated circuits were protected by copyright through drawings or photographs. Most of the masks used in the manufacture were produced photographically and would be protected as photographs. The United States of America was the driving force behind the development of specific protection for semiconductor topographies, and in 1984 the USA enacted the Semiconductor Chip Protection

Act which gave specific protection to the circuitry contained in the layers of semiconductors. The European Community felt duty bound to follow this lead on pain of loss of reciprocal protection for European designed topographies.[84] A Community Directive was issued and, under the authority of the European Communities Act 1972 s 2(2), the Semiconductor Products (Protection of Topography) Regulations 1987 were made and came into force on 7 November 1987.[85] These Regulations gave a right (called a 'topography right') in the layout of an integrated circuit. However, with the advent of the Copyright, Designs and Patents Act 1988, it was decided to replace these Regulations with an amended version of the new design right by the Design Right (Semiconductor) Regulations 1989, which came into force on 1 August 1989.[86] The new right, referred to below as the 'semiconductor design right', draws heavily on the Copyright, Designs and Patents Act 1988 Pt III which deals with the unregistered design right, but with some differences as far as semiconductor topographies are concerned. The problem with this is that we now have the situation where some sections of the 1988 Act are different, depending on whether they are being applied to semiconductor designs or to designs for other articles.

### Design Right (Semiconductor) Regulations 1989

The 1989 Regulations are similar to the 1987 Regulations in several respects, for example, it is the topography of a semiconductor which is protected, being, by reg 2(1), a design which is either:

(a) the pattern fixed, or intended to be fixed, in or upon –
  (i) a layer of a semiconductor product, or
  (ii) a layer of material in the course of and for the purpose of the manufacture of a semiconductor product; or
(b) the arrangement of the patterns fixed, or intended to be fixed, in or upon the layers of a semiconductor product in relation to one another.

'Semiconductor product' is also defined in reg 2(1) and is:

> an article the purpose, or one of the purposes, of which is the performance of an electronic function and which consists of two or more layers, at least one of which is composed of semiconducting material and in or upon one or more of which is fixed a pattern appertaining to that or another function.

To be protected, the semiconductor topography must be original, and it is not original if it is commonplace in the design field in question at the time of its creation (s 213(4) of the 1988 Act). As discussed earlier in this chapter, although 'original' is liberally interpreted in copyright law, the requirement that the topography is not commonplace is likely to lead to a much narrower interpretation. The qualification requirements are very similar to those for 'normal' designs, with some minor differences.[87] In terms of the first marketing qualification rule, normally no account is to be taken of any sale or hire, or any offer or exposure for sale or hire which is subject to an obligation of confidence.[88] On the international scene, there are reciprocity arrangements with several non-European Community countries such as the USA, Switzerland and Japan.[89]

The ownership provisions are very similar to those for the normal design right; however, the qualification provisions are slightly changed and commis-

84 For a discussion on the American approach and other possibilities for protection of computer programs, *see* Tapper, C. (1989) *Computer Law* (4th edn) Longman, at pp. 131–3.

85 SI 1987/1497.

86 SI 1989/1100 as amended by the Design Right (Semiconductor Topographies) (Amendment) Regulations 1991 and 1992, SI 1991/2237 and SI 1992/400. It is arguable that the 1987 Regulations were a model for the new design right, *see* Cornish, W. R. (1989) *Intellectual Property: Patents, Copyright, Trade Marks and Allied Rights* (2nd edn) Sweet & Maxwell, at p. 391.

87 For semiconductor products, the Regulations substitute different sections and parts of sections into the Copyright, Designs and Patents Act 1988, for example, a new s 217 is substituted.

88 The Design Right (Semicondutor) Regulations 1989, SI 1989/1100 reg 7. This does not apply if any of these things have previously been done or in terms of a Crown obligation.

89 SI 1989/1100, Sch Pt II.

sioners or employers do not have to be qualifying persons.[90] The right given is as with normal designs and on the whole infringement (primary and secondary) is similarly defined, but reproduction of the design privately for non-commercial aims is specifically excluded from the scope of the right as is an equivalent to some of the permitted acts, including fair dealing, in copyright. Section 226(1A)(b) allows reproduction for the purpose of analysing or evaluating the design, or analysing, evaluating or teaching the concepts, processes, systems or techniques embodied in it. This can be seen as paving the way for reverse analysis of existing semiconductors in the development of new, non-competing products. This is reinforced by reg 8(4), which states that it is not an infringement of the semiconductor design right to create another original topography as a result of such analysis or evaluation, or to reproduce that other topography.[91] As regards reverse analysis, a limiting factor will be the requirement for the new topography to be original and not commonplace. Regulation 8(5) retains the substantiality test for infringement. Secondary infringement does not apply if the article in question has previously been sold or hired within the UK by or with the licence of the owner of the right, or within the European Economic Community or Gibraltar by or with the consent of the person who, at the time, was entitled to import it or sell it within the appropriate territory. Thus, the doctrine of exhaustion of rights applies to semiconductor topographies.

The duration of the semiconductor design right depends on whether and when the topography is commercially exploited. A new s 216 is substituted for semiconductor products. Normally, the right endures for ten years from the end of the year in which it was first commercially exploited (anywhere in the world). However, if the right is not commercially exploited within 15 years of the creation of the topography, the right expires 15 years from the time the topography was first recorded in a design document or the time when an article was first made to the design, whichever is the earlier. Contrary to the position with other designs in which the design right subsists, licences as of right are not available during the last five years of the semiconductor design right. However, licences may be declared available as of right as a result of a report from the Monopolies and Mergers Commission as with other designs. Remedies for infringement are as for the design right generally.

The topography right is a result of international pressure, especially from the United States. However, because the Copyright, Designs and Patents Act 1988 s 51 removes protection from design documents (in effect), the protection for topographies in the UK is now significantly weaker than it was before. Although copying a topography will infringe the copyright in the photographic masks and s 236 suppresses the design right in favour of copyright, it cannot apply as s 51 means that the copyright in the photographic masks is not infringed by making a semiconductor product to the same design.

90 Ibid regs 4 and 5.

91 At first sight, this seems to defeat the whole object of the Regulations, but although reproducing the topography is permitted, reproducing by making articles is not. In some respects, this provision is similar to the decompilation right in relation to computer programs.

# Part Six

# BUSINESS GOODWILL AND REPUTATION

# 19

## Trade marks – background and prior law

### INTRODUCTION

This chapter concentrates on the basic nature and development of trade mark and the law under the Trade Marks Act 1938. This Act is considered in detail because, although now repealed, it remains very important in understanding trade mark law both generally and in the context of the Trade Marks Act 1994. Trade mark law has been substantially modified and reformed by the 1994 Act and some background to the character of previous trade mark legislation is essential to understanding the rationale of many of the provisions in the current statute. Much of what was bad about the 1938 Act has been swept aside, but parts of it remain important in the process of explaining and comprehending the new law. In particular, much of the prior case law on distinctiveness, confusion, infringement and non-use will be useful in interpreting the 1994 Act. Additionally, the law under the 1938 Act lives on to some extent under the transitional provisions. Infringements occurring before the commencement of the 1994 Act (31 October 1994) will be governed by the old law. The following chapter contains a description of the Trade Marks Act 1994, including the case law it has generated already, and a discussion of the impact of European Community law on trade marks, especially in relation to the Community trade mark and competition law.

Trade marks are a diverse and familiar feature in both industrial and commercial markets. Trade marks have long been used by manufacturers and traders to identify their goods and distinguish them from goods made or sold by others. In Roman times it was common for pottery to be embossed or impressed with a mark, for example a representation of a dolphin or the maker's initials, as a visit to the British Museum will testify. Merchants' marks were used in commerce in Britain from the thirteenth century; William Caxton used the mark W74C and gold and silver articles were hallmarked as early as the fourteenth century.[1] By the end of the sixteenth century it was very common for shopkeepers to erect signs illustrating their trade. Traders took to using cards bearing their name and address, often accompanied by a device of some sort, an early form of business card. The industrial revolution saw an enormous growth in the use of names and marks in advertising and the modern trade mark was born. Some of the nineteenth-century marks were glorious in their pictorial detail.[2]

Marks are a very valuable form of intellectual property because they become associated with quality and consumer expectations in a product or service. Some goods become almost synonymous with their trade name, for example Hovis bread, the soft drink Coca-Cola, Mars confectionery bars,

1 Hallmarking is now covered by the Hallmarking Act 1973.

2 A dated but useful practical and descriptive history of trade marks is to be found in Caplan, D. and Stewart, G. (1966) *British Trade Marks and Symbols*, Peter Owen.

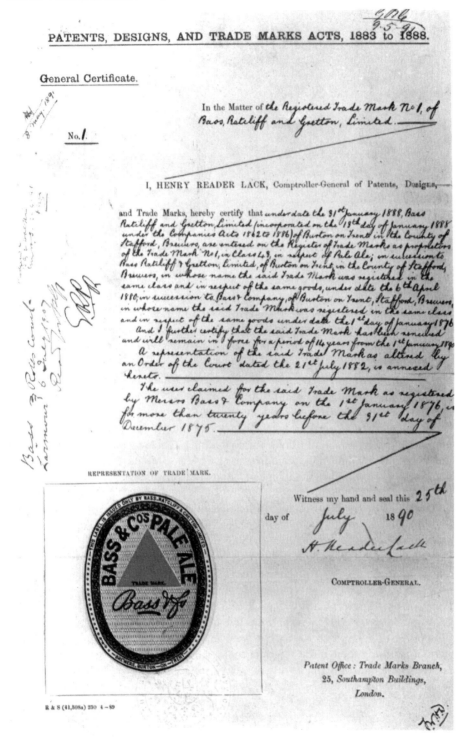

**Figure 19.1  Britain's oldest registered trade mark**

(reproduced by permission of Bass plc)

522

Nescafé coffee, Hamlet cigars, Domestos bleach, Cadbury chocolate, Levi jeans, etc. Coupled with intensive advertising campaigns, the utility of marks to their owners as marketing weapons is plain to see and trade mark rights usually will be vigorously asserted and defended.

It is difficult to estimate the economic value of the power of symbolism in marketing. For example, the value of the Coca-Cola trade mark must be immense when one considers the size of world-wide sales in what could be described as a beverage based on a formula for an unexceptional syrup. Symbolism here is also reinforced by the shape of the Coca-Cola bottle (based on the shape of the coca bean), which was designed to prevent the dissipation of the company image resulting from the variety of bottles made.[3] Why else would such an expensive and impractical form of packaging be used? As a matter of interest, an earlier attempt to register the Coca-Cola bottle itself as a trade mark in the United Kingdom failed.[4] Of course, the use of a similar shaped bottle by competitors would almost certainly amount to passing off. Advertising permits the creation of an image associated with a product that might have nothing at all to do with the qualities of the product itself. An old example was the advertising describing a particular brand of menthol tipped cigarettes as being 'fresh as a mountain stream', creating an image completely contrary to medical evidence of the harm that can be caused by smoking.[5]

A trade mark must be used or intended to be used in relation to certain goods or services.[6] A fundamental principle is that there is a connection between a trader and the goods or services in question,[7] and there can be no such connection if the mark is not being used, even though it might have been so used in the past. A mark that is dormant is susceptible to challenge on the grounds of validity and may be revoked for lack of use. Another important aspect is that the mark must be distinctive in some way, and this basic fact limits the scope of signs or symbols that can be used as marks. Ownership of a mark, referred to as proprietorship, gives what can be described as a restricted monopoly in that mark, and the proprietor of a registered trade mark has a property right in the mark. The right is limited by reference to the classes of goods or services against which the mark is registered and also by way of exceptions to the rights granted to proprietors. Trade marks are afforded legal protection through a system of examination, publication and registration. Marks can be registered in one or more of the 34 classes of goods and eight classes of services.[8]

A related area of law is called *passing off*. This can be likened to a common law version of trade mark law, and indeed both of these areas of law share a common background. Passing off, in relation to goods, can be said to be the use by a person on his own goods of an unregistered mark or get-up belonging to another person with the intention of passing off the goods as being those of that other person.[9] Quite often, a particular set of circumstances will give rise to the possibility of a cause of action in both trade mark law and passing off. Indeed, it is usual to add a claim for passing off in a trade mark action because of the risk of the registration being held invalid. The somewhat wider scope of passing off could also be important. Passing off is dealt with in Chapter 21. Another, less used area of law is trade libel, sometimes referred to as malicious falsehood. A remedy under this might be available, for example, where one trader falsely and maliciously claims that goods of another trader are not genuine.[10]

---

3 A great deal of this beverage is now sold in cans, but the shape of the bottle is still in evidence in the form of a curved white stripe alongside the name.

4 Under the 1938 Act in *Re Coca-Cola Co* [1986] 2 All ER 274, discussed post. The bottle should be registrable under the 1994 Act and an application in respect of it was submitted on 31 October 1994, the first day the new Act was in force.

5 Eisenschitz makes this point and emphasises the power of such advertising, *see* Eisenschitz, T. S. (1987) *Patents, Trade Marks and Designs in Information Work*, Croom Helm, at pp. 168–9.

6 There was an exception; defensive registration of well-known marks under the 1938 Act.

7 This principle is not as strong under the 1994 Act.

8 The classification system for trade and service marks can be seen in Appendix 1 to this book.

9 This is passing off in its traditional sense. 'Get-up' could include the appearance of goods, packaging or the general manner in which the goods are displayed, advertised or sold.

10 *Thomas v Williams* (1880) 14 ChD 864.

The law relating to trade marks is substantially civil law, but there are criminal penalties associated with the fraudulent application of marks. Other areas of criminal law may be relevant, depending on the circumstances, such as trade descriptions, theft, forgery and deception offences.

## RATIONALE

Trade marks can be seen as serving two main purposes: first, to protect business reputation and goodwill and, secondly, to protect consumers from deception, that is to prevent the buying public purchasing inferior goods or services in the mistaken belief that they originate from or are provided by another trader. As a form of consumer protection this area of law has been an effective weapon against counterfeit and inferior goods, considerably strengthened by the introduction of draconian criminal penalties for the fraudulent application of trade marks. However, as far as the control of the use of marks in the civil courts is concerned, the action lies with the proprietor of the mark and consumers are protected indirectly through the self-interest of those with property rights in trade marks. Another way of justifying a system of trade marks is that it gives effect, to some extent, to the European notion of unfair competition.

## BRIEF HISTORY

Although the application of distinguishing marks to goods has a long history, the law relating to trade marks is relatively young, going back to the early part of the nineteenth century.[11] However, an earlier example of an abuse of a mark is the case of *Southern* v *How*,[12] where one clothier applied another's mark to his own inferior cloth which gave rise to an action in deceit. Because of the importance of obtaining injunctions against infringers of marks, the Court of Chancery became popular for pursuing actions concerning marks, although the common law courts also began to hear such actions, for example in *Sykes* v *Sykes*[13] where some basic principles were laid down. However, it soon became clear that this area of law needed clarifying and strengthening, and pressure grew from traders for an effective statute which would provide for a system of registration like that adopted in France. One of the problems of litigation had been that the owner of the mark might have to prove his title to the mark every time an infringer came along, and proving title depended on establishing a goodwill associated with the mark, a problem that is still present in passing off actions. This increased the expense and the uncertainty of legal proceedings.

The first statute was the Trade Marks Registration Act 1875, which established a register for trade marks and which was extremely successful judging by the number of registrations applied for. The very first mark registered was one used for beer, a label for pale ale bearing the famous Bass red triangle (*see* Figure 19.1), the UK's No. 1 trade mark which remains registered as a trade mark today and still very much in use.[14] This particular mark has been infringed on many occasions, especially in the nineteenth century and the early part of the twentieth century. Bass plc reckons that it has had to deal with some 1900 examples of infringement of its red triangle mark. Retrospectively, this can be seen as very flattering as a measure of perceived quality and reputation of Bass ales and beers. In 1862 the Merchandise Marks Act was passed. This was a forerunner to the present Trade Descriptions Act 1968 and, *inter alia*, made it a criminal offence to forge a trade mark.

11 For a history of the legal development of trade marks and passing off, *see* Blanco White, T. A. and Jacob, R. (1986) *Kerly's Law of Trade Marks & Trade Names* (12th edn) Sweet & Maxwell.

12 (1618) Popham 144.

13 (1824) 3 B & C 541.

14 Bass also registered two similar marks and the red triangle device on its own in the same year.

After some amending legislation, trade mark law was consolidated in the Patents, Designs and Trade Marks Act 1883. A later consolidating statute, the Trade Marks Act 1905, gave a statutory definition of 'trade mark' for the first time, and a later amending statute, the Trade Marks Act 1919, divided the register into Part A and Part B marks. Registration in Part A was subject to more stringent requirements but gave better protection in terms of remedies than Part B. Then came the Trade Marks Act 1938, which consolidated the 1905 and the 1919 statutes together with the Trade Marks (Amendment) Act 1937 which was instantaneously enacted and repealed on the day the 1938 Act came into force, 27 July 1938. The 1938 Act was an outstanding example of intricate and difficult draftsmanship which has attracted judicial criticism, in particular s 4(1), dealing with rights and infringement in relation to Part A marks, being described by Mackinnon LJ as being of 'fuliginous obscurity'.[15]

The difficulty with the 1938 Act was compounded by the need to refer to earlier legislation. In *GE Trade Mark*[16] Lord Diplock said (at 325):

> My Lords it may well be a legitimate criticism of our methods of drafting legislation that in order to ascertain the meaning of an Act of Parliament passed in 1938, it should be necessary not only to consider its legislative history over the previous 63 years but also to engage in what in other systems of law might be regarded as antiquarian research, namely the state of the common law as it existed before the first Act to alter it was passed nearly 100 years ago. But, in my view, the Act of 1938 which purports to consolidate our existing law becomes intelligible only when this course ... is adopted.

The same sentiment is likely to be apposite in relation to the present legislation, the Trade Marks Act 1994. Recently, Aldous J also found it necessary to delve into the provisions in earlier law, including the Acts of 1883, 1888 and 1905 and the common law before 1875, in *Loudoun Manufacturing Co Ltd v Courtaulds plc.*[17]

Following recommendations made in a Green Paper,[18] the Trade Marks (Amendment) Act 1984 was passed, and this made amendments to the 1938 Act and extended the scheme to service marks which can be registered in respect of services such as laundries and banking.[19] These provisions came into force on 1 October 1986 and made a bad Act worse. The way the amendments were made required two copies of the 1938 Act to be used, and indeed *Kerly's Law of Trade Marks and Trade Names*[20] has the two copies on facing pages. Prior to this marks could be registered only in respect of goods. Further amendments were made by the Patents, Designs and Trade Marks Act 1986 and the Copyright, Designs and Patents Act 1988. It can be seen that the complexity of the 1938 Act was not alleviated, only added to.

The current statute is the Trade Marks Act 1994, supplemented by the Trade Mark Rules 1994.[21] This long awaited legislation brought trade mark law up to date and generally has been greatly welcomed. Primarily intended to implement the European Community Directive to approximate the laws of member states relating to trade marks,[22] the new Act makes provisions for the Community trade mark and to enable the UK to give effect to the 1989 Madrid Protocol relating to the international registration of trade marks.[23] The opportunity was taken to make some much needed improvements to trade mark law and to bring it more in line with acceptable modern trading practices. The Act came into force on 31 October 1994.

**15** *Bismag v Amblins (Chemists) Ltd* [1940] 1 Ch 667. 'Fuliginous' simply means sooty.

**16** [1973] RPC 297.

**17** *The Times*, 14 February 1994.

**18** *Intellectual Property Rights and Innovation*, Cmnd 9117 (HMSO, 1983).

**19** Previously service industries relied on the law of passing off.

**20** *See* note 11.

**21** Trade Mark Rules 1994 SI 1994/2583.

**22** OJ L40,11.2.89, p. 1.

**23** The United Kingdom ratified the Protocol in 1995.

## THE TRADE MARKS ACT 1938 (THE 'OLD' LAW)

There follows an examination of trade mark law under the Trade Marks Act 1938, as amended. Under those provisions, a distinction was made between trade marks and service marks, registrations for service marks commencing in 1986: that unnecessary and complicating distinction is not made in the Trade Marks Act 1994. Unless otherwise stated, in the remaining part of the chapter statutory references are to the Trade Marks Act 1938. First, the nature of a trade mark is discussed.

## WHAT IS A TRADE MARK?

Before the meaning of 'trade mark' under the 1938 Act can be appreciated, the scope of the word 'mark' must be established. Section 68(1), the interpretation section, defined a 'mark' as:

> a device, brand, heading, label, ticket, name, signature, word, letter, numeral or any combination thereof.[24]

A brand was added to the list of marks to cover marks made by a hot implement such as a branding iron, although there were suggestions that brand-names might also have been included in this category. A title on the top of a page of printed material is an example of a heading. Labels and tickets typically contain words and/or devices printed on a material such as paper or card, intended to be affixed to goods. It must be noted that the definition of 'mark' given in s 68(1) was not exhaustive and even the colour combination of an article was accepted for registration as a trade mark. In *Smith Kline and French Laboratories Ltd v Sterling Winthrop Group Ltd*,[25] Smith Kline and French applied to register coloured capsules for drugs as trade marks. The capsules were made in two halves, one coloured the other transparent, through which individual pellets could be seen. Registration was applied for in respect of the whole external appearance of the capsules. It was argued that a colour combination was not a trade mark within the meaning of s 68(1). It was accepted by the defendant, however, that these capsules had become sufficiently distinctive so that their use by other manufacturers would probably be actionable as passing off. It was held that there was nothing in the Trade Marks Act 1938 to exclude a mark that covers the whole surface of the goods, neither was there anything to prevent a three-dimensional object being a trade mark. The distinctiveness of the capsules was an important factor – the capsules were 'inherently adapted' to distinguish the goods of Smith Kline and French from those of other traders.[26]

Containers as such were not registrable. In *Re Coca-Cola Co*[27] an application was made to register the famous Coca-Cola bottle as a trade mark. Originally the shape of the bottle had been protected as a design under the Patents and Designs Act 1907, but the registration had expired in 1940. The House of Lords was not sympathetic. Lord Templeman said that the concept of allowing a container to be registered as a trade mark raised the spectre of a total and perpetual monopoly in such containers.[28] He thought that a rival manufacturer should be free to sell any container or article of a similar shape provided it was labelled or packaged differently in such a way as to avoid con-

24 The definition in respect of a service mark was more restrictive, omitting brands, headings, labels and tickets: the Trade Marks (Amendment) Act 1984 s 1(7).

25 [1976] RPC 511.

26 This was an important requirement for registration in Part A of the register: the Trade Marks Act 1938 s 9(3)(a).

27 [1986] 2 All ER 274.

28 Application has been made to register the Coca-Cola bottle under the Trade Marks Act 1994.

fusion as to the origin of the goods in the container. Lord Templeman was critical of the *Smith Kline & French* case, saying that it might lead to an undesirable monopoly in colours, but that the case did not create an undesirable monopoly in goods or containers. However, the argument for allowing colour combinations to be registered now seems uncontroversial and an attack on the validity of the registration of the copper and black colour combination used for Duracell batteries failed, the Patents Court treating this point as well settled in *Duracell International Inc v Ever Ready Ltd*.[29] Also, in *Smith Kline & French Laboratories Ltd's Cimetidine Trade Mark*[30] it was accepted that a colour mark was registrable in principle, although in that case it was held that an application to register the colour pale green as a trade mark for pharmaceuticals (for the drug 'Tagamet') must fail because it was not sufficiently distinctive.

A distinction which can be made between the above, apparently conflicting cases is that, in the successful applications, it was the surface of the article at issue, whereas in *Re Coca-Cola* it was the container. The drug capsule was meant to be swallowed whole, whereas the bottle would be thrown away or returned after the contents had been consumed. In all the cases, copying of the features claimed as registrable as trade marks by other traders would probably amount to passing off. The container monopoly argument is not convincing as there is room for much diversity in the shape of containers.[31]

It has already been stated that it was important that a mark was used or was intended to be used. This was borne out in the definition of 'trade mark' in s 68(1):

> a mark ... used or proposed to be used in relation to goods for the purpose of indicating, or so as to indicate, a connection in the course of trade between the goods and some person having the right either as proprietor or registered user to use the mark, whether with or without any indication of the identity of that person.[32]

The 'Batchelor Snackpot' trade mark was removed from the register for non-use and could not be saved by the fact that there was exhaustive use of the house mark 'Batchelors' in respect of other registered trade marks.[33] Token use would not suffice.[34] Intention to use had to be *bona fide* otherwise the mark was in danger of being removed from the register under s 26(1).[35] The registration of a 'ghost mark' was not bona fide and the objection under s 26(1) was not answered by token use. In *Imperial Group Ltd v Philip Morris & Co Ltd*[36] the plaintiff wished to use the name 'Merit' for a new brand of cigarettes. However, that word was not registrable as a trade mark, being a laudatory word. Nevertheless, and with the intention of protecting that name, the plaintiff registered the name 'Nerit' instead. When the defendant launched a new cigarette in the USA under the name 'Merit', the plaintiff made token use of 'Nerit' by marketing about one million cigarettes under this name in an attempt to prevent the 'Nerit' mark being expunged on the basis of non-use. This plan failed as it was held not to be *bona fide* and the mark was ordered to be removed from the register by the Court of Appeal.

The use had to be in relation to goods in the course of trade. In *Cheetah Trade Mark*[37] the defendant bought herbicide in Belgium made by the plaintiff and then imported it into the UK where he re-sold it. The herbicide was the same as that sold in the UK by the plaintiff, but it had a different mark to the plaintiff's registered trade mark on the container. However, the defendant used

29  [1989] RPC 731.

30  [1991] RPC 17.

31  In principle, containers are registrable under the new law.

32  A service mark was defined in similar terms in relation to services and a business connection with the provider of those services: the Trade Marks (Amendment) Act 1984 s 1(7).

33  *BATCHELORS SNACKPOT Trade Mark* [1995] RPC 555.

34  *See Imperial Group Ltd v Philip Morris & Co Ltd* [1982] FSR 72.

35  Section 26(1) stated that the mark 'may be removed' allowing a discretion that was, in practice, rarely exercised to allow the mark to remain: *INVERMONT Trade Mark* [1997] RPC 125.

36  [1982] FSR 72.

37  [1993] FSR 263.

the plaintiff's trade mark on delivery notes and invoices. The plaintiff sued for infringement of the trade mark, but the defendant argued that the use of the trade mark complained of was not in the course of trade. However, it was held that use on delivery notes and invoices was still use in the course of trade. This was so even though the invoices were submitted long after sale and delivery of the containers of herbicide. The marks on invoices were also used in relation to the herbicide, though not accompanying it on delivery.[38]

In *ORIENT EXPRESS Trade Mark*[39] there was no reference on orders or invoices to the trade mark of the registered proprietor. Use of the name on a label was held to be use as a company name rather than as a trade mark and it was ordered to be removed from the register. The applicant had made out a *prima facie* case of non-use which was not rebutted by showing that the mark had been used on items supplied to a friend (the 18th Duke of Valderano) of the president of the proprietor company.

Use in relation to goods did not extend to services rendered on goods. Thus, indicating a connection in the course of trade did not extend to repairers of goods. In *Aristoc v Rysta Ltd*[40] a repairer of silk stockings could not register a mark applied to stockings indicating that they had been repaired by him as there was no connection in the course of trade between the repairer and the stockings. Similarly, in respect of service marks, the provision of 'retail services', which were but an adjunct to the principal business of the applicant and not charged for as such, was not sufficient for showing a connection in the course of business between the applicant and the services provided. In *Dee Corp plc*[41] applications were made by well-known retailers Dee, Homebase and Boots for the registration of a service mark in respect of the provision of retail services such as advice and information to customers, car parking, credit facilities, etc. Even the playing of background music was included. The Court of Appeal dismissed the appeal against refusal to register the marks as service marks because the applicants were not trading in the services which were merely ancillary to their principal businesses. The services were not provided for money or money's worth as required under the Trade Marks (Amendment) Act 1984 s 1(7) when read with the Trade Marks Act 1938 s 68(1) as amended by the former Act.[42] However, it was conceded that the provision of crèche facilities could qualify as the service was charged for separately.

The person using the mark did not have to be the registered proprietor and the definition in s 68(1) shows that the connection could be between the registered user and the goods. For example, a large US corporation could have been the proprietor, while a UK subsidiary company might have been the registered user.[43] Another situation where a registered user was found was in the field of franchising, that is the contractual licensing of trade names, get-up and know-how – in other words, a licence agreement where the subject matter is the intellectual property rights connected with the form of business.[44] The franchiser may grant a series of franchises to different persons over the country and he may register a series of agreements. Under s 28(2), use by a registered user was deemed to be use by the proprietor for the purposes of s 26 (under which marks could be revoked on the grounds of non-use).

Certification trade marks were registrable in accordance with s 37 and Sch 1, being marks which associations of traders use to be applied to goods certified by them, for example, as being of a particular nature or quality, an example being 'Stilton' cheese.

38 In *Esquire Electronics Ltd v Roopanand Bros* [1985] RPC 83 it was held in the Supreme Court of South Africa that a trade mark recorded digitally on a video tape was not used in relation to the tape itself, the physical object. However, this was reversed on appeal, [1991] RPC 425.

39 [1996] RPC 25. The applicant for removal from the register hired a private investigator to find out that the proprietor had no business premises, distributors or agents in the United Kingdom and had made no use of the mark.

40 [1945] AC 68.

41 [1990] RPC 159.

42 *See also Re The Solid Fuel Advisory Service Service Mark* [1990] RPC 535.

43 Registered users and their rights were dealt with in Trade Marks Act 1938 s 28.

44 *See* Abell, M. (1989) *The Franchise Option: A Legal Guide*, Waterlow, for a description of franchising and its legal consequences.

## REQUIREMENTS FOR REGISTRATION[45]

**45** Other arrangements existed for the registration of Sheffield marks for metal goods, the register being held by the Company of Cutlers in Hallamshire: the Trade Marks Act 1938 s 38 and Sch 2. A record called 'The Manchester Record' was used for trade marks registered for textile goods: s 39.

**46** *Loudoun Manufacturing Co Ltd v Courtaulds plc*, *The Times*, 14 February 1994.

**47** *AL BASSAM Trade Mark* [1995] RPC 511.

**48** Ibid.

**49** *See AL BASSAM Trade Mark* [1994] RPC 315.

Application for registration of a trade mark or service mark was, under s 17(1), required to be made by the person claiming to be the proprietor of the mark. It appeared that it was sufficient if the applicant was acting *bona fide*,[46] even if someone else, having devised the mark, considered himself the owner of the mark in the UK and had registered the mark elsewhere.[47] In *AL BASSAM Trade Mark*[48] the applicant for a UK registered mark made headshawls for export to a third party, X, in Saudi Arabia. X was the registered proprietor of the mark in Saudi Arabia but did not trade in the UK. The applicant used X's mark in the UK with X's encouragement and consent. The Court of Appeal dismissed an opponent's appeal against the High Court decision that the applicant had a good claim to proprietorship and that the mark was registrable in Part B.[49] The Court pointed out that the applicant was the only person having business and goodwill in the UK to which the use of the mark could be incidental and, accordingly, it was the proprietor.

The register of trade marks was divided into Part A and Part B. The distinction between these was not an easy one to make and there were differences in terms of the protection afforded and the strength of the registration in terms of challenges on its validity. Registration in Part A was more desirable and almost all applications were made for this. However, if the high standards for Part A were not satisfied, Part B registration often was offered. Strong distinctiveness was an essential requirement for Part A registration of non-word marks, whereas a Part B trade mark was required to be capable of distinguishing the connection between the proprietor and his goods from goods without such a connection. In essence the difference between Part A and Part B marks was in terms of the degree of distinctiveness. Part A marks were generally more distinctive than Part B marks.

### Part A marks

Section 9 laid down the requirements for registration in Part A of the register. The mark had to contain at least one of the following:

(a) a company, individual or firm name, represented in a special or particular manner;

(b) the signature of the applicant or his predecessor in business;

(c) an invented word or words;

(d) a word or words having no direct reference to the character or quality of the goods and not being a geographical name or surname (according to its ordinary significance);

(e) any other distinctive mark – but a name, signature, word or words not falling in any of the above categories will be registrable only on evidence of distinctiveness.

Distinctiveness was expressly mentioned only in relation to the last category. However, the other categories could be said to be distinctive 'by definition', and this was borne out by the use of the phrase 'any other distinctive mark' in s 9(1)(e). 'Distinctive', under s 9(2), meant:

> ... adapted, in relation to the goods in respect of which a trade mark is registered or proposed to be registered, to distinguish goods with which the proprietor of the trade mark

is or may be connected in the course of trade from goods in the case of which no connection subsists, either generally or, where the trade mark is registered or proposed to be registered subject to limitations, in relation to use within the extent of the registration.

This is a good example of the verbosity of some of the provisions of the 1938 Act. In essence, this meant that the mark had been adapted to distinguish the proprietor's goods from those of other traders. Section 9(3) went on to suggest factors to be taken into account when determining what was distinctive, and stated that the tribunal should have regard to the extent to which:

(a) the trade mark is inherently adapted to distinguish, and
(b) by reason of the use of the trade mark or any other circumstances the trade mark is in fact adapted to distinguish.

The first part was a question of law and referred to the nature of the mark itself, while for the second part it appeared that it was a question of fact but the equivalent phrase 'in fact capable of distinguishing' was taken as meaning capable of distinguishing in law.[50] Being 'inherently adapted to distinguish' meant that the mark was '... adapted of itself, standing on its own feet'.[51] An invented word never before used would be a good example of such a mark. The Registrar and the courts generally treated with scepticism arguments that a mark was factually adapted to distinguish and registration would not automatically be afforded simply because a mark had become a household name.[52] If the applicant relied on use for other goods as 'other circumstances' to show a mark was in fact adapted to distinguish, the claimed association had to be fully demonstrated. The fact that a mark was distinctive in a particular area was not necessarily sufficient and in *Registrar of Trade Marks v W & G Du Cros Ltd*[53] two marks 'W & G', one stylised, the other simply in block letters, were refused registration even though it was recognised that the marks had become distinctive in London through their use on motor cabs. Another factor in that case was that registration would have made it difficult for other traders to use their own initials if they happened to be W & G. Each category in s 9(1) is considered below in more detail.

## Names

The name could be that of an individual, a firm or a company. It could be an adopted trade name used by, say, a sole trader or a partnership. Of course, some types of marks would be refused registration, for example if the mark was deceptive or likely to cause confusion.[54] The requirement that the name should be represented in a special or particular manner ensured that the mark was distinctive and allowed the honest use of their own names by other traders. Normally, the representation of a name in normal type would not be registered. In *Standard Cameras Ltd's Application*,[55] the name Robin Hood represented in a stylised way with the letters 'R' and 'd' showing an archer and a target respectively was accepted for registration.

A name may be unusual or even unique yet still be unregistrable because at the time the application for registration was made, the name had become so well-known through use as to be a household word. For example, in *TARZAN Trade Mark*,[56] the word 'TARZAN' was originally an invented word. However,

50 *York Trailer Holdings Ltd v Registrar of Trade Marks* [1982] FSR 111.

51 *Per* Harman LJ in *Weldmesh Trade Marks* [1966] RPC 220 at 228.

52 *Laura Ashley Trade Mark* [1990] RPC 539. The full title of the Registrar is the Comptroller-General of Patents, Designs and Trade Marks: the Trade Marks Act 1938 s 68(1).

53 [1913] AC 624.

54 The Trade Marks Act 1938 ss 11 and 12.

55 (1952) 69 RPC 125.

56 [1970] RPC 450.

by the time the estate of Edgar Rice Burroughs came to apply to register the mark in the United Kingdom, it had become so well known and had passed into everyday language that it would not serve the purpose of a trade mark as being an indication of origin. It was no longer an invented word.[57] Similarly, in *ELVIS PRESLEY Trade Marks*,[58] the name 'ELVIS' had became so well known that it had lost any inherent distinctiveness by 1989 when application was made to register the name as a mark. The application had been opposed by Mr Sid Shaw, a Londoner who traded in Elvis Presley memorabilia under the name 'ELVISLY YOURS' and had already registered that name as a trade mark.

## Signatures

A signature is, *prima facie*, distinctive, and a signature mark can be especially effective because of its personal connotations and it shows that the proprietor is very confident about the quality of his goods. Distinctiveness is not a foregone conclusion, however. The name may itself be very common or descriptive, for example, Good, Smith, Johnson, Lincoln, Perfect. All Part A marks were required to be distinctive and such common or descriptive names would have to be written in a particular stylised or distorted way to be considered distinctive.

In ELVIS PRESLEY *Trade Marks*,[59] one of the marks applied for was a signature mark, purported to be Elvis Presley's signature. It had been applied for by an organisation claiming to be carrying on merchandising of a nature that had, before the death of Elvis Presley, been carried on by him or on his behalf. However, and bearing in mind that the name itself had been held not to be distinctive for trade mark purposes, the signature had some similarity with the stylised form of 'ELVISLY YOURS' used by the opponent and the court accepted that the signature was unregistrable under ss 11 and 12 of the 1938 Act, being likely to deceive or cause confusion or nearly resembling a previously registered mark.

## Invented words

The word (or words) was required to be newly coined and convey no obvious meaning to the ordinary Englishman.[60] A slight change to an ordinary word may be insufficient to overcome an objection on this ground. For example, in *LACTEL Trade Mark*[61] it was held that 'Lactel' was not an invented word having regard to 'lacteal' (meaning related to or resembling milk) because lacteal would be known to a reasonable number of the public, and certainly to those in the milk trade.[62] An invented word would be refused if it sounded like an existing word or was suggestive of the quality of goods. However, in *Eastman Photographic Materials Co Ltd's Application*[63] the word 'Solio' was declared to be registrable by the House of Lords even though it had been refused registration as a trade mark for photographic papers because it sounded like the sun and could refer to the character of the particular goods. The Earl of Halsbury LC decided that 'Solio' was an invented word that did not indicate the character or quality of the goods, but recognised that in such cases the line is difficult to draw. He offered the made-up word 'Cheapandgood' as being an example that would clearly be unregistrable. Nevertheless, it seemed that an invented word did not have to be totally devoid of meaning. One way of predicting whether an invented word was registrable was to consider whether its registration would have made it

57 *See also Holt's Trade Mark* (1896) 13 RPC 118, where it was held that the word 'TRILBY' had become too well known to be classed as an invented word.
58 [1997] RPC 543.
59 [1997] RPC 543.
60 *Per* Parke J in *Phillipart v Whiteley Ltd* (1908) 25 RPC
61 [1994] RPC 37.
62 Compare with the mark 'BANINA' which had been accepted for registration in respect of fresh fruit.
63 [1898] AC 571.

difficult for other traders to describe their own goods, or whether it would have been an unnecessary fetter on the English language as used in business.

An invented word would not be registered as a trade or service mark if, when spoken, it sounded the same as an ordinary word. In *Re Edward Ripley and Son's Application*,[64] an application was made in respect of the word 'PIRLE' which had been formed by rearranging the applicant's surname with the 'Y' missing. The reason for refusal was that 'PIRLE' when pronounced sounded exactly like a word which had an ordinary meaning and which could not, itself, be registered. Lindley MR, in his extremely brief judgment, stressed the importance of not imposing an unjustifiable monopoly on the public.[65]

### Words not having a direct reference to the character or quality of goods

If a word had a direct reference to the character or quality of the goods in question it would not be registrable as a trade mark, otherwise the fair and honest description of his goods by another trader would have been hampered. Laudatory words (words praising the goods or services concerned) having a direct reference to the character or quality of goods or services, were not registrable in Part A, and would be registered in Part B only if the word or words did not make it difficult for other traders to describe their own goods. The phrase 'I Can't Believe it's Yoghurt' was refused registration in Part A as being a laudatory phrase.[66] Words that were descriptive without necessarily being laudatory were also refused Part A registration, as in *Re The Solid Fuel Advisory Service Service Mark*,[67] and words such as NEXT and ALWAYS that might find a use in advertising a product also were refused.[68]

Misspelling an otherwise descriptive word did not make it registrable, and in *Electrix Ltd v Electrolux Ltd*[69] a company making electrical apparatus sought to register the word 'ELECTRIX' as a trade mark. The company had used the name on their vacuum cleaners since 1933 and claimed distinctiveness on this basis, but nevertheless it was held that the word 'ELECTRICS' (correctly spelt) was inherently incapable of registration because it was a word that other traders might reasonably want to use in the course of their business. That is, it was a word which had a direct reference to the character or quality of the goods concerned. Therefore, 'ELECTRIX' was also unsuitable for registration because trade marks appeal to the ear as well as to the eye. An objection to registration of a word in its proper spelling applied equally to a word which was merely its phonetic equivalent.[70]

Geographical names and surnames were not normally permitted under this category. This was to stop a trader monopolising a particular name that would have had unduly restrictive consequences, but the registry maintained a sense of reality. Additionally, the 'bona fide use' defence could be relevant in this respect. An argument that a prefix mark 'PORTA' used with a collection of endings could prevent the use of the word 'Portadown', a town in Northern Ireland, was rejected in *Portakabin Ltd v Powerblast Ltd*[71] because it was said that any traders using the name of the town when describing his place of business or as a bona fide description of the character or quality of his goods could rely on the defence to infringement contained in s 8. Exceptionally, registration was granted if the name was very distinctive with respect to the goods, examples being 'CHARTREUSE' for liqueurs and 'APOLLINARIS' for mineral

64 (1898) 15 RPC 151.

65 *See also Electrix Ltd v Electrolux Ltd* [1960] AC 722 where the word 'Electrix' was refused registration. In *Compaq Computer Corp v Dell Computer Corp Ltd* [1992] FSR 93, Aldous J questioned whether the mark 'Compaq' was correctly registered, being phonetically similar to 'compact'.

66 *I CAN'T BELIEVE IT'S YOGHURT Trade Mark* [1992] RPC 533. It was, however, accepted for Part B of the register.

67 [1990] RPC 535. Part B registration was also refused.

68 *NEXT Trade Mark* [1992] RPC 455.

69 [1960] AC 722.

70 Pronunciation could also be relevant to the question of infringement: *see Parfums Givenchy SA v Designer Alternatives Ltd* [1994] RPC 243.

71 [1990] RPC 471.

waters from a spring of that name in Germany. The applicant had a heavy burden to discharge to show that the mark would have been recognised as a trade mark rather than as a place name[72] and it was fairly difficult to obtain registration for English and well-known foreign place names. Examples of refusals on this basis include 'LIVERPOOL' for cables, 'YORKSHIRE' for metal tubes, 'YORK' for trailers, 'KENT' for cigarettes and 'PHOENIX' for sportswear. However, 'ARCTIC' was accepted for bananas.

It was not unusual for an applicant wishing to register a name that sounded like or was the same as a geographical name to commission a survey to attempt to show that there was no danger of confusion.[73] For the evidence to be convincing, such surveys had to be statistically valid and sufficiently representative so that the results were capable of generalisation. The sample size and the questions asked were also important. For example, in *PHOENIX Trade Mark*[74] there was a survey carried out among 50 people in the Kingsway area of London by asking the question 'What does the word PHOENIX signify to you?'. Forty-two per cent said it was a bird rising from the ashes and only 8 per cent identified it as a town. However, the survey was criticised because the sample size was far too small and the location too limited to give a valid representation of the general public reaction. The survey was directed at establishing the paramount signification of the word, and in *CANNON Trade Mark*[75] this was held by the Court of Appeal to be irrelevant. To be of any assistance, apart from its other defects, the survey should have enquired about the ordinary signification of the word, followed by a second question 'And what else?'. The Supreme Court of New South Wales said that survey evidence could be admissible either as direct evidence of public impressions and opinions, or as original data which could provide the basis for expert evidence on the public opinion.[76] The Court further held that it did not need help in evaluating the survey evidence and deciding whether it could make generalisations on the basis of it.

A surname would not be registered if its ordinary signification was as a surname. Therefore, the name 'SMITH' was fundamentally unregistrable, although it might have been registered as a signature or if represented in a special manner. Surnames, as such, would be registered only upon clear evidence that the name was distinctive and not normally taken to be a surname. As regards the use of a person's own name, s 8 provided a safeguard, permitting the bona fide use by a trader of his own surname.[77] Some surnames are also geographical names and were, in principle, doubly unregistrable under s 9(1)(d).

## Any other distinctive mark

This includes device marks such as signs, symbols, pictures, labels and combinations of words and devices. They had to be sufficiently distinctive, in accordance with ss 9(2) and (3), as discussed earlier. A symbol comprising a simple pentagon on its own was not registrable. Laudatory epithets could not be registered regardless of proof of use.[78] In *Re Fantastic Sam's Service Mark*[79] it was held that the combination of 'Fantastic' with the possessive form of a familiar Christian name was not distinctive and could not be accepted under s 9(1)(e) for Part A registration. The application was made in respect of hairdressing services and the common practice of hairdressers using their Christian names reinforced the view that the phrase was not distinctive.

**72** *KENT Trade Mark* [1985] RPC 117.

**73** For example, *KENT Trade Mark* [1985] RPC 117 and *AVON Trade Mark* [1985] RPC 43. Surveys have also been used in passing off actions.

**74** [1985] RPC 122.

**75** [1980] RPC 519.

**76** The *Ritz Hotel Ltd v Charles of the Ritz* [1989] RPC 333.

**77** The law of passing off may also be important here – *see Harrods Ltd v R Harrod Ltd* (1924) 41 RPC 74.

**78** However, in *KUDOS Trade Mark* [1995] 242, it was held that Kudos was registrable in Part A because, although laudatory, it was not so in relation to the relevant goods, being paper, cardboard, etc.

**79** [1990] RPC 531.

In determining whether a composite mark, for example one made up of letters, words and symbols, was distinctive it was not permissible to dissect the mark into its individual components. The mark as a whole was judged. In *Diamond T Motor Car Company*[80] it was held that a mark comprising a large letter 'T' dissected by the word 'DIAMOND', the whole being enclosed in a diamond shape made with a double line, was distinctive and was registrable subject to the applicant disclaiming any right to the exclusive use of a diamond-shaped border and the word 'DIAMOND'.[81]

Monograms and combinations of three or more letters were usually registrable on proof of distinctiveness, examples being 'B.S.A.' and the John Player Special 'JPS' monogram. Usually at least three letters were needed and those comprising a single letter or only two letters were rarely accepted.[82] However, an attempt to have the British Petroleum 'BP' mark expunged failed because the mark, in a shield, had become very distinctive due to extensive use over the whole country for a long period of time.[83] Although the familiar green and yellow BP mark was very well-known, an application by another trader to register BP as a service mark succeeded provided that it was not used in the colours green and yellow.[84] Even numeral trade marks were possible, an example being the '4711' mark used for eau-de-Cologne, which was registered with and without a scroll and bell device.[85]

### Conclusive validity of Part A marks

One advantage a Part A mark had over a Part B mark was that of validity. For Part A marks, after the expiry of the first seven years of registration (that is, upon first renewal) the original registration of the mark was taken as being valid in all respects.[86] There were two exceptions: first, where the registration was obtained by fraud and, second, if the mark offended against s 11 by being deceptive, immoral or scandalous. Thus, the question of validity of the original registration was not just a presumption and, unless the exceptions applied, it could not be challenged in legal proceedings. Another presumption which applied to all marks facilitated the proof of title by a proprietor suing for infringement.[87]

### Part B marks

Section 10 described the standard required for registration in Part B of the register. The mark was required to be capable of distinguishing the traders goods (or services) from those of other traders. Matters which could properly be taken into account were the extent to which:

1 the trade mark was inherently capable of distinguishing, and
2 by reason of the use of the trade mark or any other circumstances the trade mark was in fact capable of distinguishing.

Where there had been no use, it was necessary to consider the inherent nature of the mark. It was held that the phrase 'I CAN'T BELIEVE IT'S YOGHURT' was registrable in Part B because, although borderline, it passed the first test in s 10.[88] The mark had been accepted against class 42 (other services) but refused against class 29 (coffee, tea, etc.) for yoghurt and yoghurt products. It was held

80 [1921] 2 Ch 583.

81 Registration could be granted subject to a disclaimer as regards common and non-distinctive material: the Trade Marks Act 1938 s 14.

82 *Registrar of Trade Marks v W & G Du Cros Ltd* [1913] AC 624, 'W & G' mark refused.

83 *British Petroleum Co v European Petroleum Distributors* [1968] RPC 54.

84 *BP Service Mark* [1996] RPC 448. The applicant had acquired distinctiveness in the very narrow field of storing, packing and distributing brochures for the travel industry, and because of this narrow field, confusion was unlikely. The application was allowed to proceed in Part B.

85 *R J Reuter & Co Ltd v Mulhens* [1954] Ch 50.

86 The Trade Marks Act 1938 s 13.

87 Ibid s 46.

88 *I CAN'T BELIEVE IT'S YOG-HURT Trade Mark* [1992] RPC 533.

that a useful test to apply was to consider how honest traders would be affected by allowing the registration and whether it would embarrass them.[89] There is a range of phrases – at one end a phrase might be a mere exhortation to buy, at the other end it was a trader's name for his goods. In between those extremes it would be necessary to show that the phrase had a branding function as well as being an advertising slogan.

89 *See also TORQ-SET Trade Mark* [1959] RPC 344, *THE CLUB Trade Marks* [1994] RPC 33 and *SAVILE Row Trade Mark* [1998] RPC 155.

The fundamental distinction between a Part A non-word mark (that is, 'any other distinctive mark') and a Part B mark was that the former had to be 'adapted to distinguish' whereas the latter was simply required to be 'capable of distinguishing'. The difference between these phrases was subject to some doubt. However, a reasonable interpretation seemed to be that the phrase 'adapted to distinguish' meant that the mark was, in fact and in law, distinctive and the phrase 'capable of distinguishing' meant that the nature of the mark was such that it was likely to become distinctive, perhaps after use of the mark. Sargant LJ described the meaning of 'capable of distinguishing' thus:

> [for Part B] ... it is not necessary for the applicant to prove that the mark has actually become distinctive. It is sufficient for him to satisfy the Registrar that it is not incapable of becoming distinctive.[90]

90 *Davies v Sussex Rubber Co* (1927) 44 RPC 412 at 425.

The requirement had generally been taken to be much less stringent than for Part A. It appeared that it was sufficient if the mark was likely to become distinctive in the sense above in the future when the mark was used in relation to the goods and services. However, if this was so, what was the meaning of 'inherently capable of distinguishing'? Although the Registrar had a discretion to accept marks in Part A and Part B (the language of ss 9 and 10 was in terms of a mark being registrable rather than saying that a complying mark must be registered), whether a mark was capable of distinguishing was, perhaps, more a matter for an opponent to disprove rather than for the applicant to demonstrate. Even though the applicant, British Airways, could show a high degree of factual distinctiveness in its use of 'Club' for airline services, it was held to have neither inherent distinctiveness nor capacity to distinguish: *CLUB Trade Mark*.[91]

91 [1994] RPC 527.

Consideration of the factual capability of distinguishing was permitted under s 10(2), for example, by use of the mark, in determining whether the mark was capable of distinguishing. However, in *York Trailer Holdings Ltd v Registrar of Trade Marks*[92] it was held that, for Part B registration, whether a mark was capable of distinguishing was also a question of law. In that case, application was made to register 'YORK' for lorry trailers and containers. It was said in the House of Lords that, being a geographical name, the word was not in law capable of distinguishing the applicant's trailers from those of other traders even though it was accepted that the word had through extensive use become 100 per cent distinctive of the applicant's trailers and containers. Such a mark could not have been registered in Part A, being a well-known geographical name, but anyone else trading in the same types of goods in relation to which the word 'YORK' was used would surely be guilty of passing off. However, the possibility of success in a passing off action was not an essential element in showing infringement of a trade mark, or in opposition proceedings.[93]

92 [1982] FSR 111.

93 *Berlei (UK) Ltd v Bali Brasserie Co Inc* [1969] 2 All ER 812.

A mark that had been registered in Part B did not necessarily qualify for Part A registration if, with the passage of time, it became 100 per cent distinctive. In *Weldmesh Trade Mark*[94] an application to register the word 'Weldmesh',

94 [1965] RPC 590.

applied to steel mesh used in the construction industry, was refused. The mark had previously been registered in Part B and had become 100 per cent distinctive through use. Nevertheless, the Court of Appeal confirmed the Registrar's decision that the mark was not registrable under Part A as the mark was too descriptive. In effect 'capable of distinguishing' did not mean 'capable of becoming distinctive within the sense required for s 9 registration'. On this basis, promotion from Part B to Part A for marks which through use have become very distinctive, was by no means to be taken for granted.

Even though the requirements for Part B were not as strict as for Part A, a mark would not be registered if to do so would interfere with the legitimate freedom of traders to describe their goods or services.[95] Furthermore, the mark still had to be capable of serving its function of distinguishing the goods of one trader from those of other traders. It was noted earlier that 'ELVIS' was not registrable in Part A. Neither was 'ELVIS PRESLEY' registrable in Part B.[96]

## UNREGISTRABLE MARKS

A trade or service mark would be refused registration if it was deceptive, disentitled to protection, contrary to law or morality, scandalous or if it conflicted with earlier marks. Further, by the Trade Marks and Service Marks Rules 1986, some marks were prohibited and others were subject to the Registrar's discretion. A mark could be deceptive in one or more of several ways. For example, it could create a misleading impression about the nature or quality of the product or services concerned, or it could be deceptive because it was likely to be confused with another similar trade mark registered by another person.

### Mark identical with or resembling a registered mark

Under s 12(1), a mark could not be registered if it was identical to a mark already registered by another proprietor in respect of the same goods or same description of goods or services. Applications software and systems software were held to be goods of the same description in *FOUNDATION Trade Mark*,[97] bearing in mind that both are machine-readable, sold in the same trade channels and, furthermore, that the distinction between the two forms of software is not clear-cut. Neither would a second mark be registered if it so nearly resembled the first mark as to be likely to deceive or cause confusion. In *UNIVER Trade Mark*[98] it was held that UNIVER for cardio-vascular preparations for humans nearly resembled UNIVET for veterinary preparations and registration was accordingly refused. The goods in relation to which the two marks were used were also in the same class.

Section 12(1) was a bar to registration only if the first mark was registered in respect of 'the same goods or description of goods'.[99] To decide whether goods were of the same description the classification used for purposes of registration was not appropriate. This may have seemed unfortunate, but the ultimate test was whether confusion was likely to follow, and the applicant would bear the onus of showing that there would be no confusion if the consequences of this would be serious.[100] The factors taken into account in deciding whether goods were of the same description were stated by Romer J (finding that shoes and shoe polish were not goods of the same description, in *Jellinek's Application*[101]) as follows:

95  *NEXT Trade Mark* [1992] RPC 455. This was a reason for refusal in both Part A and Part B. *See also Re The Solid Fuel Advisory Service Service Mark* [1990] RPC 535.

96  *ELVIS PRESLEY Trade Marks* [1997] RPC 543.

97  [1994] RPC 41.

98  [1993] RPC 239.

99  For service marks, the Trade Marks Act 1938 s 12(1) extends not only to services but to goods associated with the particular services or class of services.

100  *Univer Trade Mark* [1993] RPC 239.

101  (1946) 63 RPC 59.

(a) the nature and composition of the goods;

(b) the respective uses of the goods; and

(c) the trade channels through which the goods would be bought and sold.

102 [1992] RPC 541.

The last factor was stressed in *INVICTA Trade Marks*,[102] in which an application for registration of INVICTA for fungicide was allowed even though a similar mark already existed for a fungicide which was used for different purposes. Examples of marks refused on the grounds of s 12(1) are:

- UCOLITE – earlier mark COALITE (fuel)
- HUNTSMAN – earlier mark SPORTSMAN (both cherry brandy)
- An application showing a picture of three pigs was refused because of a prior word mark THREE PIGS BRAND (bacon).

103 (1942) 59 RPC 127.

However, in *Coca-Cola Co of Canada Ltd* v *Pepsi-Cola Co of Canada Ltd*,[103] it was held that 'PEPSI-COLA' was not too close to 'COCA-COLA', even though the suffix 'COLA' was a word that had become common and descriptive of a type of beverage.[104]

104 *See also Re Primasport Trade Mark* [1992] FSR 515.

Section 12(2) made an exception in the case of honest concurrent use, or other special circumstances, so that occasionally an identical or resembling mark could be registered in the same class of goods or services subject to any conditions or limitations imposed on the second mark or its use. If there was any doubt about the rights of the two proprietors, the Registrar could delay registration until after this had been resolved.[105] This might have applied where two persons had used identical or similar marks for at least five years or more in all honesty and had each built up goodwill in ignorance of the use of the mark by the other company.[106] Even though one mark was already registered, the second could be accepted for registration. There was no minimum period laid down as being acceptable.[107]

105 The Trade Marks Act 1938 s 12(3).

106 For example, *NUCLEUS Trade Mark* [1998] RPC 233.

107 A period of just over two years had been accepted in exceptional circumstances, *Peddie's Applications* (1944) 61 RPC 31.

108 (1933) 50 RPC 147.

Lord Tomlin set out some criteria for deciding if the second mark should be registered in such circumstances in *Pirie's Application*[108] as follows:

1 the likelihood of confusion that may arise from the use of both marks;

2 whether the original choice and subsequent use of the second mark was honest – it could be honest even if the second company knew of the existence of the first mark if it believed there would be no confusion, this being a subjective test;

3 the length of time that the second mark has been used – five years was deemed sufficient in the *Pirie* case, but normally the Registrar might expect more;

4 whether there was evidence of confusion in actual use;

5 whether the second company's trade is larger than the first company's trade – if so, this fact could help the second company's application.

This list was not exclusive – all the surrounding circumstances would be considered in addition. An example of such a registration was 'ABERMILL BOND' for paper, the earlier mark being 'HAMERHILL', also for paper. The 'ABERMILL BOND' mark had been used for six years and the owner of the mark had built up a substantial trade.

## Mark deceptive

Here we are concerned with other forms of deceptiveness under s 11, for example where it concerns the quality or nature of the goods. In particular circumstances there was an overlap between s 11 and s 12(1), as a mark that was very similar to a mark already registered in respect of the same goods would be caught by s 12(1) but could also be described as being likely to deceive or cause confusion under s 11.[109] For example, in *Berlei (UK) Ltd* v *Bali Brassière Co Inc*[110] the plaintiff who had a registered trade mark 'Berlei' complained that the defendant's mark 'Bali' would be likely to deceive or cause confusion in the sense within s 11, both marks being for brassières and corsets. The House of Lords agreed. The distinction between these two provisions was not usually important in this respect, but it should be noted that s 11 was not restricted to similarity with existing trade marks; it might, for example, apply where the prior mark had never been registered as a trade mark.

109 Failure to find confusion under one section would be an answer to the question of confusion under the other section: *JOCKEY Trade Mark* [1994] FSR 269.

110 [1969] 2 All ER 812.

The wording of s 11 was curious, stating that it would not be lawful to register a mark 'the use of which would, by reason of its being likely to deceive or cause confusion or otherwise, be disentitled to protection in a court of justice ...'. This clearly covered marks that were prohibited from registration under s 12(1) if such marks were not otherwise legally protectable, for example under the law of passing off. The origin of this provision was the Trade Marks Registration Act 1875, which spoke in terms of a court of equity. The addition of the words 'or otherwise' may have covered a situation where the owner of the mark was not entitled to the court's protection in respect of the mark because of the operation of estoppel.

Deceptiveness could relate to the origin of the goods, either by connection with the proprietor, or by false reference or implication as to the place of manufacture. For example, the use of a mark including the words 'Forrest' and 'London' by a watchmaker operating in Coventry who had no connection with London or a firm known as Forrest of London was held to be intended to deceive.[111] In *Boots Pure Drug Co's Trade Mark*[112] an application for registration of the mark 'Livron', a combination of the words 'liver' and 'iron', for a medicine was turned down because a rival company had an establishment at the town of Livron in France. The quality of the goods might be involved, such as where the word 'Dairy' was used as part of the description of a synthetic margarine, for example, 'DAIRY GOLD'.

111 *Hill's Trade Mark* (1893) 10 RPC 113.

112 (1937) 54 RPC 129.

In *Neutrogena Corp* v *Golden Ltd*,[113] the Court of Appeal stated that the correct test for deception or confusion was whether a substantial proportion of the public would be misled into buying the defendant's product, thinking it to be the plaintiff's product. Whilst the relevant confusion was that of ordinary members of the public and the nature of the confusion and required degree of awareness expected of the public, the judge was not confined to the evidence of witnesses and might make up his own mind as to the likelihood of deception and confusion.

113 [1996] RPC 473.

The Court of Appeal approved Jacob J's approach to deception and confusion at first instance, following Lord Diplock in *GE Trade Mark*,[114] where he spoke of the question being a jury question and said that, where before a judge alone (or a panel of judges), a judge is '... entitled to give effect to his own opinions as to the likelihood of deception or confusion and, in doing so, [is] not confined to the evidence of witnesses called at the trial... '.

114 [1973] RPC 297.

Where the deception or confusion related to the origin of the goods, the test to be applied to was to consider whether it would cause a number of persons to be misled as to origin on the basis of a serious and not merely fanciful possibility.

115 [1997] RPC 219.

In *SWISS MISS Trade Mark*,[115] it was held that the application to register 'SWISS MISS' for preparations for making chocolate and cocoa drinks and non-dairy cream and milk substances and the like by an American company was likely to cause some people to think the products originated in Switzerland.

Deception or confusion could arise because, although different, the goods marketed by the applicant for a trade mark and goods already sold by other traders might be associated. For example, in *SAVILE ROW Trade Mark*,[116]

116 [1998] RPC 155.

the applicant hoped to register 'SAVILE ROW' in respect of spectacle frames and eyeglasses in Class 9. Registry practice was that street names were generally registrable as trade marks in Part B provided there was no connection with the street and the goods in question. However, in this case, the mark was unregistrable, *inter alia*, on the basis of s 11 in that there could be association between eyewear and fashion clothing, Savile Row being famous for the latter, which could lead to confusion on the part of the public. In particular, sunglasses bearing the mark SAVILE ROW might be thought to come from Savile Row in London.

A mark was not registrable if its use was likely to be a danger to the public, for example if a mark used for a medicine was confusingly similar to one used for a poison. An example of such a mark was 'JARDEX' for a poisonous disinfectant when there was already a meat extract called 'JARDOX'.[117]

117 *See also Univer Trade Mark* [1993] RPC 239 concerning an application to register a mark for a medicinal preparation to be used to treat humans where there already existed a registration for a similar mark used for a preparation to treat animals.

Section 11 also prohibited the registration of marks which were contrary to law or morality and any scandalous design. This could cover something defamatory, obscene or particularly offensive, for example a mark having racist undertones. Section 11 was expressed in the imperative but, in reality, the Registrar still had an element of discretion (which could, of course, be challenged) in determining, for example, whether a mark was contrary to morality, this being a question of fact.

## REGISTRATION PROCEDURE[118]

118 Registration procedure was provided for by the Trade Marks and Service Marks Rules 1986, SI 1986/1319.

Registration was open to any person claiming to be the proprietor of the trade mark or service mark which was used or was intended to be used in the UK. Applications were made to the Trade Marks Registry at the Patent Office in London or Newport, Gwent, but applications for textile marks could be made at the Manchester branch of the Trade Marks Registry. Applications for marks for metal goods, in the case of an applicant carrying on business in or within six miles of Hallamshire, could instead be made to the Cutlers' Company of Sheffield.

119 [1932] AC 130.

120 The plaintiff was the proprietor of the famous Bass red triangle mark who had opposed the defendant's application, which was held by the House of Lords to be registrable because it was an old mark, in use since before 1875 and registrable as such under the Trade Marks Act 1905 s 9. The Registrar could also require a disclaimer in respect of certain parts of the mark.

Separate applications were required for each class of goods or services in which it was desired to register the mark. The Registrar could impose limitations, for example in respect of the colours used for the mark, as in *Bass, Ratcliff & Gretton Ltd v Nicholson & Sons Ltd*[119] where an outline triangle containing the letter 'N' inside was allowed subject to the colours being white and black only.[120] If the mark was accepted by the Registrar it was advertised in the *Trade Marks Journal*, and within one month of publication any person could give notice of his intention to oppose the mark. If this was done, the Registrar would set a date for a hearing after completing the evidence. If the mark was unopposed within the period allowed or such opposition had been unsuccessful, the mark would be entered on the register on payment of the registration fee and a certificate of registration was then issued. Initial registration was for seven years, after which time the registration could be renewed indefinitely in 14-year tranches. Usually, application was made for registration in Part A of the register. If there was any doubt as to whether the mark complied with the requirements for Part A, Part B registration could be offered instead. There was provision for restoration of a mark in respect of which the registration had lapsed.[121]

Under s 28, a person other than the proprietor of the mark could be registered as a registered user in respect of all or any of the goods (or services) for which the mark had been registered.[122] The use by the registered user was deemed under s 28(2) to be used by the proprietor. The arrangement must not have been contrary to the public interest and must not have amounted to or facilitated trafficking in trade or service marks. If the proprietor did not exercise some control over the registered user's activities the arrangement could have been deemed to be trafficking in trade marks.[123] In *Holly Hobbie Trade Mark*,[124] an application to register the Holly Hobbie mark (a drawing of a little girl in distinctive dress known as Holly Hobbie) was turned down even though the mark had previously been used by the owner of the mark in the USA for greeting cards and the like. The mark was registered in the United States as a trade mark and the owner granted licences to allow others to apply the mark to suitable goods. The House of Lords held that mark could not be registered in the UK as a trade mark because the owner intended to grant licences in such a way that the mark was being dealt with primarily as a commodity in its own right, and that there would be no real trade connection between the owner of the mark and the goods to which the mark was to be applied. The application would have facilitated trafficking in the mark. Lord Bridge of Harwich was reluctant to dismiss the appeal from the owner of the mark against the refusal to register it, and he said (at 202):

> ... though I can find no escape from section 28(6) of the Act of 1938, I do not hesitate to express my opinion that it has become a complete anachronism and that the sooner it is repealed the better.

Of course, some protection might have been available under the law of passing off.[125] Subject to any agreement between them, a registered user could call upon the proprietor to institute legal proceedings to prevent infringement, that is to apply for an injunction. If the proprietor neglected to do so within two months of the request, the registered user could institute proceedings against the proprietor for infringement.[126]

Defensive registration was possible in respect of very well-known trade and service marks.[127] This allowed a proprietor who had a registration in respect of certain classes of goods or services to register the mark for other goods or services even though he did not intend to use the mark for such other goods and services. This gave a valid registration regardless of the fact that the proprietor did not use and did not intend to use the mark in relation to the classes of goods and services to which the defensive registration applied. However, defensive registration would be granted only if the mark was so well known that there was a serious likelihood of confusion. Defensive registration could be applied for only in relation to invented word marks. A good example is the word 'KODAK'.

**121** The Trade Marks and Service Marks Rules 1986, SI 1986/1319 r 68.

**122** The Trade Marks and Service Marks Rules 1986, SI 1986/1319 rr 107–113 contained the procedural details.

**123** *Job Trade Mark* [1993] FSR 118.

**124** [1984] FSR 199.

**125** *Reform of Trade Marks Law* Cm. 1203 (HMSO, 1990) at p. 27.

**126** The Trade Marks Act 1938 s 28(3).

**127** Ibid s 27 and SI 1986/1319 r 37.

Under s 21, marks could be registered as a series. This would apply where the marks were similar, for example 'KEDS', 'PRO-KEDS' and 'KEDDETTE',[128] and were registered in respect of the same goods or description of goods. Such marks, being associated marks, were assignable or transmissible only as a whole and not separately.[129]

**128** *Re Keds Trade Mark* [1993] FSR 72.

**129** The Trade Marks Act 1938 s 23(1).

## ASSIGNMENT

Before the 1938 Act, a registered trade mark was not assignable without the business goodwill associated with it. For example, a trader might sell his business to a third party who would, naturally, wish to take an assignment of any trade mark used by the original trader. However, in recognition of the growing asset value of trade marks, s 22, subject to any rule of law or equity to the contrary, permitted the assignment or transmission of a registered mark with or without the goodwill of a business. However, this was not allowed if the result was to vest the right to use the mark in relation to the same goods or services, or the same description of goods or services in more than one person.[130] If the proposed assignment was without the goodwill of a business there was a time condition to be satisfied by s 22(7). The proposed assignee was required, within six months, to apply to the Registrar for directions about advertising the assignment. Geographically divided assignments could be made as long as they did not conflict with the public interest (s 22(6)). Under s 22(3), unregistered marks were assignable if they were assigned at the same time and to the same person as registered marks used in relation to the same business and registered for all the goods for which the unregistered mark was assigned. Assignments were notified to the Registrar by way of application to register the assignee's title and the assignee would be registered as the proprietor once the Registrar was satisfied of the assignee's title. Certain marks registered as associated marks could be assigned or transmitted only as a whole.[131] Registration of an associated mark was not complete until the fact of association had been entered in the association volume of the register. Until this had been done any assignment of the other mark only would be effective, notwithstanding that it should have been registered as an associated mark.[132]

**130** Ibid s 22(4).

**131** Section 23.

**132** *Re Keds Trade Mark* [1993] FSR 72.

## RIGHTS GIVEN BY REGISTRATION AND INFRINGEMENT

The rights given to the registered proprietor of a trade or service mark and the scope of infringement differed depending on whether registration was made in Part A or Part B of the register. Unfortunately, the provisions dealing with rights and infringement were some of the most complex on the statute book. First, the rights given and infringement of Part A marks will be discussed.

### Part A marks

The Trade Marks Act 1938 s 4 defined the rights given by registration in Part A of the register and infringement of Part A marks. The main provisions were contained in s 4(1), which was criticised strongly by the judiciary. Section 4(1) was expressed in a single sentence of some 253 words. The meaning of s 4(1) came up for examination in *Bismag Ltd v Amblins (Chemists) Ltd*,[133] an early case on comparative advertising described in more detail later in this chapter. MacKinnon LJ, giving a dissenting judgment, admitted that he was unable to discover the meaning of s 4(1), saying (at 687):

> In the course of three days hearing this case I have, I suppose, heard section 4 ... read, or I have read it for myself, dozens if not hundreds of times. Despite this iteration I must confess that, reading it through once again, I have very little notion of what the section is intended to convey ... I doubt if the entire statute book could be successfully searched for a sentence of equal length which is of more fuliginous obscurity.

Lord Greene MR, although describing the language of s 4 as turgid and diffuse, claimed to be able to discover its meaning. The difficulty in s 4 stems from the 'importing a reference' infringement in s 4(1)(b), which was intended to catch comparative advertising.

A simplistic view of the principle of infringement under the 1938 Act which has much to recommend it is that taken by Lord Greene MR in *Saville Perfumery Ltd v June Perfect Ltd*,[134] where he said:

> ... infringement consists in using the mark as a trade mark, that is, as indicating origin.

However, this failed to take into account the 'importing a reference' infringement in s 4(1)(b). The statement makes more sense in terms of the registrability of a mark, and in *Aristoc Ltd v Rysta Ltd*,[135] Lord Greene's statement was quoted with approval as one of the reasons why a trade mark, 'Rysta', could not be registered in respect of the repair of silk stockings.[136]

Normally, infringement was clear-cut, for example where a person fixed a mark on his goods identical to or nearly resembling a trade mark belonging to someone else and which was registered for the appropriate class of goods. 'Nearly resembling' meant that the mark was likely to deceive or cause confusion. As is the case in relation to registrability, the phonetic characteristics of the mark as spoken could be relevant, and in *Fisons plc v Norton Healthcare Ltd*[137] an interlocutory injunction was granted to prevent the use of EYE-CROM for eye drops which was confusingly similar to the registered mark VICROM.

Reflecting the importance and value of well-established marks, many manufacturers of alternative products are tempted to get as close as they dare to the leading brands. Lawyers have been and are being asked the question: 'How close can I get without infringing?'. This is a dangerous game and the law of passing off also may be relevant. For such alternative product manufacturers there is a real and worrying contradiction. They want to get as close as they can in the hope of capturing some of the goodwill associated with the mark, but if they succeed that is good evidence of trade mark infringement or passing off. The Court of Appeal found a serious issue to be tried in *Parfums Givenchy SA v Designer Alternatives Ltd*[138] where the defendant had used the name XEREUX for a body spray and lotion, the plaintiff being the registered proprietor of XERYUS used for perfumes and cosmetics. The Court held that evidence of pronunciation was generally unnecessary and the judge could decide the possibilities for himself. In New Zealand, a jeans manufacturer made use of a coloured tab fixed to the seam of a pocket which was held to infringe the Levi trade mark, even though placed in a different position.[139] In Saudi Arabia, it was held that the defendant's use of STELLACREAM for hair cream infringed the registered trade mark BRYLCREEM.[140] The fact that for an interlocutory

133 [1940] 1 Ch 667.

134 (1939) 58 RPC 147 at 161.

135 [1945] AC 68.

136 Another reason was that the word 'Rysta' ao nearly resembled 'Aristoc' in sound as to be likely to deceive or cause confusion.

137 [1994] FSR 745.

138 [1994] RPC 243.

139 *Levi Strauss & Co v Kimbyr Investments Ltd* [1994] FSR 685.

140 *Beecham Group plc v Mohammed Ahmed Banafi* [1994] FSR 685.

injunction to be granted, provided the balance of convenience is satisfied, it only remains to show a serious issue to be tried makes the use of similar marks by alternative product manufacturers a very dubious practice.

The 'importing a reference' example of infringement given in s 4(1)(b) was an addition to trade mark law introduced in the 1938 Act as a result of the decision in *Irving's Yeastvite Ltd v Horsenail*,[141] where it was held that the comparative advertising of the defendant's product as a substitute for the plaintiff's product 'YEASTVITE', by reference to that trade mark, was not an infringement. On this basis alone, it could be claimed that the infringement described in s 4(1)(b) was in addition to the basic exclusive right of the proprietor. It was intended to prevent comparative advertising involving the use of another's trade mark. A cynical view is that the extreme verbosity of s 4(1) compared to its prior equivalent could be explained only by saying that the legislature intended to make some change to the law.

Section 4(1)(b) was particularly relevant in terms of advertising where it was done in such a way that the goods referred to were clearly identifiable as being the goods of the proprietor of the trade mark and those actually being offered were not. Blanco White and Jacob make the point that it is not always an easy matter to identify the goods being offered and that a trap order may have been needed to prove this form of infringement.[142] The advertising circular or other advertisement issued to the public mentioned in s 4(1)(b) included a manual issued to sales distributors in *Chanel Ltd v L'Arome (UK) Ltd*.[143] Comparisons were made in the manual between the plaintiff's perfumes and the defendant's cheaper alternatives.

## Comparative advertising

Comparative advertising occurs where one manufacturer compares the specification, performance and price of his product with a rival's product. For example, a particular mark and model of car might be advertised by comparing its best features, such as acceleration times and fuel consumption, with the equivalent figures for a similar but different make of car which is mentioned by name. Such advertising might, though not always, involve the use of trade marks belonging to others. If it did, under the 1938 Act there was, in principle, a trade mark infringement. In *Bismag Ltd v Amblins (Chemists) Ltd*[144] the plaintiff owned the trade mark in the word 'bisurated' as applied to a 'patent medicine', bisurated magnesia, which was sold under a published formula. The defendant was a pharmacist and sold the plaintiff's goods, but also made up and sold a similar preparation called 'bismuthated magnesia'. The defendant published a pamphlet with a list of proprietary medicines sold by him, but opposite was printed a list of medicines made by him that were similar in all respects but much less expensive than the proprietary medicines. It was held in the Court of Appeal, by a two to one majority, that the defendant had used the plaintiff's trade name as a convenient method of describing the merits of his own products and had infringed the plaintiff's exclusive rights under s 4(1) of the Trade Marks Act 1938. Lord Greene MR applied s 4(1)(b) to the circumstances by the following steps:

1  the defendant had used the plaintiff's trade mark in two ways, one of which was legitimate as the trade mark of the plaintiff's goods, but the other use was as a mark forming by reference part of the description of his own goods

**141** (1934) 51 RPC 110.

**142** Blanco White, T. A. and Jacob, R. (1986) *Kerly's Law of Trade Marks and Trade Names* (12th edn) Sweet & Maxwell, at pp. 267–8.

**143** *The Times*, 26 November 1992.

**144** [1940] 1 Ch 667.

in the course of trade and in relation to the goods with respect to which the mark was registered;

2 the use was in an advertising circular or other advertisement;

3 the mark was used in such a manner as to render the use of the mark likely to be taken to be importing a reference;

4 the plaintiff had the right to use the mark – bisurated goods are goods with which the plaintiff had a connection in the course of trade;

5 the defendant's use manifestly imported a reference to the plaintiff's goods.

In some cases, it could have been argued that the use by the defendant of the plaintiff's trade mark in advertising did not infringe because such use did not relate to the plaintiff's product, but rather to the plaintiff's business. This argument found favour in *Pompadour Laboratories Ltd v Frazer*[145] where the phrase used by the defendant in advertising his hair lacquer – 'Frazer's Chemicals have manufactured hair lacquer for Pompadour Laboratories Limited for several years' – was held to be a reference to the plaintiff's name and not to his trade mark.[146] If this line of argument was taken by the defendant, it was a question of fact for the court to decide. So it was held in *News Group Newspapers Ltd v Mirror Group Newspapers (1986) Ltd*[147] where the defendant had used the plaintiff's masthead the *Sun*, amongst others, in an advertisement, placing it under the phrase 'Yes, Prime Minister' so as to indicate that the defendant's newspaper was the only one which opposed the Prime Minister. The advertisement was a 'knocking' advertisement indicating that the plaintiff's newspaper blindly followed the Prime Minister's views. Aldous J took the view that the advertisement must have referred to the newspaper rather than to the plaintiff's business. An injunction was awarded restraining publication of further copies of the advertisement.[148] This seems eminently sensible and it is hard to see how such advertising could do other than to have referred to the product concerned.

### Use in a trade mark sense

It is possible to use a trade mark otherwise than in a trade mark sense, and in *Mothercare UK Ltd v Penguin Books Ltd*[149] the publication of a book by the defendant with the title 'Mother Care/Other Care' was held not to infringe the plaintiff's 'Mothercare' trade mark because the words were being used in a descriptive sense and not a trade mark sense. The fact that the plaintiff had conducted surveys of the public to show evidence of confusion was criticised by Dillon LJ as being unhelpful.[150] Another example is provided by the case of *Mars GB Ltd v Cadbury Ltd*,[151] where it was held that the use by the defendant of the phrase 'Treat Size', used in relation to his packets of miniature chocolate bars, did not infringe the plaintiff's 'TREETS' trade mark, registered in Part A for confectionery. The plaintiff's use was not use as a trade mark, neither was it likely to deceive or cause confusion.

### Part B marks

The rights given by registration and infringement thereof were for Part B marks much the same as for Part A marks, with one important exception.[152] In an infringement action, if the defendant established to the satisfaction of the court that the use of which the plaintiff complained was not likely:

145 [1966] RPC 7.

146 *See also Harrods Ltd v Schartz-Sackin & Co Ltd* [1986] FSR 490. The case involved alleged passing off and breach of contract. In the Court of Appeal, allegations of trade mark infringement and passing off were dropped, leaving the question of breach of contract to be determined, [1991] FSR 209. It was held that a clause restricting the use of the plaintiff's name by the defendant in a concession agreement did not survive the termination of the agreement.

147 [1989] FSR 126.

148 However, in a later hearing, Hoffman J discharged the interlocutory injunction because of the plaintiff's inordinate and inexcusable delay in proceeding with the action, *The Times*, 18 December 1990.

149 [1988] RPC 113. This case also involved a claim in passing off and this aspect is discussed in Chapter 21.

150 *See also Smith Kline & French Laboratories Ltd's Cimetidine Trade Mark* [1991] RPC 17, where Gibson J said that survey evidence would seldom be convincing because of problems associated with sampling and the avoidance of leading questions. He suggested that it would probably be prohibitively costly to conduct a meaningful survey. In any case, whether a mark is 'in fact capable of distinguishing' was a question of law, not fact.

151 [1987] RPC 387.

152 The Trade Marks Act 1938 s 5(1) stated, in unnecessarily intricate language, that the rights given for a Part B registration were the same as for a Part A registration.

(a) to deceive or cause confusion, or

(b) to be taken as indicating a connection in the course of trade between the goods and the proprietor or registered user having the right to use the trade mark,

then injunctive or other relief would not be granted to the plaintiff.[153] In other words, if the defendant could show that his use of a mark did not cause either of the above, the trade mark right was ineffective. The provisions for service marks were similar. In view of this limitation it could be very hard to prove infringement of a Part B mark on the basis of importing a reference to it. An example might be the phrase 'If you like Everest mint chocolates you'll love our Matterhorn choice mints', where the word 'Everest' was registered in Part B for class 30 goods (including confectionery).[154] Although a technical infringement, the proprietor of the Everest mark would not be able to prevent the use of the phrase in advertising by the manufacturer of the Matterhorn mints because of the s 5(2) defence. However, it was the defendant who bore the burden of proof. As it required the proof of a negative (that the use was not likely to deceive, cause confusion or be taken to indicate a connection in the course of trade) it was a heavy onus to discharge, especially if the plaintiff filed positive evidence.[155]

## Infringement by breach of restrictions

This applied to both Part A and Part B marks.[156] However, it did not apply to service marks.[157] A proprietor or registered user of a registered trade mark might have made a written contract with another, being the purchaser or owner of goods, who agreed that he would not do any of five specified acts. If he then did one of those acts he was treated as infringing the trade mark in addition to being in breach of contract. This applied also to third parties to whom title to the goods had subsequently passed, unless that person was a *bona fide* purchaser for money or money's worth in good faith before receiving notice of the obligation.[158] The specified acts were:

(a) applying the trade mark to goods after they have been altered or repackaged;

(b) the alteration, part removal or obliteration of the trade mark;

(c) where the trade mark is on the goods and other matter (such as packaging), the total or partial removal or obliteration of the mark from the goods while leaving the mark on the other matter;

(d) where the trade mark is on the goods, applying another trade mark to the goods;

(e) where the trade mark is on the goods, adding any other matter in writing which is likely to injure the reputation of the trade mark.

## EXCEPTIONS

Certain exceptions to infringement were specifically provided for by the 1938 Act. Section 4, the Part A rights and infringement section, contained some exceptions that applied equally to Part B marks. Section 7 prevented interference by a trade mark proprietor or registered user with pre-existing rights, and s 8 permitted bona fide use of names and bona fide description of the character or quality of goods.

153 Ibid s 5(2).

154 It might not have been registrable in Part A, being a geographical name.

155 The defendant failed to discharge the burden in *Provident Financial plc* v *Halifax Building Society* [1994] FSR 81.

156 The infringement was provided for in s 6.

157 The Trade Marks (Amendment) Act 1984 Sch 1, para 4.

158 Of course, such persons would not be liable for breach of contract, not being a party to the original contract. Persons deriving title through a *bona fide* purchaser also took free of the obligation.

## Section 4 exceptions

A trade or service mark might have been entered upon the register subject to conditions or limitations. For example, a disclaimer could have been required for part of the mark that was common to the trade or service. The rights given by registration were obviously subject to any such conditions or limitations by s 4(2).[159] Section 4(3)(a) applied to goods that might have been used in the manufacture of other goods, for example a mark applied to cloth which was made into a dress by a person to whom the cloth had been supplied. This covered two situations: first, where the proprietor (or registered user) had applied the mark and not subsequently removed or obliterated it. For example, the cloth might have had the mark 'Novoweave' printed along the edge of rolls of cloth. The dressmaker buying the cloth made it up into dresses in such a way that the mark was visible on the inside of seams. The dressmaker did not infringe the trade mark by making, advertising and selling the dresses. The second situation was where the proprietor or registered user of the mark had expressly or impliedly consented to the use of the mark; for example, where the dressmaker advertised her dresses as being made from genuine 'Novoweave' cloth, the proprietor of the mark was taken to have impliedly consented by selling the material to a dressmaker.

In *Accurist Watches Ltd v King*,[160] third parties made watches for the registered user of the plaintiff's trade mark and applied the trade mark to the watches. The registered user became insolvent and the third parties took possession of quantities of the watches by virtue of retention of title clauses in their contracts with the registered user who was not to obtain good title to the watches until he had paid for them. The third parties sought to sell the watches and the plaintiff sued for trade mark infringement and passing off. Remarking that retention of title clauses could be ineffective otherwise, the court held that the makers of the watches had a complete defence under s 4(3)(a).

Section 4(3)(b) applied to goods adapted to form part of, or to be an accessory to, other goods and obviously covered both the dress examples above, spare parts and accessories. A retailer who sold replacement parts for cars would obviously have needed to refer to the make and model of the car (either of which might have been registered trade marks) in advertising and selling these parts, for example by placing a card in his shop window stating that he had for sale 'tyres for Ford Scorpios at only £33.00 each'. In terms of accessories, the advertisement might have read 'roof rack suitable for Vauxhall Vectra, only £22.50'. The use of the mark in this way was required to be 'reasonably necessary to indicate that the goods are so adapted'. It was clear that a trader could use the mark in making a bona fide description of his goods as long as he did not imply that the goods of which the adapted goods formed a part, or accessory, were not connected with the trade mark proprietor or registered user.[161]

## Section 7 – anterior marks

The continuing use of a pre-existing mark could not be restrained by subsequent registration of a similar mark (identical or nearly resembling). This

---

[159] In *Diamond T Motor Co's Application* [1921] 2 Ch 583 a disclaimer was required in respect of some of the features of the mark, such as the double line diamond border. Therefore, if another trader used a mark which included a double line diamond border, that would not infringe unless other features of the mark were the same or similar (nearly resembling).

[160] [1992] FSR 80.

[161] Advertising a film (not being one made by Kodak) for a Kodak camera was permissible as long as a connection between Kodak and the film was not imputed even though Kodak was registered for both films and cameras: *Kodak Ltd v London Stereoscopic* (1903) 20 RPC 337.

provision applied where the pre-existing mark had been continuously used from a date anterior to the use of the other mark or the date of registration of that other mark, whichever was first. Such use or registration had to be in relation to the same goods or services to which the pre-existing mark had been applied. The pre-existing mark might have been accepted for registration on the basis of honest concurrent use under s 12(2). The justification for this was that, otherwise, what was once lawful might become unlawful upon registration of the other mark. If both marks were in use in relation to the same goods or services, there could have been a possibility of a passing off action. The fact of registration did not remove this possibility because s 2 made it clear that the law of passing off was unaffected by the Trade Marks Act 1938. It was not inconceivable that, where two similar marks were involved only one of which was registered, the proprietor of one could bring a trade mark action against the other, while that other proprietor could bring a passing off action in return.

### Section 8 – bona fide use

The bona fide use by a person of his own name or that of his predecessor, or the name of his own or his predecessor's place of business was permitted. Also the bona fide description of the character or quality of goods of services was permitted provided that to do so did not import a reference as in s 4(1)(b).[162] Because of the general prohibition on the registration of a geographical name in Part A, it was unlikely that the use of names of places of business would otherwise offend. 'Bona fide' use meant essentially honest use without an intention either to deceive or to make use of another trader's goodwill.[163] Deliberately changing one's surname was not bona fide if such intention was present, for example if the owner of a small confectionery shop changed his name to 'Cadbury'.

In *Provident Financial plc* v *Halifax Building Society*[164] Aldous J, in granting an interlocutory injunction, thought there were two serious issues to be tried in relation to *bona fide* use, being:

(a) whether a person was *bona fide* within s 8 if he honestly believed that his literature was not deceiving anybody into thinking his services came from anybody else, although it might suggest that another person's services were connected; and
(b) whether the person relying on the defence had ever considered whether his expansion into the other person's field of activity would confuse the public by suggesting a connection between the parties and, if so, what was the conclusion?

### DEFENCES

A defence to an infringement action might have included a claim by the defendant that one of the exceptions, described above, applied to the alleged infringement. Other defences included claims that:

162 Or, in respect to trade marks only, as mentioned in the Trade Marks Act 1938 s 37(3) – certification marks.

163 *Baume & Co Ltd* v *A H Moore Ltd* [1958] RPC 226, *per* Romer LJ at 235.

164 [1994] FSR 81.

(a) the plaintiff did not have title to the mark allegedly infringed, that is he was not the registered proprietor (or registered user) of the mark;

(b) the mark which had allegedly been infringed was not registered or the registration was invalid and the mark ought to be expunged from the register;[165]

(c) the acts complained of did not fall within the meaning of infringement, for example the mark had not been used by the defendant as a trade mark;[166]

(d) the mark was registered in Part B of the register and the defendant was able to show that the use complained of was not likely to deceive or cause confusion, etc.[167]

Where there are two identical or similar marks on the register, use of one will not infringe the other mark under s 4(4). In *Neutrogena Corp* v *Golden Ltd*,[168] the plaintiff sold a range of soaps, shampoos and other skin and hair products under the registered trade mark 'NEUTROGENA'. The defendant sold a similar range of products under the name 'NEUTRALIA' and was the proprietor of the registered trade mark 'NUTRALIA' (without the 'E') for toiletries. The plaintiff sued for trade mark infringement and for passing off, adducing considerable evidence of deception and confusion. The defendant relied on the s 4(4) defence arguing that 'NEUTRALIA' was sufficiently close to its own registered trade mark 'NUTRALIA'. Section 30(1) allows use of a mark with additions or alterations not substantially affecting its character to be considered to be equivalent to use of the registered mark.

At first instance, Jacob J found that both trade mark infringement and passing off had been established. The defence based on s 4(4) failed. Jacob J held that there was a significant difference between 'NEUTRALIA' and 'NUTRALIA'. He considered that some persons would pronounce the words differently, the latter starting with 'nut' as in 'hazelnut'. Furthermore, the visual impression was different, 'NEUTRALIA' conjuring up neutrality and 'NUTRALIA' conveying nutrition. The Court of Appeal dismissed the appeal.

Other matters might have given rise to a defence, such as acquiescence, estoppel or delay.[169] Another situation advantageous to the defence was where the mark was being used fraudulently on the basis of the principle of *ex turpi causa non oritur actio*.[170] Unlike design law and patent law, there was no remedy for groundless threats of infringement proceedings under the 1938 Act.

## REMEDIES

The remedies available, depending upon the circumstances, were injunctions, damages or an account of profits as an alternative, and destruction of or erasure of the marks. If the marks could not be erased, an order for the destruction of the articles, advertising materials, etc. was a possibility. As has already been mentioned, in the case of an infringement of a Part B mark, injunctive and other relief was not available if the defendant could show that the act complained of was not likely to deceive or cause confusion, or be taken as indicating a connection in the course of trade between the goods or services and the proprietor or registered user of the mark.[171] In other cases, the successful plaintiff was entitled to nominal damages as a matter of course and to substantial damages if

---

165 Bearing in mind the relative safety of Part A marks after seven years (the Trade Marks Act 1938 s 13). A mark could have been removed, for example, for non-use (s 26). Other reasons included canellation of defensive marks (s 27(5)); with respect to registered users (s 28(10)) rectification under s 32 (e.g. for fraud), breach of conditions imposed: s 33.

166 Ibid s 4(1).

167 Ibid s 5(2).

168 [1996] RPC 473.

169 *See* the passing off case of *Vine Products Ltd* v *Mackenzie & Co Ltd* [1969] RPC 1, discussed in Chapter 21.

170 A right of action cannot arise from an evil deed.

171 The Trade Marks Act 1938 s 5(2).

proved based on the loss actually caused to the plaintiff, for example as a result in a downturn in sales as a consequence of the infringement. Damages were available notwithstanding the innocence of the infringer and this was treated as settled law since Eve J ordered an inquiry as to damages in *Henry Heath Ltd* v *Frederick Gorringe Ltd*.[172] In *Gillette UK Ltd* v *Edenwest Ltd*[173] the defendant contended that he was an innocent dealer in counterfeit razor cartridges imported from Italy. Blackburne J said (at 291):

> ... innocence on the part of the infringer has never at any rate in this country been found to justify denying damages to the plaintiff.

An account of profits was available as an alternative to damages.

## OFFENCES

The Trade Marks Act 1938 s 58A[174] made it a criminal offence for a person:

(a) to apply a mark identical to or nearly resembling a registered mark to goods or ancillary material, for example, labelling or packaging; or

(b) to sell, let for hire, or offer or expose for sale or hire, or distribute
   (i) goods bearing such a mark; or
   (ii) material bearing such a mark which is used or intended to be used for labelling, packaging or advertising goods; or

(c) to use material bearing such a mark in the course of a business for labelling, packaging or advertising goods; or

(d) to possess in the course of a business goods or material bearing such a mark with a view to doing any of the above mentioned things,

when the person was not entitled to use the mark in relation to the goods in question and the goods were not connected in the course of trade with a person who was so entitled.

Possession in the course of business of goods or material bearing such a mark was an offence if it was done for the purpose of enabling or assisting another to do any of the things mentioned in (a)–(c) above. For all these offences, under s 58A(3) it was required that the act was done with a view to gain or intention to cause loss to another and that the person concerned intended that the goods were accepted as being connected in the course of trade with a person entitled to use the mark. It was a defence to show a belief, on reasonable grounds, of entitlement to use the mark in question. The maximum penalty available for any of the above offences was extremely severe and reflected the growing awareness of the considerable damage caused to commerce and industry by counterfeiting, apart from public safety issues. The offences were triable either way and on indictment the maximum penalty was ten years' imprisonment and/or a fine. Under s 58A(5) a director, manager, secretary or other similar officer of a company could also have been criminally liable if he consented to or connived in the offence.

Under the Copyright, Designs and Patents Act 1988 s 283, a person or body corporate which carried on a business as, or held himself or itself out to be, a 'registered trade mark agent' when in fact that person or that body was not a

172 (1924) 51 RPC 457.
173 [1994] RPC 279.

174 Inserted by the Copyright, Designs and Patents Act 1988 s 300.

registered trade mark agent, was liable to a fine on summary conviction not exceeding £5000.[175] The Trade Marks Act 1938 s 59 concerned making or causing to be made a false entry or a forged copy of a register entry, or tendering a forged copy knowing it to be false. A person who did any of these was guilty of a summary offence.[176] Section 60 made it an offence to falsely represent that a mark was registered or was registered in respect of certain goods, etc., for example by impressing goods with the expression 'Registered Trade Mark'. The maximum penalty was a fine not exceeding level 3 on the standard scale (currently £1000).

175 This extended to allowing himself to be so described or held out.

176 However, in the Isle of Man, the offence was punishable by two years' imprisonment with or without hard labour and/or a fine not exceeding £100 (the Trade Marks Act 1938 s 59(2)).

# 20

## Trade marks – the new law

### INTRODUCTION AND BACKGROUND

The Trade Marks Act 1994 represents a milestone in trade mark law and it contains, without question, the most radical changes since the first trade mark legislation. The need for reform of trade mark law had become clear some time ago, but the opportunity to make the necessary changes was put on hold pending harmonisation of trade mark law throughout the European Community. At the end of 1988, the Council of the European Community adopted a Directive aimed at harmonising trade mark law throughout the European Community.[1] Although most of the basic principles of trade mark law were unaffected by the Directive there were, nevertheless, some significant and far-reaching changes required to be made to United Kingdom law.[2]

The Directive required compliance by 1 January 1993, but the UK failed to meet this deadline. This raised a number of issues concerning the direct effect of Directives, as in *Publicco Ministero* v *Ratti*,[3] and speculation as to the liability of the UK to individuals suffering damage as a result of non-compliance.[4] For example, a trader might claim that he has experienced loss because his application to register a trade mark has been refused because it was unregistrable, but under the law as expressed in the Directive the mark would have been registrable. However, the existence of the law of passing off substantially reduced the possibility of the trader suffering loss in practice. Consider a new trader (A) which uses a distinctive bottle for its perfume. Under the old law, following *Re Coca-Cola Co*,[5] the bottle would not be registrable. If another trader subsequently used a similar bottle, also for perfume, an action in passing off might not succeed because, being new to the market, trader A may not have had sufficient time to build up the required goodwill associated with its product. Had the bottle been registered as a trade mark, the second trader could have been stopped in its tracks as regards the use of a similar bottle.

A new Trade Marks Bill was introduced in the House of Lords in December 1993 for the primary purpose of implementing the regime of trade mark law contained in the Directive. It received the Royal Assent on 21 July 1994 and came into force on 31 October 1994. In the period between 1 January 1993 and 31 October 1994 the Registrar continued to apply the law in conformity with the 1938 Act and rules made in pursuance of it. But, in *Marleasing* v *La Commercial International de Alimentación*,[6] it was held that national courts should interpret national laws in accordance with Community law so that, in respect of registration of marks and infringement thereto in particular, there was a conflict between the position taken by the Registrar and the position likely to have been taken by the courts in respect of provisions of the Directive

1 Council Directive of 21 December 1988 to approximate the laws of member states relating to trade marks, OJ L40, 11.2.89, p. 1, A White Paper was published subsequently setting out the government's plans to conform with the Directive, *Reform of Trade Mark Law* Cm. 1203 (HMSO, 1990).

2 An early description of the changes was given in Groves, P. and Martino, T. 'Euromark: or How the EEC Bought UK Trade Mark Law into the 20th Century'(1990) 1 *European Business Law Review* 109.

3 [1980] 1 CMLR 96.

4 *Francovich & Boneface* v *Italian State* [1992] IRLR 84.

5 [1986] 2 All ER 274.

6 [1990] ECR I-4135.

that were of'direct effect'.[7] The Registrar was placed in a difficult position because of the delay in implementing the Directive, but in the event there seem to have been no major problems. Certainly, as far as the changes to registrability were concerned, it appeared that traders were satisfied to wait until the new Act was in force before applying to register marks that would have been of doubtful registrability under the 1938 Act.

The need for reform of UK trade mark law goes back to long before the Directive, and the Trade Marks Act 1938 had been subject to much judicial criticism. But difficult and obscure though the 1938 Act was, the need for change was also a reflection of a changing advertising and commercial environment. The 1938 Act sought to protect consumers from deceptive practices by making comparative advertising unlawful but it failed to take account of character merchandising (by its prohibition on trafficking in trade marks, described by Lord Bridge in *Holly Hobbie Trade Mark*[8] as a complete anachronism). Consumers are wiser now and have a far better knowledge of trading practices. In retrospect, the 1938 Act was far too restrictive in the nature of marks that could be registered and the way the legislation was altered to provide for service marks by the Trade Marks (Amendment) Act 1984 was clumsy in the extreme.

The Trade Marks Act 1994 brings a welcome breath of fresh air to trade mark law. It is fairly lengthy, comprising 106 sections and five schedules, and makes significant and substantial reforms to this important area of law. Gone is the obscure drafting of the 1938 Act. The new Act, though not without difficulty, is more clearly drafted and it paves the way for improvements in both the substantive and procedural law relating to trade marks. Greater provision is made for the international aspects of trade mark law, for example with respect to the Community trade mark, and it enabled the UK to ratify the Protocol to the Madrid Agreement on the International Registration of Marks during 1995. As was to be expected, the existing law of passing off is retained.

The Trade Marks Act 1994 heralded the possibility of registering all manner of marks that would certainly not have been registrable before. There was much speculation and excitement surrounding the possibility of registering three-dimensional marks, containers, sound, and even smells.[9] However, a meander through the *Trade Marks Journal* (in which applications to register trade marks are published) leaves one with the impression that nothing has changed, as the overwhelming proportion of applications are for marks distinctly lacking in frontier-expanding innovation. Even so, a few interesting examples can be found. An application was submitted on 31 October 1994 to register the Coca-Cola bottle as a trade mark. Applications have also been published for the Domestos bottle, the British School of Motoring's pyramid device that sits perched on top of the School's cars, a Kodak film box and, to the author's knowledge, at least one smell, being for Chanel No. 5. As we shall see, a requirement for registrability is that the trade mark should be a sign capable of being represented graphically. The course taken in the Chanel case is to describe the smell in words, following the first reported case in the USA, in *Re Clarke*,[10] which described a perfume as 'a high impact fresh floral fragrance reminiscent of plumeria blossoms'. It remains to be seen how effective such marks will be if accepted for registration in the UK. The reader is left to ponder how infringement of smell marks is to be determined!

It must be noted that the new law represents such a sea change in trade mark law that the utility of previous case law is questionable, particularly where the

7 *See* Nissen, D. and Karet, I. 'The Trade Marks Directive: Can I Prevail if the State has Failed' [1993] 3 EIPR 91.

8 [1984] FSR 199 at 202.

9 *See,* for example, Lewin, R. 'A New UK Trade Marks Law – A Godsend for Trade Mark Owners or a Goldmine for their Lawyers?' [1994] 3 EIPR 91.

10 17 USPQ 2d. 1238. For a discussion of smell marks, *see* Burton, H. 'The UK Trade Marks Act 1994: An Invitation to an Olfactory Occasion?' [1994] 8 EIPR 378.

wording in the Act closely follows that in the Directive. Of course, some of the prior case law will remain helpful in interpreting the new law, but in many cases, it will be inappropriate to rely on it to any great extent. In *Allied Domecq Spirits and Wines Ltd v Murray McDavid Ltd*,[11] Lord MacFadyen preferred the approach of Jacob J in *British Sugar plc v James Robertson & Sons Ltd*[12] where, in approaching the interpretation of s 11(2) from first principles rather than relying on earlier decided cases, he said (at 285):

> The Trade Marks Act 1994, implementing an EC Directive, has swept away the old law.

In *Bravado Merchandising Services Ltd v Mainstream Publishing (Edinburgh) Ltd*,[13] Lord McCluskey suggested that the use in a new statute of words and phrases used in earlier Acts which had been subject to judicial examination showed that the legislature, in deciding to use the same language, intended the same meaning as before. However, in *Allied Domecq*, Lord MacFadyen said that such an approach to the construction of the new Act must be severely limited. This must be right, otherwise, if each member state followed its own prior case law, the harmonising purpose of a Directive would be severely curtailed. In any case, in *Allied Domecq*, the previous equivalent statutory provision used different language and concepts. Nevertheless, Lord MacFadyen felt it inappropriate to decide whether the defender's use of the pursuer's trade mark was saved by s 11(2)(b) which permits the use in the course of trade of a trade mark by a third party to indicate, *inter alia*, geographical origin provided it is in accordance with honest practices in industrial or commercial matters. The defender had obtained a quantity of the pursuer's whisky from a third party blender. The pursuer, which distilled and matured whisky at its Laphroaig Distillery on Islay, had registered 'LAPHROAIG' as a trade mark. The defender sold the whisky as being from the Laphroaig Distillery, which indeed it was. On the basis of the balance of convenience, Lord MacFadyen discharged the interim interdict which had been granted to the pursuer.

Before looking at the provisions of the Trade Marks Act 1994 in detail, it is worth considering how the basic rationale of a registered trade mark has been subtly changed. Under the 1938 Act, the purpose of a trade mark was to indicate a connection in the course of trade between a trader and his goods. Under the 1994 Act, the primary purpose is to distinguish the goods of one undertaking from those of other undertakings.

## REGISTRABLE TRADE MARKS

The basic definition of what constitutes a registrable mark has been significantly widened. The Trade Marks Act 1994 s 1(1) defines a trade mark as being 'any sign capable of being represented graphically which is capable of distinguishing goods or services of one undertaking from those of other undertakings'. This is considerably wider than the definitions of a 'mark' and 'trade mark' in the 1938 Act.[14] However, the Registrar and the courts did not always take a particularly restrictive view of what constituted a trade mark, with the notable exception of *Re Coca-Cola*.[15] Even a two-colour combination for a capsule for a drug was held to be registrable by the House of Lords in *Smith Kline & French Laboratories Ltd v Sterling Winthrop Group Ltd*.[16]

11 [1997] FSR 864, Court of Session, Outer House.

12 [1996] RPC 281.

13 [1996] FSR 205.

14 The Trade Marks Act 1938 s 68(1) and, for Part A marks, s 9.

15 [1986] 2 All ER 274.

16 [1976] RPC 511.

The sign must be capable of distinguishing the goods or services of one under-taking from those of other undertakings and the importance of this is borne out by the recitals to the Directive.[17] The mark must serve as a guarantee of trade origin. If the sign cannot do this then it is not registrable. In *Philips Electronics NV v Remington Consumer Products*,[18] the plaintiff had registered a drawing of its three-headed shaver as a trade mark. It was held that the registration was invalid, *inter alia*, as the sign denoted function rather than trade origin.

Musical jingles, moving computer-generated images and perfumes may all potentially be registrable. Sounds, computer images and smells are all capable of graphical representation, by means of musical notation, computer data (or still frames or drawings) and chemical formulae (or written descriptions) respect-ively.[19] However, a limiting factor is the advertising of marks in the *Trade Marks Journal*, which, by the Trade Mark Rules 1994 r 65,[20] must contain a representa-tion of the mark. The application form TM3 has a square box (8cm × 8cm) in which the representation must be placed. The main purpose of advertising is to enable other traders to see if the new marks are identical to or very similar to their marks, or are otherwise unregistrable. This purpose could be defeated if the character of the mark was not readily apparent from an inspection of the journal, and while it may not be unreasonable to expect a reader to play a music mark to appreciate its character, it would be unfair to expect readers of the *Trade Marks Journal* to conduct complex chemical experiments to arrive at the mark. Scratch pads for smells, pianos and laboratory equipment are unlikely to be installed in public libraries holding copies of the *Trade Marks Journal*!

Three-dimensional marks should present no difficulty as it is a simple matter to represent the shape of an article by means of plan and elevation drawings or, even better, a perspective view. Computer-generated images can be treated in a similar manner, perhaps using a still frame, or a drawing or print out. In pract-ice, the rules made in pursuance of the new Act have to deal with the practicalities of registering new forms of marks and are expressed in an open-ended manner.[21] Rule 63 gives the Registrar a discretion to allow the filing of the application and other notices or documents by electronic means.

The Registrar has adopted guidelines as to when a sign is graphically repre-sented, being when:

(a) the sign is defined with sufficient precision so that infringement rights can be determined;

(b) the graphical representation can stand in place of the trade mark, without the need for supporting samples, etc.;

(c) it is reasonably practicable for persons inspecting the register, or reading the *Trade Marks Journal*, to understand from the graphical representation what the trade mark is.

In *Swizzels Matlow Ltd's Trade Mark Application*,[22] the sign 'The trade mark consists of a chewy sweet on a stick' was held to fail all three guidelines. A second application which had a flattened version of the sweet itself attached to the application form and which indicated that the mark was a shape, had ear-lier been withdrawn by the applicant.

Some specific examples of trade marks are given in s 1(1), being words (including personal names),[23] designs, letters, numerals, or the shape of goods or their packaging.[24] This allows the registration of distinctive containers and,

17 Seventh recital.

18 [1998] RPC 283.

19 For suggestions as to graphical representation, *see* Lyons, D. 'Sounds, Smells and Signs' [1994] 12 EIPR 540.

20 SI 1994/2583.

21 The White Paper, *Reform of Trade Marks Law*, Cm 1203 (HMSO, 1990) alluded to the fact that the open-ended definition of trade marks in the USA has not appeared to cause any particular administrative or legal problems. It is unlikely that applicants will have to deposit three-dimensional objects, computer disks or sound recordings.

22 [1998] RPC 244.

23 Thus personal names now, unlike before, have a presumption of registrability.

24 Under the previous law, a trade mark had to be some-thing distinct from the article marked. In *Re James Trade Mark* (1886) 33 ChD 392, an application to register a shape mark (a dome of blacklead) was refused.

**25** Indeed, in *Smith Kline & French Laboratories Ltd* v *Sterling Winthrop Group Ltd* [1976] RPC 511, Lord Diplock accepted that design registration and trade mark registration were not mutually exclusive.

**26** For example, a design for a shower tray including its underside in *Gardex Ltd* v *Sorata Ltd* [1986] RPC 623.

**27** [1998] RPC 69.

**28** Suggested by Peterson J in *Moore's Modern Methods Ltd's Application for a Trade Mark* (1919) 36 RPC 12, where an application had been made to register a trade mark the subject matter of a patent which was about to expire.

although there are exceptions, this could include new and aesthetic designs, normally the province of the Registered Designs Act 1949.[25] The effect of this could be to give a monopoly right in a design applied to a specific type of good for a period of potentially unlimited duration, compared with a maximum of 25 years' protection for registered designs. However, one important proviso stated in s 3(2) is that a sign will not be registered if it consists exclusively of the shape which gives substantial value to the goods, or is necessary to obtain a technical result or results from the nature of the goods themselves. It is clear that things that are acquired or used by reason of their design, such as a household ornament, will not be registrable as a trade mark, but the Design Registry has applied the eye-appeal requirement very generously in the past[26] and a great many designs do not add substantial value. Quasi-functional articles possessing an element of eye-appeal, such as food packaging, display or vending apparatus, might fall into this category and, in some cases, be registrable both as trade marks and designs.

A disadvantage some shape marks may have to overcome to be registrable is that they are not necessarily regarded by the public as trade marks. This may be the case where goods of a certain shape are well known as being from a particular manufacturer, but it is the name of the manufacturer rather than the shape of the goods which is recognised as being the trade mark by the public. For example, the shape of Lego bricks, having raised knobs which fit into tubes in the underside of the bricks, is so well known that almost everyone would instantly recognise them as Lego bricks. However, in spite of this, it was held that an application to register a brick as a trade mark must fail in *Interlego AG's Trade Mark Applications*.[27] There was no real evidence that the public recognised the bricks or the raised knobs or tubes as trade marks.

The Lego bricks had been subject to a patent which had expired. Neuberger J observed that this was a factor which should be taken into account in deciding whether to register a trade mark. He rejected the existence of a rule to the effect that dual protection could not be possible,[28] but said the decision to register required balancing the very substantial benefit to the proprietor in registering a mark with the public interest against monopolies in products (as opposed to marks).

As noted above, there are some limitations to the registrability of shape marks or functional shapes, but the 1994 Act does seem to allow dual protection by registered designs and trade marks and, exceptionally, patents and trade marks. It does seem fundamentally wrong that a design or invention that would ordinarily be limited to 25 or 20 years' protection could achieve effective protection without time limit through registration as a trade mark. The Act itself has some control in that shape marks will not be registrable if the shape results from the nature of the goods, if the shape is necessary to obtain a technical result, or if the shape gives substantial value to the goods. The Act does not expressly include a public interest prohibition on registration as suggested by Neuberger J, although other provisions could apply in relevant circumstances. For example, registration will be refused if the application in made in bad faith, and it is arguable that an applicant who now wishes to gain further protection for a registered design or patent which is about to expire could be deemed to apply in bad faith. Other hurdles may stand in the way, such as the shape not being generally appreciated by the public as a trade mark, and the interpretation of the exceptions to the registrability of shape marks.

## Single register

The two-tier system comprising Part A marks, being those adapted to distinguish, and Part B marks, being those capable of distinguishing, has been abolished and all existing marks have been transferred to the new single register. The lower threshold, capable of distinguishing, is now the test and it is likely that this will be taken to have the same meaning as before, that is capable in time of becoming distinctive with use, or not incapable of becoming distinctive, as *per* Sargant LJ in *Davies* v *Sussex Rubber Co.*[29] However, to this a proviso must be added in that the Act requires, additionally, that the trade mark is not devoid of a distinctive character: s 3(1)(b). This suggests that it is not enough that such a mark is capable of distinguishing in the future through use and that there must already have been some use of a mark which started life as devoid of distinctive character to endow it with some distinctiveness by the time of the application. This is reinforced by the proviso to s 3(1) which allows registration of marks devoid of distinctive character[30] if, at the time of the application, they have become distinctive through use. It could be argued that if a sign is capable of distinguishing the goods or services of one undertaking from those of other undertakings, it cannot be devoid of a distinctive character. This approach was rejected in *AD2000 Trade Mark*[31] where it was held that a sign is capable of distinguishing for the purposes of s 1(1) even if it is so capable only to the limited extent of being not incapable of distinguishing (as *per* Sargant J). A sign which meets that requirement must still not be devoid of a distinctive character.

Service marks are no longer treated differently to trade marks for goods and all marks, whether for goods or services, are described as trade marks.[32] Under the 1938 Act, Part A marks were conclusively valid after seven years. Pre-existing Part A marks have lost the benefit of this provision (there is no equivalent in the 1994 Act) and will be subject to the normal rules on revocation and invalidity.

## Unregistrable signs

Inevitably, there are some important exceptions to the types of signs that can be registered as trade marks. Unregistrability under the 1994 Act is tested against two types of grounds: absolute and relative. Generally, for the absolute grounds, marks caught are unregistrable *per se*, subject to some exceptions. For the relative grounds, the relationship between the mark applied for and earlier marks or other rights is important. The relative grounds for refusal have a close parallel in terms of the ways in which registered trade marks can be infringed.

## Absolute grounds for refusal

The absolute grounds for refusal are given by s 3. Section 3(1) states that the following shall not be registered:

(a) signs which do not satisfy the requirements of s 1(1);
(b) trade marks which are devoid of any distinctive character;
(c) trade marks which consist exclusively of signs or indications which may serve, in trade, to designate the kind, quality, quantity, intended purpose, value, geographical origin, the time of production of goods or of rendering of services, or other characteristics of goods or services;

---

29 (1927) 44 RPC 412 at 425.

30 The same applies to marks caught by s 3(1)(c) and (d), *see* below.

31 [1997] RPC 168.

32 There are some minor differences flowing from the differing nature of goods and services. For example, the meaning of 'using' a sign. For goods, this includes affixing the sign to goods or their packaging, and for services it includes offering or supplying services under the sign; the Trade Marks Act 1994 s 10(4).

(d) trade marks which consist exclusively of signs or indications which have become customary in the current language or in the *bona fide* and established practices of the trade.

However, registration shall not be refused by virtue of paragraphs (b), (c) or (d) above if, before the date of application, the mark has, in fact, acquired a distinctive character as a result of the use made of it. Although there is some similarity between these exceptions and the prior law, the last proviso marks a change. Under the 1938 Act the mark YORK for trailers was refused, even though it had become 100 per cent distinctive in fact,[33] although there were examples of geographical names being registered, particularly in Part B.[34]

The essence of an objection to a mark based on (b), (c) or (d) is immaturity in that there has not been sufficient use of the mark in such a way that it has become associated as an indicator of trade origin. In *AD2000 Trade Mark*,[35] in deciding that AD2000 was devoid of a distinctive character (the mark had not been used prior to the application for registration), Geoffrey Hobbs QC said (at 175):

> ... a sign possesses a distinctive character if and when it is endowed by nature and/or nurture with the capacity to communicate the fact that the goods or services with reference to which it is used recurrently are those of one and the same undertaking.

Other trade marks that have been considered to be devoid of a distinctive character are P.R.E.P.A.R.E.,[36] FROOT LOOPS,[37] a drawing showing a three-headed shaver[38] and the phrase: 'The trade mark consists of a chewy sweet on a stick.'[39]

Particular difficulty has been experienced with marks including the word 'Euro' and the Registrar has adopted guidelines to assist in determining whether such a mark fails on the basis of the absolute grounds for refusal. The guidelines are:

1 EURO (alone) – absolute grounds for refusal
2 EURO plus name of goods or services – absolute grounds for refusal
3 EURO plus invented word – accepted
4 EURO plus a word descriptive of characteristic of goods conjoined, generally accepted, but care would be required as sometimes such a combination can be descriptive.

In *EUROLAMB Trade Mark*,[40] it was held that the word 'EUROLAMB' for lamb meat was unregistrable. The mark would be understood as being Lamb from Europe and this would fall foul of s 3(1)(b) and (c) as describing the kind or geographical characteristic of the goods: The applicant cited a great many registered marks containing the word 'Euro', such as 'EUROCOOK' for cookware, 'EURO-CELL' for battery goods and 'EURODOG' for dogfood. However, most of these had been registered under the 1938 Act. The appointed person, Mr Hobbs QC, followed Jacob J in *British Sugar plc v James Robertson & Sons Ltd*[41] where he confirmed that register evidence had long since been deemed irrelevant under the 1938 Act and the same must apply to the 1994 Act.

'Shape marks' are a new departure, but there are some bars to registration in s 3(2). They will not be registered if they consist exclusively of the shape resulting from the nature of the goods themselves, or if necessary to obtain a technical result or if the shape gives substantial value to the goods.

33 *YORK Trade Mark* [1984] RPC 231.
34 For example, *Andorra Trade Mark* [1976] RPC 397 used for motor vehicles.
35 [1997] RPC 168.
36 *P.R.E.P.A.R.E. Trade Mark* [1997] RPC 884 – too close to PREPARE so as to be devoid of a distinctive character.
37 *FROOT LOOPS Trade Mark* [1998] RPC 240 – accepted as equivalent to FRUIT LOOPS and would only be registered on proof of distinctiveness through use.
38 *Philips Electronics NV v Remington Consumer Products* [1998] RPC 283.
39 *Swizzels Matlow Ltd's Trade Mark Application* [1998] RPC 244.
40 [1997] RPC 279.
41 [1996] RPC 281.

The scope of the exceptions for shape marks was considered by Jacob J in *Philips Electronics NV v Remington Consumer Products*.[42] Jacob J had already decided that the mark, comprising a drawing showing the shaving head of a three-headed shaver, was incapable of distinguishing and was also devoid of a distinctive character. Nevertheless, he went on to look at the provisions on shape marks. He decided that the shape did not result from the nature of the goods but gave substantial value to the goods, being an engineering function. Jacob J pointed out that good trade marks do add value to goods, that being one of their purposes from a trader's point of view. That being so, the exception to registrability for shapes that add substantial value must not be taken too literally. He suggested that the shape must exclusively add something of value, whether it be design or functional appearance, disregarding any value attributable to the trade mark's function of identifying the source of the goods.

As regards the shape being necessary for a technical result, Jacob J preferred the approach of Lord Reid in *Amp Inc v Utilux Pty Ltd*,[43] a registered design case, where he considered that the word 'dictated' should be viewed in a weak sense, otherwise the exception to registrability where a shape is 'dictated by function' would be reduced almost to vanishing point. Applying the same logic to the word 'necessary', Jacob J held that the sign consisted exclusively of a shape necessary to achieve a technical result. This provision could be subject to a ruling from the European Court of Justice.[44]

Section 3(3) prohibits the registration of marks that are contrary to public policy or accepted principles of morality, or if the mark is likely to deceive the public as regards the nature, quality or geographical origin of the goods or services. Marks that, by virtue of their use, are prohibited in the UK by any enactment or rule of law, or by any provision of Community law, are likewise unregistrable, by s 3(4). Thus, an application to register a word mark 'Somerset Champagne' would fail on several grounds, being deceptive in two ways regarding geographical origin and by contravening European Community regulations.[45] Certain specially protected emblems are also unregistrable, such as the Royal arms and national flags, and emblems of countries belonging to the Paris Convention and of certain international organisations (for example, the UN).[46] These provisions are similar to the exceptions provided for by the old law.[47]

A final ground for refusal on absolute grounds is given by s 3(6) where the application was made in bad faith. This could apply in the case of a 'ghost mark' such as the 'Nerit' mark in *Imperial Group Ltd v Philip Morris & Co Ltd*,[48] discussed in Chapter 19. In *Road Tech Computer Systems Ltd v Unison Software (UK) Ltd*,[49] Robert Walker J found difficulty in determining the meaning of 'bad faith'. It could have the narrow meaning of dishonesty, or a wider meaning including a lack of genuine intention or purpose. In the *Imperial Group* case, the Court of Appeal considered the application for a ghost mark was not in good faith though the Court did not regard it as dishonest. Robert Walker J found no assistance in the Directive, though in the end he did not decide the matter, the case being an application for summary judgment under Ord 14 RSC. He gave the defendant unconditional leave to defend being unpersuaded that the plaintiff's case on s 3(6) was so strong as to entitle it to summary judgment. The defendant had argued that the application for the trade mark was made in bad faith as the plaintiff had no intention to use the mark in relation to the goods for which it had been registered: 'computer software and programs; all included in Class 9; but not including any such goods relating to birds'.[50]

42 [1998] RPC 283.

43 [1972] RPC 103.

44 *See Ide Line AG v Philips Electronics NV* [1997] ETMR 377 on appeal to the Swedish Supreme Court.

45 EC 823/87 as amended. This would also amount to passing off (*see Taittinger SA v Allbey Ltd* [1993] FSR 641) which is itself a relative ground for refusing registration.

46 The Trade Marks Act 1994 ss 3(5) and 4.

47 *See* the Trade Marks Rules 1986, SI 1986/1319.

48 [1982] FSR 72.

49 [1996] FSR 805.

50 The reason for excluding goods relating to birds is that an American bird is known as a roadrunner (also known as a paisano or chaparral cock).

## Relative grounds for refusal

Section 5 contains the relative grounds for refusal. They are so described because registrability depends upon the nature of the relationship between the mark and an earlier mark or right. A mark will not be registered if identical to an earlier mark for the same goods or services (s 5(1)). In this case, there is no need to consider whether this is likely to cause confusion on the part of the public.

For marks where there is not complete identity of the mark and the goods or services, for refusal to register it is required that there exists a likelihood of confusion on the part of the public, which includes a likelihood of association with the earlier trade mark.[51] Although prior law in the Benelux countries considered this to extend to 'non-origin' association, such as where the second mark raises an association in the minds of the public without confusion as to origin, in *Sabel BV* v *Puma AG, Rudolf Dassler Sport*,[52] the European Court of Justice held that a mere association which the public might make between the two trade marks as a result of an analogous semantic content (in this case drawings showing a bounding feline) was not, by itself, sufficient to conclude that there is a likelihood of confusion.

If a likelihood of confusion exists, identical marks for similar goods or services, similar marks for identical goods or services and similar marks for similar goods or services will not be registrable. It is possible that previous case law on what constitutes a likelihood of confusion remains relevant. In *Pianotist Co's Application*,[53] Parker J suggested the following factors should be taken into account for word marks:

- the look and sound of the words
- the goods to which the marks were applied
- the nature and kind of customer (for example, trade customers would be less likely to be confused as to origin than ordinary consumers)
- the surrounding circumstances
- a consideration of what would be likely to happen if both marks were to be used.

A trade mark which is identical with or similar to an earlier trade mark and which is to be registered for dissimilar goods or services shall not be registrable if, or to the extent that, the earlier trade mark has gained reputation in the UK (or, in the case of a Community trade mark, in the European Community) and the use of the later mark without due cause would take unfair advantage of, or be detrimental to, the distinctive character or repute of that earlier trade mark (s 5(3)). Neither will a mark be registered if its use could be prevented by virtue of any rule of law (especially the law of passing off) protecting an unregistered trade mark or other sign used in the course of trade, or an earlier right such as a copyright, design right or registered design (s 5(4)). However, for all these relative grounds, registration may still be possible if the proprietor of the earlier trade mark or other right consents. Table 20.1 outlines the relative grounds for refusal.

51 For the meaning of 'likelihood of association', *see* the discussion of *Wagamama Ltd* v *City Centre Restaurants plc* [1995] FSR 713, ante.

52 [1998] RPC 199, Advocate General Jacobs approving the approach of Laddie J in *Wagamama Ltd* v *City Centre Restaurants plc* [1995] FSR 713, discussed later.

53 (1906) 23 RPC 774 at 777.

**Table 20.1 Relative grounds for refusal**

| Relationship with earlier mark | Relationship with goods or services for which earlier mark registered | Proof of likelihood of confusion | Notes |
|---|---|---|---|
| Identical | Identical | No | Unregistrable *per se*. |
| Identical | Similar | Yes | |
| Similar | Identical | Yes | |
| Similar | Similar | Yes | |
| Identical | Not similar | No* | If earlier mark has reputation, if it would take unfair advantage of, or be detrimental to distinctive character of repute of earlier mark. |
| Similar | Not similar | No* | |
| Probably similar | Probably similar | Yes | Passing off. |
| Probably similar | Similar article (if a design) | No | Copyright, design right or registered design. |

* Although, to show unfair advantage or detriment will, in most cases, probably require proof of confusion.

Consider the following examples of registrations of the mark *Splurge* for chocolate:

- *Splurge* is to be used for chocolate. There exists an earlier mark, also *Splurge*, that is also used for chocolate. The registration will be refused point blank. There is no need to consider whether there is a likelihood of confusion.
- As above, but the earlier mark is used for gum drops. Registration will not be allowed if there is a likelihood of confusion as the goods are similar (confectionery).
- As above, but the earlier mark is used for garden equipment. The new mark should be registrable because there is very little, if any, likelihood of confusion (the goods to which the two marks are applied are different and will be sold at different trade outlets), unless the first mark has a reputation which would be taken unfair advantage of or which would be detrimentally affected.
- *Splurge* is to be used for chocolate. An earlier mark also used for chocolate is *Splodge*. Registration will probably be refused because there is a likelihood of confusion.

And so on.

An earlier mark is defined in s 6. It is a UK mark, an international mark (designating the UK) or Community trade mark (CTM) having an earlier date of registration taking priority into account; a CTM with a valid claim to seniority from an earlier registered trade mark or international trade mark (designating the UK); a trade mark entitled to protection under the Paris Convention as a well-known mark. Included are marks with earlier application dates pending registration (subject to their being registered). Expired marks shall be taken into account for one year after expiry, unless the Registrar is satisfied there was no bona fide use during the two years immediately preceding the expiry.

Honest concurrent use is dealt with in s 7. Where the relative grounds for refusal would otherwise apply, the Registrar shall not refuse the application unless there is an objection from the proprietor of the earlier mark or right raised in opposition proceedings. The burden of proof is on the applicant for registration to show that there has been honest concurrent use, and this does not affect the absolute grounds for refusal or an application for a declaration of invalidity.

At the moment, opposition can be raised by anyone. Section 8 allows the possibility of limiting opposition on the basis of the relative grounds to the proprietor of the earlier mark or right by Order in Council. This is to bring UK law in line with the Community trade mark provisions. The basis of the CTM and trade mark law in a number of EC member states is that registration simply depends on lack of opposition rather than on examination by the trade mark office plus opposition. However, it will probably be a number of years before the appropriate change will be made. When this happens proprietors of existing registered marks will need to be even more vigilant and inspect the *Trade Marks Journal* regularly. This will have the effect of raising a limited presumption in favour of the mark being registrable, removing the Registrar's discretion in this respect.[54]

**54** By the Trade Marks Act 1938 s 17(2), the Registrar had a discretion to refuse or accept an application. Thus, the Registrar could refuse to register a trade mark on the ground, *inter alia*, that it would be likely to cause confusion, s 12(1).

## REGISTRATION

Under s 32, an application to register a trade mark requires the submission of the following items:

- a request for registration
- the name and address of the applicant
- a statement of goods or services in relation to which it is sought to register the trade mark
- a representation of the trade mark
- a statement that the trade mark is being used, by the applicant or with his consent, in relation to those goods or services, or that he has a *bona fide* intention of so using it
- the prescribed fee (application plus class fees)

The date of filing will be the date when all the necessary documents have been furnished to the Registrar (s 33). This is the date of application. Section 35 provides for priority from earlier filings from Paris Convention countries for up to six months.

The applicant to register a trade mark (or the proprietor of an existing mark) may disclaim the right to exclusive use of a specified element of the trade mark, or agree to a limitation (for example, a territorial limitation) under s 13. Under the Trade Marks Rules 1994 r 24, this must be by written notice, and the Registrar will make the appropriate entry in the register and publish the disclaimer or limitation. Requesting a disclaimer or limitation may be in response to advice from the Registrar. Under the old law, the Registrar could impose disclaimers himself directly; for example, as in *Diamond T Motor Car Company* [1921] 2 Ch 583.

## Registration procedure

The registration procedure is laid out in ss 37–41. The stages are as follows (*see* Figure 20.1):

- *File application.*
- *Examination* – to ensure that the requirements in the Act and rules are satisfied. This will entail a search of earlier marks as the Registrar considers necessary. The opportunity will be given to the applicant to make representations and/or amend the application if the Registrar thinks that the requirements are not met (s 37).
- *Acceptance* – if it appears to the Registrar that all the requirements for registration have been met he *shall* accept the application (under the 1938 Act, the Registrar had a discretion) (s 37(5)).
- *Publication* – in the *Trade Marks Journal* (r 61 – including particulars and such information required under the rules and any other information as the Registrar thinks fit).

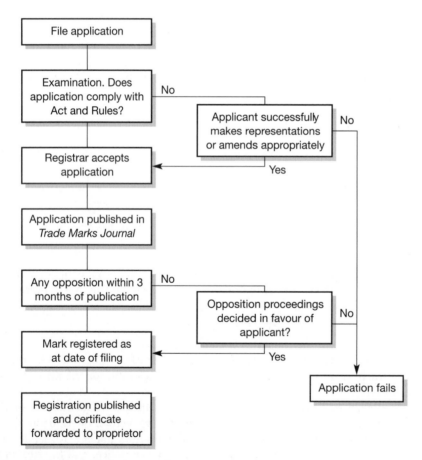

**Figure 20.1 Registration procedure**

- *Opposition* – under s 38(2), any person may give written notice of opposition within three months of the date of publication (Trade Marks Rules 1994 r 13). The grounds for opposition must be stated. Additionally, by s 38(3), any person may make observations in writing before registration without becoming a party to the proceedings on the application.
- *Registration* – where the application has been accepted and there has been no opposition (or, if there has been, the proceedings have been decided in favour of the applicant) then, unless it appears to the Registrar that the application was accepted in error, the mark shall be registered (s 40). The trade mark shall be registered as of the date of filing, which shall be deemed to be the date of registration (s 40(3)). The registration will then be published (Trade Marks Rules 1994 r 16) and a certificate issued to the applicant (s 40(4)).

The wording in s 40(1), 'the mark shall be registered', appears mandatory but this is subject to a lack of opposition and the Registrar being satisfied that the application has not been received in error. Laddie J explained the meaning of s 40(1) in *CREOLA Trade Mark*[55] where a mark had been advertised in the *Trade Marks Journal* but the word CREOLA appeared very indistinctly. There had been no opposition, but the Registrar decided to re-advertise the mark printed more clearly and, on this occasion, there was an opposition. The applicant argued that the mark should have automatically been registered after the opposition period based on the first advertisement. This was rejected by Laddie J who said that, at the end of the opposition period and in the absence of opposition, the Registrar was obliged to take steps timeously to place the mark on the register. However, until such time as the mark was placed on the register, the Registrar could take note of any material brought to his attention. Registration does not follow automatically. Had that been the intention, the statute could have provided for that in clear language.

Under s 39, the applicant may withdraw his application at any time, or restrict the goods or services covered by application. Amendment is also allowed, but only in respect of the name or address of the applicant, errors of wording or copying or obvious mistakes, provided the correction does not substantially affect the identity of the trade mark or extend the goods or services covered by the application (s 39(2)).

Applications can be divided, or merged or made in respect of a series of marks (s 41). The Trade Marks Rules, rr 19, 20 and 21 deal with the fine detail. The advantage of division might be that it is a way to isolate an objection while allowing the unchallenged aspects to proceed. Where an application is divided, each divisional application is to be treated as a separate application with the same filing date as the original application.[56] In *DUCATI Trade Mark*,[57] an original application (No. 2055227) was divided (Nos 2055227A and 2055227B). A notice of opposition incorrectly referred to No. 2055227 (it had been intended to oppose No. 2055227A) and the Trade Mark Registry pointed this out and returned the fee. The mark was then registered, there being no opposition recorded against it, and the subsequent application for rectification of the register was refused.

A series of marks means a number of trade marks resembling each other as to their material particulars and differing only as to matters of a non-distinctive character so as not substantially to affect the identity of the mark. This is equivalent to the registration of series of marks as associated marks under the old law. However, there is no limitation on the separate assignment of such marks as there was under the old law.

55 [1997] RPC 507.

56 Rule 19(1) Trade Mark Rules 1994, SI 1994/2583.

57 [1998] RPC 227.

The duration of registration has been changed. Under s 42, it is for a period of ten years from the date of registration (date of filing) and may be renewed for further ten-year periods, *ad infinitum*. Under s 43, the Registrar will send a reminder between one month and six months prior to the expiry of the last registration (r 27). Renewal shall be made on the appropriate form within six months before the expiry of the last registration. There are provisions for late renewal (if a mark has not been renewed, that fact shall be published). Renewal may take place in the six months following expiry subject to payment of an additional fee. Otherwise the mark will be removed from the register (r 29). However, within a further six months the mark may be restored subject to an additional restoration fee if the Registrar thinks it is just to do so in the circumstances (r 30).

Generally, once registered, a trade mark may not be altered (s 44). However, an alteration may be permitted where the mark includes the proprietor's name and address, for example where there is a change to the name or address of the proprietor, provided that the alteration does not substantially affect the identity of the mark. The alteration will be published and persons claiming to be affected by it may object.

Under s 72, registration of a person as proprietor of the mark is *prima facie* evidence of the validity of the original registration of a trade mark and any subsequent assignment or other transmission of it. This is equivalent to the presumption contained in s 46 of the 1938 Act.

The current fees are £225 to register a trade mark or series of trade marks, plus £50 for each additional class over one. Renewal is £250, plus £200 for each class renewal over one. A request to enter details of an assignment, or to record a licence or other registrable transaction costs £50. Serving notice of opposition costs £200.[58]

The volume of trade mark registration indicates the importance of this area of law as a means of protecting goodwill. The impact of the 1994 Act, allowing registration of a much wider range of marks, was already felt before the Act came into force. In 1994, there were 39 514 applications to register trade marks and 3058 applications for additional classes. In the previous year there were 34 764 applications in respect of trade and service marks.[59] The transitional provisions may have accounted for the increase in applications because under the Trade Marks Act 1994, Sch 3 para 11, pending applications (those that had been filed but not finally determined at commencement[60]) could be judged for registrability under the 1994 Act if the applicant gave notice not more than six months after commencement of the Act.

There were 31 241 applications to register trade marks during 1996 and 20 965 additional classes filed in that year. Just over half of the 56 531 marks registered in 1996 had been filed by United Kingdom applicants with the United States of America being the next most frequent at 8607 registrations. The most popular classes of goods were class 10 (scientific, nautical and surveying and electrical apparatus and instruments) with 7437 registrations, followed by class 16 (paper and paper articles, stationery, office requisites, etc.) with 4019 registrations and class 25 (clothing, including boots, shoes and slippers) with 3413 registrations. The most popular service was, not unexpectedly, class 42 (services that cannot be placed in other classes) with 3304 registrations.[61]

58 The Trade Marks (Fees) Rules 1996, SI 1996/1942.

59 Of which 28 460 were for trade marks. Patent Office, *Annual Report and Accounts 1994–95*, (HMSO, 1995) at p. 19.

60 The Trade Marks Act 1994, Sch 3 para 1(2).

61 Patent Office, *Annual Report and Accounts 1996-97*, (London: The Stationery Office, 1997).

## TRADE MARKS AS PROPERTY

The Act states that a registered trade mark is an item of personal property (ss 2(1) and 22, or, in Scotland, incorporeal moveable property). Under the provisions of the Act, trade marks are easily alienable. Under s 24, trade marks can be assigned, or pass by testamentary disposition or by operation of law in the same way as other personal property and with or without the goodwill of a business. Assignments may be partial in terms of:

(a) some, but not all, goods or services for which the mark is registered;
(b) use in a particular manner or in a particular locality.

This is wider than before. Under the 1938 Act, it was possible to divide a business and assign marks with that part of the goodwill which had been divested provided that the part of the business retained was in relation to different goods.[62]

Assignments or vesting assents are not effective unless in writing and signed by or on behalf of the assignor (or personal representative) (s 24(3)). This also applies to an assignment by way of security. A registered trade mark may be subject to a charge as is other personal property. Under s 23(1), each joint proprietor is entitled to an equal, undivided share. Therefore, it would appear that they are tenants in common, unlike the position under the 1938 Act which was based on a joint tenancy. However, this is subject to any agreement to the contrary, so joint proprietors could agree on a joint tenancy. The change could reflect the desire to make the property rights in trade marks more easily alienable.

A limiting factor on split assignments will probably be the desire to retain the distinctive character of a trade mark. If the mark becomes incapable of distinguishing the goods of one undertaking from those of other undertakings, this could be grounds for invalidity or revocation if the public are liable to be misled.

There are clearer rules for joint proprietorship of trade marks. Under s 23(3), each co-proprietor may do any act for his own benefit that would otherwise infringe, but may not, under s 23(4), without the consent of the other co-proprietors, grant a licence to use the mark, or assign or charge his share in the registered trade mark.

Unlike the 1938 Act, there are detailed provisions for licensing (exclusive, non-exclusive and sub-licences). Under s 28(1), a licence may be limited – in particular in terms of the goods and services for which it is registered, or in terms of use in a particular manner or locality. A licence must be in writing and signed by or on behalf of the grantor (s 28(2)). Unless otherwise provided for, a licence is binding on the grantor's successor in title. Sub-licences are recognised as possible and, under s 28(4), references in the Act to licences include sub-licences. The registered user provisions in the 1938 Act required that the proprietor must have some control over the use of the mark, for example, by exercising quality control. This is no longer required under the 1994 Act. Registered users existing at commencement were transferred to the register under the 1994 Act for transactions affecting the mark.[63]

The Trade Marks Act 1994 contemplates exclusive licensees and non-exclusive licensees commencing legal proceedings against infringers, although the right of a licensee to do this can be affected by the terms of the licence agreement. Under s 31(1), an exclusive licensee may, provided the licence agreement so provides, have the same rights and remedies as the proprietor.

62 *Sunbeam Motor Co's Application* (1916) 33 RPC 389.

63 The Trade Marks Act 1994, Sch 3 para 9(2).

However, under s 31(4), if either the proprietor or the exclusive licensee brings an infringement action, he must join the other except by leave of the court, although this does not apply to interlocutory relief.

Under s 30(2), unless the licence provides otherwise, a licensee may call upon the proprietor to take action, and if the proprietor refuses or fails to take action within two months of being called on to do so, a licensee (including a sub-licensee) may bring proceedings in his own name as if he were the proprietor. Again, the proprietor would normally be joined in the action unless the court gave leave otherwise.

In terms of an exclusive licence, it is not clear whether ss 30 and 31 are mutually exclusive or complimentary. There is an apparent contradiction in s 30 between s 30(1) and s 30(7). The former suggests that s 30 does not apply where, or to the extent that, an exclusive licensee has by virtue of s 31(1) the right to bring proceedings in his own name, whereas s 30(7) states that s 30 applies in relation to an exclusive licensee if or to the extent that he has by virtue of s 31(1) the rights and remedies of an assignee as if he were the proprietor.

In practice, the licence agreement will probably address issues dealing with rights to bring proceedings. For example, an exclusive licence may grant the licensee the same rights and remedies as if it had been an assignment. As such rights and remedies are declared by s 31(2) to be concurrent with those of the proprietor and a current proprietor with concurrent rights must be joined in the action except by leave of the court, the licence should provide for this eventuality also. The licence may state that the proprietor agrees to take part in any action as co-plaintiff subject to payment of his expenses by the licensee, and the licence may also provide for any apportionment of an award between the proprietor and licensee. Where the proprietor and exclusive licensee have concurrent rights, the court shall take into account the terms of the licence and any pecuniary remedy already awarded or available to either in respect of the infringement: s 31(6). In directing an account of profits, the court shall apportion the profits between the proprietor and exclusive licensee as the court considers just, subject to any agreement between them.

The following transactions affecting registered trade marks must be registered on application to the Registrar by a person claiming to be entitled to an interest in or under the mark concerned by virtue of any such transaction, under ss 25(1) and (2):

- an assignment of the mark or any right in it (this could include, for example, the assignment of a licence);
- the grant of a licence under the mark;
- the grant of a security interest (fixed or floating charge) over the mark, or over any right in or under it;
- the making by personal representatives of a vesting assent in relation to the mark or any right in or under it;
- a court order (or order of other competent authority – for example, the Trade Marks Registrar rectifying the register) transferring the mark or any right in or under it.

Under s 25(3), until the application for registration of the transaction has been made, it is ineffective against a person acquiring a conflicting interest in or under the mark in ignorance of the transaction, and any person claiming to be a licensee because of the transaction does not have any rights and remedies for infringement.

A person becoming a proprietor or licensee has six months to register his interest (the court has discretion to extend if it was not practicable to register within six months). Failure to register within that time will mean that the new proprietor or licensee cannot obtain damages or an account of profits in respect of infringements occurring between the date of the transaction and the date of registration of the interest (s 25(4)).

No trusts shall be entered on the register, but equities in relation to registered trade marks may be enforced as with other personal property (s 26). This permits action by beneficial owners of trade marks.

As some months may pass between application and registration, the provisions in the Act relating to assigning, licensing and registration are also effective in relation to an application to register a trade mark (s 27). Thus it is possible to grant an assignment or a licence in respect of a trade mark before it has been formally registered.

## RIGHTS CONFERRED BY REGISTRATION

The proprietor (and exclusive licensee, if there is one) has exclusive rights which are infringed by use of the trade mark without consent in the UK (s 9(1)). Section 9 continues by stating that the acts amounting to infringement are specified in s 10, but this is narrower than the basic statement – use in the UK without consent. This is contradictory and s 9(1) could be construed by considering that any use without consent in the UK infringes. In *British Sugar plc v James Robertson & Sons Ltd*,[64] it was argued that s 9(1) put a gloss upon s 10 requiring that infringing use had to be use as a trade mark. Jacob J rejected this, describing s 9(1) as no more than a 'chatty introduction to the details set out in s 10', noting that s 9(1) had no equivalent in the Directive. That being so, it is probably safe to ignore s 9(1) altogether. That leaves unresolved, however, the question as to whether infringing use must be use as a trade mark. If anything, case law has proved unhelpful (see the next section).

The rights have effect from the date of registration (s 9(3)). This is the date of filing of the application in accordance with s 40(3). However, the proprietor cannot begin infringement proceedings before the date on which the mark is in fact registered, therefore infringement proceedings cannot be brought until the day that registration is granted. The language in the two provisions is somewhat tautologous. Section 36(3) states that the date the mark is in fact registered is the date of filing. Because it is retrospective it is none the less a question of fact. But obviously no proceedings can be entertained until it is known that the mark has been registered.

The proprietor's rights will be limited if he has acquiesced in the use of a later registered trade mark for a continuous period of five years. This also applies to the owner of an earlier unregistered mark.[65] Under s 48, the proprietor of the earlier mark will not be entitled to claim that the registration of the later mark is invalid unless the later registration was applied for in bad faith. Neither will the proprietor of the earlier mark be able to oppose the use of the later mark in relation to the goods or services for which it has been used. Therefore proprietors of trade marks must scan the pages of the *Trade Marks Journal* regularly to

64 [1996] RPC 281.

65 Or, for that matter, any other earlier right such as a copyright or design right.

monitor the use of other marks that are similar and be prepared to take action. The existence of a validly registered later mark under these provisions does not affect the validity of the earlier mark in as much as the proprietor of the later mark is not allowed to oppose the use of the earlier mark or right.

## INFRINGEMENT OF A REGISTERED TRADE MARK

For an infringement to be made out, the person responsible must use a sign in the course of trade, and under s 103(1) this includes any business or profession. Use of a sign means, in particular, under s 10(4):

- affixing to goods or their packaging;
- offering or exposing goods for sale, putting them on the market or stocking them for those purposes under the sign, or offering or supplying services under the sign;[66]
- importing or exporting goods under the sign;
- use of the sign on business papers or in advertising.

The meaning of importing and exporting came up for determination in *Waterford Wedgwood plc v David Nagli Ltd*[67] in which the defendant had acquired through a third party a consignment of counterfeit Waterford Crystal valued at around £700 000 which was situated in Bilbao, Spain. The defendant gave instructions for the shipment of the crystal from Bilbao to New York. Unknown to the defendant, the crystal was loaded on a ship bound for Felixstowe where it was transferred to another ship bound for New York. Although it was held that the property in the crystal had passed to the buyer in New York, it was held that the defendant had infringed the UK trade marks of the plaintiff by importing into and exporting from the UK. The shippers were acting as agents under the instructions of the defendant as principal.

The court confirmed that importation consists of bringing goods into the territorial jurisdiction of the UK and exportation consists of their removal from territorial jurisdiction. As the crystal was imported and exported in packing cases bearing the plaintiff's trade marks, the defendant had infringed by importing and exporting under the sign, even though the crystal was only temporarily in the UK, and even though the crystal was brought into the UK *en route* for New York. As regards a claim that the defendant had infringed by using the trade marks on invoices and other papers, it was held there was no infringement as the defendant, who thought the crystal was genuine, thought it was referring to genuine Waterford Crystal. The luckless defendant had challenged the validity of some of the plaintiff's trade marks, arguing that WATERFORD was a geographical name and LISMORE was a name for a pattern in customary use in the trade. However, this was rejected as the proviso in s 3(1) allows such marks to be registered if they have become distinctive through use, which was the case here.[68]

There is some doubt as to whether the use must be use as a trade mark. In the Scottish case of *Bravado Merchandising Services Ltd v Mainstream Publishing (Edinburgh) Ltd*,[69] the respondent published a book about the pop group 'Wet Wet Wet' under the title 'A Sweet Little Mystery – Wet Wet Wet – The Inside Story'. 'Wet Wet Wet' was registered as a trade mark and the proprietor brought an action for an interdict (injunction) against this use of the name.

66 Calling a car showroom 'Autodrome' did not infringe the registered mark 'AUTODROME' used for motor cars because it was not used in relation to goods under the Trade Marks Act 1938 s 4: *AUTODROME Trade Mark* [1969] RPC 564. But compare with *CHEETAH Trade Mark* [1993] FSR 263 where use on an invoice was held to infringe.

67 [1998] FSR 92.

68 The plaintiff's request for an account of profits was not granted as the court indicated that the defendant had not made a profit!

69 [1996] FSR 205.

The respondent argued it had a defence under the Trade Marks Act 1994 s 11(2)(b), which states that a trade mark is not infringed by '... the use of indications concerning the kind, quality, quantity, intended purpose, value, geographic origin, the time of production of goods or rendering of services, or other characteristics of goods or services ...'.[70] This was accepted by the court because the respondent was using the mark as an indication of the main characteristic of the article, that is, a book about the pop group. Lord McCluskey went on to make some interesting remarks, *obiter*, about use of a trade mark in a trade mark sense. Section 10(1) sets infringement in the context of use in the course of trade. Both counsel accepted that this meant use in a trade mark sense, accepting that *Mothercare (UK) Ltd v Penguin Books Ltd*[71] still represents good law. In respect of ordinary words used as trade marks, use of the same or similar words in book titles in such as way as was descriptive of the books' contents was non-trade mark use. Lord McCluskey gave an example of a travel writer who had visited the Lake District during torrential rain and might choose to call his book about the Lake District 'Wet Wet Wet'. However, in the present case, the book had nothing to do with climate or moisture and the use was use in a trade mark sense. Also, where a trade mark was a newly coined word such as 'The Beatles', a book about the pop group entitled 'The Beatles – The Golden Years' would involve use in a trade mark sense. However, the judge said that it would be bizarre if trade mark legislation, which was designed to indicate origin, was used to prevent publishers using a trade mark in a book about the proprietor or the product.

Jacob J disagreed with Lord McCluskey's view that use must be use as a trade mark. In *British Sugar plc v James Robertson & Sons Ltd*,[72] he held that there was no such requirement in ss 10(1) or 10(2). In that case, the plaintiff had registered 'TREAT' for dessert sauces and syrups and complained of the defendant selling a sweet spread labelled 'Robertson's Toffee Treat'. The defendant claimed that it used the word descriptively and not as a trade mark. Jacob J said there was no reason to limit s 10 in such a way and purely descriptive use would not infringe because it would be within s 11(2) which states, *inter alia*, that indications of kind, quality, quantity, intended purpose etc. do not infringe if in accordance with honest practices in industrial or commercial matters. However, Jacob J held that the trade mark was invalid and, even if it was valid, it would not have been infringed and, consequently, what he said about infringing use not being required to be use as a trade mark must not be taken too seriously.[73] In *Trebor Bassett Ltd v The Football Association*,[74] Rattee J felt it unnecessary to decide the point but in *Philips Electronics NV v Remington Consumer Products*,[75] counsel cast doubt on what Jacob J had said in *British Sugar* and invited him to change his mind. He declined to do so, but he did suggest such arguments were worthy of further consideration. Displaying an uncharacteristic reticence, he said (at 312):

> The point could be important in this case if the registration were valid ... I do not think, however, this is the case where I should form a view as to whether [counsel's arguments] are right. This is because of the firm conclusion I have come to in respect of invalidity and as to a defence under s 11(2).

There must be some doubt as to whether using a trade mark but not in a trade mark sense can infringe. If it does, as Jacob J suggested, it could give a stronger monopoly than could possibly have been envisaged. As the main purpose of a

70  The defence afforded by the Trade Marks Act 1994 s 11(2)(b) is wider than the equivalent under the Trade Marks Act 1938 s 8(b) which is in terms of bona fide description of the character or quality of goods.

71  [1988] RPC 113.

72  [1996] RPC 281.

73  Nor was there any need to decide this point in *Bravado Merchandising*, as the s 11(2) defence applied there also.

74  [1997] FSR 211.

75  [1998] RPC 283.

trade mark is to denote origin (that is, in a trade mark sense) extending the rights beyond that seems unjustifiable. Of course, as Jacob J rightly points out, in most cases there will be a defence under s 11(2), but it is better to limit the rights in a trade mark to their proper sphere rather than have someone using the mark in a non-trade mark sense rely on a defence. There may be circumstances where the statutory defences do not apply. For example, the trade marks mentioned in this book are not being used in a trade mark sense. If Jacob J is right, their use in this book infringes because such use is outside the scope of s 11. The same applies to law reports of trade mark cases.

Infringement would seem to extend to the spoken use of words as well as to a visual representation as, under s 103(2), 'use' includes use otherwise than by means of a graphic representation. This should also extend to smells if such marks are registered.

One type of infringement does not require proof of a likelihood of confusion on the part of the public. This is use in the course of trade of a sign *identical* to the trade mark in relation to *identical* goods or services against which the mark is registered (s 10(1)). Other infringements require proof of likelihood of confusion (including a likelihood of association). Such infringements are use in the course of trade of a sign which is:

1 *identical* to the trade mark in relation to goods or services *similar* to those against which the mark is registered (s 10(2)(a)); or
2 *similar* to the trade mark in relation to *identical* or *similar* goods or services against which the mark is registered (s 10(2)(b));

where the similarity is the reason for the likelihood of confusion on the part of the public, which includes a likelihood of association with the trade mark.

### Similar sign

In determining whether a sign is similar to a trade mark, account is to be taken of colourable alternatives and the sound of the mark when spoken may also be relevant. In *Sir Terence Orby Conran v Mean Fiddler Holdings Ltd*[76] the plaintiff was registered proprietor of the trade mark 'Zinc' under the class of planning design and interior design of restaurants, cafes, bistros and wine bars and he planned to open a series of restaurants in London and Glasgow, under the name 'Zinc Bar'. The defendant opened a wine bar in Kilburn, London calling it 'Zincbar', using the word 'ZINCBAR' on the right-hand side of the sign on the bar's fascia and 'Zn', the chemical symbol for zinc, on the left-hand side. The defendant came up with some alternative names including Zn, ZN, Sinc or Sync.

Walker J granted summary judgment. He considered trade mark infringement to be obvious, and the same applied to the alternatives suggested by the defendant, 'ZN', 'Sinc' or 'Sync' that were sufficiently colourably similar. Evidence of confusion included a would-be customer of the plaintiff who was given the number of the defendant's bar in Kilburn.

A degree of similarity is permissible provided the sign is not confusingly similar to the trade mark. After all, a likelihood of confusion is required, mere similarity is not sufficient *per se*. In *The European Ltd v The Economist Newspaper Ltd*,[77] the plaintiff published a weekly newspaper under the masthead incorporating the word 'European'. The masthead was a registered

[76] [1997] FSR 856.

[77] [1998] FSR 283.

trade mark, but the plaintiff had disclaimed any monopoly in the word 'European'. The defendant's masthead included the phrase 'The European Voice'. The Court of Appeal confirmed the decision at first instance dismissing the plaintiff's claim for trade mark infringement. An aural comparison was eschewed by the court. The marks were visually different but phonetically similar and any aural comparison would be to disregard the distinctive features of the plaintiff's mark which could be seen but not heard. The plaintiff's mark comprised two words in upper case though with 'THE' in a smaller font and with a dove holding a copy of the newspaper and part of the globe superimposed on the letter 'O' of 'EUROPEAN'. The defendant's masthead was in lower-case type without a dove or globe, but with a star over the 'i' of 'Voice'.

### Similar goods

In determining whether goods are similar, Jacob J in *British Sugar plc v James Robertson & Sons Ltd*[78] suggested a test derived from the old test for whether goods where of the same description used under the 1938 Act.[79] He suggested the following factors were relevant:

(a) the respective uses of the respective goods or services;
(b) the respective users of the respective goods or services;
(c) the physical nature of the goods or acts of service;
(d) the respective trade channels through which the goods or services reach the market;
(e) in the case of self-service consumer items, where in practice they are respectively found or likely to be found in supermarkets and in particular whether they are, or are likely to be, found on the same or different shelves;
(f) the extent to which the respective goods or services are competitive. This inquiry may take into account how those in trade classify goods, for example, whether market research companies, which of course act for industry, put the goods or services in the same or different sectors.

Registry practice may be an important factor in determining whether the goods or services are similar. In *Avnet Inc v Isoact Ltd*,[80] the plaintiff had registered 'AVNET' in respect of advertising and promotional services within class 35. The defendant provided Internet services to the aviation industry under the names Aviation Network and Avnet, and which included the facility to allow subscribers to advertise on their own web pages. Registry practice at the time was that the defendant's activities would fall within class 42. The plaintiff's application for summary judgment was refused. In any case, what the defendant was doing, by providing customers with a facility to advertise, was not in substance providing advertising or promotional services.

The makers of the popular 'Baywatch' television series were not pleased when someone started transmitting encrypted 'adult films' under the name 'Babewatch'. In *Baywatch Production Co Inc v The Home Video Channel*,[81] it was held, *inter alia*, that the goods or services were not similar. The plaintiff had registrations for 'BAYWATCH' against video discs and tapes in class 9 and other registrations, but none that covered television programmes or broadcasting. It was also held that the signs were not similar and there was no satisfactory evidence of confusion. This must be contrasted with *NAD Electronics Inc v NAD Computer*

**78** [1996] RPC 281.

**79** Romer J in *Jellinek's Application* (1946) 63 RPC 59, approved by the House of Lords in *DAIQUIRI RUM Trade Mark* [1969] RPC 600.

**80** [1998] FSR 16.

**81** [1997] FSR 22.

*Systems Ltd*[82] in which the plaintiff had registered the trade mark 'NAD' for, *inter alia*, compact disc players. The plaintiff made high quality sound systems. The defendant used the word 'NAD' on his computer systems and this was held to infringe. Account was taken of the fact that computer technology has evolved and many computer systems come complete with CD-ROM drives and have speakers and can play music compact discs as well read CD-ROM discs.

82 [1997] FSR 380.

### Likelihood of confusion

Where there is not complete identity of sign and/or goods or services, infringement depends upon there being a likelihood of confusion which includes a likelihood of association. Under Benelux trade mark law, it had been accepted for some time that a trade mark could be infringed even if the consuming public was not misled as to origin. In *Claeryn/Klarein*,[83] Claeryn was a registered trade mark for a Dutch gin. The defendant called his liquid cleaning agent Klarein. Both words were pronounced the same in Dutch. It was held that there was an infringement on the basis of dilution and degradation of the registered mark. Persons drinking Claeryn would think of the cleaning agent as they drank, a particularly unpleasant prospect. This was sufficient to find infringement even though there was no risk that consumers would think the two products came from the same or connected companies. In other words, the association conjured up in the minds of consumers was 'non-origin' association.

83 Case A 74/1, Jur 1975, 472 (Netherlands).

The phrase 'likelihood of association' is new to UK trade mark law. Its relevance came to be considered in the Chancery Division in *Wagamama Ltd v City Centre Restaurants plc*.[84] The plaintiff had a successful Japanese restaurant in London under the registered trade mark WAGAMAMA, a Japanese word. The defendant, in April 1995, opened a restaurant in London selling Indian food under the name Rajamama. When sued, the defendant changed the name of the restaurant to Raja Mama's, but this did not satisfy the plaintiff. During the course of the trial, the question arose as to the precise meaning of the phrase 'a likelihood of confusion on the part of the public, which includes a likelihood of association with the trade mark'. The plaintiff argued that this was wider than 'classical infringement' and based the argument, in part, on the background to the EC Directive harmonising trade mark law, and in particular that the test for infringement should be that used in the Benelux countries, that is, including non-origin association (where there is no confusion as to the origin of the goods).[85] It was held that there had, indeed, been an infringement of the trade mark on the classical basis (confusion as to origin).[86] However, Laddie J refused to accept that he should follow Benelux law, especially if he was firmly of a different view. He declined to accept the importation of trade mark law as it is applied in the Benelux countries simply on the basis that they were 'first past the post'. He also refused to take account of minutes of a confidential council meeting which supported the plaintiff's contention on non-origin association. He said (at 730):

84 [1995] FSR 713.

85 For a comparison of Benelux law and the *Wagamama* decision, *see* Harris, P. 'UK Trade Mark Law: Are You Confused?' [1995] 12 EIPR 601.

86 Passing off was found also.

> ... two possible constructions which may be placed on Article 5 of the 1988 Directive and section 10(2) of the 1994 Act. The rights of the proprietor against alleged infringers may be limited to classic infringement which includes association as to origin or, following the Benelux route, it could cover not only classic infringement but also non-origin association. In my view, the former construction is preferred. If the broader

scope were to be adopted, the Directive and our Act would be creating a new type of monopoly not related to the proprietor's trade but in the trade mark itself. Such a monopoly could be likened to a quasi-copyright in the mark. However, unlike copyright, there would be no fixed duration for the right and it would be a true monopoly effective against copyist and non-copyist alike. ... Furthermore, there appears to be little commercial justification for any such extension of trade mark rights.

As noted above, non-origin association infringed in the Benelux countries and, in some respects, it is not out of step with the route now taken by the law of passing off as a result of the Elderflower Champagne case, discussed in the following chapter on passing off. That is, even though the public are not confused as to the origin of the goods or services, the unauthorised use of another's mark or sign is damaging as it tends to erode its distinctive character. However, Laddie J noted that the relevant phrase states that the likelihood of confusion *includes* a likelihood of association and, as he pointed out, the word 'includes' indicates that the latter part of the phrase cannot be more extensive than the first. In other words, a likelihood of association will infringe only if there is also a likelihood of confusion on the part of the public. The public must be confused about the origin of the goods or, as another form of confusion, assume that the infringer's trade or use of the sign is somehow associated with or consented to by the other trader.

It was not too long before the European Court of Justice had an opportunity to rule on the matter. In *Sabel BV v Puma AG, Rudolf Dassler Sport*,[87] the German court, the Bundesgerichtshof, referred a question involving non-origin association, in particular whether a coincidence in semantic content was sufficient for there to be a likelihood of confusion. Advocate General Jacobs approved the approach taken by Laddie J in *Wagamama* and the court held that a mere association which the public might make between two marks as a result of their analogous semantic content (in this case a leaping feline creature) is not, *per se*, a sufficient ground for concluding that there is a likelihood of confusion within the meaning of the Directive. Thus, Laddie J's decision has been vindicated at the highest level. It seems that the phrase 'likelihood of association' is just one example of a form of confusion. It might occur, for example, where consumers think that the defendant's goods originated from a company associated with the proprietor, perhaps as a licensee.

87 [1998] RPC 199.

### Trade marks of repute

For well-known marks, a registered trade mark is also infringed by the use of a sign in the course of trade that, without due course, takes unfair advantage of, or is detrimental to the distinctive character or repute of a registered mark enjoying a reputation in the UK (s 10(3)). For this to apply, the sign must be:

(a) *identical* or *similar* to the trade mark; and
(b) used in relation to goods or services *not similar* to those against which the mark is registered.

The Act is silent as to whether a likelihood of confusion is required to infringe under s 10(3). It could be argued that there must be confusion for the unfair advantage or detriment to the repute of the well-known mark. Indeed, in

*Baywatch Production Co Inc* v *The Home Video Channel*,[88] it was held that s 10(3) still requires a likelihood of confusion otherwise that form of infringement would give stronger protection to non-similar goods than s 10(2) gave to similar goods. However, this ignores that fact that this form of infringement is limited to marks enjoying a reputation in the United Kingdom. The parallels with passing off cannot be ignored.

If one accepts that the goodwill in a well-known name (whether or not registered as a trade mark) can be damaged by its unauthorised use by others, such as in *Taittinger SA* v *Allbev Ltd*,[89] then the same must apply to a well-known trade mark. If a trader starts selling 'Rolls-Royce Shoes' or 'Cadbury Bicycles', does that not damage the standing of those names by a process of erosion? If the use is on a large scale, it would seem entirely possible over a period of time that there would be some dilution. The distinctiveness of the registered mark, the attractive force which brings in customers, would be prejudiced. If that is so, then there is detriment to the distinctive character or repute of the mark. Even if one is not prepared fully to accept that argument, the other limb of s 10(3) permits infringement simply by taking unfair advantage of the distinctive character or repute of the registered mark. That does not need confusion. Surely it is sufficient for the other trader to use the well-known mark in an attempt to impute a feeling of quality for his goods. It is submitted that Mr Crystal QC is wrong on this point in *Baywatch*. After all, it would have been easy for the Act (and Directive) to expressly state that there must be a likelihood of confusion for this form of infringement.

Section 56 of the Act gives a right to relief for proprietors of marks which are well-known in the United Kingdom, being a mark of a person who is a national of or is domiciled in a Paris Convention country whether or not that person carries on business or has any goodwill in the United Kingdom. Such a person is entitled to injunctive relief against the use of an identical or similar mark used in relation to identical or similar goods or services where the use is likely to cause confusion. Thus, a foreign mark which is not used in the United Kingdom but is, nevertheless, well-known in the United Kingdom may be protected against non-consensual use there. This form of protection does not extend to use on non-similar goods or services. There are similar provisions for injunctive relief for national and other emblems in ss 57 and 58. Furthermore, such emblems may not be registered. An example is a national flag or state armorial bearings or such devices used by international intergovernmental organisations of which one or more Paris Convention countries are members.

## Applying mark to material etc.

Under s 10(5), a person who applies a registered mark to material intended to be used for labelling or packaging goods, as a business paper (for example, a company letterhead, or a sheet of instructions accompanying goods), or for advertising goods or services, shall be treated as a party to any infringing use if, when he applied the mark, he knew or had reason to believe that the application of the mark was not authorised by the proprietor or a licensee.

88 [1997] FSR 22.

89 [1993] FSR 641, discussed in the subsequent chapter.

## Evidential aspects

The proprietor bears the burden of proof as regards the use to which the mark has been put if the question arises (s 100). This will not normally be a problem as articles bearing infringing marks are likely to be available for sale, other materials such as advertising copy are likely to be available to be public and the use of trap orders may prove useful to winkle out other forms of infringement. If the defendant wishes to challenge the validity of the mark, or the proprietor's title or other aspects of the registration it will be he who bears the burden of proof. Under s 72, in all legal proceedings relating to a registered trade mark, the registration of a person as proprietor shall be prima facie evidence of the validity of the original registration and on any subsequent assignment or other transmission of the registered trade mark.

If the validity of a registered mark is contested and it is found to be valid, the court may give a certificate to that effect under s 73. This mirrors s 47 of the 1938 Act. Such a certificate could prove useful in any subsequent proceedings as regards an award of costs in favour of the proprietor.

## Comparative advertising

Under the 1938 Act a trade mark was infringed if it was used in comparative advertising, for example, where a trader lists his products and prices alongside those of a competitor, using the competitor's trade mark. Comparative advertising was introduced into the 1938 Act as a result of a failure to find infringement against a comparative advertiser in *Irving's Yeastvite Ltd* v *Horsenail*.[90] The 1994 Act allows comparative advertising under s 10(6) which states that nothing in the preceding provisions of s 10 shall be construed as preventing the use of a registered trade mark by any person for the purpose of identifying goods or services as those of the proprietor. However, there is a proviso to this. The use must be in accordance with honest practices in industrial or commercial matters and if it is not, such use will infringe if, without due cause, it takes unfair advantage of, or is detrimental to, the distinctive character or repute of the trade mark.

The meaning of the proviso was first considered by Laddie J in *Barclays Bank plc* v *RBS Advanta*[91] in which the plaintiff was the proprietor of the registered trade mark 'BARCLAYCARD'. The defendant was a joint venture between the Royal Bank of Scotland and the Advanta Corp of USA, which was about to launch a credit card called 'RBS Advanta Visa Card'. It distributed letters, leaflets and brochures. The leaflets contained a list of bullet points stating '15 ways the RBS Advanta Visa Card is a better card all round', and the brochure contained tables comparing the features of the RBS card with express reference to BARCLAYCARD and its features. The plaintiff applied for injunctive relief alleging that its trade mark was infringed under s 10(1) (use in the course of trade of a sign identical with the trade mark in relation to identical goods or services). The defendant argued that its advertising fell within the s 10(6) defence.

In refusing to grant an injunction, Laddie J said that the purpose of s 10(6) was to allow comparative advertising as long as it was honest. The burden was on the proprietor to show that one of the factors in the proviso to s 10(6) applied, that is, that the use was not in accordance with honest practices in

90 (1934) 51 RPC 110.

91 [1996] RPC 307.

industrial or commercial matters, or that it took unfair advantage of, or was detrimental to, the distinctive character or repute of the trade mark. He said that the question as to whether the use of the trade mark was in accordance with honest practices was an objective test, being whether it was considered honest by members of a reasonable audience. He also accepted that an amount of hyperbole was to be expected in much advertising copy. A reasonable audience would appreciate that an advertiser would select the most favourable features and might not show other features which showed his competitor's product to best effect. The amount of hyperbole which is acceptable will depend on the nature of the goods, and Laddie J contrasted second-hand cars with powerful medicines. In the latter case, to be in accordance with honest practices, comparative advertising should be more frank and forthright with much less scope for selecting features to show the advertiser's product in a more favourable light.

Laddie J in *Barclays*, stressed the importance of the phrase 'in accordance with honest practices' and suggested that the second part of the proviso, 'taking unfair advantage of, or being detrimental to, the distinctive character or repute of the trade mark' would add nothing of significance in the majority of cases. Jacob J agreed with this (and the basic test of whether the advertising was objectively misleading to a substantial proportion of a reasonable audience) in *Vodafone Group plc v Orange Personal Communications Services Ltd*.[92] In that case, which concerned an advertisement suggesting an average saving of £20 per month by switching to the defendant's mobile telephone network, Jacob J accepted that persons would generally expect some elasticity of price and usage. That is, a reasonable audience would realise that not everyone would save £20 a month and that fewer calls are generally made on a more expensive tariff.

These two cases lay down useful guidance on the scope of acceptable comparative advertising and recognise that the public have a pretty good idea that traders involved in such an activity will be selective in the choice of features that they use. This itself is not misleading. For comparative advertising to be misleading, and therefore not in accordance with honest practices, it must amount to such a distortion that the public are deceived as to the nature of one trader's goods or services in comparison with the other trader's goods or services. Such distortion could come about because the selection of features is so skewed as to misrepresent the goods or services of either trader, or because the factual information used is inaccurate to a material extent. It should be noted that there is a European Community Directive on comparative advertising that would allow it if carried out fairly.[93]

## Trap orders

If the proprietor of a registered trade mark believes that his mark is being infringed, it should not be necessary to apply for an *Anton Piller* order for the purpose of obtaining and preserving evidence of the infringement. It will usually be possible to buy examples of the product to which the alleged infringing mark has been applied. Indeed, *Anton Piller* orders are not lightly granted and alternative means of obtaining evidence should be explored first. For example, in *Systematica Ltd v London Computer Centre Ltd*[94] it was pointed out that the plaintiff could have freely walked into the defendant's shop and purchased copies of the alleged infringing computer programs.

92 [1997] FSR 34.

93 OJ L290, 23.10.97, p. 18, to be implemented by 2000.

94 [1983] FSR 313.

Several test purchases can be made to build up a pattern of infringement. It may serve a useful purpose to frame a request for goods or services in such a way as to demonstrate clearly that there is a significant chance of confusion. Such orders for goods are referred to as 'trap orders' and are commonly used as a means of obtaining evidence of infringement in relation to both trade marks and passing off actions. It is obvious that the way the order is placed is important and it should be done in a clear, unambiguous and fair way. Trap orders may indeed be essential if the trade mark infringement occurs in an advertisement, to verify that the goods or services being offered in fact are not those of the proprietor or a licensee.

## REMEDIES

Section 14(2) states that the remedies for infringement of a registered trade mark are damages, injunctions, accounts or otherwise, as are available in respect of infringement of any other property right.

Orders for delivery up of infringing goods, materials or articles from a person having them in his possession, custody or control in the course of business are available under s 16(1). But under s 18, an order for delivery up is not available after the end of the period of six years from:

- (with respect to infringing goods) the date on which the registered trade mark was applied to goods or their packaging;
- (with respect to infringing material) the date on which the registered trade mark was applied to the material;
- (with respect to infringing articles) the date on which the articles were made;

unless the proprietor of the mark was suffering from a disability, or was prevented by fraud or concealment from discovering the facts entitling him to apply for the order. In these cases, the six years run from the time when the proprietor ceased to be under a disability or when he could, with reasonable diligence, have discovered the true facts.[95]

Infringing goods, materials or articles are defined in s 17. Infringing goods are those bearing (or whose packaging bears) an identical or similar mark, the application of which was an infringement of the same in respect of goods to be imported, or where the sign has otherwise been used in relation to the goods so as to infringe. This does not affect the importation of goods that can legally be imported by virtue of any enforceable Community right (s 17(3)). Exhaustion of rights is covered under s 12: that is, it is not an infringement to use the mark in relation to goods which have been put on the market by or with the consent of the proprietor. This does not extend to a situation where the proprietor has a legitimate reason to oppose further dealings, for example where the condition of the goods has subsequently been changed or impaired.

Infringing material is material that bears an identical or similar mark and which is used (or is intended to be used) for labelling or packaging the goods, or as a business paper or for advertising goods or services so as to infringe (s 17(4)). Infringing articles are those specifically designed or adapted for making copies of a sign identical to or similar to a registered trade mark, and the person who has the article in his possession, custody or control knows or has reason to believe that the article has been or will be used to produce infringing goods or material (s 17(5)).

95 The Trade Marks Act 1994 s 18(2). A disability has, by s 18(3), the same meaning as under the relevant limitation legislation – in England and Wales, the Limitation Act 1980.

Sections 56–58 provide for injunctive relief in favour of the proprietors of well-known marks, national emblems and the like of Convention countries, and emblems, etc. of certain international organisations. Well-known marks are those entitled to protection as well-known marks under the Paris Convention for the Protection of Industrial Property, being well-known in the UK as the mark of a person who is a national of, domiciled in, or who has a real and effective industrial or commercial establishment in, a Convention country.[96]

With respect to emblems, there are some notification requirements to be fulfilled under s 59. A foreign proprietor with a foreign registration in respect of a mark well known in the above sense in the UK will be able to rely on s 56 to obtain injunctive relief even though he has no trade in the UK. In other words, a foreign mark having repute will be protected in the the UK in the absence of goodwill, unlike the case in passing off.[97]

In *Philips Electronics NV v Remington Consumer Products*,[98] Jacob J confirmed that s 56 puts a plaintiff who has a reputation but no business and, hence, no goodwill in a passing off sense, in the United Kingdom in the same position as if he did have a business and goodwill in the United Kingdom. The plaintiff was domiciled in The Netherlands (a Convention country) but was not able to rely on s 56 as there was no deceptive use. Jacob J confirmed that the provision did not extend to non-deceptive use. Section 56 implements Article 6[bis] of the Paris Convention which dates from 1927. Jacob J also made the point that the plaintiff's shape mark was not covered by this provision as he did not consider a shape mark to be a trade mark for the purposes of the Paris Convention and that it was impossible to envisage that, in 1927, anyone would have thought the provision would cover 'engineering artefacts of this sort'. Furthermore, although certain shape marks are registrable in the EC, they are not registrable in a great many other countries belonging to the Paris Convention. With this limitation in mind, what s 56 does is to cure the defect in the law of passing off that requires the plaintiff to demonstrate that he has goodwill within jurisdiction.[99]

If the application for registration of a trade mark is made by an agent of the proprietor, registration shall be refused if the proprietor opposes the application; and if the application is accepted, registration shall be refused if the proprietor applies for a declaration of the invalidity of the registration, or applies for rectification of the register so as to substitute his name as proprietor (s 60).

*TRAVELPRO Trade Mark*[100] provides an example of rectification under s 60. A sole distributor of an American company, which had several registrations for TRAVELPRO in other countries, applied to register the mark in the United Kingdom without informing the American company. It was held that the distributor was an agent within s 60 and had no claim to ownership of the mark. The American company's name was substituted for that of the distributor as registered proprietor.

## EXCEPTIONS AND DEFENCES

Compared to the 1938 Act, the defences and exceptions to infringement are expressed in much simpler language. The provisions under the old law relating to contracts between the proprietor or registered user and purchaser or owner of goods are gone. These infringements would be actionable under contract law anyway and their inclusion was somewhat of a mystery.

96 Well-known marks are defined in Article 6[bis] of the Convention.

97 Compare with *Anheuser-Busch Inc v Budejovicky Budvar NP* [1984] FSR 413, discussed in Chapter 21.

98 [1998] RPC 283.

99 A point made in the South African case of *McDonald's Corp v Joburgers Drive-In Retaurant (Pty) Ltd* [1997] (1) SA 1, approved by Jacob J in *Philips*.

100 [1997] RPC 864.

Under s 11(1), a registered trade mark is not infringed by use of another registered trade mark in relation to the goods or services for which the latter is registered. If two proprietors use similar registered trade marks in respect of the same goods, neither infringes the other's mark. This unlikely scenario could happen (that is, two very similar marks owned by different proprietors for the same or similar goods) because of the honest concurrent use provisions in s 7.[101] Honest concurrent use itself does not provide a defence, it is only when the second mark is registered that there is a defence.[102] Also, under s 47(6), if a registration is declared invalid to any extent, it shall be as if it had never been registered to that extent, and thus proving invalidity is a defence to a past infringement.

Honest practices in industrial or commercial matters are the test for non-infringing use in s 11(2), which states that a registered trade mark is not infringed, in the case of honest practices, by:

(a) the use of a person of his own name or address;
(b) indications describing the goods or services, for example kind, quality, quantity, intended purpose, value, geographical origin, the time of production of goods or rendering of services, or other characteristic of goods or services;
(c) use necessary to indicate the intended purpose of the product or service (particularly with respect to accessories or spare parts).

Section 11(2)(b) has been used on a number of occasions. For example, in *British Sugar plc* v *James Robertson & Sons Ltd*[103] it was held that the defendant's use of the phrase 'Toffee Treat' was within s 11(2)(b) although, in any event, the plaintiff's 'TREAT' trade mark was declared to be invalid. The same result occurred in *Philips Electronics NV* v *Remington Consumer Products*[104] (defendant's use within s 11(2)(b) but the plaintiff's registration declared invalid). In *Bravado Merchandising Services Ltd* v *Mainstream Publishing (Edinburgh) Ltd*,[105] the defendant published a book entitled 'A Sweet Little Mystery – Wet Wet Wet – The Inside Story'. The book was about the pop group called 'Wet Wet Wet', which had been registered as a trade mark. The defendant's use of the mark fell within s 11(2)(b) because it was descriptive of the content of the book. However, for s 11(2) to apply the use must be in accordance with honest practices in industrial or commercial matters. In *NAD Electronics Inc* v *NAD Computer Systems Ltd*,[106] Ferris J considered that this was equivalent to bona fide use under s 8 of the 1938 Act, approving Lloyd Jacob J in *George Ballantine & Sons Ltd* v *Ballantine Stewart & Co Ltd*[107] in relation to the adoption of a company name similar to an existing trade mark where it was held that the relevant aspect was the use made of the company name not the bona fides in selecting the name in the first place. In *NAD*, Ferris J accepted that the name had been selected originally in good faith but subsequent use was not in good faith and, indeed, he described the defendant's use of the name as 'unjustifiably aggressive'. A criticism of Ferris J's judgment on this point is that it is not clear that 'honest practices' is the direct equivalent of 'bona fide'. Honest practices in the cut and thrust of commercial life may not necessarily be bona fide in a strict sense. The question should be what reasonable and honest traders consider to be acceptable.

The use in the course of trade in a particular locality of an earlier right which applies only in that locality does not infringe (s 11(3)). An earlier right in this context is an unregistered trade mark or other sign continuously in use in relation to goods or services by a person or predecessor in title.

---

**101** Under the Trade Marks Act 1994 s 7(3), honest concurrent use is declared to be as under the Trade Marks Act 1938 s 12(2). The case of *Second Sight Ltd* v *Novell UK Ltd* [1995] RPC 423 affords an example of applications for registration made under this provision. It gives a defence only as from the date of registration.

**102** *Per* Jacob J in *Origins Natural Resources Inc* v *Origin Clothing Ltd* [1995] FSR 280.

**103** [1996] RPC 281.

**104** [1998] RPC 283.

**105** [1996] FSR 205.

**106** [1997] FSR 380.

**107** [1959] RPC 47.

Where the plaintiff's complaint relates to the use of a registered mark by the defendant, the defendant may be able to set up the defence of acquiescence on the part of the plaintiff if the defendant's use has been continuous for at least five years (s 48). The defendant's registration must not have been applied for in bad faith. Where a registration has been subject to a disclaimer or is limited in some other way, for example where it is restricted to a specified territory, use of the mark consistent with the disclaimer or limitation does not infringe because the rights conferred are restricted accordingly (s 13).

A defendant may apply to the Registrar or the court, as indeed may anyone else, for the mark to be revoked under s 46. However, the proprietor's rights still extend up to the date of revocation, unless the Registrar or court is satisfied that the grounds for revocation existed at an earlier date in which case that is the effective date of extinction of the proprietor's rights (s 46(6)). Alternatively, an application may be made for invalidity under s 47.

## Groundless threats of infringement proceedings

There is now, as with patents, the design right and registered designs, a remedy for groundless threats of infringement proceedings (other than in respect of the application of the mark to goods or their packaging or the importation of goods to which, or to the packaging of which, the mark has been applied or the supply of services under the mark): s 21. This remedy did not exist under previous trade mark law. Although it seems plausible that the remedy is designed to protect secondary infringers, such as distributors and retailers, rather than primary infringers because of the exceptions, s 21(1) states that 'any person aggrieved [by the threat of proceedings] may bring proceedings for relief'. Thus, if a trade mark proprietor threatens a retailer with proceedings in respect of the retailer offering to sell goods against which the mark is registered under a sign identical or similar to the registered trade mark, the retailer may bring a groundless threats action. As the retailer may cease ordering the goods from the 'primary infringer', the person making the goods and affixing the sign to the goods, he also will be a person aggrieved and may bring a groundless threats action.

Relief is a declaration that threats are unjustifiable, an injunction against continuance and damages. Under s 21(2), the plaintiff is entitled to such relief unless the defendant shows that the act in respect of which proceedings were threatened was or would be an infringement, but even then the plaintiff will be entitled to relief if he shows that the registration is invalid or liable to be revoked in any material respect: s 21(3). Mere notification that the mark is registered or that application for registration has been made does not constitute a threat of proceedings by s 21(4).

From the viewpoint of a proprietor of a registered trade mark, it is unwise to threaten proceedings in such a way as to precipitate a groundless threats action. He will have to show that the acts complained of infringe the trade mark and, in most cases, he will also have to withstand an attack on the validity of the mark. Even if the act complained of is one of those excepted from the action, for example, it alleges that the person threatened has applied the mark to goods or their packaging, the proprietor may not escape a groundless threats action if the plaintiff can show that the act does not fall within that form of infringement. For example, in *Trebor Bassett Ltd* v *The Football Association*,[108] the    108 [1997] FSR 211.

plaintiff was a sweet manufacturer which sold packets of confectionery with cards inside showing photographs of famous footballers. Some were members of the English national team and had been photographed wearing shirts with the England three-lion logo which was a registered trade mark belonging to the Football Association which complained that this was an infringement of the trade mark. The plaintiff filed a groundless threats action, seeking relief, *inter alia*, by way of a declaration that the threats were unjustifiable. The defendant responded by bringing a cross-action for infringement. The plaintiff then applied for the cross-action to be struck out as an abuse of process.

Rattee J gave summary judgment in favour of the plaintiff and awarded relief in the form of a declaration that the threats were unjustifiable and that the plaintiff's cards did not infringe the defendant's trade mark. He concluded that the plaintiff was not affixing or using the logo in respect of their cards within ss 10(4)(a) or 10(4)(b). The logo appeared on the cards only because the player was wearing the football strip with the defendant's logo on it at the time the photograph was taken and that inevitably reproduced the logo, rather as a photograph of one of the players of a team as reproduced for a newspaper. It was not even arguable that the plaintiff was using the logo in any real sense.

Foreign proprietors of trade marks might be surprised by a groundless threats action, being relatively new in trade mark law in the United Kingdom. For example, in *Prince plc v Prince Sports Group Inc,*[109] the plaintiff had registered 'prince.com' as its Internet domain name. The defendant was an American company having registered 'Prince' as a trade mark in a number of countries including the United Kingdom. The defendant's attorneys wrote to the plaintiff pointing out that its use of the domain name would prevent the defendant registering that name as its own domain name and claiming that the plaintiff was infringing the defendant's United Kingdom registered trade mark. Litigation was threatened if the plaintiff did not assign the domain name to the defendant.

The court granted a declaration that the threats were unjustified and an injunction against continuance of the threats. The basic test was held to be whether an ordinary reader would take the threat as constituting a threat of proceedings of a United Kingdom registered mark and, in the letter, reference was made to the United Kingdom registered mark. The threat was general in nature and the defendant could not take advantage of the exceptions to a threats action. A person who raised the possibility of proceedings had to take great care in expressing himself and was required to indicate precisely if he wished to rely on the exceptions. Further, where a threat was made to a person alleged to be a infringer, that person was a person aggrieved, save in exceptional circumstances.

## SURRENDER, REVOCATION AND INVALIDITY

The proprietor may surrender the registration in respect of some or all goods or services for which the mark is registered, by s 45. Rule 26 of the Trade Mark Rules 1994 requires that the proprietor certifies that any person having an interest in the mark has been given three months' notice and either is not affected or consents. The Registrar will then make the appropriate entry in the register and publish it.

109 [1998] FSR 21.

Section 46(1) lists the grounds for revocation of a registered trade mark as being:

- *non-use* – within five years of the date of completion of the registration procedure, the mark has not been put to genuine use in the UK by the proprietor or with his consent in relation to the goods or services for which it was registered and there are no proper reasons for non-use;
- *non-use* – genuine use has been suspended for an uninterrupted period of five years and there are no proper reasons for non-use;
- *that it has become a generic name* – because of the acts or inactivity of the proprietor the mark has become a common name in trade for a product or service for which it is registered (note the use of the word 'product' rather than 'goods'; presumably, the word product is narrower, being a type of or a particular species of goods);
- *it is misleading* – because of the use made by the proprietor or with his consent in relation to the goods or services for which it is registered, the mark is liable to mislead the public (particularly in respect of the nature, quality or geographical origin of the goods or services in question).

Under s 46(2), 'use' in terms of revocation includes use in a different form provided this does not alter its distinctive character, and use in the UK includes affixing the mark to goods or packaging in the UK solely for export purposes.

Where a question arises in civil proceedings as to the use to which a trade mark has been put, it is the proprietor who has the burden of proof under s 100. In *ELLE Trade Mark*,[110] the proprietor had two registrations, one for 'elle' in lower case within a circle with a cross (the female symbol) and 'ELLE' in upper case type. There was a disclaimer to any exclusive right to the use of the word 'elle'. Application had been made for the two marks to be revoked due to non-use under s 46. It was held that, although there had been some use of the word 'elle' without the device, this was not use of the trade mark as such use altered the distinctive character in a significant and substantial way.[111] Similarly, in *United Biscuits (UK) Ltd v Asda Stores Ltd*,[112] four pictorial marks depicting penguins, which had been used for Penguin biscuits in the past, were ordered to be revoked as there was no evidence of genuine use within the last five years either in the exact form of the marks or in a similar form so as to retain their distinctive character.

There have to be proper reasons for the non-use if the proprietor is to escape an application for revocation under s 46. In *INVERMONT Trade Mark*,[113] it was argued that the non-use was due to the long and complex process of introducing a new brand into the alcoholic drinks market. It was held that the phrase 'proper reason for non-use' has to be considered in a business sense. 'Proper' means 'apt, acceptable, reasonable, justifiable in all the circumstances' and proper reasons for non-use related to abnormal situations and temporary serious disruptions affecting the proprietor's business alone. It did not cover the normal difficulties to be found in trade. The mark was ordered to be revoked; apart from failing to show that such an abnormal situation or serious disruption applied, the proprietor had failed to provide evidence as to preparations to use the mark and, therefore, the prospect of imminent future use was remote.

Revocation will not be carried out on grounds of non-use if the use is commenced or resumed after five years but before application for revocation is made. However, there is a three-month period prior to the application for revocation

110 [1997] FSR 529.

111 A claim that 'ELLE' had been used in advertisements in foreign magazines failed to find sympathy as there was little practical possibility of orders being placed from the United Kingdom.

112 [1997] RPC 513.

113 [1997] RPC 125.

when use will be ignored unless preparations for a commencement or resumption of use were made before the proprietor became aware that an application for revocation might be made (s 46(3)). An application for revocation may be made by anyone to the Registrar or to the court. If proceedings before the court are pending, the application must be made to the court and, in other cases, the Registrar may refer the application to the court. Revocation may be whole or partial, under s 46(5). If a mark has been revoked, the proprietor's rights are deemed to cease from the date of the application for revocation, or at an earlier date if the Registrar or the court is satisfied that the grounds for revocation existed earlier.

Section 47 states that a registration may be declared invalid in the following circumstances:

(a) the registration was made in breach of s 3 (the absolute grounds for refusal). However, the registration shall not be declared invalid if in breach of s 3(1)(b), (c) or (d) if the mark has subsequently acquired a distinctive character in relation to the goods or services for which it was registered;
(b) the registration was contrary to s 5 (relative grounds for refusal);
(c) the proprietor acted in bad faith (the Registrar may apply to court for a declaration of invalidity).

Application may be made by anyone to the Registrar or to the court (s 47(3)). If proceedings in the court are pending, the application must be made to the court and, in other cases, the Registrar may refer the application to the court. Under s 47(5), the declaration of invalidity may be partial in terms of the goods or services for which it is registered. The effect of a declaration of invalidity is that the registration will be void *ab initio* (s 47(6)). However, this will not affect any transactions past and closed.

In terms of invalidity on the basis of the absolute grounds, if the proprietor claims that the mark has acquired a distinctive character through use, he will need to do more than simply show that there has been extensive use of the mark. The use must have been such that a substantial number of persons have come to recognise the sign as a trade mark.[114]

114 *British Sugar plc v James Robertson & Sons Ltd* [1996] RPC 281.

115 [1996] RPC 281.

In *British Sugar plc v James Robertson & Sons Ltd*,[115] Jacob J found that the plaintiff's 'TREAT' mark was invalid as being within at least some of the absolute grounds for refusal. However, he noted that, having declared the mark invalid, he did not have the power to order its revocation as the grounds for revocation are different. This would mean that an invalid mark would remain upon the register until such time as the proprietor failed to renew the registration.

## OFFENCES

The offence of fraudulent use of a trade mark and the provisions for delivery up and disposal of offending goods, as well as enforcement, are restated in language appropriate to that used elsewhere in the Trade Marks Act 1994 (ss 92–96). The offences are expressed in terms of being 'with a view to gain for himself or another or, with intent to cause loss to another, and without the consent of the proprietor'. The offences are:

• applying the mark (or one likely to be mistaken for the registered mark) to goods or their packaging, selling, hiring, etc. such goods, being in possession of such goods with intent to sell, etc., by himself or another (s 92(1));

- applying the mark to material for labelling, packaging, business papers, for advertising, using or being in possession of such material (s 92(2));
- making articles specifically designed or adapted to make copies of the mark, or being in possession of such articles (s 92(3)).

For the offences to apply, the relevant goods must be those for which the mark is registered, or the trade mark must be one with a reputation and the use of the sign would take unfair advantage of, or is or would be detrimental to, the distinctive character or the repute of the trade mark. Oddly, these offences apply only in relation to goods and not to services.

It is a defence if the person charged can show that he had reasonable grounds for believing that the use or intended use did not infringe the registered mark (s 92(5)).[116] There is also a defence, curiously placed in s 9(3), where the relevant act was done before the date of publication of registration. The maximum penalty is ten years' imprisonment and/or a fine on conviction on indictment, or, if tried summarily, six months' imprisonment and/or a fine not exceeding the statutory maximum.

The offences relating to registration, such as falsification and falsely representing a trade mark as registered, are also restated in modified language (ss 94 and 95). Using a phrase such as 'registered trade mark', or the familiar ® symbol for an unregistered mark, would be falsely representing a mark to be registered. There is a defence to the 'falsely representing' offence as, under s 95(2), the offence is not committed if 'it is shown that the reference is to registration elsewhere than in the UK and that the trade mark is in fact so registered …'. In *Second Sight Ltd* v *Novell UK Ltd*[117] the defendant used its United States registered mark TUXEDO in the UK with the word 'registered' and the ® symbol before it had registered the mark in the UK. Lightman J considered that s 95(2) ought to be construed so as to excuse if the reference is consistent with a registration elsewhere and such registration does, in fact, exist. It is unnecessary to refer to the foreign registration on the face of the material or article on which the trade mark is displayed.

The penalties for the above two offences have been updated and the offences relating to falsification of the register, etc. now become offences triable either way, with a maximum penalty on conviction on indictment of imprisonment for a term not exceeding two years, or a fine or both. Summary conviction carries a maximum of six months' imprisonment and/or a fine not exceeding the statutory maximum. The offence of falsely representing a trade mark as registered remains a summary offence with a maximum penalty of a fine on level 3 (currently £1000).

There are, under s 97 (s 98 for Scotland), extensive provisions for forfeiture of offending goods, material or articles which have come into the possession of any person in connection with the investigation or prosecution of any relevant offence (under s 92, under the Trade Descriptions Act 1968 or any offence involving dishonesty or deception). An application for an order for forfeiture must be obtained from the court where proceedings have been brought, or otherwise from a magistrates' court. The order will be granted only if the court is satisfied that the relevant offence has been committed, but the inference may be made that the offence has been committed in relation to a batch or consignment of goods from consideration of a representative sample.

116 A civil test for a criminal offence. *See* Rawlinson, P. 'The UK Trade Marks Act 1994: It's Criminal' [1995] 1 EIPR 54.

117 [1995] RPC 423.

The order may require the offending goods, materials or articles to be destroyed, or to be released to such person as the court may specify on condition that the offending sign is erased, removed or obliterated. An appeal from a forfeiture order lies to the Crown Court in England and Wales.[118]

**118** In Northern Ireland, the county court, in Scotland the High Court.

## CERTIFICATION MARKS

The purpose of certification marks is to indicate goods or services with certain objective standards, for example in respect to material, safety or quality. Examples are the Woolmark and the BSI Kitemark. The Trade Marks Act 1994 applies to certification marks subject to provisions set out in Sch 2 to the Act. The term 'certification mark' is itself defined in s 50 as:

> ... a mark indicating that the goods or services in connection with which it is used are certified by the proprietor of the mark in respect of origin, material, mode of manufacture of goods or performance of services, quality, accuracy or other characteristics.

**119** *See STILTON Trade Mark* [1967] RPC 173.

The distinctiveness required by s 1(1) must be in terms of distinguishing the goods or services certified from those which are not and, unlike the usual provisions, signs denoting geographical origin may be registered.[119] The mark must not be misleading as to the character or significance of the mark, especially if it is likely to be taken as something other than a certification mark, and to that end the Registrar may insist that the mark carries some indication that it is a certification mark and any application is amended accordingly.

An applicant for a certification mark must file regulations governing the use of the mark with the Registrar. By para 6(2), the regulations must indicate:

● who is entitled to use the mark;
● the characteristics to be certified by the mark;
● how the certifying body is to test those characteristics and supervise the use of the mark;
● what fees, if any, are to be paid in connection with the operation of the mark; and
● procedures for resolving disputes.

The mark will not be registered if the regulations do not comply with para 6(2) and further requirements imposed by rules, or are contrary to public policy or accepted principles of morality or if the applicant is not competent to certify the goods or services for which the mark is to be registered.

Publication, opposition (including opposition to the regulations) and observations procedures are broadly as for ordinary marks. Assignment also is possible, but requires the consent of the Registrar. There are a number of additional grounds for revocation and invalidity of certification marks.

## COLLECTIVE MARKS

Collective marks are new to United Kingdom trade mark law. They are defined by s 49 as:

… a mark distinguishing the goods or services of members of the association which is the proprietor of the mark from those of other undertakings.

Thus, a trade association, for example the 'Association of West Midlands Metal Bashers', may register a mark which can be used by its members on its goods or stationery. The 'Yorkshire Institute of Professional Decorators' may do likewise, as may the 'Society of Balti Restaurateurs'. At the author's place of work, Aston Business School, there is a plaque at the front of the building denoting the collective mark 'Conference Centres of Excellence'.

The Act applies to collective marks as it does to ordinary marks subject to the provisions of Sch 1 to the Act. The mark must be capable of distinguishing the goods or services of members of the association from those of other undertakings and, as with certification marks, signs indicating geographical origin may be permitted. The mark must not be misleading as to the character or significance of the mark, especially if it is likely to be taken as anything other than a collective mark. The Registrar may insist on an indication that the mark is a collective mark.

Regulations governing the use of the mark must be filed with the Registrar for approval and, by para 5(2), must specify the persons authorised to use the mark, the conditions of membership and any conditions and sanctions relating to the use of the mark. The mark will not be registered if the regulations fail to comply with the requirements of para 5(2) and any rules, or are contrary to public policy or accepted principles of morality. There are corresponding provisions to s 30 determining the rights of authorised users in cases of infringement and additional grounds of revocation and invalidity.[120]

120 For a fuller description of certification and collective marks *see* Annand, R. and Norman, H. (1994) *Blackstone's Guide to the Trade Marks Act 1994*, Blackstone Press, Chapter 13.

## TRANSITIONAL ARRANGEMENTS

Schedule 3 contains the transitional provisions. Marks registered under the 1938 Act immediately before commencement of the new Act are described as'existing registered marks' and transferred to the new register whether they were registered in Part A or Part B. Disclaimers and limitations will also be transferred to the new register, but not conditions. Any proceedings to expunge a mark will be determined under the old law.

The new law on infringement applies to existing registered marks as regards infringements occurring after the commencement of the 1994 Act (31 October 1994), but if the infringement took place earlier it will remain to be determined under the 1938 Act. However, an act done in relation to an existing registered mark before commencement that did not infringe can continue to be performed. This applies in particular with respect to marks registered under the honest concurrent use provisions in the Trade Marks Act 1938 s 12(2).

Other transitional provisions concern co-ownership, assignment and other dealings with trade marks, licensing and registered users, revocation and rectification. Pending applications were dealt with under the old law and considered to be, once registered, an existing registered mark. However, they could be converted provided they had not been published under the 1938 Act by the date of commencement. Notice was required to be given within six months of commencement.

Some existing trade marks were still classified according to the pre-1938 classification scheme, but these have been brought into line with the present system of classification. The new periods of duration took effect immediately upon commencement for new marks as well as for existing registered marks. Thus, where an existing registered mark falls due for renewal on or after 31 October 1994, it will be renewed for a period of ten years, regardless of when the fee is in fact paid.

## TRADE MARKS AND THE EUROPEAN COMMUNITY

There are several matters of interest in respect of trade marks and the European Community. As we have seen, there has been a harmonising Directive on trade marks which led to the Trade Marks Act 1994; the Community trade mark system has recently got underway; and of interest are the effects of the Treaty of Rome's prohibition on unjustifiable restrictions on imports and exports, especially in terms of 'parallel importing'.

## COMMUNITY TRADE MARK

There have been plans for some time for a Community-wide mark. The Office for the Harmonistion of the Internal Market (Trade Marks and Designs) (OHIM) was established in Alicante, Spain and commenced accepting applications on 1 January 1996. The Council Regulation for the Community Trade Mark came into force during 1994 (60 days following its publication in the *Official Journal*).[121] Only marks which can have effect throughout the entire Community will be accepted. This is one reason why existing national systems will continue to operate.

A Community trade mark (CTM) is stated, by Article 2, to have a unitary character having equal effect throughout the Community. A CTM may not be registered, transferred or surrendered, or be subject to a decision revoking the proprietor's rights or be declared invalid, neither shall its use be prohibited save in respect of the whole Community. Thus the unitary character of a CTM cannot be compromised.

Article 4 of the Regulation gives a definition of 'trade mark' which is virtually identical to that in the Trade Marks Act 1994 and the harmonisation Directive. Indeed, many of the provisions are similar or equivalent to those in the Directive. The proprietor of a CTM may be a national of a member state, a national of a Paris Convention country, or, failing either, a person domiciled or having real and effective industrial or commercial establishments in the EC or any Paris Convention country, or if that person's country otherwise gives reciprocal protection to nationals of EC member states.

There are absolute and relative grounds for refusal of registration in Articles 7 and 8 which are very similar to those in the 1994 Act. The absolute grounds will be satisfied even if the objection (for example, that the mark designates the geographical origin or characteristics of the goods or services) relates only to part of the Community. This could pose quite a hurdle. A word mark may be distinctive in one country but not in another. For example, French words might be used for marks for perfumes which would be capable of distinguishing in the UK or Sweden but which would be devoid of distinctive character in France. Consider 'le mieux' meaning 'the best'.

121 OJ L11, 14.1.94, p. 1. It was published on 14 January 1994.

A precondition for the relative grounds for refusal applying is that they depend upon the proprietor of an earlier trade mark opposing the application (Article 8(1)). At the present time that does not apply in relation to the UK trade mark, although it is expected that it will do so in due course as the Trade Marks Act 1994 s 8(1) empowers the Secretary for State to so provide. Of course, in most cases, the question of whether a mark is unregistrable on the basis of relative grounds will be raised by the owner of another mark or right. One difference between the CTM Regulation and the 1994 Act is that the former does not provide for relative grounds specifically in respect of passing off, copyright or rights in designs, but it does provide for opposition on relative grounds by owners of non-registered trade marks or signs.

Earlier trade marks include CTMs, trade marks registered in member states,[122] trade marks registered under international arrangements which have effect in member states, applications for such trade marks and well-known marks within the meaning of the Paris Convention. It will be interesting to see the level of activity in the Community Trade Mark Office in terms of applications and oppositions.

Infringement of a CTM is expressed in Articles 9 and 10. Article 9 is similar in effect to the provisions under the 1994 Act, but Article 10 is new and is designed to help to prevent trade marks becoming generic names and, as a result, being vulnerable to revocation.[123] If the reproduction of the trade mark in a dictionary, encyclopedia or similar reference work gives the impression that the mark is a generic name, the publisher must, at the request of the proprietor, ensure that the reproduction is accompanied by an indication that it is a registered trade mark by the time of the next edition at the latest. The Article does not say what should happen if the publisher fails to comply; presumably it would be treated as any other form of infringement. In any case, the provision does not apply to other forms of publication.

Defences are equivalent to those under the 1994 Act, including the doctrine of exhaustion of rights. The effects of CTMs are governed exclusively by the Regulation, but by Article 14, in other respects (for example, procedurally and in respect of remedies) infringement is to be determined by the application of national laws. As limited a number as possible of national courts must be designated for the enforcement of the CTM, by Article 91.

The duration of registration (initial and on renewal) will, by Article 46, be ten years, as it is now in respect of UK marks. There are detailed provisions for assignment and licensing and recognition of the right to use a mark as a property right. In particular, the right subsisting in the CTM may be charged as security for a loan or mortgage.[124]

The initial experience with the CTM has been very encouraging and the number of applications far exceeded initial expectations. United Kingdom applicants may apply through the Trade Mark Registry which operates as a handling forwarding office for the purposes of the CTM. Applicants need to use one of the five languages of the OHIM (Office for the Harmonisation of the Internal Market (Trade Marks and Designs)) and to specify a second language. This could be important for opposition purposes and an applicant may need to deal with oppositions in that second language.

122 Or, in the case of Belgium, the Netherlands and Luxembourg, registered at the Benelux Trade Mark Office.

123 Article 50 includes as one of the grounds for revocation where the mark, as a consequence of the inactivity of the proprietor, has become a common name in the trade for the product or service in respect of which it is registered.

124 For a fuller description of the CTM, *see* Annand, R. and Norman, H. (1994) *Blackstone's Guide to the Trade Marks Act 1994*, Blackstone Press, Chapter 14.

## PARALLEL IMPORTS AND EXHAUSTION OF RIGHTS

Exhaustion of rights can best be described by means of an example. Say that a parent company (*Bear Holdings plc*) of a group of companies making teddy bears and other fluffy animals is located in the UK. It has a subsidiary company located and trading in France, called *La Peluche SA*. The parent company uses a trade mark on its goods. The French company has the right to use the mark in France only and is not permitted to export its teddy bears to the UK. The sale price of the teddy bears is considerably less in France. A third-party entrepreneur buys a large number of the French bears and exports them to the United Kingdom where he sells them, undercutting *Bear Holdings plc* which would like to prevent the entrepreneur selling the bears in the UK.

The problem is one of reconciling the right to use a trade mark with the desirability of allowing the free movement of goods and preventing the partitioning of the market within the European Community. The European Court of Justice has not, until recently, been particularly keen on enforcing trade mark rights if there is any danger of competition being distorted. In the above example, the European Court of Justice would be unlikely to enforce the trade mark rights in favour of *Bear Holdings plc*, even though this approach seems a little unfair in that *Bear Holdings* is experiencing competition from items made by a subsidiary company in circumstances outside the contemplation of either. However, one advantage of the European approach for consumers is that it does make it difficult for undertakings to maintain unjustifiable price differentials between member states.

Articles 30–36 of the Treaty of Rome promote the free movement of goods by prohibiting unjustifiable restrictions on the import and export of goods. Article 36 permits derogations by member states on several grounds provided that they do not constitute 'a means of arbitrary discrimination or a disguised restriction on trade'. These grounds include public morality, public policy, public security, the protection of health and life of humans, animals and plants, the protection of national treasures possessing artistic, historic or archeological value, or the protection of *industrial and commercial property*.[125]

Article 7(1) of the trade mark Directive sets out the basis principle of exhaustion of rights. It states that the trade mark shall not entitle the proprietor to prohibit the use of the trade mark in relation to goods put on the market within the Community by him or with his consent. However, to this there is a proviso and Article 7(2) disapplies para (1) if there are legitimate reasons for the proprietor to oppose further commercialisation of the goods, especially where their condition is changed or impaired after they have been put on the market. To some extent, this calls for a balance to be struck. On the one hand there are the interests of the proprietor of the trade mark to protect his reputation. On the other hand, there are the interests of the reseller to be able to resell goods. The importance of this balance was addressed by the European Court of Justice in *Parfums Christian Dior SA v Evora BV*.[126] The defendant had obtained a quantity of the plaintiff's perfumes by means of parallel imports. The defendant was not an approved retailer but ran a chain of chemist's shops in the Netherlands. It advertised that it had the plaintiff's perfumes for sale by means of leaflets showing bottles and packaging of the plaintiff's perfumes. The court

125 The phrase 'industrial property' is usually taken as including patents, trade marks and designs.

126 [1998] RPC 166.

refused the relief sought by the plaintiff. The defendant habitually marketed articles of a similar kind to those of the plaintiff, though not of the same quality, in a manner of advertising customary in the defendant's sector of the trade. The proprietor of the trade mark failed to show that, in the specific circumstances, the defendant's use of the trade mark would seriously damage the reputation attaching to the trade mark.

The doctrine of exhaustion applies from the time the goods have been put on the market in the Community by or with the consent of the proprietor of the trade mark. If the goods originated from outside the Community but have subsequently been put on the market within the Community, the doctrine applies from that point in time. The doctrine applies where the owner of the mark in the country of import or export was one and the same or, where different, were economically linked such as subsidiary companies in the same group of companies.[127]

It is not unusual for commercial undertakings to use different trade marks in different countries. This, in itself, does not demonstrate a disguised restriction on trade and some further evidence is required. In *CHEETAH Trade Mark*,[128] the plaintiff, who was also the proprietor of a UK registered mark, sold herbicide in the UK and Belgium but used a different trade mark in Belgium. The defendant bought a quantity of the herbicide from the plaintiff in Belgium, bearing the Belgian mark, and imported and re-sold it in the UK without altering the packaging. He did, however, use the UK trade mark on his delivery notes and invoices. When challenged, the defendant unsuccessfully argued that the use of different trade marks by the plaintiff was a disguised restriction on trade between member states and that the rights in the UK trade mark had been exhausted by the sale of the herbicide under the Belgian mark. Of course, it would have been quite remarkable if putting goods onto the market under one trade mark exhausted the rights under another, different trade mark, even though both marks might be owned by the same company.[129]

In *Centrafarm BV v Winthrop BV*,[130] Winthrop, a Dutch company, was part of the Sterling group of companies, and Centrafarm bought and imported into The Netherlands drugs made by another company in the Sterling group in the UK. It was held that Winthrop could not exercise its trade mark rights under Dutch law to prevent this as the marketing of the drug in the UK had exhausted that right. This exhaustion principle has been applied subsequently where the importer has repackaged the goods,[131] and even where different marks were used in different countries and the importer has changed the mark accordingly. This happened in *Centrafarm BV v American Home Products Corp*,[132] where a drug was marketed in the UK under the name 'Serenid' and in the Netherlands under the name 'Seresta'. Both marks were owned by AHP and it was held that AHP could not prevent the parallel importing of the drugs as its use of several trade marks was intended to split up the market artificially contrary to Article 30.

The specific subject matter of a trade mark is the exclusive right to use the mark for the purpose of putting a product on the market for the first time, and the essential function of a trade mark is to guarantee origin of the goods or services in question. Therefore, any subsequent use which impairs that guarantee of origin, for example, by being deceptive as to origin or impairing the condition of the goods, may be actionable by the proprietor of the trade mark. In certain circumstances a parallel importer may need to repackage the goods, for example, to comply with national requirements. In such a case, a trade mark proprietor may prevent parallel imports unless:

127 *Phytheron International SA v Jean Bourdon SA* [1997] FSR 936.

128 [1993] FSR 263.

129 But, *see Centrafarm BV v American Home Products Corp* [1979] 1 CMLR 326, discussed post.

130 [1974] 2 CMLR 480.

131 *Hoffman-La Roche v Centrafarm* [1978] ECR 1139.

132 [1979] 1 CMLR 326.

- use of the trade mark to prevent imports will contribute to the artificial partitioning of markets between member states;
- the repackaging does not adversely affect the original condition of the product;
- the parallel importer complies with certain obligations as to labelling and the provision of samples; and
- the name of the person who has repackaged the product is stated on the new packaging.[133]

133 *Hoffman-La Roche* v *Centrafarm* [1978] ECR 1139.
134 [1997] FSR 102.

In *Bristol-Myers Squibb* v *Paranova*,[134] the European Court of Justice, in affirming the above principles, laid down some useful guidelines for parallel importers who repackage goods, particularly pharmaceutical products. The case involved actions brought by pharmaceutical manufacturers against Paranova A/S which imported products made by those manufacturers into Denmark. First, the European Court of Justice said that the following cannot affect the original condition of the product:

- the mere removal of blister packs, flasks, phials, ampoules or inhalers from their original external packaging and their replacement in new external packaging;
- fixing self-adhesive labels to the inner packaging, the addition of new user instructions or the insertion of an extra article;
- repackaging operations authorised and supervised by a public authority in order to ensure that the product remains intact.

An argument that repackaging might risk adversely affecting the original condition of the product, for example, by repackaging blister packs coming from different batches with different use-by dates or light-sensitive products that may be damaged by exposure to light during repackaging, was rejected by the court which said that such hypothetical risks of isolated errors could not confer on the trade mark owner the right to oppose repackaging.

It is for national courts to decide whether the cutting of blister packs or reprinting batch numbers on them or the insertion of extra articles are carried out in such a manner as to exclude any real risk of affecting the original condition of the tablets inside. In this regard, comparison with the product as imported into the member state by the trade mark owner should be made. In particular, parallel importers could indirectly affect the condition of a product where:

- the parallel importer's instructions are inaccurate or omit important information;
- any extra article inserted by the parallel importer does not comply with the method of use and dosages envisaged by the manufacturer; or
- the new packaging does not give the product adequate protection.

If repackaging is carried out in such a manner so as not to affect the original condition of the product inside the packaging, the essential function of a trade mark as a guarantee of origin is safeguarded, provided that the parallel importer complies with the following requirements:

- he must indicate on the external packaging who repackaged the product and who manufactured the product, printed in such a way as to be understood by a person with normal eyesight exercising a normal degree of attentiveness;

- if the parallel importer has added an extra article to the package, he must ensure that its origin is indicated in such a way as to dispel any impression that the trade mark owner is responsible for it;
- he must give the trade mark owner advance notice of the product being put on sale. The trade mark owner may also require the parallel importer to supply him with a specimen of the repackaged product before it goes on sale.

However, the parallel importer need not state that the repackaging was carried out without the authorisation of the trade mark owner.

If the parallel importer repackages in such a way that the product is poorly presented, this may damage the reputation of the trade mark and, if this is so, the trade mark owner may use his rights to oppose the parallel importation of the products where the repackaging is defective, untidy or of poor quality. Again, it is for national courts to decide whether cutting blister packs or inserting loose blister packs constitutes an untidy form of repackaging liable to damage the reputation of the trade mark. However, damage to the reputation of a trade mark is unlikely if the product is sold only to hospitals rather than to the public at large. In the former case, the products will be administered to patients by professionals who will have little regard for the presentation of the product. In the latter case, even if the product is prescribed by a doctor, presentation is important and gives the consumer confidence about the quality of the product.

The UK courts had the opportunity to consider parallel importing from Brazil in *Colgate-Palmolive Ltd* v *Markwell Finance Ltd*.[135] The USA parent company of the UK company and the Brazilian company owned trade marks registered in the UK and similar marks registered in Brazil. The defendant imported into the UK and sold the toothpaste made in Brazil, which was of a poorer quality than that made in the UK. The Court of Appeal held that the UK trade marks were infringed, and the defendant's argument that the parent company had expressly or impliedly consented to the importation was rejected because it would amount to a misrepresentation to consumers as to the quality of the goods.[136] This approach has found sympathy in the European Court of Justice because of the deception as to quality operating on members of the public; and this view has been borne out recently, indicating that there may be a less extremist view of trade marks than was the case previously.[137]

## SPLIT TRADE MARKS

The cases discussed above involve a common origin in terms of the goods themselves, that is the companies making the goods are associated in some way, as members of a group of companies. A rarer case involves a common origin with respect to the trade mark but the link stops there: the right to use the mark in different countries has become separated in some way. In *Van Zuylen Frères v Hag AG*,[138] Hag AG, a German company, owned the 'Kaffee Hag' trade mark in Germany, Belgium and Luxembourg. After the Second World War, the rights to the mark in Belgium and Luxembourg were sequestrated and assigned to Van Zuylen, who then attempted to use its trade mark rights to prevent the importation into Belgium of the German 'Kaffee Hag'. It

135 [1989] RPC 497.

136 The licence agreement between the parent company and the Brazilian subsidiary contained a clause declaring that no restrictions were to be placed on exports. This was held not to be equivalent to express consent and was narrowly interpreted because it was inserted so as to comply with Brazilian law.

137 Oliver, P. 'Of Split Trade Marks and Common Markets' (1991) 54 MLR 587 at 589.

138 [1974] 2 CMLR 127.

was held, in a much criticised decision, that on the doctrine of common origin the Belgian trade mark could not be relied on to prevent the marketing in one member state of a product lawfully made in another member state under an identical mark. This is not really the exhaustion principle, because the German coffee had not been marketed by or with the consent, implied or otherwise, of the owner of the Belgian trade mark. However, the European Court expressly disapproved of this decision[139] in *SA CNL-SUCAL NV v Hag GF AG*[140] ('Hag II'), in which the facts were almost the reverse of the previous *Kaffee Hag* case. This time the current owner of the Belgian mark sought to sell its *Kaffee Hag* in Germany. It was held that Articles 30–36 of the Treaty of Rome did not prevent national legislation from permitting an undertaking which owned a trade mark in one member state from restraining the importation from another member state of similar goods bearing a similar mark. The justification was that otherwise consumers would not be able to identify with any certainty the origin of the product and the owner of the mark in one member state might be blamed for the poor quality of goods for which he was not responsible. The effect of the two *Kaffee Hag* cases is that both the Belgian and the German owners can exclude the importation of the other's product into their respective countries. This accords with common sense in the very special circumstances. In its decision the European Court laid down some principles for such mutual exclusivity, being that:

1 the two marks are identical or confusingly similar;
2 the products are similar; and
3 there are no legal or economic links between the parties.[141]

This conforms with the decision in *Terrapin (Overseas) Ltd v Terranova Industrie CA Kapferer & Co*,[142] where the German owner of the 'Terranova' trade mark for building materials could prevent the UK company registering the mark 'Terrapin' for prefabricated buildings. Two themes from the above decisions can be seen in the harmonisation Directive. First, in 'Hag II' the possibility of confusion is a reason for refusing to register a mark (Article 3(1)(g) – deception as to the nature, quality or geographical origin of the goods or services). Second, Article 7(2) limits the exhaustion principle where there are legitimate reasons for a trade mark owner to oppose further commercialisation of the goods, especially where the condition of the goods is changed or impaired.

Trade marks may be split for other reasons. It is not uncommon for a group of companies to divest itself of one of its subsidiary companies. This may be as a result of normal commercial factors, or it may be as a result of a de-merger notice from the Monopolies and Mergers Commission. Where such a separation takes place, there may be provision in the necessary agreements concerning the ownership and use of intellectual property rights for mutual use of a trade mark with geographical limitations. For example, a Spanish parent company making and selling shoes has a subsidiary company in Wales which, *inter alia*, also makes and sells shoes. The same trade mark is used by both companies and is registered in several countries. The Welsh company is listed as a registered user in the United Kingdom. The Spanish parent company decides to sell the Welsh company and it is agreed that the United Kingdom

139 Express disapproval of one of its earlier decisions by the European Court of Justice is something of a rarity in itself.

140 [1990] 3 CMLR 571.

141 For a discussion of the effects of this decision, *see* Oliver, P., *op cit*.

142 [1976] 2 CMLR 482.

registration will be assigned to the Welsh company. Furthermore, it is agreed that the Spanish company will not use its mark on shoes it exports to the UK for five years and the new owner of the Welsh company agrees not to export shoes from the UK bearing the trade mark. In *Eleco* v *Mitek*,[143] the Commission took a favourable view of a similar arrangement in terms of Article 85(1). However, it leaves to be determined the question of what happens when the agreement expires. Will the territorial ban continue on the basis of mutual exclusivity, as in the latest 'Kaffee Hag' case? The issue of split trade marks is likely to cause many problems in the future and it has already been raised in a number of cases. For example, in *Job Trade Mark*,[144] it was held that it was relevant to consider, in the context of the single market, whether it would be in the public interest for a trade mark to have different proprietors in respect of the same goods in the UK and France.[145]

More recently, the European Court of Justice has confirmed that the 'Hag II' doctrine applied also where there had been a voluntary assignment of one of two identical trade marks registered in two member states. In *IHT Internationale Heiztechnik GmbH* v *Ideal-Standard GmbH*,[146] an American parent company had two subsidiaries, one in France, the other in Germany, the respondent. Each used the trade mark 'Ideal Standard' in respect of which they each were proprietors of the French and German registered marks respectively. Eventually the French company sold the French trade mark to another French company, which later assigned it to the parent company of the appellant. The German company objected to IHT importing heating equipment bearing the Ideal Standard mark into Germany. The European Court applied Hag II and confirmed that an injunction granted by the German court was not an unlawful restriction on intra-Community trade within the meaning of Articles 30 and 36 of the EC Treaty.

## REGISTRABILITY AND FREE MOVEMENT OF GOODS

The importance of ensuring the free movement of goods within the European Community is of such importance that the basic provisions for registration of marks in individual member states can be compromised. In *Re The 'Quattro' Trade Mark*,[147] the plaintiff made a motor car in Germany called the Audi Quattro, and the name 'Quattro' (meaning the numeral four in Italian) was registered as a trade mark in Germany. The defendant, a French manufacturer, started importing into Germany a model of car called 'E Quadra'. When the plaintiff objected, the defendant challenged the validity of the German registered mark. Under German law there is a presumption that a foreign numeral should not be registered as a trade mark. However, this presumption can be overcome by showing a strong identity between the word and the applicant's goods. That was so in this case. However, this could affect trade between member states, allowing the proprietor to restrict the import of goods from other countries with a numeral in their description, something that could not be registered as a trade mark in those other countries. Because of this danger and because it did not feel competent to decide the matter, the German Federal Supreme Court submitted the case to the European Court for a preliminary ruling under Article 177.

143 [1992] 4 CMLR 70.

144 [1993] FSR 118.

145 *See also Fyffes plc* v *Chiquita Brands International Inc* [1993] FSR 83.

146 [1995] FSR 59.

147 [1993] 1 CMLR 421.

148 [1995] FSR 738.

In *Deutsche Renault AG* v *Audi AG*,[148] the European Court held that, subject to Article 36 (which allows prohibitions and restrictions on the grounds of protecting industrial and commercial property provided that they do not constitute a means of arbitrary discrimination or disguised restriction on trade between member states), the conditions for protection of a mark such as 'Quattro' were a matter for national law, as were the criteria by which the risk of confusion was to be judged. In this case there was no breach of Articles 30 and 36 because German trade mark law did not distinguish between German and foreign proprietors or goods. Therefore, Audi, the owner of the 'Quattro' mark, could continue to use its trade mark rights to prevent the importation into Germany of the vehicles bearing the name 'Quadra' by Deutsche Renault.

## TRADE MARKS AND DISPARITIES IN NATIONAL LAWS

The application of the freedom of movement of goods could, in some cases, result in consumers being deceived. We have seen how the European Court of Justice finally dealt with the *Kaffee Hag* trade mark where there was a danger that consumers might be misled as to the origin of the coffee which could cause resulting damage to the reputation of a trade mark.

149 [1979] ECR 649.

Another aspect which may impact on the doctrine of exhaustion of rights is where different member states have different internal rules relating to a particular product. In *Rewe-Zentrale* v *Bundesmonopolverwaltung für Branntwein*[149] (known as the *Cassis de Dijon* case), the European Court of Justice had to grapple with such a problem. Cassis de Dijon is an alcoholic blackcurrant liqueur. It was made in France lawfully at a strength of 15–20 per cent alcohol by volume. In Germany, the law prevented the sale of spirits of the type in which Cassis de Dijon fell unless the strength was at least 32 per cent alcohol by volume. An action was brought by an importer claiming that the German law was incompatible with Article 30 and an Article 177 reference made to the European Court of Justice.

The court accepted that, pending harmonisation, it was for member states to regulate the production and marketing of alcoholic drinks on their own territory but this is subject to Community law and can only be justified if necessary to '... satisfy mandatory requirements relating in particular to the effectiveness of fiscal supervision, the protection of public health, the fairness of commercial transactions and the defence of the consumer'. German law did not discriminate against imports as such and applied to all liqueurs regardless of origin. However, such a law could clearly affect trade between member states and could only be allowed to affect trade if it was justified by the member state in accordance with the criteria above. A claim that the law helped to prevent alcohol abuse did not impress the court (banning weaker rather than stronger spirits seems an odd way of preventing alcohol abuse) and, in any case, any restriction to satisfy mandatory requirements must be proportionate and any alternative that could achieve the objective in a less onerous manner should be adopted, that being a matter for the national court following the Article 177 reference. The objective could be achieved simply by clearly labelling the drink with its alcoholic strength.

The Cassis de Dijon principle has been applied on a number of occasions, most recently in *Fratelli Graffione v Fransa*.[150] In that case, the Scott Group marketed toilet paper and paper handkerchiefs under the trade mark 'Cotonelle' in Italy. In 1993, the Italian courts declared that the trade mark was invalid as it was misleading to consumers who might think the product contained cotton. The Scott Group stopped selling the products under that name in Italy. The trade mark was challenged in other countries, including France, where it was successfully defended, and the Scott Group continued to sell the products under that trade mark in France. The defendant bought quantities of the goods in France and exported them to Italy where he sold them under the 'Cotonelle' trade mark. The plaintiff, a distributor of Scott products, sought to prevent the sales by the defendant in Italy on the basis that the use of the 'Cotonelle' trade mark was misleading. Traders who wished to sell the goods of the proprietor of the trade mark under that trade mark could do so by importing them from other member states but, if an injunction were to be granted prohibiting the marketing of those products in Italy, this would operate as an obstacle to intra-state trade.

150 [1997] FSR 538.

It was held by the European Court of Justice that obstacles to intra-state trade resulting from differences in national law were acceptable provided that:

- they were applicable to domestic and imported goods without distinction, and
- they were necessary to satisfy overriding requirements relating, *inter alia*, to consumer protection or fair trading.

Applying *Cassis de Dijon*, the court held that protection against the risk of misleading consumers by the use of a misleading trade mark could justify a barrier to the free movement of goods. The court went on to say that, before making an order, the national court must be satisfied that:

- the risk of misleading consumers was sufficiently serious to justify a barrier by preventing the use of the 'Cotonelle' trade mark, and
- the prohibition was necessary to prevent consumers being misled and was proportionate to that objective such that no other measure less restrictive of intra-Community trade would be capable of preventing consumers from being misled.

The national court must take into account factors such as the circumstances in which the goods are sold, the information on the packaging and its clarity, the presentation and content of advertising material and the risk of error in relation to the type of consumers of that product.

Although a law aimed at preventing unfair competition could justify a barrier to trade between member states, it was not so here where one trader bought goods in one member state where they were lawfully on the market and imported them into another member state under the trade mark when other traders had the same right even if they did not choose to exercise it.

Where Community law of freedom of movement of goods conflicts with domestic laws, it is for the member state to justify any obstacle to trade between member states. Freedom of movement can be seen as the overriding principle and, where there is a justifiable objective to be achieved by domestic law, careful consideration should be given as to alternative ways of achieving that objective which are less restrictive of trade. An outright ban on importation will rarely succeed as clear and appropriate information in the form of labels or advertising will usually be sufficient to achieve the objective. Of course, as more laws become harmonised, there will be less danger of conflict between domestic law and Community law as regards freedom of movement.

# 21

## *Passing off*

### INTRODUCTION

The law of passing off and trade mark law have common roots and therefore are, in many respects, similar. Passing off is a tort and can be described as the common law form of trade mark law. The Trade Marks Act 1994 s 2(2) makes it clear that the law of passing off is unaffected by the Act.[1] Business 'goodwill' is protected by passing off and, whilst this may be associated with a particular name or mark used in the course of trade, this area of law is wider than trade mark law in terms of the scope of marks, signs, materials and other aspects of a trader's 'get-up' that can be protected.[2] The owner of the goodwill has a property right that can be protected by an action in passing off. Buckley LJ described the nature of the proprietary right thus:

> A man who engages in commercial activities may acquire a valuable reputation in respect of the goods in which he deals, or of the services which he performs, or of his business as an entity. The law regards such a reputation as an incorporeal piece of property, the integrity of which the owner is entitled to protect.[3]

He went to confirm that the property right is not a right in the name, mark or get-up itself but that it is a right in the reputation or goodwill of which the name, mark or get-up is the badge or vehicle. The words 'reputation' and 'goodwill' are often used interchangeably but it is really in connection with goodwill that passing off is concerned. It is possible, after all, to have a reputation without goodwill, the Russian monk Rasputin providing a good example of this. The existence of reputation (in this case a favourable one) without any associated goodwill was fatal to a claim in passing off in *Anheuser Busch Inc* v *Budejovicky Budvar*.[4] The *Budweiser* name for beer was well known in the United Kingdom but, in the absence of a trading presence here, the plaintiff could not establish the necessary goodwill to sustain an action in passing off.[5]

A useful definition of goodwill was given by Lord Macnaghten in *The Commisioners of Inland Revenue* v *Muller & Co's Margarine Ltd*,[6] where he said (at 223):

> What is goodwill? It is a thing very easy to describe, very difficult to define. It is the benefit and advantage of the good name, reputation, and connection of a business. It is the attractive force which begins in custom. It is the one thing which distinguishes an old-established business from a new business at its first start. The goodwill of a business must emanate from a particular centre or source. However widely extended or diffused its influence may be, goodwill is worth nothing unless it has power of attraction sufficient to bring customers home to the source from which it emanates.

1 The Trade Marks Act 1994 s 2(1) also states that no action is available under the Act for the infringement of an unregistered trade mark.

2 Though the recent changes to trade mark law have brought the scope of trade mark law nearer to passing off.

3 *H P Bulmer Ltd* v *J Bollinger SA* [1978] RPC 79 at 93.

4 [1984] FSR 413.

5 However, this case should be compared with *Maxim's Ltd* v *Dye* [1977] 1 WLR 1155; and the Indian case of *Calvin Klein Inc* v *International Apparel Syndicate* [1995] FSR 515, discussed post.

6 [1901] AC 217.

The description of goodwill as the attractive force bringing in custom is very apt even though the customers may not know or care of the identity of the owner of the goodwill provided that they appreciate that there is such a person and the goods or services emanating from that person are of an expected standard.[7] This is particularly important in the context of corporate takeovers and mergers. If asked, many people would not be able to identify the maker of many products now available without referring to the product itself.

Quite often, passing off actions will be brought in respect of an unregistered trade mark, a mark that has not been registered through inertia on the part of the owner of the mark or as a result of ignorance of the advantages of trade mark law or because the mark fails to satisfy the requirements for registration. The great majority of cases will involve a mark in the wide sense, including containers and packaging, but business goodwill can be achieved and maintained in other ways and it is possible that business methods and get-up, marketing strategy and advertising themes can be protected by this useful area of law. Passing off actions have never been limited to goods and actions in respect to services have always been a possibility. However, it is clear that the tort applies in a business context, directly or indirectly, although in other circumstances a passing off type of activity could amount to defamation.[8]

The main point about passing off is that goodwill has been established by one trader and another trader tries to take advantage of that goodwill, to cash in on it to the detriment of the first trader. There are two main reasons why a trader would wish to pass off his goods or services as being those of another, established trader. The first is that by doing so, a significant portion of the established trader's custom might be captured because of confusion amongst the buying public as to whom they are dealing with. The second reason is that sales might be boosted by unjustifiably imputing a quality to the second trader's goods that is widely recognised in connection with the goods of the established trader. In both cases, the established trader suffers damage by a shortfall in trade, but in the second case the damage may be even more far-reaching in that he stands to lose his goodwill and reputation for quality goods if, because of the misrepresentation, the buying public associate the poor quality goods with him. Alternatively, the harm may be more subtle and result in a gradual degradation of the first trader's name or get-up as an indicator of origin or quality.[9]

The preservation of business goodwill is the prime concern of passing off but the protection of consumers from deception is an ancillary effect. The New Zealand case of *Plix Products Ltd* v *Frank M Whinstone (Merchants)*[10] involved pocket packs for kiwi fruit. The plaintiff had a monopoly in such packs as a result of the sole approval of the plaintiff's design for such packs by the New Zealand Kiwifruit Authority. The case turned on copyright issues in addition to passing off and in the former it was established that copyright infringement could occur through a verbal description. On the passing off claim it was held that a cause of action in passing off depended on damage to the plaintiff's reputation and not upon the premise that purchasers might confuse the plaintiff's and the defendant's packs and obtain an inferior or different product to the one they thought they were acquiring.

Passing off may overlap with other rights, especially trade marks and copyright, and a given set of circumstances may give rise to an action involving two or more different rights. For example, in *Mothercare UK Ltd* v *Penguin*

7 *United Biscuits (UK) Ltd* v *Asda Stores Ltd* [1997] RPC 513.

8 For example, *Tolley* v *J S Fry & Sons Ltd* [1931] AC 333.

9 This is a continuing concern for traders dealing with high-quality goods. *See* the discussion about the 'Champagne' cases post.

10 [1986] FSR 63.

599

*Books Ltd*[11] the defendant published a book, first published in the USA, about bringing up children, entitled 'Mother Care/Other Care'. The plaintiff, who operated a chain of retail shops selling various items for babies, small children and expectant mothers, sued for trade mark infringement and for passing off. It was held the defendant had not infringed the 'Mothercare' trade mark because it had not been used in a trade mark sense. On the passing off action it was said that, considering the title of the book as a whole, there had not been a misrepresentation by use of that title.[12] In *The Visual Connection (TVC) Ltd* v *Ashworth Associates Ltd*,[13] the plaintiff sued for infringement of copyright in photographs and for passing off resulting from the use by the defendant of the photographs, representing his business as that of the plaintiff.[14]

## BASIC REQUIREMENTS FOR A PASSING OFF ACTION

In *Perry* v *Truefitt*[15] it was said by Lord Langdale MR that, 'a man is not to sell his own goods under the pretence that they are the goods of another trader'. That is, the law would restrain one trader from passing off his goods as being those of another trader. The essence of the action is a misrepresentation, either express or implied. This was expanded to include a situation where the origin of the goods was not at issue, rather it was the quality of the goods. In *Spalding & Bros* v *A W Gamage Ltd*,[16] the plaintiff was a dealer in footballs described for some years as 'Orb' footballs and this description and descriptions including the word 'Orb' became distinctive of the plaintiff's footballs. The plaintiff sold a quantity of defective balls to a waste rubber merchant and, eventually, they fell into the hands of the defendant who advertised them as being 'Orb' balls. An injunction was granted in favour of the plaintiff and Lord Parker considered the nature of passing off, saying:

> The more general opinion appears to be that the right [that is, the right to take action to prevent passing off] is a right of property ... property in the business or goodwill likely to be injured by the misrepresentation.[17]

An important case in which the basic requirements for success in a passing off action were described in the House of Lords was *Erven Warnink Besloten Vennootschap* v *J Townend & Sons (Hull) Ltd*.[18] The plaintiffs made a liqueur called Advocaat which came to be well known.[19] It was a high quality liqueur made from brandewijn, egg yolks and sugar which acquired a substantial reputation and sold in large quantities. The defendant decided to enter this market and made a drink called 'Keeling's Old English Advocaat' which was made from Cyprus sherry and dried egg powder, an inferior but less expensive drink compared to the plaintiffs'. This captured a large part of the plaintiffs' market in the UK but it could not be shown that consumers would mistake it for the plaintiffs' drink. Nevertheless, it was held that the reputation associated with the plaintiffs' product should be protected from deceptive use of its name by competitors even though the goodwill was shared by several traders. There was a misrepresentation made by the defendant calculated to injure the plaintiffs' business or goodwill and an injunction was granted in favour of the plaintiffs, there being no exceptional grounds of public policy why an injunction should not be granted. Lord Diplock laid down the essentials for a passing off action, derived from the case of *Spalding & Bros* v *A W Gamage Ltd*[20] and subsequent cases, as being:

11  [1988] RPC 113.

12  Dillon LJ considered the recent fashion for conducting surveys to be unhelpful. He also deplored the proliferation of affidavits, assertions and counter-assertions common when wealthy companies are involved in passing off, copyright or trade mark cases.

13  (Unreported) 14 January 1986.

14  *See also Columbia Picture Industries* v *Robinson* [1987] 1 Ch 38 in which the plaintiff alleged infringement of copyright and trade marks and passing off. The defendant admitted to these and injunctive relief and an inquiry as to damages was ordered but the plaintiff had to pay £10 000 to the defendant because of an abuse of the *Anton Piller* order.

15  (1842) 49 ER 749.

16  (1915) 84 LJ Ch 449.

17  Ibid at 450.

18  [1979] AC 731.

19  The plaintiffs were representative of the Dutch manufacturers of Advocaat.

20  (1915) 84 LJ Ch 449.

- a misrepresentation
- made by a trader in the course of trade
- to prospective customers of his or ultimate consumers of goods or services supplied by him
- which is calculated to injure the business or goodwill of another trader (in the sense that this is a reasonably foreseeable consequence) and
- which causes actual damage to a business or goodwill of the trader by whom the action is brought or (in a *quia timet* action) will probably do so.

Lord Oliver reduced this list to three elements in *Reckitt & Colman Products Ltd* v *Borden Inc*[21] namely, the existence of the plaintiff's goodwill, a misrepresentation as to the goods or services offered by the defendant, and damage (or likely damage) to the plaintiff's goodwill as a result of the defendant's misrepresentation. Nevertheless, many judges still prefer Lord Diplock's authoritative test.[22] In the *Erven Warnink* case, Lord Fraser proposed a different formula to that used by Lord Diplock. Lord Fraser said:

> It is essential for the plaintiff in a passing off action to show at least the following facts:- (1) that his business consists of, or includes, selling in England a class of goods to which the particular trade name applies; (2) that the class of goods is clearly defined, and that in the minds of the public, or a section of the public, in England, the trade name distinguishes that class from other similar goods; (3) that because of the reputation of the goods, there is goodwill attached to the name; (4) that he, the plaintiff, as a member of the class of those who sell the goods, is the owner of goodwill in England which is of substantial value; (5) that he has suffered, or is really likely to suffer, substantial damage to his property in the goodwill by reason of the defendants selling goods which are falsely described by the trade name to which the goodwill is attached. Provided these conditions are satisfied ... the plaintiff is entitled to protect himself by a passing off action.[23]

The definitions given by Lords Diplock and Fraser can be seen as attempts to produce a generalised, all-purpose rule, but it is probable that their Lordships were too strongly influenced by the facts of the case before them. In particular, Lord Fraser's definition is far too narrow – being restricted to goods sold in England (although recognising that trade reputation has a specific locality) – but he does specifically mention the need for a goodwill associated with the goods although this is implicit in Lord Diplock's statement. Lord Diplock talks in terms of goods and services and it is clear that a passing off action is available in respect of services. Lord Diplock, by using the phrase 'calculated to injure' seems to suggest some fraud or malice on the part of the defendant whilst Lord Fraser makes no such inference.[24] As will be seen later, relief can be given when the misrepresentation is unintentional; the action is not limited to goods; the geographical scope can extend outside the UK as far as the trade is concerned, and passing off is not limited to trade names as indicated by Lord Fraser. On the whole, Lord Diplock's definition is probably closer to the present legal position and is the one most referred to. In subsequent cases, there has been some conflict about whether the Diplock and the Fraser test should be applied together.[25] On the whole, Lord Diplock's test is of more general application than Lord Fraser's test.

As well respected as *Erven Warnink* is, another line of definitions adopting the simpler approach in *Reckitt & Colman* has the approval of a number of judges. For example, in *Consorzio de Prosciutto di Parma* v *Marks and Spencer plc*,[26] Nourse LJ identified the ingredients of a passing off action as being comprised of:

21 [1990] 1 All ER 873.

22 *See*, for example, the judgments in *Taittinger SA* v *Allbev Ltd* [1993] FSR 641. The simpler statement of passing off is, however, preferred by the same judges; *see Consorzio de Prosciutto di Parma* v *Marks and Spencer plc* [1991] RPC 351.

23 [1979] AC 731 at 755.

24 Lord Diplock later states that 'calculated to injure' does not require actual intention to injure. It is more to do with whether injury is a reasonably foreseeable consquence.

25 *See British Broadcasting Corp* v *Talbot Motor Co Ltd* [1981] FSR 228; *Bristol Conservatories Ltd* v *Conservatories Custom Built Ltd* [1989] RPC 455. In the former case, Megarry VC suggested that the two tests may have been cumulative but, in the latter, it was held that they were not cumulative. In *Pete Waterman Ltd* v *CBS United Kingdom Ltd* [1993] EMLR 27, Browne-Wilkinson VC suggested that the Diplock and Fraser tests should be read together as the Diplock test focuses on the defendant's activities whereas the Fraser test concentrates on what the plaintiff has to show to succeed.

26 [1991] RPC 351.

- the goodwill of the plaintiff
- the misrepresentation made by the defendant and
- consequential damage.

Jacob J approved of this formula in *Hodgkinson and Corby Ltd* v *Wards Mobility Services Ltd*,[27] stressing that the essence of passing off is deception which misleads customers. This line of authorities is not inconsistent with *Erven Warnink* and can be regarded as a clearer statement of passing off, bearing in mind that Lord Diplock's phrase 'calculated to injure' appears to be redundant. However, the simpler statement of passing off ought to have some reference to the fact that it is set in the context of trade.

    In most cases, the defendant will have deliberately used some name, mark or get-up designed to capture part of the plaintiff's business but a fraudulent motive is not essential to the tort.[28] Even if the passing off is 'innocent' relief may be granted.[29] It depends mainly on whether the goodwill associated with the plaintiff's business is harmed because the nature or origin of the defendant's goods or services is misrepresented and the buying public or ultimate consumers are taken in by that misrepresentation. A statement which is true may give rise to the action. If a sole trader with a retail clothing business changes his name to Levi Strauss by deed poll, having the name signwritten above his shop is not a false misrepresentation but it is, nevertheless, likely to be restrained if the clothing manufacturer by that name sues for passing off.[30] Although it is generally accepted that honest use of one's own name is permitted, regardless of the fact that customers may be mislead, such honest use must be done in a way so as not to exaggerate the connection. For example, in *Wright, Layman & Umney Ltd* v *Wright*[31] the plaintiff had a wide reputation under the name 'Wright's', as in 'Wright's Coal Tar Soap'. The defendant, trading as 'Wright's Chemical Company', had, without any dishonesty on his part, passed off his goods as those of the plaintiff by using the name 'Wright's' in relation to them. Lord Greene MR said:

> A man may sell goods under his own name as his own goods. If he does so, he is doing no more than telling the truth. If there happens to be already on the market another trader of that name ... that is just his misfortune ... provided that a man keeps within the limit of using his own name and does so honestly and *does not go beyond that*, nobody can stop him even if the result of him doing so leads to confusion.[32]
>
> [Emphasis added]

It is apparent from the above case that a trader can easily go beyond the limit of using his own name honestly and the original injunction was extended to prevent the use by the defendant of the name 'Wright' or 'Wright's' in a descriptive phrase applied to his products. It is difficult to see what use of his own name the defendant was left with and the spirit of the sweeping and generous statement by Lord Greene does not appear to have been reflected in his judgment, bearing in mind the defendant's real surname was 'Wright'.[33]

## PLAINTIFF'S GOODWILL

Merely copying the name or style of another trader is not, *per se*, sufficient for a passing off action although it could give rise to an action for infringement of copyright if what is copied is more than a simple name, for example a logo.

27 [1995] FSR 169.

28 *Baume & Co Ltd* v *A H Moore Ltd* [1958] RPC 226.

29 *See*, for example, *Gillette UK Ltd* v *Edenwest Ltd* [1994] RPC 279.

30 *See Croft* v *Day* (1843) 7 Beav. 84. However, a true statement that the defendant had operated the fine art department in the plaintiff's store was not passing off, *Harrods Ltd* v *Schwartz-Sackin & Co Ltd* [1991] FSR 209.

31 (1949) 66 RPC 149.

32 (1949) 66 RPC 149 at 151.

33 For a discussion of the limits of honest use of a name, *see* Young, D. (1989) *Passing Off* (2nd edn) Longman, at pp. 94–7.

There must have been a goodwill associated with reputation which had been acquired by the plaintiff in relation to that name or style. Reputation comes about through consistent use, for example the phrase 'Camel Hair Belting' used by the plaintiff from 1879 to 1891 was considered by the jury in *Reddaway* v *Banham*[34] to have become distinctive of the plaintiff's belting even though it was entirely descriptive. In *County Sound plc* v *Ocean Sound plc*,[35] the phrase 'Gold AM' used in connection with broadcasts of 'golden oldies' was held not to have acquired goodwill because it was often used in conjunction with the name 'County Sound', it was immediately descriptive of a certain type of radio programme and did not indicate the source of such programmes. Nourse LJ acknowledged that, had the name been truly distinctive, that a goodwill in that name could have been acquired within a period of six months.

If a trader has just started in business or just started using an unregistered mark or 'get-up' he may be unable to succeed in a passing off action. Although a newly registered trade mark has immediate protection, with passing off the plaintiff must be able to prove that he has built up a reputation around the name, mark or 'get-up'. That is, he has acquired a property in the goodwill associated with the subject matter.[36] It is not possible to lay down hard and fast rules as to the period of time taken to acquire protectable goodwill. It depends on the circumstances. If there is a great deal of commercial activity and advertising throughout the UK, goodwill could be acquired in a relatively short period of time even prior to the availability of the goods or services to which the goodwill relates. In *Stannard* v *Reay*[37] it was held that three weeks was sufficient time to build up goodwill in the name 'Mr Chippy' for a mobile fish and chip van operating on the Isle of Wight. The central question is whether a sufficient reputation has been acquired, and it is possible for the goodwill to be shared amongst a number of traders or businesses as the *Erven Warnink* case emphatically indicates.

Goodwill can exist even if the product or service to which it relates has not yet been made available if a significant proportion of the public knew about the product or service because of a great deal of publicity. So it was held in *British Broadcasting Corp* v *Talbot Motor Co Ltd*[38] where there was evidence that a significant part of the public recognised the name CARFAX as distinctive of the BBC's traffic information system capable of being received in vehicles by special radios. Similarly, in the Singaporean case of *Pontiac Marina Pte Ltd* v *CDL Hotels International Ltd*[39] where it was held that a trader could, through extensive advertising, acquire a goodwill before he commenced trading.[40] Furthermore, goodwill is not restricted to traders having large companies or high turnovers, and a small trader may establish goodwill in a particular locality or because he is well known in a specialist field.[41]

It is important to consider how the goodwill is associated with the product or service concerned. This may, of course, be influenced by the form of an advertising campaign. In *Whitworth Foods Ltd* v *Hunni Foods (International) Ltd*[42] the defendant deliberately copied the plaintiff's containers for glacé cherries. Viewed from the top, the cartons were easily distinguishable because the two companies' names were represented differently and set on different colour backgrounds. However, from the side the cartons looked very similar (both carrying the words 'Glacé Cherries') and the plaintiff argued that if the cartons were displayed on supermarket shelves, stacked on top of one another with the plain-

34 [1896] AC 199.

35 [1991] FSR 367.

36 Just as, in the law of real property, a person may acquire property rights by continued user, for example by prescription.

37 [1967] RPC 589.

38 [1981] FSR 228.

39 [1997] FSR 725.

40 In contrast to what Lord Macnaghten suggested in *The Commisioners of Inland Revenue* v *Muller & Co's Margarine Ltd* [1901] AC 217, quoted above.

41 *NAD Electronics Inc* v *NAD Computer Systems Ltd* [1997] FSR 380. In this case, the trader made high-quality 'hi-fi' systems.

42 (Unreported) 20 October 1986.

tiff's and the defendant's cartons adjacent to each other, there was a danger of confusion. In considering the association of the plaintiff's reputation with the features of their carton, Hoffman J said that the plaintiff's goodwill was chiefly associated with their name and not the design of their containers and that this was confirmed by evidence of the plaintiff's advertising which was done in a general way without specific reference to their individual products.

Sometimes, the defendant may also have a goodwill associated with the name used by the plaintiff. If this relates to different goods or services, this may not be a problem. However, the possibility for a conflict arises if the defendant later wishes to diversify and enter the plaintiff's field of activity. In *Provident Financial plc v Halifax Building Society*,[43] the plaintiff had built up a substantial goodwill in the name Halifax which it used in respect of its motor insurance underwriting which it carried out through brokers. The defendant, one of the leading building societies, widely known as 'The Halifax' decided to launch motor insurance services under its Halifax name and 'X' logo. Granting an injunction to maintain the status quo until a full trial, it was held that it was reasonably arguable that, if the defendant was allowed to move into motor insurance, it would misrepresent that it was connected with the plaintiff. An important factor was that the defendant's goodwill and enormous public profile (it had spent over £27 million in advertising in 1991) would have been likely to have swamped and subsumed the plaintiff's goodwill.

43 [1994] FSR 81.

## DESCRIPTIVE WORDS AND GEOGRAPHICAL NAMES

As the *Halifax* case shows, it is possible to acquire goodwill in a name which includes a geographical name. However, geographical names and, *a fortiori*, descriptive words are likely to lack distinctiveness in most cases such that it will be difficult, if not impossible, for a trader to demonstrate that he has a goodwill associated with the word or words in question.

In *Office Cleaning Services Ltd v Westminster Windows and General Cleaners Ltd*,[44] the plaintiff unsuccessfully tried to restrain the defendant using the trading name 'Office Cleaning Association'. In the plaintiff's unsuccessful appeal to the House of Lords, Viscount Simonds said (at 42):

44 (1946) 63 RPC 39.

> the courts will not readily assume that the use by a trader as part of his trade name descriptive words already used by another trader as part of his trade name is likely to cause confusion and will easily accept small differences as adequate to avoid it. It is otherwise where a fancy word has been chosen as part of the name.

Other examples of descriptive words denied protection by the law of passing off include 'Oven Chips' in *McCain International Ltd v Country Fair Foods Ltd*[45] and 'Chicago Pizza' in *My Kinda Town Ltd v Soll*.[46] Where such words are used, there are two issues in effect. First, because descriptive words are unlikely to be distinctive, it is difficult for a trader to show that he has established goodwill in the words. Secondly, a trader complaining that another trader is wrongfully using the words will find it almost impossible to prove that there is a likelihood of confusion in the minds of the buying public and, that being so, proof of damage (an essential element in passing off) will not be present.

45 [1981] RPC 69.

46 [1983] RPC 407.

If things were otherwise and protection was readily afforded to descriptive words, it would become very difficult for other traders to describe their activities to potential customers. As Laddie J said in *Antec International Ltd* v *South Western Chicks (Warren) Ltd*[47] (at 285):

> As it is sometimes put, no trader will be allowed to fence in the common of the English language. From this it flows, that in some cases where a highly descriptive name has been used by a trader he will find it virtually impossible to obtain protection at all by means of passing off proceedings.

He went on to say that this is not, however, an exact science, echoing Oliver LJ in *My Kinda Town Ltd* v *Soll* who said that there was no clear dichotomy between unprotected descriptive words and fancy names. Of course, made-up words ('fancy names'), unless very similar to already known words, are distinctive *per se* and there should be little difficulty in establishing a likelihood of confusion. In *Antec*, the phrase in issue was 'Farm Fluid' used for disinfectants used at farms, and although Laddie J accepted that it was relatively descriptive, he nevertheless went on to grant an interlocutory injunction to restrain passing off. It was at least arguable that persons buying under that phrase wanted the plaintiff's product and, furthermore, no other trader, apart from the defendant, was using 'Farm Fluid' to describe their disinfectant.

Where generally descriptive words are used by one trader and another trader uses similar words, the court will tend to concentrate on the differences. Thus, in the *Office Cleaning* case, the court isolated 'Services' and 'Association' and held that there was a sufficient differentiation between them such that the defendant was not guilty of passing off. The opposite was held in *The British Diabetic Association* v *The Diabetic Society*,[48] in which Walker J accepted that 'Society' and 'Association' were similar in derivation and meaning and 'not wholly dissimilar in form'.[49] Therefore, there was not a sufficient differentiation to avoid passing off and a final injunction was granted.

A trader using a descriptive word is more likely to acquire goodwill if the word is not generally used in the trade in which the trader is involved. For example, the word 'Millenia'[50] was held not to be descriptive in the context of offices, shops and hotels.[51] Whether a word is capable of supporting goodwill depends very much on its context. Descriptive words may reach the status of fancy names if they are used in an unusual or unexpected context. For example, 'Spectrum' would be descriptive in terms or optical lens manufacture, but not when used in the field of lawnmowers. The issue is distinctiveness rather than whether the word or phrase is descriptive or fancy. Similarly with a slang term, it will be difficult to establish the presence of goodwill associated with the term. To be successful, the plaintiff must show that the term has acquired a secondary meaning, being indicative of the plaintiff's goods. Thus, in *Box Television Ltd* v *Haymarket Magazines Ltd*,[52] it was held that the plaintiff had failed to show that it had goodwill in 'The Box' for its cable TV channel. Parker J considered that 'The Box' was simply a colloquialism for a television set. That is not to say, however, that it is impossible to acquire goodwill in a slang term, merely that a trader will face an uphill task in convincing a court that the public associate the term with his goods or services.

A phrase such as 'Internet World' seems very descriptive at first sight, but in *Mecklermedia Corp* v *DC Congress Gesellschaft mbH*,[53] the plaintiff claimed extensive goodwill in the phrase as regards its activities in respect of its website and magazines. The defendant had registered the name as its trade mark in

47 [1997] FSR 278.

48 [1996] FSR 1.

49 The word 'British' was not considered as part of the plaintiff's name for the purposes of the decision.

50 The correct spelling is 'Millennia'.

51 *Pontiac Marina Pte Ltd* v *CDL Hotels International Ltd* [1997] FSR 725, High Court, Singapore.

52 *The Times*, 3 March 1997.

53 [1997] FSR 627.

Germany and had already commenced proceedings there for trade mark infringement. Jacob J held that, although 'Internet World' was to some extent descriptive, it was not so descriptive that goodwill could not exist in it and he accepted that the plaintiff had established a serious question that it had extensive goodwill in England.[54] He refused to strike out the claim, stay the action or decline jurisdiction pending the outcome in the German case. The two claims were different and there was no danger of conflicting decisions as the German case involved a trade mark whereas the English case was concerned with passing off. Jacob J considered that the English courts were the most convenient forum for hearing an English passing off case.

A geographical name used by a trade could have one of three meanings. It could indicate that:

- the trader's goods come from that place;
- the trader's goods are of a particular type associated with that place and, therefore, likely to appeal to a particular taste; or
- it is the product of a particular trader.

The third meaning has been described in the House of Lords in the 'Stone Ale' case[55] as a secondary meaning to which goodwill could attach and which could be established by evidence. However, in *Barnsley Brewery Co Ltd v RBNB*,[56] the court declined to renew an injunction against the use of 'Barnsley Bitter' by the defendant as the plaintiff did not have a strong case that the phrase had acquired such a secondary meaning. 'Barnsley Bitter' had been used by a third party at its Oakwell (near Barnsley) brewery from 1883 to 1976. Both the plaintiff and defendant were hoping to capture the historical goodwill associated with the name.

In some cases, geographical names have a special form of protection by virtue of EC regulations. For example, Council Regulation 1576/89/EEC restricting the use of geographical names for spirits such as Scotch Whisky and Council Regulation 2081/92/EEC restricting designations of origin and geographical indications for agricultural products. In the case of the former, in *Matthew Gloag & Sons Ltd v Welsh Distillers Ltd*,[57] the defendants bought Scotch Whisky and marketed it under the name Welsh Whisky. It was held that the plaintiffs had an arguable case for passing off[58] and that they also had a private right under the regulation which allowed the use of other geographical names provided that they did not mislead customers.

As regards the latter regulation, Asda Stores could not be prevented by virtue of the regulation from selling Parma ham which had been sliced and packaged outside the Parma region of Italy even though that was contrary to Italian law.[59] The ham itself came from the Parma region and was not misdescribed as the regulation was concerned with designation of origin and contained no direct reference to slicing and packaging.

## THE SCOPE OF PASSING OFF

The scope of passing off is quite wide and it can protect unregistrable business names, unregistered trade marks, advertising and general 'get-up', in fact anything that is distinctive of the plaintiff's goods, services or business. Trade mark law requires some use of the mark whereas in passing off, no express use or men-

54 The defendant's claim that 'Internet World' was too descriptive for goodwill to exist in it lay ill with its claim to have a valid registered trade mark in Germany consisting of that name.

55 *Montgomery v Thompson* [1871] AC 217.

56 [1997] FSR 462.

57 *The Times*, 27 February 1998.

58 On the basis of inverse passing off as in *British Conservatories Ltd v Conservatories Custom Built Ltd* [1989] RPC 455.

59 *Consorzio del Prosciutto di Parma v Asda Stores Ltd, The Times*, 3 February 1998.

tion of a trade name is required, mere implication is adequate. For example, in *Copydex Ltd v Noso Products Ltd*,[60] the plaintiff had given a demonstration of their glue on television although the name of the product was not mentioned (this was before the days of commercial television and great care was taken not to mention trade names, even to the extent of covering over manufacturers' names on items used in dramatic sketches). The defendant company also made glue and one of its salesmen gave a demonstration of its glue in a large retail store. During the demonstration a large card was displayed which bore the words: '"NOSO" here again! As shown on television "Women's Hour"'. When the plaintiff complained the defendant gave the court an undertaking not to do it again, otherwise an injunction would have been granted in favour of the plaintiff.

The scope of passing off can be considered in terms of the meaning of 'in the course of trade', the extent of marks and 'get-up' protected and geographical range.

### In the course of trade

Although some judges have talked about passing off in relation to trade in goods, it is clear that it applies equally to services as well. Before service marks could be registered, this was of exceptional importance as the use of another's name in relation to the provision of services could only be actionable as passing off. In *Harrods Ltd v R Harrod Ltd*,[61] the plaintiff was a well known company with a banking department, but which was precluded from operating as a moneylender by the articles of association. The defendant registered a money-lending company under the 'fancy name'[62] of R Harrod Ltd, that is a name having nothing to do with his own name. This fact together with his advertising style showed that he was acting fraudulently in an attempt to gain advantage from these similarities and the plaintiff was granted an injunction to restrain the defendant from using that name.

'Trade' does not have to be primarily associated with commercial enterprise and in *British Medical Association v Marsh*[63] the plaintiff, a professional body constituted as a non profit-making unincorporated association, was able to obtain an injunction to prevent the defendant passing off his business as that of the plaintiff's. The Association had published analyses of 'quack medicines' because of concern that they were of no medical value and were being sold at excessive prices. The defendant started making up proprietary medicines from the Association's analyses and sold them in a drug store which had the letters 'B.M.A.' displayed in the window together with other references to the Association. To describe the Association's operations as being in the course of trade shows a certain elasticity of thought but it was said that the plaintiff's 'business' would be harmed because the passing off might cause existing members to leave the Association or to discourage potential members from joining. That is, existing and potential members might think that the defendant's activities were approved of or connected with the Association.

It has been accepted that a charity too is capable of possessing goodwill indistinguishable from commercial goodwill which was equally entitled to legal protection through an action in passing off. In *The British Diabetic Association v The Diabetic Society*[64] the defendant charity was restrained from using its name, such use amounting to a deception calculated to injure (albeit unintentional) the reputation and goodwill of the plaintiff charity. Walker J expressed

60 (1952) 69 RPC 38.

61 (1924) 41 RPC 74.

62 It may have been so described because the Patents, Designs and Trade Marks Act 1883 permitted the registration of 'fancy words' although the phrase 'invented word' was soon to replace it.

63 (1931) 48 RPC 565.

64 [1996] FSR 1.

his profound regret at the failure of the parties to settle the dispute, the costs of which were £750 000. He said that it was difficult even for a lawyer to comprehend how the litigation could help diabetics whose subscriptions and gifts would ultimately be the source of payment of the lawyers' bills.[65]

Such a robust view of trade and potential harm has not readily been embraced in cases involving individuals whose names have been used without their permission. In *McCullogh* v *Lewis A May Ltd*[66] the plaintiff was a well-known children's broadcaster who used the name 'Uncle Mac'. The plaintiff had some physical infirmities. The defendant sold cereal under the name 'Uncle Mac' with indirect reference to the plaintiff's infirmities without the plaintiff's permission. It could be argued that, in such a situation, inferences might be drawn by the public seeing the cereal which might be harmful to the plaintiff. For example, it could be inferred that the plaintiff had to resort to allowing his nickname to be used in this way to earn more money and that to soil his hands with advertising was contrary to the image he was trying to maintain. However, it was held that the facts could not give rise to passing off because the plaintiff was in no way involved in the making or marketing of cereals, instead he was a broadcaster. There was no common field of activity.[67] The decision totally fails to take any account of the fact that many of the public buying and eating the cereal would assume that the plaintiff had given permission for his nickname to be used in such a fashion and the possibility that he might lose popularity as a broadcaster because of the lower regard in which media personalities involved with advertising were once held.

Where a personal name has been used without permission in order to promote a product or a service, there is always a possibility of an action in defamation.[68] 'Uncle Mac' may have stood a better chance had he sued in libel as Wynn-Parry J said: 'If it were anything, it were libel, as to which I say nothing.' In *Sim* v *H J Heinz Co Ltd*[69] Ron Moody, the actor, was engaged to read the commentaries for advertisements for the defendant's products to be broadcast on television. In making the commentaries, he mimicked the voice of another popular actor, Alistair Sim, who took objection. However, it was held that an injunction would not be granted, whether on the basis of defamation or passing off because there was no evidence of damage to the reputation of the plaintiff. Again there is no common field of activity, the plaintiff was in the business of acting and not in the business of making and selling soups and baked beans. It is certainly far less likely that the plaintiff's business goodwill would be harmed in cases such as this compared to the *Uncle Mac* case.

### Extent of marks and 'get-up' protected

Passing off goes beyond the type of mark that is registrable as a trade mark and can apply in respect of containers and packaging.[70] In a controversial case which went all the way to the House of Lords, *Reckitt & Colman Products Ltd* v *Borden Inc*,[71] it was held that the Jif lemon was protected by the law of passing off. The Jif lemon is a plastic lemon coloured and shaped receptacle in which the plaintiff's lemon juice was sold. The defendant sold lemon juice in a similar but not identical container (it was bigger, having a green cap and a flat side) and was restrained from passing off its lemon juice as that of the plaintiffs by use of a deceptively similar 'get-up'. Lord Bridge said that the result was to

---

[65] *The Times*, 14 October 1995, p. 6.

[66] (1948) 65 RPC 58.

[67] The need for the common field of activity is discussed later in this chapter.

[68] An example where the plaintiff successfully sued in defamation is *Tolley* v *J S Fry & Sons Ltd* [1931] AC 333 where the picture of the plaintiff was printed on the wrappers of chocolate bars.

[69] [1959] 1 All ER 547.

[70] Trade mark law now permits the registration of the shape of goods or their packaging, Trade Marks Act 1994 s 1(1), subject to s 3(2).

[71] [1990] 1 All ER 873.

give the plaintiff a *de facto* monopoly on the container which was just as effective as a *de jure* monopoly and he commented on the fact that a trader selling lemon juice would never be allowed to register a lemon as a trade mark but that the plaintiff had achieved that result indirectly.[72] However, Lord Bridge had to reluctantly agree that that was the outcome on the basis of the application of the law of passing off.[73] Lord Oliver said that all the main ingredients of a passing off action, namely goodwill, misrepresentation and damage, were present. The Jif lemon had been on sale since 1956 and a considerable goodwill had built up associated with it and it was likely that a good number of housewives would purchase the defendant's lemon juice in the belief that they were purchasing Jif lemons even though careful inspection would show that the defendant's lemons were not Jif lemons because of the different shape and the attached labels.[74] The essence of a passing off action was said to be a deceit practised on the public. Customers were to be taken as they were found, it being no answer to the claim that customers would not have been mistaken had they been 'more careful, more literate and more perspicacious'.

The decision seemed out of step with trade mark law at the time which, generally, denied registration to containers as in the trade mark case of *In re Coca Cola Co*[75] where the House of Lords was concerned about creating a monopoly in a container. The *Jif Lemon* decision did raise the question as to whether a greengrocer could ever be accused of passing off his natural lemons as Jif lemons! Of course, the decision stops short of this. Now, with the Trade Marks Act 1994, the congruence between the law of passing off and trade mark law is much greater.

The law of passing off does not stop short at containers. Even the shape or appearance of the article itself may be protected. In *Hodgkinson and Corby Ltd v Wards Mobility Services Ltd*,[76] the plaintiff made a cushion for use by permanently immobile persons to prevent pressure sores. It had a distinctive appearance. The defendant was planning to sell a 'lookalike' cushion though under a different trade name. It was held that passing off could occur even when the appearance of goods had been copied and that passing off was not restricted to taking a name, mark or sign. Although copying the appearance of a product is not unlawful, *per se*, in the absence of infringing an intellectual property right, in terms of passing off, the defendant must always do enough to avoid the deception.

The ability of purchasers to make subtle distinctions was considered to be a factor in the Privy Council case of *White Hudson & Co Ltd v Asian Organisation Ltd*[77] in which the plaintiff had sold cough sweets wrapped in red cellophane in Singapore since 1953. The wrapper bore the word 'Hacks' and a list of ingredients. From 1958, the defendant also sold cough sweets of a similar colour and shape which were also wrapped in red cellophane but with the name 'Pecto' printed on the wrappers. It was held that the plaintiff had established a get-up in the red coloured wrapper that was distinctive of his cough sweets and there was a danger of confusion especially as few purchasers could read the words 'Pecto' and it was shown that many customers asked for 'red paper cough sweets'. Although no deception was proved on the part of the defendant, the get-up of the defendant's sweets was calculated to deceive and the injunction granted to the plaintiff in the Court of Appeal in Singapore was confirmed. To avoid confusion the defendants could have simply used a different colour for their wrappers or used a prominent

72 Under the 1994 Act, although a representation of a lemon is descriptive of the goods, it may still be registrable if, in fact, the mark has become distinctive through use.

73 All judges from the trial judge up to and including the House of Lords judges came to the same conclusion as regards passing off.

74 However, it was accepted that the labels could easily become detached.

75 [1986] 2 All ER 274.

76 [1995] FSR 169.

77 [1964] 1 WLR 1466.

symbol on the wrapper. The use of a different colour will not always be a realistic option, for example as in the Jif lemon case.

The protection of wrappers and containers by passing off is one example of the width of this area of law compared to trade marks, although the latter has now caught up as a result of amendments to trade mark law so as to implement the European Directive on the harmonisation of trade and service marks.[78] But passing off can go even further in the subject matter protected and can protect, in principle, anything associated with goodwill such as a method of doing business or a theme used in advertising. Of course, the less tangible the subject matter is, the less likely it is that the plaintiff can show that there has been or will be damage to his goodwill as a result of the defendant's misrepresentation. In *Cadbury-Schweppes Pty Ltd* v *Pub Squash Co Pty Ltd*,[79] the plaintiff marketed a soft drink in Australia called 'Solo' which was sold in cans resembling beer cans bearing a medallion device. An intensive advertising campaign portrayed it as a drink associated with 'rugged masculine endeavour' and, in total contradiction of the popular image of the Australian male, it sold well. The defendant later started selling a comparable drink called 'Pub Squash' in similar cans with advertising in a similar vein. It was held that the plaintiff had failed to acquire an intangible property right associated with their advertising campaign because it never became a distinguishing feature of the product or generally associated with it. Although it was conceded that the defendant had deliberately taken advantage of the plaintiff's advertising campaign, the consuming public were not misled or deceived by this into thinking that Pub Squash was the plaintiff's drink. In other words, the plaintiff could show no damage resulting from the defendant's use of similar advertising and get-up.

The *Pub Squash* case shows that distinctiveness is important to success in a passing off action. If a name is descriptive this will reduce or even eliminate the possibility of it being distinctive of a particular trader's business. For example, in *Advance Magazine Publishing Inc* v *Redwood Publishing Ltd*,[80] the plaintiff published a food magazine entitled 'GOURMET'. The defendant planned to publish, as part of a series of magazines, a food magazine called 'BBC Gourmet Goodfood'. Harman J refused to grant interlocutory relief to the plaintiff. As the word 'Gourmet' was descriptive, small differences in get-up would be sufficient to avoid confusion. Furthermore, the plaintiff had failed to establish an arguable case. The magazines were different when looked at alongside each other and, even though the defendant's title might be shortened to 'Gourmet' by purchasers, magazines were not usually sold by name over the counter but from racks from which purchasers would select the magazine they wished to buy.

The use of numbers may be controlled by the law of passing off. It has become very common for motor vehicle manufacturers to use numbers as model identifiers, for example, Peugeot 306, BMW 318i, Volvo 850, Mercedes C180 and so on. The use of one maker's number by another could raise an arguable case of passing off, depending on how well established the number is. In many cases, showing goodwill should present no problem and using another manufacturers number certainly could be described as a misrepresentation. The difficulty lies in proving consequential damage. If Peugeot decided to sell a car under the name 850, would any potential buyer be deceived into thinking he was ordering a Volvo. It seems unlikely in the extreme unless the car became so well known by the number on its own without reference to the maker.

78 Even so, the law of passing off may prove wider in this respect as there are some exceptions that affect the registrability of marks.

79 [1981] 1 All ER 213 (The Judicial Committee of the Privy Council).

80 [1993] FSR 449.

However, as we shall see, the law of passing off has developed to accept erosion of goodwill as a form of damage. This could apply where one car maker uses a number that has become strongly associated with a particular manufacturer's car which is, itself, of high quality or performance.

Where the use of a number is at issue, the individual circumstances may be highly relevant. In *The Law Society of England and Wales v Griffiths*,[81] the plaintiff had launched a 'phone in advice line in respect of accidents and personal injuries. The telephone number was 0500-192939. The defendant, who was not part of the plaintiff's scheme, set up one of his own and obtained and used the telephone number 0800-192939. It was held that there was a serious issue to be tried by the court which granted an interlocutory injunction in favour of the plaintiff. By deliberately choosing a confusingly similar number, the defendant was representing that he was the plaintiff either by saying so or by failing to disabuse callers. The effect would be to cause a serious loss of business to the plaintiff who had built up a substantial goodwill associated with its scheme. It appeared that the defendant had deliberately selected his telephone number in order to divert business away from the plaintiff.

## Geographical range

If passing off by one trader is to damage another trader's interests in the goodwill he has acquired it should be reasonable to assume that there should be some overlap in the geographical location and extent of the catchment area of their respective businesses. For example, it might be assumed that a baker in Leeds operating under the name 'Melwood Bakeries' would not be able to restrain another baker using the same name in Dover but he might be able to restrain the use of the name by a baker in Bradford which lies relatively close to Leeds. Bearing in mind the basic test for passing off stated in its barest form as being a misrepresentation that causes damage to business goodwill, there is a possibility that people in Bradford will think that the bakery there and the one in Leeds are owned by the same person and the latter may lose sales as a result. Overlapping or contiguous geographical areas would seem to be precursor for a passing off action.

The narrow view above does not take account of future growth of businesses and this may be a reason for allowing passing off an expansive geographical range. For example, the baker in the above example may be ambitious and his business may grow so that eventually he has a chain of bakeries spanning the whole of England, including Dover.[82] The goodwill may even be in relation to activities in a different country. In *Maxim's Ltd v Dye*,[83] the plaintiff, an English company, owned a world-famous restaurant in Paris known as 'Maxim's'. The defendant opened a restaurant in Norwich and also named it 'Maxim's'. It was held that the plaintiff had goodwill in England derived from the business in France which might be regarded as being prospective. The plaintiff might want to commence trading in England in the future and should be able to rely on the goodwill he had in connection with the name.[84] Such international extent of goodwill will not be common, but if an international reputation has been achieved, there is a danger that another person carrying out business using the same name could cause confusion and customers might think that they were dealing with the plaintiff's business. This is particularly so in the

81 [1995] RPC 16.

82 *See*, for example, *Brestian v Try* [1958] RPC 161 where the plaintiff who had hairdressing shops in London, Wembley and Brighton succeeded in obtaining an injunction to prevent the defendant using the same name in Tunbridge Wells.

83 [1977] 1 WLR 1155.

84 Compare with *Anheuser Busch Inc v Budejovicky Budvar* [1984] FSR 413, discussed supra.

case of large multinational organisations such as 'McDonald's'. The above case is also an example of a remedy being available without proof of any actual or immediate damage; indeed, the damage is purely speculative as the plaintiff might never open a restaurant in Norwich, England or the UK. The decision can be justified on the basis that, by his choice of name, the defendant attempted to cash in on the plaintiff's goodwill. Additionally, there is always the danger that had the defendant's food not been of a high quality that the plaintiff's reputation, which it enjoyed in the UK, might have been harmed as a consequence. Dilution of goodwill is also a possible factor.

*Maxim's* v *Dye* was followed in the Calcutta High Court in *Calvin Klein Inc* v *International Apparel Syndicate*[85] where it was held that it was not necessary to have trade in India to have a reputation there. In that case, the emphasis seemed to be on reputation rather than goodwill. But we have seen that reputation without goodwill is insufficient to support an action in passing off: *Anheuser Busch Inc* v *Budejovicky Budvar*.[86] The distinction that can be made between *Maxim's* and *Anheuser Busch* is that, in the former, the plaintiff was established in the United Kingdom and persons living there might go to Maxim's in Paris on a week-end break, or whatever, attracted by its reputation.

It has been suggested that the plaintiff, wherever located, must be able to show at least a customer or customers in England. In *Panhard et Levassor SA* v *Panhard Levassor Motor Co Ltd*,[87] the French car manufacturer had goodwill in the United Kingdom even though it had no established place of business there. The goodwill was based on the fact that the plaintiff sold cars to customers in the United Kingdom either directly from Paris or through importers. There are other contrasting cases on the subject. In *Sheraton Corp of America* v *Sheraton Motels Ltd*,[88] the plaintiff was granted an interlocutory injunction on the basis that, although it had no hotels in the UK, it took bookings for its American hotels from an office in England whereas, in *Alain Bernadin et Cie* v *Pavilion Properties Ltd*,[89] an injunction was refused to the plaintiff, which owned the Crazy Horse Saloon in Paris, to prevent the defendant using the name for its establishment in London. The plaintiff did not have any place of business in the UK nor did it take bookings there. The *Crazy Horse* case was cited with approval in the *Anheuser-Busch* case, but has been criticised. One distinction between the *Crazy Horse* and *Panhard* cases is that the former was concerned with a local activity (eating, drinking and making merry) compared with the 'rather more durable enjoyment of a Panhard car'.[90] The authorities seemed in a confused state and irreconcilable.

Recent case law, albeit foreign, tends to support the approach taken in *Maxim's*. For example, in *Whirlpool Trade Mark*,[91] the Supreme Court of India held that a trader did not need to show actual sales in India to establish goodwill there. In such a case, goodwill could result from advertising in magazines which were circulated in India. In *C & A Modes* v *C & A (Waterford) Ltd*,[92] the defendant began trading under the name and symbol 'C & A' in Ireland and was held to be guilty of passing off by the Supreme Court of Ireland. The plaintiff did not have any trade outlet in Ireland, although it did in Belfast in Northern Ireland. However, many of the customers at the Belfast store had travelled from Ireland to shop there. The Supreme Court of Ireland held that goodwill does not necessarily stop at the frontier and the defendant's activities were calculated to cause confusion in the minds of existing or potential customers. Similarly in *McDonald's Corp* v

85 [1995] FSR 515.

86 [1984] FSR 413.

87 (1901) 18 RPC 405.

88 [1964] RPC 202.

89 [1967] RPC 581.

90 *Jian Tools for Sales Inc* v *Roderick Manhattan Group Ltd* [1995] FSR 924.

91 [1997] FSR 905.

92 [1978] FSR 126.

**93** [1997] FSR 760. It was held that both parties could trade under the name McDonald's. The defendant had been trading under that name in Jamaica since 1971, whereas the worldwide food chain had only recently commenced trading in Jamaica.

McDonald's Corp Ltd and Vincent Chang,[93] where the Court of Appeal in Jamaica accepted that the famous worldwide chain of fast-food restaurants had a goodwill in Jamaica before it started trading there because of intensive advertising.

The correctness of *Alain Bernadin* must now be doubted. The international nature of many business operations show that this case is no longer relevant. In many cases, the reputation of large multinational organisations precedes them as they expand their activities into other countries. Reputation in that sense must equate with goodwill because, if the reputation is harmed, the consequence is that, once established in those other countries, turnover there will also be harmed. Injuring reputation prospectively injures goodwill in future trade. That being so, *Anheuser Busch* must also be doubted.

Incidentally, there is no problem with finding passing off where the activity complained of occurs in another country, provided the defendant's misrepresentation in that other country is likely to injure the plaintiff's goodwill.[94] What matters is whether the plaintiff's goodwill has been injured and this requires consideration of a supplementary question when looking at the classic trinity of goodwill, misrepresentation and damage. That question is to ask whether the plaintiff's goodwill has extended to the territory where the defendant's activities have taken place. If the answer to this is 'No', a further question arises, being whether knowledge of the defendant's activities would reach a substantial number of persons in the territories to which the plaintiff's goodwill has extended.

**94** In which case, for jurisdictional purposes, the tort occurs in the country where the goodwill exists: *Mecklermedia Corp v DC Congress Gesellschaft mbH* [1997] FSR 627.

## THE NATURE OF THE MISREPRESENTATION

The misrepresentation or deception is not necessarily limited to an exact copy of a name, mark or 'get-up'. Similarity sufficient to result in confusion will do, an important factor being whether purchasers or consumers of the product or services have been or are likely to be misled. For trade marks, except where there is identity of the mark and the goods, the litmus test is whether the use of the second mark is likely to cause confusion on the part of the public, including a likelihood of association.[95] So too with passing off but set in the wider context of 'get-up'. In deciding whether the buying public (or the ultimate consumer) is likely to be misled or confused, it is not necessary to consider whether members of the public who are knowledgeable about the particular product or service are deceived and it may be sufficient if members of the public who have relatively little knowledge of the product or service are deceived or are likely to be deceived.

**95** The Trade Marks Act 1994 s 10(2).

There must be a misrepresentation for passing off, a likelihood of confusion will not suffice *per se*,[96] though it is not easy to think of examples of confusion absent a misrepresentation which may be direct or indirect, deliberate or innocent. Misrepresentation can take many forms. For example, it may confuse as to the origin of goods or services or the nature of the defendant's goods or services.[97] It may be made in words or pictorially,[98] or be implied from behaviour. It could be that a trader fails to disabuse customers about their mistaken beliefs which may have been encouraged by the trader.

A number of factors will affect whether the misrepresentation is likely to confuse, such as whether the traders operate in the same field of activity, the distinctiveness of the plaintiff's get-up, how well-known and familiar the get-up is and the sales outlets for the traders' goods. In *NAD Electronics Inc v NAD Computer Systems Ltd*,[99] important factors in finding passing off (and trade mark infringement) were the facts that the goodwill subsisted in 'NAD', a fancy name,

**96** *Barnsley Brewery Co Ltd v RBNB* [1997] FSR 462.

**97** For example, in *The Law Society of England & Wales v The Society of Lawyers* [1996] FSR 739, there was a risk that members of the public might believe that the defendant's members had recognised legal qualifications or even were solicitors.

**98** For example, the use of another seabird (a Puffin instead of a Penguin) and similar coloured get-up in *United Biscuits (UK) Ltd v Asda Stores Ltd* [1997] RPC 513.

**99** [1997] FSR 380.

that the goods were advertised in similar ways (the plaintiff sold hi-fi systems of high quality and the defendant sold computers) and both traders' goods were sold alongside each other in retail outlets such as Dixons.

The public are not expected to be particularly knowledgeable about the product concerned. The reasonable man is no connoisseur of fine wines and exotic foods. In *J Bollinger* v *Costa Bravo Wine Co Ltd (No. 2)*,[100] the plaintiff made the famous sparkling wine known as 'champagne' in the Champagne region of France. This drink has a very high reputation and is often bought for special occasions by people who do not purchase it regularly. The defendant imported into the UK a sparkling wine called 'Spanish Champagne' which was supposed to be like the plaintiff's product but made in Spain. The defendant claimed that by adding the word 'Spanish' this clearly indicated that the wine was not made in France and, because Champagne was such a well-known product, only a tiny portion of ignorant, ill-educated persons would be misled. The defendant further claimed that the word 'champagne' had become a generic description. An injunction was granted preventing the use of the word 'champagne' by the defendant. It was held in the High Court that a substantial number of persons, whose life and education had not taught them much about the nature and production of wine, might want to buy champagne from time to time and these people might be misled by the description of the defendant's sparkling wine as 'Spanish Champagne'. The description 'Spanish Champagne' was intended to attract to the defendant's product the goodwill connected with the reputation of champagne and amounted to dishonest trading. Danckwerts J said '... it seems to me that close resemblance makes the counterfeit not less but more calculated to deceive ...'. 'Champagne' had not become a generic name because corresponding wines made elsewhere were not described using that word.

A misrepresentation that is ineffective because the public see through it is not actionable in passing off because one important and fundamental requirement is missing.[101] In the absence of confusion there can be no harm to goodwill and, therefore, no damage to the plaintiff. In *Tamworth Herald Co Ltd* v *Thomson Free Newspapers Ltd*,[102] the plaintiff's newspaper had been published since 1868 as the *Tamworth Herald*, a weekly newspaper selling at 23 pence at the time of the action. The defendant bought the rights in a weekly free newspaper called the *Tamworth Trader* and intended to change its name to the *Tamworth Herald & Post*. Both newspapers were circulated in the same geographical area and the plaintiff commenced a *quia timet* action for passing off but was refused an injunction. It was held by Aldous J that it was improbable that the recipients of the defendant's paper would believe it was published by the plaintiff. An example of the defendant's new 'masthead' included a reference that the paper was formerly the *Tamworth Trader*. Potential advertisers would obtain the address or telephone number from the newspapers themselves or from the Yellow Pages and would in neither case be under a misapprehension as to whom they were dealing with.[103] The possibility of confusion and subsequent damage to the plaintiff's goodwill was, therefore, remote.[104]

## Parodies

In terms of passing off a parody is acceptable provided that it is clear that it is a parody and not associated with the plaintiff. There is no misrepresentation if the source is made absolutely clear.[105] However, great care must be taken because, as mentioned above, the public are not generally expected to be particularly know-

100 [1961] 1 ALL ER 561.

101 *See*, for example, *Ciba-Geigy plc* v *Parke Davis & Co Ltd* [1994] FSR 8 where it was held that a reasonable doctor, reading the defendant's advertisement for its drug which was equivalent to the plaintiff's drug and which used a picture of a green apple as used by the plaintiff, would not think the defendant's drug was associated with the plaintiff's drug, business or slow release formulation.

102 [1991] FSR 337.

103 Whether two business concerns having similar names can be easily distinguished in the Yellow Pages is a nice objective test for passing off.

104 That the word 'Herald' is commonly used in the newspaper industry was a factor. The plaintiff was also concerned about the possibility of confusion resulting from telephone canvassing but this would not happen if the canvassers followed their instructions carefully and it was wrong to assume that they would not do so.

105 Even though there is no passing off, the aggrieved party may have remedies under copyright law and the law of defamation.

ledgeable. On the same basis, the general public is not taken to be particularly careful and scrutinise the goods or services in question to determine their true origin.

Alan Clark, the famous Member of Parliament, had published his 'Diaries' which proved somewhat controversial, though very successful. The *London Evening Standard* published a weekly spoof of Alan Clark's diaries based on what a journalist imagined Alan Clark would record in his Diary. The newspaper column was headed 'Alan Clark's Secret Political Diaries' and included a photograph of Alan Clark. Below was a note identifying the journalist as the author and what the basis for the column was. In *Alan Kenneth McKenzie Clark v Associated Newspapers Ltd*,[106] the proprietor of the *Evening Standard* was held liable for passing off and for false attribution of authorship under copyright law. The court held that, to be actionable as passing off, the deception had to be more than momentary and inconsequential (as it might have been had the true fact of authorship been more prominent).

In cases where there are mixed and conflicting messages, the dominant message matters and it is not sufficient to claim that a careful sensible reader would read the 'disclaimer'. The work had to be looked at as a whole to decide whether a substantial number of readers would be misled into thinking that the column was written by Alan Clark. Nor was it a defence to claim that readers of the column would not be misled had they been more careful. The court did not prevent the continuing publication of the column but insisted that, should it continue, the identity of the true author must be made sufficiently clear.

As will be seen later, for passing off there must be a common field of activity (although it is arguable that this rule has been relaxed of late). There was a common field of activity here as Alan Clark had himself written diaries. Had he not, the passing off action might not have succeeded, although this would leave the false attribution of copyright claim intact.

## Acquiescence

A case with similar facts to the *J Bollinger* (Spanish Champagne) case demonstrates that acquiescence in an activity that could be passing off will defeat the plaintiff's claim. In *Vine Products Ltd v MacKenzie & Co Ltd*,[107] the Spanish producers of sherry tried to prevent the use of that word as in British Sherry, South African Sherry, Cyprus Sherry, etc. The genuine drink derives it name from the Jerez region in Spain and is a high-quality product. However, similar fortified wines have been produced in other countries, for example Australia, South Africa and Cyprus and sold under names including the word 'sherry', for example 'British Sherry' and 'Cyprus Sherry'. There was no evidence of confusion amongst the wine-drinking public and these other wines had been so described for a considerable period of time. It was held that the word 'Sherry', standing alone meant a wine from Jerez and others would be prevented from using the word on its own. However, the use of other descriptions such as 'British Sherry' would not be restrained because of acquiescence on the part of the plaintiffs. In practice, each type of sherry from different countries had achieved, over a long period of time, their own individual and distinct reputations. For example, it could be said that 'Cyprus Sherry' is a very pleasant and inexpensive form of the wine whilst the Spanish variant retains its high reputation as the wine of the highest quality. It is self-evident that the owner of an unregistered trade mark or other name or mark or get-up should not delay in taking action against any person copying that mark, name or get-up.

Subsequent case law confirms the importance of acquiescence as a way of defeating a claim in passing off. In *Taylor's Fashions Ltd v Liverpool Victoria Trustees Co Ltd*,[108] Oliver J said that the approach to be entertained by the court is:

> ascertaining whether, in particular individual circumstances, it would be unconscionable for a party to be permitted to deny that which, knowingly or unknowingly, he has allowed or encouraged another to assume to his detriment.[109]

If the plaintiff has been given prior warning of the defendant's planned activities and fails to object, he is less likely to be granted an injunction by the court. In *Dalgety Spillers Foods Ltd v Food Brokers Ltd*,[110] the defendant wrote to the plaintiff (which marketed 'Pot Noodles') indicating an intention to sell a similar product under the name 'Cup Noodles', enclosing an example of the container. When the plaintiff, some time later, complained and requested an injunction it was refused on the balance of convenience. An important factor was that the plaintiff could give no convincing explanation for its inactivity following the defendant's letter putting it on notice and, in the meantime, the defendant had spent time, trouble and expense in launching its 'Cup Noodles' product.

## Inverse passing off

It has been said that passing off can be one of two types:

1  classical passing off, where B represents his goods as being those of A, or
2  extended passing off, where A uses a false description for his goods to impute some quality to his goods, for example as in the *Spanish Champagne* case or the *Advocaat* case.[111]

However, passing off is not necessarily limited to these two forms and the common law should develop in such a way to reflect the higher standards of consumer protection recently legislated for. Indeed, in the *Advocaat* case, Lord Diplock said that passing off ought to proceed upon a parallel rather than diverging course to the trend in legislation.[112] Inverse passing off (if it exists as a separate species) occurs where the defendant falsely claims that the plaintiff's goods or services are actually made by, or provided by, the defendant. For example, in *Bristol Conservatories Ltd v Conservatories Custom Built Ltd*[113] the defendant's salesmen showed potential customers photographs of conservatories as a sample of the defendant's workmanship. The photographs were, in fact, of the plaintiff's conservatories. The Court of Appeal had no doubt that this constituted passing off although refusing to describe it as inverse (or reverse) passing off.[114] Nevertheless, the boundaries of passing off are not fixed and false claims as to patents or testimonials may fall within its ambit.[115]

Inverse passing off may also be committed by implicitly encouraging others to think that one is associated or responsible for material created and belonging to another. For example, in *John Robert Powers School Inc v Denyse Bernadette Tessensohn*,[116] the defendant, in her manner of leaving the plaintiff's study notes on shelves easily accessible to students and customers, was holding out that they were her notes and this misrepresentation amounted to inverse passing off.

108  [1981] 2 WLR 576.

109  *See also Habib Bank Ltd v Habib Bank AG Zurich* [1982] RPC 1; *International Business Machines Corp v Phoenix International (Computers) Ltd* [1994] RPC 251.

110  [1994] FSR 504.

111  *See* Young, D. (1989) *Passing Off* (2nd edn) Longman, at pp. 5–8.

112  *Erven Warnink Besloten Vennootschap v J Townsend & Sons (Hull) Ltd* [1979] AC 731 at 743.

113  [1989] RPC 455.

114  For a discussion of inverse passing off, *see* Carty, H. 'Inverse Passing Off: A Suitable Addition to Passing-Off?' [1993] 10 EIPR 370.

115  For example, *Copydex Ltd v Noso Products Ltd* (1952) 69 RPC 38 ('as shown on television'); *Lawrie v Baker* (1885) 2 RPC 213 where the defendant sold, as patented, articles that were not patented but the plaintiff held a patent such that the consumers would think that the defendant was selling articles made to that patent.

116  [1995] FSR 947; Court of Appeal, Republic of Singapore.

## Misrepresentation by imputing authorisation

Misrepresentation is not limited to the use of a name or a similar get-up and it can even extend to an act that implies that it is authorised or consented to by another person. Placing advertising leaflets inside magazines and newspapers is a fairly common activity nowadays and this may be done after the magazines and papers have been delivered to the newsagents with neither the permission nor the authority of the proprietors of the magazines and newspapers. An independent advertising company may approach newsagents and ask them to insert advertising leaflets and one complication is that, at this time, the title to the magazines and newspapers will have passed to the newsagent. Although such an activity by itself will not amount to passing off, it will do so if sufficient persons are likely to believe that the leaflets were inserted with the authority of the publishers of the magazines and newspapers. So it was held in the Court of Appeal in *Associated Newspapers (Holdings) plc v Insert Media Ltd*.[117] The mere fact that the advertisements had been inserted in the plaintiff's newspapers without its permission did not establish the existence of a misrepresentation and it was necessary to consider whether a substantial number of people would think that the insertion had been authorised by the proprietor of the newspaper. It had been shown that the essence of the plan to insert the advertising was the defendant's hope that it would be associated with the newspaper concerned, the *Daily Mail*, to the effect that the advertising would appear to have the newspaper's seal of approval. The plaintiff might thus suffer damage to its reputation and goodwill. The Court of Appeal rejected a suggestion that a disclaimer should be printed on the inserts on the grounds that it would not be effective.

This case represents a new extension to the law of passing off because, in the High Court, it was doubted that such an activity could amount to passing off.[118] However, it does illustrate the potential width of passing off and the way that it is capable of being developed to meet new mischiefs. Nevertheless, the case is unusual on its facts and the normal way of imputing authority will involve the use of a name or mark. For example, a person might falsely claim to be a member of a professional body and the body will be able to take action to have the claim withdrawn and not repeated.

Impliedly representing that the plaintiff's helmets would comply with safety regulations when fitted with the defendant's lens was said to be on the outer limits of passing off in *Hodge Clemco Ltd v Airblast Ltd*.[119] Helmets for use with sand-blasting had to comply with the regulations and be approved by the Health and Safety Executive. It was unlawful to use helmets which did not comply. At the time of the action, the defendant was seeking the approval of its lens and it looked like such approval would be forthcoming soon but, until it was granted, using the plaintiff's helmets fitted with the defendant's lenses was unlawful. The plaintiff claimed that the defendant, by representing that its lenses were suitable for the plaintiff's helmets was misrepresenting that the helmets when fitted with the lenses would comply with the regulations. Although it was arguable that advertising the lenses as suitable to for the plaintiff's helmets suggested that customers could lawfully use them, an injunction was refused as the balance of convenience lay in the defendant's favour, especially as it was likely to obtain approval soon as its lenses had successfully completed the required tests.

117 [1991] 3 All ER 535.

118 *Mail Newspapers plc v Insert Media Ltd* [1987] RPC 521.

119 [1995] FSR 806.

## Intention

The great majority of passing off cases involve a deliberate and calculated attempt to take advantage of the goodwill owned by another trader and associated with goods manufactured or sold by him or services supplied by him. However, a fraudulent motive is not necessary to a passing off action and, indeed, innocence is no defence,[120] the main thrust of the law of passing off being the protection of goodwill. In *Taittinger SA v Allbev Ltd*[121] Peter Gibson LJ said:

> Lord Diplock's phrase 'calculated to injure', as he himself made plain, does not import a test of actual intention to injure: it is sufficient that this should be the reasonably foreseeable consequence of the misrepresentation.

In contrast, in some cases, a person may make a deliberate misrepresentation that is intended to boost the reputation and sales of his product or services but against which there is no legal remedy under the law of passing off.[122] Some examples of this will be seen later in the section on character merchandising. A reading of the cases does, however, give the impression that intention may be an influential factor in the court's decision-making process,[123] although a deliberate and fraudulent act of copying someone else's get-up will not amount to passing off if there is little danger of the public being deceived, as in *Whitworth Foods Ltd v Hunni Foods (International) Ltd*, discussed above, where the defendant had placed an order with the company making containers for the plaintiff for containers that were similar in shape and appearance.

## Common fields of activity

In most cases, the rights associated with registered trade marks are restricted in terms of the classes of goods and services against which the marks are registered. Therefore, if Trader A has a trade mark consisting of a representation of a Harp registered for Class 2 goods (paints, varnishes, lacquers, etc.) and Trader B copies this mark but only uses it in respect of wines (falling within Class 33), Trader B does not infringe Trader A's trade mark unless it is a mark of some repute and such use would take unfair advantage of or be detrimental to Trader A's mark.[124] Apart from this latter exception, trade mark law, by reference to identical or similar goods or services, requires a 'common field of activity' between the plaintiff and defendant.

Passing off is limited in a similar way in that there must be a common field of activity between the plaintiff and the defendant. There must be some common ground, otherwise there can be no trespass to this form of intellectual property. The justification for this is that, if there is no common field of activity, there can be no damage to the plaintiff's goodwill because the public will not make a connection between the traders and their different fields of activity. For example, if Trader A uses an unregistered trade name 'Spright' for its margarine and, later, Trader B uses the same name for its bicycles there will be little danger of damage to Trader A's goodwill (irrespective of the quality of the bicycles) because the public are not likely to think that the bicycles are made by or with the licence of Trader A. An electric shaver called a 'Rolls Razor' would not normally be confused with the makers of 'Rolls-Royce' motor cars; at best it indicates that the razor is claimed, rightly or wrongly, to be of high quality.

120 *See Baume & Co Ltd v A H Moore Ltd* [1958] RPC 226. However, motive may influence the decision whether to grant an interlocutory injunction; *see The Law Society of England & Wales v Griffiths* [1995] RPC 16 where there was clear evidence that the defendant deliberately selected a similar telephone number to that of the plaintiff in order to divert business from the plaintiff.

121 [1993] FSR 641 at 667.

122 *See*, for example, *McCullogh v Lewis A May Ltd* (1948) 65 RPC 58.

123 *See*, for example, *Harrods Ltd v R Harrods Ltd* (1924) 41 RPC 74.

124 This is now an infringement under the Trade Marks Act 1994 s 10(3) where the goods or services are non-similar.

**125** [1973] RPC 49. *See also Harrods Ltd* v *The Harrodian School Ltd* [1996] RPC 697.

**126** The name 'Granada' could not have been registered in Part A of the register of trade marks, being a relatively well-known geographical name: the Trade Marks Act 1938 s 9. It was unlikely that it would have been accepted for Part B Registration.

**127** The Trade Marks Act 1994 s 10(3). Under the previous Act, defensive registration was possible.

**128** [1997] FSR 380.

**129** [1983] FSR 155, yet another case involving a survey of the public used in support of the plaintiff's argument that the public would be deceived.

**130** *See also, Annabel's (Berkeley Square)* v *Schock* [1972] RPC 838, where it was held that there was a possibility of confusion between a night club and an escort agency as both could be considered to be night-time activities.

A simple example of the common field of activity doctrine was the case of *Granada Group Ltd* v *Ford Motor Company Ltd*[125] the outcome of which was that the Granada television group, famous for making the television serial *Coronation Street*, could not prevent the Ford Motor Company naming one of its cars the 'Ford Granada'. There was no danger of confusion because of the different fields of activity (television and motor cars) and, consequently, there was little possibility of the plaintiff's goodwill being harmed.[126] This decision accords with common sense as it is highly unlikely that ordinary members of the public, even those knowing nothing about cars, would think that the car had anything whatsoever to do with the television company. The test of common field of activity is concerned with making an objective determination of the likelihood of damage to goodwill. This can only occur if there is, at least, a possibility of confusion. Yet, the test can be criticised because the diversification of business concerns and their fields of activity makes the application of the test imperfect. Many members of the public realise that some large companies have interests that are wide and disparate in nature. With a registered trade mark that has a reputation in the UK, use in respect of non-similar goods or services may infringe.[127] However, where such trade mark infringement cannot be made out, the common field of activity rule seems coarse and arbitrary in terms of well-known names, marks and get-ups. To make the issue more difficult is the general desire amongst judges not to restrict competition unduly.

Where fields of activity are converging, it is easier to accept that confusion is likely. For example, developments in computer technology have resulted in most modern personal computers having a compact disk drive capable of reading CD-ROMs and stereo speakers. They can also play audio compact discs. Therefore, the fields of audio entertainment and computers are converging. So it was held in *NAD Electronics Inc* v *NAD Computers Systems Ltd*.[128]

Showing a determined flexibility, the law of passing off has developed to embrace a situation where a name or mark is very well known, and in such cases the boundaries of the activities may be moved, dramatically enlarging the field of play. In *Lego Systems A/S* v *Lego M Lemelstrich Ltd*,[129] the very well-known Lego company, that makes coloured plastic construction bricks for children, was granted an injunction preventing the use of the name Lego by the defendant who was planning to use it for its plastic irrigation and garden equipment. The defendant had used the name Lego for its equipment in various other countries such as Israel, but the plaintiff's children's bricks had become so well known, as had the name Lego in association with these bricks, that the House of Lords was of the opinion that confusion was extremely likely. In this case, the common field of activity was, effectively, coloured plastic.[130] If the plaintiff's business had not been so successful and on such a grand scale in the UK, the plaintiff's field of activity might have been restricted to coloured children's plastic construction bricks, a much narrower field. Note that the quality of the defendant's products was not an issue: once the danger of confusion is present, it is assumed that there is a possibility that the plaintiff's reputation will be harmed. Such harm can go beyond the quality of the products concerned, and in the Lego case harm could be the result of the public thinking that the company was no longer concentrating on children's construction kits and might not continue to make the kits and additional parts for them so that it might not be feasible for a child to build up a large collection of Lego bricks and materials over a long period of time.

Although *Lego* can be said to show that the requirement for a common field of activity is not as rigidly applied as before, it was still relevant in terms of whether there existed a likelihood of confusion.[131] If the plaintiff and defendant are engaged in the same field of activity, then confusion is all the more likely. If they operate in completely different fields, there is far less likelihood of confusion though the possibility is not entirely extinguished. Given the breathtaking diversification of many large corporations, especially from the Far East, some relaxation of the rule is appropriate.

The boundaries of the plaintiff's field of activity appear to be directly proportional to the magnitude of his goodwill: the greater the goodwill, the greater the net of passing off will be cast and the more likely it is that the defendant will found to have committed passing off. However, the Lego approach was distinguished in *Fortnum & Mason plc v Fortnam Ltd*[132] where the defendant imported low price goods from the Far East, mainly for export to the rest of Europe and operated under the name Fortnam Ltd but did not apply the name to the goods. The plaintiff had a well-known and high-class store in Piccadilly and sued in passing off. Although the plaintiff was primarily known for its groceries, food and wine of high quality, it also sold fashion clothing, toys and various other articles. The defendant accepted that the plaintiff had an outstanding reputation associated with the name Fortnum and Masons, often abbreviated to Fortnums. However, in refusing the interlocutory injunction sought, Harman J considered that the defendant was not guilty of passing off. It was extremely unlikely that anyone would buy the defendant's goods thinking that they were the goods of the plaintiff. Relevant factors were the quality of the goods and the nature of the trade. Although there was some overlap in the goods the parties sold, the defendant's were mostly cheap and plastic and not likely to be associated with the plaintiff's business. Furthermore, in the main the defendant exported his goods rather than selling them in the UK. Harman J distinguished the *Lego* case which he suggested was strongly influenced by the fact that both the plaintiff's goods and the defendant's goods were made from the same raw material, being plastic. The ordinary person might think that the plaintiff had developed a further branch of its business. Thus, whilst it might be reasonable to think that Lego had diversified in such a way, it would be unreasonable to think that Fortnum and Mason had suddenly decided to sell 'cheap and nasty' goods.

### Character merchandising

A fictitious or fantastic character might be devised for a television series, a book or a film, for example, Kojak, the Wombles, Thunderbirds, Popeye, Super Mario, Teenage Mutant Hero Turtles, etc. The person who devised the character or the person commissioning the design will want to maximise the financial return on the investment involved. One way of doing this is to licence others to sell articles to which a representation of, or the name of, the character is applied. Examples are very common: Mickey Mouse watches, Captain Scarlett figures and T-shirts, Pink Panther mugs, Postman Pat toys, etc. Using fictitious characters in order to sell ordinary items is known as character merchandising and is very popular, particularly with respect to children's toys, games and stationery. It is big business. The normal way it is done is for the merchandising organisation to obtain a licence from the creator of the character permitting the application of a

131 *Nice and Safe Attitude Ltd v Piers Flook* [1997] FSR 14.

132 [1994] FSR 438.

representation of the character to the articles. In a few cases, [the]
character or the owner of the rights in the character will retail [...].
Character merchandising is not limited to fictitious character[s ...]
sportsmen and women and television personalities allow their [...]
for promotional purposes. In this case, unauthorised appropriati[on ...]
or nickname may not be remediable either under the law of pass[ing off or]
copyright law but it may be actionable as being defamatory.[133]

Character merchandising is not a new phenomenon. Walt Disney characters in particular have been used in this way for some time. However, when this operation is related to intellectual property rights subsisting in such characters, some major gaps appear. Copyright can give a fair degree of protection, for example where a representation of the character infringes the copyright in a drawing of that character. For example, if a company wishes to sell a mug to which a picture of Mickey Mouse has been applied by transfer printing, this will infringe the copyright in the original drawings of Mickey Mouse. If a photograph is made from a Mickey mouse cartoon or film, whether to be reproduced and sold as photographs or used as a medium from which to prepare a representation for transfer printing, the copyright in the film will be infringed. If a doll or three-dimensional figure is made, then the copyright in the drawings will be infringed, as it was in the case of Popeye dolls which were held to infringe the cartoon drawings of the Popeye character in *King Features Syndicate Inc v O and M Kleeman Ltd*.[134] But, difficulties arise where only the name of the character is used. We have seen in Chapter 3 that copyright will not be afforded to a title for a film or a book and that it was also denied to the word 'Exxon'.[135] Neither does copyright protect the name of a fictitious character. This can be seen as the working of the *de minimis* principle and a throwback to the judgment of Davey J in *Hollinrake v Truswell*[136] to the effect that a literary work should offer information, instruction or pleasure in the form of literary enjoyment.

All that is left to protect a name is the law of passing off, or in some cases, trade mark law. With respect to the latter, until the Trade Marks Act 1994 came into force, the question hinged simply on whether the merchandiser had applied the name to the same or similar goods. However, it was not possible to use trade mark law to promote character merchandising because the Trade Marks Act 1938 s 28(6) required the Registrar to refuse an application for registration of a registered user if it appeared to him that this would tend to facilitate trafficking in the mark. The House of Lords confirmed that trade marks law was not to be used to facilitate character merchandising in confirming the Registrar's refusal to register the 'Holly Hobbie' device including a drawing of a young girl as a trade mark.[137] This mark had been very successfully exploited in the USA but the registered user provisions in the UK were a considerable hurdle. One way over this hurdle was to show that the proprietor of the mark was able to maintain strict quality control over the articles to which the mark was applied, so demonstrating a sufficient connection in the course of trade. However, in the Holly Hobbie case, the applicant was unable to show this, partly because of the enormous scale of the planned commercial activities. Thankfully the registered user provisions and the bar over trafficking in trade marks has been swept aside to be replaced by licensing provisions which are much more suited to modern commercial practices.

---

133 *See McCullogh v Lewis A Mat* (1948) 65 RPC 58; *Tolley v J S Fry & Sons Ltd* [1931] AC 333.

134 [1941] AC 417.

135 *Exxon Corporation v Exxon Insurance Consultants International Ltd* [1981] 3 All ER 241.

136 [1894] 3 Ch 420.

137 *Holly Hobbie Trade Mark* [1984] RPC 329. This limitation does not apply under the Trade Marks Act 1994.

ing off may not be very effective in the context of character merchandis-
because of the requirement of a common field of activity and without this
there can be no harm to the owner of the name of the character. For example, if
someone buys a 'Garfield' telephone, that person would not be likely to complain to the makers of the Garfield cartoons and comic strips if the telephone
turns out to be faulty.[138] The general public probably have a much better
understanding of character merchandising than the judges have, in the past,
given them credit for.

In the South African case of *Lorimar Productions Inc v Sterling Clothing
Manufacturers (Pty) Ltd*[139] the Supreme Court considered that character
merchandising was not particularly well known and, in the absence of evidence
to the contrary, it could not be assumed that the man in the street would have
any knowledge of it. The plaintiff owned the rights in the television series
'Dallas' and failed to show an association in the minds of the public between
the goodwill in the series and clothing or restaurants owned by the defendant
which used names, locations and titles from the series.

The case of *Tavener Rutledge Ltd v Trexapalm Ltd*,[140] involving the television detective character 'Kojak', demonstrates some of the deficiencies of the
law as regards character merchandising. Kojak, played by Telly Savalas, was
often seen in the series sucking a spherical lolly. The plaintiff made similar
shaped lollies and used the word 'Kojakpops' as a brand name for these lollies
and quickly built up a substantial trade in respect of them. The plaintiff had not
obtained the permission of the makers of the *Kojak* television series to use this
name or to make similar shaped lollies. Some time later, the defendant started
making similar lollies called 'Kojak lollies' and claimed to have a licence
agreement with the owners of the television series allowing him to do this. The
plaintiff commenced an action for passing off[141] and applied for an
interlocutory injunction. The defendant claimed that there was a sufficient
connection in the course of trade between the lollies and the owners of the
Kojak name because there were provisions for quality control contained in the
licence agreement between the defendant and the owner of the name, and
because of this quality control arrangement there was a common field of
activity. Nevertheless, the injunction was granted to restrain the defendant
passing off his lollies as being those of the plaintiff. The plaintiff had built up a
considerable reputation in his lollies and the introduction of a similar lolly
would cause confusion. Walton J considered that the defendant's lollies were
not as good value as the plaintiff's and, as a consequence, the plaintiff's
reputation would be seriously harmed. The licence agreement argument failed
on the basis that there was no actual or potential field of activity between the
owners of the television series and the plaintiff's business.[142] The point had not
been reached where the fact of quality control was so well known that the
public would rely on the existence of the licence as a guarantee of the
defendant's product. Indeed, the public, in general, were not to be taken as
having any particular knowledge of character merchandising. Finally, Walton J
confirmed that there is no property in a name or a word, *per se*.

A common field of activity is the key to an action in passing off and no more
so than where character merchandising is involved. It is important for the
parties to a licence agreement to construct a connection in the course of trade
between the owner of the name, the licensor, and the goods or services to which

138 For a discussion on trafficking in marks where this point is made, *see* Pearson, H. E. and Millar, C. G. (1990) *Commercial Exploitation of Intellectual Property,* Blackstone Press, at pp. 216–17.

139 [1982] RPC 395.

140 [1977] RPC 275.

141 There was also a trade mark issue because the plaintiff had applied for a trade mark but, because the passing off action succeeded, it did not require consideration.

142 *See also Nice and Safe Attitude Ltd v Piers Flook* [1997] FSR 14, where the plaintiff, which used a logo similar to that used by the US National Aeronautics and Space Administration (NASA), succeeded in preventing a rival organisation, having a licence from NASA, using the logo.

the name is to be applied. One way to do this has been hinted at above and that is to establish a system of quality control so that the owner of the name has a part to play in the practical aspects of the marketing exercise. In this way, the reputation of the name's owner will be extended into the other fields of activity defined by the merchandising project. This approach was successful in Australia where a licence agreement for the making of soft toys of the Muppet characters contained quality control provisions,[143] but has yet to find favour in the UK. It is submitted that the exercise of quality control must be known about by the public and that appropriate advertising, marketing and labelling of the goods can do much to spread the word, thus extending the fields of activity.

Even if the field of activity can be widened by careful licensing and advertising, there will still be cases where this will not be sufficient to provide a remedy, bearing in mind that the prospect of harm to goodwill is a fundamental requirement. If there is no obvious link, regardless of any character licences, then there is no remedy under the law of passing off although there may be copyright issues, particularly if a drawing of the character is used. *Wombles Ltd v Wombles Skips Ltd*[144] shows that a wide disparity in fields of activity is fatal to a claim in passing off. The Wombles are fictitious animals from a television series and are noted for cleaning up litter and putting it to good use. The plaintiff company owned the copyright in the books and drawings of the Wombles. Its main business was granting licences in respect of the characters; for example, it granted one such licence for waste paper baskets for children. The defendant formed a company to lease builders' skips, containers used typically for building rubble. After considerable thought and remembering the Wombles' reputation for clean habits he decided to call his company Wombles Skips Ltd and registered the company name accordingly. The plaintiff argued that the use of the name would lead some persons to conclude that the defendant's business was connected with the plaintiff and that there was a common field of activity because one of the licences was for wastepaper baskets. It was held that there was no common field of activity and this was an essential ingredient in a passing off action. Without a common field of activity there is no danger of confusion and, in this case, the similarity between the making and selling of wastepaper baskets and hiring out builders' skips was not strong enough. The plain fact of the matter was that it was highly improbable that ordinary members of the public would think that the skips were associated with the Wombles in any way, just as a link between Granada Television and Ford Granada cars is quite absurd. Such an association might be made, however, in the case of waste paper baskets for children and Wombles toys and dolls.

Full legal protection of character merchandising by the law of passing off has yet to find favour in the UK courts, although there are now signs that the position is changing. There is a contradiction in the way the law has tended to dislike this form of exploitation and the way in which it has given full protection to other forms of intellectual property rights. The owner of the character has made an investment of time and money in creating and developing the character. In many cases, the character is the result of substantial flair and imagination which should be no less deserving of protection than, say, literary and artistic works. Whilst it is clear that the law gives some protection, for example copyright subsisting in drawings of characters or in written thumbnail sketches of characters[145] and other descriptive material, there are some gaps,

143 *Children's Television Workshop Inc v Woolworths (New South Wales) Pty Ltd* [1981] RPC 187.

144 [1977] RPC 99. This case may be difficult to reconcile with the *Lego* case. However, neither the *Wombles* case nor the *Kojak* case was mentioned in Falconer J's judgment.

and it is with respect to names that the law seems to be least effective. Trade mark law will only give a remedy in respect of use of a registered mark in respect of non-similar goods or services if the mark is one having a reputation in the UK.[146]

Consider the following possibilities concerning *Coronation Street* characters. What if the name 'Rover's Return' is used for a public house in the Salford area? What if a tobacco company starts marketing 'Mike Baldwin cigars' or, for those with longer memories, a trader starts selling 'Ena Sharples hairnets'? There seems to be little that the makers of the television series can do because of a lack of a common field of activity. But, there is a possibility that some portion of the public will take the use of names to indicate that the products have some seal of approval from the television company and have achieved certain standards. This might allow the traders concerned to overcharge for sub-standard goods. In attempting to cut back the degree of protection offered to the owners of fictitious characters and the like (and indeed, their licensees and franchisees), the courts may indirectly be encouraging unfair and undesirable trading practices whereby unscrupulous traders still manage to cash-in on someone else's reputation in a way which transcends the artificiality of compartmentalised fields of activity.

There have been recent signs of a change in heart. The case of *Mirage Studios* v *Counter-Feat Clothing Co Ltd*[147] is a good example, Browne-Wilkinson VC seeming to prefer the way in which Australian passing off law has developed compared to UK law. The facts of the case were that the plaintiff created the Teenage Mutant Hero Ninja Turtle characters and made and marketed cartoons, films and videos containing these characters. Part of the plaintiff's business involved licensing the reproduction of the characters on goods sold by licensees, that is character merchandising. It was almost inevitable that, in view of the success of the characters, that someone else would wish to take an unfair advantage of the immense goodwill built up by the plaintiff. The defendant, without the plaintiff's permission, made drawings of humanoid turtle characters that were similar in appearance to the plaintiff's characters. They were not exact reproductions. The defendant then began to licence these drawings to garment manufacturers for the purpose of applying them to T-shirts and the like. The defendant claimed that there was no intellectual property rights either in the name or the idea of the 'Turtles'. The Vice-Chancellor granted an interlocutory injunction to the plaintiff on the basis of an arguable case in copyright and for passing off. He found passing off to have occurred by applying Lord Diplock's test in the *Advocaat* case. The misrepresentation made by the defendant was that a substantial number of the buying public would believe that the reproduction of the figures was the result of a licence between the owner of the rights in the original drawings of the turtles. The result of the defendant's action would be that, because the public associated goods bearing the defendant's drawings with the creator of the cartoons, the plaintiff's goodwill would be harmed by fixing representations of turtles to inferior goods. The potential value of the plaintiff's licensing rights would be seriously harmed. Furthermore, there was a sufficient link between the plaintiff and the goods to found a case in passing off. At last, it seemed an English judge was prepared to accept that the public are aware of character merchandising.

Browne-Wilkinson VC considered that the law as developed in Australia was sound and applied *Children's Television Workshop Inc* v *Woolworths (New South Wales) Ltd*[148] in which it was held that the defendant, by his unlicensed use of the

---

145 This protection might be less effective. Obviously, an unauthorised photocopy will infringe, but will there be copyright infringement if the nature of the character is copied by a rival? Perhaps there might be a possibility that the restricted public performance will be relevant if the rival character faithfully follows the written description.

146 The Trade Marks Act 1994 s 10(3).

147 [1991] FSR 145.

148 [1981] RPC 187. He also approved of a similar decision, *Fido-Dido Inc* v *Venture Stores (Retailers) Pty Ltd* 16 IPR 365.

Muppet characters, had misrepresented that he had a connection with the owner of the copyright in drawings of the characters and was a *bona fide* licensee of rights in the Muppets. The Vice-Chancellor managed to distinguish three English cases involving the Wombles, Kojak and the pop group 'Abba',[149] although he seemed unduly cautious about doing so. The three English cases are distinguishable very easily because they only involved a name and not a drawing and are still good law. The question is whether the *Mirage Studios* (Turtle) case has modified the requirement of a common field of activity for an action in passing off to succeed. Certainly, there is now a greater awareness of character merchandising amongst the public but it may be insufficient to found an argument that goodwill will be harmed by unlicensed use of names and representations of characters. The public may be aware that the creator of a fictitious character will licence its use in this way, but equally may be prepared to accept that other companies can use the characters without such a licence. There may be a connection between quality products and the creator of the character, but the public may simply assume that cheaper, inferior goods are made without the creator's specific permission and the link between inferior goods and the creator, essential for a passing off action to succeed, is thus absent. Put crudely, do the public really care? Many members of the public probably think that the creator of the character has made enough money through films, books and cartoons.

One major criticism of the judgment in the *Mirage Studios* (Turtles) case is that the copyright issue alone should have been sufficient to dispose of it, and this will usually be so where representations of characters are used, whether two-dimensional or three-dimensional. In the future, fictitious names may be registrable as trade marks.[150] Browne-Wilkinson's views on passing off could be considered to be *obiter*. Where names are used, there must be a common field of activity for there to be a prospect of harm to goodwill. The only way a character merchandiser can establish a sufficient link is to exercise a form of control over the goods to which the character or its name is applied and this link must be such that sufficient numbers of the public are aware of it. This view is consistent with Australian law and prior UK law. We have not heard the last of legal actions concerning character merchandising.

## Post-sale confusion

For a passing off action to succeed there must be evidence that customers or ultimate consumers have been deceived or, if the defendant's planned activity were to come to fruition, a real likelihood of confusion. The key is confusion and it might be reasonable to assume that the confusion must occur at the time the goods are purchased, not later. For example, in *Bostick Ltd* v *Sellotape GB Ltd*[151] the plaintiff made an adhesive putty called 'Blu-tack' which was coloured blue. Apparently the colour was chosen because it might be less likely to be swallowed by children as there are very few edible materials of that colour. The defendant launched an equivalent product called 'Sellotak' which was also coloured blue. However, the 'Sellotak' was not visible in the packet it was sold in and could only be seen after it had been purchased by removing it from its packaging. Nevertheless, the plaintiff sued for passing off. It was held that, as the defendant's product could not be seen at the point of sale, there was no danger of confusion and it was highly unlikely that the similarity in colour would lead to confusion and influence future sales to the detriment of the plaintiff.

**149** *Wombles Ltd* v *Wombles Skips Ltd* [1977] RPC 99; *Tavener Rutledge Ltd* v *Trexapalm Ltd* [1977] RPC 275; *Lynstad* v *Annabast Products Ltd* [1975] FSR 488.

**150** *Reform of Trade Mark Law*, Cm 1203 (HMSO, 1990).

**151** [1994] RPC 556.

The concept of post-sales confusion, that is where the misrepresentation so essential for passing off comes after the goods have been purchased, seems, at first, difficult to accept as a possibility. Even if there is confusion post-sales, how could that lead to damage to the plaintiff? However, it must be stressed that it is business goodwill which is protected by passing off, not just trade or reputation. Damage extends beyond a straightforward and immediate loss of sales as a result of the defendant's misrepresentation. The more distinctive the name or mark used by the plaintiff, the greater the goodwill is likely to be. Even if there is no deception at the time of sale, later confusion as to the origin of the name, mark or device can still damage the goodwill by a process of dilution or erosion. So it was held in the New Zealand case of *Levi Strauss & Co v Kimbyr Investments Ltd.*[152] The defendant used a protruding tab on its jeans which was similar to the distinctive tab used by the plaintiff on its jeans. Because of the defendant's cardboard advertising labels attached to the jeans displayed for sale, there was little likelihood of confusion at the point of sale. However, the court held, *inter alia*, that it was irrelevant that the confusion took place after sale and that the owner of goodwill in a product or get up was entitled to have that goodwill protected throughout the life of the product. The plaintiff could show that the tab continued to operate as an effective badge connecting the jeans with it. The post-sale confusion would lead to a dilution of the distinctiveness of the tab and, accordingly, damage the plaintiff's goodwill.[153]

152 [1994] FSR 335.

If post-sales confusion is accepted in the UK, which it might in view of the acceptance of the principle of erosion of goodwill as being a form of damage, then manufacturers of lookalike articles who attempt to avoid allegations of passing off by the use of distinguishing labelling or disclaimers had better tread warily. However, this would represent a further extension of passing off which could result in protecting the shape of goods even where such shapes would not be registrable as trade marks, for example, by being necessary to achieve a technical result of giving substantial value to the goods.[154] This might turn out to be as effective as the old indirect copyright infringement through drawings suppressed by the Copyright, Designs and Patents Act 1988 s 51. Shapes, colours and other aspects of appearance of articles could end up with protection where those features cannot be protected by any other intellectual property right through lack of novelty or the expiry of a pre-existing right such as a registered design or patent. This could be a dangerous road to take. Imagine if the Coca-Cola company could have prevented other drinks manufacturers producing a drink having a similar colour.

153 For a discussion of this trend, *see* Karet, I. 'Passing Off and Trade Marks: Confusing Times Ahead?' [1995] 1 EIPR 3.

154 The Trade Marks Act 1994 s 3(2).

## DAMAGE TO GOODWILL

Damage to goodwill, or at least a probability that damage will ensue, is one of the essential requirements for a passing off action.[155] Damage may result in a number of ways and the diminution in the plaintiff's goodwill may be caused by:

1 lost sales because buyers confuse the defendant's products (or services) with those of the plaintiff;[156]
2 the fact that the defendant's product is inferior to the plaintiff's product and buyers think the defendant's product is the plaintiff's;[157]
3 erosion or debasement of a name that is exclusive and unique and which is used by the plaintiff (or a number of persons entitled to use it).

155 *Erven Warnink Besloten Vennootschap v J Townend & Sons (Hull) Ltd* [1973] AC 731 *per* Lords Diplock and Fraser. Lord Fraser spoke in terms of a real likelihood of suffering substantial damage to goodwill.

156 *See*, for example, *Reddaway v Banham* [1896] AC 199.

157 For example, as in *Spalding & Bros v A W Gamage Ltd* (1915) 84 LJ Ch 449.

626

**158** [1993] FSR 641. The case also hinged on EC Council Regulation 823/87 (as amended by Regulation 2043/89) which limits the use of names for wines which refer to specified regions.

**159** Other examples are provided by the *Erven Warnink* case (Advocaat) and the *Spanish Champagne* case discussed earlier.

The case of *Taittinger SA* v *Allbev Ltd*[158] provides an example of the last form of damage to goodwill.[159] The defendant, an English company, made a non-alcoholic drink called Elderflower Champagne. Not surprisingly, it attracted the attention of the French makers of champagne who have taken legal action no less than 46 times in England to protect the name 'champagne'. The High Court judge found for the defendant. He applied Lord Diplock's test and, although he found all the other elements present, he decided that there was no real likelihood of serious damage to the plaintiff's undoubted goodwill. Elderflower Champagne was only £2.45 for a 75 cl bottle and had wording on the label to the effect that it was non-alcoholic. Davies J considered that only a small number of persons would be confused even though Elderflower Champagne was sold in bottles resembling champagne bottles. A representation of the label is shown in Figure 21.1.

**Figure 21.1 Elderflower Champagne bottle label**

The Court of Appeal allowed the plaintiff's appeal because use of the word 'champagne' by those not entitled to use it would inevitably diminish the goodwill associated with it. Peter Gibson LJ said (at 670):

> ... it seems to me no less obvious that erosion of the distinctiveness of the name champagne in this country is a form of damage to the goodwill of the business of the champagne houses.

**160** [1996] RPC 697.

In *Harrods Ltd* v *The Harrodian School Ltd*,[160] Millett LJ found it difficult to accept that erosion of goodwill was sufficient, *per se*, to amount to damage for passing off. However, in that case, there was no danger that Harrods would become a generic term for retailing luxury goods by virtue of the defendant's activities. It is arguable that in *Taittinger*, the use of the word 'champagne' by the defendant for a drink would be the bridgehead by which other manufacturers of drinks would start using the name. In *Harrods*, the fields of activity (retailing and education) were very different. This was not so in *Taittinger* where the fields were alcoholic sparking drinks and non-alcoholic sparkling drinks. The 'insidious' form of damage that erosion of goodwill is recognised by some judges was evidenced again in *Chocosuisse Union des Fabricants Suisses de Chocolat v Cadbury Ltd*[161] where the name 'Swiss Chalet' was given by the defendant to a new range of bars of chocolate. The damage was that the exclusivity of the designation 'Swiss Chocolate', descriptive of chocolate made in Switzerland, would suffer, even though lesser numbers of persons might wrongly think the defendant's chocolate was made in Switzerland according to Swiss food regulations compared to the number of persons who would not be confused. As not all chocolate made by Swiss companies and described as Swiss chocolate is actually produced in Switzerland, this case must stand at the very limits of passing off. Given the enormous goodwill owned by the defendant, it is surprising that any convincing evidence of confusion could be found.

161 [1998] RPC 117.

Protection of goodwill from erosion by 'non-origin association' can be seen as an extension of the tort of passing off because in the *Erven Warnink* case there was also a substantial diminution in the sales of the plaintiff's drink.[162] However, it could be argued that the plaintiff acquiesced in the use of the name 'champagne' by others as it had been used in the UK and elsewhere for a number of years to describe a variety of locally made products. For example, 'rhubarb champagne' and 'greengage champagne', *inter alia*, have been used to describe home-made wines as the extracts below taken from *Peggy Hutchinson's Home Made Wine Secrets*, published around the time of the Second World War, demonstrate:[163]

162 Russell, F. 'The Elderflower Champagne Case: Is this a Further Expansion of the Tort of Passing Off?' [1993] 10 EIPR 379.

GREENGAGE CHAMPAGNE
*Ingredients*:
4 lbs greengages
20 vine leaves
1 gallon water
4 lbs sugar
1 slice toast; 1 oz yeast

163 Hutchinson, P. *Peggy Hutchinson's Home Made Wine Secrets* (undated) Foulsham & Co. The preface for the book starts 'The recipes for this book were orginally compiled in the days of plenty before the Second World War. Times have changed; some of the ingredients are no longer easy to obtain ...' I am indebted to Lorraine Keenan for finding this book.

*Method*:
1  Put the greengages and vine leaves in a bowl, cover with cold water. Take the vine leaves out in 3 days but mash and stir the plums for 8 days, then strain.
2  Then add the sugar and yeast spread on both sides of the toast and leave to ferment 14 days.
3  Skim and bottle.

## Proof of damage

A plaintiff must be able to satisfy the court that he has, or will, suffer substantial damage to his goodwill. Mere speculation will rarely suffice. Nor will the fact that 'only a moron in a hurry would be misled'.[164] In many cases proof of damage is not only important in quantifying damages to be awarded to the plaintiff but also it may be essential in demonstrating that there has been a

164 *Per* Foster J in *Morning Star Cooperative Society Ltd* v *Express Newspapers Ltd* [1979] FSR 113 in which the proprietor of the *Morning Star* had objected to the name *Daily Star*.

165 [1991] FSR 337.

misrepresentation calculated to injure the plaintiff's goodwill. In the case of *Tamworth Herald Co Ltd* v *Thomson Free Newspapers Ltd*,[165] the plaintiff did not put in any evidence of actual confusion on the part of persons seeking to place advertisements in its newspaper. However, in some cases, particularly in interlocutory hearings, there will be no actual damage to put before the court. The plaintiff must be able to convince the judge that there is a risk of confusion amongst the public. This will help to show that there is a serious issue to be tried and the judge can then move on to consider the balance of convenience and whether an interlocutory injunction should be granted.

Where the alleged damage is of the erosion of goodwill type, the plaintiff will be unable to show sales have been or are likely to be diverted to the defendant. Instead, it is long-term commercial damage that will ensue from the deception. Indeed, it could be argued that, if there is a deception, damage is almost certain to follow, whether in the short or longer term, as in *Kimberley-Clark Ltd* v *Fort Sterling Ltd*,[166] where the defendant placed an offer on its packs of Nouvelle toilet tissue stating:

166 [1997] FSR 877.

'Softness guaranteed (or we'll exchange it for Andrex®)'.

There was an acknowledgement under the 'Andrex®' to the effect that this was the plaintiff's registered trade mark. The case proceeded on the basis of passing off and the court was satisfied that the overall impact on normal but busy customers was that the product was that of the plaintiff or somehow associated with the plaintiff.[167] The damage would come about from the defendant taking the benefit of the plaintiff's mark and its goodwill which would strengthen the defendant's position relative to the plaintiff. The court confirmed that, in such a case, the plaintiff would not be required to point to particular examples of sales lost to the defendant as a result of the misrepresentation.

167 Confusion leading persons to believe that the defendant is connected to the plaintiff as being sufficient to prove damage was identified in *Ewing* v *Buttercup Margarine Co Ltd* (1917) 34 RPC 232 by Cozens-Hardy MR.

168 [1992] FSR 267.

In *Morgan-Grampian plc* v *Training Personnel Ltd*[168] the plaintiff published a series of magazines with titles beginning with the phrase 'What's New in...' and the defendant later changed the title of one of its publications to 'What's New in Training'. An interlocutory injunction was granted. There was a risk of confusion and the fact that it would be difficult to quantify damage in monetary terms helped to tilt the balance of convenience in favour of the plaintiff.

It may be tempting to obtain evidence of damage through surveys and trap orders. Surveys are carried out for a number of reasons but, unless they are properly carried out, they will fail to impress the court. For example, in *Imperial Group plc* v *Philip Morris Ltd*[169] it was held that there was no passing off by the defendant who used black and gold packets for 'Raffles' cigarettes. The plaintiff made John Player Specials (JPS) cigarettes in black with gold lettering and a gold monogram. The plaintiff had used surveys to show that there was a high degree of association between the colours black and gold and the JPS cigarette. Whitford J criticised the survey techniques used and he laid down some guidelines if a survey is to have validity, being:

169 [1984] RPC 293.

- the persons interviewed must be selected to represent a relevant cross-section of the public
- the sample size must be statistically significant
- the survey must be conducted fairly
- all the surveys carried out must be disclosed fully (a 'warts and all' approach)

- all the answers given must be disclosed and made available to the defendant
- no leading questions should be put to interviewees
- interviewees must not be led to embark upon a field of speculation they would not otherwise have considered
- instructions to interviewers must be disclosed
- if the answers are to be coded for computer input, the coding instructions must also be disclosed.

In other words, good statistical methods must be used coupled with complete openness and disclosure. In many cases, fulfilling these requirements will result in the survey being prohibitively expensive.

Trap orders are often used to provide evidence of passing off. For example, an order may be placed by the plaintiff (or his agent) for genuine goods in the hope that the defendant will supply other goods instead. Trap orders should be fair and, preferably, in writing where this is possible. In effect, in executing a trap order, the plaintiff is representing himself as a *bona fide* customer – in other words, he himself is making a misrepresentation. This he is allowed to do and his solicitor is allowed to advise him that he may do this and to make the necessary arrangements.[170] If the defendant had been 'caught' by a trap order, he should be put on notice immediately so that he can recall the facts clearly.[171]

## PASSING OFF AND INTERNET DOMAIN NAMES

Any person may obtain an Internet address (domain name) for their own web pages. There are certain naming conventions, the last suffix representing the country (for example, 'uk', 'jp', etc.) and the last but one represents the type of business or organisation (for example, 'co' for commercial, 'org' for non-profit making organisation, 'ac' or 'edu' for academic). Thus, an English company called Acme Trading plc might want the domain name 'acme-trading.co.uk' or 'acme-trading.plc.uk'.

Each name must be distinct from every other name. One problem is, however, that computers will distinguish between names if there is only one character different, including punctuation. Thus, 'acme.trading.co.uk' and 'acme-trading.co.uk' and 'acme_trading.co.uk' are all different from 'acme-trading.co.uk', and could all, theoretically, be registered to different persons. The opportunities for passing off and trade mark infringement are rife.

In the United Kingdom, the addresses are allocated by a body called Nominet UK. Until recently, it used to allocate names purely on a first come-first served basis, and made no checks to see if the applicant or any others were entitled to any rights in the name. Generally, bodies such as Nominet UK allocate names by automation without human intervention and do not assess the legality of a registration, or require a declaration of a right to use or operate an opposition system.[172] Past examples of domain names registered by persons not connected with the organisation whose name was used include 'mcdonalds.com', 'mtv.com' and 'harrods.com'.[173]

The first come-first served rule was shown to be unsatisfactory in *Pitman Training Ltd* v *Nominet UK*[174] in which two companies, having a common origin, Pitman Training Ltd and Pitman Publishing, a division of Pearson

170 The 'clean hands' doctrine does not appear to apply to trap orders, *see Marie Claire Albums SA* v *Hartstone Hosiery Ltd* [1993] FSR 692.

171 *Cellular Clothing Co Ltd* v *G White & Co Ltd* (1952) 70 RPC 9 where a trap order was held to be unsatisfactory for want of notice.

172 Wood, N. 'The Trouble with Domain Names' (1997) 2(3) *Intellectual Property*, p. 7, CLT Professional Publishing.

173 *See* ibid for a discussion of these and other examples. Nominet UK is introducing an 'Expert Determination' process to resolve disputes.

174 [1997] FSR 797.

175 The publisher of this book, since renamed Financial Times Management.

Professional Ltd,[175] clashed over the domain name 'pitman.co.uk'. Pitman Publishing, the second defendant, applied for and secured that name, but did not make use of it initially. Due to a mix up, the name was re-allocated to Pitman Training Ltd, the plaintiff, but following complaints from Pitman Publishing, Nominet UK, the first defendant, re-allocated the name to Pitman Publishing. The plaintiff commenced proceedings for reinstatement of the domain name, contending that its use by the second defendant amounted to passing off.[176] This was dismissed by the judge who thought it highly unlikely that the public would associate the domain name with the plaintiff; rather it was the second defendant which was more likely to have goodwill in that name as it had been trading under that name for nearly 150 years. Furthermore, when the Pitman companies were sold off in 1985, there was an express agreement that Pitman Training Ltd would not use the word Pitman without the word 'training' and the use by the plaintiff of the domain name would probably be a breach of that agreement.

176 There were also claims of unlawful interference with contract (the contract between the plaintiff and its Internet service provider) and abuse of process, neither of which was even arguable.

The registration of 'harrods.com' initiated the first case in the United Kingdom on domain names. It was registered to a person with no association with the famous Knightsbridge store and was registered through an American organisation Network Solutions Inc which provided registration services. Harrods complained to Network Solutions which suspended the domain name pending the outcome of its dispute resolution process. In the meantime, Harrods Ltd commenced proceedings for trade mark infringement and passing off. In *Harrods Ltd* v *UK Network Services Ltd*,[177] summary judgment was granted, ordering the defendants to release the domain name 'harrods.com'. However, this was an application for summary judgment only under RSC Ord 14, and the defendants were not represented so the case was not fully contested. As no use had been made of the website, it is arguable whether it was passing off. Presumably, the intention of the defendants was not to use the website but to sell the domain name to Harrods Ltd.

177 [1997] EIPR D-106.

The next case shows that, even without evidence of use of a domain name, the courts are prepared to use the law of passing off to prevent persons registering a domain name with the hope of selling it to a company that already has rights in the name as a trade mark or has established substantial goodwill in the name.

In *Marks & Spencer plc* v *One in a Million Ltd*,[178] five actions for summary judgment were brought by well-known business organisations, having substantial goodwill, against the defendants who were dealers in Internet domain names and who registered names to sell to potential users. The defendants had registered a number of names including 'bt.org', 'sainsbury.com', 'marksandspencer.co.uk'. Jonathan Sumption QC, sitting as a deputy judge, considered that threats of passing off and trade mark infringement were made out and he granted *quia timet* injunctions which went beyond normal *quia timet* injunctions in that the defendants were ordered to take the necessary steps to assign the domain names to the plaintiffs.

178 [1998] FSR 265.

At the time of the hearing, the defendants had not made any use of the domain names but, following *Singer* v *Loog*,[179] it was held to be sufficient for passing off for a person to put an 'instrument of deception' into the hands of another or to authorise another to do so. This would be the case should the defendants transfer the domain names to third parties which might or might not

179 (1880) 18 ChD 395.

have any connection with the names concerned. For example, the name 'j.sains-bury.com' could be sold to Joe Soap & Co or to someone who, by coincidence, happened to have the name John Sainsbury. In either case, use of the domain name by the third party would be highly likely to amount to passing off.

Two further possibilities were identified. First, and most obvious, the defendants might sell the domain name to the organisation with that name or trade mark. Another option might be for the defendants simply to retain the name without using it, thereby blocking the organisation from registering its own name (at least in an identical form). Neither of these possibilities would result in or involve passing off. It was not, therefore, certain that passing off would occur. Nevertheless, the judge thought it sufficient, even for a final *quia timet* injunction, that what had been done was calculated to infringe the plaintiff's rights.

Both *Directline Group Ltd* v *Directline Estate Agency*[180] and *Glaxo plc* v *Glaxowellcome Ltd*[181] were cited with approval in the *One in a Million* case. In both of those cases, injunctions were granted to restrain threatened rather than actual passing off and trade mark infringement. The companies that had been set up had not traded, but the threat of passing off was very real. In *Directline*, Laddie J accepted that the companies, which included Manchester U Ltd, Virgin Jeans Ltd, Jean Paul Gaultier Ltd and Cantona French Brandy Ltd, had been set up with the intention of trading off the plaintiffs' reputations and there was a strong case that passing off would occur. Laddie J described the defendants' activities as a 'scam'.

180 [1997] FSR 374.
181 [1996] FSR 388.

In *Glaxowellcome*, the defendant was quick off the mark to register that name as a company name when it realised that there was likely to be a takeover bid by Glaxo plc for Wellcome plc, and that the new company would be known as Glaxo-Well-come plc. When the plaintiff Glaxo discovered the registration, it tried to persuade the defendant to change the name of the defendant company or to sell it to the plain-tiff at the standard price asked for by a company registration agent of £1000 (the third defendant was a company registration agent). The defendant responded with a demand for £100 000. Lightman J granted an injunction on the basis of passing off saying that an injunction would be granted in such a case, whether or not the defen-dant's company had traded. The injunction was mandatory requiring the defendant to take steps to change or facilitate a change in name of the company.

However, in the *One in a Million* case, although the judge considered that there were four possible uses to which the domain names could be put, neither of the two most likely would amount to passing off. As the judge admitted, simply creating an instrument of deception was not in itself sufficient for passing off. This must also apply to possessing such an instrument without doing anything further with it.

Of course, the defendant's probable objective would have been to sell the domain names to the organisations having the goodwill in those names or having them as registered trade marks. That does not amount to passing off. The two possible objectives that could amount to passing off are less plausible (although an implicit threat that the name may be transferred to an uncon-nected third party might encourage the organisation to pay a high price for the name). Most third parties would realise that they would be guilty of passing off and/or trade mark infringement if they used such domain names and would be unlikely to buy them with an intention to use the names. Rather, they might buy them intending to sell them to the organisations with those names. What is clear, however, is that the courts will be quick to intervene in such cases to protect goodwill and existing trade marks.

A more plausible application of the law of passing off in the context of registration of a company name was given in *Compagnie Générale des Eaux* v *Compagnie Générale des Eaux Sdn Bhd*.[182] In that case, the plaintiff was a large company based in France and operating internationally. It had been established for 138 years and had interests in Malaysia providing training and technical services to a group of Malaysian companies. The plaintiff earned income and paid taxes in Malaysia. The defendant registered an identical name as a company name in 1991 and offered to negotiate favourable terms as to the future use of the company name by the plaintiff.

In finding that the plaintiff had goodwill in Malaysia and the existence of a likelihood of confusion, the High Court of Malaysia found that there was a probability of damage of one of two types. Either the plaintiff would suffer damage as a result of confusion, or the plaintiff would suffer damage by virtue of being unable to register its own name as its company name in Malaysia because of the defendant's prior registration. An important aspect of this case was that the actions of the defendant were clearly *mala fides* and he had refused to disclose the nature of the business he intended carrying on, in which case, the court felt entitled to assume that it was for an improper motive. The concept of suffering damage as a result of being unable to register a name as a company name or, for that matter, as a domain name, is a very real form of damage. Otherwise, why would a person try to register names of famous organisations?

## DEFENCES

Defences to a passing off action are fairly straightforward. In the case of the first (no confusion and thus no harm to goodwill), the defendant may commission a survey to demonstrate that there is no confusion although it is more likely that the plaintiff will commission such a survey to show the opposite. The utility of such surveys has been doubted, as mentioned above, and the main difficulty is ensuring objectivity. The defences to a passing off action include:

1 the defendant's activities have not harmed and are not likely to harm the plaintiff's goodwill associated with the name, mark or get-up. This may be because there is no common field of activity or because there is no danger of confusion as to the origin or quality of the goods or services;[183]

2 the passing off is not in the course of trade, that is the defendant is not using the name or get-up in the course of trade;

3 the plaintiff has no trade interest to be harmed, that is the plaintiff is not using the name or mark in the course of trade;[184]

4 the plaintiff has not established the existence of goodwill associated with the name, mark or get-up concerned;[185]

5 the defendant is simply making honest use of his own name or company name. Nevertheless, the actual use must be done carefully so as not to appear as passing off;[186]

6 the plaintiff has acquiesced in the defendant's use of the name or mark, or has expressly or impliedly granted the defendant permission to use the name or mark, for example in a contract for the sale of a business including the goodwill;[187]

7 the plaintiff is estopped from enforcing his rights under passing off because he has encouraged the defendant's act.[188]

182 [1997] FSR 610.

183 This line of defence succeeded in *Wombles Ltd* v *Wombles Skips Ltd* [1977] RPC 99.

184 *McCullogh* v *Lewis A May Ltd* (1948) 65 RPC 58.

185 *County Sound plc* v *Ocean Sound plc* [1991] FSR 367.

186 See, for example, *Wright, Layman & Umney Ltd* v *Wright* (1949) 66 RPC 149.

187 *Vine Products Ltd* v *MacKenzie & Co Ltd* [1969] RPC 1 is an example of acquiescence.

188 *Habib Bank Ltd* v *Habib Bank A G Zurich* [1982] RPC 1. This can be seen as a more positive form of acquiescence.

According to the judgment of Lord Diplock in *Erven Warnink Besloten Ven-nootschap* v *J Townend & Sons (Hull) Ltd*[189] the misrepresentation made by the defendant must be calculated to injure the plaintiff's business or goodwill. But, as mentioned earlier, innocence does not provide a defence to a passing off action[190] and whether the misrepresentation is intended or accidental should make no difference as to whether an injunction is available. One point about this is that, if knowledge was a factor, there might be difficulty concerning proof and, generally, other intellectual property rights are enforceable regardless of the defendant's state of knowledge although this may be relevant as to the availability of some of the remedies, especially damages.

189 [1979] AC 731.

190 *Baume & Co Ltd* v *A H Moore Ltd* [1958] RPC 226.

## REMEDIES

Remedies available are injunctions (especially interlocutory injunctions) and/or damages or, as an alternative, an account of profits. Additionally, an order may be granted for the delivery up or destruction of articles to which the name or mark has been applied or, if possible, an order for the obliteration of such names or marks. A declaration may be sufficient if the defendant has agreed not to continue the acts complained of.

Damages will usually be based upon the actual loss attributable to the passing off, that is resulting from the loss of sales experienced by the plaintiff. How else can harm to goodwill be measured? However, in some cases, damages may be calculated on a royalty basis, that is based on the amount that would have been payable by the defendant if he had sought a licence to use the name or mark from the plaintiff. This possibility was discussed in *Dormeuil Frères SA* v *Feraglow Ltd*[191] although it was accepted that there was no authority to that effect. However, a royalty basis could be applicable if it would yield a greater amount than that attributable to loss of sales. Of course, it will always be difficult to calculate damages resulting from a loss of sales and each sale by the defendant does not necessarily represent a sale lost by the plaintiff. A lost sale in a strict sense occurs where a purchaser buys the defendant's goods thinking that they are the plaintiff's goods. However, some of the defendant's customers will not have heard of the plaintiff, or even if they have will realise that they are not dealing with the plaintiff. In the above case, the plaintiff reckoned that 75 per cent of the defendant's sales of cloth represented sales of which the plaintiff was deprived as a result of the passing off. The plaintiff also claimed damages on a royalty basis for the remaining 25 per cent of the defendant's sales and damages for damage to goodwill because the defendant's cloth was of an inferior quality. The plaintiff was awarded a total of £20 000 damages which included interest and the unrecovered costs expended in pursuing foreign manufacturers of infringing cloth.

191 [1990] RPC 449.

If the passing off is of the extended variety as in *Erven Warnink*, the assessment of damages may prove very difficult. The same applies to inverse passing off. However, in many cases of this sort, the main remedy sought by the plaintiff will be an injunction, often at the interlocutory stage before any actual damage to the plaintiff's goodwill has been caused. In an interlocutory hearing, the fact that damages will be difficult to quantify should an injunction not be granted may be a factor, though not a conclusive one, to be taken into

**192** *See Morgan-Grampian plc* v *Training Personnel Ltd* [1992] FSR 267, cf. *Blazer plc* v *Yardley & Co Ltd* [1992] FSR 501.

**193** [1994] FSR 504.

**194** (1915) 84 LJ Ch 449.

**195** (1915) 84 LJ Ch 449 at 449.

**196** *Columbia Picture Industries* v *Robinson* [1987] 1 Ch 38.

**197** For fuller description of this tort, *see* Blanco-White, T. A. and Jacob, R. (1986) *Kerly's Law of Trade Marks and Trade Names* (12th edn) Sweet & Maxwell, Chapter 18.

**198** This might also be a personal libel, depending upon the circumstances.

**199** [1899] 1 QB 86.

**200** [1895] AC 154.

account.[192] In interlocutory hearings, the judge is entitled to take account of the behaviour of the parties as well as considering the balance of convenience as in *Dalgety Spillers Foods Ltd* v *Food Brokers Ltd*,[193] discussed earlier.

Nominal damages will be available against a trader who commits passing off innocently (an injunction almost certainly will be granted in addition). An account of profits may be a possibility in relation to the period following the time when the innocent trader is disabused of his innocence if he continues the passing off beyond this time. The position of the innocent passer off was well put by Lord Parker in *Spalding & Bros* v *A W Gamage Ltd*[194] where he said:

> Nor need the representation be made fraudulently. It is enough that it has in fact been made, whether fraudulently or otherwise, and that damages may probably ensue, though the complete innocence of the party making it may be a reason for limiting the account of profits to the period subsequent to the date at which he becomes aware of the true facts. The representation is in fact treated as the invasion of a right giving rise at any rate to nominal damages, the enquiry being granted at the plaintiff's risk if he might probably have suffered more than nominal damages.[195]

If the defendant's actions infringe a trade or service mark as well as constituting passing off, the damages that may be awarded are not cumulative. However, if passing off (or trade mark infringement) and copyright infringement both occur in relation to the same events, then the damages for passing off and copyright infringement may well be accumulated.[196]

## MALICIOUS FALSEHOOD

A tort that is related to passing off is that known as malicious falsehood, sometimes referred to as trade libel.[197] This could occur where someone publishes information that is capable of seriously damaging a trader's position or reputation. For example, one trader might unjustifiably state that another trader's goods are of poor quality or are counterfeit.[198] Advertising 'puff' and mere claims that one trader's goods are superior to those of another trader does not, *per se*, amount to malicious falsehood. For example, in *Hubbuck & Sons Ltd* v *Wilkinson, Heywood & Clerk Ltd*,[199] a published statement that the defendant's zinc paint had a slight advantage over the plaintiff's paint was held not to be a malicious falsehood, even if the statement had been made maliciously.

The basis of the action is a false statement made maliciously, that is without just cause or excuse. These two ingredients, falsity and malice, are essential if the plaintiff is to succeed. The plaintiff failed in *White* v *Mellin*[200] where the defendant sold the plaintiff's infants' food after fixing labels to the wrappers stating that the defendant's food for infants was far more nutritious and healthful than any other. There was no proof that the statement was untrue or that it had caused damage to the plaintiff. Proof of financial loss is another requirement but this was relaxed by the Defamation Act 1952 s 3 which states that proof of special damage is not necessary if the statement was calculated to cause pecuniary damage to the plaintiff:

(a) and was published in writing or some other permanent form, or
(b) was made in respect of any office, profession, calling, trade or business held or carried on by him at the time of publication.

Prior to the Defamation Act 1952, proof of special damage was not always required and general damage such as a significant fall in a trader's turnover could be sufficient. In *Ratcliffe v Evans*,[201] the plaintiff carried on business under the name 'Ratcliffe & Sons'. The defendant published a weekly newspaper circulated in the area where the plaintiff's business was situated. One week the newspaper carried a statement implying that the plaintiff had ceased trading and that the firm known as 'Ratcliffe & Sons' no longer existed. Not surprisingly, this untrue statement caused the plaintiff to experience a fall in business activity. It was held in the Court of Appeal that an untrue statement maliciously published about a plaintiff's business which is intended to produce and does indeed produce a loss is actionable as a malicious falsehood. Evidence of general loss, as was the case here, as opposed to evidence of particular loss (for example, where a named customer takes his trade elsewhere as a result of the untrue statement) was admissible in evidence and was sufficient to support the action.

Other examples of trade libel include circulars suggesting that the plaintiff's goods were not genuine[202] and claims that the plaintiff was intending to make use of a patented invention the use of which had been abandoned earlier by the defendant as being inadequate.[203] Selling one class of the plaintiff's goods as a different class can amount to malicious falsehood and passing off. The defendant in *Wilts United Dairies Ltd v Thomas Robinson Sons & Co Ltd*[204] obtained large quantities of the plaintiff's condensed milk that had been sold off by the Ministry of Food at a very low price on condition that it should be used for animal food, manufacturing or export. The milk was old (it had been stocked during the Second World War) and it was known that it deteriorated with age. The plaintiff always had required that retailers sold the cans of milk within six months. The defendant offered the old milk for sale for human consumption. It was held that the defendant had passed off one class of the plaintiff's milk (that is, old stock not fit for human consumption) as another class (normal quality) and this amounted to a malicious falsehood calculated to injure the plaintiff's reputation. In many respects, the basic principles in this case are the same as those applying to the passing off case of *Spalding & Bros v A W Gamage Ltd*,[205] discussed earlier in this chapter, where the defendant sold defective footballs made by the plaintiff as if they were of normal quality.

Malicious falsehood could be a possibility where a trader engages in comparative advertising in a way in which the stated facts concerning the other traders' goods are untrue or misleading. In *Compaq Computer Corp v Dell Computer Corp Ltd*[206] the defendant advertised using a photograph showing its computer and the plaintiff's computer side by side. Underneath were details of the two computers including price and performance. This information was selected so as to show off the defendant's computer as being the best value. However, the information was misleading, particularly as regards price. The defendant had indicated a heavily discounted price for its machine compared to the list price (undiscounted) of the plaintiff's machine. An interlocutory injunction was granted because, although the defendant intended to justify his statement, the test was whether a jury would reasonably conclude that the statement was true.[207] However, this case should be compared with *McDonald's Hamburgers Ltd v Burgerking (UK) Ltd*,[208] where it was held that an advertising campaign for 'Whopper' burgers using the slogan 'It's Not Just Big Mac' in close proximity with the phrase 'Unlike some burgers, it's 100 per cent pure beef...' did not amount to a malicious falsehood. It did, however, constitute passing off.

201 [1892] 2 QB 524.

202 *Thomas v Williams* (1880) 14 Ch D 864.

203 *London Ferro-Concrete Co Ltd v Justicz* (1951) 68 RPC 65. The statement had been made in hope that this would induce a contractor to divert a sub-contract to the defendant.

204 [1958] RPC 94.

205 (1915) 84 LJ Ch 449.

206 [1992] FSR 93.

207 However, there is no entitlement to a jury in a malicious falsehood action, unlike the case with defamation. The case also involved a trade mark infringement although the judge considered that there was an arguable case that the trade mark 'Compaq', was invalid.

208 [1987] FSR 112.

In passing off the test is whether a substantial number of people would be deceived. That is not the test to be used in malicious falsehood where the one-meaning rule is used. The judge, as notional jury, had to decide a single and natural meaning of the defendant's statement and determine its falsity on the basis of that meaning. So held Jacob J in *Vodafone Group plc v Orange Personal Communications Services Ltd*,[209] where the defendant advertised with the slogan 'On average, Orange users save £20 every month'. Jacob J decided the single meaning was that if Orange users had been using Vodafone, on the basis of the same amount of usage, on an arithmetic average they would pay £20 per monthly more including VAT. It did not mean that every single user would save £20 by switching to Orange.

In disallowing the plaintiff's claim for malicious falsehood, Jacob J held that the statement was neither misleading nor made with malice.[210] As to the plaintiff's submission that the saving was only around £15 per month, Jacob J said that the sting in the advertisement would not have been much less if that figure had been used instead. Orange would have been happy to show a saving of £10 per month.

In some cases there may be an overlap between malicious falsehood and defamation and, if that is so, it may be advantageous to bring an action in malicious falsehood as legal aid is not available for defamation. To do this is not an abuse of process even if the sole aim is to facilitate an application for legal aid and in spite of the fact that the defendant will thus be deprived of a right to elect trial by jury. So it was held in *Joyce v Sengupta*[211] in which a former lady's maid of the Princess Royal took action in respect of an allegation by the defendant (a reporter for the *Today* newspaper) that the plaintiff had stolen intimate letters belonging to the Princess Royal and handed them to the newspaper. Nicholls VC also confirmed that the effect of the Defamation Act 1952 s 3 was not to limit damages to nominal damages only.[212]

Local authorities may not sue in defamation because to allow defamation actions by local authorities and other bodies run on political lines would be an undesirable fetter on the freedom of speech. The House of Lords so held in *Derbyshire County Council v Times Newspapers Ltd*,[213] applying authorities from the USA, in particular, *New York Times Co v Sullivan*.[214] Although the United States cases were related to the American Constitution provisions securing freedom of speech, the UK principle of public interest was just as valid. Previous UK law as expressed in *Bognor Regis UDC v Campion*[215] was unsatisfactory and this case was overruled by the House of Lords. In that case, the council had been awarded £2000 in damages after the defendant had circulated a leaflet savagely attacking the Council. Of course, a personal individual such as a councillor or an officer of the council will be able to bring a libel action if his individual reputation was wrongly harmed. Indeed, the leader of Derbyshire County Council had brought a personal action based on the same facts as in the local authority action.

At the interlocutory stage where malicious falsehood is in issue and the defendant intends to plead justification a court will not normally grant an injunction if the statements are not obviously untrue.[216] Furthermore, where the balance of justice favours neither party an injunction should be refused on the grounds that it would interfere with the defendant's right of free speech.[217] In this respect, the courts behave in a similar manner as in breach of confidence cases where defamation is alleged by the confider.

209 [1997] FSR 34.

210 He also dismissed a claim of trade mark infringement.

211 [1993] All ER 897.

212 Proof of special damage unnecessary in certain cases.

213 [1993] AC 534. The Court of Appeal decision to the same effect is reported in [1992] QB 770.

214 (1964) 376 US 254.

215 [1972] 2 QB 169.

216 *Macmillan Magazines Ltd v RCN Publishing Co Ltd* [1998] FSR 9.

217 *Bestobell Paints Ltd v Bigg* [1975] FSR 421.

## SUMMARY

The establishment and development of passing off is a typically common law method of protecting traders' rights but it does have equivalents in other forms of jurisdiction, broadly falling under the heading of unfair competition. For example, in Germany, there is trade mark law like protection for the *Ausstattung* (get-up) of goods, packaging, their advertising and the like.[218] For traders contemplating operations overseas, it is obviously important to take precautions such as seeking registrations of trade marks. In terms of the Treaty of Rome, the law of passing off does not appear to pose any particular problems and, because of differences between trade mark law and the law of passing off, the difficulties experienced in respect of parallel importing and trade marks do not seem to occur. It is apparent that passing off provides a very useful remedy where there is no trade mark and the wider scope of passing off can be important in restraining unfair practices. However, the scope can sometimes appear to be too wide, as in the Jif lemon case, and there are certainly some defects and gaps, particularly in the field of character merchandising. Nevertheless, the law of passing off is alive and kicking and prevents a great deal of unfair appropriation of business goodwill. It still proves to be a useful supplement to trade mark law. In turn, the law of malicious falsehood provides a useful supplement to passing off. It should be noted that, in a significant number of cases where passing off is an issue, criminal offences may have been committed such as making a false instrument,[219] obtaining by deception,[220] going equipped to cheat[221] in addition to offences under the Trade Descriptions Act 1968 and Consumer Protection Act 1987. A local trading standards officer is likely to take an interest in an activity where a name or mark has been used without permission in circumstances where the public are likely to be deceived, as is the trader whose name or mark it is.

218 For an overview of German intellectual property law as it applies to the appearance of articles including get-up, *see* Rohnke, C. 'Protection of External Product Features in West Germany' [1990] 2 EIPR 41.

219 The Forgery and Counterfeiting Act 1981 s 1.

220 The Theft Act 1968 s 15.

221 Ibid s 25.

# Appendices

Appendix

# Appendix 1
# Trade mark classification for goods and services

## CLASSIFICATION FOR GOODS (34 classes)

1. Chemicals used in industry, science and photography, as well as in agriculture, horticulture and forestry; unprocessed artificial resins, unprocessed plastics; manures; fire extinguishing compositions; tempering and soldering preparations; chemical substances for preserving foodstuffs; tanning substances; adhesives used in industry.

2. Paints, varnishes, lacquers; preservatives against rust and against deterioration of wood; colourants; mordants; raw natural resins; metals in foil and powder form for painters, decorators, printers and artists.

3. Bleaching preparations and other substances for laundry use; cleaning, polishing, scouring and abrasive preparations; soaps; perfumery, essential oils, cosmetics, hair lotions; dentifrices.

4. Industrial oils and greases; lubricants; dust absorbing, wetting and binding compositions; fuels (including motor spirit) and illuminants; candles, wicks.

5. Pharmaceutical veterinary and sanitary preparations; dietetic substances adapted for medical use, food for babies; plasters, materials for dressings; material for stopping teeth, dental wax; disinfectants; preparations for destroying vermin; fungicides, herbicides.

6. Common metals and their alloys; metal building materials; transportable buildings of metal; materials of metal for railway tracks; non-electric cables and wires of common metal; ironmongery, small items of metal hardware; pipes and tubes of metal; safes; goods of common metal not included in other classes; ores.

7. Machines and machine tools; motors (except for land vehicles); machine coupling and belting (except for land vehicles); agricultural implements; incubators for eggs.

8. Hand tools and implements (hand operated); cutlery; side arms; razors.

9. Scientific, nautical, surveying, electric, photographic, cinematographic, optical, weighing, measuring, signalling, checking (supervision), life saving and teaching apparatus and instruments; apparatus for recording, transmission or reproduction of sound or images; magnetic data carriers, recording discs; automatic vending machines and mechanisms for coin-operated apparatus; cash registers, calculating machines, data processing equipment and computers; fire-extinguishing apparatus.

10. Surgical, medical, dental and veterinary apparatus and instruments, artificial limbs, eyes and teeth; orthopaedic articles; suture materials.

11. Apparatus for lighting, heating, steam generating, cooking, refrigerating, drying, ventilating, water supply and sanitary purposes.

12. Vehicles; apparatus for locomotion by land, air or water.

13. Firearms; ammunition and projectiles; explosives; fireworks.

14. Precious metals and their alloys and goods in precious metals or coated therewith, not included in other classes; jewellery, precious stones; horological and chronometric instruments.

15. Musical instruments.

16. Paper, cardboard and goods made from these materials, not included in other classes; printed matter; bookbinding material; photographs; stationery; adhesives for stationery or household purposes; artists' materials; paint brushes; typewriters and office requisites (except furni-

Appendix 1

ture); instructional and teaching material (except apparatus); plastic materials for packaging (not included in other classes); playing cards; printers' type; printing blocks.

17. Rubber, gutta-percha, gum, asbestos, mica and goods made from these materials and not included in other classes; plastics in extruded form for use in manufacture; packing, stopping and insulating materials; flexible pipes, not of metal.

18. Leather and imitations of leather, and goods made of these materials and not included in other classes; animal skins, hides; trunks and travelling bags; umbrellas, parasols and walking sticks; whips, harness and saddlery.

19. Building materials (non-metallic); non-metallic rigid pipes for building; asphalt, pitch and bitumen; non-metallic transportable buildings; monuments, not of metal.

20. Furniture, mirrors, picture frames; goods (not included in other classes) of wood, cork, reed, cane, wicker, horn, bone, ivory, whalebone, shell, amber, mother-of-pearl, meerschaum and substitutes for all these materials, or of plastics.

21. Household or kitchen utensils and containers (not of precious metal or coated therewith); combs and sponges; brushes (except paint brushes); brush-making materials; articles for cleaning purposes; steel wool; unworked or semi-worked glass (except glass used in building); glassware, porcelain and earthenware not included in other classes.

22. Ropes, string, nets, tents, awnings, tarpaulins, sails, sacks and bags (not included in other classes); padding and stuffing materials (except of rubber or plastics); raw fibrous textile materials.

23. Yarns and threads, for textile use.

24. Textiles and textile goods, not included in other classes; bed and table covers.

25. Clothing, footwear, headgear.

26. Lace and embroidery, ribbons and braid; buttons, hooks and eyes, pins and needles; artificial flowers.

27. Carpets, rugs, mats and matting, linoleum and other materials for covering existing floors; wall hangings (non-textile).

28. Games and playthings; gymnastic and sporting articles not included in other classes; decorations for Christmas trees.

29. Meat, fish, poultry and game; meat extracts; preserved, dried and cooked fruits and vegetables; jellies, jams, fruit sauces; eggs, milk and milk products; edible oils and fats.

30. Coffee, tea, cocoa, sugar, rice, tapioca, sago, artificial coffee; flour and preparations made from cereals, bread, pastry and confectionery, ices; honey, treacle; yeast, baking-powder; salt, mustard; vinegar, sauces (condiments); spices; ice.

31. Agricultural, horticultural and forestry products and grains not included in other classes; live animals; fresh fruits and vegetables; seeds, natural plants and flowers; foodstuffs for animals, malt.

32. Beers; mineral and aerated waters and other non-alcoholic drinks; fruit drinks and fruit juices; syrups and other preparations for making beverages.

33. Alcoholic beverages (except beers).

34. Tobacco; smokers' articles; matches.

## CLASSIFICATION FOR SERVICES (8 CLASSES)

35. Advertising, business management; business administration; office functions.

36. Insurance; financial affairs; monetary affairs; real estate affairs.

37. Building construction; repair; installation services.

38. Telecommunications.

39. Transportation; packaging and storage of goods; travel arrangement.

40. Treatment of materials.

41. Education; providing of training; entertainment; sporting and cultural activities.

42. Providing of food and drink; temporary accommodation; medical, hygienic and beauty care; veterinary and agricultural services; legal services; scientific and industrial research; computer programming; services that cannot be placed in other classes.

# Appendix 2
## Useful Internet addresses for intellectual property information

| Address | Description |
|---|---|
| http://www.open.gov.uk/ | Government Information Service with many links – try Functional Index and select Law or Acts of Parliament. There are presently links to the Lord Chancellor's Department (with access to House of Lords judgments), Hansard, etc. or try Organisational Index with many links, including The Patent Office, DTI, The Stationery Office, etc. There are also searching facilities. |
| http://www.open.gov.uk/lcd/lcdhome.htm | Lord Chancellor's Department home page with links to related sites such as Acts of Parliament, Parliamentary Bills and House of Lords judgments. |
| http://www.patent.gov.uk | The Patent Office home page. Lots of useful information about intellectual property including descriptions of rights, the work of the Patent Office and news releases. |
| http://www.hmso.gov.uk | The Stationery Office (formerly HMSO) home page. Access from here to Acts of Parliament, Statutory Instruments, Draft Statutory Instruments, information about the Copyright Unit and Crown Copyright. |
| http://www.smithbernal.com/index2.htm | Smith Bernal International – the largest court reporting and litigation support group in the world – access from here to Court of Appeal judgments. |
| http://www.european-patent-office.org | European Patent Office home page with much useful information and many links to other sites including national patent offices, patent databases, etc. |
| http://europa.eu.int/eur-lex/ | Eur-Lex – EC legislation and cases. |
| http://www.aber.ac.uk/~dgw/patent.htm | Patents on the Internet – many links to sites with patent information. |
| http://www.europa.eu.int/index-en.htm | The European Union server – news, institutions, policies, etc. with many links. |
| http://www.cla.co.uk | Copyright Licensing Agency – news releases, copyright on the Internet, etc. |

Some of the information mentioned above may be accessed via a variety of routes. For example, Acts of Parliament may be accessed from the Government Information Service or the Stationery Office. Websites and addresses may be subject to change and the information available from them and the links to other sites may change from time to time. In some cases you will need an Acrobat Reader from Adobe Systems Inc. to access or download larger files. Your computer department should be able to tell you how to obtain a copy. (It is possible to obtain a copy via the Internet!) Acrobat is a registered trade mark.

The amount of useful information now available on the Internet is impressive and it is growing at a phenomenal rate.

Most of the information outlined above may be accessed free of charge. However, this is not always so. Please ensure that you abide by the terms or conditions of use. Some allow printing or downloading for your own personal use only.

# Bibliography

## Books

Abell, M. (1989) *The Franchise Option: A Legal Guide*, Waterlow.

Annand, R. and Norman, H. (1994) *Blackstone's Guide to the Trade Marks Act 1994*, Blackstone Press.

Bainbridge, D.I. (1996) *Introduction to Computer Law* (3rd edn) Pitman Publishing.

Bentham, J., *Manual of Political Economy*, reprinted in Stark, W. (ed.) (1952) *Jeremy Bentham's Economic Writings* Vol. 1, Allen & Unwin.

Blanco White, T.A. and Jacob, R. (1985) *Kerly's Law of Trade Marks & Trade Names* (12th edn) Sweet & Maxwell.

Bowker, R.R. (1912) *Copyright: Its History and its Law*, Houghton Mifflin.

The British Copyright Council (1986) *Reprographic Copying of Books and Journals,* British Copyright Council.

Caplan, D. and Stewart, G. (1966) *British Trade Marks and Symbols*, Peter Owen.

Cawthra, B.I. (1986) *Patent Licensing in Europe* (2nd edn) Butterworths.

Coleman, A. (1992) *The Legal Protection of Trade Secrets*, Sweet & Maxwell.

Cornish, W. R. (1996) *Intellectual Property: Patents, Copyright, Trade Marks and Allied Rights* (3rd edn) Sweet & Maxwell.

Cornish, W.R. (ed.) (1990) *Materials on Intellectual Property*, ESC Publishing.

Davenport, N. (1979) *The United Kingdom Patent System: A Brief History,* Mason.

Davies, G. and Hung, M.E. (1993) *Music and Video Private Copying*, Sweet & Maxwell.

Dickens, C., *A Poor Man's Tale of a Patent*, reprinted in Phillips, J. (1984) *Charles Dickens and the 'Poor Man's Tale of a Patent'*, ESC Publishing.

Dutton, H.I. (1984) *The Patent System and Inventive Activity during the Industrial Revolution, 1750–1852*, Manchester University Press.

Drone, E.S. (1879) *A Treatise on the Law of Property in Intellectual Productions in Great Britain and the United States*, Little, Brown & Co.

Dworkin, G. and Taylor, R.D. (1989) *Blackstone's Guide to the Copyright, Designs and Patents Act 1988*, Blackstone Press.

Eisenschitz, T.S. (1987) *Patents, Trade Marks and Designs in Information Work*, Croom Helm.

Gallafent, R.J., Eastaway, N.A., Dauppe, V.A.F. (1992) *Intellectual Property: Law and Taxation* (4th edn) Longman.

Gringras, C. (1997) *The Laws of the Internet,* Butterworths.

Haselden, D. 'UK and European Patentability' in the Patent Office (1994) *Legal Protection for Software Relation Innovation*, The Patent Office.

Henry, M. (1994) *Publishing and Multimedia Law*, Butterworths.

Hohfeld, W.N. *Fundamental Legal Conceptions as Applied in Judicial Reasoning*, reprinted in part in Lloyd, Lord (of Hampstead) (1979) *Introduction to Jurisprudence* (4th edn) Stevens.

Hoptroff, C. 'Wider International Patentability' in the Patent Office (1994) *Legal Protection for Software Related Innovation*, The Patent Office.

Irish, V. (ed.) (1991) *Intellectual Property: A Manager's Guide,* McGraw-Hill.

Jacob, R. and Alexander, D. (1993) *A Guidebook to Intellectual Property* (4th edn) Sweet & Maxwell.

Johnston, D. (1989) *Design Protection* (3rd edn) The Design Council.

Laddie, H., Prescott, P. and Vittoria, M. (1995) *The Modern Law of Copyright and Designs* (2nd edn) Butterworths.

Laddie, H., Prescott, P. and Vitoria, M. (1995) *The Modern Law of Copyright and Designs* (2nd edn) Butterworths.

Lasok, D. (1994) *Lasok and Bridge: Law and Institutions of the European Union* (6th edn) Butterworths.

Lehmann, M. and Tapper, C.F. (eds) (1993) *A Handbook of European Software Law*, Clarendon Press.

Lloyd, I. (1997) *Information Technology Law* (2nd edn) Butterworths.

Marett, P. (1991) *Information Law and Practice,* Gower.

Merkin, R. (1989) *Copyright, Designs and Patents: The New Law,* Longman.

The Patent Office – various publications of interest available from the Marketing and Information Directorate, Cardiff Road, Newport, Gwent, NP9 1RH

Pearson, H. and Miller, C. (1991) *Commercial Exploitation of Intellectual Property,* Blackstone Press.

Phillips, J. (ed.) (1994) *Butterworths Intellectual Property Law Handbook* (2nd edn) Butterworths.

Phillips, J. and Firth, A. (1995) *Introduction to Intellectual Property Law* (3rd edn) Butterworths.

Phillips, J., Durie, R. and Karet, I. (1993) *Whale on Copyright* (4th edn) Sweet & Maxwell.

Prime, T. (1992) *The Law of Copyright,* Format.

Reed, C. (ed) (1996) *Computer Law* (3rd edn) Blackstone Press.

Reid, B. C. (1986) *Confidentiality and the Law,* Waterlow.

Reid, B. C. (1993) *A Practical Guide to Patent Law* (2nd edn) Sweet & Maxwell.

Schmookler, J. (1986) *Invention and Economic Growth,* Harvard University Press.

Selwyn, N. (1996) *Selwyn's Law of Employment* (9th edn) Butterworths.

Singleton, E. S. (1992) *Introduction to Competition Law,* Pitman.

Skone-James, E. P., Mummery, J., Rayner-James, J. E. & Garnett, K. M. (1991) *Copinger and Skone-James on Copyright* (13th edn) Sweet & Maxwell.

Sterling, J. A. L. (1992) *Intellectual Property Rights in Sound Recordings, Film and Video,* Sweet & Maxwell.

Stewart, S. M. (1989) *International Copyright and Neighbouring Rights* (2nd edn) Butterworths.

Tapper, C. (1989) *Computer Law* (4th edn) Longman.

Tootal, C. (1990) *The Law of Industrial Design,* CCH Editions.

Wadlow, C. (1980) *The Law of Passing Off,* Sweet & Maxwell.

Whish, R. (1992) *Competition Law* (3rd edn) Butterworths.

Young, D. (1994), *Passing Off* (3rd edn) FT Law & Tax.

Young, D., Watson, A., Thorley, S., Miller, R. (1994) *Terrell on the Law of Patents* (14th edn) Sweet & Maxwell.

## Reports

*Annual Report of the European Patent Office 1995* (Munich: European Patent Office, 1996).

*Anton Piller Orders: A Consultation Paper* Lord Chancellor's Department, 1992.

The Banks Report *Committee to Examine the Patent System and Patent Law* Cmnd 4407 (HMSO, 1970).

The Calcutt Committee *Report on Privacy and Related Matters* Cm 1102 (HMSO, 1990).

*Copyright and the Challenge of Technology – Copyright Issues Requiring Immediate Action,* COM (88) 172.

*Intellectual Property and Innovation* Cmnd 9712 (HMSO, 1986).

*Intellectual Property Rights and Innovation* Cmnd 9117 (HMSO, 1983).

The Law Commission, Law Comm No. 110 *Breach of Confidence* Cmnd 8388 (HMSO, 1981).

The Patent Office *Annual Report and Accounts 1996 to 1997* (HMSO, 1997).

*Reform of the Law Relating to Copyright, Designs and Performers' Protection* Cmnd 8302 (HMSO, 1981).

*Reform of Trade Marks Law* Cm 1203 (HMSO, 1990).

The Whitford Committee *Copyright – Copyright and Design Law* Cmnd 6732 (HMSO, 1977).

## Journal articles

Anon 'Appellate Court gives Green Light to Reverse Engineering' (1991) 2 *Intellectual Property in Business Briefing* 3.

Angel, J. and Quinn, T. 'Database Law' [1998] 14 CLSR 34.

Arnold, R. 'A New Remedy for Copyright Infringement' [1997] 12 EIPR 689.

Ashley, G. and Björk, P. 'Patenting of Alloys at the European Patent Office' (1997) 2(3) *Intellectual Property* 3.

Bainbridge, D. I. 'The Copyright Act: A Legal Red Herring' (1989) 1(8) *Computer Bulletin* 21.

Bender, D. 'Computer Programs: Should They Be Patentable?' (1968) 68 *Columbia Law Review* 241.

Benson, C. 'Fair Dealing in the United Kingdom' [1995] 6 EIPR 304.

Benson, J. R. 'Copyright Protection for Computer Screen Displays' (1988) 72 *Minnesota Law Review* 1123.

Beresford, R. 'The Patenting of Software in Europe and the UK', (1997) *Patent World*, Issue 91, p. 14.

Bull, G. 'Licensing and Distribution of Market Data' [1994] 10 CLSR 50.

Burton, H. 'The UK Trade Marks Act 1994: An Invitation to an Olfactory Occasion?' [1994] 8 EIPR 378.

Carty, H. 'Inverse Passing-Off: A Suitable Addition to Passing-Off?' [1993] 10 EIPR 370.

Chalton, S. 'Implementation of the Software Directive in the United Kingdom: The Effects of the Copyright (Computer Programs) Regulations 1992' [1993] 9 CLSR 115.

Chalton, S. 'The Effect of the Database Directive on UK Copyright Law in Relation to Databases: A Comparison of Features' [1997] 6 EIPR 278.

Cole, P. 'Purposive Construction and Inventive Step' [1995] 3 EIPR 147.

Cornish, W. R. 'Interoperable Systems and Copyright' [1989] 11 EIPR 391.

Cornish, W. R. 'Authors in Law' (1995) 58 MLR1.

Davidson, D. M. 'Protecting Computer Software: A Comprehensive Analysis' (1983) 23(4) *Jurimetrics Journal* 337.

de Freitas, D. 'The Copyright, Designs and Patents Act 1988 (2)' (1989) 133 *Solicitors Journal* 670.

de Freitas, D. 'The Copyright, Designs and Patents Act 1988 (4)' (1989) 133 *Solicitors Journal* 733.

Dutson, S. 'Actions for Infringement of a Foreign Intellectual Property Right in an English Court' (1997) 46 *The International and Comparative Law Quarterly* 918.

Dworkin, G. 'Authorship of Films and European Commission Proposals for Harmonising the Term of Copyright' [1993] 5 EIPR 151.

Goldblatt, M. 'Copyright Protection for Computer Programs in Australia: The Law since Autodesk' [1990] 5 EIPR 170.

Goltz, H. and Pritesche, K. U. 'Cable & Satellite Television – Copyright and Other Issues under German Law' [1988] 9 EIPR 261.

Gordon, S. E. 'The Very Idea! Why Copyright is an Inappropriate Way to Protect Computer Programs' [1998] 1 EIPR 10.

Groves, P. and Martino, T. 'Euromark: Or How the EEC Brought UK Trade Mark Law into the 20th Century' (1990) 1 *European Business Law Review* 109.

Günther, A. and Wuermeling, U. 'Software Protection in Germany – Recent Court Decisions in Copyright Law' [1995] 11 CLSR 12.

Hails, R., Jr. 'Liability of On-Line Service Providers Resulting from Copyright Infringement Performed by their Subscribers' [1996] 5 EIPR 304.

Harris, P. 'UK Trade Mark Law: Are You Confused?' [1995] 12 EIPR 601.

Hart, R. 'Software Patentability' [1994] 10 CLSR 296.

Hart, R. J. 'Applications of Patents to Computer Technology – UK and the EPO Harmonisation?' [1989] 2 EIPR 42.

Hoffman, G., Grossman, J., Keane, P. and Westby, J. 'Protection for Computer Software: An International Overview: Part 2' [1989] 1 EIPR 7.

Horton, A. A. 'Industrial Design Law: The Future for Europe' [1991] 12 EIPR 442.

Jacob, R. 'The Herchel Smith Lecture 1993' [1993] 9 EIPR 312.

Jehoram, H. C. 'The EC Green Paper on the Legal Protection of Industrial Design. Half Way down the Right Track – A View from the Benelux' [1992] 3 EIPR 75.

Karet, I. 'Passing Off and Trade Marks: Confusing Times Ahead?' [1995] 1 EIPR 3.

Katz, J. 'Reprography and Fair Dealing – Copying for Educational Use: Longman v Carrington [1991] 2 NZLR 574' [1993] 2 EIPR 67.

Lai, S. 'Database Protection in the UK: the New Deal and its Effects on Software Protection' [1998] 1 EIPR 32.

Lea, G. 'Database Law – Solutions beyond Copyright' [1993] 9 CLSR 127.

Lea, G. 'Passing Off and the Protection of Program Look and Feel' [1994] 10 CLSR 82.

Lewin, R. 'A New UK Trade Marks Law – A Godsend for Trade Mark Owners or a Goldmine for their Lawyers?' [1994] 3 EIPR 91.

Lyons, D. 'Sound, Smells and Signs' [1994] 12 EIPR 540.

Mamiofa, I. E. 'The Draft of a New Soviet Patent Law' [1990] 1 EIPR 21.

Markesinis, B. S. 'Our Patchy Law of Privacy – Time to Do Something about it' (1990) 53 MLR 802.

MacQueen, H. L. 'A Scottish Case on Unregistered Designs' [1994] 2 EIPR 86.

McQuaker, R. 'Software Patents' [1995] 11 CLSR 259.

Monotti, A. 'The Extent of Copyright Protection for Compilations of Artistic Works' [1993] 5 EIPR 156.

Nissen, D. and Karet, I. 'The Trade Marks Directive: Can I Prevail if the State has Failed?' [1993] 3 EIPR 91.

Oliver, P. 'Of Split Trade Marks and Common Markets' (1991) 54 MLR 587.

The Patent Office, *Combined Search and Examination*, March 1995, *Annual Reports and Accounts 1994 to 1995* (London: HMSO, 1995).

Paterson, G. D. 'The Patentability of Further Uses of a Known Product under the European Patent Convention' [1991] 1 EIPR 16.

Pessa, P. 'Evaluating the Idea-Expression Dichotomy: Rhetoric or Legal Principle?' (1991) *Computer Law & Practice* March/April, 166.

Prescott, P. 'Kaye v Robertson – a Reply' (1991) 53 MLR 451.

Rohnke, C. 'Protection of External Product Features in West Germany' [1990] 2 EIPR 41.

Sherman, B. 'Patent Claim Interpretation: The Impact of the Protocol on Interpretation' (1991) 54 MLR 499.

Snell, T. 'Pirates run Aground as UK fights IT Crime' *Computing* 21 January 1993 at 13.

Rawlinson, P. 'The UK Trade Marks Act 1994: Its Criminal' [1995] 1 EIPR 54.

Reid, B.C. 'Biogen in the EPO: The Advantage of Scintific Understanding' [1995] 2 EIPR 98.

Roberts, T. 'The European Biotechnology Patenting Directive Killed Off' [1995] 5 EIPR D-156.

Taylor, W. D. 'Copyright Protection for Computer Software after Whelan Associates v Jaslow Dental Laboratory' (1989) 54 *Missouri Law Review* 121.

Thurow, L. C. 'Needed: A New System of Intellectual Property Rights' *Harvard Business Review*, September-October 1997 at 95.

Thurston, J. 'Recent EC Developments in Biotechnology' [1993] 6 EIPR 187.

Turner, B. 'A True Design Right: C & H Engineering v Klucznik & Sons' [1993] 1 EIPR 24.

Walton, A. 'The Copyright, Designs and Patents Act 1988 (1)' (1989) 133 *Solicitors Journal* 646.

Webber, D. 'Software Patents: A New Era in Australia and the United States' [1993] 5 EIPR 181.

Whaite, R. 'The Draft Technology Transfer Block Exemption' [1994] 7 EIPR 259.

Wood, N. 'The Trouble with Domain Names' (1997) 2(3) *Intellectual Property* 7.

## Miscellaneous

Alexander, G. 'DNA holds key to explosion in computer power' *The Sunday Times*, 30 April 1995.

British Copyright Council *Reprographic Copying of Books and Journals* (British Copyright Council, 1985).

Conn, D. 'Cut-price Court in a Spin' *The Times*, 23 November 1993.

Rahn, G. 'Japanese Patent Strategy', *European Patent Office Annual Report 1995* at 9.

Smit, D. van Zyl *The Social Creation of a Legal Reality: A Study of the Emergence and Acceptance of the British Patent System as a Legal Instrument for the Control of New Technology*, unpublished Ph.D. Thesis, University of Edinburgh, 1980.

# Index

# Database of summaries of intellectual property cases and software copyright legislation

A computer database of summaries of important intellectual property cases is available from the author. The database usefully supplements this book and contains summaries of many of the cases referred to. The database comprises summaries of over 160 cases including some of the most recent ones. The database is provided complete with an easy-to-use computer program, having retrieval and editing facilities. Also included is a database of legislation relating to software copyright which includes extracts from the Copyright, Designs and Patents Act 1988, as amended, and from the Copyright and Rights in Databases Regulations 1997. The extracts, which are Crown copyright, are annotated by the author of this book and published by permission of the Stationery Office. The author updates the databases on a continuing basis.

The databases may be modified and added to and new databases can be created. The databases are in dBase III+ format and also may be used with most Windows database packages including MICROSOFT ACCESS, LOTUS APPROACH and DBASE for WINDOWS, allowing users to design their own forms and reports (you will need to have some familiarity with these packages to take full advantage to their powerful facilities). For users of MICROSOFT ACCESS Version 7 for WINDOWS 95, at no extra cost, a special version of the databases is available as an alternative with built in menus, forms and queries. If you want both the DOS and ACCESS versions, please make this clear and add £2.00 to your order.

The databases are available on a 3½ inch disk (1.44MB) suitable for an IBM personal computer or equivalent running DOS with a 1.44MB capacity disk drive. A hard disk is desirable. The system can be run from DOS or it can be run from Windows environment (as a DOS program) or used with the database packages mentioned above.

The databases are available for the price of £13.99 for students and academics or £19.99 for practitioners. If you want the Access Version 7 for Windows 95 version of the database, please specify ACCESS on your order. Send payment (cheque or postal order payable to David Bainbridge) to the address below, quoting reference **IP4**. Every effort will be made to deliver more quickly but allow 21 days. Prices include post and packaging for UK only.

> **Dr David Bainbridge**
> **Marketing and Law Group**
> **Aston Business School**
> **Aston University**
> **Aston Triangle**
> **BIRMINGHAM B4 7ET**

*Note: if entering new materials to the database or creating new databases, please take care to avoid infringing copyright (see Chapters 6 and 7 of this book). All trade marks are acknowledged.*